1,000,000 Books

are available to read at

www.ForgottenBooks.com

Read online
Download PDF
Purchase in print

ISBN 978-0-428-12512-7
PIBN 11213645

This book is a reproduction of an important historical work. Forgotten Books uses state-of-the-art technology to digitally reconstruct the work, preserving the original format whilst repairing imperfections present in the aged copy. In rare cases, an imperfection in the original, such as a blemish or missing page, may be replicated in our edition. We do, however, repair the vast majority of imperfections successfully; any imperfections that remain are intentionally left to preserve the state of such historical works.

Forgotten Books is a registered trademark of FB &c Ltd.
Copyright © 2018 FB &c Ltd.
FB &c Ltd, Dalton House, 60 Windsor Avenue, London, SW19 2RR.
Company number 08720141. Registered in England and Wales.

For support please visit www.forgottenbooks.com

1 MONTH OF FREE READING

at

www.ForgottenBooks.com

By purchasing this book you are eligible for one month membership to ForgottenBooks.com, giving you unlimited access to our entire collection of over 1,000,000 titles via our web site and mobile apps.

To claim your free month visit:
www.forgottenbooks.com/free1213645

* Offer is valid for 45 days from date of purchase. Terms and conditions apply.

English
Français
Deutsche
Italiano
Español
Português

www.forgottenbooks.com

Mythology Photography **Fiction**
Fishing Christianity **Art** Cooking
Essays Buddhism Freemasonry
Medicine **Biology** Music **Ancient Egypt** Evolution Carpentry Physics
Dance Geology **Mathematics** Fitness
Shakespeare **Folklore** Yoga Marketing
Confidence Immortality Biographies
Poetry **Psychology** Witchcraft
Electronics Chemistry History **Law**
Accounting **Philosophy** Anthropology
Alchemy Drama Quantum Mechanics
Atheism Sexual Health **Ancient History**
Entrepreneurship Languages Sport
Paleontology Needlework Islam
Metaphysics Investment Archaeology
Parenting Statistics Criminology
Motivational

C. S. WESTON, President   JAMES W. OAKFORD, Sec'y & Treas.
C. W. COLLINS, Manager of Sales

Cherry River Paper Company

Offices: Pennsylvania Building
PHILADELPHIA

Makers of High Grade

WRAPPING PAPERS, TAG and SPECIALTIES

MILLS:
RICHWOOD, WEST VIRGINIA
NICHOLAS COUNTY

Wanaque River Paper Co.
290 Broadway   NEW YORK CITY

MANUFACTURERS OF

SUPATONE
SUPERS
M. F. BOOK

PREFACE

Lockwood's Directory of the Paper, Stationery and Allied Trades for 1919 is the forty-fourth annual edition of this well-known work.

Although the largest edition in the history of the Directory was printed last year, it was exhausted before the usual time for the appearance of the new Directory. This indicates more conclusively, than could be evidenced otherwise, the constantly increasing favor with which this standard work is regarded by the members of the Paper and Allied Trades.

Because of the conditions brought about by the war, the 1919 edition will be of greater value to all buyers and sellers of paper than have been the editions of former years. Paper of practically every description is constantly becoming scarcer, and persons who wish to ascertain all the possible remaining sources of supply can find no more helpful information than is afforded by Lockwood's Directory.

Appreciating this greater need this year for the Directory, the publishers have spared no pains or expense to bring the current edition thoroughly up to date and to make it as accurate as it is humanly possible to make such a work. All the departments have been carefully revised, and some of them have been noticeably extended in the endeavor to make the Directory meet all the demands that may be reasonably made of it.

The publishers again request concerns who are eligible to be listed in the section of the Directory devoted to paper specialties to send listings of goods manufactured by them to this office. It is desired to make this list as comprehensive as possible, but it is difficult to expand the list as fully as desirable unless the manufacturers extend their co-operation. In this connection, however, it should be remembered that only *manufactures* of paper goods are eligible to be listed. The price of this edition of Lockwood's Directory is, as usual, $5.00.

THE LOCKWOOD TRADE JOURNAL CO., INC.
10 East 39th Street, New York.

Copyright, 1918, by Lockwood Trade Journal Co., Inc., New York.

TABLE OF CONTENTS

	PAGE
ALPHABETICAL LIST OF ADVERTISERS	7
CITY ADDRESS OF MILLS AND MILL SUPPLY HOUSES	447
CLASSIFIED LIST OF ADVERTISERS	9
CLASSIFIED LIST OF PAPER MILL PRODUCTS, UNITED STATES	249
CLASSIFIED LIST OF PAPER MILL PRODUCTS, CANADA	323
CLASSIFIED LIST OF PULP MILL PRODUCTS, UNITED STATES	318
CLASSIFIED LIST OF PULP MILL PRODUCTS, CANADA	331
COATED PAPER MANUFACTURERS	363
ENVELOPE MANUFACTURERS	434
GLAZED AND COATED PAPER MANUFACTURERS	363
IDLE MILLS	245
INDEX TO MILLS	57
MILL OFFICIALS	27
PAD MANUFACTURERS	437
PAPER DEALERS, UNITED STATES	367
PAPER DEALERS, CANADA	392
PAPER STOCK AND RAG DEALERS	395
PAPER BAG MANUFACTURERS	407
PAPER BOX MANUFACTURERS	411
PAPER AND PULP MILLS IN UNITED STATES	67
PAPER AND PULP MILLS IN CANADA	225
PAPER MILLS IN SOUTH AMERICA	246
PAPER SPECIALTIES	333
PAPETERIE MANUFACTURERS	446
PREFACE	3
ROOFING PAPER MANUFACTURERS	361
STATIONERS IN UNITED STATES	455
STATIONERS IN CANADA	595
STATIONERS IN CUBA	615
STATISTICAL TABLE OF MILLS	5
TABLET MANUFACTURERS	437
TAG MANUFACTURERS	439
TOILET PAPER MANUFACTURERS	360
TRADE ASSOCIATIONS	759
TWINE MANUFACTURERS IN UNITED STATES AND CANADA	442
VEGETABLE PARCHMENT PAPER MANUFACTURERS	360
WALL PAPER PRINTERS	440
WATERMARKS AND BRANDS	617
WAXED PAPER MANUFACTURERS	360

IMPORTED
PULP GRINDSTONES

MANUFACTURERS PAPER CO.
30 E. 42nd STREET
NEW YORK

Union Screen Plate Company

Fitchburg, Mass., U. S. A.   Lennoxville, Que., Canada.

Largest Manufacturers of Screen Plates in the World.

Immediate Delivery of the Largest Orders.

The Union Bronze (best phosphorized cast metal) Screen Plates.

Union Bronze Suction Plates.   Rolled Brass Screen Plates.

Union Bronze Screws for Screen Plates.

Old Plates Reclosed and Recut to Accurate Gauge.

Satisfaction Guaranteed.

Sole Mfrs. of the Witham Screen Plate Fastener (Patented).

STATISTICAL TABLE

SHOWING

Number of Firms owning Mills, together with the number of Paper and Pulp Mills in the United States, Canada and Newfoundland. Table compiled from Lockwood's Directory, 1919 Edition.

LOCATION	Number of Firms	Number of Paper Mills	Number of Pulp Mills Whether Connected With Paper Mills or Not	Number of Ground Wood Mills	Number of Sulphite Mills	Number of Soda Pulp Mills	Number of Sulphate Mills
Alabama	2	2	0	0	0	0	0
California	7	9	2	1	1	0	0
Connecticut	40	47	0	0	0	0	0
Delaware	7	7	1	0	0	1	0
District of Columbia	1	1	1	0	0	1	0
Georgia	6	6	2	0	0	1	1
Illinois	22	27	0	0	0	0	0
Indiana	23	30	0	0	0	0	0
Iowa	3	5	0	0	0	0	0
Kansas	3	3	0	0	0	0	0
Louisiana	3	3	5	0	1	1	3
Maine	21	26	42	21	14	5	2
Maryland	10	12	2	0	2	0	0
Massachusetts	65	104	6	3	2	1	0
Michigan	38	45	16	6	8	0	2
Minnesota	8	9	10	7	2	0	1
Mississippi	1	1	1	0	0	0	1
New Hampshire	25	32	14	9	5	0	0
New Jersey	37	43	1	0	0	1	0
New York	150	156	97	73	21	3	0
North Carolina	3	3	5	2	1	1	1
Ohio	48	54	3	0	1	1	1
Oregon	2	4	6	3	3	0	0
Pennsylvania	61	65	16	2	4	9	1
Rhode Island	0	1	0	0	0	0	0
South Carolina	1	1	2	1	1	0	0
Tennessee	2	1	1	0	0	1	0
Texas	2	2	1	0	0	0	1
Vermont	19	19	10	8	1	0	1
Virginia	11	12	7	2	1	2	2
Washington	6	6	7	2	3	1	1
West Virginia	9	5	5	2	3	0	0
Wisconsin	50	51	55	30	20	0	5
Total in United States	686	792	318	172	94	29	23
Canada — Brit. Columbia	4	4	9	2	5	0	2
Canada — New Brunswick	6	1	7	1	4	0	2
Canada — Nova Scotia	5	0	7	7	0	0	0
Canada — Ontario	31	29	29	16	11	1	1
Canada — Quebec	41	32	40	26	8	1	5
Total in Canada	87	66	92	52	28	2	10
Newfoundland	3	1	4	3	1	0	0
Idle Mills — United States	22	22	4	4	0	0	0
Idle Mills — Canada	1	1	1	1	0	0	0
Idle Mills — Newfoundland	0	0	0	0	0	0	0
Total	23	23	5	5	0	0	0

The Heller & Merz Co.
Main Office: New York

Branches:
Boston :: Chicago :: Philadelphia

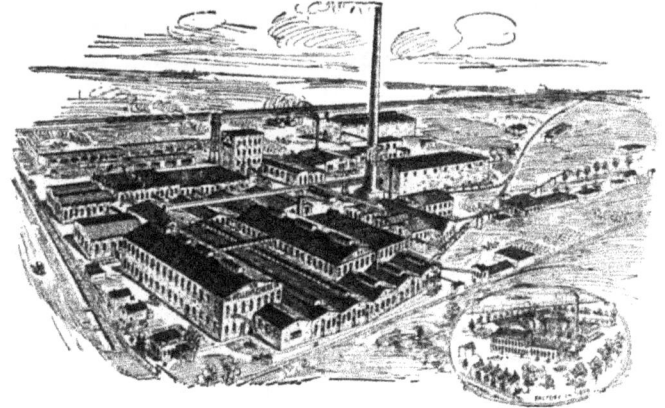

Works: Newark, N. J.

All available colors for white and colored paper

■ ■ ■

Best Values — Quality Considered

■ ■ ■

Formulae, directions, matching of product samples free to paper mills

Index to Advertisements

	PAGE
Advertisers Paper Mills	799
Albany Felt Co.	803
Albemarle Paper Manufacturing Co.	804
Allen Paper Co., A. C.	808
Alton Boxboard Co.	Opp. 192
American Writing Paper Co.	Bet. 272 and 273
Anderson & Co., J.	Opp. 367
Andrews Paper Co.	820
Appleton Machine Co.	Side Lines, 576-703
Appleton Woolen Mills	Head Lines, 576-704
Arabol Mfg. Co.	Head Lines, 66-182
	Side Lines, 71-351
Arnold, Hoffman & Co., Inc.	Opp. 32
Arnold-Roberts Co., The	817
Atterbury Bros., Inc.	8
Automatic Furnace Co.	Bet. 192 and 193
Baird & Bartlett Co.	819
Banker, J. W.	Opp. 434
Bare, D. M., Paper Co.	790
Beloit Iron Works	Opp. 48
Bennington Wax Paper Co.	798
Bermingham & Prosser Co.	Bet. 272 and 273
Black-Clawson Co., The	Bet. 296 and 297
Bowes Co., Inc., Walter H.	Opp. 9
Boyle, Luke	788
Bredt, F., & Co.	791
Brown & Co., Chas. D.	814
Brown Company	Opp. 289
Brown Paper Co., L. L.	Opp. 273
Bryant Paper Co.	Opp. 193
Buchanan & Bolt Wire Co.	775
Cabble Excelsior Wire Mfg. Co., The Wm.	Bet. 256 and 257
Cady Co., E. J.	805
Cameron Machine Co.	Opp. 257
Cantassano & Bros., V. G.	10
Carew Mfg. Co.	Third Cover
Carey, Jas. L.	790
Carter, John, & Co., Inc.	819
Carter, Rice & Co., Corp.	819
Carthage Machine Co.	Foot Lines, 72-390
Central Dyestuff & Chemical Co.	789
Central Manufacturing Co.	806
Champion-International Co.	Opp. 5
Chapman, C. A., Inc.	Head Lines, 577-703
Chemical Paper Mfg. Co.	798
Cheney Bigelow Wire Works	775
Cherry River Paper Co.	2
Claflin & Co., Inc., Wm. H.	818
Claflin Engineering Co., The	Bet. 256 and 257
Continental Paper Bag Co.	409
Cowan Truck Co.	814
Craig & Co., H. O.	Opp. 367
Crane, Z. & W. M.	794
Crane & Co.	795
Crocker-McElwain Co.	800
Croiteau, Dick	807
Darmstadt, Scott & Courtney	Side Lines, 72-384
Dean & Son, Ltd.	454
Dickinson, Thos. L.	781
Dietz Machine Works	Opp. 320
Dobler & Mudge	789
Domestic Mills Paper Co.	785
Draper Manufacturing Co., The	780
Du Pont de Nemours & Co.	801
Eagle Knife & Bar Co.	Head Lines, 11-64
Eastern Mfg. Co.	Opp. 250
Eastwood Wire Mfg. Co.	Opp. 24
Eaton-Dikeman Co., The	804
Elliott Co., W. R.	818
Elixman Paper Core Co.	Bet. 192 and 193
Esleeck Mfg. Co.	796
Falulah Paper Co.	Opp. 366
Farrel Foundry and Machine Co.	778 and 779
Feculose Co. of America	Opp. 9
Federal Paper Stock Co.	791
Ferguson, Hardy S.	Side Lines, 70-382
Fitchburg Duck Mills	790
Forsythe, Cale B.	810
Franklin Paper Co.	Bet. 362 and 363

	PAGE
Ganschow Co., Wm.	780
General Paper Stock Co.	807
Gilberts & Nash	Bet. 48 and 49
Gilbert Paper Co., Frank	Bet. 48 and 49
Gleeson, Thos. R., Inc.	Head Lines, 67-183
Glens Falls Machine Co.	Front Fly Leaf
Goldstein & Son, R.	774
Gottesman & Co., Inc., M.	Side Lines, 67-363
Guyton & Comfer Mfg. Co.	810
Hall, Ward & Walker, Inc.	Opp. 321
Hamblet Machine Co.	787
Hammermill Paper Co.	Bet. 296 and 297
Hampden Glazed Paper & Card Co.	Bet. 362 and 363
Hampden Paint & Chemical Co.	Head Lines, 417-575
Hampshire Paper Co.	Third Cover
Hardy, Geo. F.	Opp. 25
Harrisons, Inc.	Back Fly Leaf
Harrison, James H.	Foot Lines, 578-702
Hartford City Paper Company	807
Haverhill Boxboard Co.	798
Heller & Merz Co.	6
Hewitt Machine Co.	Foot Lines, 66-386
Hills Company, Geo. F.	788
Hoffman, Richard M.	803
Hoggson & Pettis Mfg. Co.	Bet. 48 and 49
Hollingsworth & Vose Co.	817
Hollingsworth & Whitney Co.	816
Hollis & Duncan	810
Holyoke Card & Paper Co.	Opp. 362
Holyoke Machine Co.	Inside Front Cover
Horne & Sons Co., The J. H.	Fourth Cover
Howard Paper Co.	806
Hudson & Sharp Machine Co.	784
Hunt Machine Co., Rodney	772
Ibbotson, Jr., Walter	784
Ideal Coated Paper Co.	Bet. 362 and 363
Illinois Envelope Co.	806
Improved Paper Machinery Co.	Bet. 88 and 89
Jaffe & Co.	788
Jointless Fire Brick Co.	786
Kalamazoo Vegetable Parchment Co.	Opp. 361
Keith Paper Co.	792
Keller Co., E. J.	Side Lines, 65-349
Kidder Press Co.	390 and 391
Klipstein, A., & Co.	Bet. 64 and 65
Knox Woolen Co.	Bet. 192 and 193
Kuttroff, Pickhardt & Co.	Opp. 33
Langston Co., Samuel M.	Opp. 360
Lennig & Co., Charles	782
Lindenmeyr & Sons, Henry	Opp. 73
Lindsay Wire Weaving Co.	Opp. 321
Linton Brothers & Co.	Opp. 363
Linton & Scott	Opp. 352
Lobdell Car Wheel Co.	778
Lockport Felt Co.	804
Lombard & Co.	Side Head Lines, 68-369
Lumen Bearing Co.	Opp. 17
McEnery Paper Co.	Foot Lines, 104-224
McEwan Bros.	Foot Lines, 65-181
McNeil Boiler Co., The	Opp. 8
Main Paper Stock Co., Inc.	788
Manchester China Clay Co., Ltd.	785
Manufacturers Paper Co.	Opp. 4
Marble & Co., J. Russel	777
Marquardt, Inc., F. G.	815
Meincke, A. M.	Opp. 16
Mendelson Bros. Paper Stock Co.	Opp. 289
Merrimac Chemical Co.	813
Merrimac Paper Co.	Opp. 362
Mid-States Gummed Paper Co.	810
Millers Falls Paper Co.	796
Miner-Edgar Co.	Foot Lines, 577-703
Moray & Co.	812
Mountain Mill Paper Co.	803
Munroe Co., D. F.	820
Munroe Felt & Paper Co.	Back Fly Leaf
Nashua Gummed & Coated Paper Co.	814
National Aniline & Chemical Co.	804
National Coated Paper Corp.	Bet. 362 and 363

Uniformly High Grade
That's What EAGLE Products Are

EAGLE KNIFE AND BAR WORKS
LAWRENCE :: :: MASS.

Index to Advertisements

	PAGE
National Waterproofing Co.	Head Lines, 69-181
Neenah Paper Co.	Bet. 212 and 213
New England Quartz Co.	Side Lines, 11-24
Newton Falls Paper Co.	Opp. 73
Newton Paper Co.	Bet. 362 and 363
New York-New England Co., The	799
N. Y. Revolving Portable Elev. Co.	783
Northern Paper Mills	Opp. 361
Norwood Engineering Co.	787
O'Malley, M. J., Co., The	789
O'Meara Co., Maurice	Foot Lines, 11-24
O'Neill Wire Works, Jos.	783
Orono Pulp & Paper Co.	796
Oswego Machine Works	784
Oxford Paper Co.	56
Parsons Trading Co.	Opp. 296
Peninsular Paper Co.	803
Penn Paper & Stock Co.	804
Pennsylvania Paper Stock Co.	774
Pennsylvania Salt Mfg. Co.	777
Perkins & Sons, Inc., B. F.	782
Perry Co., Inc., C. E.	820
Plank & Co., J. J.	797
Poland Paper Co.	Bet. 256 and 257
Potdevin Machine Co.	772
Record Foundry & Machine Co.	797
Rhode Island Cardboard Co.	Opp. 353
Rice, Barton & Fales Machine and Iron Co.	776
Rising Paper Co., B. D.	800
Robertson Paper Co.	224
Rogers Paper Mfg. Co., The	Opp. 192
Roy, B. S., & Son	811
Safepack Paper Mills	Bet. 362 and 363
Salomon, Inc., A.	Side Lines, 25-34
Savery, Thos. H., Jr.	Opp. 320
Scandinavian American Trading Co.	Opp. 297
Seaman Paper Co.	809
Shea, Sturm Co.	Back Fly Leaf
Shepard Electric Crane & Hoist Co.	Opp. 49
Sherbrooke Machinery Co.	Bet. 240 and 241
Sherman Envelope Co.	66
Shuler & Benninghofen	806
Shyrock Brothers	791
Smith Co., C. H.	797

	PAGE
Smith Paper Company	802
Snell Co., Samuel	781
Spaulding & Tewksbury Co.	Opp. 366
Standard Paper Co.	806
Standard Paper Bag Co.	410
Standard Paper Mfg. Co.	580-704
Standard Spiral Pipe Works	780
Standard Wire Co.	775
Stearns Lumber Co., The A. T.	813
Stimpson & Co.	819
Stone & Andrew, Inc.	818
Stone & Forsyth Co.	814
Storrs & Bement Co., A.	817
Stratford Paper Co.	802
Strathmore Paper Co.	797
Sutherland Paper Co.	781
Swenson Evaporator Co.	781
Taylor-Logan Co., The (Papermakers)	799
Taylor, Stiles & Company	772
Textile Finishing Machinery Co.	Front Fly Leaf
Ticonderoga Machine Works	781
Ticonderoga Pulp & Paper Co.	Bet. 362 and 363
Tileston & Hollingsworth Co.	816
Ultramarine Co., The	776
Union Screen Plate Co.	Opp. 4
Union Sulphur Co.	Foot Lines, 67-183
United States Paper Corp.	802
United States Envelope Co.	Opp. 435
Van Noorden Company, E.	Opp. 25
Von Olker-Snell Paper Co.	820
Wallace, Jos. H., & Co.	Foot Lines, 185-383
Wanaque River Paper Co.	2
Wausau Sulphate Fibre Co.	Opp. 353
Watervelit Paper Co.	802
West Virginia Pulp & Paper Co.	Bet. 224 and 225
Weston Company, Byron	793
Whiting Paper Co.	798
Whitmore Mfg. Co.	Bet. 362 and 363
Williams, C. K., & Co.	785
Williams & Co., Charles W.	Bet. 72 and 73
Williamson & Co., T.	784
Wilson, H. P. & H. F.	791
Wisconsin Wire Works	774

ATTERBURY BROTHERS, Inc.

IMPORTERS AND EXPORTERS

HIGHEST GRADES AMERICAN BLEACHED AND UNBLEACHED SULPHITE

BEST QUALITY SOUTH AMERICAN CASEINE

MADE BY

INTERNATIONAL CASEINE COMPANY OF BUENOS AIRES

FRENCH CASEINE FOREIGN AND DOMESTIC WOOD PULP RAGS AND PAPER STOCK

145 NASSAU STREET   -   -   -   NEW YORK CITY

OFFICES AT LONDON, PARIS, BUENOS AIRES

THE McNEIL BOILER COMPANY
AKRON, OHIO U S A
BUILDERS OF

DIGESTER SHELLS FOR PULP MILLS

GLOBE

CYLINDER AND GLOBE ROTARY BLEACHING BOILERS

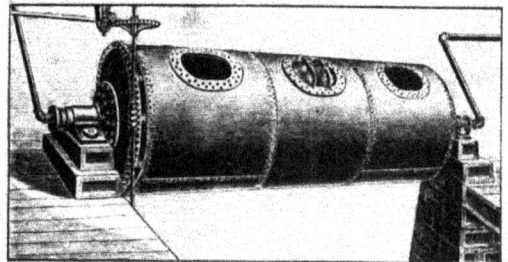

CYLINDER

HOME OF McNEIL PRODUCTS

"We Can Save You Money"

THE McNEIL BOILER COMPANY
Pioneer Builders of Rotary Bleaching Boilers
AKRON, OHIO, U. S. A.

FECULOSE

First and foremost size for fixing Coating Pigments on Paper and for Surface Sizing

SEND FOR DETAILS OF OUR
NEW TUB SIZING PROCESS

Feculose Co. of America
239 ATLANTIC AVE.   BOSTON, MASS.

Solve Your Drying Problems

THE DODGE GRAVITY EVACUATOR, by removing all water of condensation, across the entire length of the paper dryer, brings about uniform drying, which is the equivalent for fuel saving, increased production, better quality, and elimination of cockling.

The EVACUATOR carries no overhead charges, and will pay for its cost in a very short time, as the maximum possible number of heat units are always utilized.

Your selling department will appreciate our device, as the EVACUATOR will improve the quality of your paper, and insure to you a satisfied customer.

Write for Full Particulars

THE DODGE GRAVITY EVACUATOR
WALTER H. BOWES CO., Inc.
193 North Main Street   PORT CHESTER, N. Y.

HIGH GRADE STEEL PRODUCTS FOR PAPER MILLS — Eagle Knife and Bar Works, LAWRENCE :: :: MASS

Classified List of Advertisers

In Paper, Paper Stock, Paper Makers' Supplies and Machinery, also Stationery Supplies

Machinery and Paper Makers' Supplies

ACIDS. PAGE
LENNIG & CO., CHAS..................782
MERRIMAC CHEMICAL CO..........813

AGALITE.
WILLIAMS, C. K., & CO...............785

ALUM.
HARRISON, INC............Back Fly Leaf
KLIPSTEIN, A., & CO......Bet. 64 and 65
LENNIG & CO., CHAS.................782
MERRIMAC CHEMICAL CO..........813
PENNA. SALT MFG. CO...............777

AMMONIA.
MERRIMAC CHEMICAL CO..........813

ANGLE BED PLATES.
EAGLE KNIFE & BAR CO.,
 Head Lines, 11-64

ANILINE COLORS.
ARNOLD, HOFFMAN & CO., INC.,.Opp. 32
BREDT, F., & CO......................791
CENTRAL DYESTUFF & CHEMICAL CO.789
HAMPDEN PAINT & CHEMICAL CO.,
 Head Lines, 417-575
HELLER & MERZ CO., THE.............6
KLIPSTEIN, A., & CO......Bet. 64 and 65
KUTTROFF, PICKHARDT & CO...Opp. 33
NATIONAL ANILINE CHEMICAL CO..394

ARCHITECTS.
CAREY, JAS. L.......................790
CHAPMAN, C. A., INC..Head Lines, 577-703
FERGUSON, HARDY S...Side Lines, 70-382
HARDY, GEO. F..................Opp. 25
WALLACE & CO., JOS. H.,
 Foot Lines, 185-383

AUTOMATIC MACHINERY.
BOWES CO., INC., WALTER H....Opp. 8
POTDEVIN MACHINE CO..............772

BAG PRINTING PRESSES.
KIDDER PRESS CO...............330-391

BALE TIES.
WILSON, H. P. & H. F...............791

BALING PRESSES.
HUDSON-SHARP MACHINE CO........784
MOREY & CO.........................812

BALL BEARINGS.
DRAPER MANUFACTURING CO.......780

BARKER KNIVES.
EAGLE KNIFE & BAR CO..Head Lines, 11-64

BARKERS.
APPLETON MACHINE CO.,
 Side Lines, 579-703
CARTHAGE MACHINE CO.,
 Foot Lines, 72-390
HOLYOKE MACHINE CO.,
 Inside Front Cover

BARS AND PLATES. PAGE
EAGLE KNIFE & BAR CO.,
 Head Lines 11-64

BATTERY MACHINES.
IMPROVED PAPER MACHINERY CO.,
 Bet. 88 and 89

BEATER KNIVES.
LUMEN BEARING CO..............Opp. 17

BEATING ENGINES.
CLAFLIN ENGINEERING CO., THE,
 Bet. 256 and 257
HOLYOKE MACHINE CO.Inside Front Cover
HORNE & SONS CO., THE J. H.,
 Outside Back Cover
RICE, BARTON & FALES M. & I. CO...776

BED PLATES.
EAGLE KNIFE & BAR CO..Head Lines, 11-64
TAYLOR, STILES & CO...............772

BELT TIGHTENERS.
HUNT MACHINE CO., RODNEY.......772

BLANC FIXE.
KLIPSTEIN & CO..........Bet. 64 and 65

BLEACH EJECTORS.
PERKINS & SON, INC., B. F..........782

BLEACHED STRAW PULP.
ANDERSEN & CO., J.............Opp. 367
BROWN & CO., CHAS. D..............814

BLEACHING POWDERS.
ARNOLD, HOFFMAN & CO..........Opp. 32
KLIPSTEIN & CO., A......Bet. 64 and 65
MARBLE & CO., J. RUSSEL............777
PENNA. SALT MFG. CO...............777

BLOW TANKS.
RECORD FOUNDRY & MACHINE CO..797
CHAMPION-INTERNATIONAL CO..Opp. 5
 (Steam).
McNEIL BOILER CO., THE........Opp. 8

BOOK BINDERS' MACHINERY.
OSWEGO MACHINE WORKS..........784

BRASS ROLL TURNING TOOLS.
DICKINSON, THOS. L................781

BRIMSTONE.
UNION SULPHUR CO...Foot Lines, 67-183

BRONZE Y VALVES.
CARTHAGE MACHINE CO.,
 Foot Lines, 72-390
EASTWOOD WIRE MFG. CO.......Opp. 24

BURRS—STEEL SHELL.
HALL, WARD & WALKER, INC...Opp. 321

VITO G. CANTASANO & BROS.

PACKERS AND DEALERS IN

NEW AND OLD
RAGS
BAGGING
ROPE
WASTE
PAPER
ALL GRADES

...

185 South Street
NEW YORK

BRANCH AT 395 PEARL STREET

High Grade Paper Mill Knives — Eagle Knife and Bar Works, LAWRENCE :: :: MASS.

Classified List of Advertisers

CALENDERS.
BELOIT IRON WORKS............Opp. 48
BLACK-CLAWSON CO., THE
    Bet. 296 and 297
FARREL FOUNDRY AND MACHINE
  CO.........................778 and 779
GUYTON & COMFER MFG. CO.......810
HOLYOKE MACHINE CO. Inside Front Cover
LOBDELL CAR WHEEL CO............773
NORWOOD ENGINEERING CO........787
TEXTILE-FINISHING MACHINERY CO.,
    First Page, Front Fly Leaf

CALENDER ROLL GRINDER.
GUYTON & COMFER MFG. CO.......810
LOBDELL CAR WHEEL CO............773
ROY & SON, R. S..................811

CALENDER ROLL TURNING TOOLS.
DICKINSON, THOS. L..............781

CAPS (Steel Ends for Rolls).
ELIXMAN PAPER CORE CO., INC.,
    Bet. 192 and 193

CASEIN.
ATTERBURY BROS., INC............8
KLIPSTEIN & CO., A.......Bet. 64 and 65
MARBLE & CO., J. RUSSEL........777
MOREY & CO.....................812

CASTING (Iron, Brass, Bronze, Aluminum).
CENTRAL MFG. CO...............806
HUNT MACHINE CO., RODNEY......772
RECORD FOUNDRY & MACHINE CO...797

CAUSTIC SODA.
ARNOLD, HOFFMAN & CO........Opp. 32
MARBLE & CO., J. RUSSEL........777
PENNSYLVANIA SALT MFG. CO.....777

CAUSTICIZERS.
SWENSON EVAPORATOR CO.........781

CENTRIFUGAL PUMPS.
APPLETON MACHINE CO.,
    Side Lines, 579-703
CARTHAGE MACHINE CO.,
    Foot Lines, 72-390
CLAFLIN ENGINEERING CO., THE,
    Bet. 256 and 257
HUNT MACHINE CO., RODNEY......772
RECORD FOUNDRY & MACHINE CO...797

CHEMICALS.
ARNOLD, HOFFMAN & CO........Opp. 32
BROWN & CO., CHAS. D..........814
CENTRAL DYESTUFF & CHEMICAL
  CO............................789
DU PONT DE NEMOURS & CO......801
FECULOSE CO. OF AMERICA....Opp. 9
HAMPDEN PAINT & CHEMICAL CO.,
    Head Lines, 417-575
HARRISON'S, INC.......Back Fly Leaf
HELLER & MERZ CO., THE..........6
KLIPSTEIN, A., & CO......Bet. 64 and 65
KUTTROFF, PICKHARDT & CO...Opp. 33
LENNIG & CO., CHAS.............782
MERRIMAC CHEMICAL CO..........813
MOREY & CO....................812
NATIONAL ANILINE & CHEMICAL CO.394

CHEMISTS AND EXPERTS.
WALLACE & CO., JOS. H.,
    Foot Lines, 185-383

CHILLED CALENDER ROLLS.
FARREL FOUNDRY AND MACHINE
  CO.........................778 and 779
HOLYOKE MACHINE CO.
    Inside Front Cover
LOBDELL CAR WHEEL CO............773
RICE, BARTON & FALES M. & I. CO..776
TEXTILE-FINISHING MACHINERY CO.,
    First Page, Front Fly Leaf

CHILLED CALENDER ROLL TURNING TOOLS.
DICKINSON, THOS. L..............781

CHINA CLAY.
ARNOLD, HOFFMAN & CO........Opp. 32
KLIPSTEIN & CO., A.......Bet. 64 and 65
MANCHESTER CHINA CLAY CO., LTD..785
MEINCKE, A. M..............Opp. 16
MINER EDGAR CO.
MOREY & CO....................812
WILLIAMS, C. K., & CO..........785

CHIPPER KNIVES.
EAGLE KNIFE & BAR CO..Head Lines, 11-64

CHIPPERS, CRUSHERS AND SCREENS.
APPLETON MACHINE CO.,
    Side Lines, 577-703
CARTHAGE MACHINE CO.,
    Foot Lines, 72-390
HOLYOKE MACHINE CO.
    Inside Front Cover

COLORS.
ARNOLD, HOFFMAN & CO........Opp. 32
BREDT, F., & CO...............791
DU PONT DE NEMOURS & CO......801
HAMPDEN PAINT & CHEMICAL CO.,
    Head Lines, 417-575
HARRISONS, INC.......Back Fly Leaf
HELLER & MERZ CO., THE..........6
KLIPSTEIN, A., & CO......Bet. 64 and 65
KUTTROFF, PICKHARDT & CO...Opp. 33
MERRIMAC CHEMICAL CO..........813
ULTRAMARINE COMPANY, THE......776
WILLIAMS, C. K., & CO..........785

CORES.
ELIXMAN PAPER CORE CO., INC.,
    Bet. 192 and 193

CORN STARCH.
MARBLE & CO., J. RUSSEL........777

CORRUGATED PAPER MACHINERY.
LANGSTON COMPANY, S. M....Opp. 360
POTDEVIN MACHINE CO...........772

COTTON CALENDER ROLLS.
TEXTILE-FINISHING MACHINERY CO.,
    First Page, Front Fly Leaf

COTTON ROLL TURNING TOOLS.
DICKINSON, THOS. L..............781

COTTON ROLLS.
NORWOOD ENGINEERING CO........787
TEXTILE FINISHING MACHINERY CO.
    Front Fly Leaf

COUCH ROLLS.
EASTWOOD WIRE MFG. CO......Opp. 24
IMPROVED PAPER MACHINERY CO.,
    Bet. 88 and 89
SHERBROOKE MACHINERY CO.
    Bet. 240 and 241

CRANES (Electric).
SHEPARD ELECTRIC CRANE & HOIST
  CO........................Opp. 49

CREPE MACHINES.
HUDSON-SHARP MACHINE CO........784

CUTTING DIES (Paper Labels, etc.).
HOGGSON & PETTIS MFG. CO., THE
    Bet. 48 and 49

CUTTER KNIVES.
EAGLE KNIFE & BAR CO..Head Lines, 11-64
HAMBLET MACHINE CO............787

11

NEW ENGLAND QUARTZ CO. of N. Y. — 150 NASSAU STREET, NEW YORK, N. Y. — **GRANULATED QUARTZ for Digester Linings**

RAW HIDE CUTTINGS AND BOW PICKERS FOR SIZING — MAURICE O'MEARA CO., 448-450 PEARL ST., NEW YORK

PAPER TRIMMING KNIVES
of superior quality for all kinds of work

Eagle Knife and Bar Works
LAWRENCE :: :: MASS.

Left margin: NEW ENGLAND QUARTZ CO. of N. Y. — 150 NASSAU STREET, NEW YORK, N. Y. — DIGESTER LININGS--GRANULATED QUARTZ

Classified List of Advertisers

CUTTING MACHINERY.
CAMERON MACHINE CO. ....Opp. 257
DIETZ MACHINE WORKS.........Opp. 320
HAMBLET MACHINE CO. 787
LANGSTON CO., SAMUEL M.......Opp. 360
OSWEGO MACHINE WORKS............784

CYLINDER COVERS.
BUCHANAN & BOLT WIRE CO.........775
CHENEY BIGELOW WIRE WORKS....775
EASTWOOD WIRE MFG. CO.......Opp. 24
GLEESON, INC., THOS. E.,
    Head Lines, 67-183
LINDSAY WIRE WEAVING CO.....Opp. 321
O'NEILL WIRE WORKS, JOS..........783
STANDARD WIRE CO..................780
WISCONSIN WIRE WORKS.............774

CYLINDER MOULDS.
BLACK-CLAWSON CO., THE
    Bet. 296 and 297
BUCHANAN & BOLT WIRE CO.........775
CHENEY BIGELOW WIRE WORKS....775
EASTWOOD WIRE MFG. CO.......Opp. 24
GLEESON, INC., THOS. E.,
    Head Lines, 67-183
IMPROVED PAPER MACHINERY CO.,
    Bet. 88 and 89
SHERBROOKE MACHINERY CO.
    Bet. 240 and 241
STANDARD WIRE CO..................780

CYPRESS WOOD.
STEARNS LUMBER CO., A. T.........813

DANDY ROLLS.
BUCHANAN & BOLT WIRE CO.........775
CABBLE EXCELSIOR WIRE MFG. CO.,
    Bet. 256 and 257
CENTRAL MFG. CO...................806
CHENEY BIGELOW WIRE WORKS....775
EASTWOOD WIRE MFG. CO.......Opp. 24
GLEESON, INC., THOS. E.
    Head Lines, 67-183
PLANK & CO., J. J..................797
SMITH & CO., C. H..................797
STANDARD WIRE CO..................780
WISCONSIN WIRE WORKS.............774

DANDY STANDS.
GILBERTS & NASH..........Bet. 48 and 49

DECKLE WEBBING.
MOREY & CO........................812

DIAMOND TOOLS.
DICKINSON, THOS. L................781

DIE CUTTING PRESSES.
OSWEGO MACHINE WORKS.............784

DIFFUSERS.
SWENSON EVAPORATOR CO............781

DIGESTER FITTINGS.
CARTHAGE MACHINE CO.,
    Foot Lines, 72-390

DIGESTER BLOW PIPES.
RECORD FOUNDRY & MACHINE CO....797

DIGESTER, BRONZE.
EASTWOOD WIRE MFG. CO........Opp. 24

DIGESTER LININGS.
NEW ENGLAND QUARTZ CO..
    Side Lines, 11-24

DIGESTER (Sulphite).
McNEIL BOILER CO., THE.......Opp. 8

DRAINER STONES.
SNELL CO., SAMUEL.................781

DRUM WINDERS.
BELOIT IRON WORKS.............Opp. 48
TICONDEROGA MACHINE WORKS....781

DRYERS.
BOWES CO., INC., WALTER H....Opp. 9
GUYTON & COMFER MFG. CO........810

DUSTERS.
HOLYOKE MACHINE CO. Inside Front Cover
NORWOOD ENGINEERING CO..........787

DUSTER WIRES.
CHENEY BIGELOW WIRE WORKS....775

DYESTUFFS.
CENTRAL DYESTUFF & CHEMICAL
    CO...............................789
DU PONT DE NEMOURS & CO........801
HAMPDEN PAINT & CHEMICAL CO.,
    Head Lines, 417-575
HELLER & MERZ CO..................6
KLIPSTEIN, A., & CO......Bet. 64 and 65
KUTTROFF, PICKHARDT & CO....Opp. 33
MARBLE & CO., J. RUSSEL..........777
NATIONAL ANILINE & CHEMICAL
    CO...............................394

DYE TUBS.
HUNT MACHINE CO., RODNEY........772
STEARNS LUMBER CO., A. T........813

ELECTRIC HOISTS.
SHEPARD ELECTRIC CRANE & HOIST
    CO............................Opp. 49

ELEVATORS.
NORWOOD ENGINEERING CO..........787
N. Y. REVOLVING & PORTABLE ELE-
    VATOR CO........................783

ENGINE BARS AND BED-PLATES.
EAGLE KNIFE & BAR CO..Head Lines, 11-64
HORNE & SONS CO., THE J. H.,
    Outside Back Cover

ENGINE ROLL BARS.
EAGLE KNIFE & BAR CO..Head Lines, 11-64

ENGINEERS.
CAREY, JAS. L....................790
CHAPMAN, C. A., INC..Head Lines, 577-703
CLAFLIN ENGINEERING CO., THE,
    Bet. 256 and 257
FERGUSON, HARDY S.....Side Lines, 70-382
HARDY, GEO. F.................Opp. 25
HUNT MACHINE CO., RODNEY........772
WALLACE & CO., JOS. H.,
    Foot Lines, 185-383

ENVELOPE MACHINES.
DIETZ MACHINE WORKS..........Opp. 320
POTDEVIN MACHINE CO..............772

EVAPORATORS.
SWENSON EVAPORATOR CO............781

FELT ROLLS.
HEWITT MACHINE CO..Foot Lines, 66-386
IMPROVED PAPER MACHINERY CO.,
    Bet. 88 and 89
SHERBROOKE MACHINERY CO.
    Bet. 240 and 241

FELTS AND FELTING.
ALBANY FELT CO...................803
APPLETON WOOLEN MILLS,
    Head Lines, 576-704
BREDT, F. & CO...................791
BROWN & CO., CHAS. D.............814
FITCHBURG DUCK MILLS............790
KNOX WOOLEN CO.......Bet. 192 and 193
LOCKPORT FELT CO................804
MOREY & CO......................812
SHULER & BENNINGHOFEN..........806

FILTERS AND FILTRATION PLANTS.
NORWOOD ENGINEERING CO..........787

OLD AND NEW COTTON AND LINEN RAGS
WASTE PAPER OF ALL DESCRIPTIONS

MAURICE O'MEARA CO.
448-450 PEARL ST.
NEW YORK

Roll Bars for Every Kind of Work — LARGE STOCKS, QUICK SHIPMENTS

Eagle Knife and Bar Works
LAWRENCE :: :: MASS.

NEW ENGLAND QUARTZ CO. of N. Y.
150 NASSAU STREET, NEW YORK, N. Y.
GRANULATED QUARTZ for Digester Linings

Classified List of Advertisers

FILTERING MATERIALS.
NEW ENGLAND QUARTZ CO.,
    Side Lines, 11-24

FIRE BRICK.
JOINTLESS FIRE BRICK CO..........786
SNELL CO., SAMUEL................781

FIRE HYDRANTS.
NORWOOD ENGINEERING CO........787

FLY BARS.
EAGLE KNIFE & BAR CO..Head Lines, 11-64
TAYLOR, STILES & CO..............772

FRICTION CLUTCHES.
HUNT MACHINE CO., RODNEY.......772

FURNACES.
AUTOMATIC FURNACE CO.,
    Bet. 192 and 193

FURNACE LINING.
JOINTLESS FIRE BRICK CO..........786

GATES, FLUME, HEAD.
HUNT MACHINE CO., RODNEY.......772

GEARS.
GANSCHOW CO., WM................780

GRATES.
RECORD FOUNDRY & MACHINE CO..797

GRINDERS.
CARTHAGE MACHINE CO.,
    Foot Lines, 72-390
HOLYOKE MACHINE CO.
    Inside Front Cover

GRINDSTONES.
HARRISON, JAMES H..Foot Lines, 578-702
LOMBARD & CO........Head Lines, 68-359
MANUFACTURERS' PAPER CO....Opp. 4

GUMMING MACHINES.
POTDEVIN MACHINE CO.............772

HARD PINE TIMBER AND FLOORING.
STEARNS LUMBER CO., A. T........775

HOISTS (Electric Crane).
SHEPARD ELECTRIC CRANE & HOIST CO..................Opp. 49

HUSK ROLL TURNING TOOLS.
DICKINSON, THOS. L................781

HYDRAULIC AND HYDRO-ELECTRIC ENGINEERS.
CAREY, JAS. L.....................790
CHAPMAN CO., INC., C. A.,
    Head Lines, 577-703
FERGUSON, HARDY S...Side Lines, 70-382
HARDY, GEO. F..................Opp. 25
HUNT MACHINE CO., RODNEY.......772
WALLACE & CO., JOS. H.,
    Foot Lines, 185-383

HYPOSULPHITE OF SODA.
KLIPSTEIN, A., & CO......Bet. 64 and 65

INCINERATORS.
SWENSON EVAPORATOR CO..........781

JORDAN ENGINES.
BLACK-CLAWSON CO., THE
    Bet. 296 and 297
HORNE & SONS CO., THE J....Back Cover

JORDAN FILLINGS.
EAGLE KNIFE & BAR CO.,
    Head Lines, 11-64

KNIVES.
EAGLE KNIFE & BAR CO..Head Lines, 11-64
LUMEN BEARING CO..............Opp. 17

LABELING MACHINES.
POTDEVIN MACHINE CO.............772

LABEL PRINTING PRESSES.
KIDDER PRESS CO..........330 and 391

LEACH BATTERIES.
SWENSON EVAPORATOR CO..........781

LUMBER.
STEARNS LUMBER CO., A. T........813

MACHINE KNIVES.
EAGLE KNIFE & BAR CO..Head Lines, 11-64
TAYLOR, STILES CO................772

MACHINISTS AND FOUNDERS.
RECORD FOUNDRY & MACHINE CO..797

MATCH BOX MACHINERY.
DIETZ MACHINE WORKS........Opp. 320

METAL WINDOWS.
VAN NOORDEN CO., E............Opp. 25

MICROMETER GAUGE.
CADY & CO., E. J..................805
STORRS & BEMENT CO., A..........817

MILL ARCHITECTS AND ENGINEERS.
CAREY, JAS. L.....................790
CHAPMAN CO., INC., C. A.,
    Head Lines, 577-703
FERGUSON, HARDY S...Side Lines, 70-382
HARDY, GEO. F..................Opp. 25
WALLACE, JOS. H., & CO.,
    Foot Lines, 185-383

MILL FLOORS.
STEARNS LUMBER CO., A. T........813

MINERAL PULP.
WILLIAMS, C. K., & CO.............785

MOULDINGS.
STEARNS LUMBER CO., A. T........813

OFFICE RAILINGS.
CHENEY BIGELOW WIRE WORKS...775

OIL VITRIOL.
MERRIMAC CHEMICAL CO...........813

PAINTS.
HAMPDEN PAINT & CHEMICAL CO.,
    Head Lines, 417-575
HARRISONS, INC..........Back Fly Leaf

PAPER BAG MACHINERY.
DIETZ MACHINE WORKS........Opp. 320
POTDEVIN MACHINE CO.............772

PAPER CAN MACHINERY.
LANGSTON CO., S. M............Opp. 360

PAPER CORE MACHINERY.
LANGSTON CO., S. M............Opp. 360

PAPER CUTTERS.
BELOIT IRON WORKS............Opp. 48
BLACK-CLAWSON CO., THE
    Bet. 296 and 297
CAMERON MACHINE CO.........Opp. 257
DIETZ MACHINE WORKS........Opp. 320
HAMBLET MACHINE CO..............787
HORNE & SONS CO., THE, J. H.,
    Outside Back Cover
KIDDER PRESS CO..........330 and 391
OSWEGO MACHINE WORKS..........784
RICE, BARTON & FALES M. & I. CO...776

RAW HIDE CUTTINGS AND BOW PICKERS FOR SIZING

MAURICE O'MEARA CO.
448-450 PEARL ST.
NEW YORK

"EAGLE" Beater Knives
ARE UNIFORMLY HIGH GRADE

Eagle Knife and Bar Works
LAWRENCE :: :: MASS.

Quartz Flour — New England Quartz Co. of New York, 150 Nassau Street, New York, N. Y.

Classified List of Advertisers

PAPER-CUTTER KNIVES.
EAGLE KNIFE & BAR CO.,
   Head Lines, 11-64
HAMBLET MACHINE CO. 787

PAPER-MAKERS' SUPPLIES.
ALBANY FELT CO. 803
ANDERSON & CO., J. ....Opp. 367
APPLETON WOOLEN MILLS,
   Head Lines, 576-704
ARABOL MFG. CO.,
   Side Lines, 71-351, and Head Lines, 66-182
ARNOLD, HOFFMAN & CO. ......Opp. 32
ATTERBURY BROS., INC. 8
BREDT, F., & CO. 791
BROWN & CO., CHAS. D. 814
CANTASANO & BROS., V. G. 10
DARMSTADT, SCOTT & COURTNEY,
   Side Lines, 72-384
FECULOSE CO. OF AMERICA.....Opp. 9
FEDERAL PAPER STOCK CO. 791
FITCHBURG DUCK MILLS. 790
GENERAL PAPER STOCK CO. 807
GOLDSTEIN & SON, R. 774
GOTTESMAN & CO., INC., M.,
   Side Lines, 67-363
HAMPDEN PAINT & CHEMICAL CO.,
   Head Lines, 417-575
HARRISONS, INC. ....Back Fly Leaf
HELLER & MERZ CO., THE. 6
HILLS COMPANY, GEO. F. 788
JAFFE & CO. 788
KELLER & CO., E. J. ..Side Lines, 65-349
KLIPSTEIN, A., & CO. ...Bet. 64 and 65
KNOX WOOLEN CO. ...Bet. 192 and 193
KUTTROFF, PICKHARDT & CO...Opp. 33
LENNIG & CO., CHAS. 782
LOCKPORT FELT CO. 804
MAIN PAPER STOCK CO., INC. 788
MARBLE & CO., J. RUSSEL. 777
MARQUARDT, INC., F. G. 815
MEINCKE & M. ....Opp. 16
MENDELSON BROS. PAPER STOCK
   CO. ....Opp. 289
MERRIMAC CHEMICAL CO. 813
MINER-EDGAR CO. ....Foot Lines, 577-703
MOREY & CO. 812
O'MEARA, MAURICE....Foot Lines, 11-24
PARSONS TRADING CO. ......Opp. 296
PENNSYLVANIA PAPER STOCK CO...804
PENN PAPER & STOCK CO., INC...774
PENNA. SALT MFG. CO. 777
SALOMON, INC., A. .....Side Lines, 25-64
SCANDINAVIAN-AMERICAN TRADING
   CO. ....Opp. 297
SHULER & BENNINGHOFEN. 806
ULTRAMARINE CO., THE. 776
UNION SULPHUR CO...Foot Lines, 67-183

PAPER MAKING MACHINERY.
APPLETON MACHINE CO.,
   Side Lines, 579-703
BELOIT IRON WORKS. ....Opp. 48
BLACK-CLAWSON CO., THE
   Bet. 296 and 297
BOWES CO., INC., WALTER H....Opp. 9
CARTHAGE MACHINE CO.,
   Foot Lines, 72-390
CLAFLIN ENGINEERING CO., THE.
   Bet. 256 and 257
FARREL FOUNDRY AND MACHINE
   CO. ....778 and 779
GUYTON & COMFOR MFG. CO. 810
HAMBLET MACHINE CO. 787
HOLYOKE MACHINE CO. Inside Front Cover
HORNE & SONS CO., THE J. H.
   Outside Back Cover
IMPROVED PAPER MACHINERY CO.,
   Bet. 88 and 89
LOBDELL CAR WHEEL CO. 773
McNEIL BOILER CO., THE. .....Opp. 8
NORWOOD ENGINEERING CO. 787
OSWEGO MACHINE WORKS. 784
RICE, BARTON & FALES M. & I. CO...776
SHERBROOKE MACHINERY CO.,
   Bet. 240 and 241
TAYLOR, STILES & CO. 772

PAPER ROLL TURNING TOOLS.
DICKINSON, THOS. L. 781

PAPER STOCK DEALERS.
BOYLE, LUKE. 788
BROWN & CO., CHAS. D. 814
CANTASANO & BROS., V. G. 10
DARMSTADT, SCOTT & COURTNEY,
   Side Lines, 72-384
FEDERAL PAPER STOCK CO. 791
GENERAL PAPER STOCK CO. 807
GOLDSTEIN & SON, R. 774
GOTTESMAN & CO., INC., M.,
   Side Lines, 67-363
HILLS COMPANY, GEO. F. 788
JAFFE & CO. 788
KELLER & CO., E. J. ..Side Lines, 65-349
MAIN PAPER STOCK CO., INC. ...788
MARQUARDT, INC., F. G. 815
MENDELSON BROS. PAPER STOCK
   CO. ....Opp. 289
MOREY & CO. 812
O'MEARA, MAURICE....Foot Lines, 11-24
PARSONS TRADING CO. .....Opp. 296
PENNSYLVANIA PAPER STOCK CO...804
PENN PAPER & STOCK CO., INC...774
SALOMON, INC., A. ....Side Lines, 75-64

PAPER TESTER.
PERKINS & SONS, INC., R. F. 782
STORRS, BEMENT & CO., A. 817

PARAFFINE WAX.
MARBLE & CO., J. RUSSEL. 777

PENSTOCKS, IRON, WOOD.
HUNT MACHINE CO., RODNEY. ...772
McNEIL BOILER CO., THE. ....Opp. 8
RECORD FOUNDRY & MACHINE CO...797
STEARNS LUMBER CO., A. T. 813

PERFORATING MACHINERY.
DIETZ MACHINE WORKS. ......Opp. 320

PHOTO MOUNT BEVELING MACHINES.
DIETZ MACHINE WORKS. ......Opp. 320

PINIONS.
GANSCHOW CO., WM. 780

PLANER KNIVES.
EAGLE KNIFE & BAR CO..Head Lines, 11-64

PLATES.
EAGLE KNIFE & BAR CO..Head Lines, 11-64

PLAYING CARD MACHINERY.
DIETZ MACHINE WORKS. ......Opp. 320

PORTABLE ELEVATORS (REVOLVING).
N. Y. REVOLVING PORTABLE ELEVATOR CO. 783

PRESS ROLLS.
BELOIT IRON WORKS. ....Opp. 48
HEWITT MACHINE CO...Foot Lines, 66-386
IMPROVED PAPER MACHINERY CO.,
   Bet. 88 and 89
SHERBROOKE MACHINERY CO.,
   Bet. 240 and 241

PRESSES (Bundling).
POTDEVIN MACHINE CO. 772

PRESSURE GRINDER VALVES.
HUNT MACHINE CO., RODNEY. ...772

PRINTING PRESSES FOR ROLL OR SHEET PRODUCTS.
KIDDER PRESS CO. ....330 and 391

PULLEYS.
RECORD FOUNDRY & MACHINE CO...797

OLD AND NEW COTTON AND LINEN RAGS
WASTE PAPER OF ALL DESCRIPTIONS

MAURICE O'MEARA CO.
448-450 PEARL ST.
NEW YORK

KNIVES OF EVERY DESCRIPTION AND UNIFORMLY HIGH GRADE — **Eagle Knife and Bar Works** LAWRENCE :: :: MASS.

NEW ENGLAND QUARTZ CO. of N. Y.
150 NASSAU STREET, NEW YORK, N. Y.
GRANULATED QUARTZ for Water Filtration

Classified List of Advertisers — 15

PULP DRYING PLANTS.
PAGE
SWENSON EVAPORATOR CO. 781

PULP GRINDERS.
CARTHAGE MACHINE CO.,
    Foot Lines, 72-390
GLENS FALLS MACHINE CO.,
    Front Fly Leaf

PULP SCREENS.
BLACK-CLAWSON CO., THE
    Bet. 296 and 297

PULP STONES.
HARRISON, JAMES H. . Foot Lines, 578-702
LOMBARD & CO. .... Head Lines, 68-359
MANUFACTURERS' PAPER CO. .Opp. 4

PULP THICKENERS.
IMPROVED PAPER MACHINERY CO.,
    Bet. 88 and 89
SHERBROOKE MACHINERY CO.
    Bet. 240 and 241

PUMPS.
APPLETON MACHINE CO. 577-703
BELOIT IRON WORKS. .... Opp. 48
BLACK-CLAWSON CO., THE
    Bet. 296 and 297
CARTHAGE MACHINE CO.,
    Foot Lines, 72-390
CLAFLIN ENGINEERING CO., THE
    Bet. 256 and 257
HOLYOKE MACHINE CO.,
    Inside Front Cover
HUNT MACHINE CO., RODNEY. 772
RECORD FOUNDRY & MACHINE CO. .797
RICE, BARTON & FALES M. & I. CO. .776
SAVERY, THOS. H., JR. .... Opp. 320

QUARTZ (Granulated).
NEW ENGLAND QUARTZ CO.,
    Side Lines, 11-24

RAG CUTTERS.
BLACK-CLAWSON CO., THE,
    Bet. 296 and 297
HOLYOKE MACHINE CO. Inside Front Cover
NORWOOD ENGINEERING CO. 787
RICE, BARTON & FALES M. & I. CO. .776
TAYLOR, STILES & CO. 772

RAG DEALERS AND PACKERS.
ATTERBURY BROS., INC. 8
CANTASANA & BROS., V. G. 10
DARMSTADT, SCOTT & COURTNEY,
    Side Lines, 72-384
FEDERAL PAPER STOCK CO. 791
GENERAL PAPER STOCK CO. 807
GOLDSTEIN & SON, R. 774
GOTTESMAN & SON, M. .Side Lines, 67-363
JAFFE & CO. 788
KELLER & CO., E. J. .... Side Lines, 65-349
MAIN PAPER STOCK CO., INC. 788
MARQUARDT, INC., F. G. 815
MENDELSON BROS. PAPER STOCK CO.,
    Opp. 289
MOREY & CO. 812
O'MEARA, MAURICE. ..... Foot Lines, 11-24
PARSONS TRADING CO. .... Opp. 296
PENN PAPER & STOCK CO., INC. .. 804
PENNSYLVANIA PAPER STOCK CO. .774
SALOMON, INC., A. ...... Side Lines, 25-64

RAG AND PAPER-STOCK IMPORTERS—EXPORTERS.
ATTERBURY BROS., INC. 8
DARMSTADT, SCOTT & COURTNEY,
    Side Lines, 72-384
GOTTESMAN & SON, M. Side Lines, 67-363
KELLER & CO., E. J. .... Side Lines, 65-349
MARQUARDT, INC., F. G. 815
O'MEARA, MAURICE. ...... Foot Lines, 11-24
PARSONS TRADING CO. .... Opp. 296

RAG AND REFINING ENGINES.
PAGE
HOLYOKE MACHINE CO.,
    Inside Front Cover
HORNE & SONS CO., THE J. H.,
    Outside Back Cover
RICE, BARTON & FALES M. & I. CO. .776

RECLAIMING MACH'Y—SODA AND SULPHATE PULP.
SWENSON EVAPORATOR CO. 781

RED OXIDES.
WILLIAMS, C. K. & CO. 785

REFINING ENGINES.
APPLETON MACHINE CO.,
    Side Lines, 577-703

REWINDING MACHINES.
CAMERON MACHINE CO. .... Opp. 257
DIETZ MACHINE WORKS. .... Opp. 320
HUDSON MACHINE CO. 784
KIDDER PRESS CO. .... 330 and 391
LANGSTON CO., SAMUEL M. .... Opp. 360
RICE, BARTON & FALES M. & I. CO. .776

ROLL BARS AND BED PLATES.
EAGLE KNIFE & BAR CO. .Head Lines, 11-64
TAYLOR, STILES & CO. 772

ROLL GRINDING MACHINES.
FARRELL FOUNDRY & MACHINE CO.,
    778 and 779
LORDELL CAR WHEEL CO. 773
PERKINS & SON, INC., B. F. 782
ROY & SON, B. S. 811

ROLL PAPER SHEET CUTTERS.
CAMERON MACHINE CO. .... Opp. 257
DIETZ MACHINE WORKS. .... Opp. 320
KIDDER PRESS CO. .... 330 and 391
LANGSTON CO., SAMUEL. ...... Opp. 360

ROLL TURNING TOOLS.
DICKINSON, THOS. L. 781

ROSIN SIZE.
ARABOL MFG. CO.,
    Head Lines, 66-182, Side Lines, 71-351

ROTARY CARD CUTTERS.
DIETZ MACHINE WORKS. .... Opp. 320
LANGSTON CO., SAMUEL M. .... Opp. 360

ROTARY PRINTING PRESSES.
KIDDER PRESS CO. .... 330 and 391

RUBBER-COVERED ROLLS.
TEXTILE-FINISHING MACHINERY CO.,
    First Page, Front Fly Leaf

RUBBER ROLL AND TURNING TOOLS.
DICKINSON, THOS. L. 781

SALESBOOK PRINTING PRESSES.
KIDDER PRESS CO. .... 330 and 391

SATIN WHITE.
KLIPSTEIN & CO., A. ...... Bet. 64 and 65
WILLIAMS & CO., C. K. 785

SAVE ALLS.
IMPROVED PAPER MACHINERY CO.,
    Bet. 88 and 89
SAVERY, THOS. H., JR. .... Opp. 320
SHERBROOKE MACHINERY CO.
    Bet. 240 and 241

SAWING MACHINERY.
APPLETON MACHINE CO.,
    Side Lines, 577-703

RAW HIDE CUTTINGS AND BOW PICKERS FOR SIZING — **MAURICE O'MEARA CO.** 446-450 PEARL ST. NEW YORK

SUPERIOR QUALITY PROMPT SHIPMENTS — Facilities to Handle the Largest Orders

Eagle Knife and Bar Works — LAWRENCE :: :: MASS.

Classified List of Advertisers — 16

SCREEN PLATES. PAGE
CENTRAL MFG. CO. 806
EASTWOOD WIRE MFG. CO.....Opp. 24
RICE, BARTON & FALES M. & L. CO..776
UNION SCREEN PLATE CO....Opp. 4

SCREENS.
APPLETON MACHINE CO., Side Lines, 577-703
BELOIT IRON WORKS............Opp. 48

SCREENS—ROTARY.
IMPROVED PAPER MACHY. CO., Bet. 88 and 89
SAVERY, THOS. H., JR..........Opp. 320
SHERBROOKE MACHINERY CO., Bet. 240 and 241

SHAFTING.
HUNT MACHINE CO., RODNEY......772

SHEET METAL WORKERS.
VAN NOORDEN CO., E...........Opp. 25

SHINGLES—CYPRESS.
STEARNS LUMBER CO., A. T........813

SIZE PUMP.
PERKINS & SON, INC., B. F........782

SIZING.
ARABOL MFG. CO.....Head Lines, 66-182
Side Lines, 71-351
FECULOSE CO. OF AMERICA...Opp. 9

SKYLIGHTS.
VAN NOORDEN CO., E...........Opp. 25

SLITTERS AND WINDERS.
BELOIT IRON WORKS...........Opp. 48
CAMERON MACHINE CO..........Opp. 257
DIETZ MACHINE WORKS.........Opp. 320
HAMBLET MACHINE CO..............787
KIDDER PRESS CO ....330 and 391
LANGSTON CO., SAMUEL M.....Opp. 360
NORWOOD ENGINEERING CO.........787
RICE, BARTON & FALES M. & L. CO..776
TICONDEROGA MACHINE WORKS....781

SOAP POWDER.
MOREY & CO.......................812

SODA FIBRE.
ANDERSEN & CO., J............Opp. 367
BROWN COMPANY...............Opp. 289
BROWN & CO., CHAS. D............814
CHAMPION-INTERNATIONAL CO.Opp. 5
GOTTESMAN & SON, M. Side Lines, 67-363
OXFORD PAPER CO..................56
PARSONS TRADING CO.........Opp. 296
TICONDEROGA PULP AND PAPER CO., Bet. 362 and 363
WEST VIRGINIA PULP & PAPER CO..........Bet. 224 and 225

SODA RECOVERY.
SWENSON EVAPORATOR CO..........781

SPECIALTIES.
SAVERY, THOS. H., JR..........Opp. 320

SPIRAL CORE MACHINES.
LANGSTON CO., SAMUEL M.....Opp. 360

SPIRAL PIPING.
STANDARD SPIRAL PIPE WORKS....780

SPLITTER GRINDERS.
NORWOOD ENGINEERING CO........787

SPLITTERS.
APPLETON MACHINE CO., Side Lines, 577-703
CARTHAGE MACHINE CO., Foot Lines, 72-390

STEAM PRESSURE REGULATORS.
BOWES CO., INC., WALTER H..Opp. 9
RICE, BARTON & FALES M. & I. CO..776

STEAM AND WATER POWER DEVELOPMENTS. PAGE
CAREY, JAS. L....................790
CHAPMAN CO., INC., C. A.
Head Lines, 577-703
FERGUSON, HARDY S..Side Lines, 70-882
HARDY, GEO. F..............Opp. 25
WALLACE & CO., JOS. H.,
Foot Lines, 185-383

STEEL PRODUCTS.
EAGLE KNIFE & BAR CO.Head Lines, 11-64

STEEL WIRE BALE TIES.
WILSON, H. P. & H. F.............791

STOCK CUTTERS.
TAYLOR, STILES & CO.............772

STOKERS (Grate).
AUTOMATIC FURNACE CO., Bet. 192 and 193

STRAINER CLOTH.
LINDSAY WIRE WEAVING CO., Opp. 321

STRAW PULP.
ANDERSEN & CO., J............Opp. 367

STUFF CHESTS.
RECORD FOUNDRY & MACHINE CO..797
STEARNS LUMBER CO., A. T.......775

SUCTION-BOX COVERS.
EASTWOOD WIRE MFG. CO......Opp. 24
GILBERTS & NASH........Bet. 48 and 49

SULPHATE OF ALUMINA.
HARRISON'S, INC............Back Fly Leaf
KLIPSTEIN, A., & CO......Bet. 64 and 65
KUTTROFF, PICKHARDT & CO...Opp. 33
LENNIG & CO., CHAS..............782
PENNA. SALT MFG. CO.............777

SULPHATE RECOVERY.
SWENSON EVAPORATOR CO.........781

SULPHITE FIBRE.
ANDERSEN & CO., J............Opp. 367
BROWN COMPANY..............Opp. 289
BROWN & CO., CHAS. D............514
CHAMPION-INTERNATIONAL CO.Opp. 5
EASTERN MFG. CO............Opp. 256
GOTTESMAN & CO., INC., M.,
Side Lines, 67-363
ORONO PULP & PAPER CO.........796
OXFORD PAPER COMPANY...........56
PARSONS TRADING CO.........Opp. 296
WEST VIRGINIA PULP & PAPER CO., Bet. 224 and 225

SULPHUR.
UNION SULPHUR CO...Foot Lines, 67-183

SULPHUR BURNERS & OVENS.
CARTHAGE MACHINE CO., Foot Lines, 72-390
GLENS FALLS MACHINE CO., Front Fly Leaf

TANKS, WATER VATS, ETC.
HUNT MACHINE CO., RODNEY......772
STEARNS LUMBER CO., A. T.......813

TICKET PRINTING PRESSES.
KIDDER PRESS CO........330 and 391

TIES—STEEL WIRE BALE.
WILSON, H. P. & H. F............791

TIERING MACHINES.
N. Y. REVOLVING PORTABLE ELEVATOR CO......................783

TIMBER.
STEARNS LUMBER CO., A. T.......813

DIGESTER LININGS—GRANULATED QUARTZ
NEW ENGLAND QUARTZ CO. of N. Y.
150 NASSAU STREET, NEW YORK, N. Y.

OLD AND NEW COTTON AND LINEN RAGS
WASTE PAPER OF ALL DESCRIPTIONS

MAURICE O'MEARA CO.
448-450 PEARL ST.
NEW YORK

A. M. MEINCKE

Materials For

PAPERMAKING

Pearl Filler English China Clay

---

5 South Dearborn Street

CHICAGO   **ILLINOIS**

LUMEN BEARING COMPANY
BUFFALO, N. Y., U. S. A.

ACID-RESISTING CASTINGS
FOR PULP AND PAPER MILLS

BRONZE BEATER AND JORDAN KNIVES

Beater Bar   Acid Pipe   Jordan Knife after Bending

Digester Casting

HAVE YOUR ENGINEER CONSULT US

LUMEN BEARING COMPANY
BRASS FOUNDERS
BUFFALO, N. Y., U. S. A.

Classified List of Advertisers

TOILET PAPER MACHINERY.
DIETZ MACHINE WORKS......Opp. 320

TRAIN ORDERS (Blanks).
O'MALLEY CO., M. J...............789

TRANSVEYORS.
COWAN TRUCK CO................814

TRIMMING KNIVES.
EAGLE KNIFE & BAR CO.,
  Head Lines, 11-64

TRUCKS.
COWAN TRUCK CO................814

TUBS, STEEL RIVETED, WOOD.
HUNT MACHINE CO., RODNEY......772

TUBE MACHINES—AUTOMATIC TOILET ROLL.
DIETZ MACHINE WORKS......Opp. 320

TURBINES.
HOLYOKE MACHINE CO. Inside Front Cover
HUNT MACHINE CO., RODNEY......772
SAVERY, THOS. H., JR........Opp. 320

TURKEY UMBERS.
WILLIAMS, C. K., & CO...........785

ULTRAMARINE.
BREDT & CO., F..................791
KUTTROFF, PICKHARDT & CO...Opp. 33
ULTRAMARINE CO., THE............776

UNIONS—BALL.
DRAPER MANUFACTURING CO.......780

VACUUM PUMPS.
SAVERY, THOS. H., JR........Opp. 320

VALVE DISCS.
DRAPER MANUFACTURING CO.......780

VALVE FACING TOOLS.
DRAPER MANUFACTURING CO.......780

VALVES, GATE.
HUNT MACHINE CO., RODNEY......772
RECORD FOUNDRY & MACHINE CO..797

VARNISHES.
HAMPDEN PAINT & CHEMICAL CO.,
  Head Lines, 417-575

VATS.
HUNT MACHINE CO., RODNEY......772
STEARNS LUMBER CO., A. T........818

VENTILATING SYSTEMS.
PERKINS & SON, INC., B. F.......782
VAN NOORDEN CO., E.........Opp. 25

WASHER WIRES.
GLEESON, INC., THOS. E.,
  Head Lines, 67-183
LINDSAY WIRE WEAVING CO...Opp. 321
O'NEILL WIRE WORKS, JOS........783
WISCONSIN WIRE WORKS..........774

WASHERS.
HUNT MACHINE CO., RODNEY......772

WATER FILTERS.
GLENS FALLS MACHINE CO.,
  Front Fly Leaf
NORWOOD ENGINEERING CO........787

WATER SOFTENING AND PURIFYING APPARATUS.
NORWOOD ENGINEERING CO........787

WATER TANKS.
HUNT MACHINE CO., RODNEY......772
STEARNS LUMBER CO., A. T........813

WATER WHEELS—HORIZONTAL AND VERTICAL.
HUNT MACHINE CO., RODNEY......772

WAXING MACHINES.
POTDEVIN MACHINE CO............772

WEIGHT REGULATORS (Trimbey).
GLENS FALLS MACHINE CO.,
  Front Fly Leaf

WET MACHINES
CARTHAGE MACHINE CO.,
  Foot Lines, 72-390
GLENS FALLS MACHINE CO.,
  Front Fly Leaf
HOLYOKE MACHINE CO. Inside Front Cover
IMPROVED PAPER MACHINERY CO.,
  Bet. 88 and 89
RICE BARTON & FALES MACHINE & IRON CO.......................776
SHERBROOKE MACHINERY CO.
  Bet. 240 and 241

WINDERS.
TICONDEROGA MACHINE WORKS....781

WIRE BALE TIES.
WILSON, H. P. & H. F...........791

WIRE CLOTH.
BUCHANAN & BOLT WIRE CO........775
CABBLE EXCELSIOR WIRE MFG. CO.
  Bet. 256 and 257
CHENEY BIGELOW WIRE WORKS....775
EASTWOOD WIRE MFG. CO......Opp. 24
GLEESON, INC., THOS. E.,
  Head Lines, 67-183
LINDSAY WIRE WEAVING CO.,
  Opp. 321
O'NEILL WIRE WORKS, JOS........783
PARSONS TRADING CO.........Opp. 206
STANDARD WIRE WORKS...........775
WISCONSIN WIRE WORKS..........774

WIRES (Cylinder and Fourdrinier.)
BUCHANAN & BOLT WIRE CO........775
CABBLE EXCELSIOR WIRE MFG. CO.
  Bet. 256 and 257
CHENEY BIGELOW WIRE WORKS....775
EASTWOOD WIRE MFG. CO......Opp. 24
GLEESON, THOS. E., INC.,
  Head Lines, 67-183
LINDSAY WIRE WEAVING CO...Opp. 321
O'NEILL WIRE WORKS, JOS........783
PARSONS TRADING CO.........Opp. 206
STANDARD WIRE CO..............775
WISCONSIN WIRE WORKS..........774

WIRE AND FELT GUIDES.
GILBERTS & NASH........Bet. 48 and 40

WIRE SIGNS.
CHENEY BIGELOW WIRE WORKS....775

WOOD BARKER KNIVES.
EAGLE KNIFE & BAR CO..Head Lines, 11 64

WOOD BARKERS.
APPLETON MACH. CO..Side Lines, 577-703
CARTHAGE MACH. CO.,
  Foot Lines, 72-390

WOOD CHIPPER KNIVES.
EAGLE KNIFE & BAR CO.
  Head Lines, 11 64

HIGH GRADE Beater Roll Bars, Bed Plates, Jordan Fillings, Paper Mill Knives

EAGLE KNIFE AND BAR WORKS
LAWRENCE :: :: MASS.

QUARTZ FLOUR — New England Quartz Co. of New York, 150 Nassau Street, New York, N. Y.

18 Classified List of Advertisers

WOOD PULP. PAGE
ANDERSON & CO., J..........Opp. 367
ATTERBURY BROS., INC.............5
BROWN & CO., CHAS. D..........814
GOTTESMAN & CO., INC., M.,
 Side Lines, 67-363
PARSONS TRADING CO.......Opp. 296
SCANDINAVIAN-AMERICAN TRADING
 CO........................Opp. 297
WEST VIRGINIA PULP & PAPER CO.,
 Bet. 224 and 225

WOOD PULP BURNERS.
HALL, WARD & WALKER, INC...Opp. 321

WOOD-PULP KNIVES. PAGE
EAGLE KNIFE & BAR CO.,

WOOD-PULP STONES.
HARRISON, JAMES M.,
 Foot Lines, 578-702
LOMBARD & CO......Head Lines, 68-359
MANUFACTURERS PAPER CO....Opp. 4
 Head Lines, 11-64

WRAPPING PRINTING PRESSES.
KIDDER PRESS CO..........330 and 391

YELLOW OCHRE.
WILLIAMS, C. K., & CO..............785

Paper and Stationery Trades

ADDING MACHINE ROLLS. PAGE
ELLIOTT CO., W. R..................818
PERRY CO., INC., C. E..............820
SHEA, STURM CO.........Back Fly Leaf

ALBUM BOARD PAPER.
MUNROE FELT & PAPER CO.,
 Back Fly Leaf

BAG PAPER.
CRAIG & CO., H. G.............Opp. 367

BANK NOTE.
CRANE & CO........................795

BIBLE PAPERS.
SMITH PAPER CO....................802

BINDERS' BOARD.
BAIRD & BARTLETT CO..............819
BANKER, J. W..................Opp. 434
LINDENMEYR & SONS, HENRY,
 Opp. 73
SHRYOCK BROTHERS.................791

BLANKS.
FALULAH PAPER CO............Opp. 366

BLOTTING PAPER.
ALBEMARLE PAPER MFG. CO........804
EATON DIKEMAN CO................804
LINDENMEYR & SONS, HENRY,
 Opp. 73
STANDARD PAPER MFG. CO.,
 Foot Lines, 580-704

BLUEPRINT PAPER.
AMERICAN WRITING PAPER CO.,
 Bet. 272 and 273

BOARDS—OIL & STENCIL.
O'MALLEY CO., THE M. J..........789
ROGERS PAPER MFG. CO........Opp. 192

BOND PAPER.
ALLEN PAPER CO...................808
AMERICAN WRITING PAPER CO.,
 Bet. 272 and 273
BERMINGHAM & PROSSER CO...Opp. 272
CAREW MFG. CO............Third Cover
CARTER & CO., INC., JOHN.........819
CARTER, RICE & CO., CORP........819
CHEMICAL PAPER MFG. CO..........798
CRANE & CO.......................795
CROCKER-McELWAIN CO.............800
CROTTEAU, DICK...................807
DOBLER & MUDGE...................789
EASTERN MFG. CO.............Opp. 256
GILBERT PAPER CO., FRANK,
 Bet. 48 and 49
HAMMERMILL PAPER CO. Bet. 296 and 297
HAMPSHIRE PAPER CO......Third Cover

BOND PAPER—Continued.
 PAGE
HOWARD PAPER CO.................808
KALAMAZOO VEGETABLE PARCH-
 MENT PAPER CO...........Opp. 341
KEITH PAPER CO...................792
LINDENMEYR & SONS, H......Opp. 72
MILLERS FALLS PAPER CO.........796
MOREY & CO......................812
MOUNTAIN MILL PAPER CO.........803
NEENAH PAPER CO......Bet. 212 and 213
RISING PAPER CO., B. D..........800
SEAMAN PAPER CO.................808
STONE & ANDREW, INC.............814
STORRS, BEMENT & CO. A.........817
STRATHMORE PAPER CO.............797
TAYLOR-LOGAN CO. (PAPERMAK-
 ERS).........................799
U. S. PAPER CORP.................802
VON OLKER-SNELL PAPER CO.....820
WESTON CO., BYRON...............793
WHITING PAPER CO................798

BOND PAPERS IN ROLLS.
ELLIOTT & CO., W. R..............818
PERRY CO., INC., C. E............820

BOOK PAPER.
ADVERTISERS PAPER MILLS.........799
ALLEN PAPER CO., A. C...........808
AMERICAN WRITING PAPER CO.,
 Bet. 272 and 273
ARNOLD-ROBERTS CO...............817
BARE PAPER CO., THE D. M......790
BERMINGHAM & PROSSER CO..Opp. 272
BRYANT PAPER CO.............Opp. 193
CARTER & CO., JOHN..............819
CARTER, RICE & CO., CORP.......819
CHAMPION-INTERNATIONAL CO..Opp. 5
CLAFLIN & CO., INC., WM. H.....818
CROTTEAU, DICK..................807
DOBLER & MUDGE..................789
LINDENMEYR & SONS, HENRY...Opp. 73
MERRIMAC PAPER CO..........Opp. 362
MILLER FALLS PAPER CO..........796
OXFORD PAPER CO..................56
POLAND PAPER CO.......Bet. 256 and 257
SEAMAN PAPER CO.................809
STONE & ANDREW, INC.............818
STORRS, BEMENT & CO............817
STRATHMORE PAPER CO.............797
TICONDEROGA PULP & PAPER CO.,
 Bet. 362 and 363
TILESTON & HOLLINGSWORTH CO..816
UNITED STATES PAPER CORP......802
VON OLKER-SNELL PAPER CO.....820
WANAQUE RIVER PAPER CO..........2
WATERVLIET PAPER CO.............802
WEST VIRGINIA PULP & PAPER CO.,
 Bet. 224 and 225
WILLIAMS & CO., CHAS. W.,
 Bet. 72 and 73

OLD AND NEW COTTON AND LINEN RAGS
WASTE PAPER OF ALL DESCRIPTIONS

MAURICE O'MEARA CO.
448-450 PEARL ST.
NEW YORK

Classified List of Advertisers

BOX BOARDS.
ALTON BOXBOARD & PAPER CO..Opp. 192
BAIRD & BARTLETT COMPANY......819
BANKER, J. W..................Opp. 434
BOYLE, LUKE.......................788
CHEMICAL PAPER MFG. CO...........798
CHICAGO COATED BOARD CO...Opp. 192
HAVERHILL BOXBOARD CO............798
LINDENMEYR & SONS, HENRY...Opp. 73
McEWAN BROS........Foot Lines, 65-181
MOREY & CO........................812
SHRYOCK BROTHERS..................791
SPAULDING & TEWKESBURY CO.Opp. 368
STANDARD PAPER CO.................806

BOX COVERING PAPER.
HAMPDEN GLAZED PAPER & CARD
CO..................Bet. 362 and 363
WILLIAMS & CO., CHAS. W.
Bet. 72 and 73

BOX AND SHOE M'F'RS MATERIALS.
NASHUA GUMMED & COATED PAPER
CO...............................814
WILLIAMS & CO., CHAS. W.
Bet. 72 and 73

BRISTOLS AND BLANKS (WHITE).
FRANKLIN PAPER CO....Bet. 362 and 363

BRISTOLS.
CHEMICAL PAPER MFG. CO...........798
CROCKER-McELWAIN CO..............800
KEITH PAPER CO...................792
LINDENMEYR & SONS, HENRY..Opp. 73
LINTON BROS...................Opp. 363
MILLERS FALLS PAPER CO...........796
MOUNTAIN MILL PAPER CO...........803
RISING PAPER CO., B. D...........800
SEAMAN PAPER CO..................809
STANDARD PAPER CO................806

BUTTER DISHES.
STIMPSON & CO....................819
STONE & FORSYTH CO...............817

CARD CUTTING.
HAMPDEN GLAZED PAPER & CARD
CO.................Bet. 362 and 363
PERRY CO., INC., C. E............820

CARD AND CARDBOARD.
ALTON BOX BOARD & PAPER CO......192
ARNOLD ROBERTS CO., THE..........817
CARTER, JOHN, & CO., INC.........819
CARTER, RICE & CO., CORP.........819
CHICAGO COATED BOARD CO.........192
FALULAH PAPER CO............Opp. 366
HAMPDEN GLAZED PAPER AND
CARD CO...........Bet. 362 and 363
HOLYOKE CARD & PAPER CO.
Opp. 362
LINDENMEYR & SONS, HENRY...Opp. 73
LINTON BROS. & CO..........Opp. 362
NATIONAL COATED PAPER CORP.
Bet. 362 and 363
NEW YORK-NEW ENGLAND PAPER....799
RHODE ISLAND CARDBOARD CO..
Opp. 363
STORRS & BEMENT CO., A...........817
UNITED STATES PAPER CORP.........802
VON OLKER-SNELL PAPER CO.........820
WHITMORE MFG. CO....Bet. 362 and 363
WILLIAMS & CO., CHAS. W.Bet. 72 and 73

CARD MIDDLES.
STANDARD PAPER CO................806

CARPET LINING PAPER.
NEWTON PAPER CO......Bet. 362 and 363
MUNROE FELT & PAPER CO.
Back Fly Leaf

CARTONS.
HOLLIS & DUNCAN..................810

CASE LINING, WATERPROOF.
NATIONAL WATERPROOFING CO.,
Head Lines, 69-181
SAFEPACK PAPER MILLS.
Bet. 362 and 363

CASH REG. PAPER ROLLS.
ELLIOTT CO., W. R................818
PERRY CO., INC., C. E............820

CEMENT AND FLOUR SACK PAPERS.
HOLLINGSWORTH & VOSE CO..........817
ORONO PULP & PAPER CO............796

CHIP AND PAPER STOCK BOARDS.
BAIRD & BARTLETT CO..............819
BANKER, J. W................Opp. 434
BOYLE, LUKE......................788

CIGARETTE PAPER.
AMERICAN WRITING PAPER CO.,
Bet. 272 and 273
SMITH PAPER CO...................802

CLOTH BOARD.
LINDENMEYR & SONS, HENRY....Opp. 73

CLOTHS—LINING.
WILLIAMSON & CO., T..............784

CLOTH LINED STOCKS.
IDEAL COATED PAPER CO.,
Bet. 362 and 363
NASHUA GUMMED AND COATED
PAPER CO.........................814
SAFEPACK PAPER MILLS.
Bet. 362 and 363
WILLIAMS & CO., CHAS. W..Bet. 72 and 73

COATED BOARD.
BAIRD & BARTLETT CO..............819
CHICAGO COATED BOARD CO...Opp. 192
FALULAH PAPER CO............Opp. 366
SEAMAN PAPER CO..................809
STANDARD PAPER CO................806

COATED PAPER.
AMERICAN WRITING PAPER CO.,
Bet. 272 and 273
ARNOLD-ROBERTS CO., THE..........817
BRYANT PAPER CO.............Opp. 193
CHAMPION-INTERNATIONAL CO..Opp. 5
DOBLER & MUDGE...................789
FALULAH PAPER CO............Opp. 366
HAMPDEN GLAZED PAPER AND
CARD CO...........Bet. 362 and 363
HOLYOKE CARD & PAPER CO..Opp. 362
IDEAL COATED PAPER CO.,
Bet. 362 and 363
LINDENMEYR & SONS, HENRY...Opp. 73
McENERY PAPER CO.,
Foot Lines, 104-224
MERRIMAC PAPER CO..........Opp. 362
NASHUA GUMMED AND COATED PA-
PER CO...........................814
NATIONAL COATED PAPER CORP.
Bet. 362 and 363
RHODE ISLAND CARDBOARD CO..
Opp. 362 and 363
SEAMAN PAPER CO..................809
STANDARD PAPER MFG. CO.,
Foot Lines, 580-704
STONE & ANDREW, INC..............818
STORRS, BEMENT & CO., A..........817
UNITED STATES PAPER CORP.........802
WATERVLIET PAPER CO..............802
WEST VIRGINIA PULP & PAPER CO..
Bet. 224 and 225
WHITMORE MFG. CO....Bet. 362 and 363
WILLIAMS & CO., CHAS. W.
Bet. 72 and 73

COATING PAPERS.
ORONO PULP & PAPER CO............784
WEST VIRGINIA PULP & PAPER CO..
Bet. 224 and 225

CRUCIBLE JORDAN STEELS
Hard and Tough — High Tensile Strength

EAGLE KNIFE AND BAR WORKS
LAWRENCE :: :: MASS.

Classified List of Advertisers

COLLATING.
ELLIOTT CO., W. R. 818

COMBINATION BOARDS.
BAIRD & BARTLETT CO. 819
HAVERHILL BOXBOARD CO. 798

CONFETTI.
PERRY CO., INC., C. F. 820

COPYING BOOKS.
O'MALLEY CO., M. J. 789

CORDAGE.
BANKER, J. W. ....Opp. 434
STIMPSON & CO. 819

CORRUGATED
BAIRD & BARTLETT CO. 819
NEWTON PAPER CO. ....Bet. 362 and 363

COTTON SAMPLING.
NEWTON PAPER CO. ....Bet. 362 and 363

COVER PAPER.
ADVERTISERS PAPER MILLS. 799
AMERICAN WRITING PAPER CO.,
  Bet. 272 and 273
ARNOLD ROBERTS CO., THE. 817
CHEMICAL PAPER MFG. CO. 798
HAMMERMILL PAPER CO.
  Bet. 296 and 297
HAMPDEN GLAZED PAPER & CARD
  CO. ....Bet. 362 and 363
HOLYOKE CARD & PAPER CO.
  Opp. 362 and 363
KEITH PAPER CO. 792
LINDENMEYR & SONS, HENRY. .Opp. 792
MILLERS FALLS PAPER CO. 796
NEW YORK-NEW ENGLAND CO. 799
PENINSULAR PAPER CO. 805
STONE & ANDREW, INC. 818
TAYLOR-LOGAN CO. (PAPERMAK-
  ERS) 799
UNITED STATES PAPER CORP. 802
VON OLKER-SNELL PAPER CO. 786

DOUBLE AIR DRIED AND PASTED BOARDS.
BAIRD & BARTLETT CO. 819

DRAWING PAPER.
CHEMICAL PAPER MFG. CO. 798
EASTERN MFG. CO. ....Opp. 256
LINDENMEYR & SONS, HENRY. .Opp. 73
STRATHMORE PAPER CO. 797
WILLIAMS & CO., CHAS. W.,
  Bet. 72 and 73

DRINKING CUPS.
SHERMAN ENVELOPE CO. 66

DUPLEX.
NEWTON PAPER CO. ....Bet. 362 and 363

ELECTRIC BOARD.
ROGERS PAPER MFG. CO. .....Opp. 192

EMBOSSED PAPERS.
HAMPDEN GLAZED PAPER & CARD
  CO. ....Bet. 362 and 363
NATIONAL COATED PAPER CORP.,
  Bet. 362 and 363

ENAMELED BOOK.
LINDENMEYR & SONS, HENRY. .Opp. 73
MERRIMAC PAPER CO. ....Opp. 362
WILLIAMS & CO., CHAS. W.,
  Bet. 72 and 73

ENAMELED BLOTTING.
HAMPDEN GLAZED PAPER AND
  CARD CO. .....Bet. 362 and 363
WILLIAMS & CO., CHAS. W.,
  Bet. 72 and 73

ENVELOPE PAPER.
AMERICAN WRITING PAPER CO.,
  Bet. 272 and 273
CROCKER-McELWAIN CO. 800
EASTERN MFG. CO. ....Opp. 256
HOWARD PAPER CO. 808
LINDENMEYR & SONS, HENRY. .Opp. 73
NEWTON FALLS PAPER CO. ...Opp. 73
POLAND PAPER CO. ....Bet. 256 and 257
VON OLKER-SNELL PAPER CO. 820
WEST VIRGINIA PULP & PAPER CO.,
  Bet. 224 and 225

ENVELOPES.
CARTER, JOHN, & CO., INC. 819
CARTER, RICE & CO., CORP. 819
CONTINENTAL PAPER BAG CO. ...409
HOLLIS & DUNCAN. 810
ILLINOIS ENVELOPE CO. 808
SHEA, STURM CO. ....Back Fly Leaf
SHERMAN ENVELOPE CO. 66
STONE & ANDREW, INC. 818
STORRS, BEMENT & CO., A. 817
U. S. ENVELOPE CO. ....Opp. 435

EXPRESS PAPERS.
MUNROE FELT & PAPER CO.,
  Back Fly Leaf
NEWTON PAPER CO. ....Bet. 362 and 363

EYELETTING AND PUNCHING.
PERRY CO., INC., C. F. 820

FANCY PAPERS.
HAMPDEN GLAZED PAPER & CARD
  CO. ....Bet. 362 and 363
LINDENMEYR & SONS, HENRY. .Opp. 73
NASHUA GUMMED AND COATED PA-
  PER CO. 814
WILLIAMS & CO., CHAS. W. Bet. 72 and 73

FELT PAPERS.
MUNROE FELT & PAPER CO.,
  Back Fly Leaf
NEWTON PAPER CO. ....Bet. 362 and 363

FIBRE BOARDS.
BAIRD & BARTLETT CO. 819
LINDENMEYR & SONS, HENRY. .Opp. 73
ROGERS PAPER MFG. CO. .....Opp. 192

FIBRE PAPERS (SULPHITE).
BROWN COMPANY. ....Opp. 289
NEWTON FALLS PAPER CO. ...Opp. 73

FOLDING BOX BOARDS.
BAIRD & BARTLETT CO. 819
LINDENMEYR & SONS, HENRY. .Opp. 73
McEWAN BROS. ....Foot Lines, 65-181

FOLDING PAPER.
MILLERS FALLS PAPER CO. 796
ROGERS PAPER MFG. CO. .....Opp. 192

FRENCH FOLIO.
BRYANT PAPER CO. ....Opp. 193

FRICTION BOARD.
HARTFORD CITY PAPER CO. 807

FRUIT WRAPPING.
NEWTON PAPER CO. ....Bet. 362 and 363

GLASSINE PAPER.
HARTFORD CITY PAPER CO. 807
LINDENMEYR & SONS, HENRY. .Opp. 73
WILLIAMS & CO., CHAS. W. Bet. 72 and 73

NEW ENGLAND QUARTZ CO. of N. Y.
150 NASSAU STREET, NEW YORK, N. Y.
DIGESTER LININGS—GRANULATED QUARTZ

OLD AND NEW COTTON AND LINEN RAGS
WASTE PAPER OF ALL DESCRIPTIONS

MAURICE O'MEARA CO.
448-450 PEARL ST.
NEW YORK

Classified List of Advertisers

GLAZED PAPER.
BAIRD & BARTLETT CO............819
CARTER, JOHN, & CO., INC........819
DOBLER & MUDGE................789
HAMPDEN GLAZED PAPER AND
  CARD CO..........Bet. 362 and 363
HOLYOKE CARD & PAPER CO..Opp. 362
LINDENMEYR & SONS, HENRY..Opp. 73
McENERY PAPER CO..Foot Lines, 104-224
MOREY & CO....................812
NASHUA GUMMED AND COATED PAPER CO........................814
NATIONAL COATED PAPER CORP.,
  Bet. 362 and 363
ROGERS PAPER MFG. CO......Opp. 192
WILLIAMS & CO., CHAS. W.,
  Bet. 72 and 73

GREASE-PROOF PAPERS.
AMERICAN WRITING PAPER CO.,
  Bet. 272 and 273
HARTFORD CITY PAPER CO......807
RHODE ISLAND CARD BOARD CO.,
  Opp. 363
WILLIAMS & CO., CHAS. W.,
  Bet. 72 and 73

GUIDE CARDS.
ROGERS PAPER MFG. CO......Opp. 192

GUMMED CLOTH AND PAPER SPECIALTIES
IDEAL COATED PAPER CO.,
  Bet. 362 and 363
MID-STATES GUMMED PAPER CO....796
NASHUA GUMMED AND COATED PAPER CO........................814
SHEA, STURM CO........Back Fly Leaf
WILLIAMS & CO., CHAS. W.,
  Bet. 72 and 73

HANGING.
CRAIG & CO., H. G............Opp. 367
MUNROE FELT & PAPER CO.,
  Back Fly Leaf

HARDWARE PAPER.
NEWTON PAPER CO....Bet. 362 and 363

HYGIENIC PAPER SPECIALTIES.
STONE & FORSYTH CO............814

ICE BLANKETS.
KALAMAZOO VEGETABLE PARCHMENT CO...................Opp. 361

ICE CREAM AND OYSTER PAIL BOARDS.
BAIRD & BARTLETT CO............819

INSULATING PAPER.
NEWTON PAPER CO....Bet. 362 and 363
ROGERS PAPER MFG. CO......Opp. 192

JACQUARD BOARD.
BAIRD & BARTLETT CO............819
ROGERS PAPER MFG. CO......Opp. 192

JAPANESE (IMPORTED) PAPERS.
STONE & ANDREW, INC............818

JUTE MANILA.
BANKER, J. W..............Opp. 434
NEWTON PAPER CO.....Bet. 362 and 363

KRAFT PAPER.
ANDREWS PAPER CO..............820
BANKER, J. W..............Opp. 434
BROWN COMPANY............Opp. 289
CHERRY RIVER PAPER CO..........2
LINDENMEYR & SONS, HENRY..Opp. 73
MUNROE CO., D. F..............820
MUNROE FELT & PAPER CO.,
  Back Fly Leaf
NEWTON FALLS PAPER CO....Opp. 73
ORONO PULP & PAPER CO........796
UNITED STATES PAPER CORP......802
VON OLKER-SNELL PAPER CO......820
WAUSAU SULPHATE FIBRE CO..Opp. 353
WILLIAMS & CO., CHAS. W.,
  Bet. 72 and 73

KRAFT PARCHMENT.
NEWTON FALLS PAPER CO....Opp. 73

LABEL PAPER.
HAMPDEN GLAZED PAPER & CARD
  CO..............Bet. 362 and 363
HOLYOKE CARD & PAPER CO..Opp. 362
IDEAL COATED PAPER CO.,
  Bet. 362 and 363
LINDENMEYR & SONS, HENRY..Opp. 73
MERRIMAC PAPER CO........Opp. 362
NASHUA GUMMED AND COATED PAPER CO........................814
NATIONAL COATED PAPER CORP.
  Bet. 362 and 363
WEST VIRGINIA PULP & PAPER CO.,
  Bet. 224 and 225
WILLIAMS & CO., CHAS. W.,
  Bet. 72 and 73

LEATHER BOARD.
ROGERS PAPER MFG. CO......Opp. 192

LEDGER PAPERS.
AMERICAN WRITING PAPER CO.,
  Bet. 272 and 273
BROWN PAPER CO., L. L........Opp. 273
CAREW MFG. CO......Inside Back Cover
CROTTEAU, DICK................807
EASTERN MFG. CO..........Opp. 256
HAMMERMILL PAPER CO.,
  Bet. 296 and 297
HOWARD PAPER CO..............808
KEITH PAPER CO...............792
LINDENMEYR & SONS, HENRY..Opp. 73
MILLERS FALLS PAPER CO........796
MOUNTAIN MILL PAPER CO......803
NEENAH PAPER CO....Bet. 212 and 213
RISING PAPER CO., B. D.........800
STRATHMORE PAPER CO..........797
UNITED STATES PAPER CORP......802
VON OELKER-SNELL PAPER CO....820
WESTON COMPANY, BYRON......793
WHITING PAPER CO.............798

LINEN PAPERS.
AMERICAN WRITING PAPER CO.,
  Bet. 272 and 273
BROWN PAPER CO., L. L........Opp. 273
CAREW MFG. CO......Inside Back Cover
CHEMICAL PAPER MFG. CO......798
CRANE, Z. & W. M.............794
CRANE & CO...................795
CROCKER-McELWAIN CO..........800
CROTTEAU, DICK................807
EASTERN MFG. CO..........Opp. 256
ESLEECK MFG. CO..............796
HAMMERMILL PAPER CO.,
  Bet. 296 and 297
HAMPSHIRE PAPER CO..Inside Back Cover
KEITH PAPER CO...............792
LINDENMEYR & SONS, HENRY..Opp. 73
McENERY PAPER CO...Foot Lines, 104-224
MILLERS FALLS PAPER CO........796
MOUNTAIN MILL PAPER CO......803
RISING PAPER CO., D. D.........800
SEAMAN PAPER CO..............809
STORRS, BEMENT & CO., A......817
STRATHMORE PAPER CO..........797
TAYLOR-LOGAN CO., PAPER MAKERS........................799
UNITED STATES PAPER CORP......809
WESTON COMPANY, BYRON......793
WHITING PAPER CO.............798
WILLIAMS & CO., CHAS. W..Bet. 72 and 73

QUALITY SELLS The Merit of our Products, and Quick Shipments are what Developed our Business

EAGLE KNIFE AND BAR WORKS
LAWRENCE :: :: MASS.

Quartz Flour — *New England Quartz Co. of New York, 150 Nassau Street, New York, N. Y.*

Classified List of Advertisers

LINING. PAGE
KALAMAZOO VEGETABLE PARCHMENT CO. .... Opp. 361
MUNROE FELT & PAPER CO.,
 Back Fly Leaf
NEWTON PAPER CO. .... Bet. 362 and 363

LIQUID SOAP (Dispensers).
DOMESTIC MILLS PAPER CO. 785

LITHO BLOTTING PAPER.
HAMPDEN GLAZED PAPER & CARD CO. .... Bet. 362 and 363

LITHOGRAPH PAPER.
AMERICAN WRITING PAPER CO.,
 Bet. 272 and 273
BARE PAPER CO., THE D. M. 790
CHAMPION-INTERNATIONAL CO. . Opp. 5
HAMPDEN GLAZED PAPER AND CARD CO. .... Bet. 362 and 363
HOLYOKE CARD & PAPER CO. .. Opp. 362
LINDENMEYR & SONS, HENRY .. Opp. 73
MERRIMAC PAPER CO. .... Opp. 362
NASHUA GUMMED AND COATED PAPER CO. 814
NATIONAL COATED PAPER CORP.,
 Bet. 362 and 363
OXFORD PAPER CO. 56
RHODE ISLAND CARDBOARD CO. Opp. 363
TILESTON & HOLLINGSWORTH CO. .. 816
WATERVLIET PAPER CO. 802
WEST VIRGINIA PULP & PAPER CO.,
 Bet. 224 and 225
WHITMORE MFG. CO. .... Bet. 362 and 363
WILLIAMS & CO., CHAS. W. Bet. 72 and 73

LUNCH ROLLS.
HOFFMAN, RICHARD S. 803

MAGAZINE WRAPPERS.
STONE & ANDREW, INC. 818

MANIFOLD PAPERS.
DOMESTIC MILLS PAPER CO. 785
ESLEECK MFG. CO. 796
HARTFORD CITY PAPER CO. 807

MANILA LINED BOARD.
BAIRD & BARTLETT CO. 819

MANILA AND FIBRE PAPER
ANDREWS PAPER CO. 820
BANKER, J. W. .... Opp. 434
BOYLE, LUKE. 788
CLAFLIN & CO., INC., WM. H. 818
CRAIG & CO., H. G. .... Opp. 367
EASTERN MFG. CO. .... Opp. 256
HOLLINGSWORTH & VOSE CO. 817
HOLLINGSWORTH & WHITNEY CO. .. 816
LINDENMEYR & SONS, HENRY,
 Opp. 73
MOREY & CO. 812
MUNROE CO., D. F. 820
MUNROE FELT & PAPER CO.,
 Back Fly Leaf
ORONO PULP & PAPER CO. 796
ROBERTSON PAPER CO. 224
SPAULDING & TEWKESBURY CO. Opp. 366
STIMPSON & CO. 819
TICONDEROGA PULP AND PAPER CO. .... Bet. 362 and 363
UNITED STATES PAPER CORP. 802
VON OLKER-SNELL PAPER CO. 820

MANUFACTURERS' AGENTS.
CRAIG & CO., H. G. .... Opp. 367
MANUFACTURERS PAPER CO. 4
McENERY PAPER CO. . Foot Lines, 104-224

MAP PAPERS.
AMERICAN WRITING PAPER CO.,
 Bet. 272 and 273
EASTERN MFG. CO. .... Opp. 256
LINDENMEYR & SONS, HENRY,
 Opp. 73
WILLIAMS & CO., CHAS. W. Bet. 72 and 73

MAT BOARD. PAGE
STRATHMORE PAPER CO. 797

MEMORANDUM BOOK COVERS.
HAMPDEN GLAZED PAPER & CARD CO. .... Bet. 362 and 363

MILL BLANKS.
McEWAN BROS. ...... Foot Lines, 65-181

MILL WRAPPERS.
MUNROE FELT & PAPER CO.,
 Back Fly Leaf
NEWTON PAPER CO. .... Bet. 362 and 363

MIMEOGRAPH PAPER.
BARE PAPER CO., THE D. M. 790
LINDENMEYR & SONS, HENRY,
 Opp. 73

MUSIC PAPER.
TILESTON & HOLLINGSWORTH CO. 816

NAPKINS.
ANDREWS PAPER CO. 820
LINTON & SCOTT. .... Opp. 352
NORTHERN PAPER MILLS. .... Opp. 361

NEWS BOARD.
BAIRD & BARTLETT CO. 819
BOYLE, LUKE. 788
LINDENMEYR, & SONS, HENRY,
 Opp. 73
McEWAN BROS. ..... Foot Lines, 65 and 181

NEWS PAPER.
ALLEN PAPER CO., A. C. 808
BAIRD & BARTLETT CO. 819
BANKER, J. W. .... Opp. 434
BROWN COMPANY. .... Opp. 289
CLAFLIN & CO., INC., WM. H. 818
CRAIG & CO., H. G. .... Opp. 367
LINDENMEYR & SONS, HENRY,
 Opp. 73
MOREY & CO. 812
MUNROE CO., D. F. 820
VON OLKER-SNELL PAPER CO. 820

NURSERY BLANKETS.
KALAMAZOO VEGETABLE PARCHMENT CO. .... Opp. 361

OIL BOARDS AND PAPER.
O'MALLEY CO., THE M. J. 789
ROBERTSON PAPER CO. 224
ROGERS PAPER MFG. CO. ..... Opp. 192

ONION SKIN PAPERS.
BRYANT PAPER CO. .... Opp. 193
DOMESTIC MILLS PAPER CO. 785
ESLEECK MFG. CO. 796
HARTFORD CITY PAPER CO. 807
KEITH PAPER CO. 792
LINDENMEYR & SONS, HENRY,
 Opp. 73
WILLIAMS & CO., CHAS. W. Bet. 72 and 73

PAD MANUFACTURERS.
ELLIOTT CO., W. R. 818
PERRY CO., INC., C. E. 820

PAPER BAGS.
ANDREWS PAPER CO. 820
CARTER, RICE & CO., CORP. 819
CLAFLIN & CO., INC., WM. H. 818
CONTINENTAL PAPER BAG CO. 406
HOLLINGSWORTH & WHITNEY. 816
HOLLIS & DUNCAN. 810
MUNROE CO., D. F. 820
STANDARD PAPER BAG CO. 814
STIMPSON & CO. 785
STONE & FORSYTH CO. 819

PAPER BAGS ON ROLLS.
STANDARD PAPER BAG CO. 410

OLD AND NEW COTTON AND LINEN RAGS
WASTE PAPER OF ALL DESCRIPTIONS

MAURICE O'MEARA CO.
448-450 PEARL ST.
NEW YORK

BARKER & CHIPPER KNIVES For the Hard Places TRY THEM

EAGLE KNIFE AND BAR WORKS LAWRENCE :: :: MASS

Classified List of Advertisers 23

PAPER CUTTING. PAGE
PERRY CO., INC., C. E. 820

PAPER DISH CLOTHS.
KALAMAZOO VEGETABLE PARCHMENT CO. .... Opp. 361

PAPER EXPORTERS—IMPORTERS.
IBBOTSON, JR., WALTER 784
PARSONS TRADING CO. .... Opp. 296
WILLIAMS & CO., CHAS. W. ..Bet. 72 and 73

PAPER MANUFACTURERS.
ADVERTISERS PAPER MILLS 799
ALBEMARLE PAPER MFG. CO. 804
AMERICAN WRITING PAPER CO.,
Bet. 272 and 273
BARE PAPER CO., THE D. M. 790
BROWN COMPANY .... Opp. 289
BROWN PAPER CO., L. L. .... Opp. 273
CAREW MFG. CO. .... Third Cover
CHAMPION-INTERNATIONAL CO. ..Opp. 5
CHEMICAL PAPER MFG. CO. 798
CHERRY RIVER PAPER CO. 2
CONTINENTAL PAPER BAG CO. 410
CRANE & CO. 795
CRANE, Z. & W. M. 794
CROCKER-McELWAIN CO. 800
EASTERN MFG. CO. .... Opp. 256
EATON-DIKEMAN CO. 804
ESLEECK MFG. CO. 796
FALULAH PAPER CO. 366
FRANKLIN PAPER CO. ..Bet. 362 and 363
GILBERT PAPER CO., FRANK.
Bet. 48 and 49
HAMMERMILL PAPER CO.,
Bet. 296 and 297
HAMPSHIRE PAPER CO. ..Third Cover
HARTFORD CITY PAPER Co. 807
HAVERHILL BOXBOARD CO. 798
HOLLINGSWORTH & VOSE CO. 817
HOLLINGSWORTH & WHITNEY CO. . 816
HOWARD PAPER CO. 808
KALAMAZOO VEGETABLE PARCHMENT CO. .... Opp. 361
KEITH PAPER CO. 792
McEWAN BROS. .... Foot Lines, 65-181
MERRIMAC PAPER CO. .... Opp. 362
MILLERS FALLS PAPER CO. 796
MOUNTAIN MILL PAPER CO. 803
MUNROE FELT & PAPER CO.
Back Fly Leaf
NASHUA GUMMED AND COATED PAPER CO. 814
NEENAH PAPER CO. .... Bet. 212 and 213
NEWTON FALLS PAPER CO. .... Opp. 73
NEWTON PAPER CO. .. Bet. 362 and 363
NEW YORK-NEW ENGLAND CO. ... 799
NORTHERN PAPER MILLS .... Opp. 361
ORONO PULP & PAPER CO. 796
OXFORD PAPER CO. 56
PENINSULAR PAPER CO. 803
POLAND PAPER CO. ..... Bet. 256 and 257
RISING PAPER CO., B. D. 800
ROBERTSON PAPER CO. 224
ROGERS PAPER MFG. CO., THE..Opp. 192
SEAMAN PAPER CO. 809
SHRYOCK BROS. 2
SMITH PAPER CO. 791
STANDARD PAPER CO. 806
STANDARD PAPER MFG. CO.,
Foot Lines, 580-704
STRATFORD PAPER CO. 802
STRATHMORE PAPER CO. 707
TAYLOR-LOGAN CO., PAPERMAKERS 799
TILESTON & HOLLINGSWORTH CO. .816
WANAQUE RIVER PAPER CO. 2
WAUSAU SULPHATE FIBRE CO. .Opp. 353
WEST VIRGINIA PULP & PAPER CO.,
Bet. 224 and 225
WESTON COMPANY, BYRON 793
WHITING PAPER CO. 798

PAPER DEALERS. PAGE
ALLEN PAPER CO., A. C. 808
ANDREWS PAPER CO. 820
ARNOLD-ROBERTS CO., THE 817
BAIRD & BARTLETT CO. 819
BANKER, J. W. .... Opp. 434
BIRMINGHAM & PROSSER CO. ..Opp. 272
BOYLE, LUKE. 788
CARTER & CO., INC., JOHN 819
CARTER, RICE & CO., CORP. 819
CLAFLIN & CO., INC., WM. H. ... 818
CRAIG & CO., H. G. .... Opp. 367
CROTTEAU, DICK. 807
DOBLER & MUDGE. 789
DOMESTIC MILLS PAPER CO. 785
GOTTESMAN & CO., INC. Side Lines, 67-363
HILLS CO., GEO. F. 788
IBBOTSON, JR., WALTER 784
LINDENMEYR & SONS, HENRY ...Opp. 73
McENERY PAPER CO.,
Foot Lines, 104-224
MUNROE CO., D. F. 820
PENN PAPER & STOCK CO., INC. ..804
SHRYOCK BROTHERS 791
SPAULDING & TEWKESBURY CO.,
Opp. 366
STIMPSON & CO. 819
STONE & ANDREW, INC. 818
STONE & FORSYTH CO. 814
STORRS & BEMENT CO., A. 817
UNITED STATES PAPER CORP. 802
VON OLKER-SNELL PAPER CO. 820
WILLIAMS & CO., CHAS. W.,
Bet. 72 and 73

PAPETERIE PAPERS.
AMERICAN WRITING PAPER CO.,
Bet. 272 and 273
CRANE, Z. & W. M. 794
HAMMERMILL PAPER CO.,
Bet. 296 and 297
KEITH PAPER CO. 792
RISING PAPER CO., B. D. 800
WHITING PAPER CO. 798

PAPETERIES.
SHEA, STURM CO. .... Back Fly Leaf
SHERMAN ENVELOPE CO. 66
U. S. ENVELOPE CO. .... Opp. 435
WHITING PAPER CO. 798

PARAFFINE PAPER.
BENNINGTON WAX PAPER CO. 798
HOLLINGSWORTH & WHITNEY CO. . 816
WILLIAMS & CO., CHAS. W.,
Bet. 72 and 73

PARAFFINED PRODUCTS.
SUTHERLAND PAPER CO. 781

PARCHMENT PAPER.
CRANE & CO. 795
HOLLINGSWORTH & WHITNEY CO. . 816
KALAMAZOO VEGETABLE PARCHMENT CO. .... Opp. 361
KEITH PAPER CO. 792
LINDENMEYR & SONS, HENRY ...Opp. 73
ROBERTSON PAPER CO. 224
WEST VIRGINIA PULP & PAPER CO.,
Bet. 224 and 225
WILLIAMS & CO., CHAS. W.,
Bet. 72 and 73

PASTED BOARD.
BAIRD & BARTLETT CO. 819
HAMPDEN GLAZED PAPER & CARD
CO. .... Bet. 362 and 363

PATTERN AND DRAFTING PAPERS.
HOLLINGSWORTH & VOSE CO. 817
LINDENMEYR & SONS, HENRY ...Opp. 73

RAW HIDE CUTTINGS AND BOW PICKERS FOR SIZING
MAURICE O'MEARA CO
448-450 PEARL ST.
NEW YORK

Classified List of Advertisers

PHOTOGRAPH MOUNTS. PAGE
HAMPDEN GLAZED PAPER AND
CARD CO..............Bet. 362 and 363
HOLYOKE CARD & PAPER CO.,
Opp. 362
LINDENMEYR & SONS, HENRY,
Opp. 73
MILLERS FALLS PAPER CO...........796
NEW YORK-NEW ENGLAND CO.......799
PENINSULAR PAPER CO..............803
RHODE ISLAND CARDBOARD CO.,
Opp. 363
STRATHMORE PAPER CO............797

PLATE PAPER.
HAMPDEN GLAZED PAPER & CARD
CO..................Bet. 362 and 363
HOLYOKE CARD & PAPER CO..Opp. 362
LINDENMEYR & SONS, HENRY,
Opp. 73
NASHUA GUMMED AND COATED
PAPER CO..........................814
ROGERS PAPER MFG. CO..............192
STONE & ANDREW, INC...............818
WHITMORE MFG. CO....Bet. 362 and 363
WILLIAMS & CO., CHAS. W.,
Bet. 72 and 73

POSTAL CARD STOCK.
FALULAH PAPER CO............Opp. 366

PRESS BOARD.
ROGERS PAPER MFG. CO., THE,
Opp. 192
WILLIAMS & CO., CHAS. W.,
Bet. 72 and 73

PRESS-SPAHN.
ROGERS PAPER MFG. CO........Opp. 192

PRINTED BOX COVERINGS.
HAMPDEN GLAZED PAPER & CARD
CO..................Bet. 362 and 363
WILLIAMS & CO., CHAS. W.,
Bet. 72 and 73

PRINTED ROLL PAPERS.
ELLIOTT & CO., W. R...............818
PERRY CO., INC., C. E.............820

RAG WRAPPING.
NEWTON PAPER CO....Bet. 362 and 363

RAILROAD CARDBOARD.
FALULAH PAPER CO............Opp. 366

RAILROAD WRITING.
EASTERN MFG. CO.............Opp. 256

RIBBON PAPERS.
ELLIOTT & CO., W. R...............818
PERRY CO., INC., C. E.............820

ROLL PAPER.
CARTER, JOHN, & CO., INC..........819
ELLIOTT & CO., W. R...............818
HOLLINGSWORTH & WHITNEY
CO................................816
LINDENMEYR & SONS, HENRY,
Opp. 73
PERRY CO., INC., C. E.............820

**ROLL PAPER PRINTING, CUT-
TING AND REWINDING.**
ELLIOTT & CO., W. R...............818
PERRY CO., INC., C. E.............820

ROPE PAPER.
HOLLINGSWORTH & VOSE CO........817
LINDENMEYR & SONS, HENRY,
Opp. 73

SAFETY PAPERS. PAGE
HAMMERMILL PAPER CO.,
Bet. 296 and 297

SACK PAPERS.
NEWTON FALLS PAPER CO......Opp. 73

SAND PAPER.
HOLLINGSWORTH & VOSE CO........817
MUNROE FELT & PAPER CO.
Back Fly Leaf

SHEATHING PAPERS.
NEWTON PAPER CO....Bet. 362 and 363

SHEET CUTTING FROM ROLLS.
PERRY CO., INC., C. E.............820
ELLIOTT CO., W. R.................818

SHELF PAPER.
KALAMAZOO VEGETABLE PARCH-
MENT CO....................Opp. 361

SHIELD BOARD.
ROGERS PAPER MFG. CO.............192

SPECIALTIES.
ALLEN PAPER CO., A. C.............808
AMERICAN WRITING PAPER CO.,
Bet. 272 and 273
ANDREWS PAPER CO.................820
ARNOLDS-ROBERTS CO., THE........817
BANKER, J. W......................434
CHEMICAL PAPER MFG. CO.....Opp. 798
CHERRY RIVER PAPER CO.............2
CONTINENTAL PAPER BAG CO........410
CRAIG & CO., H. G............Opp. 367
CROTTEAU, DICK....................807
DOMESTIC MILLS PAPER CO..........785
EATON-DIKEMAN CO.................804
ELLIOTT CO., W. R.................818
FALULAH PAPER CO...........Opp. 366
GILBERT PAPER CO., FRANK,
Bet. 48 and 49
HAMPDEN GLAZED PAPER & CARD
CO..................Bet. 362 and 363
HOLLIS & DUNCAN...................810
HOLLINGSWORTH & VOSE CO........817
HOWARD PAPER CO..................808
KEITH PAPER CO...................792
LINDENMEYR & SONS, HENRY,
Opp. 73
MOUNTAIN MILL PAPER CO..........808
MUNROE FELT & PAPER CO.,
Back Fly Leaf
NEWTON PAPER CO....Bet. 362 and 363
NORTHERN PAPER MILLS......Opp. 361
ORONO PULP & PAPER CO............796
PENINSULAR PAPER CO..............803
POLAND PAPER CO....Bet. 188 and 189
ROGERS PAPER MFG. CO.............192
SHEA, STURM CO..........Back Fly Leaf
VON OLKER-SNELL PAPER CO........820
WEST VIRGINIA PULP & PAPER CO.,
Bet. 224 and 225
WILLIAMS & CO., CHAS. W.,
Bet. 72 and 73

STENCIL BOARDS.
O'MALLEY CO., THE M. J...........789
ROGERS PAPER MFG. CO.............192

STEREOSCOPIC MOUNTS.
RHODE ISLAND CARDBOARD CO.,
Opp. 363

STRAW BOARD.
BAIRD & BARTLETT CO...............819
BOYLE, LUKE......................788
LINDENMEYR & SONS, HENRY..Opp. 73
SHYROCK BROS.....................791
SPAULDING & TEWKESBURY CO.,
Opp. 366

NEW ENGLAND QUARTZ CO. of N. Y.
150 NASSAU STREET, NEW YORK, N. Y.
DIGESTER LININGS—GRANULATED QUARTZ

OLD AND NEW COTTON AND LINEN RAGS
WASTE PAPER OF ALL DESCRIPTIONS

MAURICE O'MEARA CO.
448-450 PEARL ST.
NEW YORK

EASTWOOD WIRE MANUFACTURING CO.

BELLEVILLE,   NEW JERSEY

We make a full line of the following goods:

Fourdrinier, Cylinder and Washer Wires
    Cylinder Moulds, also Cylinders and
        Dandy Rolls recovered and repaired

FROM PERFECTION BRONZE FOR ACID

Globe, Angle, and Y Valves, Sulphite Pattern.
    Globe, Angle, and Y Valves, Extra Heavy Pattern.
        Gland Packed Cocks and Special Tank Gauges.
Belleville Digestor Blow-off Valves, Patented.
    Fittings, all kinds, both Screwed and Flanged.
        Special Sulphite Pattern Hexagon Unions.
            Covers, Necks, Tees, Pipes, and Special Fittings.

FROM SPECIAL STEAM METAL

Extra Heavy Globe, Angle and Y Valves.
    Extra Heavy Fittings, all kinds.
        Extra Heavy and Standard Hexagon Unions.
            Boiler Blow-off Valves, Brass and Iron.
Couse Lubricators, Babbitt Metals,
    Castings in Perfection Bronze,
        Composition, Brass, Aluminum, Gun Metal,
           Iron, White Metal, Lead, etc.
              Machine and Foundry Work of every description.

Use Eastwood Damper Regulators

Orders from you will be carefully executed

GEORGE F. HARDY

M. AM. SOC. C. E.
M. AM. SOC. M. E.
M. CAN. SOC. C. E.

Mill Architect and Consulting Engineer

SPECIALTY:

Paper, Pulp and Fibre Mills
Water Power Developments
Steam Power Plants
Plans and Specifications
Valuations
Reports
Consultation

309 Broadway, New York
Langdon Building

Cable Address:
"Hardistock"
A B C 5th Edition
Bedford McNeill
Western Union

GET THE BEST LIGHT—DAYLIGHT—THROUGH

Van Noorden Skylights

E. VAN NOORDEN & COMPANY
ESTABLISHED 1873   INC. 1898

Skylights, Ventilators, Metal Windows, Etc.
100 MAGAZINE ST., BOSTON, MASS.

Uniformly High Grade
That's What EAGLE Products Are

EAGLE KNIFE AND BAR WORKS
LAWRENCE :: :: MASS.

Classified List of Advertisers 25

TAG BOARDS, MANILA AND JUTE.
	PAGE
BAIRD & BARTLETT CO.	819
LINDENMEYR & SONS, HENRY	Opp. 73
RHODE ISLAND CARDBOARD CO.	Opp. 363
WILLIAMS & CO., CHAS. W.	Bet. 72 and 73

TAG PAPER.
AMERICAN WRITING PAPER CO.	Bet. 272 and 273
CHERRY RIVER PAPER CO.	2
HOLLINGSWORTH & VOSE CO.	817

TAPES—SEALING.
MID-STATES GUMMED PAPER CO.	810
NASHUA GUMMED & COATED PAPER CO.	814

TEXTILE BOARD.
BAIRD & BARTLETT CO.	819
DOMESTIC MILLS PAPER CO.	785
LINDENMEYR & SONS, HENRY	Opp. 73
ROGERS PAPER MFG. CO.	Opp. 192
WILLIAMS & CO., CHAS. W.	Bet. 72 and 73

TISSUE PAPER.
ANDREWS PAPER CO.	820
BANKER, J. W.	Opp. 434
CARTER, RICE & CO., CORP.	819
CONTINENTAL PAPER BAG CO.	410
DOMESTIC MILLS PAPER CO.	785
HOFFMAN, RICHARD S.	803
HOLLINGSWORTH & WHITNEY CO.	816
LINDENMEYR & SONS, HENRY	Opp. 73
MUNROE CO., D. F.	820
NORTHERN PAPER MILLS	Opp. 361
SMITH PAPER CO.	802
STIMPSON & CO.	819
STORRS & BEMENT CO., A.	817
STRATFORD PAPER CO.	802
UNITED STATES PAPER CORP.	802

TOILET PAPER.
ANDREWS PAPER CO.	820
CONTINENTAL PAPER BAG CO.	410
DOMESTIC MILLS PAPER CO.	785
HOFFMAN, RICHARD S.	803
HOLLINGSWORTH & WHITNEY CO.	816
LINDENMEYR & SONS, HENRY	Opp. 73
LINTON & SCOTT	Opp. 352
MUNROE CO., D. F.	820
NORTHERN PAPER MILLS	Opp. 361
SHEA, STURM CO.	Back Fly Leaf
STIMPSON & CO.	819
U. S. ENVELOPE CO.	Opp. 435

TOILET SERVICES.
NORTHERN PAPER MILLS	Opp. 361

TOWELS.
DOMESTIC MILLS PAPER CO.	785
HAMMERMILL PAPER CO.	Bet. 296 and 297
HOLLINGSWORTH & VOSE CO.	817
LINTON & SCOTT	Opp. 352
NORTHERN PAPER MILLS	Opp. 361
STONE & FORSYTH	814

TRADE MARK PAPERS.
HAMPDEN GLAZED PAPER & CARD CO.	Bet. 362 and 363
NASHUA GUMMED AND COATED PAPER CO.	814
WILLIAMS & CO., CHAS. W.	Bet. 72 and 73

TRUNK BOARD.
BAIRD & BARTLETT CO.	819
LINDENMEYR & SONS, HENRY	Opp. 73

TWINE.
	PAGE
ANDREWS PAPER CO.	820
BANKER, J. W.	Opp. 434
CARTER, RICE & CO., CORP.	819
HOLLIS & DUNCAN	810
MUNROE CO., D. F.	820
STIMPSON & CO.	819
VON OLKER-SNELL PAPER CO.	820

TYMPAN BOARD.
ROBERTSON PAPER CO.	224
ROGERS PAPER MFG. CO.	Opp. 192

TYPEWRITER PAPER.
AMERICAN WRITING PAPER CO.	Bet. 272 and 273
CAREW MFG. CO.	Inside Back Cover
EASTERN MFG. CO.	Opp. 256
ESLEECK MFG. CO.	796
STRATFORD PAPER CO.	802

VARNISH LABEL.
WEST VIRGINIA PULP & PAPER CO.	Bet. 224 and 225

WATERPROOF.
NATIONAL WATERPROOFING CO.	Head Lines, 69-181
SAFEPACK PAPER MILLS	Bet. 362 and 363

WAXED PAPER.
BENNINGTON WAX PAPER CO.	798
HOFFMAN, RICHARD S.	803
HOLLINGSWORTH & WHITNEY CO.	816
KALAMAZOO VEGETABLE PARCHMENT CO.	Opp. 361
NASHUA GUMMED AND COATED PAPER CO.	814
ROBERTSON PAPER CO.	224
SHEA, STURM CO.	Back Fly Leaf
WILLIAMS & CO., CHAS. W.	Bet. 72 and 73

WIRE STITCHING.
ELLIOTT CO., W. R.	818
PERRY CO., INC., C. E.	820

WOOD PULP BOARDS.
BAIRD & BARTLETT CO.	819
LINDENMEYR & SONS, HENRY	Opp. 73

WOOD PULP BOX AND BARREL LAYERS.
BAIRD & BARTLETT CO.	819

WRAPPING PAPER.
ALLEN PAPER CO., A. C.	808
ANDREWS PAPER CO.	820
BANKER, J. W.	Opp. 434
BROWN COMPANY	Opp. 289
CHERRY RIVER PAPER CO.	2
CLAFLIN & CO., INC., W. H.	818
CONTINENTAL PAPER BAG CO.	410
DOMESTIC MILLS PAPER CO.	785
FRANKLIN PAPER CO.	Bet. 362 and 363
HOLLIS & DUNCAN	810
LINDENMEYR & SONS, HENRY	Opp. 73
MUNROE & CO., D. F.	820
MUNROE FELT & PAPER CO.	Back Fly Leaf
ORONO PULP & PAPER CO.	796
STIMPSON & CO.	819
WILLIAMS & CO., CHAS. W.	Bet. 72 and 73

A. SALOMON, Inc.
EMANUEL SALOMON, President
13 PARK ROW - - - NEW YORK

IMPORTED AND DOMESTIC PAPER MAKERS' SUPPLIES

Eagle Products are not the Result of Chance But the product of years of analysis, experimenting and earnest endeavor to produce something superior

EAGLE KNIFE AND BAR WORKS
LAWRENCE :: :: MASS.

Classified List of Advertisers

WRITING PAPER. PAGE
ALLEN PAPER CO.................808
AMERICAN WRITING PAPER CO.,
 Bet. 272 and 273
ARNOLD-ROBERTS CO., THE........817
BIRMINGHAM & PROSSER CO..Opp. 272
CAREW MFG. CO.....Inside Back Cover
CARTER & CO., JOHN, INC..........819
CARTER, RICE & CO., CORP.........819
CHEMICAL PAPER MFG. CO..........798
CRANE, Z. & W. M................794
CRANE & CO......................795
CROCKER, McELWAIN CO............800
DOMESTIC MILLS PAPER CO.........785
EASTERN MFG. CO..........Opp. 256
ESLEECK MFG. CO.................796
HAMMERMILL PAPER CO.
 Bet. 296 and 297
HAMPSHIRE PAPER CO. Inside Back Cover
HOWARD PAPER CO.................808

WRITING PAPER—*Continued.*
 PAGE
KEITH PAPER CO..................792
LINDENMEYR & SONS, HENRY..Opp. 73
MERRIMAC PAPER CO.........Opp. 362
MILLERS FALLS PAPER CO..........796
MOUNTAIN MILL PAPER CO..........803
POLAND PAPER CO......Bet. 256 and 257
RISING PAPER CO., B. D..........800
SEAMAN PAPER CO.................809
STORRS & BEMENT CO., A..........817
STRATHMORE PAPER CO.............797
TAYLOR-LOGAN CO., PAPERMAKERS. 799
TICONDEROGA PULP & PAPER CO.
 Bet. 362 and 363
UNITED STATES PAPER CORP........802
VON OLKER-SNELL PAPER CO........820
WEST VIRGINIA PULP & PAPER CO.,
 Bet. 224 and 225
WHITING PAPER CO................798
WILLIAMS & CO., CHAS. W.,
 Bet. 72 and 73

HIGH GRADE Beater Roll Bars, Bed Plates, Jordan Fillings, Paper Mill Knives

EAGLE KNIFE AND BAR WORKS
LAWRENCE :: :: MASS.

A. SALOMON, Inc.
EMANUEL SALOMON, President
13 PARK ROW :: NEW YORK
IMPORTED AND DOMESTIC
PAPER MAKERS' SUPPLIES

MILL OFFICIALS

Being an alphabetical list of the Presidents, Vice-Presidents, Secretaries, Treasurers, Managers, Superintendents and other officers of the Paper and Pulp Mills in the United States and Canada.

A

Abbott, Gardner, Sec., The Adams Bag Co.
Adams, Alva L., Prop. and Mgr., A. L. Adams Paper Co.
Adams, C. E., Supt.; A. L. Adams Paper Co.
Adams, G. D., Pres. and Treas., Cleveland Akron Bag Co.
Adams, John S., Asst. Mgr., High Falls Pulp & Paper Co.
Adie, John F., Pres., Advertisers Paper Co.; Pres., Taylor-Logan Co., Papermakers.
Adriance, T. F., Vice-Pres. and Gen. Mgr., Underwood Pulp & Paper Mills, Inc.
Ahles, R. L., Pres., Analomink Paper Co.
Aldrich, B., Mill Supt., Chapin & Gould Paper Co.
Aldrich, H. G., Pres., Aldrich Paper Co.
Alexander, Harry W., Asst. to Pres., of Sales; American Writing Paper Co.
Alexander, L. M., Pres. and Treas., Nekoosa-Edwards Paper Co.; Vice-Pres. and Treas., Inland Empire Paper Co.
Alexander, Walter, Pres., Wausau Paper Mills Co.; Vice-Pres., Marathon Paper Mills Co.
Alford, W. J., Pres., Continental Paper Co.; Pres., Piermont Paper Co.; Pres. and Treas., Thames River Specialty Co.; Vice Pres., Haverhill Box Co.
Alford, W. J., Jr., Treas., Continental Paper Co.; Asst. Treas., The Thames River Specialty Co.
Allen, A. D., Vice-Pres., Mengel Box Co. Branch.
Allen, C. H., Sec., Saranac Co.
Allen, E. B., Vice-Pres., The Adams Bag Co.
Allen, Harold A., Sec. and Treas., Burmus Paper Co., Inc.
Allen, H. B., Mgr., Niagara Falls, N. Y., Certain-Teed Products Corp.
Allen, J. R., Pres., Wrenn Paper Co.
Allen, Kenneth L., Treas., The Adams Bag Co.
Allen, Philip R., Pres., Bird & Son, Ltd.
Allen, T. E., Supt., Munroe Felt & Paper Co.
Allison, S. E., Vice-Pres., Certain-Teed Product Corp.
Alsted, L. L., Pres., Combined Locks Paper Co.
Altick, C. D., Gen. Supt., Bogalusa Paper Co., Inc.
Atland, D. F., Vice-Pres., Kalamazoo Paper. Co.
Alward, F. E., Gen. Mgr., and Pur. Agt., Lancaster Board & Paper Co.
Amerine, D. C., Vice-Pres. and Mill Mgr., Indiana Board & Filler Co.
Amos, J. F., Sec. and Treas., Taggart Bros. Co.
Anderson, A. O., Sec., The James Maclaren Co., Ltd.
Anderson, C., Asst. Sec. and Treas., Marinette & Menominee Paper Co.
Anderson, D. M., 2nd Vice-Pres., St. Regis Paper Co.
Anderson, F. R., Sec., Sail Mountain Co.
Anderson, Harry W., Cost Acct., American Writing Paper Co.
Anderson, J. F., Mgr., Piqua and Tippacanoe City Ohio American Straw Board Co.
Anderson, James H., Vice-Pres., Albemarle Paper Mfg. Co.
Anderson, J. M., Treas., Astoria Pulp & Paper Co.
Anderson, L. C., Sec., Paul A. Sorg Paper Co.; Treas., W. B. Oglesby Paper Co.
Anderson, R. H., Third Vice-Pres., Keasbey & Mattison Co.
Anderson, W. A., Supt., Kinleith Paper Mills, Ltd.
Anderson, W. H., Sec., New Elkhart Paper Mills Co.
Andre, W. L., Vice-Pres., Analomink Paper Co.
Andrews, C. K., Mgr., Itasca Paper Co.
Andrews, Clarence R., Sec. and Treas., John T. Andrews & Co., Inc.
Andrews, Charles T., Pres., John T. Andrews & Co., Inc.
Andrews, Edwin C., Vice-Pres., John T. Andrews & Co., Inc.
Anson, F. H., Pres., Abitibi Power & Paper Co., Ltd.
Anson, L. N., Pres., Grandfather's Falls Co.
Argy, M. J., Supt., Cliff Paper Co.
Armstrong, Louis, Asst. Treas., Laurentide Co., Ltd.
Armstrong, W. H., Sec., H. F. Watson Co.
Artman, Wm., Sec., The Ohio Box Board Co.
Ash, C. D., Gen. Mgr., Crescent Paper & Machine Co.
Ash, Clinton D., Co-partner, Crescent Paper & Machine Co.
Ash, F. C., Sec., Oswego Falls Pulp & Paper Co.
Atkins, F. C., Treas., Taylor-Atkins Co.
Atland, D. F., Vice-Pres., Kalamazoo Paper Co.
Auer, J. F., Treas., Phila. Wax Paper Co.
Aull, J. A., Pres., Paul A. Sorg Paper Co.; Pres., W. B. Oglesby Paper Co.; Vice-Pres., Carso Paper Co.
Ault, Robt. A. G., Gen. Mgr., Schmidt & Ault Paper Co.
Austin, C. R., Supt., Ball Bros. Co.
Ayer, F. R., Pres., Eastern Mfg. Co.
Ayers, P. W., Vice-Pres. and Sec., Mountain Mill Paper Co.

Eagle Products Do the Work
They Are Designed For It

EAGLE KNIFE AND BAR WORKS
LAWRENCE :: :: MASS.

Mill Officials in the United States and Canada

B

Babbitt, Frederick H., Pres., Robertson Paper Co.
Babbitt, John, Treas., Robertson Paper Co.
Babcock, C. A., Pres. and Treas., Wisconsin River Paper & Pulp Co.
Babcock, F. R., Vice-Pres., S. George Co.
Babcock, H. K., Vice-Pres., Fox River Paper Co.
Bache-Wiig, O., Vice-Pres., and Gen. Mgr., Wausau Sulphate Fibre Co.
Bachert, E. A., Vice-Pres., Coshocton Straw Paper Co.
Bachert, K. W., Sec. and Treas., Coshocton Straw Paper Co.
Bachert, W. H., Pres., Coshocton Straw Paper Co.
Backus, E. W., Pres., Fort Frances Pulp & Paper Co., Ltd.; Pres., Minnesota & Ontario Power Co.
Backus, S. W., First Vice-Pres., Fort Frances Pulp & Paper Co., Ltd.; Vice-Pres., Minnesota & Ontario Power Co.
Bagg, Aaron C., Sec., Parsons Paper Co.
Bagg, Aaron, Jr., Pres., Parsons Paper Co.; Pres., Valley Paper Co.
Bagg, Edward P., Pres., Millers Falls Paper Co.; Treas., Parsons Paper Co.
Bailey, Robt., Supt., Pettebone-Cataract Paper Co.
Bailly, Edward C., Sec. and Treas., Kingsport Pulp Corp.
Baker, C. W., Mill Supt., Bedford Pulp & Paper Co.
Baker, E., Supt., Lindale Mills.
Baker, Frank S., Pres., Cascade Paper Co.
Baker, H. M., Mgr., Winchester, Va., American Straw Board Co.
Baker, Wm. T., Vice-Pres., Mutual Box Board Co.
Balch, Chas. A., Supt., Colonial Board Co.
Ball, E. B., Vice-Pres., Ball Bros,. Co.
Ball, F. C., Pres., Ball Bros. Co.
Ball, G. A., Treas., Ball Bros. Co.
Ball, John, Mgr., The Jonquieres Pulp Co., Ltd.; Mgr. Price Bros. & Co., Ltd; Mgr., Price-Porritt Pulp & Paper Co.
Ball, W. C., Sec., Ball Bros. Co.
Ballou, Harry, Treas., Menasha Paper Co.
Ballou, M. E., Vice-Pres. and Gen. Mgr. Menasha Paper Co.
Banyon, R., Sec., Mullen Bros. Paper Co.
Barbour, D. S., Sec. and Mgr., Patent Vulcanite Roofing Co.
Barchard, J. L., Mgr., Chicago Mill & Lumber Co.
Bardeen, G. E., Pres., Bardeen Paper Co.; First Vice-Pres., Lee Paper Co.; Treas., Mac Sim Bar Paper Co.
Bardeen, H. A., Vice-Pres., Sec. and Gen. Mgr., Wheat Paper Co.
Bardeen, Norman, Sec., Treas. and Gen. Mgr., Lee Paper Co.
Bare, D. M., Vice-Pres., D. M. Bare Paper Co.
Barnes, Clayton, C., Prop., Barnes Paper Mill.
Barnes, Clyde, Vice-Pres., Dresden Paper Mills Co.
Barnes, H. P., Asst. Treas., Keasbey & Mattison Co.
Baron, J. V., Sec., and Treas., Taggarts Paper Co.

Barratt, Edgar G., Pres., Hadley Paper Corp.
Barrett, Thos., Supt., Noble Mfg. Co.
Baseler, H. C., Gen. Mgr., Carthage Board & Paper Co.
Bates, John S., Supt., Forest Products Laboratories of Canada.
Bauer, Thomas, Vice-Pres., Alton Box Board & Paper Co.; Pres. and Mgr., Lafayette Box Board & Paper Co.
Bayless, Geo. C., Chairman, Board of Directors, Bayless Mfg. Corp.
Bayless, Stanley C., Sec. and Treas., Bayless Mfg. Corp.
Beach, Andrew Y., Pres., S. Y. Beach Paper Co.
Beach, R. S., Sec., S. Y. Beach Paper Co.
Beach, S. M., Treas. and Supt., S. Y. Beach Paper Co.
Beal, J. E., Vice-Pres., Peninsular Paper Co.
Beale, J. B., Sales Mgr., Chesapeake Paperboard Co.
Beatty, Charles S., Treas., General Fibre Board Co.
Beatty, J. D., Supt., Patent Vulcanite Roofing Co.
Beauclerk, H. W., Vice-Pres., Claremont Paper Co., Inc.
Bechard, A., Treas., Compagnie de Pulpe de Chicoutimi; Treas., St. Lawrence Pulp & Lumber Corp.
Bechthold, M., Sec., United Paperboard Co.
Becker, F., Pres., Ha! Ha! Bay Sulphite Co., Ltd.
Becker, John A., Vice-Pres., Iriquois Pulp & Paper Co.
Beckett, T., Pres., Beckett Paper Co.
Beckwith, W. H., Sec. and Gen. Mgr., Morris Paper Mills.
Becraft, W. E., Sec., Hinkley Fibre Co.
Beggs, G. E., Sec. and Treas., Mumford Paper Mills, Inc.
Begin, F. F., Supt., General Fibre Co.
Behnke, J. H., Sec., Detroit Sulphite Pulp & Paper Co.
Behrend, Ernst R., Pres. and Gen. Mgr., Hammermill Paper Co.
Behrend, Otto, F., Treas., Hammermill Paper Co.
Bell, Edw. C., Sec., Case Mfg. Co.
Bell, Rae, F., Sec., Kaukauna Pulp Co.
Belleau, Ray, Sec., Compagnie de Pulpe de Chicoutimi.
Benn, A. Shirley, First Vice-Pres., Southern Paper Co.
Bennett, W. T., Mgr., Chestertown, Md., American Straw Board Co.
Bensing, W. M., Gen. Mgr., The Sterling Paper Co.
Berg, H. O., Sec. and Treas., Kenyon Paper Corp.
Bergstrom, D. W., Pres. and Sec., Bergstrom Paper Co.
Bergstrom, J. N., Treas., Bergstrom Paper Co.
Berkey, Geo. P., Sec. and Mgr., Interlake Pulp & Paper Co.
Bertschy, R. D., Vice-Pres., Miamisburg Paper Co.
Betz, E. C., Sec., Monroe Binder Board Co.
Beveridge, F. N., Mill Supt., Dryden Timber & Power Co., Ltd.
Beveridge, H. L., Pres., Beveridge Paper Co.
Beveridge, J. B., Gen. Mgr., Dryden Timber & Power Co., Ltd.
Beyer, A. D., Pleasant Mills Paper Co.

Mill Officials in the United States and Canada

Bickford, L. M., Vice-Pres., Nashwaak Pulp & Paper Co.; Vice-Pres. and Gen. Mgr., Oxford Paper Co.
Bicking, B. F., Supt., General Paper Co., Inc.
Bicking, D. Purke, Supt., S. Austin Bicking Paper Mfg. Co.
Bicking, Edwin, Vice-Pres., S. Austin Bicking Paper Mfg. Co.
Bicking, Frank S., Sec. and Treas., S. Austin Bicking Mfg. Co.
Bicking, Jos. A., Pres., S. Austin Bicking Paper Mfg. Co.
Biermans, H., Gen. Mgr., Belgo-Canadian Pulp & Paper Co., Ltd.
Bigelow, Bernard, L., Pres., Colonial Board Co.
Bigelow, W. E., Vice-Pres., Colonial Board Co.
Billingham, F. A., Treas. and Supt., Rockford Paper Mills.
Bingham, John, Mill Supt., Dill & Collins Co.
Bingham, S. H., Pres., American Tar Products Co.
Bird, Charles S., Pres., Bird & Son, Inc.
Bishop, Alf., Supt., Montreal Paper Co., Ltd.
Bishop, D. A., Sec. and Mgr., Clyde River Pulp & Paper Co., Ltd.
Bishop, L. P., Vice-Pres., Montreal Paper Co., Ltd.
Bishop, R. K., Dir., Horwood Lumber Co., Ltd.
Bishop, T. Parkin, Pres., Montreal Paper Co., Ltd.
Blaier, G. A., Vice-Pres., Phila. Paper Mfg. Co.
Bird, Charles S., Pres., Bird & Son, Inc.
Bixby, W. E., Pres., Lee Fibre Co.
Black, Sullivan, Supt., The Brere Pulp & Paper Co.
Blake, C. M., Blake & Higgins.
Blake, W. S., Pres., Senoso Paper Co., Inc., Phoenix, N. Y.
Blanchard, Denman, Treas., Acme Paper & Paper Box Co. (Trust.)
Blandin, Amos. N., Pres., Aroostook Pulp & Paper Co.; Pres., Deerfield Pulp & Paper Co.; Pres., Howland Pulp & Paper Corp.
Blandin, C. K., Pres., Itasca Paper Co.
Blandy, Graham, Sec., American Wood Board Co.
Blandy, I. C., Pres., American Wood Board Co.; Treas., Blandy Paper Co.
Blaney, A. Charles, Vice-Pres., Rex Paper Co.
Bleyker, D. Den, Vice-Pres., Cascade Paper Co.
Briggs, F. A., Supt., Aldrich Paper Co.
Bliss, Edgar S., Pres., Worthy Paper Co. Ass'n.
Bloch, Louis, Vice-Pres. and Gen. Mgr., Crown Willamette Paper Co.
Bloomer, Charles T., Pres., Bloomer Bros. Co.
Bloomer, R. A., Sec. and Treas., Bloomer Bros. Co.
Bobb, E. G., Pres., D. M. Bare Paper Co.
Boggs, Eugene, Mgr., Waverly Paper Board Co.
Boland, J. C., Sec. and Treas., Marcellus Paper Co.
Boldt, Charles, Pres., The Charles Boldt Paper Mills.

Bollinger, George H., Pres., New Castle Paper Mills.
Bond, D. W., Treas., Dill & Collins Co.
Bond, S. D., Treas., Fort Wayne Corrugated Paper Co.
Bond, W. H., Treas., Japanese Tissue Mills.
Bonning, Carl, Treas., Port Huron Sulphite & Paper Co.
Bonthrone, Barclay, Pres., Western Paper Mills, Ltd.
Booth, B. O., Auditor, International Paper Co.
Booth, C. J., J. R. Booth.
Booth, J. F., J. R. Booth.
Booth, J. R., J. R. Booth.
Borden, J. Parker, Sec. and Treas., Union Mills Paper Mfg. Co.
Borland, Charles, Vice-Pres., Fort Orange Paper Co.
Boswell, L. P., Mgr., Aetna Paper Co.
Bothwell, J. A., Gen. Mgr., Brompton Pulp & Paper Co.; Gen. Mgr., Claremont Paper Co., Inc.
Botsford, N. H., Treas., De Grasse Paper Co.; Treas., High Falls Pulp & Paper Co.
Bottum, F. H., Sec., Combined Locks Paper Co.
Bounds, S. J., Treas., Halifax Paper Corp.
Bowers, George, W., Pres., S. George Co.
Bowers, O. H., Vice-Pres., Wanaque River Paper Co.
Bowersock, J. D., Pres., Lawrence Paper Mfg. Co.
Bowker, N. J., Treas., Mgr., Pettebone-Cataract Paper Co.
Bowman, J. N., Treas., Clayville Paper Mills Co.
Boyer, F. M., Sec., Harmon Paper Co.; Sec., Warren Puchment Co.
Boykin, Wm. E., The Metalite Co.
Boyle, J. F., Pres. and Treas. John F. Boyle Co.
Bradley, G. E., Supt., Alex. McArthur & Co., Ltd.
Bradt, W. D., Mgr., The Thompson & Norris Co., of Indiana.
Bragg, Charles F., Pres., Orono Pulp & Paper Co.
Brainard, Newton Case, Sec., Hartford Paper Co.
Branerd, Amaziah, Pres. and Treas., Hartford Paper Co.
Brannan, Daniel, Pres., North End Paper Co.
Brannan, John, Treas., North End Paper Co.; Vice-Pres. and Mgr. Mars Paper Corp.
Brantingham, F. W., Vice-Pres., Union Paper Mill Co.
Brashear, Peter C., Pres., Fort Orange Paper Co.
Brazeau, W. A., Sec., Inland Empire Paper Co.
Breck, Joseph, H., Supt., Mason-Perkins Paper Company.
Brewer, Frank, Treas. and Mgr., E-Z Opener Bag. Co.
Briggs, A. W., Sec., Toronto Paper Mfg. Co., Ltd.
Briggs, Walter, Sec., Cherry River Paper Co.
Brigham, J. J., Sec., East Hartford, Mfg. Co.
Bronson, E. H., Pres., The Bronson Co.
Bronson, Frederick E., Mng. Dir., The Bronson Co.

BARKER & CHIPPER KNIVES For the Hard Places TRY THEM

EAGLE KNIFE AND BAR WORKS LAWRENCE :: :: MASS.

30   Mill Officials in the United States and Canada

Bronson, J. P., Treas., **The Boehme & Rauch Co.**
Brooks, A. S., Treas., Powell River Co., Ltd.
Brooks, D. F., Pres., Powell River Co., Ltd.
Brooks, H. K., Sec., Powell River Co., Ltd.
Brooks, W. A., Sec., Menasha Printing & Carton Co.
Brooks, Wm. F., Treas., Fort Frances Pulp & Paper Co., Ltd.; Treas., Minnesota & Ontario Power Co.
Brooks, William S., Asst. Gen. Supt., American Writing Paper Co.
Brooksbank, C. B., Supt., Cherry River Paper Co.
Brown, A., Mill Supt., Iroquis Pulp & Paper Co.
Brown, A. G., Prop., Brown Paper Co.
Brown, A. P., Pres. and Treas., The Brown Paper Co.
Brown, A. W., Rhinelander Paper Co.
Brown, D. L., Supt., Salt Mountain Co.
Brown, D. P., Local Mgr., La Toque, Brown Corp.
Brown, E. E., Sec. and Treas., E. M. Brown Paper Co.
Brown, E. M., Pres., E. M. **Brown Paper Co.**
Brown, **Frank K.**, owner, Medway Pulp & Power Co.
Brown, **Geo. M.**, Pres., Certain-Teed Products Corp.
Brown, H. J., Pres., Brown Co.; Pres., Brown Corp.
Brown, H. M., Mill Supt., The E. M. Brown Paper Co.
Brown, H. M., Vice-Pres., Anson-Eldred Co.
Brown, H. T., Pres., Monroe Bridge Paper Co.; Vice-Pres., Federal Paper Board Co., Inc.
Brown, Joseph, Pres., Los Angeles Paper Mfg. Co.
Brown, Joseph, Jr., Vice-Pres., Los Angeles Paper Mfg. Co.
Brown, L. M., Sec., Finch, Pruyn & Co., Inc.
Brown, Martin A., Treas., Parker-Young Co.; Henry Paper Co., Branch.
Brown, O. B., Vice-Pres. and Treas., Brown Co.; Sec. and Treas., Brown Corp.
Brown, Robert, Supt., Monroe Bridge Paper Co.
Brown, Robert E., Sec., Los Angeles Paper Mfg. Co.
Brown, R. G., Vice-Pres., Manistique Pulp & Paper Co.
Brown, S. H., Asst. Sec., Union Bag & Paper Corp.
Brown, W. R., Asst. Treas., Brown Co.
Browne, Paul, Sec., Rhinelander Paper Co.
Browne, P. B., Auditor, American Writing Paper Co.
Brunalle, Ellie, Mgr., Hydro-Electric Power Commission, Pulp Mill.
Brunner, W. I., Supt., Bristol, Va., Columbian Paper Co.
Buescher, F. A., Vice-Pres., New Elkhart Paper Mills Co.
Burnside, G. W., Gen. Mgr., Lakeside Paper Co.
Brunt, J. P., Vice-Pres. and Sales Mgr., Mid-West Box Co.
Bryan, V. H., Treas., Mengel Box Co., Branch.

Bryant, Chas. C., Sec. and Treas., Champion Fibre Co.
Bryant, Noah, Vice-Pres., Bryant Paper Co.
Bryant, O. F., Supt., Bennett, Ltd.
Buck, R. J., Vice-Pres., Hall & Richter Paper Co.
Buehler, Hy., Treas., Atlas Leather Mfg. Co.
Buehler, Jr., H., Vice-Pres., Sec. and Supt., Atlas Leather Mfg. Co.
Buell, Martha M., Oswego River Paper Mills.
Bulkley, Jonathan, Treas., Union Mill; Vice-Pres., Keith Paper Co.
Bull, Karhl, Sec., Franklin Board & Paper Co.
Bupp, L. A., Owner and Mgr., The Springets Mills.
Burbank, L. A., Mill Supt., Hydro-Electric Power Commission, Pulp Mill.
Burby, John M., Pres. and Supt., Burmus Paper Co., Inc.
Burch, Arthur J., Treas., Big Falls Paper Co., Inc.
Burgstresser, A. K., Supt., Norristown Magnesia & Asbestos Co.
Burkhardt, C. R., Gen. Supt., National Asbestos Mfg. Co.
Burrows, A. A., Supt., Crescent Paper Machine Co.
Burrows, C. H., Pres., Mohawk Valley Paper Co., Inc.
Burrows, M. O., Mrs., Sec., Mohawk Valley Paper Co., Inc.
Buse, E. L., Sec., The Philip Carey Mfg. Co.
Bush, S. L., Asst. Treas., Chemical Paper Mfg. Co.
Bush, Thos. J., Supt., Mutual Box Board Co.
Bushong, I. N., Pres., Watab Pulp & Paper Co.
Buskirk, C. A., Vice-Pres. and Treas., Wolverine Paper Co.
Buss, Charles F., Supt., Provincial Paper Mills Co., Ltd.
Butler, B. F., Vice-Pres., New Castle Paper Mills.
Butler, Frederick M., Sec. and Treas., Clifton Paper Mills.
Buzby, J. B., Treas., William Mann Co.
Bye, Harry, Vice-Pres., Marcellus Paper Co.
Byrne, J. F., Sec. and Supt., Michigan Carton Co.
Byrne, P., Supt., Riordon Pulp & Paper Co., Ltd.
Byrne, W. E., Roanoke Fibre Board Co.

C

Cabell, W. Carrington, Sec., Wanaque River Paper Co.
Calder, John, Supt., Wreen Paper Co.
Cameron, Angus, Treas., Millers Falls Paper Co.
Cameron, E. B., Treas., J. G. Cherry Co.
Campbell, C. S., Treas., Kalamazoo Vegetable Parchment Co.
Campbell, G. D., Sr., Pres., Campbell Lumber Co., Ltd.
Campbell, G. D., Jr., Vice-Pres., Campbell Lumber Co., Ltd.
Campbell, Palmer, Sec. and Treas.; Hoboken Paper Mill Co.
Campbell, Raymond R., Asst. to Pres. on Production, American Writing Paper Co.
Campbell, A. H., Traffic Mgr., International Paper Co.

QUALITY SELLS The Merit of our Products, and Quick Shipments are what Developed our Business

EAGLE KNIFE AND BAR WORKS
LAWRENCE :: :: MASS.

Mill Officials in the United States and Canada

Campbell, C. W., Vice-Pres. and Gen. Mgr., Dexter Sulphite Pulp & Paper Co.
Campbell, F. J., Gen. Mgr., Canada Paper Co., Ltd.
Campbell, F. P., Supt., Wilder, Vt., International Paper Co.
Campbell, J. E., Pres. and Treas., Dexter Sulphite Pulp & Paper Co.
Campbell, Ross, Acting Mgr., Dept of Research & Tests.
Cape, Ed., Supt., Creamery Package Mfg. Co.
Carey, Chas. E., Sec. and Gen. Mgr., The Hutchinson Box Board Co.
Carey, Emerson, Pres., The Hutchinson Box Board & Paper Co.
Carey, Howard J., Vice-Pres., The Hutchinson Box Board & Paper Co.
Carlisle, F. L., Pres., St. Regis Paper Co.
Carney, Daniel, Mgr., Carney Paper Co.; Mgr., Simplex Paper Co.
Carney, P. J., Supt., Fitzdale Paper Co.
Caron, Joseph Ed., Sec. and Treas., Metabetchouan Co.
Carpenter, A. B., Treas., Amoskeag Paper Mills Co.
Carpenter, F. P., Pres., Amoskeag Paper Mills Co.
Carpenter, N. H., Gen. Mgr., Coshocton Straw Paper Co.
Carruthers, Geo., Pres., Interlake Tissue Mills, Ltd.
Carter, J. R., Supt., J. G. Cherry Co.
Carter, James Richard, Pres., Carso Paper Co.
Carter, Robt. D., Pres. and Treas., Wanaque River Paper Co.
Carter, W. L., Sec., Carso Paper Co.
Case, A. Willard, Treas., Case Bros.; Pres., Case Mfg.; Pres., A. Willard Case Co.
Case, C. C., Vice-Pres. and Supt., Case Board Co.
Case, C. H., Prop. and Gen. Mgr., Case & Risley Press Paper Co.
Case, L. W., Pres., Case Board Co.; Pres., Riverton Co.; Pres., Case Bros.; Vice-Pres., Case & Marshall, Inc.
Case, R. S., Vice-Pres. and Treas., Case Mfg. Co.; Pres., Case & Marshall Inc.; Treas., Riverton Co.
Caskey, Paul D., Clerk, Claremont Paper Co., Inc.
Cass, Charles A., Vice-Pres., West Va. Pulp Products Co., Inc.; Sec., West Va. Pulp & Paper Co.
Caswell, Nelson, R., Treas., Aldrich Paper Co.
Caswell, W. W., Treas., Arthur D. Little, Inc.
Cathcart, P., Agent. Niagara Falls, N. Y., International Paper Co.
Catto, F. S., Vice-Pres., MacAndrews & Forbes Co.
Cauthorne, R. A., Pres., Dixie Paper Mills, Inc.
Cayford, A. F., Sec. & Treas., Hartje Paper Mfg. Co.
Cayford, J. H., Supt., Hartje Paper Mfg. Co.
Chahoon, George, Vice-Pres., J. & J. Rogers Co.
Chahoon, George, Jr., Pres. and Mgr., Laurentide Co., Ltd.
Chahoon, I. H., Paper Mill Supt., J. & J. Rogers Co.
Challes, George E., Sales Mgr., Riordon Pulp & Paper Co., Inc.
Chalmers, John, Sec., West Jersey Paper Mfg. Co.

Champion, Chas., Supt., Berkshire Hills Paper Co.
Chandler, E. W., Vice-Pres. & Gen. Mgr., Creamery Package Mfg. Co.
Chapin, Charles L., Pres. and Treas., Chapin & Gould Paper Co.
Chapin, W. G., Pres., The Pynetree Paper Co.; Sec., The Thompson & Norris Co. of Indiana.
Chapman, F. B., Treas., Finch, Pruyn & Co., Inc.
Chase, Stephnen, Pres. and Mgr., Passumpsic Fibre Leather Co.
Chase, Theo. W., Treas. and Supt., Passumpsic Fibre Leather Co.
Cass, Chas. A., Sec., West Virginia Pulp & Paper Co.
Chatfield, M. E., Pres., New Haven Pulp & Board Co.
Chauncey, G. G., Pres. and Treas., Three Rivers Paper Co.
Cheney, Howard L., Mgr., Srere Bros. & Co.; Treas., Srere Pulp & Paper Co.
Cherry, H. H., Sec., J. G. Cherry Co.
Cherry, H. T., Vice-Pres., J. G. Cherry Co.
Cherry, W. L., Pres., J. G. Cherry Co.
Chilcott, A., Supt., Continental Paper Bag Co.
Child, Sam, Sec., Aldrich Paper Co.
Childs, F. W., Vice-Pres., Ashuelot Paper Co.
Childs, Horace H., Prop., Childsdale Paper Mills.
Childs, Wm. Hamlin, Pres., Barrett Co.
Chippendale, A. W., Treas., Lindale Mills.
Chisholm, Duncan, Pres., Mattagami Pulp & Paper Co., Ltd.
Chisolhm, H. J., pres., Nashwaak Pulp & Paper Co.; Pres., Oxford Paper Co.
Chitty, A. H., Treas., Spanish River Pulp & Paper Mills, Ltd.
Claflin, W. N., Vice-Pres. and Mgr., Lancaster Leather Co.
Clapp, Eugene H., Treas., Penobscot Chemical Fibre Co.
Clapp, E. H., Vice-Pres. and Treas., Tileston & Hollingsworth Co.
Clark, Alex. L., Sec., Standard Paper Co.
Clark, B. R., Treas. and Gen. Mgr., Malone Paper Co.
Clark, C. M., Pres., Sall Mountain Co.
Clark, F. B., Prop., Naubuc Co.; Sec., Malone Paper Co.
Clark, F. C., in charge of paper work, Bureau of Standards, Dept. of Commerce.
Clark, George F., Sec. and Treas., Brownville Paper Co.
Clark, H. V., Pres., Malone Paper Co.
Clark, W., Treas., The Terre Haute Paper Co.
Clark, W. G., Treas. and Gen. Mgr., The Anglaise Box Board Co.; Vice-Pres., Rockford Mills.
Clark, Wm. H., Mgr. Sales, The Aetna Paper Co.
Clark, W. H., Sec., The Jessup & Moore Paper Co.
Clarke, George, Sec. and Treas., Gulf Pulp & Paper Co.
Clarke, James, Pres., Gulf Pulp & Paper Co.
Clarke, Wm., Vice-Pres., Gulf Pulp & Paper Co.
Clay, C. M., Mgr., Circleville, Ohio, American Straw Board Co.
Cleary, J. J., Vice-Pres., Escanaba Pulp & Paper Co.
Clinedinst, S. H., Pres., Menasha Printing & Carton Co.

RAG CUTTER KNIVES
TRY SOME EAGLE KNIVES NEXT TIME

EAGLE KNIFE AND BAR WORKS
LAWRENCE :: :: MASS.

Mill Officials in the United States and Canada

Clough, C. A., Gen. Sales-Mgr., New York & Pennsylvania Co.
Clough, Geo. H., Treas., Androscoggin Pulp Co.; Treas. and Clerk, Mount Tom Sulphite Co.
Clute, Charles E., Pres. and Gen. Mgr., Acme Paper & Paper Box Co. (Trust).
Coffin, Arthur D., Pres. and Treas., C. H. Dexter & Sons, Inc.
Coffin, Herbert R., Vice-Pres., C. H. Dexter & Sons, Inc.
Coffin, J. D. Mgr., Tidewater Paper Mills Co.
Cofrin, A. E., Gen. Supt., Northern Paper Mills.
Cohen, I. D., Vice-Pres., The Fairfield Paper Co.
Cohn, M. M., Treas., Nation Paper Products Co.
Coll, W. D., Pres., Indiana Board & Filler Co.
Coker, J. L., Pres., Carolina Fibre Co.
Coker, J. L. Jr., Vice-Pres., Carolina Fibre Co.
Colby, A. H., Pres., Taylor-Atkins Paper Co.
Coleman, J. B., Supt., Cascade Paper Co.
Collins, Grellet, Pres., Dill & Collins Co.
Collins, J. C., Vice-Pres., Certain-Teed Products Corp.
Comfort, George O., Vice-Pres., Carthage Sulphite Pulp & Paper Co.
Connelly, John A., Supt., Contoocook Valley Paper Co.
Connelly, R. J., Pres., Ohio Paper Co.
Connor, Walter A., Treas., Contoocook Valley Paper Co.
Conrad, W. L., Sec., Fitzdale Paper Co.
Constatime, H. A., Sec. and Treas., Peerless Pulp Co., Ltd.; Sec. and Treas., Foley-Rieger Pulp & Paper Co., Ltd.
Cook, Clarence A., Treas., Pairpoint Corp.
Cook, C. E., Vice-Pres. and Treas., Sall Mountain Co.
Cook, C. S., Sec., Empire Paper Co.
Cook, H. H., Pres. and Gen. Mgr., Alexandria Paper Co.
Cooke, H. S., Sec., Outagamie Paper Co.
Cooke, Walter P., Pres., Bogalusa Paper Co., Inc.
Coombs, C. A., Sec. and Treas., Natick Box & Board Co.
Cooney, R. A., Supt., H. F. Watson Co.
Coons, Fred M., Pres. and Treas., Beloit Box Board Co.
Copeland, S. B., Vice-Pres., Eastern Mfg. Co.
Corcoran, W. P., Asst. Treas., Hall & Richter Paper Co.
Cornwall, A. R., Asst. Sec., Malone Paper Co.
Cornwell, E. C., Sec. and Treas., Peninsular Paper Co.
Cornell, T. L., First Vice-Pres., National Folding Box & Paper Co.
Corwin, H. J., Sec. and Treas., Union Waxed & Parchment Paper Co.; Sec. and Treas., Ulster Tissue Mills, Inc.
Costello, Maurice, Pres., Nixon & Costello Co.
Costello, M. B., Sec. and Treas., Nixon & Costello Co.
Costello, R. M., Vice-Pres., Nixon & Costello Co.
Cota, Frank, Asst. Sec., Falls Mfg. Co.; Sec., Union Mfg. Co.
Cottingham, Walter H., Pres., Adams Bag Co.

Courtney, J. I., Sec., Bergen Paper Co.
Cowan, C. P., Supt., Bird & Son, Ltd.
Cowles, C. P., Mgr. Dept. of Woodlands, Pejepscot Paper Co.
Cowles, Justus A. B., Pres., Pejepscot Paper Co.
Cowley, John, London Mgr., Anglo-Newfoundland Development Co., Ltd.
Coxe, W. Griscom, Pres., Reading Paper Mills.
Coy, F. E., Sec. and Treas., Coy Paper Co.
Coy, John H., Treas., Underwood Pulp & Paper Mills, Inc.
Coye, Chas. H., Sec., C. H. Dexter & Sons, Inc.
Crabbs, G. D., Pres., The Philip Carey Mfg. Co.
Crabbs, R. B., Vice-Pres. and Treas., The Philip Carey Mfg. Co.
Crabtree, H., Gen. Mgr., Adams Paper Co., Inc.; Sec. and Treas., Howard Smith Paper Mills, Ltd.
Crabtree, Harold, Sec., Treas. and Mang. Dir., New Brunswick Sulphate Fibre Co., Ltd.
Crafts, Geo. E., Treas., Orono Pulp & Paper Co.
Cramer, Martin L., Gen. Pur. Agt., American Writing Paper Co.
Cramer, William, Supt., Clayville Paper Mills Co.
Crandall, Willis S., Supt., A. P. W. Paper Co.
Crane, F. G., Crane & Co.
Crane, W. Murray, Z. & W. M. Crane; Crane & Co.
Crane, W. M., Jr., Crane & Co.
Crane, Zenas, Z. & W. M. Crane; Crane & Co.
Cree, J. F., Sec., S. George Co.
Crehore, Frederic M., Charles F. Crehore & Son.
Crocker, Alvah, Pres. and Treas., Crocker, Burbank & Co. Ass'n.; Sec. and Treas., The Highland Paper Co.
Crocker, Bartow, Sec., Crocker, Burbank & Co. Ass'n.
Crocker, C. A., Pres., Chemical Paper Mfg. Co.; Pres. and Treas., Crocker-McElwain Co.
Crocker, C. T., Vice-Pres., Crocker, Burbank & Co. Ass'n.
Crocker, Charles T., Jr., Vice-Pres., The Highland Paper Co.
Crocker, D. A., Vice-Pres., Eastern Mfg. Co.
Croft, W. H., Mill Supt., Esleeck Mfg. Co.
Crooney, J. P., Supt., Peninsular Paper Co.
Crowell, A. L., Sec., Case & Marshall, Inc.; Treas., Case Board Co.
Crowell, Albert L., Vice-Pres., Case Bros.; Vice-Pres., A. Willard Case Co.
Crump, R. S., Pres. Richmond Paper Mfg. Co.
Cudlip, C. W., Supt., Rogers Paper Mfg. Co.
Cullen, G. M., Sec., Taylor-Atkins Paper Co.
Cullen, R. J., Gen. Supt., Louisiana Fibre Board Co.
Cullet, G. F., Supt., The Jonquieres Pulp Co., Ltd.
Currie, F. P., Pres., Dominion Paper Co.
Currie, Robert, Vice-Pres. and Gen. Mgr., Dominion Paper Co.
Currier, M. D., Mill Supt., Champion-International Co.

Arnold, Hoffman & Co., Inc.

PROVIDENCE, NEW YORK, BOSTON, PHILADELPHIA AND CHARLOTTE, N. C.

SOLE AGENTS FOR

The Mathieson Alkali Works, Inc.
SALTVILLE, VIRGINIA
AND
NIAGARA FALLS, NEW YORK

MANUFACTURERS OF

EAGLE and THISTLE BRAND
Bleaching Powder

CAUSTIC SODA, 70, 74 and 78 per cent.
REFINED ALKALI, 48 and 58 per cent.

PROPRIETORS OF THE

Anchor Color and Gum Works
DIGHTON, MASS.

Paper Makers' Colors

to match any shade or tint desired. We invite inquiries and shall be pleased to furnish a match for any sample submitted.

Brown Sugar of Lead   *Yellow Prussiate of Potash*
Starch

COLORS

FOR

PAPER MAKERS

We offer the Paper Industry of the United States all colors for the Beater, Calender and for coating, and place at the disposal of Paper Makers our well equipped Paper Laboratories for the accurate and expeditious solution of problems relating to the application and cost of colors for Paper.

□ □ □

KUTTROFF, PICKHARDT & CO.
INCORPORATED

128 Duane Street, New York

BRANCH OFFICES:

BOSTON: 86 Federal Street   PHILADELPHIA: 111 Arch Street
PROVIDENCE: 52 Exchange Place   CHICAGO: 305 W. Randolph Street

Curtenius, A. E., Treas., Kalamazoo Paper Co.; Pres., Western Board & Paper Co.
Curtis, Alfred A., Pres., Curtis & Bro., Inc.
Curtis, Allen, Mgr. Dept. of Manufacture, International Paper Co.
Curtis, F. Lindsey, Sec. and Treas., Curtis & Bro., Inc.
Curtis, Geo. M., Vice-Pres., Louisiana Fibre Board Co.
Curtis, H. H., Pres., Creamery Package Mfg. Co.
Curtis, Warren, Jr., Pres. and Mgr., The Ontario Paper Co., Ltd.
Cushing, D. T., Treas., Bogalusa Paper Co., Inc.
Custer, M. D., Sec. and Treas., Dresden Paper Mills Co.; Sec. and Treas., The Fairfield Paper Co.
Cutler, M. H., Treas., Herkimer Fibre Co.

D

Datewyler, R., Pres., Economic Power & Products Co.
Dahlberg, B. G., Second Vice-Pres., Fort Frances Pulp & Paper Co., Ltd.; Second Vice-Pres., Minnesota & Ontario Pulp & Paper Co.
Daley, John E., Supt. Paper Div., Port Huron Sulphite & Paper Co.
Dance, L. A., Sales Agt., Kinleith Paper Mills, Ltd.
Daniel, Charles E., Treas., United Paperboard Co.
Daniels, Arthur B., Treas. and Mgr., L. L. Brown Paper Co.
Daniels, Dr. A. D., Vice-Pres., Rhinelander Paper Co.
Daniels, A. Millard, Gen. Supt., L. L. Brown Paper Co.
Dantzler, A. F., Treas., Southern Paper Co.
Dantzler, J. L., Pres., Southern Paper Co.
Darmstadt, L. F., Vice-Pres. and Treas., Bergen Paper Co.
Davenport, H. E., Sec. and Treas., Bird & Son, Ltd.
Daverin, D., Supt., Provincial Paper Mills Co., Ltd.
Davey, E. S., Sec., W. O. Davey & Sons.
Davey, Leigh H., Pres., W. O. Davey & Sons.
Davidson, F. B., Mgr., National Biscuit Co.
Davidson, H. N., Mgr. & Supt., Clifton Paper Mills.
Davies, A. J., Supt., Price Bros. & Co., Ltd.
Davies, W., Vice-Pres., Don Valley Paper Co., Ltd.
Davis, G. S., Sec. and Treas., King Paper Co.
Davis, Geo. F., Vice-Pres., Bennett, Ltd.
Davis, H. A., Sec., Wm. Mann Co.
Davis, H. C., Pres., Davis Paper Co.
Davis, H. J., Treas., Davis Paper Co.
Davis, John A., Vice-Pres., St. Croix Paper Co.
Davis, N. F., Sec., Davis Paper Co.
Davis, S. E., Vice-Pres., Dells Paper & Pulp Co.
Davis, T. J., Vice-Pres., Fox Paper Co.
Davis, W. L., Pres. and Supt., Dells Paper & Pulp Co.
Dawson, S. F., Jr., Pres. and Treas., Milton Leather Board Co.

Dawson, W. C., Treas., Claremont Paper Co., Inc.
Day, John O., Vice-Pres., Grandfather's Falls Co.
Day, Martin H., Treas. and Vice-Pres., The Thompson & Norris Co. of Indiana; Treas., The Pynetree Paper Co.
Dean, J. E., Sec., Mars Paper Corporation.
De Cant, L. G., Second Vice-Pres., Malone Paper Co.; Treas., Carthage Sulphite Pulp & Paper Co.
DeCant, Wood, Mgr. of Sales, Carthage Sulphite Pulp & Paper Co.
DeLano, Clayton H., Pres., Penobscot Chemical Fibre Co.
Delbridge, J. H., Pres., Falls Mfg. Co.; Pres. and Gen. Mgr., Union Mfg. Co.
Dessert, Louis, Vice-Pres., Wausau Sulphate Fibre Co.
Dew, J. H., Sec., Chesapeake Paperboard Co.
Dewing, Chas. A., Pres., Monarch Paper Co.
Dewing, J. H., Vice-Pres., Standard Paper Co.
Dice, J. P., Sec., Hagar Straw Board & Paper Co.
Dickinson, B. C., Pres., Standard Paper Co.
Dickinson, F. M., Sales Mgr., E-Z Opener Bag Co.
Dickinson, Isabel R., Pres., Fisk Paper Co., Inc.
Dickinson, L. W., Asst. Sec., Eddy Paper Co.
Dickinson, O. H., Treas., Fisk Paper Co., Inc.
Dinsmoor, P. A., Sec. and Asst. Mgr., Lawrence Paper Mfg. Co.
Dodd, Allison, Pres., E. H. Davey Co.
Dodd, E. Davey, Sec. and Treas., E. H. Davey Co.
Dodge, O. F., Supt., Taggarts Paper Co.
Dodge, Philip T., Pres., International Paper Co.; Pres., Herkimer Paper Co.
Dolan, W. J., Supt., Rhinelander Paper Co.
Dole, C. T., Mgr. Sales, Champion-International Co.
Dole, W. T., Asst. Gen. Mgr., Champion-International Co.
Donnelly, M. R., Sec., Merion Paper Co.
Donoghue, Thomas W., Mgr., Empire Paper Co.
Donohue, Chas., Mng. Dir., Nairn Falls Power & Pulp Co., Ltd.
Donohue, J. T., Pres., Nairn Falls Power & Pulp Co., Ltd.
Donovan, H. B., Mgr. of Sales, Canada Paper Co., Ltd.
Dooley, P. F., Supt., Buena Vista, Va., Columbian Paper Co.
Door, William H., Vice-Pres., Sugar Cane By-Products Co.
Dougall, A. H., Jr., Gen. Mgr., Board & Paper Div., The Paraffine Companies, Inc.
Downey, R. A., Sec., Arrowhead Mills, Inc.
Doyle, J. W., Plant Mgr., Nat'l Folding Box & Paper Co.
Dozier, Lewis, Supt., Westfield River Paper Co.
Drew, A. C., Supt., Pairpoint Corp.
Drew, L. L., Supt., Clyde River Pulp Co.
Drolet, F. X., Vice-Pres., Metabetchouan Co.
Drummond, J. H., Sec., Nashwaak Pulp & Paper Co.; Sec., Oxford Paper Co.

Dubuc, J. E. A., Mng. Dir., Compagnie de Pulpe de Chicoutimi; Pres. and Mng. Dir., St. Lawrence Pulp & Lumber Corp.; Vice-Pres., Ha! Ha! Bay Sulphite Co., Ltd.
Duff, C. C., Sec., New Castle Paper Mills.
Dugay, J. O., Supt., Nairn Falls Power & Pulp Co., Ltd.
Dunifer, J. F., Asst. Gen. Mgr., Miami Paper Co.
Duncan, S. F., Sec. and Treas., Port Arthur Pulp & Paper Co., Ltd.; Sec.-Treas. & Mgr. Provincial Paper Mills Co., Ltd.; Sec., Interlake Tissue Mills, Ltd.
Dunham, Geo. M., Mgr., Franklin, N. H., International Paper Co.
Dunklee, C. A., Pres. and Treas., Cleveland Paper Mfg. Co.
Dunn, T. W., Vice-Pres. and Gen. Mgr., Detroit Sulphite Pulp & Paper Co.
Durand, J. P., Sec. and Asst. Treas., Port Huron Sulphite & Paper Co.
Durgin, Prof. A. G., in Charge of Pulp Works; University of Maine Paper & Pulp School.
Durkee, Wm. L. R., Sec., Schroon River Pulp & Paper Co.
Dwight, A. H., Pres. and Mgr., Hawthorne Paper Co.
Dyke, C. H., Supt., Decatur Strawboard Co.

E

Earhart, E. E., Vice-Pres. and Supt., Continental Paper Co.
Easley, Prof. Charles W., in General Charge, University of Maine Paper & Pulp School.
Eaton, Wm. H., Vice-Pres. and Treas., Eaton, Dikeman Co.
Eckhardt, L. C., Sec., Acme Paper Co.; Asst. Treas., Monroe Bridge Paper Co.; Treas., Federal Paper Co.
Edmonds, W. L., Sec.-Treas. and Mgr., Wausau Paper Mills Co.
Edwards, Hon. W. C., Pres., Bathurst Lumber Co., Ltd.
Eibel, Wm., Treas. and Mgr., Rhinelander Paper Co.
Eichelberger, W. H., Mgr., Dresden Paper Mills Co.
Elder, John, Treas., New Castle Paper Mills.
Eldred, H. S., Pres., Anson Eldred Co.
Eldridge, Herbert W., Treas., Walloomsac Paper Co.
Elkins, T. F., Supt., Stevens Point Pulp & Paper Co.
Ellerson, H. W., Pres., Albemarle Paper Mfg. Co.
Elsas, Herman, Pres., Continental Paper Bag Co.
Embree, Royal B., Pres., Kingsport Pulp Corp.
Emerick, F. A., Pres., Arrowhead Mills, Inc.
Emerick, S. P., Vice-Pres., Arrowhead Mills, Inc.
Emerson, James A., Pres., Schroon River Pulp & Paper Co.
Emigh, O. R., Vice-Pres. and Gen. Mgr., Baltimore Roofing & Asbestos Mfg. Co.
Emmons, Fred, Sec., Hinde & Dauch Paper Co.; Sec., Southern Paper Co.
Empsall, F. A., Sec. and Treas., St. Regis Paper Co.
Emmons, Fred, Sec., Hinde & Dauche Paper Co.
Endicott, H. B., Pres., Endicott, Johnson & Co.

Endress, Frank, Pres., Mt. Vernon Straw Board Co.
Esleeck, A. W., Pres., Esleeck Mfg. Co.
Esleeck, I. N., Vice-Pres., Esleeck Mfg. Co.
Evans, Arthur S., Pres., Blossvale Paper Co.
Evans, H. C., Resident Mgr., Alton Box Board & Paper Co.
Evans, Henry, Vice-Pres., American Writing Paper Co.
Everard, A. C., First Vice-Pres., Detroit Sulphite Pulp & Paper Co.
Everest, D. C., Sec. and Gen. Mgr., Marathon Paper Mills Co.
Everhard, N. S., Pres., The Ohio Box Board Co.

F

Failey, Bruce F., Treas., Lafayette Box Board & Paper Co.; Sec. and Treas., Alton Box Board & Paper Co.
Fairbanks, Crawford, Pres., Alton Box Board & Paper Co.; Pres., Chicago Coated Board Co.; Pres., Haverhill Box Board Co.; Vice-Pres., Piermont Paper Co.
Fairbanks, Grant, Vice-Pres., Columbia Box Board Mills, Inc.; Sec. and Treas., Haverhill Box Board Co.
Fairburn, W. A., Pres., Diamond Match Co.
Fairchild, W. H., Pres., Mid-West Box Co.
Fales, H. E., Treas., Hollingsworth & Whitney Co.
Farley, D. E., Amboy Paper Co.
Farley, H. I., Amboy Paper Co.
Farnsworth, R. L., Supt., Cadyville, N. Y., International Paper Co.
Farwell, F. H., Sec. and Treas., Yellow Pine Paper Mill Co.
Farwell, R. E., Mgr., Ryegate Paper Co.
Fell, W. I., Pres. Michigan Carton Co.
Felton, Albert, Gen. Mgr., Quebec & Saguanay Pulp Co.
Ferguson, Joseph, Pres. and Mgr., The F. H. Whittelsey Co.
Ferris, T. H., Treas., Hinckley Fibre Co.
Fetty, I. H., Pres., Atlantic Paper and Pulp Corp.
Field, F. E., Supt., Hinsdale Paper Mfg. Co.
Fields, S. H., Sec. and Treas., American Tar Products Co.
Filer, E. G., Pres., Filer Fibre Co.
Filleul, H. P., Sec. and Treas., Campbell Lumber Co., Ltd.
Fillmore, H. D., Fillmore & Slade.
Finlay, G. R., The Strathcona Paper Co.
Finlay, W. J., The Strathcona Paper Co.
Fisher, J. A., Vice-Pres., Sec. and Supt., Beloit Box Board Co.
Fisk, I. T., Supt., Stevens & Thompson.
Flanders, L. P., Treas., Michigan Carton Co.
Fleming, E. T., John G. Fleming & Sons.
Fleming, S. B., Treas., Acme Paper Co.; Treas., Indiana Board & Filler Co.
Fleming, Walter L., John G. Fleming & Sons.
Fletcher, Allan M., Pres., Fletcher Paper Co.
Fletcher, Henry E., Treas., Fletcher Paper Co.
Fletcher, J. S., Sec., Tennessee Paper Mills, Inc.
Fletcher, Philip K., Sec., Fletcher Paper Co.

Mill Officials in the United States and Canada

Flint, Lester E., Treas., Westfield River Paper Co.
Flynn, Michael, Supt., John T. Andrews & Co., Inc.
Foley, Ed. P., Vice-Pres. and Mang. Dir., Foley-Rieger Pulp & Paper Co., Ltd.; Vice-Pres. and Mgr., Peerless Pulp Co., Ltd.
Foley, Joseph M., Asst. Mgr., Foley-Rieger Pulp & Paper Co., Ltd.
Foley, T. J., Gen. Mgr., Mumford Paper Mills, Inc.
Forbes, L. S., Pres. and Treas., East Hartford Mfg. Co.
Forbes, R. S., Asst. Treas., East Hartford Mfg. Co.
Ford, Albert, Mill Supt., Lazier Paper Mills, Ltd.
Ford, Jos., Jr., Joseph Ford & Co.
Ford, J. W., Jr., Pres., Ford Mfg. Co.
Ford, L. M., Treas., Ford Mfg. Co.
Ford, Rowland, Jr., Rowland Ford & Son.
Ford, Rowland, Sr., Rowland Ford & Son.
Ford, Thos. F., Joseph Ford & Co.
Ford, W. O., Vice-Pres. and Sec., Ford Mfg. Co.
Forman, W. A., Mgr. Paper Mill Div., Barrett Co.
Forsyth, W. L., Sec., Victoria Paper Mills Co.
Foster, Geo. A., Sec. and Treas., Grandfather's Falls Co.
Foster, Theodore, Treas., Foster Box Board Co.
Foster, T. S., Sec., Foster Box Board Co.
Foster, W. B., Vice-Pres., Foster Box Board Co.
Foster, W. S., Pres., Foster Box Board Co.
Foulds, Wm., Jr., Pres. and Sec., Wm. Foulds & Co., Inc.; Sec., Colonial Board Co.
Foulds, William, Treas., Colonial Board Co.
Foulds, Wm., Sr., Treas., Wm Foulds & Co., Inc.
Foulds, Wm., Pres., Lydall & Foulds Paper Co., Inc.
Fowler, Geo. F., Treas., Valley Paper Co.
Fowler, Wm. S., Asst. Treas., Valley Paper Co.
Fox, C. A., Sec. and Treas., Bryant Paper Co.
Fox, G. B., Sec. and Mgr. Sales, Fox Paper Co.
Fox, J. C., W. H. Fox & Sons.
Fox, Louis, Pres., Hartford City Paper Co.
Fox, Oscar W., Sec., Hartford City Paper Co.
Fox, W. D., Mill Supt., W. H. Fox & Sons.
Fraga, J. M., Mgr., Norwich, Conn., American Straw Board Co.
France, R. A., Pres. and Mgr., Joseph Parker & Son Co.
Franck, B. C., Sec. and Treas., Tidewater Paper Mills Co.
Frank, Edward W., Traveling Auditor, American Writing Paper Co.
Frank, Alfred, Pres., Ancram Paper Mills.
Frank, Jerome W., Vice-Pres., Ancram Paper Mills.
Franklin, B. A., Vice-Pres., Strathmore Paper Co.
Fraser, Archibald, Pres., Fraser Companies, Ltd.
Fraser, Donald, Vice-Pres., Fraser Companies, Ltd.
Freeman, Eben W., Sec., Rogers Fibre Co., National Div.
Freeman, H. G., Treas., Fox River Paper Co.
Freeman, Lewis C., Sec., Columbia Box Board Mills, Inc.
Frelday, Wm., Vice-Pres., Mount Tom Sulphite Pulp Co.
French, F. J., Treas., French Paper Co.
French, J. E., Pres., French Paper Co.
Frey, Andrew, Pres., Mutual Box Board Co.
Friend, H. W., Vice-Pres., The Sterling Paper Co.
Frisbie, C. O., Pres., Cornell Wood Products Co.
Frisbie, H. C., Vice-Pres. and Gen Mgr., Cornell Wood Products Co.
Frohman, Sidney, Treas., Hinde & Dauch Paper Co.; Sec., Hinde & Dauch Paper Co. of Canada, Ltd.; Treas., Southern Fibre Co.
Frost, Horace W., Sec., Westfield River Paper Co.
Fry, Eugene W., Pres., The Jessup & Moore Paper Co.
Fulks, E. B., Vice-Pres., American Tar Products Co.
Fuller, F. H., Supt. and Gen. Mgr., Hall & Richter Paper Co.
Funk, U. F., Treas., Keasbey & Mattison Co.
Funke, Ferd. A., Supt., Ferdinand Funke's Sons.
Funke, John M. F., Ferdinand Funke's Sons.
Funke, Jos. H. F., Ferdinand Funke's Sons.
Furlong, J., Supt., Patent Vulcanite Roofing Co.
Furminger, H. S., Supt., Fox River Paper Co.
Fynes, Thomas, Sec. and Asst. Treas., Continental Paper Bag Co.; Sec., Falls Mfg. Co.

G

Gable, J. L., Treas., Marion Paper Co.
Gabmle, J Munson, Pres. and Treas., Brownville Board Co.
Gage, W. J., Pres., Kinleith Paper Mills, Ltd.
Gain, C. Nelson, Supt., Don Valley Paper Co., Ltd.
Gallagher, J. E., Pres. and Treas., Beaver Brook Paper Mills, Inc.
Gallagher, L. P., Pres., Dresden Paper Mills Co.
Galliver, George A., Pres. and Gen. Mgr., American Writing Paper Co.
Gannon, J. J., Treas., The Ohio Box Board Co.
Garabrant, D. G., Pres., Union Mill.
Garber, L. F., Treas., D. M. Bare Paper Co.
Gardner, A. B., Second Vice-Pres., Lee Paper Co.
Gardner, A. H., Treas., Fox Paper Co.
Gardner, Chas. H., Treas., Albia Box & Paper Co.
Gardner, C. H., Asst. Treas., Advertisers Paper Mills; Asst. Treas., Taylor-Logan Co., Papermakers.
Gardner, Colin, Chairman, The Gardner-Harvey Paper Co.; Chairman, The Colin-Gardner Paper Co.; Chairman, The Gardner Paper Board Co.

Gardner, Colin, Jr., Vice-Pres., The Gardner-Harvey Paper Co.; Vice-Pres., The Colin Gardner Paper Co.; Vice-Pres., The Gardner Paper Board Co.
Gardner, E. T., Pres., The Gardner-Harvey Paper Co.; Pres., The Colin Gardner Paper Co.; Pres., The Gardner Paper Board Co.
Gardner, L. H., Pres., Garden City Paper Mills Co., Ltd.
Gardner, W. J., Supt., Mountain Paper Co.
Garfield, H. S., Asst. Treas., Ashuelot Paper Co.
Garneau, N., Pres., Campagnie de Pulpe de Chicoutimi.
Garrett, C. S., Supt., Marley Paper Mfg. Co.
Gerrett, Casper S., Vice-Pres., Edwin T. Garrett Co.
Garrett, Elmer E., Pres., Edwin T. Garrett Co.
Garrett, Harvey, Sec., Treas. and Gen. Mgr., Edwin T. Garrett Co.
Garvin, J. F., Sec. and Treas., Western Paper Mills, Ltd.
Garvan, T. F., Owner, Thomas F. Garvan Co. and Hartford Board Co.
Gault, Arthur C., Asst. Gen. Supt., American Writing Paper Co.
Gaylord, Geo. S., Vice-Pres. and Mgr., Menasha Printing & Carton Co.
Geddes, E. J., Sec., Central Paper Co.
Geddes, W. L., Vice-Pres., MacAndrews & Forbes Co.
Gee, Forest R., Comptroller, American Writing Paper Co.
Geer, William C., Pres., Albin Box & Paper Co.
Geiger, Fred., Treas. and Gen. Mgr., John Lang Paper Co.
George, S., Gen. Mgr., George & Sherrard Paper Co.
George, T. H., Treas. and Gen. Mgr., S. George Co.
Gerphelde, G. H., Sec., Bardeen Paper Co.
Getten, F. W., Gen. Mgr., The Adams Bag Co.
Gibson, Jno., Jr., Sec. and Treas., Wrenn Paper Co.
Gibson, T., Sec., Spanish River Pulp & Paper Mills, Ltd.
Gilbert, A. C., Treas., Gilbert Paper Co.
Gilbert, Jay, Vice-Pres., Frank Gilbert Paper Co.
Gilbert, J. J., Vice-Pres., Mohawk Valley Paper Co., Inc.
Gilbert, L. L., Pres., Ulster Tissue Mills, Inc.; Pres., Union Waxed and Parchment Paper Co.
Gilbert, Theo. M., Vice-Pres., Gilbert Paper Co.
Gilbert, W. H., Sec., American Box Board Co.
Gilbert, W. M., Pres., Gilbert Paper Co.; Pres., Riverside Fibre & Paper Co.
Gilchrist, F. D., Asst. Mgr. and Asst. Sec., Watervliet Paper Co.
Gilchrist, F. H., Supt., Standard Paint Co., Joliet, Ill.
Ikey, Geo. W., Sec. and Mgr., Michigan Paper Co. of Plainwell.
Il, George C., Pres., Missisquoi Pulp & Paper Co.; Pres., Erving Paper Mills, Erving, Mass.
Gill, I. V. H., Treas. and Sec., Mohican Pulp & Paper Co.
Gill, John M., Asst. Treas., Iroquois Pulp & Paper Co.
Gilman, Alex. G., Vice-Pres., Monarch Paper Co.

Gilman, Frank N., Treasurer, Mason-Perkins Paper Company.
Gilman, Isaac, Pres., Fitzdale Paper Co.
Glasson, Wm., Treas., Pejepscot Paper Co.
Glatfelter, P. H., Treas., P. H. Glatfelter Co.
Glatfelter, W. L., Pres., P. H. Glatfelter Co.
Glendinning, R., Pres., Patent Vulcanite Roofing Co.
Gleasner, M. F., Sec. and Treas., Megargee Paper Mills.
Godhelp, J. C., Vice-Pres., Morris Paper Mills.
Goethe, Henry, Sec., The John Hoberg Co.
Goldberg, J. D., Vice-Pres., Hammerschlag Mfg. Co.
Goldsword, James, Vice-Pres., Cleveland-Akron Bag Co.
Goodell, E. G., Vice-Pres., Stevens Point Pulp & Paper Co.
Goodenough, C. F., Supt., The Aetna Paper Co.
Goodfellow, J., Pres., St. George Pulp & Paper Co.
Goodman, Robert F., Vice-Pres., Marinette & Menominee Paper Co.
Goodnow, Westen W., Treas., Fort Orange Paper Co.
Goodrich, A. B., Pres. and Treas., Riverside Paper Mfg. Co.
Goodspeed, J. W., Treas., American Box Board Co.
Goodspeed, T. H., Pres., American Box Board Co.
Goodspeed, W. P., Vice-Pres., Moore Paper Mill Corp.
Goodwyn, W. L., Mgr., Richmond Paper Mfg. Co.
Gore, Frederic E., Mgr., Forest Paper Co.
Gotualt, W. K., Supt., The Springets Mills.
Goulard, Thomas, Asst. Treas., Ballston Fibre Products Co.
Gould, G. H. P., Pres., Donnacona Paper Co., Ltd.; Pres. and Treas., Gould Paper Co.
Gould, George H., Vice-Pres., Sugar Cane By-Products Co.
Gould, Harry P., Sec. and Asst. Treas., Gould Paper Co.
Gould, W. H., Vice-Pres., Hoboken Paper Mill Co.
Gouldman, W. Clyde, Asst. Mgr., Chesapeake Pulp & Paper Co., Inc.
Gradner, R. B., Treas., The Gardner-Harvey Paper Co.; Treas., The Colon Gardner Paper Co.; Treas., The Gardner Paper Board Co.
Graham, J. A., Gen. Mgr., Bergen Paper Co.; Pres., Lancaster Board & Paper Co.
Grandsen, V. T., Sec. and Sales-Mgr., The Auglaize Box Board Co.
Grant, J. S., Vice-Pres., Clayville Paper Mills Co.
Gray, F. D., Gen. Mgr. and Supt., Herkimer Fibre Co.
Gray, Guy F., Supt., Rogers Fibre Co., National Div.
Gray, H. C., Mobican Pulp & Paper Co.
Greason, E. P., Vice-Pres., Greasonia Paper Mills Co., Inc.
Greason, E. T., Treas., Greasonia Paper Mills Co., Inc.
Greason, W. H., Pres., Greasonia Paper Mills Co., Inc.
Greene, D. H., Vice-Pres. and Gen. Mgr., Gulf Paper Mills Co.

Greene, George E., Sec. and Treas., Niagara Paper Mills.
Greene, H., Sec. and Treas., The Bronson Co.
Greenfield, C. M., Supt., George O. Jenkins Co.
Gregor, W. D., Gen. Supt., Remington Paper & Power Co.
Gridley, Philip W., Asst. Treas., Crocker-McElwain Co.
Grieve, Edmond, Auditor, The Adams Bag Co.
Griffin, P. F., Sec., Fort Wayne Corrugated Paper Co.
Griffin, Solomon B., Pres., Hampshire Paper Co.
Grigg, E. M., Vice-Pres., Cliff Paper Co.
Griley, T. D., Gen. Mgr., The Fairfield Paper Co.
Guilbord, R. H., Treas. and Mgr., Saranac Co.
Guilbord, S. H., Pres., Saranac Co.
Guild, H. J., Vice-Pres., Eastern Mfg. Co.
Gumbinsky, Oscar, Vice-Pres., Eddy Paper Co.
Gundy, W. P., Vice-Pres., Kinleith Paper Mills, Ltd.
Gzowski, C. S., Pres., Canada Boxboard Co., Ltd.
Gzowski, N. G., Sec. and Treas., Canada Boxboard Co., Ltd.

H

Hacking, Edwin, H., Sec., Rex Paper Co.
Hager, George, Supt., Whiting-Plover Paper Co.
Haggerty, J. F., Vice-Pres., Beaver Wood Fibre Co., Ltd.
Hagar, Albert F., Pres., Franklin Board & Paper Co.
Hagar, M. G., Treas., Hagar Straw Board & Paper Co.
Hair, Clarence, Sec., D. M. Bare Paper Co.
Hall, B. F., Sec., Shortsville Paper Co.
Hall, E. M., Vice-Pres., Taggarts Paper Co.; Pres., Shortsville Paper Co.
Hall, George, Supt., Mountain Mill Paper Co.
Hall, H. F., Pres., Harper's Ferry Paper Co.; Vice-Pres., Shenandoah Pulp Co.
Hall, H. H., Vice-Pres., Senoso Paper Co., Inc.
Hall, S. C., Vice-Pres., Underwood Pulp & Paper Mills, Inc.
Halloch, Dr., E. C., Sec. and Treas., Lindauer Pulp Co.
Hamilton, Charles L., Pres. and Gen. Mgr., W. C. Hamilton & Sons, Inc.
Hamilton, Russell D., Sec., W. C. Hamilton & Sons, Inc.
Hamilton, Wilbur F., Vice-Pres. and Treas., W. C. Hamilton & Sons, Inc.
Hammer, Samuel L., Pres., Columbian Paper Co.
Hammerschlag, C. S., Pres., Hammerschlag Mfg. Co.
Hammerschlag, G. W., Sec. and Treas., Hammerschlag Mfg. Co.
Hammond, O. L., Sec., E-Z Opener Bag Co.
Hammond, P. A., Sec. and Treas., Champion-International Co.
Hammond, R. F., Sec. and Treas., Ha! Ha! Bay Sulphite Co., Ltd.
Hammond, T. H., Mill Supt., Taggart Bros. Co.
Hancock, George H., Supt., Columbia Box Board Mills, Inc.
Hankins, Edward R., Vice-Pres. and Treas., Mid-West Box Co.
Hanna, C. H., Vice-Pres., Remington Paper & Power Co.
Hanna, M. A., Pres., Champion Paper Co.
Hanna, M. H., Vice-Pres., Remington Paper & Power Co.
Hanson, G., Supt., Ha! Ha! Bay Sulphite Co., Ltd.
Harbison, R. B., Sec., The Sterling Paper Co.
Harbrecht, W. F., Gen. Supt., Hinde & Dauch Paper Co.; Vice-Pres., Southern Fibre Co.
Hardin, R. A., Sec., Riverside Paper Mfg. Co.
Harlan, D. E., Sec., Treas. and Mgr., Crystal Paper Co.
Harmon, Herbert E., Sec., Knowlton Bros., Inc.
Harrigan, W. T., Supt., Hartje Bros. Paper Co.
Harrington, H. L., Treas., Berkshire Hills Paper Co.
Harrington, T. R., Mgr., Marseilles Plant, Certain-Teed Products Corp.
Harris, A. B., Gen. Mgr., Albert E. Reed & Co.
Harris, J. W., Mill Mgr., Oxford Paper Co.
Harris, Robert H., Sec., Fort Orange Paper Co.
Harrison, A. McL., Vice-Pres., Halltown Paper Board Co.
Harrison, F. S., Pres. and Gen. Mgr., Halltown Paper Board Co.
Hart, Alfaretta M., Vice-Pres., T. F. Hart Paper Co.
Hart, T. F., Pres., T. F. Hart Paper Co.
Hartje, Augustus, Pres., Hartje Paper Mfg. Co.
Hartje, Chas. G., Pres., Hartje Bros. Paper Co.
Hartje, Richard, Vice-Pres. and Treas., Hartje Bros. Paper Co.
Hartley, M. T., Vice-Pres. and Treas., Paul A. Sorg Paper Co.; Sec., W. B. Oglesby Paper Co.
Hartman, Gunnar, Vice-Pres., Westfield River Paper Co.
Hartnett, W. J., Vice-Pres., North End Paper Co.
Harvey, Alexander J., Pres., Agasote Millboard Co.
Harvey, E. G. Supt., Columbia Paper Mills Co.
Harvey, Harold, Treas., Agasote Millboard Co.
Harvey, Tom, Gen. Mgr., The Gardner-Harvey Paper Co.; Gen. Mgr., The Colin Gardner Paper Co.; Gen. Mgr., The Gardner Paper Board Co.
Haskell, W. E., Asst. to Pres., International Paper Co.
Hastings, A. C., Gen. Mgr., Cliff Paper Co.
Hastings, Frederick E., Sec., Dill & Collins Co.
Hawley, Willard P., Pres., Hawley Pulp & Paper Co.
Hawley, Willard P., Jr., Vice-Pres. and Gen. Mgr., Hawley Pulp & Paper Co.
Hayden, W. B., Treas., Miami Paper Co.
Haynes, E. A., Second Vice-Pres., Port Huron Sulphite & Paper Co.
Haynes, S. B., Vice-Pres., Taylor-Atkins Paper Co.
Hays, C. B., Vice-Pres., Watervliet Paper Co.

Hazel, Wm. F., Gen. Supt., St. Regis Paper Co.
Hazen, J. N., Sec., Advertisers Paper Mills; Asst. Treas., Taylor-Logan Co., Papermakers.
Heberly, Thos. F., Mill Supt., Schmidt & Ault Paper Co.
Hecht, Louis, Sec., Cornwall Paper Mfg. Co.
Heckscher, August, Chairman of the Board, Union Bag & Paper Corp.
Heebner, Wm. D., Treas., The Jessup & Moore Paper Co.
Heisler, G. W., Treas., Menasha Printing & Carton Co.
Helmer, F. T., Treas., Newton Falls Paper Co.
Helwig, Edward, Sec. and Treas., The Beckett Paper Co.
Henderson, A. L., Fandango Mills.
Henderson, J. O., Vice-Pres., Lafayette Box Board & Paper Co.
Henderson, T. G., Supt., Bird & Son, Inc.
Hendrickson, C. F., Pres., Astoria Pulp & Paper Co.
Henry, H. B., Prop., Perseverance Paper Mills.
Hercher, John, Supt., John Strange Paper Co.
Herman, K. I., Sec. and Gen. Mgr., Mid-West Box Co.
Herrick, Robert F., Vice-Pres., Aroostook Pulp & Paper Co.
Hervey, H. C., Pres., Harvey Paper Co.
Heselton, H. B., Sec., Otter River Board Co.
Hewton, James, Supt., J. R. Walker & Co., Ltd.
Heywood, Frank, Pres., Rockford Paper Box Board Co.
Hibbard, E. A., Supt., French Paper Co.
Hidden, Edward, Vice-Pres., The Terre Haute Paper Co.
Higgins, C. D., Blake & Higgins.
Higgins, M. R., Pres., National Paper Products Co.
High, J. M., Sec., Agasote Millboard Co.
Hildreth, Horace E., Treas., C. M. Robertson Co.
Hiles, H. N., Asst. Sec., The Beaver Wood Fibre Co., Ltd.
Hill, Arthur H., Second Vice-Pres., Crocker-McElwain Co.
Hill, Irving, Vice-Pres. and Mgr., Lawrence Paper Mfg. Co.
Hillegass, Dr. Chas. Q., Pres. and Treas., Perkiomen Paper Co.
Hillegass, Foster C., Sec., Perkiomen Paper Co.
Hilton, Geo., Sec., Fox River Paper Co.
Hinnenthal, W. W., Treas., Union Mfg. Co.
Hinzke, A. G., Gen. Supt., Port Arthur Pulp & Paper Co., Ltd.
Hitchcock, A. W., Treas., American Wood Board Co.; Pres. Blandy Paper Co.
Hixon, Harold W., Sec., Chapin & Gould Paper Co.
Hobble, E. W., Treas., The Phœnix Paper Co.
Hobble, P. W., Vice-Pres., The Phœnix Paper Co.
Hobble, W. R., Pres., The Phœnix Paper Co.
Hoberg, Anton, Vice-Pres., The John Hoberg Co.
Hoberg, A. E., Vice-Pres., Crivitz Pulp & Paper Co.
Hoberg, Frank H., Pres. and Gen. Mgr., The John Hoberg Co.; Vice-Pres., Green Bay Paper & Fibre Co.

Hoberg, Wm., Pres., Crivitz Pulp & Paper Co.; Treas., John Hoberg Co.
Hobson, Arthur L., Treas., St. Croix Paper Co.
Hodge, F. M., Pres., Kalamazoo Paper Co.; Treas., Western Board & Paper Co.; Vice-Pres., Hawthorne Paper Co.
Hoefler, F. W., Mgr., Oswego River Paper Mills.
Hoes, Guy M., Treas., Columbia Box Board Mills, Inc.
Hoffman, A. E., Vice-Pres., Saxer Paper Mills.
Hoffman, C. E., Vice-Pres., The Aetna Paper Co.
Hoffman, H. H., Pres., Aetna Paper Co.
Hofstra, W. S., Second Vice-Pres., Southern Paper Co.
Holden, A. F., Pres., Holden Paper Co.; Prop., Little Falls Paper Co.
Holliday, Wm. P., Chairman of Board, Detroit Sulphite Pulp & Paper Co.
Hollingsworth, Amor, Pres., Tileston & Hollingsworth Co.; Vice-Pres., Penobscot Chemical Fibre Co.
Hollingsworth, J. H., Mill Supt., Oswego Falls Pulp & Paper Co.
Hollingsworth, V., Treas., Hollingsworth & Vose Co.
Hollingsworth, Zachary T., Pres., Hollingsworth & Vose Co.
Hollister, R. A., Sec., Wisconsin River Paper & Pulp Co.
Holman, H. F., Sec., Diamond Match Co.
Holmes, Geo. S., Gen. Mgr., Yellow Pine Paper Mill Co.
Hoopes, Maurice, Pres., Finch, Pruyn & Co., Inc.
Horn, Wm. E., Mgr., East St. Louis Plant, Certain-Teed Products Corp.
Horwood, R. F., Dir., Horwood Lumber Co., Ltd.
Horwood, W. F., Dir., Horwood Lumber Co., Ltd.
Hosford, I. B., Pres., St. Croix Paper Co.
Hoskin, R. W. S., Mgr., Marinette & Menominee Paper Co.
Hosmer, Charles R., Vice-Pres., Laurentide Co., Ltd.
Houk, R. T., Sec., The Mead Pulp & Paper Co.; Vice-Pres., The Peerless Paper Co.
Howard, H. M., Sec. and Treas., The Aetna Paper Co.
Howard, Lucius S., Sec. and Treas., The Howard Paper Co.
Howard, Maxwell, Pres., Howard Paper Co.
Howard, Ward R., Vice-Pres., The Howard Paper Co.
Howarth, William, Pres. and Treas., Everett Pulp & Paper Co.
Howe, Albert E., Sec., George La Monte & Son.
Howe, J. H., Treas., Arrowhead Mills, Inc.
Howe, W. H., Pres., Mumford Paper Mills, Inc.
Howell, C. F., Sec. and Treas., Cornell Wood Products Co.
Howes, Willis H., Vice-Pres., Knowlton Bros., Inc.
Howland, Arthur V., Asst. Treas., Tileston & Hollingsworth Co.
Howland, Frank C., Treas. and Gen. Mgr., The Thomas Phillips Co.
Howland, Fred D., Pres., The Thomas Phillips Co.
Howland, Geo. S., Sec., The Thomas Phillips Co.

Hubbard, Fred, Supt., Gilbert Paper Co.
Hummel, J. P., Pres., Hummel & Downing Co.
Humphrey, F. W., Vice-Pres., Wolf River Paper & Fibre Co.
Hunter, Dard, Dard Hunter Paper Mill.
Huntington, E. H., Sec., Ontario Paper Co., Ltd.
Huppuch, W. A., Vice-Pres., Iroquois Pulp & Paper Co.
Hussey, W. J., Supt., Espanola, Spanish River Pulp & Paper Mills, Ltd.
Hutchinson, B. E., Treas., American Writing Paper Co.
Hutchinson, C. S., Sec. and Treas., Lancaster Board & Paper Co.; Sec. and Treas., Lancaster Leather Co.
Hutchinson, Dwight, Hutchinson-Puttaert Co.
Hyde, C. B., Pres., Niagara River Mfg. Co.
Hyde, Geo. E., Sec. and Treas., Eastern Mfg. Co.
Hyde, L. F., Vice-Pres., Finch, Pruyn & Co., Inc.

I

Ingalls, H. H. G., Sec. and Treas., Ingalls & Co.
Ingersoll, Mrs. E. S., Ingersoll Paper Co.
Ingersoll, N. C., Ingersoll Paper Co.
Inwood, E. Buyer, Riordon Pulp & Paper Co., Ltd.
Irving, S. C., Treas., The Paraffine Co's., Inc.

J

Jack, Allan M., Supt., Lockport Paper Co.
Jack, John M., Mgr., The Barrett Co.
Jack, W. A., Gen. Mgr., American Box Board Co.
Jackman, Charles L., Pres., Contoocook Valley Paper Co.
Jackson, J. G., Vice-Pres., De Grasse Paper Co.; Vice-Pres., High Falls Pulp & Paper Co.
Jacobs, John, Pres., Pioneer Paper Co.
Jacobs, John, Jr., Pres., Phila. Paper Mfg. Co.
Jaite, C. H., Pres. and Gen. Mgr., The Jaite Co.
Jaite, E. W., Sec., The Jaite Co.
Jaite, Robert, Vice-Pres., The Jaite Co.
James, Lee Warren, Pres., Hinckley Fibre Co.
James, Wm. B., Sec., Baltimore Roofing & Asbestos Mfg. Co.
Jansen, J. J., Sec., A. P. W. Paper Co.
Jarvis, H. St. J., Sec. and Treas., Don Valley Paper Co., Ltd.
Jarvis, Russell, Jarvis Paper Mills.
Jasperson, C. A., Sec., Nekoosa-Edwards Paper Co.
Jay, G. D., Sec., Lafayette Box Board & Paper Co.
Jefferson, G. H., Sec. and Treas., Kineleith Paper Mills, Ltd.
Jelenick, F. J., Sec.-Treas., Standard Paint Co., Joliet, Ill.
Jenkins, H. Loring, Treas. & Mgr., George O. Jenkins Co.
Jenkins, Robert A., Pres., George O. Jenkins Co.
Jenks, Charles C., Pres., L. L. Brown Paper Co.
Johnson, Augustus, Sec., Everett Pulp & Paper Co.

Johnson, C. S., Vice-Pres., Lake Champlain Pulp & Paper Co.
Johnson, E. E., Supt., Wheat Paper Co.
Johnson, H. L., Mgr., Endicott Johnson & Co.
Johnson, M. B., Pres., Winona Pulp & Paper Co.
Johnson, N. C., Treas., Diamond Match Co.
Johnson, Wm. Pierce, Pres., Crown Williamette Paper Co.
Johnson, W. R., Pres., George & Sherrard Paper Co.
Johnston, A. O., Pres., Treas. and Gen. Mgr., Chateaugay Pulp Co.
Johnston, J. E., Johnston & Son.
Johnston, M. S., Sec., The Gardner-Harvey Paper Co.; Sec., The Colin Gardner Paper Co.; Sec., The Gardner Paper Board Co.
Jones, E. A., Sec. and Treas., Tarentum Paper Mills.
Jones, G. D., Sec., Wausau Sulpate Fibre Co.
Jones, Guy, C., Sec., Carthage Sulphite Pulp & Paper Co.
Jones, M. E., Pres., Pettebone-Cataract Paper Co.
Jones, N. M., Mgr., Nashwaak Pulp & Paper Co.
Jones, W. O., Vice-Pres., Kalamazoo Vegetable Parchment Co.
Jordan, A. H. B., Vice-Pres. and Mill Supt., Everett Pulp & Paper Co.
Jourdain, L. T., Sec. and Treas., Lakeside Paper Co.
Joyce, H. Merton, Treas., Great Northern Paper Co.
Joyce, J. T., Treas., Dells Paper & Pulp Co.
Judd, W. D., Pres. and Treas., Carew Mfg. Co.; Treas., Hampshire Paper Co.
Judge, Thos. F., Supt., Anglo-Newfoundland Development Co., Ltd.
Jungbluth, Karl, Pres., MacAndrews & Forbes Co.

K

Kading, E. N., Sec., B. F. Nelson Mfg. Co.
Kain, John G., Treas., Tennessee Paper Mills, Inc.
Kappler, G. E., Sec., Cleveland-Akron Bag Co.
Karasik, Charles I., Business Mgr., Ravenswood Paper Mill Co.
Kaufman, Geo., Supt., Lafayette Box Board & Paper Co.
Kavenaugh, A., Supt., Sault Ste Marie Spanish River Pulp & Paper Mills, Ltd.
Keating, J. M., Supt., Merion Paper Co.
Keegan, Edward J., Supt., Flower City Tissue Mills Co.
Keeler, H. G., Treas., Lee Fibre Co.
Keens, F. R., Sec., Japanese Tissue Mills.
Keep, Wallace I., Pres. and Treas., Lockport Paper Co.
Kehew, H. T., Treas., Cargo Paper Co.
Keith, W. F., Treas., John Roberts & Son, Inc.
Kelley, Erwin W., Vice-Pres., Robertson Paper Co.
Kelley, Herbert, T., Sec., Robertson Paper Co.
Kelley, M. J., Supt., P. H. Glatfelter Co.
Kellogg, H. J., Supt., Turners Falls, Mass., International Paper Co.

Kellogg, V. K., Sec., **Newton Falls Paper Co.**
Kelly, W. A., Gen. Supt., **Marathon Paper Mills Co.**
Kelso, J. A., Treas., **Crescent Paper Co.**
Kennedy, S. Ward, Sec., **Kalamazoo Vegetable Parchment Co.**
Kenny, R. M., Mgr., **The James Maclaren Co., Ltd.**
Kent, H. F. E., Mng. Dir., **Kinleith Paper Mills, Ltd.**
Kenyon, Jacob C., Vice-Pres. and Mgr., **Kenyon Paper Corp.**
Keogh, Thos. H., Supt., **Wanaque River Paper Co.**
Kerry, J. G. G., Pres., **Northumberland Paper & Electric Co., Ltd.**
Kesson, W. M., Treas., **Fraser Companies, Ltd.**
Ketcham, A. E., Mill Supt., **Saxer Paper Mills.**
Keyes, C. W., Vice-Pres. and Sec., **Nashua River Paper Co.**
Keyes, George T., Pres. and Treas., Nashua River Paper Co.
Kieckhefer, J. W., Pres., **Kaukauna Pulp Co.**
Kiefer, E. W., First Vice-Pres., **Port Huron Sulphite & Paper Co.**
Kieffer, John E., Sec. and Gen. Mgr., Kieffer Paper Co.
Kieren, C. A., Supt., **Rainy River Pulp & Paper Co.**
Kilgour, Joseph, Pres., **Canada Paper Co., Ltd.**
Kimberland, W. H., Sec., **Hartje Bros. Paper Co.**
Kimberly, J. A., Pres., **Kimberly-Clark Co.**; Pres., Neenah Paper Co.
Kimberly, J. C., Second Vice-Pres., Kimberly-Clark Co.; Vice-Pres., **Neenah Paper Co.**
Kindleberger, J., Pres. **and Gen. Mgr.**, Kalamazoo Vegetable Parchment Co.
King, F. E., Supt., Orono, Me., International Paper Co.
King, G. F., Vice-Pres., **Fletcher Paper Co.**
King, J. B., Factory Mgr., **Diamond Match Co.**
King, John F., Pres., **Rex Paper Co.**; Treas. **Fitzdale Paper Co.**
King, Merrill B., Treas., **Rex Paper Co.**
Kingsbury, A. L., Pres., **South Coventry Paper Co.**
Kingsbury, L. A., Sec. and Treas., **South Coventry Paper Co.**
Kingston, Perry, Vice-Pres., Gen. Mgr. and Supt., Kingston Paper Co., Inc.
Kinley, Wm., Vice-Pres., **The Metalite Co.**
Kinsman, A. J., Pres., **American Fibre Chair Seat Corp.**
Kissinger, W. G., Supt., Acme Paper Co.
Kitzinger, Gus., Treas., Filer Fibre Co.
Klauser, Karl, Sec. and Treas., **Anson-Eldred Co.**
Klefeker, Charles B., Vice-Pres., **Bloomer Bros. Co.**
Kline, E. A., Plant Mgr., **The Adams Bag Co.**
Kline, J. G., Sec., Miamisburg Paper Co.
Knapp, L. C., Vice-Pres., **Monroe Binder Board Co.**
Kneeland, H. L., Vice-Pres., **Michigan Carton Co.**
Knickerbocker, H. McC., Treas., **Esleeck Mfg. Co.**
Knott, M. F., Pres., Crescent Paper Co.
Knowlton, Geo. S., Pres. and Treas., **Knowlton Bros., Inc.**

Kobeesen, John, Supt., **Lindauer Pulp Co.**
Koehler, C. W., Roofing Dept. Supt., National Asbestos Mfg. Co.
Kohl, J. L., Sec., **Phila. Wax Paper Co.**
Kowalsky, Robert, Pres. and Treas., Kingston Paper Co., Inc.
Krathge, H. F., Pur. Agt., **Baltimore Roofing & Asbestos Mfg. Co.**
Kraus, R. L., Vice-Pres., **Consolidated Water Power & Paper Co.**
Krebs, B. A., Supt., **Unity Paper Mills.**
Kreckel, Julius, Treas., **The Jalte Co.**
Kuehn, A. L., Gen. Supt., **American Tar Products Co.**
Kuhe, I., Vice-Pres., Continental **Paper Bag Co.**; Vice-Pres., **Falls Mfg. Co.**; Vice-Pres., Union Mfg. Co.

L

Labbe, V. E., Sec., **Tomahawk Pulp & Paper Co.**
Lachmann, E. J., Pres., **Lakeside Paper Co.**
Lafean, Carl, Mgr., **York Paper Mfg. Co.**
Lafore, J. A., Pres., **Merion Paper Co.**
Lafore, P. J., Treas., **Merion Paper Co.**
La Monte, Geo. M., Pres., **George La Monte & Son.**
La Monte, Geo. V., Vice-Pres., George La Monte & Son.
Lancaster, C. F., Vice-Pres., **Alexandria Paper Co.**
Landis, D. B., Supt., **Davis, W. Va., West Va. Pulp & Paper Co.**
Lane, W. R., Sec. and Treas., **Union Paper Mill Co.**
Lange, N. R., Mng. Dir., **Powell River Co., Ltd.**
Langtry, W. W., Sales-Mgr., D. of C. Paper Mfg. Co.
Lapointe, J. A., Mill Supt., **Compagnie de Pulpe de Chicoutimi.**
Lappen, J. E., Sec. and Treas., **Winona Pulp & Paper Co.**
La Rue, W. S., Sec., **Richardson Paper Co.**
Law, C. A., Supt., **Wisconsin River Paper & Pulp Co.**
Lawless, C. H., Sec., **Onondaga Paper Co.**
Lawless, David F., Pres., **Lawless Bros. Paper Mills**, Lawless Paper Co.
Lawless, D. J., Gen. Mgr., **Onondaga Paper Co.**
Lawless, D. T., Lawless Paper Co.
Lawless, F. J., Treas., **Onondaga Paper Co.**
Lawless, M. J., Lawless Paper Co.
Lawless, Matthew D., Sec., **Lawless Bros. Paper Mills.**
Lawless, Michael J., Vice-Pres., Lawless Bros. Paper Mills; Vice-Pres., Onondaga Paper Co.
Lawless, T. E., Pres., **Onondaga Paper Co.**
Lawrence, Jas., Vice-Pres., **Wardlow-Thomas Paper Co.**
Lawrence, S. C., Sec., **Atlantic Paper & Pulp Corporation.**
Lawrence, Wm. A., Pres., **Groton Leather Board Co.**
Lawson, J. H., Asst. Sec., **Powell River Co., Ltd.**
Lazier, R. E., Sec. and Treas., **Lazier Paper Mills, Ltd.**
Lazier, S. A., Pres., **Lazier Paper Mills, Ltd.**
Leadbetter, C. H., Sec., **Astoria Pulp & Paper Co.**

Leadbetter, L. C., Vice-Pres., Astoria Pulp & Paper Co.
Leahy, F. A., Vice-Pres., Eastern Mfg. Co.
Leathers, Don., Treas., Monroe Binder Board Co.
Leathers, L. W., Pres., Monroe Binder Board Co.
Lee, Arthur E., Vice-Pres., Ulster Tissue Mills, Inc.; Vice-Pres., Union Wax & Parchment Paper Co.
Lee, F. E., Pres., Lee Paper Co.
Leeds, Alfred, Treas., Worthy Paper Co. Ass'n.
LeFerve, H. I., Pres. and Treas., The Lewis Slocum & LeFevre Co., Inc.
Leggett, Joseph A., Pres., Big Falls Paper Co., Inc.
Lehr, L. F., First Vice-Pres., Malone Paper Co.
Leishman, John, Supt., C. H. Dexter & Sons, Inc.
Lennox, Robert W., Asst. Treas., Hollingsworth & Vose Co.
Leo, James, Pres., James Leo Co.
Leo, James, Jr., Vice-Pres., James Leo Co.
Leo, Stephen, Sec., James Leo Co.
Leonard, Fred'k S., Pres., Ashuelot Paper Co.
Leonhard, A. F., Vice-Pres., Megargee Paper Mills.
Leopold, N. F., Pres., Morris Paper Mills.
Levis, Chas., Sec. and Treas., Carlyle Paper Co.
Levis, Chas. M., Vice-Pres., Curtis & Bro., Inc.
Levis, E. H., Pres., Carlyle Paper Co.
Lewis, E. C., Prop., Chicago Folding Box Co.
Lewis, Geo. S., Treas., Aroostook Pulp & Paper Co.
Lewis, George S., Treas., Deerfield Pulp Co.; Treas., Haviland Pulp & Paper Corp.
Lewis, H. S., Pres. and Gen. Mgr., The J. P. Lewis Co., Inc.; First Vice-Pres. and Sec., The Lewis, Slocum & LeFevre Co., Inc.
Lewis, H. S., Sec. and Treas., Beaver Wood Fibre Co., Ltd.
Lewis, R. R., Pres., Bayless Mfg. Corp.
Lewis, T. E., Sec. and Treas., Mountain Paper Co.
Liebeck, Harry, Supt., Chester Paper Co.
Lincoln, C. E., Sales Mgr., Peninsular Paper Co.
Lincoln, E. Ellsworth, L. Lincoln & Co.
Lincoln, N. R., L. Lincoln & Co.
Lindauer, L., Pres., Lindauer Pulp Co.
Lindauer, Mrs. L., Vice-Pres., Lindauer Pulp Co.
Lindsay, David, Pres., Keystone Paper Mills Co.
Lindsay, David, Jr., Sec., Keystone Paper Mills Co.
Lindsay, E. W., Supt., Wasuc Mills Co.
Lindsay, J. Horace, Treas., Keystone Paper Mills Co.
Lindsay, W. Allan, Vice-Pres., Keystone Paper Mills Co.
Little, Arthur D., Pres., Arthur D. Little, Inc.
Little, George, Pres. and Gen. Mgr., Hagar Straw Board & Paper Co.; Vice-Pres., Brown Paper Co.; Vice-Pres., Franklin Board & Paper Co.
Littleton, W. B., Vice-Pres. and Gen. Mgr., Antietam Paper Co.

Livermore, R. B., Supt., Beaver Book Paper Mills, Inc.
Lloyd, Robert McAllister, Pres., Kenyon Paper Corp.
Locke, Frank, Pres., Mt. Holly Paper Mills, Inc.
Locke, H. A. G., Treas., Mt. Holly Paper Mills, Inc.
Locklin, L. C., Gen. Mgr. & Supt., Ashland Paper Co.
Logan, D. B., Treas., Advertisers Paper Mills; Treas., Taylor-Logan Co., Papermakers.
Logan, J., Vice-Pres., Patent Vulcantie Roofing Co.
Long, H. A., Sec., Dexter Sulphite Pulp. & Paper Co.
Long, John R., Gen. Supt., Tarentum Paper Mills.
Long, L. M., Asst. Sec., Chesapeake Pulp & Paper Co., Inc.
Long, Milton, Sec. and Treas., U. S. Paper Mills, Inc.
Longlaw, P. H., Mill Supt., Holden Paper Co.
Loosen, A. E., Treas., Bathurst Lumber Co., Ltd.
Loucks, Wm. D., Treas., Pioneer Paper Co.
Loveland, W. M., Pres., Watervliet Paper Co.
Lowe, Ernest P., Pres., Falulah Paper Co.
Lowe, Erving F., Sec., Falulah Paper Co.
Lowe, Joseph A., Treas., Falulah Paper Co.
Luke, Adam K., Treas., West Virginia Pulp & Paper Co.; Treas., West Virginia Pulp Co.
Luke, Allan L., Res. Mgr., West Virginia Pulp & Paper Co.
Luke, David L., Vice-Pres., West Virginia Pulp & Paper Co.; Pres., West Virginia Pulp Products Co., Inc.
Luke, John G., Pres., West Virginia Pulp & Paper Co.
Luke, Thomas, Vice-Pres., West Virginia Pulp & Paper Co.
Luke, Wm. L., Res. Mgr., West Virginia Pulp & Paper Co.
Lutz, A. George, Pres. and Treas., Cornwall Paper Mfg. Co.
Lydall, E. A., Sec., Lydall & Foulds Paper Co., Inc.
Lyle, J. T. S., Sec. and Treas., Cascade Paper Co.
Lyman, C. W., Vice-Pres. and Mgr. Dept. of Sales, International Paper Co.; Treas., Continental Paper Bag Co.; Treas., Falls Mfg. Co.
Lyman, Frederick S., Vice-Pres., Cushnoc Paper Co.
Lysle, Mary R., Sec. and Treas., Estate of Wilson Lysle.
Lysle, N. C., Supt., Estate of Wilson Lysle.

M

MacArthur, H. H., Sec. and Treas., News Pulp & Paper Co., Ltd.
MacGlashan, W. F., Pres., Beaver Wood Fibre Co., Ltd.
MacPherson, F. H., Pres. and Treas., Detroit Sulphite Pulp & Paper Co.
McAdam, Quentin, Treas., Mutual Box Board Co.
McAlpine, C. W., Supt., La Salle Paper Co.
McAlpine, W. T., Gen. Mgr., Munroe Felt & Paper Co.

McAneny, George, Vice-Pres., Tidewater Paper Mills Co.
McCarthy, J. M., Vice-Pres., The Jonquieres Pulp Co., Ltd.; Price Bros. & Co., Ltd.
McCarthy, P. E., Supt., Rumford, Me., International Paper Co.
McClellan, John R., Pres., Skowhegan Pulp Co.
McClellan, M. R., Pres., Mac Sim Bar Paper Co.; Pres., Wolverine Paper Co.
McClelland, R. L., Treas., Chicago Mill & Lumber Co.
McClenathan, R. C., Vice-Pres. and Treas., H. F. Watson Co.
McColl, Arch., Pres., Clyde River Pulp & Paper Co., Ltd.
McCook, Thomas, Mill Supt., Northumberland Paper & Electric Co., Ltd.
McCormick, D. T., Supt., Fort Edward, N. Y., International Paper Co.
McCormick, R. R., Vice-Pres. and Treas., The Ontario Paper Co., Ltd.
McCoy, H. C., Pur. Agent, Spanish River Pulp & Paper Mills, Ltd.
McCrea, F. N., Pres., Brompton Pulp & Paper Co.; Pres., Claremont Paper Co., Inc.
McCulloch, J. L., Vice-Pres. and Sec., Marion Paper Co.
McCurdy, Dr. H. R., Pres., The Fairfield Paper Co.
McDaniel, H. C., Mill Mgr., Waldorf Paper Products Co.
McDermott, Thos., Supt., Greenwich Leatherboard Co.
McDonald, Donald, Supt., Lawless Bros. Paper Mills.
McDowell, Charles, McDowell Paper Mills.
McDuffee, C. H., Gen. Supt., Claremont Paper Co., Inc.
McElwain, J. F., Pres., W. H. McElwain Co.
McElwain, R. F., Vice-Pres., Chemical Paper Mfg. Co.; First Vice-Pres., Crocker-McElwain Co.
McEvoy, Thomas, Supt., Cornwall Paper Mfg. Co.
McEwan, Arthur, Treas. and Mgr., McEwan Bros.
McEwan, Frank, Sec. and Treas., Newark Boxboard Co.
McEwan, Fred, Pres., Newark Boxboard Co.
McEwan, J. L., Vice-Pres., McEwan Bros.
McEwan, R. B., Pres., McEwan Bros.
McEwan, R. W., Sec., McEwan Bros.
McGinley, James, Supt., Ticonderoga, N. Y., International Paper Co.
McIfree, D. J., Asst. Treas., Falls Mfg. Co.
McIlvain, Hugh, Vice-Pres., Frank P. Miller Paper Co.
McIlvain, J. Gibson, Pres., Frank P. Miller Paper Co.
McIlvary, W. N., Vice-Pres., Barrett Co.
McInnis, R. A., Supt., Abitibi Power & Paper Co., Ltd.
McIntyre, L. N., Vice-Pres. and Sec., McIntyre Bros. Paper Co., Inc.
McIntyre, W. E., Pres. and Treas., McIntyre Bros. Paper Co., Inc.
McKay, A. J., Mgr., Combined Locks Paper Co.
McKee, Geo. M., Gen. Mgr., The Donnacona Paper Co., Ltd.
McKee, Wm. A., Supt., Hinckley Fibre Co.
McKernon, Charles, Treas., B. D. Rising Paper Co.
McKinstry, D. E., Vice-Pres., Holden Paper Co.
McKowen, G. E., Sec., Hummel & Downing Co.
McLaren, Thomas, Sec., Fort Frances Pulp & Paper Co., Ltd.; Sec., Minnesota & Ontario Power Co.
McLean, Augustus, Vice-Pres. and Gen. Mgr., Bathurst Lumber Co., Ltd.
McLean, Charles F., Sec., Louisiana Fibre Board Co.
McMillan, B. F., Treas., Wausau Sulphate Fibre Co.
McMiller, C. R., Vice-Pres., Union Bag & Paper Corp.
McMillian, E. A., Pres., Lindale Mills.
McNair, C. I., Second Vice-Pres. and Gen. Mgr., Northwest Paper Co.
McNair, C. I., Jr., Sec., Northwest Paper Co.
McNair, W. K., Supt. and Asst. Treas., Northwest Paper Co.
McNaughton, John, Treas., Outagamie Paper Co., Vice-Pres., Potters Paper Co., Ltd.
McNaughton, W. G., Gen. Mgr., Inland Empire Paper Co.
McNevins, James W., Sec. and Treas., Crivitz Pulp & Paper Co.
McPherson, Wm. R., Supt., Eddy Paper Co.
McVicker, H., Mill Mgr., The Mead. Pulp & Paper Co.
Mabee, D. W., Asst. Sec., Nat'l Folding Box & Paper Co.
Mabee, G. W., Sec., Nat'l Folding Box & Paper Co.
Macke, B. H., Sec., Gulf Paper Mills Co.
Mackinnon, D. T. H., Pres., Island Paper Co.
Maclaren, Albert, Pres., The James Maclaren Co., Ltd.
Maclaren, Alexander, Vice-Pres., The James Maclaren Co., Ltd.
Macleod, J. R., Pres., Macleod Pulp Co., Ltd.
Macy, C. B., Mgr., Nobleville, Ind., American Straw Board Co.
Madden, M. L., Vice-Pres., Hollingsworth & Whitney Co.
Maeder, James, Supt., Menasha Printing & Carton Co.
Mahaffey, E. C., Sec., Lewis Mfg. Co.
Mahler, Ernst, Gen. Supt., Kimberly-Clark Co.
Mallory, H. S., Vice-Pres., Monroe Bridge Paper Co.
Maltby, R. B., Sec. and Treas., Champion Paper Co.; Sec. and Treas., Remington Paper & Power Co.
Mandel, A. E., Gen. Mgr., National Paper Products Co.
Manhall, T. E., Supt., Marshall Bros., Inc.
Manning, John A., Pres. and Treas., John A. Manning Paper Co.
Manning, William H., Vice-Pres., John A. Manning Paper Co.
Mansfield, E. E., Asst. Sec., Cliff Paper Co.
Mansfield, Edw. F., Vice-Pres., New Haven Pulp & Board Co.
Manville, C. R., Vice-Pres., H. W. Johns-Manville Co.
Manville, H. E., Sec. and Treas., H. W. Johns-Manville Co.
Manville, T. F., Pres., H. W. Johns-Manville Co.; Treas., Fibre Corp.

Marcuse, M. E., Vice-Pres., Dixie Paper Mills, Inc.; Vice-Pres. and Treas., Bedford Pulp & Paper Co.
Marks, L. S., Vice-Pres., Tonawanda Board & Paper Co.
Marsden, John W., Treas., Economic Power & Products Co.; Treas., Sugar Cane By-Products Co.
Marsden, M. W., First Vice-Pres. and Gen. Mgr., Economic Power & Paper Co.
Marsh, Egbert, Vice-Pres., Tait & Sons Paper Co.
Marshall, H. W., Vice-Pres., National Fibre & Insulation Co.
Marshall, J. A., Sec. and Treas., National Fibre & Insulation Co.; Vice-Pres., Marshall Bros., Inc.; Supt. Marshall & Mitchell.
Marshall, J. W., Pres., National Fibre & Insulation Co.; Sec., Marshall Bros., Inc.
Marshall, T. C., Supt., National Fibre & Insulation Co.; Treas. Marshall Bros., Inc.; Vice-Pres., National Fibre & Insulation Co.
Marshall, T. Elwood, Marshall & Mitchell; Pres., Marshall Bros, Inc.
Marshall, Wm., Supt., Mohawk Valley Paper Co., Inc.
Martin, A. H., Treas., Martin Pulp & Paper Co.
Martin, H. W., Sec., Martin Pulp & Paper Co.
Martin, M. J., Vice-Pres., Martin Pulp & Paper Co.
Martin, O. E., Pres., Martin Pulp & Paper Co.
Martin, Thomas M., Fandango Mills.
Marx, John, Vice-Pres., John Strange Paper Co.
Mason, H. W., Treas., S. D. Warren Co.
Mather, D. L., Pres., Dryden Timber & Power Co., Ltd.
Mather, John, Sales-Mgr., Wayagamack Pulp & Paper Co.
Mather, S. L., Treas., Munising Paper Co.
Mather, Wm. G., Pres., Munising Paper Co.
Matheson, Wm., Sec., Fraser Companies, Ltd.
Martinson, H., Supt., Brown Corp.
Matthews, F. R., Supt., Taylor-Atkins Paper Co.
Mattison, Richard V., M. D., Pres., Keasbey & Mattison Co.
Mattison, Richard V., Jr., Vice-Pres. and Gen. Mgr., Keasbey & Mattison Co.
Mattison, Royal, Second Vice-Pres., Keasbey & Mattison Co.
May, F. H., Sec. and Treas., T. F. Hart Paper Co.
Mayer, Dr. John B., Second Vice-Pres., Economic Power & Products Co.
Maynard, Geo., Supt., South Coventry Paper Co.
Maynard, H. T., Vice-Pres., Mt. Holly Paper Mills, Inc.
Maynes, A. W., Sec. and Mgr. Sales, Fox Paper Co.
Mayo, E. H., Gen. Mgr., Southern Paper Co.
Mead, George H., Pres., Mead Pulp & Paper Co.; Pres., Spanish River Pulp & Paper Mills, Ltd.; Pres., Peerless Paper Co.
Mead, George W., Pres. and Mgr., Consolidated Water Power & Paper Co.; Pres., Interlake Pulp Co.

Meader, Henry J., Pres., Ballston Fibre Products Co.
Meagher, Charles, Supt., Astoria Pulp & Paper Co.
Meehan, Andrew, Supt., Srere Bros. & Co.
Megargee, M. B., Pres., Megargee Paper Mills.
Mellor, Alfred, Vice-Pres., MacAndrews & Forbes Co.
Melson, W. W., Supt., Delaware Hard Fibre Co.
Mendsen, E. B., Sales-Mgr., Michigan Paper Co. of Plainwell.
Mengel, C. C., Pres.; Mengel Box Co., Branch.
Merrill, O. B., Treas., Sec. and Mgr., Poland Paper Co.
Merritt, N. A., Pres., Lehigh Paper Mills, Inc.
Merry, A. D., Oswego River Paper Mills.
Merwin, G. J., Pres., Merwin Paper Co.
Messer, G. E., Vice-Pres., Bird & Son. Ltd.
Meurer, E., Pres., Central Paper Co.
Meyers, C. N., Vice-Pres., Winona Pulp & Paper Co.
Meyer, H. H., Pres., Hall & Richter Paper Co.
Milham, Frank H., Pres. and Gen. Mgr., Bryant Paper Co.; Mng. Dir., Munising Paper Co.; Pres., Eddy Paper Co.
Millen, Geo. H., Pres. and Mgr., The E. B. Eddy Co., Ltd.
Miller, Alvah, First Vice-Pres., St. Regis Paper Co.
Miller, Frank P., Sec. and Treas., Frank P. Miller Paper Co.
Miller, George E., Supt., Mattagami Pulp & Paper Co., Ltd.
Miller, H. H., Sec. and Treas., Bird & Son, Inc.
Miller, Henry J., Vice-Pres., Hartford City Paper Co.
Miller, James M., Vice-Pres. and Gen. Mgr., Reading Paper Mills.
Miller, L., Vice-Pres., Yellow Pine Paper Mill Co.
Miller, O. A., Pres., B. D. Rising Paper Co.
Miller, P., Mill Mgr., The Miller Brothers Co., Ltd.
Miller, W. A., Pres., Lancaster Leather Co.
Miller, William T., Pres., Miller Brothers Co., Ltd.
Millhiser, Clarence, Pres., Bedford Pulp & Paper Co.
Mills, Ogden, Vice-Pres., International Paper Co.
Milne, William, Treas., James Leo Co.
Mitchell, Emil, Sec. and Treas., Monroe Paper Co.
Mitchell, Leonard, Pres., Monroe Paper Co.
Mitchell, Sidney, Pres., United Paperboard Co.
Moeller, Wm. J., Supt., The Philip Carey Mfg. Co.
Mohn, E. L., Vice-Pres. and Treas., Rainy River Pulp & Paper Co.
Moles, John, Chief Engineer, American Writing Paper Co.
Monroe, S. B., Vice-Pres., Bardeen Paper Co.; Treas., Hawthorne Paper Co.; Sec., Wolverine Paper Co.
Monroe, W. S., Dir., Horwood Lumber Co., Ltd.
Montague, M. F., Mgr.-Sales, Standard Paper Mfg. Co.

Montgomery, John, Gen. Supt., Machine Drying Mills, American Writing Paper Co.
Moon, Owen, Sec., Chester Paper Co.
Mooney, Dr. M. T., Pres., Quebec & Saguanay Pulp Co.
Moore, B. S., Sec. and Treas., Moore Paper Mill Corp.
Moore, Chas. G., Pres., Moore Paper Mill Corp.
Moore, F. A., Pres. and Supt., Moore & Thompson Paper Co., Inc.
Moore, F. L., Pres. and Gen. Mgr., Newton Falls Paper Co.
Moore, J. T., Vice-Pres. and Mng. Dir. The Pynetree Paper Co.
Moore, John W., Owner, Felt Paper Co.
Moore, O. H., Treas. and Mgr., Hinde & Dauch Paper Co. of Canada, Ltd.
Moore, R. A., Vice-Pres., Yellow Pine Paper Mill Co.
Moore, R. S., Pres., The Paraffine Companies, Inc.
Moore, Stephen, Treas., Rogers Fibre Co., National Div.
Moore, Warner, Pres., Manchester Board & Paper Co.
Moorhouse, R. T., Pres., R. T. Moorhouse Paper Co.
Moorhouse, R. W., Sec., Treas. and Supt., R. T. Moorhouse Paper Co.
Morfey, M. W., Sec., Rainy River Pulp & Paper Co.
Morin, Laurent G., Sec. and Treas., Nairn Falls Power & Pulp Co., Ltd.
Morman, S. A., Vice-Pres., American Box Board Co.
Morrell, Herbert P., Vice-Pres., Empire Paper Co.
Morris, E. H., Pres., John Lang Paper Co.; Pres., Thorold Pulp Co., Ltd.; Treas., Hall & Richter Paper Co.; Vice-Pres., Merion Paper Co.
Morse, G. Stanley, Vice-Pres., Valley Paper Co.
Mortenson, Jacob, Vice-Pres., Watab Pulp & Paper Co.
Moses, H. A., Pres. and Treas., Strathmore Paper Co.
Moul, C. E., Vice-Pres. and Sec., P. H. Glatfelter Co.
Moulton, H. B., Pres., Parker-Young Co.-Henry Paper Co. Branch.
Mousley, Frank Co., Supt., The Thames River Specialties Co.
Mowry, J. S., Supt., Albemarle Paper Mfg. Co.
Moyer, J. W., Moyer & Pratt.
Muir, W. E., Pres., Treas. and Supt., Muir Board Co., Inc.
Muirhead, Andrew, Pres., Columbia Box Board Mills, Inc.; Vice-Pres., The Thames River Specialties Co.
Mullen, J. A., Pres., Mullen Bros. Paper Co.
Mullen, W. T., Vice-Pres. and Treas., Mullen Bros. Paper Co.
Mullin, T. J., Supt., Richardson Paper Co.
Munn, D. J., Pres., Alex. McArthur & Co., Ltd.
Munro, W. A., Escanaba Pulp & Paper Co.
Munroe, James P., Pres. and Treas., Munroe Felt & Paper Co.
Munroe, W. N., Treas., Brompton Pulp & Paper Co.; Treas. and Sec., Odell Mfg. Co.
Murgittroyd, Smith N., Co-partner, Crescent Paper & Machine Co.

Murphey, E. W., Treas., St. George Pulp & Paper Co.
Murphy, E. G., Vice-Pres., St. George Pulp & Paper Co.
Murphy, John, Local Supt., Claremont Paper Co., Inc.
Murphy, J. J., Supt., Barrett Co.
Murphy, L. T., Supt., Tennessee Paper Mills, Inc.
Murphy, S. W., Sec. and Treas., Riverside Fibre & Paper Co.
Murphy, T. A., Vice-Pres. and Supt., Walsh Paper Co., Inc.
Murphy, W. J., Pres., Manistique Pulp & Paper Corp.
Murray, D. C., Vice-Pres., The Donnacona Paper Co., Ltd.
Murray, E. B., Vice-Pres., Union Bag & Paper Corp.
Murray, James M., Supt., Berlin, N. H., International Paper Co.
Murray, Richard F., Supt., Thomson, N. Y., Iroquois Pulp & Paper Co.
Murray, Wm. A., Supt., Chisholm, Me., Livermore Falls, Me., and Riley, Me., International Paper Co.
Musser, R. D., First Vice-Pres. and Treas., Northwest Paper Co.
Myer, Jas. D., Supt. of Paper Mill, Finch, Pruyn & Co., Inc.
Myers, J. E., Mgr., Bellows Falls, Vt., International Paper Co.
Myers, Paul N., Vice-Pres., Waldorf Paper Products Co.
Myers, R. E., Vice-Pres., Garden City Paper Mills Co., Ltd.

N

Naber, F. D., Pres., Wolf River Pulp & Fibre Co.
Nash, W. C., Supt., Lakeside Paper Co.
Nathan, A., Sec., Kingston Paper Co., Inc.
Nau, George D., Pres., Green Bay Paper & Fibre Co.
Nauman, Layton M., Treas., Analomink Paper Co.
Nearing, W. W., Vice-Pres., Pejepscot Paper Co.
Nelson, B. F., Pres., Hennepin Paper Co.; Treas., B. F. Nelson Mfg. Co.
Nelson, C. E., Sec. and Gen. Mgr., Eddy Paper Co.
Nelson, George E., Sec., West Va. Pulp Products Co., Inc.
Nelson, G. H., Vice-Pres., B. F. Nelson Mfg. Co.
Nelson, C. M., Supt., Neenah Paper Co.
Nelson, N. Supt., Harvey Paper Co.
Nelson, P. P., Treas. and Supt., Halltown Paper Board Co.
Nelson, R. M., Sec. and Treas., Certain-Teed Products Corp.
Nelson, W. E., Pres., B. F. Nelson Mfg. Co.; Sec., Hennepin Paper Co.
Nevill, T. H., Supt., The Beaver Wood Fibre Co., Ltd.
Nevius, A. H., Vice-Pres. and Gen. Mgr., Miami Paper Co.
Newell, H. L., Treas., Miamisburg Paper Co.
Newman, Louis, Pres. and Treas., Tonawanda Board & Paper Co.
Newton, Herbert B., Sec. and Treas., Newton Paper Co.
Newton, James H., Vice. Pres., Newton Paper Co.
Nicely, F. P., Prop., La Salle Paper Co.
Nicely, R. S., Sec., La Salle Paper Co.
Nicholls, Henry M., Sec., Lockport Paper Co.

Nichols, H. W., Pres. and Gen. Mgr. Fox Paper Co.; Vice-Pres., Baltimore Roofing & Asbestos Mfg. Co.; Pres. and Treas., Chesapeake Pulp & Paper Co., Inc.
Nichols, M. T., Vice-Pres. and Supt., Atlantic Paper and Pulp Corp.
Nichols, R. M., Pres. Baltimore Roofing & Asbestos Mfg. Co.
Nicolson, G. L., Pres. District of Columbia Paper Mfg. Co.
Nixon, W. L., Gen. Supt., Chemical Paper Mfg. Co.
Noble, F. D., Pres., Noble Mfg. Co.
Norris, Beverly A., Vice-Pres., The Thompson & Norris Co. of Indiana.
Norris, Frederick A., Vice-Pres., The Thompson & Norris Co. of Indiana.
Northcliffe, Viscount, Pres., Anglo-Newfoundland Development Co., Ltd.
Norton, F. E., Supt., Bennett, Ltd.
Norton, Frank, E., Pres., Bennett, Ltd.
Nugent, J. S., Second Vice-Pres., Nat'l Folding Box & Paper Co.
Nutting, M. D., Vice-Pres. and Treas., Shortsville Paper Co.
Nye, W. B., Vice-Pres., S. D. Warren Co.

O

O'Brien, F. L., Traffic Mgr., Spanish River Pulp & Paper Mills, Ltd.
O'Brien, Josephine, Oswego River Paper Mills.
O'Brien, J. H., Asst. Treas. and Mgr., Otter River Board Co.
O'Brien, J. P., Pres. and Treas., Otter River Board Co.
O'Brien, W. M., Sec. and Treas., Unity Paper Mills.
O'Connell, J. H., Supt., King Paper Co.
O'Meara, Maurice, Pres., Mars Paper Corp.
O'Meara, Wm., Treas., Ballston Fibre Products Co.
O'Neil, A. S., Treas., Cascade Wood Products Co.
O'Neil, H. E., Pres. and Mgr., Cascade Wood Products Co.
O'Neill, Thos. J., Treas., George La Monte & Son.
Oakford, Jas. W., Vice-Pres. and Treas., Cherry River Paper Co.
Oatman, A. A., Asst. Treas., Cliff Paper Co.
Oberdorfer, Max, Supt., Filer Fibre Co.
Oberley, C. G., Gen. Mgr., Munising Paper Co.
Oberweiser, E. A., Sec. and Treas., Whiting-Plover Paper Co.
Oblinger, Daniel B., Supt., Union Mills Paper Mfg. Co.
Ochs, Adolph S., Pres., Tidewater Paper Mills Co.
Odell, W. H., Sec., St. George Pulp & Paper Co.
Ogilvie, Shirley, Vice-Pres., Abitibi Power & Paper Co., Ltd.
Oldham, F. H., Pres., General Paper Co., Inc.; Gen. Mgr., Thomas F. Garvan Co.
Oliner, L. E., Sec. and Treas., Tolland Leather Board Co.
Oliver, R. R., Supt., Southern Fibre Co.
Oliver, Wm., Mgr., Southern Fibre Co.
Oppenheimer, D. E., Sec. and Treas., Ancram Paper Mills.
Orbison, T. W., Vice-Pres., Riverside Fibre & Paper Co.
Orde, John F., K. C., Solicitor Director, The E. B. Eddy Co., Ltd.

Osmund, Theo., Sec. and Treas., Hawley Pulp & Paper Co.
Ouellet, Frank, Sec., Macleod Pulp Co., Ltd.
Outerbridge, E. H., Vice-Pres., Agasote Millboard Co.
Outterson, C. E., Pres., Union Paper Mills Co.
Outterson, J. A., Pres., De Grasse Paper Co.; Pres., High Falls Pulp & Paper Co.; Pres., Carthage Sulphite Pulp & Paper Co.

P

Paddock, H. L., Pres., Oswego Falls Pulp & Paper Co.; Pres., Skaneateles Paper Co.
Paepke, H., Pres., Chicago Mill & Lumber Co.
Page, B. W., Treas., Skowhegan Pulp Co.
Page, Wm. B., Asst. Treas. and Agt., Geo. W. Wheelwright Paper Co.
Pagenstecher, A. Pres., Keith Paper Co.
Pagenstecher, A., Jr., Vice-Pres., Central Paper Co.
Pagenstecher, F., Sec., Kalamazoo Paper Co.
Paine, A. G., Jr., Pres., New York & Pennsylvania Co.; Pres., The Highland Paper Co.
Paine, A. G., 3rd, Second Vice-Pres. and Gen. Mgr., New York & Pennsylvania Co.
Paine, Geo. E., Asst. Sec. and Treas., New York & Pennsylvania Co.
Painter, John, Supt., Mars Paper Corporation.
Palmer, G. H., Sec. and Treas., Blossvale Paper Co.
Palmer, J. C., Jr., Sec. and Treas., Harvey Paper Co.
Palmer, R. W., Vice-Pres. and Mgr., Harvey Paper Co.
Pankhard, H. I., Pres., Frank Gilbert Paper Co.
Parant, L. J., Gen. Supt., St. Croix Paper Co.
Parent, John, Sr., Supt., Crivits Pulp & Paper Co.
Parker, H. O., Sec., French Paper Co.
Parnell, W. E., Res. Mgr., La Have Pulp Co.
Parsons, Wm. H., Pres. & Treas., Roanoke Fibre Board Co.
Partington, S., Mill Supt., Greenwich, Continental Paper Bag Co.
Paterson, Allan, Sec., Whalen Pulp & Paper Mills, Ltd.
Patton, W. J., Supt., Price-Porritt Pulp & Paper Co.
Paul, Henry C., Pres., Fort Wayne Corrugated Paper Co.
Payne, F. C., Supt., River Raisin Paper Co.
Pearson, Frank, Supt., Munising Paper Co.
Pease, R. L., Sec., Hawthorne Paper Co.
Peck, Chas. A., Treas., Bardeen Co.
Penfield, E. J., Vice-Pres., Eureka Paper Co.
Pepin, E. M. R., Pres. and Gen. Mgr., Eastern Paper Co., Ltd.
Pepin, J. E., Sec. and Treas., Eastern Paper Co., Ltd.
Perkins, J. L., Pres., Japanese Tissue Mills.
Perry, E. L., Supt., The Metalite Co.
Perry, F. J., Coy Paper Co.
Perry, Ray P., Vice-Pres., Barrett Co.

Perry, W. P., Sec., Esleeck Mfg. Co.
Peters, H. C., Pres. and Mgr., Marcellus Paper Co.
Peters, R. R., Asst. Mgr., Lancaster Board & Paper Co.
Peterson, A., Supt., Shortsville Paper Co.
Peterson, Edw., Sec. and Treas., Manistique Pulp & Paper Co.
Peterson, T. L., Sec. and Supt., Brown Paper Co.
Pfister, John, Mill Supt., Waldorf Paper Products Co.
Phillips, D. F., Sec., Brownville Board Co.
Piatt, K. R., Sec., Analomink Paper Co.
Picker, John M., Mgr., Dept. of Insurance & Taxes, International Paper Co.
Pierce, Andrew G., Jr., Pres., Fairpoint Corp.
Pierce, Arthur J., Pres. and Treas., Monadnock Paper Mills.
Pierce, Freeman A., Pierce Bros.
Pierce, E. W., Agt., Geo. W. Wheelwright Paper Co.
Pierce, Josiah W., Pierce Bros.
Pierson, H. J., Pres. and Gen. Mgr., Consumers' Box Board & Paper Co.
Pilz, W. J., Asst. Mgr. and Asst. Treas., Everett Pulp & Paper Co.
Plamondon, Paul, Sec. and Treas., Montreal Paper Co., Ltd.
Plowman, William L., Asst. Pur. Agt., American Writing Paper Co.
Plum, Matthias, Vice-Pres. and Gen. Mgr., United Paperboard Co.; Prop., Waverly Paper Board Co.
Poland, C. A., Sec. and Supt., Wm. A. Cole Paper Co.
Pomeroy, F. W., Sec. and Treas., Frank Gilbert Paper Co.
Pomeroy, G. M., Supt., Frank Gilbert Paper Co.
Pooler, E. J., Treas., Central Paper Co.
Pope, R. H., Sec. and Treas., Wayagamack Pulp & Paper Co.
Porritt, O. A., Vice-Pres., Canada Boxboard Co., Ltd.
Porter, J. S., Vice-Pres., Certain-Teed Products Corp.
Post, Robt. W., Pres. and Treas., Westport Paper Co.
Potter, R. W., Pres., H. F. Watson Co.
Pounsford, A. G., Gen. Mgr., Port Arthur Pulp & Paper Co., Ltd.
Powell, Frank, Mgr., News Pulp & Paper Co., Ltd.
Powers, W. C., Mgr. of Sales, Great Northern Paper Co.
Pratt, A. L., Pres. and Gen. Mgr., King Paper Co.
Pratt, Chas. W., Moyer & Pratt; Pres. and Treas., Island Paper Co.; Vice-Pres., Gould Paper Co.
Pratt, R. K., Supt. of Ground Wood Mill, Finch, Pruyn & Co., Inc.
Pratt, Waldo E., Pres., Hollingsworth & Whitney Co.
Pratt, Walter, Vice-Pres. and Sec., The Island Paper Co.
Preisch, Maurice, Sec. and Treas., Bathurst Lumber Co., Ltd.
Prescott, C. J., Vice-Pres., W. H. McElwain Co.
Prescott, E. L., Treas., W. H. McElwain Co.
Preu, J. A., Pur. Agt., Thomas F. Garvan Co.
Prevost, Gabe, Supt., Fletcher Paper Co.
Price, Harry, Sec., Kimberly-Clark Co.
Price, H. E., Sec. and Treas., The Jonquieres Pulp Co., Ltd.; Sec. and Treas., Price-Porritt Pulp & Paper Co.; Sec. and Treas., Price Bros. & Co., Ltd.
Price, Sir William, Pres., The Jonquieres Pulp Co., Ltd.; Pres., Price Bros. & Co., Ltd.; Pres., Price-Porritt Pulp & Paper Co.
Prickitt, C. H., Asst. Treas., William Mann Co.
Pride, B. A., Vice-Pres., Treas. and Mgr., Tomahawk Pulp & Paper Co.
Pride, C. B., Pres., Tomahawk Pulp & Paper Co.
Priest, A. W., Pres., Outagamie Paper Co.
Pringle, Alex., Vice-Pres., Wayagamack Pulp & Paper Co.
Prior, Wm. G., Sec., Tait & Sons Paper Co.
Prizer, H. A., Pres., William Mann Co.
Prouty, C. A., Pres., Clyde River Pulp Co.
Prouty, J. A., Treas., Clyde River Pulp Co.
Purtill, J. W., Jr., Sec., Wasuc Mills Co.
Purtill, J. W., Pres. and Treas., Wasuc Mills Co.
Pusey, George E., Supt., Hawley Pulp & Paper Co.
Putnam, Douglas, Sec. and Treas., Waldorf Paper Products Co.
Puttaert, F., Hutchinson-Puttaert Co.
Pyke, J. W., Vice-Pres., Howard Smith Paper Mills, Ltd.; Vice-Pres., Wayagamack Pulp & Paper Co.
Pyl, John A., Sec. and Treas., Monarch Paper Co.

Q

Quayle, W. E., Asst. Treas., Union Bag & Paper Corp.
Quinlan, William J., Supt., Schroon River Pulp & Paper Co.
Quirk, D. L., Jr., Pres., Peninsular Paper Co.

R

Ramage, Archibald P., Treas. and Gen. Mgr., Missisquoi Pulp & Paper Co.
Ramage, James M., Pres. and Treas., Franklin Paper Co.
Ramage, Robt. A., Sec., Franklin Paper Co.
Ramsey, S. M., Vice-Pres., Phila. Wax Paper Co.
Ranck, Z. W., Vice-Pres., Crystal Paper Co.
Randall, Charles P., Asst. Treas., Parsons Paper Co.
Randall, J. Edwin, Clerk, Millers Falls Paper Co.
Randall, Walter D., Sec. and Treas., Champion Coated Paper Co.; Asst. Sec. and Asst. Treas., Champion Fibre Co.
Raney, E., Supt., Chicago Mill & Lumber Co.
Rankin, E. S., Vice-Pres., King Paper Co.
Ranson, W. E., Sec. and Treas., MacAndrews & Forbes Co.
Rantoul, E. L., Sec. and Clerk, Androscoggin Pulp Co.; Sec. and Clerk, Mt. Tom Sulphite Pulp Co.
Rauch, E. C., Pres., The Boehme & Rauch Co.
Rauch, H. Lee, Vice-Pres., The Boehme & Rauch Co.

Ray, Charles, Sec., John A. Manning Paper Co.
Raybold, W. J., Sec., B. D. Rising Paper Co.
Raymond, H. E., Vice-Pres., Missisquoi Pulp & Paper Co.
Read, N. G., Vice-Pres., Japanese Tissue Mills.
Reddick, W. B., Supt., Watertown, N. Y., Continental Paper Bag Co.
Redford, E. B., Sec., Consolidated Water Power & Paper Co.; Treas., Interlake Pulp & Paper Co.
Redhead, E. R., Pres., Victoria Paper Mills Co.
Reed, Albert E., Chairman Board of Directors, Albert E. Reed & Co.
Reed, Stanley, Sec. and Treas., Manchester Board & Paper Co.
Reed, John S., Asst. Treas., St. Croix Paper Co.
Reese, D. E., Treas., Combined Locks Paper Co.
Rehine, Wm. D., Supt., Bogota Paper & Board Co.
Remington, J. A., Asst. Sec., Remington Paper & Power Co.
Reoux, Louis E., Treas., Schroon River Pulp & Paper Co.
Rexford, L. P., Pres. and Treas., Carthage Board & Paper Co.
Reynolds, J. J., Supt., Federal Paper Board Co.
Reynolds, W. B., Sales-Mgr., Cascade Paper Co.
Rianhard, T. M., Vice-Pres., Barrett Co.
Rice, Philip E., Vice-Pres., Schroon River Pulp & Paper Co.
Richard, Louis, Mgr. and Supt., Richard & Co.
Richardson, A. V., Sec., Gilbert Paper Co.
Richardson, J. M., Pres., Richardson Paper Co.
Richardson, Paul, Treas., Richardson Paper Co.
Richardson, W. H., Vice-Pres., Richardson Paper Co.
Ricker, Edward P., Pres., Empire Paper Co.
Rieg, J. B., Mgr. of Sales, Detroit Sulphite Pulp & Paper Co.
Riegel, Benj. D., Vice-Pres., Warren Mfg. Co.
Riegel, J. M., Vice-Pres., Itasca Paper Co.
Rieger, A. L., Treas. and Gen. Mgr., The Peerless Paper Co.; Treas., The Mead Pulp & Paper Co.
Rieger, Herman M., Pres., Foley-Rieger Pulp & Paper Co.; Pres., Peerless Pulp Co., Ltd.
Rieger, L. P., Sec., The Peerless Paper Co.
Riley, Philip J., Sec., Underwood Pulp & Paper Mills, Inc.
Riordan, Carl, Vice-Pres. and Mng. Dir., Riordan Pulp & Paper Co., Ltd.; Vice-Pres. and Mng. Dir., Ticonderoga Pulp & Paper Co.
Riordan, Charles, Pres., Riordan Pulp & Paper Co., Ltd.; Pres., Ticonderoga Pulp & Paper Co.
Risser, C. B., Treas., Consumer's Box Board & Paper Co.
Ritchie, F. I., Supt. of Lumber Dept., Wayagamack Pulp & Paper Co.
Robb, W. D., Vice- Pres., New Brunswick Sulphate Fibre Co., Ltd.
Roberts, Ernst B., Mgr., Illinois Paper Co. Plant; Bemis Bro. Bag Co.

Roberts, H. P., Sec., Mengel Box Co., Branch.
Roberts, W. Leslie, Sec., Mutual Box Board Co.
Robertson, A. F., Sec. and Treas., Albemarle Paper Mfg. Co.
Robertson, Col. D. M., Sec. and Treas., Mattagami Pulp & Paper Co., Ltd.
Robertson, David F., Gen. Mgr., Northumberland Paper & Electric Co., Ltd.
Robertson, E. C., E. C. Robertson & Son; Robertson Bros.; W. F. Robertson & Co.
Robertson, Frank, M., Wm. Robertson's Sons.
Robertson, Fred E., Wm. Robertson's Sons.
Robertson, F. W. R., Robertson Bros.
Robertson, G. A., George A. Robertson & Co.
Robertson, H. H., Pres., John Roberts & Son Co., Inc.
Robertson, J. E., Pres., Emerson Paper Co.
Robertson, O. C. R., G. A. Robertson & Co.
Robertson, Reuben B., Gen. Mgr., Champion Fibre Co.
Robertson, S. J., Sec., Itasca Paper Co.
Robertson, W. F. R., W. F. Robertson & Co.; E. C. Robertson & Son.
Robinson, B. S., Treas., Empire Paper Co.
Robinson, W. F., Sec., Laurentide Co., Ltd.
Robinson, W. T., Vice-Pres., Quebec & Saguanay Pulp Co.
Rochester, R. A., Mgr. Quincy, Ill., American Straw Board Co.
Rockwood, H. E., Supt., Champion Paper Co.
Roebling, Ferdinand W., Pres., Union Mills Paper Mfg. Co.
Roether, H. E., Mgr., Wardway Paper Mills.
Rogers, C. B., Treas., Donnacona Paper Co., Ltd.
Rogers, Dudley P., Pres., Androscoggin Pulp Co.; Pres., McTom Sulphite Pulp Co.
Rogers, Elliot, Pres., Rogers Fibre Co., National Div.
Rogers, F. S., Sec. and Treas., Hadley Paper Corp.
Rogers, G. H., Pres. and Treas., Rogers Paper Mfg. Co.
Rogers, Henry G., Sulphite Mill Supt., J. & J. Rogers Co.
Rogers, James, Pres., J. & J. Rogers Co.
Rogers, James P., Pres. The Metalite Co.
Rogers, Louis, Vice-Pres. and Mgr., Rogers Fibre Co. National Div.
Rogers, P. H., Jr., Sec. and Treas., Carolina Fibre Co.
Rogers, S. S., Vice-Pres. and Mgr., Chemical Paper Mfg. Co.
Rogers, Wm. R., Pres., The Metalite Co.
Rolfe, A. O., Paper Mill Supt., Champion Coated Paper Co.
Rolland, Olivier, Mgr., Rolland Paper Co.
Rolland, S. J. B., Pres., Rolland Paper Co.
Romberger, R. E., Asst. Treas., Norristown Magnesia & Asbestos Co.
Rosebush, Judson G., Pres., Inland Empire Paper Co.; Vice-Pres., Outagamie Paper Co.; Pres. and Treas., Patten Paper Co., Ltd.; Vice-Pres., Neekoosa-Edwards Paper Co.

Rosebush, Waldo, E., Sec., Patten Paper Co., Ltd.
Rosenthal, Dunbar A., Pres., U. S. Paper Mills, Inc.
Rosevear, Edmund B., Sec. and Treas., Field & White Co.
Ross, O. H., Sec., Rockford Paper Mills.
Ross, T. W., Vice-Pres., Hummel & Downing Co.
Ross, Wm. Supt., Beveridge Paper Co.
Roth, Jacob, Vice-Pres., Unity Paper Mills.
Rouse, Guy W., Vice-Pres., Michigan Paper Co. of Plainwell.
Rowe, Bertha B., Vice-Pres., Thorold Pulp Co., Ltd.
Rowe, Elmer E., Sec. and Treas., Thorold Pulp Co., Ltd.
Rowlands, E. J., Sec. and Treas., Alex. McArthur & Co., Ltd.
Royse, Fred A., Supt., Underwood Pulp & Paper Mills, Inc.
Ruhl, E. J., Supt., Bloomsburg Paper Co.
Runkle, John C., Barrett Co.
Rupert, A. S., Pres., Delaware Hard Fibre Co.
Rupert, Chas. G., Treas., Sec. and Mgr., Delaware Hard Fibre Co.
Russell, G. F., Pres. and Gen. Mgr., Champion International Co.
Russell, G. C., Mgr. Elizabeth, N. J., The Barrett Co.
Russell, H. C., Sec. and Treas., The Miller Brothers Co., Ltd.
Russell, Henry L., Pres., Newton Paper Co.
Russell, J. R., Sales-Mgr., Marathon Paper Mills Co.
Russell, W. D., Vice-Pres., International Paper Co.; Treas., Lake Megantic Pulp Co.
Ryan, John, Supt., The Ontario Paper Co. Ltd.
Ryland, J. F., Sec. and Treas., Standard Paper Mfg. Co.

S

Sackett, J. D., Sec., Cleveland Paper Mfg. Co.
Safford, T. S., Pres. and Treas., West Jersey Paper Mfg. Co.
Sager, R. G., Mgr., Wilmington, Ill. American Straw Board Co.
Salmonson, V., Supt., Sulp Mill, Marathon Paper Mills Co.
Saltonstall, Philip, L., Pres., Westfield River Paper Co.
Samson, H. L., Gen. Mgr., Eastern Div., National Paper Products Co.
Sanburn, W. H., Asst. Treas., Strathmore Paper Co.
Sanders, C. B., Sec., Union Bag & Paper Corp.
Saunders, G. W., Asst. Sec., Mattagami Pulp & Paper Co., Ltd.
Savage, C. E., Pres., Savage Mfg. Co.
Savage, E. L., Treas., Savage Mfg. Co.
Savage, J. O., Vice-Pres., Savage Mfg. Co.
Savery, Wm. H., Pres., Shenandoah Pulp Co.; Vice-Pres. and Gen. Mgr., Harper's Ferry Paper Co.
Saville, W. G., Vice-Pres., Cornell Wood Products Co.
Sawyer, C. J., Pres., Natick Box & Board Co.
Saxer, Leonard A., Pres., Saxer Paper Mills.
Scanlon, M. J., Vice-Pres., Powell River Co., Ltd.

Scharwath, John A., Owner, National Asbestos Mfg. Co.
Scheid, A. B., Sec. and Treas., Watervliet Paper Co.
Schenck, Garrett, Pres., Great Northern Paper Co.
Schenk, Wm., Coating Mill Supt., Champion Coated Paper Co.
Schieble, H. W., Sec. and Treas., Ohio Paper Co.
Schmidt, Henry D., Sec. and Treas., Schmidt & Ault Paper Co.
Schmidt, John C., Pres., Schmidt & Ault Paper Co.
Schnorbach, P. P., Sec., Filer Fibre Co.
Schoellkopf, J. F., Pres., Cliff Paper Co.
Schoellkopf, Paul A., Sec. and Treas., Cliff Paper Co.
Scholz, Walter V., Vice-Pres., Mt. Vernon Straw Board Co.
Schreiter, Henry, Pres. and Treas., Ravenswood Paper Mills Co.
Schwabacher, Frank, Treas., Crown Willamette Paper Co.
Schwenk, F., Vice-Pres., The Charles Boldt Paper Mills.
Scott, A. H., Vice-Pres. and Treas., Chester Paper Co.
Scott, B. H., Treas., Gulf Paper Mills Co.
Scott, D. E., Supt., Arthur D. Little, Inc.
Scott, E. Irwin, Pres., Chester Paper Co.
Scott, F. O., Supt., Southworth Co.
Scott, William, Vice-Pres., Anglo-Newfoundland Development Co., Ltd.
Scott, W. H., Vice-Pres., Western Board & Paper Co.
Screven, M. L., Sec., Southern Paper Co.
Seaman, G. M., Vice-Pres., Combined Locks Paper Co.
Seasholtz, Charles, Supt., Perkiomen Paper Co.
Seelye, Bryan, Clerk & Auditor, Great Northern Paper Co.
Seiberling, Chas. W., The Thomas Phillips Co.
Seigle, W. R., Pres., Fibre Corp.
Seiler, J. L., Sec., Warren Mfg. Co.
Seits, T. J., Asst. Treas., The Beaver Wood Fibre Co., Ltd.
Senn, Chas., Vice-Pres., The Munroe Falls Paper Co.
Sensenbrenner, F. J., First Vice-Pres., Kimberly-Clark Co.; Sec., Neenah Paper Co.
Sensenbrenner, R. M., Sec., Menasha Paper Co.
Servass, F. C., Sec., Western Board & Paper Co.
Server, H. W., Supt., Miami Paper Co.
Shaffer, Wm. R., Sec., Treas. and Gen. Mgr., New Haven Pulp & Board Co.
Shainwald, R. L., Pres., Standard Paint Co.
Shainwald, R. S., Vice-Pres., The Paraffine Co.'s, Inc.
Sharpley, R. C., Mgr. of Sales, Belgo-Canadian Pulp & Paper Co., Ltd.
Shattuck, A. E., Clerk, Strathmore Paper Co.
Shattuck, Edwin P., Sec., Pejepscot Paper Co.
Shattuck, F. S., Treas., Kimberly-Clark Co.
Shaw, Chas. H., Sec., Norristown Magnesia & Asbestos Co.
Shaw, Edwin, Treas., Atlantic Paper & Pulp Corp.

Beloit Iron Works
Builders of Paper Mill Machinery

Fourdrinier Machines, Cylinder Machines, Strawboard Machines, Harper Fourdriniers, Tissue Machines, Flying Dutchman Machines, Pulp Machines, Wet Machines, Wax Coating Machines, Patented Adjustable Fourdriniers, Sheet Liners, Container Pasting Machines, Wall Board Machines, Improved Noiseless Screens, Granite Press Rolls, Chilled Calenders, Double Drum Winders, Patented Steam Joints

Tompkins-Hawley-Fuller Patent Pick Up Felt
King-Neary Patent Revolving Suction Roll

Beloit Iron Works
Beloit, - - - - Wis., U. S. A.

Frank Gilbert Paper Company

PAPER MILLS: Waterford and Cohoes, N. Y.
PULP MILLS: Cohoes, N. Y.

* * *

Manufacturers of

High Grade Papers

SULPHITE BOND in White and Colors and COLORED SPECIAL PAPERS

CUTTING DIES

FOR EVERYTHING IN
PAPER, ENVELOPES, LITHOGRAPHS, LABELS, GASKETS,
ETC., ETC.

THE HOGGSON & PETTIS MFG. CO.
NEW HAVEN, CONN., U. S. A.

Reduce Your Wire and Felt Costs

GILBERTS & NASH WIRE GUIDE has proven by actual tests that it increases the life of wires 25 per cent. It prevents side travel of wire over suction boxes, cracked edges and loss of selvage, which shorten the life of wires.

OUR AUTOMATIC WET FELT GUIDE does away with guide straps—holds the felt in any position—in fact, does away with all guide strap difficulties and increases the wearing qualities of the felt.

We will send you our guide—freight prepaid—subject to a satisfactory trial. Write us now for Illustrated Catalogue and Quotations.

GILBERTS & NASH
MENASHA, WISCONSIN

Makers of
Wire and Felt Guides, Suction Box Covers, Patent Dandy Stands.

Shaw, F. R., Pres., Berkshire Hills Paper Co.
Shea, Wm. M., Sec. and Treas., Lincoln Paper Mills Co., Ltd.
Sheedy, Harold, R., Supt., Groton Leather Board Co.
Sheedy, Michael, Sec. and Treas., Groton Leather Board Co.
Sheedy, Winthrop L., Vice-Pres., Groton Leather Board Co.
Sheehy, J. C., Sec. and Treas., Lehigh Paper Mills, Inc.
Sheffield, J. M., Sec., J. & J. Rogers Co.
Shellington, H. S., Supt., Stratford Paper Co.
Shepard, A. M., Vice-Pres. and Gen. Mgr., Tennessee Paper Mills, Inc.
Shepard, G. G., Sec. and Treas., Niagara River Mfg. Co.
Shepherd, Owen, Treas., International Paper Co.
Sheppard, W. J., Vice-Pres., Toronto Paper Mfg. Co., Ltd.
Sheperd, E. S., Supt., The Hutchinson Box Board & Paper Co.
Sherman, Elmer, Sec., Blandy Paper Co.
Sherman, Elmer A., Mgr., Sherman & Co.
Sherman, Geo. C., Pres., Taggarts Paper Co.; Vice-Pres., Brownville Paper Co.
Sherman Raymond R., Supt., Sherman & Co.
Sherrard, T. J., Sec. and Treas., George & Sherrard Paper Co.
Sherry, E. P., Pres. and Treas., Flambeau Paper Co.
Shirreff, J. T., Vice-Pres., The E. B. Eddy Co., Ltd.
Shortess, W. G., Pres., Acme Paper Co.; Sec. and Treas., Monroe Bridge Paper Co.; Sec., The Thames River Specialties Co.; Pres., Federal Paper Board Co., Inc.
Shove, E. P., Vice-Pres., Mattagami Pulp & Paper Co., Ltd.
Shryock, O. A., Sec. and Treas., Shryock Bros.
Shryock, S. S., Pres., Shryock Bros.
Shryock, S. S., Jr., Vice-Pres., Shryock Bros.
Shuttleworth, Walter E., Treas., Cushnoc Paper Co.
Silberman, S., Vice-Pres., Lancaster Board & Paper Co.
Silk, C. B., Pres., The Munroe Falls Paper Co.; Pres., Massillon Paper Co.
Silk, F. B., Sec. and Treas., Massillon Paper Co.; Sec. and Treas., The Munroe Falls Paper Co.
Silk, J. R., Vice-Pres., Massillon Paper Co.
Sill, J. P., Asst. Sec. and Treas., Wausau Sulphate Fibre Co.
Sillman, F. A., Treas. and Sec., Marinette & Menominee Paper Co.
Simon, M. W., Sec. and Mgr. of Sales, Tonawanda Board & Paper Co.
Simons, F. G., Sec., International Paper Co.; Sec., Herkimer Fibre Co.
Simonson, E., Supt., Sulphite Mill, Bathurst Lumber Co., Ltd.
Simpson, S. W., Vice-Pres., MacSim Bar Paper Co.; Supt., Bardeen Paper Co.
Sisson, Chas. H., Vice-Pres., Racquette River Paper Co.
Sisson, Geo. W., Jr., Pres., Racquette River Paper Co.
Sisson, Rufus L., Treas., Racquette River Paper Co.
Sisson, F. T. E., Sec. and Mgr., Racquette River Paper Co.

Skinner, H. J., Vice-Pres., Arthur D. Little, Inc.
Slade, B. G., Co-Partner and Supt., Fillmore & Slade.
Slater, Joseph H., Sec. and Mgr., Chesapeake Pulp & Paper Co., Inc.
Slickty, Geo. D., Supt. and Vice-Pres., Weis Paper Mill Co.
Sloat, M. B., Sec. and Treas., New York & Pennsylvania Co.
Slocum, F. E., Second Vice-Pres., The Lewis Slocum & LeFevre Co., Inc.
Slotnick, Mitchell N., Gen. Counsel, American Writing Paper Co.
Smeallie, P. H., Smeallie & Voorhees.
Smith, Austin, Vice-Pres., Wrenn Paper Co.
Smith, A. B., Pres., Treas. and Gen. Mgr., New Elkhart Paper Mills Co.
Smith, A. C., Dr., Vice-Pres., Beaver Brook Paper Mills, Inc.
Smith, A. F., Vice-Pres. and Gen. Supt., Paul A. Sorg Paper Co.; Vice-Pres., W. B. Oglesby Paper Co.
Smith, Albert E., Treas. and Gen. Mgr., Keith Paper Co.
Smith, C. A., Pres., Coos Bay Pulp & Paper Co.
Smith, C. Howard, Pres., Howard Smith Paper Mills, Ltd.; Pres., New Brunswick Sulphite Fibre Co., Ltd.
Smith, D. A., Vice-Pres., Sec., Treas. and Gen. Mgr., D. of C. Paper Mfg. Co.
Smith, Edwin S., Sec., American Writing Paper Co.
Smith, Ernest E., Pres., C. M. Robertson Co.
Smith, F. A., Supt., Mullen Bros. Paper Co.
Smith, Forrest E., Sec., Crescent Paper Co.
Smith, G. E., Mgr., Purchasing Dept., International Paper Co.
Smith, W. H., Treas., Abitibi Power & Paper Co., Ltd.
Smith, H. F., Sec. and Supt., Lee Fibre Co.
Smith, Harold S., Vice-Pres., Bogota Paper & Board Co.; Sec., and Treas., General Paper Co., Inc.
Smith, H. W., Supt., Ryegate Paper Co.
Smith, J. E., Pres., Marley Paper Mfg. Co.; Pres. and Gen. Mgr., Chesapeake Paperboard Co.
Smith, M. N., Treas., Escanaba Pulp & Paper Co.
Smith, N. J., Pres., Menasha Paper Co.
Smith, P. A., Supt., Combined Locks Paper Co.
Smith, R. D., Vice-Pres., S. D. Warren Co.
Smith, Richard H., Pres., Cushnoc Paper Co.
Smith, R. W., Vice-Pres., Filer Fibre Co.
Smith, Thompson, Gen. Mgr., St. Croix Paper Co.
Smith, T. L., Treas., The Hutchinson Box Board & Paper Co.
Smith, V. A., Vice-Pres., Coos Bay Pulp & Paper Co.
Smith, Waldo R., Treas., York Haven Paper Co.
Smith, Willard F., Pres., Smith Paper Co.
Smith, Wm. N., Pres., Bogota Paper & Board Co.
Snell, Jno. B., Mgr., Garoga Creek Mill.
Snyder, F. W., Vice-Pres. and Treas., Victoria Paper Mills Co.
Snyder, J. Leslie, Sec., Albia Box & Paper Co.

Snyder, M. A., Pres., W. W. Snyder Mfg. Co., Inc.
Snyder, William, Supt., U. S. Paper Mills, Inc.
Snyder, W. W., Treas., W. W. Snyder Mfg. Co., Inc.
Somers, Henry W. Pres., Iroquois Pulp & Paper Co.
Soule, R. L., Treas., Michigan Paper Co. of Plainwell.
Southworth, Edw., Sales-Mgr., Southworth Co.
Southworth, Melvin D., Treas. and Mgr., Southwoth Co.
Southworth, M. S., Clerk, Southworth Co.
Southworth, T. S., Pres., Southworth Co.
Spalding, Eliot, Treas., Endicott, Johnson & Co.
Sparks, Samuel, Pres., California Tissue Mill, Inc.
Spaulding, H. M., Pres., Atlas Leather Mfg. Co.
Spaulding, H. N., J. Spaulding & Sons, J. Spaulding & Sons Co.
Spaulding, L. C., J. Spaulding & Sons Co.
Spaulding, R. H., J. Spaulding & Sons Co.
Spencer, B. T., Pres. and Treas., Warren Mfg. Co.
Spencer, R. W., Treas., Holden Paper Co.
Springer, Chas. C., Vice-Pres., Mount Tom Sulphite Pulp Co.
Srere, Abraham, Sec., The Srere Pulp & Paper Co.
Srere, Alfred A., Pres., Srere Pulp & Paper Co., Srere Bros. & Co.; Pres., Unity Paper Mills.
Srere, Harry, Vice-Pres., The Srere Pulp & Paper Co., Srere Bros. & Co.
Sroufe, S. W., Supt., Dresden Paper Mills Co.
Stack, J. K., Pres.; Escanaba Pulp & Paper Co.
Stadler, John, Chief Engineer, Belgo-Canadian Pulp & Paper Co., Ltd.
Stagmaier, John, Pres., Tehnessee Paper Mills, Inc.
Stalker, David E., Sec. and Treas., Bogota Paper & Board Co.
Stanger, Wm. D., Gen. Mgr., National Metal Edge Box Co.
Stanley, Alfred, Supt., Parker-Young Co. —Henry Paper Co., Branch.
Stanley, Edward C., Asst. Sec., Case Bros.
Stanley, Robert N., Sec., Case Bros.
Stansbury, K. E., Sec., Thilmany Pulp & Paper Co.
Stanton, James F., Supt., Rogers Fibre Co., National Div.
Stanton, William B., Supt., Paper Mill, Bathurst Lumber Co., Ltd.
Stark, W. H., Pres., Yellow Pine Paper Mill Co.
Staub, Elmer, Supt., Holden Paper Co.
Stearns, Geo. M., Pres., Sec. and Supt., Lake Megantic Pulp Co.
Stearns, L. N., Vice-Pres., Hinsdale Paper Mfg. Co.
Stebbins, J. C., Vice-Pres., West End Paper Co.
Steer, E. J., Sec. and Treas., Barrett Co.
Steers, N. I., Mgr., Newhall Pulp Mill, E. I. Du Pont De Nemours & Co.
Sterling, E. B., Pres. and Gen. Mgr., West End Paper Co.
Stevens, A. J., Pres., Parsons Pulp & Lumber Co.

Stevens, Frank L., Pres., Stevens & Thompson Paper Co.; Pres., Walloomsac Paper Co.; Vice-Pres., Stevens & Thompson.
Stevens, Fred N., Vice-Pres., Stevens & Thompson Paper Co.; Pres., Stevens & Thompson; Vice-Pres., Walloomsac Paper Co.
Stevens, Richard, Pres.; Hoboken Paper Mill Co.
Stevens, Robert, Supt., Nat'l Folding Box & Paper Co.
Stevens, T. J., Elbridge Strawboard Mill.
Stevens, W. G., Mgr., Dominion Pulp Co., Ltd.
Stevenson, J. M., Pres., Mountain Mill Paper Co.
Stevenson, L. T., Treas. and Mgr., Mountain Mill Paper Co.
Stevenson, T. J., Sales Mgr., Riordan Pulp & Paper Co., Ltd.
Stewart, Chas., Supt., Collins Mfg. Co.
Stiles, W. J., Supt., Richmond Paper Mfg. Co.; Supt., Standard Paper Mfg. Co.
Stilp, J. A., Sec., Dells Paper & Pulp Co.
Stinchfield, J. H., Supt., Orano, Me., International Paper Co.
Stirling, Thos. H., Res. Mgr., Mechanicville, N. Y., West Virginia Pulp & Paper Co.
Stitt, A. W., Sec. and Treas., River Raisin Paper Co.
Stoehr, G. F., Treas., Hinsdale Paper Mfg. Co.
Stoeser, Edward J., Sec. and Treas., Phila. Paper Mfg. Co.
Stokes, C. M., Sales Mgr., Norristown Magnesia & Asbestos Co.
Stokes, Henry W., Pres., York Haven Paper Co.
Stone, Avery J., Treas., Mohawk Valley Paper Co., Inc.
Stone, F. P., Pres., Wausau Sulphate Fibre Co.; Treas., Watab Pulp & Paper Co.
Stone, J. C., Vice-Pres., Kingsport Pulp Corp.
Stone, J. F., Sec., Consumer's Box Board & Paper Co.
Stonebraker, John E., Jr., Sec., Antietam Paper Co.
Stonebraker, J. Elsworth, Pres., Antietam Paper Co.
Stoppenbach, W. E., Res. Mgr., Wolf River Paper & Fibre Co.
Storb, John W., Vice-Pres., Columbian Paper Co.
Storrs, L. J., Vice-Pres., South Coventry Paper Co.
Stovel, C. J., Mgr., York, Pa., Certain-Teed Products Corp.
Stowe, Charles E., Sec. and Treas., Stowe & Sons, Inc., J. D.
Stowe, Geo. W., Pres., Stowe & Sons, Inc., J. D.
Stowe, Wm. H., Vice-Pres., Stowe & Sons, Inc., J. D.
Strain, E. W., Sec. Economic Power & Products Co.; Sec., Sugar Cane By-Products Co.
Strange, A. N., Sec., Treas. and Mgr., Island Paper Co.; Treas. and Gen. Mgr., Wolf River Paper & Fibre Co.
Strange, Hugh, Sec. and Treas., John Strange Paper Co.; Sec. and Treas., Stevens Point Pulp & Paper Co.
Strange, John, Pres., John Strange Paper Co.; Pres., Stevens Point Pulp & Paper Co.

Strange, William, Vice-Pres., Island Paper Co.
Stratford, A. C., Pres., Stratford Paper Co.
Stratford, E. H., Vice-Pres., Stratford Paper Co.
Stratford, F. B., Sec. and Treas., Stratford Paper Co.
Stratton, S. W., Director, Bureau of Standards, Dept. of Commerce.
Straub, S. C., Mgr., Certain-Teed Products Corp.
Straus, Eli M., Treas., Morris Paper Mills.
Straus, Raymond I., Sec. Bedford Pulp & Paper Co.; Sec. and Treas., Dixie Paper Mills, Inc.
Straw, A. J., Treas., Lydall & Foulds Paper Co., Inc.
Stribley, C. W., Treas., Thilmany Pulp & Paper Co.
Strickland, L., Sec., Westport Paper Co.
Stringer, Charles H., Sales Agt., National Asbestos Mfg. Co.
Strong, E. P., Sec., Munising Paper Co.
Stuart, W. Z., Treas. and Mgr., Neenah Paper Co.
Sturtevant, Fred. H., Gen. Supt., Loft Drying Mills; American Writing Paper Co.
Stutt, F. E., James Stutt & Sons.
Stutt, Geo., James Stutt & Sons.
Stutt, W. J., James Stutt & Sons.
Sugden, B. W., Sec., Stevens & Thompson.

Sullivan, W. H., Vice-Pres., Bogalusa Paper Co., Inc.
Sullivan, W. J., Mgr., Grandfather's Falls Co.
Sunderland, W. W., Pres., Miami Paper Co.
Sursham, E. A., Sec., Anglo-Newfoundland Development Co.
Sutherland, D. M., Jr., Mgr., Agasote Millboard Co.
Sutherland, William, Supt., Hadley Paper Corp.
Sutphin, S. B., Sec. and Treas., Beveridge Paper Co.
Sutton, C. H., Vice-Pres., Standard Paper Mfg. Co.
Sweeny, Robert, Pres., Rainy River Pulp & Paper Co.
Sweet, K. N., Sweet Bros. Paper Mfg. Co.
Sweet, T. C., Sweet Bros. Paper Mfg. Co.
Syrett, Charles V., Sec. and Treas., Garden City Paper Mills Co., Ltd.

T

Taggart, B. B., Pres., Taggart Bros. Co.
Taggart, J. W., Vice-Pres., Taggart Bros. Co.
Tait, Andrew, Treas., Tait & Sons Paper Co.
Tait, George, Pres., Underwood Pulp & Paper Mills, Inc.
Tait, Wm. F., Pres., Tait & Sons Paper Co., The.
Talbott, H. E., Sr., Vice-Pres., The Mead Pulp & Paper Co.
Taylor, B. E., Gen. Mgr., Rainy River Pulp & Paper Co.
Taylor, E. M., Pres., Diamond State Fibre Co.
Taylor, F. E., Vice-Pres., Advertisers Paper Mills; Vice-Pres., Taylor-Logan Co., Papermakers.

Taylor, Howard W., Vice-Pres. and Mill Mgr., Dill & Collins Co.
Taylor, Job, Pres. and Gen. Mgr., Halifax Paper Corp.; Vice-Pres., Roanoke Fibre Board Co.
Taylor, John F., Sec., The E. B. Eddy Co., Ltd.
Taylor, R. J., Supt., Campbell Lumber Co., Ltd.
Temple, F. M., Pres. and Gen. Mgr., Merrimac Paper Co.
Terreau, Ls., Pres., Metabetchouan Co.
Thatcher, E. E., Sec. and Treas., Harper's Ferry Paper Co.; Sec. and Treas. Shenandoah Pulp Co.
Thickens, J. H., Mgr. of Pulp & Paper Mills, Bathurst Lumber Co., Ltd.
Thomas, A. B., Sec., Mac Sim Bar Paper Co.
Thomas, J. E., Vice-Pres., Thilmany Pulp & Paper Co.
Thomas, M. A., Wardlow-Thomas Paper Co.
Thomas, Wm., Supt., Michigan Paper Co. of Plainwell.
Thompson, C. D., Sec. and Treas., Merrimac Paper Co.
Thompson, F. L., Treas., Moore & Thompson Paper Co., Inc.
Thompson, Howard B., Sec. and Treas., Stevens & Thompson Paper Co.; Sec., Walloomsac Paper Co.
Thompson, H. B., Treas., Stevens & Thompson.
Thompson, J. Linton, Pres., The Thompson & Norris Co. of Indiana.
Thompson, L. G., Vice-Pres., Mohican Pulp & Paper Co.
Thompson, R. H., Pres., Diamond Mills Paper Co.
Thompson, Robert H., Vice-Pres., The Thompson & Norris Co., of Indiana.
Thompson, R. W., Sec. and Treas., Merwin Paper Co.
Thompson, W., Treas., Patent Vulcanite Roofing Co.
Thomson, Geo. H., Vice-Pres., The Jonquieres Pulp Co., Ltd.; Vice-Pres. Price Bros. & Co., Ltd.
Thomson, Peter G., Pres., Champion Coated Paper Co.; Pres., Champion Fibre Co.
Thomson, Peter G., Jr., Vice-Pres., Champion Coated Paper Co.; Vice-Pres., Champion Fibre Co.
Thornburg, G. C., Sec. and Asst. Treas., Miami Paper Co.
Thorne, C. B., Mgr. of Manufacturing, Riordan Pulp & Paper Co., Ltd.
Thorne, H. M., Sec. and Treas., Canada Paper Co., Ltd.
Thorpe, A. B., Sec. and Treas. and Gen. Mgr., Fort Miller Pulp & Paper Co.
Thorpe, A. B., Vice-Pres. and Supt., Franklin Paper Co.
Tilley, David, Treas., The E. B. Eddy Co., Ltd.
Tilton, Wesley N., Supt., Toronto Paper Mfg. Co., Ltd.
Tinker, Francis, Pres., Columbia Paper Mills Co.
Tinker, Uriah W., Treas., Columbia Paper Mills Co.
Tomczak, S. E., Supt., Menasha Printing & Carton Co.
Tomskey, Geo., Supt., Winona Pulp & Paper Co.
Tooke, C. W., Treas., Oswego Falls Pulp & Paper Co.; Sec., Skaneateles Paper Co.
Trabert, C. L., Sec., Coos Bay Pulp & Paper Co.

Tripp, Thos. A., Mgr., Pairpoint Corp.
Trondsen, D. C., Vice-Pres., Blandy Paper Co.; Vice-Pres., American Wood Board Co.
Trumbower, Howard, Sec. and Treas., Columbian Paper Co.
True, F. D., Pres., Poland Paper Co.
Tschudi, S. W., Treas., Chesapeake Paperboard Co.
Tucker, Thomas, Gen. Supt., Crescent Paper Co.
Tucker, W. S., Supt., Wardway Paper Mills.
Tufts, F. E., Treas., Nashwaak Pulp & Paper Co.; Treas., Oxford Paper Co.
Tufts, Wm. L., Sec., Ravenswood Paper Mill Co.
Tullis, W. C., Sec., The Boehme & Rauch Co.
Turner, Noble B., Vice-Pres., Berkshire Hills Paper Co.
Tuttle, A. T., Pres., Ashland Paper Co.
Tuttle, Geo. F., Pres., Lake Champlain Pulp & Paper Co.
Tyson, H. B., Vice-Pres., Norristown Magnesia & Asbestos Co.

U

Ullrich, F. H. von, Crescent Paper & Machine Co.
Underwood, George F., Chairman of Board of Directors, Underwood Pulp & Paper Mills, Inc.
Unkle, C. W., Supt., The Fairfield Paper Co.
Upham, H. A. J., Pres., Marinette & Menominee Paper Co.
Upham, S. A., Pres., Brownville Paper Co.
Upson, Charles A., Pres., The Upson Co.
Upson, W. Harrison, Sec. and Treas., The Upson Co.
Uptegraff, J. M., Treas., Defiance Paper Co.
Uptegraff, T. M., Sec. and Mgr., Defiance Paper Co.
Uptegraff, W. D., Pres., Defiance Paper Co.
Utley, P. L., Sec. and Mgr., Escanaba Pulp & Paper Co.

V

Vail, D. R., Pres., Decatur Strawboard Co.; Pres., Delphi Strawboard Co.
Vail, F. E., Sec. and Treas., Decatur Strawboard Co.; Sec. and Treas., Delphi Strawboard Co.
Vail, H. J., Sec., Monroe Bridge Paper Co.
Vail, J. W., Vice-Pres., Decatur Strawboard Co.
Valkenburg, E. C. Van, Gen. Mgr., Flower City Tissue Mills Co.
Van Alstyne, J. W., Supt., Fraser Companies, Ltd.
Van Arnam, H. L., Asst. Treas., The Lewis Slocum & LeFevre Co., Inc.
Van de Carr, C. R., Pres. and Treas., Van de Carr Paper Co.
Van de Carr, C. R., Jr., Vice-Pres., Van de Carr Paper Co.
Van de Carr, J. W., Sec. and Supt., Van de Carr Paper Co.
Van Dyke, J. W., Pres., Crystal Paper Co.
Van Gilder, C. G., Sec., Diamond Mills Paper Co.
Van Voorhis, E., Treas., Diamond Mills Paper Co.

Van Winkle, B. A., Treas. and Gen. Mgr., Hartford City Paper Co.
Van Zandt, Clarence E., Vice-Pres., Albia Box & Paper Co.
Veeder, Garrett S., Vice-Pres., Pioneer Paper Co.
Vernon, Benjamin & Thomas P., Proprietors, The Rainbow Mills.
Viets, W. A., Sec., Indiana Board & Filler Co.
Vinton, W. B., Wm., H. Vinton & Son.
Viot, J. N., Treas., Case & Marshall, Inc.
Viot, J. N., Treas. and Sec., A. Willard Case Co.
Voight, Edward W., Pres., Port Huron Sulphite & Paper Co.
Voorhees, J. L., Sneallie & Voorhees.
Vose, Chas., Vice-Pres., Hollingsworth & Vose Co.

W

Wagg, W. E., Gen. Mgr., Wm. Mann Co.
Wagner, C. C., Asst. Sec., Michigan Paper Co. of Plainwell.
Wagner, J. D., Pres., Michigan Paper Co. of Plainwell.
Wagner, P. S., Sec., Treas. and Sales-Mgr., Northern Paper Mills.
Wagner, W. P., Pres., Northern Paper Mills.
Wait, Luther A., Sec. and Treas., Iroquois Pulp & Paper Co.
Waite, C. H., Treas., Erving Paper Mills.
Waldie, R. S., Pres. and Mang. Dir., Toronto Paper Mfg. Co., Ltd.
Waldo, Guy, Sec. and Mgr., Flambeau Paper Co.
Waldorf, M. W., Pres., Waldorf Paper Products Co.
Walker, C. W., Supt., Palmer, N. Y., International Paper Co.
Walker, E. C., Mgr. of Sales, Collins Mfg. Co.
Walker, E. H., Vice-Pres. and Treas., Kaukauna Pulp Co.
Walker, F. E., Treas., J. R. Walker & Co., Ltd.
Walker, Geo., Sec. and Treas., Creamery Package Mfg. Co.
Walker, Geo. I., Vice-Pres., Erving Paper Mills.
Walker, Geo. K., Mgr., De Grasse Paper Co.
Walker, Gilbert M., Vice-Pres., Hennepin Paper Co.
Walker, G. P., Vice-Pres., J. R. Walker & Co., Ltd.
Walker, H. E., Sec., Bennett, Ltd.; Sec., J. R. Walker & Co., Ltd.
Walker, J. R., Pres., J. R. Walker & Co., Ltd.; Vice-Pres., The Miller Bros. Co., Ltd.
Walker, O. D., Supt., Senoso Paper Co., Inc., Phoenix, N. Y.
Walker, W. J., Treas., Hennepin Paper Co.
Wallace, George R., Pres. and Treas., Fitchburg Paper Co.
Wallace, M. B., Pres. and Treas., Union Bag & Paper Corp.
Wallace, Robert B., Sec., Carthage Board & Paper Co.
Wallace, W. J., Treas., Toronto Paper Mfg. Co., Ltd.
Walsh, C. M., Pres., Walsh Paper Co., Inc.
Walsh, J. M., Pres., Gulp Paper Mills Co.
Walter, F. P., Vice-Pres., River Raisin Paper Co.

Mill Officials in the United States and Canada 53

Walters, Christian, Vice-Pres., Lakeside Paper Co.
Walton, D. S., Pres., National Folding Box & Paper Co.
Walton, D. S., Jr., Treas., Nat'l Folding Box & Paper Co.
Wants, R. E., Sec. and Mgr., Rockford Paper Box Board Co.
Ward, Benj. I., Pres., Clifton Paper Mills.
Wardner, W. A., Sec., Cascade Wood Products Co.
Wardwell, S. B., Sec. and Treas., West End Paper Co.
Waring, A. N., Mgr. of Sales, Bayless Mfg. Corp.; Mgr. of Sales, Odell Mfg. Co.
Warnock, Henry C., Pres. and Treas., Wm. A. Cole Paper Co.
Warnock, Una Winchester, Vice-Pres., Wm. A. Cole Paper Co.
Warren, Clifford P., Sec., W. H. McElwain Co.
Warren, Eugene, Asst. Treas., John A. Manning Paper Co.
Warren, Fiske, Pres., S. D. Warren Co.
Warren, J. J., Pres. and Treas., Harmon Paper Co.; Pres. and Treas., Warren Parchment Co.
Warren, S. D., Sec., S. D. Warren Co.
Warren, T. E., Mgr., Ticonderoga Pulp & Paper Co.
Washburn, S. R., Sec., The Phœnix Paper Co.
Waters, P. J., Sec., Beaver Brook Paper Mills, Inc.
Weaver, Dr., J. K., Pres., Norristown Magnesia & Asbestos Co.
Webb, G. C., Sec., Eureka Paper Co.
Webb, Richard A., Supt., Albia Box & Paper Co.
Webb, S. W., Chairman, Eastern Mfg. Co.
Wemm, Thomas F., Supt., Chesapeake Paperboard Co.
Webb, T. H., Pres. and Treas., Eureka Paper Co.
Weber, O. L. E., Sec. and Gen. Mgr., Watab Pulp & Paper Co.
Weber, W. A. O., Pres. Phila. Wax Paper Co.
Webster, Alden P., Sec. and Treas., Nekonegan Paper Co.
Webster, J. Fred, Pres., Nekonegan Paper Co.
Weed, C. E., Supt., Ashuelot Paper Co.
Weeks, Forest G., Treas., Skaneateles Paper Co.
Weeks, F. G., Vice-Pres., Oswego Falls Pulp & Paper Co.
Weeks, Fred P., Pres., Mason-Perkins Paper Co.
Weeks, John, Vice-Pres., Diana Paper Co.
Weeks, N. W., Vice-Pres., Skaneateles Paper Co.
Weihenmayer, E. A., Vice-Pres., Jessup & Moore Paper Co.
Weinkauf, F. C., Mill Supt., Thilmany Pulp & Paper Co.
Weir, C. S., Sec., Hammermill Paper Co.
Weir, Robert T., Mgr., Constantine Board & Paper Co.
Weis, A. W. D., Sec. and Treas., Weis Paper Mill Co.
Weis, F. O., Mgr., Creamery Package Mfg. Co.
Weis, Henry, Pres., Weis Paper Mill Co.
Weiser, Irving, Sec. and Treas., American Fibre Chair Seat Corp.

Weldon, I. H., Pres., Port Arthur Pulp & Paper Co., Ltd.; Pres. and Mgr. of Sales, Provincila Paper Mills Co., Ltd.; Treas., Interlake Tissue Mills, Ltd.
Weldon, T. A., Vice-Pres., Provincial Paper Mills Co., Ltd.
Welling, E. D., Pres., Stark Paper Co.
Welling, G. B., Treas., Stark Paper Co.
Wells, Clifford, Treas., Bennett, Ltd.
Welsh, John, Sec., Treas. and Gen. Mgr., Green Bay Paper & Fibre Co.
Wentworth, Walter V., Mgr., Penobscot Chemical Fibre Co.
Wertheimer, M. A., Pres., Thilmany Pulp & Paper Co.
Westervelt, E. C., Vice-Pres., E-Z Opener Bag Co.
Westervelt H. E., Pres., E-Z Opener Bag Co.
Weston, Chas. S., Pres., Cherry River Paper Co.
Weston, E. R., Pres., Auglaize Box Board Co.; Pres., Rockford Paper Mills; Pres., Terre Haute Paper Co.
Weston, Franklin, Pres., Byron Weston Co.
Weston, Philip, Treas., Byron Weston Co.
Wetherbee, J. E., Mill Mgr., Kingsport Pulp Corp.
Wethill, Robert, First Vice-Pres., New York & Pennsylvania Co.
Wetmore, G. M., Sales-Mgr., Schmidt & Ault Paper Co.
Whalen, George F., Vice-Pres. and Gen. Mgr., Whalen Pulp & Paper Mills, Ltd.
Whalen, James, Pres., Whalen Pulp & Paper Mills, Ltd.
Whalen, M. F., Pres., Mountain Paper Co.
Whalen, Mrs. M. F., Vice-Pres., Mountain Paper Co.
Wharfield, W. C., Asst. Treas., American Writing Paper Co.
Wheat, A. A., Treas., Wheat Paper Co.
Whedon, S. A., Sec. and Treas., Ashland Paper Co.
Wheeler, Seth, Pres., A. P. W. Paper Co.
Wheeler, Seth, Jr., Vice-Pres., A. P. W. Paper Co.
Wheeler, Wm. A., Treas., A. P. W. Paper Co.
Wheelwright, George W., Jr., Pres. and Treas., Geo. W. Wheelwright Paper Co.
Wheelwright, H. M., Vice-Pres. and Clerk, Geo. W. Wheelwright Paper Co.
Whitaker, W. O., Supt., Natick Box & Board Co.
Whitcomb, William A., Vice-Pres. and Gen. Mgr., Great Northern Paper Co.
White, A. H., Chief Engr., International Paper Co.
White, Colonel J. B., Wood Dept. Mgr., Riordan Pulp & Paper Co., Ltd.
White, Fred S., Pres., Pequannock Valley Paper Co.
White, John, Supt. Board Mill, Chesapeake Pulp & Paper Co., Inc.
White, J. B., Treas., Mars Paper Corp.; Vice Pres., Dallston Fibre Products Co.; Vice-Pres., Pequannock Valley Paper Co.
White, L. H., Sec. and Treas., California Tissue Mill, Inc.
White, L. J., Sec., Holden Paper Co.
White, M. E., Treas., Norristown Magnesia & Asbestos Co.; Pleasant Mills Paper Co.

White, R. B., Pres., Hinsdale Paper Mfg. Co.
White, S. George, Treas, Antietam Paper Co.
White, W. C., Sec. and Treas., Pequannock Valley Paper Co.
White, Wm. S., Pres., Field & White Co.
Whitehead, C. R., Pres., Waygamack Pulp & Paper Co.
Whiting, C. W., Sec. Erving Paper Mills.
Whiting, F. B., Vice-Pres., Whiting-Plover Paper Co.; Vice-Pres. and Sec., Geo. A. Whiting Paper Co.
Whiting, George A., Pres., Whiting-Plover Paper Co.; Pres. and Treas., Geo. A. Whiting Paper Co.
Whiting, Samuel R., Pres. and Treas., Collins Mfg. Co.
Whiting, Wm., Treas., Whiting Paper Co.
Whiting, Wm. F., Pres. Whiting Paper Co.
Whiting, W. T., Vice-Pres., Wisconsin River Paper & Pulp Co.
Whitlet, F. B., Sec. and Treas., Ticonderoga Pulp & Paper Co.
Whitney, Charles M., Sec., Crown Willamette Paper Co.
Whitney, W. A., Treas. and Mgr., Emerson Paper Co.
Whittelsey, Mrs. F. H., Sec. and Treas., The F. H. Whittelsey Co.
Whittemore, A., Vice-Pres., Certain-Teed Products Corp.
Whittemore, Howard, Sec., Roanoke Fibre Board Co.
Wickham, A. W., Supt., MacAndrews & Forbes Co.
Wiedemann, C. F., Sec., Chicago Mill & Lumber Co.
Wightman, A. G., Supt., Hawthorne Paper Co.
Wightman, W. H., Supt., Lee Paper Co.
Wilcox, F. L., Vice-Pres., Merwin Paper Co.
Wilcox, H. A., Asst. Mgr. and Supt., Case & Risley Press Paper Co.
Wilcox, H. B., Vice-Pres., Chesapeake Paperboard Co.
Wilder, F. P., Sec., Treas. and Gen. Mgr., Diana Paper Co.
Wilder, M. S., Pres., Diana Paper Co.; Pres., Remington Paper & Power Co.; Vice-Pres., Champion Paper Co.
Wilds, Jos. S., Asst. Sec., Wm. Mann Co.
Wilkins, Edward H., Sec. Acme Paper & Paper Box Co. (Trust).
Williams, C. E., Treas., Piermont Paper Co.; Vice-Pres., Chicago Coated Board Co.
Williams, C. M., Gen. Mgr., Alton Box Board & Paper Co.; Sec., Piermont Paper Co.; Sec., Treas. and Gen. Mgr., Chicago Coated Board Co.
Williams, E. T., Treas., Mt. Vernon Straw Board Co.
Williams, F. M., Mill Supt., Certain-Teed Products Corp.
Williams, L. M., Sec., Halifax Paper Corp.
Williams, S. A., Sec., Fibre Corp.
Williamson, F. E., Vice-Pres., The Boehme & Rauch Co.
Willis, F. L., Vice-Pres. and Asst. Treas., Moore & Thompson Paper Co., Inc.
Willock, F. S., Pres., Tarentum Paper Mills.
Wilson, B. F., Treas., Marathon Paper Mills Co.
Wilson, Chas. C., Pres., Odell Mfg. Co.
Wilson, D. G., Sec. and Treas., Parsons Pulp & Lumber Co.
Wilson, F. H., Sec., Halltown Paper Board Co.
Wilson, L. G., Supt., Glens Falls, N. Y., International Paper Co.
Wilson, Lee L., Supt., Morris Paper Mills.
Wilson, L. R., Sec., Abitibi Power & Paper Co., Ltd.
Wilson, N. W. Vice-Pres. and Mgr.-Sales. Hammermill Paper Co.
Wilson, P. B., Vice-Pres., Spanish River Pulp & Paper Mills, Ltd.
Wilson, P. M., Asst. Sec., Marathon Paper Mills Co.
Wilson, S. L., Sec., Mt. Vernon Straw Board Co.
Wilson, Wm., Supt., Peerless Pulp Co., Ltd.
Wilson, W. J., Jr., Sales-Mgr., Ticonderoga Pulp & Paper Co.
Wilt, J. B., Supt., Parsons Pulp & Lumber Co.
Wing, Wm. C., Pres., Fox River Paper Co.
Winslow, Carlisle P., Dir., Forest Products Laboratory, Forest Service, United States Dept. of Agriculture, University of Wisconsin.
Witter, Isaac P., Treas., Consolidated Water Power & Paper Co.; Vice-Pres., Interlake Pulp & Paper Co.
Whittet, F. B., Sec. and Treas., Riordon Pulp & Paper Co., Ltd.
Wohnsiedler, J., Asst. Treas., Union Bag & Paper Corp.
Wolf, Geo. T., Treas., Eddy Paper Co.
Wolf, R. B., Mgr., Spanish River Pulp & Paper Mills, Ltd.
Wolf, L. E., Sec., De Grasse Paper Co.
Wolfe, Lynn E., Sec., High Falls Pulp & Paper Co.
Wood, Forbes, Supt., Nixon & Costello Co.
Wood, G. H., Pres. and Gen. Mgr., River Raisin Paper Co.; Gen. Mgr., Bogalusa Paper Co., Inc.
Wood, H. D., Owner, Phoenix Toilet & Paper Mfg. Co.; Pres., Clayville Paper Mills Co.
Wood, H. J., Sec., Big Falls Paper Co., Inc.
Wood, Irving S., Sec. and Treas., Phoenix Toilet & Paper Mfg. Co.; Sec., Clayville Paper Mills Co.
Wood, M. O., Mgr., Piercefield, International Paper Co.
Wood, N. F., Fourth Vice-Pres., Keasbey & Mattison Co.
Woodhead, Robt., Supt., Chesapeake Pulp & Paper Co., Inc.
Woodruff, A. S., Vice-Pres., Lincoln Paper Co., Ltd.
Woodruff, W. D., Pres., Lincoln Paper Mills Co., Ltd.
Woodward, E. C., Sec. and Treas., Wardlow-Thomas Paper Co.
Woodward, W. H., Paper Mill Supt., National Asbestos Mfg. Co.
Woodworth, E. K., Vice-Pres., Parker-Young Co.—Henry Paper Co. Branch.
Wood, Robert J., Vice-Pres. and Mgr., Big Falls Paper Co.
Woods, C. F., Sec., Arthur D. Little, Inc.
Woods, Thomas, Supt., West End Paper Co.
Woolworth, C. C., Pres., Ingalls Co.
Worcester, C. H., Vice-Pres., Munising Paper Co.
Worts, J. G., Pres., Don Valley Paper Co., Ltd.

Wright, C. T., Asst. Sec., Champion Paper Co.
Wright, Edward, Supt. and Mgr., High Falls Pulp & Paper Co.
Wright, George R., Pres. and Treas., Louisiana Fibre Board Co.
Wright, James, Supt., Newton Paper Co.
Wright, M. E., Sec. and Treas., Walsh Paper Co., Inc.
Wuescher, M. L., Sec., Bogalusa Paper Co., Inc.
Wyerhaeuser, R. M., Pres., Northwest Paper Co.
Wyman, G. R., Vice-Pres. and Mfg. Mgr., Bird & Son, Inc.

Y

Yarwood, W. H., Vice-Pres., Three Rivers Paper Co.
Yates, Calvin C., Pres., Eaton, Dikeman Co.
Yates, Olen V., Sec. and Supt., Eaton, Dikeman Co.
Yawkey, C. C., Pres., Marathon Paper Mills Co.; Vice-Pres., Wausau Paper Mills Co.
Yoder, Isaac C., Prop., West Branch Paper Mill.
Yordy, Jno., Supt., The Howard Paper Co.
Yost, Heber Y., Sec. and Treas., Reading Paper Mills.
Young, Charles E., Supt., Skowhegan Pulp Co.
Young, E. J., Vice-Pres. and Gen. Mgr., The Ohio Box Board Co.
Young, Herman D., Pres., Daniel & James B. Young.
Young, Robert, Sec., Ballston Fibre Products Co.
Young, S. A., Treas., Itasca Paper Co.
Yule, E. W., Sec. and Treas., Alexandria Paper Co.

Z

Zartman, Fred B., Treas. and Gen. Mgr., Franklin Board & Paper Co.
Zellerbach, I., Vice-Pres., National Paper Products Co.
Zellerbach, J. D., Sec., National Paper Products Co.
Zellerbach, T., Vice-Pres., National Paper Products Co.
Zerbe, H. C., Gen. Mgr., Mt. Vernon Straw Board Co.
Zigler, E. B., Pres., Wheat Paper Co.
Zimmerman, Max, Mgr., The Charles Boldt Paper Mills.
Zucker, Max, Pres., Toll and Leather Board Co.
Zurawski, Max, Supt., Federal Paper Board Co., Inc.

Oxford Paper Company

OFFICE:
FIFTH AVENUE BUILDING, 200 FIFTH AVENUE
NEW YORK

MILLS AT RUMFORD, MAINE

MANUFACTURERS OF

Machine Finish & Super Calendered Book Papers

Capacity of Paper Mill 275 Tons Daily

ALSO

Bleached Spruce Sulphite and Soda Pulp

Eagle Products Do the Work
They Are Designed For It

EAGLE KNIFE AND BAR WORKS
LAWRENCE :: :: MASS.

A. SALOMON, Inc.
EMANUEL SALOMON, President
13 PARK ROW — NEW YORK

IMPORTED AND DOMESTIC

PAPER MAKERS' SUPPLIES

INDEX TO MILLS

	PAGE
Abenaquis Mill	97
Abitibi Power and Paper Co.	231
Acme Paper Co.	198
Acme Paper and Paper Box Co.	106
Adams Bag Co.	178
Adams Paper Co.	206
Adams Paper Co., A. L.	104
Adriatic Mill, So. Manchester, Conn.	75
Advertisers Paper Mills	107
Aetna Paper Co.	180
Agasote Millboard Co.	136
Akron Paper Mill	177
Albemarle Paper Mfg. Co.	208
Albey Bros.	140
Albia Box and Paper Co.	173
Albion Mill	109
Aldrich Paper Co.	150, 160
Alexandria Paper Co.	85
Algonquin Sulphite Mill	100
Allen Division	155
Alton Box Board and Paper Co.	81
Amboy Paper Co.	189
American Box Board Co.	121
American Fibre Chair Seat Corp.	163
American Straw Board Co., 73, 82, 83, 85, 89, 101, 177, 179, 180, 185, 209	
American Tar Products Co.	84
American Wood Board Co.	170
American Writing Paper Co., 71, 75, 76, 108, 112, 113, 117, 180, 186, 215	
Amoskeag Paper Mills Co.	133
Analomink Paper Co.	195
Anchor Paper Co., Inc., The	76
Aneram Paper Mills	143
Andover Mill	102
Andrews, John T., & Co.	166
Androscoggin Pulp Co.	99
Anglo-Newfoundland Development Co., Ltd.	244
Ansen-Eldred Co., The	223
Antistam Paper Co.	102
A. P. W. Paper Co.	143
Aroostook Mill	95
Aroostook Pulp & Paper Co.	100
Arrow Head Mill, Inc.	152
Ashland Mills	130
Ashland Paper Co.	213
Ashuelot Paper Co.	132
Astoria Pulp & Paper Co.	187
Atlantic Mill, So. Manchester, Conn.	75
Atlantic Paper & Pulp Corp.	80
Atlas Leather Mfg. Co.	80
Atlas Mill, Appleton, Wis.	213
Auglaise Box Board Co., The	186
Augusta Pulp Mill	93
Augustine Mill	77

B

	PAGE
Baeder, Adamson & Co.	196
Ball Bros. Co.	88
Ballston Fibre Products Co., Inc.	144
Baltimore Mill	115
Baltimore Roofing & Asbestos Mfg. Co.	100
Bar Mills Mill	93
Bardeen Paper Co.	125
Bare Co., D. M.	198
Barnes Paper Mill	126
Barrett Co.	83, 137, 193
Bathurst Lumber Co.	226
Bayless Mfg. Corporation	189
Bay State Mill	105
Beach Paper Co., S. Y.	74
Beaver Brook Mill	70
Beaver Brook Paper Mills	70
Beaver Dam Mill	190
Beaver Falls Pulp Mills	144
Beaver Wood Fibre Co., Ltd.	233
Beckett Paper Co.	181
Bedford Pulp and Paper Co.	206, 207
Beebe & Holbrook Div.	109
Belfast Mills	93
Belgo-Canadian Pulp and Paper Co.	243
Beloit Box Board Co.	214
Bemis Bro. Bag Co.	83
Bennett, Ltd.	236
Benton Falls Mill	94
Bergen Paper Co.	140
Bergstrom Paper Co.	220
Berkshire Box and Paper Co.	159
Berkshire Hills Paper Co.	103
Beveridge Paper Co.	87
Bicking, S. Austin Paper Mfg. Co.	191
Big Falls Paper Co.	169
Bird & Son, Inc.	106, 201
Bird & Son, Ltd.	240
Biron Mill	215
Blake & Higgins	203
Blandy Paper Co.	153
Bloomer Bros. Co.	160
Bloomsburg Paper Co.	189
Blossvale Paper Co.	145
Boehme & Rauch Co.	123
Bogalua Paper Co.	92
Bogota Paper and Board Co.	136
Boldt, The Chas., Paper Mills	178
Booth, J. R.	232
Boston Mill	178
Bowdoin Mills	94
Boyle Co., John F.	138
Brainard Mill	173
Brainerd Pulp Mill	128
Braithwaite Paper Mill	92
Bridesburg Mill	197

Index to Mills

	PAGE		PAGE
Brightwood Mill	132	Charter Oak Mill	69
Bristol Paper Mills	131	Chateaugay Pulp Co.	147
Brompton Pulp and Paper Co.	235, 237	Cheboygan Paper Co. Plant	120
Bronson Company, The	232	Chemical Paper Mfg. Co.	110
Brookside Paper Co.	75	Cherry Co., J. G.	91
Brown Co.	131	Cherry River Paper Co.	212
Brown Corp.	239	Chesapeake Paperboard Co.	101
Brown, Howard C., Est.	70	Chesapeake Pulp & Paper Co., Inc.	209
Brown Paper Co., Fort Madison, Ia.	90	Chester Paper Co.	190
Brown Paper Co., Ithaca, N. Y.	155	Chestertown Mill	101
Brown Paper Co., L. L.	103	Chicago Coated Board Co.	80
Brown Paper Co., The E. M.	169	Chicago Folding Box Co.	81
Brownville Board Co.	145	Chicago Mill & Lumber Co.	81
Brownville Paper Co.	145	Chicoutimi Pulp Co.	236, 243
Bryant Paper Co.	121	Childsdale Paper Mills	120
Buck Run Mill	190	Circleville Mill	179
Buena Vista Mill	207	Claremont Paper Co., Inc.	132, 203
Bureau of Standards, Dept. of Commerce	78	Clayville Paper Mills Co.	148
		Cleveland-Akron Bag Co.	177, 179
Burmus Paper Co., Inc.	118	Cleveland Paper Mfg. Co.	179
		Cliff Paper Co.	164
C		Clifton Paper Mills	137
Cadyville Mills	146	Climax Mills	138
Caledonian Mill	142	Clyde River Pulp Co.	206
California Tissue Mills, Inc.	68	Clyde River Pulp & Paper Co.	227
Camillus Paper Mills	143	Cobbossee Mill	95
Campbell Lumber Co.	228	Codorus Mill	200
Canada Paper Co., Ltd.	243	Cole Paper Co., W. A.	205
Canada Boxboard Co., Ltd.	230, 239	Coleman's Mill	207
Carew Mfg. Co.	117	Collins Mfg. Co.	116
Carey Mfg. Co., Philip	182	Colonial Board Co.	71
Carlyle Paper Co.	80	Colonial Pulp Mills	93
Carney Paper Co.	183	Columbia Box Board Mills, Inc.	148
Carolina Fibre Co.	201	Columbia Mill, Lee, Mass.	113
Carso Paper Co.	149	Columbia Mills, Chatham Centre, N. Y.	148
Carthage Board and Paper Co.	86	Columbia Paper Mills Co.	195
Carthage Mill	86	Columbian Paper Co.	207
Carthage Sulphite Pulp and Paper Co.	146	Combined Locks Paper Co.	214
Cascade Mill, Berlin, N. H.	131	Compagnie de Pulpe de Chicoutimi, La.	236, 243
Cascade Paper Co.	210	Congress Mill, Rainbow, Conn.	74
Cascade Wood Products Co.	172	Consolidated Water Power and Paper Co.	215
Case & Marshall	69		
Case & Risley Press Paper Co.	73	Constantine Board & Paper Co.	120
Case Board Co.	60	Consumers Box Board & Paper Co.	193
Case Bros., Inc.	75	Continental Paper Bag Co.	130, 153, 161, 175
Case Co., A. Willard	71	Continental Paper Co.	136
Case Manufacturing Co.	75	Contoocook Valley Paper Co.	135
Cecil Mill	103	Coos Bay Pulp and Paper Co.	188
Centennial Mill, Dalton, Mass.	105	Copsecook Mill	95
Centennial Mill, Lee, Mass.	113	Cornell Wood Products Co.	214
Centennial Mill, Valatie, N. Y.	174	Cornwall Paper Mfg. Co.	148
Central Paper Co.	124	Coshocton Straw Paper Co.	179
Certain-teed Products Corp.	68, 81, 82, 164, 200	Covington Mill	207
		Cowies Falls Mill	228
Champion Coated Paper Co.	181	Coy Paper Co.	135
Champion Fibre Co.	176	Crabtree, Edwin S.	151
Champion-International Co.	112	Crane & Co.	105
Champion Paper Co.	146	Crane Bros.	118
Champlain Mills	176	Crane, Z. & W. M.	105
Chapin & Gould Paper Co.	116	Creamery Package Mfg. Co.	91

Index to Mills

	PAGE
Crehore, Chas. F., & Son	115
Crescent Mill, Marseilles, Ill.	82
Crescent Mills, Russell, Mass.	116
Crescent Paper & Machine Co.	166
Crescent Paper Co.	82
Crescentville Mill	182
Crivits Pulp & Paper Co.	215
Crocker, Burbank & Co. Assn.	107
Crocker-McElwain Co.	111
Crocker Mfg. Co. Div.	109
Crown Willamette Paper Co.	67, 187, 188, 209
Crystal Paper Co.	183
Cullen, L. C.	200
Cumberland Mills	94
Curtis & Bro., Inc.	77
Cushman-Rankin Co.	130
Cushnoc Paper Co.	93

D

	PAGE
Darby Mill	193
Davey Co., E. H.	136
Davey, W. O., & Sons	139
Davis Mill	211
Davis Paper Co.	135
Davy Mills	234
Decatur Strawboard Co.	88
Deerfield Pulp Co., Mountain Mills, Vt.	204
Deferiet Mill	148
Defiance Mill, Dalton, Mass.	105
Defiance Paper Co.	164
De Grasse Paper Co.	169
Delaware Hard Fibre Co.	77
Delaware Mills, Wilmington, Del.	78
Delaware Paper Mill	196
Dells Paper and Pulp Co.	215
Delphi Straw Board Co.	86
Delray Mill	120
Detroit Sulphite Pulp and Paper Co.	120, 149
Dexter, C. H., & Sons, Inc.	76
Diana Paper Co.	154
Diamond Match Co.	75
Diamond Mills Paper Co.	136, 140, 160, 170
Diamond State Fibre Co.	189
Dill & Collins Co.	196
District of Columbia Paper Mfg. Co.	79
Dixie Paper Mills, Inc.	208
Dominion Paper Co.	239
Dominion Pulp Co., Ltd.	226
Don Valley Paper Co., Ltd.	234
Donnacona Paper Co., Ltd., The	237, 241
Draycott Mill	171
Dresden Paper Mills Co.	180
Dryden Pulp & Paper Co., Ltd.	220
Du Pont De Nemours & Co., E. I.	73, 97, 142

E

	PAGE
Eagle Mill, Bentley's Springs, Md.	101
Eagle Mill, Ballston Spa, N. Y.	144
Eagle Mill, Burnside, Conn.	70
Eagle Mill, Lee, Mass.	113
Eagle Mill, Marcellus Falls, N. Y.	158
Eagle Mill, Putney, Vt.	205
Eagle Paper Mills, Downingtown	191
East Angus Boxboard Mill	237
East Hartford Manufacturing Co.	69
East Lake Mill	68
East Walpole Mill	106
Eastern Mfg. Co.	93, 96
Eastern Paper Co., Ltd.	242
Eastman Kodak Co.	169
Eaton, Dikeman Co., The	113
Eddy Co., The E. B.	238
Eddy Paper Co.	126, 127
Eden Mill	142
Edwards, John, Mill	222
Eldridge Strawboard Mill	150
Emerson Paper Co.	135
Empire Mill	169
Empire Paper Co., Ithaca, N. Y.	155
Endicott, Johnson & Co.	155
Erving Paper Mills	106
Escanaba Pulp & Paper Co.	121
Estcock Manufacturing Co.	117
Eureka Mill	172
Eureka Paper Co.	152
Evansville Paper Mill	87
Everett Pulp and Paper Co.	209
Ewing, Everest Pulp Co.	219
Excelsior Mill	180
E-Z Opener Bag Co.	84, 92

F

	PAGE
Fairfield Ground Wood Mill	95
Fairfield Paper Co., The	177
Fairfield Pulp Mills	95
Fall Mountain Mills	203
Falls Mfg. Co.	221
Falleburgh Mill	150
Falulah Paper Co.	107
Fandango Mills	140
Fawn Mill	120
Federal Mill	81
Federal Paper Board Co.	76, 136
Felt Paper Co.	103
Felts Mills	150
Fenimore Paper Mill	155
Fibre Conduit Co.	165
Fibre Corporation	156
Fibre Products, Ltd.	232
Field & White Co.	137
Filer Fibre Co.	120
Fillmore & Slade	204
Finch, Pruyn & Co., Inc.	153
Fisher, John, & Son	229
Fisk Paper Co.	132
Fitchburg Paper Co.	107
Fitsdale Paper Co.	204
Flambeau Paper Co.	222
Fleming, John G., & Sons	202
Fletcher Paper Co.	119

Index to Mills

	PAGE
Flower City Tissue Mills Co.	169, 171
Foley-Rieger Pulp & Paper Co., Ltd.	234
Ford, Joseph, & Co.	241
Ford Mfg. Co.	84, 90
Ford, Rowland & Son	241
Forest Mill, Willistown Inn, Pa.	200
Forest Paper Co.	100
Forest Products Laboratory	218
Forest Products Laboratory of Canada	240
Fort Edward Mill	151
Fort Frances Pulp and Paper Co.	230
Fort Miller Pulp and Paper Co.	151
Fort Orange Paper Co.	147
Fort Wayne Corrugated Paper Co.	87, 89
Foster Box Board Co.	174
Foulds & Co., William, Inc.	71
Fox & Sons, W. H.	166
Fox Paper Co.	182
Fox River Paper Co.	212
Franklin Board and Paper Co.	180
Franklin Mill, Chesterville, Pa.	190
Franklin Mill, Franklin, O.	180
Franklin Mill, Poquonock, Conn.	73
Franklin Paper Co., Holyoke, Mass.	111
Franklin Paper Mills	199
Franklin Pulp Mill	157
Fraser Companies, Ltd.	226
French Paper Co.	124
Frontenac Mill	149
Funke's Sons, Ferdinand	87

G

	PAGE
Gandey, Est. of W. H.	139
Garden City Paper Mills Co., Ltd.	232
Gardner-Harvey Paper Co., The	183
Gardner Paper Co., The Colin	184
Gardner, The, Paper Board Co.	184
Garoga Creek Mill	171
Garrett, Edwin	77
Garrett, E. T., Co.	193
Garvan, Thomas F., Co.	70
General Fibre Board Co.	105
General Paper Co., Inc.	190
George Co., S.	212
George & Sherrard Paper Co.	212
Gilbert Paper Co.	218
Gilbert Paper Co., Frank	148, 174
Glatfelter, P. H., Co.	199
Glen Mills, Berlin, N. H.	131
Glen Mills Paper Co.	192
Glen Rock Mills	78
Glens Falls Mills	153
Globe Mills, Neenah, Wis.	220
Gore, H. M.	102
Gould Paper Co.	157, 168
Government Mill	121
Granby Plant	152
Grandfather's Falls Co.	219
Grand Rapids Mill	215
Grant Mill	218

	PAGE
Graves, W. L.	195
Greasonia Paper Mills Co.	151
Great Eastern Paper Co.	237
Great Northern Paper Co.	95, 96, 97
Green Bay Paper and Fibre Co.	216
Green Island Mill	173
Green Mountain Pulp Co.	204
Greenwich Leatherboard Co.	159
Greylock Paper Mills	103
Groton Leather Board Co.	118
Groton Mill	105
Gulf Paper Mills Co.	67
Gulf Pulp and Paper Co.	236
Gunpowder Paper Mill	102

H

	PAGE
Hadley Mill	154
Hadley Paper Corp.	154
Hagar Straw Board and Paper Co.	178
Ha! Ha! Bay Sulphite Co.	235
Halifax Paper Corporation	176
Hall & Richter Paper Co.	134
Halltown Paper Board Co.	211
Hamilton, W. C., & Sons	196
Hammermill Paper Co.	191
Hammerschlag Mfg. Co.	138
Hampshire Paper Co., Inc.	117
Hampton Mill	160
Haner, Sanford Co.	148
Hannawa Falls Water Power Co.	154
Hanover Mills	142
Hardwick Mill	119
Harmon Paper Co.	146
Harpers Ferry Paper Co.	211
Hart Paper Co.	85
Hartford Board Co.	70, 72
Hartford City Paper Co.	87
Hartford Paper Co.	73
Hartje Bros. Paper Co.	186
Hartje Paper Mfg. Co.	186
Harvey Paper Co.	212
Haverhill Box Board Co.	107
Hawley Pulp and Paper Co.	188
Hawthorne Paper Co.	121
Hennepin Paper Co.	129
Hercules Mills Nos. 1 and 2	196, 197
Herkimer Fibre Co.	154
Herrings Mills	154
High Falls Pulp and Paper Co.	147
Highland Lake Mill	115
Highland Mill	192
Highland Mills, So. Manchester, Conn.	75
Highland Paper Co.	192
Hinckley Fibre Co.	154
Hinde & Dauch Paper Co.	89, 138, 175, 180, 185
Hinde & Dauch Paper Co. of Canada, Ltd.	235
Hinsdale Mill	133
Hinsdale Paper Co.	133
Hoberg Co., The John	216

Index to Mills

	PAGE
Hoboken Paper Mill Co.	138, 170
Hoffman, R. S.	143
Holden Paper Co.	160, 170
Hollingsworth & Vose Co.	106, 118
Hollingsworth & Whitney Co.	95, 97, 100
Hollywood Mills	208
Home Pulp & Paper Mills Co.	67
Hoornbeek's Sons, John C.	159
Houpt Paper Mill, Ltd.	228
Horwood Lumber Co.	244
Housatonic Mill	113
Howard Paper Co.	187
Howland Pulp & Paper Corp.	96
Hudson Paper Mill	175
Hudson River Mills	165
Hughesville Mill	141
Hummel & Downing Co.	219
Humphrey & Young	159
Hunter's, Dard, Paper Mill	158
Huntington Paper Mill	192
Hutchinson Box Board & Paper Co., The	91
Hutchinson-Puttaert Co.	68
Hydro-Electric Power Commission Pulp Mill	229

I

Indiana Board & Filler Co.	90
Ingalls & Co.	147
Ingersoll Paper Co.	173
Inland Empire Paper Co.	210
Interlake Pulp & Paper Co.	213
Interlake Tissue Mills, Ltd.	231
International Paper Co., 94, 96, 97, 98, 99, 100, 117, 132, 146, 148, 151, 153, 161, 164, 165, 167, 172, 175, 203, 204, 206	
Iroquois Pulp & Paper Co.	158, 172
Irving—See Erving Paper Mills	106
Island Mill, Ticonderoga, N. Y.	173
Island Paper Co., Menasha, Wis.	219
Island Paper Co., The, Carthage, N. Y.	146
Itasca Paper Co.	128

Jaite Co., The	178
James River Mills	206
Japanese Mills	118
Japanese Tissue Mills	116
Jarvis Paper Mills	135
Jenkins, Geo. O., Co.	104
Jessup & Moore Paper Co.	77, 101, 102, 190
Johns-Manville Co., H. W.	140, 220
Johnston & Son	168
Joliette Paper Mill	238
Jonquieres Pulp Co.	238

K

Kalamazoo Paper Co.	121
Kalamazoo Vegetable Parchment Co.	122
Kamargo Mills	175

	PAGE
Katahdin Mill	96
Kaukauna Pulp Co.	216
Keasbey & Mattison Co.	189
Keith Paper Co.	118
Kenmore Mills	103
Kennesaw Paper Co.	80
Kenogami Mills	238
Kenyon Paper Corp.	197
Kerr Paper Mill Co.	191
Keuka Mill	166
Keystone Paper Mills Co.	200
Kieffer Paper Co.	85
Kimberly-Clark Co.	213, 217, 220, 221
King Paper Co.	122
Kingsey Falls Mills	239
Kingsley Wood Pulp Co.	205
Kingsport Pulp Corp.	202
Kingston Paper Co.	156
Kinleith Paper Co.	232
Kitsmiller & Bro., S. M.	194
Klein Paper Co.	90
Knife Falls Pulp Mill	128
Knowlton Bros., Inc.	175

L

La Chute Paper Mills	239
Ladysmith Mill	217
Lafayette Box Board and Paper Co.	88
La Have Pulp Co., Ltd.	228
Lake Champlain Pulp and Paper Co.	167
Lake George Mills	172
Lake Megantic Pulp Co.	239
Lake Sunapee Mill	135
Lakeside Mill	171
Lakeside Paper Co.	220
La Monte, Geo., & Son	141
Lancaster Board and Paper Co.	181
Lancaster Leather Co.	182
Lang Paper Co., John	196
La Salle Paper Co.	89
Laurentide Co., Ltd.	237
Lawless Bros. Paper Mills	150
Lawless Paper Co.	166
Lawrence Paper Mfg. Co.	91
Lawrenceville Paper Mills	79
Lazier Paper Mills, Ltd.	228
Lee Fibre Co.	135
Lee Paper Co.	127
Lefebvre, Edward Y.	150
Lehigh Paper Mills, Inc.	198
Leo Co., James	139
Leominster Mill	115
Lewis Co., J. P., Inc.	144
Lewis Mfg. Co., F. J.	82
Lewis, Slocum & Lefevre Co., Inc.	145
Lincoln, L., & Co.	115
Lincoln Mill	212
Lincoln Paper Mills Co., Ltd.	231
Lindale Mills	106

Index to Mills

	PAGE		PAGE
Lindauer Pulp Co.	216	Merwin Paper Co.	74
Lisbon Falls Mills	96	Metabetchouan Pulp Co.	242
Little Androscoggin Mill	95	Metalite Co.	104
Little Falls Paper Co.	156, 160	Meyers, Jr., J. E.	92
Little Arthur D., Inc.	104	Miami Paper Co., The	187
Livermore Falls Pulp Co.	134	Miamisburg Paper Co.	183
Livermore Mill	96	Michigan Bag and Paper Co.	121
Livingston Pulp Mill	128	Michigan Carton Co.	119
Lock Haven Mills	193	Michigan Paper Co., Plainwell, Mich.	126
Lockland Mill (Fox Paper Co.)	182	Midland Paper Mills	85
Lockland Mills (Richardson Paper Co.)	182	Mid-West Box Co.	87
Lockport Paper Co.	156	Milford Mill	140
Los Angeles Paper Mfg. Co.	68	Millburn Mill	140
Lotbiniere Lumber Co.	240	Miller Bros. Co., Ltd.	230
Louisiana Fibre Board Co.	92	Miller Paper Co., Frank P.	191
Lydall & Foulds Paper Co.	71	Millers Falls Paper Co.	113
Lyonsdale Mills	157	Millinockett Mill	97
Lysle, Wilson, Estate of	190	Milo Paper Mills	166
		Milton Leather Board Co.	134
		Milton Mills	204
		Minnesota & Ontario Power Co.	128
M		Missisquoi Pulp and Paper Co.	206
McArthur, Alexander & Co.	238	Mohawk Improvement Co., Inc.	151
McDowell Paper Mills	196	Mohawk Mill	175
McElwain Company, W. H.	134	Mohawk Valley Paper Co., Inc.	156
McEwan Bros.	142	Mohican Pulp and Paper Co.	153
McIntyre Bros., Inc.	150	Moira Mill	228
Mac Andrews & Forbes Co.	137	Monadnock Paper Mills	131
MacLaren Co., Ltd., The James	235	Monarch Paper Co.	122
MacLeod Pulp Co., Ltd.	228	Monroe Binder Board Co.	80, 123
MacSim Bar Paper Co.	125	Monroe Bridge Paper Co.	114
Madison Mill, Madison, Me.	97	Monroe Felt & Paper Co.	113
Malone Paper Co.	157	Monroe Paper Co.	124
Manchester Board & Paper Co.	208	Montague Mills	117
Manistique Pulp & Paper Co.	123	Montreal Paper Co.	241
Mann Co., Wm.	139	Montrose Mill	234
Manning Paper Co., John A.	173	Montville Mill	71
Marathon Paper Mills Co.	224	Moore Paper Mill Corp.	166
Marcellus Falls Mill	158	Moore & Thompson Paper Co.	203
Marcellus Paper Co.	158	Moorhouse, R. T., Paper Co.	197
Marinette & Menominee Paper Co.	123, 218	Morgan Falls Mill	228
Marion Paper Co.	88	Morley Button Co.	134
Marley Paper Mfg. Co.	101	Morris Paper Mills	82
Mars Paper Corp.	118	Mt. Carmel Mill	82
Marseilles Wrapping Paper Co.	82	Mt. Holly Paper Mills	194
Marshall Bros., Inc.	78	Mt. Ida Mill	173
Marshall & Mitchell	78	Mt. Tom Sulphite Pulp Co.	114
Martin Pulp & Paper Co., Ltd.	165	Mt. Vernon Straw Board Co.	88
Mason-Perkins Paper Co.	131	Mountain Mill Paper Co.	113
Massillon Paper Co.	183	Mountain Paper Co.	192
Mattagami Pulp and Paper Co., Ltd.	233	Mountain Spring Paper Mill	139
Mead Pulp & Paper Co.	178	Moyer & Pratt	157
Mechanicville Mills	158	Muckle Bros. Mfg. Co.	128
Medway Pulp & Power Co.	227	Muir Board Co.	194
Megargee Paper Mills	194	Muir, Jas. A.	142
Menasha Mill	219	Mullen Bros. Paper Co.	126
Menasha Paper Co.	217	Mumford Paper Mills, Inc.	159
Menasha Printing & Carton Co.	214, 219	Munising Paper Co.	124
Mengel Boxboard Co., Branch	86	Munroe Falls Paper Co.	185
Merion Paper Co.	188	Munroe Felt and Paper Co.	113
Merrimac Paper Co.	112		

Index to Mills

	PAGE		PAGE
Munroe Mill	185	Norton, C. H.	73
Mutual Box Board Co.	174	Norwalk Paper Mill	73

N

	PAGE
Nairn Falls Power and Pulp Co., Ltd.	240
Napanoch Mills	159
Nashua River Paper Company	105
Nashwaak Pulp & Paper Co.	227
Nassau Mills Corporation	190
Natick Box and Board Co.	114
National Asbestos Mfg. Co.	139
National Biscuit Co.	82
National Cellulose Co.	80
National Fibre and Insulation Co.	78
National Folding Box and Paper Co.	72, 144
National Metal Edge Box Co.	205
National Mill, Ballston Spa, N. Y.	144
National Paper Co.	79
National Paper Products Co.	68, 147
Naubuc Mill	70
Naubuc Paper Co.	70
Neenah Paper Co.	221
Neenah Paper Mill	220
Nekonagan Paper Co.	97
Nekoosa-Edwards Paper Co.	216, 221, 222
Nekoosa Mill	221
Nelson, B. F., Mfg. Co.	129
Newark Box Board Co.	140
New Brunswick Sulphate Fibre Co., Ltd.	227
New Castle Paper Co.	194
New Elkhart Paper Mills Co.	86
New Found Pulp Mill	131
New Haven Pulp and Board Co.	72
News Pulp and Paper Co., Ltd.	242
Newton Falls Paper Co.	160
Newton Paper Co.	111
New York & Pennsylvania Co.	176, 192, 193
Niagara Falls Mill (International Paper Co.)	164
Niagara Falls Mills (Certain-teed Products Corp.)	164
Niagara Mill, Lee, Mass.	113
Niagara Mill, Niagara, Wis.	221
Niagara Paper Mills	156
Niagara Pulp Mill	157
Niagara River Mfg. Co.	164
Nissitissitt Mill	106
Nixon Paper Co., Martin & Wm. H.	197
Noble Mfg. Co.	79
Noblesville Mill	89
Nonantum Paper Mills	77
Norristown Magnesia and Asbestos Co.	195
North End Paper Co.	152
Northern Michigan Pulp Co.	125
Northern Paper Mills	216
North Hoosick Mills	165
Northumberland Paper and Electric Co., Ltd.	229
Northwest Paper Co.	128

O

	PAGE
Oak Cliff Paper Mill	202
Oak Grove Mill	147
Oakland Mill	71
Odell Mfg. Co.	132
Oglesby Paper Co., The W. B.	184
Ohio Box Board Co.	185
Ohio Paper Co.	183
Old Berkshire Mills	105
Old Dominion Mill	209
Old Reliable Mills	139
Onondaga Paper Co.	158
Ontario Paper Co., Ltd.	234
Orange County Paper Mill	160
Orono Pulp and Paper Co.	98
Oswego Falls Pulp and Paper Co.	152
Oswego River Paper Mills	166
Otis Mills	94
Otter River Board Co.	116
Outagamie Paper Co.	217
Outterson, James A.	144
Oxford Paper Co.	98

P

	PAGE
Pacific Mills, Ltd.	225
Packwack Mill	198
Pairpoint Corporation	115
Palisade Mill	74
Palmer, Willis B.	191
Paraffine Companies, Inc.	67, 68, 69, 210, 211
Paran Creek Mill	205
Park Mills	218
Parker & Son Co., Jos.	76
Parker-Young Co. (Henry Paper Co. Branch)	133
Parksville Mill	41
Parsons Paper Co.	111
Parsons Pulp and Lumber Co.	211
Passumpsic Fibre Leather Co.	205
Patent Vulcanite Roofing Co.	85, 181
Patten Paper Co., Ltd.	213
Peerless Paper Co.	180
Peerless Pulp Co., Ltd.	234
Pejepscot Paper Co.	94, 96
Pemble Mills	172
Peninsular Paper Co.	127
Penobscot Chemical Fibre Co.	95
Peoria Mill	83
Pepperell Mills	105
Pequannock Valley Paper Co.	137
Perkiomen Paper Co.	195
Perseverance Paper Mills	139
Pettebone-Cataract Paper Co.	165
Philadelphia Paper Mfg. Co.	197
Philadelphia Wax Paper Co.	199

Index to Mills

	PAGE		PAGE
Phillips Co., The Thomas	177	Riverside Paper Mfg. Co., The	70
Phoenix Mill	158	Riverton Co	74
Phoenix Paper Co., The	144	Riverview Coated Paper Co	122
Phoenix Tissue Mills	167	Roanoke Fibre Board Co	176
Phoenix Toilet and Paper Mfg. Co	167	Roaring Spring Mill	198
Pierce Bros	205	Roberts & Son Co., John	118
Piercefield Mill	167	Robertson Bros	133
Piermont Paper Co	167	Robertson Co., The C. M.	71
Pioneer Mill, Dalton, Mass	105	Robertson, E. C., & Son	133
Pioneer Paper Co	176	Robertson, G. A., & Co	133
Pleasant Mills Paper Co	141	Robertson, W. F., & Co	133
Poland Paper Co	97	Robertson Paper Co	203
Pont Rouge Pulp Mill	241	Robertson's Sons, William	205
Port Arthur Pulp & Paper Co., Ltd	232	Rock Falls Board Co	84
Port Edwards Fibre Mill	222	Rockford Paper Box Board Co	84
Port Huron Sulphite and Paper Co	126	Rockford Paper Mills	84
Powell River Paper Co	225	Rockland Mill, Montville, Conn	71
Powerville Mills	137	Rockland Mill, Wilmington, Del	77
Price Brothers & Co., Ltd	238	Rockport Mill	89
Price-Porritt Pulp and Paper Co	241	Rogers Co., J. & J	143
Provincial Paper Mills Co., Ltd	230, 231, 234	Rogers Fibre Co	93, 95
Pynetree Paper Co	79	Rogers Paper Mfg. Co	75
		Rolland Paper Co	241, 242
Q		Rollstone Mill	107
		Rudolph, F. M., & Son	191
Quaker Oats Co., The	83	Rumford Falls Mill	98
Quebec & Saguanay Pulp Co	242	Rushmore Paper Co	161
		Ryegate Paper Co	204
R			
		S	
Raquette River Paper Co	155, 168		
Radnor Pulp Mill	102	St. Croix Paper Co	100
Rainbow Mills, The	74	St. Croix Paper Co., Ltd	227
Rainy River Pulp & Paper Co	225	St. Francis Mill	243
Rapid Falls Mills	228	St. George Pulp and Paper Co	73, 227
Ravenswood Paper Mill Co	164	St. Lawrence Pulp & Lumber Corp	236
Ravine Mills	212	St. Maurice Paper Co., Ltd	236
Reading Mill	198	St. Regis Paper Co	145, 149, 154
Reading Paper Mills	198	Sall Mountain Asbestos Mfg. Co	185
Red Mill	167	Sandusky Paper Mill	185
Reed & Co., Albert E., Newfoundland, Ltd	243	Saranac Co	168
Remington Paper & Power Co	149, 165, 169	Sault au Recollet Paper Mill	240
Rex Paper Co	122	Savage Mfg. Co	99
Reynolds Mill	89	Saxer Paper Mills	171
Rhinelander Paper Co	222	Schmidt & Ault Paper Co	200
Rialto Mill	182	Schroon River Pulp and Paper Co	174
Richard & Co	239	Sears, Roebuck & Co	81
Richardson Paper Co	182	Seneco Paper Co., Inc	167
Richmond Paper Mfg. Co	208	Shawmut Mfg. Co	99
Richmond, Robert P	174	Sheeder's Paper Mill	198
Richwood Mill	212	Shenandoah Pulp Co	211
Riegelsville Mill	141	Sherman & Co	93
Riley Mill	98	Shortville Paper Co	171
Riordon Pulp & Paper Co., Ltd	230, 231	Shryock Bros	191
Rising Paper Co., B. D	112	Silver Spring Mill	136
River du Loup Pulp Co., Ltd	237	Simplex Paper Co	125
River Raisin Paper Co	124	Skaneateles Mill	171
Riverside Fibre and Paper Co	213, 218	Skaneateles Paper Co	171
Riverside Mills, Berlin, N. H	131	Skowhegan Pulp Co	99

SPECIALTIES
FOR THE PAPER MANUFACTURERS

Auramine   Methyl Violet

Ozo Rubine   Methylene Blue

Brilliant Scarlet   Vegetable Tallow

Croceine Scarlet   Alizarine Assistant

Basic News Blue BS   Soluble Oils

Metanil Yellow   Orange

Bismarck Browns   Crysoidine

A. KLIPSTEIN & COMPANY
644-652 GREENWICH STREET
NEW YORK CITY

See Other Side

A. KLIPSTEIN & COMPANY
644-54 GREENWICH STREET
NEW YORK

BRANCHES:
- 283-85 Congress Street, Boston
- 50-52 North Front Street, Philadelphia
- 145-47 West Kinzie Street, Chicago
- 130 Fountain Street, Providence
- Com'l Nat'l Bank Bldg., Charlotte, N. C.

CANADIAN REPRESENTATIVES

A. KLIPSTEIN & COMPANY, Ltd.
12 ST. PETER STREET, MONTREAL

Chemicals, Colors and Dye Stuffs
FOR PAPER MAKERS

CASEIN—SODA ASH
High Grade Electrolytic Bleaching Powder

CHEMICAL SPECIALTIES

Alum,	Formaldehyde, 40%
Alumina Sulphate	Potato Flour, Starch and Dextrine
Bichromate Potash	Borax
Bichromate Soda	Blanc Fixe, Aqua Ammonia
Permanganate Potash	Satin White
Barium Chloride	Zinc Oxide (Imported)
Glauber's Salt	Trisodium Phosphate

VEGETABLE TALLOW
(FOR PREVENTING FOAM)

See Other Side

National Duplex Waterproof Case Lining
IS WATERPROOF—CLEAN TO HANDLE   **NATIONAL WATERPROOFING CO.,** 1054 DREXEL BLDG. PHILADELPHIA

Index to Mills

	PAGE		PAGE
Smeallie & Voorhees	143	Three Rivers Paper Co.	167
Smith, Howard Paper Mills, Ltd.	235, 236	Ticonderoga Pulp and Paper Co.	172
Smith Paper Co.	113	Tidewater Paper Mills Co.	161
Snyder Mfg. Co., Inc., W. W.	148	Tileston & Hollingsworth Co.	104
Solon Mill	99	Tobacco Production Co.	72
Sorg Paper Co., Paul A.	184	Tolland Leather Board Co.	71
Soucy, F. Florentin	242	Tomahawk Pulp and Paper Co.	217, 223
South Coventry Paper Co.	74	Tonawanda Board and Paper Co.	173
Southern Fibre Co.	208	Topsham Mill	94
Southern Paper Co.	130	Toronto Paper Mfg. Co.	229
Southford Mill	75	Traders Mill	136
Southworth Co.	114	Trent Valley Paper Mills	230
Spanish River Pulp and Paper Mills, Ltd.	229, 233	Troy Mill	173
Spaulding & Sons Co., J.	117, 134	Troy City Mill	173
Spring Grove Paper Mills	199	Tulpehocken Mill	198
Springets Mills, The	201	Tunxis Mill	75
Srere Bros & Co.	181	Twin Falls Mills	141
Srere Pulp and Paper Co.	181	Tyrone Mill	199
Standard Mill	179		
Standard Paint Co.	81	**U**	
Standard Paper Co.	123		
Standard Paper Mfg. Co.	208	Ulster Tissue Mills, Inc.	159
Stark Paper Co.	205	Uncas Mill	73
Star Mills, Windsor Locks, Conn.	76	Underwood Pulp and Paper Mills, Inc.	168
State Line Mill	205	Union Bag and Paper Corp.	120, 155, 162, 217
Sterling Paper Co.	181	Union Mfg. Co.	221
Stevens Point Pulp & Paper Co.	223	Union Mill, Bancroft, Mass.	104
Stevens & Thompson	165	Union Mills, New Hope, Pa.	195
Stevens & Thompson Paper Co.	159	Union Mills Paper Mfg. Co.	195
Stever, George	145	Union Paper Mill Co.	194
Stowe & Sons, Inc., J. D.	74	Unionville Mill	75
Strange Paper Co., The John	219	Union Waxed and Parchment Paper Co.	138
Stratford Paper Co.	139	United Paperboard Co.	82, 83, 86, 89, 90, 94, 95, 142, 156, 163, 170, 187
Strathoona Paper Co.	233		
Strathmore Paper Co.	114, 119	United Paper Co.	144
Stutt, James, & Son	235	United States Paper Mills, Inc.	190
Sugar Cane By-Products Co.	92	Unity Paper Mills	168
Sunny Dale Mill	77	University of Maine Paper Pulp School	98
Sweet Bros. Paper Mfg. Co.	167	Upson Co.	157
		Urbana Mill	187
T			
		Valley Falls Mills	205
Taconnet Mill	100	Valley Mill, Bentley's Springs, Md.	101
Taggart Bros. Co.	175	Valley Mill, Cleveland, O.	179
Taggarts Paper Co.	150, 153	Valley Mill, Lee, Mass.	113
Tait & Sons Paper Co., The	69	Valley Paper Co., Holyoke, Mass.	111
Tama Paper Mill	91	Van Buren, J. M., & Co.	159
Tarentum Paper Mills	199	Vandalia Paper Mill	84
Taylor-Atkins Paper Co.	70	Van de Carr Paper Co.	172
Taylor-Logan Co. Papermakers	112	Victoria Paper Mills Co.	152
Telulah Mill	213	Vinton, Wm. H., & Son	203
Tennessee Paper Mills, Inc.	202	Voluey Plant	152
Terre Haute Paper Co.	89		
Thames River Specialties Co., The	72	**W**	
Thilmany Pulp and Paper Co.	213, 217		
Thompson & Norris Co. of Indiana, The	85	Wabash Mill	90
Thornapple Ground Wood Mills	218	Wagner's Hollow Mill	151
Thorold Pulp Co., Ltd.	234	Waldorf Box Board Co.	129

E. J. KELLER CO., INC.
380 FIFTH AVENUE   E. J. KELLER, Pres.   NEW YORK
FOREIGN AND DOMESTIC

Ropes AND Bagging

Rags, Linen, Flax and Cotton Wastes, Paper Stock, Wood Pulp and Rag Pulp.

R. H. McEwan, Pres.   J. L. McEwan, Vice-Pres.   Arthur McEwan, Treas. and Mgr.   R. W. McEwan, Secy.
Sheet Lining Plant, Office and Mills at WHIPPANY, N. J.

McEWAN BROS., Inc. MANUFACTURERS OF ALL GRADES **PAPER BOX BOARD**

DRY ROSIN SIZE Brittle, easy soluble, cheapest size out; cheaper than mill made size. Ask us about it. Also all other grades. **ARABOL M'F'G CO.** 100 William St., N. Y.

Index to Mills

	PAGE
Walker, J. R., & Co.	240
Wall & Son, J. F.	115
Walloomsac Paper Co.	174
Walsh Paper Co., Inc.	179
Wanaque River Paper Co.	142
Wardlow-Thomas Paper Co.	184
Wardway Paper Mills.	91
Warren Mfg. Co.	140, 141
Warren Mill.	141
Warren Parchment Company	149
Warren, S. D., Co.	94, 95
Washington Pulp & Paper Corp.	210
Wasuc Mills Co.	75
Watab Pulp and Paper Co.	129
Watertown Mills.	175
Watervliet Paper Co.	127
Watson Co., H. F.	192
Wausau Paper Mills Co.	214
Wausau Sulphate Fibre Co.	220
Waverly Paper Box Board Co.	141
Wayagamack Pulp & Paper Co.	243
Webster Mill.	87
Webster Mills.	97
Wels Paper Mill Co.	83
Wells River Mills.	206
Wellsburg Mill.	212
Wentworth Paper Mill.	235
West Branch Paper Mill.	189
West End Paper Co.	147
West Enfield Mill.	100
Western Board & Paper Co.	123
Western Paper Mills, Ltd.	225
Westfield River Paper Co.	116
West Groton Mill-Groton Leather Board Co.	118
West Groton Mill-Hollingsworth & Vose	118
West Jersey Paper Mfg. Co.	137
Weston Co., Byron.	105
Westport Paper Co.	76
West Rock Paper Mill.	76

	PAGE
West Virginia Pulp and Paper Co.	102, 158, 199, 200, 207, 211
West Virginia Pulp Product Co., Inc.	207
Weymouth Falls Mill.	228
Whalen Pulp & Paper Mills, Ltd.	225, 226
Wheat Paper Co.	86
Wheelwright Paper Co., Geo. W.	107, 115, 119
White Oak Mills.	84
Whiting Paper Co.	112
Whiting Paper Co., Geo. A.	219
Whiting-Plover Paper Co.	223
Whittelsey Co., F. H.	76
Wilder Mill.	206
Williamsburg Mill.	200
Willow Glen Mills.	190
Wilson, J. C., Ltd.	139, 242
Windham Mill.	99
Windsor Mill.	243
Winnipiseogee Mills.	132
Winona Pulp & Paper Co.	130
Wisconsin River Paper and Pulp Co.	223
Wolf River Paper and Fibre Co.	222
Wolverine Paper Co.	125
Wood & Nellis.	151
Wooddale Paper Mill.	78
Woodland Mill.	69
Woods Falls Mills.	175
Worthy Paper Co. Association.	114
Wrenn Paper Co.	184
Wyoming Valley Paper Mill.	197

Y

	PAGE
Yellow Pine Paper Mill Co.	202
York Haven Paper Co., The.	201
York Paper Mfg. Co.	201
Yorktown Mill.	90
Young, Daniel & James B.	101
Young, Jos. W.	101

SHERMAN ENVELOPE CO. Cor. **PRESCOTT** and **OTIS** STS. Office and Factory: **WORCESTER, MASS.**

Manufacturers of all kinds **Envelopes** Lithographed Printed or Plain

Sherman's Double Tongue Metal Clasp and Tension Fastener Envelope for mailing packages under second class postage.

All Our ENVELOPES are made from Standard Grades of Paper.

Also Manufacturers of the Seco Safety Edge Sanitary Drinking Cup

PRESS ROLLS Maple and Gum White Wood Felt Rolls **J. W. HEWITT MACHINE CO.** Neenah, Wis.

THOMAS E. GLEESON, Inc., 411-413 John St., E. NEWARK, N. J
CYLINDER MOULDS and DANDY ROLLS Made and Repaired
LETTERING and MONOGRAMS for WATERMARKS

PAPER and PULP MILLS
IN THE
UNITED STATES

ALABAMA.

MOBILE—Mobile Co.

Pop. 51,521. On Mobile & Ohio; Gulf, Mobile & Northern; L. & N.; Southern; Mobile & Bay Shore and Tombigbee Valley RR. So. Ex.

GULF PAPER MILLS CO. (J. M. Walsh, Pres.; D. H. Greene, Vice-Pres. and Gen. Mgr.; B. H. Scott, Treas.; B. H. Mack, Sec.) Four Beaters and one Refining engine; one 62-inch Single Cylinder and one 62-inch Four Cylinder Machines. Widest trimmed sheet, 58 inches. Steam. Chip, Lined and Plain, and Binders' Board. 24,000 lbs. 24 hours.

HOME PULP & PAPER MILLS CO., INC. (William Dennon, Pres.; William B. Dennon, Treas.; W. J. Armstrong, Vice-Pres. and Gen. Mgr.) Three 800-lb. Beaters and two Jordans. Two 72-inch Wet Machines. Binders Board. 30,000 lbs. 24 hours.

CALIFORNIA.

ANTIOCH—Contra Costa Co.

Pop. 2,000. Santa Fe & S. P. RR. steamer from San Francisco. M. O. and Tel. office; Wells Fargo & Co. Ex.

PARAFFINE, THE, COMPANIES, INC. California Paper and Board Mills Plant. Two mills. (R. S. Moore, Pres.; A. H. Dougall, Jr., Gen. Mgr. Board and Paper Div.) San Francisco office, 40 First street. S. P., Antioch. One 100-inch and one 120-inch Board Machines. Widest trimmed sheets, 90 and 109 inches. Steam and Electricity. 200,000 lbs. 24 hours. All Grades Paper, Box Boards, Tag Boards, Wood Boards, Container Boards, Amiwud Wall Boards, Litho Blanks and Specialties in boards and papers.

FLORISTON—Nevada Co.

Pop. 350. On C. P. RR. Tel. office; nearest bank, Reno, Nev., 27 miles; M. O.; Wells Fargo & Co. Ex.

CROWN WILLAMETTE PAPER CO. Office, Alaska Commercial Bldg., San Francisco, Cal. (Wm. Pierce Johnson, Pres.; Louis Bloch, Vice-Pres. & Gen. Mgr.; Charles M. Whitney, Sec.; Frank Schwabacher, Treas.) S. P., at mill. Eight Beating and three Refining engines; two 110-inch and one 112-inch Fourdriniers. Widest trimmed sheet, 100 inches. Water. Manila, Express, News, Fibre and Tissue. 70,000 lbs. 24 hours. PULP MILLS. S. P., at mill. Four Grinders; three Digesters; six Wet machines. Ground Wood Pulp, 40,000 lbs. 24 hours; Sulphite Fibre, 50,000 lbs. 24 hours.

BRIMSTONE MAKES THE VERY BEST SULPHITE.
If you are looking for a high-grade Brimstone write to
THE UNION SULPHUR CO., Main Office, 17 Battery Pl., New York. Mines, Calcasieu Parish, L

DRY ROSIN SIZE Brittle, easy soluble, cheapest size out; cheaper than mill made size. Ask us about it. Also all other grades. **ARABOL M'F'G CO.** 100 William St., N. Y.

California

LOS ANGELES—Los Angeles Co.

Pop. 600,000. S. P., Cal. Div. S. F., L. A. Terminal, and L. A. & R. RR. M. O. and Tel. office; Wells Fargo & Co. Ex.

CALIFORNIA TISSUE MILL, INC. 55th and Alameda Streets. (Samuel Sparks, Pres.; L. H. White, Sec. and Treas.) Nine Refining engines; three Fourdriniers. Widest trimmed sheet, 80 inches. White, Manila, Tissue, Fruit and Waxed Bread Wraps.

LOS ANGELES PAPER MANUFACTURING CO. (Joseph Brown, Pres.; Joseph Brown, Jr., Vice-Pres.; Robert E. Brown, Sec.) EAST LAKE MILL. Alhambra avenue and San Pablo street, opposite Lincoln Park. S. P., at mill. Six 1000-lb. Beating and one Refining engines; and one 84-inch Two Cylinder. Widest trimmed sheet, 72 inches. Steam and Electricity. Saturating and Deadening Felt, Red and Gray Sheathing, Heavy Wrappers and Car Lining. 42,000 lbs. 24 hours.

PARAFFINE STATION—Alameda Co.
On Southern Pacific.

PARAFFINE COMPANIES, INC. Office, 34 First Street, San Francisco, Cal. (Robert S. Moore, Pres.; R. S. Shainwald, Vice-Pres. and Gen. Mgr.; R. H. Obea, Sec.; A. H. Irving, Treas.) S. P., Paraffine Station. Fourteen Beating and three Jordan engines; one 84-inch Single Cylinder and one 120-inch Three Cylinder Machine. Steam and Electricity. Deadening and Saturating Felts and Sheathing. 120,000 lbs. 24 hours.

RICHMOND—Contra Costa.

Pop. 22,000. On Atch., Topeka & Sante Fe R.R. M. O., Tel.; bank. Wells, Fargo & Co. Ex.

CERTAIN-TEED PRODUCTS CORP. General Offices, St. Louis, Mo. (George M. Brown, Pres.; Smith E. Allison, Vice-Pres.; J. S. Porter, Vice-Pres.; Audenried Whittemore, Vice-Pres.; J. C. Collins, Vice-Pres.; Robert M. Nelson, Sec.-Treas.; S. C. Straub, Mgr.; F. M. Williams, Mill Supt.) Six 1000-lb. Beaters and two Refining engines. Two 86-inch Cylinders. Widest trimmed sheet, 72 inches. Hydro-Electric. Roofing Felt and Sheathing. 70,000 lbs. 24 hours.

SAN FRANCISCO—San Francisco Co.

Pop. 463,516. On So. Pac.; Atch., Topeka & Santa Fe; Western Pac. and Northwestern Pac. RR.

HUTCHINSON-PUTTAERT CO. (Dwight Hutchinson and F. Puttaert.) Office and mill, 526 Bay Street, San Francisco. One 1500-lb. Beater, one Jordan and one Wet Machine. Boards.

STOCKTON—San Joaquin Co.

Pop. 35,358. On So. Pacific; Western Pacific; Santa Fe RR. M. O., Tel., Bank. Wells Fargo and Am. Ex.

NATIONAL PAPER PRODUCTS CO. (M. R. Higgins, Pres.; I. Zellerbach, Vice-Pres.; J. D. Zellerbach, Sec.; M. M. Cohn, Treas.; A. E. Mandel, Gen. Mgr.) Ten 2000-lb. Beating and six Refining engines. Six 124-inch Cylinders. Widest trimmed sheet, 114 inches. Steam and Electricity. All Grades Box Boards and Fibre Shipping Cases. 160,000 lbs. 24 hours.

LOMBARD'S ENGLISH NEWCASTLE PULP STONES ARE SUPERIOR TO ALL OTHERS. ALL SIZES IN STOCK. LOMBARD & CO., Importers & Manufacturers, 236 & 238 A Street, Boston.

Paper and Pulp Mills in the United States 69

VERNON—Los Angeles Co.
On A. T. & Santa Fe.

PARAFFINE, THE, COMPANIES, INC. Southern Board and Paper Mills Plant. R. F. D. No. 2, Box 596, Los Angeles. (A. H. Dougall, Jr., Gen. Mgr. Board and Paper Div.) S. P., Los Angeles. Four 1200-lb., five 1800-lb. Beating and six Refining engines; one 84-inch and one 108-inch Dowingtown Five Cylinders. Widest trimmed sheets, 80 inches and 102 inches. Electricity and Steam. Box Board, Bristol Boards, Container Boards, Patent Coated Boards and Test Boards for fibre boxes, Sheathing and Heavy Cylinder Papers, Sheet Lining and Graining a specialty. 110,000 lbs. 24 hours.

CONNECTICUT.

ANDOVER—Tolland Co.
Pop. 385. On Highland Div. N. Y., N. H. & H. RR. M. O. and Tel. office; nearest bank, Willimantic, 9 miles; Adams Ex.

CASE BOARD CO. (L. W. Case, Pres.; C. C. Case, Vice-Pres. and Supt.; A. L. Crowell, Sec.-Treas.) S. P., Andover. Three 600-lb. and two 800-lb. Beating and two Jordan engines; two Single and two Double Cylinder Machines. Steam and Water. Fibre Board and Specialties. 15,000 lbs. 24 hours.

BRIDGEPORT—Fairfield Co.
Pop. 102,054. On N. Y., N. H. & H. RR. M. O. and Tel. office; Adams Ex.

TAIT & SONS PAPER CO., THE. (Wm. F. Tait, Pres.; Egbert Marsh, Vice-Pres.; Andrew Tait, Treas.; William G. Prior, Sec.) Siding at mill. Three 1200-lb. Beating; one Claflin and two Jordan engines; one 66-inch Six Cylinder Machine; widest trimmed sheet 60 inches. Steam and Electricity. Box Boards. 60,000 lbs. 24 hours.

BURNSIDE—Hartford Co.
Pop. 1,856. On Highland Div. N. Y., N. H. & H. Tel. office, Burnside; Adams Ex.

CASE & MARSHALL. Incorporated. (Raymond S. Case, Pres.; Lawrence W. Case, Vice-Pres.; Albert L. Crowell, Sec.; Joseph N. Viot, Treas.) P. O. address, Box 1332, Hartford, Conn. WOODLAND MILL. S. P., at mill. Four 1000-lb. and one 1200-lb. Beating and six Jordan engines; one 62-inch Five and one 76-inch Five Cylinders; one 51-inch, one 52-inch and one 52-inch Wet machines. Widest trimmed sheets, 44, 45, 52, 57 and 70 inches. Water and Steam. Specialties in Papers and Boards. 40,000 lbs. 24 hours.

EAST HARTFORD MANUFACTURING CO. (L. S. Forbes, Pres. and Treas.; R. S. Forbes, Asst. Treas.; J. J. Brigham, Sec.) CHARTER OAK MILL. S. P., at mill. Three 500-lb. and one 600-lb. engines; one 68-inch Fourdrinier. Width of Super Calenders, 26 and 40 inches. Widest trimmed sheet made, 25 x 37 inches. Water and Steam. Bonds, Linens, Ledgers, Folding Writing, Wedding and Specialties. 2500 lbs. 24 hours. *East Hartford Linens; Damask Linene; East Hartford Ledger; Belford Parchment; Charter Oak Bond; Pequot Bond; Penmans Linen, Lisle Parchment Bond; Old Scotland Mills; Half-Tone Writing, Extra Quality, Artistic Wedding Paper and Bristols.*

DRY ROSIN SIZE Brittle, easy soluble, cheapest size out; cheaper than mill made size. Ask us about it. Also all other grades. **ARABOL M'F'G CO.** 100 William St., N. Y.

Connecticut

Water and Steam. Folding Box Boards. 20,000 lbs. 24 hours. BANK MILL. Two 800-lb. and one 1000-lb. engines; one Jordan engine; one 72-inch three Cylinder. Widest trimmed sheet made, 64 inches. Water and Steam. Folding Box Boards and Colored Specialties. 20,000 lbs. 24 hours.

THAMES RIVER SPECIALTIES CO., THE. (W. J. Alford, Pres. and Treas.; Andrew Muirhead, Vice-Pres.; W. G. Shortess, Sec.; W. J. Alford, Jr., Asst. Treas.; Frank C. Mousley, Supt.) P. O. address, Uncasville. S. P., at mill. Twelve 1800-lb. Beating engines; one 130 and one 134-inch Six Cylinder Board Machines. Widest trimmed sheet, 121 inches. Steam. Card Middles, Patent Coated White and High Grade Carton Stock. 200,000 lbs. 24 hours.

NEW HAVEN—New Haven Co.

Pop. 108,027. N. Y., N. H. & H. RR. M. O. and Tel. office; Adams and N. Y. & Bos. Dis. Ex.

NATIONAL FOLDING BOX AND PAPER CO. Office, James and Alton streets, New Haven. New York Salesroom, 132 and 134 Franklin street. (D. S. Walton, Pres.; T. L. Cornell, First Vice-Pres.; J. S. Nugent, Second Vice-Pres.; G. W. Mabee, Sec.; D. S. Walton, Jr., Treas.; David W. Mabee, Asst. Sec.; John W. Doyle, Plant Mgr.; Robert Stevens, Supt.) Four 1500-lb. and two 2000-lb. Beating and three Refining engines; one Six Cylinder; widest trimmed sheet, 132 inches. Electric. Folding Paper Box Board, all used in Company's own factory. 120,000 lbs. 24 hours.

NEW HAVEN PULP AND BOARD CO. (Minotte E. Chatfield, Pres.; Edw. F. Mansfield, Vice-Pres.; William R. Shaffer, Sec., Treas. and Gen. Mgr.) S. P., at mill. Six 1200-lb., seven 1800-lb. and one 2000-lb. Beating and six Jordan engines; one 106-inch Five Cylinder and one 126-inch Five Cylinder. Widest trimmed sheets, 96 and 114 inches. Steam and Electricity. Manila and White Folding Box Boards, Specialties. 200,000 lbs. 24 hours.

NEWINGTON—Hartford Co.

Pop. 1,041. On H. & H. Div. N. Y., N. H. & H. RR. Tel. office; nearest bank, Hartford, 5 miles; Adams Ex.

HARTFORD BOARD CO., successor to Thomas F. Garvan Co. Mail address Hartford, Conn. (Thomas F. Garvan, owner; James A. Preu, Mgr.) ROCKDALE MILL. S. P., Newington Junction, 1¼ miles. Four 1000-lb. Beating engines. Three 50-inch Wet Machines and two Refining engines. Widest trimmed sheet, 48 inches. Water and Steam. Binders' Board and Chair Seat Fibre Board. 30,000 lbs. 24 hours.

NEW MILFORD—Litchfield Co.

Pop. 5,010. On Berkshire Div. N. Y., N.H. & H. RR. M. O. and Tel. Office; Adams Ex.

TOBACCO PRODUCTION CO., THE. (Mill formerly operated by New Milford Paper Co.) S. P., at mill. One 800-lb. Beating engine; two 42-inch Wet machines. Widest trimmed sheet 40 inches. Water and Steam. The product of this company is not used in the paper business.

DARMSTADT, SCOTT & COURTNEY, Inc. Importers, Exporters and Dealers in **PAPER MAKERS' SUPPLIES** Also Mfrs. of DEADENING and SATURATING FELTS. NEW YORK. 178 and 184 SOUTH STREET

Ground Pulp & Sulphite Fibre Mill Machinery OUR SPECIALTY | **CARTHAGE MACHINE CO.** CARTHAGE, N. Y.

PAPER

Buy Right—Buy from Headquarters

As Paper Headquarters, we offer you a splendid range of selections. We carry in our warehouses, in different parts of the country, at all times, a big stock of paper ready for shipment.

Especially noteworthy is our justly famous line of plain, embossed, printed and fancy box covering papers.

Get in touch with us on your paper needs. If you can buy better paper at the price, you surely want to know it.

• • •

Charles W. Williams & Co.

309 Lafayette St.,  538 So. Clark St.,
New York, N.Y.   Chicago, Ill.

Bourse Building, Machinery Dept., Philadelphia, Pa.

Everything in Paper for the Paper Box Maker
"Penn Paste Flour makes your Paste Dollars go further"

FRANK L. MOORE, President and General Manager
F. T. HELMER, Treasurer

Newton Falls Paper Company

MANUFACTURERS OF

Kraft, Parchment, Bag, Sack, Envelope

and High-Grade Sulphite Fibre Papers

Mills at
NEWTON FALLS, N. Y.

General Offices
WATERTOWN, N. Y.

LINDENMEYR LINES

It is almost impossible to comprehend the large line of papers of every description carried in our Warehouses for the benefit of our many customers.

To give a brief idea of the large number of different kinds of paper carried, we are listing the lines below:

News	Coated Box Board	Car Sign	Drawing and Pattern Papers
Colored Poster	Overlay Papers	Tag Manila	Tissues
Machine Finish Book	Cover Papers	Blotting Papers	Memorandum and Check Book Covers
English Finish Book	Writing Papers	Parchment and Transparent Papers	Waterproof Coated Fibre
Antique Wove Book	Mimeograph Papers	Boards	Glazed and Fancy Box Covers
Offset Papers	Bonds	Card Middle	Fancy Papers
Bible Papers	Map Papers	Manila and Fibre Wrappings	Imitation Leather Papers
Music Paper	Onion Skin and Manifold Papers	Corrugated Board	Plated Papers
Steel Plate	Ledger Papers	Twines	
Super Book	Bristol Boards	Advertising Tape	
Coated Book	Post Card		
Litho Coated	Blanks		
Cloth Lined			

ESTABLISHED 1859

HENRY LINDENMEYR & SONS.

"PAPERS OF MERIT"

32-34-36 BLEECKER STREET, NEW YORK

16-18 BEEKMAN STREET
NEW YORK

54-56 CLINTON STREET
NEWARK, N. J.

530 ASYLUM STREET
HARTFORD, CONN.

Paper and Pulp Mills in the United States 73

NORTH WESTCHESTER—New London Co.

Pop. 150. On N. Y., N. H. & H. Air Line. Tel. office; nearest bank, Willimantic, 15 miles; Adams Ex.

NORTON, C. H. S. P., Westchester Station. One 500-lb., two 800-lb. and one 1000-lb. Beating and two Jordan engines; three 48-inch Wet Machine engines. Steam, Water and Electricity. Binders, Box, Shoe and Trunk Board. 20,000 lbs. 24 hours.

NORWALK—Fairfield Co.

Pop. 6,125. On N. Y., N. H. & H. R.R. M. O. and Tel. office; Adams Ex.

ST. GEORGE PULP AND PAPER CO. (J. Goodfellow, Pres.; E. G. Murphy, Vice-Pres.; W. H. Odell, Sec.; E. W. Murphey, Treas.) NORWALK PAPER MILL. S. P., at mill. Three 1500-lb. Beating and two Refining engines; one 115-inch Fourdrinier. Widest trimmed sheet, 105½ inches. Steam. News Print. 56,000 lbs. 24 hours. Also Ground Wood at St. George, New Brunswick.

NORWICH—New London Co.

Pop. 20,367. On Cent. Vt. and Norwich Br. N. Y., N. H. & H. RR. M. O. and Tel. office; Adams and Am. Ex.

AMERICAN STRAW BOARD CO. Executive Offices, Akron, O. UNCAS MILL. Location, Thamesville. (J. M. Fraga, Mgr.) S. P., at mill. Nine 1500-lb. and four 1800-lb. Beating and nine Refining engines; one 76-inch and one 122-inch Five Cylinder and one 132-inch Five Cylinder. Steam. Box Board and Card Middles. 200,000 lbs. 24 hours.

DU PONT DE NEMOURS, E. I., & CO. NORWICH PLANT. Successors to The Arlington Co. (foot of Tenth Street). New York office, 725-727 Broadway. This mill is now being operated in the manufacture of tissue paper, but no material is being made for outside consumption.

ONECO—Windham Co.

Pop. 409. On Worcester Div. N. Y., N. H. & H. RR. M. O. and Tel.; nearest bank, Plainfield, 8 miles; Adams Ex.

CASE & RISLEY PRESS PAPER CO. (C. H. Case, Prop. and Gen. Mgr.; H. A. Wilcox, Asst. Mgr. and Supt.) S. P., at mill. Two 1000-lb. Beating engines; one 48-inch Wet Machine. Widest trimmed sheet, 38 inches. Water and Steam. Press Boards for Electric and Office Filing Devices; also high grade, hand finished boards. 6000 lbs. 24 hours.

POQUONOCK—Hartford Co.

Pop. 900. Electric cars from Hartford. M. O. office; Tel. and Ex. office, Windsor, 4 miles; nearest bank, Hartford.

HARTFORD PAPER CO. (Amaziah Brainerd, Pres. and Treas.; Newton Case Brainard, Sec.) P. O. address, Hartford. FRANKLIN MILL. S. P., Windsor, 4 miles. One 500-lb. and one 1200-lb. Beating engines; one 1200-lb. Washing engine; one 84-inch Fourdrinier. Widest trimmed sheet, 72 inches. Water and Steam. Book, Catalogue, French Folio and Colored Papers. 6000 lbs. 24 hours.

Connecticut

RAINBOW—Hartford Co.

Pop. 312. Electric cars from Hartford. M. O. office, Tel. and Ex. office, Windsor, 5 miles; nearest bank, Hartford.

MERWIN PAPER CO. (G. J. Merwin, Pres.; F. L. Wilcox, Vice-Pres.; R. W. Thompson, Sec. and Treas.) P. O. address, Windsor, Conn. S. P., Windsor, 5 miles. Two 1000-lb. and one 750-lb. Beating and one Jordan engines. One 54-inch Four Cylinder. Widest trimmed sheet, 45 inches. Steam. 6000 lbs. 24 hours. Glazed Press Boards, Jacquard Cards and Specialties.

THE RAINBOW MILLS. (Not Inc.) Office, 239 Broadway, New York City. (Benjamin and Thomas P. Vernon, Proprietors.) CONGRESS MILL. S. P., Windsor, 5 miles. Three 1000-lb. and one Jordan engines; one 76-inch Harper Fourdrinier. Water and Steam. Tissue and Copying and Manifold Papers in Colors. 4000 lbs. 24 hours. RAINBOW MILLS. S. P., Windsor, 5 miles. Three 700-lb. and one 800-lb. engines; one 48-inch and one 56-inch Cylinders. Water. "O. Y." and "T. O. Y." (trade marked) brands of R.R. Impression Paper. 2000 lbs. 24 hours.

RIVERTON—Litchfield Co.

Pop. 200. Four miles from Winsted. M. O., Tel., Ex. and nearest bank, Winsted.

RIVERTON CO., THE PALISADE MILL. Lawrence W. Case, Pres.; Raymond S. Case, Treas.; J. N. Viot, Sec.; E. C. Bell, Asst. Treas.) S. P., Winsted. Two 600-lb., one 1200-lb., Beating and one Refining engines; one 62-inch Single Cylinder. Water and Steam. (Mill makes pulp for the other mills in which the Messrs. Case are interested.)

SCITICO—Hartford Co.

Pop. 534. On S. Branch, Highland Div. N. Y., N. H. & H. RR. Tel. office, Thompsonville. Adams Ex.

STOWE & SONS, INC., J. D. (George W. Stowe, Pres.; William H. Stowe, Vice-Pres.; Charles E. Stowe, Sec. and Treas.; William H. Stowe, Supt.) S. P., Hazardville. Two 600-lb. Beating engines and two Wet Machines. Water and Steam. Leather Boards. 3000 lbs. 24 hours.

SEYMOUR—New Haven Co.

Pop. 4,850. On N. Div. N. Y., N. H. & H. RR. M. O. and Tel. office; Adams Ex.

BEACH, S. Y., PAPER CO. (Andrew Y. Beach, Pres.; Ralph S. Beach, Sec.; Sharon M. Beach, Treas. and Supt.) S. P., Naugatuck R.R., ¾ mile. One 350-lb. and one 600-lb. Beating engine and one 56-inch Cylinder. Widest trimmed sheet, 51 inches. Water and Steam. Specialties. 3000 lbs. 24 hours.

SOUTH COVENTRY—Tolland Co.

Pop. 950. On N. L. Div. C. V. RR. M. O., Tel. and Am. Ex., So. Coventry, Conn.

SOUTH COVENTRY PAPER CO. P. O. and S. P., South Coventry. (A. L. Kingsbury, Pres.; L. J. Storrs, Vice-Pres.; L. A Kingsbury, Sec. and Treas.; Geo. Maynard, Supt.) One 800-lb. and one 1000-lb. Beating and one Jordan engines; one 40-inch and one 50-inch Cylinders. Steam. Counter, Shank, Inner Sole and Suit Boards. 8000 lbs. 24 hours.

THOMAS E. GLEESON, Inc., 411-413 John St., E. NEWARK, N. J
CYLINDER MOULDS and DANDY ROLLS Made and Repaired
LETTERING and MONOGRAMS for WATERMARKS

Paper and Pulp Mills in the United States 75

SOUTHFORD—New Haven Co.

Pop. 225. On W. Div. N. Y., N. H. & H. RR. M. O., Tel. and Adams Ex., Oxford Station ¾ mile; nearest bank, Waterbury, 12 miles.

DIAMOND MATCH COMPANY, SOUTHFORD MILL. (W. A. Fairburn, Pres.; N. C. Johnson, Treas.; H. F. Holman, Sec.; J. B. King, Factory Mgr.) S. P., Southford Station, ¾ mile. Three 900-lb. and one 1000-lb. Beating and three Jordan engines; one 72-inch Five Cylinder Machine. Widest trimmed sheet, 68 inches. Water and Steam. Bleached Manila, Colored and Manila Lined Board. 41,000 lbs. 24 hours.

SOUTH GLASTONBURY—Hartford Co.

Pop. 960. Electric Road from Hartford. M. O. and Ex., Rocky Hill; Tel. office, Hartford; nearest bank, Hartford, 9 miles.

WASUC MILLS COMPANY. (J. W. Purtill, Pres., and J. W. Purtill, Jr., Sec.-Treas.; E. W. Lindsay, Supt.) WASUC MILLS. S. P., Rocky Hill, Conn. RR. Two 1000-lb. Beating Engines; two 44-inch Cylinders. Water and Steam. Binders', Album, Leather, Trunk, Tar, Friction, Fibre, Wagon, Insulating, Heeling, Button, Pattern, Cloth and Specialties.

SOUTH MANCHESTER—Hartford Co.

Pop. 14,000. On S. M. Branch of N. Y., N. H. & H. RR. and electric cars from Hartford. M. O. office; bank, Manchester; Adams Ex.

BROOKSIDE PAPER CO. (Company dissolved and mill dismantled.)

CASE BROTHERS. (Incorporated.) (Lawrence W. Case, Pres.; Albert L. Crowell, Vice-Pres.; A. Willard Case, Treas.; Robert N. Stanley, Sec.; Edward C. Stanley, Asst. Sec.) P. O. address, Highland Park. HIGHLAND MILLS. S. P., Manchester. Two 600-lb., four 6-cwt. Umpherston and two Jordan engines; one 48-inch Wet, one 52-inch Four Cylinder and one 46-inch Four Cylinder Machines. Steam. Press Board, Jacquard Cards, Insulating Board and Specialties. 16,000 lbs. 24 hours.

ROGERS PAPER MANUFACTURING CO. (G. H. Rogers, Pres. and Treas.; C. W. Cudlipp, Supt.) Two mills. ATLANTIC and ADRIATIC MILLS. S. P., South Manchester. One 300-lb., two 600-lb. and four 1200-lb. Beating engines; one 52, one 56 single and one 64-inch double cylinder Wet Machines. Widest trimmed sheet, 60 inches. Water and Steam. Press, Insulating, Jacquard, Shield and Leather Boards. 15,000 lbs. 24 hours. *Rogers Press Boards, Rogers Press Spahn.*

UNIONVILLE—Hartford Co.

Pop. 1,998. On N. H. Branch N. Div. N. Y., N. H. & H. RR.; nearest bank, Collinsville, 5 miles; M. O. and Tel. office; Adams Ex.

AMERICAN WRITING PAPER COMPANY.—Platner & Porter Paper Manufacturing Company Division. TUNXIS MILL. S. P., Unionville. Three 800-lb. and four 1200-lb. engines; one 72-inch Machine. Water. 7000 lbs. 24 hours. *Coupon Bond.*

CASE MANUFACTURING CO. (A. Willard Case, Pres.; Raymond S. Case, Vice-Pres. and Treas., and Edward C. Bell, Sec.) UNIONVILLE MILL. S. P., Unionville. Four 800-lb. and one 1000-lb. Beating and two Refining engines; one 48-inch Three and one 68-inch Four Cylinders. Widest trimmed sheet, 60 inches. Water, Steam and Electricity. Colored, Hardware, Pattern, Rope and Specialties. 20,000 lbs. 24 hours.

SULPHUR—CRUDE. GUARANTEED 99% PURE.
The average analysis of our high-grade brimstone is in itself a guarantee. Write us for quotation
THE UNION SULPHUR CO., Main Office, 17 Battery Pl., New York. Mines, Calcasieu Parish, La

)RY ROSIN SIZE Brittle, easy soluble, cheapest size out; cheaper than mill made size. Ask us about it. Also all other grades. **ARABOL M'F'G CO.** 100 William St., N. Y.

Connecticut

VERSAILLES—New London Co.

Pop. 147. On C. Div. N. Y., N. H. & H. RR.; nearest bank, Norwich, 6 miles; M. O. and Tel. office; Adams Ex.

FEDERAL PAPER BOARD CO. (W. G. Shortess, Pres.; H. T. Brown, Vice-Pres.; L. C. Eckhardt, Sec. and Treas.; Max Zurawski, Supt.) One 1000-lb. and two 1400-lb. Beating and three Jordan engines; one 96-inch Five-Cylinder. Widest trimmed sheet, 83 inches. Water and Steam. Chip, News, Manila Lined, Patent Coated Jute, Container Board Specialties, Graining, News and Book Lining. 60,000 lbs. 24 hours.

WESTPORT—Fairfield Co.

Pop. 4,017. On N. Y. Div. N. Y., N. H. & H. RR. M. O. and Tel. office; Adams Ex.

WESTPORT PAPER CO. (Robt. W. Post, Pres. and Treas.; L. Strickland, Sec.) Two 800-lb., one 600-lb. and two 1000-lb. Beating engines; three 40-inch Wet Machines; one 48-inch Wet Machine. Steam. Binders' Leather, Press and News Boards. 25,000 lbs. 24 hours.

WESTVILLE—New Haven Co.

Street cars from New Haven, 3 miles; M. O. office; Tel. office, Ex. and nearest bank, New Haven.

PARKER & SON CO., JOSEPH. Office, Whalley Avenue, near Dayton Street, New Haven. (R. A. France, Pres. and Mgr.) WEST ROCK PAPER MILL. S. P., New Haven, 3 miles. One 500-lb. and one 700-lb. Beating, three 700-lb. Washing and one Jordan engines; one 66-inch Fourdrinier. Water and Steam. Blotting. 12,000 lbs. 24 hours

WINDSOR LOCKS—Hartford Co.

Pop. 2,997. On H. Div. N. Y., N. H. & H. RR. M. O. and Tel. office; nearest bank, Suffield, 4 miles; Adams Ex.

AMERICAN WRITING PAPER CO.—Windsor Paper Company Division. Nineteen engines, 700 to 2000 lbs.; one 76-inch, one 88-inch and one 100-inch Cylinders. Water. Boards and Manilas. Rope and Jute Manilas. 130,000 lbs. 24 hours.

ANCHOR PAPER CO., INC. Mill totally destroyed by fire February 1, 1916.

DEXTER, C. H., & SONS, INC. (Arthur D. Coffin, Pres. and Treas.; Herbert R. Coffin, Vice-Pres.; Chas. H. Coye, Sec.; John Leishman, Supt.) STAR MILLS. S. P., at mill. Twelve 1000-lb. and three 1500-lb. Beating and four Refining engines; one 100-inch Combination Cylinder and Fourdrinier; three Fourdriniers. Widest trimmed sheet, two 60 inches and two 80 inches. Union Screens. Water. Steam and Electricity. Cover Paper, Tissues and Specialties. 20,000 lbs. 24 hours. "*Star*" *Grass-bleached Silver Tissue;* "*Star*" *White and Colored Tissues;* "*Star*" *Stereotype;* "*Star*" *Manifold Linen, and Thin Typewriter Papers;* "*Star Mills*" *and* "*Congress Mills*" *Toilet Paper;* "*Princess*" *and* "*Levant*" *Cover Papers;* "*Star*" *Patterns and Specialties.*

WHITTELSEY CO., THE F. H. (Joseph Ferguson, Pres. and Mgr.; Mrs. F. H. Whittelsey, Sec. and Treas.) S. P. ¼ mile. Five 1000-lb. and one Refining engines; one 56-inch Cylinder and one 76-inch Harper Fourdrinier.

)HIPPERS We make a specialty of GROUND WOOD PULP and SULPHITE FIBRE MACHINERY || **Carthage Machine Co.** CARTHAGE, N. Y.

National Duplex Waterproof Case-Lining
IS WATERPROOF—
CLEAN TO HANDLE   **NATIONAL WATERPROOFING CO.,** 1054 DREXEL BLDG., PHILADELPHIA

Paper and Pulp Mills in the United States 77

Widest trimmed sheet, 60 inches. Water and Steam. 6000 lbs. 24 hours. R. R. Yellow Way Bill Copying, Manila, White and Parchment Copying; Oiled Train Order Tissue; Oiled Stencil Board; Way Bill Copying Books; Train Order Pads; Jute Anti-Tarnish; No. 1 Jute Manila, White and Colored Tissues; Billing Machine Tissue; Crepe Paper. (August 28, 1918. Went into hands of receiver July 5, 1918. Mill not operating. J. A. Turnbull, trustee in bankruptcy.)

DELAWARE.

BEAVER VALLEY—New Castle Co.

Pop. 307. M. O. and Tel. office, Brandywine Summit, Pa., 2½ miles; nearest bank, Wilmington, 7 miles; U. S. Ex. at Granogue, ¾ mile.

GARRETT, EDWIN. Office and warehouse, 516 and 518 Welsh street, Chester, Pa. SUNNY DALE MILL. S. P., Granogue. Two 300-lb. Beating and two Refining engines; one 36-inch Cylinder. Widest trimmed sheet, 30 inches. Width of Super Calenders, 40 inches. Water and Steam. Fine Tissue, Manila and Colored. 1000 lbs. 24 hours.

MARSHALLTON—New Castle Co.

Pop. 424. On B. & O. R.R. M. O. and Tel. office. Nearest bank Newport, 2½ miles.

DELAWARE HARD FIBRE CO. Office, Wilmington, Del. (A. S. Rupert, Pres.; Chas. G. Rupert, Treas., Sec. and Mgr.; W. W. Melson, Supt.) Three 1500-lb. and four 1000-lb. Beating engines. One Fourdrinier and one Wet Machine. Steam and Water. Paper for Vulcanized Fibre only.

NEWARK—New Castle Co.

Pop. 2,200. On Penn. RR. M. O. and Tel. office; Adams and W. F. Ex.

CURTIS & BROTHER, INCORPORATED. (Alfred A. Curtis, Pres.; Chas. M. Levis, Vice-Pres.; F. Lindsey Curtis, Sec. and Treas.) NONANTUM PAPER MILLS. S. P., Newark Centre. Three 1200-lb., one 2200-lb. Beating, three Rag Washing and two Jordan engines; one 66-inch and one 83-inch Fourdriniers. Width of Super Calenders, 42 inches. Widest trimmed sheet, 76 inches. Steam and Water. Rag Book, Envelopes, Specialties and Writings. 25,000 lbs. 24 hours.

WILMINGTON—New Castle Co.

Pop. 76,508. On B. & O.; B. & P.; P., W. & B.; W. & N. RR.; also vessels. M. O. and Tel. office; Adams and B. & O. Ex.

JESSUP & MOORE PAPER CO., THE. (Eugene W. Fry, Pres.; E. A. Weihenmayer, Vice-Pres.; Wm. D. Heebner, Treas.; W. H. Clark, Sec.) Offices, 16 S. Broad Street, Philadelphia, Pa., and 50 E. 42d Street, New York City. AUGUSTINE MILLS on the Brandywine—Wilmington, 1 mile. Twelve Beating and three Refining engines; one 76-inch, one 90-inch and one 120-inch Fourdriniers. Widest trimmed sheet, 117 inches. Width of Super Calenders, 72 inches. Water and Steam. Book. 65,000 lbs. 24 hours. ROCKLAND MILLS, Wilmington, 3 miles. Eleven Beating and three Refining engines. Two 86-inch and one 108-inch Fourdriniers. Widest trimmed sheet, 96 inches. Width of Super Calenders, 58 inches. Water

R. B. McEwan, Pres't.   J. L. McEwan, Vice-Pres't.   Arthur McEwan, Treas. and Mgr.   R. W. McEwan, Sec'y.
Sheet Lining Plant, Office and Mills at WHIPPANY, N. J.

McEWAN BROS., Inc. MANUFACTURERS OF ALL GRADES **PAPER BOX BOARD**

Delaware and District of Columbia

and Steam. Book. 60,000 lbs. 24 hours. PULP MILL—DELAWARE MILLS, Wilmington, 1 mile. Seven Digesters, three Wet machines, one Dry machine. Soda Fibre. 135,000 lbs. 24 hours.

WOODDALE—New Castle Co.

Pop. 57. On B. & O. RR. M.O. and Tel. office, Marshallton, 3 miles; nearest bank, Wilmington, 6 miles.

MARSHALL & MITCHELL. (T. Elwood Marshall, Dr. T. S. Mitchell estate and J. A. Marshall, Supt.) WOODDALE PAPER MILL. S. P., at mill. Four 600-lb. Beating and one Jordan engines. Widest trimmed sheet, 58 inches. Water and Steam. Filter Paper and Special Paper for making Vulcanized Fibre for Electrical and Mechanical Purposes. 4000 lbs. 24 hours.

YORKLYN—New Castle Co.

Pop. 300. On L. Div. of B. & O. RR. Nearest bank, Kennett Square, Pa., 4 miles; Tel. office, Yorklyn, 1 mile.

MARSHALL BROTHERS, INC. (T. Elwood Marshall, Pres.; J. A. Marshall, Vice-Pres.; T. Clarence Marshall, Treas.; J. W. Marshall, Sec.; T. E. Manhall, Supt.) GLEN ROCK MILLS. S. P., ¼ mile. Two 1000-lb. Washers. Two 600-lb. and two 800-lb. Beating engines and one 600-lb. Umpherson; one 66-inch Fourdrinier. Widest trimmed sheet, 60 inches. Water and Steam. All Rag Papers and Specialties. 6000 lbs. 24 hours.

NATIONAL FIBRE & INSULATION CO. (J. W. Marshall, Pres.; T. C. and H. W. Marshall, Vice-Presidents; J. A. Marshall, Treas.; J. A. Marshall, Sec.; T. C. Marshall, Supt.) S. P., Yorklyn. Two Beaters and seven Washers. One 72-inch Downingtown machine. Steam. Rag Specialties. 16,000 lbs. 24 hours.

DISTRICT OF COLUMBIA.

WASHINGTON.

Pop. 350,000. On B. & O. RR. M. O. and Tel. offices; Adams Ex.

BUREAU OF STANDARDS, DEPARTMENT OF COMMERCE, Connecticut Avenue and Pierce Mill Road. Paper testing laboratory and semi-commercial experimental paper making equipment, capable of making practically all grades of paper. (S. W. Stratton, Director; F. C. Clark in charge of paper work.) S. P., Washington. One 150-lb. Manitowoc Rotary boiler; one 15-lb. and one 75-lb. Noble & Wood Beating engines, both equipped with cylindrical washers; one Noble & Wood Baby Jordan; one two-plate Packer Screen; one 31-inch Pusey & Jones Combination Fourdrinier and Cylinder Machine, equipped with one 24-inch diameter cylinder mold, length of Fourdrinier wire 33 feet, two presses, nine 15-inch diameter Dryers, Seven-Roll Machine Calender Stack, Two-Drum Reel and Combination Slitter and Rewinder; machine speed, 5 to 90 feet; capacity, maximum, 150 lbs. per hour; trim, 12 to 25 inches; one 14-inch Waldron Flat Bed Brush Coater, with Festoon Dryer and Rewinder; Tub Sizing Vat; Mixing Tanks, etc. Equipped throughout with Copper and Brass Stock Pipes, Pumps, Agitators. Electrically driven. Experimental work only.

THOMAS E. GLEESON, Inc., **FOURDRINIER WIRES**
411-413 John St., E. NEWARK, N. J. For Tissue and Fine Grade Papers

Paper and Pulp Mills in the United States 79

DISTRICT OF COLUMBIA PAPER MANUFACTURING COMPANY.
(G. L. Nicolson, Pres.; D. A. Smith, Vice-Pres., Sec., Treas. and Gen. Mgr.;
W. W. Langtry, Sales Mgr.) Location, Potomac and K Streets, N. W. S. P.,
Washington, D. C. One 68-inch Fourdrinier and two Special Machines.
Widest trimmed sheet, 62 inches. Water and Steam. Blotting, Cover, Box
Cover, Rag Book and Specialties. 50,000 lbs. 24 hours. PULP MILL. Two
Digesters. Soda Pulp. 70,000 lbs. 24 hours. Blotting. *Official; National; Congress, Executive; Flora, Plain Finish; Flora, Embossed Patterns; Artillery; Potomac Half Tone; No. 1 Photographic.* Cover: *Potomac, Antique Finish; Potomac, Crash Finish; Potomac, Embossed Patterns; Modern, Ripple Finish; Modern, Stucco Finish; Congress, Parchment Finish; Cabinet, Antique Finish; Cirrus, Ripple Antique Finish; Artillery, Cloud Effect; White House, Cloud Effect; White House, Ripple Antique Finish; National, Laid Antique; Flora, Parchment Finish; Aerial, Smooth Antique Finish; Washington, Two Tone Effect; Allied Duplex Folder, Antique and Finishes; Executive Parchment Finish.* Book Papers: *Congress Text, Laid, D. E.; Executive Text, Laid, D. E.; National Book, Laid, D. E.; Aerial.* Box Coverings: *Executive; Artillery, Cloud Effect; National, Cobble Effect; Washington Brilliant; Radio, American; Anslaston, Congress, Ribbed Two-tone, Washington; Flora; Grained. All the Box Coverings in Antique and Embossed Patterns.*

GEORGIA.

BOLTON—Fulton Co.

Pop. 190. On N. C. & St. L. RR. M. O. and Tel. Nearest bank and ex., Atlanta, 7 miles.
NATIONAL PAPER CO. Office, Atlanta. (S. P., Bolton.) Two Beaters and one Jordan. One 72-inch double Cylinder; widest trimmed sheet, 64 inches. Bogus, Furniture, Car Lining, Rag Wrapping, Cone and Tube, Ham Paper and Specialties. 20,000 lbs. 24 hours.

CEDARTOWN—Polk Co.

Pop. 3,551. On Seaboard Air Line and Central of Georgia RR. M. O.; Tel.; Bank. So. Ex.
NOBLE MFG. CO. (F. D. Noble, Pres.; Thomas Barrett, Supt.) Two Beaters and one Refining engine. One Four Cylinder machine. Steam. Paper for cones and tubes. 14,000 lbs. 24 hours.

GORDON—Wilkinson Co.

Pop. 509. On Central of Georgia R. R.; M. O. Tel office; Bank and So. Ex.
PYNETREE PAPER CO., THE. (W. G. Chapin, Pres.; J. T. Moore, Vice-Pres. and Mng. Dir.; M. H. Day, Treas.) S. P., Gordon, Ga. Seven Beating and five Jordan engines; one 120-inch Cylinder; sixty-one Dryers. Steam and Electricity. Container Board. 100,000 lbs. 24 hours. PULP MILL. One Chipper, four Digesters. Soda Pulp. 40,000 to 50,000 lbs. 24 hours.

LAWRENCEVILLE—Gwinnett Co.

Pop. 2,000. Seaboard Air Line & Lawrenceville RR. M. O. and Tel. Office; So. Ex.
LAWRENCEVILLE PAPER MILLS. (Atlanta Paper Co., Owner.) One 68-inch Cylinder. Widest trimmed sheet, 60 inches. Wrapping, Ham, Car Lining and Furniture Felt. 10,000 lbs. 24 hours.

DRY ROSIN SIZE
Brittle, easy soluble.
Cheapest size out; cheaper than mill made size. Ask us about it.
Also all other grades.

ARABOL M'F'G CO.
100 William St., New York

HIGHEST GRADE BRIMSTONE—GUARANTEED 99% PURE
free from Arsenic or Selenium. Write for particulars to
THE UNION SULPHUR CO., Main Office, 17 Battery Pl., New York. Mines, Calcasieu Parish, La.

Georgia and Illinois

MARIETTA—Cobb Co.

Pop. 7,814. On W. & A.; L. & N. RR. M. O. and Tel. office; Southern and Adams Ex.

KENNESAW PAPER CO. (Clarence E. Power, Custodian.) S. P., at mill. Ten 1200-lb. and two 1500-lb. Beating and six Refining engines; one 70-inch and one 72-inch Fourdriniers. Widest trimmed sheet, 72 inches. Steam. News, Manila, Bag, Gray, Rag, Sheathing, Carpet Lining and Water Finish Fibre. 40,000 lbs. 24 hours. July 5, 1918. (Not in operation; some of the machines sold.)

ST. MARYS—Camden Co.

Pop. 529. Connect daily with Fernandina by steamer.

NATIONAL CELLULOSE CO. Butchers' Fibre.

SAVANNAH—Chatham Co.—PULP MILL.

Pop. 67,917. On C. of Ga. RR., S, A, L. S. & Atlanta, O. S. S. Co.; M. & M. T. Co. M. O., Tel., bank and So. Ex.

ATLANTIC PAPER AND PULP CORPORATION. (Price & Pierce, Ltd., 30 E. 42d, New York, Selling Agents. I. H. Fetty, Pres.; M. T. Nichols, Vice-Pres.; S. C. Lawrence, Sec.; Edwin Shaw, Treas.) S. P., Port Wentworth. Four Digesters, three Wet Machines. Steam and Electricity. Sulphate Fibre. 120,000 lbs. 24 hours.

ILLINOIS.

AURORA—Kane Co.

Pop. 29,807. On C. B. & Q.; C. & N. W.; Ill., Ia. & Minn.; Elgin, Joliet & Eastern; A. E. & Ch. RR. M. O. and Tel.; Adams, Am. and U. S. Ex.

MONROE BINDER BOARD CO. (L. W. Leathers, Pres.; L. C. Knapp, Vice-Pres.; Don Leathers, Treas.; E. C. Betz, Sec.) S. P., at mill. Two 1200-lb., three 1500-lb. and two Refining engines. Three 60-inch and one 66-inch Wet machines. Steam. Chip, Binders', Templet, Backing, Fibre and Leather Boards. 60,000 lbs. 24 hours.

CARLYLE—Clinton Co.

Pop. 1,874. On B. & O. RR. M. O. and Tel. office; U. S. Ex.

CARLYLE PAPER CO. P. O. address, Alton, Ill. (R. H. Levis, Pres.; Chas. Levis, Sec. and Treas.) S. P., Carlyle. Four 1200-lb. and two 1500-lb. Beating and two Refining engines; one 86-inch Cylinder. Widest trimmed sheet, 80 inches. Steam. Straw Board and Chip Board for Corrugating and Indented Packing Paper. 48,000 lbs. 24 hours.

CASEYVILLE.

On B. & O. S. W. RR. M. O., Tel. Wells, Fargo Ex., nearest bank, Collinsville.

ATLAS LEATHER MFG. CO. (H. N. Spaulding, Pres.; H. Buehler, Jr., Vice-Pres., Sec. and Supt.; Hy. Buehler, Treas.) Eight Beaters and six Wet Machines. Leather Board. 45,000 lbs. 24 hours.

CHICAGO—Cook Co.

CHICAGO COATED BOARD CO. 422 E. North Water Street. (C. Fairbanks, Pres.; C. E. Williams, Vice-Pres.; Carl M. Williams, Sec., Treas. and Gen. Mgr.) S. P., at mill. Eighteen 1500-lb. Beating and nine Jordan engines; two 122-inch Six and one 94-inch Five Cylinder. Steam. Paper Box Boards. 360,000 lbs. 24 hours.

CHICAGO FOLDING BOX CO., 2539-61 W. Taylor Street. (E. C. Lewis, Prop.) Four 1200-lbs. Beating engines; one 90-inch Five Cylinder Machine. Widest trimmed sheet, 81 inches. Electricity and Steam. Chip, Filled News and Combination Boards. 80,000 lbs. 24 hours.

CHICAGO MILL AND LUMBER CO. (H. Paepke, Pres.; C. F. Wiedemann, Sec.; R. L. McClelland, Treas.; J. L. Barchard, Mgr.; E. Raney, Supt.) Seven 1800-lb. Beating and four Refining engines; one 136-inch Seven Cylinder Machine. Widest trimmed sheet, 120 inches. Steam and Electricity. Container Linen and Chip. 160,000 lbs. 24 hours.

SEARS, ROEBUCK & CO., 1012 S. Spaulding Avenue. One 1200-lb. Beater and two 1750-lb. Mixers; one Fourdrinier. Widest trimmed sheet, 70 inches. Steam and Electricity. Hangings and Wrappers. 36,000 lbs. 24 hours.

EAST ST. LOUIS—St. Clair Co., Ill.

Pop. 75,000. On So.; C. & A.; C. B. & Q.; B. & O. So. W.; C. P. St. L.; C., C., O. & St. L. RR. M. O., Tel. office. U. S., Am., Pas., Natl., So., Adams Ex

CERTAIN-TEED PRODUCTS CORPORATION, Successors to General Roofing Mfg. Co. General Offices, Boatmen's Bank Bldg., St. Louis, Mo. (Geo. M. Brown, Pres.; S. E. Allison, Vice-Pres.; J. S. Porter, Vice-Pres.; A. Whittemore, Vice-Pres.; J. C. Collins, Vice-Pres.; R. M. Nelson, Sec.-Treas.; Wm. E. Horn, Local Mgr.) S. P., East St. Louis. Thirteen 1000-lb. Beating and one Refining, one 80-inch Cylinder and one 84-inch Three Cylinders. Widest trimmed sheet, 80 inches. Steam. Roofing, Saturating and Deadening Felts, Carpet Lining and Building Papers. 100,000 lbs. 24 hours. *Insulating Paper. Asphalt Roofings and Shingles; Tarred Felts; Asphalt Felts; Asphalt and Coal Tar Products. Roofing Factory in connection.*

FEDERAL—Madison Co.

Pop. 38. On Illinois Terminal RR., connecting with C. & A.; C., B. & Q.; C. P. & St. L.; C., C., C. & St. L.; Wabash, L. & M.; Penn. and T., St. L. & W. M. O., Tel., Exp. and nearest bank, Alton, 2½ miles.

ALTON BOX BOARD AND PAPER CO. P. O. address, Alton, Ill. (Crawford Fairbanks, Pres.; Thomas Bauer, Vice-Pres.; B. F. Failey, Sec. and Treas.; C. M. Williams, Gen. Mgr.; H. C. Evans, Resident Manager; G. R. Stewart, Cashier.) FEDERAL MILL. S. P., Federal. Ten 1500-lb. Beating and five Refining engines; one 145-inch Beloit Six Cylinder machine. Widest trimmed sheet, 134 inches. Union Screens. Steam. Straw and Paper Stock Boards. 180,000 lbs. 24 hours.

JOLIET—Will Co.

Pop. 36,170. On Chic. & Alton; Chic., R. I. & Pacific; Joliet Div. Mich. Central; Atch., Topeka & Santa Fe.; Illinois, Iowa & Minnesota, and Elgin, Joliet & Eastern RR.; Am., Nat. and Wells Fargo Ex.

STANDARD PAINT CO. (R. L. Shainwald, Pres.; F. J. Jelenick, Sec. and Treas.; F. H. Gilchrist, Supt.) Nine 1000-lb. Beating and two Refining engines. One 128-inch cylinder machine; widest trimmed sheet, 112 inches. Steam and electricity. Roofing Felts and Box Board. 100,000 lbs. 24 hours.

DRY ROSIN SIZE Brittle, easy soluble, cheapest size out; cheaper than mill made size. Ask us about it. Also all other grades. **ARABOL M'F'G CO.** 100 William St., N. Y.

Illinois

ROCK FALLS—Whiteside Co.

Pop. 2,176. On C., B. & Q. and C. & N. W. RR. M. O. and Tel. office; Am. and Ad: Ex.

ROCK FALLS BOX BOARD CO., successor to Central Boxboard Company. S. P., at mill. Eight 1200-lb., four Refining engines and five Rotary boilers; one 72-inch Four Cylinder and one 86-inch Five Cylinder Machines. Widest trimmed sheets, 68 and 81 inches. Water and Steam. Plain and Test Chip and Combination Box Boards, Express, Ham and Rag Wrapping. 100,000 lbs. 24 hours.

ROCKFORD—Winnebago Co.

Pop. 60,000. On C. & N. W.; C., B. & Q.; C., M. & St. P.; I. C. RR.; C. M. & G. RR. M. O. and Tel. office; Am., Adams and U. S. Ex.

ROCKFORD PAPER BOX BOARD CO. (Frank Heywood, Pres.; R. E. Wantz, Sec. and Mgr.) S. P., at mill. One 1500-lb. and four 1200-lb. Beating and four Jordan engines; one 96-inch Six Cylinder. Widest sheet made, 86 inches. Steam and Electricity. Chip, Jute, Built-Up Fibre and Container Boards. 80,000 lbs. 24 hours.

ROCKFORD PAPER MILLS. S. P., at mill. (E. B. Weston, Pres.; W. G. Clark, Vice-Pres.; O. H. Ross, Sec.; F. A. Billingham, Treas. and Supt.) Three 1400-lb. and two Refining engines; six Washers and five Rotary boilers; one 94-inch Cylinder. Widest trimmed sheet, 86 inches. Water and Steam. Straw Wrapping, Straw Corrugating and Chip Papers. 50,000 lbs. 24 hours.

ROCKTON—Winnebago Co.

Pop. 936. On R. & S. Div. of C., M. & St. P. RR.; nearest bank, Beloit, Wis., 3 miles; M. O. and Tel. office; W. F. Ex.

AMERICAN TAR PRODUCTS CO., Successors to Rockton Paper Co. S. P., 208 So. La Salle Street, Chicago. (S. H. Bingham, Pres.; E. B. Fulke, Vice-Pres.; S. H. Fields, Sec. and Treas.; A. L. Kuehn, Supt.) Five 1000-lb. Beating and one Refining engines; one 80-inch Three-Cylinder. Widest trimmed sheet, 72 inches. Water and Steam. Wool Deadening Felt, Dry Felt, Indented Packing Paper, Plain and Corrugated Carpet Lining, Red and Gray Rosin Sized Sheathing and Building. 40,000 lbs. 24 hours.

TAYLORVILLE—Christian Co.

Pop. 8,000. On B. Div. of B. & O. S. W.; St. L. Div. of W. RR. M. O. and Tel. office; U. S. and Pac. Ex.

E.-Z. OPENER BAG CO. (H. E. Westervelt, Pres.; E. C. Westervelt, Vice-Pres.; O. L. Hammond, Sec.; Frank Brewer, Treas. and Mgr.; F. M. Dickinson, Sales Mgr.) WHITE OAK MILLS. S. P., side track at mill. Six 1200-lb. Beating and two Jordan engines; one 125-inch Fourdrinier. Widest trimmed sheet, 115 inches. Steam. Bag papers. 50,000 lbs. 24 hours.

VANDALIA—Fayette Co.

Pop. 3,500. On Vandalia and I. C. RR. M. O. and Tel. office; Adams and Am. Ex.

FORD MANUFACTURING CO., Chicago, Ill.; St. Louis, Mo.; Kansas City, Mo.; Buffalo, N. Y.; Atlanta, Ga. Factories: St. Paul, Minn.; Clinton, Iowa; Vandalia, Ill. (J. W. Ford, Jr., Pres.; W. O. Ford, Sec.; L. M. Ford, Treas., Mgr. of Plants and Pur. Agt.) VANDALIA PAPER MILL. (Destroyed by fire.)

LOMBARD'S ENGLISH NEWCASTLE PULP STONES ARE SUPERIOR TO ALL OTHERS. ALL SIZES IN STOCK. LOMBARD & CO., Importers & Manufacturers, 226 & 228 A Street, Boston.

CHIP CRUSHER We make a specialty of GROUND WOOD PULP and SULPHITE FIBRE MACHINERY **Carthage Machine Co.** CARTHAGE, N. Y.

National Duplex Waterproof Case Lining
IS WATERPROOF— NATIONAL WATERPROOFING CO., 1054 DREXEL BLDG.
CLEAN TO HANDLE   PHILADELPHIA

Paper and Pulp Mills in the United States 85

WILMINGTON—Fayette Co.
Pop. 1,420. On Chicago & Alton RR. M. O. and Tel. office; U. S. Ex.
AMERICAN STRAW BOARD CO., Akron, Ohio. S. P., side track at mill. (R. G. Sager, Mgr.) Six 1200-lb. Beating and six Jordan engines; one 110-inch Cylinders. Widest sheet made, 104 inches. Water and Steam. Chip, Paper Stock, News and Combination Boards. 80,000 lbs. 24 hours.

INDIANA.
ALBANY—Delaware Co.
Pop. 2,116. On L. E. & W. RR. M. O. and Tel. office; Am. Ex.
HART PAPER CO., T. F. Main Office, Muncie. (T. F. Hart, Pres.; Alfaretta M. Hart, Vice-Pres.; F. H. May, Sec. and Treas.) S. P., at mill. Five 1200-lb. Beating and one Jordan engines; one 68-inch Five Cylinder. Widest trimmed sheet, 65 inches. Steam. Plain, Refined Straw Board for tube and cap work. 38,000 lbs. 24 hours.

ALEXANDRIA—Madison Co.
Pop. 7,221. On L. E. & W.; C. C. C. & St. L. RR. M. O. and Tel. offices; Am. and U. S. Ex.
ALEXANDRIA PAPER CO. (H. H. Cook, Pres. and Gen. Mgr.; C. F. Lancaster, Vice-Pres.; E. W. Yule, Sec. and Treas.) S. P., at mill. Six 1200-lb. and two Refining engines; one 114-inch and one 118-inch Fourdriniers. Widest trimmed sheets, 105 and 108 inches. Steam. Machine Finished Book and News. 100,000 lbs. 24 hours.

ANDERSON—Madison Co.
Pop. 28,000. On C. C. C. & St. L.; P. C. C. & St. L.; C. & E. RR. M. O. and Tel. office; Am., Adams and U. S. Ex.
PATENT VULCANITE ROOFING CO. S. P., at mill. (R. Glendinning, Pres.; J. Logan, Vice-Pres.; D. S. Barbour, Sec. and Mgr.; W. Thompson, Treas.; J. Furlong, Supt.) Twelve 800-lb., eight 1000-lb. engines; two 72-inch and one 86-inch Cylinders. Widest sheet made, 80 inches. Steam. Roofing Felt. 150,000 lbs. 24 hours.

BROOKVILLE—Franklin Co.
Pop. 2,037. On White Water Valley Division of C. C. C. & St. L. RR. M. O. and Tel. office; Am. Ex.
THOMPSON & NORRIS CO. OF INDIANA, THE. (J. Linton Thompson, Pres.; Frederick A. Norris, Vice-Pres.; Robert H. Thompson, Vice-Pres.; Beverly A. Norris, Vice-Pres.; Martin H. Day, Vice-Pres. and Treas.; William G. Chapin, Sec.; W. D. Bradt, Mgr.) Office, Concord and Prince Streets, Brooklyn, N. Y.—also office at Paper Mills, Brookville, Ind. MIDLAND PAPER MILLS. S. P., side track to mills. Two 1000-lb., two 1400-lb. and three 1000-lb. Beating and two Jordan engines; one 72-inch and one 96-inch Cylinder. Widest trimmed sheet, 85 inches. Water and Steam. Straw and Fibre Papers for Corrugating. 50,000 lbs. 24 hours.

BROWNSTOWN—Jackson Co.
Pop. 1,685. B. & O. S. W. RR. M. O. and Tel. office; U. S. Ex.
KIEFFER PAPER CO. (John E. Kieffer, Sec. & Gen. Mgr.) P. O. address, Ewing. Two 900-lb. and one 1500-lb. Beating and one Refining

R. B. McEwan, Pres. J. L. McEwan, Vice-Pres. Arthur McEwan, Treas. and Mgr. R. W. McEwan, Secy.
Sheet Lining Plant, Office and Mills at WHIPPANY, N. J.
McEWAN BROS., Inc. MANUFACTURERS OF ALL GRADES **PAPER BOX BOARD**

engines, one 44-inch Single and one 62-inch Cylinder. Widest trimmed sheet, 57 inches. Steam. Rag Wrapping, Rag Lining, Macaroni and Starch Paper, Indented Packing, Carpet Lining and Papier Maché Boards and Specialties. 84,000 lbs. 24 hours.

CARTHAGE—Rush Co.

Pop. 1,028. On Michigan Div. Big Four Line—C., C., C. & St. L. RR. M. O. and Tel. office; Am. Ex.

CARTHAGE BOARD AND PAPER CO. (Ley P. Rexford, Pres. and Treas.; Robert B. Wallace, Sec.; H. C. Baseler, Gen. Mgr.) CARTHAGE MILL. S. P., Carthage. Twelve 1000-lb. Beating engines; six Jordans, six Washers and six Rotary boilers, one 99-inch, one 80-inch, one 44-inch and one 102-inch Cylinders. Widest trimmed sheets, 94 inches, 68 inches, 40 inches and 96 inches. Steam. Corrugating Straw Board, Test Fibre Board, Test Chip Board and Fibre Container Board. 200,000 lbs. 24 hours.

DELPHI—Carroll Co.

Pop. 2,600. On Toledo & Tilton Br., Wabash; Monon & Indianapolis Br., Chicago, Indianapolis & Louisville & Ft. Wayne & Wabash Valley Traction. M. O. and Tel.; Am., Ad. & W. F. & Co. Ex.

DELPHI STRAW BOARD CO. Office, Decatur. (Dan R. Vail, Pres.; F. C. Vail, Sec. and Treas.) S. P., at mill. Three 1200-lb. Beating and one Refining engines. One 72-inch Machine, trims 70 inches. Steam and Electricity. Egg Case Filler Straw Board Exclusively. 30,000 lbs. 24 hours.

EATON—Delaware Co.

Pop. 1,567. On F. W., C. & L. Branch L. E. & W. RR. M. O. and Tel. office; Am. Ex.

UNITED PAPERBOARD COMPANY, INC. General Office, 171 Madison Avenue, New York. S. P., switch to mill. Six Beating (48x48 inches) and two Jordan engines; one 86-inch Cylinder. Widest trimmed sheet, 80½ inches. Steam. Straw Corrugating. 50,000 lbs. 24 hours.

ELKHART—Elkhart Co.

Pop. 25,000. On C. C. C. & St. L.; L. S. & M. S.; and E. & W. RR. M. O. and Tel. office; Am., Adams and Wells Fargo & Co. Ex.

MENGEL BOX COMPANY BRANCH. (C. C. Mengel, Pres.; A. D. Allen, Vice-Pres.; H. P. Roberts, Sec.; V. H. Bryan, Treas.; Wm. P. B. Hamilton, Mgr.) S. P. at mill. Four 1800-lb. Beating and four Refining engines; one Five Cylinder. Widest trimmed sheet, 62 inches. Water, Steam and Electricity. Container Board. 60,000 lbs. 24 hours.

NEW ELKHART PAPER MILLS CO. (a common law company). (A. B. Smith, Pres., Treas. and Gen Mgr.; F. A. Buescher, Vice-Pres.; W. H. Anderson, Sec.) Four 1500-lb. Beating and two Refining engines; one 76-inch double Cylinder. Widest trimmed sheet, 72 inches. Steam. Heavy Tissue, Heavy Chip Wrapping and Light Weight Chip Board. 20,000 lbs. 24 hours. One Double Cylinder machine to trim 105 inches has been purchased, and will probably be installed during the winter of 1918-19.

WHEAT PAPER CO. (E. B. Zigler, Pres.; H. A. Bardeen, Vice-Pres., Sec. and Gen. Mgr.; A. A. Wheat, Treas.; E. E. Johnson, Supt.) Six 1200 Beaters, three Jordans, six Washers and two Rotary boilers. One 78-inch, one 86-inch and one 100-inch Fourdriniers; widest trimmed sheets,

THOMAS E. GLEESON, Inc., } **FOURDRINIER WIRES**
411-413 John St., E. NEWARK, N. J. } For Tissue and Fine Grade Papers

Paper and Pulp Mills in the United States 87

70, 80 and 90 inches. Width of Super Calenders, 80 inches. Super-Calendered and M. F. Book, White and Colored; M. F. Bond and Superfine Writing, Tablet. Mill equipped for Rewinding Adding Machine and Counter Roll. 60,000 lbs. 24 hours.

EVANSVILLE—Vanderburg Co.

Pop. 59,007. On E. & T. H., E. H. & N. Div. of L. & N.; E. Div. S.; P. Div. I. C.; E. & I.; L. H. & St. L.; Ohio Valley Branch I. C. and E. Sub. & N. RR. M. O. and Tel. office; Adams, Am., U. S. and Southern Ex.

FUNKE'S SONS, FERDINAND. (John M. F., Ferdinand A. F. and Jos. H. F.; Ferd. A. Funke, Supt.) EVANSVILLE PAPER MILL. S. P., at mill. Two 900-lb. and one 1000-lb. Beating and one Jordan engines; one 66-inch Double Cylinder. Widest trimmed sheet, 60 inches. Steam. Heavy Cloth, Mill Wrapper, Absorbent and Common Ham Wrapper and Feather Edge Fire Work. 20,000 lbs. 24 hours.

HARTFORD CITY—Blackford Co.

Pop. 5,912. On Ft. W., C. & L. Div. of L. E. & W.; P., C., C. & St. L. RR. M. O. and Tel. office; U. S. and Adams Ex.

FORT WAYNE CORRUGATED PAPER CO. (Henry C. Paul, Pres.; P. F. Griffin, Sec.) General Offices, Fort Wayne, Ind. Twelve 1000-lb. Beating and four Refining engines; one 114-inch Five Cylinder machine. Widest trimmed sheet, 100 inches. Steam. Jute Board and Box Board. 70,000 lbs. 24 hours.

HARTFORD CITY PAPER CO. (Louis Fox, Pres.; Oscar W. Fox, Sec.; B. A. Van Winkle, Treas. and Gen. Mgr.; Henry J. Miller, V. P.) S. P., track at mill. Thirteen 1000-lb. Beating and two Refining engines; one 94 and one 120-inch Fourdrinier. Widest trimmed sheet, 100 inches. Steam. Greaseproof Parchment, Glassine (Plain and Embossed), Onion Skin and Manifold Paper. 36,000 lbs. 24 hours.

INDIANAPOLIS—Marion Co.

Pop. 169,164. On C. H. & I.; I. D. & W.; L. E. & W.; C. I. & L.; I. C. & I.; I. & C.; C. C. C. & St. L.; P. C. C. & St. L.; I. & V.; T. H. & I. RR. M. O. and Tel. office; Adams, Am., Nat., G. N., Pac., Tex., U. S., B. & O., Southern and Wells, Fargo & Co. Ex.

BEVERIDGE PAPER CO. (H. L. Beveridge, Pres.; S. B. Sutphin, Sec. and Treas.; Wm. Ross, Supt.) S. P., at mill. Four 1200-lb. and five 1000-lb. Beating and five Jordan engines; one 54-inch Six and one 72-inch Five Cylinders. Widest trimmed sheets, 52 inches and 70 inches. Steam. Post Card, White and Tinted Bristols, Bogus Bristols, Mill Blanks, White and Colored Patent Coated Box Board and Specialties in Bristols, Bogus Press Boards, Tablet Cover Papers, Duplex and other Ticket stock. The mill has facilities for rewinding narrow rolls. 70,000 lbs. 24 hours.

KOKOMO—Howard Co.

Pop. 10,609. On P., C., C. & St. L.; I. & M. C. Div. of L. E. & W. and T.; St. L. & K. C. RR. M. O. and Tel. office; Adams, Nat. and U. S. Ex.

MID-WEST BOX COMPANY. Office, Conway Bldg., Chicago. (W. H. Fairchild, Pres.; J. P. Brunt, Vice-Pres.; Edward R. Hankins, Vice-Pres. and Treas.; K. I. Herman, Sec. and Gen. Mgr. S. P., at mill. Five 1200-lb. Beating engines; one 96-inch Five Cylinder Board Machine. Widest

DRY ROSIN SIZE

Brittle, easy soluble. Cheapest size out; cheaper than mill made size. Ask us about it. Also all other grades.

ARABOL M'F'G CO.
100 William St., New York

THE UNION SULPHUR CO.
Main Office: 17 Battery Pl., New York. Mines: Calcasieu Parish, La.
Producers of **The Only Arsenic Free Sulphur on the Market**

trimmed sheet, 82 inches. Container, Backing and Box Boards. 80,000 lbs. 24 hours.

LAFAYETTE—Tippecanoe Co.

Pop. 18,116. On W., L. E. & W.; C. I. & L.; C., C., C. & St. L. and Wabash RR. M. O. and Tel.; Am., U. S. and Pac. Ex.

LAFAYETTE BOX BOARD AND PAPER CO. Sales Agents, The C. L. La Boiteaux Co., Cincinnati, Chicago, New York, Cleveland. (Thomas Bauer, Pres.; J. O. Henderson, Vice-Pres.; G. D. Jay, Sec.; Bruce F. Failey, Treas.; Thomas Bauer, Mgr.; Geo. Kaufman, Supt.) S. P., at mill. Nine 1500-lb. Beating and four Jordan engines; one 122-inch Five Cylinder. Widest trimmed sheet, 110 inches. Steam. Straw and Chip Boards, plain and mill and sheet lined. 180,000 lbs. 24 hours.

MARION—Grant Co.

Pop. 17,337. On M. Div. of C. C. C. & St. L.; C. Div. of P. C. C. & St. L.; T., St. L. & K. C. and C. & O. RR. of Ind. M. O. and Tel. office; Am., Adams and Nat. Ex.

DECATUR STRAWBOARD CO. (D. R. Vail, Pres.; J. W. Vail, Vice-Pres.; F. E. Vail, Sec. and Treas.; C. H. Dyke, Supt.) Four 600-lb. Beating and two Refining engines; four Washers and four Rotary boilers; one 62-inch Four Cylinder. Widest trimmed sheet, 57 inches. Electricity. Plain Straw and Chip Board. 40,000 lbs. 24 hours.

MARION PAPER CO. (J. L. McCulloch, Vice-Pres. and Sec.; J. L. Gable, Treas.) S. P., Marion. Four 1000-lb. and four 1500-lb. Beating engines; one 72-inch and one 86-inch Cylinders. Widest trimmed sheets, 66 and 82 inches. Union Screens. Steam. Test, Jute and Folding Box Board. 100,000 lbs. 24 hours.

MT. VERNON—Posey Co.

Pop. 8,000. On Ohio River; St. L. Div L. & N. and Mt. V. Br. O. & E. P. RR. M. O. and Tel. office; American, Adams and W. F. Ex.

MT. VERNON STRAW BOARD CO., Sales Office, Graham Paper Co., St. Louis. (Frank Endress, Pres.; Walter V. Scholz, Vice-Pres.; S. L. Wilson, Sec.; E. T. Williams, Treas.; H. C. Zerbe, Gen. Mgr.) S. P., at mill. Nine 1500-lb. Beating, four Refining engines and eight Rotary boilers; one 72-inch Five Cylinder and one 86-inch Four Cylinder. Widest trimmed sheets, 69 and 84 inches. Steam and Electricity. Plain and Manila Lined Chip, Plain and Lined Straw Board, Egg Case Flats and Rolls. 125,000 lbs. 24 hours.

MUNCIE—Delaware Co.

Pop. 20,942. On C. C. C. & St. L.; L. E. & W.; P. C. C. & St. L.; C. & O. of I.; Central Ind. M. O. and Tel. office; Am. and U. S. Ex.

BALL BROS. CO. Paper Mill Department. Communications for mill should be addressed: C. R. Austin, Supt., R.R. No. 12, Box 164A, Muncie, Ind.; and for General Offices, Ball Bros. Co., Muncie, Ind. (F. C. Ball, Pres.; E. B. Ball, Vice-Pres.; W. C. Ball, Sec.; G. A. Ball, Treas.; C. R. Austin, Supt.) S. P., at mill. Eight 1000-lb. Beating engines; three Refining engines; one 118-inch Five Cylinder Machine. Widest trimmed sheet, 104 inches. Steam and Electricity. Jute and Test Chip for Containers. 70,000 to 80,000 lbs. 24 hours.

IMPCo

WE SPECIALIZE IN MACHINERY FOR HANDLING

PULP

OUR SYSTEM AND MACHINES REPRESENT THE LATEST

METHODS

FOR SCREENING AND THICKENING

Ground Wood, Sulphite or Sulphate

STOCK
(SEE REVERSE PAGE)

IMPROVED PAPER MACHINERY CO.
NASHUA, N. H., U. S. A.

SHERBROOKE MACHINERY CO., Limited
SHERBROOKE, CANADA

IMPROVED PAPER MACHINERY CO.

MANUFACTURERS OF

Pulp and Paper Making Machinery

INCLUDING

PNEUMATIC MACHINES — Built in single units or in batteries for use as

    SAVE-ALLS — a money maker when used to remove the valuable fibre in the waste water from blow pits, wet machines, thickeners, cylinder and fourdrinier machines.

    THICKENERS — The best means of thickening sulphite or other free stock, will deliver uniform stock continuously, at minimum running expense.

    FILTERS — Mechanical, of large capacity, can be used in connection with sand filters.

"IMPCO" KNOTTERS, KNOT SCREENS, SLIVER SCREENS — For sulphite, sulphate soda, ground wood and paper stock. Less than 1 H. P. required for one machine. Capacity up to 50 tons. Simple belt drive. No gears or sprockets. No packings. Slow speed. Quickly detachable plates. The ideal machine for removing larger shives, slivers, knots and foreign material from the stock.

"IMPCO" CENTRIFUGAL SCREENS — For screening sulphite, sulphate soda, Kraft, ground wood and straw pulp.

PULP THICKENERS OR DECKERS — Built in single units or in batteries for use as

    THICKENERS
    FILTERS — the standard machine for thickening ground wood or other slow stock.

SPECIAL DECKERS WITH PRESS ROLL — Furnish stock about 18% dry.

    AS SAVE-ALLS AND THICKENERS

"IMPCO" RECLAIMER — For recovering waste of any kind.

VARIABLE SPEED COUCH ROLL DRIVES — For Deckers and Decker-Save-Alls. Insures greatest efficiency of decker machines. Allows the use of fine wire. Speed of couch can be made to correspond exactly with wire speed.

WASHING MACHINES — Very effective to remove dirt and coloring matter in suspension and solution. For sulphite, soda and waste paper stock.

CYLINDER MOULDS — Made in all sizes, absolutely non-sagging, of exact construction.

IMPROVED BUILT-UP PRESS ROLLS — Can be built in large diameter.

SUCTION ROLLS — Of rigid construction. May be run with press roll. No packings of any kind, very small power.

FELT COUCH ROLLS — Patent spiral winding insures uniform elastic surface of long life.

SPECIAL MACHINES — Designed and built to order.

REPAIRING — We make a specialty of repairing cylinder moulds.

Correspondence a Pleasure

IMPROVED PAPER MACHINERY CO.
NASHUA, N. H., U. S. A.
Sherbrooke Machinery Co., Ltd., Sherbrooke, Que.

HINDE & DAUCH PAPER CO., THE. (Sidney Frohman, Pres.; W. F. Harbrecht, Vice-Pres.; Fred Emmons, Sec.) Office, Sandusky, Ohio. S. P., at mill. Three 1200-lb. and 1500-lb. Beating and three Jordan engines; one 86-inch Cylinder machine. Widest trimmed sheet, 80 inches. Steam and Electricity. Chip and Container Boards. 58,000 lbs. 24 hours.

NOBLESVILLE—Hamilton Co.

Pop. 4,792. On L. E. & W.; C. & S. E. RR. M. O. and Tel. office; U. S. Ex.

AMERICAN STRAW BOARD CO., Akron, O. (C. B. Macy, Mgr.) NOBLESVILLE MILL. S. P., at mill. Twenty 1200-lb. and four Jordan engines; one 86-inch and one 96-inch Cylinder Machines. Widest sheet made, 90 inches. Steam. Steam Dried Straw Board, Plain and Straw Board for Corrugating. 100,000 lbs. 24 hours.

ROCKPORT—Spencer Co.

Pop. 2,382. On Ohio River; Southern RR. M. O. and Tel. office; Adams, Am. and U. S. Ex.

UNITED PAPERBOARD COMPANY. General Office, 171 Madison Ave., New York. ROCKPORT MILL. S. P., at mill. Four 1500-lb. Beating and two Jordan engines; one 66-inch Three Cylinder. Widest trimmed sheet, 62 inches. Steam. Straw Boards and Straw Corrugating. 38,000 lbs. 24 hours.

SOUTH BEND—St. Joseph Co.

Pop. 55,000. On Western Div. of L. S. & M. S.; C. & G. T.; C. & S. B.; T. H. & I.; S. B. Div. of M. C.; C. I. & S. RR. M. O. and Tel. office; Am., Ad., Nat., Northern & Wells Fargo and U. S. Ex.

LA SALLE PAPER CO., THE. (F. P. Nicely, Prop.; R. S. Nicely, Sec.; C. W. McAlpine, Supt.) REYNOLDS MILL. S. P., at mill. One 700-lb. and one 1000-lb. Beating and one Jordan engines; one 76-inch Double Cylinder. Widest trimmed sheet, 70 inches. Water, Steam and Electricity. Express, Wrapping, Light Chip Board, Mill Wrappers, Ham Wrappers, Rag Lining and Specialties. 24,000 lbs. 24 hours.

TERRE HAUTE—Vigo Co.

Pop. 60,000. On Penn., Big 4, C. & E. I. and C. T. H. & S. R. Adams, American and Wells Fargo Ex.

THE TERRE HAUTE PAPER CO. (E. B. Weston, Pres.; Edward Hidden, Vice-Pres.; H. J. Wantland, Sec.; W. G. Clark, Treas.) S. P., at mills. **No. 1 Mill.**—Eight 1500-lb., one 1200-lb. Beating and four Refining engines. One 78-inch and one 86-inch Cylinders. Widest trimmed sheet, 80 inches. Steam. Straw, Jute and Chip for Corrugating; Tube and Egg Case Boards; Straw and Rag Wrappings. 100,000 lbs. 24 hours. **No. 2 Mill.**—Eight 1500-lb. Beating and Two Refining engines. Eight Globe Rotary boilers, one 120-inch Cylinder. Widest trimmed sheet, 110 inches. Steam. Straw Board for Corrugating. 75,000 lbs. 24 hours.

VINCENNES—Knox Co.

Pop. 10,249. On B. & O. S. W.; O., C. & St. L.; P., C., C. & St. L.; C. & E. J. RR. M. O. and Tel. office. Am., Adams and W. F. Ex.

FORT WAYNE CORRUGATED PAPER CO. VINCENNES MILL. General Offices, Fort Wayne, Ind. (H. C. Paul, Pres.; P. F. Griffin, Sec.;

Indiana and Iowa

S. D. Bond, Treas.) S. P., at mill. Eight 1500-lb. Beating and two Refining engines; one 96-inch Cylinder. Widest trimmed sheet, 89 inches. Steam. Straw Board for Corrugating. 60,000 lbs. 24 hours.

INDIANA BOARD AND FILLER CO. (W. D. Coil, Pres.; D. C. Amerine, Vice-Pres. and Mill Mgr.; S. B. Fleming, Treas.; W. A. Viets, Sec.) S. P., at mill. Five 1200-lb. Beating and two Jordan engines; one 72-inch Five Cylinder. Widest trimmed sheet, 65 inches. Steam. Plain and Mill Lined Straw and Chip Board. 50,000 lbs. 24 hours.

WABASH—Wabash Co.

Pop. 8,618. On Wabash; C., C., C. & St. L. W. RR. M. O. and Tel. office; Am. and Pac. Ex.

UNITED PAPERBOARD COMPANY. General Office, 171 Madison Ave., New York. WABASH MILL. S. P., at mill. Eight 1000-lb. and five 1200-lb. Beating and seven Jordan engines; one 118-inch Five Cylinder and one 96-inch Five Cylinder machines. Widest trimmed sheet, 105 inches. Steam. Straw Board, Doubled Straw and Paper Stock Boards, Chip, News and Combination Boards; also specialties. Coated Box Boards of all kinds. 120,000 lbs. 24 hours.

YORKTOWN—Delaware Co.

Pop. 1,100. On Indianap. Div. C., C. C. & St. L. M. O., Tel. and bank. Am. and Wells, Fargo & Co. Ex.

UNITED PAPERBOARD COMPANY. General Office, 171 Madison Ave., New York. YORKTOWN MILL. S. P., Yorktown. Six 1250-lb. and one Refining engines; one 68-inch Cylinder. Widest trimmed sheet, 66 inches. Steam. Straw Board. 45,000 lbs. 24 hours.

IOWA.

CLINTON—Clinton Co.

Pop. 25,689. On C. & N. W.; C. M. & St. P.; C. B. & Q.; C., R. I. & P. RR. M. O. and Tel. office; Adams, Am. and W. F. Ex.

FORD MANUFACTURING CO. General Office, Chicago. (J. W. Ford, Jr., Pres.; W. O. Ford, Vice-Pres. and Sec.; L. M. Ford, Treas.) S. P., at mill. Eight 800-lb. and one 2000-lb. Beating and three Refining engines; one 72-inch Cylinder. Widest trimmed sheet, 72 inches. Steam. Roofing Deadening Felts and Red Rosins. 60,000 lbs. 24 hours. Offices, Chicago, Ill.; St. Louis, Mo.; Clinton, Iowa; Vandalia, Ill.; Kansas City, Mo.; Buffalo, N. Y.; Atlanta, Ga. Factories, Clinton, Iowa; Vandalia, Ill.; York, Pa.; St. Louis, Mo.

KLEIN PAPER CO. One 800-lb., one 1200-lb. and one 1500-lb. Beating and two Refining engines; one 68-inch Cylinder. Widest trimmed sheet, 64 inches. Steam. Gray Rag Wrapping and Lining and Bogus Drawing Paper. 25,000 lbs. 24 hours.

FORT MADISON—Lee Co.

Pop. 9,278. On C., B. & Q.; A. T. & S. F.; Mississippi River. M. O. and Tel. office; Adams and Wells Fargo & Co. Ex.

BROWN PAPER CO., THE. (A. P. Brown, Pres.; Geo. Little, Vice-Pres.; T. L. Peterson, Sec.; A. P. Brown, Treas.; T. L. Peterson, Supt.)

THOMAS E. GLEESON, Inc., 411-413 John St., E. NEWARK, N. J.
CYLINDER MOULDS and DANDY ROLLS Made and Repaired
LETTERING and MONOGRAMS for WATERMARKS

Paper and Pulp Mills in the United States 91

S. P., at mill. Four 1100-lb. Beating, one Jordan and one Claflin Refining engines, eight Washers and four Rotary boilers; one 78-inch Cylinder. Widest trimmed sheet, 73 inches. Light Weight Straw Board. 38,000 lbs. 24 hours.

WARDWAY PAPER MILLS. Montgomery Ward & Co. (H. E. Roether, Mgr.; W. S. Tucker, Supt.) Two 1200-lb. and one 1000-lb. Beating and one 50-ton Refining engines; one 50-inch Double Cylinder. Widest trimmed sheet, 45 inches. Electricity. Rosin Sized Sheathing, Rag Wrapping, Chip Board, Kraft Wrapping. 15,000 lbs. 24 hours. Single Faced Corrugated Paper. 8000 lbs. 24 hours.

TAMA—Tama Co.

Pop. 2,649. On C. & N. W.; C., M. & St. P. RR. M. O. and Tel. office; Am. and Wells Fargo & Co. Ex.

CHERRY, J. G., COMPANY. (W. L. Cherry, Pres., H. T. Cherry, Vice-Pres. and Mgr.; H. H. Cherry, Sec.; E. B. Cameron, Treas.; J. R. Carter, Supt.) TAMA PAPER MILL. S. P., at mill. Two 1200-lb. and three 1500-lb. Beating and two Refining engines; five Rotary boilers; one Cylinder machine. Widest trimmed sheet, 86 inches. Steam. Strawboard. 65,000 lbs. 24 hours.

KANSAS.

COFFEYVILLE—Montgomery Co.

Pop. 18,500. On M. P.; A. T. & S. F.; M. K. & T. RR. M. O. and Tel. office; Am., Pac. and Wells Fargo & Co. Ex.

CREAMERY PACKAGE MANUFACTURING CO., Successors to North Star Manufacturing Co. Chicago Office, 61 West Kinzie Street. (H. H. Curtis, Pres.; E. W. Chandler, Vice-Pres. and Gen. Mgr.; Geo. Walker, Sec. and Treas.; F. O. Weis, Mgr.; Ed. Cape, Supt.) S. P., switch at mill. Three 1500-lb. Beating and one Refining engines; three Washers and three Rotary boilers; one 90-inch Double Cylinder. Widest trimmed sheet, 82 inches. Steam. Plain Straw Board. 35,000 lbs. 24 hours.

HUTCHINSON—Reno Co.

On A. T. & S. F., C. R. I. & P. & Mo. Pac.

HUTCHINSON BOX BOARD & PAPER CO., THE. (Emerson Carey, Pres.; Howard J. Carey, Vice-Pres.; Charles E. Carey, Sec. and Genl. Mgr.; T. S. Smith, Treas.; E. S. Shepherd, Supt.) S. P., Hutchinson. Eight 1500-lb. Beating engines. One 100-inch machine. Widest trimmed sheet, 102 inches. Steam. Straw Board, News Board, Chip Board, Vat Lined, etc. 80,000 lbs. 24 hours.

LAWRENCE—Douglas Co.

Pop. 12,700. On U. P., A., T. & S. F.; K. C.-K. V. & W. RR. M. O. and Tel. office; Am. and Wells Fargo & Co. Ex.

LAWRENCE PAPER MANUFACTURING CO. (J. D. Bowersock, Pres.; Irving Hill, Vice-Pres. and Mgr.; P. A. Dinsmoor, Sec. and Asst. Mgr.) S. P., side track to mill. One 1200-lb., two 1500-lb. and one 2000-lb. Beating and three Refining engines; one 72-inch Five Cylinder. Widest

SULPHUR—CRUDE. GUARANTEED 99% PURE.
The average analysis of our high-grade brimstone is in itself a guarantee. Write us for quotations.
THE UNION SULPHUR CO., Main Office, 17 Battery Pl., New York. Mines, Calcasieu Parish, La.

'trimmed sheet, 67 inches. Water, Electricity and Steam. Straw and Liners for Corrugated Containers; Corrugated Boxes and Packing. 30,000 lbs. 24 hours.

LOUISIANA.

BOGALUSA—Washington Parish.

Pop. 10,000. On N. O. and Great Northern R.R.; M. O., Tel. office, Banks and Southern Express, Bogalusa.

BOGALUSA PAPER CO., INC. (Walter P. Cooke, Pres.; G. H. Wood, Gen. Mgr.; W. H. Sullivan, Vice-Pres.; M. L. Wuescher, Sec.; D. T. Cushing, Treas.; C. D. Altick, Gen. Supt.) Sixteen 1500-lb. Beating and eight Refining engines; one 112-inch and one 118-inch Cylinder machines. Widest trimmed sheets, 106 and 112 inches. Steam. Container Liner. 250,000 lbs. 24 hours. PULP MILL. Eight Digesters and six Wet Machines. Sulphate Pulp. 150,000 lbs. 24 hours.

LOUISIANA FIBRE BOARD CO., Successor to Southern Wood Distillates & Fibre Co. (George R. Wright, Pres. and Treas.; Geo. M. Curtis, Vice-Pres.; Charles F. McLean, Sec.; R. J. Cullen, Genl. Supt.) S. P., at mill. Six 2000-lb. Beating and three Refining engines. One 108-inch Five Cylinder Board Machine. Steam. Container Liner. 150,000 lbs. 24 hours. PULP MILL. Sulphate Pulp. 80,000 lbs. 24 hours.

BRAITHWAITE—Plaquemine Parish.

Pop. 75. On La. So. RR. M. O. and Tel. and nearest bank, New Orleans, 21 miles.

E. Z. OPENER BAG CO., Taylorville, Ill. Lessee from United Railway & Trading Co. Sales Office, Decatur, Ill. (H. E. Westervelt, Pres.; E. C. Westervelt, Vice-Pres.; O. L. Hammond, Sec.; Frank Brewer, Treas. and Mgr.) BRAITHWAITE PAPER MILL. S. P., Braithwaite. Eight 2000-lb. Beating, three Claflin and one Jordan engines. One 136-inch Fourdrinier. Widest trimmed sheet, 126 inches. Width of Super Calenders, 134 inches. Steam. Kraft Bag Paper. 50,000 lbs. 24 hours. PULP MILL. Four Digesters. Steam. Yellow Pine, Sulphate Pulp. 50,000 lbs. 24 hours.

NEW IBERIA—Iberia Co.—PULP MILL.

Pop. 7,499. So. Pacific & New Iberia, Northern & Frisco RR. M. O., Tel., Wells, Fargo and Am. Ex.

SUGAR CANE BY-PRODUCTS CO. Office, Widener Bldg., Philadelphia. (George H. Gould, Vice-Pres.; William H. Door, Vice-Pres.; John W. Marsden, Treas.; E. W. Strain, Sec.) Eight Large Digesters, Soda Process; five Digesters, Sulphite Process. Pulp. 100,000 lbs. 24 hours.

MAINE.

AUBURN—Androscoggin Co.

Pop. 12,951. On M. C.; P. & R. F.; G. T. RR. M. O. and Tel. office; Am. and Merchants' Ex.

MYERS, JR., J. E., Successor to The Stevens Mills Paper Co. P. O. Address, Box 314 Lewiston, Me. S. P., at mill. Two Beating engines; one 52-inch Three Cylinder Paper Machine. Water and Steam. Specialties. 6000 lbs. 24 hours. (Sept. 9, 1918. Idle. Expected to be running in a short time.)

National Duplex Waterproof Case Lining
IS WATERPROOF— **NATIONAL WATERPROOFING CO.,** 1054 DREXEL BLDG.
CLEAN TO HANDLE PHILADELPHIA

Paper and Pulp Mills in the United States 93

AUGUSTA—Kennebec Co.

Pop. 11,683. On M. C. RR. M. O. and Tel. office; Am. and Atlantic Ex.

CUSHNOC PAPER CO. Richard Smith, Pres.; Frederick S. Lyman, Vice-Pres.; Walter E. Shuttleworth, Treas.) S. P., side track at mill, and wharf ½ mile. One 1000-lb. and five 1800-lb. Beating and three Refining engines; one 86-inch and one 100-inch Fourdriniers. Widest trimmed sheet, 90 inches. Water and Steam. Manila Envelope, Bag and Sack, Manila Wrapping, Yellow Writing, laid and wove, and White Sulphite papers. *Our Specialties are Envelope papers, Bag and Sack papers, White Sulphite papers, Manila Wrappings, Yellow Writing, Bleached Ground Wood papers, laid and wove, sheets and rolls.* 90,000 lbs. 24 hours. PULP MILLS.—SULPHITE MILL. S. P., at mills. Three Digesters; two 76-inch Wet Machines. Water. Sulphite Fibre. 60,000 lbs. 24 hours. AUGUSTA PULP MILL. Nine Grinders, four 80-inch Wet Machines. Water. Ground Wood, Bleached and Unbleached. 90,000 lbs. 24 hours.

BANGOR—Penobscot Co.

Pop. 24,867. On Maine Central & Bangor and Aroostook RR.; and Steamers from Boston and Portland M. O. and Tel. Hoyts Ex.

EASTERN MANUFACTURING CO. P. O. address, 92 Exchange St., Bangor. Eastern Office, 501 Fifth Avenue, New York. Western Office, Chicago. (F. R. Ayer, Pres.; S. W. Webb, Chairman; F. A. Leahy, Vice-Pres.; S. B. Copeland, Vice-Pres.; H. J. Guild, Vice-Pres.; D. A. Crocker, Vice-Pres.; Geo. E. Hyde, Sec. and Treas.) S. P., at mill at South Brewer, 2½ miles from Bangor. Fifteen 1200-lb. Beaters, six Refining engines; four Washers and two Rotary boilers; one 100-inch, one 112-inch and one 116-inch Fourdriniers. Widest trimmed sheets, 90 inches, 102 inches and 104 inches. Widest Super Calendered sheet, 60 inches. Steam and Electricity. Loft and Machine Dried, Ledger, Writing, Bond and Envelope. 100,000 lbs. 24 hours. PULP MILL. S. P., at mill. Five Digesters; one 72-inch and one 84-inch Wet Machine; one 100-inch Dry Machine. Steam and Electricity. Sulphite Fibre, 130,000 lbs. 24 hours.

BAR MILLS—York Co.

Pop. 140. Saco River Station. W. N. & P. Div. B. & M. Am. Ex.

COLONIAL PULP MILL. (Theodore W. Law, Portsmouth, N. H.) S. P., at mill. Six Grinders and four Wet Machines. Ground Wood. 70,000 lbs. 24 hours. Bought in under mortgage foreclosure by Equitable Trust Co. of New York City. (Idle.)

ROGERS FIBRE CO. NATIONAL DIV., successors to National Fibre Board Co. BAR MILLS MILL. 121 Beach Street, Boston, Mass. (Elliot Rogers, Pres.; Louis Rogers, Vice-Pres. and Mgr.; Stephen Moore, Treas.; Eben W. Freeman, Sec.; James F. Stanton, Supt.) Twenty-eight Beating engines; eight Cylinder Wet machines. Water. Fibre Board. 30,000 lbs. 24 hours.

BELFAST—Waldo Co.

Pop. 4,615. On Belfast Div. of M. C. RR.; also vessels. M. O. and Tel. office; Am. Ex.

SHERMAN & CO. BELFAST MILLS. Two mills. S. P., Belfast. Elmer A. Sherman, Mgr.; Raymond R. Sherman, Supt. Six 800-lb. engines; two 44-inch machines. Water. Leather Board. 8000 lbs. 24 hours.

R. S. McEwan, *Pres.* J. L. McEwan, *Vice-Pres.* Arthur McEwan, *Treas. and Mgr.* R. W. McEwan, *Secy*
Sheet Lining Plant, Office and Mills at WHIPPANY, N. J.
McEWAN BROS., Inc. MANUFACTURERS OF ALL GRADES **PAPER BOX BOARD**

E. J. KELLER CO., INC.
200 FIFTH AVENUE E.J.KELLER, Pres. NEW YORK
FOREIGN AND DOMESTIC
Rags AND Wastes
Gunny Bagging, Burlap Bagging, Ropes, Flax, Hemp, Cotton Wastes, Paper Stock, Wood Pulp and Rag Pulp.

DRY ROSIN SIZE Brittle, easy soluble, cheapest size out; cheaper than mill made size. Ask us about it. Also all other grades. **ARABOL M'F'G CO.** 100 William St., N. Y.

Maine

BENTON FALLS—Kennebec Co.

Pop. 240. Electric cars from Fairfield. Nearest bank and Tel. office, Fairfield, 3 miles; Am. Ex.

UNITED PAPERBOARD COMPANY. General Office, 171 Madison Ave., New York. BENTON FALLS MILL. S. P., at mill. Five 1200-lb. and four Jordan engines; one 84-inch Cylinder. Widest trimmed sheet, 80 inches. Water. Jute Board for Containers. 40,000 lbs. 24 hours. PULP MILL. S. P., at mill. Two Grinders, three Wet Machines. Water. Ground Wood. 20,000 lbs. 24 hours.

BRUNSWICK—Cumberland Co.

Pop. 6,306. On M. C. RR. M. O. and Tel. office; Am. and Hoyt Ex.

PEJEPSCOT PAPER CO. BOWDOIN MILL. S. P., at mills. (Justus A. B. Cowles, Pres.; W. W. Nearing, Vice-Pres.; William Glasson, Treas.; C. P. Cowles, Mgr., Dept. of Woodlands; Edward P. Shattuck, Sec.) Three 450-lb., four 500-lb., three 600-lb., two 1000-lb. Beating and four Jordan engines; one 70-inch Harper, one 60-inch Cylinder, and one 84-inch and one 94-inch Fourdriniers. Widest trimmed sheet, 88 inches. Water. News, Poster, Cover and Wrapping. 70,000 lbs. 24 hours.

PEJEPSCOT PAPER CO. PEJEPSCOT MILL located at Pejepscot, 4½ miles from Brunswick. S. P., at mill. Six 1500-lb. Beating and two Refining engines; one 124-inch and one 144-inch Fourdriniers. Water, Steam and Electricity. News. 150,000 lbs. 24 hours. PULP MILL. S. P., at mill. Fourteen Grinders, six Wet and six Feltless Machines. Three "Impco" Screens. Water. Ground Wood. 160,000 lbs. 24 hours.

PEJEPSCOT PAPER CO. TOPSHAM MILL located at Topsham, ½ mile from Brunswick. S. P., at mill. Twelve Grinders; thirteen Wet machines; four "Impco" Screens. Water. Ground Wood. 140,000 lbs. 24 hours.

CHISHOLM—Franklin Co.

Pop. 200. M. C. RR. M. O., Tel. and nearest bank, Livermore Falls, 1 mile; Am. Ex.

INTERNATIONAL PAPER CO. Office, 30 Broad street, New York. OTIS MILLS. (Wm. A. Murray, Supt.) S. P., at mill. Ten Beating and seven Refining engines; one 86-inch, one 97-inch, one 110-inch, two 120-inch, two 126-inch, one 135-inch, two 152-inch Fourdriniers and one 90-inch Cylinder. Water and Steam. News and Wrappers. 604,000 lbs. 24 hours. PULP MILL. Nineteen Grinders; seventeen Wet Machines. Water and Steam. Ground Wood. 160,000 lbs. 24 hours. SULPHITE MILL. Three Digesters, 130,000 lbs.

CUMBERLAND MILLS—Cumberland Co.

Pop. 860. On B. & M.; M. C. RR. Tel. office; nearest bank, Westbrook, 1½ miles; Am. Ex.

WARREN, S. D. CO. (Fiske Warren, Pres.; R. D. Smith, Vice-Pres.; W. B. Nye, Vice-Pres.; H. W. Mason, Treas.; S. D. Warren, Sec.) P. O. Address, Boston, Mass. Two mills. CUMBERLAND MILLS. On Presumpscot River. S. P., at mill. Two 700-lb., seven 1200-lb., two 1300-lb., three 1500-lb., twenty-nine 1600-lb., two 1800-lb. Beaters and nineteen Refining engines; one 56-inch, two 68-inch, one 82-inch, one 84-inch, one 90-inch, one 96-inch, two 105-inch, one 119-inch and two 145-inch Four-

HARDY S. FERGUSON CONSULTING ENGINEER 200 FIFTH AVENUE NEW YORK CITY

PAPER, PULP AND FIBRE MILLS WATER POWER DEVELOPMENT DAMS, STORAGE RESERVOIRS AND OTHER HYDRAULIC STRUCTURES

PRESS ROLLS Maple and Gum White Wood Felt Rolls **J. W. HEWITT MACHINE CO.** Neenah, Wis.

THOMAS E. GLEESON, Inc., **FOURDRINIER WIRES**
411-413 John St., E. NEWARK, N. J. For Tissue and Fine Grade Papers

Paper and Pulp Mills in the United States 95

driniers. Widest trimmed sheet, 137 inches. Width of Super Calenders up to 82 inches. Union Screens. Water, Steam and Electricity. Book and Coated. 400,000 lbs. 24 hours. CHEMICAL FIBRE MILL. Steam and Electricity. Soda Fibre. 200,000 lbs. 24 hours.

EAST POLAND—Androscoggin Co.

Pop. 347. On G. T. RR. M. O. and Tel. office, Poland, 3 miles; nearest bank, Auburn, 7 miles; Am. Ex.

ROGERS FIBRE CO. NATIONAL DIV. S. P., Empire Road. (Elliott Rogers, Pres.; Stephen Moore, Treas.; Eben W. Freeman, Sec.; Guy F. Davis, Supt.) Boston Office, 121 Beach Street. LITTLE ANDROSCOGGIN MILL. S. P. ½ mile. Eleven 400-lb., two 700-lb. and one 1000-lb. Beating engines; six 48-inch Wet machines. Water and Steam. Fibre Board and Horn Fibre. 14,000 lbs. 24 hours.

EAST MILLINOCKET.
(See Millinocket.)

GREAT NORTHERN PAPER CO. LOWER MILL. Four 158-inch News machines. 400,000 lbs. 24 hours. PULP MILL. Thirty-nine Grinders; ten "Impco" Rotary Screens. Ground Wood. 320,000 lbs. 24 hours.

FAIRFIELD—Somerset Co.—PULP MILL.

Pop. 3,878. On Skowhegan Branch of M. C. RR. M. O. and Tel. office; Am. Ex.

UNITED PAPERBOARD COMPANY. General Office, 171 Madison Ave., New York. FAIRFIELD SODA PULP MILL. S. P., at mill. Five Digesters; two Wet Machines and one Drying Machine. Water. Soda Fibre. 60,000 lbs. 24 hours. FAIRFIELD GROUND WOOD MILL. Four Grinders; three Wet Machines. Water. Ground Wood. 30,000 lbs. 24 hours.

GARDINER—Kennebec Co.

Pop. 5,501. On M. C. RR. M. O. and Tel. office; Am. Ex.

HOLLINGSWORTH & WHITNEY CO. (Waldo E. Pratt, Pres.; M. L. Madden, Vice-Pres.; H. E. Fales, Treas.) P. O. address, Boston, Mass., 111 W. Washington, Chicago, and 299 Broadway, New York. Two mills. COBBOSSEE MILL. One 94-inch Fourdrinier and one 62-inch Double Cylinder. Water and Steam. Writings, Colors, White and Special Papers. 40,000 lbs. 24 hours. AROOSTOOK MILL. One 90-inch Fourdrinier. Water and Steam. Fine Manilas, White and Colors. 30,000 lbs. 24 hours. (See advertisement in back of Directory.)

WARREN, S. D. CO. P. O. address, Boston, Mass. COPSECOOK MILL. Eight 600-lb., one 1200-lb., one 1500-lb. Beating and three Refining engines; one 84-inch and one 90-inch Fourdriniers. Widest trimmed sheet, 70 inches. Width of Super-Calenders, up to 72 inches. Water and Steam. Specialties. 20,000 lbs. 24 hours.

GREAT WORKS—Penobscot Co.—PULP MILL.

Pop. 600. On M. C. RR. M. O. and Tel. office; nearest bank, Oldtown, 1 mile; Am. Ex.

PENOBSCOT CHEMICAL FIBRE CO. (Clayton H. De Lano, Pres.; Amos Hollingsworth; Eugene H. Clapp, Treas.; Walter V. Wentworth,

DRY ROSIN SIZE
Brittle, easy soluble. Cheapest, also out; cheaper than mill made size. Ask us about it. Also all other grades.
ARABOL MF'G CO.
100 William St., New York

HIGHEST GRADE BRIMSTONE—GUARANTEED 99% PURE
free from Arsenic or Selenium. Write for particulars to
THE UNION SULPHUR CO., Main Office, 17 Battery Pl., New York. Mines, Calcasieu Parish, La.

DRY ROSIN SIZE Brittle, easy soluble, cheapest size out; cheaper than mill made size. Ask us about it. Also all other grades. **ARABOL M'F'G CO.** 100 William St., N. Y.

Mgr.) Boston office, 49 Federal street. S. P., at mill. Eight Digesters; two Dry Machines; one 86-inch and one 118-inch Cylinder machines. Water and Steam. Soda Fibre (dry). 160,000 lbs. 24 hours. SULPHITE FIBRE MILL. Three Digesters and one 128-inch Drying machine. Water. Sulphite Fibre. 150,000 lbs. 24 hours.

HOWLAND—Penobscot Co.

Pop. 500. Stage from Enfield. M. O. and Tel. office, Enfield, 4 miles; nearest bank, Oldtown, 26 miles; Am. Ex.

HOWLAND PULP & PAPER CORP. (A. N. Blandin, Pres.; Geo. S. Lewis, Treas.; Edwin P. Lindsay, Sales Agent, 301 Congress St., Boston.) S. P., Enfield, Me. Two 1500-lb. Beating and one Refining engines. One 112-inch Fourdrinier. Widest trimmed sheet, 103 inches. Water and Electricity. Bag. 48,000 lbs. 24 hours. PULP MILL. S. P., Enfield. Six Sulphite and four Sulphate Digesters; four Wet Machines. Water and Steam. Sulphite Fibre. 80,000 lbs. 24 hours. Sulphate Fibre. 80,000 lbs. 24 hours.

LINCOLN—Penobscot Co.

Pop. 1,731. On M. C. RR. M. O. and Tel. office; Am. Ex.

EASTERN MANUFACTURING CO., KATAHDIN DIVISION. P. O. Address, 92 Exchange St., Bangor, Me. Eastern Office, 501 Fifth Avenue. Western Office, Chicago. (F. R. Ayer, Pres.; S. W. Webb, Chairman; F. A. Leahy, Vice-Pres.; S. B. Copeland, Vice-Pres.; H. J. Guild, Vice-Pres.; D. A. Crocker, Vice-Pres.; Geo. E. Hyde, Sec. and Treas.) PAPER MILL. S. P., Lincoln, Me. Six 1400-lb. Beaters and two Refining engines. One 112-inch Fourdrinier. Widest trimmed sheet, 102 inches. Steam and Electric. Union Screens. Sulphite Papers and White Paper Specialties. 50,000 lbs. 24 hours. SULPHITE (KATAHDIN) MILL. S. P., Lincoln, Me. Seven Digesters; one 112-inch Drying Machine and one 84-inch Wet Machine. Steam and Electric. Dry Sulphite Fibre. 100,000 lbs. 24 hours.

LISBON FALLS—Androscoggin Co.

Pop. 3,603. On A. Div. of M. C. RR. M. O. and Tel. office; Am. Ex.

PEJEPSCOT PAPER CO. LISBON FALLS MILL. S. P., siding at mill. Five 1000-lb. and one 800-lb. Beating and three Jordan engines; one 84-inch and one 104-inch Fourdriniers. Widest trimmed sheet, 94 inches. Water, Electricity and Steam. News. 100,000 lbs. 24 hours. PULP MILL. S. P., siding at mill. Four Digesters; four Wet Machines. Water. Sulphite Fibre. 70,000 lbs. 24 hours.

LIVERMORE FALLS—Androscoggin Co.—PULP MILL.

Pop. 791. On Androscoggin Branch of M. C. RR. M. O. and Tel. office; Am. Ex.

INTERNATIONAL PAPER CO. Office, 30 Broad Street, New York. LIVERMORE MILL. Wm. A. Murray, Supt. Sixteen Grinders. Ground Wood. 180,000 lbs. 24 hours.

MADISON—Somerset Co.

Pop. 3,879. Maine Central RR. M. O. and Tel. office; Am. Ex.

GREAT NORTHERN PAPER CO. (Garrett Schenck, Pres.; William A. Whitcomb, Vice-Pres. and Gen. Mgr.; H. Merton Joyce, Treas.; Bryan L.

National Duplex Waterproof Case Lining
IS WATERPROOF—
CLEAN TO HANDLE **NATIONAL WATERPROOFING CO.,** 1054 DREXEL BLDG. PHILADELPHIA

Paper and Pulp Mills in the United States

Seelye, Clerk and Auditor; W. C. Powers, Manager of Sales.) New York office, 30 East 42d street. MADISON MILL. S. P., at mill. Six 1000-lb. Beating engines; two 136-inch Fourdriniers. Widest trimmed sheet, 120 inches. Water. News and Bag Paper. 140,000 lbs. 24 hours. PULP MILL. MADISON MILL. Ten Digesters; eight Grinders; four "Improved" Rotary Screens, and two "Impco" Knotters. Water. Sulphite Fibre and Ground Wood. Mitscherlich Sulphite Fibre 120,000 lbs. and Ground Wood 80,000 lbs. 24 hours.

HOLLINGSWORTH & WHITNEY CO. ABENAQUIS MILL. Office, 185 Devonshire Street, Boston. (Waldo E. Pratt, Pres.; M. L. Madden, Vice-Pres.; Herbert E. Fales, Treas.) S. P., Madison. Water. Ground Wood. 250,000 lbs. 24 hours.

MECHANIC FALLS—Androscoggin Co.

Pop. 1,687. On P. Div. of G. T. and M. C. RR. M. O., Tel. office and bank; Am. Merchants' and Can. Ex.

POLAND PAPER CO. (F. D. True, Pres.; O. B. Merrill, Treas., Secy. and Mgr.) S. P., at mill. Fourteen 1000-lb. and two 1500-lb. and four Refining Beating engines; one 68-inch, one 88-inch and two 90-inch Fourdriniers. Width of Super-Calenders, up to 64 inches. Water and Steam. Book, Bond, Ledger and Writing. 80,000 lbs. 24 hours.

MILLINOCKET—Penobscot Co.

Pop. 3,500. B. & A. RR. M. O. and Tel. office; Millinocket Trust Co.; Am. Ex.

GREAT NORTHERN PAPER CO. (Garret Schenck, Pres.; William A. Whitcomb, Vice-Pres. and Gen. Mgr.; H. Merton Joyce, Treas.; Bryan L. Seelye, Clerk and Auditor; W. C. Powers, Manager of Sales.) New York office, 30 East 42d street. MILLINOCKET MILL. S. P., at mill. Sixteen 1500-lb. engines; eight 152-inch and two 168-inch Fourdriniers and one 84-inch Cylinder. Widest trimmed sheet, 146 inches. Water. News. 900,000 lbs. and 40,000 Wrappers 24 hours. PULP MILL. S. P., at mill. Sixty Grinders; seven Digesters; six "Impco" Knotters. Water. Ground Wood and Sulphite. 720,000 lbs. 24 hours.

NEWHALL—Cumberland Co.—PULP MILL.

Pop. 216. On M. C. RR. M. O. and Tel. office; Ex. So. Windham, 1 mile; bank at Gorham, 4 miles.

DU PONT DE NEMOURS, E. I., & CO. P. O. Address, South Windham, Me. (Sales office, Wilmington, Del.; N. I. Steers, Wilmington, Del., Mgr.) Eight Grinders. Water. Ground Wood for Dynamite and Linoleoum. 75,000 lbs. 24 hours.

OLDTOWN—Penobscot Co.—PULP MILL.

Pop. 3,000. On B. & A.; M. C. RR. M. O. and Tel. office; Am. Ex.

NEKONEGAN PAPER CO. (J. Fred Webster, Pres.; Alden P. Webster, Sec. and Treas.) S. P., at mill. Eight Grinders; six Wet Machines. Water. Ground Wood. 80,000 lbs. 24 hours.

ORONO—Penobscot Co.

Pop. 3,257. On M. C. RR. M. O. and Tel. office; nearest bank, Bangor, 10 miles; Am. Ex.

INTERNATIONAL PAPER CO. Office, 30 Broad street, New York. WEBSTER MILL. Location, Orono, Me. (F. E. King, Supt.) S. P.,

---

E. J. KELLER CO., INC. 280 FIFTH AVENUE, E. J. KELLER, Pres., NEW YORK FOREIGN AND DOMESTIC **Wood Pulp and Rag Pulp** Gunny Bagging, Burlap Bagging, Ropes, Flax, Linen and Cotton Wastes, Paper Stock, Rags.

R. B. McEwan, Prest.   J. L. McEwan, Vice-Prest.   Arthur McEwan, Treas. and Mgr.   R. W. McEwan, Secy.
Sheet Lining Plant, Office and Mills at WHIPPANY, N. J.
McEWAN BROS., Inc. MANUFACTURERS OF ALL GRADES **PAPER BOX BOARD**

DRY ROSIN SIZE Brittle, easy soluble, cheapest size out; cheaper than mill made size. Ask us about it. Also all other grades. **ARABOL M'F'G CO.** 100 William St., N.Y.

98   *Maine*

Webster Station. Two 1000-lb., two 1400-lb. and two Jordan engines; one 96-inch and one 110-inch Fourdriniers. Water and Steam. News. 56,000 lbs. 24 hours. PULP MILL. Three Grinders; three Wet Machines. Water and Steam. Ground Wood. 60,000 lbs. 24 hours.

ORONO PULP & PAPER CO. (Charles F. Bragg, Pres.; Geo. E. Crafts, Treas.) P. O. Address, Bangor, Orono Mill. Location, Basin Mills. S. P., Basin Mills. Fourteen Beating and four Jordan engines, one 98-inch, one 100-inch and one 110-inch Fourdrinier. Hydro Electric. Bag, Wrapping Kraft, Tissue and Specialties, basis 24x36—10 to 150. 120,000 lbs. 24 hours. Also Sulphite Fibre. We make a specialty of extra strong, clean Sulphite Papers, for all purposes where such a paper is desired. PULP MILL. P. O. Address, Bangor. S. P., at mill. Five Digesters; three Wet Machines. Hydro Electric. Sulphite Fibre. 100,000 lbs. 24 hours.

UNIVERSITY OF MAINE PAPER & PULP SCHOOL. (Prof. Charles W. Easley in General Charge. PAPER MILL. (Chemical Bldg.) Hand Moulds. Widest trimmed sheet, 7 inches. Electricity. Rag and Sulphite Papers. 15 lbs. 24 hours. PUMP MILL. (Chemical Bldg.) Two Sulphite and one Soda Digesters. Electricity. Soda Fibre 20 lbs. and Sulphite Fibre 300 lbs. 24 hours.

RILEY—Franklin Co.—PULP MILL.
Pop. 175. M. C. RR. M. O., Riley; Ex. office, Jay, 2 miles; Tel. and nearest bank, Livermore Falls, 4 miles.

INTERNATIONAL PAPER CO. Office, 30 Broad street, New York. RILEY MILL. Wm. A. Murray, Supt. S. P., at mill. Twenty-one Grinders; seventeen Wet Machines. Water and Steam. Ground Wood. 160,000 lbs. 24 hours.

RUMFORD—Oxford Co.
Pop. 8,770. On M. C. RR. M. O. and Tel. office; Am. Ex.

INTERNATIONAL PAPER CO. Office, 30 Broad street, New York. RUMFORD FALLS MILL. P. E. McCarthy, Supt. S. P., at mill. Twenty-six Beating and eleven Refining engines; one 85-inch, one 98-inch, one 107-inch, one 109-inch, one 119-inch, two 124-inch, one 134-inch, one 153-inch Fourdriniers. Water and Steam. Manila, Kraft, Screenings and M. G. Fibre. 378,000 lbs. 24 hours. PULP MILL. Sixteen Grinders; eight Digesters; twenty-one Wet Machines. Water and Steam. Ground Wood, 180,000 lbs. Sulphite Fibre, 240,000 lbs. 24 hours.

OXFORD PAPER CO. Office, 200 Fifth Avenue, New York. (H. J. Chisholm, Pres.; L. M. Bickford, Vice-Pres. and Gen. Mgr.; F. E. Tufts, Treas.; J. H. Drummond, Sec.; J. W. Harris, Mill Mgr.) Fifty-eight 1800-lb. Beating and ten Refining engines; one 87-inch, one 89-inch, one 118-inch, one 128-inch, two 138-inch, one 146-inch, one 148-inch and two 152-inch Fourdriniers. Widest trimmed sheets, one 77 inches, one 79 inches, one 108 inches, one 117 inches, two 126 inches, one 134 inches, one 136 inches, two 140 inches. Four 48-inch, three 60-inch, five 72-inch, one 76-inch and two 80-inch Super Calenders. Steam, Water and Electric. Super Calender Machine Finish Book and Paper for Coating. 500,000 lbs.

PRESS ROLLS   Maple and Gum White Wood Felt Rolls   **J. W. HEWITT MACHINE CO.** Neenah, Wis.

THOMAS E. GLEESON, Inc., 411-413 John St., E. NEWARK, N. J.
CYLINDER MOULDS and DANDY ROLLS Made and Repaired
LETTERING and MONOGRAMS for WATERMARKS

Paper and Pulp Mills in the United States 99

24 hours. PULP MILLS. S. P., at mill. Seven Soda and three Sulphite Digesters, 124-inch Drying Machine, three Sulphite Digesters, six Wet Machines. Steam, Water and Electric. Soda Pulp, 275,000 lbs.; Sulphite Pulp, 220,000 lbs. 24 hours. Makes own Bleach.

SHAWMUT—Somerset Co.—PULP MILL.
Pop. 205. On S. Br. of M. C. RR. M. O. and Tel. office; Am. Ex.

SHAWMUT MANUFACTURING CO. P. O. Address, Fairfield, Me. (R. Pagenstecher, Pres. and Treas.; G. Pagenstecher, Sec., New York; G. M. Stearns, Vice-Pres. and Gen. Mgr., Shawmut, Me.) S. P., at mill. Five Wet Machines. Water. Ground Wood. 50,000 lbs. 24 hours. (Idle.)

SKOWHEGAN—Somerset Co.
Pop. 5,810. On M. C. RR. M. O. and eTl. Office; Am. xE.

SAVAGE MANUFACTURING CO. (C. E. Savage, Pres.; J. O. Savage, Vice-Pres.; E. L. Savage, Treas.) S. P., station one block from mill. Three 1500-lb. Patent Double Roll Beating Engines; one Washing and one Refining Engine; one 90-inch Cylinder Machine. Widest trimmed sheet, 81 inches. Water and Steam. Cheviot, Felt and Specialties in colors. 6000 lbs. 24 hours. (Mill destroyed by fire February 8, 1916. Expected to be in operation November 1, 1918.)

SKOWHEGAN PULP CO. (John R. McClellan, Pres.; B. W. Page, Treas.; Charles E. Young, Supt.) Three Grinders; four 72-inch Wet Machines. Water. Ground Wood. 40,000 lbs. 24 hours. (Power sold to Central Maine Power Co., but mill has right to complete present contracts expiring Dec. 31, 1918.)

SOLON—Somerset Co.—PULP MILL.
Pop. 700. On S. RR. M. O. and Tel office; nearest bank, Madison, 11 miles; Am. Ex.

INTERNATIONAL PAPER CO. Office, 30 Broad Street, New York. SOLON MILL, six Grinders, nine Wet Machines. Water and Steam. Ground Wood. 90,000 lbs. 24 hours.

SOUTH WINDHAM—Cumberland Co.
Pop. 1,309. On M. C. R. R. M. O. and Tel. office; nearest bank, Gorham, 4 miles; Am. Ex.

ANDROSCOGGIN PULP COMPANY, 50 State Street, Boston, Mass. (Dudley P. Rogers, Pres.; Geo. H. Clough, Treas.; E. L. Rantoul, Sec. and Clerk.) WINDHAM MILL. S. P., at mill. Twelve 1500-lb. Beating and eight Refining engines; two 72-inch Five Cylinder and one 120-inch Six Cylinder. Widest trimmed sheet, 110 inches. Union Screens. Water and Steam. Wood Pulp Board. 160,000 lbs. 24 hours. PULP MILL. S. P., siding at mill. Seven Grinders; five Wet Machines. Water. Ground Wood. 50,000 lbs. 24 hours.

STEEP FALLS—Cumberland Co.—PULP MILL.
Pop. 400. White Mt. Div. M. C. RR. Am Ex.

ANDROSCOGGIN PULP COMPANY. Office, 50 State Street, Boston, Mass. (Dudley P. Rogers, Pres.; Geo. H. Clough, Treas.; E. L. Rantoul, Sec. and Clerk.) S. P., at mill. Six Grinders, five Wet Machines. Water. Ground Wood. 80,000 lbs. 24 hours.

M. GOTTESMAN & CO., Inc., 18 E. 41st STREET, NEW YORK. Cable Address "Namettor" EUROPEAN OFFICES: Stockholm, Sweden. BLEACHED and UNBLEACHED **WOOD PULP OF ALL KINDS**

BRIMSTONE MAKES THE VERY BEST SULPHITE.
If you are looking for a high-grade Brimstone write to
THE UNION SULPHUR CO., Main Office, 17 Battery Pl., New York. Mines, Calcasieu Parish, La.

851648

DRY ROSIN SIZE Brittle, easy soluble, cheapest size out; cheaper than mill made size. Ask us about it. Also all other grades. **ARABOL M'F'G CO.** 100 William St., N. Y.

Maine and Maryland

VAN BUREN—Aroostook Co.—PULP MILL.

Pop. 3,500. On Bangor & Aroostook RR. M. O., bank, Tel. and Am. Ex.

AROOSTOOK PULP AND PAPER CO. (Selling Agent, Edwin P. Lindsay, 301 Congress Street, Boston, Mass.; Amos N. Blandin, Pres.; Robert F. Herrick, Vice-Pres.; George S. Lewis, Treas.) Four Digesters; four Wet Machines. Steam. Sulphate Pulp. 100,000 lbs. 24 hours.

WEST ENFIELD—Penobscot Co.—PULP MILL.

Pop. 389. On M. C. RR. Tel. office, Enfield; Am. Ex., Enfield; M. O.; nearest bank, Oldtown, 23 miles.

INTERNATIONAL PAPER CO. Office, 30 Broad Street, New York. WEST ENFIELD MILL. P. O. Address, West Enfield. Eleven Grinders. Eight Wet Machines. Water. Ground Wood. 70,000 lbs. 24 hours.

WINSLOW—Kennebec Co.

Pop. 2,277. On M. C. RR. M. O. office; Tel. office and nearest bank, Waterville, 1 mile; Am. Ex.

HOLLINGSWORTH & WHITNEY CO. (Waldo E. Pratt, Pres.; M. L. Madden, Vice-Pres.; H. E. Fales, Treas.) Address, Boston, Mass.; 111 W. Washington Street, Chicago, and 299 Broadway, New York. TACONNET MILL. S. P., Winslow. Four 136-inch and two 158-inch Fourdriniers. Water, Electricity and Steam. Fine Manilas, Fibres, Writings, white and colors, Special Papers and Waxed Papers. 470,000 lbs. 24 hours. ALGONQUIN SULPHITE MILL. Water, Steam and Electricity. Sulphite Fibre. 270,000 lbs. 24 hours. (See advertisement in back of Directory.)

WOODLAND—Washington Co.

Pop. 800. On Wash. Co. Div. of Maine Central RR. Am. Ex.; M. O. and Tel. office; nearest bank, Calais, 10 miles.

ST. CROIX PAPER CO. (I. B. Hosford, Pres.; John A. Davis, Vice-Pres.; Arthur L. Hobson, Treas.; John S. Reed, Asst. Treas.; Thompson Smith, Gen. Mgr.; L. J. Parant, Gen. Supt.) Boston office, 244 Washington street. S. P., at mill. Eight Beating and three Jordans. One 158-inch and two 166-inch Fourdriniers. Water, Steam and Electricity. News, 250,000 lbs., bag, 40,000 lbs. 24 hours. PULP MILL. S. P., at mill. Twenty-two Grinders; two Digesters; fifteen Wet Machines; five "Impco" Screens and three "Impco" Knotters. Water, Steam and Electricity. Ground Wood, 290,000 lbs.; Sulphite Fibre, 120,000 lbs. 24 hours.

YARMOUTH—Cumberland Co.—PULP MILL.

Pop. 2,400. On G. T.; M. C. RR. M. O. and Tel. office; nearest bank, Portland, 11 miles; Am. Ex.

FOREST PAPER CO. (S. D. Warren Co., Boston, Mass., Owners.) (Frederic E. Gore, Mgr.) S. P., at mill. Five Digesters; one 62-inch and one 118-inch Dry Machines. Water and Steam. Soda Fibre (dry), 160,000 lbs. 24 hours.

MARYLAND.

ASBESTOS—Carroll Co.

Pop. 100. On West Md. RR. Tel., nearest bank, Reistertown, 3 miles; Am. Ex.

BALTIMORE ROOFING & ASBESTOS MFG. CO. (R. M. Nichols, Pres.; O. R. Emigh, Vice-Pres. and Gen. Mgr.; H. M. Nichols, Vice-Pres.;

LOMBARD'S ENGLISH NEWCASTLE PULP STONES ARE SUPERIOR TO ALL OTHERS. ALL SIZES IN STOCK. LOMBARD & CO., Importers & Manufacturers, 236 & 238 A Street, Boston.

National Duplex Waterproof Case Lining
IS WATERPROOF— NATIONAL WATERPROOFING CO., 1064 DREXEL BLDG.
CLEAN TO HANDLE PHILADELPHIA

Paper and Pulp Mills in the United States 101

Wm. B. James, Sec.; H. F. Krathge, Pur. Agt.) "BRAMCO" MILL. S. P., at mill. Twelve 1500-lb. Beating engines; one 82 and one 120-inch Cylinders; five Wet Machines. Widest sheet, 108 inches. Steam and Electricity. Asbestos Paper and Asbestos Millboard, Saturating and Dry Felts, Building Paper, Carpet Lining. Asbestos Paper, 80,000 lbs.; Wool Felt 50,000 lbs. 24 hours. The company also has a complete roofing plant attached. *Asbestos Paper, Asbestos Millboard, Ready Roofings, Asphalt and Coal Tar Products, Asbestos Cement and Pipe Coverings.*

BALTIMORE—Baltimore Co.

CHESAPEAKE PAPERBOARD CO. (J. E. Smith, Pres. and Gen. Mgr.; H. B. Wilcox, Vice-Pres.; S. W. Tschudi, Treas.; J. H. Dew, Sec.; Thomas F. Webb, Supt.; J. B. Beale, Sales Mgr.) S. P., at mill. One 62-inch Beloit, forty-nine Dryers; five 1000-lb. Beating and two Jordan engines. Widest trimmed sheet, 57 inches. Steam. Plain Chip Board, Mill-lined Chip Board, Single Manila Lined Chip and News Board. 50,000 lbs. 24 hours.

BENTLEY'S SPRINGS—Baltimore Co.

Pop. 100. On N. C. RR. M. O. and Adams Ex., Bentley's Springs, Md.; nearest bank and Tel. office, Parkton, Md. C. & P. Telephone, Parkton, 3—2.

YOUNG, DANIEL & JAMES B. (Herman D. Young, Pres.) S. P., Bentley's Springs, ½ mile. EAGLE MILL. Two 500-lb. Beating engines; two Washers and one Rotary. One 48-inch Double Cylinder. Widest trimmed sheet, 40 inches. Water and Steam. Rag Wrapping. 8000 lbs. 24 hours.

YOUNG, JOSEPH W., VALLEY MILL. P. O. Address, Freelands. S. P., at mill. Two 300-lb. Beating engines; one 48-inch Machine. Widest trimmed sheet, 40 inches. Gray Wrapping. 4000 lbs. 24 hours.

CHESTERTOWN—Kent Co.

Pop. 3,008. On K. C.; S. & D. B. RR. M. O. and Tel. office; Adams and U. S. Ex.

AMERICAN STRAW BOARD CO. Executive Office, Akron, Ohio. CHESTERTOWN MILL. (W. D. Bennett, Mgr.) S. P., at mill. Six 800-lb., one 1000-lb. and two Jordan engines; one 72-inch Cylinder. Widest sheet made, 66 inches. Steam Dried Straw Board, Plain, Mill Lined and Sheet Lined. 40,000 lbs. 24 hours.

CHILDS—Cecil Co.

Pop. 150. On B. & O. RR. Tel. office; M. O., Childs; nearest bank, Elkton, 4 miles; Wells Fargo & Co. Ex.

MARLEY PAPER MFG. CO., successor to Marley Mills Corporation. MARLEY MILLS. (J. E. Smith, Pres.; C. S. Garrett, Supt.) S. P., at mill. Philadelphia Office, 122 South 13th Street. Five 1000-lb. Beating and one Jordan engines; one 96-inch Harper Fourdrinier. Widest trimmed sheet, 84 inches. Water and Steam. Wood Tissues and Towels. 24,000 lbs. 24 hours.

ELKTON—Cecil Co.—PULP MILL.

Pop. 3,000. On Phila., Balt. & Wash. RR. M. O., Tel.; Bank; Ad. Ex.

JESSUP & MOORE PAPER CO., THE. (Eugene W. Fry, Pres.; E. A. Weihenmayer, Vice-Pres.; Wm. D. Heebner, Treas.; W. H. Clark, Sec.)

R. B. McEwan, Prest. J. L. McEwan, Vice-Prest. Arthur McEwan, Treas. and Mgr. R. W. McEwan, Secy.
Sheet Lining Plant, Office and Mills at WHIPPANY, N. J.
McEWAN BROS., Inc. MANUFACTURERS OF ALL GRADES **PAPER BOX BOARD**

DRY ROSIN SIZE Brittle, easy soluble, cheapest size out; cheaper than mill made size. Ask us about it. Also all other grades. **ARABOL M'F'G CO.** 100 William St., N. Y.

Maryland

Offices 16 S. Broad Street, Philadelphia, Pa.; and 50 E. 42d Street, New York City. PULP MILL-RADNOR MILLS. Eight Digesters; three Wet Machines; one Dry Machine. Steam. Soda Fibre. 90,000 lbs. 24 hours.

FREELAND—Baltimore Co.

Pop. 40. On Baltimore Div. of N. C. RR. M. O. and nearest bank, Parkton, Md., 4 miles; Adams Ex.

GORE, H. M. ANDOVER MILL. S. P., Freeland. One 250-lb. Beating engine; one Jordan engine; one 44-inch Cylinder. Widest trimmed sheet, 36 inches. Water and Steam. Manila and Rag Wrapping. 3500 lbs. 24 hours. ☉

HAGERSTOWN—Washington Co.

Pop. 13,591. On N. & W.; B. & O.; C. V.; W. M. RR. M. O. and Tel. office; Adams and U. S. Ex.

ANTIETAM PAPER CO. (J. Elsworth Stonebraker, Pres.; W. B. Littleton, Vice-Pres. and Gen. Mgr.; S. George White, Treas.; John E. Stonebraker, Jr., Sec.) ANTIETAM MILL. S. P., switch at mill. Seven 450-lb. and one Jordan engines; one 62-inch Fourdrinier. Width of Super-Calenders, 50 inches. Widest trimmed sheet, 58 inches. Water and Steam. Machine Finished and Super-Calendered Book. 8000 lbs. 24 hours

LUKE—Allegany Co.

Pop. 1,100. On W. M. and B. & O. RR. M. O. Tel. office and nearest bank, Piedmont, W. Va., ½ mile. Wells Fargo Ex.

WEST VIRGINIA PULP AND PAPER CO. (John G. Luke, Pres.; David L. Luke, Vice-Pres.; Thomas Luke, Vice-Pres.; Adam K. Luke, Treas.; Chas. A. Cass, Sec.; Allan L. Luke, Res. Mgr.) Office, 200 Fifth avenue, New York. Western Sales Office, 732 Sherman Street, Chicago. Sixteen 1000-lb., twelve 1800-lb. and fourteen 2500-lb. Umpherson Beating and twelve Refining engines; one 92-inch, one 102-inch, one 110-inch, one 116-inch, one 136-inch, one 142-inch and one 152-inch Fourdrinier. Union Screens. Widest trimmed sheet, 138 inches. Width of Super-Calenders, 52, 62, 66, 72 and 86 inches. Steam. Super-Calendered and Machine Finished Book, Envelope and White Writing, Lithograph and Varnish Label and Blank Book Papers. 275,000 lbs. 24 hours. PULP MILL. Five Digesters; one 84-inch Wet, one 90-inch Dry Machines. Steam. Bleached Soda Fibre. 150,000 lbs. 24 hours. Coating Plant: One Single and five Double Coaters. Coated Book, Litho and Lithograph Label. 40 tons 24 hours.

PARKTON—Baltimore Co.

Pop. 60. On Baltimore Div. of N. C. RR. M. O. Tel. office; nearest bank, Cockeysville, 14 miles; Adams Ex.

GUNPOWDER PAPER MILL. (Levin Mitchell Estate. L. Mitchel.) S. P., at mill. Two 300-lb. and one 500-lb. engines; one 48-inch Cylinder. Water. Gray Wrapping and Butchers' Manila. 3000 lbs. 24 hours. (Idle.)

PROVIDENCE—Cecil Co.

Pop. 50. Five miles from Elkton. M. O., Tel., Ex. and nearest bank, Elkton.

JESSUP & MOORE PAPER CO., THE. (Eugene W. Fry, Pres.; E. A. Weihenmayer, Vice-Pres.; Wm. D. Heebner, Treas.; W. H. Clark, Sec.) Offices, 16 So. Broad Street, Philadelphia, Pa., and 50 E. 42d Street, New

PRESS ROLLS Maple and Gum White Wood Felt Rolls **J. W. HEWITT MACHINE CO.** Neenah, Wis.

THOMAS E. GLEESON, Inc., 411-413 John St., E. NEWARK, N. J. — **FOURDRINIER WIRES** For Tissue and Fine Grade Papers

Paper and Pulp Mills in the United States

York City. **KENMORE MILLS.** Thirteen Beating engines and six Refining engines; two 86-inch, one 96-inch and one 110-inch Fourdriniers. Widest trimmed sheet, 100 inches. Width of Calenders, 72 inches. Steam. Book and Specialties ("*Old English*" *Laid;* "*Kenmore*" *Deckle Edge*). 85,000 lbs. 24 hours.

RISING SUN—Cecil Co.
Pop. 500. On Central Div. P. B. & W. RR. Tel. and Adams Ex.

CECIL MILL. Until recently leased by Nixon & Costello Co., but now given up. (Idle.)

ROWLANDVILLE—Cecil Co.
Pop. 300. On C. Div. P. B. & W. RR. M. O. and Tel. office; nearest bank, Port Deposit or Rising Sun, 5 miles. Ad. Ex.

FELT PAPER COMPANY, THE. (John W. Moore, Owner.) S. P., at mill. Seven 1000-lb. Beating and one Refining engines; one 86-inch Cylinder. Widest trimmed sheet, 76 inches. Water and Steam. Deadening and Dry Saturating Felt. 36,000 lbs. 24 hours.

WHITE HALL—Baltimore Co.
Pop. 200. On N. C. RR. M. O., Tel. office, bank and Adams Ex.

NIXON & COSTELLO CO., Successors to Fibre Fabric Corporation. (Maurice Costello, Pres.; R. M. Costello, Vice-Pres.; M. B. Costello, Sec. and Treas.; Forbes Wood, Supt.) Two 1200-lb. Beating and one Refining engines; one 68-inch Three Cylinder Machine. Widest trimmed sheet, 58 inches. Water and Steam. Chip Wrapping. 20,000 lbs. 24 hours.

MASSACHUSETTS.
ADAMS—Berkshire Co.
Pop. 11,134. On B. & A. RR. M. O. and Tel. office; Am. Ex.

BERKSHIRE HILLS PAPER CO. (F. R. Shaw, Pres.; Noble B. Turner, Vice-Pres.; H. L. Harrington, Treas.; Chas. Champion, Supt.) Berkshire Co., 626 Federal Street, Chicago. S. P., Zylonite Station. Five 800-lb. and 1000-lb. Beating engines; three 1000-lb. and one 1500-lb. Washing engines; two Refining engines; one 80-inch and one 90-inch Fourdrinier, one Patented Hinging Machine for Making Loose Leaf Ledger. Widest trimmed sheet, 72 inches. Width of Calenders, 40 inches. Water and Steam. Ledgers, Bonds, Linens, Papeteries, Weddings, Index Bristols and Typewriter Paper. 24,000 lbs. 24 hours.

BROWN, L. L., PAPER CO. GREYLOCK PAPER MILLS (two mills). (Charles C. Jenks, Pres.; Arthur B. Daniels, Treas. and Mgr.; A. Millard Daniels, Gen. Supt.) UPPER MILL. Two 600-lb. Washing engines; two 900-lb. Washing engines; six 900-lb. Beating engines; one 64½-inch Fourdrinier Machine; one 77-inch Fourdrinier Machine. Widest trimmed sheets, 58 and 71 inches. Electricity and Water. 7500 lbs. 24 hours. LOWER MILL. Six 400-lb. Washing engines; five 800-lb. Beating engines; two 1000-lb. Beating engines; two 64½-inch Fourdrinier Machines. Widest trimmed sheets, 57 and 58 inches. Electricity and Water. 7500 lbs. 24 hours. (*Since 1850 these mills have made a specialty of Linen Ledger Papers for County Records, Merchants' and Bankers' Ledgers, Loose Leaf*

DRY ROSIN SIZE
Brittle, easy soluble. Cheapest, also cut; cheaper than mill made size. Ask us about it. Also all other grades.

ARABOL M'F'G CO.
100 William St., New York

THE UNION SULPHUR CO.
Main Office: 17 Battery Pl., New York. Mines: Calcasieu Parish, La.
Producers of **The Only Arsenic Free Sulphur on the Market**

Massachusetts

Systems, etc. Also manufacturers of All Linen, Typewriter, Bond, Bank Note and Parchment Papers of highest quality.

AMESBURY—Essex Co.

Pop. 8,543. On Portland Div. Boston & Maine RR. M. O., Tel., Bank. Am. and Adams Ex.

METALITE CO., THE. (Wm. R. Rogers, Pres.; Wm. Kinley, Vice-Pres.; Wm. E. Boykin, Sec.; James P. Rogers, Treas.; E. L. Perry, Supt.) Eight 2000-lb. Beating and two Refining engines; one Rotary boiler. One Dry and seven Wet Machines. Electricity. Shoe, Trunk and Container Fibre Board. 20,000 lbs. 24 hours.

BALDWINSVILLE—Worcester Co.

On Ware River Branch of B. & A.; Fitchburg Div. B. & M. RR. Tel. and M. O. office; nearest bank, Gardner and Winchendon, 6 miles each; Nat. Ex.

ADAMS, A. L., PAPER CO. (Alva L. Adams, Prop.; A. L. Adams, Mgr.; C. E. Adams, Supt.) S. P., at mill. Three 1000-lb. Beating and one Refining engines; one 74-inch Cylinder Machine. Widest trimmed sheet, 67 inches. Water and Steam. No. 2 White and Manila Crepe in Drum-Wound Rolls for Toilet Papers. 6000 lbs. 24 hours.

BANCROFT—Hampshire Co.

Pop. 210. On B. & A. RR. M. O. and Am. Ex.; Tel. office, Middlefield Station; nearest bank, Pittsfield.

UNION MILL. P. O. address, 75 Duane Street, New York. (D. G. Garabrant, Pres.; Jonathan Bulkley, Treas.) S. P., Middlefield. Three 1000-lb. and one 1500-lb. Beating engines; one 76-inch Fourdrinier. Widest sheet made, 70 inches. Water and Steam. Tissue. 6000 lbs. 24 hours.

BOSTON.

Pop. 688,136. On N. Y., N. H. & H. M. O. and Tel. office; Am. and Adams. Ex.

TILESTON & HOLLINGSWORTH CO. (Amor Hollingsworth, Pres.; E. H. Clapp, Vice-Pres. and Treas.; Arthur V. Howland, Asst. Treas.) S. P., Fairmount. Thirteen 1200-lb. Umpherston engines; one 76-inch, one 104-inch and one 120-inch Fourdriniers. Width of Super Calenders, 66 inches. Water and Steam. Book, Lithograph, Bible, Music, Half-Tone, Folder, Coating, Catalog, Card and Specialties. 75,000 lbs. 24 hours.

BRIDGEWATER—Plymouth Co.

Pop. 6,806. On O. C. System. N. Y., N. H. & H. RR. M. O. and Tel. office; Adams Ex.

JENKINS CO., GEORGE O. (Robert A. Jenkins, Pres.; Mrs. G. O. Jenkins, Vice-Pres. and Sec.; H. Loring Jenkins, Treas. and Mgr.; C. M. Greenfield, Supt.) S. P., 2 miles. Four 2000-lb. Beating and one Jordan engines; six Wet Machines. Water and Steam. Leather and "Heeling" Board. 36,000 lbs. 24 hours.

CAMBRIDGE, MASS.

Pop. 108,822. On Fitchburg and So. Div. M. & M. M. O. and Tel. office. Nat. and Am. Ex.

LITTLE, ARTHUR D., INC. Experimental Paper and Pulp Mill, 30 Charles River Road. (Arthur D. Little, Pres.; H. J. Skinner, Vice-Pres.; W. W. Caswell, Treas.; C. F. Woods, Sec.; D. E. Scott, Supt.) One 29-inch Combination Fourdrinier and Cylinder Machine. Widest trimmed sheet, 24 inches. Two 50-lb. Beating and one Jordan engines and two Digesters. Electricity. Experimental Work Only.

DALTON—Berkshire Co.

Pop. 3,500. On B. & A. RR. Tel. office; nearest bank, Pittsfield, 5 miles; Am. Ex.

BAY STATE MILL. (Zenas and W. Murray Crane.) S. P., Dalton, ¾ mile. Five 750-lb. Beating, two 750-lb. and one 1000-lb. Washing engines; one 80-inch Fourdrinier. Union Screens. Water, Steam and Electricity. Extra-fine Writing. 7500 lbs. 24 hours.

CRANE & CO. (F. G. & W. M., Zenas & W. M. Crane, Jr.) Two mills. PIONEER MILL. Ten 600-lb. engines; one 54-inch and one 66-inch Fourdriniers. Leith Walk Screens. Water and Steam. Bank Note, Parchment and Bond. 4500 lbs. 24 hours. GOVERNMENT MILL. S. P., Dalton. Fourteen 600-lb. engines; two 66-inch Fourdriniers. Water and Steam. Bank Note, Parchment and Bond. 6000 lbs. 24 hours.

OLD BERKSHIRE MILL. (Zenas and W. Murray Crane.) OLD BERKSHIRE MILLS. S. P., Dalton, ¾ mile. Four 800-lb. Beating engines; three 800-lb. Washers; one 80-inch Fourdrinier. Widest trimmed sheet, 48 inches. Water, Steam and Electricity. Superfine Writings and Pasted Bristols. 6000 lbs. 24 hours.

WESTON CO., BYRON. (Franklin Weston, Pres.; Philip Weston, Treas.) Two mills. DEFIANCE and CENTENNIAL. S. P., at mills. Fourteen 600-lb., two 1000-lb. and five 800-lb. engines; two 66-inch and one 84-inch Fourdriniers. Widest trimmed sheet, 56 inches. Water, Steam and Electricity. Byron Weston Co.'s Linen Ledger, B. W. Defiance Bond, Flexo Loose Leaf Ledger, Waverly Ledger and Typocount Linen Ledger Loose Leaf Papers. 15,000 lbs. 24 hours. *Twenty-four Medals have been awarded, including Highest Award at the World's Fair; California Midwinter Gold Medal; Trans Mississippi Gold Medal and Pan-American Gold Medal.*

DANVERS—Essex Co.

Pop. 9,814. On Portland Div. B. & M. RR. M. O., Tel., bank and Ex.

GENERAL FIBRE BOARD CO., successor to Danvers Leather Company. (Charles S. Beatty, Owner; T. H. Begin, Supt.) S. P., Danvers. Two 1500-lb. Beating and one Refining engines; two Cylinder Machines. Widest trimmed sheet, 46 inches. Steam. Leather Board, Counter, Shank and Veneer. 13,000 lbs. 24 hours.

EAST PEPPERELL—Middlesex Co.

On W. N. & P. Div. ; B. & M.; F. RR. M. O. and Tel. office; nearest bank, E. Pepperell; Am., Nat. and Morrill Ex.

NASHUA RIVER PAPER COMPANY. (George T. Keyes, Pres. and Treas.; C. W. Keyes, Vice-Pres. and Sec.) Two mills. PEPPERELL MILLS. S. P., at mills. Eight 500-lb., six 1200-lb., four 10-cwt Umpherston, two 2000-lb. Beating and seven Jordan engines; one 86-inch, one 91-inch, one 96-inch and one 123-inch Fourdriniers. Width of Super-Calenders up to 66 inches; Platers, 34x44. Water and Steam. Bond, Writing, High Grade Book and Specialties. 120,000 lbs. 24 hours. GROTON MILL.

DRY ROSIN SIZE Brittle, easy soluble, cheapest size out; cheaper than mill made size. Ask us about it. Also all other grades. **ARABOL M'F'G CO.** 100 William St., N. Y.

Massachusetts

Location, Groton Centre. One 1000-lb., two 1500-lb., one 6-cwt. Umpherston Beating and one Jordan engines; one 87-inch Fourdrinier. Water and Steam. Book and Specialties. 30,000 lbs. 24 hours.

ACME PAPER & PAPER BOX CO. (TRUST). (Charles E. Clute, Pres. and Gen. Mgr.; Denman Blanchard, Treas.; Edward H. Wilkins, Sec.) NISSITISSITT MILL. Two 500-lb. Beating engines; one 62-inch Three Cylinder. Widest trimmed sheet, 54 inches. Water and Steam. Mill and Bogus Wrappers, Egg Box, Cap Tube, Fire Works and Mailing Tube Board and Sheathing. 8000 lbs. 24 hours. (September 19, 1918, No. 1 now used as paper mill. Plant being demolished.)

EAST WALPOLE—Norfolk Co.

On P. Div. of N. Y., N. H., & H. RR. M. O. and Tel.; nearest bank, Norwood, 2 miles; Earle & Prew's Ex.

BIRD & SON, INC. (Charles S. Bird, Pres.; Philip R. Allen, Vice-Pres.; H. H. Miller, Sec. and Treas.; G. R. Wyman, Mfrg. Mgr.) S. P., at mill. Nineteen 1800-lb. Beating and ten Jordan engines; two 90-inch and one 120-inch Cylinders; one 90-inch Fourdrinier. Widest trimmed sheet, 112 inches. Water and Steam. Roofing, Building, Sheathing, Hardware, Wrapping, Insulating and Special Papers of all kinds. 220,000 lbs. 24 hours.

HOLLINGSWORTH & VOSE CO. Address, Boston. (Zackary T. Hollingsworth, Pres.; Charles Vose, Vice-Pres.; V. Hollingsworth, Treas.; Robert W. Lennox, Asst. Treas.) EAST WALPOLE MILL. On N. Y., N. H. & H. RR. S. P., at mill. Three 1500-lb., eighteen 1000-lb. Beating and three Refining engines; one 56-inch and one 110-inch Four Cylinders and one 90-inch Fourdrinier. Widest sheet made, 100 inches. Steam and Water. All grades Electric Insulating—Fourdrinier and Cylinder. Sand, Norfolk Towels, all and part Rope Tag, Pattern, Box Stay, Flour and Cement Sack, Jute Manila and Specialties. 50,000 lbs. 24 hours.

ERVING—Franklin Co.

Pop. 1,148. Fitchburg Div. B. & M. RR. Nearest bank, Orange; Nat. Ex.

ERVING PAPER MILLS. (Geo. C. Gill, Pres.; C. H. Waite, Treas.; Geo. I. Walker, Vice-Pres.; C. W. Whiting, Sec.) S P., at mill. Seven Beating and three Refining engines; one 36-inch and one 72-inch Cylinders. Widest trimmed sheets, 31 inches and 60 inches; one 100-inch Yankee Fourdrinier. Widest trimmed sheet, 90 inches. Water and Electricity. M. G., Carpet, Folded Tissue, Waxing and Tissue Specialties. 24,000 lbs. 24 hours.

FARLEY—Franklin Co.

Pop. 70. On Boston & Maine RR. Tel.; nearest bank, North Adams; Am. Ex.

LINDALE MILLS, Successors to The Farley Paper Co. General, Purchasing and Sales Offices, North Adams. (E. A. McMillian, Pres.; A. W. Chippendale, Treas.; E. Baker, Supt.) S. P., at mill. One 500-lb., four 800-lb. and two 1500-lb. Beating engines; one 74-inch Four Cylinder and one 88-inch Five Cylinder. Widest trimmed sheets, 68 and 79 inches. Hydro-Electric. Box Boards. 80,000 lbs. 24 hours.

PRESS ROLLS Maple and Gum White Wood Felt Rolls **J. W. HEWITT MACHINE CO.** Neenah, Wis.

THOMAS E. GLEESON, Inc., 411-413 John St., E. NEWARK, N. J.
CYLINDER MOULDS and DANDY ROLLS Made and Repaired
LETTERING and MONOGRAMS for WATERMARKS

Paper and Pulp Mills in the United States 107

FITCHBURG—Worcester Co.

Pop. 31,531. On F., Northern Div. of N. Y., N. H. & H. RR. M. O. and Tel. office; Am., Ad., Nat. and N. Y. & B. D. Ex.

CROCKER, BURBANK & CO. ASS'N. (Alvah Crocker, Pres. and Treas.; C. T. Crocker, Vice-Pres. and Asst. Treas.; Barto Crocker, Sec.) Eight mills. All located on Nashua River, 2 miles above Fitchburg. S. P., Wachusett Station, ¼ mile from six mills, 1 mile from two mills. Fourteen 1000-lb., fourteen 1200-lb. Beating and thirty-three Jordan engines; twenty-six Rotary boilers; one 72-inch, one 74-inch, one 100-inch and one 102-inch Cylinders; widest trimmed sheet, 66 and 92 inches; one 112-inch, one 125-inch, two 134-inch, and two 156-inch Fourdriniers. Widest trimmed sheets, 72 inches, 76 inches, 84 inches, 92 inches, 110 inches, 76 inches and 86 inches. Width of Super-Calenders: two 42, one 50, two 52, one 66, two 72 and one 100 inches. Union Screens. Water and Steam. Book, Bristol and Index Coating Paper. 500,000 lbs. 24 hours.

FALULAH PAPER CO. (Ernest P. Lowe, Pres.; Joseph A. Lowe, Treas.; Erving F. Lowe, Sec.) New York Office, 233 Broadway. Mill located at Fitchburg. Twelve 1200-lb. Beating and eight Jordan engines; one 96-inch Eight Cylinder and one 112-inch Eight Cylinder. Widest trimmed sheet, 100 inches. Union Screens. Water, Steam and Electricity. Coated Mill Blanks. 90,000 lbs. 24 hours.

FITCHBURG PAPER CO. (George R. Wallace, Pres. and Treas.) Mills Nos. I, II, III and IV. S. P., at mills. Six 600-lb., one 700-lb., two 800-lb., six 1000-lb., one 1400-lb., six 1500-lb. Beating and eight Jordan engines; one 76-inch, one 85-inch, three 90-inch and one 110-inch Fourdriniers. Widest trimmed sheet 102 inches. Union Screens. Water and Steam. Foundation stock for Glazing, Coating and Special Wall Papers. 140,000 lbs. 24 hours.

WHEELWRIGHT PAPER CO., GEO. W. (George W. Wheelwright, Jr., Pres. and Treas.; H. M. Wheelwright, Vice-Pres. & Clerk.; Wm. B. Page, Asst. Treas.; Wm. B. Page, Agt.) P. O. Address, 95 Milk Street, Boston. ROLLSTONE MILL. Location, Fitchburg Div. B. & M. RR. S. P., at mill. Seven rag engines; one 100-inch Fourdrinier. Water and Steam. Coating Paper. 24,000 lbs. 24 hours.

HAVERHILL—Essex Co.

Pop. 37,175. On B. & M. RR. M. O. and Tel. office; Am. Ex.

HAVERHILL BOX BOARD CO. (Crawford Fairbanks, Pres.; W. J. Alford, Vice-Pres.; Grant H. Fairbanks, Sec.-Treas.; Andrew Murlhead, Supt.) S. P., at mill. Eighteen 1200-lb. Beating and ten Jordan engines; one 90-inch, one 112-inch and one 126-inch Five Cylinders. Widest trimmed sheets, 81, 100 and 118 inches. Steam. Box Boards. 300,000 lbs. 24 hours.

HOLYOKE—Hampden Co.

Pop. 51,609. On C. R. Div. B. & M.; N. Y., N. H. & H. RR. M. O. and Tel. office. Adams and Am., Ex.

ADVERTISERS PAPER MILLS. (John F. Adee, Pres.; F. E. Taylor, First Vice-Pres.; R. A. Wright, Second Vice-Pres.; J. N. Hazen, Sec.; D.

SULPHUR—CRUDE. GUARANTEED 99% PURE.
The average analysis of our high-grade brimstone is in itself a guarantee. Write us for quotations.
THE UNION SULPHUR CO., Main Office, 17 Battery Pl., New York. Mines, Calcasieu Parish, La.

DRY ROSIN SIZE Brittle, easy soluble, cheapest size out; cheaper than mill made size. Ask us about it. Also all other grades. **ARABOL M'F'G CO.** 100 William St., N. Y.

LOMBARD'S ENGLISH NEWCASTLE PULP STONES ARE SUPERIOR TO ALL OTHERS. ALL SIZES IN STOCK. LOMBARD & CO., Importers & Manufacturers, 226 & 228 A Street, Boston.

108   Massachusetts

B. Logan, Treas.; C. H. Gardner, Asst. Treas.) Four 1000-lb. Beating engines; one special Vat Machine. Widest trimmed sheet, 60 inches. Electricity. Deckle Edge Covers, Texts and Vellum Papers. 8000 lbs. 24 hours. *Chippendale, Cloth-of-Gold, Advertisers, Aeolian, Antiquarian, Cadmus and Advertisers, Holyoke Covers, Holyoke Text, Broadcloth Papers.*

AMERICAN WRITING PAPER COMPANY. Organized under the laws of the State of New Jersey, July, 1899. General Offices, Holyoke, Mass.

OFFICERS.—George A. Galliver, Pres. and Gen. Mgr.; Henry Evans, Vice-Pres.; Raymond R. Campbell, Asst. to Pres. on Production; Harry W. Alexander, Asst. to Pres. on Sales; Forest R. Gee, Compt.; B. E. Hutchinson, Treas.; W. C. Wharfield, Asst. Treas.; Edwin S. Smith, Sec.; Michael N. Slotnick, Gen. Counsel; Martin L. Cramer, Gen. Purch. Agt.; William L. Plowman, Asst. Purch. Agt.; P. R. Browne, Auditor; Harry W. Anderson, Cost Accountant; Edward H. Frank, Traveling Auditor.

DEPARTMENT OF PRODUCTION. ————————, Gen. Supt. Machine Drying Mills; Arthur C. Gault, Asst. Gen. Supt.; Fred H. Sturtevant, Gen. Supt. Loft Drying Mills; William S. Brooks, Asst. Gen. Supt.; John Moles, Chief Eng.; Ross Campbell, Act. Mgr. Department of Research and Tests.

DEPARTMENT OF SALES.—Augustus C. Lamb, Gen. Sales Mgr.; Downer H. Newell, Asst. Gen. Sales Mgr.; John T. Wolohan, Mgr. Writing & Ledger Paper Section; James C. De Coster, Mgr. Papeterie & Book Paper Section; Charles B. Foster, Mgr. Specialties & Cover Paper Section; Richard C. Chapin, Mgr. Envelope Paper Section; Charles Drury Jacobs, Mgr. Drury Water Marked Paper Section; Lewis F. Hayward, Mgr. New York Br.; William B. Snyder, Mgr. Philadelphia Br.; James A. Lemmon, Mgr. Chicago Br.; Charles P. Armstrong, Mgr. San Francisco Br.; Frederick M. Webster, Mgr. Dept. of Adv.

BOARD OF DIRECTORS. *Term expiring* 1919.—J. K. Branch, Richmond, Va.; Geo. A. Galliver, Holyoke, Mass.; J. S. Gittins, De Pere, Wis.; T. A. Jones, Franklin, Ohio; Otto Marx, Birmingham, Ala.; Galen L. Stone, Boston, Mass.; G. W. Vaillant, Boston, Mass.

Term expiring 1920.—Henry Evans, New York, N. Y.; G. B. Holbrook, Springfield, Mass.; H. B. Lake, New York, N. Y.; M. E. Marcuse, Richmond, Va.; Edwin Packard, Brooklyn, N. Y.; C. J. Schmidlapp, New York, N. Y.; J. N. Wallace, New York, N. Y.

Term expiring 1921.—Walter T. Rosen, *Chairman,* New York, N. Y.; James D. Callery, Pittsburgh, Pa.; Parmely W. Herrick, Cleveland, Ohio; W. C. Loree, New York, N. Y.; F. M. Tait, New York, N. Y.; F. B. Van Vorst, Hackensack, N. J.

EXECUTIVE COMMITTEE.—Walter T. Rosen, *Chairman;* Henry Evans, G. B. Holbrook, H. B. Lake, M. E. Marcuse, Otto Marx, G. W. Vaillant, Geo. A. Galliver, *ex officio.*

ADVISORY COMMITTEE.—Walter T. Rosen, *Chairman;* Henry Evans, H. B. Lake, Otto Marx, George A. Galliver.

McEnery Paper Company Practically All Grades
Manufacturers' Sales Agency   112 W. ADAMS ST., CHICAGO

Paper and Pulp Mills in the United States

LIST OF PAPER MILLS OWNED BY COMPANY

Division.	Capacity Pounds per 24 hours.
Agawam Paper Co., Mittineague, Mass.	20,000
Albion Paper Co., Holyoke, Mass.	50,000
G. K. Baird Co., Lee, Mass.	3,000
Beebe & Holbrook Co., Holyoke, Mass.	50,000
Chester Paper Co., Huntington,, Mass.	6,000
Crocker Mfg. Co., Holyoke, Mass.	100,000
Geo. R. Dickinson Paper Co., Holyoke, Mass.	75,000
The Geo. C. Gill Paper Co., Holyoke, Mass.	80,000
Harding Paper Co., Franklin, Ohio	19,000
Holyoke Paper Co., Holyoke, Mass.	30,000
Hurlbut Paper Co., South Lee, Mass.	12,000
Linden Paper Co., Holyoke, Mass.	36,000
Mt. Tom Paper Co., Holyoke, Mass.	38,000
Nonotuck Paper Co., Holyoke, Mass.	75,000
Norman Paper Co., Holyoke, Mass.	70,000
Oakland Paper Co., Manchester, Conn.	12,000
Parsons Paper Co., Holyoke, Mass.	30,000
Platner & Porter Paper Mfg. Co., Unionville, Conn.	7,500
Riverside Paper Co., Holyoke, Mass., 1, 2, 3.	80,000
Shattuck & Babcock Co., De Pere, Wis.	40,000
Wauregan Paper Co., Holyoke, Mass.	24,000
Windsor Paper Co., Windsor Locks, Conn.	130,000

AMERICAN WRITING PAPER CO.—Albion Paper Company Division. S. P., Holyoke. Two 10-cwt. Umpherson, sixteen 1000-lb. Beaters and three Jordan engines; one 78-inch, one 84-inch and one 90-inch Fourdriniers. Width of Super-Calenders, 36 to 66 inches. Water and Steam. Offset, Book, Envelope and Writing. 50,000 lbs. 24 hours. *Extra Quality S. & S. C. Book, Half-Tone and English Finished Book.*

AMERICAN WRITING PAPER CO.—Beebe & Holbrook Company Division. Two mills. S. P., depot, 100 rods. Eight 600-lb., nine 1000-lb., three 1200-lb. and three 1500-lb. Beaters; three Jordans; two 84-inch and one 80-inch Fourdriniers. Water and Steam. Writing. 50,000 lbs. 24 hours. The MASSASOIT MILL has been consolidated with this division. *Wedding Folios, Calender and High Plate Finish, Bond, Linen and Ledger Papers, Government Bond, Government Record Ledger, Old Hempstead Bond, Indenture Bond.*

AMERICAN WRITING PAPER CO.—Crocker Manufacturing Company Division. S. P., at mill. Two 1000-lb., three 2000-lb., five 2500-lb. and four Marshall engines; one 48-inch, one 76-inch, one 96-inch Fourdriniers and one 107-inch M. G. Machine. Width of Super Calenders, 38 to 50 inches. Water and Steam. Book and Colored Mediums. 100,000 lbs. 24 hours. *Covers and Colored Specialties.*

AMERICAN WRITING PAPER CO.—George R. Dickinson Paper Company Division. S. P., at mill. Ten 1000-lb., eleven 2000-lb. Beaters and five Jordans; one 90-inch, one 88-inch and one 110-inch Fourdriniers. Width of Super Calenders, 36 to 56 inches. Water and Steam. Book and Envelope. 75,000 lbs. 24 hours.

AMERICAN WRITING PAPER CO.—The George C. Gill Paper Company Division. S. P., at mill. Six 2000-lb. Beaters and three Jordans;

one 152-inch Fourdrinier. Width of Super Calenders, 48 and 52 inches. Water and Steam. Book, Writing and Envelope. 80,000 lbs. 24 hours.

AMERICAN WRITING PAPER CO.—Holyoke Paper Company Division. S. P., at mill. Twenty 700-lb. Beaters; three Jordans; two 62-inch and one 84-inch Fourdriniers. Water. Writing. 30,000 lbs. 24 hours. *Security Trust Bond, American Linen and Linen Finished Papers.*

AMERICAN WRITING PAPER CO.—Linden Paper Company Division. S. P., Holyoke. Eleven 1500-lb. and two Marshall engines; two 98-inch Fourdriniers. Water and Steam. Pole-dried Writing, Bonds and Linen Ledgers. 36,000 lbs. 24 hours. *Map Paper a Specialty.*

AMERICAN WRITING PAPER CO.—Mt. Tom Paper Company Division. S. P., at mill. Nine 1200-lb., three 1500-lb. Beating and four Refining engines; one 80-inch and one 86-inch Fourdriniers. Width of Super Calenders, 30 to 42 inches. Water. Bonds, Ledgers and Writings. 38,000 lbs. 24 hours.

AMERICAN WRITING PAPER CO.—Nonotuck Paper Company Division. (S. P., at mill. Nine 1200-lb., three 1500-lb. Beating and three Jordan engines. Two 122-inch Fourdriniers. Width of Super-Calenders, 36 to 115 inches. Water. Offset, Book and Writing. 75,000 lbs. 24 hours.

AMERICAN WRITING PAPER CO.—Norman Paper Company Division. S. P., at mill. Ten 2000-lb. and three Marshall engines; one 86-inch and one 116-inch Fourdriniers. Width of Super-Calenders, 42 to 56 inches. Water and Steam. Writing, Sulphite Bonds and Envelope. 70,000 lbs. 24 hours.

AMERICAN WRITING PAPER CO.—Parsons Paper Company Division. MILL NO. 1. Ten 600-lb. and sixteen 700-lb. Beaters; three Jordans; two 66-inch and one 84-inch Fourdriniers. Water and Steam. Writing. 28,000 lbs. 24 hours. *White and Colored Envelope, Superfine White and Colored Writings, White and Colored Bristols.*

AMERICAN WRITING PAPER CO.—Riverside Paper Company Division. Seven spur tracks in yards from B. & M. and N. Y., N. H. & H. R. R. NO. 1. One Marshall and nine engines; one 72-inch and one 80-inch Fourdriniers. Water. Specialties. 12,000 lbs. 24 hours. NO. II. Twelve 1200-lb. and three Marshall engines; two 100-inch Fourdriniers. Width of sheet Calenders, 26, 30, 36, 38 and 40 inches. Water and Steam. Writing. 56,000 lbs. 24 hours. NO. III. Ten 750-lb. and one Marshall engines; one 62-inch and one 72-inch Fourdriniers. Steam and Water. Writing. 8000 lbs. 24 hours. *High Grade Specialty Papers.*

AMERICAN WRITING PAPER CO.—Wauregan Paper Company Division. WAUREGAN MILL. Location, Dwight Street. S. P., depot, ½ mile. Seven 1000-lb. and one Jordan engines; one 86-inch Fourdrinier. Width of Super-Calenders, 42 and 46 inches. Water. Writing and Bonds. 24,000 lbs. 24 hours. *Papeterie Papers and Colored Envelope.*

CHEMICAL PAPER MFG. CO. (C. A. Crocker, Pres.; R. F. McElwain, Vice-Pres.; S. S. Rogers, Vice-Pres. and Mgr.; S. L. Bush, Asst.

THOMAS E. GLEESON, Inc., **FOURDRINIER WIRES**
411-413 John St., E. NEWARK, N. J. For Tissue and Fine Grade Papers

Paper and Pulp Mills in the United States

Treas.; W. L. Nixon, Gen. Supt.) S. P., at mill. Nine 1000-lb., four 1200-lb. and one 1500-lb. Beating; eight Washing and eleven Jordan engines; four 1000-lb., two 1500-lb. and two 2000-lb. Washers; one 78-inch and two 84-inch Fourdriniers; one 72-inch and one 84-inch Cylinders. Width of Super-Calenders, 40 and 72 inches. Width of Sheet Calenders, 32 inches. Widest trimmed sheets, Cylinder 60 and 72 inches and Fourdrinier 68 and 72 inches. Water and Steam. Tub-sized Writing. Envelope, Papeterie, Bonds, Linens, Index Bristols and Covers, White and Colored Patent Coated Folding Box Boards, Silk Boards, White Blanks and Bristols, Cover and Specialties; Sphinx Bond, Cretonne Bond, Old Holyoke Bond and Cabinet Bond, all Linen Finished; also Specialties in Linen Finish, Climax Detail Drawing, No Protest Bond, Buyers Ledger, Interwoven Cover, Offset Paper and Bristol Mimeograph Paper, Manifold, Onion Skin, Uwanta Cover and Wicker Covers. 100,000 lbs. 24 hours.

CROCKER-McELWAIN CO. (C. A. Crocker, Pres. and Treas.; R. F. McElwain, 1st Vice-Pres.; Arthur H. Hill, 2d Vice-Pres.; Philip W. Gridley, Asst. Treas.; Walter E. Perry, Chicago Representative.) S. P., at mill. Twelve 1500-lb. Beating and two Refining engines; two 102-inch Fourdriniers. Width of Super-Calenders, 28, 36, 42 and 52 inches. Water. Loft-Dried and Machine-Dried Writings. 52,000 lbs. 24 hours. *"Bonds,"* *"Card Index Bristols." Envelope Paper.*

FRANKLIN PAPER CO. (James M. Ramage, Pres. and Treas.; A. B. Thorpe, Vice-Pres. and Supt.; Robt. A. Ramage, Sec.) S. P., siding at mill. Seven 500-lb. Beating and two Jordan engines; one 66-inch Cylinder. Widest trimmed sheet, 58 inches. Water and Steam. White and Colored Bristol Boards. White and Colored Index Bristols, National Post Card Bristol, Sample Card Bristol and White Blanks. 30,000 lbs. 24 hours.

NEWTON PAPER CO. (Henry L. Russell, Pres.; James H. Newton, Vice-Pres.; Herbert B. Newton, Sec. and Treas.; James Wright, Supt.) Four 1000-lb., twelve 1200-lb. Beating and two Jordan engines; sixteen Washers, three Rotary Boilers; one 42-inch, one 58-inch and one 64-inch Cylinders. Widest trimmed sheets, 36 inches, 50 inches and 59½ inches. Water and Steam. Carpet Lining, Sheathing, Deadening, Mill Wrapping, Felt, Jute, Manila, Duplex and Specialties. 50,000 lbs. 24 hours. *"Medal Brand" Blue Corrugated Carpet Lining Felt, "Elegant Brand" 12 Square Sheathing.*

PARSONS PAPER CO. (Aaron Bagg, Jr., Pres.; Edward P. Bagg, Treas.; Charles P. Randall, Asst. Treas.; Aaron C. Bagg, Sec.) Sergeant Street. S. P., at mill. Thirteen 1000-lb. and nine 1200-lb. engines; one 68-inch, one 84-inch and one 98-inch Fourdriniers. Widest trimmed sheet, 68 inches. Water and Steam. Bonds, Ledgers, Bristols and Linens. 22,000 lbs. 24 hours.

TAYLOR-LOGAN CO. PAPERMAKERS. (John F. Adie, Pres.; F. E. Taylor, First Vice-Pres.; R. A. Wright, Second Vice-Pres.; D. B. Logan, Treas.; J. N. Hazen, Sec.; C. H. Gardner, Asst. Treas.) Office, Fifth Avenue Building, New York S. P., at mill. One 700-lb. and five 1000-lb. Beating and one Jordan engines; one 66-inch Fourdrinier. Widest trimmed sheet,

DRY ROSIN SIZE

Brittle, easy soluble. Cheapest size out; cheaper than mill made sizes. Ask us about it. Also all other grades.

ARABOL M'F'G CO.
100 William St., New York

HIGHEST GRADE BRIMSTONE—GUARANTEED 99% PURE
free from Arsenic or Selenium. Write for particulars to
THE UNION SULPHUR CO., Main Office, 17 Battery Pl., New York. Mines, Calcasieu Parish, La.

Massachusetts

59 inches. Water, Steam and Electricity. Bond. 10,000 lbs. 24 hours. *"Mail Order Bond," "Public Service Bond," "Royal Mail Bond," "Administration Bond," "Market Place Bond."*

VALLEY PAPER CO. (Geo. F. Fowler, Treas.; Wm. S. Fowler, Asst. Treas.; Aaron Bagg, Jr., Pres.; G. Stanley Morse, Vice-Pres.) Five 1200-lb., two 2000-lb. Beating and two Jordan engines; two Rotary boilers; two 68-inch Fourdriniers. Widest trimmed sheet, 58 inches. Water and Steam. Bond, Ledgers, Writing and High Grade Specialties. 12,000 lbs. 24 hours.

WHITING PAPER CO. Fourteenth St. and Seventh Ave., New York; 619 Chestnut St., Philadelphia; 318 W. Washington St., Chicago. (William F. Whiting, Pres.; William Whiting, Treas.) Two mills. No. 1 MILL. Seven 1000-lb. engines; one 1000-lb. and two 1500-lb. Washers; one 62-inch and one 80-inch Fourdriniers. Water and Steam. Writing. 15,000 lbs. 24 hours. No. II MILL. Eight 1000-lb. engines and six 1000-lb. Washers; two 66-inch and one 76-inch Fourdriniers. Water. Writing. 10,000 lbs. 24 hours.

HOUSATONIC—Berkshire Co.
On N. Y., N. H. & H. RR. M. O. and Tel. office; nearest bank, Great Barrington, 4 miles; Adams Ex.

RISING PAPER CO., B. D. (O. A. Miller, Pres.; Charles McKernon, Treas., and W. J. Raybold, Sec.) S. P., at mill. Sixteen 800-lb. and two 1200-lb. Beating and Washing engines; two 94-inch Fourdriniers. Widest trimmed sheet, 78 inches. Eleven Sheet Calenders, three Platers. Width of Super-Calenders, 44 inches. Water and Steam. Bond, Linen and Ledgers, Wedding and Index Bristols. 30,000 lbs. 24 hours. *Our Specialties: "Housatonic," "Danish" and Finance Bond and Ledger, Twentieth Century Bond, Reference Linen Ledger, Twenty Carat Linen, Wedding and Index Bristols.*

HUNTINGTON—Hampshire Co.
Pop. 1,673. On B. & A. RR. M. O. and Tel. office; nearest bank, Westfield, 11 miles; Am. Ex.

AMERICAN WRITING PAPER CO.—Chester Paper Company Division. S. P., Huntington. Two 500-lb. and four 700-lb. engines; one 72-inch Fourdrinier. Water and Steam. Writing. 6000 lbs. 24 hours. *No. 1 Loft-dried Papeterie Papers.*

LAWRENCE—Essex Co.
Pop. 90,250. On B. & M. RR. M. O. and Tel. office; Am., People's, Lawrence and Union Ex.

CHAMPION-INTERNATIONAL CO. (G. F. Russell, Pres. and Gen. Mgr.; P. A. Hammond, Secy. and Treas.; C. T. Dole, Mgr. Sales; W. T. Dole, Asst. Gen. Mgr.; M. D. Currier, Mill Supt.) Ten Beating and six Jordan engines; two 62-inch and two 72-inch Fourdriniers. Widest trimmed sheet, 70 inches. Water and Steam. Surface Coated Papers. 200,000 lbs. 24 hours. PULP MILL. Twelve Digesters. Water and Steam. Soda Fibre 24,000 lbs. Sulphite Fibre 40,000 lbs. 24 hours. Coating mills at Lawrence and East Pepperell.

MERRIMAC PAPER CO. (F. M. Temple, Pres. and Gen. Mgr.; C. D. Thompson, Sec. and Treas.; John Johnson, Supt.) S. P., at mill. Twelve 1000-lb., one 1800-lb. and two Jordan engines; one 88-inch and one 112-

inch Fourdriniers. Width of Super Calenders, 44 and 52 inches. Widest trimmed sheet, 100 inches. Water and Steam. Super Calendered and Machine Finished and Enameled Book, Coated and Uncoated Lithograph, Offset Writing and Music. 50,000 lbs. 24 hours. *Enameled Book and Lithographic Papers.*

MUNROE FELT AND PAPER CO. (James P. Munroe, Pres. and Treas.; W. T. McAlpine, Gen. Mgr.; T. E. Allen, Supt.) P. O. address, Lawrence. S. P., at mill. Four 600-lb., three 800-lb. and three 1200-lb. Beating and two Refining engines; two 92-inch Fourdriniers. Widest trimmed sheet, 80 inches. Union Screens. Water and Steam. Kraft and Specialties. 30,000 lbs. 24 hours.

LEE—Berkshire Co.

Pop. 3,596. On B. Div. N. Y., N. H. & H. RR. M. O. and Tel. office; Adams Ex.

AMERICAN WRITING PAPER CO.—G. K. Baird Paper Company Division. Three mills. CONGRESS, NATIONAL and New MILLS. (Plants dismantled.)

EATON, DIKEMAN CO., THE. (Calvin C. Yates, Pres.; Wm. H. Eaton, Vice-Pres. and Treas.; Olen V. Yates, Sec. and Supt.) HOUSATONIC MILL. S. P., Lee. Five 1000-lb. Washing, one 1200-lb. and one 1500-lb. Beating, one Umpherston and two Jordan engines; one 72-inch and one 90-inch Fourdriniers. Water and Steam. Blotting. 24,000 lbs. 24 hours. *"Magnet," "Columbian" and "Lenox" Blotting and all grades of absorbent papers.*

MOUNTAIN MILL PAPER CO. (J. M. Stevenson, P. W. Ayers, Vice-Pres. and Sec.; Louis T. Stevenson, Treas.; George Hall, Supt.) Three 450-lb. and two 600-lb. Beaters; one Refining engine, three 600-lb. Washers and one Rotary Boiler. One 62-inch Fourdrinier. Widest trimmed sheet, 54 inches. Steam and Water. Wedding Paper and Wedding Bristol. 8,000 lbs. 24 hours.

SMITH PAPER CO, THE. (Willard F. Smith, Pres.) Five mills. EAGLE, COLUMBIA, VALLEY, CENTENNIAL AND NIAGARA. Thirty-one Beating and seven Refining engines; fifteen Washers; eight Rotary boilers; one 76-inch, two 84-inch, three 90-inch and two 100-inch Fourdriniers. Water, Steam and Electricity. Tissues and Specialties. 30,000 lbs. 24 hours.

MILLERS FALLS—Franklin Co.

Crossing Fitchburg and New London Div. of C. Vt. RR. Tel. and M. O.; nearest bank, Turners Falls, 4 miles; Am. and Nat. Ex.

MILLERS FALLS PAPER CO. (Edward P. Bagg, Pres.; Angus Cameron, Treas.; J. Edwin Randall, Clerk.) S. P., at mill. Three 1000-lb., seven 1200-lb. Beating and two Refining engines; two 90-inch Fourdriniers. Water. Bonds, Ledgers, Index Bristol, Extra Fines. 24,000 lbs. 24 hours.

MITTINEAGUE—Hampden Co.

On B. & A. RR. M. O. and Tel. office; nearest bank, Springfield, 3 miles; Am. Ex.

AMERICAN WRITING PAPER CO.—Agawam Paper Company Division. Two mills. S. P., B. & A. R.R., at mills. Four 500-lb., thirteen

DRY ROSIN SIZE Brittle, easy soluble, cheapest size out; cheaper than mill made size. Ask us about it. Also all other grades. **ARABOL M'F'G CO.** 100 William St., N. Y.

114   Massachusetts

1000-lb. and three Marshall engines; three 84-inch Fourdriniers. Water and Steam. Writing. 20,000 lbs. 24 hours. *Specialties are Agawam Bond, Russian Linen Ledger, Wedding Board.*

SOUTHWORTH CO. (T. S. Southworth, Pres.; Melvin D. Southworth, Treas. and Mgr.; Edward Southworth, Sales Mgr.; M. S. Southworth, Clerk; F. O. Scott, Supt.) S. P., at mill. Five 500-lb. Beating engines; one 50-inch and one 80-inch Fourdriniers. Widest trimmed sheet, 56 inches. Water and Steam. Bonds, Linens, Ledgers, Typewriter Papers and DeLuxe Bonds, with individual watermarks. 8000 lbs. 24 hours.

STRATHMORE PAPER CO. (H. A. Moses, Pres. and Treas.; B. A. Franklin, Vice-Pres.; W. H. Sanburn, Asst. Treas.; A. E. Shattuck, Clerk.) S. P., Mittineague. Sixteen 1100-lb. and twelve 1000-lb. engines; six 500-lb. Washers; one 66-inch, one 76-inch, one 86-inch and one 106-inch Fourdriniers and two Special. Widest trimmed sheet, 62 inches. Water and Steam. Bond, Typewriter, Book, Cover, Drawing Paper and Board, Wedding and Stationery Papers and Pasted Bristol Boards, Photographic Mounting Paper and Board, Box Cover Paper and Specialties. Loft, Air and Cylinder Dried. All above varieties finished in sheets or rolls.

WORTHY PAPER CO. ASSOCIATION. (Edgar S. Bliss, Pres.; Alfred Leeds, Treas.) S. P., Mittineague. Six 800-lb. Beating engines; one 66-inch Fourdrinier. Water and Steam. Bond, Ledger, Linen, Fine, Superfine, Pasted and Wedding Bristol. 9000 lbs. 24 hours.

MONROE BRIDGE—Franklin Co.

Pop. 300. On H. T. & W. RR. M. O. and Tel. office; nearest bank, North Adams, 12 miles; Nat. Ex.

MONROE BRIDGE PAPER CO. (H. Y. Brown, Pres.; H. S. Mallory, Vice-Pres.; H. J. Vail, Sec.; Wm. G. Shortress, Treas.; L. C. Eckhardt, Asst. Treas.; Robert Brown, Supt.) S. P., at mill. Seven 500-lb. Beating and three Jordan engines; one 72-inch Five Cylinder. Widest trimmed sheet, 64 inches. Water, Steam and Electricity. Tag Board, Ticket Bristol, Solid Manila, Manila Lined, Patent Coated, Container Board and High Grade Specialties. 36,000 lbs. 24 hours. PULP MILL. Two mills. Four Grinders; two 72-inch Wet Machines. Steam and Electricity. Ground Wood. 20,000 lbs. 24 hours.

MOUNT TOM—Hampshire Co.—PULP MILL.

On C. R. Div. B. & M. RR. M. O., Tel. office and nearest bank, Northampton, 8 miles; Am. Ex.

MOUNT TOM SULPHITE PULP CO. (Dudley P. Rogers, Pres.; Chas. S. Springer, Vice-Pres.; Wm. Freiday, Vice-Pres.; Edward L. Rantoul, Sec. and Clerk; Geo. H. Clough, Treas.) Address, 50 State Street, Boston. S. P., at mill. Seven Digesters; two 72-inch Rogers Wet Machines. Bleached Sulphite Fibre. 90,000 lbs. 24 hours.

NATICK—Middlesex Co.

Pop. 9,886. B. & A. RR. M. O. and Tel. office.

NATICK BOX AND BOARD CO. (C. J. Sawyer, Pres.; C. A. Coombs, Sec. and Treas.; W. O. Whitaker, Supt.) Four 1000-lb. Beating and three

PRESS ROLLS Maple and Gum White Wood Felt Rolls **J. W. HEWITT MACHINE CO.** Neenah, Wis.

THOMAS E. GLEESON, Inc., 411-413 John St., E. NEWARK, N. J.
CYLINDER MOULDS and DANDY ROLLS Made and Repaired
LETTERING and MONOGRAMS for WATERMARKS

Paper and Pulp Mills in the United States 115

Refining engines; one 96-inch Five Cylinder Machine. Mill Lining and Pasting Machines. Widest trimmed sheet, 81 inches. Steam. Chip, News, Manila Lined and Solid. Jute and Colored Boards. 70,000 lbs. 24 hours.

NEW BEDFORD—Bristol Co.

Pop. 110,000. On N. Y., N. H. & H. RR. M. O. and Tel. office; Adams Ex.

PAIRPOINT CORPORATION, THE. (Andrew G. Pierce, Jr., Pres.; Clarence A. Cook, Treas.; Thos. A. Tripp, Mgr.; A. C. Drew, Supt.) Five 1000-lb. Beating engines; one 60 and 65-inch Cylinders. Steam. Box Board, Heavy Baling and Case Lining Papers. 30,000 lbs. 24 hours. (Makes paper mainly for own manufacturing purposes.)

NEWTON LOWER FALLS—Middlesex Co.

On B. & A. Div. of N. Y. C. & H. R. RR. M. O. and Tel. office; nearest bank, Newton, 2 miles; Am. Ex.

CREHORE, CHARLES F., & SON. P. O. address, 87 Milk street, Boston. (Frederic M. Crehore.) Four engines; 30-inch Roll; one 40-inch Cylinder. Water and Steam. Press Board and Jacquard Cards. 2000 lbs. 24 hours.

NORFOLK—Norfolk Co.

Pop. 960. N. Y., N. H. & H. RR. M. O. and Tel. office; nearest bank, Franklin, 5 miles; Adams Ex.

J. F. WALL & SON. P. O. address, Walpole, Mass. Two mills. BALTIMORE MILL. S. P., at mill. Two 400-lb. Beating and one Jordan engines; one 60-inch Cylinder. Widest trimmed sheet, 58 inches. Water and Steam. Sheathing, Wrapping, Cone and Duplex. 8000 lbs. 24 hours. HIGHLAND LAKE MILL. Two 500-lb. Beating and one Jordan engines; one 66-inch Three Cylinder. Widest trimmed sheet, 54 inches. Water, Steam and Electricity. Sheathing, Wrapping, Red Rope Roofing, Black Waterproof Building Paper, Ponwal and Aero Roofing. 10,000 lbs. 24 hours.

NORTH DIGHTON—Bristol Co.

Pop. 743. On O. C. RR. Div. N. Y., N. H. & H. RR. Tel. office; nearest bank, Taunton, 3½ miles; Adams Ex.

LINCOLN, L., & CO. (E. Ellsworth Lincoln and N. R. Lincoln.) S. P., station, ¾ mile. Four 600-lb. Beating and one Jordan engines; one 68-inch Double Cylinder; one 56-inch Three Cylinder. Widest trimmed sheet, 64 inches. Water and Steam. Manila, Sheathing, Tack and Tailors' Pattern. 18,000 lbs. 24 hours.

NORTH LEOMINSTER—Worcester Co.

On Fitchburg Div. B. & M. RR. M. O. and Tel. office; nearest bank, Leominster, 1 mile; Nat. Ex.

WHEELWRIGHT PAPER CO., GEO. W. (Geo. W. Wheelwright, Jr., Pres. and Treas.; H. M. Wheelwright, Vice-Pres. and Clerk; Wm. B. Page, Asst. Treas. and Agt.) P. O. Address, 95 Milk Street, Boston. LEOMINSTER MILL. S. P., North Leominster. Eleven rag engines; one 102-inch and one 114-inch Cylinder; widest trimmed sheets, 96 inches. Water and Steam. "Dove Mill." Bristol Boards, White and Tinted, Coating and Book. 50,000 lbs. 24 hours.

M. GOTTESMAN & CO., Inc., 18 E. 41st STREET, NEW YORK. Cable Address "Nammettco" EUROPEAN OFFICES: Stockholm, Sweden

Finest Mitscherlich Sulphite

BRIMSTONE MAKES THE VERY BEST SULPHITE.
If you are looking for a high-grade Brimstone write to
THE UNION SULPHUR CO., Main Office, 17 Battery Pl., New York. Mines, Calcasieu Parish.

DRY ROSIN SIZE Brittle, easy soluble, cheapest size out; cheaper than mill made size. Ask us about it. Also all other grades. **ARABOL M'F'G CO.** 100 William St., N. Y.

LOMBARD'S ENGLISH NEWCASTLE PULP STONES ARE SUPERIOR TO ALL OTHERS. ALL SIZES IN STOCK. LOMBARD & CO., Importers & Manufacturers, 226 & 228 A Street, Boston.

116 *Massachusetts*

NORTH WILBRAHAM—Hampden Co.

Pop. 1,789. On B. & A. RR. Tel. and M. O. office; nearest bank, Springfield, 10 miles; Am. Ex.

COLLINS MANUFACTURING CO. (Samuel R. Whiting, Pres. and Treas.; Charles Stewart Supt.; E. C. Walker, Mgr. of Sales.) Nine Beating and three Refining engines; ten Washers; one 68-inch, one 82-inch and one 102-inch Fourdriniers. Widest trimmed sheets, 58 inches, 79 inches and 90 inches. Water and Steam. Loft Dried Bonds, Ledger and Writing Papers, Index Bristol, Papeterie Paper and Specialties. 30,000 lbs. 24 hours.

OTTER RIVER—Worcester Co.

Pop. 550. On Fitchburg Div. B. & M. M. O. and Tel. office; nearest bank, Gardner, 4 miles.

OTTER RIVER BOARD CO. (J. P. O'Brien, Pres. and Treas.; H. B. Heselton, Sec.; J. H. O'Brien, Asst. Treas. and Mgr.) Two 1000 Beating engines and one Jordan; one 60- and one 72-inch Machines. Binders', Trunk and Special Button Boards. 36,000 lbs. 24 hours.

RUSSELL—Hampden Co.

Pop. 792. On B. & A. RR. M. O. and Tel. office; nearest bank, Westfield, 3 miles; Am. Ex.

CHAPIN & GOULD PAPER CO. (Charles L. Chapin, Pres. and Treas.; Harold W. Hixon, Sec.; B. Aldrich, Mill Supt.) P. O. Address, Springfield, Mass. CRESCENT MILLS. S. P., Huntington Station, 1¼ miles. Four 1000-lb., one 1200-lb., two 1500-lb. and one 2000 lb. Beating and two Refining engines; one 76-inch and one 88-inch Fourdriniers. Union Screens. Water and Steam. Superfines, Specialties, Bonds, Ledger and Writing. 16,000 lbs. 24 hours.

WESTFIELD RIVER PAPER CO. (Philip L. Saltonstall, Pres.; Gunnar Hartmann, Vice-Pres.; Horace W. Frost, Sec.; L. E. Flint, Treas.; N. Folke Becker, Mill Mgr.; Lewis Dozier, Supt.) Two 1200-lb. Beating, one Refining engine; two Washers; one 96-inch Fourdrinier. Widest trimmed sheet, 76 inches. Water and Steam. Glassine. 15,000 lbs. 24 hours.

SOUTH HADLEY—Hampshire Co.

Pop. 4,526. Stage from Holyoke. M. O. and Tel. office; nearest bank, Holyoke, 4 miles; Adams and Am. Ex.

JAPANESE TISSUE MILLS. Pearl City Division. P. O. Address, 12 Crescent Street, Holyoke. (J. L. Perkins, Pres.; N. G. Read, Vice-Pres.; F. R. Keens, Sec.; W. H. Bond, Treas.) S. P., at mill. Six 1000-lb. Beating engines. Two 72-inch Fourdriniers. Water and Electricity. Tissue. 12,000 lbs. 24 hours.

JAPANESE TISSUE MILLS. Mt. Holyoke Division. P. O. Address, 12 Crescent Street, Holyoke. (J. L. Perkins, Pres.; N. G. Read, Vice-Pres.; F. R. Keens, Sec.; Wm. H. Bond, Treas.) S. P., Holyoke. Seven 1000-lb. Beating engines; two 72-inch Cylinders and one 96-inch Fourdrinier. Electricity. Tissue. 16,000 lbs. 24 hours.

McEnery Paper Company Practically All Grades
Manufacturers' Sales Agency 112 W. ADAMS ST., CHICAGO

SOUTH HADLEY FALLS—Hampshire Co.

On Conn. River opposite Holyoke. M. O. and Tel. office; nearest bank, Holyoke, 1 mile; Adams and Am. Ex.

CAREW MANUFACTURING CO. (W. D. Judd, Pres. and Treas.) S. P., Holyoke, 1 mile. Eleven 1200-lb. Beating and Two Jordan engines; one 84-inch and one 86-inch Fourdriniers. Water and Steam. Writing. 24,000 lbs. 24 hours. *High Grade Ledgers, Bonds, Linens, Typewriter Papers and Superfine Writings.*

HAMPSHIRE PAPER CO. Incorporated. (Solomon B. Griffin, Pres., and W. D. Judd, Treas.) S. P., Holyoke, 1 mile. Two 1000-lb. and four 1200-lb. Beating and two Jordan engines; two Rotary boilers; one 86-inch and one 78-inch Fourdriniers. Water and Steam. Bonds only. 12,000 lbs. 24 hours.

SOUTH LEE—Berkshire Co.

On B. Div. of N. Y., N. H. & H. RR. M. O. and Tel. office; nearest bank, Lee, 3 miles; Adams Ex.

AMERICAN WRITING PAPER CO.—Hurlbut Paper Manufacturing Company Division. S. P., 2 rods. Eight 500-lb., four 700-lb. and two Marshall engines; one 66-inch and one 80-inch Fourdriniers. Water and Steam. Writing. 10,000 lbs. 24 hours. *Bond, Linen and Ex-Super.*

TOWNSEND HARBOR—Middlesex Co.

On F. Div. B. & M. RR. M. O. office; Tel. and nearest bank, Townsend, 2 miles; Nat. Ex.

SPAULDING, J., & SONS CO. (Copartnership.) New York Office, 449 Broome Street; Chicago Office, 166 North Clinton Street. Boston Office, 203 Albany Bldg. (L. C. Spaulding; R. H. Spaulding; H. N. Spaulding.) Address, North Rochester, N. H. Four mills, Townsend Harbor, Mass. North Rochester and Milton, N. H. Forty-four 500-lb. engines; four 40-inch and six 48-inch and four 52-inch Wet Machines. Widest trimmed sheet, 40 inches. Water and Steam. Leather Board. 48,000 lbs. 24 hours.

TURNERS FALLS—Franklin Co.

Pop. 6,000. On Fitchburg and N. Y., N. H. & H. RR. M. O. and Tel. office; Am. and Nat. Ex.

ESLEECK MANUFACTURING CO. (A. W. Esleeck, Pres.; I. N. Esleeck, Vice-Pres.; H. McC. Knickerbocker, Treas.; W. P. Perry, Sec.; W. H. Croft, Mill Supt.) S. P., at mill. Five 1200-lb. Beating and two Refining engines; three Washers and one Rotary boiler; one 120-inch Fourdrinier. Widest trimmed sheet, 106 inches. Width of Super-Calenders, 48 inches. Water and Steam. Fine Onion Skin and Thin Typewriter Papers in White and Colors. 12,000 lbs. 24 hours. *The company's speciality is loft dried, white and colored onion skin papers of the highest quality.*

INTERNATIONAL PAPER CO. Office, 30 Broad street, New York. MONTAGUE MILL. (H. J. Kellogg, Supt.) S. P., at mill. Six Beating and four Refining engines; one 84-inch, one 88-inch, one 118-inch Fourdriniers. Water and Steam. Half-Tone. Secial Supplement, Colored Poster, Topaz Writing. 94,000 lbs. 24 hours. PULP MILL. Eight Grinders; two Wet Machines. Ground Wood. 72,000 lbs. 24 hours.

Massachusetts

KEITH PAPER COMPANY. (A. Pagenstecher, Pres.; Jonathan Bulkley, Vice-Pres.; Albert R. Smith, Treas. and Gen. Mgr.) Twenty-one Beating and Washing engines; one 66-inch, two 80-inch, one 86-inch Fourdrinier Machines. Water, Steam and Electricity. Bonds, Linens, Ledgers, Flats, Wedding and Correspondence Papers, Wedding Bristols and High-Grade Specialties. 30,000 lbs. 24 hours.

WALTHAM—Middlesex Co.
Pop. 23,481. On F. & Mass. C. RR. M. O. and Tel. office; Am. and Nat. Ex.

ROBERTS & SON CO., JOHN, Incorporated. Head Office, 1606 First National Bank Bldg., Pittsburgh, Pa. P. O. Box 546. (H. H. Robertson, Pres.; W. F. Keith, Treas.) S. P., Roberts' Station. Four 500-lb. and one Jordan engines; one 70-inch Cylinder. Widest trimmed sheet, 66 inches. Water and Steam. Asbestos. 16,000 lbs. 24 hours.

WEST DUDLEY—Worcester Co.
On N. Y., N. H. & H. RR. M. O., Tel. and nearest bank, Southbridge, 3½ miles; Adams Ex.

BURMUS PAPER CO., INC. (John M. Burby, Pres. and Supt.; Harold A. Allen, Sec. and Treas.) West Dudley Mill. S. P., at mill. One 600-lb. Beating engine; three Washers and one Rotary boiler; one 92-inch Three-Cylinder Machine. Widest trimmed sheet, 87 inches. Water and Electricity. Tag, Card Middles, Bristols and Colored Specialties. 16,000 lbs. 24 hours.

WESTFIELD—Hampden Co.
Pop. 17,000. On N. Y., N. H. & H. and B. & A. R.R. M. O. and Tel. office; Adams and Am. Ex.

CRANE BROTHERS. S. P., Westfield Depot, 1½ miles; spur track to mills. JAPANESE MILLS. Four Beaters and three Washers; one 66-inch Fourdrinier. Water and Steam. "Japanese Linen." 4,000 lbs. 24 hours.

MARS PAPER CORPORATION. New York Office, 448 Pearl Street. (Maurice O'Meara, Pres.; John Brannan, Vice-Pres. and Mgr.; J. E. Dean, Sec.; J. B. White, Treas.; John Painter, Supt.) Two 800-lb. Beating and one Marshall Perfecting engines; two 800-lb. Washers and one Rotary; one 66-inch Fourdrinier. Widest trimmed sheet, 60 inches. Water and Steam. Carton Tissue. 4000 lbs. 24 hours.

WEST GROTON—Middlesex Co.
On Fitchburg Div. B. & M. R.R. Nearest bank, Ayer, 4 miles. Am. Ex.

GROTON LEATHER BOARD CO. (William A. Lawrence, Pres.; Winthrop L. Sheedy, Vice-Pres.; Michael Sheedy, Jr., Sec. and Treas.; Harold Sheedy, Supt.) WEST GROTON MILLS. S. P., at mill. Four 1500-lb. Beaters. Four 48-inch Board Machines. Water, Steam and Electricity. Heeling, Board and Leather Board. 24,000 lbs. 24 hours.

HOLLINGSWORTH & VOSE CO. Address, Boston. (Zachary T. Hollingsworth, Pres.; Chas. Vose, Vice-Pres.; V. Hollingsworth, Treas.; Robert W. Lennox, Asst. Treas.) WEST GROTON MILL. On Boston & Maine RR. S. P., at mill. One 600-lb. and twenty 1200-lb. Beaters; three Refining engines; one 56-inch Double Cylinder, one 86-inch Four Cylinder

THOMAS E. GLEESON, Inc., **FOURDRINIER WIRES**
411-413 John St., E. NEWARK, N. J. For Tissue and Fine Grade Papers

and one 62-inch Fourdrinier. Widest trimmed sheet, 78 inches. Water and Steam. Red Rope Roofing and Insulating—Fourdrinier and Cylinder Sand—all and part Rope Tag, Pattern, Box Stay, Flour and Cement Sack, Jute Manila, Rope and Jute Duplex, also Specialties. 40,000 lbs. 24 hours.

WHEELWRIGHT—Worcester Co.
On C. M. Div. B. & M. RR. M. O. and Tel. office; nearest bank, Ware, 10 miles; Am. Ex.

WHEELWRIGHT PAPER CO., GEO. W. (George W. Wheelwright, Jr., Pres. and Treas.; H. M. Wheelwright, Vice-Pres. and Clerk; Wm. B. Page, Asst. Treas.; E. W. Pierce, Agt.) Address, 95 Milk Street, Boston. HARDWICK MILL. S. P., at mill. Eleven rag engines; one 86-inch and one 102-inch Fourdriniers. Width of Super Calender, 50 inches. Water and Steam, Book, Coating and Music. 40,000 lbs. 24 hours. *Makers "Best Plate Finish" (B. P. F.) Dull Finish Book.*

WORONOCO—Hampden Co.
On B. & A. RR.; also on Western Mass. St. Ry. M. O. and Tel. office; nearest bank, Westfield, 5 miles; Am. Ex.

STRATHMORE PAPER CO. (H. A. Moses, Pres. and Treas.; B. A. Franklin, Vice-Pres.; W. H. Sanburn, Asst. Treas.; A. E. Shattuck, Clerk.) Bond, Ledger, Superfine Wedding, Pasted Bristol, Typewriter, Book and Cover Papers and Specialties. Loft, Air and Machine Dried. (See Mittineague for Equipment.)

MICHIGAN.
ALPENA—Alpena Co.
Pop. 11,802. On D. & M. RR. M. O. and Tel. office; Am. Ex.

FLETCHER PAPER CO. (Allan M. Fletcher, Pres.; G. F. King, Vice-Pres.; Philip K. Fletcher, Sec.; Henry E. Fletcher, Treas.; Gabe Prevost, Supt.) S. P., Alpena. New York Office, 5 Beekman Street. Eight 1000-lb. Beating and four Jordan engines; two 112-inch Fourdriniers. Widest trimmed sheet, 102 inches. Steam and Water. Fibre Specials. 70,000 lbs. 24 hours. PULP MILL. S. P., Alpena. Four Grinders; four Wet Machines. Steam and Water. Ground Wood, 50,000 lbs.; Sulphite Fibre; also Bleached Mitscherlich Fibre, 30,000 lbs. 24 hours.

BATTLE CREEK—Calhoun Co.
Pop. 25,267. On G. T. W. & M. C. RR. M. O. and Tel. office.

MICHIGAN CARTON CO. (W. I. Fell, Pres.; H. L. Kneeland, Vice-Pres.; J. F. Byrne, Sec. and Supt.; L. P. Flanders, Treas.) No. 1. Five 1500-lb. Beating and three Refining engines; one 106-inch Black & Clawson Machine. Widest trimmed sheet, 96 inches. No. 2. 132-inch Black & Clawson. Eight 1500-lb. Beating engines. Four Refining engines. Widest trim 120 inches. Steam. Box Boards, Combination and Patent Coated Boards. 90,000 lbs. 24 hours.

CAPAC—St. Clair Co.
Pop. 761. On Grand Trunk W. RR. M. O. and Tel. office; Nat. Ex.

UPSON CO., successors to St. Clair Paper Co. (Plant being dismantled and being removed to Lockport, N. Y.)

DRY ROSIN SIZE

Brittle, easy soluble. Cheapest size out; cheaper than mill made size. Ask us about it. Also all other grades.

ARABOL M'F'G CO.
100 William St., New York

THE UNION SULPHUR CO.
Main Office: 17 Battery Pl., New York.
Mines: Calcasieu Parish, La.
Producers of **The Only Arsenic Free Sulphur on the Market**

Michigan

CHEYBOYGAN—Cheyboygan Co.

Pop. 6,489. M. Div. M. C. RR. M. O. and Tel. office; Am. Ex.

UNION BAG AND PAPER CORPORATION. Cheyboggan Paper Co. plant. Six 1500-lb. Beating and two Jordan engines; two 136-inch Fourdriniers. Widest trimmed sheet, 123½ inches. No. 1 and No. 2 Manilas, Butchers'. All Sulphite, Bag. 120,000 lbs. 24 hours. PULP AND FIBRE MILL. S. P., at mill. Four Ontario Grinder Co. Grinders; two Digesters; five Wet Machines. Water. Ground Wood, 16,000 lbs. 24 hours. Sulphite. 100,000 lbs. 24 hours.

CHILDSDALE—Kent Co.

Pop. 102. On G. R. & I. RR. M. O. Tel. (Grand Rapids) and Ex. office and nearest bank, Rockford, 2 miles.

CHILDSDALE PAPER MILLS. (Horace H. Childs, Prop.) S. P., at mill. Four 1200-lb. Beating and three Refining engines; one 36-inch and one 42-inch Wet Machines and one 64-inch Four Cylinder. Widest sheet made, 60 inches. Water. Air-dried Straw Boards; Double Pasted Boards, Straw and Chip, Manila lined; Plain Straw and Chip, Colored Boards, Pulp Boards. 80,000 lbs. 24 hours.

CONSTANTINE—St. Joseph Co.

Pop. 1,919. On Grand Rapids Branch of N. Y. C. RR. M. O. and Tel. office; Am. Ex.

CONSTANTINE BOARD AND PAPER CO. (Robert T. Weir, Mgr.) FAWN MILL. S. P., at mill. Two 900-lb. and three 1200-lb. Beating and two Jordan engines; one 108-inch Four Cylinder. Water and Steam. Box Board. 50,000 lbs. 24 hours.

DETROIT—Wayne Co.

Pop. 600,000. On M. C.; D. T. & I.; P. M.; L. S. & M. S.; C. P. RR. M. O. and Tel. office; Am., Can. and Nat. Ex.

DETROIT SULPHITE PULP & PAPER CO. (William P. Holliday, Chairman of Board; F. H. MacPherson, Pres. and Treas.; A. C. Everard, First Vice-Pres.; T. W. Dunn, Vice-Pres. and Gen. Supt.; J. H. Behnke, Sec.; J. B. Rieg, Mgr. of Sales.) DELRAY MILL. S. P., at mill. Nineteen Beating and five Refining engines; one 48-inch and one 72-inch Cylinders; one 80-inch Fourdrinier and two 120-inch "Yankee" Fourdrinier. Widest trimmed sheet, 75 inches. Steam. High Grade Mitchfibre Wrapping, Cordage Document Manila, Swederope Tag, Cordovan Bristols, Cover and Specialties, Platine Tympan, Tissues, Machine Glazed Envelope and Wrapping. 100,000 lbs. 24 hours. PULP MILL. Seven Digesters; two Wet Machines. Steam. Sulphite Fibre (dry). 100,000 lbs. 24 hours.

FILER CITY—Manistee Co.—PULP MILL.

Pop. 400. On Mich. East & West RR. M. O., Adams and Am. Ex., nearest bank and Tel. Manistee, 2½ miles.

FILER FIBRE CO. (E. G. Filer, Pres.; R. W. Smith, Vice-Pres.; P. P. Schnorbach, Sec. and Mgr.; Gus Kitzinger, Treas.; Max Oberdorfer, Supt.) Three Digesters; two Wet Machines. Steam and Electricity. Sulphate Fibre. 90,000 lbs. 24 hours.

National Duplex Waterproof Case Lining
IS WATERPROOF—
CLEAN TO HANDLE **NATIONAL WATERPROOFING CO.,** 1054 DREXEL BLDG. PHILADELPHIA

Paper and Pulp Mills in the United States 121

GRAND RAPIDS—Kent Co.

Pop. 101,700. On G. R. & I. and P. M. RR.

AMERICAN BOX BOARD CO. (T. H. Goodspeed, Pres.; S. A. Morman, Vice-Pres.; J. W. Goodspeed, Treas.; W. H. Gilbert, Sec.; W. A. Jack, Gen. Mgr.) Twenty 1800-lb. Beating engines. One Fourdrinier for Corrugating Straw. Widest trimmed sheet, 70 inches. Two 122-inch Cylinder Machines. Widest trimmed sheet, 116 inches. Steam and Electricity. High Grade Box Boards and Corrugated Boards and Test Liners. 250,000 lbs. 24 hours.

GROOS—Delta Co.—PULP MILL.

Pop. 18. On M. L. & S. RR. M. O. Tel. and Bank at Escanaba.

ESCANABA WOOD FIBRE CO. P. O. address, Escanaba, Delta Co. (J. K. Stack, Pres.; P. L. Utley, Sec. and Mgr.; M. N. Smith, Treas.; G. F. Germanson, Supt.) S. P., Groos. Five Grinders and six Wet Machines. Ground Wood. 100,000 lbs. 24 hours.

JACKSON—Jackson Co.

Pop. 25,180. On M. C.; F. W. & J. Branch of L. S. & M. S.; G. T. & C. N. RR. M. O. and Tel. office; Am., Nat. and U. S. Ex.

MICHIGAN BAG AND PAPER CO. GRAND RIVER MILLS. (Has discontinued making Paper. Machinery removed.)

KALAMAZOO—Kalamazoo Co.

Pop. 50,000. On M. C., S. Div. G. R. & I.; K. Div. of L. S. & M. S.; C. K. & S. & G. T. RR. M. O. and Tel. office; Am., U. S. and Adams Ex.

BRYANT PAPER COMPANY. (Frank H. Milham, Pres. and Gen. Mgr.; Noah Bryant, Vice-Pres.; C. A. Fox, Sec. and Treas.) FOUR MILLS. BRYANT DIVISION. S. P., at mill. One 116-inch, two 126-inch, one 136-inch and one 188-inch Fourdriniers. Widest trimmed sheet, 128 inches. Super Calenders from 36 to 74 inches. Steam. Machine Finish and Super Calendered Book, Map, Lithograph, Label, Music, Folder, Drawing, Rag and Wood Envelope, and Tub and Engine-sized Writings. 200,000 lbs. 24 hours. SUPERIOR DIVISION. S. P., at mill. One 110-inch Harper Fourdrinier and one 136-inch Fourdrinier. Widest trimmed sheet, 128 inches. Width of Super Calenders, 40 to 60 inches. Steam. Super Calendered and Machine-finished Book, Catalogue, Lithograph, French Folio and Specialties. 50,000 lbs. 24 hours. MILHAM DIVISION. S. P., at mill. One 154-inch Fourdrinier, one 140-inch Fourdrinier and one 136-inch Harper Super Calenders 66 inches wide. Steam. Book and Magazine. 150,000 lbs. 24 hours. IMPERIAL DIVISION. Coated Papers. 100,000 lbs. 24 hours.

HAWTHORNE PAPER CO. (On M. C. R. R., 2 miles east of Kalamazoo.) (A. H. Dwight, Pres. and Mgr.; F. M. Hodge, Vice-Pres.; R. L. Pease, Sec.; S. B. Monroe, Treas.; A. G. Wightman, Supt.) Eight 1000-lb. Beating, two Refining engines; five Washers and two Rotary Boilers; two Fourdriniers. Widest trimmed sheets, 78 and 88 inches. Steam. Bonds and Ledgers. 24,000 lbs. 24 hours.

KALAMAZOO PAPER CO. (F. M. Hodge, Pres.; D. F. Altland, Vice-Pres.; F. Pagenstecher, Sec.; A. F. Curtenius, Treas.) MILL NO. 1. Six

R. B. McEwan, *Pres.* J. L. McEwan, *Vice-Pres.* Arthur McEwan, *Treas. and Mgr.* R. W. McEwan, *Secy.*
Sheet Lining Plant, Office and Mills at WHIPPANY, N. J.
McEWAN BROS., Inc. MANUFACTURERS OF ALL GRADES **PAPER BOX BOARD**

1500-lb. Beaters, four Jordans, seven Washers and four Rotary boilers. Two 130-inch Fourdriniers; widest trimmed sheet, 120 inches. MILL NO. 2. Four 1500-lb. Beaters, two Jordans, five Washers and two Rotary boilers. One 90-inch and one 114-inch Fourdriniers; widest trimmed sheet, 105 inches. MILL NO. 3. Four 1500-lb. Beaters, two Jordans, five Washers and three Rotary boilers. One 146-inch Fourdriniers; widest trimmed sheet, 135 inches. Steam and Electricity. Map, Writing, Book, Envelope and Coating. 150,000 lbs. 24 hours.

KALAMAZOO VEGETABLE PARCHMENT CO. (J. Kindleberger, Pres. and Gen. Mgr.; W. O. Jones, Vice-Pres.; S. Ward Kennedy, Sec.; O. S. Campbell, Treas.) S. P., Kalamazoo. Two Parchment Machines. Widest trimmed sheets 80 and 110 inches. Six Waxing Machines. Steam. Vegetable Parchment and Wax Paper. *Kalamazoo Ice Blanket, Parchment Dish Cloths, Nursery Blanket.* NEW MILL. Fourteen 1000-lb. Beating engines; four Washers and two Rotary boilers; one 165 and one 116-inch Fourdriniers. Widest trimmed sheets, 156 and 105 inches. Steam. Waterleaf and Waxing, Sulphite Bond. 84,000 lbs. 24 hours.

KING PAPER CO. (A. L. Pratt, Pres. and Gen. Mgr.; E. S. Rankin, Vice-Pres.; G. S. Davis, Sec. and Treas.; J. H. O'Connell, Supt.) S. P., at mill. Thirteen 1200-lb. Beating and seven Refining engines; eleven Washers and two Rotary boilers; one 120, one 130, one 126 and one 140-inch Fourdriniers. Widest trimmed sheets, 108, 120, 116 and 132 inches. Width of Super-Calenders up to 68 inches. Steam and Electricity. M. F., S. & S. C. Laid Book, Map, Music, Eggshell, Mimeograph, Catalogue, Bible, Offset, Litho, Label, Envelope and Writing. *King Dependable Offset, King Superior, King Superba, King Superfine, King Durable Folder, Victory Dull Finish.* 120,000 lbs. 24 hours. The company also operates a Nine-Coater Coating Plant.

MONARCH PAPER CO. (Chas. A. Dewing, Pres.; Alex. G. Gilman, Vice-Pres.; John A. Pyl, Sec. and Treas.) S. P., at mill. Two 600-lb. and six 1200-lb. Beating; seven 1800-lb. Washington and three Refining engines; one 65-inch, one 124-inch and one 132-inch Fourdriniers. Widest trimmed sheets, 54 inches, 110 inches and 117 inches. Width of Super Calenders, 40, 52, 58 and 72 inches. Union Screens. Water and Steam. Machine-finished, Super Calendered and Coated Book, Lithograph, Card and Folders. 100,000 lbs. 24 hours.

REX PAPER CO. (John F. King, Pres.; Chas. A. Blaney, Vice-Pres.; Edwin H. Hacking, Sec.; Merrill B. King, Treas.) S. P., 3½ miles east of Kalamazoo. Five 1200 J. H. Horne & Sons Beaters and two 1800-lb. Downingtons Rag Washers; two Horne Jordans; four Valley Iron Works Paper Washers; one McNeal Rotary boiler; one 114-inch Fourdrinier. Widest trimmed sheet, 105 inches. Steam. Offset and Mimeograph. 34,000 lbs. 24 hours.

RIVERVIEW COATED PAPER CO. Combined with the Kalamazoo Paper Co.

THOMAS E. GLEESON, Inc., 411-413 John St., E. NEWARK, N. J.
CYLINDER MOULDS and DANDY ROLLS Made and Repaired
LETTERING and MONOGRAMS for WATERMARKS

Paper and Pulp Mills in the United States

STANDARD PAPER CO. (B. C. Dickinson, Pres.; J. H. Dewing, Vice-Pres.; Alex. L. Clark, Sec.) S. P., at mill. Fourteen 1500-lb. Beating and ten Refining engines. One 100-inch, one 115-inch and one 132-inch Cylinder machines. Trims 92, 103 and 120 inches. Steam. High Grade Box Boards, Bristols and Blanks. 150,000 lbs. 24 hours.

WESTERN BOARD AND PAPER CO. (A. E. Curtenius, Pres.; W. H. Scott, Vice-Pres.; F. M. Hodge, Treas.; P. C. Servass, Sec.) S. P., at mill. Five 1500-lb. Beating and three Jordan engines. One 104-inch Five Cylinder Machine. Widest trimmed sheet, 96 inches. Steam. Card Middles, Patent White, Silk Wrappers, Combination Boards, News Boards and Mill Wrappers. 60,000 lbs. 24 hours.

MANISTIQUE—Schoolcraft Co.—PULP MILL.
Pop. 5,000. On Minn., St. Paul & S. Ste. Marie and Manistique and Naillom. M. O., Tel. and Bank. West Ex.

MANISTIQUE PULP & PAPER CO. (W. J. Murphy, Pres.; R. G. Brown, Vice-Pres.; Edw. Peterson, Sec.-Treas.) Six automatic Grinders; twelve Wet machines. Water. Ground Wood. 200,000 lbs. 24 hours. (Aug. 21, 1918. Pulp mill will be in operation in fall. Firm will also erect a paper mill for which there has already been purchased one 164-inch wire Pusey & Jones Fourdrinier; four Horne beaters; two Jordans; one Langston Slitter and Winder and two Voith Paper Machine Screens.

MENOMINEE—Menominee Co.
Pop. 12,818. On P. Div. C. & N. W.; L. S. Div. C., M. & St. P.; W. & M. RR. M. O. and Tel. office; Am. and U. S. Ex.

MARINETTE AND MENOMINEE PAPER CO. (H. A. J. Upham, Pres.; R. F. Goodman, Vice-Pres.; R. W. S. Hoskin, Mgr.; Frank A. Sillman, Sec. and Treas.; Christian Anderson, Asst. Sec. and Treas.) S. P., at mill. Four 1500-lb. Beating and three Refining engines; one 108-inch Beloit Paper Machine. Widest trimmed sheet, 105 inches. Water and Steam. Manila and Fibre Papers. PULP MILL. Three 7-ton Grinders. Water. SULPHITE MILL. Two Digesters. 20,000 lbs. 24 hours.

MONROE—Monroe Co.
Pop. 8,000. Detroit Div. L. S. & M. S.; Toledo Div. M. C.; Toledo Div. G. T.; P. M. and D. M. & T. RR. M. O. and Telegraph and Long Distance Telephone; Am., Ad. and Electric Ex.

THE BOEHME & RAUCH CO. (E. C. Rauch, Pres.; H. Lee Rauch, F. E. Williamson, Vice-Prests.; J. P. Bronson, Treas.; W. C. Tullis, Sec.) Three Mills. S. P., R. R. sidings at mills. Eighteen Beating and twelve Jordan engines. One 90-inch, one 114-inch and one 124-inch Six-Cylinder Board Machines. Folding Paper Boxes and Fibre Shipping Containers. 314,000 lbs. 24 hours.

MONROE BINDER BOARD CO., THE. (L. W. Leathers, Pres.; L. C. Knapp, Vice-Pres.; Don Leathers, Treas.; E. C. Betz, Sec.) S. P., at mill. One 52-inch, three 62-inch and two 96-inch Wet Machines and four Jordans. Five 1200-lb., four 1500-lb. Beating engines; one 1000-lb. Breaker engine. Steam. Binders', Buggy, Templet and Wall Board and Backing Board. 110,000 lbs. 24 hours. NEW MILL. Eight 1500-lb. and two 1800-lb.

M. GOTTESMAN & CO., Inc.
18 E. 41st STREET, NEW YORK. Cable Address "Namector"
EUROPEAN OFFICES: Stockholm, Sweden

HIGHEST GRADE KRAFT PULPS

SULPHUR—CRUDE. GUARANTEED 99% PURE.
The average analysis of our high-grade brimstone is in itself a guarantee. Write us for quotations.
THE UNION SULPHUR CO., Main Office, 17 Battery Pl., New York. Mines, Calcasieu Parish, La.

DRY ROSIN SIZE Brittle, easy soluble, cheapest size out; cheaper than mill made size. Ask us about it. Also all other grades. **ARABOL M'F'G CO.** 100 William St., N. Y.

124   *Michigan*

Beaters and four Jordans. One 124-inch Black-Clawson Machine. Widest trim, 114 inches. Ninety-six Dryers. All kinds of Chip and Container Board.

MONROE PAPER CO. (Leonard Mitchell, Pres.; Emil Mitchell, Sec. and Treas.) Location, First Ward. S. P., at mill. Two 800-lb. Beating one Refining and two Washing engines; one 54-inch Cylinder. Widest trimmed sheet, 44½ inches. Steam. Red and Gray Express, Bag Wrapping, Bag Lining, Straw Wrapping, and Straw Paper for Corrugating Purposes. Bogus, Light Weight Chip and Black Hardware. 10,000 lbs. 24 hours.

RIVER RAISIN PAPER CO. (G. H. Wood, Pres. and Gen. Mgr.; F. P. Walter, Vice-Pres.; A. W. Stitt, Sec. and Treas.; F. C. Payne, Supt.) MILL NO. 1. One 104-inch Five Cylinder Board Machine. MILL NO. 2. One 112-inch Six Cylinder Board Machine. MILL NO. 3. One 124-inch Cylinder. MILL No. 4. One 124-inch Cylinder; Forty-two 1500-lb. Beating engines. Steam. Solid Fibre Board and Shipping Cases. 600,000 lbs. 24 hours.

MUNISING—Alger Co.

Pop. 4,500. On M. M. & S. E. Ry. M. O. and Tel. office; Am. Ex.

MUNISING PAPER CO. (Wm. G. Mather, Pres.; C. H. Worcester, Vice-Pres.; E. P. Strong, Sec.; S. L. Mather, Treas.; Frank H. Milham, Mng. Dir.; C. G. Oberley, Gen. Mgr.; Frank Pearson, Supt.) S. P., at mills. No. 1 MILL. Ten 1800-lb. Beating and two Refining engines; two 136-inch Fourdriniers. Widest trimmed sheet, 120 inches. Steam and electricity. Bonds, Writing, Envelope, Offset, Waxing and Bleached Specialties and Dry Finish Sulphite Fibre Papers. 110,000 lbs. 24 hours. PULP MILL. Three Digesters; one 84-inch and three 72-inch Wet Machines. Steam and Electricity. Unbleached and Bleached Sulphite Fibre. 120,000 lbs. 24 hours.

MUSKEGON—Muskegon Co.

Pop. 20,818. On P. M.; T. S. & M.; M. G. R. & I. RR. M. O. and Tel. office; Am., Ad. and Nat. Ex.

CENTRAL PAPER CO. (E. Meurer, Pres.; A. Pagenstecher, Jr., Vice-Pres.; E. J. Geddes, Sec.; E. J. Pooler, Treas.) S. P., at mill. Sixteen 1000-lb. Beating engines; two 112-inch and one 136-inch Fourdriniers. Widest trimmed sheet, 120 inches. Steam. Fibre Manila Kraft Papers. 110,000 lbs. 24 hours. PULP MILL. S. P., at mill. Two Digesters; three Wet Machines. Steam. Sulphite, 70,000 lbs., Sulphate Pulp 30,000 lbs. 24 hours.

NILES—Berrien Co.

Pop. 4,287. On M. C.; C., C. C. & St. L. RR. M. O. and Tel. office; Am. and Wells, Fargo & Co. Ex.

FRENCH PAPER COMPANY. (J. E. French, Pres.; H. O. Parker, Sec.; F. J. French, Treas.; E. A. Hibbard, Supt.) S. P., at mill. Six 1300-lb., four 500-lb. Beating; three Refining and ten Washing engines; one Cylinder on Board. Widest trimmed sheet, 64 inches. One 86-inch and one 118-inch Fourdriniers. Widest trimmed sheets, 80 and 102 inches. Width of Super Calenders, 42, 44, 62 and 73 inches. Water and Steam. No. 1 and No. 2 Machine Finished and Super Calendered Book, Litho and Poster Papers,

LOMBARD'S ENGLISH NEWCASTLE PULP STONES ARE SUPERIOR TO ALL OTHERS. ALL SIZES IN STOCK. LOMBARD & CO., Importers & Manufacturers, 226 & 228 A Street, Boston.

McEnery Paper Company Practically All Grades
Manufacturers' Sales Agency   112 W. ADAMS ST., CHICAGO

Paper and Pulp Mills in the United States

50,000 lbs. 24 hours; Filled and Solid Wood Pulp Board, Chip Board, 40,000 lbs. 24 hours. PULP MILL. S. P., at mill. Four Grinders; two Wet Machines.

OTSEGO—Allegan Co.

Pop. 2,100. On K. Div. L. S. & M. S. RR. M. O. and Tel. office. Am. Long distance phone.

BARDEEN PAPER CO. (Geo. E. Bardeen, Pres.; S. B. Monroe, Vice-Pres.; G. H. Gerphelde, Sec.; Chas. A. Peck, Treas.; S. B. Monroe, Gen. Mgr.; S. W. Simpson, Supt.) Three mills. MILL NO. 1. S. P., at mill. Six 600-lb., two 1000-lb. and one 1500-lb. Beating and two Jordan engines; one 96-inch (trims 86) Fourdrinier. Water and Steam. Width of Super Calenders, 50 inches, 63 inches and 71 inches. Book, Interleaving, Blotting, Cover, French Folio, Matrix, Map, Poster and Writing. 70,000 lbs. 24 hours. MILL NO. II. S. P., at mill. Four 800-lb. and two 1000-lb. Beating and two Jordan engines; one 110-inch Fourdrinier. Widest trimmed sheet, 100 inches. Width of Super Calenders, 50 and 65 inches. Water and Steam. Book, Interleaving, Blotting, Label, Map, Ticket, Bible, Drug, Mimeograph, Poster, Parchment, Railroad Manila, Music, Coupon, Colors and Writing. 40,000 lbs. 24 hours. *French Folios, Machine Finish and Super-Calendered, White and Colors carried in stock for immediate shipment.*

MAC SIM BAR PAPER CO. (M. B. McClellan, Pres. and Mgr. of Sales; S. W. Simpson, Vice-Pres.; G. E. Bardeen, Treas.; A. B. Thomas, Sec. and Asst. Mgr.) MAC SIM BAR MILL. S. P., at mill. Seventeen 1000-lb. Beating and ten Refining engines; two Rotary Boilers; one 126-inch Six and one 142-inch Seven Cylinders. Widest trimmed sheets, 115 and 130 inches. Steam. Marble and Oak Graining. High Grade Bending and non-Bending Combination Boards. 250,000 lbs. 24 hours.

WOLVERINE PAPER CO. (M. B. McClellan, Pres.; C. A. Buskirk, Vice-Pres. and Treas.; S. B. Monroe, Sec.) Office, Elkhart, Ind. One 88-inch Single Cylinder; one 96-inch Fourdrinier; ten 1000-lb. Beating engines; three Jordan engines. Widest trimmed cylinder sheet, 76 inches; widest Fourdrinier, 84 inches. Manifold Bond, Waxed, Printed and Plain, Waxing, Tissue Papers and Light-weight Book. Steam. Cylinder Tissue, 7000 lbs. 24 hours; on Fourdrinier, 20,000 lbs. 24 hours.

PALMYRA—Lenawee Co.

Pop. 600. On L. S. & M. S.; T. & W. and Wabash RR. Tel. and M. O. office; nearest banks, Adrian and Blissfield. Am. and W. F. Ex.

SIMPLEX PAPER CO., Successor to Mitchell & Sons Co. Main Office, Maumee, Ohio. (Daniel Carney, Mgr.) S. P., Palmyra. One 1200-lb. and one Jordan engine; one 48-inch Double Cylinder. Widest trimmed sheet, 46 inches. Water and Steam. Rag Wrapping, Sheathing and Mill Wrappers. 9000 lbs. 24 hours.

PETOSKEY—Emmett Co.—PULP MILL.

Pop. 5,285. On P. M.; G. R. & I. RR. M. O. and Tel. office; Ad. Ex.

NORTHERN MICHIGAN PULP CO., Successor to Wheat Paper Co. S. P., at mill. PULP MILL. S. P., at mill. Three Digesters; two Wet Machines. Water and Steam. Bleached Sulphite Fibre. 40,000 lbs. 24 hours.

Michigan

PLAINWELL—Allegan Co.

Pop. 1,318. On L. S. & M. S.; G. R. & I. RR. M. O. and Tel. office; Adams and U. S. Ex.

MICHIGAN PAPER CO. OF PLAINWELL, THE. (J. D. Wagner, Pres.; Guy W. Rouse, Vice-Pres.; R. S. Soule, Treas.; Geo. W. Gilkey, Sec. and Mgr.; C. C. Wagner, Asst. Sec.; E. B. Mendsen, Sales Mgr.; William Thomas, Supt.) S. P., at mill. Twenty-six 1100-lb. Beating and four Refining engines; one 76-inch Harper, one 110-inch and two 130-inch Fourdriniers. Widest trimmed sheets, 72 inches, 100 inches and 120 inches. Widest Super-Calender, 80 inches. Water and Steam. White and Colored M. F. and S. C., Book, French Folio, Non-Fading Poster, Catalogue and Bible Papers, Writing, Mimeograph, Colored Covers and Specialties. 100,000 lbs. 24 hours.

PORT HURON—St. Clair Co.

Pop. 25,000. On G. T.; C. & G. T.; P. M. R.R.; D., B. C. & W. M. O. and Tel. office; Can. and Nat. Ex.

PORT HURON SULPHITE AND PAPER CO. (Edward W. Voight, Pres.; E. W. Kiefer, First Vice-Pres.; E. A. Haynes, Second Vice-Pres.; Carl Bonning, Treas.; J. P. Durand, Sec. and Asst. Treas.; John E. Daley, Supt. Paper Div.) One 500-lb. and four 1200-lb. Beating engines; two Refining engines; one 120-inch "Yankee" Fourdrinier; two 72-inch Cylinders. Steam and Electricity. Bleached and Unbleached Mitscherlich M. G. Fibres, Waxing Papers, Building and Trunk Wrap. 30,000 lbs. 24 hours. PULP MILL. Five Digesters; two Wet Machines. Genuine Mitscherlich Sulphite. 60,000 lbs. 24 hours.

ROCHESTER—Oakland Co.

Pop. 1,535. On M. A. L. of G. T.; M. C. RR. M. O. and Tel. office; Am. and Nat. Ex.

BARNES PAPER MILL. (Clayton C. Barnes, Proprietor.) S. P., at mill. Four 500-lb. Beating and one Jordan engines; one 54-inch Two-Cylinder. Widest trimmed sheet, 46 inches. Water, Steam and Electricity. Tobacco, Chip Board and Wrapping Papers. 12,000 lbs. 24 hours.

ST. JOSEPH—Berrien Co.

Pop. 6,000. On P. M. & M. C. RR.; St. J. C. SS. Co. M. O. and Tel. office; Am., Adams and Wells, Fargo & Co. Ex.

MULLEN BROS. PAPER CO. (James A. Mullen, Pres.; W. T. Mullen, Vice-Pres.; Treas. and Gen. Mgr.; R. Banyon, Sec.; F. A. Smith, Supt.) S. P., at mill. Three 1000-lb. Beating and two Jordan engines; one 90-inch Four-Cylinder. Widest trimmed sheet, 81 inches. Steam. Red Rosin Sized Sheathing, Light-Weight Plain Chip, Light-Weight Straw Chip, Chip and Felt Saturating, Paper Butter Dishes, Paper Sugar Bags. 40,000 lbs. 24 hours.

THREE RIVERS—St. Joseph Co.

Pop. 5,213. K. Div. L. S. & M. S. and M. S. A. Div. M. C. M. O. Tel.; Am. and U. S. Ex.

EDDY PAPER CO. MILL No. 1. (Frank H. Milham, Pres.; Oscar Gumbinsky, Vice-Pres.; Geo. T. Wolf, Treas.; C. E. Nelson, Sec. and Gen. Mgr.; L. W. Dickinson, Asst. Sec.; Wm. R. McPherson, Supt.) S. P., at mill. Four 1200-lb. Beating and two Jordan engines. One 80-inch Five

THOMAS E. GLEESON, Inc., **FOURDRINIER WIRES**
411-413 John St., E. NEWARK, N. J. For Tissue and Fine Grade Papers

Cylinder. Widest trimmed sheet, 72 inches. Card Middles, Bogus Bristols, Box Boards, Blanks and Colored Specialties. Steam and Electricity. 50,000 lbs. 24 hours.

VICKSBURG—Kalamazoo Co.
Pop. 1,624. At Junc. G. R. & I. and G. T. W. RR. M. O. and Tel. office. Nat. and Ad. Ex.

LEE PAPER CO. (F. E. Lee, Pres.; Geo. E. Bardeen, First Vice-Pres.; A. B. Gardner, Second Vice-Pres.; Norman Bardeen, Sec.-Treas. and Gen. Mgr.; W. H. Wightman, Supt.) S. P., at mill. Thirteen Beating and two Refining engines; two 118-inch Fourdriniers. Widest trimmed sheet, 108 inches. Steam. Loft-Dried, Air-Dried and Machine-Dried Bonds, Writings, Linens, Ledgers, Envelops and Plated Papers. 30,000 lbs. 24 hours.

WATERVLIET—Berrien Co.
Pop. 1,200. Pere Marquette RR. M. O., Tel., Bank and Ex.

WATERVLIET PAPER CO. (W. M. Loveland, Pres.; C. B. Hays, Vice-Pres.; A. B. Scheld, Sec. and Treas.; F. D. Gilchrist, Asst. Sec. and Asst. Mgr.) S. P., at mill. Four 1500-lb. Beating and two Refining engines; one 138-inch Fourdrinier. Widest trimmed sheet, 126 inches. Width of Super Calenders, 52 and 60 inches. Water and Steam. Book, Lithograph and Folder Papers. 40,000 lbs. 24 hours. COATING DIVISION—Five Single 54-inch and two Single 64-inch Coaters, one 54-inch Cylinder Coater, two 54-inch and two 64-inch Super Calenders. Capacity, 50,000 lbs. 24 hours.

WHITE PIGEON—St. Joseph Co.
Pop. 705. On L. S. & M. S. RR. M. O. and Tel. office; Am. Ex.

EDDY PAPER CO. MILL NO. 2. Main Office, Three Rivers. (Frank H. Milham, Pres.; Oscar Gumbinsky, Vice-Pres.; Geo. T. Wolf, Treas.; C. E. Nelson, Sec. and Gen. Mgr.; L. W. Dickinson, Asst. Sec.; C. F. Sisson, Res. Mgr.; H. E. Eurich, Supt.) S. P., at mill. Fourteen Beating and six Refining engines. One 100-inch and one 122-inch Cylinder Machines. Widest trimmed sheets, 92 and 110 inches. Water, Steam and Electricity. Card Middles, Bogus Bristols, Box Boards, Blanks and Colored Specialties. 150,000 lbs. 24 hours.

YPSILANTI—Washtenaw Co.
Pop. 7,378. On N. Y. C. RR. M. O. and Tel. office. Am. and U. S. Ex.

PENINSULAR PAPER CO. (D. L. Quirk, Jr., Pres.; J. E. Beal, Vice-Pres.; E. C. Cornwell, Sec. and Treas.; C. E. Lincoln, Sales Mgr.; J. P. Cooney, Supt.) S. P., at mill. Four 1000-lb. Beating, two Jordan; one 1500-lb. Washing engines and one Rotary; one 64-inch and one 78-inch Fourdriniers. Widest trimmed sheets, 56 and 75 inches. Width of Super-Calenders, 48 inches. Width of Paster, 51 inches. Three 36-inch Platters. Water, Steam and Electricity. Cover and Colored Specialties. 36,000 lbs. 24 hours. *"Orkin," "Onimbo," "Gibraltar," "Highlight," "Patrician," "Neapolitan"* Covers, and *"The Covenant Papers," "Platefold"* and *"Publicity."*

DRY ROSIN SIZE

Brittle, easy soluble. Cheapest size out; cheaper than mill made size. Ask us about it. Also all other grades.

ARABOL M'F'G CO.
100 William St., New York

HIGHEST GRADE BRIMSTONE—GUARANTEED 99% PURE
free from Arsenic or Selenium. Write for particulars to
THE UNION SULPHUR CO., Main Office, 17 Battery Pl., New York. Mines, Calcasieu Parish, La.

DRY ROSIN SIZE Brittle, easy soluble, cheapest size out; cheaper than mill made size. Ask us about it. Also all other grades. **ARABOL M'F'G CO.** 109 William St., N. Y.

128 *Minnesota*

MINNESOTA.

BRAINERD—Crow Wing Co.

Pop. 9,524. N. P. and M. & I. RR. M. O. and Tel. office; N. P. Ex.

NORTHWEST PAPER CO., THE. (R. M. Wyerhaeuser, Pres.; R. D. Musser, 1st Vice-Pres. and Treas.; C. I. McNair, 2d Vice-Pres. and Gen. Mgr.; C. I. McNair, Jr., Sec.; W. K. McNair, Supt. and Asst. Treas.) Office, Cloquet. FREDERICK MILL. Three 1200-lb. Beating and one Refining engines; one Fourdrinier. Widest trimmed sheet, 115 inches. Water, Steam and Electricity. News, Book and Manila. 80,000 lbs. 24 hours. BRAINERD PULP MILL. S. P., at mill. Eight Grinders; four Wet, three Feltless Machines; four "Impco" Screens and one "Impco" Knotter. Water and Electricity. Ground Wood Pulp. 106,000 lbs. 24 hours.

CLEARWATER—Wright Co.—PULP MILL.

Pop. 287. On M. & N. W. Div. of G. N. RR. M. O., Tel., Gr. North. Ex., Clearwater.

MUCKLE BROS. MFG. CO. S. P., at mill. One Grinder, one Wet and Insulator Machine combined. Water and Steam. Econ-o-Flax Insulator. 16 000 lbs. 24 hours. (Idle and for sale.)

CLOQUET—Carlton Co.

Pop. 8,031. On Gt. N.; N. P.; C., M. & St. P. RR.; D. & N. R. RR. M. O. and Tel. office. Adams, N. P. and Great Northern Ex.

NORTHWEST PAPER CO., THE. (R. M. Weyerhaeuser, Pres.; R. D. Musser, 1st Vice-Pres. and Treas.; C. I. McNair, 2d Vice-Pres. and Gen. Mgr.; C. I. McNair, Jr., Sec.; W. K. McNair, Asst. Treas. and Supt.) S. P., at mill. One 1000-lb. and five 1200-lb. Beating and two Refining engines; two Fourdriniers. Widest trimmed sheets, 110 and 111 inches. Water, Steam and Electricity. News, Book and Manila. 130,000 lbs. 24 hours. PULP MILL. Two mills. S. P., at mills. LIVINGSTON PULP MILL. Fourteen Grinders; six Wet and five Feltless Machines, five "Impco" Screens. Water and Electricity. Ground Wood. 160,000 lbs. 24 hours. KNIFE FALLS PULP MILL. Three Grinders; two Wet Machines. Water. Ground Wood. 24,000 lbs. 24 hours. NORTHSTAR SULPHITE MILL. Two Digesters, two Rogers Wet Machines, three "Impco" Screens. Water, Steam and Electricity. 100,000 lbs. 24 hours.

GRAND RAPIDS—Itasca Co.

Pop. 1,428. On G. N. RR. M. O. and Tel. office; G. N. Ex.

ITASCA PAPER CO. (C. K. Blandin, Pres.; J. M. Riegel, Vice-Pres.; S. J. Robertson, Sec.; S. A. Young, St. Paul, Minn., Treas.; C. K. Andrews, Mgr.) S. P., at mill. Three 1250-lb. Beating and one Jordan engines; one 120-inch Fourdrinier; widest trimmed sheet, 112 inches. Water and Steam. News. 65,000 lbs. 24 hours. PULP MILL. S. P., at mill. Seven Grinders; five Wet and two Decker Machines. Water. Ground Wood. 50,000 lbs. 24 hours.

INTERNATIONAL FALLS—Koochiching Co.

Pop. 5,500. On N. P.; M. D. & W.; C. N. and D. R. L. & W. RR.

MINNESOTA AND ONTARIO POWER CO. (General Office, International Falls.) (E. W. Backus, Pres.; S. W. Backus, Vice-Pres.; B. G.

DARMSTADT, SCOTT & COURTNEY, Inc. Importers, Exporters and Dealers in **PAPER MAKERS' SUPPLIES** Also Mfrs. of DEADENING and SATURATING FELTS 178 and 184 SOUTH STREET NEW YORK

McENERY PAPER COMPANY 112 W. ADAMS ST., CHICAGO MANUFACTURERS' SALES AGENCY PRACTICALLY ALL GRADES

Dahlberg, Second Vice-Pres.; William F. Brooks, Treas.; Thomas McLaren, Sec.) Four Beating engines; two Mixing tanks; two 154-inch and two 184-inch Fourdriniers. Water and Electricity. News Print, 450,000 lbs. 24 hours. PULP MILL. Twenty-four 24-inch Grinders; nine "Impco" Rotary Screens. Water. Ground Wood, 340,000 lbs. 24 hours; Sulphite, 280,000 lbs. 24 hours; Insulite Plant, 45,000 sq. ft. 24 hours. Kraft Mill—15,000 lbs. 24 hours.

LITTLE FALLS—Morrison Co.

Pop. 6,774. On N. P. RR. M. O. and Tel. office; N. Pac. Ex.

HENNEPIN PAPER CO. (B. F. Nelson, Pres.; Gilbert M. Walker, Vice-Pres.; W. E. Nelson, Sec.; W. J. Walker, Treas.) General office, 1128 Plymouth Building, Minneapolis, Minn. S. P., at mill. Three 1000-lb., one 1200-lb. and two Jordan engines; one 122-inch Fourdrinier. Widest trimmed sheet, 111 inches. Union Screens. Water and Steam. News and Manila. 64,000 lbs. 24 hours. PULP MILL. S. P., at mill. Six Grinders; two Wet Machines. Water and Electricity. Ground Wood. 50,000 lbs. (dry) 24 hours.

MINNEAPOLIS—Hennepin Co.

Pop. 400,000. On N. P.; W. C.; G. N.; C. M. & St. P.; M. & St. L.; C., St. P., M. & O.; C. R. I. P. Ry.; M., S. P. & S. M.; C. G. W.; C. B. & N. RR. M. O. and Tel. office; Am., Adams, Gt. Northern, Nat., N. Pac., U. S., W., F. & Co. and West Ex.

B. F. NELSON MANUFACTURING COMPANY, THE. (W. E. Nelson, Pres.; G. H. Nelson, Vice-Pres.; B. F. Nelson, Treas.; E. N. Kading, Sec.) Twenty-three 1200-lb. Beating engines and four Refining engines; one 42-inch Cylinder; widest trimmed sheet, 40 inches; one 80-inch Five Cylinder; widest trimmed sheet, 78 inches; one 140-inch Five-Cylinder; widest trimmed sheet, 132 inches. Steam and Electricity. News Board, Mill Wrappers, Combination Boards, Mist Gray, Suit Boards, Building Paper, Dry Felt Roofing and Asphalt Shingles. 250,000 lbs. 24 hours.

ST. PAUL—Ramsey Co.

Pop. 247,232. On C. B. & Q.; C. G. W.; C. M. & St. P.; M. & O.; M., St. P. & Ste. M.; No. P.; G. N.; M. & St. L. and C., R. I. & P. RR. West, National and Wells Fargo Ex.

WALDORF PAPER PRODUCTS CO., Successors to Waldorf Box Board Co. (M. W. Waldorf, Pres.; Paul N. Myers, Vice-Pres.; Douglas Putnam, Sec. and Treas.; H. C. McDaniel, Mill Mgr.; John Pfister, Mill Supt.) S. P., "Minnesota Transfer, Minnesota." Twelve 1500-lb. E. D. Jones & Sons Co. Beating and six Jordan engines; one Beloit Iron Works 120-inch Five Cylinder and one 145-inch six Cylinder Machines. Electricity. Widest trimmed sheets, 112 and 134 inches. Plain and Vat Lined Chip Boards, News Board, Cracker Shell, Manila Lined Chip and News, Colored Suit Box Board, Solid Manila, Fibre Container Board, Pasted Binders' Board, Mill Wrappers and all calipers of single and double lined Patent Coated Board, Wall Board, Test Chips and Jute. Capacity 250,000 lbs. 24 hours.

SARTELL—Benton Co.

Pop. 200. On Miss. River and N. P. RR. M. O. and Tel. offices; Northern P. Ex.

WATAB PULP AND PAPER CO. P. O. Address, Sartell. (I. N. Bushong, Pres.; Jacob Mortenson, Vice-Pres.; O. L. E. Weber, Sec. and

DRY ROSIN SIZE Brittle, easy soluble, cheapest size out; cheaper than mill made size. Ask us about it. Also all other grades. **ARABOL M'F'G CO.** 100 William St., N. Y.

Minnesota, Mississippi and New Hampshire

Gen. Mgr.; F. P. Stone, Treas.) S. P., at Sartell. Eleven 1000-lb. Beating, three Wagg Majestic Refining, four 2000-lb. Washing and two 2000-lb. Cooking engines; two 154-inch Fourdriniers. Widest trimmed sheet, 140 inches. Electricity. High Grade News, Ground Wood, M. F. and S. & S. C. Book Papers in Sheets and Rolls, Light Weight Catalogue Papers. 180,000 lbs. 24 hours. PULP MILL. S. P., at mill. Seventeen Grinders; nine Wet Machines. Water. Ground Wood. 170,000 lbs. 24 hours.

WINONA—Winona Co.

Pop. 18,583. On River Div. Chic., Milw. & St. Paul; St. Paul Div. Chic., Burl. & Quincy. Eastern Term. Winona & St. Peter Div. Chicago & Northwestern; Western Term. Green Bay & Western and Chicago Great Western RR. M. O., Tel., Bank. Wells Fargo, Adams and Am. Ex.

WINONA PULP & PAPER CO. (M. B. Johnson, Pres.; C. N. Weyer, Vice-Pres.; J. E. Lappen, Sec.-Treas.; George Tomskey, Supt.) One 500-lb. and three 1000-lb. Beaters, two Refining engines and one Rotary Boiler. One 68-inch Fourdrinier. Widest trimmed sheet, 64 inches. Steam. Straw Kraft Butchers Fibre, Sulphite Wrapper, No. 2 Book and Gray Car Lining. 20,000 lbs. 24 hours.

MISSISSIPPI.

MOSS POINT—Jackson Co.

Pop. 4,500. On Moss Point & Pascagoula RR. M. O. and Tel. office (Postal and W. U.). So. Ex.; two local banks.

SOUTHERN PAPER CO. Office, Moss Point. S. P., Kreole and Moss Point. (J. L. Dantzler, Pres.; A. Shirley Benn, M. P., First Vice-Pres.; W. S. Hofstra, Second Vice-Pres.; A. F. Dantzler, Treas.; M. L. Screven, Sec.; E. H. Mayo, Gen. Mgr.) Eight 1500-lb. Horne Beaters, four Claflin Continuous Beaters; one Marshall Continuous and one E. D. Jones' Refiner; one 106-inch Flying Dutchman; one 136-inch Fourdrinier. Widest trimmed sheets, 96 and 120 inches. Steam. "KREOLEKRAFT" Sulphate Wrapping, Bag, Envelope and Specialties, Glazed and Unglazed. 80,000 lbs. 24 hours. PULP MILL. Three Digesters. Steam. Sulphate pulp 80,000 lbs. 24 hours.

NEW HAMPSHIRE.

ASHLAND—Grafton Co.

Pop. 1,289. On W. M. Div. of B. & M. RR. M. O. and Tel. office; nearest bank, Plymouth, 6 miles; Am. Ex.

CONTINENTAL PAPER BAG CO. Office, 17 Battery Place, New York. (H. Elsas, Pres.; I. Kuhe, Vice-Pres.; C. W. Lyman, Treas.; A. Chilcott, Supt.) ASHLAND MILLS. (A. Chilcott, Supt.) S. P., at mill. Six 500-lb., two 800-lb. Beating and three Jordan engines; one 84-inch and two 66-inch Fourdriniers. Widest trimmed sheets, 72 and 60 inches. Water and Steam. Toilet Papers and Tissues. 30,000 lbs. 24 hours.

BATH—Grafton Co.

Pop. 906. On White Mountain Div. of B. & M. RR. M. O. and Tel. office; Am. Ex.; nearest bank, Lisbon, N. H., 5 miles.

CUSHMAN-RANKIN CO., THE. Three Noble & Wood 1200-lb. and one Emerson Beating engines; one Jordan and three Wet Machines. Water and Steam. Heeling Board. 16,000 lbs. 24 hours.

PRESS ROLLS Maple and Gum White Wood Felt Rolls **J. W. HEWITT MACHINE CO.** Neenah, Wis.

THOMAS E. GLEESON, Inc., 411-413 John St., E. NEWARK, N. J.
CYLINDER MOULDS and DANDY ROLLS Made and Repaired
LETTERING and MONOGRAMS for WATERMARKS

BENNINGTON—Hillsboro Co.

Pop. 667. On Concord Div. B. & M. RR. M. O. and Tel. office. Nearest bank, Hillsboro Bridge, 10 miles; Am. Ex.

MONADNOCK PAPER MILLS. (Arthur J. Pierce, Pres. and Treas.) P. O. address, 201 Devonshire street, Boston. MONADNOCK MILL. Seven 1700-lb. Beating and four Jordan engines; one 96-inch and one 110-inch Fourdriniers. Width of Super Calenders, up to 50 inches. Widest trimmed sheet, 100 inches. Water and Steam. Machine-finished and Super Calendered Book. English finish, Music, Lithograph, Envelope and Coating. 65,000 lbs. 24 hours.

BERLIN—Coos Co.

Pop. 8,886. On G. T. Div. of B. & M. M. O. and Tel. office; Am. and Can. Ex.

BROWN CO., successors to BERLIN MILLS CO. (H. J. Brown, Pres.; O. B. Brown, Vice-Pres. and Treas.; W. R. Brown, Asst. Treas.; D. P. Brown.) Main Office, 404 Commercial Street, Portland, Me. RIVERSIDE MILLS. One 100-inch and 102-inch Fourdriniers. Widest trimmed sheet, 90 inches. Kraft. 100,000 lbs. 24 hours. CASCADE MILL. Four 104-inch Fourdriniers; one 94-inch Fourdrinier. Widest trimmed sheets, 150 inches and 80 inches. Kraft, 200,000 lbs., Fibre, 100,000 lbs., Bond, 80,000 lbs. and Sheathing 50,000 lbs. 24 hours. PULP MILL. Eight Digesters. Bleached and Unbleached Sulphite. 350,000 lbs. 24 hours.

BROWN CO., successors to Burgess Sulphite Fibre Co. Office, 404 Commercial Street, Portland, Me. (H. J. Brown, Pres.; O. B. Brown, Treas.) S. P., at mill. Eighteen Digesters; fourteen 72-inch Wet Machines and one 132-inch Drying Machine. Water, Steam and Electricity. Bleached Sulphite Fibre (dry). 900,000 lbs. 24 hours.

INTERNATIONAL PAPER CO. Office, 30 Broad street, New York. GLENN MILL. (James M. Murray, Supt.) S. P., at mill. Twelve Beating and six Refining engines; one 88-inch, one 96-inch, one 103-inch, two 122-inch Fourdriniers. Water and Steam. News and Catalogue and Wrappers. 206,000 lbs. 24 hours. PULP MILL. Six Digesters; twenty-one Grinders; eighteen Wet Machines. Water and Steam. Sulphite Fibre 120,000 lbs., Ground Wood 160,000 lbs. 24 hours.

BRISTOL—Grafton Co.

Pop. 1,600. On So. Div. of B. & M. RR. M. O. and Tel. office; Am. Ex.

MASON-PERKINS PAPER COMPANY. (Fred P. Weeks, Pres.; F. N. Gilman, Treas.; Joseph H. Breck, Supt.) PAPER MILL. S. P., station, ¾ mile. Three 500-lb. and three 700-lb. Beating engines; two Refining engines; one 62-inch Cylinder. Widest trimmed sheet, 56 inches. Water. Toilet Tissue, 4,000 lbs. 24 hours. PULP MILL. S. P., station ⅛ mile. Two Grinders; one 76-inch Dry Machine. Water. Ground Wood (dry). 12,000 lbs. 24 hours. BRISTOL PAPER MILLS. S. P., 1 mile. Five 500lb., one 600-lb. Beating and one Jordan engines; one 68-inch Fourdrinier. Widest trimmed sheet, 61 inches. Water. Colored, Poster and Box Lining. 18,000 lbs. 24 hours. PULP MILL. NEW-FOUND PULP MILL. S. P., at mill. Two New England Grinders; one 64-inch Wet Machine. Water. Ground Wood. 10,000 lbs. 24 hours.

BRIMSTONE MAKES THE VERY BEST SULPHITE.
If you are looking for a high-grade Brimstone write to
THE UNION SULPHUR CO., Main Office, 17 Battery Pl., New York. Mines, Calcasieu Parish, La.

M. GOTTESMAN & CO., Inc., 18 E. 41st STREET, NEW YORK, Cable Address "Namsettog" EUROPEAN OFFICES: Stockholm, Sweden — Strong and Easy Bleaching SULPHITE PULP

DRY ROSIN SIZE Brittle, easy soluble, cheapest size out; cheaper than mill made size. Ask us about it. Also all other grades. **ARABOL M'F'G CO.** 109 William St., N. Y.

New Hampshire

CLAREMONT—Sullivan Co.
Pop. 6,498. On C. R. & O. Div. of B. & M. RR. M. O. and Tel. office; Am. Ex.

CLAREMONT PAPER CO., INC. (F. N. McCrea, Pres.; H. W. Beauclerk, Vice-Pres.; W. C. Dawson, Treas.; Paul D. Caskey, Clerk; J. A. Bothwell, Gen. Mgr.; C. H. McDuffee, Supt.; E. P. Lindsay, Selling Agt., 299 Congress Street, Boston, Mass.) S. P., at mill. Six 1000-lb., two 1500-lb., eight 2000-lb. Beating and four Jordan engines; one 62-inch, one 102-inch and one 136-inch Fourdriniers. Widest trimmed sheet, 128 inches. Water. Manila and Kraft. 120,000 lbs. 24 hours.

FRANKLIN—Merrimac Co.
Pop. 5,846. On F. & T.; B. & M. RR. M. O. and Tel. office; nearest bank, Franklin Falls, 1 mile; Am. Ex.

INTERNATIONAL PAPER COMPANY. Office, 30 Broad Street, New York. WINNIPISEOGEE MILL. (Geo. M. Dunham, Mgr.) S. P., Franklin. Ten Beating and five Refining engines; one 84-inch, one 95-inch and one 106-inch Fourdriniers. Union Screens. Water and Steam. Special Super Half-tone, M. F. Book, Rotograph. 90,000 lbs. 24 hours. PULP MILL. Eighteen Grinders; five Wet Machines. Ground Wood. 70,000 lbs. 24 hours.

GROVETON—Coos Co.
On W. M. Div. B. & M. and G. T. RR. Tel. office and M. O. Am. and Can. Ex.

ODELL MANUFACTURING CO. (Charles C. Wilson, Pres., Groveton, N. H.; W. N. Munroe, Treas., Groveton, N. H.; A. N. Waring, Mgr. of Sales, 527 Fifth Avenue, New York City, N. Y.) S. P., at mills. MILL NO. 1. Nine Beating and two Jordan engines; one 112-inch Bagley & Sewall and one 112-inch J. H. Horne & Sons Fourdriniers. Steam and Electricity. Dello Bond and Ledger and Bleached Sulphite Specialties. 95,000 lbs. 24 hours. MILL NO. II. Nine Beating and one Jordan engines; one 158-inch Pusey & Jones Fourdrinier. Steam. High grade Manila and Fibre, Tag, Textile and Sealing Wrappers. 100,000 lbs. 24 hours. All above grades furnished Waxed or Oiled; also Waxed and Oiled Specialties. PULP MILL. Four Digesters; six Wet machines; three "Impco Knotters." Steam and Water. Sulphite Fibre. 160,000 lbs. 24 hours.

HINSDALE—Cheshire Co.
Pop. 1,500. On Ashuelot Div. of B. & M. RR. M. O. and Tel. office; nearest bank, Brattleboro, Vt., and Winchester, N. H., 6 miles; Am. Ex.

ASHUELOT PAPER CO. (Fred'k S. Leonard, Pres.; F. W. Childs, Vice-Pres.; H. S. Garfield, Asst. Treas.; C. E. Weed, Supt.) ASHUELOT MILL. S. P., at mill. Seven 1000-lb. and one 1250-lb. Beating engines; one 2000-lb. Washing engine; two Refining engines; two 29-inch Cylinder Machines. Widest trimmed sheet, 81 inches. Water and Steam. Tissue. 12,000 lbs. 24 hours. *Yellow Copying and High Grade Tissues.*

FISK PAPER CO., INC., THE. (Mrs. Isabel R. Dickinson, Pres.; O. H. Dickinson, Treas.; Frederick S. Leonard, Agt.) BRIGHTWOOD MILL. Two 800-lb. Beating and one Jordan engines; one 62-inch Cylinder. Widest trimmed sheet, 55 inches. Water and Steam. White and Manila (wood), Flat and Folded and Cased (flat package) Toilet. 4000 lbs. 24 hours.

LOMBARD'S ENGLISH NEWCASTLE PULP STONES ARE SUPERIOR TO ALL OTHERS. ALL SIZES IN STOCK. LOMBARD & CO., Importers & Manufacturers, 226 & 228 A Street, Boston.

National Duplex Waterproof Case Lining
IS WATERPROOF— NATIONAL WATERPROOFING CO., 1054 DREXEL BLDG.
CLEAN TO HANDLE PHILADELPHIA

Paper and Pulp Mills in the United States 133

HINSDALE PAPER MFG. CO., succeeds Orren C. Robertson Co. (R. W. White, Pres.; L. N. Stearns, Vice-Pres.; G. F. Stoehr, Treas.; F. E. Field, Supt.) S. P., at mill. Three 1200-lb. Beating and two Refining engines; two 84-inch Cylinder machines. Widest trimmed rolls, 76 inches. Water and Steam. Manila and White and Crêpe Tissues. 20,000- lbs. 24 hours.

ROBERTSON BROTHERS. (E. C. and Est. of F. W. R.) S. P., at mill. Four 800-lb. Beating and one 1500-lb. Washing and one Refining engines; one 72-inch Cylinder. Widest trimmed sheet, 63 inches. Water and Steam. Manila and Kraft Tissue in Rolls. 6000 lbs. 24 hours.

ROBERTSON, E. C., & SON. (E. C. and W. F. R.) S. P., at mill. Two 900-lb. Beating and one Refining engines; one 86-inch Cylinder. Widest trimmed sheet, 76 inches. Water and Steam. Tissue Manila, and White and Colored Tissue in rolls and large sheets. 6000 lbs. 24 hours.

ROBERTSON, G. A., & CO. (G. A. and O. C. R.) HINSDALE MILL. S. P., Hinsdale Station, ½ mile. Two 550-lb., two 1000-lb. Beating and two Jordan engines; one 72-inch and one 90-inch Cylinder. Widest trimmed sheets, 68 and 80 inches. Water and Steam. Manila Tissue and Toilet. Rolls only. 15,000 lbs. 24 hours.

ROBERTSON, W. F., & CO. (W. F. R. and E. C.) S. P., at mill. Two 900-lb. Beating and one Refining engines; one 86-inch Cylinder. Widest trimmed sheet, 76 inches. Water and Steam. Tissue Manila, and White and Colored Tissue in rolls and large sheets. 5000 lbs. 24 hours. *Perforated Crêpe Papers and Towels a Specialty.*

LINCOLN—Grafton Co.
Pop. 1,540. On P. V. Branch B. & M. RR. M. O. and Tel. office; nearest bank, Plymouth, 21 miles; Am. Ex.

PARKER-YOUNG CO.—HENRY PAPER CO., BRANCH, 181 State St., Boston, Mass. (H. B. Moulton, Pres.; E. K. Woodworth, Vice-Pres.; Martin A. Brown, Treas.; Alfred Stanley, Supt.) S. P., at mill. Thirteen 1400-lb. Beating and four Refining engines; three 135-inch Fourdriniers. Widest trimmed sheet, 120 inches. Union Screens; one "Impco" Screen. Steam and Water. Bond and Manilas. 160,000 lbs. 24 hours. PULP MILL. Four Grinders, two Wet Machines and two Digesters. Steam and Water. Ground Wood, 40,000 tons 24 hours. Sulphite, 120,000 tons 24 hours.

PARKER-YOUNG CO.—HENRY PAPER CO., BRANCH. SULPHITE MILL. Two Digesters; four Wet Machines; one "Improved" Knotter. Steam and Electricity. Sulphite Fibre. 110,000 lbs. 24 hours. GROUND WOOD MILL. Four Grinders; two Deckers. Water and Electricity. Ground Wood. 50,000 lbs. (dry) 24 hours.

MANCHESTER—Hillsborough Co.
Pop. 70,000. On S. Div. of B. & M. RR. M. O. and Tel. office. Am. Ex.

AMOSKEAG PAPER MILLS CO. (F. P. Carpenter, Pres.; A. B. Carpenter, Treas.) AMOSKEAG PAPER MILLS. S. P., at mill. Six 800-lb., one 1000-lb. and three Jordan engines; one 68-inch and one 88-inch Fourdriniers. Water and Steam. Book. 20,000 lbs. 24 hours.

R. B. McEwan, *Pres.* J. L. McEwan, *Vice-Pres.* Arthur McEwan, *Treas. and Mgr.* R. W. McEwan, *Secy.*
Sheet Lining Plant, Office and Mills at WHIPPANY, N. J.
McEWAN BROS., Inc. MANUFACTURERS OF ALL GRADES **PAPER BOX BOARD**

DRY ROSIN SIZE Brittle, easy soluble, cheapest size out; cheaper than mill made size. Ask us about it. Also all other grades. **ARABOL M'F'G CO.** 100 William St., N. Y.

New Hampshire

MERRIMACK—Hillsboro Co.

Pop. 1,089. On B. & M. Banking town, Manchester or Nashua.

McELWAIN COMPANY, W. H. Office, 354 Congress Street, Boston, Mass. (J. F. McElwain, Pres.; C. J. Prescott, Vice-Pres.; E. L. Prescott, Treas.; Clifford P. Warren, Sec.) S. P., Merrimack. Eight 1000-lb. Beating engines; five 52-inch Noble & Wood Wet Machines. Water and Electricity. Granosole. 24,000 lbs. 24 hours.

MILTON—Strafford Co.

Pop. 1,625. On B. & M. RR. M. O and Tel. office; nearest bank, Rochester, 8 miles; Am. Ex.

MILTON LEATHER BOARD CO. (S. F. Dawson, Jr., Pres.; S. F. Dawson, Treas.) S. P., at mill. Five 3500-lb. Beating and three Jordan engines; six Wet Machines. Water and Steam. Sole Leather Heeling. 30,000 lbs. 24 hours.

SPAULDING, J., & SONS. (Co-partnership.) New York Office, 449 Broome Street; Chicago Office, 166 North Clinton Street. Boston Office, 203 Albany Bldg. (L. C. Spaulding, R. H. Spaulding and H. N. Spaulding.) Address, North Rochester, N. H. Four Mills, North Rochester and Milton, N. H., and Townsend Harbor, Mass. Leatherboard. (For equipment, see Townsend Harbor, Mass.)

NORTH ROCHESTER—Strafford Co.

Pop. 7,800. On P. & W. and N. & P. Divisions B. & M. RR. M. O. and Tel. office.

SPAULDING, J., & SONS. (Co-partnership.) New York Office, 449 Broome Street; Chicago Office, 106 North Clinton Street. Boston Office, 203 Albany Bldg. (L. C. Spaulding, R. H. Spaulding and H. N. Spaulding.) Address, North Rochester, N. H. Four Mills. Townsend Harbor, Mass., North Rochester and Milton, N. H. Leatherboard. (For equipment, see Townsend Harbor, Mass.)

NORTHUMBERLAND—Coos Co.

Pop. 200. On White Mt. Div. B. & M. RR. M. O.; nearest Tel. and bank, Lancaster, 5 miles.

HALL & RICHTER PAPER CO. (H. H. Meyer, Pres.; R. J. Buck, Vice-Pres.; E. H. Morris, Treas.; W. P. Corcoran, Asst. Treas.; F. L. Fuller, Supt. and Gen. Mgr.) Three 800-lb. Beaters and one Jordan; one 72-inch Fourdrinier. Widest trimmed sheet, 65 inches. Water and Steam. Manila Tissue. 9,000 lbs. 24 hours. PULP MILL. Two Grinders; two Wet Machines. Water. Ground Wood. 10,000 lbs. 24 hours.

PLYMOUTH—Grafton Co.—PULP MILL.

Pop. 1,972. On B. & M. RR. M. O. and Tel. office; Am. Ex.

LIVERMORE FALLS PULP CO. (Parker-Young Co. Henry Paper Co. Branch, Lincoln, N. H., Owner.) S. P., at mill. Four Grinders; six Wet Machines. Water. Ground Wood (dry). 50,000 lbs. 24 hours.

PORTSMOUTH—Rockingham Co.

Pop. 11,269. Portland and Southern Div. Boston and Maine. Tel., M. O., Bank. Am. Ex.

MORLEY BUTTON MFG. CO. All paper made is used by the company.

HARDY S. FERGUSON CONSULTING ENGINEER 200 FIFTH AVENUE NEW YORK CITY
PAPER, PULP AND FIBRE MILLS WATER POWER DEVELOPMENT DAMS, STORAGE RESERVOIRS AND OTHER HYDRAULIC STRUCTURES

PRESS ROLLS Maple and Gum White Wood Felt Rolls **J. W. HEWITT MACHINE CO.** Neenah, Wis.

THOMAS E. GLEESON, Inc., **FOURDRINIER WIRES**
411-413 John St., E. NEWARK, N. J. For Tissue and Fine Grade Papers

Paper and Pulp Mills in the United States

SUNAPEE—Sullivan Co.
Pop. 946. On C. Div. of B. & M. RR. M. O. and Tel. office, Newport, and nearest bank, Claremont; Am. Ex.

EMERSON PAPER CO. (J. E. Robertson, Pres.; W. A. Whitney, Treas. and Mgr.) P. O. Address, Wendell, N. H. EMERSON PAPER MILL. S. P., ¼ mile. Two 1000-lb. and one 1400-lb. Beating, one Jordan engines; one 84-inch Fourdrinier. Widest trimmed sheet, 76 inches. Water and Steam. Book Paper and Specialties. 20,000 lbs. 24 hours. PULP MILL. LAKE SUNAPEE MILL. S. P., Sunapee, 3 miles. Two Grinders; two 66-inch Wet Machines. Water. Ground Wood (dry). 10,000 lbs. 24 hours.

WADLEY'S FALLS—Strafford Co.
Pop. 45. Tel. connection. M. O. office, Ex. and nearest bank, Newmarket.

LEE FIBRE CO. P. O. address, Newmarket, N. H. (W. E. Bixby, Pres.; H. F. Smith, Sec. and Supt.; H. G. Keeler, Treas.) S. P., Lee, 1¾ miles. Two 1000-lb. Beating engines; two 50-inch Wet Machines. Widest trimmed sheet, 42 inches. Water and Steam. Heeling Board. 6000 lbs. 24 hours.

WEST CLAREMONT—Sullivan Co.
On Conn. River Div. of B. & M. RR. Tel. office, M. O. and nearest bank, Claremont, 2½ miles; Am. Ex.

COY PAPER CO. (F. J. Perry, Pres.; F. E. Coy, Sec. and Treas.) S. P., Claremont. Six 800-lb. Beating, one 1500-lb. Washing and one Refining engines; two 66-inch Cylinders. Widest trimmed sheet, 58 inches. Water, Steam and Electricity. Tissue Manila. No. 1 Pattern Tissue a Specialty. 7000 lbs. 24 hours.

JARVIS PAPER MILLS. (Russell Jarvis.) P. O. address, Claremont, N. H. S. P., Claremont Junction. Four 1000-lb. Beating, one 1500-lb. Washing and one Refining engines; one 68-inch Cylinder. Widest trimmed sheet, 60 inches. Water and Steam. Pattern Tissue; all Rag Toilet, Sheets and Jumbo Rolls. 6000 lbs. 24 hours.

WEST HENNIKER—Merrimac Co.
On W. N. & P. Div. of B. & M. RR., P. O. and M. O. office West Henniker; Station, Emerson, N. H.; Tel. office, Henniker, 1½ miles; nearest bank, Hillsboro Bridge, 5 miles; Am. Ex.

CONTOOCOOK VALLEY PAPER CO. (Charles L. Jackman, Pres.; Walter A. Connor, Treas.; John A. Connelly, Supt.) CONTOOCOOK MILL. S. P., at mill. One 1200-lb. Beating and one Jordan engines; three 400-lb Washers and one Rotary boiler; one 62-inch Fourdrinier. Widest trimmed sheet, 58 inches. Water. Card, Coating, Gumming and Specialties in Strong Papers. 6000 to 8000 lbs. 24 hours.

WEST HOPKINTON—Merrimac Co.
Pop. 100. On W. N. & P. Div. B. & M. R.R. M. O. and Tel. office; Ex. at W. Hopkinton; bank, Hillsboro, 11 miles, or Concord, 12 miles.

DAVIS PAPER CO. P. O. Address, West Hopkinton, N. H. (H. C. Davis, Pres.; N. F. Davis; H. J. Davis, Treas.) Nine 1000-lb. Emerson Beaters and three Jordan engines, one 64-inch Board Machine, four 48-inch Wet Machines. Water and Steam. Leather Boards and Paper Box Boards. Leather Board, 20,000 lbs.; Box Boards, 48,000 lbs. 24 hours.

DRY ROSIN SIZE

Brittle, easy soluble. Cheapest size out; cheaper than mill made size. Ask us about it. Also all other grades.

ARABOL M'F'G CO.
100 William St., New York

THE UNION SULPHUR CO.
Main Office: 17 Battery Pl., New York. Mines: Calcasieu Parish, La.

Producers of
The Only Arsenic Free Sulphur on the Market

NEW JERSEY.

AGASOTE—Mercer Co.
A suburb of the City of Trenton.

AGASOTE MILLBOARD CO. P. O. address, Trenton. (Alexander J. Harvey, Pres.; E .H. Outerbridge, Vice-Pres.; Harold Harvey, Treas.; J. M. High, Sec.;. D. M. Sutherland, Jr., Mgr.) New York Office, Bowling Green Building, 11 Broadway. S. P., Trenton. Steam. Millboards. All Kinds of Specialties in Pulp Products. 40,000 lbs. 24 hours.

BLOOMFIELD—Essex Co.
Pop. 17,000. On Erie & D. L. & W. RR. M. O. and Tel. office; Adams and Wells Fargo Ex.

E. H. DAVEY CO. (Allison Dodd, Pres.; E. Davey Dodd, Sec. and Treas.) S. P., ½ mile. One 600-lb. and two 800-lb. engines; one 74-inch Cylinder. Water and Steam. Trunk, Binders and Friction Boards. 8000 lbs. 24 hours. *"Highgrade Tar Boards."*

DIAMOND MILLS PAPER CO. (R. H. Thompson, Pres.; C. G. Van Gilder, Sec.; E. Van Voorhis, Treas.) Office, 44 Murray street, New York. SILVER SPRING MILL. S. P., Bloomfield. Two 500-lb., two 1000-lb. and one 10-cwt. Umpherston Beating and two Jordan engines; one 62-inch and one 84-inch Fourdriniers. Width of Super Calenders, 36 inches. Widest trimmed sheet, 78 inches. Water and Steam. Copying, Carbon, Cigarette and Tissues. 5000 lbs. 24 hours.

BOGOTA—Bergen Co.
Pop. 2,000. On Hackensack River; N. Y., S. & W.; W. S. RR.; M. O. and Tel. office; nearest bank, Hackensack, 1 mile; Nat. and Wells Fargo Ex.

BOGOTA PAPER AND BOARD CO. (William N. Smith, Pres.; Harold S. Smith, Vice-Pres.; David E. Stalker, Sec. and Treas.; Wm. D. Rehine, Supt.) General Office, at mill. S. P., at mill. Six 1500-lb. Beaters; three Jordans; one 104-inch Six Cylinder Machine. Widest trimmed sheet, 93 inches. Union Screens. Steam and Electricity. News, Chip and Combination Boards. 100,000 lbs. 24 hours.

CONTINENTAL PAPER CO. Office and S. P., at mill. (W. J. Alford, Pres.; E. E. Earhart, Vice-Pres.; W. J. Alford, Jr., Treas.) TRADERS MILL. Eight 1200-lb. Beating, five Refining and one Washing engines; one 136-inch six Cylinder Machine. Widest trimmed sheet, 122 inches. Steam and Electricity. Stiff and Folding Box Boards; also Jute Boards. 150,000 lbs. 24 hours. *Pasted Boards a Specialty; Sheet Lining.*

FEDERAL PAPER BOARD CO., INC. P. O. Address, Box 57, Hackensack, N. J. (W. G. Shortess, Pres.; H. T. Brown, Vice-Pres.; L. C. Eckhardt, Sec. and Treas.; J. J. Reynolds, Supt.) S. P., at mill. Three 1500-lb., three 2000-lb. Beating and four Jordan engines; one 115-inch Six Cylinder Machine. Widest trimmed sheet, 105 inches. Steam and Electricity. News, Chip and Combination Boards. 130,000 lbs. 24 hours.

Paper and Pulp Mills in the United States

BOONTON—Morris Co.

Pop. 3,901. On D., L. & W. RR. M. O. and Tel. office; U. S. Ex.

FIELD & WHITE CO. New York office, 116 Nassau street. (Wm. S. White, Pres.; Edmund B. Rosevear, Sec. and Treas.) POWERVILLE MILLS. S. P., Boonton. Six 900-lb. Beating engines; one 44-inch Single Cylinder. Widest trimmed sheet, 40 inches. Water and Steam. Roofing, Saturating and Deadening Felts (Rolls or Sheets). 16,000 lbs. 24 hours.

BUTLER—Morris Co.

Pop. 875. On N. Y., S. & W. RR. M. O. and Tel. office; nearest bank, Paterson, 11 miles; Nat. Ex.

PEQUANNOCK VALLEY PAPER CO., THE. (Fred. S. White, Pres.; J. B. White, Vice-Pres.; W. C. White, Sec. and Treas.) PEQUANNOCK VALLEY PAPER MILLS. Two mills. On Pequannock River, 1 mile above Butler, on N. Y., S. & W. RR. Three 350-lb., two 500-lb., eight 800-lb. and one 1800-lb. Beating and three Jordan engines; two 62-inch and one 68-inch Cylinders. Widest sheet made, 60 inches. Water and Steam. Tissue Manila. 12,000 lbs. 24 hours.

CAMDEN—Camden Co.

Pop. 75,935. On Amboy Div. of Penn.; P. & A. C.; W. J., C. & A.; P. & R. RR. M. O. and Tel. office; Adams, U. S., W. J., Camden and Atlantic Ex.

MACANDREWS & FORBES CO. P. O. address, Third street and Jefferson avenue. S. P., siding on P. & R. R. (Karl Jungbluth, Pres.; Alfred Mellor, T. S. Catto and W. L. Geddes, Vice-Pres.; W. E. Ransom, Sec. and Treas.; A. W. Wickham, Supt.) Six 1000-lb. and four 1500-lb. Beating and six Refining engines. One 106-inch six Cylinder Board Machine and one 102-inch six Cylinder Board Machine. Widest trimmed sheets, 100 inches and 96 inches. Steam. High Grade Box Board, Patent White Folding Box, Container, Card Mounting, Easel Boards and Jacquard Cards, Fibrelic Wall Board. 160,000 lbs. 24 hours. PULP MILL. Five Digesters. Steam. Soda Fibre. 40,000 lbs. 24 hours.

WEST JERSEY PAPER MANUFACTURING CO., THE. (T. S. Safford, Pres. and Treas.; John Chalmers, Sec.) S. P., Camden. One 120-inch Three Cylinder. Widest trimmed sheet, 108 inches. All grades of Rope Manilas. 24,000 lbs. 24 hours.

CLIFTON—Passaic Co.

Pop. 10,037. N. Y., S. & W. RR. M. O. and Tel. office. W. F. and Ad. Ex.; nearest bank, Passaic, 1½ miles.

CLIFTON PAPER MILLS. P. O. Address, Passaic, N. J. (Benj. I. Ward, Pres.; Frederick M. Butler, Sec. and Treas.; H. N. Davidson, Mgr. and Supt.) CLIFTON PAPER MILLS. S. P., at mill. Five 1200-lb. Beating and three Jordan engines. One Five Cylinder. Widest trimmed sheet, 80 inches. Steam. Box Boards, Test Jute and Chip for Corrugating. 60,000 lbs. 24 hours.

ELIZABETH—Union Co.

Pop. 70,000. C. RR. of N. J.; P. RR. M. O. and Tel. office; Adams and Am. Ex.

BARRETT CO., THE. (William Hamlin Childs, Pres.; T. M. Rianhard, Vice-Pres.; W. N. McIlravy, Vice-Pres.; A. T. Perry, Vice-Pres.; John C.

Runkle, Vice-Pres.; E. J. Steer, Sec. and Treas.; G. C. Russell, Mgr.; W. A. Forman, Mgr. Paper Mill Div., 17 Battery Pl., New York.) S. P., Elizabethport. Twenty-three 600-lb. and six 1000-lb. Beating engines; three 84-inch Cylinders. Steam and Electricity. Roofing, Deadening and Sheathing. 120,000 lbs. 24 hours.

GARFIELD—Bergen Co.

Pop. 15,455. On Erie RR. Tel. office; M. O. and bank; Wells Fargo & Co. and Adams Ex.

HAMMERSCHLAG MFG. CO. P. O. Address, 234 Greenwich Street, New York. (C. S. Hammerschlag, Pres.; J. D. Goldberg, Vice-Pres.; G. W. Hammerschlag, Sec. and Treas.) Eight Machines. Company uses entire product in its waxed paper factory.

GLOUCESTER—Camden Co.

Pop. 6,840. On West Jersey & Seashore RR., and via boat from Philadelphia. M. O. and Tel. offices; Adams and U. S. Ex.

HINDE & DAUCH PAPER CO., THE. (Sidney Frohman, Pres.; W. F. Harbrecht, Vice-Pres.; Fred Emmons, Sec.; V. H. Wendt, Local Mgr.) Main Office, Sandusky, Ohio. S. P., at mill. No. 1 MILL. Six 1200-lb. Beating and four Jordan engines; one 94-inch Four Cylinder Downingtown machine. Widest trimmed sheet, 87 inches. Steam and Electricity. Chip and Jute for Corrugating. 70,000 lbs. 24 hours. No. 2 MILL. One 84-inch Three Cylinder machine. Widest trimmed sheet, 76 inches. Steam and electricity. Bogus, Felt, Chip and Indented Board. 40,000 lbs. 24 hours. Corrugated and Indented Felt Papers.

HAMBURG—Sussex Co.

Pop. 800. On N. Y., Susq. & West.; L. & H. R. RR. M. O. and Tel. office; W. F. Ex.

UNION WAXED AND PARCHMENT PAPER CO. (L. L. Gilbert, Pres.; Arthur E. Lee, Vice-Pres.; H. J. Corwin, Sec. and Treas.) New York office, 45 Cedar Street. CLIMAX MILLS. S. P. mill switch. Two 66-inch and one 76-inch Cylinders. Widest trimmed sheets, 60 and 72 inches. One 66-inch and two 76-inch and two 96-inch Fourdriniers. Widest trimmed sheets, 60 inches, 72 inches and 80 inches. Water and Steam. Tissue and Waxed Papers.

HOBOKEN—Hudson Co.

Pop. 59,364. On M. & E. Div. and B. Branch of D., L. & W. RR; also vessels. M. O. and Tel. office; Am., Nat. and U. S. Ex.

HOBOKEN PAPER MILL CO. (Richard Stevens, Pres.; W. H. Gould, Vice-Pres. and Gen. Mgr.; Palmer Campbell, Sec. and Treas.) HOBOKEN PAPER MILL. S. P., at mill. Two 1600-lb. and four 1000-lb. Beaters; three Noble & Wood Refining engines; two 90-inch Double Cylinder Machines. Widest sheet made, 82 inches. Steam. Wrapping, Container and Specialties. 75,000 lbs. 24 hours.

JERSEY CITY—Hudson Co.

Pop. 206,433. On Penn.; Erie; N. Y., S. & W.; N. Y. & G. L.; L. & V.; C. RR. of N. J.; N. N. J.; N. J. & N. Y. RR. M. O. and Tel. office; Adams, Am., U. S., Nat. and Wells Fargo & Co. Ex.

BOYLE CO., JOHN F. (J. F. Boyle, Pres. and Treas.) S. P., Jersey City. Six 2000-lb. and four Refining engines; one 96-inch Machine. Steam.

THOMAS E. GLEESON, Inc., 411-413 John St., E. NEWARK, N. J.
CYLINDER MOULDS and DANDY ROLLS Made and Repaired
LETTERING and MONOGRAMS for WATERMARKS

Paper and Pulp Mills in the United States 139

Chip Board, Lined and Plain, News Board, Paper Stock Board, Vat Lined and Combination Boards. 100,000 lbs. 24 hours.

DAVEY, W. O., & SONS. (Leigh H. Davey, Pres.; E. S. Davey, Sec.) Four 500-lb. engines; four 62-inch Cylinders. Steam. Binders, Friction and Trunk and Counter Board. 8000 lbs. 10 hours. *Jacquard Pattern Cards.*

LEO CO., JAMES, 257 Varick. (James Leo, Pres.; James Leo, Jr., Vice-Pres.; Stephen Leo, Sec.; William Milne, Treas.) S. P., at mill. One 500-lb., two 1000-lb., one 2000-lb. Beating and two Jordan engines; one 70-inch Board Machine. Widest trimmed sheet, 68 inches. Steam. Chip and Combination Box Boards. 40,000 lbs. 24 hours.

NATIONAL ASBESTOS MFG. CO., 163-193 Henderson St. (John A. Scharwath, Owner; C. R. Burkhardt, Gen. Supt.; W. H. Woodward, Paper Mill Supt.; C. W. Koehler, Roofing Dept. Supt.; Charles H. Stringer, Sales Agent.) Two 2000-lb. Beaters. One 90-inch Cylinder; widest trimmed sheet, 84 inches. Steam. Asbestos Paper, Asbesto Felt, Dry and Saturating Felts; Asbestos, Asphalt, Slate Surface Shingles; Asbestos Roof Papers. 40,000 lbs. 24 hours.

STRATFORD PAPER CO. (A. C. Stratford, Pres.; E. H. Stratford, Vice-Pres.; F. B. Stratford, Sec. and Treas.; H. S. Shellington, Supt.) P. O. address, 170 Cornelius Avenue. Four 500-lb. and five 1000-lb. and one 1800-lb. Mills Universal Beating, three Refining Engines and two Rotary Boilers; one 60-inch Fourdrinier, one 76-inch Edwards and one 90-inch Harper Fourdriniers. Widest trimmed sheets, 60, 62 and 80 inches. Steam. White, Colored, GB Silver, Manifold, Celluloid, Cigarette and Specialties in Fine Papers. 12,000 lbs. 24 hours.

LAMBERTVILLE—Hunterdon Co.
Pop. 4,687. On Belvidere Div. P. RR. M. O. and Tel. office; Adams Ex.

GANDEY, EST. OF WM. H. MOUNTAIN SPRING PAPER MILL. S. P., at mill. Three 250-lb. and one 400-lb. Beating, and one 800-lb. Washing engines; one 56-inch Cylinder. Water and Steam. Parchment Copying, Yellow Copying, Tissue and Manifold Typewriting Papers in White and Colors and America Stereotype Tissue. 2000 lbs. 24 hours.

MANN CO., WILLIAM. Philadelphia Office, 529 Market Street. (H. A. Prizer, Pres.; J. B. Buzby, Treas.; C. H. Prickitt, Asst. Treas.; H. A. Davis, Sec.; Jos. S. Wilds, Asst. Sec.; W. E. Wagg, Gen. Mgr.) OLD RELIABLE MILLS. S. P., station, ½ mile. One 1200, one 1000 and six 800-lb. Beating and Washing engines; two 60 and one 68-inch Cylinders. Widest trimmed sheet, 50 inches. Water and Steam. Railroad Copying and Manifold Papers. 800 reams, 20x30, 24 hours.

PERSEVERANCE PAPER MILLS. (H. B. Henry, Prop.) Office, Produce Exchange Bldg., New York City. S. P., at mill. Two 800-lb., three 500-lb. and one 650-lb. Beating and one Jordan Engines. One 76-inch Harper Fourdrinier. Widest trimmed sheet, 69 inches. Water and Steam. 6000 lbs. 24 hours. *"Sanitary Crêpe Paper Specialties, Towels, Napkins, Tablecloths and Toilet Paper. Oiled Boards. Anti-Tarnish Paper and Hand Rolls."*

SULPHUR—CRUDE. GUARANTEED 99% PURE.
The average analysis of our high-grade brimstone is in itself a guarantee. Write us for quotations.
THE UNION SULPHUR CO., Main Office, 17 Battery Pl., New York. Mines, Calcasieu Parish, La.

New Jersey

WANAQUE—Passaic Co.

Pop. 6,000. On N. Y. & G. L. R.R. (branch of Erie R.R.). Tel. and M. O. office; nearest bank, Pompton Lakes, 8 miles; Wells, Fargo & Co. Ex.

WANAQUE RIVER PAPER CO. (Robt. D. Carter, Pres. and Treas.; O. H. Bowers, Vice-Pres.; W. Carrington Cabell, Sec.; Thos. H. Keogh, Supt.) S. P., Wanaque. One 800-lb. and six 1200-lb. Beating and two Refining engines; eight 4000-lb. Washing tubs, four 4000-lb. Boiling tubs and five 48-96 feltless Wet Machines for washing. Two Kidder Slitting Machines for making rolls, all widths. One 86-inch Fourdrinier. Widest trimmed sheet, 78 inches. Width of Super Calenders, 40, 45 and 60 inches. Five Screens. Water, Steam, Internal combustion crude oil engine. *Supatone* Super-Calendered and Machine Finished Book. 40,000 lbs. 24 hours.

WEST NUTLEY—Passaic Co.

DU PONT DE NEMOURS, E. I., & CO., Successors to The Arlington Co., Nutley Plant. New York office, 725-727 Broadway. This plant is now being operated in the manufacture of tissue paper, but no material is being made for outside consumption.

WHIPPANY—Morris Co.

Pop. 961. On Morristown & Erie RR. M. O. and Tel. office; nearest bank and Ex., Morristown, 4 miles.

McEWAN BROTHERS. (R. B. McEwan, Pres.; J. L. McEwan, Vice-Pres.; Arthur McEwan, Treas. and Mgr.; R. W. McEwan, Sec.) Main office, Whippany, N. J. Three mills. NO. I MILL. S. P., at mill. Three 1000-lb. Beating and two Refining engines; one 68-inch Six Cylinder. Widest trimmed sheet 65 inches. Union Screens. Water, Steam and Electricity. News and Folding Paper Box Boards, 50,000 lbs. 24 hours. No. II MILL. S. P., at mill. Five 1000-lb. Beating and three Refining engines; one 86-inch Board Machine. Widest trimmed sheet, 81 inches. Water, Steam and Electricity. News and Folding Paper Box Boards. 70,000 lbs. 24 hours. EDEN MILL. S. P., at mill. Six 1500-lb. Beating and four Refining engines. One 113-inch Six Cylinder. Widest trimmed sheet, 105 inches. Water, Steam and Electricity. News and Folding Paper Box Boards. 100,000 lbs. 24 hours; also Lining Plant for Sheet Lining and Rewinding Rolls.

MUIR, JAMES A. Office, Morristown, N. J. S. P., Whippany. Two 500-lb. engines; one 60-inch Cylinder. Widest trimmed sheet, 56 inches. Water. Binders' and Leather Board. 8000 lbs. 24 hours.

UNITED PAPERBOARD COMPANY. General Office, 171 Madison avenue, N. Y. CALEDONIAN MILL. S. P., at mill. Two 1100-lb., one 1300-lb. and two Jordan engines; one 68-inch Four Cylinder. Widest trimmed sheet, 64 inches. Steam. News Board and Chip Board. 60,000 lbs. 24 hours. HANOVER MILLS. S. P., at mill. Four 1000-lb., two 1200-lb. Beating and four Jordan engines; one 120-inch Four Cylinder. Widest trimmed sheet, 110 inches. Steam. News, Chip and Combination Board. 112,000 lbs. 24 hours.

THOMAS E. GLEESON, Inc.,) **FOURDRINIER WIRES**
411-413 John St., E. NEWARK, N. J.) For Tissue and Fine Grade Pape

NEW YORK.

ALBANY—Albany Co.

Pop. 107,979. On Mohawk Div. N. Y. & Albany Div. N. Y., West Shore & Buf., Boston & Albany and Del. Hudson RR. Bank, M. O. and Tel.; Am. and Natl. Ex.

A. P. W. PAPER CO. 12 Lumber Dist. (Seth Wheeler, Pres.; Seth Wheeler, Jr., Vice-Pres.; J. J. Jansen, Sec.; Wm. A. Wheeler, Treas.; Willis S. Crandell, Supt.) Six 1000-lb. Beating and four Refining engines. Four 86-inch Cylinders. Widest trimmed sheet, 76 inches. Steam and Electricity. Tissues and Toilets. 30,000 lbs. 24 hours.

AMBOY—Onondaga Co.

Pop. 840. On Auburn Branch N. Y. C. RR. M. O. and Tel. office; nearest bank, Syracuse, 8 miles.

CAMILLUS PAPER MILLS. P. O. Address, Camillus, N. Y. Two 500-lb. Beating and one Rotary engines. One 48-inch Cylinder; widest trimmed sheet, 40 inches. Water and Steam. Wrapping and Tube. 10,000 lbs. 24 hours. (Idle.)

AMSTERDAM—Montgomery Co.

Pop. 31,207. On N. Y. C. & H. R. RR. M. O. and Tel. office; Am. and Nat. Ex.

SMEALLIE & VOORHEES. (P. H. Smeallie, J. L. Voorhees.) S. P., at mill. Four 800-lb. Beating and two Jordan engines; one 76-inch Five Cylinder. Widest trimmed sheet, 70 inches. Water and Steam. Lined and unlined Chip Boards. 70,000 lbs. 24 hours.

ANCRAM—Columbia Co.

Pop. 1,332. On C. N. E. RR. M. O. and Tel. office; nearest bank, Pine Plains, 6 miles; Adams Ex.

ANCRAM PAPER MILLS. (Alfred Frank, Pres.; Jerome W. Frank, Vice-Pres.; D. E. Oppenheimer, Sec. and Treas.) New York Office, 150-154 W. Twenty-second Street. S. P., at mill. Three 500-lb., five 800-lb. and one 1000-lb. Beating and two Jordan engines; one 72-inch Cylinder and one 90-inch Fourdrinier. Widest trimmed sheet, 80 inches. Water and Steam. White, Colored, Manila and Anti-Rust Tissue, and Specialties in Tissue. 8000 lbs. 24 hours.

AUSABLE FORKS—Essex Co.

Pop. 2,509. On D. & H. C. Co. RR. M. O. and Tel. office; nearest bank. Ausable Forks. 11½ miles; Nat. Ex.

ROGERS, J. & J., Co. (James Rogers, Pres.; George Chahoon, Vice-Pres.; J. M. Sheffield, Sec.; I. H. Chahoon Paper Mill, Supt.; Henry G. Rogers, Sulphite Mill Supt.) S. P., at mill. Six 1800-lb. Beating and three Refining engines; one 90-inch Cylinder and one 126-inch Fourdrinier. Widest trimmed sheet, 116 inches. Water, Steam and Electricity. Bond, Offset, Embossing and Writings; also Manilas, Hardware and Boards. 80,000 lbs. 24 hours. Ausable Forks. SULPHITE MILL. Five Digesters; four Wet Machines. Steam. Sulphite. 100,000 lbs. 24 hours.

BALDWINSVILLE—Onondaga Co.

Pop. 3,040. On O. & S. Div. of D., L. & W.; S. & B. R.R. M. O. and Tel. office; Adams, Wells Fargo & Co. Ex.

R. S. HOFFMAN. (Earl Bort, Supt.) HOFFMAN-YOUMAN'S MILLS. S. P., at mill. Three 800-lb., two 1000-lb., one 1500-lb. Beating and six

---

HIGHEST GRADE BRIMSTONE—GUARANTEED 99% PURE
free from Arsenic or Selenium. Write for particulars to
THE UNION SULPHUR CO., Main Office, 17 Battery Pl., New York. Mines, Calcasieu Parish,

DRY ROSIN SIZE Brittle, easy soluble, cheapest size out; cheaper than mill made size. Ask us about it. Also all other grades. **ARABOL M'F'G CO.** 100 William St N. Y.

PAPER MAKERS' SUPPLIES
Also Mfrs. of DEADENING and SATURATING FELTS

DARMSTADT, SCOTT & COURTNEY, Inc., Importers, Exporters and Dealers in
178 and 184 SOUTH STREET, NEW YORK

---

144   New York

Refining engines; one 72-inch and one 90-inch Cylinders. Widest trimmed sheets, 62 and 80 inches. Water, Electricity and Steam. No. 2 White and No. 1 Manila, Manila and Crêpe Toilet and Wax Papers. 13,000 lbs. 24 hours.

BALLSTON SPA— Saratoga Co.
Pop. 5,000. On S. & R. Div. D. & H. C. Co. RR. M. O. and Tel. office; Nat. Ex.

BALLSTON FIBRE PRODUCTS CO. (Henry J. Meader, Pres., Gen. Mgr. and Supt.; J. B. White, Vice-Pres.; Robert Young, Sec.; Wm. O'Meara, Treas.; Thomas Goulard, Asst. Treas.) S. P., at mill. Two Jones 1500-lb. and two Mills Beaters with Meader Beater Attachment; two Refining engines; one Meaders Patent Machine Combination, 96-inch Cylinder and Fourdrinier. Widest trimmed sheet, 86 inches. Water, Steam and Electricity. Light-Weight Box Boards and Wrappers, Chip and News Board and Plyless Container Board in Sheets and Rolls.

NATIONAL FOLDING BOX AND PAPER CO. Office, James and Alton streets, New Haven, Conn. New York salesroom, 132 and 134 Franklin Street. NATIONAL MILL. Fred Rooney. S. P., at Ballston Spa. Two 500-lb., two 1000-lb. and two Jordan engines; one 76-inch Five Cylinder. Widest trimmed sheet, 67 inches. Water and Steam. Manila Board and Single and Double Lined Chip Box Board. 30,000 lbs. 24 hours.

OUTTERSON, JAMES A. EAGLE MILL. S. P., at mill. Five Beating and one Jordan engines; one 72-inch Harper Fourdrinier. Water and Steam. Bag and Manila. 18,000 lbs. 24 hours. (Idle. Mill damaged by fire. Is being offered for sale.)

UNITED PAPER CO., Successor to Riverside Pulp & Paper Corp. Office, 1309-1315 Third National Bank Bldg., Atlanta, Ga. S. P., at mill. August 7, 1918. Idle. Mill destroyed by fire in April, 1917. Company is considering rebuilding as soon as machinery, etc., can be obtained.)

BATTENVILLE—Washington Co.
Pop. 150. On G. & J. RR. M. O. and Tel. offices and nearest bank, Salem.

PHŒNIX PAPER CO., THE. (W. R. Hobbie, Pres.; P. W. Hobbie, Vice-Pres.; S. R. Washburn, Sec.; E. W. Hobbie, Treas.) P. O. Address, Greenwich. S. P., Battenville. Three 600-lb. Beating and one Jordan engines; two 72-inch Cylinders Widest trimmed sheet, 67½ inches. Water. Width of Super Calenders, 70 inches. White and Manila Tissue and Jumbo Rolls. 15,000 to 20,000 lbs. 24 hours.

BEAVER FALLS—Lewis Co.
Pop. 600. On L. & B. RR. M. O.; nearest bank, Lowville, 10 miles; Tel. and Ex.

LEWIS CO., THE J. P. Incorporated. (H. S. Lewis, Pres. and Gen Mgr.) S. P., Beaver Falls. Six 1000-lb. Beating and five Jordan engines; one 72-inch Six Cylinder and one 92-inch Five Cylinder. Widest trimmed sheet, 80 inches. Water, Steam and Electricity. Wood Pulp, Manila, Jute, Fibre and Combination Boards. 90,000 lbs. 24 hours. PULP MILLS. Two mills. BEAVER FALLS PULP MILLS. S. P., Beaver Falls. Ten Grinders. Water. Ground Wood (dry). 100,000 lbs. 24 hours. HAMPTON DIVISION. One 72-inch Four Cylinder, four 1000-lb. Beating and two

---

McENERY PAPER COMPANY 112 W. ADAMS ST., CHICAGO — MANUFACTURERS' SALES AGENCY PRACTICALLY ALL GRADES

Jordan engines. Widest trimmed sheet, 64 inches. Electricity. Album, Coating, Cover, Tough Check, Cartridge, High Grade Blacks and Special Papers. 12,000 lbs. 24 hours.

LEWIS SLOCUM & LE FEVRE CO., INC., THE. PAPER MILL. (H. L. LeFevre, Pres. and Treas.; H. S. Lewis, First Vice-Pres. and Sec.; F. E. Slocum, Second Vice-Pres.; H. L. Van Arnam, Asst. Treas.) S. P., at mill. Two 1000-lb. engines; one 66-inch Five Cylinder. Widest trimmed sheet, 58 inches. Water and Steam. Wood Pulp and Sulphite Boards in natural colors and tints, and Milk Bottle Cap Stock. 20,000 lbs. 24 hours. PULP MILL. S. P., at mill. Four Grinders; three 72-inch Wet Machines. Water. Ground Wood. 40,000 lbs. 24 hours.

BLACK RIVER—Jefferson Co.

Pop. 949. St. Lawrence Division, N. Y. C. RR. M. O. and Tel. office; nearest bank, Watertown, 7 miles; Am. Ex.

ST. REGIS PAPER CO. (F. L. Carlisle, Pres.; Alvah Miller, 1st Vice-Pres.; D. M. Anderson, 2nd Vice-Pres.; F. A. Empsall, Sec.-Treas.) Two 1300-lb., one 1500-lb. Beaters; one Jordan; one 90-inch Fourdrinier. Widest trimmed sheet, 80 inches. Water and Steam. Manila. 40,000 lbs. 24 hours. *Hanging.* PULP MILL. S. P., Black River. Two Grinders. Water. Ground Wood (dry). 16,000 lbs. 24 hours.

BLOSSVALE—Oneida Co.

Pop. 120. On R., W. & O. RR. M. O. office; Tel. and bank, Camden, 8 miles; Am. Ex.

BLOSSVALE PAPER CO. (Arthur S. Evans, Pres.; G. H. Palmer, Sec. and Treas.) S. P., at mill. One 700-lb. Beating and one Refining engines; one 48-inch Cylinder. Widest trimmed sheet, 46-inches. White and Manila Tissue. 4000 lbs. 24 hours.

BROADALBIN—Fulton Co.

Pop. 1,946. On F. J. & G. RR. M. O. and Tel. office; nearest bank, Gloversville, 7 miles; Am. Ex.

STEVER, GEORGE. STEVER'S MILLS. Successor to Isaac Allen. S. P., Broadalbin, 1½ miles. One 48-inch Cylinder Machine (Trim 40 inches); one 600-lb. Beating and one Refining engines. Width of Super-Calenders, 48 inches. Water and Steam. Butchers' Manila and Kraft. 8000 lbs. 24 hours. (Mill idle and for sale.)

BROWNVILLE—Jefferson Co.

Pop. 666. On Cape Vincent Branch of R., W. & O. RR. M. O. and Tel. office; nearest bank, Watertown, 4 miles; Am. Ex.

BROWNVILLE BOARD CO., THE. (J. Munson Gamble, Pres. and Treas.; D. F. Phillips, Sec.) S. P., at mill. Five 1100-lbs. and two Jordan engines; one 112-inch Four Cylinder. Widest trimmed sheet, 102 inches. Union Screens. Water and Steam. Tag Board, Document Manila and Manila Folding Box Boards. 60,000 lbs. 24 hours. PULP MILL. S. P., Brownville. Six Grinders; four Wet Machines. Water. Ground Wood. 50,000 lbs. 24 hours.

BROWNVILLE PAPER CO. (S. A. Upham, Pres.; George C. Sherman, Vice-Pres.; George F. Clark, Sec. and Treas.) S. P., Brownville. Six

DRY ROSIN SIZE Brittle, easy soluble, cheapest size out; cheaper than mill made size. Ask us about it. Also all other grades. **ARABOL M'F'G CO.** 100 William St., N. Y.

146 — New York

600-lb. Beating and two Refining engines; two 70-inch Fourdriniers. Widest trimmed sheet, 63 inches. Water and Steam. Railroad Manila, Colored Poster, Glazed Fibre and Colored Specialties and Light-Weight "Sea Foam" Bond. 35,000 lbs. 24 hours. PULP MILL. S. P., Brownville. Four Grinders; three Wet Machines. Water. Ground Wood (dry). 30,000 lbs. 24 hours.

HARMON PAPER CO. (J. J. Warren, Pres. and Treas.; F. M. Boyer, Sec.) S. P., Brownville Station. Four 600-lb., one 1200-lb. and two Jordan engines; one 66-inch Combination and one 86-inch Fourdrinier. Widest sheet made, 78 inches. Water and Steam. Wall Papers and Colored Specialties. 40,000 lbs. 24 hours. PULP MILL. S. P., Brownville. Six Grinders; three Wet and one Decker machines. Water. Ground Wood. 35,000 lbs. 24 hours.

CADYVILLE—Clinton Co.—PULP MILL.

Pop. 550. On D. & H. RR. Tel. and M. O. office; nearest bank, Plattsburgh, 10 miles; Nat. Ex.

INTERNATIONAL PAPER CO. Office, 30 Broad Street, New York. CADYVILLE MILLS. (R. L. Farnsworth, Supt.) Twenty-three Grinders; thirty-one Wet Machines. Water. Ground Wood. 210,000 lbs. 24 hours.

CARTHAGE—Jefferson Co.

Pop. 2,895. On Junction R., W. & O., C. & A. RR. M. O. and Tel. office; Am. Ex.

CARTHAGE SULPHITE PULP & PAPER CO. (J. A. Outterson, Pres.; George O. Comfort, Vice-Pres.; Guy C. Jones, Sec.; L. G. DeCant, Treas.; Wood DeCant, Mgr. of Sales.) PAPER MILL. S. P., at mill. Four 1500-lb. Beating engines; one 72-inch and one 112-inch Five Cylinders. Widest trimmed sheet, 102 inches. Harmon Screens. Water, Electricity and Steam. Tag Board, Single and Double Manila Lined News, Heavy Manilas, also Solid Manila Folding Box Boards, Ice Cream and Oyster Pail Waterproof Boards. 90,000 lbs. 24 hours. GROUND WOOD MILL. Four Grinders; one "Impco" Screen. Electricity. 50,000 lbs. (dry) 24 hours. SULPHITE MILL. Six Digesters; six Wet Machines. Water and Electricity. Sulphite Fibre. 100,000 lbs. 24 hours.

CHAMPION PAPER CO. (M. A. Hanna, Pres.; M. S. Wilder, Vice-Pres.; R. B. Maltby, Sec.-Treas.; C. T. Wright, Asst. Sec.; H. E. Rockwood, Supt.) S. P., at mill. One 1000-lb. and two 1500-lb. Beating and one Refining engines; one 132-inch Fourdrinier. Widest trimmed sheet, 124 inches. Water and Steam. News. 80,000 lbs. 24 hours. PULP MILL. S. P., at mill. Eight Grinders; eight Wet Machines. Water. Ground Wood. 100,000 lbs. 24 hours.

ISLAND PAPER CO., THE. (Chas. W. Pratt, Pres. and Treas.; Walter Pratt, Vice-Pres. and Sec.) S. P., at mill. Two 1000-lb. and three 1500-lb. Beating and two Refining engines; one 66-inch and one 114-inch Fourdriniers. Widest trimmed sheet, 104 inches. Water and Steam. Manila, Bag and Dry Fibre. 50,000 lbs. 24 hours. GROUND WOOD MILL. S. P., at mill. Three Grinders; two Wet Machines. Water. Ground Wood (dry). 30,000 lbs. 24 hours. SULPHITE MILL. Two Digesters. Electricity. Sulphite, 80,000 lbs. 24 hours.

PRESS ROLLS Maple and Gum White Wood Felt Rolls **J. W. HEWITT MACHINE CO.** Neenah, Wis.

THOMAS E. GLEESON, Inc., 411-413 John St., E. NEWARK, N. J.
CYLINDER MOULDS and DANDY ROLLS Made and Repaired
LETTERING and MONOGRAMS for WATERMARKS

Paper and Pulp Mills in the United States 147

NATIONAL PAPER PRODUCTS CO., successors to Carthage Tissue Paper Mills. (M. R. Higgins, Pres.; I. Zellerbach, Vice-Pres.; J. D. Zellerbach, Sec.; Max M. Cohn, Treas.; H. L. Sampson, Gen. Mgr., Eastern Div.) S. P., at mill. Five 1200-lb. Beating and four Jordan engines; one 72-inch Cylinder; widest trimmed sheet, 62 inches; and three 90-inch Harper Fourdriniers; widest trimmed sheet, 81 inches. Water and Steam. Manila and White Tissue, Commercial Toilet Paper, packages and rolls. *Folded Specialties, Public Service Towels and No Waste Toilet Tissues.* 50,000 lbs. 24 hours. SULPHITE MILL. S. P., at mill. One Digester, one Wet Machine. Water. 14,000 lbs. 24 hours. GROUND WOOD MILL. S. P., at mill. Two Grinders and two Wet Machines; one "Impco" Screen. Electricity. Ground Wood (dry). 28,000 lbs. 24 hours.

WEST END PAPER CO. (E. B. Sterling, Pres. and Gen. Mgr.; J. C. Stebbins, Vice-Pres.; S. B. Wardwell, Sec. and Treas.; Thomas Woods, Supt.) S. P., at mill. One 1000-lb. and two 1500-lb. Beating engines; one 132-inch Fourdrinier. Widest trimmed sheet, 123 inches. Water, Steam and Electricity. News. 72,000 lbs. 24 hours. PULP MILL. Eight Grinders; six Wet Machines. Water and Electricity. Ground Wood. 70,000 lbs. 24 hours.

CASTLETON—Rensselaer Co.
Pop. 1,600. On H. R. Div. of N. Y. C. & H. R. RR.; also vessels. M. O. and Tel. office; Am. Ex.

FORT ORANGE PAPER CO. (Peter C. Brashear, Pres.; Charles Borland, Vice-Pres.; Weston W. Goodnow, Treas.; Robert H. Harris, Sec.) FORT ORANGE MILL. P. O. Address, Castleton, N. Y. New York Office, 200 Fifth Avenue, New York City. S. P., at mill. Two 1000-lb., one 1200-lb., three 1500-lb. and five Jordan engines; one 74-inch Fourdrinier and one 101-inch Four Cylinder. Widest trimmed sheet, Fourdrinier 67½ inches; Cylinder 88 inches. Water and Steam. Buckskin, Patent Coated, News and Columbia Box Boards, Card Middles, Bristols, Colored Ticket, Cash Register, Silk Wrappers, Jacquard Boards and other Specialties; complete Folding Box Department. 70,000 lbs. 24 hours.

INGALLS & CO. (C. C. Woolworth, Pres.; H. H. G. Ingalls, Sec. and Treas.) OAK GROVE MILL. S. P., at mill. One 600-lb. and one 800-lb. Beating and one Refining engines; one 36-inch and two 44-inch Cylinders. Widest trimmed sheet, 38 inches. Steam. Binders', Friction, Trunk, Wagon, Pattern, Leather, Album, Suit Case and Box Boards.

CHATEAUGAY—Franklin Co.—PULP MILL.
Pop. 1,200. On Rutland RR. M. O. and Tel. office; Am. Ex.

CHATEAUGAY PULP CO. (A. O. Johnston, Pres., Treas. and Gen. Mgr.) CHATEAUGAY PULP MILL. S. P., Chateangay. Two Grinders; two Wet Machines. Water. Ground Wood. 30,000 lbs. 24 hours.

HIGH FALLS PULP & PAPER CO. (James A. Outterson, Pres.; J. G. Jackson, Vice-Pres.; Lynn E. Wolfe, Sec.; N. H. Botsford, Treas.; Edward Wright, Supt. and Mgr.; John S. Adams, Asst. Mgr.) S. P., at mill. Two 1500-lb. Dillon Beaters; one Refining engine; 113-inch Fourdrinier. Widest

M. GOTTESMAN & CO., Inc.
18 E. 41st STREET, NEW YORK. Cable Address "Nausettor"
EUROPEAN OFFICES: Stockholm, Sweden

BLEACHED and UNBLEACHED GROUND WOOD PULP

BRIMSTONE MAKES THE VERY BEST SULPHITE.
If you are looking for a high-grade Brimstone write to
THE UNION SULPHUR CO., Main Office, 17 Battery Pl., New York. Mines, Calcasieu Parish, La.

DRY ROSIN SIZE Brittle, easy soluble, cheapest size out; cheaper than mill made size. Ask us about it. Also all other grades. **ARABOL M'F'G CO.** 100 William St., N. Y.

150   *New York*

R. B. Maltby, Sec. and Treas.; J. A. Remington, Asst. Sec.; W. D. Gregor, Gen. Supt.) S. P., at mill. Fourteen Grinders; Ten Wet Machines. Water and Steam. Ground Wood. 100,000 lbs. 24 hours.

EAST ROCHESTER—Monroe Co.

Pop. 3,471. On N. Y. Central RR. Tel.; Am. and Wells Fargo & Co. Ex.

LAWLESS BROS. PAPER MILLS. (David F. Lawless, Pres.; Michael J. Lawless, Vice-Pres.; Matthew D. Lawless, Sec.; Donald McDonald, Supt.) Three 1000-lb. Beating and two Refining engines; one 100-inch Four Cylinder. Widest trimmed sheet, 92 inches. Steam and Electricity. Corrugated Board, Box Boards, Mill Wrappers, Screenings, Express and Specialties. 80,000 lbs. 24 hours.

ELBRIDGE—Onondaga Co.

Pop. 549. On Auburn Branch of N. Y. C. & H. R.; M. O.; nearest bank, Syracuse, 16 miles. Tel. and Ex. Skaneateles Junction.

ELBRIDGE STRAWBOARD MILL, Successor to Paddock Tube Paper Co. (T. J. Stevens.) S. P., Skaneateles Junction, 2 miles. Two 500-lb. Beaters and one 1000-lb. Dilts Beater; one Washer; one 36-inch Double Cylinder. Widest trimmed sheet, 30 inches. Water and Steam. Straw Board especially for fireworks, Double Deckle Feather edge. 6000 lbs. 24 hours.

EMERYVILLE—St. Lawrence Co.—PULP MILL.

Pop. 200. On R., W. & O. RR. Tel. and M. O. office; nearest bank, Gouverneur, 9 miles; Am. Ex.

ALDRICH PAPER CO. (See also Natural Dam, N. Y.) S. P., at mill. Five Grinders; six 72-inch Wet Machines. Water. Ground Wood (dry). 80,000 lbs. 24 hours.

FALLSBURGH—Sullivan Co.

Pop. 2,974. On N. Y., O. & W. RR. Nearest bank, Monticello, 7 miles. Tel., M. O. and Ex., South Fallsburgh.

LEFEVRE, EDWARD Y. FALLSBURGH MILL. S. P., station. Two 800-lb. and three 1200-lb. Beating and two Jordan engines; one 64-inch Double Cylinder and one 90-inch Cylinder. Widest trimmed sheet, 86 inches. Water and Steam. Crêpe Tissue for Toilet and Towels, Crinkled and Light Weight Manila. 12,000 lbs. 24 hours.

FAYETTEVILLE—Onondaga Co.

Pop. 1,380. On West Shore RR., Chenango Branch. M. O. and Tel. office; Nat. Ex.; nearest bank, Syracuse.

McINTYRE BROS. PAPER CO., INC. (W. E. McIntyre, Pres.; L. N. McIntyre, Vice-Pres. and Sec.; W. E. McIntyre, Treas.) Two 1000-lb. and 1500-lb. Beaters, two Refining engines, one Washer and one Rotary boiler. One 86-inch Cylinder; widest trimmed sheet, 80 inches. Water and Steam. White, Manila and Anti-Tarnish Kraft Tissues. 8000 lbs. 24 hours.

FELT'S MILLS—Jefferson Co.—PULP MILL.

Pop. 400. On C. & W. Branch of N. Y. C. RR. M. O. and Tel. office; nearest bank, Watertown, 8 miles; Am. Ex.

TAGGARTS PAPER CO. (Geo. C. Sherman, Pres.; E. M. Hall, Vice-Pres.; J. V. Baron, Sec. and Treas.) Office, Watertown. FELT'S MILLS.

PRESS ROLLS   Maple and Gum White Wood Felt Rolls   **J. W. HEWITT MACHINE CO.** Neenah, Wis.

THOMAS E. GLEESON, Inc., **FOURDRINIER WIRES**
411-413 John St., E. NEWARK, N. J. For Tissue and Fine Grade Paper

---

Paper and Pulp Mills in the United States 151

S. P., at mill. Four 1200-lb. and two Jordan engines; one 84-inch and one 90-inch Fourdriniers. Widest trimmed sheet, 80 inches. Water and Steam. News, Catalogue, Light-Weight Manila and Specialties. 60,000 lbs. 24 hours. PULP MILL. S. P., at mill. Eight Grinders; two Wet Machines; one "Impco" Rotary Screen. Water. Ground Wood. 50,000 lbs. 24 hours. PULP MILL. Formerly A. H. LeFebvre. S. P., Great Bend. Four Grinders; two Wet Machines. Water. Ground Wood. 20,000 lbs. 24 hours.

FORESTPORT—Oneida Co.—PULP MILL.

Pop. 600. On M. & M. Div. of N. Y. C. & H. R. RR. M. O. and Tel. office; nearest bank, Boonville, 5 miles; Am. Ex.

CRABTREE, EDWIN S., Successor to A. R. Pennington & Co. S. P., at mill. Two Grinders; two Wet Machines. Water. Ground Wood. 12,000 lbs. 24 hours.

FORT EDWARD—Washington Co.

Pop. 3531. On R. & S. Div. of D. & H. Co. RR. M. O. and Tel. office; Nat. Ex.

INTERNATIONAL PAPER CO. Office, 30 Broad street, New York. FORT EDWARD MILL. (D. T. McCormick, Supt.) S. P., at mill. Fourteen Beating and nine Refining engines; two 88-inch, two 110-inch, two 122-inch Fourdriniers; one 90-inch Cylinder; one 76-inch Harper. Water and Steam. News, Kraft, Bag Manila, Wrapping Manila, Wrappers and Screenings. 296,000 lbs. 24 hours. PULP MILL. Eleven Grinders, eight Digesters; four Wet Machines. Water and Steam. Ground Wood. 100,000 lbs.; Sulphite Fibre. 160,000 lbs. 24 hours.

FORT MILLER—Washington Co.

Pop. 150. On H. R. Ry. & Barge Canal. M. O., Tel. and nearest bank, Schuylerville, 5 miles; Nat. Ex.

FORT MILLER PULP AND PAPER CO. (A. M. Thorpe, Sec., Treas. and Gen. Mgr.) FORT MILLER PAPER MILL. S. P., Schuylerville. Two 1000-lb. Beating and one Jordan engines; one 72-inch Harper Fourdrinier. Widest trimmed sheet, 60 inches. Water. Hanging. 24,000 lbs. 24 hours. PULP MILL. S. P., canal and trolley near mill. Four Grinders; three Wet Machines. Water. Ground Wood. 28,000 lbs. 24 hours.

FORT PLAIN—Montgomery Co.

Pop. 2,444. On N. Y. C. & H. R.; N. Y., W. S. & B. RR. M. O. and Tel. office; Am. and Nat. Ex.

MOHAWK IMPROVEMENT CO., INC., successor to Levi Yoran, Cooper Hill Paper Mill. S. P., Fort Plain, 4 miles. Two 500-lb. engines; one 40-inch Cylinder. Widest trimmed sheet, 36 inches. Width of Super Calenders, 36 inches. Water. Air-dried Straw Board. 3000 lbs. 24 hours. (Idle.)

WOOD & NELLIS. WAGNER'S HOLLOW MILL. Wagner's Hollow, 3 miles. S. P., Fort Plain. Two 600-lb. engines; one 46-inch Cylinder. Water. Air-Dried Straw Board. 6000 lbs. 24 hours. (Idle.)

FRANKFORT—Herkimer Co.

Pop. 2,870. On Erie Canal, also on N. Y. C. & H. R. and N. Y., West Shore & Buffalo RR. M. O., Tel. office, Am. and Nat. Ex., Bank.

GREASONIA PAPER MILLS CO., INC. (W. H. Greason, Pres.; E. P. Greason, Vice-Pres.; E. T. Greason, Treas.) S. P., at mill. Four 1000-lb.

THE UNION SULPHUR CO.   Producers of
Main Office: Mines:
17 Battery Pl., New York. Calcasieu Parish, La.   **The Only Arsenic Free Sulphur on the Market**

Beating and two Jordan engines; one 76-inch and one 84-inch Single Cylinder Machines. Steam. Tissue Papers. 12,000 lbs. 24 hours. (Idle.)

FULTON—Oswego Co.

Pop. 12,000. On O. & S. Div. of D., L. & W.; N. Y., O. & W.; N. Y. C. & H. R. RR., and Oswego Canal. M. O. and Tel. office; Adams, Am., Nat. and U. S. Ex.

ARROWHEAD MILLS, INC. (F. A. Emerick, Pres.; S. P. Emerick, Vice-Pres.; J. H. Howe, Treas.; R. A. Downey, Sec.) S. P., at mill. Eight Beaters, two Jordans, one 100-inch Fourdrinier. Kraft and all Sulphite papers. PULP MILL. Three Digesters; six Wet Machines. Water and Steam. Sulphite Fibre (dry). 100,000 lbs. 24 hours. GRANBY PLANT. Two 1500-lb. Beaters and one Jordan. One 90-inch Harper Fourdrinier. Widest trimmed sheet, 82 inches. Water and Steam. Lightweight Manila, News and White Lining. 25,000 lbs. 24 hours. PULP MILL. Ten Grinders and eight 84-inch Wet Machines. Water. Ground Wood (dry), 100,000 lbs. 24 hours. VOLNEY PLANT. Fourteen 1000-lb. Beaters and six Refiners. Two 90-inch Cylinders. Water, Steam and Electricity. Saturating Felts. 110,000 lbs. 24 hours.

EUREKA PAPER CO. (T. H. Webb, Pres. and Treas.; E. J. Penfield, Vice-Pres.; G. C. Webb, Sec.) S. P., at mill. Two 1000-lb. and four 1500-lb. Beating and Refining engines; one 90-inch Three Cylinder. Widest trimmed sheet, 81 inches. Water, Steam and Electricity. Rope, Fibre, Express, Manila, Insulating, Building, Rocket, Bag, Saturating and Specialties. 32,000 lbs. 24 hours.

NORTH END PAPER CO. (Daniel Brannan, Pres.; W. J. Hartnett, Vice-Pres.; John Brannan, Treas.; J. L. Sullivan, Sec.) S. P., at mill. Two 1000-lb. Beating and one Jordan; one Bageley and Sewall 94-inch Cylinder Machine. Widest trimmed sheet, 81 inches. Steam and Electricity. Manila and No. 1 and No. 2 White Tissue; also Colors. 8000 lbs. 24 hours.

OSWEGO FALLS PULP AND PAPER CO. (H. L. Paddock, Pres.; F. G. Weeks, Vice-Pres.; C. W. Tooke, Treas.; F. C. Ash, Sec.; J. H. Hollingsworth, Mill Supt.) S. P., at mill. Six 1200-lb. engines; one 102-inch Six Cylinder and one 185-inch Fourdrinier. Widest trimmed sheet, 128 inches. Water and Steam. News-Print, Ice Cream Pail Board, Milk Bottle Caps, Oyster Pail Board, Wood Pulp Board, Match Board and Box Board. 140,000 lbs. 24 hours. PULP MILL. S. P., at mill. Eight Grinders; four 96-inch Wet Machines, three "Impco" Screens and two "Impco" Knotters. Hydro-Electric and Steam. Ground Wood. 120,000 lbs. 24 hours.

VICTORIA PAPER MILLS CO., THE. (E. R. Redhead, Pres.; F. W. Snyder, Vice-Pres. and Treas.; W. L. Forsyth, Sec.) Three paper mills and one bag factory. S. P., at mills. Four 600-lb., seven 1200-lb. Beating and four Refining engines; two 76-inch, one 90-inch and one 72-inch Single Cylinders. Electricity, Steam and Water. White and Manila Tissue, in sheets and rolls and Tissue Specialties. Flour Sacks, Nail Bags and Sugar Bags. 30,000 lbs. 24 hours. *Drum Wound Jumbo Rolls for Toilet Manufacturers a Specialty.*

National Duplex Waterproof Case Lining
IS WATERPROOF— NATIONAL WATERPROOFING CO., 1054 DREXEL BLDG.
CLEAN TO HANDLE PHILADELPHIA

Paper and Pulp Mills in the United States 153

GLENS FALLS— Warren Co.

Pop. 18,200. On D. & H. C. Co. RR. M. O. and Tel. office; Nat. Ex.

FINCH, PRUYN & CO., INC. (Maurice Hoopes, Pres.; L. F. Hyde, Vice-Pres.; F. B. Chapman, Treas.; L. M. Brown, Sec.; Jas. D. Myer, Supt. of Paper Mill; R. K. Pratt, Supt. of Ground Wood Mill.) S. P., at station. Seven 1500-lb. and one 2000-lb. Beating engines; one 68-inch, one 116-inch and one 148-inch Fourdriniers. Widest trimmed sheet, 139 inches. Water and Steam. News, Half-tone and Hangings. 220,000 lbs. 24 hours. PULP MILL. S. P., at mill. Twenty-four Grinders; thirteen Wet Machines. Water. Ground Wood. 260,000 lbs. 24 hours.

INTERNATIONAL PAPER CO. Office, 30 Broad street, New York. GLENS FALLS MILL. L. G. Willson, Supt. S. P., at mill. Twelve Beating and seven Refining engines; two 88-inch, one 98-inch, one 104-inch, two 144-inch Fourdriniers. Water and Steam. News, Poster, Hanging and Tablet Transfer Ticket. 284,000 lbs. 24 hours. PULP MILL. Eleven Grinders. Water and Steam. Ground Wood. 120,000 lbs. 24 hours.

GREAT BEND—Jefferson Co.

Pop. 800. On St. Lawrence Division of N. Y. C. RR. M. O. and Tel. office; bank. Watertown; Am. Ex.

TAGGARTS PAPER CO. P. O. Address, Watertown. (George C. Sherman, Pres.; E. M. Hall, Vice-Pres.; J. V. Baron, Sec. and Treas.; O. F. Dodge, Supt.) Two 1000-lb. and one Jordan engines; one 72-inch Fourdrinier. Widest trimmed sheet, 62 inches. Water. Hanging and Tablet, Light-weight Catalogue and News. 32,000 lbs. 24 hours. PULP MILL. S. P., Great Bend. Three Grinders; two Wet Machines; one "Impco" Screen. Ground Wood (dry). 30,000 lbs. 24 hours.

GREENWICH—Washington Co.

Pop. 1,869. On Greenwich & Johnsville RR. M. O. and Tel. office; Nat. Ex.

BLANDY PAPER CO. (A. W. Hitchcock, Pres.; D. C. Trondsen, Vice-Pres.; Elmer Sherman, Sec.; I. C. Blandy, Treas.) Office, Schuylerville. S. P., Center Falls, N. Y., on Greenwich and Johnsonville Ry. Three 1000-lb. engines; one 76-inch Cylinder. Widest trimmed sheet, 68 inches. Water. Tag Manila and Special Papers for Glazed Paper and Cardboard Manufacturers. 16,000 lbs. 24 hours. PULP MILL. Office, Schuylerville. S. P., at mill. Two Grinders; three Wet Machines. Water. Ground Wood. 30,000 lbs. 24 hours.

CONTINENTAL PAPER BAG CO. Office, 17 Battery place, New York. (S. Partington, Mill Supt.) S. P., Greenwich, N. Y. One 800-lb., two 500-lb. Beating and one Refining engines; one 76-inch Cylinder. Widest trimmed sheet, 65 inches. Water and Steam. High Grade White, Colored and Manila Tissues. 5000 lbs. 24 hours.

MOHICAN PULP AND PAPER CO. Office, Greenwich, N. Y. (H. C. Gray, Pres.; L. G. Thompson, Vice-Pres.; I, V. H. Gill, Treas. and Sec.) S. P., Greenwich. Two Grinders; three Wet Machines. Water. Ground Wood (dry). 24,000 lbs. 24 hours.

R. B. McEwan, Pres. J. L. McEwan, Vice-Pres. Arthur McEwan, Treas. and Mgr. R. W. McEwan, Secy.
Sheet Lining Plant, Office and Mills at WHIPPANY, N. J.

McEWAN BROS., Inc. MANUFACTURERS OF ALL GRADES **PAPER BOX BOARD**

E. J. KELLER CO., INC.
290 FIFTH AVENUE, NEW YORK
E. J. KELLER, Pres.
FOREIGN AND DOMESTIC
Rags AND Wastes
Gunny Bagging, Burlap Bagging, Ropes, Flax, Hemp, Cotton Wastes, Paper Stock, Wood Pulp and Rag Pulp.

DRY ROSIN SIZE Brittle, easy soluble, cheapest size out; cheaper than mill made size. Ask us about it. Also all other grades. **ARABOL M'F'G CO.** 100 William St., N. Y.

New York

HADLEY—Saratoga Co.

Pop. 914. On D. & H. R.R. Tel. office, M. O. and nearest bank, Corinth; Nat. Ex.

HADLEY PAPER CORPORATION, Successor to Union Bag and Paper Corp. Main Office, Woolworth Bldg., New York. (Edgar G. Barratt, Pres.; F. S. Rogers, Sec. and Treas.; William Sutherland, Supt.) HADLEY MILL. S. P., at mill. Six 1400-lb. Beating and three Jordan; six Rotary; one 100-inch Four Cylinder. Widest trimmed sheet, 92 inches. One 64-inch and one 74-inch Fourdrinier. Widest trimmed sheets, 56 and 65 inches. Water and Steam. Bogus, Carpet Lining, Chip and Box Boards. 54,000 lbs. 24 hours.

HANNAWA FALLS—St. Lawrence Co.—PULP MILL.

Pop. 300. Four miles from Potsdam. Tel., M. O., Ex. and nearest bank, Potsdam.

HANNAWA FALLS WATER POWER CO. Ground Wood. (Mill has been dismantled. Machinery sold. Power now used in hydro electric operation.)

HARRISVILLE—Lewis Co.

Pop. 1,000. On C. & A. RR. M. O. and Tel. offices; bank, Harrisville; Am. Ex.

DIANA PAPER CO. (M. S. Wilder, Pres.; John Weeks, Vice-Pres.; F. P. Wilder, Sec.-Treas. and Gen. Mgr.) S. P., at mill. Seven 1000-lb. Beating engines, electrically driven; two 110-inch Fourdriniers. Widest trimmed sheet, 102 inches. Union Screen. Water. Catalogue Papers and Light Weight News. 70,000 lbs. 24 hours. PULP MILL. S. P., at mill. Four Grinders, water wheel connection; six Grinders, electrically driven; seven Wet Machines. Water. Ground Wood. 60,000 lbs. 24 hours.

HERKIMER—Herkimer Co.

Pop. 6,596. On N. Y. C. Div. of N. Y. C. & H. R.; A. & St. L. line of M. & M. RR. M. O. and Tel. office; Am. and Electric Ex.

HERKIMER FIBRE CO., THE. HERKIMER MILLS. Office, 51 Lincoln Street, Boston, Mass. (Philip T. Dodge, Pres.; M. H. Cutler, Treas.; F. G. Simons, Sec.; F. D. Gray, Gen. Mgr. and Supt.) Six Beating and four Jordan engines; eleven 50-inch Cylinder Wet Machines. Water and Steam. Leather and Fibre Board. 65,000 lbs. 24 hours.

HERRINGS—Jefferson Co.

Pop. 150. On St. Lawrence Division, N. Y. C. RR. M. O., Ex., Tel. office and nearest bank, Carthage, 3½ miles.

ST. REGIS PAPER CO. Office, Watertown. HERRINGS MILLS. S. P., Carthage. PAPER MILL. One 87-inch Five Cylinder. Water and Steam. Container Board. 80,000 lbs. 24 hours. GROUND WOOD MILL. Eight Grinders; six Wet Machines. Water and Steam. Ground Wood (dry). 80,000 lbs. 24 hours. SULPHITE MILL. Four Digesters. Water and Steam. Sulphite Fibre. 72,000 lbs. 24 hours.

HINCKLEY—Oneida Co.—PULP MILL.

Pop. 600. On M. & M. RR. M. O. and Tel. office; nearest bank, Remsen, 5 miles; Am. Ex.

HINCKLEY FIBRE COMPANY. Lee Warren James, Pres.; J. H. Friend, Vice-Pres.; W. E. Becraft, Sec.; T. H. Ferris, Treas.; Wm. A. McKee,

PRESS ROLLS Maple and Gum White Wood Felt Rolls — J. W. HEWITT MACHINE CO. Neenah, Wis.

THOMAS E. GLEESON, Inc., 411-413 John St., E. NEWARK, N. J.
CYLINDER MOULDS and DANDY ROLLS Made and Repaired
LETTERING and MONOGRAMS for WATERMARKS

Paper and Pulp Mills in the United States 155

Supt.) HINCKLEY MILL. S. P., Hinckley. Nine Digesters; one Dry and five Wet Machines. One 90-inch Cylinder Drying Machine. Union Screens. Water and Electricity. Sulphite Fibre, Bleached and Unbleached. 180,000 lbs. 24 hours.

HEWITTVILLE—St. Lawrence Co.—PULP MILL.

Pop. 359. Three miles from Potsdam, N. Y. M. O., Tel. and bank, Potsdam, N. Y.

RACQUETTE RIVER PAPER CO. S. P., at Potsdam. Three Grinders; four Wet Machines. Water. Ground Wood. 30,000 lbs. 24 hours.

HUDSON FALLS—Washington Co.

Pop. 4,473. On Glens Falls Branch D. & H. RR.; Champlain Canal. M. O. and Tel. office; Nat. Ex.

UNION BAG AND PAPER CORPORATION. Main Office, Woolworth Bldg., New York. FENIMORE PAPER MILL. Eleven 1500-lb. Beating and three Jordan engines; two 158-inch Fourdriniers. Widest trimmed sheet, 146 inches. Bag and Kraft. ALLEN MILL. Seven 1500 and six 950-lbs. Beaters; two Jordans and one Claflin; one 96-inch Cylinder and one 112-inch Fourdrinier. Widest trimmed sheets, 88 and 102 inches. Bag, Kraft, Wrapping. PULP MILL. Seven Grinders; three Wet Machines. Water. Ground Wood. 30,000 lbs. 24 hours. MILL No. 5. Six 1200-lb. Beaters and one Jordan; one 158-inch Fourdriniers. Widest trimmed sheet, 146 inches. Bag. PULP MILL No. 1. Four Grinders; two Wet Machines. Water. Ground Wood. 20,000 lbs. 24 hours. MOREAU PULP MILL. Five Grinders; four Wet Machines. Water. Ground Wood. 30,000 lbs. 24 hours. SULPHITE MILL. Four Digesters. Sulphite. 220,000 lbs. 24 hours.

ITHACA—Tompkins Co.

Pop. 13,136. On D., L. & W.; L. V. RR; also canal lines. M. O. and Tel. office; U. S. Ex.

BROWN PAPER CO. Successor to Ithaca Paper Co. (A. G. Brown, Prop.) S. P., 100 yards. Two 500-lb. Beating engines; one 62-inch Single Cylinder. Water and Steam. Bogus Wrapping and Building Paper. 8000 lbs. 24 hours.

EMPIRE PAPER CO. Office, Fidelity Bldg., Portland, Me. (Edward P. Ricker, Pres.; Herbert P. Morrell, Vice-Pres.; B. S. Robinson, Treas.; C. S. Cook, Sec.; Thomas W. Donoghue, Mgr.) S. P., ¼ mile. Three 800-lb. Beating and one Refining engines; one Cylinder Machine. Width of Super Calenders, 72 inches. Widest trimmed sheet, 62 inches. Water and Steam. White, Colored and Manila Tissue. 8000 lbs. 24 hours.

JOHNSON CITY—Broome Co.

Pop. 5,600. On D. L. & W. and Erie RR. Tel. and M. O., bank; Adams and Wells Fargo Ex.

ENDICOTT, JOHNSON & CO. (H. B. Endicott, Pres.; Eliot Spalding, Treas.; H. L. Johnson, Mgr.) FIBRE BOARD MILL. Eight 1500-lb. Beaters and one Rotary Boiler. Ten 50-inch Wet Machines. Steam and Electricity. 21,000 lbs. 24 hours. COUNTER BOARD MILL. Four 1500-lb. Beaters and two Rotary Boilers. Six 50-inch Cylinder Wet Machines. Electricity. 12,000 lbs. 24 hours. HEELING BOARD MILL. Two 2400-lb. Beaters and two Jordans. Six 50-inch Cylinder Wet Machines. Electricity. 22,000 lbs. 24 hours.

M. GOTTESMAN & CO., Inc.
18 E. 41st STREET, NEW YORK. Cable Address "Namsettog"
EUROPEAN OFFICES: Stockholm, Sweden

Finest Mitscherlich Sulphite

SULPHUR—CRUDE. GUARANTEED 99% PURE.
The average analysis of our high-grade brimstone is in itself a guarantee. Write us for quotations.
THE UNION SULPHUR CO., Main Office, 17 Battery Pl., New York. Mines, Calcasieu Parish, La.

MARCELLUS FALLS—Onondaga Co.

Pop. 589. On N. Y. C. RR. Nearest bank, Marcellus; M. O., Tel. and Ex., Marcellus Station, 1½ miles.

MARCELLUS PAPER CO. (H. C. Peters, Pres. and Mgr.; Harry Bye, Vice-Pres.; J. C. Boland, Sec. and Treas.) Office, 511 S. A. & K. Bldg., Syracuse, N. Y. MARCELLUS FALLS MILL. S. P., Marcellus Falls. Three 1200-lb. Beating and two Horne Jordan engines; one 66-inch Two Cylinder. Widest trimmed sheet, 60 inches. Water and Steam. Express, Fibres, Screenings, Light-Weight Mill Wrappers, Hardware and Butchers' Waterproof. 14,000 lbs. 24 hours.

ONONDAGA PAPER CO. (T. E. Lawless, Pres.; M. J. Lawless, Vice-Pres.; C. H. Lawless, Sec.; F. J. Lawless, Treas.; D. J. Lawless, Gen. Mgr.) EAGLE AND PHOENIX MILL. S. P., at mill. Six 1000-lb. Beating and four Jordan engines; one 72-inch Fourdrinier and one 90-inch Cylinder. Widest trimmed sheet, 65 inches and 80 inches. Water, Steam and Electricity. Screening, Express, Fibre, Manila. Kraft Tissue and Colored Specialties. 34,000 lbs. 24 hours. *"Screenings, Express, all weights."*

McKEEVER—Herkimer Co.—PULP MILL.

Adirondack Branch of N. Y. C. & H. R. RR. P. O.; Am. Ex.; Telephone; Telegraph.

IROQUOIS PULP AND PAPER CO. (Henry W. Somers, Pres.; W. A. Huppuch, Vice-Pres.; John A. Becker, Vice-Pres.; Luther A. Wait, Sec. and Treas.; John M. Gill, Asst. Treas.; A. Brown, Mill Supt.) Head office, Thomson, Washington Co., N. Y. Four Grinders, five Wet Machines and two Hydraulic Pulp Presses. Capacity, Ground Wood, 40,000 lbs. 24 hours.

MARLBOROUGH-ON-HUDSON—Orange Co.

HUNTER'S, DARD, PAPER MILL. (Dard Hunter, Owner.) S. P., Newburgh. Water. Hand-made Book and Writing. (Aug. 14, 1918. Mill discontinued for duration of war as Mr. Dard Hunter is about to enter service.)

MECHANICVILLE—Saratoga Co.

Pop. 8,000. On D. & H. C. Co.; B. & M. RR.; Hudson Valley Electric Ry.; Champlain Canal. M. O. and Tel. office; Nat. Ex.

WEST VIRGINIA PULP AND PAPER CO. Office, 200 Fifth avenue, New York. Western Sales Office, 732 Sherman street, Chicago. (John G. Luke, Pres.; David L. Luke, Vice-Pres.; Thomas Luke, Vice-Pres.; Adam K. Luke, Treas.; Chas. A. Cass, Sec.; Thos. H. Stirling, Res. Mgr.) MECHANICVILLE MILL. Thirty-seven 1500-lb. Beating and six Refining engines; one 99-inch, two 112-inch, one 119-inch and two 137-inch Fourdriniers. Widest trimmed sheet, 125 inches. Width of Super-Calenders, 44, 52, 66, 72, 90 and 100 inches. Water and Steam. Machine finished and Super-Calendered Book, Lithograph and Varnish Label. 240,000 lbs. 24 hours. PULP MILLS. MECHANICVILLE SODA FIBRE MILL. Ten Digesters; one 84-inch Cylinder. Water and Steam. Bleached Soda Fibre (dry). 150,000 lbs. 24 hours. MECHANICVILLE SULPHITE FIBRE MILL. Five Digesters; one 84-inch and one 72-inch Wet Machine. Water and Steam. Bleached Sulphite Fibre. 150,000 lbs. 24 hours.

THOMAS E. GLEESON, Inc., **FOURDRINIER WIRES**
411-413 John St., E. NEWARK, N. J. For Tissue and Fine Grade Papers

Paper and Pulp Mills in the United States 159

MELLENVILLE—Columbia Co.

Pop. 564. On H. & C. Branch of B. & A. R.R. M. O. and Tel. office; nearest bank, Philmont; Am. Ex.

BERKSHIRE BOX AND PAPER CO., THE. Hallett Bros. Co., Lessees. Boston Office, 35 Sleeper Street. S. P., Mellenville or Philmont. One 600-lb., one 1000-lb. and one 1500-lb. Beating engines; one 70-inch Four Cylinder. Widest trimmed sheet, 62 inches. Electricity. Box Board, Wrapper, Card Middles, Lined and Unlined Folding Box Board and Manila Lined Board. 20,000 lbs. 24 hours.

VAN BUREN & CO., J. MYERS. Three 1000-lb. Beating and one Jordan engines; one Two Cylinder Machine and one Screen. Widest trimmed sheet, 48 inches. Water and Steam. Wrapping. 20,000 lbs. 24 hours.

MIDDLE FALLS—Washington Co.

Pop. 420. On G. & J. RR. Tel. office, Nat. Ex. and nearest bank, Greenwich.

GREENWICH LEATHERBOARD CO., Successor to Bossom Manufacturing Co. (Thos. McDermott, Supt.) Office, Boston, Mass. Eight 1000-lb. Beating and one Jordan engines; four 48-inch Wet Machines. Water. Leather Board. 30,000 lbs. 24 hours.

STEVENS & THOMPSON PAPER CO. (Frank L. Stevens, Pres.; Fred N. Stevens, Vice-Pres.; Howard B. Thompson, Sec. & Treas.) S. P., at mill. Twelve 600-lb. and one 1000-lb. Beating engines; one 68-inch and two 72-inch and three 76-inch Cylinder machines. Widest trimmed sheet, 72 inches. Water, Steam and Electricity. Manila Tissue. 36,000 lbs. 24 hours. PULP MILL. Four Grinders; four Wet Machines. Water. Ground Wood.

MUMFORD—Monroe Co.

Pop. 455. On B. R. & P. RR. M. O. and Tel. office; Am. Ex.

MUMFORD PAPER MILLS, INC. Buffalo Office, 495 Seneca Street. (Wm. H. Howe, Pres.; G. E. Beggs, Sec. and Treas.; T. J. Foley, Gen. Mgr.) TROUT MILLS. S. P., at mill. Two 800-lb. Beating and one Jordan engines; one 76-inch Cylinder. Widest trimmed sheet, 68 inches. Water and Steam. Manila Tissue and Toilet. 9000 lbs. 24 hours.

NAPANOCH—Ulster Co.

Pop. 650. On Port Jervis and Kingston Div. of N. Y. O. & W. RR. Nearest bank, Ellenville, 2 miles.

HOORNBEEK'S SONS, JOHN C. Wood Flour for Explosives.

HUMPHREY & YOUNG, INC. NAPANOCH MILLS. S. P., ½ mile to railroad. Five 400-lb. Beaters and one Jordan engine; one 62-inch machine. Water. Light and Heavy Bogus Wrappings and Butchers' Manila. 10,000 lbs. 24 hours.

ULSTER TISSUE MILLS, INC. (L. L. Gilbert, Pres.; Arthur E. Lee, Vice-Pres.; H. J. Corwin, Sec. and Treas.) New York Office, 45 Cedar Street. S. P., ¼ mile. One 800-lb., one 1000-lb., two 1200-lb. Beating and three Refining engines; two 84-inch Cylinder Machines. Widest trimmed sheet, 72 inches. Water and Steam. Manila Sheet and Roll Tissue. 8000 lbs. 24 hours.

DRY ROSIN SIZE

Brittle, easy soluble. Cheaper, size out; cheaper than mill made size. Ask us about it. Also all other grades.

ARABOL M'F'G CO.
100 William St., New York

HIGHEST GRADE BRIMSTONE—GUARANTEED 99% PURE
free from Arsenic or Selenium. Write for particulars to
THE UNION SULPHUR CO., Main Office, 17 Battery Pl., New York. Mines, Calcasieu Parish, La.

DRY ROSIN SIZE Brittle, easy soluble, cheapest size out; cheaper than mill made size. Ask us about it. Also all other grades. **ARABOL M'F'G CO.** 100 William St., N. Y.

New York

NATURAL DAM—St. Lawrence Co.

Two miles from Gouverneur. Tel., M. O., Ex. and nearest bank, Gouverneur.

ALDRICH PAPER CO. (H. G. Aldrich, Pres.; Sam. Child, Sec.; Nelson R. Caswell, Treas.; F. A. Briggs, Supt.) S. P., Gouverneur. One 1000-lb. and two 2000-lb. Beating engines; one 132-inch Bagley. Widest trimmed sheet, 123 inches. Water and Steam. News, Manila and Hanging. 60,000 lbs. 24 hours. PULP MILL. Five Grinders. Water. Ground Wood. 30,000 lbs. 24 hours. SULPHITE MILL. Two Digesters, two Wet Machines. Water. Sulphite Fibre. 40,000 lbs. 24 hours.

NEWBURGH—Orange Co.

Pop. 24,943. On Erie; N. Y., L. E. & W.; N. Y., W. S. & B.; N. Y., O. & W.; H. Div. N. Y., N. H. & H. RR.; also vessels. M. O. and Tel. office; Am., Ad., Nat. and W., F. & Co. Ex.

HOLDEN PAPER COMPANY. (A. F. Holden, Pres.; D. E. McKinstry, Vice-Pres.; R. W. Spencer, Treas.; L. J. White, Sec.; Elmer Staub, Mill Supt.) Location, New Windsor No. 1 Mill. S. P., New Windsor, via Erie R. R. Two 1200-lb. Beating and one Refining engines; one 700-lb., two 1500-lb. and four 1000-lb. Washing engines; one 88-inch Fourdrinier. Widest trimmed sheet, 82 inches. Width of Super-Calenders, 54 inches. Steam. M. F. & S. C. Book and Writing. 30,000 lbs. 24 hours.

LITTLE FALLS PAPER CO. (A. F. Holden, Prop.) ORANGE COUNTY PAPER MILL. S. P., at mill. One 500-lb., one 800-lb., five 1000-lb. and one 1200-lb. Beating; three Refining engines and one Rotary boiler; one 84-inch and two 88-inch Cylinders. Widest trimmed sheet, 72 inches. Steam. White and Manila Tissue. 17,000 lbs. 24 hours.

NEWARK—Wayne Co.

Pop. 6,227. On N. Y. Central, Sodus Bay Div. No. Central; West Shore and Newark & Marion RR. M. O., Tel., Bank. Ad., Am., Nat. and Wells Fargo Ex.

BLOOMER BROS. CO. (Charles T. Bloomer, Pres.; Charles B. Kiefeker, Vice-Pres.; R. A. S. Bloomer, Sec. and Treas.) One 72-inch Machine. Combination Box Boards. 50,000 lbs. 24 hours. (Sell no stock on the open market.)

NEW HAMPTON—Orange Co.

Pop. 260. On Eastern Div. of Erie RR. M. O. and Tel. office; nearest bank, Middletown, 3 miles; Wells, Fargo & Co. Ex.

DIAMOND MILLS PAPER CO. (R. H. Thompson, Pres.; C. G. Van Gilder, Sec.; E. Van Voorhis, Treas.) P. O. address, 44 Murray street, New York. HAMPTON MILL. S. P., at mill. Four 700-lb., one 1200-lb. Beating, two Jordan engines; one 62-inch and one 58-inch Cylinder machines. Widest trimmed sheet, 56 inches. Water and Steam. Tissue. 5000 lbs. 24 hours. (Idle.)

NEWTON FALLS—St. Lawrence Co.

On C. & A. Div. N. Y. C. RR. Tel. and Am. Ex.; nearest bank, Carthage, 45 miles.

NEWTON FALLS PAPER CO. (F. L. Moore, Pres. and Gen. Mgr.; F. T. Helmer, Treas.; V. K. Kellogg, Sec.) S. P., at mill. Six 1500-lb. Beating and three Jordan engines; one 90-inch and one 113-inch Four-

DARMSTADT, SCOTT & COURTNEY, Inc. Importers, Exporters and Dealers in **PAPER MAKERS' SUPPLIES** Also Mfrs. of DEADENING and SATURATING FELTS 178 and 184 SOUTH STREET, NEW YORK

McENERY PAPER COMPANY 112 W. ADAMS ST., CHICAGO — MANUFACTURERS' SALES AGENCY PRACTICALLY ALL GRADES

driniers. Widest trimmed sheet, 104 inches. Union Screens. Water and Steam. High Grade Sulphite and Colored Specialties. 68,000 lbs. 24 hours. PULP MILL. S. P., at mill. Two Grinders; three Digesters; eight Wet Machines. Water and Steam. Ground Wood 14,000 lbs., Sulphite Fibre 80,000 lbs. 24 hours.

NEW YORK CITY.
Brooklyn Borough.

RUSHMORE PAPER CO. New York Office, 61 Beekman Street. Four 1000-lb. Beating and two Refining engines; one 64-inch and one 76-inch Cylinder Machines. Widest trimmed sheets, 60 and 72 inches. Steam. Toilet Paper, Paper Towels and Creped Specialties. 24,000 lbs. 24 hours.

TIDEWATER PAPER MILLS CO. Office at mill, 32 Thirty-third Street, Bush Terminal, South Brooklyn. (Adolph S. Ochs, Pres.; Geo. McAneny, Vice-Pres.; B. C. Franck, Sec. and Treas.; J .D. Coffin, Mgr.) Six 2000-lb. Beating engines; two 154-inch Fourdriniers. Widest trimmed sheet, 146½ inches. Union Screens. Steam and Electricity. News. 190,000 lbs. 24 hours.

Manhattan Borough.

The following list includes the paper manufacturing companies the head offices of which are located in New York City (for location of plants see index to mills):

CONTINENTAL PAPER BAG CO. Main Office, 17 Battery place, New York. Incorporated under the laws of the State of New York, May 8, 1899.

Authorized Capital Stock, $5,000,000: Preferred, $2,500,000; Common, $2,500,000.

OFFICERS.—Herman Elsas, Pres.; I. Kuhe, Vice-Pres.; Chester W. Lyman, Treas.; Thomas Fynes, Sec. and Asst. Treas.

LIST OF MILLS OF THE COMPANY.

Name of Mill	Location	Daily Capacity in Pounds	
		Tissue paper	Ground wood
Watertown	Watertown, N. Y.	25,000	15,000
Ashland	Ashland, N. H.	30,000	
Greenwich	Greenwich, N. Y.	5,000	
Totals		60,000	15,000

Bag Factory at Rumford, Me.
Egg Carton Factory, Cincinnati, O.

INTERNATIONAL PAPER COMPANY. Main Office, 30 Broad Street. Incorporated under the laws of the State of New York, January, 1898.

Authorized capital stock: Preferred 6 per cent. cumulative, $25,000,000 (issued $25,000,000); Common, $20,000,000 (issued $19,828,000); Bonds: December 31, 1917, 6% Consolidated, First Mortgage, $10,000,000 (outstanding $3,272,000); Divisional Mortgage, $1,311,000, 5% Convertible Gold Bonds, $10,000,000 (outstanding $940,000). First and Rfdg. Mtg. 5% Bonds, $6,419,000. Dividends payable quarterly on preferred stock. (Last dividend of 1 per cent. on common, July, 1899.)

New York

OFFICERS.—Philip T. Dodge, Pres.; Ogden Mills, Vice-Pres.; W. D. Russell, Vice-Pres.; C. W. Lyman, Vice-Pres.; W. E. Haskell, Asst. to Pres.; Owen Shepherd, Treas.; F. G. Simons, Sec.; John M. Picker, Mgr. Dept. of Insurance and Taxes; Allen Curtis, Mgr. Dept. of Manufacture; A. H. White, Chief Engr.; G. E. Smith, Mgr. Purchasing Dept.; Geo. M. Stearns, Mgr. Dept. of Woodlands; B. O. Booth, Auditor; C. W. Lyman, Mgr. Dept. of Sales; A. H. Campbell, Traffic Mgr.

LIST OF MILLS OF THE COMPANY.

	NAME OF MILL.	LOCATION.	Paper.	Ground wood.	Sulphite
1	Glens Falls	Glens Falls, N. Y.	142	60	..
2	Fort Edward	Fort Edward, N. Y.	148	50	80
3	Hudson River	Palmer, N. Y.	262	230	62
4	Otis	Chisholm, Me.	302	80	65
5	Glen	Berlin, N. H.	103	80	60
6	Niagara Falls	Niagara Falls, N. Y.	154	64	45
7	Rumford Falls	Rumford, Me.	189	90	120
8	Curtis	Corinth	..	85	..
9	Webster	Orono, Me.	28	30	..
10	Winnipiseogee	Franklin Falls, N. H.	45	35	..
11	Livermore	Livermore Falls, Me.	..	90	..
13	Montague	Turners Falls, Mass.	47	36	..
14	Lake George	Ticonderoga, N. Y.	54	40	..
15	Fall Mountain	Bellows Falls, Vt.	94	42	35
17	Piercefield	Piercefield, N. Y.	47	40	35
19	Solon	Solon, Me.	..	45	..
22	Cadyville	Cadyville, N. Y.	..	105	..
23	Riley	Riley, Me.	..	80	..
24	Wilder	Wilder, Vt.	53	55	..
27	West Enfield	West Enfield, Me.	..	35	..
28	Milton	Milton, Vt.	..	36	..
29	Watertown	Watertown, N. Y.	..	9	..
31	Woods Falls	Watertown, N. Y.	120	95	..
	Totals		1,788	1,512	502

UNION BAG AND PAPER CORPORATION. Main Office, Woolworth Bldg., New York, Incorporated under the laws of the State of New Jersey, October 4, 1916.

Authorized capital stock, $10,000,000. First Mortgage 5 per cent. Gold Bonds (authorized), $5,000,000; outstanding, $3,023,000.

OFFICERS.—President and Treasurer, M. B. Wallace, Chairman of the Board, August Heckscher; Vice-Presidents, E. B. Murray and C. R. McMillen; Secretary, C. B. Sanders; Asst. Secretary, S. H. Brown; Asst. Treasurers, W. E. Quayle and J. Wohnsiedler.

BOARD OF DIRECTORS.—August Heckscher, M. B. Wallace, C. R. McMillen, John H. Derby, James B. Marsh, Alexander MacLaurin, John A. Sleicher, D. S. Walton, Niel A. Weathers, E. B. Murray, R. T. Spencer, C. B. Sanders, C. B. Jaqua, Chas. B. Osborne and Thomas M. Day.

THOMAS E. GLEESON, Inc., } **FOURDRINIER WIRES**
411-413 John St., E. NEWARK, N. J. } For Tissue and Fine Grade Papers

LIST OF MILLS OF THE COMPANY.

NAME OF MILL.	LOCATION.	Paper.	Ground wood.	Sulphite
Fenimore	Hudson Falls, N. Y.	85	..	110
Allen Division	Hudson Falls, N. Y.	45	15	..
No. 5, Hudson Falls	Hudson Falls, N. Y.	40	..	..
No. 1 Pulp	Hudson Falls, N. Y.	..	10	..
Moreau Pulp	Hudson Falls, N. Y.	..	15	..
Kaukauna	Kaukauna, Wis.	20	..	..
Pulp	Kaukauna, Wis.	..	7	..
Cheboygan	Cheboygan, Mich.	60	8	50

Daily Capacity in Tons

BAG FACTORIES.—Hudson Falls, N. Y.; Kaukauna, Wis.; Chicago, Ill.; Wausau, Wis.

SUBSIDIARY COMPANY.—Badger Bag & Paper Company, Wausau, Wis.

Union Bag and Paper Corporation also owns three-quarters of the stock of the St. Maurice Paper Co., Limited, Board of Trade Bldg., Montreal, Quebec.

UNITED PAPERBOARD COMPANY. General Offices, 171 Madison avenue, New York City. Incorporated under the laws of New Jersey, February, 1912.

Capitalization: $14,100,000. Underlying Liens Outstanding: $325,000.

OFFICERS—Sidney Mitchell, Pres.; Matthias Plum, Vice-Pres. and Gen. Mgr.; Albion W. Boothby, Vice-Pres. and Mgr. Sales; M. Bechthold, Sec.; Charles E. Daniel, Treas.

Mills Owned by Company	Paper-board.	Ground wood.	Soda.	
Benton Falls Board Mill	40,000	20,000	.....	....
Fairfield Ground Wood Mill	.....	30,000	.....	....
Fairfield Soda Mill	.....	.....	60,000	....
Caledonian (Whippany)	60,000	.....	.....	....
Eaton	50,000	.....	.....	....
Hanover (Whippany)	.....	.....	.....	....
Urbana Mill	70,000	.....	.....	....
Peoria Mill	100,000	.....	.....	....
Rockport Mill	38,000	.....	.....	....
Thomson Board Mill	80,000	.....	.....	....
Thomson Pulp Mill	.....	50,000	.....	....
Lockport Board Mill	140,000	.....	.....	....
Lockport Niagara Pulp	.....	10,000	.....	....
Lockport Pulp	.....	60,000	.....	....
Lockport Franklin Pulp	.....	16,000	.....	....
Lockport Sulphite Mill	.....	.....	.....	60,000
Mt. Carmel Mill	55,000	.....	.....	....
Wabash Mill	120,000	.....	.....	....
Yorktown Mill	45,000	.....	.....	....
Total	910,000	186,000	60,000	60,000

Capacity in Pounds Per 24 Hours.

Borough of Queens (Long Island City).

AMERICAN FIBRE CHAIR SEAT CORP., 540 Van Alst Ave. (A. J. Kinsman, Pres.; Irving Weiser, Sec.-Treas.) Two 800-lb. Beaters and one

BRIMSTONE MAKES THE VERY BEST SULPHITE.
If you are looking for a high-grade Brimstone write to
THE UNION SULPHUR CO., Main Office, 17 Battery Pl., New York. Mines, Calcasieu Parish, La.

M. GOTTESMAN & CO., Inc. 18 E. 41st STREET, NEW YORK. Cable Address "Namestog". EUROPEAN OFFICES: Stockholm, Sweden — **HIGHEST GRADE KRAFT PULPS**

DRY ROSIN SIZE Brittle, easy soluble, cheapest size out; cheaper than mill made size. Ask us about it. Also all other grades. **ARABOL M'F'G CO.** 100 William St., N. Y.

New York

Refining engine. One 42-inch Cylinder Machine; one Wet Machine. Widest trimmed sheet, 42 inches. Steam and Electricity. Chair Seat Board, Binders' Board and Specialties. 10,000 lbs. 24 hours.

RAVENSWOOD PAPER MILL CO. (Henry Schreiter, Pres. and Treas.; Charles I. Karasik, Business Manager; Wm. L. Tufts, Sec.; J. F. Baker, Supt.) Location, 545 to 575 Van Alst Avenue, Long Island City. S. P., at mill. Four 1000-lb. Beating and two Refining engines; one 86-inch Five Cylinder. Widest trimmed sheet, 84 inches. Steam and Electricity. Plain and Colored and Coated Chip and News Boards, Vat Lined, Combination and other Special Boards, Plain and Lined. 60,000 lbs. 24 hours.

NIAGARA FALLS—Niagara Co.

Pop. 35,000. On N. F. Branch of E. & L.; N. Y. C. & H. R. RR.; W. & O.; W. S.; E. Div. of M. C.; G. T. RR. M. O. and Tel. office; Am., R., U. S. and Wells, Fargo & Co. Ex.

CERTAIN-TEED PRODUCTS CORPORATION, Successors to Lockport Paper Company. NIAGARA FALLS MILL. Elizabeth Street. General Office, Boatmen's Bank Bldg., St. Louis, Mo. (Geo. M. Brown, Pres.; S. E. Allison, Vice-Pres.; J. S. Porter, Vice-Pres.; A. Whittenmore, Vice-Pres.; J. C. Collins, Vice-Pres.; R. M. Nelson, Sec. and Treas.; H. B. Allen, Mgr.) S. P., at mill. Two 1200-lb., eight 1000-lb. Beating and two Jordans; three 94-inch Cylinders. Widest trimmed sheet, 90 inches. Union Screens. Electricity. 70,000 lbs. 24 hours. Building, Roofing, Wrapping and Deadening Felts. (Roofing factory in connection.)

CLIFF PAPER CO. (J. F. Schoellkopf, Pres.; E. M. Grigg, Vice-Pres.; Paul A. Schoellkopf, Sec. and Treas.; A. C. Hastings, Gen. Mgr.; E. E. Mansfield, Asst. Sec.; A. A. Oatman, Asst. Treas.; M. J. Argy, Supt.) CLIFF PAPER MILLS. S. P., at mills. Five 1000-lb. Beating and two Jordan engines; one 92-inch and one 102-inch Fourdriniers. Widest trimmed sheet, 94 inches. Electricity. News in rolls and sheets. 80,000 lbs. 24 hours. PULP MILL. S. P., at mill. Two Voith Magazine Grinders; two Wet Machines. Electricity. Ground Wood (dry). 80,000 lbs. 24 hours. (Mill shut down Jan. 1, 1918, and electric power delivered to war industries for duration of war.)

DEFIANCE PAPER CO. (W. D. Uptegraff, Pres.; J. M. Uptegraff, Treas.; T. M. Uptegraff, Sec. & Mgr. DEFIANCE MILL. S. P., at mill. Three 1200-lb. Beating and one Refining engines; one 90-inch machine. Electricity. Hanging and News. 60,000 lbs. 24 hours. PULP MILL. S. P., at mill. Four Grinders and four Wet Machines. Electricity.

INTERNATIONAL PAPER CO. Office, 30 Broad street, New York. NIAGARA FALLS MILL. (F. Cathcart, Agt.) S. P., at mill. Two Beating and two Refining engines; five 120-inch, one 135-inch Fourdriniers. Water and Steam. News. 38,000 lbs. 24 hours. PULP MILL. Six Digesters; eight Grinders; eight Wet Machines. Ground Wood, 128,000 lbs.; Sulphite Fibre, 90,000 lbs. 24 hours. (Mill down; Government orders.)

NIAGARA RIVER MANUFACTURING CO. (C. B. Hyde, Pres.; G. G. Shepard, Sec. and Treas.) S. P., at mill. Five Wet Machines; two Grinders. Electricity. Ground Wood. 30,000 lbs. 24 hours.

LOMBARD'S ENGLISH NEWCASTLE PULP STONES ARE SUPERIOR TO ALL OTHERS. ALL SIZES IN STOCK. LOMBARD & CO., Importers & Manufacturers, 226 & 228 A Street, Boston.

McEnery Paper Company Practically All Grades
Manufacturers' Sales Agency 112 W. ADAMS ST., CHICAGO

Paper and Pulp Mills in the United States 165

PETTEBONE-CATARACT PAPER CO., THE. (M. E. Jones, Pres.; N. J. Bowker, Treas.-Mgr.; Robt. Bailey, Supt.) Mill on the Hydraulic Basin. S. P., at mill. Three 1000-lb. and two Jordan engines; two 90-inch Fourdriniers. Widest trimmed sheet, 80 inches. Water. Roll and Sheet News. 60,000 lbs. 24 hours. PULP MILL. S. P., at mill. Three Grinders; three Wet Machines. Water. Ground Wood (dry). 36,000 lbs. 24 hours.

NORFOLK—St. Lawrence Co.
Pop. 1,500. On Norwood & St. Lawrence RR; 3 miles from Norwood. M. O., Tel. Ex. and bank.

REMINGTON PAPER AND POWER CO. Offices, Watertown, N. Y. (M. S. Wilder, Pres.; M. A. Hanna, Vice-Pres.; C. H. Hanna, Vice-Pres.; R. B. Maltby, Sec. and Treas.; J. A. Remington, Asst. Sec.; W. D. Gregor, Gen. Supt.) S. P., at mill. Six Beater and two Jordan engines; one 100-inch and one 163-inch Fourdriniers. Water, Steam and Electricity. News and Catalogue. 150,000 lbs. 24 hours. PULP MILLS. Ten Grinders, Water Power; four Grinders, Electric Power. Ground Wood. 100,000 lbs. 24 hours. Three Manitowac Digesters; eight Wet Machines. Sulphite. 85,000 lbs. 24 hours.

NORWOOD—St. Lawrence Co.
Pop. 2,000. At Junction of R. W. & O., Rutland & Norwood and St. Lawrence R.R. M. O. and Ex.

MARTIN PULP & PAPER CO., THE. (O. E. Martin, Pres.; M. J. Martin, Vice-Pres.; A. H. Martin, Treas.; H. W. Martin, Sec.) One mile north of Norwood on N. Y. C. & Rutland R.R. Two Grinders, three Wet Machines. Ground Wood. 16,000 lbs. 24 hours.

REMINGTON PAPER AND POWER CO. Office, Watertown, N. Y. (M. S. Wilder, Pres.; M. A. Hanna, Vice-Pres.; C. H. Hanna, Vice-Pres.; R. B. Maltby, Sec. and Treas.; J. A. Remington, Asst. Sec.; W. D. Gregor, Gen. Supt.) Four Beating and one Jordan engines; one 120-inch Fourdrinier. Water and Steam. News and Catalogue. 50,000 lbs. 24 hours. PULP MILL. Seven Grinders and four Wet Machines. Ground Wood. 70,000 lbs. 24 hours.

NORTH HOOSICK—Rensselaer Co.
Pop. 491. On B. & M. RR. M. O. and Tel. office; nearest bank, Hoosick Falls, 2 miles; Nat. Ex.

STEVENS & THOMPSON. (F. N. Stevens, Pres.; F. L. Stevens, Vice-Pres.; H. B. Thompson, Treas.; B. W. Sugden, Sec.; I. T. Fisk, Supt.) NORTH HOOSICK MILLS. S. P., at mill. Eight 800-lb. Beating engines; one 80-inch Fourdrinier. Widest sheet made, 74 inches. Union Screens. Water and Steam. Specialties in Colors. 24,000 lbs. 24 hours.

ORANGEBURG—Rockland Co.
Pop. 300. On West Shore and Piermont Br. of Erie RR. M. O. and Tel. office; Wells Fargo & Co. and Nat. Ex.

FIBRE CONDUIT COMPANY, THE. Conduits made from wood pulp.

PALMER—Saratoga Co.
Pop. 1,200. On A. Div. D. & H. RR. M. O. and Tel. office; bank, Corinth, ½ mile; Nat. Ex.

INTERNATIONAL PAPER CO. Office, 30 Broad Street, New York. HUDSON RIVER MILL. (C. W. Walker, Supt.) S. P., at mill. Fourteen

Beating and six Refining engines (large size); one 84-inch Cylinder; three 86-inch, one 92-inch, one 108-inch, one 122-inch, one 145-inch and two 152-inch Fourdriniers. Water and Steam. News and Mill Wrappers. 524,000 lbs. 24 hours. PULP MILL. Thirty-four Grinders; five Digesters; thirty Wet Machines. Ground Wood, 400,000 lbs.; Sulphite Fibre, 124,000 lbs. 24 hours.

PENFIELD—Monroe Co.

Pop. 2,857. On O. Div. of N. Y. C. & H. R. RR. Bank, Fairport, 8 miles; Am. Ex.

LAWLESS PAPER CO. (D. T., D. F. and M. J. L.) P. O. address, Rochester. Four 500-lb. Beating and two Jordan engines; one 88-inch Double Cylinder. Widest trimmed sheet, 80 inches. Water and Steam. Corrugating Boards, Mill Wrappers, Screenings, Express, Rag Wrappings and Specialties. 40,000 lbs. 24 hours.

PENN YAN—Yates Co.

Pop. 4,650. On P. Div. of N. Y. C. & H. R. RR. M. O. and Tel. office; Adams and Am. Ex.

ANDREWS, JOHN T., & CO., INC. (Charles T. Andrews, Pres.; Edwin C. Andrews, Vice-Pres.; Clarence R. Andrews, Sec. and Treas.; Michael Flynn, Supt.) MILO PAPER MILLS. S. P., Milo Mills. Three 1000-lb. and two 1200-lb. and two Jordan engines; one 68-inch and one 88-inch Cylinders. Widest trimmed sheet, 80 inches. Water and Steam. Butchers' Fibre, Bogus Wrapping, Black Hardware, Express and Sheathing, Car Lining and Carpet Lining. 40,000 lbs. 24 hours.

FOX, W. H., & SONS. (W. D. Fox, Mill Supt., and J. C. Fox.) KEUKA MILL. S. P., side track at mill. Three 1200-lb. Beating engines; two Jordans. Two 50-inch Cylinder Machines; widest trimmed sheet, 45 inches. Water and Steam. Straw Wrapping, Corrugating, etc. 24,000 to 30,000 lbs. 24 hours.

MOORE PAPER MILL CORP., Successor to Yates Paper Mill. (Charles G. Moore, Pres.; W. P. Goodspeed, Vice-Pres.; B. S. Moore, Sec. and Treas.) S. P., at mill. Three 1500-lb. Beating and two Jordan engines; one 76-inch Four Cylinder Machine. Widest trimmed sheet, 68 inches. Box Board, Container Board and Specialties. Water and Steam. 40,000 lbs. 24 hours.

PHOENIX—Oswego Co.

Pop. 1,532. On N. Y. C. & H. R. RR.; Barge Canal. M. O. and Tel. office; Am. Ex.

CRESCENT PAPER & MACHINE CO. (Co-Partnership, Clinton D. Ash and Smith N. Murgittroyd; C. D. Ash, Gen. Mgr.; A. A. Burrows, Supt.; F. H. von Ullrich, Mgr.) S. P., at mill. Three 800-lb. Beating and two Refining engines. One 69-inch and one 92-inch Double Deck Cylinder Machines. Widest trimmed sheets, 61¾ and 80 inches. Water, Steam and Electricity. No. 2 White and Manila Tissues 10 to 15. 10,000 lbs. 24 hours.

OSWEGO RIVER PAPER MILLS. (Martha M. Buell, A. D. Merry, Josephine O'Brien, F. W. Hoefler, Mgr.) S. P., Phœnix. Three 500-lb. Beating and one Jordan engines; one Rotary boiler; one 72-inch Cylinder.

THOMAS E. GLEESON, Inc., 411-413 John St., E. NEWARK, N..
CYLINDER MOULDS and DANDY ROLLS Made and Repaired
LETTERING and MONOGRAMS for WATERMARKS

Paper and Pulp Mills in the United States 167

Widest trimmed sheet, 63½ Inches. Water and Steam. Tissues 10 to 16 and Crepe. 6000 to 10,000 lbs. 24 hours. *All kinds of Packages and Roll Toilet Papers a Specialty.*

PHŒNIX TOILET AND PAPER MANUFACTURING CO. (H. D. Wood, owner; Irving S. Wood, Sec. and Treas.) THE RED MILL. S. P., at mill. Three 800-lb. Beating and one Jordan engines; one 66-inch Cylinder. Widest trimmed sheet, 60 Inches. Water and Steam. Toilet 12,000 lbs. 24 hours.

SENOSO PAPER CO., INC. (W. S. Blake, Pres. and Gen. Mgr.; H. R. Hall, Vice-Pres.; E. R. Spencer, Sec. and Treas.; Isaac Allen, Supt.) One 800-lb. and one 900-lb. Beaters and one Jordan. One 98-inch Cylinder; widest trimmed sheet, 82 inches. Water and Electricity. Tissue and Crêpe.

SWEET BROS. PAPER MANUFACTURING CO. (T. C. S., K. N. S.) S. P., Phœnix. Three 700-lb. and two 1000-lb. Beating and two Jordan engines; one 68-inch and one 72-inch Cylinders. Water. White, Colored and Manila Tissue.

THREE RIVERS PAPER CO. (G. G. Chauncey, Pres. and Treas.; W. H. Yarwood, Vice-Pres.) PHŒNIX TISSUE MILLS. Three 1000-lb. Beating and two Refining engines. One 80-inch and one 60-inch Cylinder Machine. Widest trimmed sheets, 68 and 50 inches. Water and Steam. Tissue, Manila, White Roll Toilet and Fruit Wrappers. 10,000 lbs. 24 hours.

PIERCEFIELD—St. Lawrence Co.
Pop. 500. On N. Y. C. & H. R. RR. M. O. and Tel. office; Am. Ex.

INTERNATIONAL PAPER CO. Office, 30 Broad Street, New York. PIERCEFIELD MILL. (M. O. Wood, Mgr.) S. P., at mill. Eight Beating and two Refining engines; one 110-inch and one 123-inch Fourdriniers. Water and Steam. Wrapping Manila, Envelope Manila, Bag, Express, Screenings. 94,000 lbs. 24 hours. PULP MILL. Eight Grinders; four Digesters; twelve Wet Machines. Water and Steam. Ground Wood, 80,000 lbs.; Sulphite Fibre, 70,000 lbs. 24 hours.

PIERMONT—Rockland Co.
Pop. 1,153. On N. RR. of N. J. and E. RR. M. O. and Tel. office; nearest bank, Nyack, 3½ miles; Ex. Sparkill, 1 mile.

PIERMONT PAPER CO. (W. J. Alford, Pres.; Crawford Fairbanks, Vice-Pres.; C. E. Williams, Treas.; C. M. Williams, Sec.) Nineteen 1500-lb. Beating and ten Jordans; one 104-inch Six, one 120-inch Five and one 130-inch Five Cylinder Board Machines. Widest trimmed sheet, 118 inches. Steam and Electricity. Patent Coated, Pulp Lined and other Folding Box Boards. 350,000 lbs. 24 hours.

PLATTSBURG—Clinton Co.
Pop. 11,612. On D. & H. RR. M. O. and Tel. office; Nat. Ex.

LAKE CHAMPLAIN PULP AND PAPER CO. (Geo. F. Tuttle, Pres.; C. S. Johnson, Vice-Pres.) S. P., at mill. One 800-lb., two 1000-lb. and two Claflin Beating and two Refining engines; two 72-inch and one 76-inch Cylinders. Widest trimmed sheet, 69 inches. Water and Steam. Tissue

---

THE UNION SULPHUR CO.
Main Office: Mines:
17 Battery Pl., New York. Calcasieu Parish, La.

Producers of
The Only Arsenic Free Sulphur on the Marke

and Light-Weight Manila. 24,000 lbs. 24 hours. PULP MILL. S. P., at mill. Three Grinders; two Wet Machines. Water. Ground Wood (dry). 15,000 lbs. 24 hours.

UNDERWOOD PULP AND PAPER MILLS, INC. (George F. Underwood, Chairman of Board of Directors; George Tait, Pres.; Thomas F. Adriance, Vice-Pres. and Gen. Mgr.; S. C. Hall, Vice-Pres.; Philip J. Riley, Sec.; John S. Coy, Treas.; Fred'k Royse, Supt.) S. P., at mill. Three 500-lb. and two 1000-lb. Beating and two Refining engines; one 90-inch Combination Harper Fourdrinier and Cylinder. Widest trimmed sheet, 80 inches. Water and Steam. Hanging and Specialties, Duplex and Ingrains. 40,000 lbs. 24 hours. PULP MILL. Four Grinders; two Wet and two Dry Machines. Water. Ground Wood (dry). 40,000 lbs. 24 hours. (This Company is affiliated with the Imperial, Wm. Campbell and Plattsburg Wall Paper Companies, Inc.)

SARANAC CO. (S. H. Guibord, Pres.; R. H. Guibord, Treas. and Mgr.; C. H. Allen, Sec.) S. P., Morrisonville. Seven Grinders; six Wet Machines. Water. Ground Wood. 40,000 lbs. 24 hours.

PORT LEYDEN—Lewis Co.

Pop. 746. On R., W. & O. RR. M. O. and Tel. office; nearest bank, Boonville, 7 miles; Am. Ex.

GOULD PAPER CO. P. O. address, Lyon Falls. (G. H. P. Gould, Pres. and Treas.; Charles W. Pratt, Vice-Pres.; Harry P. Gould, Sec. and Asst. Treas.) NO. II. S. P., Port Leyden. Two 800-lb. Beating and one Refining engines; one 52-inch Cylinder. Widest trimmed sheet, 50 inches. Water. Manila, Express and Wrapping. 12,000 lbs. 24 hours.

JOHNSTON & SON. (M. L. J. and J. E. J.) S. P., Port Leyden. Two Grinders; two Wet Machines. Water. Ground Wood (dry). 16,000 lbs. 24 hours.

POTSDAM—St. Lawrence Co.

Pop. 4,500. On R., W. & O. Branch N. Y. C. RR. M. O. and Tel. office; Am. Ex.

UNITY PAPER MILLS. P. O., Potsdam, N. Y. (A. A. Srere, Pres., Franklin, Ohio; Jacob Roth, Vice-Pres., Erie, Pa.; W. M. O'Brien, Sec. and Treas.; B. A. Krebs, Supt.) S. P., at mill. Four Beating engines; two Refining engines; one 76-inch Fourdrinier. Widest trimmed sheet, 68 inches. Width of Super-Calenders, 68 inches. Electricity and Steam. Bond, Book, Writing and Ledger Papers. 20,000 lbs. 24 hours.

RACQUETTE RIVER PAPER CO. (Geo. W. Sisson, Jr., Pres.; Chas. H. Sisson, Vice-Pres.; Rufus L. Sisson, Treas.; F. T. E. Sisson, Sec. and Mgr.) S. P., at mill. Eight 1000-lb. and six 1500-lb. Beating and four Refining engines; one 76-inch, one 110-inch and one 136-inch Fourdriniers. Widest trimmed sheet, 124 inches. Water, Steam and Electricity. Manila, Manila Envelope, Fibre, Bag, Express and Parchment. 140,000 lbs. 24 hours. SULPHITE MILL. Four Digesters; six Wet Machines. Sulphite Fibre. 100,000 lbs. (dry) 24 hours. GROUND WOOD MILL. Two Grinders; two Wet Machines. 10,000 lbs. (dry).

PYRITES—St. Lawrence Co.

DE GRASSE PAPER CO. Office, Pyrites. (J. A. Outterson, Pres.; J. G. Jackson, Vice-Pres.; L. E. Wolf, Sec.; N. H. Botsford, Treas.; Geo. K. Walker, Mgr.) S. P., Canton. Six 1500-lb. Beating and one Refining engines; one 120-inch, one 132-inch and two 160-inch Fourdriniers. Widest trimmed sheets, 109½ and 146 inches. Union Screens. Water and Steam. News. 325,000 lbs. 24 hours. PULP MILL. S. P., Canton. Twenty-four Grinders, four Digesters; fifteen Wet Machines; eight "Impco" Rotary Screens and two "Impco" Knotters. Water, Steam and Electricity. Sulphite Fibre (dry), 70,000 lbs. 24 hours. Ground Wood. 250,000 lbs. 24 hours.

RAYMONDVILLE—St. Lawrence Co.

Pop. 700. On Norwood & St. Lawrence RR. 7 miles from Norwood. M. O., Tel. and Ex. Nearest bank, Norfolk, 3 miles.

REMINGTON PAPER AND POWER CO. Office, Watertown, N. Y. (M. S. Wilder, Pres.; M. A. Hanna, Vice-Pres.; C. H. Hanna, Vice-Pres.; R. B. Maltby, Sec. and Treas.; J. A. Remington, Asst. Sec.; W. D. Gregor, Gen. Supt.) S. P., at mill. Five Beating and two Jordan engines; one 114-inch and one 120-inch Fourdriniers. Water, Steam and Electricity. News and Catalogue. 125,000 lbs. 24 hours. PULP MILL. Six Grinders; two Wet Machines. Ground Wood. 60,000 lbs. 24 hours.

ROCHESTER—Monroe Co.

Pop. 235,000. On N. Y. C. & H. R., Rochester Br. Erie, R., W. & O., R. Br. Lehigh Valley and Buff., Roch. & Pitt. RR. M. O., Tel. A., Nat., W., F. & Co. and U. S. Ex.

EASTMAN KODAK CO. This company operates its mill for the production of photographers' raw stock for its own use only.

FLOWER CITY TISSUE MILLS CO. (E. C. Van Valkenberg, Gen. Mgr.; Edward J. Keegan, Supt.) S. P., at mill. Three 1000-lb. Beating engines, two Jordans, one 84-inch Harper Fourdrinier. Widest trimmed sheet, 74 inches. Steam. Tissue Papers of the Medium and Better Class. 8000 lbs. 24 hours.

ROCK CITY FALLS— Saratoga Co.

Pop. 220. On S. Branch of D. & H. C. Co. RR. M. O. and Tel. office; nearest bank, Ballston, 6 miles; Nat. Ex.

BIG FALLS PAPER CO., INC., Successor to H. S. Chalfant Paper Co. (Joseph A. Leggett, Pres.; Robert J. Wood, Vice-Pres. and Mgr.; Arthur J. Burch, Treas.; H. J. Wood, Sec.) S. P., at mill. Five 500-lb. Beating engines and four Rotaries; one Five Cylinder Machine. Widest trimmed sheet, 62 inches. Water and Steam. Box Board. 30,000 lbs. 24 hours.

BROWN PAPER CO., THE E. M. (E. M. Brown, Pres.; E. E. Brown, Sec. and Treas.; H. M. Brown, Mill Supt.) EXCELSIOR MILL. S. P., Ballston Spa. Three 800-lb. Beating engines; one 74-inch Four Cylinder Paster Machine. Widest trimmed sheet, 69 inches. Water and Steam. Card Middles, Coating, Manila and Duplex. 16,000 lbs. 24 hours. EMPIRE MILL. Two 800-lb. and one 1200-lb. Beating engines; one 64-inch Four Cylinder. Widest trimmed sheet, 61 inches. Water and Steam. Card Middles, Coating, Manila and Duplex. 16,000 lbs. 24 hours.

ROSSMANS—Columbia Co.

Pop. 150. On Albany Southern RR. Tel. and Telegraph office; nearest bank, Hudson, 8 miles. Am. Ex.

HOBOKEN PAPER MILL CO., INC. (Richard Stevens, Pres.; W. H. Gould, Vice-Pres. and Gen. Mgr.; Palmer Campbell, Treas. and Sec.) S. P., Gould Station. Two 2000-lb. and three 1000-lb. Beaters; two Noble & Wood Refining engines; one 62-inch and one 90-inch Three Cylinder Machine; widest trimmed sheets, 60 and 82 inches. Water and Electricity. Wrapping Container and Specialties. 50,000 lbs. 24 hours.

SALISBURY MILLS—Orange Co.

Pop. 350. On Newburgh Branch of Erie RR. M. O. and Tel. office; nearest bank, Newburgh, 8½ miles; Wells Fargo & Co. Ex.

HOLDEN PAPER CO., THE, Office, Newburgh, N. Y. (A. F. Holden, Pres.; D. E. McKinstry, Vice-Pres.; L. J. White, Sec.; R. W. Spencer, Treas.; P. H. Longlaw, Mill Supt.) No. II MILL. S. P., at mill. Two 600-lb., seven 900-lb., three 750-lb., four 1000-lb. Beating; two 15,000 lb. Washing and Beating and two Jordan engines; two 88-inch Fourdriniers. Widest sheet made, 80 inches. Water and Steam. Book and Writing. 40,000 lbs. 24 hours.

SAUGERTIES—Ulster Co.

Pop. 3,697. On W. S. RR.; Saugerties and N. Y. Steamboat Co. M. O. and Tel. office; U. S. and Nat. Ex.

DIAMOND MILLS PAPER CO. (R. H. Thompson, Pres.; C. G. Van Gilder, Sec.; E. Van Voorhis, Treas.) P. O. address, 44 Murray street, New York. S. P., at mill. Five 700-lb., three 1000-lb., one 1500-lb. Beating and four Jordan engines; one 76-inch Cylinder; two 80-inch, one 90-inch and one 92-inch Fourdriniers. Widest trimmed sheet, 84 inches. Water and Steam. Typewriter, Copying, Carbon, Silver Tissue and Cigarette. 12,000 lbs. 24 hours.

SCHUYLERVILLE—Saratoga Co.

Pop. 1,601. On Greenwich & Johnsonville RR.; Champlain Canal. M. O. and Tel. office; Nat. Ex.

AMERICAN WOOD BOARD CO. (I. C. Blandy, Pres.; D. C. Trondsen, Vice-Pres.; A. W. Hitchcock, Treas.; Graham Blandy, Sec.) S. P., Trionda. Two 500-lb. and five 1000-lb. engines; one 72-inch and one 90-inch Four Cylinders. Widest trimmed sheet, 81 inches. Water and Steam. Tag Manila and Special Paper for Glazed Paper and Cardboard Manufacturers. 50,000 lbs. 24 hours. *We manufacture the following grades of Tag Boards:* "Bill," "Railroad," "Program," "Arctic," "Saratoga." PULP MILLS. Two mills. S. P., Trionda. Six Grinders; six Wet Machines; two "Impco" Rotary Screens. Water. Ground wood. 58,000 lbs. 24 hours.

UNITED PAPERBOARD CO. General Office, 171 Madison Avenue, N. Y. THOMSON BOARD MILL. S. P., Thomson. Five 1200-lb. engines; one 126-inch Nine Cylinder. Widest trimmed sheet, 108 inches. Water and Steam. Jute Fibre and Jute Jacquard Boards. 80,000 lbs. 24 hours. PULP MILL. Eight Grinders; six Wet Machines; two "Impco" Screens. Water and Steam. 50,000 lbs. 24 hours.

THOMAS E. GLEESON, Inc., } FOURDRINIER WIRES
411-413 John St., E. NEWARK, N. J. } For Tissue and Fine Grade Papers

SCOTTSVILLE—Monroe Co.

Pop. 900. On B. R. & P. and Rochester Div. P. RR. M. O. and Tel. office; nearest bank, Rochester; Adams and Am. Ex.

FLOWER CITY TISSUE MILLS CO. P. O. Address, Rochester, N. Y. (E. C. Van Valkenberg, Gen. Mgr.; James C. Renwick, Supt.) S. P., at mill. Two 1500-lb. Beaters and two Jordans; one 92-inch two-mould Cylinder. Widest trimmed sheet, 80 inches. Water and Steam. Tag Board, Folder Stock and Colored Wrappers. 30,000 lbs. 24 hours.

SHORTSVILLE—Ontario Co.

Pop. 957. On Auburn Branch N. Y. C. & Buffalo Div. Lehigh Valley RR. M. O. and Tel. office; bank and Am. Ex.

SHORTSVILLE PAPER CO. (E. M. Hall, Pres.; M. D. Nutting, Vice-Pres. and Treas.; B. F. Hall, Sec.; A. Peterson, Supt.) Two 1000-lb. Boston Machine Co. Beaters; one J. H. Horne & Sons Co. Refining engine; two Washers; one 84-inch Cylinder. Widest trimmed sheet, 78½ inches. Steam and Water. White, Manila and Anti-Tarnish Kraft Tissues. 6000 lbs. 24 hours.

SKANEATELES—Onondaga Co.

Pop. 1,495. On Skaneateles RR. M. O. and Tel. office; Am. Ex.

SKANEATELES PAPER CO. LAKESIDE MILL. (H. Lester Paddock, Pres.; N. W. Weeks, Vice-Pres.; Charles W. Tooke, Sec.; Forest G. Weeks, Treas.) Location, 2 miles north of Skaneateles. S. P., at mill. Three 1200-lb. Beating engines; one 70-inch Three Cylinder. Widest trimmed sheet, 68 inches. Water and Steam. Mill Wrappers. 24,000 lbs. 24 hours.

SKANEATELES PAPER CO. SKANEATELES MILL. (H. Lester Paddock, Pres.; N. W. Weeks, Vice-Pres.; Charles W. Tooke, Sec.; Forest G. Weeks, Treas.) Five 1500-lb. Beating and three Jordan engines; one 104-inch Five Cylinder. Widest trimmed sheet, 92 inches. Water and Steam. Jute Corrugating Board, Chip Board and Box Board and Mill Wrappers. 100,000 lbs. 24 hours.

SKANEATELES FALLS—Onondaga Co.

Pop. 500. On S. RR. M. O. and Tel. offices; nearest bank, Skaneateles, 2 miles; Am. Ex.

SAXER PAPER MILLS. Office, 100 W. Division street, Syracuse, N. Y. (Leonard A. Saxer, Pres.; A. E. Hoffman, Vice-Pres.; A. E. Ketcham, Mill Supt.) S. P., at mill. Four 1000-lb. Beating and one Refining engines; one 72-inch Harper Fourdrinier. Widest trimmed sheet, 62 inches. Water and Steam. Hanging. 26,000 lbs. 24 hours.

SKANEATELES PAPER CO., THE. DRAYCOTT MILL. Office, Skaneateles, N. Y. S. P., at mill. Three 1000-lb. Beating and one Refining engines; one 76-inch Cylinder. Widest trimmed sheet, 70 inches. Water and Steam. Mill Wrappers and Box Boards. 50,000 lbs. 24 hours.

ST. JOHNSVILLE—Montgomery Co.

GAROGA CREEK MILL. (Jno. B. Snell, Mgr.) Office, St. Johnsville S. P., St. Johnsville. Two 500-lb. Beating engines; one 36-inch Cylinder. Widest trimmed sheet, 30 inches. Width of Super-Calenders, 38 inches. Water. Air dried Straw Board. 3000 lbs. 24 hours.

SULPHUR—CRUDE. GUARANTEED 99% PURE.
The average analysis of our high-grade brimstone is in itself a guarantee. Write us for quotations.
THE UNION SULPHUR CO., Main Office, 17 Battery Pl., New York. Mines, Calcasieu Parish, La.

ST. REGIS FALLS—Franklin Co.

Pop. 1,323. On N. Y. & Ottawa Branch Adirondack Div. N. Y. Central RR. Tel., M. O. and bank; Am. Ex.

CASCADE WOOD PRODUCTS CO. (H. E. O'Neil, Pres. and Mgr.; A. S. O'Neil, Treas.; W. A. Wardner, Sec.) S. P., at mill. Two Grinders and three Wet Machines. Water. Ground Wood. 20,000 lbs. 24 hours.

STILLWATER—Saratoga Co.

Pop. 1,007. On B. & M. RR. M O., Tel. and nearest bank, Mechanicville, 8 miles; Nat. Ex.

PEMBLE MILLS. (Wood Flong Corp., owners.) Water. LEATHER BOARD MILL. S. P., at mill. Three 500-lb., one 800-lb. and three 1000-lb. Beating engines; two Rotary Boilers; two 50-inch Wet Machines. Water. Counter Board and Chair Seat. 6000 lbs. 24 hours.

STOCKPORT—Columbia Co.

Pop. 2,719. On A. S. RR. Tel. and Telegraph office; nearest bank, Hudson.

VAN de CARR PAPER CO. (C. R. Van de Carr, Pres. and Treas.; C. R. Van de Carr, Jr., Vice-Pres.; J. W. Van de Carr, Sec. and Supt.) EUREKA MILL. S. P., Stockport Station. Two 600-lb. and two 800-lb. Beating and two Refining engines; two 48-inch Cylinders. Widest trimmed sheet, 44 inches. Water and Steam. Carpet Lining, Light Weight Bogus Wrappings and Colored for Export. 36,000 lbs. 24 hours.

THOMSON—Washington Co.

Pop. 100. On G. & J. RR. and H. V. Electric RR.; Champlain Canal. M. O. office; Tel. and bank; Nat. Ex. Schuylerville, N. Y.

IROQUOIS PULP AND PAPER CO. (Henry W. Somers, Pres.; Jno. A. Becker, Vice-Pres.; W. A. Huppuch, Vice-Pres.; Luther A. Walt, Sec. and Treas.; Jno. M. Gill, Asst. Treas.; Richard F. Murray, Supt.) S. P., at mill. Five 1500-lb. Beating and two Jordan engines; two 90-inch Fourdriniers. Widest trimmed sheet, 80 inches. Union Screens. Steam. 100,000 lbs. 24 hours. Hanging, News Print and Bag. PULP MILL. S. P., at mill. Three Grinders; one Wet Machine; one Double Cylinder Decker. Water. Ground Wood. 30,000 lbs. 24 hours.

TICONDEROGA—Essex Co.

Pop. 5,048. On Lake George Branch of D. & H. C. Co. RR. M. O. and Tel. office; Nat. Ex.

INTERNATIONAL PAPER CO. Office, 30 Broad Street, New York. LAKE GEORGE MILL. (James McGinley, Supt.) S. P., at mill. Six Beating and four Refining engines; one 85-inch, one 94-inch and one 119-inch Fourdriniers. Water and Steam. News, Half Tone and Special Supplement, Colored Poster, Topaz Writing. 108,000 lbs. 24 hours. PULP MILL. Sixteen Grinders; seven Wet Machines. Water and Steam. Ground Wood. 80,000 lbs. 24 hours.

TICONDEROGA PULP AND PAPER CO. (Chas. Riordan, Pres.; Carl Riordan, Vice-Pres. and Mng. Dir.; F. B. Whitlet, Sec. and Treas.; T. E. Warren, Mgr.; W. J. Wilson, Jr., Sales Mgr.) New York Office, Room 934, No. 200 Fifth Avenue. LOWER MILL. S. P., at mill. Two 1200-lb., nine 1500-lb. Beating and two Jordan engines; one 88-inch and one 94-

inch Fourdriniers. Widest trimmed sheet, 84 inches. Water, Steam and Electricity. High Grade Book, Magazine, Music, Lithograph and Coating. 44,000 lbs. 24 hours. ISLAND MILL. S. P., at mill. Ten 1700-lb. Beating and four Jordan engines; one 102-inch and one 125-inch Fourdriniers. Widest trimmed sheet, 116 inches. High Grade Book, Magazine, Music, Lithograph, Coating and Super Calendered. 64,000 lbs. 24 hours. PULP MILL. CHEMICAL FIBRE MILL. Eight Digesters; one 84-inch Drying Machine. Water and Steam. Soda Fibre (dry), 120,000 lbs. 24 hours.

TONAWANDA—Erie Co.

Pop. 7,421. On W. Div. L. & B. Br. of N. Y. C. & H. R. RR. M. O. and Tel. office.

TONAWANDA BOARD AND PAPER CO. (Louis Newman, Pres. and Treas.; L. S. Marks, Vice-Pres.; M. W. Simon, Sec. and Mgr. of Sales.) TONAWANDA MILL. S. P., at mill. Ten 1500-lb. Beating and eight Refining engines; one 110-inch and one 135-inch Cylinders. Widest trimmed sheet, 120 inches. Union Screens. Electricity and Steam. Chip Board, News, Book and Litho Sheet Lining. Solid and Filled Jute Boards, Oak, Cedar and Marble Graining, Three-Ply Container Board, Plain and White Pulp Lined Eureka Boards, Pasted Boards, Binders' Boards, Textile Boards, Cloth Boards, Straw Chip, Solid and Filled News Boards, Solid and Filled Pulp Boards, Box and Barrel Layers, Combination Boards, Manila Lined Chip, Patent Coated Boards, Colored Box Boards, Solid Fibre Shipping Containers and Milk Cap Pulp. 300,000 lbs. 24 hours.

TROY—Rensselaer Co.

Pop. 77,060. On N. Y. C. & H. R., D. & H. and B. & M. RR. M. O. and Tel. office. Am. and Nat. Ex.

ALBIA BOX AND PAPER CO. (William C. Geer, Pres.; Clarence E. Van Zandt, Vice-Pres.; J. Leslie Snyder, Sec.; Chas. H. Gardner, Treas.; Richard A. Webb, Supt.) Office, Troy, N. Y. Mills at Troy and Brainard, N. Y. TROY MILL. S. P., 2 miles. Four 1000-lb. and one 1500-lb. Beating and three Jordan engines; one 72-inch Six Cylinder machine. Widest trimmed sheet, 69 inches. Water, Steam and Electric Power. Box Boards, plain, combination pulp mill and sheet lined. 40,000 lbs. 24 hours. Also all kinds stiff paper boxes. BRAINARD MILL. S. P., 1 mile, Lebanon Springs R.R. Three 1000-lb. and three Jordan engines; one 68-inch Five Cylinder machine. Widest trimmed sheet, 65 inches. Water and Steam. Box Boards, plain, combination and mill sheet lined. 46,000 lbs. 24 hours.

INGERSOLL PAPER COMPANY. TROY CITY MILL. (Mrs. E. S. Ingersoll and N. C. Ingersoll.) S. P., 1 mile. Two 600-lb. Beating and one Jordan engines; one 66-inch Cylinder Machine. Widest trimmed sheet, 60 inches. Water and Steam. Manila Tissue. 4000 lbs. 24 hours.

MANNING, JOHN A., PAPER CO. (John A. Manning, Pres. and Treas.; William H. Manning, Vice-Pres.; Charles Ray, Sec.; Eugene Warren, Asst. Treas.) Two mills. S. P., at mills. MOUNT IDA MILL. Two 60-inch Wet machines. Widest trimmed sheet, 50 inches. Rag Press, Counter and Insulating Board. Water and Steam. 12,000 lbs. 24 hours. GREEN ISLAND MILL. One 66-inch Three Cylinder and one 101-inch Five Cylinder. Widest trimmed sheet, 90 inches. Steam and Electricity.

New York

Rope Manila Papers for Sand Paper; Flour and Cement Sacks and Insulating Cable. 30,000 lbs. 24 hours.

UTICA—Oneida Co.

Pop. 60,007. On N. Y. C. & H. R.; R., W. & O.; D. L. & W.; N. W., W. S. & B., and N Y., O. W. & R. R. M. O. & Tel. offices; Adams, Am., Nat. and U. S. Ex.

FOSTER BOX BOARD CO. (William S. Foster, Pres.; William B. Foster, Vice-Pres.; T. S. Foster, Sec.; Theodore Foster, Treas.) S. P., at mill. Four 1000-lb. Beating and two Refining engines; one 74-inch Cylinder. Widest trimmed sheet, 67 inches. Union Screens. Steam. Box Board and Mill Wrappers. 60,000 lbs. 24 hours.

MUTUAL BOX BOARD CO. (Andrew Frey, Pres.; W. T. Baker, Vice-Pres.; Quentin McAdam, Treas. and Gen. Mgr.; W. Leslie Roberts, Sec.; T. J. Bush, Supt.) Five 1000-lb. Beating and four Noble & Wood engines; one 108-inch Five Cylinder Machine. Widest trimmed sheet, 98 inches. Steam. Plain Chip, News Vat Lined Chip, Filled News, News Board, White Pulp Lined Chip, Double Pulp Lined Chip, Oak Grained Jute, Mill Lined Chip and Wrappers. 100,000 lbs. 24 hours.

VALATIE—Columbia Co.

Pop. 1,400. On Albany Southern RR. M. O. and Tel. office; nearest bank, Kinderhook, 3 miles; Am. Ex.

ROBERT P. RICHMOND. CENTENNIAL MILL. S. P.; ½ mile. Two 600-lb. Beating and one Jordan engines; two 48-inch Cylinders. Widest trimmed sheet, 40 inches. Water. Light Straw Wrapping. 10,000 lbs. 24 hours.

WALLOOMSAC—Rensselaer Co.

On B. R. & F. Div. B. & M. Tel. office and M. O. Walloomsac. Nearest bank, Hoosic Falls, 3 miles. Nat. Ex.

WALLOOMSAC PAPER CO. (Frank L. Stevens, Pres.; Fred N. Stevens, Vice-Pres.; Howard B. Thompson, Sec.; Herbert Q. Eldridge, Treas.) WALLOOMSAC PAPER MILL. S. P., Walloomsac. Twelve Beating, three Refining engines and two Rotary Boilers; two 90-inch Harper Fourdriniers. Widest trimmed sheet, 80 inches. Water, Steam and Electricity. Towel Paper, Colored Wall Papers, Ingrains and Specialties. 70,000 lbs. 24 hours.

WARRENSBURGH—Warren Co.

Pop. 2,852. D. & H. RR. M. O. and Tel. office; Nat. Ex.

SCHROON RIVER PULP AND PAPER CO. (James A. Emerson, Pres.; Philip E. Rice, Vice-Pres.; Wm. L. R. Durkee, Sec.; Louis E. Reoux, Treas.; William Quinlan, Supt.) S. P., at Company's mill. Two 1200-lb. Beating and one Refining engines; one 90-inch Fourdrinier. Widest trimmed sheet, 80 inches. Water and Steam. Hanging and News. 40,000 lbs. 24 hours. PULP MILL. Six Grinders; eight Wet Machines. Water. Ground Wood (dry). 90,000 lbs. 24 hours.

WATERFORD—Saratoga Co.

Pop. 3,146. On D. & H. C. Co. RR. and Champlain Canal. M. O. and Tel. office; Nat. Ex.

GILBERT, FRANK, PAPER CO. (H. I. Prankard, Pres.; Jay Gilbert, Vice-Pres.; F. W. Pomeroy, Sec. and Treas.; G. M. Pomeroy, Supt.) MO-

THOMAS E. GLEESON, Inc., 411-413 John St., E. NEWARK, N. J.
CYLINDER MOULDS and DANDY ROLLS Made and Repaired
LETTERING and MONOGRAMS for WATERMARKS

Paper and Pulp Mills in the United States

HAWK AND HUDSON PAPER MILL. One 500-lb., seven 1000-lb. Beating, two Refining, two Washing engines and one Rotary boiler; one 62-inch and one 74-inch Fourdriniers. Widest trimmed sheets, 53 and 66 inches. Union Screens. Water and Steam. 35,000 lbs. 24 hours. *White and Colored Coating and Glazing, Blasting, Cash Register, Ribbon, Sales Book, Ticker, Hanging in White and Colors, Book, Tablet, Novel, Interleaving, Poster, Blotting, Black Papers for many purposes, including Album, Coating, etc. Also Colored Specialties, Bag, Pattern, No. 2 Book, Box Lining, Card Middles, Catalogue, Cop Tube, Cotton Batting, Cover, R.R. Manila, Envelope, Ticket, Music.*

WATERTOWN—Jefferson Co.

Pop. 21,696. On R., W. & O. Div. of N. Y. C. RR. M. O. and Tel. office; Am. Ex.

CONTINENTAL PAPER BAG CO. Office, 17 Battery place, New York. MILL B. (W. B. Reddick, Supt.) S. P., at mill. Three 1000-lb. Beating and two Refining engines; one 65-inch and one 80-inch Harper Fourdriniers. Widest trimmed sheet, 72 inches. Water and Steam. Manila Tissue, Roll Toilet and Light Weight Specialties. 25,000 lbs. 24 hours. PULP MILL. Ground Wood. 16,000 lbs. 24 hours.

HINDE & DAUCH PAPER CO. General Offices, Sandusky, Ohio. S. P., at mill. (Sidney Frohman, Pres.; W. F. Harbrecht, Vice-Pres.; Fred Emmons, Sec.) CYLINDER PAPER MILL. Four 1000-lb. and one 1500-lb. Beating and five Jordan engines; one 6 by 12 Rag Cooker; one 106-inch Five Cylinder and one 96-inch Five Cylinder Bagley & Sewall Machine. Trim, 96 and 86 inches. Water, Electricity and Steam. Test Boards, Chip Boards and Container Boards. 120,000 lbs. 24 hours.

INTERNATIONAL PAPER CO. Office, 30 Broad Street, New York. WOODS FALLS MILLS A, B and C. (J. H. Stinchfield, Supt.) S. P., Brownville. Ten Beating, six Refining; one 86-inch, one 87-inch, one 88-inch, one 98-inch, one 131-inch Fourdriniers. Water and Steam. News Print, Poster, Tablet and Manila. 240,000 lbs. 24 hours. WATERTOWN MILL. Watertown. (Destroyed by fire.) PULP MILLS. WOODS FALLS MILLS A, B and C. S. P., Brownville. Twenty Grinders; thirteen Wet Machines. Water and Steam. Ground Wood Pulp, 190,000 lbs. 24 hours. WATERTOWN MILL. S. P., Watertown. Four Grinders; four Wet Machines. Water and Steam. Ground Wood, 18,000 lbs.

KNOWLTON BROTHERS, INC. (Geo. W. Knowlton, Pres.; Willis H. Howes, Vice-Pres.; Geo. S. Knowlton, Treas.; Herbert E. Harmon, Sec.) KAMARGO MILLS. On Black River, in the City of Watertown. S. P., at mill. Five 1200-lb., two 600-lb. Beating and three 2000-lb. Washing engines; three Jordan engines; one 66-inch and one 90-inch special Fourdriniers. Widest trimmed sheet, 80 inches. Width of Super Calenders, 50 inches. Union Screens. Water, Steam and Electricity. Standard Covers, Colored Flats and Specialties. 40,000 lbs. 24 hours. *Liberty, Alhambra and Conqueror Covers.*

TAGGART BROTHERS CO. (B. B. Taggart, Pres.; J. W. Taggart, Vice-Pres.; J. F. Amos, Sec. and Treas.; T. H. Hammond, Mill Supt.) STONE MILL. S. P., at mill. Nine 500-lb., two 600-lb., two 1000-lb. and six 1200-lb. Beating and two Refining engines; one 66-inch Three Cylinder, one 70-

HIGHEST GRADE BRIMSTONE—GUARANTEED 99% PURE
free from Arsenic or Selenium. Write for particulars to
THE UNION SULPHUR CO., Main Office, 17 Battery Pl., New York. Mines, Calcasieu Parish, La.

DRY ROSIN SIZE

Brittle, easy soluble. Cheapest size out; cheaper than mill made size. Ask us about it. Also all other grades.

ARABOL M'F'G CO.
100 William St., New York

inch Three Cylinder, one 84-inch Three Cylinder Machines. Widest trimmed sheet, 74 inches. Water. 40,000 lbs. 24 hours. Rope Papers, Flour and Cement Paper Sacks.

WEST MILTON—Saratoga Co.

Pop. 241. Five miles from Ballston Spa. M. O., Tel. and nearest bank, Ballston Spa; Nat. Ex.

PIONEER PAPER CO. (John Jacobs, Pres.; Garrett S. Veeder, Vice-Pres.; Wm. D. Loucks, Treas.) Post Office Address, Ballston Spa. S. P., Ballston Spa. Seven 600-lb., two 1200-lb. Beating and two Jordan engines; two Harper Fourdriniers. Widest trimmed sheet, 80 inches. Water and Steam. Tissues, White and Colors. 12,000 lbs. 24 hours.

WILLSBORO—Essex Co.—PULP MILL.

Pop. 1,522. On D. & H. RR. M. O. and Tel. Office; nearest bank, Keeseville, 18 miles; Nat. Ex.

NEW YORK AND PENNSYLVANIA CO. CHAMPLAIN MILLS. New York Office, 200 Fifth Avenue. (A. G. Paine, Jr., Pres.; Robert Wetherill, First Vice-Pres.; A. G. Paine, 3d, Second Vice-Pres. and Gen. Mgr.; M. B. Sloat, Sec. and Treas.; Geo. E. Paine, Asst. Sec. and Treas.; C. A. Clough, Gen. Sales Mgr.) S. P., at mill. One 62-inch Cylinder Machine; five Digesters. Water. Soda Fibre. 110,000 lbs. (dry in rolls) 24 hours. Also Paper.

NORTH CAROLINA.

CANTON—Haywood Co.

Pop. 4,000. Branch Southern RR. Southern Ex., M. O. and Tel. office, Canton; bank at Canton.

CHAMPION FIBRE CO. (Peter G. Thomson, Pres.; Peter G. Thomson, Jr., Vice-Pres.; Reuben B. Robertson, Gen. Mgr.; Chas. S. Bryant, Sec. and Treas.; Walter D. Randall, Asst. Sec. and Asst. Treas.) S. P., at mill. Thirteen Digesters, six Wet Machines and three Dry Machines; one 65-inch Five Cylinder. Steam. Water and Electricity. Container Board. 28,000 lbs. 24 hours. FIBRE MILL. Thirteen Digesters. Soda Fibre, 250,000 lbs., and Sulphite Fibre, 200,000 lbs. 24 hours.

ROANOKE RAPIDS—Halifax Co.

Pop. 3,000. Seaboard RR. M. O., Tel. and Southern Ex.

HALIFAX PAPER CORPORATION. Office, Roanoke Rapids. (Job Taylor, Pres. and Gen. Mgr.; L. M. Williams, Sec.; S. J. Bounds, Treas.) S. P., at mill. Eight 1500-lb. Beating and three Refining engines; one 102-inch Fourdrinier. Widest trimmed sheet, 90 inches. Water, Steam and Electricity. Kraft. 40,000 lbs. 24 hours. SULPHATE MILL. Two Digesters. Water and Electricity. Sulphate Pulp. 50,000 lbs. 24 hours. GROUND WOOD MILL. Two Grinders. 24,000 lbs. 24 hours.

ROANOKE FIBRE BOARD CO. New York Office, 174 Fulton Street. (Wm. H. Parsons, Pres. and Treas.; Job Taylor, Vice-Pres.; Howard Whittemore, Sec.; W. E. Byrne.) S. P., at mill. BOARD MILL. Four 1000-lb. Beating and three Refining engines; one 90-inch Four Cylinder Machine. Widest trimmed sheet, 84 inches. Water, Steam and Electricity.

National Duplex Waterproof Case Lining
IS WATERPROOF—
CLEAN TO HANDLE **NATIONAL WATERPROOFING CO.,** 1054 DREXEL BLDG. PHILADELPHIA

Paper and Pulp Mills in the United States   177

Container Jute, Roanoke Fibre and Special Kraft Board. 40,000 lbs. 24 hours. PULP MILL. Three Grinders; two Digesters; one Wet Machine. Water. Ground Wood. 20,000 lbs. 24 hours.

OHIO.

AKRON—Summit Co.

Pop. 150,000. On C. A. & C.; P. A. & W.; P. & W.; B. & O.; E.; C. T. & V. RR.; A. C. & Y.; Ohio Canal. M. O. and Tel. office; Adams, Am. and Wells Fargo & Co. Ex.

AMERICAN STRAW BOARD CO. General offices, Akron, Ohio.

OFFICERS.—President, O. C. Barber; Vice-President and Treasurer, C. H. Palmer; Secretary, K. S. Smith; Directors, O. C. Barber, Frederick Davenport, C. H. Palmer, L. A. Wiley, K. S. Smith and C. E. Hawkins. Chas. E. Hawkins, Gen. Mgr., Akron, Ohio.

Incorporated under the laws of Illinois in 1889. Capital stock $8,000,000, all one issue and all issued. Bonds—$600,000. Interest payable January 1 and July 1.

LIST OF MILLS OWNED BY THE COMPANY.	Capacity pounds per 24 hours.
Lockport, Ill. (Idle)	......
Quincy, Ill.	240,000
Wilmington, Ill.	180,000
Noblesville, Ind.	100,000
Chestertown, Md.	40,000
Circleville, Ohio	150,000
Dayton, Ohio (Idle)	......
Piqua, Ohio	20,000
Tiffin, Ohio (Idle)	......
Tippecanoe City, Ohio	24,000
Winchester, Va.	24,000
Norwich, Conn. (Uncas)	200,000

PHILLIPS CO., THE THOMAS. (Fred D. Howland, Pres.; Chas. W. Seiberling, Vice-Pres.; George S. Howland, Sec.; Frank C. Howland, Treas. and Gen. Mgr.) AKRON PAPER MILL. S. P., ½ mile. Five 1000-lb., four 1500-lb. Beating engines; one 64-inch and one 84-inch Three Cylinders. Widest trimmed sheet, 75¼ inches. Steam. Rope, Cement, Flour, Feed, and Lime Sack Papers; Rope, Sand and Sign Paper. 22,000 lbs. 24 hours.

BALTIMORE—Fairfield Co.

Pop. 650. On T. & O. C. RR. Bank, Baltimore; U. S. Ex.

FAIRFIELD, THE, PAPER CO. (Dr. H. R. McCurdy, Pres.; I. D. Cohen, Vice-Pres.; M. D. Custer, Sec. and Treas.; T. D. Griley, Gen. Mgr.; C. W. Unkle, Supt.) S. P., at mill. Three 1500-lb. Beating and two Refining engines; one 80-inch Four Cylinder. Widest trimmed sheet, 75 inches. Electricity. Container Liners. 40,000 lbs. 24 hours.

BOSTON—Summit Co.

Pop. 260. On the Cuyahoga River; B. & O. RR. M. O. and Tel. office, Boston, O.; bank, Cleveland, O.

CLEVELAND-AKRON BAG CO. (G. D. Adams, Pres. and Treas.; James Goldsword, Vice-Pres.; G. E. Kappler, Sec.) Main Office, Cleveland, O.

E. J. KELLER CO., INC. 290 FIFTH AVENUE E.J.KELLER, Pres. NEW YORK — FOREIGN AND DOMESTIC **Rags AND Wastes** Gunny Bagging, Burlap Bagging, Ropes, Flax, Hemp, Cotton Wastes, Paper Stock, Wood Pulp and Rag Pulp.

R. B. McEwan, Pres.   J. L. McEwan, Vice-Pres.   Arthur McEwan, Treas. and Mgr.   R. W. McEwan, Secy
Sheet Lining Plant, Office and Mills at WHIPPANY, N. J.
McEWAN BROS., Inc. MANUFACTURERS OF ALL GRADES **PAPER BOX BOARD**

DRY ROSIN SIZE Brittle, easy soluble, cheapest size out; cheaper than mill made size. Ask us about it. Also all other grades. **ARABOL M'F'G CO.** 100 William St., N. Y.

Ohio

BOSTON MILL. S. P., Boston. Three 1000-lb. and nine 1500-lb. Beating engines; one 86-inch and one 120-inch Three Cylinders. Widest trimmed sheet, 112 inches. Water and Steam. Rope, Flour Sack, Manilas and Roofing. 30,000 lbs. 24 hours.

JAITE, THE, CO. (C. H. Jaite, Pres. and Gen. Mgr.; Robert Jaite, Vice-Pres.; E. W. Jaite, Sec.; Julius Kreckel, Treas.) P. O. Address, Jaite, Ohio. S. P., at mill. Six 1000-lb. and five 1200-lb. Beating engines, and three Rotary Boilers; two Cylinder Machines. Widest trimmed sheet, 56 inches. Steam and Electricity. Rope Specialties, Cement, Flour, Charcoal Bag Paper and Bag. 10,000 lbs. 24 hours. SULPHATE MILL. Two Digesters; one Wet Machine. 40,000 to 50,000 lbs. 24 hours.

CEDARVILLE—Greene Co.

Pop. 1,189. On L. M. Div. of P., C., C. & St. L. RR. M. O. and Tel. office; Adams Ex.

HAGAR STRAW BOARD AND PAPER CO., THE. (George Little, Pres. and Gen. Mgr.; M. G. Hagar, Treas.; J. P. Dice, Sec.) Office, Xenia, O. S. P., at mill. Seven 1200-lb. Beating, two Jordan engines and six Rotary Boilers; one 86-inch Three Cylinder. Widest trimmed sheet, 81 inches. Steam. Light Straw Board, Straw Wrapping and Corrugating. 50,000 lbs. 24 hours.

CHAGRIN FALLS—Cuyahoga Co.

Pop. 2,100. On W. & L. E. RR. M. O. and Tel. office; Wells Fargo & Co. Ex.

ADAMS BAG COMPANY, THE. (Walter H. Cottingham, Pres.; E. B. Allen, Vice-Pres.; Gardner Abbott, Sec.; Kenneth L. Allen, Treas.; Edmond Grieve, Auditor; F. W. Getten, Gen. Mgr.; E. A. Kline, Plant Mgr.) Office, 502, The 1900 Euclid Building, Cleveland. S. P., station, ¼ mile. Two 600-lb., two 800-lb. and six 1000-lb. Beating engines; two 62-inch Two Cylinders. Widest trimmed sheet, 56½ inches. Water and Steam. Manila Rope Shipping Containers for Cereal and Fertilizer and Building Products. 20,000 lbs. 24 hours.

CHILLICOTHE—Ross Co.

Pop. 14,965. On Ohio and Toledo Div. of B. & O. S. W.; Scioto Valley Div. of N. & W.; M. O. and Tel. office; Wells Fargo and Southern Ex.

MEAD PULP & PAPER CO. (George H. Mead, Pres.; H. E. Talbott, Sr., Vice-Pres.; R. T. Houk, Sec.; A. L. Rieger, Treas. and Sales Mgr.; Hector McVicker, Mill Mgr.) Office, Dayton. SCIOTO MILL. S. P., at mills. Fourteen 2000-lb. and five 800-lb. Beating and eight Jordan engines; four Washers and two Rotary boilers; one 60-inch, one 80-inch, one 92-inch, one 100-inch and one 120-inch Fourdriniers. Widest trimmed sheets, 52, 72, 80, 90 and 107 inches. Width of Super Calenders, up to 76 inches. Steam. Book, Lithograph Offset and Magazine Papers. 150,000 lbs. 24 hours. SCIOTO PULP MILL. Four Digesters; one 68-inch and one 92-inch Wet Machines. Steam. Soda Fibre. 50,000 lbs. 24 hours.

CINCINNATI—Hamilton Co.

Pop. 416,119. Erie; Balt. & Ohio and Chesapeake and Ohio RR. Adams, Am., So. and Wells Fargo & Co. Ex.

BOLDT, THE CHARLES, PAPER MILLS. (Charles Boldt, Pres.; F. Schwenk, Vice-Pres.; Max Zimmerman, Mgr.) S. P., Redbank, Cin-

PRESS ROLLS Maple and Gum White Wood Felt Rolls **J. W. HEWITT MACHINE CO.** Neenah, Wis.

THOMAS E. GLEESON, Inc., } **FOURDRINIER WIRES**
411-413 John St., E. NEWARK, N. J. } For Tissue and Fine Grade Paper

Paper and Pulp Mills in the United States

cinnati. Five 1800-lb. Beating and Three Refining engines; one Beloit 120-inch Six Cylinder. Widest trimmed sheet, 108 inches. Steam. Container. 100,000 lbs. 24 hours.

CIRCLEVILLE—Pickaway Co.

Pop. 6,991. On C. & M. V. Div., N. & W. RR. M. O. and Tel. office; Adams Ex.

AMERICAN STRAW BOARD CO. Executive Office, Akron, Ohio. CIRCLEVILLE MILL. (C. M. Clay, Mgr.) Twenty-two 1200-lb. and eight Jordan engines; one 66-inch and three 86-inch Cylinders. Widest sheet made, 80 inches. Steam. Steam Dried Straw Board, Plain, Mill Lined and Sheet Lined and Straw Board for Corrugating. 150,000 lbs. 24 hours.

CLEVELAND—Cuyahoga Co.

Pop. 650,000. On L. S. & M. S.; N. Y., C. & St. L; P., C., C. & St. L.; C. L. & W.; E.; C. T. & V.; C. C. & S. RR. M. O. and Tel. office. Adams, Am., Nat., U. S. and W. F. & Co. Ex.

CLEVELAND-AKRON BAG CO. (G. D. Adams, Pres. and Treas.; James Goldsword, Vice-Pres.; G. E. Kappler, Sec.) STANDARD MILL. S. P., at mill. Four 500-lb., four 750-lb. and four 1000-lb. Beating and one Refining engines; one 66-inch Three Cylinder and one 74-inch Fourdrinier. Widest trimmed sheet, 66 inches. Steam and Water. Express, Manila and Rope. 20,000 lbs. 24 hours. *Our Specialties are: Signal and Cartridge Papers; Cotton Sampling, Rope, Box Stay, Manilas; Bag Papers; Cement and Flour Sack Papers.*

CLEVELAND PAPER MFG. CO. (C. A. Dunklee, Pres. and Treas.; J. D. Sackett, Sec.) Office, 209 St. Clair Avenue, East. VALLEY MILL. S. P., at mill. Seven 900-lb. Beating engines; one 66-inch and one 76-inch Fourdriniers. Widest trimmed sheet, 70 inches. Steam. News, Book and Colored. 30,000 lbs. 24 hours. PULP MILL. VALLEY MILL. S. P., at mill. Two Grinders; three Wet Machines. Steam. Ground Wood (dry). 24,000 lbs. 24 hours. (Mill destroyed by fire 1918.)

COSHOCTON—Coshocton Co.

Pop. 9,631. On P., C., C. & St. L.; W. & L. E.; T. C. & O. R. RR. M. O. and Tel. office; Adams and Wells Fargo & Co. Ex.

COSHOCTON STRAW PAPER CO., THE. (W. H. Bachert, Pres.; E. A. Bachert, Vice-Pres.; K. W. Bachert, Sec. and Treas.; N. H. Carpenter, Gen. Mgr.) COSHOCTON MILL. S. P., siding at mill. Two 1500-lb. and one 1000-lb. Beating and Two Refining engines; five Rotary boilers; one 88-inch Double Cylinder. Widest trimmed sheet, 82 inches. Steam. Light Straw Board for Corrugating. 50,000 lbs. 24 hours.

CUYAHOGA FALLS—Summit Co.

Pop. 12,000. On C., A. & C.; B. & O.; A. B. & C.; A. & C. F. Electric Street RR. M. O. and Tel. office; Adams and U. S. Ex.

WALSH PAPER CO., INC. (C. M. Walsh, Pres.; T. A. Murphy, Vice-Pres. and Supt.; M. E. Wright, Sec.-Treas.) S. P., at mill. Three 400-lb., one 1000-lb. and one 800-lb. Beating and two Refining engines; one 82-inch Fourdrinier. Widest trimmed sheet, 60 inches. Water and Steam. Album, Tobacco, Cheviot, Starch, Macaroni, Tailors' Pattern, Colored Specialties. 15,000 lbs. 24 hours.

BRIMSTONE MAKES THE VERY BEST SULPHITE.
If you are looking for a high-grade Brimstone write to
THE UNION SULPHUR CO., Main Office, 17 Battery Pl., New York. Mines, Calcasieu Parish, La

DRY ROSIN SIZE Brittle, easy soluble, cheapest size out; cheaper than mill made size. Ask us about it. Also all other grades. **ARABOL M'F'G CO.** 100 William St., N. Y.

LOMBARD'S ENGLISH NEWCASTLE PULP STONES ARE SUPERIOR TO ALL OTHERS. ALL SIZES IN STOCK. LOMBARD & CO., Importer & Manufacturers, 236 & 238 A Street, Boston.

Ohio

DAYTON—Montgomery Co.

Pop. 120,000. On B.; C., C., C. & St. L.; C., H. & D.; D. & M.; P., C., C. & St. L.; C. D. & C.; D. & U. RR. M. O. and Tel. office; Am., Adams.

ÆTNA PAPER CO., THE. (H. H. Hoffman, Pres.; C. E. Hoffman, Vice-Pres.; H. M. Howard, Sec. and Treas.; L. P. Boswell, Mgr.; C. F. Goodenough, Supt.; Wm. H. Clark, Mgr. Sales, 251 W. 92d Street, New York.) Two mills. NOS. I and II. S. P., at mills. Five 1000-lb. Beating, two Refining engines and eight Washers; one 86-inch and one 88-inch Fourdriniers. Widest trimmed sheet, 80 inches. Union Screens. Steam. Loft Dried, Bonds, Ledgers and Linens. 60,000 lbs. 24 hours.

AMERICAN STRAW BOARD CO. General offices, Akron, Ohio. (Idle.)

PEERLESS PAPER CO. (Geo. H. Mead, Pres. and Gen. Mgr.; R. T. Houk, Vice-Pres.; A. L. Rieger, Treas. and Gen. Mgr.; L. P. Rieger, Supt.) Nine Beating and four Jordan engines; one 94-inch and one 116-inch Fourdriniers. Steam and Electricity. Mecopa Bond, Peerless Writing, Lithograph, Offset, Text, English Finish and M. F. Book. 70,000 lbs. 24 hours.

DELPHOS—Allen Co.

Pop. 4,517. On P., Ft. W. & C.; N. O.; O., H. & D.; T., St. L. & W. RR., M. & B. Canal. M. O. and Tel. office; Adams, Nat. and U. S. Ex.

HINDE & DAUCH PAPER CO., THE. General Offices, Sandusky, Ohio. (Sidney Frohman, Pres.; W. F. Harbrecht, Vice-Pres.; Fred Emmons, Sec.) DELPHOS PAPER MILLS. S. P., at mills. Two 1000-lb., one 1200-lb. Beating and two Jordan engines; one 72-inch Cylinder. Trims 64 inches. Steam. Straw Wrapping and Light Strawboard. 30,000 lbs. 24 hours.

DRESDEN.

Pop. 1,549. On Zanesville Div. Penna. & Wheeling and Lake Erie RR. Tel., M. O., and bank; Adams and Wells Fargo Ex.

DRESDEN PAPER MILLS CO. (L. P. Gallagher, Pres.; Clyde Barnes, Vice-Pres.; M. D. Custer, Sec. and Treas.; S. W. Sroufe, Supt.; W. H. Eichelberger, Mgr.) Four 1200-lb. Beaters and two 2500-lb. Claflin Beaters; eight Washers and six Globe Rotaries; one 102-inch Cylinder. Widest trimmed sheet, 88 inches. Steam. Special Straw Board for Corrugating Purposes. 60,000 lbs. 24 hours.

FRANKLIN—Warren Co.

Pop. 2,724. On C. Div. of C., C., C. & St. L.; C., M. & M. V. RR. M. O. and Tel. office; Am. Ex.

AMERICAN WRITING PAPER CO.—Harding Paper Company, Division. (T. A. Jones, Mgr.) Two mills. EXCELLO MILL. Location, Excello, 3 miles south. Four 800-lb. and two 1000-lb. Umpherston engines; one 84-inch Fourdrinier. Water and Steam. Writing. 5000 lbs. 24 hours. FRANKLIN MILL. S. P., Franklin. Four 750-lb., three 1000-lb. and one Marshall engines; one 66-inch and one 80-inch Fourdriniers. Water and Steam. Writing. 14,000 lbs. 24 hours. *Tub-sized and Loft-dried Papers exclusively.*

FRANKLIN BOARD AND PAPER CO., THE. (Albert F. Hagar, Pres.; George Little, Vice-Pres.; Karhl Bull, Sec.; Fred B. Zartman, Treas. and

McEnery Paper Company Practically All Grades
Manufacturers' Sales Agency 112 W. ADAMS ST., CHICAGO

Gen. Mgr.) S. P., at mill. Four 800-lb., one 1000-lb. and one 2000-lb. Beating and four Refining engines; one 102-inch Six Cylinder. Widest trimmed sheet, 92 inches. Steam. News, Manila Lined, Chip, Paper Stock, Jute, Pulp and Combination Boards. 90,000 lbs. 24 hours.

PATENT VULCANITE ROOFING CO. (R. Glendinning, Pres.; J. Logan, Vice-Pres.; D. S. Barbour, Sec.; W. Thompson, Treas.; D. S. Barbour, Mgr.; J. D. Beatty, Supt.) Five 1500-lb. and one 1000-lb. Beating engines; one 72-inch Single Cylinder. Roofing papers for own use. 50,000 lbs. 24 hours.

SRERE BROS. & CO. (Alfred A. and Harry Srere, Co-partners; Howard L. Cheney, Mgr.; Andrew Meehan, Supt.) Branch Office, Detroit, Mich. S. P., Franklin. Two Beating and Washing engines; two Digesters and one Wet Machine. Steam. Rag and Jute Pulp and Hemp Specialties. 8000 lbs. 24 hours.

SRERE, THE, PULP & PAPER CO. (Alfred A. Srere, Pres.; Harry Srere, Vice-Pres.; Abraham Srere, Sec.; Howard L. Cheney, Treas.; Sullivan Black, Supt.) S. P., Park. Six Combination Washing and Beating engines, two Wet Machines, three Rotaries. Steam. Rag and Jute Pulp. 24,000 lbs. 24 hours.

HAMILTON—Butler Co.

Pop. 35,400. On B. & O. R. Div. of P., C., C. & St. L. and M. V. T. Co. R.R.

BECKETT PAPER CO., THE. (T. Beckett, Pres., Edward Helwig, Sec.-Treas.) S. P., at mill. Twelve 1200-lb. Beating and two Jordan engines; one 68-inch and one 118-inch Fourdriniers. Width of Super Calenders, 36, 44 and 74 inches. Widest trimmed sheet, 110 inches. Steam. Bonds, Writing and Cover. 50,000 lbs. 24 hours.

CHAMPION COATED PAPER CO. (Peter G. Thomson, Pres.; Peter G. Thomson, Jr., Vice-Pres.; Walter D. Randall, Sec. and Treas.; A. O. Rolfe, Paper Mill Supt; and Wm. Schenk, Coating Mill Supt.) S. P., at mill. Sixty-nine 1500-lb. Beating and fifteen Jordan engines; two 106-inch, two 126-inch, two 138-inch and three 152-inch Fourdriniers and one 128-inch Five Cylinder. Widest trimmed sheet, 140 inches. Steam and Electricity. Super-Calendered, Machine Finish and Coated Book, Coated Manila and Cardboard. 525,000 lbs. 24 hours.

STERLING, THE, PAPER CO. (H. W. Friend, Vice-Pres.; R. B. Harbison, Sec.; W. M. Benzing, Gen. Mgr.) S. P., at mill. Six 1000-lb. Beating and two Jordan engines; one 94-inch Fourdrinier, trims 81 inches. Water and Steam. Waterleaf and Absorbent Specialties. 28,000 lbs. 24 hours.

LANCASTER—Fairfield Co.

Pop. 13,093. On Penn Hocking Valley RR. M. O. and Tel.; Adams and Wells Fargo Ex.

LANCASTER BOARD & PAPER CO. (J. L. Graham, Pres.; S. Silberman, Vice-Pres.; C. S. Hutchinson, Sec. and Treas.; F. E. Alward, Gen. Mgr. and Pur. Agt.; R. R. Peters, Asst. Mgr.) One 1200-lb. and one 1500-lb. Beating and two Refining engines; one 62-inch Five Cylinder Machine. Widest trimmed sheet, 53 inches. Steam. Solid News and Plain Chip. 40,000 lbs. 24 hours. (July 29, 1918. Will add new machine soon to trim 84 inches.)

LANCASTER LEATHER CO. (W. A. Miller, Pres.; W. N. Claflin, Vice-Pres. and Mgr.; C. S. Hutchinson, Sec. and Treas.) S. P., at mill. Three Beaters; one 48-inch and one 60-inch Cylinders. Electricity. Leather Heeling Board. 14,000 lbs. 24 hours.

LOCKLAND—Hamilton Co.

Pop. 2,695. On C., H. & D.; C., C., C. & St. L. and M. C. V. T. Co. RR. M. O. and Tel. office; Am. Ex.

CAREY, THE PHILIP, MFG. CO. P. O. Address, Cincinnati. (G. D. Crabbs, Pres.; R. B. Crabbs, Vice-Pres. and Treas.; E. L. Buse, Sec.; W. J. Moeller, Gen. Supt.) ASBESTOS PAPER MILL. One 82-inch asbestos paper machine. Capacity, 25 tons every 24 hours. Widest trimmed sheet, 76 inches. Two 3000-lb. Beaters. Two Board Machines—capacity, 10 tons 24 hours. FELT MILL. Eighteen 800-lb. Beaters. One 86-inch Felt Paper Machine. Widest trimmed sheet, 76 inches. Capacity, 32 tons 24 hours. One 92-inch Felt Paper Machine. Widest trimmed, 86 inches. Capacity, 48 tons every 24 hours.

FOX PAPER CO. (H. W. Nichols, Pres. and Gen. Mgr.; T. J. Davis, Vice-Pres.; G. B. Fox, A. W. Maynes, Sec. and Mgr. Sales; A. H. Gardner, Treas.) LOCKLAND MILL. Location, Lockland. Eight 1500-lb. Dilts Holland engines, four 1600-lb. Jones engines, one Majestic and one Imperial Wagg Jordan, one 136-inch Fourdrinier and one 130-inch Dutchman, trimming 120 inches each. Water and Steam. High-Grade Anti-Tarnish Pure Kraft, Antique and Machine Glazed Kraft and Sulphite and Specialties Tape, Gummed and Ungummed, Kraft and Sulphite Hand Rolls, all Widths and Diameter. 70,000 lbs. 24 hours. CRESCENTVILLE MILL. Location, Crescentville. Seven 1500-lb. Beaters and two Rotary Refiners; one 90-inch Four Cylinder. Widest trimmed sheet, 84 inches. Water and Steam. Carpet, Building, Rag Wrapping, Plain and Duplex Chip Board, Test Chip and Jute, and Chip Express Mill Wrappers, Bottle Wrapper Paper, Candy Paper and Specialties. 50,000 lbs. 24 hours. RIALTO MILL. Location, Rialto. Four 1500-lb. Beating and one Rotary Refiner; one 90-inch Fourdrinier, trims 80 inches. Water and Steam. No. 2 and Butchers' Manila, Butchers' Fibre, Dry and Water Finish, Duplex and Solid Colored Specialties, Black Hardware, Blue Macaroni, Ham and Rag Wrapping, Light Weight Non-Test Chip for Corrugating, Express and Saturating Paper. 50,000 lbs. 24 hours.

RICHARDSON PAPER CO., THE. (J. M. Richardson, Pres.; W. H. Richardson, Vice-Pres.; Paul Richardson, Treas.; W. S. LaRue, Sec.; T. J. Mullin, Supt.) S. P., at mill. LOCKLAND MILLS. Twenty-four Beating and eight Jordan engines; one 80-inch and one 86-inch Single Cylinders; one 128-inch Six Cylinders and one 132-inch Six Cylinders. Widest trimmed sheet, 128 inches. Water, Steam and Electricity. Wrapping, Roofing, Specialties in Felt, Bottle and Rag Wrapper, Carpet Lining, Saturating Felts, Deadening Felts, Fly Felts; Asphalt Roofing and Shingles

THOMAS E. GLEESON, Inc., 411-413 John St., E. NEWARK, N. J.
CYLINDER MOULDS and DANDY ROLLS Made and Repaired
LETTERING and MONOGRAMS for WATERMARKS

Paper and Pulp Mills in the United States 183

and Prepared Roofings; Box Boards, Chip, Container, White Patent Coated and Colored Boards; Cracker Shell, Folding Box and Jute Boards; Black Tack and Pulp Board; Pasted Boards, Wall Board and Jacquard Boards. 400,000 lbs. 24 hours. Manufacturers of Fibre Shipping Cases, Cartons and Folding Paper Boxes.

MASSILLON—Stark Co.

Pop. 16,000. On Penn., B. & O. and W. & L. R.R. M. O. and Tel. office; Ad., Am. and U. S. Ex.

MASSILLON PAPER CO. (C. B. Silk, Pres.; J. R. Silk, Vice-Pres.; F. B. Silk, Sec. and Treas.) MASSILLON MILL. S. P., at mill. Two 600-lb., two 800-lb. and one 1500-lb. Beating and two Refining engines; one 48-inch and one 56-inch Cylinders. Widest trimmed sheet, 52 inches. Steam. Straw and Rag Wrapping. Light-Weight Straw and Chip Board for Corrugating. 30,000 lbs. 24 hours.

MAUMEE—Lucas Co.

Pop. 1,856. On T., St. L. & W.; T., B. B. & F.; T. & M. V. Electric RR. M. O. and Tel. office; Nat. and Pac. Ex.

CARNEY PAPER CO. (Daniel Carney, Mgr.) S. P., at mill. Three 1000-lb. Beating and two Refining engines; one 70-inch Double Cylinder. Widest trimmed sheet, 65 inches. Steam. Rag Wrapping, Mill Wrappers, Duplex, Card Middles, Ham Paper and Specialties. 24,000 lbs. 24 hours.

MIAMISBURG—Montgomery Co.

Pop. 3,941. On C. H. & D.; Cincinnati Branch of C., C., C. & St. L.; Erie and S. O. T. RR. M. O. and Tel. office; Am. and U. S. Ex.

MIAMISBURG PAPER CO. (J. H. Friend, Pres.; R. D. Bertschy, Vice-Pres.; H. L. Newell, Treas.; J. G. Kline, Sec.) S. P., railroad, ¼ mile. Four 1200-lb. Beating and two Refining engines; one 76-inch and one 90-inch Fourdriniers. Widest trimmed sheet, 78 inches. Width of Super Calenders, 42 inches. Water and Steam. Envelope, Bond and Ledger. 40,000 lbs. 24 hours.

OHIO PAPER CO. (R. J. Connelly, Pres.; H. W. Schieble, Sec. and Treas.) Four 800-lb. Beating engines and one 44-inch Cylinder machines. Widest trimmed sheet, 36 inches. Water and Steam. Roofing Felt. 20,000 lbs. 24 hours.

MIDDLETOWN—Butler Co.

Pop. 25,000. On C. H. & D.; C. & N.; M. & C.; C., C., C. & St. L. RR.; Miami and Erie Canal. M. O. and Tel. office; Adams, Am. and U. S. Ex.

CRYSTAL PAPER CO. (J. W. Van Dyke, Pres.; Z. W. Ranck, Vice-Pres.; D. E. Harlan, Sec., Treas. and Mgr.) Location, 2 miles south. S. P., at mill. C. H. & D. R. R. and M. & E. Canal. Four 800-lb., three 1200-lb. and four 1800-lb. Beating and four Jordan engines; one 68-inch, one 94-inch, one 120-inch and one 140-inch Cylinders. Widest trimmed sheet, 120 inches. Water and Steam. White, Colored, Manila, Kraft, Tissue and Waxing Paper. 32,000 lbs. 24 hours.

GARDNER-HARVEY PAPER CO., THE. (Colin Gardner, Chairman; E. T. Gardner, Pres.; Colin Gardner, Jr., Vice-Pres.; R. B. Gardner, Treas.; M. S. Johnston, Sec.; Tom Harvey, Gen. Mgr.) S. P., at mill. Six 1500-lb.

THE UNION SULPHUR CO.
Producers of
Main Office: Mines:
17 Battery Pl., New York. Calcasieu Parish, La.
The Only Arsenic Free Sulphur on the Market

DRY ROSIN SIZE
Brittle, easy soluble. Cheaper, size cut; cheaper than mill made size. Ask us about it. Also all other grades.

ARABOL M'F'G CO.
100 William St., New York

Ohio

Beating and five Jordan engines; one 136-inch Seven Cylinder Machine. Widest trimmed sheet, 124 inches. Bleached Manila Lined Chip, Manila Lined Chip, Single Vat Lined Chip, Colored Suit Box Boards and Combination Boards of all grades. 180,000 lbs. 24 hours. Address all communications to The Gardner & Harvey Co., Middletown, O.

GARDNER PAPER CO., THE COLIN. (Colin Gardner, Chairman; E. T. Gardner, Pres.; Colin Gardner, Jr., Vice-Pres. R;. B. Gardner, Treas., M. S. Johnston, Sec.; Geo. H. Harvey, Gen. Mgr.) S. P., at mill. Ten 1800-lb. Beating and eight Refining engines; one 98-inch Six and one 120-inch Six Cylinders. Widest trimmed sheets, 86 and 110 inches. Steam. Patent Coated Boards, Bleached Manila Lined Chip Board, Manila Lined Chip Boards, Combination Boards of all kinds, and White Blanks. 200,000 lbs. 24 hours. We make a specialty of all grades of Patent Coated Boards. Address all communications to The Gardner & Harvey Co., Middletown, Ohio.

GARDNER PAPER BOARD CO., THE. (Colin Gardner, Chairman; E. T. Gardner, Pres.; Colin Gardner, Jr., Vice-Pres.; R. B. Gardner, Treas.; M. S. Johnston, Sec.; Tom Harvey, Gen. Mgr.) S. P., at mill. Four 1200-lb. Beating and three Jordan engines; one 82-inch Six Cylinder Machine. Widest trimmed sheet, 72 inches. Plain Chip, Single Manila Lined Chip, Manila Lined Chip, Single News Vat Lined Chip, White Van Lined Chip. Address all communications to The Gardner & Harvey Co., Middleton, Ohio.

OGLESBY, THE W. B., PAPER CO. (J. A. Aull, Pres.; A. F. Smith, Vice-Pres.; M. T. Hartley, Sec.; L. C. Anderson, Treas.) S. P., at mill. Eight 10-cwt. Beating, six 8-cwt. Washing and two Refining engines; two Rotary boilers; one 112-inch and 118-inch Fourdriniers. Widest trimmed sheets, 102 and 108 inches. Water and Steam. Bonds, Writings, Ledgers and High Grade Offset Papers. 60,000 lbs. 24 hours. *The company specializes in Offset Papers and guarantees them to give satisfaction.*

PAUL A. SORG PAPER CO., THE (J. A. Aull, Pres.; M. T. Hartley, Vice-Pres. and Treas.; A. F. Smith, Vice-Pres. and Gen. Supt.; L. C. Anderson, Sec.) S. P., at mill. Five 1200-lb., eleven 1000-lb. Beating and three Refining engines; one 124-inch Fourdrinier; one 92-inch Four Cylinder and one Two Cylinders. Widest trimmed sheet, Fourdrinier, 112 inches; Four Cylinder, 78 inches; Two Cylinder, 102 inches. Water and Steam. Capacity, 62,000 lbs. 24 hours. Jute and Manila Rope Specialties, Tissues and Bleached White Sulphates for Waxing.

WARDLOW-THOMAS PAPER CO., THE. (M. A. Thomas, Pres.; Jas. Lawrence, Vice-Pres.; E. C. Woodward, Sec. and Treas.) S. P., railroad and canal at mill. Four 800-lb., six 1200-lb., two 10-cwt. Umpherston and two Jordan engines; one 76-inch Three and one 92-inch Four Cylinders. Widest trimmed sheet, 80 inches. Water and Steam. Rope and Jute Manilas. 20,000 lbs. 24 hours.

WRENN PAPER CO., THE. (Jno. Gibson, Jr., Pres. and Treas.; Austin Smith, Vice-Pres.; J. J. Hallowell, Sec.; John Calder, Supt.) S. P., at mill. Two 800-lb., one 1000-lb. and one 1200-lb. Beating and one Refining engines; one 84-inch Fourdrinier. Widest trimmed sheet, 76 inches. Water and

ARE SUPERIOR TO ALL OTHERS. ALL SIZES IN STOCK.
LOMBARD & CO., Importers & Manufacturers, 236 & 238 A Street, Boston.

Paper and Pulp Mills in the United States 185

Steam. Blotting. 25,000 lbs. 24 hours. *Wrenn's Royal High Colors. Wrenn's Best Blotting—pure cotton. Wrenn's Record Blotting. Wrenn's Mosaic Blotting. Wrenn's Basket Weave Blotting. Wrenn's Antlers Blotting. "Porcelain" Halftone Blotting.*

MUNROE FALLS—Summit Co.

Pop. 900. On P. & W.; B. & O. RR. Tel. office, M. O. and nearest bank, Cuyahoga Falls, 3 miles; U. S. Ex.

MUNROE FALLS PAPER CO., THE. (C. B. Silk, Pres.; Charles Senn, Vice-Pres.; F. B. Silk, Sec. and Treas.) Office, Massillon. MUNROE MILL. S. P., at mill. Four 800-lb., two 1000-lb. and two Jordan engines; one 44-inch and one 64-inch Double Cylinders. Water and Steam. Carpet Lining, Express, Straw and Rag Wrapping, Building, Absorbent, Fly Paper, Fireworks Paper, Deadening Felt and Roofing. 30,000 lbs. 24 hours.

PIQUA—Miami Co.

Pop. 12,172. On P., C., C. & St. L.; C., H. & D. RR. M. O. and Tel. office; Adams, Am. and U. S. Ex.

AMERICAN STRAW BOARD CO. Executive Office, Akron, Ohio. (J. F. Anderson, Mgr.) S. P., at mill. UPPER MILL. Three 800-lb. and two 1200-lb. Beating and one Jordan engines; one 62-inch Cylinder. Widest sheet made, 56 inches. Water and Steam. Straw Board, Combination Board, Pulp Lined Board, News Board and Chip Board Cap Stock for Tubes and Paper Cans. 20,000 lbs. 24 hours.

RITTMAN—Wayne Co.

Pop. 2,000. On B. & O. and Erie RR. M. O. and Tel. office. W. F. & Co. Ex.

THE OHIO BOX BOARD CO. (N. S. Everhard, Pres.; E. J. Young, Vice-Pres. and Gen. Mgr.; Wm. Artman, Sec.; J. J. Gannon, Treas.) S. P., at mill. Seven 2000-lb. and seven 1500-lb. Beating and nine Jordan engines; one 132-inch Six Cylinder, and one 105-inch Five Cylinder Board Machine and one 120-inch Roll Pasting Machine. Widest trimmed sheets, 122 and 97 inches. Electricity and Steam. Box Boards of all Grades, including Patent Coated, Jute, Wood Pulp, Manila Lined, News Board, Chip and Three-Ply Fibre Container Board. 220,000 lbs. 24 hours.

ROCKDALE—Butler Co.

Pop. 60. On B. & O. RR. 7 miles east of Hamilton; 7 miles west of Middletown. M. O., Tel., bank and Wells Fargo & Co. Ex. at Hamilton.

SALL MOUNTAIN CO. Office, 230 So. La Salle Street, Chicago, Ill, and Scranton, Pa. (C. M. Clark, Pres.; C. E. Cook, Vice-Pres. and Treas.; F. R. Anderson, Sec.; D. L. Brown, Supt.) Three 1500-lb. Beating and two Refining engines; one 84-inch Five Cylinder Machine. Widest trimmed sheet, 80 inches. Water and Steam. Asbestos Building Paper, Asbestos Mill Board, Asbestos Roll Board and Special Asbestos Paper for Electrolysis. 60,000 lbs. 24 hours.

SANDUSKY—Erie Co.

Pop. 19,664. On L. S. & M. S.; C., C., C. & St. L.; B. & O.; L. E. & W.; S. & O. S. L. RR. M. O. and Tel. office; U. S., Am. and Wells Fargo & Co. Ex.

HINDE & DAUCH PAPER CO., THE. (Sidney Frohman, Pres.; W. F. Harbrecht, Vice-Pres. Fred Emmons, Sec.) SANDUSKY PAPER MILL.

ENGINEERING FOR PULP, PAPER AND POWER PLANTS

JOSEPH H. WALLACE & CO.
INDUSTRIAL ENGINEERS
Temple Court Building, NEW YORK
71 Bay Street, TORONTO, CAN.

S. P., at mill. One 1000 lb., one 1200-lb. and two Jordan engines; one 56-inch Cylinder. Widest trimmed sheet, 52 inches. Steam. Straw Wrapping and Light Strawboard. 20,000 lbs. 24 hours. No. 2 MILL. One 96-inch Beloit Cylinder and one 96-inch Dowingtown Fourdrinier; six Beating engines; six Jordans and Claflins. Straw Wrapping and Corrugated Straw. 100,000 lbs. 24 hours. *"Corrugated Paper Specialties."*

ST. MARYS—Auglaize Co.

Pop. 6,000. On M. & E. Canal; L. E. & W. T. & O. C. RR. Western Union. Tel. office; Am. and Wells Fargo Ex.

AUGLAIZE, THE, BOX BOARD CO. (E. B. Weston, Pres.; W. G. Clark, Treas. and Gen. Mgr.; V. T. Gransden, Sec. and Sales Mgr.) S. P., at St. Marys. Eight 2000-lb. Beating and six Jordan engines; one 86-inch Six Cylinder and one 96-inch Five Cylinder. Widest trimmed sheet, 91 inches. Steam. Boards for Corrugating and Solid Fibre Containers, Folding Box Boards, Straw and Plain Chip and Pulp Lined Straw Board. 144,000 lbs. 24 hours.

STEUBENVILLE—Jefferson Co.

Pop. 14,349. On P., C., C. & St. L.; R. Div. C. & P.; Wheeling & L. E. & Ohio River RR. M. O. and Tel. office; Adams and W. F. & Co. Ex.

HARTJE PAPER MANUFACTURING CO. (Augustus Hartje, Pres.; A. F. Cayford, Sec. and Treas.; J. H. Cayford, Supt.) P. O. address, 113 and 115 Wood street, Pittsburgh, Pa. S. P., at mill. Six 1000-lb., four 1200-lb., four 1500-lb. and six Refining engines; one 96-inch Four Cylinder Board Machine and two 120-inch Fourdriniers. Steam. No. 1 and No. 2 Water Finished Fibres, Butcher's Manila, News, No. 2. Manila, No. 1 and No. 2 Kraft, Paper Board, Mill Wrappers, Sheathing Papers, Carpet Lining, Indented Packing Paper. 220,000 lbs. 24 hours. PULP MILL. Three Digesters and three Wet Machines. Steam. Sulphite, 70,000 lbs. 24 hours.

TIFFIN—Seneca Co.

AMERICAN STRAW BOARD CO. General offices, Akron, Ohio. (Idle.)

TIPPECANOE CITY—Miami Co.

Pop. 1,703. On C., H. & D. RR. M. O. and Tel. office; U. S. Ex.

AMERICAN STRAW BOARD CO. Executive Office, Akron, Ohio. (J. F. Anderson, Mgr.) Five 800-lb. Beating and two Jordan engines; one 72-inch Four Cylinder. Widest sheet made, 66 inches. Steam. Steam Dried Straw Board, extra smooth; Cap Stock for Paper Cans; Pulp Lined Boards. 24,000 lbs. 24 hours.

TORONTO—Jefferson Co.

Pop. 4,271. On River Div. Cleveland & Pittsburgh RR. M. O., Tel., bank and Ad. Ex.

HARTJE BROS. PAPER CO. (Chas. G. Hartje, Pres.; Richard Hartje, Vice-Pres. and Treas.; W. H. Kimberland, Sec.; W. T. Harrigan, Supt.) Three 1500-lb. Beating and two Refining engines. One 94-inch Cylinder. Widest trimmed sheet, 80 inches. Steam. Box Board, Mill Wrappers, Indented Boards and Building Paper.. 50,000 lbs. 24 hours.

URBANA—Champaign Co.

Pop. 6,906. On P. C. C. & St. L. Ry Co.; Big Four; Erie and Ohio Electric. M. O. and Tel. office; Adams, Am. and Wells Fargo & Co. Ex.

HOWARD PAPER CO., THE. Branch Office, Dayton, Ohio. (Maxwell Howard, Pres.; Ward R. Howard, Vice-Pres.; Lucius S. Howard, Sec. and Treas.; Jno. Yardy, Supt.) S. P., at mill. Ten Beating and two Noble & Wood engines; two 90-inch Pusey & Jones Fourdriniers. Widest trimmed sheet, 76 inches. Steam. Writings, Linens, Ledgers, Envelope and Bonds. Specialty Bonds. 60,000 lbs. 24 hours. *Watermarked Bonds and Designs (Howard Patent Process).*

UNITED PAPERBOARD COMPANY. General Offices, 171 Madison avenue, New York. URBANA MILL. S. P., at mill. Seven 1200-lb. and two Jordan engines; one 100-inch Four Cylinder. Widest trimmed sheet, 96 inches. Steam. Straw, Chip, News and Container Boards. 70,000 lbs. 24 hours.

WEST CARROLLTON—Montgomery Co.

Pop. 2,500. On C., C., C. & St. L. RR. M. O. and Tel. office; nearest bank, Dayton, 6 miles; Am. and Adams Ex.

MIAMI PAPER CO., THE. (W. W. Sunderland, Pres.; A. H. Nevius, Vice-Pres. and Gen. Mgr.; J. F. Dunifer, Asst. Gen. Mgr.; W. S. Hayden, Treas.; G. C. Thornburg, Sec. and Asst. Treas.; H. W. Server, Supt.) S. P., at mill. Thirteen 2000-lb. Beating, eight Refining engines; one 120-inch, two 140-inch, one 165-inch Fourdrinier Machines; six Super Calenders, 46, 52, 58 and 85 inches wide. Machine Finish and S. & S. C. Book, Laid Papers, Eggshell. Railroad Folders, Ledger, Bond, White Writings, Canary Writings and Mimeograph. 200,000 lbs. 24 hours.

OREGON.

ASTORIA—Clatsop Co.

Pop. 10,363. On Spokane, Portland & Seattle RR. No.; Wells Fargo & Co. and Am. Ex.

ASTORIA PULP & PAPER CO. (C. F. Hendrickson, Pres.; L. C. Leadbetter, Vice-Pres.; C. H. Leadbetter, Sec.; J. M. Anderson, Treas.; Charles Meagher, Supt.) Two 600-lb. and one 1000-lb. Beating and one Refining engines; one washer and one Rotary boiler; one 68-inch Four Cylinder Machine. Widest trimmed sheet, 60 inches. Steam and Electricity. Chip Board. 40,000 lbs. 24 hours. (Aug. 28, 1918. Company in process of reorganization.)

LEBANON—Linn Co.

Pop. 922. Lebanon Branch of S. P. RR. M. O. and Tel. office; Wells Fargo & Co. Ex.

CROWN WILLAMETTE PAPER CO. Office, Alaska Commercial Bldg., San Francisco. (Wm. Pierce Johnson, Pres.; Louis Bloch, Vice-Pres. and Gen. Mgr.; Chas. M. Whitney, Sec.; Frank Schwabacher, Treas.) LEBAPAPER MILLS. Six 1000-lb. Beating and Three Refining engines; one 70-inch and one 76-inch Fourdriniers. Water and Steam. Fibre and Manila. 35,000 lbs. 24 hours. LEBANON PULP MILL. S. P., at mill. Two Digesters; one Wet Machine. Water and Steam. Sulphite. 40,000 lbs. 24 hours.

Oregon and Pennsylvania

MARSHFIELD CITY—Coos Co.—**PULP MILL.**
COOS BAY PULP & PAPER CO. (Mill dismantled and out of business.)

OREGON CITY—Clackamas Co.
Pop. 4,500. On W. River, S. P. RR. M. O. and Tel. office; Wells Fargo & Co. Ex.
CROWN WILLAMETTE PAPER CO. EAST SIDE MILL. Ten Four Pocket Bagley and Sewall Grinders; nine 90-inch and one 72-inch Wet Machines. Ground Wood. 120,000 lbs. 24 hours.

HAWLEY PULP AND PAPER COMPANY. (Willard P. Hawley, Pres.; Willard P. Hawley, Jr., Vice-Pres. and Gen. Mgr.; Theo. Osmund, Sec. and Treas.; George E. Pusey, Supt.) NO. 1 MACHINE. 120-inch Fourdrinier (110-inch trim); six Beating engines and one Jordan engine. Water and Steam. NO. 2 MACHINE. 114-inch Harper Fourdrinier (104-inch trim); two 1000-lb. Beating engines and one Jordan engine. Water and Steam. NO. 3 MACHINE. 116-inch Harper Fourdrinier (107-inch trim); two 1700-lb. Beating engines and one Jordan engine. Water and Steam. NO. 4 MACHINE. 165-inch Fourdrinier (152-inch trim); seven Beating engines and one Jordan engine. Electricity. Wrapping, News, Fruit Wraps, Tissue, Towelling. 200,000 lbs. 24 hours. PULP MILLS. Sulphite. 140,000 lbs. Ground Wood. 150,000 lbs. 24 hours.

WARRENDALE—Multnomah Co.—**PULP MILL.**
Pop. 75. On O. R. & N. C. RR. Tel., Bonneville, 3 miles; Ex. Cascades Locks, 7 miles; M. O., Hood River, 16 miles; nearest bank, Portland, 37 miles.
CROWN WILLAMETTE PAPER CO. Office, Alaska Commercial Bldg., San Francisco, Cal. S. P., at mill. Seven Grinders; three Wet Machines. Water. Ground Wood (dry). 32,000 lbs. 24 hours. (Plant no longer in operation and has been partly dismantled.)

WEST LINN.
CROWN WILLAMETTE PAPER CO. Office, Alaska Commercial Bldg. (Wm. Pierce Johnson, Pres.; Louis Bloch, Vice-Pres. and Gen. Mgr.; Charles M. Whitney, Sec.; Frank Schwabacher, Treas.; A. J. Lewthwaite, Res. Mgr., Portland, Ore.) WEST LINN MILLS. S. P., at Pulp Station above plant on river bank. One 65-inch, one 74-inch, two 84-inch, one 102-inch, two 150-inch and one 158-inch Fourdriniers. Widest trimmed sheet, 146 inches. Water. News. 400,000 lbs. 24 hours. PULP MILL NO. 1. Forty-eight Grinders; twenty-five 72-inch Wet Machines; twenty "Improved" Rotary Screens. Water. Ground Wood (dry). 500,000 lbs. 24 hours. MILL NO. 2. Six Digesters; four 72-inch Wet Machines. Water. Sulphite Fibre (dry). 200,000 lbs. 24 hours.

PENNSYLVANIA.

ABRAMS—Montgomery Co.
Pop. 150. On Phila. & Reading RR. Tel. and Am. Ex.; nearest M. O. and bank, Norristown, 2 miles.
MERION PAPER CO. (J. A. Lafore, Pres.; E. H. Morris, Vice-Pres.; M. R. Donnelly, Sec.; P. J. Lafore, Treas.; J. M. Keating, Supt.) Two 800-lb. Beaters, one Breaker and one Jordan; one 75-inch Wet Machine.

Widest trimmed sheet, 65 inches. Steam. Binders' Board, Shell Packing Board, Chair Seat Board, Trunk and Suit Case. 16,000 lbs. 24 hours.

AMBLER—Montgomery Co.

Pop. 3,000. On N. P. RR. M. O. and Tel.; U. S. Ex.

KEASBEY & MATTISON CO. (Richard V. Mattison, M. D., Pres.; Richard V. Mattison, Jr., Vice-Pres. and Gen. Mgr.; Royal Mattison, Second Vice-Pres.; R. H. Anderson, Third Vice-Pres.; N. F. Wood, Fourth Vice-Pres.; H. P. Barnes, Act. Sec.; U. F. Funk, Treas.; H. P. Barnes, Asst. Treas.) Four 2500-lb. Beating engines; one 54-inch and two 78-inch Cylinders. Widest trimmed sheets, 48 and 73 inches. Steam and Electricity. Asbestos Paper and Asbestos Mill Board. Paper 100,000 lbs. and Mill Board 15,000 lbs. 24 hours.

AUSTIN—Potter Co.

Pop. 2,300. On B. & S. RR. M. O. and Tel.; Am. Ex.; also bank.

BAYLESS MFG. CORPORATION. Sales office, 527 1fth Ave., New York. (R. R. Lewis, Pres.; Stanley C. Bayless, Sec. and Treas.; Geo. C. Bayless, Chairman, Board of Directors; A. N. Waring, Mgr. of Sales.) Thirteen Beating and five Jordan engines. Three Kollergangs. One 66-inch, one 114-inch and one 136-inch Fourdriniers. Steam. Fibre, Bag and Kraft. 140,000 lbs. 24 hours. SULPHITE MILL. Four Digesters, five Wet Machines. Steam. Sulphite Fibre. 140,000 lbs. 24 hours.

BARTO—Berks Co.

Pop. 82. On Colebrookdale Br. of Phila. & Read. RR. M. O. and Tel. Am. Ex.; nearest bank, Bally, 2 miles.

WEST BRANCH PAPER MILL. (Isaac C. Yoder, Proprietor.) Three Beating engines. One 40-inch Cylinder. Water. Gray Bogus Wrapping. 3000 lbs. 24 hours.

BLOOMSBURG—Columbia Co.

Pop. 6,170. On D., L. & W.; P. & R.; B. & S.; P. RR. M. O. and Tel. office; Adams and U. S. Ex.

BLOOMSBURG PAPER CO. P. O. address, Bloomsburg R. D. No. 3. (R. J. Ruhl and Mark Cressy, Executors and Trustees.) Four 500-lb. Beating and one Kingsland Refining engines, one 56-inch Double Cylinder. Widest trimmed sheet, 48 inches. Water and Steam. Waterproof Cartridge. 4000 lbs. 24 hours.

BRIDGEPORT—Montgomery Co.

Pop. 3,500. On P. & R. RR. M. O. and Tel. office; bank, Bridgeport. Nat. Ex.

AMBOY PAPER CO. (D. E. and H. I. Farley, Proprietors.) Three 800-lb. Beating and three Jordan engines; one 72-inch Machine. Widest trimmed sheet, 70 inches. Bristols and Chocolate Layer Board. 20,000 lbs. 24 hours.

DIAMOND STATE FIBRE CO. (E. M. Taylor, Pres.) S. P., at mill. Three 66-inch and one 136-inch Fourdriniers. Steam. Waterleaf, Vulcanized Fibre, Insulating Papers, Glassine, Greaseproof Vegetable Parchment and Parchmold; also Trunk, Counter and Press Boards, Filter Paper.

Pennsylvania

BUCK RUN—Chester Co.
Four miles from Pomeroy. M. O., Ex. and Tel. office, Pomeroy, 4 miles; nearest bank, Coatesville, 8 miles.

GENERAL PAPER CO., INC., successors to Marley Mill Corporation. BEAVER DAM MILL. (P. O. address, Pomeroy. New York Office, 175 Fifth Ave. (F. B. Oldham, Pres.; Harold S. Smith, Sec.-Treas.; B. F. Bicking, Supt.) S. P., Beaver Dam Siding. Three 750-lb. and two 1000-lb. Beating and two Refining engines; three Washers and one Rotary Boiler; one 72-inch Harper Fourdrinier. Widest trimmed sheet, 64 inches. Steam and Water. Hanging, Writing, Mimeograph and Specialties. 20,000 lbs. 24 hours.

NASSAU MILLS CORPORATION. BUCK RUN MILL. (Idle.)

CHAMBERSBURG—Franklin Co.
Pop. 12,000. On Cumberland Valley and B. & H. Div. of W. M. RR. M. O. and Tel. office; Adams and Am. Ex.

UNITED STATES PAPER MILLS, INC. (Dunbar A. Rosenthal, Pres.; Milton Long, Sec.-Treas.; William Snyder, Supt.) Three 600-lb. and one 1000-lb. Beating engines; one Refining engine; one Rotary boiler; one 64-inch Cylinder. Widest trimmed sheet, 60 inches. Water and Steam. Paper Towels, Toilet Paper and Crepe Paper Specialties. 15,00 lbs. 24 hours.

CHESTER—Chester Co.
Pop. 38,537. On Penn. RR.; P. & R. RR. and Delaware River. M. O., Tel., bank and Wells Fargo & Co and Adams Ex.

CHESTER PAPER CO. P. O. Address, Seventh and Glenwood Avenues, Philadelphia. (E. Irvin Scott, Pres.; A. H. Scott, Vice-Pres. and Treas.; Owen Moon, Jr., Sec.; Harry Liebeck, Supt.) S. P., at mill. Sixteen 1000-lb. Beating and six Refining engines; two 86-inch Cylinders. Widest trimmed sheet, 78 inches. One 147-inch ourdrinier. Widest trimmed sheet, 78 inches. One 147-inch Fourdrinier. Widest trimmed sheet, 138 inches. Two 86-inch Harpers. Widest trimmed sheet, 78 inches. Steam and Electricity. Tissue and Towel. 80,000 lbs. 24 hours.

CHESTERVILLE—Chester Co.
Pop. 30. Two miles from Landenberg. M. O. and Tel., Landenberg; nearest bank, Avondale. Ex. at Kelton.

LYSLE, WILSON, ESTATE OF. P. O. Address, Landenberg. Mary R. Lysle, Sec. and Treas.; H. C. Lysle, Supt.) FRANKLIN MILLS. S. P., Kelton Station, 3 miles. Two 400-lb. engines; one 48-inch Harper. Water and Steam. Filter Paper. 2000 lbs. 24 hours.

COATESVILLE—Chester Co.
JESSUP & MOORE PAPER CO., THE. (Eugene W. Fry, Pres.; E. A. Weihenmayer, Vice-Pres.; Wm. D. Heebner, Treas.; W. H. Clark, Sec.) Offices, 16 S. Broad Street, Philadelphia, Pa., and 50 E. 42d Street, New York City. CHESTER MILLS. (Idle.)

DOE RUN—Chester Co.

Pop. 215. Two miles from Gum Tree. M. O. office; Ex. Gum Tree. Tel. and nearest bank, Coatesville, 5 miles.

PALMER, WILLIS B. WILLOW GLEN MILLS. P. O. Address, Coatesville, Route D. S. P., at mill. One 500-lb. Beating engine; one 36-inch Machine. Widest trimmed sheet, 32 inches. Water. Binders' and Jacquard Boards. 2000 lbs. 24 hours.

DOWNINGTOWN—Chester Co.

Pop. 4,000. On Penn.; C. V. Branch of P. & R. R.R. M. O. and Tel. office; Adams and American Ex.

BICKING, S. AUSTIN, PAPER MFG. CO. P. O. address, East Downingtown. Two mills. NO. 1 MILL. Three 1000-lb., one 2000-lb. Beating and two Jordan engines; one 84-inch Four Cylinder. Widest trimmed sheet, 74 inches. NO. 2 MILL. One 1000-lb., two 2000-lb. Beating and two Jordan engines; one 92-inch Four Cylinder. Trims 84 inches. Water and Steam for both mills. Rosin-Sized Building, Indented Bottle Cover and Packing Paper, Indented Carpet Lining, Mill Wrappers, Test and No Test Chip and Box Board. 100,000 lbs. 24 hours.

KERR PAPER MILL CO. P. O. address, Box 52, East Downingtown, Pa. BRANDYWINE MILLS. S. P., Downingtown. Two 800-lb. engines; one 900-lb Breaker; two Wet Machines; one Jordan. Widest trimmed sheet, 48x80 inches. Water and Steam. Box, Binders', Tar Boards, Air Dried Straw and Leather Boards. 24,000 lbs. 24 hours.

FRANK P. MILLER PAPER CO. (J. Gibson McIlvain, Pres.; Hugh McIlvain, Vice-Pres.; Frank P. Miller, Sec. and Treas.) P. O. Address, East Downingtown. S. P., siding at mill. One 96-inch Seven Cylinder and one 132-inch Six Cylinder. Widest trimmed sheets, 88 and 120 inches. Steam. Patent Coated, Folding Box, News, Vat Lined Chip and Pasted Boards. 200,000 lbs. 24 hours.

RUDOLPH, F. M., & SON, Successors to James Guie Estate & Sons. EAGLE PAPER MILLS. Four 700-lb. engines; one 60-inch Double Cylinder. Water and Steam. Roofing, Sheathing and Corrugating. 16,000 lbs. 24 hours.

SHRYOCK BROS. P. O. Address, 924, 926 and 928 Cherry Street, Philadelphia. (S. S. Shryock, Pres.; S. S. Shryock, Jr., Vice-Pres.; O. A. Shryock, Sec. and Treas.) DORLAN MILL. S. P., at mill. One 800-lb., one 1000-lb. Beating and one Refining engines; one 62-inch Cylinder. Trims 59 inches. Steam and Water. Binders' Trunk, Air-Dried Straw and Box Boards. 20,000 lbs. 24 hours.

ERIE—Erie Co.

Pop. 110,000. On L. S. & M. S.; P. & E.; E. & P.; P., B. & L. E. and N. Y., C. & St. L. RR. M. O. and Tel. office; W., F. & Co., Nat., Adams and Am. Ex.

HAMMERMILL PAPER CO. (Ernst R. Behrend, Pres. and Gen. Mgr.; Otto F. Behrend, Treas.; C. S. Weir, Sec.; N. W. Wilson, Vice-Pres. and Mgr. Sales.) Eastern Office, 291 Broadway, New York. S. P., at mill. Twenty-seven Beating and five Refining engines; one 100-inch, one 108-inch,

Pennsylvania

one 128-inch and one 184-inch Fourdriniers; one 108-inch Yankee Fourdrinier. Widest sheet made, 120 inches. Width of Super-Calenders 44, 54 and 64-inch. Platers, Folders, Ruling and Punching Machines. Hammermill Bond, Ledger, Cover, Safety Paper, M. G. Wrappings, Writings, etc. 200,000 lbs. 24 hours. Also 100 tons Sulphite Fibre.

WATSON CO., H. F. Chicago Office, 319 Wells Street; Boston Office, 79 Milk Street. (R. W. Potter, Pres.; R. C. McClenathan, Vice-Pres. and Treas.; W. Henry Armstrong, Sec.; R. A. Cooney, Supt.) ERIE MILL. S. P., at mill. Thirty-six 1200-lb. to 2000-lb. Beating and four Refining engines; one Rotary Boiler; one 80-inch and four 84-inch Cylinders. Widest trimmed sheet, 75 inches. Steam. Dry Felt, Deadening Felt, Rosin-sized Sheathings, Insulating Papers, Asbestos Felt, Asbestos Mill Board, Corrugated Papers and all kinds of Building Papers. 250,000 lbs. 24 hours.

GLEN MILLS—Delaware Co.

Pop. 275. On P. W. & B. RR. M. O. and Tel. office; nearest bank, Media, 4½ miles; Adams Ex.

GLEN MILLS PAPER CO. Philadelphia office, 1005 Stephen Girard Building. GLEN MILLS. S. P., at mill. Two 12-cwt. Umpherston and two Downingtown Washing and one Smith & Winchester Jordan engines; three Rotary boilers; 12,000 lb. combined capacity; one 76-inch Fourdrinier. Widest trimmed sheet, 68½ inches. Steam. Genuine Vegetable Parchment. 10,000 lbs. 24 hours. Specialties: Vegetable Parchment, Rag Specialties.

HUNTINGTON MILLS—Luzerne Co.

Pop. 150. On D., L. & W. RR. M. O. office; nearest bank and Tel., Wilkes-Barre; Ex. Shickshinny, 5 miles.

MOUNTAIN PAPER CO., THE. HUNTINGTON PAPER MILL. P. O Address, Wilkes-Barre, Pa. (M. F. Whalen, Pres.; Mrs. M. F. Whalen, Vice-Pres.; T. E. Lewis, Sec. and Treas.; W. J. Gardner, Supt.) S. P., Shickshinny, 5 miles. Two 1400-lb. Beating and two Washing engines; one 48-inch Cylinder. Widest trimmed sheet, 44 inches. Water and Steam. Paper Napkins and Specialties. 2500 lbs. 24 hours.

JOHNSONBURG—Elk Co.

Pop. 2,894. On P. & E.; J. Div. of P.; B., R. & P.; E. RR. M. O. and Tel. office; Adams, Am. and Wells Fargo & Co. Ex.

HIGHLAND PAPER CO., THE. (A. G. Paine, Jr., Pres.; Charles T. Crocker, Jr., Vice-Pres.; Alvah Crocker, Sec. and Treas.) New York office, 200 Fifth avenue. HIGHLAND MILL. S. P., at mill. Five Digesters; one 90-inch Cylinder. Steam. Soda Fibre (dry), 110,000 lbs. 24 hours.

NEW YORK AND PENNSYLVANIA CO. New York office, 200 Fifth Avenue. (A. G. Paine, Jr., Pres.; Robert Wetherill, First Vice-Pres.; A. G. Paine, 3d, Second Vice-Pres. and Gen. Mgr.; M. B. Sloat, Sec. and Treas.; G. E. Paine, Asst. Sec. and Treas.; C. A. Clough, Gen. Sales Mgr.) CLARION MILLS. S. P., at mill. Thirty-one 2000-lb. Beating and fifteen Refining engines; one 96-inch Cylinder and one 106-inch, two 114-inch, one 125-inch, two 137-inch and one 158-inch Fourdriniers. Widest trimmed sheet, 148 inches. Width of Super-Calenders, 44, 54, 66 and 72 inches.

ESTABLISHED IN 1832

THE ROGERS PAPER MFG. CO.
INCORPORATED
SOUTH MANCHESTER, CONN., U. S. A.

MANUFACTURERS OF
INSULATING BOARD **PRESS-SPAHN** TEXTILE BOARD

SPECIALTIES

Alton Box Board & Paper Co.
FEDERAL, ILL.

Chicago Coated Board Co.
CHICAGO, ILL.

MANUFACTURERS OF

Paper Box Boards

SALES DEPARTMENT
Office, 1520 Lumber Exchange Bldg.   CHICAGO, ILL.

F. D. WILSON, Sales Manager

Address all Communications Regarding Sales to this Office

300 TONS DAILY CAPACITY

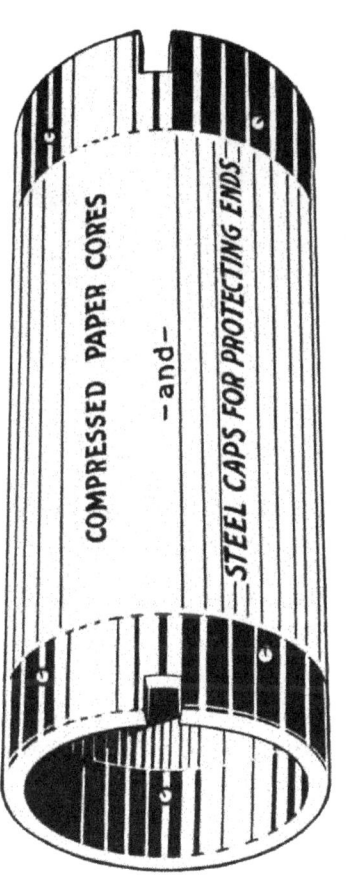

"Excelsior" Felts and Jackets

FOR EVERY GRADE OF PAPER

MANUFACTURED BY

KNOX WOOLEN CO.   CAMDEN, MAINE

The Model Automatic Smokeless Furnace
The Model-Chicago Chain Grate Stoker

Equip your boilers with suitable stokers and be prepared to burn the poor grades of coal you are likely to receive. Highest capacities and efficiency. Requires only natural draft.

THE MODEL-ACME ENGINE in units from 1 to 50 Horse Power.

Write for Catalogue E

THE AUTOMATIC FURNACE COMPANY
DAYTON, OHIO

FRANK H. MILHAM, *President* C. A. FOX, *Secretary and Treasurer*
NOAH BRYANT, *Vice-President* C. A. HUBBARD, *Manager of Sales*
JAMES H. WRIGHT, *Assistant to President*

Bryant Paper Company

Kalamazoo, Michigan

• • •

Daily Capacity
200 Tons Book Paper
50 Tons Coated Papers

• • •

BRYANT DIVISION
   Super-Calendered and Machine Finish Book Papers

SUPERIOR DIVISION
   Silverleaf   Onion Skin   MF Book

MILHAM DIVISION
   British Opaque   English Finish Opacity

IMPERIAL DIVISION
   Silverleaf Coated Bond and Surface Coated Papers

• • •

Specialties in Light Weight for Mail Order Catalogues

Steam. Bond, White and Colored; M. F. and S. C. Book; Cover, Envelope, Label, Lithograph, Railroad Manila, Mimeograph and Writing. 300,000 lbs. 24 hours. PULP MILL. Two mills. CHEMICAL FIBRE MILL. S. P., at mill. Thirteen Digesters; four Wet Machines; one 96-inch Cylinder. Steam. Soda Fibre. 200,000 lbs. 24 hours. CLARION SULPHITE MILL No. 1. S. P., at mill. Four Digesters; two Wet Machines. Steam. Bleached Sulphite. 190,000 lbs. 24 hours

LANCASTER—Lancaster Co.

Pop. 41,459. On P.; P. & R. RR. M. O. and Tel. office; Adams and U. S. Ex.

CONSUMERS' BOX BOARD AND PAPER CO. Formerly Lancaster Paper Co., Inc. P. O., Lititz, Pa. (H. J. Pierson, Pres. and Gen. Mgr.; C. B. Risser, Treas.; J. F. Stone, Sec.) S. P., Lancaster. Three 650-lb. Beating and two 650-lb. Washing and one Jordan engines; one 72-inch Cylinder. Widest trimmed sheet, 66 inches. Water and Steam. Tissue. 20,000 lbs. 24 hours.

LANSDOWNE—Delaware Co.

GARRETT, EDWIN T. (Elmer E. Garrett, Pres.; Casper S. Garrett, Vice-Pres.; Harvey Garrett, Sec., Treas. and Gen. Mgr.) DARBY MILL. S. P., Lansdowne Station, ½ mile. One 600-lb. and one 1000-lb. Umpherstons, one 500-lb. and one 800-lb. Beating engines; one 54-inch Cylinder. Water and Steam. Tissue Manila and Railroad Copying. 4000 lbs. 24 hours.

LATROBE—Westmoreland Co.

Pop. 8,000. On Penn. RR. M. O. and Tel. office; Adams Ex.

BARRETT CO., Successors to Peters Paper Co. (William Hamlin Childs, Pres.; T. M. Rianhart, Vice-Pres.; W. N. McIlravy, Vice-Pres.; John C. Runkle, Vice-Pres.; R. P. Perry, Vice-Pres.; E. J. Steer, Sec. and Treas.; J. J. Murphy, Supt.; W. A. Forman, Mgr. Paper Mill Div., 17 Battery Pl., New York.) S. P., at mill. Twenty 100-lb. Beating and three Jordan engines; two Cylinders. Widest trimmed sheets, 74 and 84 inches. Steam. Carpet Lining, Roofing and Sheathing. 100,000 lbs. 24 hours.

LITITZ—Lancaster Co.

Pop. 1,637. On W. & C. Br. P. & R. and L. & L. E. RR. M. O. and Tel. office; U. S. Ex.

CONSUMERS' BOX BOARD AND PAPER CO. (H. J. Pierson, Pres. and Gen. Mgr.; C. B. Risser, Treas.; J. F. Stoner, Sec.; H. J. Pierson, Gen. Mgr.) Two 84-inch Cylinder Machines. Widest trimmed sheet, 75 inches. Tissues in Rolls.

LOCK HAVEN—Clinton Co.

Pop. 8,210. On P. & E. Div. of P. RR. M. O. and Tel. office; Adams Ex.

NEW YORK AND PENNSYLVANIA CO. New York office, 200 Fifth Avenue. (A. G. Paine, Jr., Pres.; Robert Wetherill, First Vice-Pres.; A. G. Paine, 3d, Second Vice-Pres. and Gen. Mgr.; M. B. Sloat, Sec. and Treas.; G. E. Paine, Asst. Sec. and Treas.; C. A. Clough, Gen. Sales Mgr.) Two mills. LOCK HAVEN MILLS. S. P., at mills. Seventeen 1200-lb. Beaters and nine Jordans; one 72-inch, one 86-inch, one 92-inch and one

Lombard's English Newcastle Pulp Stones

Pennsylvania

110-inch Fourdriniers; one 62-inch and one 72-inch Cylinders. Widest trimmed sheet, 102 inches. Water and Steam. Kraft, Bag, Pure Soda Express and Fibre Papers. Hardware, Pressboard, Drug, Parchment, Cover and Specialties. 170,000 lbs. 24 hours. PULP MILL. LOCK HAVEN MILLS. S. P., at mills. Twelve Digesters; three Wet Machines. Water and Steam. Sulphate and Soda Pulp. 190,000 lbs. 24 hours.

LYNDELL—Chester Co.

Pop. 50. On Penn. RR. Tel. and Ex., Glen Moore; nearest bank, Downingtown.

MUIR BOARD CO., INC., successor to Lyndell Mill. (W. E. Muir, Pres., Treas. and Supt.) S. P., Lyndell. One 400-lb. and one 600-lb. Beating and one Jordan engines; one 68-inch Wet Machine. Widest trimmed sheet, 66 inches. Width of Super-Calenders, 37 inches. Steam. Leather, Counter, Friction, Pattern and Fibre Specialties. 8,000 lbs. 24 hours.

MODENA—Chester Co.

Pop. 126. On Phila. & Reading RR. Tel.; nearest bank, Coatesville, 2 miles; Am. Ex.

MEGARGEE PAPER MILLS. (M. B. Megargee Pres.; A. F. Leonhard, Vice-Pres.; M. F. Glessner, Sec. and Treas.) P. O. address, at mill. S. P., at mill. Fifteen 1000-lb. Beating, three 500-lb. and ten 2000-lb. Washing and Beating and four Jordan engines; ten Rotary Boilers; three 72-inch and one 80-inch Fourdrinier Machines. Widest trimmed sheets, 64 and 72 inches. Electricity and Steam. Rag Waterleaf for Fibre and Parchmentising. 60,000 lbs. 24 hours.

MONONGAHELA—Washington Co.

On P. RR. and P. & L. E. RR. Adams and Am. Ex.

UNION PAPER MILL CO. (C. E. Outterson, Pres.; F. W. Brautigam, Vice-Pres.; W. R. Lane, Sec. and Treas.) S. P., at mill. Two 800-lb. and two 1200-lb. Beating engines; one Rotary Boiler; one Two Cylinder Machine. Widest trimmed sheet, 52 inches. Electricity and Steam. Kraft and Colors. 10,000 lbs. 24 hours.

MOUNT HOLLY SPRINGS—Cumberland Co.

Pop. 1325. On Philadelphia & Reading RR. M. O. and Tel. and Ex.

KITZMILLER & BRO., S. M. Office, Shippensburg, Pa. S. P., at mill. UPPER MILL. Two 600-lb., two 1000-lb. and one Jordan engines; one 64-inch Fourdrinier. Water and Steam. Writing. 5000 lbs. 24 hours. (Idle.)

MT. HOLLY PAPER MILLS, INC. Boston office, 17 Tremont place. (Frank Locke, Pres.; H. T. Maynard, Vice-Pres.; H. A. G. Locke, Treas.) LOWER MILL. S. P., at mill. Three 1200-lb. Beaters and two 1000-lb. Washers; one 64-inch and one 82-inch Fourdrinier. Width of Super-Calenders, 32 inches; Platers, 36 and 42 inches. Water and Steam. High Grade Loft Dried and Tub Sized Bonds, Ledgers, etc. 10,000 24 hours. August 28, 1918. Installing additional beaters and washers.)

NEW CASTLE—Lawrence Co.

NEW CASTLE PAPER MILLS, successor to Dilworth Paper Co. (George H. Bollinger, Pres.; B. F. Butler, Vice-Pres.; C. C. Duff, Sec.; John Elder, Treas.) S. P., at mill. Four 750-lb. and two 1000-lb. Beating and one

PRESS ROLLS Maple and Gum White Wood Felt Rolls — J. W. HEWITT MACHINE CO. Neenah, Wis.

Jordan engines; one 62-inch Cylinder. Widest trimmed sheet, 60 inches. Water and Steam. Glazed and Calendered Rope Express. Kraft (50-lb. and heavier). 16,000 lbs. 24 hours.

NEW HOPE—Bucks Co.

Pop. 1,250. On P. & R. RR. M. O. and Tel. office; bank, New Hope, Pa.

UNION MILLS PAPER MANUFACTURING CO. (Ferdinand W. Roebling, Pres.; J. Parker Borden, Sec. and Treas.; Daniel B. Oblinger, Supt.) UNION MILLS. S. P., at mill. Eleven 600-lb., one Claflin Continuous Beating and one Jordan engines; one 62-inch Double and one 84-inch Three Cylinders. Widest trimmed sheet, 79 inches. Water and Steam. No. 1 Manila Rope, Insulating Sack and Rope Specialties. 24,000 lbs. 24 hours.

NORRISTOWN—Montgomery Co.

Pop. 28,500. On Schuylkill Div. Penn. and Phila. & Reading, Germantown & Norristown Div. P. & R. RR. Tel. and M. O.; Adams and U. S. Ex.

NORRISTOWN MAGNESIA AND ASBESTOS CO. (Dr. J. K. Weaver, Pres.; H. B. Tyson, Vice-Pres.; Chas. H. Shaw, Sec.; M. E. White, Treas.; R. E. Romberger, Asst. Treas.; C. M. Stokes, Sales Mgr.; A. K. Burgstresser, Supt.) Three Beaters; one 40-inch Machine; also one Mill Board Machine. Asbestos and Wool Felt. 24,000 lbs. 24 hours.

NORTH WATER GAP—Monroe Co.

Pop. 200. On D., L. & W. and N. Y., S. & W. RR.; Freight and Ex., North Water Gap. Tel., Delaware Water Gap, and nearest bank, Stroudsburg, 3 miles; Wells Fargo Ex.

ANALOMINK PAPER CO. (R. L. Ahles, Pres.; W. L. Andre, Vice-Pres.; Layton M. Nauman, Treas.; K. R. Platt, Sec.; C. Bartron.) S. P., sidings at mill. Five 1000-lb. Beating and two Jordan engines; one 52-inch and one 76-inch Fourdriniers. Widest trimmed sheet, 68 inches. Water, Steam and Electricity. Manila, Fibre and Colored Specialties. 40,000 lbs. 24 hours. PULP MILL. S. P., at mill. Two Grinders; one Digester; two Wet Machines. Water, Electricity and Steam. Ground Wood, 20,000 lbs.; Sulphite Fibre, 12,000 lbs. 24 hours.

NOTTINGHAM—Chester Co.

Pop. 150. On C. Div. P., W. & B. R. RR. M. O. and Tel. office; nearest bank, Oxford, 4 miles; Adams Ex.

GRAVES, W. L. SILVERMERE MILL. S. P., Nottingham Station, 1⅔ miles. (Mill dismantled and out of business.)

OAKMONT—Allegheny Co.

Pop. 4,000. On Buffalo & Allegheny Valley Div. P. RR. Tel., M. O. and Ex.

COLUMBIA PAPER MILLS CO. (Francis Tinker, Pres.; Uriah W. Tinker, Treas.; E. G. Harvey, Supt.) Five 1200-lb. Beating engines; one 76-inch Sandy Hill Paper Machine. Widest trimmed sheet, 72 inches. Electricity and Steam. Manila Rope Papers for Cement, Lime, Plaster, Coke and Lamp Black Bags, etc. 10,000 lbs. 24 hours.

PENNSBURG—Montgomery Co.

Pop. 1,032. On P. Br. P. & R. RR. M. O. and Tel. office; U. S. Ex.

PERKIOMEN PAPER CO. (Dr. Chas. Q. Hillegass, Pres. and Treas.; Foster C. Hillegass, Sec.; Charles Seasholtz, Supt.) PERKIOMEN PAPER

Lombard's English Newcastle Pulp Stones

Pennsylvania

MILL. S. P., at mill. Two 800-lb. Beating engines and one Jordan. One 66-inch Wet Machine. Widest trimmed sheet, 65 inches. Steam. Binder, Trunk and Box Boards. 12,000 to 16,000 lbs. 24 hours.

PHILADELPHIA—Philadelphia Co.

BAEDER, ADAMSON & CO. RIVERSIDE MILL. S. P., Delaware River and Allegheny Ave. Eight Beating engines and Jordans. Two double Cylinders. Steam. All Rope Manila for Sand Paper. Rope and Jute for Cement and Lime Sacks.

DILL & COLLINS CO. 140 North 6th Street, Philadelphia. (Grellet Collins, Pres.; Howard W. Taylor, Vice-Pres. and Mill Mgr.; D. W. Bond, Treas.; Frederick E. Hastings, Sec.; John Bingham, Mill Supt.) DELAWARE PAPER MILL. Location, Tioga and Richmond Streets. S. P., Tioga Street Station, opposite Penna. R.R.; Port Richmond on P. & R. and B. & O. R.R. Nineteen 1000-lb. Beating and five Jordan engines; five Washers and six Rotaries; one 76-inch, two 86-inch, one 96-inch and one 113-inch Fourdriniers. Widest trimmed sheets, 66 inches, 76 inches, 86 inches and 107 inches. Steam. Book and Coated Papers. 100,000 lbs. 24 hours. PULP MILL. Nine Digesters; one 104-inch Cylinder for Dry Soda Pulp; three Wet Machines. Steam. Soda Fibre. 90,000 lbs. 24 hours. FLAT ROCK MILL. *High Grade Machine Finish, English Finish, Music, Super Calendered Book and Surface Coated Papers for Printing from Half-tone Engravings, Color Plates, Aluminum Offset and Lithographic Stone, Bonds, Writing, Envelope and Mimeograph.*

HAMILTON, W. C., & SONS, INC. (Charles L. Hamilton, Pres. and Gen. Mgr.; Wilbur F. Hamilton, Vice-Pres. and Treas.; Russell D. Hamilton, Sec.) Address, Wm. Penn P. O., Montgomery Co. RIVERSIDE MILLS. S. P., Lafayette Station. Four 1000-lb., seven 2000-lb. Beating and four Refining engines; one 82-inch, one 86-inch, one 100-inch and one 116-inch Fourdriniers. Widest trimmed sheets, 72, 78, 88 and 100 inches. Width of Super-Calenders, 36, 39 and 45 inches. Moore & White Screens. Steam. Book, Tablet, Writing, Bond and Offset. ·80,000 lbs. 24 hours. PULP MILL. Six Digesters; two Wet Machines. Steam. Soda Fibre. 40,000 lbs. 24 hours.

LANG PAPER CO., JOHN. (E. H. Morris, Pres.; Fred. Geiger, Treas. and Gen. Mgr.) Twenty-fourth and Vine streets. PARK PAPER MILLS. Thirty-one 1000-lb. Beating engines; four Jordans; one 84-inch Three Cylinder, two 84-inch Cylinders, one 124-inch Cylinder. Steam. Roofing, Saturating and Deadening Felt. 260,000 lbs. 24 hours.

McDOWELL PAPER MILLS. (Charles McDowell.) Office and Mills, Manayunk, Philadelphia, Pa. Two mills. S. P., Pencoyd, Pa. (Venice Branch, care of P. & R. Ry. Co.) Both mills on same siding. HERCULES MILL NO. 1. Five 1000-lb. Beating, three 1000-lb. Washing and Beating, and one Jordan and one Marshall Refining engine. One 90-inch Special Fourdrinier. (Trims 72 to 78 inches.) Water and Steam. Heavy and Light Weight, Colored Fibre, Express, Specialties in Colors of all

Ground Pulp & Sulphite Fibre Mill Machinery — OUR SPECIALTY | **CARTHAGE MACHINE CO.** CARTHAGE, N. Y.

Kinds, Rough and Glazed Finish for Finishers, Textile, Leather and General Wrapping, Glassine, Greaseproof, Parchment and Covers. 20,000 lbs. 24 hours. HERCULES MILL No. 2. One 1000-lb. and three 2000-lb. Beating and Washing engines, two Jordan Refining engines; one 114-inch Special Fourdrinier (trims 96 to 105 inches.) Widest sheet Super Calendered, 53 inches. Water, Steam and Hydro-Electric. Hercules Fibre, Drug Bond, Soft White Drug, Hercules Grade for Writing, Envelope, Coating, Waxing, Bag, M. F. and Super Calendered Book, Catalogue, French Folio, Tracing, Light and Heavy Weight Specialties of all kinds. 35,000 lbs. 24 hours. Three Special Washers and Bleachers, one Rotary boiler and 72-inch Wet Machine, in separate building, used to supply stock to both mills; one Hydraulic Baling Press for Export.

MOORHOUSE PAPER CO., R. T. Post Office Address, Bridge and Thompson Streets, Bridesburg, Philadelphia. (R. I. Moorhouse, Pres.; R. W. Moorhouse, Sec., Treas. and Supt.) BRIDESBURG MILL. S. P., at mill. Nine 500-lb., six 1600-lb. Beating and three Jordan engines; one 66-inch, one 72-inch and one 86-inch Fourdriniers. Widest trimmed sheet, 78 inches. Width of Super Calenders, 83 inches. 36-inch, 48-inch, 60-inch and 100-inch Rewinders. Steam. White Colored Machine-Finished and Super Calendered Book, Colored Book Covers, Melton Box Covering, Manila, Poster, Wrappings, Cop Tube, Drug, Macaroni, Pattern, Ticket, Tobacco and Colored Specialties. 40,000 lbs. 24 hours. *A complete Stock of Colored Covers, Posters and Manilas always ready for prompt shipment.*

NIXON PAPER CO., MARTIN & WILLIAM H. (Dill & Collins Co., Successors.) FLAT ROCK MILLS. Phila. & Reading R.R. Twenty 1200-lb. Beaters and six Jordan engines; four Fourdriniers, 114-inch, 106-inch, 90-inch and 68-inch. Width of Super-Calenders, 42 and 60 inches. M. F. and S. and S. C. Book, English Finish, Mimeograph, Sulphite Bonds and Writings, White and Tints. Steam. 100,000 lbs. 24 hours.

PHILADELPHIA PAPER MANUFACTURING CO. (John Jacobs, Jr., Pres.; G. A. Bisler, Vice-Pres.; Edward J. Stoeser, Sec. and Treas.) Post Office Address, Manayunk. S. P., Pencoyd, Pa. Twenty-six Beating and eighteen Jordan engines; five Board Machines. Widest trimmed sheets, 80, 84, 114, 119 and 132 inches. Steam. Box Boards. 600,000 lbs. 24 hours. *News, Chip, Jute, Fibre, News Lined, White Vat Lined, Manila Lined Chip, Container Boards and Specialties.*

PITTSTON—Lucerne Co.

Pop. 12,556. On L. V.; L. & B. Branch of D., L. & W.; L. & S. Branch of C. N. J.; D. & H.; E. & W. V. RR. M. O. and Tel. office; Ad., W. F. & Co., U. S. & Nat. Ex.

KENYON PAPER CORP. (Robert McAllister Lloyd, Pres.; Jacob C. Kenyon, Vice-Pres. and Mgr.; H. O. Berg, Sec and Treas.) One 1000-lb. and two 1500-lb. Beating and one Jordan Refining engines; one 104-inch Yankee Fourdrinier. Widest trimmed sheet, 96 inches. Electricity. White and Colored Tissue. 8000 lbs. 24 hours.

WYOMING VALLEY PAPER MILL. New York Office, 61 Beekman Street. Four 1000-lb. Beating and two Refining engines; one Cylinder and one Fourdrinier. Steam. Paper Towels and Toilet Paper, Crepe Specialties. 24,000 lbs. 24 hours.

Pennsylvania

RAUBSVILLE—Northampton Co.

Pop. 100. On Delaware River, near Easton Pa. M. O. office; Tel., Ex. and nearest bank at Easton. Am., Adams and Wells Fargo & Co. Ex.

LEHIGH PAPER MILLS, INC. New York Office, 41 Park Row. (N. A. Merritt, Pres.; J. C. Sheehy, Sec. and Treas.) S. P., at Carpenterville, N. J. Two 450-lb., three 600-lb., one 1000-lb. Downingtown Beating and two Jordan engines; two Washers and two Rotaries; one 66-inch and one 110-inch Cylinder. Widest trimmed sheets, 58 inches and 102 inches. Steam. Crepe Papers, 18 lbs. and upward; Paper Towels, Toilet Paper and Furniture Paper. 20,000 lbs. 24 hours.

READING—Berks Co.

Pop. 100,000. On P. & R.; W. & C.; and S. V. Div. of P. RR. M. O. and Tel. office; U. S. and Adams Ex.

ACME PAPER CO. P. O. Address, Reading, Berks Co., Pa. S. P., Reading. (W. G. Shortess, Pres.; L. C. Eckhardt, Sec.; S. B. Fleming, Treas.; W. G. Kissinger, Supt.) Three 600-lb. Beating and two Refining engines; one 48-inch Four Cylinder. Widest trimmed sheet, 41 inches. Water and Steam. Box Board, Container Board and Specialties. 18,000 lbs. 24 hours.

READING PAPER MILLS. (W. Griscom Coxe, Pres.; James M. Miller, Vice-Pres. and Gen. Mgr.; Heber Y. Yost, Sec. and Treas.) Main Office, Reading, Pa.; Sales Office, 308 Chestnut Street, Philadelphia, Pa. Three mills. READING MILL. Two 1200-lb. Umpherston and one 1000-lb. Beaters, two 1200-lb. Washing engines and one Jordan engine; one 82-inch Fourdrinier. Steam. Book, Lithograph, Map and Plate. 12,000 lbs. 24 hours. PACKERACK MILL. Five 2000-lb. Beating and one Jordan engines; one 100-inch Fourdrinier. Steam and Electricity. Book, Lithograph and Coated. Width of Super Calenders, 50 inches. Widest trimmed sheet, 92 inches. 20,000 lbs. 24 hours. TULPEHOCKEN MILL. S. P., Reading, ½ mile. Three 500-lb., two 850-lb. and two 1000-lb. Beating and two Refining engines; one 72-inch Fourdrinier. Water and Steam. Manila and Rope. 10,000 lbs. 24 hours. *We make a specialty of Lithograph, Map, Plate, Deckel Edge Water Marked and Coated Papers. Also Rope Papers for Sandpaper Purposes.*

ROARING SPRING—Blair Co.

Pop. 3,000. On M. C. Branch of Penn. RR. M. O. and Tel. office; Adams Ex.

D. M. BARE PAPER CO., THE. (E. G. Bobb, Pres.; D. M. Bare, Vice-Pres.; L. F. Garber, Treas.; Clarence Hair, Sec.) ROARING SPRING MILL. S. P., siding to mill. Twelve 1000-lb. and six Jordan engines; one 76-inch, one 80-inch and one 86-inch Fourdriniers. Width of Super-Calenders, 36, 40 and 60 inches. Widest trimmed sheet, 60 inches. Steam. Super-Calendered and Machine Finished Book, Lithograph, White Flats and Mimeograph. 60,000 lbs. 24 hours. PULP MILL. S. P., at mill. Eight Digesters; one 100-inch Wet Machine. Steam. Soda Fibre. 45,000 lbs. 24 hours.

SHEEDER—Chester Co.

On P. & R. RR. Tel. and Ex. offices, Kimberton; M. O. and nearest bank, Spring City. 6½ miles.

SHEEDER, A. M. SHEEDER'S PAPER MILL. (Mill dismantled.)

SPRING GROVE—York Co.

Pop. 1,005. Balt. Div. P. RR. and B. & H. Div. of W. M. RR. M. O. and Tel. offices; two banks; Adams and Am. Ex.

GLATFELTER, P. H., CO. (W. L. Glatfelter, Pres.; C. E. Moul, Vice-Pres. and Sec.; P. H. Glatfelter, Treas.; M. J. Kelly, Supt.) SPRING GROVE PAPER MILLS. S. P., Spring Grove. Twelve 1200-lb. Beating and seven Refining engines; one 62-inch, one 82-inch, one 90-inch and one 104-inch Fourdriniers. Width of Super Calenders, 44, 54, 68 and 70 inches. Widest trimmed sheet, 93 inches. Water and Steam. Machine Finished and Super-Calendered Book and Writing, Label, Bond and Blank Book Papers. 100,000 lbs. 24 hours. PULP MILL. Eighteen Digesters. Steam. Soda Fibre. 75,000 lbs. 24 hours. *S. S. & C. and M. F. Book, Varnish Label Paper, Writing and Music Paper; Bond, Mimeograph and Drawing Paper; Blank Book Papers a Specialty.*

SWARTHMORE—Delaware Co.

Pop. 1,800. On C. Div. P., B. & W. RR. Branch of Penn. RR. M. O., Tel. office and Adams Ex.

PHILADELPHIA WAX PAPER CO. (W. A. O. Webber, Pres.; S. M. Ramsey, Vice-Pres.; J. F. Auer, Treas.; J. L. Kohl, Sec.) FRANKLIN PAPER MILLS. S. P., Swarthmore, 1½ miles. One 500-lb. and two 900-lb. Beaters and two Jordans; two 1000-lb. and one 1500-lb. Washers and two Rotary boilers. One 90-inch Fourdrinier. Widest trimmed sheet, 80 inches. Steam and Water. Manifold, Greaseproof. 8000 lbs. 24 hours.

TARENTUM—Allegheny Co.

Pop. 7,414. On W. P. Div. P. RR. M. O. and Tel. office; Adams Ex.

TARENTUM PAPER MILLS. (F. S. Willock, Pres.; E. A. Jones, Sec. and Treas.; John R. Long, Gen. Supt.) Office, 2d Nat. Bank Bldg., Pittsburg. TARENTUM PAPER MILLS. S. P., Tarentum. Twenty-three Beating and five Refining engines; one 70-inch Double and one 96-inch Three Cylinder Machines, and one 114-inch Fourdrinier. Widest trimmed sheet, 104 inches. Steam. Express and Rope Wrapping Papers, Insulating and Rope Sack Papers, Paper Flour, Lime and Cement Sacks. 75,000 lbs. 24 hours.

TYRONE—Blair Co.

Pop. 8,000. On Middle Division P. RR. M. O. and Tel. office. Adams Ex.

WEST VIRGINIA PULP AND PAPER CO. Office, 200 Fifth avenue, New York. Western Sales Office, 782 Sherman street, Chicago. (John G. Luke, Pres.; David L. Luke, Vice-Pres.; Thomas Luke, Vice-Pres.; Adam K. Luke, Treas.; Chas. A. Cass, Sec.; Jno. G. Anderson, Res. Mgr.) TYRONE MILL. Ten 1000-lb. and eight 2000-lb. Beating and four Refining engines; one 80-inch, one 86-inch, one 96-inch and one 114-inch Fourdriniers. Widest trimmed sheet, 102 inches. Width of Super-Calenders, 42, 54, 72, 86 and 108 inches. Union Screens. Steam. Super Calendered and Machine Finished Book, Lithograph and Varnish Label, White Writing, Blank Book, Tablet. 110,000 lbs. 24 hours. PULP MILL. Ten Digesters; one 100-inch Wet Machine. Steam. Bleached Soda Fibre. 80,000 lbs. 24 hours.

Lombard's English Newcastle Pulp Stones

200 *Pennsylvania*

UPPER DARBY—Delaware Co.

Pop. 8,831. One mile from Philadelphia. M. O. office Upper Darby; Tel. office, Philadelphia. and Ex., Millbourn Mills, 63d and Market Sts., Philadelphia, ¼ mile. Nearest bank, Philadelphia.

KEYSTONE PAPER MILLS CO. (David Lindsay, Pres.; W. Allan Lindsay, Vice-Pres.; J. Horace Lindsay, Treas.; David Lindsay, Jr., Sec.) KEYSTONE MILL. R. R. Siding into mill. One 800-lb. and two 1000-lb. Umpherstons, two 1500-lb. and one 2000-lb. Washing and one Jordan engines; three Rotaries; one 86-inch Fourdrinier. Widest trimmed sheet, 72 inches. Steam. Waterleaf for Vulcanized Fibre and Rag Specialties. 20,000 lbs. 24 hours.

WILLIAMSBURG—Blair Co.

Pop. 1,500. On Middle Div. Petersburg Branch P. RR. M. O. and Tel. Adams Ex.

WEST VIRGINIA PULP & PAPER CO. New York office, 200 Fifth avenue. (John G. Luke, Pres.; David L. Luke, Vice-Pres.; Thomas Luke, Vice-Pres.; Adam K. Luke, Treas.; Chas. A. Cass, Sec.) WILLIAMSBURG MILL. Ten 1000-lb. and two 2000-lb. Beaters and two Refining engines; one 112-inch and one 126-inch Fourdriniers. Widest trimmed sheet, 116 inches. Width of Super-Calenders, up to 76 inches. Steam and Electricity. Writing, Book and Specialties. 90,000 lbs. 24 hours. PULP MILL. Four Digesters. Steam. Bleached Soda Fibre. 70,000 lbs. 24 hours.

WILLISTOWN INN—Chester Co.

Pop. 35. On P. & W. C. electric RR. M. O. and Ex. office, Cheyney, 4 miles; Tel. and nearest bank, West Chester, 6 miles.

CULLEN, LEWIS C. P. O. Address, West Chester, Route B. FOREST MILL. S. P., Cheyney, 4 miles. Three 400-lb. Beating engines; one 44-inch Cylinder. Widest trimmed sheet, 36 inches. Water and Steam. Sheathing, Carpet Lining, Plain and Corrugated Deadening Felt, and Building. 6000 lbs. 24 hours. (Idle.)

YORK—York Co.

Pop. 50,000. On Penn.; W. M. RR. M. O. and Tel. office; Adams Ex.

CERTAIN-TEED PRODUCTS CORPORATION, Successor to General Roofing Mfg. Co. General Offices, Boatmen's Bank Bldg. (Geo. M. Brown, Pres.; S. E. Allison, Vice-Pres.; J. S. Porter, Vice-Pres.; A. Whittemore, Vice-Pres.; J. C. Collins, Vice-Pres.; R. M. Nelson, Sec.-Treas.; C. J. Stovel, Mgr.) S. P., York. Sixteen 1000-lb. Beating and three Refining engines; one 120-inch Four Cylinder. Widest trimmed sheet, 108 inches. Electricity and Steam. Roofing, Saturating Felts, Deadening Felt, Building Paper, Carpet Lining, Insulating Paper and Asphalt and Coal Tar Products. 90,000 lbs. 24 hours. *Roofing factory in connection.*

SCHMIDT & AULT PAPER CO. (John C. Schmidt, Pres.; Henry D. Schmidt, Sec. and Treas.; Robt. A. G. Ault, Gen. Mgr.; G. M. Wetmore, Sales Mgr.; Thos. F. Heberly, Mill Supt.) CODORUS MILL. S. P, at mill. Three 2000-lb., six 1500-lb., two 1000-lb. and one 600-lb. Beating engines, and four Jordan engines; one 48-inch Cylinder. Widest trim, 40 inches; minimum weight 90 lbs.; maximum weight 230 lbs. One 72-inch Fourdrinier. Widest trim, 64 inches; minimum weight, 40 lbs.; maximum, 120 lbs. One 90-inch Fourdrinier. Widest trim, 80 inches; minimum weight, 40 lbs.; maximum, 120 lbs. One 90-inch Cylinder. Widest trim, 80 inches; minimum caliper, .011; maximum, .036. Water, Steam and Electricity. Bogus, Box and Barrel Layers, Building, Butchers' Manila, Card Middles, Carpet Lining (plain and corrugated), Chip Board (light weight) for Backing Corrugated Board, Crepe Sheathing (heavy), Crinkled Sheathing (heavy), News, Bogus, Drawing, Duplex Board, Ham, Black Hardware, Heavy Wrapper, Indented Packing, Macaroni, Mill Wrappers, News Board, Paper Stock Board, Black and Green Tailors' Pattern, Rag Wrapping, Screenings, Sheathing, Ice Wrappers, Car Lining and Specialties. 120,000 lbs. 24 hours.

SPRINGETS MILLS, THE. (L. A. Bupp, Owner and Mgr.; W. K. Gotwalt, Supt.) S. P., York. Two Downington and four 1000-lb. Noble & Wood Beaters. Three Jordans and two Washers. One Three Cylinder Machine. Widest trimmed sheet, 74 inches. Steam. Building, Chip, Plaster Board, Felt and Specialties. 36,000 to 40,000 lbs. 24 hours.

YORK PAPER MFG. CO. (Carl Lafean, Mgr.) S. P., at mill. Four 1000-lb. Beating engines. One 84-inch Three Cylinder. Widest trimmed sheet, 72 inches. Steam. Sheathing. 30,000 lbs. 24 hours.

YORK HAVEN—York Co.

Pop. 824. On N. C. RR. Tel. office; M. O. and nearest bank, York, 12 miles; Adams Ex.

YORK HAVEN PAPER CO., THE. (Henry W. Stokes, Pres.; Waldo R. Smith, Treas.) Land Title Building, Philadelphia. YORK HAVEN PAPER MILL. Seven 1500-lb. Beating and three Jordan engines; one 72-inch, one 94-inch and one 104-inch Fourdriniers. Widest trimmed sheet, 96 inches. Water and Steam. Colored Fibre, Light and Dark Express. *Green Band Fibre.* 140,000 lbs. 24 hours. PULP MILL. Two Grinders; seven Digesters; six 72-inch Wet machines. Water. Ground Wood (dry), 20,000 lbs.; Sulphite Fibre (dry), 100,000 lbs. 24 hours.

RHODE ISLAND.
PHILLIPSDALE.

Pop. 700. On Worcester Div. N. Y., N. H. & H. RR. M. O. and Tel., Ex. and bank, Providence, 3 miles.

BIRD & SON, INC. Main Office, East Walpole, Mass.—Chas. S. Bird, Pres.; Philip Allen, Vice-Pres.; H. H. Miller, Sec.-Treas.; George R. Wyman, Mfg. Mgr.; T. G. Henderson, Supt.) S. P., at mill. One 120-inch Machine. Steam. Felt and Sheathing. 100,000 lbs. 24 hours.

SOUTH CAROLINA.
HARTSVILLE—Darlington Co.

Pop. 2,000. On A. Coast Line and C. A. & W. RR. M. O. and Tel. office; Southern Ex.

CAROLINA FIBRE CO. (J. L. Coker, Pres.; J. L. Coker, Jr., Vice-Pres.; P. H. Rogers, Jr., Sec. and Treas.) S. P., at mill. Four 1500-lb.

and two 800-lb. Beating and two Refining engines; one 90-inch Fourdrinier, one 60-inch Fourdrinier and one 72-inch Cylinder. Widest trimmed sheets, 80 inches. Steam and Water. Water Finish Fibre. 50,000 lbs. 24 hours. PULP MILL. S. P., at mill. Two Grinders, three Digesters; two 72-inch Wet Machines. Water and Steam. Ground Wood (dry), 18,000 lbs.; Sulphite Fibre, 30,000 lbs. 24 hours.

TENNESSEE.

CHATTANOOGA—Hamilton Co.

Pop. 44,604. On Southern; Alabama Great Southern; Western and Atlantic; Tennessee, Alabama and Georgia, and Central of Georgia RR. M. O.; Tel.; Bank. So. and Adams Ex.

TENNESSEE PAPER MILLS, INC. (John Stagmaier, Pres.; A. M. Sheperd, Vice-Pres. and Gen. Mgr.; J. S. Fletcher, Sec.; John G. Kain, Treas.; L. T. Murphy, Supt.) Six 1500-lb. Beaters, four Refining engines and four Rotary boilers. One 132-inch Five Cylinder. Widest trimmed sheet, 124 inches. Folding Box Boards. 100,000 lbs. 24 hours.

KINGSPORT—Sullivan Co.—PULP MILL.

Pop. 10,000. On C., C. & O. Ry. M. O., Tel and Ex.

KINGSPORT PULP CORPORATION. (Royal B. Embree, Pres.; J. C. Stone, Vice-Pres.; Edward C. Bailly, Sec. and Treas.) Ten Digesters; one 120-inch Dry Machine. Steam. Soda Fibre. 120,000 lbs. 24 hours.

TEXAS.

DALLAS—Dallas Co.

On G. C. & S. F. RR. M. O., Tel., Ex. and nearest bank, Dallas, 1½ miles.

FLEMING, JOHN G., & SONS. (Walter L. and E. T.) OAK CLIFF PAPER MILL. P. O. address, Station A, Dallas. S. P., at mill. Two 1000-lb., one 1250-lb. and one 1500-lb. Beating and one Jordan engines; one 72-inch Double Cylinder. Widest trimmed sheet, 68 inches. Steam. Butchers' Manila, No. 2 Manila, Rag Wrapping, Roofing and Sheathing. 28,000 lbs. 24 hours.

ORANGE—Orange Co.

Pop. 6,000. On T. & N. O. Div. So. Pac. and O. & N. W. Div. of Frisco RR. M. O. and Tel. Wells Fargo & Co. and Am. Ex.

YELLOW PINE PAPER MILL CO. (W. H. Stark, Pres.; L. Miller, Vice-Pres.; R. A. Moore, Vice-Pres.; F. H. Farwell, Sec.-Treas.; Geo. S. Holmes, Gen. Mgr.) YELLOW PINE PAPER MILL. S. P., at mill. Eight 1200-lb. and two 2000-lb. Beating and five Refining engines; one 64-inch and one 108-inch Fourdriniers. Widest trimmed sheet, 96 inches. Steam and Electricity. Genuine Sulphate Kraft, Bag and Envelope. 60,000 lbs. 24 hours. PULP MILL. S. P., at mill. Five Digesters, two Wet Machines. Steam. Sulphate Fibre. 60,000 lbs. 24 hours.

Paper and Pulp Mills in the United States

VERMONT.

BELLOWS FALLS—Windham Co.

Pop. 4,337. On R.; F.; S.; B. & M. RR. M. O. and Tel. office; Am. Ex.

BLAKE & HIGGINS. (C. M. B., C. D. H.) S. P., at mill. Three 800-lb. engines; one 72-inch Fourdrinier. Water and Steam. Manila, 20,000 lbs. 24 hours.

CLAREMONT PAPER CO., INC., successors to Flint, Wyman & Sons Co. (F. N. McCrea, Pres. and Treas.; H. W. Beauclerk, Vice-Pres.; W. C. Dawson, Treas.; Paul Caskey, Clerk; J. A. Bothwell, Gen. Mgr.; C. H. McDuffee, Gen. Supt.; John Murphy, Local Supt.; E. P. Lindsay, Selling Agent, 229 Congress Street, Boston, Mass.) S. P., railroad, ⅛ mile. Seven 800-lb. Beating and two Jordan engines; one 62-inch and one 72-inch Harper Fourdriniers. Widest trimmed sheet, 62 inches. Water. Kraft and Fibre. 90,000 lbs. 24 hours.

INTERNATIONAL PAPER COMPANY. Office, 30 Broad street, New York. FALL MOUNTAIN MILLS. (J. E. Myers, Mgr.) S. P., at mill. Twenty-nine Beating and fourteen Refining engines; one 59-inch, one 62½-inch, one 65½-inch, one 69-inch, one 76-inch, one 94-inch, one 106-inch Cylinders; one 84-inch, one 92-inch and one 104-inch Fourdriniers. Water and Steam. Tablets, Blank Boards, Box Boards, Bristol, Card, Chip Board, Manila, Card Boards, Card Middles and Specialties. 188,000 lbs. 24 hours. PULP MILLS. FALL MOUNTAIN MILLS. Thirteen Grinders, six Digesters, thirteen Wet Machines. Water and Steam. Ground Wood, 84,000 lbs.; Sulphite Fibre, 70,000 lbs. 24 hours.

INTERNATIONAL PAPER CO., Successor to John T. Moore & Son. Office, 30 Broad Street, New York.

MOORE & THOMPSON PAPER CO. Incorporated. F. A. Moore, Pres.; F. L. Willis, 1st Vice-Pres. and Asst. Treas.; Albert C. Moore, 2nd Vice-Pres.; F. L. Thompson, Treas.) S. P., at mill. Twelve 1000-lb. Beating and four Jordan engines; one 76-inch Fourdrinier and one 90-inch Harper Fourdrinier. Widest trimmed sheet, 80 inches. Water and Steam. Manila Wrapping, Kraft, Railroad Manila, Parchment and Coating Envelope. 40,000 lbs. 24 hours.

ROBERTSON PAPER CO. (Frederick H. Babbitt, Pres.; Erwin W. Kelley, Vice-Pres.; John E. Babbitt, Treas.; Herbert T. Kelley, Sec.) Four Beating and one Jordan engines; one 92-inch (80-inch sheet) Fourdrinier. Water and Steam. Envelope, Manila Railroad and Telegraph Writing. 24,000 lbs. 24 hours. Waxing Plant of Nine Waxing Machines and New Printing Plant. Specialty: Plain and Printed Waxed Papers, Both Heavy and Light Weights, for Packers, Bakers, Confectioners, Florists, Creameries, etc. Waxed Paper Capacity. 50,000 lbs. 24 hours.

BRATTLEBORO—Windham Co.

Pop. 8,200. On Junction B. & M. with N. L. and C. V. RR. M. O. and Tel. office. Am. Ex.

VINTON, WM. H., & SON. (W. B. V.) S. P., railroad, 50 rods. Two 750-lb. Beating engines; one Rotary boiler; one 62-inch Fourdrinier.

Lombard's English Newcastle Pulp Stones

Vermont and Virginia

SHELDON SPRINGS—Franklin Co.

On Mississippi Div. C. V. RR. Tel. and M. O. office; nearest bank, St. Albans, 9 miles; Am. Ex.

MISSISQUOI PULP AND PAPER CO. (George C. Gill, Pres.; H. E. Raymond, Vice-Pres.; Archibald P. Ramage, Treas. and Gen. Mgr.) MISSISQUOI MILL. S. P., at mill. PAPER MILL. Six Beating and two Refining engines; one 99-inch Five Cylinder Machine. Widest trimmed sheet, 87 inches. Water, Electricity and Steam. White and Colored Bristol, Index Bristol, White Blanks and Specialties. 50,000 lbs. 24 hours. PULP MILL. Eight Grinders; ten Wet Machines. Water. Ground Wood. 120,000 lbs. (dry) 24 hours.

WELLS RIVER—Orange Co.

Pop. 565. On M. & W. R.; B. & M. RR. M. O. and Tel. office; Am. Ex.

ADAMS PAPER CO., INC. (H. Crabtree, Gen. Mgr.) WELLS RIVER MILLS. S. P., ½ mile. Three 1000-lb. Beating, two Jordan engines, one Rotary boiler, and one 86-inch Fourdrinier. Widest trimmed sheet, 72 inches. Water, Steam and Electricity. Manila Tissues, Kraft, Anti-Tarnish Tissues from 9 to 20 lbs. 10,000 lbs. 24 hours.

WEST DERBY—Orleans Co.—PULP MILL.

Pop. 913. Tel. and Ex. Newport.

CLYDE RIVER PULP CO. P. O. Address, Newport, Vt. (C. A. Prouty, Pres.; Ward Prouty; J. A. Prouty, Treas.; L. L. Drew, Supt.) S. P., Newport. Two 24-inch Grinders; two Wet Machines. Water and Electricity. Ground Wood (dry). 14,000 lbs. 24 hours. *Fine grade spruce tissue pulp a specialty.*

WILDER—Windsor Co.

On P. Div. of B. & M. RR. M. O.; Tel. and Ex. offices and nearest bank, White River Junction, 2 miles.

INTERNATIONAL PAPER CO. Office, 30 Broad street, New York. WILDER MILL. (F. P. Campbell, Supt.) S. P., at mill. Ten Beating, four Refining engines; one 82-inch, one 84-inch, two 97-inch Fourdriniers. Water and Steam. News. 106,000 lbs. 24 hours. PULP MILL. Twelve Grinders; six Wet Machines. Water and Steam. Ground Wood. 180,000 lbs. 24 hours.

VIRGINIA.

BIG ISLAND—Bedford Co.

Pop. 700. On C. & O. R.R. M. O. and Tel. offices; nearest bank, Big Island; Adams Ex.

BEDFORD PULP AND PAPER CO. Office, 419 Mutual Bldg., Richmond, Va. (Clarence Millhiser, Pres.; Milton E. Marcuse, Vice-Pres. and Treas.; Raymond I. Straus, Sec.; C. W. Baker, Mill Supt.) S. P., Big Island. Six 2000-lb. Beating engines; two 114-inch Fourdriniers. Widest sheet made, 105 inches. Water and Steam. Water Finish Fibres and Transfer Ticket Paper. 140,000 lbs. 24 hours. PULP MILL. Two Glen Falls Grinders; one Wet Machine. Water and Steam. Ground Wood (dry). 16,000 lbs. 24 hours.

HARDY S. FERGUSON, CONSULTING ENGINEER, 200 FIFTH AVENUE, NEW YORK CITY

PAPER, PULP AND FIBRE MILLS, WATER POWER DEVELOPMENT, DAMS, STORAGE RESERVOIRS AND OTHER HYDRAULIC STRUCTURES

PRESS ROLLS Maple and Gum White Wood Felt Rolls — J. W. HEWITT MACHINE CO. Neenah, Wis.

BRISTOL—Washington Co.—PULP MILL.
Pop. 15,000. On N. & W., V. & S. and So. Ry. M. O. and Tel.; Southern Ex.

COLUMBIAN PAPER CO. (Samuel L. Hammer, Pres.; John W. Storb, Vice-Pres.; Howard Trumbower, Sec. and Treas.; W. I. Brummer, Supt.) Office, Buena Vista, Va. S. P., at mill. Eight Digesters; six 72-inch Wet Machines; one 120-inch Cylinder. Steam. Soda Fibre. 95,000 lbs. 24 hours.

BUENA VISTA—Rockbridge Co.
Pop. 3,500. On Shenandoah Valley Div. of N. W.; James River Div. of C. & O. RR. M. O. and Tel. office; Southern Ex.

COLUMBIAN PAPER CO. (Saml. L. Hammer, Pres.; John W. Storb, Vice-Pres.; Howard Trumbower, Sec. and Treas.; P. F. Dooley, Supt.) BUENA VISTA MILL. S. P., siding at mill. Six 1000-lb. Horne Beating and two Horne Refining engines; one 92-inch and one 112-inch Four-driniers. Water and Steam. *Card and Bristol Board, Linen Finished Papeterie in White and Colors, Tablet and Flat Writing.* 50,000 lbs. 24 hours. PULP MILL. S. P., siding at mill. Six Digesters; one Wet Machine. Water and Steam. Soda Fibre. 40,000 lbs. 24 hours.

COLEMANS—Bedford Co.—PULP MILL.
Pop. 100. On J. R. Div. C. & O. RR. M. O.; nearest bank and Tel., Big Island, 4 miles; Adams Ex.

BEDFORD PULP AND PAPER CO. Office, 419 Mutual Bldg., Richmond, Va. (Clarence Millhiser, Pres.; M. E. Marcuse, Vice-Pres. and Treas.; Raymond I. Straus, Sec.; C. W. Baker, Supt.) COLEMANS MILL. S. P., at mill. Six Grinders; seven Wet Machines. Water and Steam. Ground Wood. 50,000 lbs. 24 hours.

COVINGTON—Alleghany Co.
Pop. 4,500. C. & O. RR. M. O. and Tel. office; Adams Ex.

WEST VIRGINIA PULP AND PAPER CO. Office, 200 Fifth avenue, New York. Western Sales Office, 732 Sherman street, Chicago. (John G. Luke, Pres.; David L. Luke, Vice-Pres.; Thomas Luke, Vice-Pres.; Adam K. Luke, Treas.; Chas. A. Cass, Sec.; Wm. A. Luke, Res. Mgr.) COVINGTON MILL. Twenty-six 2000-lb. Beating and eight Refining engines; one 120-inch, one 132-inch, one 136-inch and one 148-inch Fourdriniers. Widest trimmed sheet, 134 inches. Width of Super-Calenders, 48, 66, 72, 86 and 100 inches. Union Screens. Steam. Super-Calendered and Machine-finished Book, Lithograph and Varnish Label, 200,000 lbs. 24 hours. PULP MILL. Five Digesters; one 112-inch Dry and two 86-inch and one 90-inch Wet Machines. Steam. Bleached Sulphite Fibre. 240,000 lbs. 24 hours.

WEST VIRGINIA PULP PRODUCTS CO., INC. New York Office, 200 Fifth Avenue. Chicago Office, 732 Sherman Street. (David L. Luke, Pres.; Charles A. Cass, Vice-Pres.; George E. Nelson, Sec.; Adam K. Luke, Treas.) Two Digesters; eight Beaters; four Wet Machines. Steam. High Grade Fibre Board, made from Special Vegetable Fibre by Patented Process, for Shoe Counter, Innersole, Sample Case, Suit Case and Friction Board and Board Specialties. 20,000 lbs. 24 hours.

Virginia

PORTSMOUTH—Norfolk Co.

Pop. 33,190. On S. A. L. & A. C. L. M. O. and Tel. office; Adams, So. and U. S. Ex.

SOUTHERN FIBRE CO. (W. F. Harbrecht, Vice-Pres.; Fred Emmons, Sec.; Sidney Frohman, Treas.; R. R. Oliver, Supt.; Wm. Oliver, Mgr.) S. P., at mill on N. & P. Belt Line R. R. Three 1000-lb. and two 1500-lb. Beating and one Refining engines; one 60-inch Fourdrinier. Width of Super-Calenders, 80 inches. Kraft. 16,000 lbs. 24 hours. PULP MILL. S. P., at mill. Two Wet Machines; two Digesters. Kraft Pulp. 48,000 lbs. 24 hours.

RICHMOND—Henrico Co.

Pop. 146,000. On S.; C. & O.; R., F. & P.; A. C. L. and S. A. L. RR. M. O. and Tel. office; Adams and Southern Ex.

ALBEMARLE PAPER MANUFACTURING CO. (H. W. Ellerson, Pres.; James H. Anderson, Vice-Pres.; A. F. Robertson, Sec. and Treas.; J. S. Mowry, Supt.) HOLLYWOOD MILLS. S. P., Richmond. One 500-lb., two 1000-lb. Beating, one Jordan and four 1000-lb. Washing engines; two 12,000-lb. and one 5000-lb. Rotary Boilers; one 90-inch Rice, Barton & Fales Fourdrinier. Widest trimmed sheet, 80 inches. Union Screens. Water, Steam and Electricity. Blotting and Absorptive Papers. 30,000 lbs. 24 hours. *"World," "Hollyrood," "Reliance," "Vienna Moire," "Directoire," "Albemarle Enameled" Blotting and Albemarle "Half-Tone" Blottings.*

DIXIE PAPER MILLS, INC. Brown's Island, foot Seventh Street. (R. A. Cauthorne, Pres.; M. E. Marcuse, Vice-Pres.; Raymond I. Straus, Sec.; E. C. Anderson, Treas.) Two 2000-lb. Beating an dtwo Refining engines; one 80-inch Fourdrinier. Widest trimmed sheet, 72 inches. Electricity and Steam. Absorbent, Black Paper, Bogus, Bottle Wrapper, Box and Barrel Layers, Building, Butchers' Manila, Card Middles, News Bogus, Drawing, Fibre, Furniture, Ham, Hardware, Heavy and Mill Wrappers, Car Lining, Tailors' Patterns, Rag Wrapping, Screenings and Specialties. 36,000 lbs. 24 hours.

MANCHESTER BOARD AND PAPER CO. (Warner Moore, Pres.; Stanley Reed, Sec. and Treas.) MANCHESTER PAPER MILL. S. P., at mill. Two 1000-lb. and two 500-lb. Beating and three Refining engines; one 110-inch Four Cylinder. Widest trimmed sheet, 102 inches. Water and Steam. Chip and Folding Box Board and Mill Wrappers. 60,000 lbs. 24 hours.

RICHMOND PAPER MANUFACTURING CO. (Owned by Standard Paper Mfg. Co.) JAMES RIVER MILLS. (R. S. Crump, Pres.; W. L. Goodwyn, Mgr.; W. J. Stiles, Supt.) Location, First and Hull Streets. S. P., Richmond. Six Beating and two Jordan engines; one 90-inch Fourdrinier. Water and Steam. Blotting. 28,000 lbs. 24 hours. *Manufacturers of the Celebrated "Climax," "Star" and "Bank" Plain Blottings; "Perfection" and "Ivory" Enameled Blottings; also "Fairfax" Plate and "Princess" Plain and Cloth-finish Blottings.*

STANDARD PAPER MANUFACTURING CO. (R. S. Crump, Pres.; C. H. Sutton, Vice-Pres.; J. F. Ryland, Sec. and Treas.; M. F. Montague,

ARE SUPERIOR TO ALL OTHERS. ALL SIZES IN STOCK.
LOMBARD & CO., Importers & Manufacturers, 236 & 238 A Street, Boston.

Paper and Pulp Mills in the United States 209

Mgr. Sales; W. J. Stiles, Supt.) OLD DOMINION MILL. Six 1200-lb. Combination Beating and Washing and two Jordan engines; one 90-inch Fourdrinier. Widest trimmed sheet, 80 inches. Union Screens. Water and Steam. Blotting, 30,000 lbs. 24 hours. "*Coating Mill, four machines making Enameled Blotting and Coated Specialties.*" "*Standard,*" "*Imperial,*" "*Sterling,*" *United States' Plain Blotting,* "*Royal Worcester,*" "*Defender*" *Enameled Blotting,* "*Curl Curl,*" "*Prismatic*" *Embossed Blotting.*

WEST POINT—King William Co.—PULP MILL.

Pop. 1,397. On So. RR., also Chesapeake Steamship Co.'s Line.

CHESAPEAKE PULP & PAPER CO., INC. General Offices, Lockland, Ohio. Eastern Sales and Operating Offices, West Point, Va. (Harold W. Nichols, Pres. and Treas.; Joseph H. Slater, Sec. and Mgr.; L. M. Long, Asst. Sec.; W. Clyde Gouldman, Assistant to Mgr.; Robert Woodhead, Supt.; John White, Supt. Board Mill.) BOARD MILL. Black-Clawson Five Cylinder Board Machine. Trims 99 inches. Steam. Test Board, Heavy Felt and Kraft Specialties. PULP MILL. Three Digesters; three Wet Machines. Steam. Sulphate pulp. 40 to 50 tons pulp board and paper combined 24 hours.

WINCHESTER—Frederick Co.

Pop. 5,161. On B. & O.; C. V. RR. M. O. and Tel. office; Adams and U. S. Ex.

AMERICAN STRAW BOARD CO. General Offices, Akron, Ohio. S. P., at mill. (H. M. Baker, Mgr.) Two 800-lb. and two 1000-lb. Beating and two Jordan engines; one 62-inch Four Cylinder. Widest sheet made, 58 inches. Steam. News Board and Chip Board 40,000 lbs. 24 hours.

WASHINGTON.

CAMAS—Clarke Co.

Pop. 1,000. On S. P. RR. Boat Landing on Columbia River. M. O., Tel. office and Ex. Frostdale, 3 miles; nearest bank, Vancouver, 14 miles.

CROWN WILLAMETTE PAPER CO. Address, Alaska Commercial Bldg., San Francisco, Cal. (Wm. Pierce Johnson, Pres.; Louis Bloch, Vice Pres. and Gen. Mgr.; Charles M. Whitney, Sec.; Frank Schwabacher, Treas.; A. J. Lewthwaite, Res. Mgr., Portland, Ore.) S. P., at mill. Twenty-five Beating and nine Jordan engines; one 84-inch, one 124-inch, one 152-inch and one 186-inch Fourdriniers; one 86-inch, one 114-inch, one 134-inch and one 186-inch Harper Fourdriniers. Widest trimmed sheet, 175 inches. Water, Steam and Electricity. News, Manila, Bag, Wrapping, Tissue, Hanging and Sheathing. 360,000 lbs. 24 hours. PULP MILL. Twelve Four Pocket Bagley & Sewall Grinders; one Pusey & Jones, two Willamette and two Manitowoc Digesters; eight Wet Machines. Water. Ground Wood 200,000 lbs., Sulphite Fibre 200,000 lbs. 24 hours.

EVERETT—Snohomish Co.

Pop. 30,000. On G. N.; C. M. & P. S.; N. P. RR. M. O. and Tel. office; W. F. & Co., N. Pac. and Gt. Northern Ex., American.

EVERETT PULP AND PAPER CO. (William Howarth, Pres. and Treas.; A. H. B. Jordan, Vice-Pres.; Augustus Johnson, Sec.; W. J. Pils,

ENGINEERING FOR **PULP, PAPER AND POWER PLANTS**

JOSEPH H. WALLACE & CO.
INDUSTRIAL ENGINEERS
Temple Court Building, NEW YORK
71 Bay Street, TORONTO, CAN.

Washington

Asst. Mgr. and Asst. Treas.; A. H. B. Jordan, Mill Supt.) S. P., Lowell. Six 1000-lb. Beating and four Jordan engines; one 96-inch and one 106-inch Fourdriniers. Width of Super Calenders, 52 inches. Widest trimmed sheets, 80 and 96 inches. Steam and Electricity. Machine Finished and Super Calendered Book, Varnish Label, Chemical, Railroad Writing, Folded Writing, Filing Sheets, Cartridge Tablets, Composition Books and School Supplies. 70,000 lbs. 24 hours. PULP MILL. Six Digesters. Steam. Soda Fibre. 60,000 lbs. 24 hours. "O. P. S." *Railroad Writing and "Tereve" Trade Mark.*

PORT ANGELES—Clallam Co.

Pop. 6,000. Seattle, Port Angeles & Western RR. Steamers to all points of world. M. O. and Tel. offices.

PARAFFINE, THE, COMPANIES, INC. Crescent Boxboard Plant. (R. S. Moore, Pres.; A. H. Dougall, Jr., Gen. Mgr. Board and Paper Division.) Six Beaters and one Cylinder Machine. Widest trimmed sheet, 104 inches. Steam and Electricity. Wood Fibre Boards and Container Boards, 100,000 lbs. PULP MILL. Four 4-pocket Grinders, one Digester and one Dry Machine. Steam. Ground Wood, 80,000 lbs. 24 hours. Sulphite, 40,000 lbs. 24 hours. Sulphate, 20,000 lbs. 24 hours.

WASHINGTON PULP & PAPER CORP. Office, Merchants Bank Bldg., Vancouver, B. C. (Aug. 20, 1918. Company has purchased equipment to the value of about $250,000, including paper machine, boilers, superheaters, stokers, beaters and all electrical equipment, but it is not the intention to proceed with the construction for a short period at least.)

SPOKANE—Spokane Co.

Pop. 104, 402. On N. P.; Gt. N.; Ore.-Wash. RR. & Nav.; Sp. & Int.; Sp. Falls & No.; Sp.-Idaho; Sp. & Inland Empire; Sp.; Port Seattle and Wash. & No. Idaho RR. M. O. and Tel.; No., Gt. N. and West Ex.

INLAND EMPIRE PAPER CO. (Judson G. Rosebush, Pres.; L. M. Alexander, Vice-Pres. and Treas.; W. A. Brazeau, Sec.; W. G. McNaughton, Gen. Mgr.) Mill located at Millwood, six miles east of Spokane. Five 1000-lb., six 1400-lb. Beating; two Refining and one Washing engines; one Rotary Boiler; one 90-inch and one 158-inch Fourdriniers. Widest trimmed sheets, 81 and 146 inches. Steam and Electricity. Bond, Writing, Book and News. 110,000 lbs. 24 hours. PULP MILL. Seven Grinders; eight Wet Machines; two Digesters. Electricity. Sulphite. 40,000 lbs. 24 hours. Ground Wood. 80,000 lbs. 24 hours.

STEILACOOM—Pierce Co.

Pop. 630. No. Pacific and Oregon-Washington RR. & Nav. Co. Tel. M. O. Nearest bank Tacoma, 12 miles.

CASCADE PAPER CO. P. O. Address, Perkins Bldg., Tacoma. General Sales Office, Balboa Bldg., San Francisco, Cal. (Frank S. Baker, Pres.; D. Den Bleyker, Vice-Pres.; J. T. S. Lyle, Sec.-Treas.; J. B. Coleman, Supt.; W. B. Reynolds, Sales Mgr.) S. P., West Tacoma. Four 1200-lb. Beaters, two Refining engines, four 2400-lb. Washers and five 2400-lb. Tub Cookers. One 122-inch Fourdrinier. Widest trimmed sheet, 115½ inches. Steam and Electricity. Book and Writing. 40,000 lbs. 24 hours.

SUMNER—Pierce Co.

Pop. 362. On Cascade Div. P. O. W. RR. and Nav. Co. & Great Northern; M. O. and Tel.; No Ex.

PARAFFINE, THE, COMPANIES, INC. Northern Board and Paper Mills Plant. Mill office, Sumner; Sales office, 815 White Bldg., Seattle, Wash. (R. S. Moore, Pres.; A. H. Dougall, Jr., Gen. Mgr. Board and Paper Div.) Six 1200-lb. Beating and three Refining engines; one machine trims 84-inch sheet. Steam and Electricity. All Grades of Box Boards and Heavy Papers. 80,000 lbs. 24 hours.

WEST VIRGINIA.

DAVIS—Tucker Co.—PULP MILL.

Pop. 1,700. On W. M. Ry. M. O. and Tel. office. Am. Ex.

WEST VIRGINIA PULP AND PAPER CO. New York office, 200 Fifth avenue. Western Sales Office, 732 Sherman street, Chicago. DAVIS MILL. (D. B. Landis, Supt.) Two Digesters; one 76-inch Dry and one 60-inch Wet Machines. Union Screens. Steam. Bleached Sulphite Fibre. 90,000 lbs. 24 hours.

HALLTOWN—Jefferson Co.

Pop. 300. On Shenandoah Valley Branch of B. & O. RR. M. O. office; Tel. and nearest bank, Charles Town, 4 miles; Wells Fargo & Co. Ex.

HALLTOWN PAPER BOARD CO. (F. S. Harrison, Pres. and Gen. Mgr.; A. McL. Harrison, Vice-Pres.; F. H. Wilson, Sec.; P. P. Nelson, Treas. and Supt.) S. P., at mill. Five Beating and four Jordan engines; two 76-inch Five Cylinders. Widest trimmed sheets, 60 and 62 inches. Steam and Electricity. Plain Mill Lined and Vat Lined Chip and News Board. 100,000 lbs. 24 hours.

HARPER'S FERRY—Jefferson Co.—PULP MILL.

Pop. 896. On B. & O.; S. V. Branch B. & O. RR. M. O. and Tel. office; U. S. Ex

HARPER'S FERRY PAPER CO. (H. F. Hall, Pres.; Wm. H. Savery, Vice-Pres. and Gen. Mgr.; E. E. Thatcher, Sec.-Treas.) S. P., Harper's Ferry. Four Grinders; six Wet Machines. Water. Ground Wood (dry). 40,000 lbs. 24 hours.

SHENANDOAH PULP CO. (William H. Savery, Pres. and Gen. Mgr.; H. F. Hall, Vice-Pres.; E. E. Thatcher, Sec.-Treas.) S. P., Harper's Ferry. Four Grinders; six 62-inch Wet Machines. Water. Ground Wood (dry). 40,000 lbs. 24 hours.

PARSONS—Tucker Co.

Pop. 1,800. On W. M. RR. M. O. and Tel. offices. Adams Ex.

PARSONS PULP AND LUMBER CO. (A. J. Stevens, Pres.; D. G. Wilson, Sec. and Treas.; J. Wilt, Supt.) Office, Finance Building, Philadelphia, Pa.; E. A. Hays, Supt. S. P., at mill. Two Digesters; one Wet Machine; one 100-inch Dry Machine. Steam and Natural Gas, Bleached Sulphite Pulp. 120,000 lbs. 24 hours.

West Virginia and Wisconsin

RICHWOOD—Nicholas Co.

Pop. 4,000. On B. & O. RR. M. O. and Tel. office; Wells Fargo & Co. Ex.

CHERRY RIVER PAPER CO. RICHWOOD MILL. (Chas. S. Weston, Pres.; Jas. W. Oakford, Vice-Pres. and Treas.; Walter Briggs, Sec.; C. B. Brooksbank, Supt.) S. P., Richwood, 1 mile. Ten 1000-lb., four 1500-lb. Beating and five Refining engines; one 86-inch and one 186-inch Fourdriniers. Widest trimmed sheets, 75 and 120 inches. One 112-inch Cylinder. Widest trimmed sheet, 100 inches. Union Screens. Steam. Manila, White and Colored Fibre, and Specialties. Tag Board, Container. 140,000 lbs. 24 hours. PULP MILL. S. P., Richwood, 1 mile. Two Digesters, five Wet Machines and one Decker Machine. Steam. Sulphite. 120,000 lbs. 24 hours.

WELLSBURG—Brooke Co.

Pop. 8,000. On P., W. & K. Branch of.P., C., C. & St. L. RR. M. O. and Tel. office; Adams Ex.

GEORGE, S., CO. (George W. Bowers, Pres.; F. R. Babcock, Vice-Pres.; J. F. Cree, Sec.; T. H. George, Treas. and Gen. Mgr.) Nine 1200-lb. Beating engines; one 72-inch and one 44-inch Cylinder Machines. Widest trimmed sheet, 68 inches. Steam and Electricity. Flour, Cement and Lime Bags. 30,000 lbs. 24 hours.

GEORGE AND SHERRARD PAPER CO. (W. R. Johnson, Pres.; T. J. Sherrard, Sec. and Treas.; S. George, Gen. Mgr.) Ten 1000-lb. Beating engines; five 1500-lb. Beating engines; one 84-inch Four Cylinder Machine; one 48-inch Three Cylinder Machine. Steam and Natural Gas. Rope Papers and Paper Shipping Sacks. 25,000 lbs. Rope Paper in 24 hours.

HARVEY PAPER CO. (H. C. Hervey, Pres.; R. W. Palmer, Vice-Pres. and Mgr.; J. C. Palmer, Jr., Sec. and Treas.; N. Nelson, Supt.) WELLSBURG MILL. S. P., at mill. Six 1000-lb. Beating and six Washing engines; one Rotary boiler; one 62-inch Three Cylinder Machine. Widest trimmed sheet, 58 inches. Steam and Electricity. Rope, Flour, Cement Sack, Insulating, Saturating and Specialties. 18,000 lbs. 24 hours.

WISCONSIN.

APPLETON—Outagamie Co.

Pop. 17,000. On C., M. & St. P.; C. & N. W. RR. M. O. and Tel. office. Am. and Wells Fargo. Ex.

FOX RIVER PAPER CO. (Wm. C. Wing, Pres.; H. K. Babcock, Vice-Pres.; George Hilton, Sec.; H. G. Freeman, Treas.; H. S. Furminger, Supt.) RAVINE MILLS. S. P., at mill. Four 1300-lb. Beating and one Jordan; one Rotary Boiler; one 86-inch Fourdrinier. Width of Super Calenders, 36 and 39 inches. Water. Bonds and Ledgers. 16,000 lbs. 24 hours. LINCOLN MILL. S. P., at mill. Four 1100-lb. Beating, three 1200-lb. Washing and one Jordan engines; one Rotary Boiler; one 81-inch Fourdrinier. Width of Super-Calenders, 36 inches. Water and Steam. Fine Writing. Drawing, Folded and Ruled. 18,000 lbs. 24 hours. FOX RIVER MILL. S. P., at mill. Four 1300-lb. Beating, four 1200-lb. Washing and one Jordan engines; one Rotary Boiler; one 82-inch Fourdrinier. Width of

Our Bonds and Ledgers Require No Explanations

" NOTE THE TEAR AS WELL AS THE TEST "

EACH GRADE GUARANTEED TO SATISFY
— USER TO BE THE JUDGE —

NEENAH PAPER COMPANY
LOFT DRIED BONDS AND LEDGERS ONLY
NEENAH, WISCONSIN

MEMBER
PAPER MAKERS
ADVERTISING CLUB

See Other Side

**Loft-Dried-*Quality* Made by Modern Processes
In a Mill of "*Safety-First*"**

NEENAH PAPER COMPANY

LOFT DRIED BONDS AND LEDGERS ONLY
Follow Your Inclination and Adopt One
"We are always doing something to keep our Customers in the Lead"

  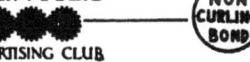 

See Other Side

Super Calenders, 36 and 41 inches. Water and Steam. Bond and Ledgers. 16,000 lbs. 24 hours.

INTERLAKE PULP AND PAPER CO. (George W. Mead, Pres.; Isaac P. Witter, Vice-Pres.; George P. Berkey, Sec. and Mgr.; E. B. Redford, Treas.; Geo. F. Adams, Sales Agt.) SULPHITE MILL. S. P., at mill. Nine Digesters; one 94-inch Double Cylinder and one 56-inch Cylinder Machines. Water. Mitscherlich Process Sulphite Fibre. 120,000 lbs. 24 hours. GROUND WOOD MILL. Two Grinders; one Wet Machine. Water. Ground Wood. 10,000 lbs. 24 hours.

KIMBERLY-CLARK CO. (J. A. Kimberly, Pres.; F. J. Sensenbrenner, 1st Vice-Pres.; J. C. Kimberly, 2d Vice-Pres.; F. S. Shattuck, Treas.; Harry Price, Sec.; Ernst Mahler, Gen. Supt.) P. O. Address, Neenah. ATLAS MILL (formerly operated by the Atlas Paper Co.). S. P., side track to mill. Ten 1000-lb. Beating and three Jordan engines; two 82-inch Fourdriniers. Widest trimmed sheet, 72 inches. Union Screens. Water and Steam. Specialties. 60,000 lbs. 24 hours. TELULAH MILL (formerly operated by the TELULAH PAPER Co.) S. P., at mill. Twelve 1000-lb. Beating and three Refining engines; one 110-inch and one 90-inch Fourdriniers. Widest trimmed sheet, 100 inches. Width of Super Calenders, 45 and 69 inches. Water and Steam. Book, Envelope, Writing and Railroad Manila. 56,000 lbs. 24 hours.

PATTEN PAPER CO., LIMITED. (Judson G. Rosebush, Pres. and Treas.; John McNaughton, Vice-Pres.; Waldo E. Rosebush, Sec.) S. P., at mill. Fourteen 700-lb. and two Jordan engines; one 62-inch and one 72-inch Fourdriniers. Widest trimmed sheet, 72 inches. Water and Steam. M. F. Book, Rag Print, Railroad and Envelope Manila. 36,000 lbs. 24 hours.

RIVERSIDE FIBRE AND PAPER CO. (W. M. Gilbert, Pres.; T. W. Orbison, Vice-Pres.; S. W. Murphy, Sec. and Treas.) S. P., at mill. Three 1200-lb. Beating and two Refining engines; one 106-inch Fourdrinier. Widest trimmed sheet, 100 inches. Width of Super Calenders, 64 inches. Bonds and Ledgers. 32,000 lbs. 24 hours. Water and Steam. PULP MILL. S. P., Appleton. Five Digesters; four Wet Machines. Steam. Bleached and Unbleached Sulphite Fibre, 70,000 lbs. 24 hours.

THILMANY PULP & PAPER CO. WISCONSIN TISSUE DIVISION. (M. A. Wertheimer, Pres.; J. E. Thomas, Vice-Pres.; C. W. Stribley, Treas.; K. E. Stansbury, Sec.; F. C. Weinkauf, Mill Supt.) S. P., at mill. Six 1000-lb. Beating and two Jordan engines; one 98-inch and one 106-inch Fourdriniers. Widest trimmed sheet, 100 inches. Water and Steam. Light Weight Special Wrappings. 40,000 lbs. 24 hours.

ASHLAND—Ashland Co.

Pop. 13,074. C. & N. W.; C. S. & P. M. O.; Soo Line N. P. Lake Superior Steamers. M. O., Tel. office.

ASHLAND PAPER CO. (A. F. Tuttle, Pres.; S. A. Whedon, Sec.-Treas.; L. C. Locklin, Gen. Mgr.) One 600-lb., three 1000-lb. Beating; two Claflin, one Standard Jordan engines; one Cylinder Machine. Widest trimmed sheet, 96 inches; one Yankee Fourdrinier. Widest trimmed sheet, 84 inches. Hydro-Electro, Steam. Tissue Wrappings, Crepe, Napkins, Mill Rolls for Conversion Plant. 20,000 lbs. 24 hours.

MENASHA PRINTING & CARTON CO. Main Office, Menasha, Wis. (S. H. Clinedinst, Pres.; Geo. S. Gaylord, Vice-Pres. and Mgr.; W. A. Brooks, Sec.; G. W. Heisler, Treas.; S. E. Tomczak, Supt.) SULPHITE MILL. Two Digesters, two Wet Machines. Steam and Electricity.

BELOIT—Rock Co.

Pop. 17,436. On C. & N. W.; C., M. & St. P. RR. Am. and Wells Fargo Ex.

BELOIT BOX BOARD CO. (Fred M. Coons, Pres. and Treas.; J. A. Fisher, Vice-Pres., Sec. and Supt.) Eight 1000-lb. Beating and two Jordan engines; one 78-inch Machine. Water and Steam. Building, Box and Straw Board. 60,000 lbs. 24 hours.

BROKAW—Marathon Co.

Pop. 500. On W. V. Div. C., M. & St. P. RR. M. O. and Tel. office; nearest bank, Wausau, 5 miles; Wells Fargo Ex.

WAUSAU PAPER MILLS CO. (Walter Alexander, Pres.; C. C. Yawkey, Vice-Pres.; W. L. Edmonds, Sec., Treas. and Mgr.) S. P., at mill. Nine 1200-lb. Beating and six Jordan engines; one 92-inch and three 110-inch Fourdriniers. Widest trimmed sheet, 100 inches. Union Screens. Water and Steam. All grades Fibre and Manila; also Drug Bond Papers and genuine Kraft Papers. 130,000 lbs. 24 hours. PULP MILL. S. P., at mill. Six Grinders; three Digesters; six Wet Machines and two Deckers. Water. Ground Wood, 50,000 lbs.; Sulphite, 100,000 lbs. 24 hours.

BUCHANAN—Outagamie Co.—PULP MILL.

Pop. 2,096. M. O., Tel., Ex. and nearest bank, Little Chute, 3 miles.

COMBINED LOCKS PAPER CO., Successor to The Little Chute Pulp Co. Office at Combined Locks. (L. L. Alsted, Pres.; G. M. Seaman, Vice-Pres.; D. E. Reese, Treas.; F. H. Bottum, Sec.) Ground Wood.

COMBINED LOCKS—Outagamie Co.

On C. & N. W. RR. Tel. office; M. O.; nearest bank, Appleton; Am. Ex.

COMBINED LOCKS PAPER CO. Office at Combined Locks. (L. L. Alsted, Pres.; G. M. Seaman, Vice-Pres.; D. E. Reese, Treas.; F. H. Bottum, Sec.; A. J. McKay, Mgr.; P. A. Smith, Supt.) Seventeen 1000-lb. and two 1500-lb. Beating, five Refining and one Washing engines; five Fourdriniers. Widest trimmed sheets, one 88 inches, two 98 inches, one 112 inches and one 164 inches. Water, Steam and Electricity. Catalogue, Envelope, Manilas and Specialties. 220,000 lbs. 24 hours. GROUND WOOD MILL. Thirty-eight Grinders; fifteen Wet Machines. Water. Ground Wood. 150,000 lbs. 24 hours. SULPHITE FIBRE MILL. Four Digesters; three Wet Machines. Water and Steam. Sulphite Fibre. 110,000 lbs. 24 hours.

CORNELL, Chippewa Co.

Pop. 1,150. On C. St. P.; M. & O. RR. M. O. and Tel. office; American Ex.

CORNELL WOOD PRODUCTS CO. Chicago Office, 173 W. Jackson Bldg. (C. O. Frisbie, Pres., Chicago; H. C. Frisbie, Vice-Pres. and Gen.

Paper and Pulp Mills in the United States 215

Mgr.; W. G. Sarville, Vice-Pres.; C. F. Howell, Sec. and Treas.) Six 1500-lb. Beating and two Jordan engines; one 146-inch Seven Cylinder. Widest trimmed sheet, 134½ inches. Water and Electricity. Pure Wood Fibre Wall Board, Solid Pulp and Jute Container Board. 200,000 lbs. 24 hours. PULP MILL. Twenty-one Grinders, nine Wet Machines and five Digesters. Water and Electricity. Ground Wood. 275,000 lbs. 24 hours.

CRIVITZ—Marinette Co.—PULP MILL.

Pop. 176. On S. Div. C.; M. & St. P. RR. M. O. and Tel. office. W., F. Ex.

CRIVITZ PULP AND PAPER CO. General Offices, Green Bay, Wis. (Wm. Hoberg, Pres.; A. E. Hoberg, Vice-Pres.; James W. McNevins, Sec.-Treas.; John Parent, Supt.) S. P., Ellis Junction. Four Grinders; three Wet Machines. Water. Ground Wood. 50,000 lbs. 24 hours.

DE PERE—Brown Co.

Pop. 4,038. On C. & N. W.; C., M. & St. P. RR.; also Lake vessels. M. O. and Tel. office; Am. and U. S. Ex.

AMERICAN WRITING PAPER CO.—Shattuck & Babcock Company Division. (J. S. Gittins, Mgr.) DE PERE MILLS. S. P., at mill. Fourteen 1000-lb. and four Marshall engines; one 78-inch, one 82-inch and one 116-inch Fourdriniers. Twelve Stacks Sheet Super Calenders, 26, 82, 36 and 42 inches wide, and two Stacks Web Super Calenders, 56 inches wide. Water and Steam. Writing. 32,000 lbs. 24 hours. *Loft-dried and Machine-dried Bonds, Linens and Ledgers.*

EAU CLAIRE—Eau Claire Co.

Pop. 22,000. On C., St. P., M. & O.; C., M. & St. P. M. O. and Tel. office; Am. and Nat. Ex.

DELLS PAPER AND PULP CO. (W. L. Davis, Pres.; S. R. Davis, Vice-Pres.; J. A. Stilp, Sec.; J. T. Joyce, Treas.; W. L. Davis, Jr., Supt.) S. P., at mill. One 850-lb. and ten 1250-lb. Beating and four Jordan engines; one 76-inch, one 104-inch and one 182-inch Fourdriniers. Widest trimmed sheets, 72, 96 and 120 inches. Water and Steam. Manilas, Fibre, Novel, News and Hanging. 150,000 lbs. 24 hours. PULP MILL. S. P., side track at mill. Sixteen Grinders; four Digesters; thirteen Wet Machines; one "Improved" Knotter. Water and Steam. Ground Wood, 150,000 lbs.; Sulphite Fibre, 100,000 lbs. 24 hours.

GRAND RAPIDS—Wood Co.

Pop. 7,261. On C., M. & St. P.; G. B. & W.; C. & N. W.; Sou. Line. M. O. and Tel. office; U. S., Am., Nat. and Wells Fargo & Co. Ex.

CONSOLIDATED WATER POWER AND PAPER CO. (George W. Mead, Pres. and Mgr.; R. L. Kraus, Vice-Pres.; Isaac P. Witter, Treas.; E. B. Redford, Sec.) GRAND RAPIDS MILL. S. P., at mill. Six 1000-lb. Beating engines; two 130-inch Fourdriniers. Widest trimmed sheet, 122 inches. Water and Electricity. News Print and Railroad Writing. 156,000 lbs. 24 hours. One 102-inch Cylinder, 15 tons Wrapping daily. BIRON MILL. S. P., Grand Rapids. Six Beating engines; one 86-inch and one 108-inch Fourdriniers (80 and 100½-inch sheets). Water, Steam and Electricity. News Print and Wallpaper. 110,000 lbs. 24 hours. PULP MILL. S. P., at mill. Twenty-four Grinders; ten Wet Machines; four

Lombard's English Newcastle Pulp Stones

Wisconsin

"Impco" Screens. Water and Electricity. Ground Wood. 240,000 lbs. 24 hours.

NEKOOSA-EDWARDS PAPER CO., Successor to Centralia Pulp and Water Power Co. (L. M. Alexander, Pres. and Treas.; Judson G. Rosebush, Vice-Pres.; C. A. Jasperson, Sec.) PULP MILL. S. P., Grand Rapids. Five Grinders; two Wet Machines. Water and Hydro-Electric Power. Ground Wood (dry). 36,000 lbs. 24 hours.

GREEN BAY—Brown Co.

Pop. 25,236. On C. & N. W.; C., M. & St. P.; G., B. & W., and K., G., B. & W. RR. Steamship line; M. O. and Tel. office. Am., U. S. and Wells Fargo Ex.

GREEN BAY PAPER AND FIBRE CO. (George D. Nau, Pres.; Frank H. Hoberg, Vice-Pres.; John Welsh, Sec., Treas. and Gen. Mgr.) PAPER MILL. Eight 1000-lb. Beating engines; three Jordan Refining engines; one 95-inch Fourdrinier Machine. Widest trimmed sheet, 82 inches. One 112-inch Harper Fourdrinier Machine. Widest trimmed sheet, 102 inches. Fibres and Manilas; also Bag Papers. Steam. 70,000 lbs. 24 hours. SULPHITE MILL. Three Manitowoc Digesters; five Wet Machines; three "Impco" Screens. Steam. Sulphite Pulp. 100,000 lbs. 24 hours.

HOBERG CO., THE JOHN. (Frank H. Hoberg, Pres.; Anton Hoberg, Vice-Pres.; Henry Goethe, Sec.; Wm. Hoberg, Treas.) S. P., Green Bay. Four 800-lb. and five 1000-lb. Beating and four Refining engines; one 74-inch Cylinder, and one 98-inch, one 104-inch and one 132-inch Fourdriniers. Electricity and Steam. White, Manila and Colored Tissue, Paper Napkins, Fruit Wrappers, Tissue Excelsior, Roll and Package Toilet Paper, Paper Towels, Cotton Batting, Paper Printed Tissues and White Sulphite Fibre Papers. 50,000 lbs. 24 hours.

NORTHERN PAPER MILLS. (W. P. Wagner, Pres.; P. S. Wagner, Sec., Treas. and Sales Mgr.; A. E. Cofrin, Gen. Supt.) S. P., at mill. Eleven Beaters, ten Refining and three Washing engines; one 96-inch and one 114-inch Cylinders. Widest trimmed sheets, 82 and 100 inches; one 111-inch and one 130-inch Harper Fourdrinier, and one 111-inch Yankee Fourdrinier, trimming 100, 118 and 102 inches, respectively. Steam and Electricity. Toilet, Towels, Duplex Tissue and Napkins. Production 95,000 lbs. 24 hours. PULP MILL. Two Digesters; three Wet Machines; three "Impco" Screens and two "Impco" Knotters. Steam and Electricity. Bleached and Unbleached Hemlock Sulphite. 70,000 lbs. 24 hours.

KAUKAUNA—Outagamie Co.

Pop. 5,115. On C. & N. W. RR. M. O. and Tel. office; Am. Ex.

KAUKAUNA PULP CO. General Office, Milwaukee, Wis. (J. W. Kleckhefer, Pres.; E. L. Walker, Vice-Pres. and Treas.; Rae F. Bell, Treas.) S. P., at mill. Three Digesters; two 76-inch Wet Machines. Water and Steam. Sulphite Fibre (dry). 45,000 lbs. 24 hours.

LINDAUER PULP CO. (Luther Lindauer, Pres.; Mrs. L. Lindauer, Vice-Pres.; Dr. E. C. Halloch, Sec.-Treas.; John Kobeesen, Supt.) Three Grinders; three Wet Machines. Water. Ground Wood. 30,000 lbs. 24 hours.

DARMSTADT, SCOTT & COURTNEY, Inc. 178 and 184 SOUTH STREET, NEW YORK. Importers, Exporters and Dealers in **PAPER MAKERS' SUPPLIES**. Also Mfrs. of DEADENING and SATURATING FELTS.

McEnery Paper Company Practically All Grades
Manufacturers' Sales Agency 112 W. ADAMS ST., CHICAGO

Paper and Pulp Mills in the United States

OUTAGAMIE PAPER CO. (A. W. Priest, Pres.; J. G. Rosebush, Vice-Pres.; H. S. Cooke, Sec.; John McNaughton, Treas.) S. P., at mill. Eight 700-lb. and two Jordan engines; one 70-inch and one 80-inch Fourdriniers. Water. No. 1 Bag Print. 34,000 lbs. 24 hours. PULP MILL. S. P., at mill. Eight Grinders; four Wet Machines. Water. Ground Wood. 34,000 lbs. 24 hours.

THILMANY PULP AND PAPER CO. (M. A. Wertheimer, Pres.; J. E. Thomas, Vice-Pres.; C. W. Stribley, Treas.; K. E. Stansbury, Sec.; F. C. Weinkauf, Mill Supt.) S. P., at mill. Twelve 1000-lb. and two 1500-lb. Beating and five Refining engines; two 86-inch and three 96-inch Fourdriniers. Widest trimmed sheet, 90 inches. Water and Steam. Light Weight Wrappings and Specialties. 65,000 lbs. 24 hours; also Sulphate Pulp, 80,000 lbs. 24 hours.

UNION BAG AND PAPER CORP. Main Office, Woolworth Bldg., New York. S. P., at mill. Six 1000-lb. and two Jordan engines; one 74-inch and one 84-inch Fourdriniers. Water and Steam. Bag Paper. 40,000 lbs. 24 hours. PULP MILL. S. P., at mill. Four Grinders; one Wet Machine. Water. Ground Wood Pulp. 14,000 lbs. 24 hours.

KIMBERLY—Outagamie Co.

Pop. 3,000. On C. & N. W. RR. M. O. and Tel. office; Am. Ex.

KIMBERLY-CLARK CO. (J. A. Kimberly, Pres.; F. J. Sensenbrenner, First Vice-Pres.; J. C. Kimberly, Second Vice-Pres.; S. F. Shattuck, Treas.; Harry Price, Sec.; Ernst Mahler.) P. O. Address, Neenah. S. P., at mill. Four 1000-lb. and four 1500-lb. Beating and six Jordan engines; one 84-inch Cylinder; one 120-inch, one 138-inch, one 140-inch and one 156-inch Fourdriniers. Widest trimmed sheet, 141 inches for Book and 70 inches for Wrappings. Water and Steam. Book and Wrapping. 220,000 lbs. Book, 20,000 lbs. Wrapping, 24 hours. FIBRE MILL. S. P., at mill. Six Digesters. Water and Steam. Sulphite Fibre. 150,000 lbs. 24 hours.

KINGS—Lincoln Co.—PULP MILL.

King Dam Station on M. T. & W. RR., 3½ miles from Tomahawk.

TOMAHAWK PULP AND PAPER CO. KING PULP MILL. P. O. address, Tomahawk. S. P., King Dam Station. Six Four Pocket International Grinders; five 86-inch Wet Machines. Water. Ground Wood. 50,000 lbs. 24 hours.

LADYSMITH—Rusk Co.

Pop. 2,000. On Mpls., St. P. & St. M. & W. C. RR. M. O. and Tel. office; Western and Nat. Ex.

MENASHA PAPER CO. (N. J. Smith, Pres.; M. H. Ballou, Vice-Pres. and Gen. Mgr.; Harry Ballou, Treas.; R. M. Sensenbrenner, Sec.) LADYSMITH MILLS. S. P., at mill. Five 1000-lb. Beating and two Refining engines; one 88-inch, one 108-inch and one 118-inch Fourdriniers; also Bleaching Plant. Water and Steam. Manila, Special Magazine, Bleached Sulphite Bonds, R. R. Manilas, Opaque Catalogue Papers, Poster and Specialties. 100,000 lbs. 24 hours. GROUND WOOD MILL. S. P., at mill. Five Grinders; three Wet Machines. Water. Ground Wood. 48,000 lbs. 24 hours. SULPHITE MILL. Three 10x32 Digesters; five Wet machines. Steam and

Lombard's English Newcastle Pulp Stones

Water. Sulphite Fibre, 40,000 lbs. 24 hours. GRANT GROUND WOOD MILL. Located in Grant Township, five miles from Ladysmith on Flambeau River. S. P., Ladysmith via private railroad of the company. Six Grinders; five Wet machines. Water. Ground Wood. 70,000 lbs. 24 hours. THORNAPPLE GROUND WOOD MILL. Located on Flambeau River, in Thornapple township, Rusk County, ten miles from Ladysmith. S. P., Ladysmith via company's private railroad. Six Grinders; four Wet machines. Water. Ground Wood. 60,000 lbs. 24 hours. Also 20-ton Bleaching Plant.

LITTLE RAPIDS—Brown Co.—PULP MILL.

Pop. 75. On Wisconsin Div. Chic. & North; Am. Ex. M. O. and Tel; nearest bank, Wrightstown, 4 miles.

RIVERSIDE FIBRE & PAPER CO., Successors to Lindauer-O'Connell Co. (W. M. Gilbert, Pres.; T. W. Orbison, Vice-Pres.; S. W. Murphy, Sec. and Treas. S. P., at mill. Eight Grinders; four Wet Machines. Water, Ground Wood. 50,000 lbs. 24 hours.

MADISON—Dane Co.

FOREST PRODUCTS LABORATORY, FOREST SERVICE, UNITED STATES DEP'T OF AGRICULTURE, UNIVERSITY OF WISCONSIN. (Carlisle P. Winslow, Director.) S. P., at Madison. One 25-lb. and one 60-lb. Beating and one Refining engine; one 14-inch Fourdrinier and Cylinder Machine (trim 12 inches). PULP MILL. One 20-inch Wet Machine; one 50-lb. Sulphite Digester; one 50-lb. Soda Digester and two Two Pocket Grinder. Electric. Experimental work only.

MARINETTE—Marinette Co.

Pop. 16,195. On C. & N. W.; L. S. Div. of C., M. & St. P. and W. & M. RR.; also vessels. M. O. and Tel. office; Am. and U. S. Ex.

MARINETTE AND MENOMINEE PAPER CO. (H. A. J. Upham, Pres.; Robert F. Goodman, Vice-Pres.; F. A. Silliman, Treas. and Sec.; C. Anderson, Asst. Sec. and Treas.; R. W. S. Hoskin, Mgr.) Two mills. S. P., at mill. No. I MILL. Four 1200-lb. and one Jordan engines; one 96-inch Fourdrinier. Widest trimmed sheet, 81 inches. Water and Steam. Manila. 18,000 lbs. 24 hours. PARK MILLS. Eight 1000-lb., four 1200-lb. and two Jordan engines; two 96-inch Fourdriniers. Water and Steam. Fibre and Jute Manila and Kraft, 55,000 lbs. 24 hours. PARK GROUND WOOD MILL. Eight New England Grinders. Ground Wood (dry). 30,000 lbs. 24 hours. SULPHITE MILL. Three Digesters. Sulphite Fibre. 25,000 lbs. 24 hours.

MENASHA—Winnebago Co.

Pop. 7,000. On C. & N. W.; C. M. & St. P.; Soo Line RR.; also vessels. M. O. and Tel. office; Am. and Wells, Fargo & Co. Ex.

GILBERT PAPER CO. (W. M. Gilbert, Pres.; Theo. M. Gilbert, Vice-Pres.; A. C. Gilbert, Treas.; A. V. Richardson, Sec.; Fred Hubbard, Supt.) S. P., at mill. Four 800-lb. and four 1000-lb. Beating; four 1200-lb. Washing and two Refining engines; two Rotary Boilers; one 86-inch and one 102-inch Fourdriniers. Widest trimmed sheets, 76 and 88 inches. Width of Super Calenders, up to 50 inches. Water and Steam. Bond, Ledger and Writing. 34,000 lbs. 24 hours.

PRESS ROLLS — Maple and Gum White Wood Felt Rolls — J. W. HEWITT MACHINE CO. Neenah, Wis.

ISLAND PAPER CO. (D. T. H. Mackinnon, Pres.; William Strange, Vice-Pres.; A. N. Strange, Sec.-Treas. and Mgr.) S. P., at mill. Ten 500-lb. Beating engines; two 68-inch and one 82-inch Fourdriniers. Widest trimmed sheet, 72 inches. Steam and Water. White and Colored Fibre. 70,000 lbs. 24 hours. PULP MILL. S. P., at mill. Three Digesters; two Wet machines. Water and Steam. Sulphite Fibre. 60,000 lbs. 24 hours.

MENASHA PRINTING & CARTON CO., Successors to Menasha Printing Co. (S. H. Clinedinst, Pres. and Treas.; G. S. Gaylord, Vice-Pres.; W. A. Brooks, Sec.; G. W. Heisler, Treas.; James Maeder, Supt.) MENASHA MILL. S. P., at mill. Four 1000-lb. Beating; two Fourdriniers. Widest trimmed sheets, 62 and 72 inches. One large size Lanoye Pulper. Steam and Electricity. Writing, Sulphite, Bleached Wax, Book and Specialties. Wax papers plain and printed, Adding Machine Rolls and Special Roll. 32,000 lbs. 24 hours.

STRANGE, JOHN, PAPER CO. (John Strange, Pres.; John Marx, Vice-Pres.; Hugh Strange, Sec. and Treas.; John Hercher, Supt.) Nine 1000-lb. Beating and seven Jordan engines; one 110-inch, and one 144-inch Cylinders; widest trimmed sheet, 132 inches. One 84-inch Fourdrinier. Widest trimmed sheet, 72 inches. Water and Steam. High Grade Dry Finish, Kraft, Mill Wrappers, Boards and Express. 80,000 lbs. 24 hours. NEW MILL. Seven 1500-lb. Beaters; four 3000-lb. Auxiliary Beaters; one 144-inch Six Cylinder Machine. Board, 200,000 lbs. 24 hours.

WHITING PAPER CO., GEO. A. (Geo. A. Whiting, Pres. and Treas.; F. B. Whiting. Vice-Pres. and Sec.) S. P., at mill. Five 600-lb. Beating and one Refining engines; one 84-inch Fourdrinier. Widest trimmed sheet, 76 inches. Width of Super-Calenders, 48 inches. Norwood Plater. Water and Steam. Loft and Machine Dried Bonds, Flat Writings, Linen Fabric Bond and Check Papers. 24,000 lbs. 24 hours.

MERRILL—Lincoln Co.

Pop. 8,537. On Wis. Val. Br. C., M. & St. P. RR. M. O. and Tel. office; Wells Fargo Ex.

GRANDFATHER'S FALLS CO. (L. N. Anson, Pres.; John O. Day, Vice-Pres.; Geo. A. Foster, Sec. and Treas.; W. J. Sullivan, Mgr.) S. P., at mill. Three 1000-lb. Beating engines; one 130-inch Fourdrinier. Water, Electricity and Steam. Widest trimmed sheet, 122 inches. News, Hanging, Tablet, Novel. 60,000 lbs. 24 hours. PULP MILL. S. P., at mill. Six Grinders; four Wet Machines. Electricity. Ground Wood. 70,000 lbs. 24 hours.

EWING EVEREST PULP CO., Successor to Lindauer Pulp and Manufacturing Co. S. P., at mill. Five Grinders; three Wet Machines. Ground Wood. 20,000 to 24,000 lbs. 24 hours.

MILWAUKEE—Milwaukee Co.

Pop. 500,000. On C. & N. W.; C., M. & St. P.; St. Paul & S. Ste. Marie RR. M. O., Tel., Am., U. S., Adams, Pac. & Natl. Express.

HUMMEL & DOWNING CO. (J. P. Hummel, Pres.; T. W. Ross, Vice-Pres.; G. E. McKowen, Sec.) Twelve 1600-lb. Beating and eight Jordan engines; one 130-inch Six Cylinder and one 140-inch Fixe Cylinder Board

Lombard's English Newcastle Pulp Stones

222 Wisconsin

reaux, Supt.) S. P., at mill. Three Grinders; two Wet Machines. Water. Ground Wood. 30,000 lbs. 24 hours.

PARK FALLS—Price Co.

Pop. 2,500. On "Soo" Line and Chicago, St. Paul, Minneapolis and Omaha RR. M. O., bank and Tel. office; Western and Am. Ex.

FLAMBEAU PAPER CO. Chicago Office, 111 W. Washington Street. (E. P. Sherry, Pres. and Treas.; Guy Waldo, Sec. and Mgr.) FLAMBEAU MILL. S. P., at mill. Six 1000-lb. Beating and two Refining engines; one 107-inch Fourdrinier and one 132-inch Harper Fourdrinier. Widest trimmed sheets, 99 inches and 120 inches. Water and Steam. No. 1 News, No. 3 Book and Light Weight Catalogue and Specialties. Railroad Manila and Poster. 70,000 lbs. 24 hours. PULP MILL. S. P., at mill. Eleven Grinders; eight Wet Machines; one Decker Machine; three "Impco" Screens and two "Impco" Knotters. Water. Ground Wood. 80,000 lbs. 24 hours.

PORT EDWARDS—Wood Co.

Pop. 1,200. On C., M. & St. P.; M. St. P. & S. Ste. M. & C. & N. W. RR. M. O. and Tel. office; nearest bank, Grand Rapids, 4 miles; Am., West. and W., F. & Co. Ex.

NEKOOSA-EDWARDS PAPER CO. Incorporated. (L. M. Alexander, Pres. and Treas.; Judson G. Rosebush, Vice-Pres. C. A. Jasperson, Sec.) JOHN EDWARDS MILL. Six 2000-lb. Beating engines, and three Jordan engines; one 104-inch and one 110-inch machines. Water and Steam. News, Manila and Fibre. 120,000 lbs. 24 hours. PULP MILL. Twelve Sandy Hill Grinders; seven 80-inch Wet Machines; one "Impco" Rotary Screen. Water. Spruce Ground Wood. 100,000 lbs. 24 hours. PORT EDWARDS FIBRE MILL. Three Digesters. Six 84-inch Wet Machines. Steam. Unbleached and Bleached Sulphite Fibre. 150,000 lbs. 24 hours.

RHINELANDER—Oneida Co.

Pop. 4,998. On Ash. Div. C. & N. W. and M. St. P. and S. Ste. Marie RR. M. O. and Tel. office.

RHINELANDER PAPER CO. (A. W. Brown, Pres.; Dr. A. D. Daniels, Vice-Pres.; Paul Browne, Sec.; Wm. Eibel, Treas. and Mgr.; W. J. Dolan, Supt.) Ten 1000-lb. Beating and four Refining engines; four Fourdriniers. Widest trimmed sheets, two 100 inches and two 126 inches. Also two 132-inch Duplex Tissue Machine. Water and Steam. Glassine, Grease-proof Wrapping, M. G. Wrapping and M. G. Tissue, 57,000 lbs.; Dry Finish Wrapping, 65,000 lbs. 24 hours. PULP MILL. Four Grinders; four Digesters; eight Wet Machines. Water and Steam. Sulphite Fibre, 110,000 lbs. 24 hours.

SHAWANO—Shawano Co.

Pop. 3,500. On O. Branch of C. & N. and Wis. & Northern Ry. M. O. and Tel. office; Am. Ex.

WOLF RIVER PAPER AND FIBRE CO. (F. D. Naber, Pres.; F. W. Humphrey, Vice-Pres.; A. N. Strange, Sec., Treas. and Gen. Mgr.; W. E. Stoppenbach, Res. Mgr.) PAPER MILL. S. P., at mill. Five 1000-lb. Beating and two Refining engines; one 108-inch Fourdrinier, trims 96 inches, and one 132-inch "Yankee" Tissue Machine, trims 120 inches. Steam and Electricity. Fibre, Manila Wrapping, Machine Glazed Fibres and Specialties. 70,000 lbs. 24 hours. PULP MILLS. Two mills. S. P., at mills.

HARDY S. FERGUSON, CONSULTING ENGINEER, 200 FIFTH AVENUE, NEW YORK CITY. PAPER, PULP AND FIBRE MILLS, WATER POWER DEVELOPMENT, DAMS, STORAGE RESERVOIRS AND OTHER HYDRAULIC STRUCTURES.

PRESS ROLLS Maple and Gum White Wood Felt Rolls — J. W. HEWITT MACHINE CO., Neenah, Wis.

PULP MILLS. Four Grinders; two 84-inch Wet Machines; one "Impco" Screen and one "Impco" Knotter. Water. Ground Wood. 20,000 lbs. 24 hours. SULPHITE MILL. Three Digesters; two Wet Machines. Water Sulphite Fibre (dry). 60,000 lbs. 24 hours.

STEVENS POINT—Portage Co.

Pop. 9,524. On "Soo" Line; G. B. & W. RR. M. O. and Tel. office; Western and Wells Fargo Ex.

STEVENS POINT PULP AND PAPER CO. (John Strange, Pres.; E. G. Goodell, Vice-Pres.; Hugh Strange, Sec. and Treas.; T. F. Elkins, Supt.) PULP MILL. One Digester; two Wet Machines. Water. Sulphate Pulp. 40,000 lbs. 24 hours.

WHITING-PLOVER PAPER CO. (Geo. A. Whiting, Pres.; F. B. Whiting, Vice-Pres.; E. A. Oberweiser, Sec. and Treas.; Geo. Hager, Supt.) S. P., Stevens Point. Nine 1200-lb. Beating and two Refining engines; five 1200-lb. Washers and two Rotary boilers; one 112-inch and one 115-inch Fourdrinier. Widest trimmed sheets, 99 and 102 inches. Width of Super-Calenders, up to 64 inches. Water, Steam and Electricity. Bonds, Ledgers and Writings. 43,000 lbs. 24 hours. *International Bond, Yankee Bond and Artesian Bond.*

WISCONSIN RIVER PAPER AND PULP CO. P. O. address, Neenah. (C. A. Babcock, Pres. and Treas.; W. T. Whiting, Vice-Pres.; R. A. Hollister, Sec.; O. A. Law, Supt.) S. P., at mill. Six 1200-lb. Beating and two Refining engines; one 106-inch and one 120-inch Fourdriniers. Widest trimmed sheet, 110 inches. Water and Steam. Hanging and News. 110,000 lbs. 24 hours. PULP MILL. S. P., at mill. Eleven Grinders, Six Four Decker Wet Machines; three "Improved" Rotary Screens. Water. Ground Wood (dry). 120,000 lbs. 24 hours.

STILES—Oconto Co.—PULP MILL.

Pop. 897. On C., M. & St. P., C. N. W. RR; Tel. office; Am. and Wells, Fargo Ex.; nearest bank, Oconto, 10 miles.

ANSON-ELDRED, THE, CO. (H. S. Eldred, Pres.; Karl Klauser, Sec. and Treas.; H. M. Brown, Vice-Pres.) S. P., at mill. One Grinder; one Wet Machine. Water. Ground Wood. 12,000 lbs. 24 hours.

TOMAHAWK—Lincoln Co.

Pop. 3,000. On C. M. & St. P. and M. T. & W. Rys. Also connections with C. & N. W. and Soo Lines and Western Ex. M. O. and Tel. office; Wells, Fargo Ex.

TOMAHAWK PULP AND PAPER CO. (C. B. Pride, Pres.; B. A. Pride, Vice-Pres., Treas. and Mgr.; V. E. Labbe, Sec.) S. P., Wisconsin Dam Station, on M. T. & W. RR. MILL NO. 1. Three 600-lb. engines; one 76-inch Fourdrinier. Widest trimmed sheet, 70 inches. Water. M. F. Book. 16,000 lbs. 24 hours. MILL NO. 2. Four 1000-lb. engines; one 118-inch Fourdrinier. Widest trimmed sheet, 112 inches. M. F. Book. 34,000 lbs. 24 hours. PULP MILL. One Green Bay, two E. F. Millard Grinders; one 86-inch Wet Machine. Water. Ground Wood. 12,000 lbs. 24 hours.

Lombard's English Newcastle Pulp Stones

224　　　　　　　　*Wisconsin*

WAUSAU—Marathon Co.

Pop. 14,000.　C., M. & St. P. RR. and C. & N. W. RR.　Am. and W., F. & Co. Ex.
MARATHON PAPER MILLS CO. (On street car line, 4½ miles south of Wausau.) (C. C. Yawkey, Pres.; Walter Alexander, Vice-Pres.; D. C. Everest, Sec. and Gen. Mgr.; B. F. Wilson, Treas.; P. M. Wilson, Asst. Sec.; J. R. Russell, Sales Mgr.; W. A. Kelly, Gen. Supt.; V. Salmonson, Supt.) Sulphite Mill. S. P., Electricity and Steam at Rothschild. Sixteen 1800-lb. Beating and five Refining engines; one Four Cylinder (trims 100 inches), one Fourdrinier (trims 120 inches) an dtwo Yankee Fourdriniers (trim 120 inches). Union Screens. Electricity. Machine Glazed and Dry Finish. Fancy Wrapping, Tag, Offset, Bristols, Bonds, Covers and Specialties, 150,000 lbs. 24 hours. PULP MILL. Four Grinders, ten 84-inch Wet Machines and four 16x52 Digesters. Water and Electricity. Ground Wood, 40,000 lbs. 24 hours. Sulphite (Mitscherlich), 170,000 lbs. 24 hours. Bleached Sulphite, 100,000 lbs. 24 hours. *Watermarked Specialties in Machine-Glazed and Dry Finish. Extra Water Finish Fibres, twenty-five pounds and heavier. Sulphite Bonds, Bleached Bristols and Heavy Weight Offset, High Finish Bleached Waxing.*

DARMSTADT, SCOTT & COURTNEY, Inc., Importers, Exporters and Dealers in
178 and 184 SOUTH STREET　NEW YORK
PAPER MAKERS' SUPPLIES
Also Mfrs. of DEADENING and SATURATING FELTS

ROBERTSON PAPER CO.
MANUFACTURERS OF
PLAIN AND PRINTED WAXED PAPERS
BELLOWS FALLS, VERMONT

ESTABLISHED 1892　　　　　DAILY CAPACITY, 60 TONS
SPECIALTIES:

BREAD WRAPPERS In Copyrighted Designs.　　LUNCH ROLLS, for Specialty and Department Stores
TYMPAN PAPER, for Printing Trade.　　　　　SELF-SEALING PAPERS in Sheets or Rolls.
WRAPPING MACHINE ROLLS, for Bakers, Chewing　DIPPING PAPER, for Confectionery Manufacturers.
Gum Manufacturers and Confectioners.

McEnery Paper Company Practically All Grades
Manufacturers' Sales Agency　112 W. ADAMS ST., CHICAGO

The West Virginia Pulp & Paper Co.

with a daily production of over 600 tons of Book and Coated Paper manufactured at its six mills located in four states, offers to users of paper a service unexcelled in promptness of delivery as well as in ability to take care of contracts, no matter of what size.

MAKERS OF THE

Well Known Coated Book Paper

"VELVO-ENAMEL"

A Paper Built to Fit the Needs of Direct Advertising

West Virginia Pulp and Paper Co.

New York Office - - - 200 Fifth Avenue
Chicago Office - - - 732 Sherman Street

This paper is a sample of our Velvo-Enamel

See Other Side

West Virginia Pulp and Paper Company

MANUFACTURERS OF

SUPERCALENDERED and MACHINE FINISHED

BOOK and LITHOGRAPHIC PAPERS

OFFSET, ENVELOPE and MUSIC PAPER

HIGH GRADE COATED BOOK
and LABEL PAPERS

ALSO

BLEACHED SPRUCE SULPHITE and SODA PULP

OFFICE:

200 Fifth Avenue, New York
732 Sherman Street, Chicago

Mills at: Tyrone, Pa.
Williamsburg, Pa.
Piedmont, W. Va.
Luke, Md.
Covington, Va.
Davis, W. Va.
Mechanicville, N. Y.

Cable Address
" PULPMONT NEW YORK "
A1 and A, B, C Codes Used

This paper is a sample of our Velvo-Enamel

See Other Side

ARE SUPERIOR TO ALL OTHERS. ALL SIZES IN STOCK.
LOMBARD & CO., Importers & Manufacturers, 236 & 238 A Street, Boston.

PAPER and PULP MILLS
IN THE
DOMINION of CANADA

BRITISH COLUMBIA.

MILL CREEK—HOWE SOUND.

On Mill Creek, 30 miles from the City of Vancouver.

WHALEN PULP & PAPER MILLS, LTD., Successor to The British Columbia Sulphite Fibre Co., Ltd. Office, Merchants' Bank Bldg., Vancouver. (James Whalen, Pres.; George F. Whalen, Vice-Pres. and Gen. Mgr.; Allan Paterson, Sec.) One 100-inch and one 112-inch Fourdrinier. SULPHITE MILL. Four Digesters. Easy Bleaching and Strong Sulphite. 160,000 lbs. 24 hours.

OCEAN FALLS.

In Cousin's Inlet. Tel., Vancouver, 300 miles.

PACIFIC MILLS, LTD. S. P., at mill. General Office, Standard Bank Building, Vancouver, B. C. One 174-inch News Machine; one 122-inch Kraft Machine; two 204-inch News Machines. PULP AND FIBRE MILLS. Twenty-four Grinders; twenty Wet Machines. Water. Ground Wood. 300,000 lbs. 24 hours. Sulphite. 100,000 lbs. 24 hours. Sulphate. 80,000 lbs. 24 hours.

PORT ALICE—QUATSINO SOUND—Vancouver Co.—PULP MILL.

WHALEN PULP & PAPER MILLS, LTD. Office, Merchants' Bank Bldg., Vancouver, B. C. (James Whalen, Pres.; George F. Whalen, Vice-Pres. and Gen. Mgr.; Allan Paterson, Sec.) Bleached Sulphite Fibre. 160,000 lbs. 24 hours.

PORT MELLON, HOWE SOUND.

Nearest M. O. and bank, Vancouver, B. C., 25 miles. Tel.

RAINY RIVER PULP AND PAPER CO. General offices, Standard Bank Bldg., Vancouver, B. C. New York Office, 52 Broadway. (Robert Sweeny, Pres.; E. L. Mohn, Vice-Pres. and Treas.; M. W. Morfey, Sec.; C. A. Kieren, Supt.; B. F. Taylor, Gen. Mgr.) Two Beating and two Refining engines. One 66-inch Fourdrinier. Widest trimmed sheet, 62 inches. Steam. PULP MILL. Three digesters and one Wet and one Dry Machine. Sulphate Fibre. 50,000 lbs. 24 hours.

POWELL RIVER.

On Powell River, 80 miles north of Vancouver.

POWELL RIVER CO., LTD. General Offices at mill; Eastern Office at 1120 Plymouth Bldg., Minneapolis, Minn.; Registered Office, 804 Standard Bank Bldg., Vancouver, B. C. (D. F. Brooks, Pres.; M. J. Scanlon, Vice-

---

ENGINEERING FOR
PULP, PAPER AND POWER PLANTS

JOSEPH H. WALLACE & CO.
INDUSTRIAL ENGINEERS
Temple Court Building, NEW YORK
71 Bay Street, TORONTO, CAN.

Lombard's English Newcastle Pulp Stones

British Columbia and New Brunswick

Pres.; H. K. Brooks, Sec.; A. S. Brooks, Treas., Minneapolis, Minn.; N. R. Lang, Managing Director; J. H. Lawson, Asst. Sec., Vancouver, B. C.; Wm. McBain, Mill Mgr., Powell River.) Six 1400-lb. Beaters, four Majestic Jordans and Six Mixing Tanks; one 148-inch, one 156-inch and two 184-inch Pusey & Jones Fourdriniers. Water, Steam and Electricity. News. 450,000 lbs. 24 hours. PULP MILL. Five Marx Refiners; four Wet Machines for ground wood, and three Wet Machines for Sulphite; three Digesters. Ground Wood, 200 tons; Sulphite, 170,000 lbs. 24 hours.

SAPPERTON—Westminster Co.

Pop. 1,200. On Great Northern RR. Ex. and Tel. office. Sapperton; M. O. and nearest bank, New Westminster, 1 mile.

WESTERN PAPER MILLS, LIMITED. (Barclay Bonthrone, Pres.; J. F. Garvin, Sec. and Treas.) (Machinery removed. Building for sale.)

SWANSON BAY—PULP MILL.

On Tolmie Channel, 350 miles north from Vancouver. Wireless; nearest bank, Prince Rupert.

WHALEN PULP & PAPER MILLS, LTD., Successor to Empire Pulp & Paper Mills, Ltd. (Office, Merchants' Bank Bldg., Vancouver, B. C. (James Whalen, Pres.; George F. Whalen, Vice-Pres. and Gen. Mgr.; Allan Paterson, Sec.) One 100-inch Cylinder Machine; three Digesters. Easy Bleaching and Strong Sulphite. 80,000 lbs. 24 hours.

NEW BRUNSWICK.

BATHURST—Gloucester Co.

Pop. 4,000. Port of Entry and County Seat. On Intercolonial and Term. Caraquet & Gulf Shore RR. M. O. and Tel. office; Dom. and Can. Ex.

BATHURST LUMBER CO., LTD. Pulp and Paper Division. (Hon. W. C. Edwards, Pres.; Angus McLean, Vice-Pres. and Gen. Mgr.; A. E. Loosen, Treas.; Maurice Preisch, Sec. and Treas.; J. H. Thickens, Mgr. of Pulp and Paper Mills; E. Simonson, Supt. Sulphite Mill; O. J. Oleson, Supt. of Sulphate Mill; William B. Stanton, Supt. of Paper Mill.) BATHURST PAPER MILL. S. P., Bathurst. One 130-inch Board Machine, trim 120 inches; ten 2000-lb. Beating and two Refining engines. Steam. PULP MILL. S. P., Bathurst. Five Digesters, two Wet and one 100-inch Dry Machines. Sulphite. 100,000 lbs. 24 hours. Sulphate. 120,000 lbs. 24 hours. Rolls or Bales.

CHATHAM—Northumberland Co.—PULP MILL.

Pop. 5,000 On I. C. RR. M. O. and Tel. office; Dom. Ex.

DOMINION PULP CO., LIMITED. (W. G. Stevens, Manager.) DOMINION MILL. S. P., at mill. Four Digesters; one 120-inch Fourdrinier Machine. Steam. Sulphite Fibre. 100,000 lbs. 24 hours.

EDMUNDSTON—Madawaska—PULP MILL.

Pop. 1,821. On Edmundston Branch Canadian Pacific Ry. M. O. Tel., bank and Dominion Ex.

FRASER COMPANIES, LIMITED. (Archibald Fraser, Pres.; Donald Fraser, Vice-Pres.; William Matheson, Sec.; W. M. Kesson, Treas.; J. W. Van Alstyne, Supt.) Four Digesters. Two 128-inch Rice, Barton & Fales

PRESS ROLLS Maple and Gum White Wood Felt Rolls — J. W. HEWITT MACHINE CO. Neenah, Wis.

Drying Machines; one Wet Machine. 1000 kw. Hydraulic Turbo Generator Tower Acid System. Bleaching System. Sulphite Fibre. 240,000 lbs. 24 hours.

MILLERTON—Northumberland Co—PULP MILL.

Pop. 400.   On Indiantown Branch Intercolonial RR.   Tel., Dom. and Can. Ex. Newcastle, 8 miles.

NEW BRUNSWICK SULPHATE FIBRE CO., LTD. Head Office, McGill BLDG., Montreal. (C. Howard Smith, Pres.; W. D. Robb, Vice-Pres.; Harold Crabtree, Sec., Treas. and Mang. Dir.) Two Digesters; two Wet Machines. Steam. Sulphate Fibre. 40,000 lbs. 24 hours.

ST. GEORGE—Charlotte Co.—PULP MILL.

On N. B. Southern RR.

ST. GEORGE PULP AND PAPER CO. Office, Norwalk, Conn., U. S. Six Grinders; five Wet Machines. Water and Electricity. Ground Wood. 60,000 lbs. 24 hours. Also Paper at Norwalk, Conn., U. S.

ST. JOHN—St. John Co.—PULP MILL.

Pop. 55,000.   On Can. Pacific and International RR.   M. O. Nearest Tel. and Bank, St. John; Can. and Dom. Ex.

NASHWAAK PULP AND PAPER CO., Successor to The Edward Partington Pulp & Paper Co. New York Office, 200 Fifth Avenue. (H. J. Chisholm, Pres.; L. M. Bickford, Vice-Pres.; J. H. Drummond, Sec.; F. E. Tufts, Treas.; N. M. Jones, Mgr.) S .P., airville Station. Four Digesters. Steam. Bleached Sulphite Fibre. 150,000 lbs. 24 hours

NOVA SCOTIA.

CLYDE RIVER—Shelburne Co.

Pop. 304.   Tel. and nearest bank, Barrington, 9 miles.   Southwest Ex.

CLYDE RIVER PULP AND PAPER CO., LTD. (Arch. McColl, Pres.; D. A. Bishop, Sec. and Mgr.) S. P., Port Clyde. Three Grinders and four Wet Machines. Water. Ground Wood. 40,000 lbs. 24 hours.

HARTVILLE—Hants Co.

Pop. 75.   On D. A. RR.   M. O. and bank, Windsor; West. Ex.

ST. CROIX PAPER CO., LTD. P. O. address, Ellershouse. Four Beating and one Refining engines; one 60-inch Paper Machine. Water and Steam. News, Manila, Box Boards. 12,000 lbs. 24 hours. PULP MILL. One Grinder, one Wet Machine. Ground Wood. 10,000 lbs. 24 hours. (Idle.)

MILL VILLAGE—Queens Co.—PULP MILL.

Pop. 400.   On H. & S. W. Ry.   M. O. and Tel. office; nearest bank, Winsor; West. Ex.

MEDWAY PULP & POWER CO., Successor to Nova Scotia Wood Pulp & Paper Co., Limited. (Frank K. Brown, Owner.) S. P., Port Medway. Four New England Grinders; three Wet Machines. Water. Ground Wood (dry). 40,000 lbs. 24 hours.

Lombard's English Newcastle Pulp Stones

Nova Scotia and Ontario

MILTON—Queens Co.

Pop. 2,500. H. & S. W. RR. M. O., Tel. and Ex. offices. Royal Bank of Canada and Bank of Nova Scotia.

MACLEOD PULP CO., LTD. (J. R. Macleod, Pres.; Frank Ouellet, Sec.) P. O. address, Liverpool, N. S. PAPER MILL at Rapid Falls, Milton, Queens Co. (four miles above Liverpool). (Paper mill destroyed by fire. Pulp mill running as usual.) PULP MILLS. Water. Ground Wood. 150,000 lbs. (dry) 24 hours. RAPID FALLS MILL at Milton. Six Grinders; six Wet Machines. COWIES FALLS MILL at Milton. Three Grinders; four Wet Machines.

NEW GERMANY—Lunenburg Co.—PULP MILL.

Pop. 1,500. On H. & S. W. Ry. M. O. Tel. office, Ex. and bank.

LA HAVE PULP CO., LIMITED. Stock owned by New Haven Pulp & Board Co. (W. E. Parnell, Resident Mgr.) MORGAN FALLS MILL. S. P., mill. Four Grinders; four 72-inch Wet Machines. Water. Ground Wood. 32,000 lbs. (dry) 24 hours.

WEYMOUTH—Digby Co.—PULP MILL.

Pop. 1,200. On D. A. RR. and Company's docks. M. O. and Tel. office; Maritime Ex.

CAMPBELL LUMBER CO., LTD. Two mills. (G. D. Campbell, Sr., Pres.; G. D. Campbell, Jr., Vice-Pres.; H. P. Filleul, Sec. and Treas.; R. J. Taylor, Supt.) WEYMOUTH FALLS MILL (Mill No. 2). Located at Weymouth Falls and at Tide Water. S. P., at mill. Six Grinders, six 72-inch Wet Machines. Water. Wood Pulp. 140,000 lbs. (50 per cent. dry) 24 hours. Mill No. 1 out of commission; 70,000 lbs. 24 hours.

ONTARIO.

BELLEVILLE—Hastings Co.

Pop. 9,914. On G. T. RR. M. O. and Tel. office; Can. and Dom. Ex.

LAZIER PAPER MILLS, LIMITED. (S. A. Lazier, Pres.; R. E. Lazier, Sec. and Treas.; Albert Ford, Mill Supt.) MOIRA MILL. S. P., Belleville, ½ mile. Two 500-lb. engines; one 56-inch Double Cylinder. Widest trimmed sheet, 54 inches. Water. Straw Paper for Corrugating and Corrugated Paper Carpet Lining and Stair Pads. 5000 lbs. 24 hours.

CAMDEN EAST—Addington Co.

Pop. 600. On Can. No. RR. Tel. office, Newburgh, Ont.; Can. No. Ex.

HOUPT PAPER MILLS, LIMITED. (L. F. Houpt, Pres.; W. E. Houpt, Vice-Pres. and Treas.; E. A. Crippen, Sec. and Sales Mgr.; George B. Thomson, Resident Mgr.; C. M. Nealy, Auditor.) Sales Office, 79 Spadina Avenue, Toronto. Two 1000-lb. Horne Beating; one Rag and one 1200-lb. Horne Washing and one Horne Jordan engine; one Rotary; one Paper Cooker; one Rice Barton & Fales Harper Fourdrinier, 80-inch wire. Widest trimmed sheet, 72 inches. Water, Electricity and Steam. Pure Vegetable Parchment, Grease Proof, Bleached Light Weight for Waxing, Light-Weight Catalogue, French Folio, Glazed and Unglazed Onion Skin, Feather Weight Bond, Crepe Toilet and Towelling and Specialties. 40,000 lbs. 24 hours. (Aug. 19, 1918. Affairs of company being wound up under order of court.)

WET MACHINES — We make a specialty of GROUND WOOD PULP and SULPHITE FIBRE MACHINERY — **Carthage Machine Co.** CARTHAGE, N. Y.

ARE SUPERIOR TO ALL OTHERS. ALL SIZES IN STOCK.
LOMBARD & CO., Importers & Manufacturers, 236 & 238 A Street, Boston.

Paper and Pulp Mills in Canada

CAMPBELLFORD—Northumberland Co.
Pop. 3,424. On Midland Div. G. T. RR. M. O. and Tel. office; Can. and Dom. Ex.

HYDRO-ELECTRIC POWER COMMISSION. PULP MILL, Successor to Northumberland Pulp Co., Limited. (Elie Brunelle, Mgr.; L. A. Burbank, Mill Supt.) S. P., at mill. Four Jenckes Grinders; six Wet Machines; four Hydraulic Presses. Electricity. Ground Wood Pulp. 60,000 lbs. 24 hours.

NORTHUMBERLAND PAPER AND ELECTRIC CO., LIMITED. PAPER MILL. (J. G. G. Kerry, Pres.; David F. Robertson, Gen. Mgr.; Thomas McCook, Mill Supt.) S. P., at mill. Four 1500-lb. Beating and three Jordan engines; one 70-inch Six Cylinder Machine. Widest trimmed sheet, 66 inches. Water and Electricity. Straw Board, Chip Board, News Board, Filled Wood Board, Pulp Board, Building Paper, Folding Board and Specialties. 50,000 lbs. 24 hours.

CORNWALL—Stormont Co.
Pop. 7,000. On G. T.; N. Y. & O. and C. P. RR. Cornwall Canal. M. O. and Tel. office; Can., Dom. and Am. Ex.

TORONTO PAPER MFG. COMPANY, LIMITED. (R. S. Waldie, Pres. and Managing Director, Toronto; W. J. Sheppard, Vice-Pres.; W. J. Wallace, Treas., Cornwall; A. W. Briggs, Sec.; Toronto; Wesley N. Tilton, Supt., Cornwall.) S. P., at mill. Six 800-lb., five 900-lb., two 1000-lb., four 1400-lb. Beating and six Jordan engines; one 72-inch, two 82-inch and one 90-inch Fourdriniers. Width of Super Calenders, up to 52 inches. Widest trimmed sheet, 82 inches. Water, Steam and Electricity. Writing, Bond, Ledgers, Cover, White and Colored Envelope, Lithograph and Book. Loft Drying and Linen Finishing. 62,000 lbs. 24 hours. PULP MILL. Three Digesters; one Wet Machine. Water, Steam and Electricity. Sulphite Fibre. 30,000 lbs. 24 hours.

DRYDEN—District of Kenora.
Pop. 1,000. Canadian Pacific RR. Dominion Ex.

DRYDEN PULP AND PAPER CO., LTD. (J. B. Beveridge, Gen. Mgr.; H. Humphreys, Sec. and Treas.; F. N. Beveridge, Gen. Supt.). S. P., Dryden. Water, Electricity and Steam. Four Beating and two Refining engines; one Cylinder Machine and one Fourdrinier Machine, trimming 132 and 100 inches respectively. Kraft Sheathing and Kraft Wrapping Papers. PULP MILL. Two Wet Machines; four Digesters. Sulphate of Soda (Kraft) Pulp. 120,000 lbs. 24 hours.

DUNDAS—Wentworth Co.
Pop. 5,000. On S. Div. of G. T.; T. H. & B. RR. M. O. and Tel. office; Can. and Dom. Ex.

FISHER, JOHN, & SON, LTD. GORE PAPER MILLS. One 700-lb. and two 900-lb. and two Refining engines; one 72-inch Double Cylinder. Water and Steam. Hardware, Manila Rope, Wrapping and Wax. 12,000 lbs. 24 hours.

ESPANOLA—Algoma District.
Pop. 1,700. On C. P. R., Algoma Eastern Ry. M. O. and Tel. office; nearest bank, Webbwood, 6 miles. Dom. Ex.

SPANISH RIVER PULP AND PAPER MILLS, LIMITED, THE. General Offices at Sault Ste. Marie. For officers, see Sault Ste. Marie.

ENGINEERING FOR PULP, PAPER AND POWER PLANTS

JOSEPH H. WALLACE & CO.
INDUSTRIAL ENGINEERS
Temple Court Building, NEW YORK
71 Bay Street, ___, CAN.

Ontario

(W. J. Hussey, Supt.) PAPER MILL. Eight 2000-lb. Beating and four Jones Jordan engines; two 120-inch Rice, Barton & Fales and two 164-inch Pusey & Jones Fourdriniers. News. 170 tons 24 hours. PULP MILL. S. P., at Espanola. Twenty-nine Grinders; eighteen Wet Machines. Twelve 400-ton Hydraulic Presses. Water. Ground Wood. 350,000 lbs. 24 hours.

FORT FRANCES.
On D. R. L. & W.; C. N.; M. D. & W. and N. P.

FORT FRANCES PULP AND PAPER CO., LTD. (E. W. Backus, Pres.; S. W. Backus, 1st Vice-Pres.; B. G. Dahlberg, 2nd Vice-Pres.; Wm. F. Brooks, Treas.; Thomas McLaren, Sec.) PAPER MILL. Two 186-inch Fourdriniers. Water and Electricity. News. 300,000 lbs. 24 hours. Fifteen Grinders and twelve Wet Machines; eight "Impco" Screens. Water. Ground Wood.

FRANKFORD—Hastings Co.
Pop. 700. On C. N. R. M. O. and Tel. office; Can. Ex.

CANADA BOXBOARD COMPANY, LIMITED. P. O. Address, 182 Shearer Street, Montreal, P. Q. (C. S. Gzowski, Pres.; O. A. Porritt, Vice-Pres.; N. G. Gzowski, Sec. and Treas.) S. P., at mill. Four 1800-lb. Beating and two Jordan engines; one 102-inch Six Cylinder. Widest trimmed sheet, 92 inches. Water. Straw and Wood Board. 80,000 lbs. 24 hours. PULP MILL. S. P., at mill. One New England Grinder. Water. Ground Wood. 12,000 lbs. 24 hours. (All used in company's paper mill.)

GEORGETOWN—Halton Co.
Pop. 1,500. On G. T. RR. M. O. and Tel. office; Can. Ex.

PROVINCIAL PAPER MILLS CO., LTD. BARBER DIVISION. Head office, Toronto. (I. H. Weldon, Pres.; T. A. Weldon, Vice-Pres.; S. F. Duncan, Sec. and Treas.) PAPER MILL. S. P., ½ mile. Four 1000-lb. Beating and two Refining engines; one 60-inch and one 72-inch Fourdriniers. Widest trimmed sheet, 70 inches. Water, Steam and Electricity. Machine Finished Book, Laid and Wove Envelope, Lithograph, Label, Cover and Poster. 25,000 lbs. 24 hours. PULP MILL. S. P., ½ mile. Three Digesters; one Wet Machine. Steam. Soda Fibre. 12,000 lbs. 24 hours. COATING PLANT. All kinds of Coated Book, Litho, Cover, Box Boards and Blanks.

GLEN MILLER—Hastings Co.
Pop. 1,000. On C. O. RR. Tel., M. O. and Ex. offices and nearest bank, Trenton, 3 miles.

MILLER BROTHERS CO., LIMITED, THE. (William T. Miller, Pres.; J. R. Walker, Vice-Pres.; H. C. Russell, Sec. and Treas.; P. Miller, Mill Mgr.) TRENT VALLEY PAPER MILLS. S. P., at mill. Four 750-lb. and two Jordan engines; one 68-inch Board Machine. Widest trimmed sheet, 66 inches. Water. Straw Board, Wood Pulp Board and Egg-Case Fillers. 50,000 lbs. 24 hours.

HAWKESBURY—Prescott Co.—PULP MILL.
Pop. 4,600. On G. T. R.; Can. N. RR. and Ottawa River. M. O. and Tel. office and Ex.

RIORDON PULP AND PAPER COMPANY, LIMITED, THE. Office, No. 355 Beaver Hall Square, Montreal. (Charles Riordon, Pres.; Carl

Riordon, Vice-Pres. and Managing Director; F. B. Whittet, Sec. and Treas.;
T. J. Stevenson and George E. Challes, Sales Mgrs.; E. Inwood, Buyer;
C. B. Thorne, Mgr. of Manufacturing; Col. J. B. White, Wood Dept. Mgr.)
S. P., at mill. Nine Digesters; three Dry Machines, and three Wet Machines. Steam and Electricity. Spruce Fibre. 400,000 lbs. 24 hours.
Specialty, High Color, Easy Bleaching and Strong Bleached Sulphite.

IROQUOIS FALLS—NIPISSING DIST.
On T. & N. O. R.R. Bank, M. O. and Tel. office.

ABITIBI POWER & PAPER CO., LTD. Main Office, Montreal. (F. H. Anson, Pres.; Shirley Ogilvie, Vice-Pres.; L. R. Wilson, Sec.; W. H. Smith, Treas.; R. A. McInnis, Supt.) S. P., Iroquois Falls. PAPER MILL. (News). Two 1600 broke Beaters; four Jordans. One 186-inch Pusey & Jones Machine, two 158-inch Pusey & Jones Machines and one 202-inch Walmsley Machine. Widest trimmed sheets, 148 and 176 inches. Steam and Electricity. 450,000 lbs. 24 hours. SULPHITE MILL. Four Digesters; one "Impco" Knotter. Electricity. Capacity, 260,000 lbs. 24 hours. GROUND WOOD MILL. Thirty Grinders; twenty 86-inch Wet Machines; eighteen "Impco" Screens. Electricity. 660,000 lbs. 24 hours.

MERRITTON—Lincoln Co.
Pop. 2,100. On G. T.; N. St. C. & T. RR. M. O. and Tel. office; Can. and Dom. Ex.

INTERLAKE TISSUE MILLS, LTD. (Geo. Carruthers, Pres.; S. F. Duncan, Sec.; I. H. Weldon, Treas.) S. P., Merritton. Two 1000-lb. and one Double Roll 2500-lb. Beating engines; one 116-inch Yankee Tissue Machine. Widest trimmed sheet, 110 inches. Steam and Electricity. M. G. Tissues and Light Weight Wrappings, Plain and Crepe Toilet Paper. Paper Napkins and Specialties. 20,000 lbs. 24 hours.

LINCOLN PAPER MILLS CO., LIMITED. (W. D. Woodruff, Pres.; A. S. Woodruff, Vice-Pres.; Wm. M. Shea, Sec.-Treas.) Eight 1200-lb. Beaters and one Jordan; one 112-inch Fourdrinier. Water. Manila, Fibre, Jute, Kraft, Greaseproof and Glassine. 40,000 lbs. 24 hours. Six 1000-lb. and two 1500-lb. Beaters and one Jordan. One 92-inch Three Cylinder. Water. Rôpe Manila and Wrapping. 14,000 lbs. 24 hours. SULPHITE MILL. Special Extra Strong Sulphite. 80,000 lbs. 24 hours.

RIORDON PULP AND PAPER COMPANY, LIMITED, THE. Office, No. 355 Beaver Hall Square, Montreal. (Charles Riordon, Pres.; Carl Riordon, Vice-Pres. and Managing Director; Fred B. Whittet, Sec. and Treas.; T. J. Stevenson and George E. Challes, Sales Mgrs.; E. Inwood, Buyer; P. Byrne, Supt.) SULPHITE MILL. Four Digesters; three Wet Machines. Bleached Sulphite Fibre. 80,000 lbs. 24 hours. Sulphite Screenings.

MILLE ROCHES—Stormont Co.
Pop. 500. On G. T. RR. Tel. and M. O.

PROVINCIAL PAPER MILLS CO., LTD. ST. LAWRENCE DIVISION. Office, Bell Telephone Bldg., Toronto. (I. H. Weldon, Pres. and Mgr. of Sales; T. A. Weldon, Vice-Pres.; S. F. Duncan, Sec., Treas. and Mgr.; Charles F. Buss, Supt.) S. P., Mille Roches. Five 1000-lb. Beating, five 2000-lb. Washing and three Refining engines; one 120-inch and one 136-inch

Lombard's English Newcastle Pulp Stones

Ontario

Fourdriniers. Widest trimmed sheet, 126 inches. Width of Super Calenders, 64 inches. Steam and Electricity. Book, Lithograph, Envelope and Catalogue. 60,000 lbs. 24 hours.

OTTAWA—Carleton Co.

Pop. 100,000. On Ottawa River; C. P.; G. T.; C. N.; O. & N. Y. RR.; M. O. and Tel. office. Am., Can. and Dom. Exp.

BOOTH, J. R. (J. R. Booth, J. F. Booth, C. J. Booth. S. P., Ottawa. Ten Beating and three Jordan engines; three Pusey & Jones Fourdriniers, one trimming 122 inches, and two trimming 142 inches each. Water and Electricity. News and Hanging. 260,000 lbs. 24 hours. BOARD MILL. Twelve Beating and three Jordan engines; one Black-Clawson Board Machine, trimming 112 inches. Wood Pulp, Folding Box Boards, Test Boards, Tag Boards and Mill Wrappers. 110,000 lbs. 24 hours. Also Ground Wood and Sulphite Fibre. GROUND WOOD MILL. Twelve International Type, four Sandy Hill and ten Jencks Grinders; twenty-two Wet Machines. Ground Wood 320,000 lbs. 24 hours. SULPHITE MILL. Four Manitowoc Steam Boiler, Works Digesters; seven Wet Machines, Sulphite Fibre, 140,000 lbs. 24 hours.

BRONSON, THE, COMPANY. (E. H. Bronson, Pres.; Frederic E. Bronson, Mng. Dir.; H. Greene, Sec. and Treas.) Three Grinders, three Wet Machines. Water. Ground Wood. 40,000 lbs. 24 hours.

PENETANGUISHENE—Simcoe Co.

Pop. 3,568. On Grand Trunk RR. Tel. and M. O. office. Can. Ex.

FIBRE PRODUCTS, LTD. (Out of business.)

PORT ARTHUR—Thunder Bay District—PULP MILL.

Pop. 11,216. Canadian Pacific and Canadian Northern RR. M. O., Tel., bank and Dom. and Can. No. Ex.

PORT ARTHUR PULP AND PAPER CO., LTD. (I. H. Weldon, Pres.; S. F. Duncan, Sec. and Treas.; A. G. Pounsford, Gen. Mgr.; A. G. Hinzke, Gen. Supt.) Two Digesters; Three Wet Machines. Steam and Electricity. Sulphite. 100,000 lbs. 24 hours.

ST. CATHARINES—Lincoln Co.

Pop. 12,000. On G. T.; N, C. RR.; Welland Canal. M. O. and Tel. office; Can. and Dom. Ex.

GARDEN CITY PAPER MILLS CO., LTD. (L. H. Gardner, Pres.; R. E. Myers, Vice-Pres.; Charles V. Syrett, Sec. and Treas.) On Lock No. 7, Old Welland Canal. S. P., St. Catherines and Merritton. Two 1000-lb. Beaters; one 84-inch Harper Fourdrinier. Widest trimmed sheet, 76 inches. Water and Electricity. Tissues and Toilet Papers; all kinds of Tissue Specialties. 18,000 lbs. 24 hours.

KINLEITH PAPER MILLS, LIMITED. (W. J. Gage, Pres.; W. P. Gundy, Vice-Pres.; H. F. E. Kent, Mng. Dir.; G. H. Jefferson, Sec. and Treas.; L. A. Dance, Sales Agent; W. A. Anderson, Supt.) S. P., N. C. and G. T. Railways and Welland Canal. Three 900-lb., two 1000-lb., four 1200-lb., three 1300-lb. and two 1800-lb. Beating and three Refining engines; one 76-inch and one 96-inch Fourdriniers. Widest trimmed sheet, 87 inches. Union Screens. Width of Super-Calenders, 42, 56 and 75

DARMSTADT, SCOTT & COURTNEY, Inc., Importers, Exporters and Dealers in **PAPER MAKERS' SUPPLIES**, Also Mfrs. of DEADENING and SATURATING FELTS. 178 and 184 SOUTH STREET, NEW YORK

Ground Pulp & Sulphite Fibre Mill Machinery OUR SPECIALTY | **CARTHAGE MACHINE CO.** CARTHAGE, N. Y.

inches. Water, Steam and Electricity. Book, Bond, Lithograph and Writing. 40,000 lbs. 24 hours.

SAULT STE. MARIE—Algoma District.

Pop. 13,000. On C. P. R.; A. C. & H. B. Ry. M. O. and Tel. Offices; Dom. and B. A. Ex.

SPANISH RIVER PULP & PAPER MILLS., LTD., THE. (G. H. Mead, Pres.; P. B. Wilson, Vice-Pres.; R. B. Wolf, Mgr.; A. H. Chitty, Treas.; T. Gibson, Sec.; F. L. O'Brien, Traffic Mgr.; H. C. McCoy, Pur. Agt.) General Offices, Sault Ste. Marie, Ontario. Mills at Sault Ste. Marie, Espanola and Sturgeon Falls, Ontario. SAULT STE. MARIE. S. P., at mills. C. Mackey, Supt. PAPER MILL. Two 156-inch Black-Clawson and one 186-inch and one 198-inch Pusey & Jones Fourdriniers. News. 220 tons 24 hours. One 106-inch Black & Clawson Board Machine. 70,000 lbs. 24 hours. GROUND-WOOD MILL. Thirty Grinders. 450,000 lbs. 24 hours. SULPHITE MILL. Four Digesters. 340,000 lbs. 24 hours.

SMOOTH ROCK FALLS—Ont.—PULP MILL.

On Canadian Government Railways, Transcontinental Div. M. O. and Tel.; nearest bank, Cochrane, 30 miles; Canadian and Dominion Ex.

MATTAGAMI PULP AND PAPER CO., LTD. Office, Bank of Hamilton Bldg., Toronto. (Duncan Chisholm, Pres.; E. P. Shove, Vice-Pres.; Col. D. M. Robertson, Sec. and Treas.; G. W. Saunders, Asst. Sec.; George E. Miller, Supt.) Three Digesters; one Dry Machine; two Wet Machines. Hydro-Electric. Sulphite Fibre. 300,000 lbs. 24 hours.

STRATHCONA—Addington Co.

Pop. 350. On C. W. R. RR. Tel. office; M. O. and Ex. office and nearest bank, Napanee, 5 miles.

STRATHCONA PAPER CO., THE. (G. R. Finlay and W. J. Finlay.) S. P., at mill. One 500-lb. and three 700-lb. Beating and one Jordan engines; one 84-inch Fourdrinier. Widest trimmed sheet, 72 inches. Water and Steam and Electricity. Specialty of all kinds of Sheathing. 30,000 lbs. 24 hours.

STURGEON FALLS—Nipissing District.

Pop. 3,000. On C. P. R. M. O. and Tel. office; Dom. Ex.

SPANISH RIVER PULP & PAPER MILLS, LIMITED, THE. General Offices, Sault Ste. Marie. For officers, see Sault Ste. Marie. (A. Kavenaugh, Supt.) PAPER MILL. Four 1500-lb. Beating and two Refining engines; two 120-inch Rice, Barton & Fales Fourdriniers. News and Hanging. 120,000 lbs. 24 hours. GROUND WOOD MILL. S. P., at mill. Twenty-four Grinders. Water. Ground Wood. 240,000 lbs. 24 hours. SULPHITE MILL. Two Digesters and eight Wet Machines. 130,000 lbs. 24 hours.

THOROLD—Welland Co.

Pop. 4,000. On G. T.; N. S. & T. RR.; also Welland Canal. M. O. and Tel. office; Can. Ex.

BEAVER WOOD FIBRE CO., THE, LIMITED. Main Office, Buffalo, N. Y. (W. F. MacGlashan, Pres.; J. F. Haggerty, Vice-Pres.; H. S. Lewis, Sec. and Treas.; H. N. Hiles, Asst. Sec.; T. J. Seitz, Asst. Treas.; T. H Nevill, Supt.) S. P., at mill Eight 1500-lb. Beating and three Howard Refining engines; two six 112-inch Cylinder Machines; widest trimmed sheet, 102 inches. Steam and Electricity. Wood Pulp, Fibre for Wall

Lombard's English·Newcastle Pulp Stones

Quebec

CAP MAGDELEINE—Champlain Co.—PULP MILL.

Pop. 4,000. Three miles from Three Rivers. M. O. and Tel. office. Ex. and bank at Three Rivers.

ST. MAURICE PAPER CO., LTD. Office, Board of Trade Bldg., Montreal, P. Q. One Beating and two Jordan engines; two Fourdriniers; widest trimmed sheets, 152 inches. Steam and Electricity. News. 200,000 lbs. 24 hours. GROUND WOOD MILL. Fifteen Grinders, sixteen Wet Machines. Electricity. Ground Wood. 200,000 lbs. 24 hours. SULPHITE MILL. Two Digesters. Sulphite Fibre. 120,000 lbs. 24 hours. SULPHATE MILL. Two Digesters. Sulphate Fibre. 100,000 lbs. 24 hours.

CHAMBLY CANTON—Chambly.

Pop. 857. On Cent. Vt. RR. M. O. and Tel. office. Can. Ex. Nearest bank, Chambly Basin, 1 mile.

BENNETT, LTD., successor to Canadian Leatherboard Co., Ltd. (F. E. Norton, Pres.; Geo. F. Davis, Vice-Pres.; Clifford Wells, Treas.; H. E. Walker, Sec.; F. E. Norton and O. F. Bryant, Supts.) S. P., Chambly, ¼ mile. Fifteen 900-lb. and one 600-lb. Beating engines; three Refining engines; two Rotary boilers; seven 32-inch Cylinder Machines. Widest trimmed sheet, 46 inches. Width of Super Calenders, 52 inches. Electricity. Binders', Counter, Fibre and Shoe Board. 32,000 lbs. 24 hours.

CHANDLER—Gaspe—PULP MILL.

Pop. 1,200. On Atlantic, Quebec & Western RR. M. O. & Tel. office. Ex.

ST. LAWRENCE PULP AND LUMBER CORP. Office, Chicoutimi. J. E. A. Dubuc, Pres. and Gen. Mgr.; A. Bechard, Treas.) This company is controlled by the North American Pulp & Paper Co. Office, Chicoutimi. ST. LAWRENCE SULPHITE MILL. S. P., at mill. Four Digesters; four Wet and one Drying Machine. Sulphite (dry). Steam and Electricity. 240,000 lbs. 24 hours.

CHICOUTIMI—Chicoutimi Co.—PULP MILL.

Pop. 6,000. On Q. & Lake St. J. RR.; steamer from Quebec. M. O. and Tel. office.

COMPAGNIE DE PULPE DE CHICOUTIMI, LA. (N. Garneau, Pres.; J. E. A. Dubuc, Managing Director; A. Bechard, Treas.; Ray Belleau, Sec.; Edouard Lavoie, Mill Supt.) This company is controlled by the North American Pulp & Paper Co. Office, 33 West 42d Street, New York. Three mills. S. P., at mills. Fifty Grinders; forty-eight Wet Machines. Water. Ground Wood. 720,000 lbs. (dry) 24 hours.

CLARKE CITY—Saguenay Co.—PULP MILL.

GULF PULP & PAPER CO. 17 St. James Street, Quebec, and Clarke City, Quebec, Canada. (James Clarke, Pres.; William Clarke, Vice-Pres.; George Clarke, Sec.-Treas.) Location on St. Marguerite River, Bay of Seven Islands. S. P., at mill. Twenty-four Grinders. Water. Ground Wood. 300,000 lbs. 24 hours.

CRABTREE MILLS—Joliette Co.

On C. N. Que. RR. M. O., Tel., Ex. and nearest bank, Joliette, 4 miles.

HOWARD SMITH PAPER MILLS, LTD., Successor to Edwin Crabtree & Sons, Ltd. Offices, 138 McGill Street, Montreal. (C. Howard Smith,

Pres.; J. W. Pyke, Vice-Pres.; Alex. Cameron, H. C. Courtney, J. M. M. Pangman, D. W. Campbell and J. Anderson, Directors; H. Crabtree, Sec. and Treas.) S. P., at mill. Six Beating engines; one 100-inch Fourdrinier. Water and Steam. Sulphite Bonds and High Grade Writings. 20,000 lbs. 24 hours.

DONNACONA—Portneuf Co.

Pop. 600. On Can. Northern Quebec R.R. Tel., G. N. W. Ex., C. N. R. M. O. and bank.

DONNACONA PAPER CO., LTD., THE. (G. H. P. Gould, Lyons Falls, N. Y., Pres.; D. C. Murray, Utica, N. Y., Vice-Pres.; C. B. Rogers, Utica, N. Y., Treas.; Geo. M. McKee, Donnacona, Gen. Mgr.) S. P., at mill. Three 2000-lb. Beating engines and two Majestic Jordans; two Bagley & Sewall 160-inch Fourdrinier. Widest trimmed sheet, 150 inches. Water and Electricity. News. 200,000 lbs. 24 hours. GROUND WOOD MILL. Eighteen Grinders; four Wet Machines. Water. 200,000 lbs. 24 hours. SULPHITE MILL. Two 15x54 Digesters. 100,000 lbs. 24 hours.

EAST ANGUS—Compton Co.

Pop. 3,000. On Quebec Central R.R. M. O. and Tel. office; Dominion Ex.

BROMPTON PULP AND PAPER CO. (F. N. McCrea, Pres.; W. N. Munroe, Treas.; J. A. Bothwell, Gen. Mgr.) ANGUS MILLS. S. P., East Angus. Two 1000-lb. and nine 2000-lb. Beating and two Jordan engines; one 84-inch and one 96-inch Fourdriniers. Widest trimmed sheet, 85 inches. Water and Steam. Kraft and Manilas. 50,000 lbs. 24 hours. EAST ANGUS BOXBOARD MILL. One 112-inch Cylinder machine and three Beating engines. Boxboard, 80,000 lbs. 24 hours. NEWS MILL. One 162-inch Fourdrinier, four Beating engines and two Jordans. News. 120,000 lbs. 24 hours. CHEMICAL PULP MILL. S. P., at mill. Six Digesters; one 85-inch Drying Machine; four 2000-lb. Beaters; one 112-inch Board Machine; two "Impco" Knotters. Sulphate Fibre. 120,000 lbs. 24 hours. GROUND WOOD MILL. Twenty Grinders; fourteen Wet Presses, four Hydraulic Presses; one "Impco" Screen. Water and Electricity. 200,000 lbs. (dry) 24 hours. (July 6, 1918. Putting in a second 162-inch News Machine which will be installed this fall.)

FRASERVILLE—Temiscouata Co.

Pop. 9,000. On Intercolonial and Temiscouata Railroads. M. O. and Tel. offices; Can. Ex. Three Banks.

RIVER DU LOUP PULP CO., LIMITED, THE. S. P., at mill. Six Grinders; eight "Warren-Hughes" Patent New Process Wet Machines. Water. Ground Wood (dry). 80,000 lbs. 24 hours.

GRAND FALLS, Madeleine River, Gaspe.

M. O. and bank, Ste. Anne, Des Monts. Tel., Madeleine East; Ex. connections, Matane.

GREAT EASTERN PAPER CO. Eight Grinders, seven Wet Machines. Water and Electricity. Ground Wood. 40,000 lbs. 24 hours.

GRAND MERE—Champlain Co.

Pop. 5,000. On C. P. and C. N. Q. RR. M. O. and Tel. offices; Dom. and Can. N. Ex.

LAURENTIDE COMPANY, LIMITED. (George Chahoon, Jr., Pres. and Mgr.; Charles R. Hosmer, Vice-Pres.; W. F. Robinson, Sec.; Louis

Lombard's English Newcastle Pulp Stones

Hardy S. Ferguson, Consulting Engineer — 200 Fifth Avenue, New York City — Paper, Pulp and Fibre Mills, Water Power Development, Dams, Storage Reservoirs and Other Hydraulic Structures

238   *Quebec*

Armstrong, Asst. Treas.) S. P., Grand Mere. Nineteen 1300-lb. Horne Beating and six Jordan engines; one 90-inch, one 100-inch, one 110-inch, one 120-inch, two 124-inch Fourdriniers, and one 120-inch Cylinder. Widest trimmed sheet, 115 inches. Electricity. News, Folding Wood Boards, Sulphite and Ground Wood. News, 420,000 lbs.; Boards, 100,000 lbs. 24 hours. PULP MILL. S. P., Grand Mere. Fourteen Magazine Grinders; six Digesters; Twenty Wet Machines. Electricity. Ground Wood Pulp (dry), 560,000 lbs. Sulphite Fibre, 350,000 lbs. 24 hours.

HULL—Wright Co.

Pop. 25,422. On C. P.; C. A.; O. & N. Y.; O. A. & P.; O. & G. RR. M. O. and Tel. office; Dom. and Canadian Ex.; Cable and Long Distance Tel.

EDDY CO., THE E. B., LIMITED. Incorporated. (Geo. H. Millen, Pres. and Mgr.; J. T. Shirreff, Vice-Pres.; David Tilley, Treas.; John F. Taylor, Sec.; John F. Orde, K. C., Solicitor Director.) S. P., at mills and at Ottawa. Twenty-four Beating, four Washing and six Jordan engines; one 86-inch Harper Fourdrinier, three 100-inch and one 116-inch Fourdriniers; one 86-inch Tissue and one 100-inch Cylinder Board Machine. Width of Super-Calenders, 50 inches. Water, Steam and Electricity, but mostly Electricity. Ledger, Writing, Litho, Book, News, Poster, Drug, Tea, Cover, Manila, Brown Wrapping, Tissues and Tissue Toilet, Cardboard, Wood Pulp Board, Flour Sack. Also Binders' and Box Boards. Boards and Papers, 200,000 lbs. 24 hours. PULP MILL. S. P., at mills. Fifteen Grinders; four Refiner Grinders and one Silver Grinder; eight Wet Machines. Steam, Water and Electricity, but mostly Electricity. Ground Wood, 200,000; and Sulphite, 120,000 lbs. 24 hours.

JOLIETTE—Joliette Co.

Pop. 2,347. On C. P. and G. N. RR. M. O. and Tel. office; Dom. Ex.

McARTHUR, ALEX., & CO., LTD. (D. J. Munn, Pres.; E. J. Rowlands, Sec. and Treas.; G. E. Bradley, Supt.) P. O. address, 82 McGill street, Montreal. JOLIETTE PAPER MILLS. S. P., station. Four 750-lb., two 800-lb. Horne Beating and two Jordan engines; one 68-inch Three Cylinder and one 84-inch Fourdriniers. Widest trimmed sheet, 76 inches. Water, Steam and Electricity. Hanging, Fibre, Wrapping, Building, Manila and News and Poster Paper. 45,000 lbs. 24 hours.

JONQUIERES—Chicoutimi Co.

Q. & L. St. J. RR. Tel. office.

PRICE BROTHERS & COMPANY, LTD. (Sir William Price, Pres.; J. M. McCarthy, Vice-Pres.; Geo. H. Thomson, Vice-Pres.; H. E. Price, Sec. and Treas.; John Ball, Mgr.; A. J. Davies, Supt.) KENOGAMI MILLS. S. P., at mills. Eight 2000-lb. Beating and three Refining engines; four 156-inch Machines. Widest trimmed sheet, 146 inches. Union Screens. Water. News Print. 220 tons 24 hours. PULP MILL. Forty-two Grinders; Four Digesters. Water. 500,000 lbs. Ground Wood; 180,000 lbs. Sulphite 24 hours.

THE JONQUIERES PULP CO., LTD. (Sir William Price, Pres.; J. M. McCarthy, Vice-Pres.; Geo. H. Thomson, Vice-Pres.; H. E. Price, Sec. and Treas.; John Ball, Mgr.; G. F. Cullet, Supt.) S. P., at mill. Three 1000-lb.

PRESS ROLLS Maple and Gum White Wood Felt Rolls — J. W. HEWITT MACHINE CO. Neenah, Wis.

and three 1200-lb. Beating engines; one 78-inch Six Cylinder. Widest trimmed sheet, 70 inches. One 110-inch Bagley and Sewell Machine. Widest trimmed sheet, 102 inches. Water, Steam and Electricity. Cardboard of all kinds, Sheathing and Fancy Colored Folding Box Board, Manila, News and Bond. 110,000 lbs. 24 hours. PULP MILL. JONQUIERES PULP MILL. S. P., at mill. Nine Grinders; nine Wet Machines. Water. Ground Wood (dry). 120,000 lbs. 24 hours.

LAKE MEGANTIC—Compton Co.—PULP MILL.

Pop. 1,875. On I. Div. C. P. and Q. C. RR. Tel. office; M. O.; Dom. and Am. Express.

LAKE MEGANTIC PULP CO. (Geo. M. Stearns, Pres.; W. D. Russell, Treas.; G. M. Stearns, Sec. and Supt.) Four Grinders; three Wet Machines. Water. Ground Wood. 30,000 lbs. 24 hours.

LACHUTE MILLS—Argenteuil Co.

Pop. 2,500. On C. P. & C. N. RR. M. O., Tel. office and bank; Dom. Ex.

WILSON, LIMITED, J. C. Office, 61 St. Alexander street, Montreal. LACHUTE PAPER MILLS. S. P., at mill. Three 500-lb., nine 1000-lb. and four Jordan engines; two 76-inch Harper, one 84-inch Fourdrinier, one 94-inch Harper Fourdrinier. Water and Steam. Manila, Wrappings, Bag, Tissue, Fibre and Browns. 100,000 lbs. 24 hours.

L'ANGE GARDIEN—Montgomery Co.

RICHARD & CO. (Louis Richard, Mgr. and Supt.) Office, 161 Arago Street, Quebec. Five Beating and one Refining engines. Four Wet Machines. Water. Leather, Counter, Friction and Fibre Board. 6,000 lbs. 24 hours.

LA TUQUE—Champlain Co.—PULP MILL.

115 miles from Quebec City. C. N. Ry. Tel. office. Canadian North. Ex.

BROWN CORPORATION. Office, 404 Commercial Street, Portland, Me. (H. J. Brown, Pres.; O. B. Brown, Sec. and Treas.; H. Martinson, Supt.; D. P. Brown, Local Mgr.) Eight Digesters; three Dry Machines; two Wet Machines. Four "Impco" Screens. Electric. Sulphate Kraft Pulp. Production all used by parent company at Berlin, N. H.

LES SAULES—Quebec Co.

3 miles from Ancienne Lorette. Tel., M. O. and Ex. Ancienne Lorette. Nearest bank, Quebec, 6 miles.

RICHARD & CO. Office, 161 Arago Street, Quebec. Two Wet Machines. Water. Leather Board. 6,000 lbs. 24 hours.

MONTREAL—Hochelaga Co.

Pop. 600,000. On G. T.; C. P.; D. & H.; C. V.; N. Y. C. RR. M. O. and Tel. office; U. S., & Can., Dom. and Nat. Ex.

CANADA BOXBOARD COMPANY, LTD., 182 Shearer Street. (C. S. Gzowski, Pres.; O. A. Porritt, Vice-Pres.; N. G. Gzowski, Sec. and Treas.) Four 1500-lb. Beating and four Jordan engines; one Six Cylinder Machine. Widest trimmed sheet, 83 inches. Water, Electricity and Steam. All Lines of Chip and Folding Boxboards. 70,000 lbs. 24 hours.

DOMINION PAPER CO. (F. P. Currie, Pres.; Robert Currie, Vice-Pres. and Gen. Mgr.) KINGSEY FALLS MILLS. S. P., Kingsey Station.

Three 800-lb. and one 1200-lb. Beating engines; one 92-inch Fourdrinier Machine. Widest trimmed sheet, 84 inches. Water and Steam. Brown and Manila Wrapping, Fibre, Hardware and Sheathing; also Kraft Brown. 30,000 lbs. 24 hours. PULP MILLS. Two mills. KINGSEY FALLS CHEMICAL FIBRE MILLS. Three Digesters. Sulphate Pulp. 12,000 lbs. 24 hours. KINGSEY FALLS WOOD PULP MILL. One Grinder; three 72-inch Wet Machines. Ground Wood Pulp (dry). 14,000 lbs. 24 hours.

FOREST PRODUCTS LABORATORIES OF CANADA. (John S. Bates, Supt.) Organized under Department of the Interior, Forestry Branch. Located at McGill University, Montreal. Experimental Pulp and Paper Mill on a semi-commercial basis. One 40-lb. Marx Single Beater and one 60-lb. Marx Double Beater; one Noble and Woods Baby Jordan; one Four Plate Packer Screen; one Pusey and Jones Experimental Paper Machine with 25 feet wire 33 inches wide; two Wet Presses with Granite Top Rolls; Smoothing Press; twenty Dryers 15 inches diameter; Tub-Sizing Vat; Machine Glaze Dryer 5-foot diameter; eight Roll Calendar Stock, etc.; one 47-inch Carthage Chipper; Erfurt Sizing System; small Sulphite and Soda Digesters, etc. Equipped to make practically all kinds and grades of Pulp and Paper for experimental purposes. Chemical Laboratory especially equipped for Research Work on Wood and Pulp.

WALKER & CO., LTD., J. R., 35 Common Street, Montreal. (J. R. Walker, G. P. Walker, H. E. Walker, Sec.; F. E. Walker, Treas.; James Hewton, Mgr.) SAULT AU RECOLLET PAPER MILL. S. P., at mill. Six 600-lb. and four 700-lb. Beating engines; two Washing engines and one Rotary Boiler; two 48-inch and one 84-inch Cylinders. Widest trimmed sheet, 76 inches. Water and Steam. Roofing and Sheathing, Trunk, Friction and Fibre Boards. 25,000 lbs. 24 hours.

MURRAY BAY—Charlevoix Co.—PULP MILL.
On Q. & S. RR. M. O. and Tel. office. Also Ex.

NAIRN FALLS POWER & PULP CO., LTD. (J. T. Donohue Pres.; Chas. Donohue, Mng. Dir.; Laurent G. Morin, Sec. and Treas.; J. O. Dugay, Supt.) S. P., at mill. Twelve Grinders for 30-inch wood; fourteen Wet Machines. Water, Steam and Electricity. Ground Wood. 240,000 lbs. 24 hours.

NICOLET FALLS—Richmond Co.—PULP MILL.
Pop. 500. On G. T. RR. Two miles from Danville. Tel., Ex. and bank, Danville.

LOTBINIERE LUMBER CO., THE. Head office, Lyster, Que. (E. W. Tobin, M. P., Pres.; F. N. McCrea, M. P., Vice-Pres.; F. C. Baker, Sec. and Treas.; W. H. Mitchell, Mgr.) P. O. address, Nicolet Falls, Que. S. P., Danville. Four Grinders; four Wet Machines. Water. Ground Wood. 50,000 lbs. 24 hours. (Destroyed by fire; undecided as to rebuilding.)

PONT ROUGE—Portneuf Co.
Pop. 1,800. On Q. Div. of C. P. RR. M. O. and Tel. office; nearest bank, Quebec, 25 miles; Dom. Ex.

BIRD & SON, LTD. (Philip R. Allen, Pres.; G. E. Messer and G. R. Wyman, Vice-Pres.; H. E. Davenport, Sec. and Treas.; C. P. Cowan, Supt.) Office, Hamilton, Ont. S. P., at mill. One 84-inch Cylinder machine.

WE SPECIALIZE

In Pulp and Paper Mill Machinery therefore our service is of the greatest value to you

It will pay you to investigate the merits of our

Centrifugal Screens, "Improved Design"
Knotter, "Sulphite Knot Screen"
Pneumatic Save-alls
Pneumatic Sulphite Thickeners
Pneumatic Water Filters
Wet Machines, "Several Designs"
Pulp Thickeners or Deckers
Suction Pumps
Blowers, "Positive Pressure"
North Beater Filling, "Patented"
Warren Improved Calender Doctors, "Patented"
Nuttall's Patent Doctors
Cylinder Moulds, "Non-Sagging"
Couch Rolls, "Spirally Wound," Patented
Suction Rolls
Rock Maple Press Rolls
Special Machinery, "Your Design"
Repair Work, Etc., Etc.

Ask us for everything you may need.   Correspondence a pleasure

Sherbrooke Machinery Co., Limited
Sherbrooke, Quebec

Parent Company
Improved Paper Machinery Company, Nashua, N. H., U. S. A.

See Other Side

WE BUILD <IMPCO> SPECIALIZED

PULP MACHINERY

Knotters, Knot Screens or Sliver Screens
  For sulphite, sulphate, soda or ground wood. Capacity up to 50 tons, less than 1 H.P. per machine, single belt drive, no gears or sprockets, no packings, slow speed, quick detachable plates. The standard machine for removing knots, shives and foreign matter.

Centrifugal Screens
  For screening sulphite, sulphate, soda, kraft or ground wood. Highest quality of stock produced at minimum power, revolving screen plates, mechanically correct.

Thickeners Pneumatic or Decker Design
  Built as single machines or in batteries, "Patented" to suit individual mills

Pneumatic Save-alls

Pneumatic Water Filters

Vacuum Pumps and Wet Machines

Your Investigation Warranted

Sherbrooke Machinery Co., Limited
Sherbrooke, Quebec, Canada

Parent Company
Improved Paper Machinery Company, Nashua, N. H., U. S. A.

See Other Side

Widest trimmed sheet, 74 inches. Water. Building, Carpet Lining, Felts, Roofing, Sheathing and Wrapping. 50,000 lbs. 24 hours.

DONNACONA PAPER CO., LTD. P. O. address, Donnacona, P. Q. PONT ROUGE PULP MILL. S. P., Pont Rouge. Two Grinders; three 72-inch Wet Machines. Water. Ground Wood. 30,000 lbs. 24 hours.

PORTNEUF STATION—Portneuf Co.

Pop. 200. On Que. Div. C. P. RR. M. O., Tel. office and Dom. Ex. Nearest bank, Portneuf, 2 miles.

FORD, JOSEPH, & CO. P. O. Address, Portneuf Station, P. Q. (Jos., Jr., and Thos. F.) Three mills. NO. 1 MILL. S. P., C. P. RR., ½ mile. One 600-lb. Beating and one Refining engines; one 72-inch Fourdrinier. Widest trimmed sheet, 66 inches. Water and Steam. Hanging, News and Wrapping. 12,000 lbs. 24 hours. NO. 2 MILL. S. P., siding, ¼ mile. Two 600-lb. Beating and one Refining engines; one 64-inch Fourdrinier. Widest trimmed sheet, 59 inches. Water and Steam. Hanging, News and Wrapping. 14,000 lbs. 24 hours. NO. 3 MILL. Four 600-lb. Beaters, four 84-inch Cylinders. Widest trimmed sheet, 74 inches. Water. Roofing Felt. 20,000 lbs. 24 hours.

FORD, ROWLAND, & SON. (Rowland Ford, Sr., and Rowland Ford, Jr.) P. O. Address, Portneuf Station. Three 500-lb. Beating engines and one Rotary boiler; one 70-inch Cylinder. Widest trimmed sheet, 68 inches. Water. Roofing Felt, Carpet Felt and Sheathing. 10,000 lbs. 24 hours.

MONTREAL PAPER CO., LTD. Office, Portneuf Station, Portneuf Co. (T. Parkin, Bishop, Pres.; L. P. Bishop, Vice-Pres.; Paul Plamondon, Sec. and Treas.; Alf. Bishop, Supt.) S. P., at mill. Four 500-lb. Beating engines; one 84-inch Double Cylinder. Widest trimmed sheet, 72 inches. Water and Electricity. Saturating Felts, Carpet Felt, Deadening Felts, Straw and Gray Sheathing. 24,000 lbs. 24 hours.

RIMOUSKI—PULP MILL.

Pop. 3,800. On C. G. RR. Intercolonial Div. M. O. and Tel. office. Dom. and Can. Ex.

PRICE-PORRITT PULP AND PAPER CO. A subsidiary of Price Brothers & Co., Ltd. Quebec. (Sir William Price, M. P., Pres.; H. E. Price, Sec. and Treas.; John Ball, Gen. Mgr.; W. J. Patton, Supt. of Pulp Mill.) S. P., Rimouski. Six Grinders; six Wet Machines. Water and Electricity. Ground Wood. 84,500 lbs. (dry) 24 hours. *Manufacturers of Fine Ground Wood Pulp.*

ST. ADELE—Terrebonne Co.

Pop. 2,050. On C. P. RR. M. O. and Tel. office; nearest bank, St. Jerome.

ROLLAND PAPER CO., THE. NORTHERN DIVISION. P. O. address, Mont Rolland, Terrebonne Co., Que.; Montreal Office, 142 St. Paul Street W. (S. J. B. Rolland, Pres.; Olivier Rolland, Mgr.) S. P., at mill. Ten 1500-lb. Beating and two Refining engines; one 87-inch and one 100-inch Fourdrinier. Widest trimmed sheet, 94 inches. Width of Super Calenders, 41 and 52 inches. Water and Steam. Tub Sized and Loft Dried Bond, Ledger, Writing, Envelope, Book and Lithographed. 40,000 lbs. 24 hours.

Quebec

ST. AMEDEE DE PERRIBONKA—Lake St. John—PULP MILL.
Nearest bank and Tel., Roberval.

QUEBEC & SAGUANAY PULP CO., Successors to Perribonka Co., Ltd. S. P., Roberval. (Dr. M. J. Mooney, Pres.; W. T. Robinson, Vice-Pres.; Albert Felton, Gen. Mgr.) Three Grinders; four 80-inch Wet Machines. Water and Steam. Ground Wood, 60,000 lbs. 24 hours.

ST. ANDRE—Lake St. John Co.—PULP MILL.
Pop. 1,816. On Lake St. John Railway. Tel. office; M. O., Std Jerome, 9½ miles; Ex. Lake Bouchette Station; nearest bank, Quebec.

METABETCHOUAN CO. Office, 216 St. Paul Street, Quebec. (La. Terreau, Pres.; F. X. Drolet, Vice-Pres.; Joseph Ed. Caron, Sec. and Treas.) Water.

ST. ANTONIN—Temiscouata Co.—PULP MILL.
Pop. 1,500. M. O., Ex. and nearest bank, Fraserville, 6 miles; Tel., Old Road, 1¼ miles.

SOUCY, F. FLORENTIN. P. O. Address, Old Lake Road. S. P., Old Lake Road. Two Grinders; three Wet Machines. Water. Ground Wood. 30,000 lbs. 24 hours.

ST. BASILE—Portneuf Co.
Pop. 2,500. On Que. Div. C. P. RR. and T. C. RR. M. O., Tel. office. Dom. and Can. Ex.

EASTERN PAPER CO., LTD. Office, St. Basile Station, Portneuf Co. (E. M. R. Pepin, Pres. and Gen. Mgr.; J. E. Pepin, Sec.-Treas.) Six 500-lb. Beating engines; one 92-inch Cylinder. Widest trimmed sheet, 84 inches. Water, Steam and Electric Motors. Carpet Lining, Deadening Felt, Sheathing, Colored Felt, Insulating Felt, Thick Felt for Export, Tarred Sheathing and Tarred Papers; also Boards of all Kinds. 30,000 lbs. 24 hours.

ST. JEROME—Terrebonne Co.
Pop. 4,479. On C. P. and C. N. Q. M. O., bank and Tel. office; Dom. and Can. Ex.

ROLLAND PAPER CO., THE. Montreal Office, 142 St. Paul Street W. (S. J. B. Rolland, Pres.; J. P. Rolland, Vice-Pres.; Jean Rolland, Gen. Mgr.) ROLLAND MILLS. S. P., at mill. Twelve 1000-lb. Beating and two Jordan engines; one 66-inch and one 87-inch Fourdriniers. Width of Super-Calenders, 42 inches. Water and Steam. Loft Dried Papers, Bristol, Ledger, Bond, Wedding and Linen. 14,000 lbs. 24 hours.

WILSON, LTD., J. C. Three Grinders. Three 73-inch Wet Machines. Water. Ground Wood. 30,000 lbs. 24 hours.

ST. RAYMOND—Portneuf Co.
Pop. 4,000. On Q. & L. St. J. RR. M. O. and Tel. office.

NEWS PULP AND PAPER CO., LTD. Office, 31 Herald Bldg., 275 Craig Street W, Montreal. (Frank Powell, Mgr.; H. H. MacArthur, Sec. and Treas.) S. P., at mill. Three 1200-lb. Beating and one Refining engines; one 118-inch Fourdrinier. Widest trimmed sheet, 109½ inches. Width of Super Calenders, 112 inches. Water and Steam. News, 60,000 lbs. 24 hours. PULP MILL. S. P., at mill. Eight Grinders; six Wet Machines. Water. Ground Wood (dry). 80,000 lbs. 24 hours.

SHAWINIGAN FALLS—St. Maurice Co.

Pop. 8,500. On Can., North Que. & Can. Pac. RR. M. O. and Tel. office; Ex.

BELGO-CANADIAN PULP AND PAPER CO., LTD. (H. Biermans, Gen. Mgr.; John Stadler, Chief Engineer; R. C. Sharpley, Mgr. of Sales.) S. P., at mill. Eight 2000-lb. Beating engines; two 127-inch, one 152-inch and one 202-inch Fourdriniers. Widest trimmed sheet, 192 inches. Water, Steam and Electricity. News. 380,000 lbs. 24 hours. PULP MILL. S. P., at mill. Twenty-four Grinders; twelve Wet Machines; three Digesters. Water. Ground Wood. 280,000 lbs. (dry); Sulphite, 180,000 lbs. 24 hours.

THREE RIVERS.

WAYAGAMACK PULP AND PAPER CO. (C. R. Whitehead, Pres.; James W. Pyke, Vice-Pres.; Alex. Pringle, Vice-Pres.; R. H. Pope, Sec. and Treas.; F. I. Ritchie, Supt. of Lumber Dept.; John Mather, Sales Mgr.; Directors: J. N. Greenshields, K. C.; Sir Wm. Price, Hugh Markey, K. C.; G. H. Duggan, Alexander Maclaren.) Located on Baptist Island. Kraft Wrapping and Sulphate Pulp. 300,000 lbs. 24 hours.

VAL-JALBERT—Lake St. John Co.—PULP MILL.

Pop. 1,000. On C. N. RR. System. M. O., Tel. and Ex. offices, Reberval, 6 miles.

COMPAGNIE DE PULPE DE CHICOUTIMI, LA. Head office at Chicoutimi. (N. Garneau, Pres.; J. E. A. Dubuc, Managing Director; A. Bechard, Treas.; Ray Belleau, Sec.; J. A. Lapointe, Mill Supt.) Ten Grinders; fifteen Wet Machines. Water. Ground Wood. 240,000 lbs. (dry) 24 hours.

WINDSOR MILLS—Richmond Co.

Pop. 2,800. On G. T.; C. P. RR. M. O. and Tel. office; Can. and Dom. Ex.

CANADA PAPER CO., LIMITED. (Joseph Kilgour, Pres.; F. J. Campbell, Gen. Mgr.; H. M. Thorne, Sec.-Treas.; H. B. Donovan, Mgr. of Sales.) Two mills. WINDSOR and ST. FRANCIS. Four 600-lb., seven 800-lb., two 1000-lb., four 2000-lb. and five Refining engines; two 72-inch, one 92-inch and one 156-inch Fourdriniers. Widest trimmed sheet, 146 inches. Width of Super-Calenders, 84 inches. Water, Steam and Electricity. News, Manilas, Colors and Book. 140,000 lbs. 24 hours. PULP MILL. Two mills. WINDSOR and ST. FRANCIS. S. P., at mill. Twelve Grinders; four Digesters; ten 72-inch Wet Machines. Water and Steam. Ground Wood, 120,000 lbs.; Soda Fibre, 30,000 lbs. 24 hours.

COLONY OF NEWFOUNDLAND.

BISHOPS' FALLS.

ALBERT E. REED & CO., NEWFOUNDLAND, LIMITED. (Albert E. Reed, Chairman Board of Directors; A. E. Harris, General Manager.) S. P., Botwood. Eighteen Grinders, for 30-inch wood; twenty-four 72-inch Wet Machines. Ground Wood. 280,000 lbs. 24 hours.

Colony of Newfoundland

CAMPBELLTOWN—Twillingate Dist.—PULP MILL.

Pop. 90. M. O. and Tel., Lewisport, 9 miles; Ex. and nearest bank, Twillingate, 30 miles.

HORWOOD LUMBER CO., LTD. Head Office, St. John. (Directors, W. F. Horwood, R. F. Horwood, W. S. Monroe and R. K. Bishop.) Three Grinders; three Wet Machines; five Twelve-plate Screens Hydraulic Presses. Ground Wood. 40,000 lbs. 24 hours.

GRAND FALLS

Pop. 2,000. Grand Falls R. N. Railway and A. N. D. RR. to Botwood. Nearest M. O. and Tel., Grand Falls; nearest bank, Bank of Montreal.

ANGLO-NEWFOUNDLAND DEVELOPMENT CO., LTD. HARMSWORTH'S MILL. (Viscount Northcliffe, Pres.; Wm. Scott, Vice-Pres. and Mgr.; John Cowley, London Mgr., "The Fleetway House," Farringdon Street, E. C., London; E. A. Sursham, Sec.; T. F. Judge, Supt.) S. P., Botwood, Heart's Content, St. John's. Ten 1800-lb. Beating and five Majestic Jordan engines; one 124, one 134, two 156 and one 164-inch Fourdrinier Machines Electricity. 205 tons News. PULP MILLS. Twenty-four Grinders for 32-inch wood; five Digesters; sixteen 84-inch Wet Machines for ground wood and five 84-inch Wet Machines for sulphite. Water and Electricity. 240 tons Ground Wood, 135 tons Sulphite 24 hours.

ARE SUPERIOR TO ALL OTHERS. ALL SIZES IN STOCK.
LOMBARD & CO., Importers & Manufacturers, 236 & 238 A Street, Boston.

IDLE MILLS
See Mill Section for Equipment

UNITED STATES

WHITTELSEY CO., THE F. H., Windsor Locks, Conn.
KENNESAW PAPER CO., Marietta, Ga.
AMERICAN STRAW BOARD CO., Lockport, Ill.
COLONIAL PULP MILL, Bar Mills, Me.
SHAWMUT MFG. CO., Shawmut, Me.
GUNPOWDER PAPER MILL, Parkton, Md.
CECIL MILL, Rising Sun, Md.
MUCKLE BROS. MFG. CO., Clearwater, Minn.
TWIN FALLS MILLS, Scotch Plains, N. J.
CAMILLUS PAPER MILLS, Camillus, N. Y.
OUTTERSON, JAMES H., Eagle Mill, Ballston Spa, N. Y.
UNITED PAPER CO., Ballston Spa, N. Y.
SEVER'S MILL, Broadalbin, N. Y.
MOHAWK IMPROVEMENT CO., Fort Plain, N. Y.
WOOD & NELLIS, Fort Plain, N. Y.
GREASONIA PAPER MILLS CO., INC., Frankfort, N. Y.
CLIFF PAPER CO., Niagara Falls, N. Y. (Closed by Government order.)
INTERNATIONAL PAPER CO., Niagara Falls, N. Y. (Closed by Government order.)
CLEVELAND PAPER MFG. CO., Cleveland, Ohio.
AMERICAN STRAW BOARD CO., Dayton, Ohio.
AMERICAN STRAW BOARD CO., Tiffin, Ohio.
NASSAU MILLS CORP., Buck Run, Pa.
JESSUP & MOORE PAPER CO., THE, Coatesville, Pa.
KITZMILLER, S. M., & BROS., Mt. Holly Springs, Pa.
CULLEN, LEWIS C., Willistown Inn, Pa.

CANADA

ST. CROIX PULP & PAPER CO., LTD., Hartville, N. S.

ENGINEERING FOR
PULP, PAPER AND POWER PLANTS

JOSEPH H. WALLACE & CO.
INDUSTRIAL ENGINEERS
Temple Court Building, NEW YORK
71 Bay Street, TORONTO, CAN.

Lombard's English Newcastle Pulp Stones

HARDY S. FERGUSON
CONSULTING ENGINEER
200 FIFTH AVENUE
NEW YORK CITY
PAPER, PULP AND FIBRE MILLS
WATER POWER DEVELOPMENT
DAMS, STORAGE RESERVOIRS AND
OTHER HYDRAULIC STRUCTURES

PAPER AND PULP MILLS
IN
South America and Mexico

ARGENTINE REPUBLIC.

COMPAÑIA GENERAL DE FOSFOROS. Main offices, Calle Lima 239, Buenos Aires; mill at Bernal, 6 miles from Buenos Aires on Argentine Southern Railway. Two machines. All kinds of paper.

FABRICA DE PAPEL (CASATI) DE SAN NICOLAS (S. A.). Main offices and mill at San Nicolas on Argentine Central Railway and Paraná River, 148 miles from Buenos Aires. Colored Wrappings and Boards.

FABRICA DE PAPEL EL FENIX (S. A.). Main offices, Calle Reconquista 46, Buenos Aires; Campaña mill at Campaña on Argentine Central Railway and Paraná River, 50 miles from Buenos Aires; Vicente Lopez mill (not in operation) at Vicente Lopez, 8 miles from Buenos Aires on Argentine Central Railway. Book; some better grade News; Wrappings.

GAZZO, BLAZIO, Cordoba. Wrappings. Two machines. 20 tons per week. Electric power.

GILCHRIST & CO. Main offices, Calle Lavalle 333, Buenos Aires. Mill at Dock Sur, Buenos Aires.

ITURRAT, MANASSERO & CO. Main offices, Pozos 841, Buenos Aires. Mill at Andino, 34 miles from Rosario on Argentine Central Railway.

LA ARGENTINA (S. A.) PARA LA FABRICACIÓN DE PAPEL. Main offices, Calle Bolivar 393, Buenos Aires. Mill at Zarate, 57 miles from Buenos Aires on Argentine Central Railway and Paraná River. News, Book, Writing, Wrappings and Boards. Nine machines.

OLIVA & CO., Cordoba.

PAROVI & RODRIGUEZ CANEDO. Main offices and mill at Bancalari, 15 miles from Rosario on Argentine Central Railway.

SANTIAGO MARIETTA, Pasaje Ayacucho 3810, Saladillo, 4 miles from Rosario.

BRAZIL.

AGRA & CO., Estrella, near Rio de Janeiro. One machine. News, Printing and Wrappings.

ANDOUIN, H., Estrella, near Rio de Janeiro. Three vats. Hand-made Papers.

ANGLO-BRAZILIAN PULP AND PAPER MILLS, LTD., Morretes, Parana.

ARAUJO, JOSÉ DA SILVA, Avenida Passos 32, Rio de Janeiro. Wrapping.

CACONDA PAPER MILL, Caconda. Wrappings. 3 tons per day.

CAMPANEMA, Strela, near Rio de Janeiro. One machine. White Paper and News.

CIA INDUSTRIAL PAPEIS E CARTONAGEM, Rua Washington Luis, Sao Paulo.

PRESS ROLLS Maple and Gum White Wood Felt Rolls J. W. HEWITT MACHINE CO. Neenah, Wis.

Paper and Pulp Mills in South America and Mexico

COMPANHIA FABRICA DE PAPEL, Sao Paulo.
DA SILVA (FRANCISCO BORES), 89, Rua General Camara, Rio de Janeiro. Cardboard and Wrappings.
DE OLIVEIRA (José Pereira Gomez), 101, Rua de Hospicio, Rio de Janeiro. Cardboards and Wrappings.
ESTACAO DE MENDES PAPER MILL, Estacão de Mendes, Rio de Janeiro. Wrappings.
FABRICA DE PAPEL, Pernambucana, Jaboatao, Pernambuco.
FABRICA DE PAPEL E PAPELAO, Pedros Brancas Via Parto Alcyre. Sebastian de Brito, Mng. Dir.; Enrique Brockmann, Tech. Dir. Coarse Wrapping and Cardboard.
GUTENBERG PAPER MILLS, Mendes. One machine.
ITACOLOMY, COMPANIA INDUSTRIAL (Sociedad Anonima), Mendes. Esdado de Rio de Janeiro. Passengers and Goods—Ottoni, ½ mile. Cellulose Paper, Manila and Wrappings, etc. Two Machines, one 180 cm. and one 210 cm. (about 70 and 82 in.). 50 tons per week. Water Power. Telegraphic Address—"Itacolomy-Rio."
KLABIM, IRMAOS & CIA, Rua Marechal Deodoro 2, Sao Paulo.
LUIS STRINA & CIA, Galeria Crystal 13 e 16, Sao Paulo.
MELHORAMENTOS DE S. PAULO, COMPANHIA, Fabrica do Papel. Cayeiras, Estado de S. Paulo. Passengers and Goods—Cayeiras, 2½ miles. All kinds of Wrappings. Four Machines, two 200 cm., one 250 cm. and one 275 cm. (about 78, 98 and 106½ in.). 41 tons per week. Electric and Water Power. Telegraphic Address—"Melhoralus, S. Paulo."

CHILI.

AVARIA & RIVERA, Talca.
BECKDORF & CO., La Cruz.
BESA & CO., Quillota. Railroad station at Quillota. One machine, 180 cm. Fifteen tons a week. Water Power. Packings and Wrappings. Main office at Valparaiso.
EBBINGHAUS, HANSEL & CO., La Esperanza Mill, Puerto Alto, near Santiago. Packings and Pasteboards. Water Power.
FABRICA DE PAPEL, La Cruz.
FABRICA DE PAPEL, SOCIEDAD ANONIMA, Puerto Alto.
FABRICA DE PAPEL, Talca.
NACIONALES DE PAPEL Y CARTON, FABRICAS, Quillota. Passenger and freight station—Quillota, ½ m. Main office—Valparaiso. All sorts of White and Colored Papers. One machine, 180 cm. (about 70¾ in.) Thirty tons per week. Steam and Water Power. Telegraphic address —"Fapapel, Quillota, Chili."
PAPEN, PEDRO, Peñon, La Calera. Passenger station at La Calera. Wrappings and Packings. One machine. 120 cm. (about 47¼ in.) 8 tons per week. Water Power.
PASCAL HEGUY, Quillota.
PASTOR INFANTE CONCHA, Buin. Main office at Santiago. Packing Paper. One machine.
PEUMO PAPER MILL, Peumo, Cachapoal. Passenger station at Peumo, 1¼ m. All sorts of Papers and Cardboards. Two machines.

Lombard's English Newcastle Pulp Stones

Paper and Pulp Mills in South America and Mexico

SCHORR, CONCHA I CIA, El Palaccio, Talca. Passenger and freight station. Talca Packings. One machine, 160 cm. (about 62 in.). 6 tons per week. Steam and Water Power.

SPELLMAN, C. W., Llalllal. Wrappings. One machine.

MEXICO.

ANCIRA HERMANOS & CO., El Batan Mill, Atemajac, Jalisco. Printings, Writings and Wrappings. Two machines.

DE GUTIERREZ MERCEDES, RULFO, La Constancia, Tapalpa, Jalisco. Various papers.

SAN RAFAEL Y ANEXAS, COMPANIA DE LAS FABRICAS DE PAPEL DE, Ave Uruguay 71, Mexico City. Two mills—"San Rafael" and "El Progreso Industrial." Passenger and Freight Station (San Rafael Mill, Zavaleta, San Rafael, 1 m.; El Progreso Mill, El Progreso Industrial). Writings, Printings, News, Wrappings. Boards, Coated, Cover, Rag, Bond and other Papers. Mechanical Ground Wood Pulp, Sulphite, etc. Ten Paper machines, one 56-inch, two 60-inch, one 80-inch, four 85-inch, one 132-inch and one 154-inch. 700 tons per week. Electric, Steam and Water Power. Telegraphic address—"Saraico, Mexico."

SANTA TERESA, FABRICA DE, San Angel, Federal District. Passenger and Freight Station—Contreras, 2 m. Proprietors—Donnadieu, Veyan, y Cia. All sorts of papers. Two machines. 25 tons per week.

YNDUSTRIAL SALTILLERA, COMPANHIA, Coahuia, Saltillo. Wrappings. One machine, 36 inches.

URUGUAY.

FABRICA NACIONAL DE PAPEL, Sociedad Anonima, (Ing. S. A. Calcagno, Pres.; Sr. Juan Cavajani, Vice-Pres.; Sr. Romeo Puppo, Sec.) Railroad station at Puerto del Sauce (close to mill). Telegraphic address, "Capubaco, Montevideo." Six Beating and six Refining engines; two Fourdriniers, one 2.25 cm. and one 2.45 cm. Steam. Packings, Printing, News, etc. 25,000 to 50,000 lbs. 24 hours. Office, Calle Colonia 1222-28, Montevideo.

VENEZUELA.

CALAXTO (MADRID), La Quebradita. One machine. Printing, Wrapping Papers and Boards.

FABRICA NACIONAL DE PAPEL, Caracas. (Tomas Reyna, Pres.) Passengers and Goods—El Encantado (close to mill). One Fourdrinier, 184 cm. (about 72 in.). Electric. Wrapping. 5000 lbs. 24 hours.

MARACAY PAPER MILL, Maracay. Wrappings, Cardboard and Printing Paper.

CUBA.

PAPELERA CUBANA, S. A., Fabrica de Papel, Real Numero 68, Puentes Grandes, Havana. Passengers' Station, ¼ m.; Goods, Havana, 2½ m. (José Marimon, Pres.; Armando Godoy, Vice-Pres.; Dr. Domingo Mendez Capote, Sec.; Paulino Vladero, Treas.; Juliot Blanco, Supt.) Printings, Writings, Wrappings and Cardboard. One Board machine, 30 inches, and two Paper machines, one 60-inch and one 70-inch. Ten Vats. 50 to 60 tons per week. Steam and Water Power. Telegraphic address, "Castro, Habana."

DARMSTADT, SCOTT & COURTNEY, Inc. Importers, Exporters and Dealers in **PAPER MAKERS' SUPPLIES** Also Mfrs. of DEADENING and SATURATING FELTS
178 and 184 SOUTH STREET, NEW YORK

Ground Pulp & Sulphite Fibre Mill Machinery OUR SPECIALTY | **CARTHAGE MACHINE CO.** CARTHAGE, N. Y.

A LIST OF PAPER MILLS
IN
THE UNITED STATES
CLASSIFIED ACCORDING TO GOODS MADE

IDLE MILLS ARE NOT INCLUDED IN THIS LIST

NOTE SPECIALLY—That after consulting this section the MILL REPORTS should be referred to, where more DETAILED information will be found. The addresses given are those of the Main or Sales Offices. For list of manufacturers of goods made from paper, consult Table of Contents under "SPECIALTIES."

ABSORBENT.

Dixie Paper Mills, Inc., Richmond, Va.
Eaton, Dikeman Co., Lee, Mass.
Funke's Sons, Ferd., Evansville, Ill.
Lawless Paper Co., Rochester, N. Y.
Monroe Falls Paper Co., Massillon, Ohio.
Schmidt & Ault Paper Co., York, Pa.
Sterling Paper Co., Hamilton, Ohio.
United States Paper Mills, Pittston, Pa.

ACID PROOF PAPERS.

American Writing Paper Co., Holyoke, Mass.

ALBUM BOARDS.

Albey Bros., Newark, N. J.
American Straw Board Co., Akron, Ohio.
Ingalls & Co., Castleton, N. Y.
Naubuc Paper Co., Glastonbury, Conn.
Wasuc Mills Co., South Glastonbury, Conn.

ALBUM PAPERS.

Gilbert, Frank, Paper Co., Waterford, N. Y.
Lewis, J. P., Co., Beaver Falls, N. Y.
Munroe Felt & Paper Co., Boston, Mass.
Strathmore Paper Co., Mittineague, Mass.
Walsh Paper Co., Inc., Cuyahoga Falls, Ohio.

ANTI-RUST.

American Writing Paper Co., Holyoke, Mass.
Ancram Paper Mills, 150 W. 22d, New York.
Beaver Brook Paper Mills, Danbury, Conn.
Dexter & Sons, C. H., Inc., Windsor Locks, Conn.
Lewis, J. P., Co., Beaver Falls, N. Y. (Black).
Perseverance Paper Mills, Produce Exch. Bldg., New York.
Schmidt & Ault Paper Co., York, Pa.

Lombard's English Newcastle Pulp Stones

Classified List—United States

ANTI-TARNISH.

Adams Paper Co., Wells River, Vt.
American Writing Paper Co., Holyoke, Mass.
Ancram Paper Mills, 150 W. 22d, New York. (Tissue.)
Fox Paper Co., Lockland, Ohio. (Kraft.)
Jersey City Paper Co., Jersey City, N. J. (Tissues.)
Lewis, J. P., Co., Beaver Falls, N. Y. (Black.)
McIntyre Bros., Inc., Fayetteville, N. Y.
Mohawk Valley Paper Co., Inc., Little Falls, N. Y.
Perseverance Paper Mills, Produce Exch. Bldg., New York.
Shortsville Paper Co., Shortsville, N. Y.
Standard Paper Co., Kalamazoo, Mich.

ASBESTOS PAPER AND BOARD.

Baltimore Roofing & Asbestos Mfg. Co., Asbestos, Md.
Carey, Philip, Mfg. Co., Lockland, Ohio.
H. W. Johns-Manville Co., Madison ave. and 41st, New York.
Keasbey & Mattison Co., Ambler, Pa.
Norristown Magnesia and Asbestos Co., Morristown, Pa.
National Asbestos Mfg. Co., Jersey City, N. J.
Pleasant Mills Paper Co., Pleasant Mills, N. J.
Roberts & Son Co., John, Pittsburgh, Pa.
Sall Mountain Co., Chicago, Ill.
Watson, H. F., Co., Erie, Pa.

BACKING PAPER AND BOARD.

John T. Andrews & Co., Penn Yan, N. Y. (Corrugated.)
Lawless Paper Co., Rochester, N. Y.
Mid-West Box Co., Kokomo, Ind.
Monroe Binder Board Co., Monroe, Mich.
Moorhouse, R. T., Paper Co., Bridesburg, Pa.
Schmidt & Ault Paper Co., York, Pa.
United Paperboard Co., New York.
Wasuc Mills Co., So. Glastonbury, Conn.

BAG PAPER.
(See also under SACK, ETC.)

American Writing Paper Co., Holyoke, Mass.
Bayless Mfg. Corporation, 527 Fifth ave., New York.
Bemis Bros. Bag Co., Peoria, Ill.
Carthage Tissue Paper Mills, Carthage, N. Y. (Lightweight.)
Cleveland-Akron Bag Co., Cleveland, Ohio.
Crown-Willamette Paper Co., Alaska Commercial Bldg., San Francisco, Cal.
Cushnoc Paper Co., Augusta, Me.
Dexter Sulphite Pulp & Paper Co., Dexter, N. Y.
Eureka Paper Co., Fulton, N. Y.
E-Z Opener Bag Co., Taylorville, Ill.
Fletcher Paper Co., Alpena, Mich.
Gilbert, Frank, Paper Co., Waterford, N. Y.
Great Northern Paper Co., 30 E. 42d, New York.
Green Bay Paper & Fibre Co., Green Bay, Wis.
Howland Pulp & Paper Corp., Boston, Mass.
International Paper Co., 30 Broad, New York.
Iroquois Pulp & Paper Co., Thomson, N. Y.
Island Paper Co., Carthage, N. Y.
Jaite Co., Boston, Ohio.
Malone Paper Co., Malone, N. Y.
McDowell Paper Mills, Manayunk, Pa.
Munroe Felt & Paper Co., Boston, Mass.
New York and Pennsylvania Co., 200 Fifth ave., New York.
Orono Pulp and Paper Co., Bangor, Me.
Racquette River Paper Co., Potsdam, N. Y.
St. Croix Paper Co., 244 Washington St., Boston, Mass.
Southern Paper Co., Moss Point, Miss.
Union Bag and Paper Corp., Woolworth Bldg., New York.
Yellow Pine Paper Mill Co., Orange, Texas.

PRESS ROLLS — Maple and Gum White Wood Felt Rolls — J. W. HEWITT MACHINE CO. Neenah, Wis.

ARE SUPERIOR TO ALL OTHERS. ALL SIZES IN STOCK.
LOMBARD & CO., Importers & Manufacturers, 236 & 238 A Street, Boston.

Classified List—United States

BANK NOTE.
Brown Paper Co., L. L., Adams, Mass.
Berkshire Hills Paper Co., Adams, Mass.
Crane & Co., Dalton, Mass.

BIBLE.
Bardeen Paper Co., Otsego, Mich.
King Paper Co., Kalamazoo, Mich.
Lakeside Paper Co., Neenah, Wis.
Michigan Paper Co., Plainwell, Mich.
Moorhouse, R. T., Paper Co., Bridesburg, Pa.
Tileston & Hollingsworth Co., Boston, Mass.

BINDERS' BOARD.
Albey Bros., 149 to 177 Meeker ave., Newark, N. J.
American Fibre Seat Corp., Long Island City, N. Y.
Carthage Board & Paper Co., Carthage, Ind.
Case & Risley Press Paper Co., Oneco, Conn.
Colonial Board Co., Manchester, Conn.
Davey, E. H., Co., Bloomfield, N. J.
Davey, W. O., & Sons, Jersey City, N. J.
Fandango Mills, Millburn, N. J.
Foulds & Co., Inc., William, Manchester, Conn.
Gulf Paper Mills Co., Mobile, Ala.
Hartford Board Co., Newington, Conn.
Ingalls & Co., Castleton, N. Y.
Kerr Paper Mill Co., East Downingtown, Pa.
Merion Paper Co., Abrams, Pa.
Monroe Binder Board Co., Monroe, Mich.
Muir Board Co., Inc., Lyndell, Pa.
Muir, James A., Morristown, N. J.
Naubuc Paper Co., Glastonbury, Conn.
Norton, C. H., North Westchester, Conn.
Otter River Board Co., Otter River, Mass.
Palmer, Willis B., Coatesville, Pa.
Perkiomen Paper Co., Pennsburg, Pa.
Riverside Paper Mfg. Co., The, Glastonbury, Conn.
Shryock Bros., 924 Cherry, Philadelphia.
Tonawanda Board & Paper Co., Tonawanda, N. Y.
United Paperboard Co., 171 Madison av., New York.
Waldorf Box Board Co., St. Paul, Minn.
Wasuc Mills Co., South Glastonbury, Conn.
Westport Paper Co., Westport, Conn.

BLACK PAPER.
American Writing Paper Co., Holyoke, Mass.
Andrews, John T. & Co., Penn Yan, N. Y. (Hardware.)
Dixie Paper Mills, Inc., Richmond, Va.
Fox Paper Co., Lockland, Ohio. (Hardware.)
Gilbert Paper Co., Frank, Waterford, N. Y.
Lawless Paper Co., Rochester, N. Y.
Lewis, J. P., Co., Beaver Falls, N. Y.
Richardson Paper Co., Lockland, Ohio.
Schmidt & Ault Paper Co., York, Pa. (Hardware and Black Pattern.)
Strathmore Paper Co., Mittineague, Mass.

BLANKS.
Beveridge Paper Co., Indianapolis, Ind. (Mill.)
California Paper & Board Mills, 40 First St., San Francisco, Cal. (Litho.)
Chemical Paper Mfg. Co., Holyoke, Mass.
Eddy Paper Co., Three Rivers, Mich.
Falulah Paper Co., Fitchburg, Mass. (Mill.)
Franklin Paper Co., Holyoke, Mass.
Gardner Paper Co., The Colin, Middletown, Ohio. (White.)
International Paper Co., 30 Broad, New York.
Missisquoi Pulp & Paper Co., Sheldon Springs, Vt.
Munroe Felt & Paper Co., Boston, Mass.
Standard Paper Co., Kalamazoo, Mich.
United Paperboard Co., New York.

M. GOTTESMAN & CO., Inc.
18 E. 41st STREET, NEW YORK. Cable Address "Namsettog"
EUROPEAN OFFICES: Stockholm, Sweden

Strong and Easy Bleaching SULPHITE PULP

ENGINEERING FOR PULP, PAPER AND POWER PLANTS

JOSEPH H. WALLACE & CO.
INDUSTRIAL ENGINEERS
Temple Court Building, NEW YORK
71 Bay Street, TORONTO, CAN.

Lombard's English Newcastle Pulp Stones

Classified List—United States

BLASTING.

Gilbert, Frank, Paper Co., Waterford, N. Y.
National Paper Co., Atlanta, Ga.
Unity Paper Mills, Potsdam, N. Y.

BLOTTING.

Albemarle Paper Mfg. Co., Richmond, Va.
District of Columbia Paper Mfg. Co., Washington, D. C.
Eaton, Dikeman Co., The, Lee, Mass.
Gilbert Paper Co., Frank, Waterford, N. Y. (Interleaving.)
Parker, Joseph, & Son, Co., office Whalley Ave., near Dayton, New Haven, Conn.
Richmond Paper Mfg. Co., Richmond, Va.
Standard Paper Mfg. Co., Richmond, Va.
Wrenn Paper Co., Middletown, Ohio.

BOARDS.

Acme Paper Co., Reading, Pa.
Albey Bros., Newark, N. J.
Albia Box & Paper Co., Troy, N. Y.
Alton Box Board & Paper Co., Federal, Ill.
American Box Board Co., Grand Rapids, Mich.
American Fibre Seat Corp., Long Island City, N. Y.
American Straw Board Co., Akron, Ohio.
American Wood Board Co., Schuylerville, N. Y.
American Writing Paper Co., Holyoke, Mass.
Androscoggin Pulp Co., South Windham, Me.
Auglaize Box Board Co., St. Mary's, Ohio.
Ballston Fibre Products Co., Ballston Spa, N. Y.
Beloit Box Board Co., Beloit, Wis.
Berkshire Box & Paper Co., Mellenville, N. Y.
Beveridge Paper Co., Indianapolis, Ind.
Big Falls Paper Co., Inc., Rock City Falls, N. Y.
Boehme & Rauch Co., The, Monroe, Mich.
Bogota Paper & Board Co., Bogota, N. J.
Boldt, The Charles, Paper Mills, Cincinnati, Ohio.
Boyle Company, John F., Jersey City, N. J.
Brown Paper Co., Fort Madison, Ia.
Brownville Board Co., Brownville, N. Y.
Carlyle Paper Co., Alton, Ill.
Carthage Board & Paper Co., Carthage, Ind.
Carthage Pulp & Paper Co., Carthage, N. Y.
Carthage Sulphite Pulp & Paper Co., Carthage, N. Y.
Case & Marshall, Inc., Burnside, Conn.
Case & Risley Press Paper Co., Oneco, Conn.
Case Board Co., Andover, Conn.
Case Bros., Inc., So. Manchester, Conn.
Case Co., A. Willard, Manchester, Conn. (Decorated.)
Champion Fibre Co., Canton, N. C.
Chemical Paper Mfg. Co., Holyoke, Mass.
Cherry, J. G. Co., Tama, Ia.
Chesapeake Paperboard Co., Baltimore, Md.
Chicago Coated Board Co., Chicago, Ill.
Chicago Folding Box Co., Chicago.
Chicago Mill & Lumber Co., Chicago.
Childsdale Paper Mills, Childsdale, Mich.
Clifton Paper Mills, Passaic, N. J.
Colonial Board Co., Manchester, Conn.
Columbian Box Board Mills, Inc., Chatham, N. Y.
Constantine Board & Paper Co., Constantine, Mich.
Continental Paper Co., Bogota, N. J.
Cornell Wood Products Co., Cornell, Wis.
Coshocton Straw Paper Co., Coshocton, Ohio.
Creamery Package Mfg. Co., Coffeyville, Kans.
Crehore, Chas. F., & Son, Boston, Mass.
Crescent Paper Co., Marseilles, Ill.
Cushman-Rankin Co., Bath, N. H.
Davey, E. H., Co., Bloomfield, N. J.
Davey, W. O., & Sons, Jersey City, N. J.
Davis Paper Co., West Hopkinton, N. H.
Decatur Strawboard Co., Marion, Ind.

LOMBARD'S ENGLISH NEWCASTLE PULP STONES ARE SUPERIOR TO ALL OTHERS. ALL SIZES IN STOCK. LOMBARD & CO., Importers & Manufacturers, 226 & 228 A Street, Boston.

WET MACHINES — We make a specialty of GROUND WOOD PULP and SULPHITE FIBRE MACHINERY

Carthage Machine Co.
CARTHAGE, N. Y.

Classified List—United States 253

BOARDS.
(CONTINUED.)

Delphi Straw Board Co., Decatur, Ind.
Diamond Match Co., Southford, Conn.
Diamond State Fibre Co., Bridgeport, Pa.
Eddy Paper Co., Three Rivers, Mich.
Fandango Mills, Milburn, N. J.
Federal Paper Board Co., Bogota, N. J.
Flower City Tissue Mills Co., Rochester, N. Y.
Fort Orange Paper Co., Castleton, N. Y.
Fort Wayne Corrugated Paper Co., Fort Wayne, Ind.
Fort Wayne Paper Co., Eaton, Ind.
Foster Box Board Co., Utica, N. Y.
Foulds & Co., Inc., William, Manchester, Conn.
Franklin Board & Paper Co., Franklin, Ohio.
Franklin Paper Co., Holyoke, Mass.
French Paper Co., Niles, Mich.
Gardner-Harvey Paper Co. (The), Middletown, Ohio.
Gardner Paper Board Co., Middletown, Ohio.
Gardner, The Colin, Paper Co., Middletown, Ohio.
Gulf Paper Mills Co., Holyoke, Ala.
Hadley Paper Corp., Hadley, N. Y.
Hagar Straw Board & Paper Co., Xenia, Ohio.
Halltown Paper Board Co., Halltown, W. Va.
Hartford Board Co., Newington, Conn.
Hartje Bros. Paper Co., Toronto, Ohio.
Hartje Paper Mfg. Co., Pittsburgh, Pa.
Haverhill Box Board Co., Haverhill, Mass.
Herkimer Fibre Co., Herkimer, N. Y.
Hinde & Dauch Paper Co., Sandusky, O.
Hummel & Downing Co., Milwaukee, Wis.
Hutchinson Box Board & Paper Co., Hutchinson, Kan.
Hutchinson & Puttaert Co., San Francisco, Cal.
Independent Paper Co., Independence, Kan.
Indiana Board & Filler Co., Vincennes, Ind.
Ingalls & Co., Castleton, N. Y.
International Paper Co., 30 Broad, New York.
James Leo Co., Jersey City, N. J.
Jenkins, Geo. O., Co., Bridgewater, Mass.
Kerr Paper Mills Co., East Downingtown, Pa.
Keyes Products Co., The, 120 Broadway, New York City. (Specialties.)
Kieffer Paper Co., Brownstown, Ind.
Lafayette Box Board Co., Lafayette, Ind.
Lancaster Board & Paper Co., Lancaster, Ohio.
Lawless Bros. Paper Mills, East Rochester, N. Y.
Lawless Paper Co., Rochester, N. Y.
Lawrence Paper Mfg. Co., Lawrence, Kan.
Leo, James, Co., Jersey City, N. J.
Lewis Co., Inc., The J. P., Beaver Falls, N. Y.
Lydell & Foulds Paper Co., Inc., Manchester, Conn.
MacAndrews & Forbes Co., Camden, N. J.
McElwain Company, Merrimack, N. H.
McEwan Brothers, Whippany, N. J.
Mac-Sim-Bar Paper Co., Otsego, Mich.
Manchester Board and Paper Co., Richmond, Pa.
Marion Paper Co., Marion, Ind.
Merion Paper Co., Abrams, Pa.
Merwin Paper Co., Rainbow, Conn.
Michigan Carton Co., Battle Creek, Mich.
Mid-West Box Co., Kokomo, Ind.
Miller, Frank P., Paper Co., East Downingtown, Pa.
Monroe Binder Board Co., Aurora, Ill.
Monroe Binder Board Co., Monroe, Mich.
Monroe Bridge Paper Co., Monroe Bridge, Mass.
Moore Paper Mill Corp., Penn Yan, N. Y.
Morris Paper Mills, Morris, Ill.
Mt. Vernon Straw Board & Paper Co., Mt. Vernon, Ind.
Muir Board Co., Inc., Lyndell, Pa.
Muir, James A., Morristown, N. J.
Mullen Bros. Paper Co., St. Joseph, Mich.
Mutual Box Board Co., Utica, N. Y.

Lombard's English Newcastle Pulp Stones

Classified List—United States

BOARDS.
(CONTINUED.)

Natick Box & Board Co., Natick, Mass.
National Folding Box & Paper Co., New Haven, Conn.
National Metal Edge Box Co., Philadelphia.
National Paper Products Co., Stockton, Cal.
Naubuc Paper Co., Glastonbury, Conn.
Nelson, B. F., Mfg. Co., Minneapolis, Minn.
Newark Box Board Co., Newark, N. J.
New Haven Pulp & Board Co., New Haven, Conn. (Folding.)
North Star Mfg. Co., Coffeyville, Kan.
Norton, C. H., North Westchester, Conn.
Ohio Box Board Co., Cleveland, Ohio.
Oswego Falls Pulp & Paper Co., Fulton, N. Y.
Otter River Board Co., Otter River, Mass.
Pairpoint Corporation, The, New Bedford, Mass.
Palmer, Willis B., Coatesville, Pa.
Paraffine Companies, Inc., San Francisco, Cal.
Perkiomen Paper Co., Pennsburg, Pa.
Philadelphia Paper Manufacturing Co., Philadelphia, Pa. (White Vat Lined.)
Piermont Paper Co., Piermont, N. Y.
Pynetree Paper Co., Gordon, Ga.
Quaker Oats Co., Pekin, Ill.
Ravenswood Paper Mill Co., 545 Van Alst Ave., Long Island City, N. Y.
Richardson Paper Co., Lockland, Ohio. (Container, etc.)
River Raisin Paper Co., Monroe, Mich.
Riverside Paper Mfg. Co., Glastonbury, Conn.
Roanoke Fibre Board Co., Roanoke Rapids, N. C.
Robertson, C. M., Co., Montville, Conn.
Rock Falls Box Board Co., Rock Falls, Ill.
Rockford Paper Box Co., Rockford, Ill.
Rogers Co., J. & J., Ausable Forks, N. Y.
Rogers Fibre Co., 121 Beach St., Boston, Mass.
Rogers Paper Mfg. Co., South Manchester, Conn. (Press, Insulating, Jacquard, etc.)
Schmidt & Ault Paper Co., York, Pa.
Sherman & Co., Belfast, Me.
Shryock Bros., Philadelphia, Pa.
Skaneateles Paper Co., Skaneateles, N. Y.
Smeallie & Vorhees, Amsterdam, N. Y. (Pasted Boards a Specialty.)
Snyder Mfg. Co., Cohoes, N. Y.
South Coventry Paper Co., South Coventry, Conn.
Spaulding & Sons, J., North Rochester, N. H.
Springets Mills, The, York, Pa.
Standard Paper Co., Kalamazoo, Mich.
Stowe, J. D., & Sons, Inc., Scitico, Conn.
Strange Paper Co., John, Menasha, Wis.
Tait & Sons Paper Co., Bridgeport, Conn.
Terre Haute Paper Co., Terre Haute, Ind.
Thames River Specialties Co., Uncasville, Conn. (High Grade.)
Thompson & Norris Co. of Ind., Brookville, Ind.
Tonawanda Board & Paper Co., Tonawanda, N. Y.
United Paperboard Co., New York.
Vincennes Board & Paper Co., Vincennes, Ind.
Waldorf Box Board Co., St. Paul, Minn.
Wardway Paper Mills, Ft. Madison, Ia.
Wasuc Mills Co., So. Glastonbury, Conn.
Waverly Paper Box Board Co., Newark, N. J.
Weis Paper Mill Co., Quincy, Ill.
Western Board & Paper Co., Kalamazoo, Mich.
Westport Paper Co., Westport, Conn.
West Virginia Pulp Products Co., 200 Fifth ave., New York; 732 Sherman St., Chicago.
Wheelwright, Geo. W., Paper Co., Boston, Mass.

HARDY S. FERGUSON, CONSULTING ENGINEER, 200 FIFTH AVENUE, NEW YORK CITY. PAPER, PULP AND FIBRE MILLS, WATER POWER DEVELOPMENT, DAMS, STORAGE RESERVOIRS AND OTHER HYDRAULIC STRUCTURES

PRESS ROLLS Maple and Gum White Wood Felt Rolls — J. W. HEWITT MACHINE CO., Neenah, Wis.

Classified List—United States

BOGUS.

Andrews, John T., & Co., Penn Yan, N. Y.
Clinton Paper Co., Clinton, Iowa.
Columbia Mills, Chatham Centre, N. Y.
Dixie Paper Mills, Inc., Richmond, Va.
Hadley Paper Corp., Hadley, N. Y.
Hinde & Dauch Paper Co., The, Sandusky, Ohio.
Humphrey & Young, Inc., Napanoch, N. Y.
Klein Paper Co., Clinton, Iowa.
Lawless Paper Co., Rochester, N. Y.
Monroe Paper Co., Monroe, Mich.
National Paper Co., Atlanta, Ga.
Schmidt & Ault Paper Co., York, Pa.
Van de Carr Paper Co., Stockport, N. Y.

BOND.

Aetna Paper Co., Dayton, Ohio.
American Writing Paper Co., Holyoke, Mass.
Beckett Paper Co., Hamilton, Ohio.
Berkshire Hills Paper Co., Adams, Mass.
Brown Co., Portland, Me.
Brown Paper Co., L. L., Adams, Mass.
Brownsville Paper Co., Brownsville, N. Y.
Carew Mfg. Co., South Hadley Falls, Mass.
Chapin & Gould Paper Co., Springfield, Mass.
Chemical Paper Mfg. Co., Holyoke, Mass.
Collins Mfg. Co., North Wilbraham, Mass.
Cornwall Paper Mfg. Co., Cornwall-on-Hudson, N. Y.
Crane & Co., Dalton, Mass.
Crocker-McElwain Co., Holyoke, Mass.
East Hartford Mfg. Co., Burnside, Conn.
Eastern Mfg. Co., Bangor, Me. New York Sales Office, 200 Fifth Ave.
Fox River Paper Co., Appleton, Wis.
Gilbert Paper Co., Menasha, Wis.
Glatfelter, P. H., Co., Spring Grove, Pa.
Hamilton, W. C., & Sons, Inc., Wm. Penn P. O., Pa.
Hammermill Paper Co., Erie, Pa.
Hampshire Paper Co., South Hadley Falls, Mass.
Hawthorne Paper Co., Kalamazoo, Mich.
Howard Paper Co., The, Urbana, O.
Inland Empire Paper Co., Spokane, Wash.
Kalamazoo Vegetable Parchment Co., Kalamazoo, Mich.
Keith Paper Co., Turners Falls, Mass.
Kimberly-Clark Co., Neenah, Wis.
King Paper Co., Kalamazoo, Mich.
Lakeside Paper Co., Neenah, Wis.
La Monte, Geo., & Son, 61 Broadway, New York.
Lee Paper Co., Vicksburg, Mich.
McDowell Paper Mills, Manayunk, Pa.
Marathon Paper Mills Co., Wausau, Wis.
Menasha Paper Co., Ladysmith, Wis. (Bleached Sulphite Bonds.)
Miami Paper Co., The, West Carrollton, Ohio.
Miamisburg Paper Co., Miamisburg, Ohio.
Millers Falls Paper Co., Millers Falls, Mass.
Mt. Holly Paper Mills, Inc., Mt. Holly Springs, Pa.
Munising Paper Co., Munising, Mich.
Nashua River Paper Co., East Pepperell, Mass.
Neenah Paper Co., Neenah, Wis.
New York and Pennsylvania Co., 200 Fifth ave., New York.
Nixon, Martin & William H., Paper Co., Philadelphia.
Odell Mfg. Co., Groveton, N. H.
Oglesby Paper Co., The W. B., Middletown, Ohio.
Parker-Young Co., Lincoln, N. H.
Parsons Paper Co., Holyoke, Mass.
Peerless Paper Co., Dayton, Ohio.
Poland Paper Co., Mechanics Falls, Me.
Rising Paper Co., B. D., Housatonic, Mass.
Riverside Fibre & Paper Co., Appleton, Wis.
Rogers Co., J. & J., Ausable Forks, N. Y.
Southworth Co., Mittineague, Mass.
Sterling Paper Co., Dayton, Ohio.
Strathmore Paper Co., Mittineague, Mass.
Taylor-Atkins Paper Co., Burnside, Conn.
Taylor-Logan Co. Papermakers, Holyoke, Mass.
Unity Paper Mills, Potsdam, N. Y.

ombard's English Newcastle Pulp Stones

Classified List—United States

BOND.
(CONTINUED.)

Valley Paper Co., Holyoke, Mass.
Wausau Paper Mills Co., Brokaw, Wis. (Drug.)
Weston Co., Byron, Dalton, Mass.
Wheat Paper Co., Elkhart, Ind.
Whiting Paper Co., Geo. A., Menasha, Wis. (Plain and Linen Fabric.)
Whiting-Plover Paper Co., Stevens Point, Wis.
Wolverine Paper Co., Elkhart, Ind. (Manifold.)
Worthy Paper Co., Mittineague, Mass.

BOOK.

Alexandria Paper Co., Alexandria, Ind.
American Writing Paper Co., Holyoke, Mass.
Amoskeag Paper Mills Co., Manchester, N. H.
Antietam Paper Co., Hagerstown, Md.
Bardeen Paper Co., Otsego, Mich.
Bare Paper Co., D. M., Roaring Spring, Pa.
Bergstrom Paper Co., Neenah, Wis. (S. S. C. & M. F.)
Bryant Paper Co., Kalamazoo, Mich.
Cascade Paper Co., Balboa Bldg., San Francisco, Cal.
Champion Coated Paper Co., Hamilton, Ohio.
Chemical Paper Mfg. Co., Holyoke, Mass.
Combined Locks Paper Co., Combined Locks, Wis.
Consolidated Water Power & Paper Co., Grand Rapids, Wis.
Cornwall Paper Mfg. Co., Cornwall-on-Hudson, N. Y.
Crocker, Burbank & Co. Ass'n, Fitchburg, Mass.
Curtis & Bro., Inc., Newark, Del. (Rag.)
Dill & Collins Co., 140 North 6th St., Philadelphia, Pa.
Dist. of Columbia Paper Mfg. Co., Washington, D. C. (Rag.)
Emerson Paper Co., Wendell, N. H.
Everett Pulp and Paper Co., Everett, Wash.
Fitchburg Paper Co., Fitchburg, Mass.
Flambeau Paper Co., Park Falls, Wis.
Fox River Paper Co., Appleton, Wis.
French Paper Co., Niles, Mich.
Gilbert, Frank, Paper Co., Waterford, N. Y.
Glatfelter Co., P. H., Spring Grove, Pa.
Hamilton, W. C., & Sons, Wm. Penn P. O., Pa.
Hartford Paper Co., Hartford, Conn.
Holden Paper Co., Newburgh, N. Y.
Inland Empire Paper Co., Spokane, Wash.
International Paper Co., 30 Broad, New York.
Jessup & Moore Paper Co., Philadelphia, Pa.
Kalamazoo Paper Co., Kalamazoo, Mich.
Kimberly-Clark Co., Neenah, Wis.
King Paper Co., Kalamazoo, Mich.
Lakeside Paper Co., Neenah, Wis.
McDowell Paper Mills, Manayunk, Pa. (M. F.)
Mead Pulp & Paper Co., Dayton, Ohio.
Menasha Paper Co., Ladysmith, Wis.
Menasha Printing & Carton Co., Menasha, Wis.
Merrimac Paper Co., Lawrence, Mass.
Miami Paper Co., West Carrollton, Ohio.
Michigan Paper Co., Plainwell, Mich.
Monadnock Paper Mills, Boston, Mass.
Monarch Paper Co., Kalamazoo, Mich.
Moorhouse, R. T., Paper Co., Bridesburg, Pa.
Nashua River Paper Co., East Pepperell, Mass.
New York and Pennsylvania Co., 200 Fifth ave., New York.
Nixon Paper Co., Martin & William H., Manayunk, Philadelphia, Pa.
Northwest Paper Co., Cloquet, Minn.
Oxford Paper Co., 200 Fifth ave., New York.
Patten Paper Co., Appleton, Wis. (M. F.)
Peerless Paper Co., Dayton, Ohio.
Peninsular Paper Co., Ypsilanti, Mich.

Ground Pulp & Sulphite Fibre Mill Machinery | **CARTHAGE MACHINE CO.**
OUR SPECIALTY | CARTHAGE, N. Y.

Eastern Manufacturing Company

S. W. WEBB, *Chairman*   H. J. GUILD, *Vice-President*
F. R. AYER, *President*   FRED. A. LEAHY, *Vice-President*

MANUFACTURERS OF

BONDS
LEDGERS
WRITINGS

Linen Finish Papers a Specialty

DAILY OUTPUT:
100 TONS PAPER
100 TONS BLEACHED SULPHITE PULP

GENERAL SALES OFFICE
501 Fifth Avenue, New York City

MILLS
Bangor, Maine
Lincoln, Maine

WESTERN SALES OFFICE
1223 Conway Building
Chicago, Ill.

POLAND PAPER COMPANY

MANUFACTURERS OF { **BONDS** **LEDGERS** **WRITINGS** }

Envelope, High Grade Book Papers and Specialties

MILLS and MAIN OFFICE: MECHANIC FALLS, MAINE
SALES OFFICE: JOHN HANCOCK BUILDING

BOSTON, MASS.

ESTABLISHED 1846 INCORPORATED 1870-1896

THE WM. CABBLE EXCELSIOR WIRE MFG. CO.

74-90 AINSLIE STREET - - BROOKLYN, N. Y.

MANUFACTURERS OF **SUPERIOR FOURDRINIER WIRES.**

WASHER AND CYLINDER WIRES

Brass, Copper and Iron Wire Cloth,
Brass, Copper and Iron Wire, Etc.

CABBLE'S WIRES ARE THE BEST

CAMERON WINDERS

of the Universal Type 6 series are especially useful for the Finishing Rooms of Paper Mills and for Paper Dealers and Manufacturers doing a variety of work. A few features of our Type 6 Machines are as follows:

1. These machines will handle any kind of paper made, including fabrics.
2. They give a clean, smooth cut without distorting the paper.
3. They can be operated at practically unlimited speed, as there is scarcely any friction or wear on the cutting edge of knives.
4. A large variety of work from the thinnest tissue to boxboard can be handled with perfect results.
5. Any width or assortment of widths can be cut from $\frac{1}{4}$ inch and upwards.
6. Re-spacing of cutters requires only a few minutes' time.
7. Injury to the operator by our method of slitting is impossible.
8. The waste or trim at the edges may be extremely narrow.
9. Machine is of simple construction and can be operated by anyone without special skill.

Send for catalog and further interesting features

CAMERON MACHINE COMPANY
57-61 POPLAR ST., BROOKLYN, N. Y.

CHICAGO OFFICE	CINCINNATI OFFICE
10 South La Salle Street	First National Bank Building

ARE SUPERIOR TO ALL OTHERS. ALL SIZES IN STOCK.
LOMBARD & CO., Importers & Manufacturers, 236 & 238 A Street, Boston.

BOOK.
(CONTINUED.)

Poland Paper Co., Mechanic Falls, Me
Reading Paper Mills, 808 Chestnut, Philadelphia, Pa.
Richmond Paper Mfg. Co., Richmond, Va.
Sterling Paper Co., Dayton, Ohio.
Strathmore Paper Co., Mittineague, Mass.
Ticonderoga Pulp and Paper Co., 200 Fifth ave., New York.
Tileston & Hollingsworth Co., Boston, Mass.
Tomahawk Pulp & Paper Co., Tomahawk, Wis.
Unity Paper Mills, Potsdam, N. Y.
Wanaque River Paper Co., 290 Broadway, New York.
Warren, S. D., Co., Boston, Mass.
Watab Pulp and Paper Co., Sartell, Minn. (M. F. & S. & S. C.)
Watervliet Paper Co., Watervliet, Mich.
West Virginia Pulp and Paper Co., 200 Fifth ave., New York, and 732 Sherman, Chicago.
Wheat Paper Co., Elkhart, Ind. (M. F. & S. & S. C. and Colored.)
Wheelwright Paper Co., George W., Boston, Mass.
Winona Pulp & Paper Co., Winona, Minn.
Wolverine Paper Co., Otsego, Mich.

BOTTLE WRAPPER.

American Writing Paper Co., Holyoke, Mass.
Bicking, S. Austin, Paper Mfg. Co., E. Downington, Pa.
Dixie Paper Mills, Inc., Richmond, Va.
Fox Paper Co., Lockland, Ohio.
National Paper Co., Atlanta, Ga.
Richardson Paper Co., The, Lockland, Ohio.

BOX AND BARREL LAYERS.

American Straw Board Co., Akron, Ohio.
Dixie Paper Mills, Inc., Richmond, Va.
Lawless Paper Co., Rochester, N. Y.
Perseverance Paper Mills, Produce Exchange Bldg., New York.
Schmidt & Ault Paper Co., York, Pa.
Tonawanda Board and Paper Co., Tonawanda, N. Y.
United Paperboard Co., New York.

BOX BOARD.

Acme Paper Co., Reading, Pa.
Albey Bros., Newark, N. J.
Albia Box & Paper Co., Troy, N. Y.
American Box Board Co., Grand Rapids, Mich.
American Paper Co., Bogota, N. J.
American Straw Board Co., Akron, Ohio.
American Box Board Co., Grand Rapids, Mich.
Auglaize Box Board Co., St. Marys, Ohio.
Ballston Fibre Products Co., Inc., Ballston Spa, N. Y.
Beloit Box Board Co., Beloit, Wis.
Berkshire Box and Paper Co., Mellenville, N. Y.
Beveridge Paper Co., Indianapolis, Ind.
Bicking, S. Austin, Paper Mfg. Co., East Downingtown, Pa.
Big Falls Paper Co., Rock City Falls, N. Y.
Boehme & Rauch Co., Monroe, Mich.
Case & Marshall, Hartford, Conn.
Chemical Paper Mfg. Co., Holyoke, Mass.
Chicago Coated Board Co., Chicago, Ill.
Childsdale Paper Mill. Childsdale. Mich.
Clifton Paper Mills, Passaic, N. J.
Columbian Box Board Mills, Inc., Chatham, N .Y.
Constantine Board & Paper Co., Constantine, Mich.
Continental Paper Co., Bogota, N. J.
Crescent Paper Co., Marseilles, Ill.
Davis Paper Co., West Hopkinton, N. H.
Diamond Match Co., Southford, Conn.
Eddy Paper Co., Three Rivers, Mich.
Federal Paper Board Co., Versailles, Conn.
Fort Orange Paper Co., Castleton, N. Y.
Fort Wayne Corrugated Paper Co., Fort Wayne, Ind.

E. J. KELLER CO., INC.
200 FIFTH AVENUE E. J. KELLER, Pres. NEW YORK
FOREIGN AND DOMESTIC
Ropes AND Bagging
Rags, Linen, Flax and Cotton Wastes, Paper Stock, Wood Pulp and Rag Pulp.

ENGINEERING FOR PULP, PAPER AND POWER PLANTS

JOSEPH H. WALLACE & CO.
INDUSTRIAL ENGINEERS
Temple Court Building, NEW YORK
71 Bay Street, TORONTO, CAN.

Lombard's English Newcastle Pulp Stones

Classified List—United States

BOX BOARD.
(CONTINUED.)

Foster Box Board Co., Utica, N. Y.
Franklin Board and Paper Co., Franklin, Ohio.
Gardner Paper Co., The Colin, Middletown, O.
Gardner-Harvey Paper Co., Middletown, Ohio. (Colored Suit.)
Hadley Paper Corp., Hadley, N. Y.
Hartje Bros. Paper Co., Toronto, Ohio.
Haverhill Box Board Co., Haverhill, Mass.
Hutchinson Box Board & Paper Co., Hutchinson, Kan.
Ingalls & Co., Castleton, N. Y.
International Paper Co., 80 Broad, New York.
Kerr Paper Mill Co., East Downingtown, Pa.
Lawless Paper Co., Rochester, N. Y.
Lawrence Paper Mfg. Co., Lawrence, Kan.
Leo Co., James, Jersey City, N. J.
Lewis & Slocum, Beaver Falls, N. Y.
Lindale Mills, Farley, Mass.
Los Angeles Paper Mfg. Co., Los Angeles, Cal.
MacAndrews & Forbes Co., Camden, N. J.
Mac-Sim-Bar Paper Co., Otsego, Mich.
Manchester Board & Paper Co., Richmond, Va. (Folding.)
MacAndrews & Forbes Co., Camden, N. J.
Marion Paper Co., Marion, Ind.
McEwan Bros., Whippany, N. J.
Mid-West Box Co., Kokomo, Ind.
Michigan Carton Co., Battle Creek, Mich.
Miller Paper Co., Frank P., East Downington, Pa.
Moore Paper Mill, Penn Yan, N. Y.
Morris Paper Mills Co., Morris, Ill.
National Folding Box & Paper Co., New Haven, Conn.
National Metal Edge Box Co., 8th and Willow Sts., Philadelphia, Pa.
National Paper Products Co., Stockton, Cal.
Naubuc Paper Co., Glastonbury, Conn.
Nelson Mfg. Co., The B. F., Minneapolis, Minn.
New Haven Pulp and Board Co., New Haven, Conn.
Norton, C. H., North Westchester, Conn.
Ohio Box Board Co., Cleveland, Ohio.
Oswego Falls Pulp & Paper Co., Fulton, N. Y.
Pairpoint Corporation, The, New Bedford, Mass.
Paraffine Companies, Inc., San Francisco.
Perkiomen Paper Co., Pennsburg, Pa.
Philadelphia Paper Mfg. Co., Philadelphia, Pa.
Piermont Paper Co., Piermont, N. Y.
Richardson Paper Co., Lockland, Ohio.
River Raisin Paper Co., Monroe, Mich.
Robertson Co., C. M., Montville, Conn.
Rock Falls Box Board Co., Rock Falls, Ill.
Schmidt & Ault Paper Co., York, Pa.
Shryock Bros., 924 Cherry, Philadelphia, Pa.
Skaneateles Paper Co., Skaneateles, N. Y.
Standard Paint Co., Joliet, Ill.
Standard Paper Co., Kalamazoo, Mich.
Tait & Sons Paper Co., Bridgeport, Conn.
Tennessee Paper Mills, Inc., Chattanooga, Tenn.
Tonawanda Board and Paper Co., Tonawanda, N. Y.
United Paperboard Co., New York.
Waldorf Box Board Co., St. Paul, Minn.
Waverly Paper Box Board Co., Newark, N. J.
Westport Paper Co., Westport, Conn.

BOX COVER.

American Writing Paper Co., Holyoke, Mass.
District of Columbia Paper Mfg. Co., Washington, D. C.
Moorhouse, R. T., Paper Co., Bridesburg, Pa.
Savage Mfg. Co., Skowhegan, Me.
Strathmore Paper Co., Mittineague, Mass.

PRESS ROLLS Maple and Gum White Wood Felt Rolls — J. W. HEWITT MACHINE CO. Neenah, Wis.

ARE SUPERIOR TO ALL OTHERS. ALL SIZES IN STOCK.
LOMBARD & CO., Importers & Manufacturers, 236 & 238 A Street, Boston.

Classified List—United States

BOX STAY.

Cleveland-Akron Bag Co., Cleveland, Ohio.
Hollingsworth & Vose Co., Boston, Mass.
National Metal Edge Box Co., Philadelphia, Pa.

BRISTOL.

Amboy Paper Co., Bridgeport, Pa.
American Writing Paper Co., Holyoke, Mass. (White and Colored.)
Bardeen Paper Co., Otsego, Mich. (Index.)
Berkshire Hills Paper Co., Adams, Mass. (Index.)
Beveridge Paper Co., Indianapolis, Ind. (Bogus, and White and Tinted.)
Burmus Paper Co., Inc., West Dudley, Mass.
Chemical Paper Mfg. Co., Holyoke, Mass. (Index and White.)
Collins Mfg. Co., North Wilbraham, Mass.
Columbian Paper Co., Buena Vista, Va.
Crocker, Burbank & Co. Ass'n, Fitchburg, Mass.
Crocker-McElwain Co., Holyoke, Mass. (Index.)
Detroit Sulphite Pulp and Paper Co., Detroit, Mich.
Dexter, C. H., & Sons, Windsor Locks, Conn.
East Hartford Mfg. Co., Burnside, Conn.
Eddy Paper Co., Three Rivers, Mich.
Fort Orange Paper Co., Castleton, N. Y.
Franklin Paper Co., Holyoke, Mass.
Garvan, Thomas F., Co., Burnside, Conn.
International Paper Co., 30 Broad, New York.
Keith Paper Co., Turners' Falls, Mass. (Wedding.)
Lewis, J. P., Co., Beaver Falls, N. Y.
Marathon Paper Mills Co., Wausau, Wis.
Millers Falls Paper Co., Millers Falls, Mass. (Index.)
Missisquoi Pulp & Paper Co., Sheldon Springs, Vt.
Monroe Bridge Paper Co., Monroe Bridge, Mass. (Ticket.)
Mountain Paper Co., Lee, Mass.
Old Berkshire Mill, Dalton, Mass. (Pasted.)
Paraffine Companies, Inc., 40 First, San Francisco, Cal.
Parsons Paper Co., Holyoke, Mass.
Rising Paper Co., B. D., Housatonic, Mass.
Standard Paper Co., Kalamazoo, Mich.
Strathmore Paper Co., Mittineague, Mass.
Tileston & Hollingsworth Co., Boston, Mass.
United Paperboard Co., New York.
Warren Mfg. Co., New York. (Rope.)
Wheelwright Paper Co., Geo. W., Boston, Mass.
Worthy Paper Co., Mittineague, Mass. (Pasted Wedding.)

BUGGY BOARDS.

Merwin Paper Co., Hartford, Conn.
Monroe Binder Board Co., Monroe, Mich.
Shryock Bros., Philadelphia, Pa.
Tonawanda Board & Paper Co., Tonawanda, N. Y.
United Paperboard Co., New York.
Wasuc Mills Co., So. Glastonbury, Conn.

BUILDING.

American Tar Products Co., Rocklin, Ill.
Auglaize Box Board Co., St. Mary's Ohio.
Baltimore Roofing & Asbestos Mfg. Co., Asbestos, Carroll Co., Md.
Beloit Box Board Co., Beloit, Wis.
Bicking, S. Austin, Paper Mfg. Co., East Downingtown, Pa.
Bird & Son, Inc., East Walpole, Mass.
Brown Paper Co., Ithaca, N. Y.
Certain-Teed Products Corp., St Louis, Mo.
Crescent Paper Co., Marseilles, Ill.
Dixie Paper Mills, Inc., Richmond, Va.
Eureka Paper Co., Fulton, N. Y.
Fox Paper Co., Lockland, Ohio.
Hartje Bros. Paper Co., Toronto, Ohio.

ENGINEERING FOR
PULP, PAPER AND POWER PLANTS

JOSEPH H. WALLACE & CO
INDUSTRIAL ENGINEERS
Temple Court Building, NEW YORK
71 Bay Street, TORONTO, CAN

BUILDING.
(CONTINUED.)

Hartje Paper Mfg. Co., Pittsburg, Pa.
Harvey Paper Co., Wellsburg, W. Va.
Hoboken Paper Mill Co., Hoboken, N. J.
International Paper Co., New York.
Kingston's Son, Wm., Little Falls, N. Y. (Felts.)
Lawless Paper Co., Rochester, N. Y.
Lockport Paper Co., Lockport, N. Y.
Mullen Bros. Paper Co., St. Joseph, Mich.
Munroe Falls Paper Co., Massillon, Ohio.
Nelson Mfg. Co., The B. F., Minneapolis, Minn.
Newton Paper Co., Holyoke, Mass.
Parker, F. H., East Pepperell, Mass.
Port Huron Sulphite & Paper Co., Port Huron, Mich.
Ravenswood Paper Mill Co., 545 Van Alst ave., Long Island City, N. Y.
Schmidt & Ault Paper Co., York, Pa.
Springets Mills, York, Pa.
Standard Paint Co., Woolworth Bldg., New York.
United Paperboard Co., New York.
Wall, J. F., & Son, Walpole, Mass.
Watson Co., The H. F., Erie, Pa.

BUILDING BOARD.

American Straw Board Co., Akron, Ohio.
Eastern Straw Board Co., Inc., Manchester, Conn.
Rockton Paper Co., Rockton, Ill.
Springets Mills, York, Pa.
United Paperboard Co., New York.

BUTCHERS' MANILA.

Andrews, John T., & Co., Penn Yan, N. Y. (Fibre.)
Dixie Paper Mills, Inc., Richmond, Va.
Fleming, J. G., & Sons, Dallas, Tex.
Fox Paper Co., Lockland, Ohio.
Hartje Paper Mfg. Co., Pittsburg, Pa.
Humphrey & Young, Inc., Napanoch, N. Y.
Independent Paper Co., Independence, Kan.
Marcellus Paper Co., Syracuse, N. Y. (Waterproof.)
Schmidt & Ault Paper Co., York, Pa.
Winona Pulp & Paper Co., Winona, Minn.

BUTTON BOARD.

Albey Bros., Newark, N. J.
Foulds & Co., Inc., William, Manchester, Conn.
Naubuc Paper Co., Glastonbury, Conn.
Otter River Board Co., Otter River, Mass.
Wasuc Mills Co., South Glastonbury, Conn.

CANDY PAPER.

American Writing Paper Co., Holyoke, Mass.
Fox Paper Co., Lockland, Ohio.

CARBON TISSUE.

Ancram Paper Mill, 150 W. 22d, New York.
Dexter & Sons, C. H., Windsor Locks, Conn.
Diamond Mills Paper Co., 44 Murray, New York.
Mars Paper Corp., Westfield, Mass.
Smith Paper Co., Lee, Mass.

CARD BOARD.

American Wood Board Co., Schuylerville, N. Y.
American Writing Paper Co., Holyoke, Mass.
Bardeen Paper Co., Otsego, Mich.
Beveridge Paper Co., Indianapolis, Ind.
Blandy Paper Co., Schuylerville, N. Y.
Brown Paper Co., The E. M., Rock City Falls, N. Y.
Burmus Paper Co., Inc., West Dudley, Mass.
Champion Coated Paper Co., Hamilton, Ohio.
Columbian Paper Co., Buena Vista, Va.

CARD BOARD
(CONTINUED.)

Contoocook Valley Paper Co., West Henniker, N. H.
Eddy Paper Co., Three Rivers, Mich.
Fitchburg Paper Co., Fitchburg, Mass.
Haverhill Box Board Co., Haverhill, Mass.
International Paper Co., 30 Broad, New York.
Monarch Paper Co., Kalamazoo, Mich.
Tileston & Hollingsworth Co., Boston, Mass.
United Paperboard Co., New York.
Wasuc Mills Co., So. Glastonbury, Conn.

CARD MIDDLES.

American Straw Board Co., Akron, Ohio.
Berkshire Box and Paper Co., Mellenville, N. Y.
Beveridge Paper Co., Indianapolis, Ind.
Blandy Paper Co., Schuylerville, N. Y.
Brown, Howard C., Est., East Hampton, Conn.
Brown Paper Co., The E. M., Rock City Falls, N. Y.
Burmus Paper Co., Inc., West Dudley, Mass.
Carney Paper Co., Maumee, O.
Dixie Paper Mills, Inc., Richmond, Va.
Eddy Paper Co., Three Rivers, Mich.
Fort Orange Paper Co., Castleton, N. Y.
Gilbert, Frank, Paper Co., Waterford, N. Y.
International Paper Co., 30 Broad, New York.
Mac-Sim-Bar Paper Co., Otsego, Mich.
Moorhouse, R. T., Paper Co., Bridesburg, Pa.
Piermont Paper Co., Piermont, N. Y.
Schmidt & Ault Paper Co., York, Pa.
Standard Paper Co., Kalamazoo, Mich.
Thames River Specialties Co., The, Uncasville, Conn.
United Paperboard Co., New York.
Western Board & Paper Co., Kalamazoo, Mich.

CAR LINING.

Andrews, John T., & Co., Penn Yan, N. Y.
Dixie Paper Mills, Inc., Richmond, Va.
Lawless Paper Co., Rochester, N. Y.
Los Angeles Paper Mfg. Co., Los Angeles, Cal.
National Paper Co., Atlanta, Ga.
Rockton Paper Co., Rockton, Ill.
Schmidt & Ault Paper Co., York, Pa.
Standard Paint Co., Woolworth Bldg., New York.
Winona Pulp & Paper Co., Winona, Minn.

CARPET LINING.

American Tar Products Co., Rockton, Ill.
Andrews, John T., & Co., Penn Yan, N. Y.
Baltimore Roofing & Asbestos Mfg. Co., Asbestos, Carroll Co., Md.
Barrett Co., 17 Battery Place, New York.
Bicking, Estate of S. Austin, Downingtown, Pa.
Certain-Teed Products Corp., St. Louis, Mo.
Fox Paper Co., Lockland, Ohio.
Hadley Paper Corp., Hadley, N. Y.
Hartje Paper Mfg. Co., Pittsburgh, Pa.
Kieffer Paper Co., Ewing, Ind.
Lawrenceville Paper Mills, Lawrenceville, Ga.
Munroe Falls Paper Co., Massillon, Ohio.
Munroe Felt & Paper Co., Boston, Mass.
Newton Paper Co., Holyoke, Mass.
Ohio Paper Co., Miamisburg, Ohio.
Richardson Paper Co., Lockland, Ohio.
Robertson, C. M., Co., Montville, Conn.
Schmidt & Ault Paper Co., York, Pa.
Van de Carr, C. R., Stockport, N. Y.
Watson Co., H. F., Erie, Pa.

Lombard's English Newcastle Pulp Stones

Classified List—United States

CARTRIDGE.

American Writing Paper Co., Holyoke, Mass.
Bloomsburg Paper Co., Bloomsburg, Pa. (Waterproof.)
Cleveland-Akron Bag Co., Cleveland, Ohio.
Everett Pulp and Paper Co., Everett, Wash.
Lewis, J. P., Co., Beaver Falls, N. Y.

CASH REGISTER.

Fort Orange Paper Co., Castleton, N. Y.
Gilbert, Frank, Paper Co., Waterford, N. Y.

CATALOGUE.

American Writing Paper Co., Holyoke, Mass.
Bardeen Paper Co., Otsego, Mich.
Bryant Paper Co., Kalamazoo, Mich.
Combined Locks Paper Co., Combined Locks, Wis.
Dexter & Sons, C. H., Windsor Locks, Conn.
Diana Paper Co., Harrisville, N. Y.
Everett Pulp & Paper Co., Everett, Wash.
Flambeau Paper Co., Park Falls, Wis. (Light Weight.)
Gilbert, Frank, Paper Co., Waterford, N. Y.
Hartford Paper Co., Hartford, Conn.
International Paper Co., 30 Broad, New York.
King Paper Co., Kalamazoo, Mich.
Lakeside Paper Co., Neenah, Wis.
McDowell Paper Mills, Manayunk, Philadelphia, Pa.
Menasha Paper Co., Ladysmith, Wis.
Menasha Printing Co., Menasha, Wis.
Michigan Paper Co., Plainwell, Mich.
Moorhouse, R. T., Paper Co., Bridesburg, Pa.
Nixon Paper Co., Martin & Wm. H., Manayunk, Philadelphia, Pa.
Patten Paper Co., Ltd., Appleton, Wis.
Remington Paper & Power Co., Watertown, N. Y.
Taggarts Paper Co., Watertown, N. Y.
Tileston & Hollingsworth Co., Boston, Mass.
Watab Pulp and Paper Co., Sartell, Minn.

CHAIR SEAT BOARD.

American Fibre Seat Corp., Long Island City, N. Y.
Merlon Paper Co., Abrams, Pa.
Wasuc Mills Co., So. Glastonbury, Conn.

CHALK.

Clinton Paper Co., Clinton, Iowa. (Blue Express.)

CHART.

Strathmore Paper Co., Mittineague, Mass.

CHECK PAPERS.

Lewis, J. P., Co., Inc., Beaver Falls, N. Y.
Whiting, Geo. A., Paper Co., Menasha, Wis.

CHEVIOT.

Gilbert Paper Co., Frank, Waterford, N. Y.
Lewis, J. P., Co., Inc., Beaver Falls, N. Y.
Moorhouse, R. T., Paper Co., Bridesburg, Pa.
Munroe Felt & Paper Co., Boston, Mass.
Savage Mfg. Co., Skowhegan, Me.
Walsh Paper Co., Inc., Cuyahoga, Ohio.

CHIP BOARD.

Albany Paper Products Co., Albany, Ind.
American Straw Board Co., Akron, Ohio.
Astoria Pulp & Paper Co., Astoria, Ore.
Auglaize Box Board Co., St. Mary's, Ohio.
Barnes Paper Mill, Rochester, Mich.
Ballston Fibre Product Co., Inc., Ballston, N. Y.
Bicking, S. Austin, Paper Mfg. Co., E. Downingtown, Pa.
Bogota Paper & Board Co., Bogota, N. J.
Boyle Company, John F., Jersey City, N. J.
Boldt, Chas., Paper Mills, Cincinnati, Ohio.
Carthage Board & Paper Co., Carthage, Ind.
Carlyle Paper Co., Alton, Ill.
Chesapeake Paperboard Co., Baltimore, Md. (Plain, Mill Lined and Manila Lined.)
Chicago Coated Board Co., 545 N. Water, Chicago, Ill.
Chicago Folding Box Co., Chicago, Ill.
Chicago Mill & Lumber Co., Chicago.
Childsdale Paper Mill, Childsdale, Mich.
Clifton Paper Mills, Passaic, N. J.
Continental Paper Co., Bogota, N. J.
Crescent Paper Co., Marseilles, Ill.
Davis Paper Co., Contoocook, N. H.
Decatur Straw Board Co., Marion, Ind.
Federal Paper Board Co., Bogota, N. J.
Fox Paper Co., Lockland, Ohio.
Franklin Board & Paper Co., Franklin, Ohio.
French Paper Co., Niles, Mich.
Gardner-Harvey Paper Co., Middletown, Ohio. (Manila Lined.)
Gardner Paper Co., Middletown, Ohio.
Gardner Paper Co., The Colin, Middletown, Ohio. (Manila Lined.)
Gulf Paper Mills Co., Mobile, Ala.
Hadley Paper Corp., Hadley, N. Y.
Halltown Paper Board Co., Halltown, W. Va. (Mill and Vat Lined.)
Hartje Paper Mfg. Co., Pittsburgh, Pa.
Haverhill Box Board Co., Haverhill, Mass.
Hinde & Dauch Paper Co., Sandusky, Ohio.
Hutchinson Box Board & Paper Co., Hutchinson, Kan.
Independent Paper Co., Independence, Kan.
Indiana Board & Filler Co., Vincennes, Ind.
International Paper Co., 30 Broad, New York.
Lafayette Box Board & Paper Co., Lafayette, Ind.
Lancaster Board & Paper Co., Lancaster, Ohio.
La Salle Paper Co., South Bend, Ind.
Lawless Paper Co., Rochester, N. Y.
Leo Co., James, Jersey City, N. J.
Lydall & Foulds Paper Co., Inc., Manchester, Conn.
Manchester Board and Paper Co., Richmond, Va.
Marion Paper Co., Marion, Ind.
Massillon Paper Co., Massillon, Ohio. (For Corrugating.)
Mid-West Box Co., Kokomo, Ind.
Mt. Vernon Straw Board Co., Mt. Vernon, Ind. (Plain and Manila Lined.)
Miller Paper Co., Frank P., East Downingtown, Pa.
Monroe Binder Board Co., Monroe, Mich.
Monroe Paper Co., Monroe, Mich. (Light Weight.)
Mullen Bros. Paper Co., St. Joseph, Mich.
Mutual Box Board Co., Utica, N. Y.
Natick Box & Board Co., Natick, Mass.
National Folding Box and Paper Co., New Haven, Conn.
National Metal Edge Box Co., 8th and Willow Sts., Phila., Pa.
Newark Box Board Co., Newark, N. J.
New Elkhart Paper Mills Co., Elkhart, Ind.
Ohio Box Board Co., Cleveland, Ohio.
Philadelphia Paper Mfg. Co., Philadelphia, Pa.
Quaker Oats Co., Pekin, Ill.
Ravenswood Paper Mill Co., 545 Van Alst ave., Long Island City, N. Y. (Plain, colored and coated.)
Richardson Paper Co., Lockland, Ohio.
Rock Falls Box Board Co., Rock Falls, Ill. (Plain and Test.)

Lombard's English Newcastle Pulp Stones

Classified List—United States

CHIP BOARD.
(CONTINUED.)

Rockford Paper Box Board Co., Rockford, Ill.
Schmidt & Ault Paper Co., York, Pa.
Shryock Bros., Philadelphia, Pa.
Skaneateles Paper Co., Skaneateles, N. Y.
Smeallie & Voorhees, Amsterdam, N. Y. (Lined and Unlined.)
Snyder Mfg. Co., W. W., Cohoes, N. Y.
Springlets Mills, York, Pa.
Standard Paper Co., Kalamazoo, Mich.
Strange Paper Co., John, Menasha, Wis.
Tait & Sons Paper Co., The, Bridgeport, Conn.
Terre Haute Paper Co., Terre Haute, Ind.
Tonawanda Board & Paper Co., Tonawanda, N. Y. (Straw.)
United Paperboard Co., New York.
Waldorf Box Board Co., St. Paul, Minn. (Plain and Vat Lined.)
Wardway Paper Mills, Ft. Madison, Ia.
Weis Paper Mill Co., Quincy, Ill.

CHOCOLATE LAYER BOARD.
Amboy Paper Co., Bridgeport, Pa.

CIGARETTE.
American Writing Paper Co., Holyoke, Mass.
Columbia Mills, Chatham Centre, N. Y. (Straw.)
Diamond Mills Paper Co., 44 Murray, New York.
Smith Paper Co., Lee, Mass.
Stratford Paper Co., Jersey City, N. J.

CLOTH BOARD.
American Straw Board Co., Akron, Ohio.
Auglaize Box Board Co., St. Mary's, Ohio.
Funke's Sons, Ferd., Evansville, Ind.
Haverhill Box Board Co., Haverhill, Mass.
Ingalls & Co., Castleton, N. Y.
Naubuc Paper Co., Glastonbury, Conn.
Shryock Bros., Philadelphia, Pa.
Tait & Sons Co., The, Bridgeport, Conn.
Tonawanda Board & Paper Co., Tonawanda, N. Y.
United Paperboard Co., New York.
Wasuc Mills Co., South Glastonbury, Conn.

COATED BOOK.
Bryant Paper Co., Kalamazoo, Mich.
Champion Coated Paper Co., Hamilton, Ohio.
Champion-International Co., Lawrence, Mass.
Dill & Collins Co., 140 N. 6th st., Philadelphia, Pa.
King Paper Co., Kalamazoo, Mich.
Merrimac Paper Co., Lawrence, Mass.
Monarch Paper Co., Kalamazoo, Mich.
Reading Paper Mills, 808 Chestnut, Philadelphia, Pa.
Warren, S. D., Co., Boston, Mass.
West Virginia Pulp & Paper Co., 200 Fifth ave., New York, and 782 Sherman, Chicago.

COATED MILL BLANKS.
Falulah Paper Co., Fitchburg, Mass.

COATING AND GLAZING.
American Wood Board Co., Schuylerville, N. Y.
American Writing Paper Co., Holyoke, Mass.
Blandy Paper Co., Schuylerville, N. Y.
Brown, E. M., Paper Co., Rock City Falls, N. Y.
Brown, Howard C., Est., East Hampton, Conn.
Champion International Co., Lawrence, Mass.

DARNSTADT, SCOTT & COURTNEY, Inc., Importers, Exporters and Dealers in **PAPER MAKERS' SUPPLIES** Also Mfrs. of DEADENING and SATURATING FELTS
173 and 184 SOUTH STREET, NEW YORK

Ground Pulp & Sulphite Fibre Mill Machinery OUR SPECIALTY | **CARTHAGE MACHINE CO.** CARTHAGE, N. Y.

ARE SUPERIOR TO ALL OTHERS. ALL SIZES IN STOCK.
LOMBARD & CO., Importers & Manufacturers, 236 & 238 A Street, Boston.

Classified List—United States 265

COATING AND GLAZING.
(CONTINUED.)

Contoocook Valley Paper Co., West Henniker, N. H.
Crocker, Burbank & Co. Assn., Fitchburg, Mass.
Fitchburg Paper Co., Fitchburg, Mass.
Gilbert Paper Co., Frank, Waterford, N. Y.
International Paper Co., 80 Broad, New York.
Kalamazoo Paper Co., Kalamazoo, Mich.
Lewis, J. P., Co., Inc., Beaver Falls, N. Y.
McDowell Paper Mills, Manayunk, Philadelphia, Pa.
Monadnock Paper Mills, Boston, Mass.
Moore & Thompson Paper Co., Bellows Falls, Vt. (Manila.)
Nashua River Paper Co., East Pepperell, Mass.
Oxford Paper Co., 200 Fifth av., New York.
Rex Paper Co., Kalamazoo, Mich.
Ticonderoga Pulp & Paper Co., 200 Fifth ave., New York.
Tileston & Hollingsworth Co., Boston, Mass.
Wheelwright Paper Co., Geo. W., 95 Milk, Boston, Mass.

COLORED PAPERS AND BOARDS.

American Writing Paper Co., Holyoke, Mass.
Analomink Paper Co., North Water Gap, Pa.
Bardeen Paper Co., Otsego, Mich.
Beach Paper Co., The S. Y., Seymour, Conn.
Bear River Paper Co., Petoskey, Mich.
Beaver Brook Paper Mills, Danbury, Conn.
Beveridge Paper Co., Indianapolis, Ind.
Brownville Paper Co., Brownville, N. Y.
Bryant Paper Co., Kalamazoo, Mich.
Carney Paper Co., Maumee, O.
Carolina Fibre Co., Hartsville, S. C. (Wrapping.)
Case Mfg. Co., Unionville, Conn.
Chemical Paper Mfg. Co., Holyoke, Mass.
Childsdale Paper Mills, Childsdale, Mich.
Danville Pulp & Paper Mills, Danville, N. Y.
Dexter & Sons, Inc., C. H., Windsor Locks, Conn.
Diamond Match Co., Southford, Conn.
Eddy Paper Co., Three Rivers, Mich.
Esleeck Mfg. Co., Turners Falls, Mass. (Typewriter.)
Eureka Paper Co., Fulton, N. Y.
Fort Orange Paper Co., Castleton, N. Y.
Franklin Paper Co., Holyoke, Mass.
Gilbert Paper Co., Frank, Waterford, N. Y.
Harmon Paper Co., Brownville, N. Y.
Hartford Paper Co., Hartford, Conn.
Hollingsworth & Whitney, Boston, Mass.
Kalamazoo Paper Co., Kalamazoo, Mich.
Kieffer Paper Co., Ewing, Ind.
Knowlton Bros., Watertown, N. Y.
Lewis, J. P., Co., Beaver Falls, N. Y.
McDowell Paper Mills, Manayunk, Pa.
Mac-Sim-Bar Paper Co., Otsego, Mich.
Mason-Perkins Paper Co., Bristol, N. H.
Menasha Paper Co., Ladysmith, Wis. (Colored Laid Writings.)
Michigan Paper Co., Plainwell, Mich.
Moorhouse, R. T., Paper Co., Bridesburg, Pa.
Natick Box & Board Co., Natick, Mass.
Newton Falls Paper Co., Newton Falls, N. Y.
Nelson, The B. F., Mfg. Co., Minneapolis, Minn. (Lint.)
Onondaga Paper Co., Marcellus Falls, N. Y.
Oswego Falls Pulp & Paper Co., Fulton, N. Y. (Specialties.)
Rainbow Mills, The, 239 B'way, New York. (Manifold.)
Richardson Paper Co., Lockland, Ohio.
Robertson Co., C. M., The, Montville, Conn. (Specialties.)
Savage Mfg. Co., Skowhegan, Me.
Schmidt & Ault Paper Co., York, Pa.
Stevens & Thompson, Inc., North Hoosic, N. Y.
Strange Paper Co., John, Menasha, Wis.

E. J. KELLER CO., INC.
200 FIFTH AVENUE E. J. KELLER, Pres. NEW YORK
FOREIGN AND DOMESTIC
Wood Pulp and Rag Pulp
Gunny Bagging, Burlap Bagging, Ropes, Flax, Linen and Cotton Wastes, Paper Stock, Rags.

ENGINEERING FOR
PULP, PAPER AND POWER PLANTS

JOSEPH H. WALLACE & CO.
INDUSTRIAL ENGINEERS
Temple Court Building, NEW YORK
71 Bay Street, TORONTO, CAN.

COLORED PAPERS AND BOARDS.
(CONTINUED.)

Strathmore Paper Co., Mittineague, Mass.
Sweet Bros. Paper Mfg. Co., Phoenix, N. Y.
Van de Carr Paper Co., Stockport, N. Y.
Walsh Paper Co., Cuyahoga Falls, Ohio.
Walloomsac Paper Co., Walloomsac, N. Y.
Wheat Paper Co., Elkhart, Ind.
Yellow Pine Paper Mill Co., Orange, Texas. (Fibres.)
York Haven Paper Co., York Haven, Pa.

COMBINATION BOARD.

Albia Box and Paper Co., Troy, N. Y.
American Straw Board Co., Akron, Ohio.
Auglaize Box Board Co., The, St. Mary's, Ohio.
Boehme & Rauch Co., The, Monroe, Mich.
Bogota Paper & Board Co., Bogota, N. J.
Boyle Company, John F., Jersey City, N. J.
Chicago Coated Board Co., 545 N. Water St., Chicago, Ill.
Chicago Folding Box Co., Chicago.
Childsdale Paper Mills, Childsdale, Mich.
Continental Paper Co., Bogota, N. J.
Crescent Paper Co., Marseilles, Ill.
Eddy Paper Co., Three Rivers, Mich.
Federal Paper Board Co., Bogota, N. J.
Franklin Board & Paper Co., Franklin, Ohio.
Gardner-Harvey Paper Co., Middletown, Ohio.
Gardner Paper Co., The Colin, Middletown, Ohio.
Hummel & Downing Co., Milwaukee, Wis.
Hutchinson Box Board & Paper Co., Hutchinson, Kan.
International Paper Co., 30 Broad, New York
Leo Co., James, Jersey City, N. J.
Lewis, J. P., Co., Beaver Falls, N. Y.
Lydall & Foulds Paper Co., Inc., Manchester, Conn.
Mac-Sim-Bar Paper Co., Otsego, Mich.
Michigan Boxboard Co., White Pigeon, Mich.
Michigan Carton Co., Battle Creek, Mich.
Mid-West Box Co., Kokomo, Ind.
Morris Paper Mills, Morris, Ill.
Nelson, The B. F., Mfg. Co., Minneapolis, Minn.
Piermont Paper Co., Piermont, N. Y.
Ravenswood Paper Mills Co., 545 Van Alst ave., Long Island City, N. Y. (Vat-lined and Special Boards.)
Richardson Paper Co., Lockland, Ohio.
Rock Falls Box Board Co., Rock Falls, Ill.
Rockford Paper Box Board Co., Rockford, Ill.
Standard Paper Co., Kalamazoo, Mich.
Strange Paper Co., John, Menasha, Wis.
Tait & Sons Paper Co., Bridgeport, Conn.
Tonawanda Board & Paper Co., Tonawanda, N. Y.
United Paperboard Co., New York.
Waldorf Box Board Co., St. Paul, Minn.
Western Board & Paper Co., Kalamazoo, Mich.

CONDENSER.

Adams Paper Co., Wells River, Vt.
American Writing Paper Co., Holyoke, Mass.
Smith Paper Co., Lee, Mass.

CONE.

National Paper Co., Atlanta, Ga.
Noble Mfg. Co., Cedartown, Ga.
Wall, J. F., & Son, Walpole, Mass.

CONTAINER BOARDS.

Acme Paper Co., Reading, Pa.
American Straw Board Co., Akron, Ohio.
Auglaize Box Board Co., St. Marys, Ohio. (All Grades.)

ARE SUPERIOR TO ALL OTHERS. ALL SIZES IN STOCK.
LOMBARD & CO., Importers & Manufacturers, 236 & 238 A Street, Boston.

CONTAINER BOARDS.
(CONTINUED.)

Ballston Fibre Products Co., Inc., Ballston Spa, N. Y. (Plyless.)
Boldt, Chas., Paper Mills, Cincinnati, Ohio.
Carthage Board & Paper Co., Carthage, Ind.
Champion Fibre Co., Canton, N. C.
Cherry River Paper Co., Richwood, W. Va.
Chicago Coated Board Co., Chicago, Ill.
Continental Paper Co., Bogota, N. J.
Cornell Wood Products Co., Cornell, Wis. (Solid, Pulp, Jute.)
Crescent Paper Co., Marseilles, Ill.
Eddy Paper Co., Three Rivers, Mich.
Eureka Paper Co., Fulton, N. Y.
Hinde & Dauch Paper Co., Sandusky, Ohio.
Hoboken Paper Mill Co., Hoboken, N. J.
Hummel & Downing Co., Milwaukee, Wis. (High Grade Fibre.)
Hutchinson Box Board & Paper Co., Hutchinson, Kan.
Lawless Paper Co., Rochester, N. Y.
MacAndrews & Forbes Co., Camden, N. J.
Mac-Sim-Bar Paper Co., Otsego, Mich. (Pasted.)
Mengel Box Co., Elkhart, Ind.
Metalite Co., Amesbury, Mass.
Mid-West Box Co., Kokomo, Ind.
Monroe Binder Board Co., Monroe, Mich.
Moore Paper Mill Corp., Penn Yan, N. Y.
Mullen Bros. Paper Co., St. Joseph, Mich.
Ohio Box Board Co., Cleveland, Ohio. (Three Ply Fibre.)
Paraffine Companies, Inc., San Francisco.
Philadelphia Paper Mfg. Co., Philadelphia, Pa.
Pynetree Paper Co., Gordon, Ga.
Richardson Paper Co., Lockland, Ohio.
River Raisin Paper Co., Monroe, Mich.
Roanoke Fibre Board Co., Roanoke Rapids, N. C.
Rockford Paper Box Board Co., Rockford, Ill.
St. Regis Paper Co., Watertown, N. Y.
Strange Paper Co., John, Menasha, Wis.
Tonawanda Board & Paper Co., Tonawanda, N. Y.
United Paperboard Co., New York.
Waldorf Box Board Co., St. Paul, Minn. (Fibre.)

CONTAINER LINER.

Bogalusa Paper Co., Inc., Bogalusa, La.
Chicago Mill & Lumber Co., Chicago.
Fairfield Paper Co., Baltimore, Ohio.
Louisiana Fibre Board Co., Bogalusa, La.

COP TUBE.

Acme Paper & Paper Box Co. (Trust), East Pepperell, Mass.
American Straw Board Co., Akron, Ohio.
Bedford Pulp & Paper Co., Richmond, Va.
Gilbert, Frank, Paper Co., Waterford, N. Y.
Moorhouse, R. T., Paper Co., Bridesburg, Pa.

COPYING.

Ashuelot Paper Co., Hinsdale, N. H. (Yellow.)
Dexter & Sons, C. H., Windsor Locks, Conn.
Diamond Mills Paper Co., 44 Murray St., New York.
Flower City Tissue Mills Co., Rochester, N. Y.
Gandey, W. H., Lambertville, N. J. (Parchments and Yellow and Copying Tissue.)
Garrett Co., Edwin T., Lansdowne, Pa.
International Paper Co., 30 Broad, New York.
Mann Co., William, Lambertville, N. J.
Rainbow Mills, Rainbow, Conn.
Smith Paper Co., Lee, Mass.
Stratford Paper Co., Jersey City, N. J.

ENGINEERING FOR PULP, PAPER AND POWER PLANTS

JOSEPH H. WALLACE & CO.
INDUSTRIAL ENGINEERS
Temple Court Building   NEW YORK
71 Bay Street,   ONTO, CAN.

Lombard's English-Newcastle Pulp Stones

Classified List—United States

CORRUGATED.

American Box Board Co., Grand Rapids, Mich. (Liners.)
American Straw Board Co., Akron, Ohio.
Andrews, John T., & Co., Penn Yan, N. Y.
Fort Wayne Corrugated Paper Co., Eaton, Ind.
Hinde & Dauch Paper Co., The, Sandusky, Ohio. (Straw and Felt.)
Lawless Bros. Paper Mills, East Rochester, N. Y.
Lawrence Paper Mfg. Co., Lawrence, Kan.
Newton Paper Co., Holyoke, Mass.
Ravenswood Paper Mill Co., Long Island City, N. Y.
Rockford Paper Mills Co., Rockford, Ill.
Rockton Paper Co., Rockton, Ill.
Schmidt & Ault Paper Co., York, Pa. (Packing.)
Thompson & Norris Co., Concord and Prince, Brooklyn, N. Y.
Wardway Paper Mills, Fort Madison, Ia.
Watson, H. F., Co., Erie, Pa.

CORRUGATING.

American Straw Board Co., Akron, Ohio.
Auglaize Box Board Co., St. Mary's, Ohio. (All Grades.)
Brown Paper Co., Ft. Madison, Iowa.
Carlyle Paper Co., Alton, Ill.
Carthage Board & Paper Co., Carthage, Ind.
Clifton Paper Mills, Passaic, N. J.
Coshocton Straw Paper Co., Coshocton, Ohio.
Dresden Paper Mills Co., Dresden, Ohio.
Fairfield Paper Co., The, Baltimore, Ohio.
Fort Wayne Corrugated Paper Co., Fort Wayne, Ind.
Fox, W. H., & Son, Penn Yan, N. Y. (Straw.)
Hagar Straw Board & Paper Co., Xenia, Ohio.
Hinde & Dauch Paper Co., The, Sandusky, Ohio. (Chip and Jute.)
Lawless Paper Co., Rochester, N. Y.
Massillon Paper Co., Massillon, Ohio. (Straw and Chip Boards.)
Monroe Paper Co., Monroe, Mich. (Straw.)
Rockford Paper Mills, Rockford, Ill.
Schmidt & Ault Paper Co., York, Pa.
Skaneateles Paper Co., Skaneateles, N. Y. (Jute.)
Terre Haute Paper Co., Terre Haute, Ind. (Straw, Jute and Chip.)
Thompson & Norris Co., Concord and Prince, Brooklyn, N. Y. (Straw and Fibre.)
United Paperboard Co., New York. (Straw.)

COTTON BATTING.

Dexter & Sons, Inc., C. H., Windsor Locks, Conn.
Gilbert, Frank, Paper Co., Waterford, N. Y.
Hoberg Co., The John, Green Bay, Wis.

COTTON SAMPLING.

Cleveland-Akron Bag Co., Cleveland, Ohio.

COUNTER BOARD.

Davey, W. O., & Sons, Jersey City, N. J.
Diamond State Fibre Co., Bridgeport, Pa.
Groton Leather Board Co., West Groton, Mass.
Manning, John A., Paper Co., Troy, N. Y.
Muir Board Co., Inc., Lyndell, Pa.
South Coventry Paper Co., South Coventry, Conn.
Wasuc Mills Co., So. Glastonbury, Conn.
West Virginia Pulp Products Co., 200 Fifth Ave., New York; 732 Sherman St., Chicago.

COUPON.

American Writing Paper Co., Holyoke, Mass.
Bardeen Paper Co., Otsego, Mich
La Monte, Geo., & Son, New York.

LOMBARD'S ENGLISH NEWCASTLE PULP STONES ARE SUPERIOR TO ALL OTHERS. ALL SIZES IN STOCK. LOMBARD & CO., Importers & Manufacturers, 236 & 238 A Street, Boston.

CHIP CRUSHER — We make a specialty of GROUND WOOD PULP and SULPHITE FIBRE MACHINERY. Carthage Machine Co., CARTHAGE, N. Y.

COVER.

Advertisers' Paper Mills, Holyoke, Mass. (Deckle Edge.)
American Writing Paper Co., Holyoke, Mass.
Bardeen Paper Co., Otsego, Mich.
Beckett Paper Co., Hamilton, Ohio.
Bergstrom Paper Co., Neenah, Wis.
Beveridge Paper Co., The, Indianapolis, Ind. (Tablet.)
Boyd, Chas. S., Paper Co., Appleton, Wis.
Case, A. Willard, Co., Manchester, Conn.
Chemical Paper Mfg. Co., Holyoke, Mass.
Detroit Sulphite Pulp and Paper Co., Detroit, Mich.
Dexter & Sons, C. H., Windsor Locks, Conn.
District of Columbia Paper Mfg. Co., Washington, D. C.
Eureka Paper Co., Fulton, N. Y.
Hammermill Paper Co., Erie, Pa.
International Paper Co., 30 Broad, New York.
King Paper Co., Kalamazoo, Mich.
Knowlton Bros., Watertown, N. Y.
Lewis, J. P., Co., Beaver Falls, N. Y.
Marathon Paper Mills Co., Wausau, Wis.
McDowell Paper Mills, Manayunk, Philadelphia, Pa.
Michigan Paper Co., Plainwell, Mich. (Colored.)
Monroe Bridge Paper Co., Monroe Bridge, Mass. (Duplex.)
Moorhouse, R. T., Paper Co., Bridesburg, Pa.
New York and Pennsylvania Co., 200 Fifth ave., New York.
Niagara Paper Mills, Lockport, N. Y.
Pejepscot Paper Co., 111 B'dway, New York.
Peninsular Paper Co., Ypsilanti, Mich.
Rogers Paper Mfg. Co., South Manchester, Conn.
Strathmore Paper Co., Mittineague, Mass.
Tileston & Hollingsworth Co., Boston, Mass.

CRACKER SHELL BOARD.

American Straw Board Co., Akron, Ohio.
Anglaize Box Board Co., St. Mary's, Ohio.
Chicago Coated Board Co., Chicago, Ill.
Crescent Paper Co., Marseilles, Ill.
Gardner-Harvey Paper Co., Middletown, Ohio.
Gardner Paper Co., The Colin, Middletown, Ohio.
Haverhill Box Board Co., Haverhill, Mass.
Richardson Paper Co., Lockland, Ohio.
Strange Paper Co., John, Menasha, Wis.
United Paperboard Co., New York.
Waldorf Box Board Co., St. Paul, Minn.

CREPE.

Ashland Paper Co., Ashland, Wis.
Diamond Mills Paper Co., New York.
Erving Mills, Erving, Mass.
Lefevre, Edward Y., Fallsburgh, N. Y.
Lehigh Paper Mills, Inc., Raubsville, Pa.
Mt. Holyoke Tissue Mills, Holyoke, Mass.
Northern Paper Mills, Green Bay, Wis.
Oswego River Paper Mills, Phoenix, N. Y.
Perseverance Mills, Produce Exchange Bldg., New York.
Robertson Co., Orren C., Hinsdale, N. H.
Robertson & Co., W. F., Hinsdale, N. H. (Perforated.)
Rushmore Paper Co., Brooklyn, N. Y.
Schmidt & Ault Paper Co., York, Pa.
United States Paper Mills, Inc., Chamsberburg, Pa.
Wyoming Valley Paper Mill, Pittston, Pa.

CREPE TISSUE.

Diamond Mills Paper Co., N. Y.
Hinsdale Paper Mfg. Co., Hinsdale, N. H.
Mumford Paper Mills, Inc., Mumford, N. Y.
Northern Paper Mills, Green Bay, Wis.
Oswego River Paper Mills, Phoenix, N. Y.
Smith Paper Co., Lee, Mass.

Classified List—United States

CRINKLED.

Adams Paper Co., A. L., Baldwinsville, Mass.
Erving Mills, Erving, Mass.
Le Fevre, Edward Y., Fallsburgh, N. Y.
Northern Paper Mills, Green Bay, Wis.
Perseverance Paper Mills, Produce Exchange Bldg., New York.
Robertson Bros., Hinsdale, N. H.
Schmidt & Ault Paper Co., York, Pa.

DECORATED BOARDS.

American Straw Board Co., Akron, Ohio.
Case, A. Willard Co., Manchester, Conn.

DOCUMENT MANILA.
(See Manila and Tag Board.)

DRAWING.

American Writing Paper Co., Holyoke, Mass.
Bardeen Paper Co., Otsego, Mich.
Bedford Pulp & Paper Co., Richmond, Va.
Bryant Paper Co., Kalamazoo, Mich.
Chemical Paper Mfg. Co., Holyoke, Mass.
Dixie Paper Mills, Inc., Richmond, Va.
Fox River Paper Co., Appleton, Wis.
Gilbert Paper Co., Frank, Waterford, N. Y.
Glatfelter, P. H., Co., Spring Grove, Pa.
International Paper Co., 30 Broad, New York.
Lawless Paper Co., Rochester, N. Y.
Klein Paper Co., Clinton, Ia.
Mason-Perkins Paper Co., Bristol, N. H.
Moorhouse, R. T., Paper Co., Bridesburg, Pa.
Parsons Paper Co., Holyoke, Mass.
Schmidt & Ault Paper Co., York, Pa.
Strathmore Paper Co., Mittineague, Mass. (Also Board.)
Tileston & Hollingsworth Co., Boston, Mass.
Whiting Paper Co., Geo. A., Menasha, Wis.

DRUG.

American Writing Paper Co., Holyoke, Mass.
Bardeen Paper Co., Otsego, Mich.
Bedford Pulp & Paper Co., Richmond, Va.
McDowell Paper Mills, Manayunk, Pa.
Marathon Paper Mills Co., Wausau, Wis.
Moorhouse, R. T., Paper Co., Bridesburg, Pa.
New York & Pennsylvania Co., 200 Fifth av., New York.
Wausau Paper Mills Co., Brokaw, Wis. (Bond.)

DUPLEX.

American Writing Paper Co., Holyoke, Mass.
Beveridge Paper Co., The, Indianapolis, Ind.
Brown, The E. M., Paper Co., Rock City Falls, N. Y.
Carney Paper Co., Maumee, O.
Dexter & Sons, Inc., C. H., Windsor Locks, Conn.
Eddy Paper Co., Three Rivers, Mich.
Fox Paper Co., Lockland, Ohio.
Haverhill Box Board Co., Haverhill, Mass.
Hollingsworth & Vose Co., Boston, Mass. (Jute and Rope.)
International Paper Co., 30 Broad, New York.
Lewis, J. P., Co., Inc., Beaver Falls, N. Y.
Newton Paper Co., Holyoke, Mass.
Northern Paper Mills, Green Bay, Wis.
Schmidt & Ault Paper Co., York, Pa.
Standard Paper Co., Kalamazoo, Mich.
Stark Paper Co., North Bennington, Vt.
Strange Paper Co., John, Menasha, Wis.
Underwood Pulp & Paper Mills, Inc., Plattsburg, N. Y.
Wall, J. F., & Son, Walpole, Mass.
Warren Mfg. Co., New York.

Classified List—United States

DUPLEX BOARD.

American Straw Board Co., Akron, Ohio.
Brown Paper Co., Rock City Falls, N. Y.
Carney Paper Co., Maumee, Ohio.
Dexter & Sons, Inc., C. H., Windsor Locks, Conn.
Fox Paper Co., Lockland, Ohio. (Chip.)
Hollingsworth & Vose Co., Boston, Mass. (Rope and Jute.)
International Paper Co., New York.
Miller Paper Co., Frank P., East Downingtown, Pa. (Pasted.)
Schmidt & Ault Paper Co., York, Pa.
Strange Paper Co., John, Menasha, Wis.
United Paperboard Co., New York.

EASEL BOARD.

American Straw Board Co., Akron, Ohio.
MacAndrews & Forbes Co., Camden, N. J.

EGG CASE BOARD.

Acme Paper & Paper Box Co. (Trust), East Pepperell, Mass.
American Straw Board Co., Akron, Ohio.
Auglaize Box Board Co., St. Mary's, Ohio.
Delphi Straw Board Co., Decatur, Ind.
Hutchinson Box Board & Paper Co., Hutchinson, Kan.
Lawless Paper Co., Rochester, N. Y.
Mt. Vernon Strawboard Co., Mt. Vernon, Ind.
Terre Haute Paper Co., Terre Haute, Ind.
United Paperboard Co., New York.

EGG CASE FILLERS.

American Straw Board Co., Akron, Ohio.
Crescent Paper Co., Marseilles, Ill.
Delphi Straw Board Co., Decatur, Ind.

EGG SHELL.

King Paper Co., Kalamazoo, Mich.
Lakeside Paper Co., Neenah, Wis.
Miami Paper Co., West Carrollton, Ohio.

ELECTRIC BOARD.

Case & Risley Press Paper Co., Oneco, Conn.
Diamond State Fibre Co., Bridgeport, Pa.
Lewis, J. P., Co., Inc., Beaver Falls, N. Y.
Rogers Paper Mfg. Co., So. Manchester, Conn.

EMBOSSING.

Rogers Co., J. & J., Ausable Forks, N. Y.

ENGLISH FINISH.

Monadnock Paper Mills, Bennington, Vt.
Nixon, Martin & William H., Dill & Collins Co., successors, Philadelphia.

ENGLISH OPACITY.

Lakeside Paper Co., Neenah, Wis.

ENVELOPE.

Ætna Paper Co., The, Dayton, Ohio.
American Writing Paper Co., Holyoke, Mass.
Bryant Paper Co., Kalamazoo, Mich.
Chemical Paper Mfg. Co., Holyoke, Mass.
Combined Locks Paper Co., Combined Locks, Wis.
Crocker-McElwain Co., Holyoke, Mass.
Curtis & Bro., Inc., Newark, Del.
Cushnoc Paper Co., Augusta, Me. (Manila.)
Detroit Sulphite Pulp & Paper Co., Detroit, Mich. (Machine-Glazed.)
Dexter & Sons, Inc., C. H., Windsor Locks, Conn.

Classified List—United States

ENVELOPE.
(CONTINUED.)

Dill & Collins Co., Philadelphia.
Eastern Mfg. Co., Bangor, Me.; New York Office, 200 Fifth av.
Garvan, Thomas F., Co., Burnside, Conn.
Gilbert, Frank, Paper Co., Waterford, N. Y.
Howard Paper Co., The, Urbana, Ohio.
International Paper Co., 30 Broad, New York.
Kalamazoo Paper Co., Kalamazoo, Mich.
Kimberly-Clark Co., Neenah, Wis.
King Paper Co., Kalamazoo, Mich.
Lee Paper Co., Vicksburg, Mich.
Lewis, J. P., Co., Inc., Beaver Falls, N. Y. (Black.)
McDowell Paper Mills, Manayunk, Pa.
Miamisburg Paper Co., Miamisburg, Ohio.
Monadnock Paper Mills, Boston, Mass.
Moore & Thompson Paper Co., Inc., Bellows Falls, Vt.
Moorhouse, R. T., Paper Co., Bridesburg, Pa.
Munising Paper Co., Munising, Mich.
New York and Pennsylvania Co., 200 Fifth ave., New York.
Orono Pulp and Paper Co., Bangor, Me.
Parker-Young Co., Lincoln, N. H.
Racquette River Paper Co., Potsdam, N. Y. (Manila.)
Robertson Paper Co., Bellows Falls, Vt.
Southern Paper Co., Moss Point, Miss.
Southworth Co., Mittineague, Mass.
Strange Paper Co., John, Menasha, Wis.
Taylor-Logan Co. Papermakers, Holyoke, Mass.
Tileston & Hollingsworth Co., Boston, Mass.
Warren Mfg. Co., New York. (Jute.)
West Virginia Pulp and Paper Co., 200 Fifth av., New York, and 732 Sherman, Chicago.
Yellow Pine Paper Mill Co., Orange, Tex.

EXPRESS.

American Writing Paper Co., Holyoke, Mass.
Andrews & Co., John T., Penn Yan.
Bardeen Paper Co., Otsego, Mich.
Beaver Brook Paper Mill, Danbury, Conn.
Cleveland-Akron Bag Co., Cleveland, Ohio.
Clinton Paper Co., Clinton, Iowa. (No. 2 Red and Blue.)
Crown-Willamette Paper Co., Alaska Commercial Bldg., San Francisco, Cal.
Eureka Paper Co., Fulton, N. Y.
Fairfield Paper Co., The, Baltimore, Ohio.
Fox Paper Co., Lockland, Ohio.
Gould Paper Co., Lyons Falls, N. Y.
Hawley Pulp & Paper Co., Oregon City, Ore.
International Paper Co., New York.
Kieffer Paper Co., Ewing, Ind.
LaSalle Paper Co., South Bend, Ind.
Lawless Bros. Paper Mills, East Rochester, N. Y.
Lawless Paper Co., Rochester, N. Y.
Marcellus Paper Co., Marcellus Falls, N. Y.
McDowell Paper Mills, Manayunk, Pa.
Monroe Paper Co., Monroe, Mich. (Red and Gray.)
Munroe Falls Paper Co., Massillon, Ohio.
Munroe Felt & Paper Co., Boston, Mass.
New Castle Paper Mill, New Castle, Pa.
New York and Pennsylvania Co., 200 Fifth ave., New York.
Onondaga Paper Co., Marcellus Falls, N. Y.
Racquette River Paper Co., Potsdam, N. Y.
Robertson Paper Co., Bellows Falls, Vt.
Rock Falls Box Board Co., Rock Falls, Ill.
Schmidt & Ault Paper Co., York, Pa.
Shryock Bros., Philadelphia, Pa.
Strange Paper Co., John, Menasha, Wis.
Tarentum Paper Mills, Pittsburg, Pa.
Union Bag & Paper Corp., New York
Yellow Pine Paper Mill Co., Orange, Texas. (Drab.)
York Haven Paper Co., Philadelphia, Pa.

Arthur T. Bermingham
President

Walter P. Bermingham
Vice-President

Louis P. Simon
Secretary

Henry G. Prosser
Treasurer

Bermingham & Prosser Company

Paper Dealers

AND SPECIALISTS IN MAIL ORDER CATALOGUE PAPERS

■ ■

In Kalamazoo we carry in stock a full line of

Bonds, Flat Writings, Ledger, Coated and Uncoated Book, Tissue, Cardboard, Tag, Envelopes, Etc., and Coated Paper Seconds

■ ■

KALAMAZOO
402-404 East Kalamazoo Avenue

CHICAGO
10 South La Salle Street

NEW YORK
501 Fifth Avenue

Specialty Products
MANUFACTURED BY
AMERICAN WRITING PAPER COMPANY

Machine Finished and Super-Calendered
Book Papers
    For Publications
High-Grade Halftone Papers
    For Fine Catalogs, Books and House Organs
Antique Book Papers
    For Books, Booklets and General Advertising Matter
Halftone Covers
    For Magazines, Trade Papers, House Organs, etc.
Cover Papers
    For Catalogs, Booklets, Brochures, etc.
Offset Papers
Typewriter Papers and Manuscript Covers
Mimeograph Papers
Drawing Papers
Tracing Papers
Index Bristols
Rope Bristols
    For strong envelopes, mailing containers, etc.
Rope Pattern Papers
Blue Print Papers
Buff and Manila Drafting Papers
Map Papers
Coating Papers
Jute and Manila Tag
Bag Papers
Grease-Proof Papers
Gumming Papers
Hard Fibre Papers
    For making vulcanized fibre for electrical purposes
Duplex Papers

Papers for Pho
    *Photographic Pa
    Paper, Photo Mou*
Autographic Dupl
Black Papers of F
Special Wrapping
Bottle Wrapping
Candy Wrapping
Envelope Papers
    For Phonograph
Drug Powder Pa
Matrix Papers
Condenser Papers
Filter Papers
Acid Proof Papers
Mat Facing Papers
Papers for Va
Box Cover Papers
Anti-Tarnish Pape
Anti-Rust Papers
Ticker Papers
Music Papers
Music Roll Papers
Ribbon Papers
Cartridge Papers
Ice Cream and Oy
Hanging Papers
Single and Double
    Boards
Single and Double
    For Coating and F
All Grades of Colo
    For Special Pur

With our "26 Mill Organization," including a large Department of Research and Tests, we are in a position to make Specialties to meet the most exacting demands. We welcome your inquiries.

American Wri
HOLYOKE

Also
Manufacturers *of the* Famous
"Eagle A" Writing Papers

For Commercial Use

**BOND, LINEN, LEDGER
SUPERFINE AND TINTED
WRITING PAPERS**

A grade for every business requirement —from factory forms to high-grade stationery—affording a wide selection of qualities in each respective product.

Each paper is water-marked with the quality assuring "Eagle A"—the service and satisfaction mark of the World's Largest Makers of Fine Writing Paper.

SOLICITORS' OFFICES
NEW YORK CITY - - - - 41 *Park Row*
PHILADELPHIA - - - - *The Bourse*
CHICAGO - - - - - *The Otis Building*

BROWN'S
Linen Ledger Paper

Insures Permanency of Records

Records written on poor quality paper are like scratches on the sand. Inscribed on Brown's Linen Ledger Paper, they are as annals deeply carved into the solid rock.

For 68 years Brown's Linen Ledger Paper has been the highest standard of quality. It is made in a scientific way from pure white rags—made to endure for generations and in any climate. It is the paper of absolute reliability. It never grows yellow, never cracks, never tears away from the binding. Yet it makes the cost of a ledger only a fraction more. Write for Sample Book of Brown's Linen Ledger Paper.

L. L. BROWN PAPER COMPANY
Established 1850.   ADAMS, MASS., U. S. A.

FELTS.

Baltimore Roofing & Asbestos Mfg. Co., Asbestos, Carroll Co., Md.
Bardeen Paper Co., Otsego, Mich.
Barrett Mfg. Co., 17 Battery pl., New York. (Roofing.)
Bergen Paper Co., 178 South st., New York.
Bird & Son, Inc., East Walpole, Mass.
Carey, Philip, Mfg. Co., Lockland, Ohio.
Certain-Teed Products Corp., St. Louis, Mo.
Chesapeake Pulp & Paper Co., West Point, Va.
Eureka Paper Co., Fulton, N. Y.
Felt Paper Co., Rowlandville, Md.
Field & White Co., 116 Nassau st., New York. (Rolls and sheets.)
Ford Mfg. Co., Chicago, Ill.
Hinde & Dauch Paper Co., The, Sandusky, Ohio. (Corrugated and Indented Felt Papers.)
Johns-Manville Co., H. W., New York.
Kingston Paper Co., Inc., Little Falls, N. Y.
Lang Paper Co., John, Philadelphia, Pa.
Lewis, J. P., Co., Inc., Beaver Falls, N. Y.
Lockport Paper Co., Lockport, N. Y.
Los Angeles Paper Mfg. Co., Los Angeles, Cal.
Munroe Falls Paper Co., Massillon, Ohio.
National Asbestos Mfg. Co., Jersey City, N. J. (Asbestos.)
Munroe Felt & Paper Co., Boston, Mass.
Nelson, The B. F., Mfg. Co., Minneapolis, Minn.
Newton Paper Co., Holyoke, Mass.
Ohio Paper Mfg. Co., Miamisburg, Ohio.
Pleasant Mills Paper Co., Pleasant Mills, N. J.
Paraffine Companies, Inc., San Francisco, Cal.
Patent Vulcanite Roofing Co., Anderson, Ind. (Roofing.)
Richardson Paper Co., Lockland, Ohio. (Specialties.)
Savage Mfg. Co., Skowhegan, Me.
Schmidt & Ault Paper Co., York, Pa.
Springets Mills. The. York. Pa.
Standard Paint Co., Woolworth Bldg., New York.
Watson, H. F., Co., Erie, Pa.

FELTS—DEADENING.

American Tar Products Co., Rockton, Ill.
Barrett, The, Co., New York.
Bergen Paper Co., Little Ferry, N. J.
Certain-Teed Products Corp., St. Louis, Mo.
Felt Paper Co., Rowlandville, Md.
Field & White Co., 116 Nassau st., New York.
Ford Mfg. Co., Chicago, Ill.
Kingston Paper Co., Inc., Little Falls, N. Y.
Lang Paper Co., The John, Philadelphia, Pa.
Lockport Paper Co., Lockport, N. Y.
Los Angeles Paper Mfg. Co., Los Angeles, Cal.
Munroe Falls Paper Co., Massillon, Ohio.
National Asbestos Mfg. Co., Jersey City, N. J.
Newton Paper Co., Holyoke, Mass.
Paraffine Companies, Inc., San Francisco, Cal.
Richardson Paper Co., Lockland, Ohio.
Savage Mfg. Co., Skowhegan, Me.
Watson Co., H. F., Erie, Pa.

FELTS—SATURATING.

Arrowhead Mills, Inc., Fulton, N. Y.
Baltimore Roofing & Asbestos Mfg. Co., Asbestos, Md.
Bergen Paper Co., Little Ferry, N. J.
Bird & Son, Inc., East Walpole, Mass.
Certain-Teed Products Corp., St. Louis, Mo.
Eureka Paper Co., Fulton, N. Y.
Felt Paper Co., Rowlandville, Md.
Field & White Co., 116 Nassau st., New York.
Harvey Paper Co., Wellsburg, W. Va.
Johns-Manville Co., H. W., Manville, N. J.
Kingston Paper Co., Inc., Little Falls, N. Y.
Lang Paper Co., The John, Philadelphia, Pa.
Lockport Paper Co., Lockport, N. Y.
Los Angeles Paper Mfg. Co., Los Angeles, Cal.
Mullen Bros. Paper Co., St. Joseph, Mich.

Lombard's English Newcastle Pulp Stones

274   *Classified List—United States*

FELTS—SATURATING.
(CONTINUED.)

National Asbestos Mfg. Co., Jersey City, N. J.
Ohio Paper Co., Miamisburg, Ohio.
Paraffine Companies, Inc., San Francisco, Cal.
Richardson Paper Co., Lockland, Ohio.
Standard Paint Co., Woolworth Bldg., New York.
Wardway Paper Mills, Fort Madison, Ia.
Watson Co., H. F., Erie, Pa.

FIBRE.—

American Vulcanized Fibre Co., Wilmington, Del. (Hard.)
Analomink Paper Co., North Water Gap, Pa.
Andrews & Co., John T., Penn Yan, N. Y.
Arrowhead Mills, Inc., Fulton, N. Y.
Bayless Mfg. Corporation, 527 Fifth Ave., New York.
Bedford Pulp & Paper Co., 419 Mutual Bldg., Richmond, Va. (Water Finished.)
Boehme & Rauch Co., The, Monroe, Mich.
Brown Co., Portland, Me.
Brownville Paper Co., Brownville, N. Y. (Glazed.)
Carolina Fibre Co., Hartsville, S. C. (Water Finish.)
Central Paper Co., Muskegon, Mich.
Cherry River Paper Co., Richwood, W. Va.
Claremont Paper Co., Claremont, N. H.
Crown-Willamette Paper Co., Alaska Commercial Bldg., San Francisco, Cal.
Dells Paper and Pulp Co., Eau Claire, Wis.
Dexter Sulphite Pulp and Paper Co., Dexter, N. Y.
Diamond State Fibre Co., Bridgeport, Pa.
Dixie Paper Mills, Inc., Richmond, Va.
Eureka Paper Co., Fulton, N. Y.
Falls Mfg. Co., Oconto Falls, Wis.
Fibre Corporation, Lockport, N. Y. (Hard.)
Fletcher Paper Co., Alpena, Mich.
Fox Paper Co., Lockland, O.
Green Bay Paper & Fibre Co., Green Bay, Wis.
Halifax Paper Corporation, Richmond, Va. (Kraft.)
Hartje Paper Mfg. Co., Pittsburg, Pa.
Hoboken Paper Mill Co., Hoboken, N. J.
Hoberg, The John, Co., Green Bay, Wis.
Hollingsworth & Whitney Co., Boston, Mass.
International Paper Co., 30 Broad, New York.
Island Paper Co., The, Carthage, N. Y. (Dry.)
Island Paper Co., Menasha, Wis.
Lebanon Paper Co., 722 Montgomery st., San Francisco, Cal.
Malone Paper Co., Malone, N. Y. (Dry Finish.)
Marathon Paper Mills Co., Wausau, Wis.
Marcellus Paper Co., Marcellus Falls, N. Y.
Marinette & Menominee Paper Co., Menominee, Mich.
McDowell Paper Mills, Manayunk, Pa. (Colored.)
Megargee Paper Mills, Modena, Pa.
Menasha Paper Co., Ladysmith, Wis. (Striped, Dry and Sulphite.)
Moorhouse, R. T., Paper Co., Bridesburg, Pa.
Moyer & Pratt, Lyons Falls, N. Y.
Munising Paper Co., Munising, Mich.
Monroe Binder Board Co., Monroe, Mich.
Munroe Felt & Paper Co., Boston, Mass.
Nekoosa-Edwards Paper Co., Nekoosa, Wis.
New York and Pennsylvania Co., 200 Fifth ave., New York.
Odell Mfg. Co., Groveton, N. H.
Onondaga Paper Co., Marcellus Falls, N. Y.
Port Huron Sulphite & Paper Co., Port Huron, Mich.
Racquette River Paper Co., Potsdam, N. Y.
Strange Paper Co., John, Menasha, Wis.
Tennessee Fibre Co., Inc., Memphis, Tenn. (Cotton Hull.)
Thompson & Norris Co., Prince and Concord, Brooklyn. (For Corrugating.)

PRESS ROLLS   Maple and Gum   White Wood Felt Rolls   **J. W. HEWITT MACHINE CO.** Neenah, Wis.

ARE SUPERIOR TO ALL OTHERS. ALL SIZES IN STOCK.
LOMBARD & CO., Importers & Manufacturers, 236 & 238 A Street, Boston.

Classified List—United States 275

FIBRE.
(CONTINUED.)

Union Bag & Paper Corp., New York.
Volney Paper Co., Fulton, N. Y.
Waldorf Box Board Co., St. Paul, Minn.
Wasuc Mills Company, South Glastonbury, Conn.
Wausau Paper Mills Co., Brokaw, Wis.
West Virginia Pulp Products Co., 200 Fifth Ave., New York; 732 Sherman St., Chicago.
Wolf River Paper and Fibre Co., Shawano, Wis. (Machine-Glazed.)
Yellow Pine Paper Mill Co., Orange, Texas.
York Haven Paper Co., Philadelphia, Pa. (Colored.)

FIBRE BOARDS.

American Hard Fibre Co., Newark, Del.
American Straw Board Co., New York.
Auglaize Box Board Co., St. Mary's, Ohio.
Boehme & Rauch Co., The, Monroe, Mich. (Pasted Container Boards.)
Chicago Coated Board Co., Chicago, Ill.
Continental Paper Co., Bogota, N. J.
Crescent Paper Co., Marseilles, Ill.
Davis Paper Co., Contoocook, N. H.
Garvan, Thomas F., Co., Hartford, Conn.
Haverhill Box Board Co., Haverhill, Mass.
Herkimer Fibre Co., Herkimer, N. Y.
Hummel & Downing Co., Milwaukee, Wis. (High Grade Container.)
Keyes Products Co., 120 Broadway, New York. (Hard.)
Lewis, J. P. Co., Inc., Beaver Falls, N. Y.
Louisiana Fibre Board Co., Bogalusa, La.
Manning Paper Co., John A., Troy, N. Y.
Monroe Binder Board Co., Monroe, Mich.
Ohio Box Board Co., Cleveland, O.
Philadelphia Paper Mfg. Co., Philadelphia, Pa.
River Raisin Paper Co., Monroe, Mich.
Roanoke Fibre Board Co., Roanoke Rapids, N. C.
Rockford Paper Box Board, Co., Rockford, Ill. (Built up.)
Rogers Fibre Co., 121 Beach St., Boston, Mass.
Rogers Paper Mfg. Co., So. Manchester, Conn.
Stowe, J. D., & Sons, Inc., Scitico, Conn.
Tolland Leather Board Co., Hop River, Conn.
United Paperboard Co., New York.
Waldorf Box Board Co., St. Paul, Minn. (For Shipping Cases.)
Wasuc Mills Co., South Glastonbury, Conn.
West Virginia Pulp Product Co., 200 Fifth Av., New York; 732 Sherman, Chicago.

FILTER.

American Writing Paper Co., Holyoke, Mass.
Diamond State Fibre Co., Bridgeport, Pa.
Eaton-Dikemann Co., Lee, Mass.
Lylse, Wilson, Estate of, Landenberg, Pa.
Lewis, J. P., Co., Inc., Beaver Falls, N. Y.
Marshall & Mitchell, Wooddale, Del.

FINE.

Millers Falls Paper Co., Millers Falls, Mass. (Extra.)
Worthy Paper Co., Mittineague, Mass.

FIRE WORK AND TUBE.

Acme Paper & Paper Box Co. (Trust), East Pepperell, Mass.
American Straw Board Co., Akron, Ohio.
Elridge Strawboard Mill, Eldridge, N. Y.
Eureka Paper Co., Fulton, N. Y.
Fairfield Paper Co., The, Baltimore, Ohio.
Funke's Sons, Ferdinand, Evansville, Ind.
Hartje Paper Mfg. Co., Pittsburgh, Pa.
Lawless Paper Co., Rochester, N. Y.

ENGINEERING FOR
PULP, PAPER AND POWER PLANTS

JOSEPH H. WALLACE & CO.
INDUSTRIAL ENGINEERS
Temple Court Building, NEW YORK
71 Bay Street, TORONTO, CAN.

M. GOTTESMAN & CO., Inc.
18 E. 41st STREET, NEW YORK. Cable Address "Samsetcog"
EUROPEAN OFFICES: Stockholm, Sweden

Finest Mitscherlich Sulphite

Classified List—United States

FIRE WORK AND TUBE.
(CONTINUED.)

Munroe Falls Paper Co., Massillon, Ohio.
Schmidt & Ault Paper Co., York, Pa.
Terre Haute Paper Co., Terre Haute, Ind.
United Boxboard Co., New York.

FLATS.

Aetna Paper Co., Dayton, Ohio.
American Writing Paper Co., Holyoke, Mass.
Bardeen Paper Co., Otsego, Mich.
Bare Paper Co., D. M., Roaring Springs, Pa. (White.)
Bryant Paper Co., Kalamazoo, Mich.
Chemical Paper Mfg. Co., Holyoke, Mass.
Fox River Paper Co., Appleton, Wis. (Engine size.)
King Paper Co., Kalamazoo, Mich.
Knowlton Bros., Watertown, N. Y.
Peninsular Paper Co., Ypsilanti, Mich.
Southworth Co., Mittineague, Mass.
Whiting Paper Co., Geo. A., Menasha, Wis.

FLY PAPER.

Munroe Falls Paper Co., Massillon, Ohio.
Richardson Paper Co., Lockland, Ohio.

FOLDER.

Bryant Paper Co., Kalamazoo, Mich.
Chemical Paper Mfg. Co., Holyoke, Mass.
Flower City Tissue Mills Co., Rochester, N. Y.
King Paper Co., Kalamazoo, Mich.
Monarch Paper Co., Kalamazoo, Mich.
Tileston & Hollingsworth Co., Boston, Mass.
Rogers Paper Mfg. Co., So. Manchester, Conn.
Watervliet Paper Co., Watervliet, Mich.

FOLDED WRITINGS.

American Writing Paper Co., Holyoke, Mass.
East Hartford Mfg. Co., Burnside, Conn.
Everett Pulp & Paper Co., Everett, Wash.
Fox River Paper Co., Appleton, Wis. (Ruled.)
Southworth Co., Mittineague, Mass.
Watervliet Paper Co., Watervliet, Mich.

FOLDING BOX BOARD.

American Straw Board Co., Akron, Ohio.
Auglaize Box Board Co., St. Mary's Ohio.
Berkshire Box & Paper Co., Mellenville, N. Y.
Boehme & Rauch Co., Monroe, Mich.
Brownville Board Co., Brownville, N. Y.
Carthage Sulphite Pulp & Paper Co., Carthage, N. Y. (Solid Manila.)
Chemical Paper Mfg. Co., Holyoke, Mass. (White and Colored.)
Chicago Coated Board Co., Chicago, Ill.
Continental Paper Co., Bogota, N. J.
Crescent Paper Co., Marseilles, Ill.
Eddy Paper Co., Three Rivers, Mich.
Haverhill Box Board Co., Haverhill, Mass.
Lawless Paper Co., Rochester, N. Y.
MacAndrews & Forbes Co., Camden, N. J. (Patent White.)
McEwan Bros., Whippany, N. J.
Manchester Board & Paper Co., Richmond, Va.
Marathon Paper Mills Co., Wausau, Wis.
Marion Paper Co., Marion, Ind.
Miller Paper Co., Frank P., East Downingtown, Pa.
Morris Paper Mills, Morris, Ill.
National Folding Box & Paper Co., New Haven, Conn.
National Metal Edge Box Co., Philadelphia.
New Haven Pulp and Board Co., New Haven, Conn.
Ohio Box Board Co., Cleveland, Ohio.
Piermont Paper Co., Piermont, N. Y.

Classified List—United States

FOLDING BOX BOARD.
(CONTINUED.)

Richardson Paper Co., Lockland, Ohio.
River Raisin Paper Co., Monroe, Mich.
Robertson, C. M., Co., Montville, Conn.
Schmidt & Ault Paper Co., York, Pa.
Standard Paper Co., Kalamazoo, Mich.
Strange Paper Co., John, Menasha, Wis.
Tennessee Paper Mills,, Inc., Chattanooga, Tenn.
United Paperboard Co., New York.
Waldorf Box Board Co., St. Paul, Minn.

FRENCH FOLIO.

American Writing Paper Co., Holyoke, Mass.
Bardeen Paper Co., Otsego, Mich.
Bryant Paper Co., Kalamazoo, Mich.
Hartford Paper Co., Hartford, Conn.
Lakeside Paper Co., Neenah, Wis. (Glazed and Unglazed.)
McDowell Paper Mills. Manayunk, Pa.
Michigan Paper Co., Plainwell, Mich.

FRICTION BOARDS.

Davey Co., E. H., Bloomfield, N. J.
Davey, W. O., & Sons, Jersey City, N. J.
Haverhill Box Board Co., Haverhill, Mass.
Ingalls & Co., Castleton, N. Y.
Monroe Binder Board Co., Monroe, Mich.
Muir Board Co., Inc., Lyndell, Pa.
Wasuc Mills Co., South Glastonbury, Conn.
West Virginia Pulp Products Co., Inc., 200 Fifth Ave., New York; 732 Sherman St., Chicago.

FRUIT WRAPPING.

Andrews, John T., & Co., Penn Yan, N. Y.
Ashland Paper Co., Ashland, Wis.
California Tissue Mills, Inc., Los Angeles, Cal.
Everett Pulp & Paper Co., Everett, Wash.
Hawley Pulp & Paper Co., Oregon City, Ore.
Hoberg Co., The John, Green Bay, Wis.
Lawless Paper Co., Rochester, N. Y.
McDowell Paper Mills, Manayunk, Pa.
Mullen Bros. Paper Co., St. Joseph, Mich.
Robertson Paper Co., Bellows Falls, Vt.
Schmidt & Ault Paper Co., York, Pa.
Three Rivers Paper Co., Phoenix, N. Y.

FURNITURE.

Dixie Paper Mills, Inc., Richmond, Va.
Eureka Paper Co., Fulton, N. Y.
Lawless Paper Co., Rochester, N. Y.
Lawrence Paper Mills, Lawrenceville, Ga.
Lehigh Paper Mills, Inc., Raubsville, Pa.
Monroe Paper Co., Monroe, Mich.
National Paper Co., Atlanta, Ga.
Perseverance Paper Mills, Produce Exchange Bldg., New York.
Rockport Paper Mills Co., Rockport, Ill.
Shryock Bros., Philadelphia, Pa.
Standard Paper Mills, Lawrenceville, Ga.
Tonawanda Board & Paper Co., Tonawanda, N. Y.

GLASSINE.

Diamond State Fibre Co., Bridgeport, Pa.
Hartford City Paper Co., Hartford City, Ind. (Plain and Embossed.)
McDowell Paper Mills, Manayunk, Pa.
Rhinelander Paper Co., Rhinelander, Wis.
Warren Manufacturing Co., Woolworth Bldg., New York.
Warren Parchment Co., Dexter, N. Y.
Westfield River Paper Co., Russell, Mass.

Lombard's English-Newcastle Pulp Stones

Classified List—United States

HEELING.
(CONTINUED.)

Lancaster Leather Co., Lancaster, Ohio.
Lee Fibre Co., Newmarket, N. H.
Milton Leatherboard Co., Milton, N. H.
Wasuc Mills Co., South Glastonbury, Conn.

ICE CREAM PAIL BOARDS.

American Straw Board Co., New York.
American Writing Paper Co., Holyoke, Mass.
Brownville Board Co., Brownville, N. Y.
Carthage Sulphite Pulp & Paper Co., Carthage, N. Y.
Continental Paper Co., Bogota, N. J.
Eddy Paper Co., Three Rivers, Mich.
Marathon Paper Mills Co., Wausau, Wis.
Oswego Falls Pulp & Paper Co., Fulton, N. Y.
Richardson Paper Co., Lockland, Ohio.
Standard Paper Co., Kalamazoo, Mich.
The Thames River Specialty Co., Uncasville, Conn.
United Paperboard Co., New York.

IMPRESSION PAPER.

Dexter & Sons, Inc., C. H., Windsor Locks, Conn.
King Paper Co., Kalamazoo, Mich.
Rainbow Mills, 239 Broadway, N. Y.

INDENTED BOARDS.

American Straw Board Co., Akron, Ohio.
American Tar Products Co., Rockton, Ill.
Bicking, S. Austin, Paper Mfg. Co., E. Downingtown, Pa.
Carlyle Paper Co., Alton, Ill.
Hartje Bros. Paper Co., Toronto, Ohio.
Hartje Paper Mfg. Co., Pittsburgh, Pa.
Hinde & Dauch Paper Co., The, Sandusky, Ohio.
Kieffer Paper Co., Ewing, Ind.
Rockford Paper Mills Co., Rockford, Ill.
Schmidt & Ault Paper Co., York, Pa.

INDURATED.

Fibre Corporation, Lockport, N. Y.

INGRAIN WALL PAPERS.

Stark Paper Co., North Bennington, Vt.
Underwood Pulp & Paper Mills, Inc., Plattsburg, N. Y.
Walloomsac Paper Co., Walloomsac, N. Y.

INSULATING.

Bird & Son, Inc., East Walpole, Mass.
Case Bros., Inc., So. Manchester, Conn.
Certain-Teed Products Corp., St. Louis, Mo.
Diamond State Fibre Co., Bridgeport, Pa.
Eureka Paper Co., Fulton, N. Y.
Harvey Paper Co., Wellsburg, W. Va.
Hollingsworth & Vose Co., Boston, Mass.
Lewis, J. P., Co., Inc., Beaver Falls, N. Y.
Manning Paper Co., John A., Troy, N. Y.
Marshall & Mitchell, Wooddale, Del.
National Fibre & Insulation Co., Yorklyn, Del. (Rag Specialties.)
Newton Paper Co., Holyoke, Mass.
Ramsey, E. R., Co., Penn Yan, N. Y.
Rogers Paper Mfg. Co., South Manchester, Conn.
Standard Paint Co., Woolworth Bldg., New York.
Tarentum Paper Mills, Pittsburgh, Pa.
Union Mills Paper Mfg. Co., New Hope, Pa.
Warren Mfg. Co., Woolworth Bldg., New York City.
Wasuc Mills Co., South Glastonbury, Conn.
Watson Co., H. F., Erie, Pa.

Ground Pulp & Sulphite Fibre Mill Machinery — OUR SPECIALTY — CARTHAGE MACHINE CO., CARTHAGE, N. Y.

INTERLEAVING.

Ancram Paper Mills, 150 W. 22d, New York.
Bardeen Paper Co., Otsego, Mich.
Dexter & Sons Inc., C. H., Windsor Locks, Conn.
Eaton-Dikeman Co., Lee, Mass.
Gilbert Paper Co., Frank, Waterford, N. Y.
International Paper Co., New York.
Michigan Paper Co., Plainwell, Mich.

JACQUARD CARDS.

American Straw Board Co., Akron, Ohio.
Case Bros., Inc., So. Manchester, Conn.
Continental Paper Co., Bogota, N. J.
Crebore, C. F., & Son, 87 Milk, Boston, Mass.
Davey & Sons, W. O., Jersey City, N. J. (Boards.)
Fort Orange Paper Co., Castleton, N. Y.
Ingalls & Co., Castleton, N. Y.
International Paper Co., 30 Broad, New York.
MacAndrews & Forbes Co., Camden, N. J.
Merwin Paper Co., Rainbow, Conn.
National Metal Edge Box Co., 8th and Willow, Phila, Pa.
Palmer, Willis B., Coatesville, Pa.
Richardson Paper Co., Lockland, Ohio.
Rogers Paper Mfg. Co., South Manchester, Conn.
United Paperboard Co., New York. (Jute.)
Wauc Mills Co., So. Glastonbury, Conn.

JUTE BOARDS.

American Straw Board Co., Akron, Ohio.
American Writing Paper Co., Holyoke, Mass.
Bemis Bros. Bag Co., Peoria, Ill.
Boldt, Chas., Paper Mills, Cincinnati, Ohio.
Chicago Coated Board Co., Chicago, Ill.
Clifton Paper Mills, Passaic, N. J.
Continental Paper Co., Bogota, N. J.
Cornell Wood Products Co., Cornell, Wis.
Eddy Paper Co., Three Rivers, Mich.
Fort Wayne Corrugated Paper Co., Fort Wayne, Ind.
Fox Paper Co., Lockland, Ohio. (Test.)
Franklin Board & Paper Co., Franklin, Ohio.
Gardner-Harvey Paper Co. (The), Middletown, Ohio. (Plain and Oak Grain.)
Harvey Paper Co., Wellsburg, W. Va.
Haverhill Box Board Co., Haverhill, Mass.
Hinde & Dauch Paper Co., Sandusky, Ohio.
Lewis Co., J. P., Inc., Beaver Falls, N. Y.
Mac-Sim-Bar Paper Co., Otsego, Mich.
Marion Paper Co., Marion, Ind.
Mutual Box Board Co., Utica, N. Y. (Oak Grained.)
Natick Book & Board Co., Natick, Mass.
National Metal Edge Box Co., Philadelphia, Pa.
Ohio Box Board Co., Cleveland, Ohio.
Philadelphia Paper Mfg. Co., Philadelphia, Pa.
Richardson Paper Co., Lockland, Ohio.
Roanoke Fibre Board Co., Roanoke Rapids, N. C.
Rockford Paper Box Board Co., Rockford, Ill.
Skaneateles Paper Co., Skaneateles, N. Y.
Terre Haute Paper Co., The, Terre Haute, Ind.
Tonawanda Board Paper Co. Tonawanda, N. Y.
United Paperboard Co., New York.
Waldorf Box Board Co., St. Paul, Minn.

JUTE MANILA.

American Writing Paper Co., Holyoke, Mass.
Ancram Paper Mills, 150 W. 22d, New York.
Bemis Bro. Bag Co., Peoria, Ill.
Continental Paper Co., Bogota, N. J.
Eureka Paper Co., Fulton, N. Y.
Hollingsworth & Vose Co., Boston, Mass.

Classified List—United States

JUTE MANILA.
(CONTINUED.)

Marinette & Menominee Paper Co., Menominee, Mich.
Natick Box & Board Co., Natick, Mass.
National Metal Edge Box Co., 8th and Willow sts., Phila., Pa.
Newton Paper Co., Holyoke, Mass.
Sorg Paper Co., Paul A., Middletown, Ohio.
Warren Mfg. Co., Woolworth Bldg., New York.
Wardlow-Thomas Paper Co., Middletown, Ohio.

KRAFT.

Adams Paper Co., Wells River, Vt. (Lightweight.)
Bayless Mfg. Corporation, 527 Fifth Ave., New York.
Bloomsburg Paper Co., Bloomsburg, Pa.
Brown Co., Portland, Me.
Central Paper Co., Muskegon, Mich.
Chesapeake Pulp & Paper Co., West Point, Va.
Claremont Paper Co., Claremont, N. H.
Crystal Paper Co., Middletown, Ohio.
Dexter Sulphite Pulp & Paper Co., Dexter, N. Y.
Diamond Mills Paper Co., New York.
Eureka Paper Co., Fulton, N. Y.
Falls Mfg. Co., Oconto Falls, Wis.
Fox Paper Co., Lockland, Ohio. (Anti-Tarnish and Machine Glazed.)
Halifax Paper Corporation, Roanoke Rapids, N. C.
Hartje Paper Mfg. Co., Pittsburgh, Pa.
International Paper Co., 30 Broad, New York.
Lewis, J. P., Co., Inc., Beaver Falls, N. Y.
Marinette & Menominee Paper Co., Marinette, Wis.
McDowell Paper Mills, Manayunk, Philadelphia, Pa.
McIntyre Bros., Inc., Fayetteville, N. Y. (Light Weight.)
Mohawk Valley Paper Co., Inc., Little Falls, N. Y.
Moore & Thompson Paper Co., Inc., Bellows Falls, Vt.
Munroe Felt & Paper Co., Lawrence, Mass.
New Castle Paper Mills, New Castle, Pa.
New York & Pennsylvania Co., 200 Fifth av., New York.
Orono Pulp and Paper Co., Bangor, Me.
Paper Products Co., 2405 W. Franklin st., Baltimore, Md.
Perseverance Paper Mills, Produce Exchange Bldg, New York.
Savage Mfg. Co., Skowhegan, Me.
Southern Fibre Co., Portsmouth, Va.
Strange, John, Paper Co., Menasha, Wis.
Union Bag & Paper Corp., Woolworth Bldg., New York.
Union Paper Mills Co., Monongahela, Pa.
Wardway Paper Mills, Ft. Madison, Ia.
Wausau Paper Mills Co., Brokaw, Wis.
Wausau Sulphate Fibre Co., Mosines, Wis.
Wasuc Mills Co., South Glastonbury, Conn.
Winona Pulp & Paper Co., Winona, Minn.
Yellow Pine Paper Mill Co., Orange, Tex.

KRAFT BOARD.

American Straw Board Co., Akron, Ohio.
Auglaize Box Board Co., St. Mary's, Ohio.
Continental Paper Co., Bogota, N. J.
Haverhill Box Board Co., Haverhill, Mass.
National Metal Edge Box Co., Phila., Pa.
Roanoke Fibre Board Co., Roanoke Rapids, N. C.
West Virginia Pulp Products Co., Inc., 200 Fifth Av., New York; 732 Sherman, Chicago.

LABEL.

Bardeen Paper Co., Otsego, Mich.
Bryant Paper Co., Kalamazoo, Mich.
Estes, Herbert, Ausable Chasm, N.Y.
Everett Pulp and Paper Co., Everett, Wash. (Varnish.)
Glatfelter, P. H., Co., Spring Grove, Pa. (Varnish.)
International Paper Co., 30 Broad, New York.
King Paper Co., Kalamazoo, Mich.
New York and Pennsylvania Co., 200 Fifth ave., New York.
Oxford Paper Co., 200 Fifth ave., New York. (Varnish.)
Tileston & Hollingsworth Co., Boston, Mass.
West Virginia Pulp and Paper Co., 200 Fifth ave., New York, and 732 Sherman, Chicago. (Varnish.)

LEATHER BOARD.

Atlas Leather Mfg. Co., Caseyville, Ill.
Auburn Leather Board Supply Co., Auburn, Me.
Case Board Co., Andover, Conn.
Cushman & Rankin Co., Bath, N. H.
Davis Paper Co., West Hopkinton, N. H.
Endicott, Johnson & Co., Johnson City, N. Y.
Foulds, William, & Co., Inc., Manchester, Conn.
General Fibre Board Co., Danvers, Mass.
Greenwich Leatherboard Co., Middle Falls, N. Y.
Herkimer Fibre Co., Herkimer, N. Y.
Ingalls & Co., Castleton, N. Y.
Jenkins, George O., Co., Bridgewater, Mass.
Kerr Paper Mill Co., East Downingtown, Pa.
McElwain Co., Boston, Mass.
McKinnon Leatherboard Co., Oriskany, N. Y.
Milton Leather Board Co., Milton, N. H.
Monroe Binder Board Co., Monroe, Mich.
Muir Board Co., Inc., Lyndell, Pa.
Muir, James A., Morristown, N. J.
National Fibre Board Co., 121 Beach, Boston. (Horn Fibre.)
Passumpsic Fibre Leather Co., Passumpsic, Vt.
Pierce Bros., St. Johnsbury, Vt.
Rogers Paper Mfg. Co., South Manchester, Conn.
Sherman & Co., Belfast, Me.
South Coventry Paper Co., South Coventry, Conn.
Spaulding & Sons Co., J., North Rochester, N. H.
Stowe, J. D., & Sons, Inc., Scitico, Conn.
Tolland Leather Board Co., Hop River, Conn.
Wasuc Mills Co., South Glastonbury, Conn.
Wausau Sulphate Fibre Co., Mosinee, Wis.
Westport Paper Co., Westport, Conn.

LEDGER.

Ætna Paper Co., Dayton, Ohio.
American Writing Paper Co., Holyoke, Mass.
Berkshire Hills Paper Co., Adams, Mass.
Brown Paper Co., L. L., Adams, Mass.
Carew Mfg. Co., South Hadley Falls, Mass.
Chapin & Gould Paper Co., Springfield, Mass.
Chemical Paper Mfg. Co., Holyoke, Mass.
Collins Mfg. Co., North Wilbraham, Mass.
Crane Bros., Westfield, Mass.
Crocker-McElwain Co., Holyoke, Mass.
Eastern Mfg. Co., Bangor, Me.
East Hartford Mfg. Co., Burnside, Conn.
Fox River Paper Co., Appleton, Wis.
Garvan, Thomas F., Co., Burnside, Conn.
Gilbert Paper Co., Menasha, Wis.
Hamilton, W. C., & Sons, Wm. Penn P. O., Pa.
Hammermill Paper Co., Erie, Pa.
Hampshire Paper Co., South Hadley Falls, Mass.
Hawthorne Paper Co., Kalamazoo, Mich. (Ledger Bond.)
Howard Paper Co., The, Urbana, Ohio.
Keith Paper Co., Turners Falls, Mass.
Lee Paper Co., Vicksburg, Mich.

Lombard's English Newcastle Pulp Stones

Classified List—United States

LEDGER.
(CONTINUED.)

Miami Paper Co., West Carrollton, Ohio.
Miamisburg Paper Co., Miamisburg, Ohio.
Millers Falls Paper Co., Millers Falls, Mass.
Mt. Holly Paper Mills, Inc., Mt. Holly Springs, Pa.
Nashua River Paper Corporation, East Pepperell, Mass.
Neenah Paper Co., Neenah, Wis.
Odell Mfg. Co., Groveton, N. H.
Oglesby Paper Co., The W. B., Middletown, Ohio.
Parsons Paper Co., Holyoke, Mass.
Poland Paper Co., Mechanics Falls, Me.
Rising Paper Co., B. D., Housatonic, Mass.
Riverside Paper & Fibre Co., Appleton, Wis.
Southworth Co., Mittineague, Mass.
Strathmore Paper Co., Mittineague, Mass.
Unity Paper Mills, Potsdam, N. Y.
Valley Paper Co., Holyoke, Mass.
Weston Co., Byron, Dalton, Mass. (Linen.)
Whiting Ploover Paper Co., Stevens Point, Wis.
Whiting Paper Co., Geo. A., Menasha, Wis.
Whiting Paper Co.. Holyoke, Mass.
Worthy Paper Co., Mitteneague, Mass.

LINED BOARD.

Albany Paper Co., Albany, Ind.
Albia Box & Paper Co., Troy, N. Y.
American Straw Board Co., Akron, Ohio.
American Writing Paper Co., Holyoke, Mass.
Berkshire Box & Paper Co., Mellenville, N. Y.
Boyle Company, John F., Jersey City, N. J.
Carthage Sulphite Pulp & Paper Co., Carthage, N. Y.
Childsdale Paper Mills, Childsdale, Mich. (Manila.)
Crescent Paper Co.. Marseilles, Ill.
Davis Paper Co., West Hopkinton, N. H.
Diamond Match Co., Southford, Conn. (Bleached Manila Lined.)
Franklin Board & Paper Co., Franklin, Ohio.
Gardner Paper Co., The Colin, Middletown, Ohio.
Gardner-Harvey Paper Co., Middletown, Ohio.
Halltown Paper Board Co., Halltown, W. Va.
Haverhill Box Board Co., Haverhill, Mass.
Hutchinson Box Board & Paper Co., Hutchinson, Kans.
Lafayette Box Board Co., Transportation Bldg., Chicago, Ill.
Mac-Sim-Bar Paper Co., Otsego, Mich. (Sheet.)
Ohio Box Board Co., Miamisburg, Ohio. (Manila.)
Piermont Paper Co., Piermont, N. Y.
Ravenswood Paper Mill Co., Long Island, N. Y.
Richardson Paper Co., Lockland, Ohio.
Standard Paper Co., Kalamazoo, Mich.
Strange Paper Co., John, Menasha, Wis.
Tait & Sons Paper Co., Bridgeport, Conn.
Tonawanda Board & Paper Co., Tonawanda, N. Y.
United Paperboard Co., New York.
Waldorf Box Board Co., St. Paul, Minn. (Plain and Vat, Manila, Chip and News.)

LINEN.

Ætna Paper Co., Dayton, Ohio.
American Writing Paper Co., Holyoke, Mass.
Berkshire Hills Paper Co., Adams, Mass.
Brown Paper Co., L. L., Adams, Mass.
Carew Mfg. Co., South Hadley Falls, Mass.
Chemical Paper Mfg. Co., Holyoke, Mass.
Crane Bros., Westfield, Mass.
East Hartford Mfg. Co., Burnside, Conn.
Fox River Paper Co., Appleton, Wis.
Howard Paper Co., The, Urbana, Ohio.
Keith Paper Co., Turners Falls, Mass.
Lee Paper Co., Vicksburg, Mich.
Parsons Paper Co., Holyoke, Mass.

LOMBARD'S ENGLISH NEWCASTLE PULP STONES ARE SUPERIOR TO ALL OTHERS. ALL SIZES IN STOCK. LOMBARD & CO., Importer & Manufacturer, 236 & 238 A Street, Boston.

WET MACHINES We make a specialty of GROUND WOOD PULP and SULPHITE FIBRE MACHINERY

Carthage Machine Co. CARTHAGE, N. Y.

LINEN.
(CONTINUED.)

Peninsular Paper Co., Ypsilanti, Mich.
Rising Paper Co., B. D., Housatonic, Mass.
Southworth Co., Mittineague, Mass.
Strathmore Paper Co., Mittineague, Mass. (Box Cover.)
Taylor-Atkins Paper Co., Burnside, Conn.
Valley Paper Co., Holyoke, Mass.
Weston Co., Byron, Dalton, Mass.
Worthy Paper Co., Mittineague, Mass.

LINEN FINISHED.

American Writing Paper Co., Holyoke, Mass.
Eastern Mfg. Co., Bangor, Me.
Millers Falls Paper Co., Millers Falls, Mass.
Southworth Co., Mittineague, Mass.
Whiting Paper Co., Menasha, Wis.

LINENOID GOODS.

Berkshire Box & Paper Co., Mellenville, N. Y. (Folding.)
Crane Bros., Westfield, Mass.

LINING.

American Straw Board Co., Akron, Ohio.
Arrowhead Mills, Inc., Fulton, N. Y.
Auglaize Box Board Co., St. Mary's, Ohio.
Barnes Paper Mill, Rochester, Mich.
Clinton Paper Co., Clinton, Iowa. (Rag.)
Continental Paper Co., Bogota, N. J.
Fairfield Paper Co., Baltimore, Ohio.
High Falls Pulp & Paper Co., Chateaugay, N. Y.
Hoboken Paper Mill Co., Hoboken, N. J.
Hutchinson Box Board & Paper Co., Hutchinson, Kan.
Kieffer Paper Co., Ewing, Ind. (Rag.)
Klein Paper Co., Clinton, Ia. (Rag.)
La Salle Paper Co., South Bend, Ind. (Rag.)
Lawless Paper Co., Rochester, N. Y.
Mason-Perkins Paper Co., Bristol, N. H. (Box.)
McEwan Bros., Whippany, N. J.
Monroe Paper Co., Monroe, Mich. (Rag.)
Munroe Felt & Paper Co., Boston, Mass.
Pairpoint Corporation, New Bedford, Mass. (Case.)
Paraffine Companies, Inc., San Francisco.
Robertson Paper Co., Bellows Falls, Vt.
Standard Paint Co., Woolworth Bldg., New York.
Terre Haute Paper Co., Terre Haute, Ind.

LITHOGRAPH.

American Writing Paper Co., Holyoke, Mass.
Bare Paper Co., D. M., Roaring Spring, Pa.
Brown, Howard C., Est., East Hampton.
Bryant Paper Co., Kalamazoo, Mich.
Columbian Paper Co., Buena Vista, Va. (Card.)
Dill & Collins Co., 140 6th st., Philadelphia, Pa.
Everett Pulp & Paper Co., Everett, Wash.
French Paper Co., Niles, Mich.
King Paper Co., Kalamazoo, Mich.
Mead Pulp & Paper Co., Dayton, Ohio.
Merrimac Paper Co., Lawrence, Mass. (Coated and Uncoated.)
Monadnock Paper Mills, Boston, Mass.
Monarch Paper Co., Kalamazoo, Mich.
Nashua River Paper Co., East Pepperell, Mass.
New York and Pennsylvania Co., 200 Fifth ave., New York.
Nixon Paper Co., Martin & Wm. H., Manayunk, Philadelphia, Pa.
Oxford Paper Co., 200 Fifth ave., New York.
Peerless Paper Co., Dayton, Ohio.
Reading Paper Mills, 806 Chestnut, Philadelphia, Pa.
Southworth Co., Mittineague, Mass.

ENGINEERING FOR **PULP, PAPER AND POWER PLANTS**

JOSEPH H. WALLACE & CO.
INDUSTRIAL ENGINEERS
Temple Court Building, NEW YORK
71 Bay Street, TORONTO, CAN.

Classified List—United States

LITHOGRAPH.
(CONTINUED.)

Ticonderoga Pulp & Paper Co., 200 Fifth ave., New York.
Tileston & Hollingsworth Co., Boston, Mass.
Watervliet Paper Co., Watervliet, Mich.
West Virginia Pulp and Paper Co., 200 Fifth ave., New York, and 732 Sherman, Chicago.

LOFT DRIED.

Aetna Paper Co., Dayton, Ohio. (Bonds, Linens, Ledgers and Flats.)
American Writing Paper Co., Holyoke, Mass.
Crocker-McElwain Co., Holyoke, Mass. (Writings.)
Eastern Mfg. Co., The, Bangor, Me. (Ledger.)
Esleeck Mfg. Co., Turners Falls, Mass.
Lee Paper Co., Vicksburg, Mich.
Mountain Mill Paper Co., Lee, Mass.
Neenah Paper Co., Neenah, Wis. (Board and Flats.)
Southworth Co., Mittineague, Mass.
Strathmore Paper Co., Mittineague, Mass.
Whiting, Geo. A., Paper Co., Menasha, Wis.
Whiting-Plover Paper Co., Stevens Point, Wis. (Bond.)

LOOSE LEAF.

American Writing Paper Co., Holyoke, Mass.
Brown Paper Co., L. L., Adams, Mass.
Berkshire Hill Paper Co., Adams, Mass.
Southworth Co., Mittineague, Mass.
Weston Paper Co., Byron, Dalton, Mass.

MACARONI.

Eureka Paper Co., Fulton, N. Y.
Fox Paper Co., Lockland, Ohio.
Kieffer Paper Co., Ewing, Ind.
Lawless Paper Co., Rochester, N. Y.
Moorhouse, R. T., Paper Co., Bridesburg, Pa.
Schmidt & Ault Paper Co., York, Pa.
Walsh Paper Co., Cuyahoga Falls, Ohio.

MAGAZINE.

American Writing Paper Co., Holyoke, Mass. (Special.)
Bardeen Paper Co., Otsego, Mich.
Bryant Paper Co., Kalamazoo, Mich.
Everett Pulp & Paper Co., Everett, Wash.
King Paper Co., Kalamazoo, Mich.
Mead Pulp & Paper Co., Dayton, Ohio.
Menasha Paper Co., Ladysmith, Wis.
Moorhouse, R. T., Paper Co., Bridesburg, Pa.
Nixon Paper Co., Martin & Wm. H., Manayunk, Philadelphia, Pa.
Ticonderoga Pulp & Paper Co., 200 Fifth ave., New York City.

MANIFOLD.

Chemical Paper Mfg. Co., Holyoke, Mass.
Dexter, C. H., & Sons, Windsor Locks, Conn. (Linens.)
Esleeck Mfg. Co., Turner's Falls, Mass.
Everett Pulp & Paper Co., Everett, Wash.
Gandey, Est. of Wm. H., Lambertville, N. J.
Hartford City Paper Co., Hartford City, Ind.
Lakeside Paper Co., Neenah, Wis.
Mann Co., Wm., Lambertsville, N. J.
McDowell Paper Mills, Manayunk, Pa.
Philadelphia Wax Paper Co., Swarthmore, Pa.
Rainbow Mills, The, 239 B'way, New York.
Smith Paper Co., Lee, Mass.
Stratford Paper Co., Jersey City, N. J.
Wolverine Paper Co., Elkhart, Ind.

Classified List—United States

MANILA.

American Writing Paper Co., Holyoke, Mass.
Adams Bag Co., Cleveland, Ohio.
Adams Paper Co., Wells River, Vt.
Adams Paper Co., A. L., Baldwinsville, Mass. (Light Weight.)
Aldrich Paper Co., Natural Dam, N. Y.
Analomink Paper Co., North Water Gap, Pa.
Ancram Paper Mills, 150 W. 22d, New York.
Arrowhead Mills, Inc., Fulton, N. Y.
Ashland Paper Co., Ashland, Wis. (Nos. 1 and 2 White.)
Bergstrom Paper Co., Neenah, Wis.
Blake & Higgins, Bellows Falls, Vt.
Brown, The E. M., Paper Co., Rock City Falls, N. Y.
California Paper & Board Mills, Antioch, Cal.
Carthage Sulphite Pulp & Paper Co., Carthage, N. Y. (Heavy.)
Carthage Tissue Paper Co., Carthage, N. Y.
Central Paper Co., Muskegon, Mich.
Champion Coated Paper Co., Hamilton, Ohio. (Coated.)
Chemical Paper Mfg. Co., Holyoke, Mass.
Cherry River Paper Co., Richwood, W. Va.
Claremont Paper Co., Claremont, N. H.
Cleveland-Akron Bag Co., Cleveland, Ohio.
Cleveland Paper Mfg. Co., Cleveland, Ohio.
Combined Locks Paper Co., Combined Locks, Wis.
Continental Bag & Paper Co., 17 Battery pl., New York.
Coy Paper Co., West Claremont, N. H. (Tissue.)
Crown Willamette Paper Co., Alaska Com. Bldg., San Francisco, Cal.
Crystal Paper Co., Middletown, Ohio.
Cushnoc Paper Co., Augusta, Me.
Dells Paper and Pulp Co., Eau Claire, Wis.
Detroit Sulphite Pulp & Paper Co., Detroit, Mich.
Diamond Match Co., Southford, Conn. (Bleached.)
Eureka Paper Co., Fulton, N. Y.
Everett Pulp and Paper Co., Everett, Wash.
Falls Mfg. Co., Oconto Falls, Wis.

Fleming, John G., & Sons, Dallas, Tex.
Fletcher Paper Co., Alpena, Mich.
Fox Paper Co., Lockland, Ohio.
General Paper Co., 175 Fifth Ave., New York.
Gore, H. M., Freeland, Md.
Gould Paper Co., Lyons Falls, N. Y.
Great Northern Paper Co., New York.
Green Bay Paper & Fibre Co., Green Bay, Wis.
Hartje Paper Mfg. Co., Pittsburgh, Pa.
Hawley Pulp & Paper Co., Oregon City, Oregon. (All grades.)
Hennepin Paper Co., Minneapolis, Minn.
Hollingsworth & Whitney Co., Boston, Mass. (White and Colors.)
International Paper Co., 30 Broad, New York.
Island Paper Co., Carthage, N. Y.
Kieffer Paper Co., Ewing, Ind. (No. 2.)
Lake Champlain Pulp & Paper Co., Plattsburg, N. Y.
Lefevre, Edw. Y., Fallsburg, N. Y.
Lincoln & Co., L., North Dighton, Mass.
Marinette & Menominee Paper Co., Menominee, Mich., and Marinette, Wis.
Mason-Perkins Paper Co., Bristol, N. H.
McIntyre Bros., Inc., Fayetteville, N. Y.
Menasha Paper Co., Ladysmith, Wis.
Menasha Printing & Carton Co., Menasha, Wis.
Mohawk Valley Paper Co., Inc., Little Falls, N. Y.
Moore & Thompson Paper Co., Inc., Bellows Falls, Vt.
Moorhouse, R. T., Paper Co., Bridesburg, Pa.
Moyer & Pratt, Lyons Falls, N. Y.
Munising Paper Co., Munising, Mich.
Munroe Felt & Paper Co., Boston, Mass.
Nekoosa-Edwards Paper Co., Nekoosa, Wis.
Newton Falls Paper Co., Newton Falls, N. Y.
Newton Paper Co., Holyoke, Mass.
New York & Pennsylvania Co., 200 Fifth ave., New York.
North End Paper Co., Fulton, N. Y.

MANILA
(CONTINUED.)

Northwest Paper Co., Cloquet, Minn.
Odell Mfg. Co., Groveton, N. H.
Onondaga Paper Co., Marcellus Falls, N. Y.
Orono Pulp and Paper Co., Bangor, Me.
Parker-Young Co., Lincoln, N. H.
Racquette River Paper Co., Potsdam, N. Y.
Reading Paper Mills, 808 Chestnut, Philadelphia, Pa.
Robertson Paper Co., Bellows Falls, Vt.
Rogers Co., J. & J., Au Sable Forks, N. Y.
St. Regis Paper Co., Watertown, N. Y.
Schmidt & Ault Paper Co., York, Pa.
Shortsville Paper Co., Shortsville, N. Y.
Taggarts Paper Co., Watertown, N. Y. (Lightweight.)
Union Bag and Paper Corp., New York.
Wardlow-Thomas Paper Co., Middletown, Ohio.
Wausau Paper Mills Co., Brokaw, Wis.
West Jersey Paper Mfg. Co., Camden, N. J.
Wolf River Paper & Fibre Co., Shawano, Wis.

MANILA AND TAG BOARD.

American Straw Board Co., Akron, Ohio.
American Wood Board Co., Schuylerville, N. Y.
American Writing Paper Co., Holyoke, Mass.
Blandy Paper Co., Schuylerville, N. Y. (Tag.)
Brown Paper Co., The E. M., Rock City Falls, N. Y.
Brownville Board Co., Brownville, N. Y. (Tag.)
Burmus Paper Co., Inc., West Dudley, Mass. (Tag.)
Carthage Sulphite Pulp & Paper Co., Carthage, N. Y.
Cherry River Paper Co., Richmond, W. Va.
Crescent Paper Co., Marseilles, Ill. (Lined.)
Detroit Sulphite Pulp and Paper Co., Detroit, Mich.
Eddy Paper Co., Three Rivers, Mich.
Eureka Paper Co., Fulton, N. Y.
Flower City Tissue Mills Co., Rochester, N. Y.
Haverhill Box Board Co., Haverhill, Mass.
Hollingsworth & Vose Co., Boston, Mass. (Rag Tag.)
International Paper Co., 30 Broad, New York.
Lewis Co., The J. P., Inc., Beaver Falls, N. Y.
Mac-Sim-Bar Paper Co., Otsego, Mich.
Marathon Paper Mills Co., Wausau, Wis. (Tag.)
Monroe Bridge Paper Co., Monroe Bridge, Mass.
National Folding Box & Paper Co., New Haven, Conn.
Odell Mfg. Co., Groveton, N. H.
Paraffine Companies, Inc., San Francisco, Cal.
Quaker Oats, Pekin, Ill.
Standard Paper Co., Kalamazoo, Mich.
Strange Paper Co., John, Menasha, Wis.
United Paperboard Co., New York.
Waldorf Box Board Co., St. Paul, Minn.
Warren Mfg. Co., New York.

MANILA WRITING.

American Writing Paper Co., Holyoke, Mass.
Bardeen Paper Co., Otsego, Mich.
Everett Pulp & Paper Co., Everett, Wash.
Hollingsworth & Whitney Co., Boston, Mass.
King Paper Co., Kalamazoo, Mich.
Lakeside Paper Co., Neenah, Wis.
Robertson Paper Co., Bellows Falls, Vt.
Whiting Paper Co., Geo. A., Menasha, Wis.

ESTABLISHED 1885

MENDELSON BROS. PAPER STOCK CO.

PACKERS OF ALL GRADES OF

PAPER STOCK SUPPLIES

General Offices
Suite 317, 910 So. Michigan Boulevard   CHICAGO, ILL.
Warehouses—Chicago, Ill.

Exclusive Representatives
MISSOURI PAPER STOCK COMPANY
22d and Scott Avenue   ST. LOUIS, MO.
On Terminal Railway

Berlin Mills Company
and
Burgess Sulphite Fibre Company

are now associated
under the name

Brown Company

Sales and General Offices, Portland, Maine

New York Office
Woolworth Building

Chicago Office
110 South Dearborn Street

* * *

Business founded 1852
Mills at Berlin, New Hampshire

* * *

In addition to a daily output of six hundred tons of Bleached Sulphite Fibre, the Company and its subsidiaries produce a large tonnage of Nibroc Kraft, Bermico Sheathing Paper, Mill Wrappers, Turpentine and other by-products associated with the pulp and paper industries.

Inquiries for samples and quotations receive prompt and careful attention

The Company's large producing capacity and excellent shipping facilities, together with the established quality of its products, offer to the prospective customer the same service which has held its existing clientele through sixty-six years of sustained growth.

ARE SUPERIOR TO ALL OTHERS. ALL SIZES IN STOCK.
LOMBARD & CO., Importers & Manufacturers, 236 & 238 A Street, Boston.

Classified List—United States 289

MAP.

American Writing Paper Co., Holyoke, Mass.
Bardeen Paper Co., Otsego, Mich.
Bryant Paper Co., Kalamazoo, Mich.
Chemical Paper Mfg. Co., Holyoke, Mass.
Kalamazoo Paper Co., Kalamazoo, Mich.
King Paper Co., Kalamazoo, Mich.
Reading Paper Mills, 808 Chestnut, Philadelphia, Pa.
Southworth Co., Mittineague, Mass.
Strathmore Paper Co., Mittineague, Mass.
Tileston & Hollingsworth Co., Boston, Mass.
Valley Paper Co., Holyoke, Mass.

MAT BOARDS.

American Straw Board Co., Akron, Ohio.
American Writing Paper Co., Holyoke, Mass.
Case Co., The A. Willard, Manchester, Conn.
Hurlock Bros. Co., Philadelphia, Pa.
Strathmore Paper Co., Mittineague, Mass.
United Paperboard Co., New York.
Wasuc Mills Co., So. Glastonbury, Conn.

MATRIX.

American Writing Paper Co., Holyoke, Mass.
Bardeen Paper Co., Otsego, Mich.
District of Columbia Paper Mfg. Co., Washington, D. C.
Eaton-Dikeman Co., Lee, Mass.
Vinton, Wm. H., & Son, Brattleboro, Vt.

MILK BOTTLE CAP.

American Straw Board Co., Akron, Ohio.
Continental Paper Co., Bogota, N. J.
Haverhill Box Board Co., Haverhill, Mass.
Lewis, Slocum & Lefevre Co., Inc., Beaver Falls, N. Y.
Mac-Sim-Bar Paper Co., Otsego, Mich.
Oswego Falls Pulp & Paper Co., Fulton, N. Y.
Strange Paper Co., John, Menasha, Wis.
Tonawanda Board & Paper Co., Tonawanda, N. Y.
United Paperboard Co., New York.

MILL BOARDS.

Agasote Mill Board Co., Trenton, N. J.
Albey Bros., Newark, N. J.
American Writing Paper Co., Holyoke, Mass.
American Straw Board Co., Akron, Ohio.
Haverhill Box Board Co., Haverhill, Mass.
Ingalls & Co., Castleton, N. Y.
Johns-Manville Co., H. W., Madison ave. and 41st st., New York City.
Illinois Box Board Co., Pekin, Ill.
Keasbey & Mattison Co., Ambler, Pa.
Lawless Paper Co., Rochester, N. Y.
Lydell & Foulds Paper Co., Inc., Manchester, Conn.
Naubuc Paper Co., Glastonbury, Conn.
Schmidt & Ault Paper Co., York, Pa.
Wasuc Mills Co., So. Glastonbury, Conn.
Watson Co., H. F., Erie, Pa.

MILL WRAPPERS.

Acme Paper & Paper Box Co. (Trust), East Pepperell, Mass.
Ballston Fibre Products Co., Inc., Ballston Spa, N. Y.
Beaver Brook Paper Mill, Danbury, Conn.
Bicking, S. Austin, Paper Mfg. Co., East Downingtown, Pa.
Carney Paper Co., Maumee, Ohio.
Chicago Coated Board Co., Chicago, Ill.
Dixie Paper Mills, Inc., Richmond, Va.

ENGINEERING FOR
PULP, PAPER AND POWER PLANTS

JOSEPH H. WALLACE & CO.
INDUSTRIAL ENGINEERS
Temple Court Building, NEW YORK
71 Bay Street, TORONTO, CAN.

E. J. KELLER CO., INC.
200 FIFTH AVENUE E. J. KELLER, Pres. NEW YORK
FOREIGN AND DOMESTIC
Wood Pulp and Rag Pulp
Gunny Bagging, Burlap Bagging, Ropes, Flax, Linen and Cotton Wastes, Paper Stock, Rags.

Lombard's English Newcastle Pulp Stones

Classified List—United States

MILK WRAPPERS.
(CONTINUED.)

Foster Box Board Co., Utica, N. Y.
Fox Paper Co., Lockland, Ohio.
Funke's Sons, Ferdinand, Evansville, Ind.
Hartje Bros. Paper Co., Toronto, Ohio.
Hartje Paper Mfg. Co., Pittsburgh, Pa.
Haverhill Box Board Co., Haverhill, Mass.
International Paper Co., 30 Broad, New York.
La Salle Paper Co., South Bend, Ind.
Lawless Bros. Paper Mills, East Rochester, N. Y.
Lawless Paper Co., Rochester, N. Y.
Mac-Sim-Bar Paper Co., Otsego, Mich.
Manchester Board & Paper Co., Richmond, Va.
Marcellus Paper Co., Marcellus Falls, N. Y. (Lightweight.)
Munroe Felt & Paper Co., Boston, Mass.
Nelson, B. F., Mfg. Co., Minneapolis, Minn.
Newton Paper Co., Holyoke, Mass.
Schmidt & Ault Paper Co., York, Pa.
Simplex Paper Co., Palmyra, Mich.
Skaneateles Paper Co., Skaneateles, N. Y.
Springets Mills, York, Pa.
Strange, John, Paper Co., Menasha, Wis.
Waldorf Box Board Co., St. Paul, Minn.
Western Board & Paper Co., Kalamazoo, Mich.

MIMEOGRAPH.

American Writing Paper Co., Holyoke, Mass.
Bardeen Paper Co., Otsego, Mich.
Bare, D. M., Paper Co., Roaring Springs, Pa.
Bryant Paper Co., Kalamazoo, Mich.
Chemical Paper Mfg. Co., Holyoke, Mass.
Cornwall Paper Mfg. Co., Cornwall-on-Hudson, N. Y.
Dill & Collins Co., Philadelphia, Pa.
Garvan, Thomas F., Co., Burnside, Conn.
General Paper Co., 175 Fifth Ave., New York.
Glatfelter, P. H., Co., Spring Grove, Pa.
King Paper Co., Kalamazoo, Mich.
Miami Paper Co., West Carrollton, Ohio.
Michigan Paper Co., Plainwell, Mich.
Moorhouse, R. T., Paper Co., Bridesburg, Pa.
New York & Pennsylvania Co., New York.
Nixon Paper Co., Martin & William H., Dill & Collins Co., successors, Philadelphia.
Rex Paper Co., Kalamazoo, Mich.
Whiting Paper Co., Geo. A., Menasha, Wis.

MOUNTING BOARD.

American Straw Board Co., Akron, Ohio.
Hurlock Bros. Co., Philadelphia, Pa.
Ingalls & Co., Castleton, N. Y.
Lewis, J. P., Co., Inc., Beaver Falls, N. Y.
MacAndrews & Forbes Co., Camden, N. J.
Strathmore Paper Co., Mittineague, Mass.
United Paperboard Co., New York.

MUSIC.

American Writing Paper Co., Holyoke, Mass.
Bardeen Paper Co., Otsego, Mich.
Bryant Paper Co., Kalamazoo, Mich.
Gilbert, Frank, Paper Co., Waterford, N. Y.
Glatfelter, P. H., Co., Spring Grove, Pa.
King Paper Co., Kalamazoo, Mich.
McDowell Paper Mills, Manayunk, Pa.
Merrimac Paper Co., Lawrence, Mass.
Michigan Paper Co., Plainwell, Mich.
Monadnock Paper Mills, Boston, Mass.
Ticonderoga Pulp & Paper Co., 200 Fifth av., New York.
Tileston & Hollingsworth Co., Boston, Mass.
Wheelwright Paper Co., G. W., 95 Milk St., Boston, Mass.

PRESS ROLLS — Maple and Gum White Wood Felt Rolls — J. W. HEWITT MACHINE CO. Neenah, Wis.

NAPKIN PAPER.
(See Paper Napkins.)

NEWS.

Aldrich Paper Co., Natural Dam, N. Y.
Alexandria Paper Co., Alexandria, Ind.
Arrowhead Mills, Inc., Fulton, N. Y.
Champion Paper Co., Carthage, N.Y.
Combined Locks Paper Co., Combined Locks, Wis.
Consolidated Water Power and Paper Co., Grand Rapids, Wis.
Crown Willamette Paper Co., Alaska Commercial Bldg., San Francisco, Cal.
De Grasse Paper Co., Pyrites, N. Y.
Defiance Paper Co., Niagara Falls, N. Y.
Dells Paper and Pulp Co., Eau Claire, Wis.
Diana Paper Co., Harrisville, N. Y. (Light Weight.)
Finch, Pruyn & Co., Inc., Glens Falls, N. Y.
Fitzdale Paper Co., Fitzdale, Vt.
Flambeau Paper Co., Park Falls, Wis.
Gould Paper Co., Lyons Falls, N. Y.
Grandfather's Fall Co., Merrill, Wis.
Great Northern Paper Co., 30 E. 42d, New York.
Hawley Pulp & Paper Co., Oregon City, Ore.
Hennepin Paper Co., Minneapolis, Minn.
High Falls Pulp & Paper Co., Chateaugay, N. Y.
Hutchinson Box Board & Paper Co., Hutchinson, Kan.
Inland Empire Paper Co., Spokane, Wash.
International Paper Co., 30 Broad, New York.
Iroquois Pulp & Paper Co., Thomson, N. Y.
Itasca Paper Co., Grand Rapids, Minn.
Lake Champlain Pulp and Paper Co., Plattsburg, N. Y.
Malone Paper Co., Malone, N. Y.
Mason-Perkins Paper Co., Bristol, N. H.
Menasha Paper Co., Ladysmith, Wis.
Menasha Printing Co., Menasha, Wis.
Minnesota and Ontario Power Co., International Falls, Minn.
Northwest Paper Co., Cloquet, Minn.
Norwood Paper Co., Norwood, N. Y.
Oswego Falls Pulp & Paper Co., Fulton, N. Y.
Outagamie Paper Co., Kaukauna, Wis. (No. 1 Rag.)
Patten Paper Co., Appleton, Wis. (No. 1 Rag Print.)
Pejepscot Paper Co., 111 Broadway, New York.
Pettebone-Cataract Paper Co., Niagara Falls, N. Y.
Remington Paper & Power Co., Watertown, N. Y.
Rhinelander Paper Co., Rhinelander, Wis.
Richmond Paper Mfg. Co., Richmond, Va.
St. Croix Paper Co., Boston, Mass.
St. George Pulp and Paper Co., Norwalk, Conn.
St. Regis Paper Co., Watertown, N. Y.
Schroon River Pulp and Paper Co., Warrensburg, N. Y.
Standard Paper Co., Kalamazoo, Mich.
Taggarts Paper Co., Watertown, N. Y.
Tidewater Paper Mills Co., 82 83d st., So. Brooklyn, N. Y.
Unity Paper Mills, Potsdam, N. Y.
Watab Pulp & Paper Co., Sartell, Minn.
West End Paper Co., Carthage, N. Y.
Wisconsin River Paper and Pulp Co., Neenah, Wis.

NEWS BOARD.
(See also Paper Stock Boards.)

American Straw Board Co., Akron, Ohio.
Ballston Fibre Products Co., Inc., Ballston Spa, N. Y.
Boyle Co., John F., Jersey City, N. J.
Bogota Paper & Pulp Co., Bogota N. J.
Carthage Sulphite Pulp & Paper Co., Carthage, N. Y. (Single and Double Manila Lined.)

Lombard's English Newcastle Pulp Stones

Classified List—United States

NEWS BOARD.
(CONTINUED.)

Chesapeake Paperboard Co., Baltimore, Md.
Chicago Coated Board Co., Chicago, Ill.
Chicago Folding Box Co., Chicago, Ill.
Continental Paper Co., Bogota, N. J.
Davis Paper Co., Contoocook, N. H.
Eddy Paper Co., Three Rivers, Mich.
Federal Paper Board Co., Bogota, N. J.
Fort Orange Paper Co., Castleton, N. Y.
Franklin Board & Paper Co., Franklin, Ohio.
Gardner Paper Co., The Colin, Middletown, Ohio.
Halltown Paper Board Co., Halltown, W. Va.
Hartje Paper Mfg. Co., Pittsburgh, Pa.
Haverhill Box Board Co., Haverhill, Mass.
Hutchinson Box Board & Paper Co., Hutchinson, Kan.
International Paper Co., New York.
Lancaster Board & Paper Co., Lancaster, Ohio.
Lawless Paper Co., Rochester, N. Y.
McEwan Bros., Whippany, N. J.
Mac-Sim-Bar Paper Co., Otsego, Mich.
Mid-West Box Co., Kokomo, Ind.
Miller Paper Co., Frank P., East Downingtown, Pa.
Mutual Box Board Co., Utica, N. Y.
Natick Box & Board Co., Natick, Mass. (Manila Lined and Solid.)
National Metal Edge Box Co., Phila., Pa.
Nelson, The B. F., Mfg. Co., Minneapolis, Minn.
Newark Boxboard Co., Newark, N. J.
Ohio Box Board Co., Cleveland, Ohio.
Philadelphia Paper Mfg. Co., Philadelphia, Pa.
Ravenswood Paper Mill Co., 545 Van Alst ave., Long Island City, N. Y. (Plain, Colored and Coated.)
Richardson Paper Co., Lockland, Ohio.
Schmidt & Ault Paper Co., York, Pa.
Strange Paper Co., John, Menasha, Wis.
Tait & Sons Paper Co., Bridgeport, Conn.
Thames River Specialties Co., The, Uncasville, Conn.
Tonawanda Board and Paper Co., Tonawanda, N. Y.
United Paperboard Co., New York.
Waldorf Box Board Co., St. Paul, Minn. (Also Manila Lined.)
Western Board & Paper Co., Kalamazoo, Mich.
Westport Paper Co., Westport, Conn.

NOVEL.

Dells Paper and Pulp Co., Eau Claire, Wis.
Flambeau Paper Co., Park Falls, Wis.
Gilbert, Frank, Paper Co., Waterford, N. Y.
Grandfather's Fall Co., Merrill, Wis.
International Paper Co., 30 Broad, New York.
Menasha Paper Co., Ladysmith, Wis.
Moorhouse, R. T., Paper Co., Bridesburg, Pa.
Tileston & Hollingsworth Co., Boston, Mass.

OAK GRAINED BOARDS.

American Straw Board Co., Akron, Ohio.
Chicago Coated Board Co., Chicago, Ill.
Haverhill Box Board Co., Haverhill, Mass.
Mac-Sim-Bar Paper Co., Otsego, Mich.
Mutual Box Board Co., Utica, N. Y.
National Metal Edge Box Co., Phila., Pa.
Tonawanda Board and Paper Co., Tonawanda, N. Y.

OFFSET PAPERS.

American Writing Paper Co., Holyoke, Mass.
Bryant Paper Co., Kalamazoo, Mich.
Chemical Paper Mfg. Co., Holyoke, Mass.
Dill & Collins Co., 140 N. 6th st., Philadelphia, Pa.

WET MACHINES — We make a specialty of GROUND WOOD PULP and SULPHITE FIBRE MACHINERY — **Carthage Machine Co.** CARTHAGE, N. Y.

OFFSET PAPERS.
(CONTINUED.)

Eureka Paper Co., Fulton, N. Y.
Hamilton, W. C., & Sons, Inc., Wm. Penn P. O., Pa.
International Paper Co., 30 Broad, New York.
King Paper Co., Kalamazoo, Mich.
Marathon Paper Mills Co., Wausau, Wis.
Mead Pulp & Paper Co., Dayton, Ohio.
Merrimac Paper Co., Lawrence, Mass.
Mountain Mill Paper Co., Lee, Mass.
Munising Paper Co., Munising, Mich.
Oglesby Paper Co., W. B., Middletown, Ohio.
Peerless Paper Co., Dayton, Ohio.
Rex Paper Co., Kalamazoo, Mich.
Robertson Paper Co., Bellows Falls, Vt.
Rogers Co., J. & J., Ausable Forks, N. Y.
Southworth Co., Mittineague, Mass.
Tileston & Hollingsworth Co., Boston, Mass.
Warren Mfg. Co., New York.

OILED BOARDS.

Perseverance Paper Mills, Produce Exchange Bldg, New York.
Rogers Paper Mfg. Co., South Manchester, Conn.

ONION SKIN.

Ancram Paper Mills, 150 W. 22d, New York.
Bryant Paper Co., Kalamazoo, Mich.
Chemical Paper Mfg. Co., Holyoke, Mass.
Dexter & Sons, Inc., C. H., Windsor Locks, Conn.
Esleeck Mfg. Co., Turner's Falls, Mass.
Hartford City Paper Co., Hartford City, Ind.
Lakeside Paper Co., Neenah, Wis.
Parsons Paper Co., Holyoke, Mass.
Southworth Co., Mittineague, Mass.
Strathmore Paper Co., Mittineague, Mass.

OYSTER PAIL BOARD.

American Straw Board Co., Akron, Ohio.
American Writing Paper Co., Holyoke, Mass.
Brownville Board Co., Brownville, N. Y.
Carthage Sulphite Pulp & Paper Co., Carthage, N. Y.
Haverhill Box Board Co., Haverhill, Mass.
Marathon Paper Mills Co., Wausau, Wis.
Oswego Falls Pulp & Paper Co., Fulton, N. Y.
Standard Paper Co., Kalamazoo, Mich.
United Paperboard Co., New York.

PACKING PAPER.

American Tar Products Co., Rockton, Ill.
Bicking, S. Austin, Paper Mfg. Co., East Downingtown, Pa.
Carlyle Paper Co., Carlyle, Ill.
Eureka Paper Co., Fulton, N. Y.
Kieffer Paper Co., Ewing, Ind.
Lawrence Paper Mfg. Co., Lawrence, Kans.
Monroe Paper Co., Monroe, Mich.
Schmidt & Ault Paper Co., York, Pa.

PAPER NAPKINS.

Ashland Paper Co., Ashland, Wis.
Hoberg Co., The John, Green Bay, Wis.
Mountain Paper Co., Wilkes-Barre, Pa.
Northern Paper Mills, Green Bay, Wis.
Perseverance Paper Mills, Produce Exchange Bldg., New York.
Wardway Paper Mills, Fort Madison, Ia.

PAPER STOCK BOARDS.
(See also News Boards.)

Albia Box and Paper Co., Troy, N. Y.
Alton Box Board & Paper Co., Alton, Ill.

294   Classified List—United States

PAPER STOCK BOARDS.
(CONTINUED.)

American Straw Board Co., Akron, Ohio.
Auglaize Box Board Co., St. Mary's, Ohio.
Boyle Company, John F., Jersey City, N. J.
Chemical Paper Mfg. Co., Holyoke, Mass.
Chicago Coated Board Co., 545 North Water, Chicago.
Continental Paper Co., Bogota, N. J.
Eastern Straw Board Co., Manchester, Conn.
Franklin Board & Paper Co., Franklin, Ohio.
Gardner-Harvey Paper Co., Middletown, Ohio.
Gardner Paper Co., The Colin, Middletown, Ohio.
Hartje Paper Mfg. Co., Pittsburgh, Pa.
Haverhill Box Board Co., Haverhill, Mass.
Hummel & Downing Co., Milwaukee, Wis.
Hutchinson Box Board & Paper Co., Hutchinson, Kan.
Lawless Paper Co., Rochester, N. Y.
Leo Co., James, Jersey City, N. J.
Mid-West Box Co., Kokomo, Ind.
Miller Paper Co., Frank P., East Downingtown, Pa.
Mutual Box Board Co., Utica, N. Y.
National Metal Edge Box Co., Phila. Pa.
Ohio Box Board Co., Cleveland, Ohio.
Philadelphia Paper Mfg. Co., Philadelphia, Pa.
Richardson Paper Co., Lockland, Ohio.
Robertson Co., C. M., Montville, Conn.
Schmidt & Ault Paper Co., York, Pa.
Shryock Bros., Philadelphia, Pa.
Strange Paper Co., John, Menasha, Wis.
Tait & Sons Paper Co., The, Bridgeport, Conn.
United Paperboard Co., New York.
Waldorf Box Board Co., St. Paul, Minn.

PAPETERIE.

American Writing Paper Co., Holyoke, Mass.
Berkshire Hills Paper Co., Adams, Mass.
Chemical Paper Mfg. Co., Holyoke, Mass.
Collins Mfg. Co., North Wilbraham, Mass.
Columbian Paper Co., Buena Vista, Va.
Crocker-McElwain Co., Holyoke, Mass.
Hollingsworth & Vose Co., Boston, Mass.
Millers Falls Paper Co., Millers Falls, Mass.
Mountain Mill Paper Co., Lee, Mass.
Southworth Co., Mittineague, Mass.
Strathmore Paper Co., Mittineague, Mass.

PAPIER-MACHE BOARD.

American Straw Board Co., Akron, Ohio.
Kieffer Paper Co., Ewing, Ind.

PARCHMENT.
(Also see Table of Contents for list of Manufacturers of Vegetable Parchment.)

Bardeen Paper Co., Otsego, Mich.
Berkshire Hills Paper Co., Adams, Mass.
Brown Paper Co., L. L., Adams, Mass.
Crane & Co., Dalton, Mass.
Diamond Mills Paper Co., 44 Murray st., New York.
Diamond State Fibre Co., Bridgeport, Pa.
Glen Mills Paper Co., 1005 Stephen Girard Building, Philadelphia, Pa. (Vegetable.)
Hartford City Paper Co., Hartford City, Ind. (Grease-proof.)
International Paper Co., 30 Broad, New York.
Kalamazoo Vegetable Parchment Co., Kalamazoo, Mich. (Vegetable only.)
Mann Co., Wm., Lambertville, N. J.
McDowell Paper Mills, Manayunk, Pa.
Megargee Paper Mills, Modena, Pa.
Moore & Thompson Paper Co., Inc., Bellows Falls, Vt.
New York and Pennsylvania Co., 200 Fifth ave., New York.
Parsons Paper Co., Holyoke, Mass.

Classified List—United States

PARCHMENT.
(CONTINUED.)

Philadelphia Wax Paper Co., Swarthmore, Pa.
Racquette River Paper Co., Potsdam, N. Y.
Rhinelander Paper Co., Rhinelander, Wis.
Robertson Paper Co., Bellows Falls, Vt. (Writing and Greaseproof.)
Southworth Co., Mittineague, Mass.
Union Waxed and Parchment Paper Co., 277 Broadway, New York.
Warren Manufacturing Co., Woolworth Bldg., New York. (Greaseproof.)
Warren Parchment Co., Dexter, N. Y.
Whiting, Geo. A., Menasha, Wis. (Manila.)

PARCHMENTIZING.
Megargee Paper Co., Philadelphia, Pa.

PARAFFIN.
Robertson Paper Co., Bellows Falls, Vt.

PATENT COATED BOARDS.

American Straw Board Co., Akron, Ohio.
American Writing Paper Co., Holyoke, Mass.
Beveridge Paper Co., Indianapolis, Ind. (White and Colors.)
Chemical Paper Mfg. Co., Holyoke, Mass.
Chicago Coated Board Co., 547 N. Water, Chicago.
Eddy Paper Co., Three Rivers, Mich.
Elkhart Bristol Board & Paper Co., Elkhart, Ind.
Fort Orange Paper Co., Castleton, N. Y.
Gardner Paper Co., The Colin, Middletown, Ohio.
International Paper Co., 30 Broad, New York.
MacAndrews & Forbes, Camden, N. J.
Michigan Carton Co., Battle Creek, Mich.
Miller Paper Co., Frank P., East Downingtown, Pa.
Monroe Bridge Paper Co., Monroe Bridge, Mass.
Ohio Box Board Co., Cleveland, Ohio.
Paraffine Cos., San Francisco, Cal.
Piermont Paper Co., Piermont, N. Y.
Richardson Paper Co., Lockland, Ohio. (Colored.)
Thames River Specialties Co., The, Uncasville, Conn.
Tonawanda Board & Paper Co., Tonawanda, N. Y.
United Paperboard Co., New York.
Waldorf Box Board Co., St. Paul, Minn.
Western Board & Paper Co., Kalamazoo, Mich.

PATTERN.

American Writing Paper Co., Holyoke, Mass.
Case Mfg. Co., Unionville, Conn.
Coy Paper Co., West Claremont, N. H.
Dexter & Sons, Inc., C. H., Windsor Locks, Conn.
Diamond Mills Paper Co., 44 Murray, New York.
Dixie Paper Mills, Inc., Richmond, Va.
Garrett Co., Edwin T., Lansdowne, Pa. (Tissue.)
Gilbert, Frank, Paper Co., Waterford, N. Y.
Hollingsworth & Vose Co., Boston, Mass.
Ingalls & Co., Castleton, N. Y.
Jarvis Paper Mills, Claremont, N. H.
Lewis, J. P., Co., Inc., Beaver Falls, N. Y.
Lincoln, L., & Co., North Dighton, Mass. (Tack and Tailors'.)
Marathon Paper Mills Co., Wausau, Wis.
Moorhouse, R. T., Paper Co., Bridesburg, Pa.
Muir Board Co., Inc., Lyndell, Pa.
Schmidt & Ault Paper Co., York, Pa.
Smith Paper Co., Lee, Mass.
Strange Paper Co., John, Menasha, Wis.
Walsh Paper Co., Cuyahoga Falls, Ohio.
Warren Mfg. Co., New York.
Wasuc Mills Company, South Glastonbury, Conn.

Lombard's English Newcastle Pulp Stones

Classified List—United States

PAPER STOCK BOARDS.
(CONTINUED.)

American Straw Board Co., Akron, Ohio.
Auglaize Box Board Co., St. Mary's, Ohio.
Boyle Company, John F., Jersey City, N. J.
Chemical Paper Mfg. Co., Holyoke, Mass.
Chicago Coated Board Co., 545 North Water, Chicago.
Continental Paper Co., Bogota, N. J.
Eastern Straw Board Co., Manchester, Conn.
Franklin Board & Paper Co., Franklin, Ohio.
Gardner-Harvey Paper Co., Middletown, Ohio.
Gardner Paper Co., The Colin, Middletown, Ohio.
Hartje Paper Mfg. Co., Pittsburgh, Pa.
Haverhill Box Board Co., Haverhill, Mass.
Hummel & Downing Co., Milwaukee, Wis.
Hutchinson Box Board & Paper Co., Hutchinson, Kan.
Lawless Paper Co., Rochester, N. Y.
Leo Co., James, Jersey City, N. J.
Mid-West Box Co., Kokomo, Ind.
Miller Paper Co., Frank P., East Downingtown, Pa.
Mutual Box Board Co., Utica, N. Y.
National Metal Edge Box Co., Phila., Pa.
Ohio Box Board Co., Cleveland, Ohio.
Philadelphia Paper Mfg. Co., Philadelphia, Pa.
Richardson Paper Co., Lockland, Ohio.
Robertson Co., C. M., Montville, Conn.
Schmidt & Ault Paper Co., York, Pa.
Shryock Bros., Philadelphia, Pa.
Strange Paper Co., John, Menasha, Wis.
Tait & Sons Paper Co., The, Bridgeport, Conn.
United Paperboard Co., New York.
Waldorf Box Board Co., St. Paul, Minn.

PAPETERIE.

American Writing Paper Co., Holyoke, Mass.
Berkshire Hills Paper Co., Adams, Mass.
Chemical Paper Mfg. Co., Holyoke, Mass.
Collins Mfg. Co., North Wilbraham, Mass.
Columbian Paper Co., Buena Vista, Va.
Crocker-McElwain Co., Holyoke, Mass.
Hollingsworth & Vose Co., Boston, Mass.
Millers Falls Paper Co., Millers Falls, Mass.
Mountain Mill Paper Co., Lee, Mass.
Southworth Co., Mittineague, Mass.
Strathmore Paper Co., Mittineague, Mass.

PAPIER-MACHE BOARD.

American Straw Board Co., Akron, Ohio.
Kieffer Paper Co., Ewing, Ind.

PARCHMENT.
(Also see Table of Contents for list of Manufacturers of Vegetable Parchment.)

Bardeen Paper Co., Otsego, Mich.
Berkshire Hills Paper Co., Adams, Mass.
Brown Paper Co., L. L., Adams, Mass.
Crane & Co., Dalton, Mass.
Diamond Mills Paper Co., 44 Murray st., New York.
Diamond State Fibre Co., Bridgeport, Pa.
Glen Mills Paper Co., 1005 Stephen Girard Building, Philadelphia, Pa. (Vegetable.)
Hartford City Paper Co., Hartford City, Ind. (Grease-proof.)
International Paper Co., 30 Broad, New York.
Kalamazoo Vegetable Parchment Co., Kalamazoo, Mich. (Vegetable only.)
Mann Co., Wm., Lambertville, N. J.
McDowell Paper Mills, Manayunk, Pa.
Megargee Paper Mills, Modena, Pa.
Moore & Thompson Paper Co., Inc., Bellows Falls, Vt.
New York and Pennsylvania Co., 200 Fifth ave., New York.
Parsons Paper Co., Holyoke, Mass.

HARDY S. FERGUSON
CONSULTING ENGINEER
200 FIFTH AVENUE
NEW YORK CITY
PAPER, PULP AND FIBRE MILLS, WATER POWER DEVELOPMENT, DAMS, STORAGE RESERVOIRS AND OTHER HYDRAULIC STRUCTURES

PRESS ROLLS Maple and Gum White Wood Felt Rolls J. W. HEWITT MACHINE CO. Neenah, Wis.

ARE SUPERIOR TO ALL OTHERS. ALL SIZES IN STOCK.
LOMBARD & CO., Importers & Manufacturers, 236 & 238 A Street, Boston.

PARCHMENT.
(CONTINUED.)

Philadelphia Wax Paper Co., Swarthmore, Pa.
Racquette River Paper Co., Potsdam, N. Y.
Rhinelander Paper Co., Rhinelander, Wis.
Robertson Paper Co., Bellows Falls, Vt. (Writing and Greaseproof.)
Southworth Co., Mittineague, Mass.
Union Waxed and Parchment Paper Co., 277 Broadway, New York.
Warren Manufacturing Co., Woolworth Bldg., New York. (Greaseproof.)
Warren Parchment Co., Dexter, N. Y.
Whiting, Geo. A., Menasha, Wis. (Manila.)

PARCHMENTIZING.
Megargee Paper Co., Philadelphia, Pa.

PARAFFIN.
Robertson Paper Co., Bellows Falls, Vt.

PATENT COATED BOARDS.

American Straw Board Co., Akron, Ohio.
American Writing Paper Co., Holyoke, Mass.
Beveridge Paper Co., Indianapolis, Ind. (White and Colors.)
Chemical Paper Mfg. Co., Holyoke, Mass.
Chicago Coated Board Co., 547 N. Water, Chicago.
Eddy Paper Co., Three Rivers, Mich.
Elkhart Bristol Board & Paper Co., Elkhart, Ind.
Fort Orange Paper Co., Castleton, N. Y.
Gardner Paper Co., The Colin, Middletown, Ohio.
International Paper Co., 30 Broad, New York.
MacAndrews & Forbes, Camden, N. J.
Michigan Carton Co., Battle Creek, Mich.
Miller Paper Co., Frank P., East Downingtown, Pa.
Monroe Bridge Paper Co., Monroe Bridge, Mass.
Ohio Box Board Co., Cleveland, Ohio.
Paraffine Cos., San Francisco, Cal.
Piermont Paper Co., Piermont, N. Y.
Richardson Paper Co., Lockland, Ohio. (Colored.)
Thames River Specialties Co., The, Uncasville, Conn.
Tonawanda Board & Paper Co., Tonawanda, N. Y.
United Paperboard Co., New York.
Waldorf Box Board Co., St. Paul, Minn.
Western Board & Paper Co., Kalamazoo, Mich.

PATTERN.

American Writing Paper Co., Holyoke, Mass.
Case Mfg. Co., Unionville, Conn.
Coy Paper Co., West Claremont, N. H.
Dexter & Sons, Inc., C. H., Windsor Locks, Conn.
Diamond Mills Paper Co., 44 Murray, New York.
Dixie Paper Mills, Inc., Richmond, Va.
Garrett Co., Edwin T., Lansdowne, Pa. (Tissue.)
Gilbert, Frank, Paper Co., Waterford, N. Y.
Hollingsworth & Vose Co., Boston, Mass.
Ingalls & Co., Castleton, N. Y.
Jarvis Paper Mills, Claremont, N. H.
Lewis, J. P., Co., Inc., Beaver Falls, N. Y.
Lincoln, L., & Co., North Dighton, Mass. (Tack and Tailors'.)
Marathon Paper Mills Co., Wausau, Wis.
Moorhouse, R. T., Paper Co., Bridesburg, Pa.
Muir Board Co., Inc., Lyndell, Pa.
Schmidt & Ault Paper Co., York, Pa.
Smith Paper Co., Lee, Mass.
Strange Paper Co., John, Menasha, Wis.
Walsh Paper Co., Cuyahoga Falls, Ohio.
Warren Mfg. Co., New York.
Wasuc Mills Company, South Glastonbury, Conn.

DRY ROSIN SIZE
Brittle, easy soluble. Cheapest size out; cheaper than mill made size. Ask us about it. Also all other grades.
ARABOL MF'G CO.
100 William St., New York

ENGINEERING FOR
JOSEPH H. WALLACE & CO
INDUSTRIAL ENGINEERS
Temple Court Building, NEW YORK

PATTERN BOARD.

Ingalls & Co., Castleton, N. Y.
Muir, Jas. A., Morristown, N. J.
United Paperboard Co., New York.
Wasuc Mills Co., South Glastonbury, Conn.

PHOTOGRAPHIC.

American Photographic Paper Co., Boston, Mass. (Paper made at mills of Hurlbut Paper Mfg. Co., Division of American Writing Paper Co., South Lee, Mass.)
American Writing Paper Co., Holyoke, Mass.
Lewis, J. P., Co., Inc., Beaver Falls, N. Y. (Black.)
Strathmore Paper Co., Mittineague, Mass.
United Paperboard Co., New York.

PHOTOGRAVURE.

American Writing Paper Co., Holyoke, Mass.
International Paper Co., 30 Broad, New York.
Mountain Mill Paper Co., Lee, Mass.
Strathmore Paper Co., Mittineague, Mass.

PHOTO MOUNTS.

Dexter & Sons, Inc., C. H., Windsor Locks, Conn.
Hurlock Bros. Co., Philadelphia, Pa.
Peninsular Paper Co., Ypsilanti, Mich.
Strathmore Paper Co., Mittineague, Mass. (Paper and Boards.)
Tonawanda Board & Paper Co., Tonawanda, N. Y.
United Paperboard Co., New York.

PICTURE BOARD.

American Straw Board Co., Akron, Ohio.
Hurlock Bros. Co., Philadelphia, Pa.
Tonawanda Board & Paper Co., Tonawanda, N. Y.
United Paperboard Co., New York.

PLATE.

American Writing Paper Co., Holyoke, Mass.
Lee Paper Co., Vicksburg, Mich.
Reading Paper Mills, 808 Chestnut, Philadelphia, Pa.
Southworth Co., Mittineague, Mass.
Taylor-Atkins Paper Co., Burnside, Conn.
Tileston & Hollingsworth Co., Boston, Mass.
Wheelwright Paper Co., Geo. W., 95 Milk st., Boston, Mass. (Dull Finish Book.)

PLATER BOARD.

Rogers Paper Mfg. Co., So. Manchester, Conn.

POSTAL CARDS.

American Writing Paper Co., Holyoke, Mass.
Beveridge Paper Co., Indianapolis, Ind.
Falulah Paper Co., Fitchburg, Mass.
Marathon Paper Mills Co., Wausau, Wis.
United Paperboard Co., New York.
Wabash Coating Mills, Wabash, Ind.

POSTER.

Bardeen Paper Co., Otsego, Mich.
Brownville Paper Co., Brownville, N. Y.
Cleveland Paper Mfg. Co., Cleveland, Ohio.
Everett Pulp & Paper Co., Everett, Wash.
Flambeau Paper Co., Park Falls, Wis.
French Paper Co., Niles, Mich.
Gilbert, Frank, Paper Co., Waterford, N. Y.
International Paper Co., 30 Broad St., New York.
King Paper Co., Kalamazoo, Mich.
Malone Paper Co., Malone, N. Y. (Colored.)
Mason-Perkins Paper Co., Bristol, N. H.
Menasha Paper Co., Ladysmith, Wis.

Is Your Paper Sold Abroad

A foreign demand for the products of your mills not only establishes their reputation 'round the world, but, as the Federal Trade Commission has shown, tends to stabilize business and create permanent prosperity.

The Parsons Trading Company has specialized in the exportation of paper for many years, and through its highly organized system of branch houses and selling connections has built up a demand in all parts of the world for the American-made papers which it handles. Are yours among them? Correspondence solicited.

Also Exporters and Importers of Pulp

PARSONS TRADING COMPANY

LONDON	17 BATTERY PLACE	SYDNEY
BUENOS AIRES		MELBOURNE
MEXICO	NEW YORK	WELLINGTON
HABANA		CAPE TOWN
BOMBAY		STOCKHOLM

Travelers and Selling Representatives Throughout Europe, Central and South America, West Indies, India, Australasia, South Africa, The Orient, Etc.

The Black-Clawson Co.
HAMILTON, OHIO

BUILDERS OF A COMPLETE LINE OF

PAPER AND PULP MILL MACHINERY

From New Patterns, Embracing the Best and Latest Improvements

Machine for Saturating and Waxing Papers

OUR SPECIALTY

Is HIGH-GRADE and Efficient Fourdrinier and Cylinder Paper Making Machines

OF EVERY TYPE

IT IS WELL WORTH YOUR WHILE TO WRITE US FOR PARTICULARS

HAMMERMILL BOND
HAMMERMILL LEDGER
HAMMERMILL COVER

HAMMERMILL SAFETY

HAMMERMILL PAPER CO.
ERIE, PENNSYLVANIA

Eastern Office   291 BROADWAY   NEW YORK CITY

Lombard's English Newcastle Pulp Stones

Classified List—United States

RAILROAD COPYING.
Garrett, E. T., Co., Lansdowne, Pa.
Mann, Wm., Co., Lambertville, N. J.
Rainbow Mills, The, Rainbow, Conn.
Smith Paper Co., Lee, Mass.

RAILROAD MANIFOLDING.
Everett Pulp & Paper Co., Everett, Wash.
Mann Co., Wm., Lambertville, N. J.
Robertson Paper Co., Bellows Falls, Vt.

RAILROAD MANILA AND WRITING.
American Writing Paper Co., Holyoke, Mass.
Bardeen Paper Co., Otsego, Mich.
Brownville Paper Co., Brownville, N. Y.
Consolidated Water Power & Paper Co., Grand Rapids, Wis.
Everett Pulp and Paper Co., Everett, Wash.
Flambeau Paper Co., Park Falls, Wis.
Gilbert, Frank, Paper Co., Waterford, N. Y.
Hollingsworth & Whitney Co., Boston, Mass. (White and Colored.)
International Paper Co., 30 Broad, New York.
Kimberly-Clark Co., Neenah, Wis.
King Paper Co., Kalamazoo, Mich.
Lakeside Paper Co., Neenah, Wis.
Menasha Paper Co., Ladysmith, Wis.
Moore & Thompson Paper Co., Inc., Bellows Falls, Vt.
New York and Pennsylvania Co., 200 Fifth ave., New York.
Patten Paper Co., Ltd., Appleton, Wis.
Robertson Paper Co., Bellows Falls, Vt.
Whiting Paper Co., Geo. A., Menasha, Wis.

RECORD.
American Writing Paper Co., Holyoke, Mass.
Brown Paper Co., L. L., Adams, Mass.
Parsons Paper Co., Holyoke, Mass. (Writing.)
Southworth Co., Mittineague, Mass.
Tileston & Hollingsworth Co., Boston, Mass.
Weston Co., Byron, Dalton, Mass.

REFINED WOOD.
The Keyes Products Co., 120 Broadway, New York.

RIBBON.
American Writing Paper Co., Holyoke, Mass.
International Paper Co., 30 Broad, New York.

ROCKET.
Eureka Paper Co., Fulton, N. Y.

ROOFING.
Baltimore Roofing & Asbestos Mfg. Co., Asbestos, Md.
Barrett, The, Co., New York.
Bird & Son, Inc., East Walpole, Mass.
Carey Mfg. Co., The Philip, Cincinnati, Ohio. (Felts.)
Certain-Teed Products Corp., St. Louis, Mo.
Cleveland-Akron Bag Co., Boston, Ohio.
Field & White Co., 116 Nassau, New York.
Fleming & Sons, John G., Dallas, Tex.
Ford Mfg. Co., Chicago, Ill.
Foster Box Board Co., Utica, N. Y.
Hollingsworth & Vose Co., Boston, Mass.
Kingston's Son, William, Little Falls, N. Y.
Lang Paper Co., John, Philadelphia, Pa.
Lockport Paper Co., Lockport, N. Y.
Mac-Sim-Bar Paper Co., Otsego, Mich.
Munroe Falls Paper Co., Massillon, Ohio.
National Asbestos Mfg. Co., Jersey City, N. J.
Nelson, The B. F., Mfg. Co., Minneapolis, Minn.

PRESS ROLLS — Maple and Gum White Wood Felt Rolls — **J. W. HEWITT MACHINE CO.** Neenah, Wis.

Classified List—United States

ROOFING.
(CONTINUED.)

Ohio Paper Co., Miamisburg, Ohio.
Patent Vulcanite Roofing Co., Anderson, Ind. (Felt.)
Richardson Paper Co., Lockland, Ohio.
Rudolph, F. M., & Son, Downingtown, Pa.
Standard Paint Co., Woolworth Bldg., New York.
Wall, J. F., & Son, Walpole, Mass.
Watson Co., H. F., Erie, Pa.

ROPE.

Adams Bag Co., 609 Caxton Bldg., Cleveland, Ohio.
American Writing Paper Co., Holyoke, Mass.
Bemis Bro. Bag Co., Peoria, Ill.
Case Mfg. Co., Unionville, Conn.
Case & Marshall, Inc., Hartford, Conn.
Cleveland-Akron Bag Co., Cleveland, Ohio.
Columbia Paper Mills Co., Oakmont, Pa.
Detroit Sulphite Pulp & Paper Co., Detroit, Mich.
Eureka Paper Co., Fulton, N. Y.
George & Sherrard Paper Co., Wellsburg, W. Va.
Harvey Paper Co., Wellsburg, W. Va.
Hollingsworth & Vose Co., Boston, Mass.
Jaite Co., Boston, Ohio.
Lewis, J. P., Co., Inc., Beaver Falls, N. Y.
Manning Paper Co., John A., Troy, N. Y.
Phillips Co., The Thomas, Akron, Ohio.
Reading Paper Mills, 308 Chestnut, Philadelphia, Pa.
Sorg Paper Co., Paul A., Middletown, Ohio. (Jute and Manila.)
Taggart Bros. Co., Watertown, N. Y.
Tarentum Paper Mills, Pittsburg, Pa.
Union Mills Paper Mfg. Co., New Hope, Pa. (No. 1 Manila.)
Wardlow-Thomas Paper Co., Middletown, Ohio.
Warren Mfg. Co., New York.
West Jersey Paper Mfg. Co., Camden, N. J.

SACK, FLOUR, CEMENT, CHARCOAL, SUGAR AND NAIL BAG, ETC.

Adams Bag Co., 609 Caxton Bldg., Cleveland, Ohio.
American Writing Paper Co., Holyoke, Mass.
Baeder, Adamson & Co., Philadelphia.
Bemis Bro. Bag Co., Peoria, Ill.
Cleveland-Akron Bag Co., Cleveland, Ohio.
Columbia Paper Mills Co., Oakmont, Pa.
Cushnoc Paper Co., Augusta, Me.
Eureka Paper Co., Fulton, N. Y.
George Co., S. Wellsburg, W. Va.
George & Sherrard Paper Co., Wellsburg, W. Va.
Harvey Paper Co., Wellsburg, W. Va.
Hollingsworth & Vose Co., Boston, Mass.
Jaite Co., Boston, Ohio.
Manning Paper Co., John A., Troy, N. Y.
Phillips Co., The Thomas, Akron, Ohio.
Sorg Paper Co., Paul A., Middletown, Ohio.
Taggart Bros. Co., Watertown, N. Y.
Tarentum Paper Mill, Pittsburg, Pa.
Union Bag & Paper Corp., New York.
Union Mills Paper Mfg. Co., New Hope, Pa.
Victoria Paper Mills Co., Fulton, N. Y.

SAFETY PAPER.

American Writing Paper Co., Holyoke, Mass.
Hammermill Paper Co., Erie, Pa.
La Monte, Geo., & Son, 61 Broadway, New York.

SALES BOOK.

Gilbert, Frank, Paper Co., Waterford, N. Y.

Classified List—United States

SAND.

American Writing Paper Co., Holyoke, Mass.
Baeder, Adamson & Co., Philadelphia.
Eureka Paper Co., Fulton, N. Y.
Hollingsworth & Vose Co., Boston, Mass.
Manning Paper Co., John A., Troy, N. Y.
Munroe Felt & Paper Co., Boston, Mass.
Phillips Co., The Thos., Akron, O.
Reading Paper Mills, 308 Chestnut, Philadelphia.
Sorg Paper Co., Paul A., Middletown, Ohio.

SATURATING FELT.
(See Felt.)

SCREENING.

Carney Paper Co., Maumee, Ohio.
Dixie Paper Mills, Inc., Richmond, Va.
Fox Paper Co., Lockland, Ohio. (Sulphite.)
Hoboken Paper Mills Co., Hoboken, N. J.
International Paper Co., 30 Broad, New York.
Lawless Paper Co., Rochester, N. Y.
Lawless Paper Mills, East Rochester, N. Y.
Marcellus Paper Co., Marcellus Falls, N. Y.
Onondaga Paper Co., Marcellus Falls, N. Y.
Parsons Pulp & Paper Co., Franklin Bank Bldg., Philadelphia, Pa.
Schmidt & Ault Paper Co., York, Pa.
Union Bag & Paper Corp., New York.
United Paperboard Co., New York.

SHEATHING.

Acme Paper & Paper Box Co. (Trust), East Pepperell, Mass.
American Tar Products Co., Rockton, Ill.
Andrews, John T., & Co., Penn Yan, N. Y.
Barrett, The, Co., New York.
Bird & Son, Inc., East Walpole, Mass.
Brown Co., Portland, Me.
Certain-teed Products Corp., St. Louis, Mo.
Crown Willamette Paper Co., Alaska Coml. Bldg., San Francisco, Cal.
Fairfield Paper Co., The, Baltimore, Md.
Fleming, John G., & Son, Dallas, Tex.
Fox Paper Co., Lockland, Ohio.
Hartje Paper Mfg. Co., Pittsburg, Pa.
Harvey Paper Co., Wellsburg, W. Va.
Keasbey & Mattison Co., Ambler, Pa.
Lewis Mfg. Co., F. J., Moline, Ill.
Lincoln, L., & Co., No. Dighton, Mass.
Lockport Paper Co., Lockport, N. Y.
Los Angeles Paper Mfg. Co., Los Angeles, Cal. (Red and Gray.)
Monroe Paper Co., Monroe, Mich. (Red Rosin.)
Mullen Bros. Paper Co., St. Joseph, Mich.
Newton Paper Co., Holyoke, Mass.
Paraffine Companies, Inc., San Francisco, Cal.
Pleasant Mills Paper Co., Pleasant Mills, N. J.
Rudolph, F. M., & Son, Downingtown, Pa.
Schmidt & Ault Paper Co., York, Pa. (Crepe and Crinkled.)
Simplex Paper Co., Palmyra, Mich.
Standard Paint Co., Woolworth Bldg., New York.
Wall, J. F., & Son, Walpole, Mass.
Wardway Paper Mills, Ft. Madison, Ia.
Watson Co., H. F., Erie, Pa.
York Paper Mfg. Co., York, Pa.

SHIELD BOARD.

American Straw Board Co., Akron, Ohio.
Rogers Paper Mfg. Co., South Manchester, Conn.

Classified List—United States

SHOE BOARDS.

American Straw Board Co., Akron, Ohio.
Ingalls & Co., Castleton, N. Y.
Metalite Co., Amesbury, Mass.
Norton, C. H., North Westchester, Conn.
West Virginia Pulp Products Co., Inc., 200 Fifth Ave., New York; 732 Sherman, Chicago.

SIGN.

Beveridge Paper Co., Indianapolis, Ind.
Phillips Co., The Thos. Akron, Ohio.

SILK WRAPPERS.

Beaver Brook Paper Mills, Danbury, Conn.
Chemical Paper Mfg. Co., Holyoke, Mass.
Eddy Paper Co., Three Rivers, Mich.
Fort Orange Paper Co., Castleton, N. Y.
International Paper Co., New York.
Lawless Paper Co., Rochester, N. Y.
MacAndrews & Forbes Co., Camden, N. J.
Mac-Sim-Bar Paper Co., Otsego, Mich.
McDowell Paper Mills, Manayunk, Pa.
Western Board & Paper Co., Kalamazoo, Mich.

SILVER TISSUE, see Grass Bleached.

SPECIALTIES.

Acme Paper Co., Reading, Pa.
American Fibre Seat Corp., Long Island City, N. Y.
American Writing Paper Co., Holyoke, Mass.
Analomink Paper Co., North Water Gap, Pa. (Colored.)
Ancram Paper Mills, 150 W. 22d, New York. (Tissues.)
Beach Paper Co., The S. Y., Seymour, Conn.
Beaver Brook Paper Mills, Danbury, Conn.
Beveridge Paper Co., Indianapolis, Ind.
Bird & Son, Inc., East Walpole, Mass.
Blandy Paper Co., Schuylerville, N. Y.
Brown Paper Co., Ft. Madison, Iowa.
Brownville Paper Co., Brownville, N. Y.
Bryant Paper Co., Kalamazoo, Mich.
Burmus Paper Co., Inc., West Dudley, Mass.
Carney Paper Co., Maumee, Ohio.
Case Bros., Inc., South Manchester, Conn.
Case Board Co., Andover, Conn.
Case Co., A. Willard, Manchester, Conn.
Case & Marshall, Inc., Hartford, Conn.
Chapin & Gould Paper Co., Springfield, Mass.
Chemical Paper Mfg. Co., Holyoke, Mass.
Cherry River Paper Co., Richmond, W. Va.
Collins Mfg. Co., North Wilbraham, Mass.
Combined Locks Paper Co., Combined Locks, Wis.
Consolidated Water Power & Paper Co., Grand Rapids, Wis.
Continental Paper Bag Co., 17 Battery Pl., N. Y. (Light Weight.)
Contoocook Valley Paper Co., West Henniker, N. H.
Curtis & Bro., Inc., Newark, Del.
Detroit Sulphite Pulp and Paper Co., Detroit, Mich.
Dexter & Sons, C. H., Windsor Locks, Conn.
Dexter Sulphite Pulp & Paper Co., Dexter, N. Y.
District of Columbia Paper Mfg. Co., Washington, D. C.
Dixie Paper Mills, Inc., Richmond, Va.
East Hartford Paper Mfg. Co., Burnside, Conn.
Eastern Mfg. Co., 200 Fifth ave., New York.
Eddy Paper Co., Three Rivers, Mich.
Emerson Paper Co., Wendell, N. H.
Erving Mills, Erving, Mass. (Tissues.)
Eureka Paper Co., Fulton, N. Y.
Federal Paper Board Co., Bogota, N. J.

Classified List—United States

SPECIALTIES.
(CONTINUED.)

Flambeau Paper Co., Park Falls, Wis.
Fort Orange Paper Co., Castleton, N. Y. (Boards.)
Fox Paper Co., Lockland, Ohio.
Garven, Thomas F., Co., Burnside, Conn.
Gilbert Paper Co., Frank, Waterford, N. Y. (Colored.)
Glen Mills Paper Co., 1005 Stephen Girard Bldg., Philadelphia, Pa.
Green Bay Paper & Fibre Co., Green Bay, Wis.
Hammermill Paper Co., Erie, Pa.
Harmon Paper Co., Brownville, N. Y. (Colored.)
Harvey Paper Co., Wellsburg, W. Va.
Hoboken Mills Paper Co., Hoboken, N. J.
Hollingsworth & Vose Co., Boston, Mass.
International Paper Co., New York.
Jaite Co., The, Boston, Ohio.
Jessup & Moore, Philadelphia.
Keyes Products Co., The, 120 B'way, New York.
Kieffer Paper Co., Ewing, Ind.
Kimberly-Clark Co., Neenah, Wis.
Knowlton Bros., Watertown, N. Y.
La Monte & Son, Geo., 61 Broadway, New York.
La Salle Paper Co., South Bend, Ind.
Lawless Bros. Paper Mills, East Rochester, N. Y.
Lawless Paper Co., Rochester, N. Y.
Lewis, J. P., Co., Inc., Beaver Falls, N. Y.
Mac-Sim-Bar Paper Co., Otsego, Mich.
McDowell Paper Mills, Manayunk, Pa. (Colored.)
Marathon Paper Mills Co., Wausau, Wis.
Marshall Bros., Inc., Yorklyn, Del. (Rag.)
Marshall & Mitchell, Woodale, Del. (Sulphite.)
Menasha Paper Co., Ladysmith, Wis.
Menasha Printing & Carton Co., Menasha, Wis.
Merwin Paper Co., Rainbow, Conn.
Michigan Paper Co., Plainville, Mich.
Miller's Falls Paper Co., Miller's Falls, Mass.
Missisquoi Pulp & Paper Co., Sheldon Springs, Vt.
Mohawk Valley Paper Co., Inc., Little Falls, N. Y.
Monroe Bridge Paper Co., Monroe Bridge, Mass. (High Grade.)
Moore Paper Mill Corp., Penn Yan, N. Y.
Moorhouse, R. T., Paper Co., Bridesburg, Pa. (Colored.)
Mountain Mill Paper Co., Lee, Mass.
Mountain Paper Co., Wilkes-Barre, Pa.
Muir Board Co., Inc., Lyndell, Pa.
Mullen Bros. Paper Co., St. Joseph, Mich.
Munising Paper Co., Munising, Mich.
Munroe Felt & Paper Co., Lawrence, Mass.
Nashua River Paper Co., East Pepperell, Mass.
National Fibre & Insulation Co., Yorklyn, Del. (Rag.)
National Paper Co., Atlanta, Ga.
New Haven Pulp & Board Co., New Haven, Conn.
New York and Pennsylvania Co., 200 Fifth ave., New York.
Newton Falls Paper Co., Newton Falls, N. Y.
Newton Paper Co., Holyoke, Mass.
Niagara Paper Mills, Lockport, N. Y.
Northern Paper Mills, Green Bay, Wis. (Toilet.)
Onondaga Paper Co., Marcellus Falls, N. Y. (Colored.)
Orono Pulp & Paper Co., Bangor, Me.
Paraffine Companies, Inc., 40 First, San Francisco.
Peninsular Paper Co., Ypsilanti, Mich. (Pasted.)
Perseverance Paper Mills, Produce Exchange Bldg., New York.
Philadelphia Paper Mfg. Co., Philadelphia, Pa.
Richardson Paper Co., Lockland, Ohio.
Robertson, C. M., Co., Montville, Conn. (Colored.)
Robertson Paper Co., Bellows Falls, Vt.
Rogers Paper Mfg. Co., South Manchester, Conn.
Savage Mfg. Co., Skowhegan, Me.
Schmidt & Ault Paper Co., York, Pa.
Seneca Falls Paper Co., Seneca Falls, N. Y. (Light Weight.)
Smith Paper Co., Lee, Mass.
Southern Paper Co., Moss Point, Miss.

SPECIALTIES.
(CONTINUED.)

Southworth Co., Mittineague, Mass.
Stratford Paper Co., Jersey City, N. J. (Tissue.)
Springlet Mills, York, Pa.
Srere Bros. & Co., Franklin, Ohio. (Rag, Jute, Hemp.)
Srere Pulp & Paper Co., Franklin, Ohio. (Rag and Jute Pulp.)
Sterling Paper Co., Hamilton, Ohio.
Stevens Mills Paper Co., Auburn, Me.
Stevens & Thompson, Inc., North Hoosick, N. Y. (Colored.)
Strange Paper Co., John, Menasha, Wis.
Stratford Paper Co., Jersey City, N. J.
Strathmore Paper Co., Mittineague, Mass.
Taggarts Paper Co., Watertown, N. Y.
Thilmany Pulp & Paper Co., Kaukauna, Wis.
Tileston & Hollingsworth Co., Boston, Mass.
Tolland Leather Board Co., Hop River, Conn.
Underwood Paper Mills, Inc., Plattsburg, N. Y.
United Paperboard Co., New York.
Valley Paper Co., Holyoke, Mass.
Victoria Paper Co., Fulton, N. Y. (Tissue.)
Walloomsac Paper Co., Walloomsac, N. Y.
Walsh Paper Co., Cuyahoga Falls, Ohio. (Colored.)
Warren Mfg. Co., New York.
Warren, S. D., Co., Boston, Mass.
Wasuc Mills Co., South Glastonbury, Conn.
Wheat Paper Co., Elkhart, Ind.
Whiting Paper Co., Geo. A., Menasha, Wis.
West Virginia Pulp & Paper Co., 200 Fifth ave., New York, and 732 Sherman, Chicago.
Wolf River Paper & Fibre Co., Shawano, Wis.

STARCH.

Kieffer Paper Co., Ewing, Ind.
Walsh Paper Co., Cuyahoga Falls, Ohio.

STENCIL BOARD.

Rogers Paper Mfg. Co., South Manchester, Conn.

STEREOTYPE TISSUE.

Dexter & Sons, Inc., C. H., Windsor Locks, Conn.
Diamond Mills Paper Co., 44 Murray st., New York City.
Gandey, Estate of Wm. H., Lambertville, N. J.

STRAW BOARD.

Albany Paper Products Co., Inc., Albany, Ind.
Alton Box Board & Paper Co., Federal, Ill.
American Straw Board Co., Akron, Ohio.
Auglaize Box Board Co., St. Mary's, Ohio.
Beloit Box Board Co., Beloit, Wis.
Boyle Co., John F., Jersey City, N. J.
Brown Paper Co., Ft. Madison, Iowa.
Creamery Package Mfg. Co., Coffeyville, Kans.
Carthage Board & Paper Co., Carthage, Ind.
Carlyle Paper Co., Alton, Ill.
Cherry Co., J. G., Cedar Rapids, Iowa.
Childsdale Paper Mills, Childsdale, Mich.
Coshocton Straw Paper Co., Coshocton, Ohio.
Crescent Paper Co., Marseilles, Ill.
Decatur Strawboard Co., Marion, Ind.
Delphi Straw Board Co., Decatur, Ind.
Dresden Paper Mills Co., Dresden, Ohio.
Elridge Strawboard Mill, Elridge, N. Y.
Fort Wayne Corrugated Paper Co., Ft. Wayne, Ind.
Foulds & Co., William, Inc., Manchester, Conn.
Garoga Creek Mill, St. Johnsville, N. Y.

Classified List—United States

STRAW BOARD.
(CONTINUED.)

Hagar Straw Board & Paper Co., Xenia, Ohio.
Hart Paper Co., Albany, Ind. (For Tube and Cap Work.)
Hartje Paper Mfg. Co., Pittsburg, Pa.
Hinde & Dauch Paper Co., Sandusky, Ohio. (Light Weight.)
Hutchinson Box Board & Paper Co., Hutchinson, Kan.
Independent Paper Co., Independence, Kan.
Indiana Board & Filler Co., Vincennes, Ind.
Kerr Paper Mill Co., East Downingtown, Pa.
Lafayette Box Board Co., Lafayette, Ind.
Lawrence Paper Mfg. Co., Lawrence, Kan.
Lydall & Foulds Paper Co., Inc., Manchester, Conn.
Massillon Paper Co., Massillon, O. (For Corrugating.)
Monroe Paper Co., Monroe, Mich.
Mt. Vernon Straw Board Co., Mt. Vernon, Ind.
Mullen Bros. Paper Co., St. Joseph, Mich. (Chip.)
North Star Mfg. Co., Coffeyville, Kan. (Plain.)
Quaker Oats Co., Pekin, Ill.
Rock Falls Box Board Co., Rock Falls, Ill.
Rockford Paper Box Board Co., Rockford, Ill.
Shryock Bros., 924 Cherry st., Philadelphia.
South Coventry Paper Co., South Coventry, Conn.
Standard Paper Mfg. Co., Richmond, Va. (Coated.)
Terre Haute Paper Co., The, Terre Haute, Ind.
Thompson & Norris Co. of Ind., Brookville, Ind.
United Paper Board Co., New York.
Weis Paper Mill Co., Quincy, Ill.

STRAW WRAPPING.

American Straw Board Co., Akron, Ohio.
Brown Paper Co., Fort Madison, Iowa.
Carlyle Paper Co., Carlyle, Ill.
Clinton Paper Co., Clinton, Iowa.
Columbia Mills, Chatham Centre, N. Y.
Coshocton Straw Paper Co., Coshocton, Ohio.
Fox, W. H., & Son, Penn Yan, N. Y.
Hagar Straw Board Co., Xenia, O.
Hinde & Dauch Paper Co., Sandusky, Ohio. (Light Weight.)
Independent Paper Co., Independence, Kan.
Massillon Paper Co., Massillon, Ohio.
Mitchell & Sons Co., Palmyra, Mich.
Monroe Paper Co., Monroe, Mich.
Munroe Falls Paper Co., Massillon, Ohio.
Northwest Paper Co., The, Cloquet, Minn.
Richmond, Robert P., Valatie, N. Y.
Rockford Paper Mills, Rockford, Ill.
Terre Haute Paper Co., Terre Haute, Ind.
Winona Pulp & Paper Co., Winona, Minn.

SUIT BOARDS.

Gardner-Harvey Paper Co., Middletown, Ohio. (Colored Box.)
Nelson, B. F., Mfg. Co., Minneapolis, Minn. (Gray Mist.)
South Coventry Paper Co., South Coventry, Conn.
Waldorf Box Board Co., St. Paul. Minn. (Colored Box.)
West Virginia Pulp Products Co., Inc., 200 Fifth Ave., New York; 732 Sherman St., Chicago.

SUIT CASE BOARDS.

Ingalls & Co., Castelton, N. Y.
Merion Paper Co., Abrams, Pa.

SULPHITE BOARDS.

American Straw Board Co., Akron, Ohio.
Carthage Sulphite Pulp & Paper Co., Carthage, N. Y.
Chicago Coated Board Co., Chicago, Ill.
Haverhill Box Board Co., Haverhill, Mass.

ARE SUPERIOR TO ALL OTHERS. ALL SIZES IN STOCK.

LOMBARD & CO., Importers & Manufacturers, 236 & 238 A Street, Boston.

Classified List—United States

SULPHITE BOARDS.
(CONTINUED.)

Lewis, Slocum & LeFevre Co., Inc., Beaver Falls, N. Y.
Marathon Paper Mills Co., Wausau, Wis.
Strange Paper Co., Menasha, Wis.
United Paperboard Co., New York.

SULPHITE PAPERS.

American Writing Paper Co., Holyoke, Mass.
Cushnoc Paper Co., Augusta, Me. (White.)
Eastern Mfg. Co., Bangor, Me.; New York office, 501 Fifth av.
Fox Paper Co., Lockland, Ohio.
Hoberg, The John, Co., Green Bay, Wis.
International Paper Co., 30 Broad, New York.
Marathon Paper Mills Co., Wausau, Wis.
Menasha Paper Co., Steger Bldg., Chicago, Ill.
Menasha Printing Co., Menasha, Wis. (Bleached.)
Munising Paper Co., Munising, Mich.
Newton Falls Paper Co., Newton Falls, N. Y.
Odell Mfg. Co., Groveton, N. H. (Bleached Specialties.)
Orono Pulp & Paper Co., Bangor, Me.
Parker-Young Co., Lincoln, N. H.
Port Huron Sulphite & Paper Co., Port Huron, Mich. (Dry Finish and M. G. Mitscherlich Papers.)
Sorg Paper Co., The Paul A., Middletown, Ohio. (Bleached White for Waxing.)
Strange Paper Co., John, Menasha, Wis.
Union Bag & Paper Corp., New York.

SULPHITE MANILA.

American Writing Paper Co., Holyoke, Mass.
Eureka Paper Co., Fulton, N. Y.
Malone Paper Co., Malone, N. Y.
Union Bag & Paper Corp., New York.

SUPERFINE.

American Writing Paper Co., Holyoke, Mass.
Carew Mfg. Co., South Hadley Falls, Mass.
Chapin & Gould Paper Co., Springfield, Mass.
Elkhart Paper Co., Elkhart, Ind.
Everett Pulp & Paper Co., Everett, Wash.
Fox River Paper Co., Appleton, Wis.
Hammermill Paper Co., Erie, Pa.
Millers Falls Paper Co., Millers Falls, Mass. (Tinted.)
Old Berkshire Mills Co., Dalton, Mass.
Southworth Co., Mittineague, Mass.
Strathmore Paper Co., Woronoco, Mass.
Worthy Paper Co., Mittineague, Mass.

SUPPLEMENT.
International Paper Co., 30 Broad, New York.

TABLET.

American Writing Paper Co., Holyoke, Mass.
Beveridge Paper Co., Indianapolis, Ind.
Columbian Paper Co., Buena Vista, Va.
Everett Pulp & Paper Co., Everett, Wash.
Gilbert Paper Co., Frank, Waterford, N. Y.
Grandfather's Fall Co., Merrill, Wis.
Hamilton, W. C., & Sons, Inc., Wm. Penn P. O., Pa.
Hutchinson Box Board & Paper Co., Hutchinson, Kan.
International Paper Co., 30 Broad, New York.
King Paper Co., Kalamazoo, Mich.
McDowell Paper Mills, Manayunk, Pa.
Michigan Paper Co., Plainwell, Mich.
Pattern Paper Co., Ltd., Appleton, Wis.
Ryegate Paper Co., E. Ryegate, Vt.
Strathmore Paper Co., Mittineague, Mass.

ENGINEERING FOR
PULP, PAPER AND POWER PLANTS

JOSEPH H. WALLACE & C(
INDUSTRIAL ENGINEERS
Temple Court Building, NEW YOR
71 Bay Street. TORONTO, CA

Lombard's English Newcastle Pulp Stones

Classified List—United States

TABLET.
(CONTINUED.)

Taggarts Paper Co., Watertown, N. Y.
United Paperboard Co., New York.
West Virginia Pulp and Paper Co., 200 Fifth ave., N. Y., and 732 Sherman, Chicago.
Wheat Paper Co., Elkhart, Ind.

TACK.

American Straw Board Co., Akron, Ohio.
Lincoln & Co., L., North Dighton, Mass.
Richardson Paper Co., Lockland, Ohio. (Black.)
United Paperboard Co., New York.

TAG BOARD.
(See Manila and Tag.)

TAR BOARD.

American Straw Board Co., Akron, Ohio.
Davey Co., E. H., Bloomfield, N. J.
Dyson, Jas. N., Phila., Pa.
Ingalls & Co., Castleton, N. Y.
International Paper Co., 30 Broad, New York.
Kerr Paper Mill Co., East Downingtown, Pa.
Monroe Binders Board Co., Monroe, Mich.
Wasuc Mills Co., South Glastonbury, Conn.

TELEGRAPH.

American Writing Paper Co., Holyoke, Mass.
International Paper Co., 30 Broad, New York.
King Paper Co., Kalamazoo, Mich.
Robertson Paper Co., Bellows Falls, Vt.
Whiting Paper Co., Geo. A., Menasha, Wis.

TEMPLET BOARD.

American Straw Board Co., Akron, Ohio.
Ingalls & Co., Castleton, N. Y.
Monroe Binder Board Co., Monroe, Mich.

TEST BOARDS.

American Box Board Co., Grand Rapids, Mich.
Auglaize, The, Box Board Co., St. Mary's, Ohio.
Ball Bros. Co., Muncie, Ind.
Bicking, S. Austin, Paper Mfg. Co., E. Downington, Pa.
Carthage Board & Paper Co., Carthage, Ind.
Chesapeake Pulp & Paper Co., Inc., West Point, Va.
Clifton Paper Mills, Passaic, N. J.
Fox Paper Co., Lockland, Ohio.
Hinde & Dauch Paper Co., Sandusky, Ohio.
Marion Paper Co., Marion, Ind.
Paraffine Companies, Inc., San Francisco, Cal.
Waldorf Box Board Co., St. Paul, Minn. (Chip and Jute.)

TEXTILE.

Odell Mfg. Co., Groveton, N. H.

TEXTILE BOARD.

American Straw Board Co., Akron, Ohio.
Beaver Brook Paper Mills, Inc., Danbury, Conn.
Chicago Coated Board Co., Chicago, Ill.
Continental Paper Co., Bogota, N. J.
Fort Orange Paper Co., Castleton, N. Y. (Feather Weight.)
Haverhill Box Board Co., Haverhill, Mass.
Ingalls & Co., Castleton, N. Y.

PRESS ROLLS Maple and Gum White Wood Felt Rolls J. W. HEWITT MACHINE CO. Neenah, Wis.

Classified List—United States

TEXTILE BOARD.
(CONTINUED.)

Rogers Paper Mfg. Co., South Manchester, Conn.
Tonawanda Board & Paper Co., Tonawanda, N. Y.
United Paperboard Co., New York.

TEXTS.

Advertisers Paper Mills, Holyoke, Mass.
Nixon Paper Co., Martin & Wm. H., Dill & Collins Co., successors, Philadelphia.
Peerless Paper Co., Dayton, Ohio.
Tileston & Hollingsworth Co., Boston, Mass.

TICKER.

Gilbert Paper Co., Waterford, N. Y.

TICKET.

American Writing Paper Co., Holyoke, Mass.
Bardeen Paper Co., Otsego, Mich.
Bedford Pulp & Paper Co., Mutual Bldg., Richmond, Va. (Transfer.)
Beveridge Paper Co., Indianapolis, Ind.
Burmus Paper Co., Inc., West Dudley, Mass.
Eddy Paper Co., Three Rivers, Mich.
Elkhart Bristol Board & Paper Co., Elkhart, Ind.
Flower City Tissue Mills Co., Rochester, N. Y.
Fort Orange Paper Co., Castleton, N. Y. (Colored.)
Gilbert, Frank, Paper Co., Waterford, N. Y.
International Paper Co., 30 Broad, New York.
La Monte, Geo., & Son, 61 Broadway, New York. (Safety.)
Lewis, J. P., Co., Inc., Beaver Falls, N. Y.
Monroe Bridge Paper Co., Monroe Bridge, Mass.
Moorhouse, R. T., Paper Co., Bridesburg, Pa.
Ramage Paper Co., James, Monroe Bridge, Mass. (Bristol.)
Tileston & Hollingsworth Co., Boston, Mass.

TISSUE.

Adams Paper Co., Wells River, Vt.
Ancram Paper Mills, 150 W. 22d, New York.
A. P. W. Paper Co., Albany, N. Y.
Arlington Co., 727 Broadway, N. Y.
Ashland Paper Co., Ashland, Wis. (Wrappings.)
Ashuelot Paper Co., Hinsdale, N. H.
Blossvale Paper Co., Blossvale, N. Y.
California Tissue Mills, Inc., Los Angeles, Cal.
Carthage Tissue Paper Mills, Carthage, N. Y. (Packages and Rolls.)
Chester Paper Co., Chester, Pa.
Clayville Paper Mills Co., Clayville, N. Y.
Cole Paper Co., W. A., Putney, Vt.
Consumers Box Board & Paper Co., Lititz, Pa.
Continental Paper Bag Co., 17 Battery Place, New York.
Coy Paper Co., West Claremont, N. H. (No. 1 Pattern Tissue.)
Crescent Paper & Machine Co., Phoenix, N. Y.
Crown Willamette Paper Co., Alaska Com'l Bldg., San Francisco, Cal.
Crystal Paper Co., Middletown, Ohio.
Detroit Sulphite Pulp & Paper Co., Detroit, Mich.
Dexter & Sons, C. H., Windsor Locks, Conn.
Diamond Mills Paper Co., 44 Murray St., New York.
Empire Paper Co., Empire Trust Bldg., Portland, Me.
Erving Mills, Erving, Mass. (Specialties.)
Fillmore & Slade, Bennington, Vt.
Fisk Paper Co., Inc., Hinsdale, N. H. (White, Manila and Toilet.)
Flambeau Paper Co., Park Falls, Wis.
Flower City Tissue Mills Co., Rochester, N. Y.
Gandey, Est. of Wm. H., Lambertville, N. J.
Gardner Paper Co., L. H., Mumford, N. Y.
Garrett, Edwin, Chester, Pa.

Classified List—United States

TISSUE.
(CONTINUED.)

Garrett, E. T., Co., Lansdowne, Pa.
Hawley Pulp & Paper Co., Oregon City, Ore.
Hinsdale Paper Mfg. Co., Hinsdale, N. H.
Hoberg, The John, Co., Green Bay, Wis.
Hoffman, R. S., Baldwinsville, N. Y.
Ingersoll Paper Co., Troy, N. Y. (Manila.)
International Paper Co., 30 Broad, New York.
Japanese Tissue Mills, Holyoke, Mass.
Lake Champlain Pulp & Paper Co., Plattsburg, N. Y.
Lefevre, Edward Y., Fallsburgh, N.Y.
Little Falls Paper Co., Newburgh, N. Y.
Marley Paper Mfg. Co., Childs, Md.
Mason-Perkins Paper Co., Bristol, N. H.
McIntyre Bros., Inc., Fayetteville, N. Y.
Mohawk Valley Paper Co., Inc., Little Falls, N. Y.
Moyer & Pratt, Lyons Falls, N. Y. (Manila and White.)
New Elkhart Paper Mills Co., Elkhart, Ind.
North End Paper Co., Fulton, N. Y.
Northern Paper Mills, Green Bay, Wis. (Duplex.)
Onondaga Paper Co., Marcellus Falls, N. Y. (Kraft.)
Orono Pulp & Paper Co., Bangor, Me.
Oswego River Paper Mills, Phoenix, N. Y. (Toilet.)
Perseverance Paper Mills, Produce Exchange Bldg., New York.
Phoenix Paper Co., Greenwich, N.Y.
Phoenix Toilet and Paper Mfg. Co., Phoenix, N. Y.
Pioneer Paper Mills, Ballston Spa, N. Y.
Rainbow Mills, The, 239 Broadway, New York.
Rhinelander Paper Co., Rhinelander, Wis. (M. G.)
Robertson Bros., Hinsdale, N. H.
Robertson, E. C., & Son, Hinsdale, N. H.
Robertson, W. F., & Co., Hinsdale, N. H.
Robertson Paper Co., Bellows Falls, Vt.
Robertson's Sons, Wm., Putney, Vt.
Shortsville Paper Co., Shortsville, N. Y. (Kraft.)
Smith Paper Co., Lee, Mass.
Sorg Paper Co., Paul A., Middletown, Ohio.
Southworth Co., Mittineague, Mass.
Stratford Paper Co., Jersey City, N. J.
Sweet Bros. Paper Mfg. Co., Phoenix, N. Y.
Thilmany Pulp and Paper Co., Kaukauna, Wis.
Three Rivers Paper Co., Phoenix, N. Y. (White and Manila.)
Ulster Tissue Mills, Inc., Napanoch, N. Y.
Union Mill, 75 Duane, New York.
Union Waxed and Parchment Paper Co., New York.
Victoria Mills Paper Co., Fulton, N. Y. (Also Roll.)
Wisconsin Tissue Paper Co., Appleton, Wis.
Wolverine Paper Co., Elkhart, Ind.

TISSUE MANILA.

Adams Paper Co., A. L., Baldwinsville, Mass. (In Rolls for Toilet Paper.)
Adams Paper Co., Wells River, Vt.
Ancram Paper Mills, 150 W. 22d, New York.
Ashland Paper Co., Ashland, Wis.
Blossvale Paper Co., Blossvale, N. Y. (White.)
California Tissue Mills, Inc., Los Angeles, Cal.
Chester Paper Co., 7th and Glenwood ave., Philadelphia, Pa.
Cole Paper Co., W. A., Putney, Vt.
Continental Paper Bag Co., 17 Battery Place, New York.
Coy Paper Co., West Claremont, N. H.
Crescent Paper & Machine Co., Phoenix, N. Y.
Crystal Paper Co., Middletown, O.
Diamond Mills Paper Co., New York.
Empire Paper Co., Portland, Me.
Fisk Paper Co., Inc., Hinsdale, N. H.
Gandey, W. H., Lambertville, N. J.
Gardner Paper Co., L. H., Mumford, N. Y.
Garrett, Edwin, Chester, Pa.
Garrett Co., E. T., Lansdowne, Pa.
Hall & Richter Paper Co., Northumberland, N. H.

Classified List—United States

TISSUE MANILA.
(CONTINUED.)

Hoberg Co., The John, Green Bay, Wis.
Hoffman, R. S., Baldwinsville, N. Y.
Ingersoll Paper Co., Troy, N. Y.
Jarvis Paper Mills, West Claremont, N. H.
Lake Champlain Pulp & Paper Co., Plattsburg, N. Y.
Lancaster Paper Co., Lancaster, Pa.
Lawless Paper Co., Rochester. N. Y.
Little Falls Paper Co., Newburgh, N. Y.
Mason-Perkins Paper Co., Bristol, N. H.
Mohawk Valley Paper Co., Little Falls, N. Y.
Moyer & Pratt, Lyons Falls, N. Y.
National Paper Products Co., Carthage, N. Y.
North End Paper Co., Fulton, N. Y.
Northern Paper Mills, Green Bay, Wis.
Onondaga Paper Co., Marcellus Falls, N. Y.
Oswego River Paper Mills, Phœnix, N. Y.
Peerless Paper Co., Troy, N. Y.
Pequannock Valley Paper Co., Butler, N. J.
Phœnix Paper Co., Greenwich, N. Y.
Ramsey, E. R., Co., Penn Yan, N. Y.
Robertson Bros., Hinsdale, N. H.
Robertson, E. C., & Son, Hinsdale, N. H.
Robertson, G. A., & Co., Hinsdale, N. H.
Robertson, Orren C., Co., Hinsdale, N. H.
Robertson, W. F., & Co., Hinsdale, N. H.
Robertson Paper Co., Bellows Falls, Vt.
Stevens & Thompson Paper Co., North Hoosick, N. Y.
Sweet Bros. Paper Mfg. Co., Phœnix, N. Y.
Three Rivers Paper Co., Phœnix, N. Y.
Ulster Tissue Mills, Inc., Napanoch, N. Y.
Victoria Paper Mills Co., Fulton, N. Y.

TISSUE (WHITE AND COLORED).

Adams Paper Co., Wells River, Vt.
Ancram Paper Mills, 150 W. 22d, New York City.
Ashland Paper Co., Ashland, Wis. (Colors.)
Ashuelot Paper Co., Hinsdale, N. H. (White.)
Blossvale Paper Co., Blossvale, N. Y.
Carthage Tissue Paper Mills, Carthage, N. Y.
Continental Paper Bag Co., 17 Battery pl., New York.
Crystal Paper Co., Middletown, Ohio.
Dexter & Sons, C. H., Windsor Locks, Conn.
Diamond Mills Paper Co., New York.
Empire Paper Co., Portland, Me.
Fisk Paper Co., Inc., Hinsdale, N. H. (White.)
Flower City Tissue Mills Co., Rochester, N. Y. (Light Weight.)
Garrett, Edwin, Chester, Pa.
Hoberg Co., The John, Green Bay, Wis.
Hoffman, R. S., Baldwinsville, N. Y. (No. 2 White.)
Kenyan Paper Corp., Pittston, Pa.
Little Falls Paper Co., Newburgh, N. Y.
Moyer & Pratt, Lyons Falls, N. Y. (White.)
North End Paper Co., Fulton, N. Y. (Nos. 1 and 2 White and Colored.)
Onondaga Paper Co., Marcellus Falls, N. Y. (White.)
Phœnix Paper Co., Greenwich, N. Y. (Toilet.)
Pioneer Paper Co., Ballston Spa, N. Y.
Robertson Bros., Hinsdale, N. H. (Roll.)
Robertson, E. C., & Son, Hinsdale, N. H.
Robertson, W. F., & Co., Hinsdale, N. H. (Rolls and Sheets.)
Robertson's Sons, Wm., Putney, Vt.
Smith Paper Co., Lee, Mass.
Stratford Paper Co., Jersey City, N. J.
Sweet Bros. Paper Mfg. Co., Phœnix, N. Y.
Three Rivers Paper Co., Phœnix, N. Y. (No. 2 White.)
Victoria Paper Mills Co., Fulton, N. Y. (White, Sheets and Rolls.)

Classified List—United States

TOBACCO.

Barnes Paper Mill, Rochester, Mich.
Eureka Paper Co., Fulton, N. Y.
International Paper Co., 30 Broad, New York.
Moorhouse, R. T., Paper Co., Bridesburg, Pa.
Robertson Paper Co., Bellows Falls, Vt.
Strange Paper Co., John, Menasha, Wis.
Walsh Paper Co., Inc., Cuyahoga Falls, Ohio.

TOILET.

Adams Paper Co., A. L., Baldwinsville, Mass.
Adams Paper Co., Wells River, Vt.
A. P. W. Paper Co., Albany, N. Y.
Ashland Paper Co., Ashland, Wis.
Clayville Paper Mills Co., Clayville, N. Y. (Tissue and Crepe Roll.)
Cole, Wm. A., Paper Co., Putney, Vt.
Continental Paper Bag Co., 17 Battery pl., New York.
Dexter & Sons, Inc., C. H., Windsor Locks, Conn.
Diamond Mills Paper Co., New York.
Fisk Paper Co., Inc., Hinsdale, N. H.
Gardner Paper Co., L. H., Mumford, N. Y.
Hoberg Co., The John, Green Bay, Wis. (Roll and Pack.)
Hoffman, R. S., Baldwinsville, N. Y.
Ingersoll Paper Co., Troy, N. Y.
Jarvis Paper Mills, Claremont, N. H. (All Rag.)
Lefevre, Edward Y., Fallsburgh, N. Y.
Lehigh Paper Mills, Inc., Raubsville, Pa.
Mt. Holyoke Tissue Mills, Holyoke, Mass.
National Paper Products Co., Carthage, N. Y.
Northern Paper Mills, Green Bay, Wis.
Oswego River Paper Mills, Phoenix, N. Y. (Rolls & Packages.)
Perseverance Paper Mills, Produce Exchange Bldg., New York.
Phoenix Paper Co., Battenville, N. Y.
Phoenix Toilet & Paper Mfg. Co., Inc., Phoenix, N. Y.
Rhinelander Paper Co., Rhinelander, Wis.
Robertson, G. A., & Co., Hinsdale, N. H.
Rushmore Paper Co., Brooklyn, N. Y.
Three Rivers Paper Co., Phoenix, N. Y.
United States Paper Mills, Inc., Chambersburg, Pa.
Victoria Paper Co., Fulton, N. Y. (Jumbo Rolls.)
Wyoming Valley Paper Mill, Pittston, Pa.

TOWELING.

Chester Paper Co., Chester, Pa.
Hawley Pulp & Paper Co., Oregon City, Ore.
Hoberg, The John, Co., Green Bay, Wis.
Hollingsworth & Vose Co., Oliver Bldg., Boston, Mass.
Lefevre, Edward Y., Fallsburgh, N. Y.
Lehigh Paper Mills, Inc., Raubsville, Pa.
Mt. Holyoke Tissue Mills, Holyoke, Mass.
Marley Paper Mfg. Co., Childs, Md.
Northern Paper Mills, Green Bay, Wis.
Perseverance Paper Mills, Produce Exchange Bldg., New York.
Robertson Bros., Hinsdale, N. H.
Rushmore Paper Co., Brooklyn, N. Y.
Smith Paper Co., Lee, Mass.
Walloomsac Paper Co., Walloomsac, N. Y.
United States Paper Mills, Inc., Chambersburg, Pa.
Wyoming Valley Paper Mill, Pittston, Pa.

TRUNK BOARDS.

American Straw Board Co., Akron, Ohio.
Albey Bros., 149 to 177 Meeker Ave., Newark, N. J.
Davey Co., E. H., Bloomfield, N. J.
Davey, W. O., & Sons, Jersey City, N. J.
Diamond State Fibre Co., Bridgeport, Pa.
Eureka Paper Co., Fulton, N. Y.
Haverhill Box Board Co., Haverhill, Mass.
Ingalls & Co., Castleton, N. Y.
Merion Paper Co., Abrams, Pa.

ARE SUPERIOR TO ALL OTHERS. ALL SIZES IN STOCK.

LOMBARD & CO., Importers & Manufacturers, 236 & 238 A Street, Boston.

Classified List—United States   311

TRUNK BOARDS.
(CONTINUED.)

Metalite Co., Amesbury, Mass.
Naubuc Paper Co., Glastonbury, Conn.
Norton, C. H., N. Westchester, Conn.
Otter River Board Co., Otter River, Mass.
Paddock Tube Paper Co., Syracuse, N. Y.
Perkiomen Paper Co., Pennsburg, Pa.
River Raisin Paper Co., Monroe, Mich.
Richardson Paper Co., Lockland, O.
Shryock Bros., Philadelphia, Pa.
Tonawanda Board & Paper Co., Tonawanda, N. Y.
Waldorf Box Board Co., St. Paul, Minn.
Wasuc Mills Co., South Glastonbury, Conn.
Westport Paper Co., Westport, Conn.

TUBE BOARDS.

Acme Paper & Paper Box Co. (Trust), East Pepperell, Mass.
American Straw Board Co., Akron, Ohio.
Brown Paper Co., Ft. Madison, Iowa.
National Paper Co., Atlanta, Ga.
Noble Mfg. Co., Cedartown, Ga.
Paddock Tube Paper Co., Syracuse, N. Y.
Port Huron Sulphite & Paper Co., Port Huron, Mich.
Standard Paper Mills, Lawrenceville, Ga. (Featheredge.)
Terre Haute Paper Co., The, Terre Haute, Ind.
United Paperboard Co., New York.

TYMPAN.

Detroit Sulphite Pulp & Paper Co., Detroit, Mich. (Platine.)
Eureka Paper Co., Fulton, N. Y.
Robertson Paper Co., Bellows Falls, Vt.
Rogers Paper Mfg. Co., So. Manchester, Conn.
Warren Mfg. Co., New York.

TYPEWRITER.

American Writing Paper Co., Holyoke, Mass.
Berkshire Hills Paper Co., Adams, Mass.
Brown, L. L., Paper Co., Adams, Mass.
Carew Mfg. Co., South Hadley, Mass.
Dexter, C. H., & Sons, Windsor Locks, Conn.
Diamond Mills Paper Co., 44 Murray, New York.
Esleeck Mfg. Co., Turner's Falls, Mass. (White and Colored.)
Everett Pulp & Paper Co., Everett, Wash.
Gandey, Est. of Wm. H., Lambertville, N. J. (Tissue and Manifold.)
King Paper Co., Kalamazoo, Mich.
Smith Paper Co., Lee, Mass.
Southworth Co., Mittineague, Mass.
Strathmore Paper Co., Mittineague, Mass.

TYPEWRITER MANIFOLD.

American Writing Paper Co., Holyoke, Mass.
Dexter & Sons, Inc., C. H., Windsor Locks, Conn.
Diamond Mills Paper Co., New York.
Esleeck Mfg. Co., Turner's Falls, Mass.
Everett Pulp & Paper Co., Everett, Wash.
Mann Co., Wm., Lambertville, N. J.
Smith Paper Co., Lee, Mass.
Southworth Co., Mittineague, Mass.

VARNISH LABEL.

American Writing Paper Co., Holyoke, Mass.
Everett Pulp & Paper Co., Everett, Wash.
West Virginia Pulp & Paper Co., 200 Fifth av., New York, and 732 Sherman, Chicago.

DRY ROSIN SIZE

Brittle, easy soluble. Cheapest per mill made size. Ask us about it. Also all other grades.

ARABOL M'F'G CO., 100 William St., New York

ENGINEERING FOR PULP, PAPER AND POWER PLANTS

JOSEPH H. WALLACE & CO.
INDUSTRIAL ENGINEERS
Temple Court Building, NEW YORK
71 Bay Street,   TORONTO, CAN

VULCANIZING.

Delaware Hard Fibre Co., Wilmington, Del.
Diamond State Fibre Co., Bridgeport, Pa.
Fibre Corporation, Lockport, N. Y.
Marshall Bros., Inc., Yorklyn, Del.
Marshall & Mitchell, Wooddale, Del.
Megargee Paper Mills, Philadelphia, Pa.

VELLUM.

Advertisers' Paper Mills, Holyoke, Mass.
Southworth Co., Mittineague, Mass.
Strathmore Paper Co., Mittineague, Mass.
Taylor-Logan Co. Papermakers, Holyoke, Mass.

WAGON BOARD.

American Straw Board Co., New York.
Dyson, Jas. N., Philadelphia, Pa.
Ingalls & Co., Castleton, N. Y.
United Paperboard Co., New York.
Wasuc Mills Co., South Glastonbury, Conn.

WALL BOARDS.
(See also List of Paper Specialties.)

Bird & Son, Inc., East Walpole, Mass.
Continental Paper Co., Bogota, N. J.
Cornell Wood Products Co., Cornell, Wis.
Crescent Paper Co., Marseilles, Ill.
Hurlock Bros. Co., Philadelphia, Pa.
Haverhill Box Board Co., Haverhill, Mass.
MacAndrews & Forbes Co., Camden, N. J.
Monroe Binder Board Co., Monroe, Mich.
Paraffine Companies, Inc., 40 First, San Francisco, Cal.
Richardson Paper Co., Lockland, Ohio.
Rockford Paper Box Board Co., Rockford, Ill.
Waldorf Box Board Co., St. Paul, Minn.

WALL PAPER.
(See Hanging.)

WATER MARKED MANILA.

International Paper Co., 30 Broad, New York.

WATERLEAF.

American Writing Paper Co., Holyoke, Mass.
Dexter & Sons, Inc., C. H., Windsor Locks, Conn.
Diamond State Fibre Co., Bridgeport, Pa.
Kalamazoo Vegetable Parchment Co., Kalamazoo, Mich.
Keystone Paper Mills Co., Upper Darby, Pa.
King Paper Co., Kalamazoo, Mich.
Lewis, J. P., Co., Inc., Beaver Falls, N. Y.
Megargee Paper Mills, Modena, Pa. (All Rag.)
Moorhouse, R. T., Paper Co., Bridesburg, Pa.
Nixon Paper Co., Martin & Wm. H., Dill & Collins Co., successors, Philadelphia.
Sterling Paper Co., The, Hamilton, Ohio.

WATERPROOF.

Bird & Son, Inc., East Walpole, Mass.
Bloomsburg Paper Co., Bloomsburg, Pa.
Carthage Sulphite Pulp & Paper Co., Carthage, N. Y.
Case & Marshall, Inc., Hartford, Conn.
Chesapeake Pulp & Paper Co., West Point, Va.
Diamond State Fibre Co., Bridgeport, Pa.

ARE SUPERIOR TO ALL OTHERS. ALL SIZES IN STOCK.
LOMBARD & CO., Importers & Manufacturers, 236 & 238 A Street, Boston.

WATERPROOF.
(CONTINUED.)

Hartje Paper Mfg. Co., Pittsburg, Pa.
Marcellus Paper Co., Syracuse, N. Y. (Butchers.)
McDowell Paper Mills, Manayunk, Pa.
Moorhouse, R. T., Paper Co., Bridesburg, Pa.
Parker, F. H., East Pepperell, Mass. (Bogus.)
St. Regis Paper Co., Watertown, N. Y.
Watson Co., H. F., Erie, Pa.

WAXED.
(Also see Table of Contents for list of concerns that wax paper, some of which do not make their own raw stock.)

Hammerschlag Mfg. Co., New York.
Hollingsworth & Whitney Co., Boston, Mass.
Howe & Davidson Co., Marseilles, Ill.
Kalamazoo Vegetable Parchment Co., Kalamazoo, Mich.
Menasha Printing & Carton Co., Menasha. (Plain and Printed.)
Sorg Paper Co., The Paul A., Middletown, Ohio.
Union Bag & Paper Corp., New York.
Union Waxed and Parchment Paper Co., New York.
Wolverine Paper Co., Elkhart, Ind. (Printed and Plain.)

WAXING.

Carso Paper Co., Dansville, N. Y.
Crystal Paper Co., Middletown, Ohio.
Empire Paper Co., 158 Franklin st., Boston, Mass. (Tissues.)
Erving Paper Mills, Erving, Mass.
Hoffman, R. S., Baldwinsville, N. Y.
Kalamazoo Vegetable Parchment Co., Kalamazoo, Mich.
Lakeside Paper Co., Neenah, Wis. (Rolls.)
Marathon Paper Mills Co., Wausau, Wis.
McDowell Paper Mills, Manayunk, Pa.
Munising Paper Co., Munising, Mich.
Robertson Bros., Hinsdale, N. H.
Robertson Paper Co., Bellows Falls, Vt.
Port Huron Sulphite & Paper Co., Port Huron, Mich.
Smith Paper Co., Lee, Mass.
Sorg, P. A., Paper Co., Middletown, Ohio. (Bleached White Sulphate.)
Union Bag & Paper Corp., New York.
Wolverine Paper Co., Elkhart, Ind.

WEDDING.

American Writing Paper Co., Holyoke, Mass. (Folios.)
Berkshire Hills Paper Co., Adams, Mass.
Chemical Paper Mfg. Co., Holyoke, Mass.
East Hartford Mfg. Co., Burnside, Conn.
Keith Paper Co., Turners Falls, Mass.
Mountain Mill Paper Co., Lee, Mass.
Rising, B. D., Paper Co., Housatonic, Mass.
Southworth Co., Mittineague, Mass.
Strathmore Paper Co., Mittineague, Mass.

WHITE SULPHITE.

Cushnoc Paper Co., Augusta, Me.
Eastern Mfg. Co., Bangor, Me.
Hoberg Co., The John, Green Bay, Wis.
Marathon Paper Mills Co., Wausau, Wis.
McDowell Paper Mills, Manayunk, Pa.
Smith Paper Co., Lee, Mass.
Strange Paper Co., John, Menasha, Wis.
United Paperboard Co., New York.

WOOD PULP BOARDS.

American Straw Board Co., Akron, Ohio.
Androscoggin Pulp Co., 50 State st., Boston, Mass.

ENGINEERING FOR

JOSEPH H. WALLACE & CO.
INDUSTRIAL ENGINEERS
Temple Court Building, NEW YORK

Classified List—United States

WOOD PULP BOARDS.
(CONTINUED.)

Chilsdale Paper Mills, Chilsdale, Mich.
Continental Paper Co., Bogota, N. J.
Cornell Wood Products Co., Cornell, Wis.
Franklin Board and Paper Co., Franklin, Ohio.
French Paper Co., Niles, Mich. (Filled and Solid.)
Hartje Paper Mfg. Co., Pittsburg, Pa.
Hutchinson Box Board & Paper Co., Hutchinson, Kan.
Keyes Products Co., 120 Broadway, New York. (Refined Boards.)
Lewis Co., Inc., The J. P., Beaver Falls, N. Y.
Lewis, Slocum & Lefevre Co., Inc., Beaver Falls, N. Y.
Mac-Sim-Bar Paper Co., Otsego, Mich.
Marion Paper Co., Marion, Ind.
Mutual Box Board Co., Utica, N. Y.
National Metal Edge Box Co., Philadelphia, Pa.
Niagara Pulp Board Co., Niagara Falls, N. Y.
Ohio Box Board Co., Cleveland, Ohio.
Oswego Falls Pulp & Paper Co., Fulton, N. Y.
Paraffine Companies, Inc., San Francisco, Cal.
Piermont Paper Co., Piermont, N. Y.
Richardson Paper Co., Lockland, Ohio.
Roanoke Fibre Board Co., Roanoke Rapids, N. C.
Strange Paper Co., John, Menasha, Wis.
Tait & Sons Paper Co., The, Bridgeport, Conn.
Tonawanda Board & Paper Co., Tonawanda, N. Y.
United Paperboard Co., New York.

WRAPPING.
(See also Rag Wrapping.)

Acme Paper & Paper Box Co. (Trust), East Pepperell, Mass.
American Straw Board Co., Akron, Ohio.
American Writing Paper Co., Holyoke, Mass.
Andrews & Co., John T., Penn Yan, N. Y.
Ashland Paper Co., Ashland, Wis. (Fruit.)
Ballston Fibre Products Co., Ballston Spa, N. Y.
Barnes Paper Mill, Rochester, Mich.
Beaver Brook Paper Mills, Danbury, Conn. (Textile and Mill.)
Bedford Pulp & Paper Co., Richmond, Va.
Berkshire Box and Paper Co., Mellenville, N. Y.
Bird & Son, Inc., East Walpole, Mass.
Brown Paper Co., Ithaca, N. Y.
Carney Paper Co., Maumee, Ohio. (Sealing.)
Certain-feed Products Corp., St. Louis.
Chemical Paper Mfg. Co., Holyoke, Mass.
Consolidated Water Power and Paper Co., Grand Rapids, Wis.
Crown Willamette Paper Co., Alaska Coml. Bldg., San Francisco, Cal.
Cushnoc Paper Co., Augusta, Me.
Davis & Richmond, Valatie, N. Y.
Detroit Sulphite Pulp & Paper Co., Detroit, Mich.
Dexter Sulphite Pulp & Paper Co., Dexter, N. Y.
Eureka Paper Co., Fulton, N. Y.
Fleming & Sons, John G., Dallas, Tex.
Flower City Tissue Mills Co., Rochester, N. Y.
Fox Paper Co., Lockland, Ohio. (Rag.)
Fox, W. H., & Son, Penn Yan, N. Y. (Straw.)
Funke's Sons, Ferd., Evansville, Ind.
Gould Paper Co., Lyon Falls, N. Y.
Great Northern Paper Co., 80 E. 42d St., New York.
Hagar Straw Board & Paper Co., Xenia, Ohio.
Hammermill Paper Co., Erie, Pa.
Hartje Paper Mfg. Co., Pittsburg, Pa.
Harvey Paper Co., Wellsburg, W. Va.
Hawley Pulp & Paper Co., Oregon City, Ore.

Classified List—United States

WRAPPING.
(CONTINUED.)

Hinde & Dauch Paper Co., The, Sandusky, O.
Hoboken Paper Mills Co., Hoboken, N. J.
Humphrey & Young, Inc., Napanoch, N. Y.
Inland Empire Paper Co., Spokane, Wash.
International Paper Co., 30 Broad, New York.
Kimberly-Clark Co., Neenah, Wis.
Lawless Paper Co., Rochester, N. Y.
Lawrenceville Paper Mills, Lawrenceville, Ga.
Lockport Paper Co., Lockport, N. Y.
Los Angeles Paper Mfg. Co., Los Angeles, Cal.
McDowell Paper Mills, Manayunk, Pa.
Mac-Sim-Bar Paper Co., Otsego, Mich.
Marathon Paper Mills Co., Wausau, Wis. (Fancy.)
Marcellus Paper Co., Marcellus Falls, N. Y.
Massillon Paper Co., Massillon, O.
Monroe Paper Co., Monroe, Mich. (Straw.)
Moorhouse, R. T., Paper Co., Bridesburg, Pa.
Munroe Falls Paper Co., Massillon, Ohio.
Munroe Felt & Paper Co., Boston, Mass.
Mutual Box Board Co., Utica, N. Y.
New Elkhart Paper Mills Co., Elkhart, Ind.
Newton Falls Paper Co., Newton Falls, N. Y. (Sulphite.)
Newton Paper Co., Holyoke, Mass.
Nixon & Costello Co., White Hall, Md.
Odell Mfg. Co., Groveton, N. H. Sealing.
Orono Pulp & Paper Co., Bangor, Me.
Pejepscot Paper Co., 111 Broadway, New York.
Pleasant Mills Paper Co., Pleasant Mills, N. J.
Ravenswood Paper Mill Co., 545 Van Alst ave., Long Island City, N. Y.
Rhinelander Paper Co., Rhinelander, Wis.
Richardson Paper Co., Lockland, Ohio.
Richmond, R. P., Valatie, N. Y.
Robertson, C. M., Co., Montville, Conn.
Rockford Paper Mills, Rockford, Ill.
Schmidt & Ault Paper Co., York, Pa.
Sears, Roebuck & Co., Chicago.
Smith Paper Co., Lee, Mass.
Southern Paper Co., Moss Point, Miss.
Standard Paper Co., Kalamazoo, Mich.
Strange Paper Co., John, Menasha, Wis.
Tarentum Paper Mills, Pittsburg, Pa.
Terre Haute Paper Co., Terre Haute, Ind.
Thilmany Pulp and Paper Co., Kaukauna, Wis. (Special.)
Union Bag & Paper Corp., New York.
Van Buren, J. M., & Co., Mellenville, N. Y.
Van de Carr Paper Co., Stockport, N. Y. (Bogus.)
Wall, J. F., & Son, Walpole, Mass.
Wardway Paper Mills, Ft. Madison, Ga.
West Branch Paper Mill, Barto, Pa.
Winona Pulp & Paper Co., Winona, Minn.
Wolf River Paper and Fibre Co., Shawano, Wis.
Young, J. W., Bentleys Springs, Md. (Gray.)

WRAPPING BOARDS.

American Straw Board Co., Akron, Ohio.
International Paper Co., New York.
Naubuc Paper Co., Glastonbury, Conn.
Terre Haute Paper Co., Terre Haute, Ind.
United Paperboard Co., New York.

WRITING.

Advertisers Paper Mills, Holyoke, Mass. (Feather Edge.)
Ætna Paper Co., The, Dayton, Ohio.
American Writing Paper Co., Holyoke, Mass.
Bardeen Paper Co., Otsego, Mich.
Bay State Mill, Dalton, Mass.
Beckett Paper Co., Hamilton, Ohio.
Berkshire Hills Paper Co., Adams, Mass.

Lombard's English Newcastle Pulp Stones

Classified List—United States

WRITING.
(CONTINUED.)

Bryant Paper Co., Kalamazoo, Mich.
Carew Mfg. Co., South Hadley Falls, Mass.
Cascade Paper Co., Balboa Bldg., San Francisco, Cal.
Chapin & Gould Paper Co., Springfield, Mass.
Chemical Paper Mfg. Co., Holyoke, Mass.
Collins Mfg. Co., North Wilbraham, Mass.
Columbian Paper Co., Buena Vista, Va.
Cornwall Paper Mfg. Co., Cornwall-on-Hudson, N. Y.
Crane & Co., Dalton, Mass.
Crane Bros., Westfield, Mass.
Crocker-McElwain Co., Holyoke, Mass.
Cushnoc Paper Co., Augusta, Me. (Yellow.)
Curtis & Bro., Inc., Newark, Del.
Eastern Mfg. Co., Bangor, Me.
East Hartford Mfg. Co., Burnside, Conn.
Everett Pulp and Paper Co., Everett, Wash.
Fox River Paper Co., Appleton, Wis.
Garvan, Thomas F., Co., Burnside, Conn.
General Paper Co., 175 Fifth Ave., New York.
Gilbert Paper Co., Menasha, Wis.
Glatfelter, P. H., Co., Spring Grove, Pa.
Hamilton, W. C., & Sons, William Penn P. O., Pa.
Hammermill Paper Co., Erie, Pa.
Hawthorne Paper Co., Kalamazoo, Mich.
Holden Paper Co., Newburgh, N. Y.
Hollingsworth & Whitney, Boston, Mass.
Howard Paper Co., The, Urbana, Ohio.
Inland Empire Paper Co., Spokane, Wash.
International Paper Co., 30 Broad, New York.
Jessup & Moore Paper Co., New York.
Kalamazoo Paper Co., Kalamazoo, Mich.
Keith Paper Co., Turners Falls, Mass.
Kimberly-Clark Co., Neenah, Wis.
King Paper Co., Kalamazoo, Mich.
Kitzmiller, S. M., & Bro., Shippensburg, Pa.
La Monte, Geo., & Sons, 61 Broadway, New York.
Lee Paper Co., Vicksburg, Mich.
Malone Paper Co., Malone, N. Y. (Yellow and White.)
McDowell Paper Mills, Manayunk, Pa.
Menasha Paper Co., Ladysmith, Wis. (Colored Laid.)
Menasha Printing & Carton Co., Menasha, Wis.
Merrimac Paper Co., Lawrence, Mass.
Miami Paper Co., West Carrollton, Ohio. (White and Canary.)
Miamisburg Paper Co., Miamisburg, Ohio.
Michigan Paper Co., Plainwell, Mich.
Moorhouse, R. T., Paper Co., Bridesburg, Pa.
Mountain Mill Paper Co., Lee, Mass.
Munising Paper Co., Munising, Mich.
Nashua River Paper Co., East Pepperell, Mass.
New York and Pennsylvania Co., 200 Fifth ave., New York.
Nixon Paper Co., Martin & William H. Dill & Collins Co., successors, Philadelphia.
Oglesby Paper Co., The W. B., Middletown, Ohio.
Old Berkshire Mill, Dalton, Mass.
Parsons Paper Co., Holyoke, Mass. (Record.)
Peerless Paper Co., Dayton, Ohio.
Peninsular Paper Co., Ypsilanti, Mich.
Poland Paper Co., Mechanic Falls, Me.
Rogers Co., J. & J., Ausable Forks, N. Y.
Southworth Co., Mittineague, Mass.
Strathmore Paper Co., Mittineague, Mass.

NET MACHINES — We make a specialty of GROUND WOOD PULP and SULPHITE FIBRE MACHINERY — **Carthage Machine Co., CARTHAGE, N. Y.**

Classified List—United States

WRITING.
(CONTINUED.)

Taylor-Atkins Paper Co., Burnside, Conn.
Ticonderoga Pulp and Paper Co., 200 Fifth ave., New York.
Unity Paper Mills, Potsdam, N. Y.
Valley Paper Co., Holyoke, Mass.
West Virginia Pulp and Paper Co., 200 Fifth ave., New York, and 732 Sherman, Chicago.
Weston Co., Byron, Dalton, Mass.
Wheat Paper Co., Elkhart, Ind.
Whiting Paper Co., George A., Menasha, Wis.
Whiting Paper Co., Holyoke, Mass.
Whiting-Plover Paper Co., Stevens Point, Wis.
Worthy Paper Co., Mittineague, Mass.

YELLOW WAY-BILL COPYING.
(See also Railroad Copying.)

Garrett Co., E. T., Lansdowne, Pa.
Mann Co., Wm., Lambertville, N. J.
McDowell Paper Mills, Manayunk, Pa.
Smith Paper Co., Lee, Mass.

GROUND WOOD.
(CONTINUED.)

Underwood Paper Mills, Inc., Plattsburg, N. Y.
Union Bag and Paper Corp., N. Y.
Union Mfg. Co., Oconto Falls, Wis.
United Indurated Fibre Co. of New Jersey, Lockport, N. Y.
United Paperboard Co., 171 Madison av., New York.
Watab Pulp & Paper Co., Sartell, Minn.
Wausau Paper Mills Co., Brokaw, Wis.
West End Paper Co., Carthage, N. Y.
Wisconsin River Paper and Pulp Co., Neenah, Wis.
Wolf River Paper and Fibre Co., Shawano, Wis.
York Haven Paper Co., 290 Broadway, New York City.

SODA FIBRE.

Bare Paper Co., D. M., Roaring Spring, Pa.
Champion Fibre Co., Canton, N. C.
Champion-International Co., Lawrence, Mass.
Columbian Paper Co., Buena Vista, Va.
Dill & Collins Co., 140 6th st., Philadelphia, Pa.
District of Columbia Paper Mfg. Co., Washington, D. C.
Everett Pulp and Paper Co., Everett, Wash.
Forest Paper Co., Yarmouth, Me.
Glatfelter Co., P. H., Spring Grove, Pa.
Hamilton, W. C., & Sons, William Penn P. O., Pa.
Highland Paper Co., 200 Fifth ave., New York City.
Jessup & Moore Paper Co., 16 South Broad, Philadelphia, Pa.
Kingsport Pulp Corp., Kingsport, Tenn.
MacAndrews & Forbes Co., Camden, N. J.
Mead Pulp & Paper Co., Dayton, O.
New York and Pennsylvania Co., 200 Fifth ave., New York.
Oxford Paper Co., 200 Fifth ave., New York.
Penobscot Chemical Fibre Co., 49 Federal st., Boston, Mass.
Pynetree Paper Co., Gordon, Ga.
Sugar Cane By-Products Co., New Iberia, La.
Ticonderoga Pulp and Paper Co., 200 Fifth ave., New York.
United Paperboard Co., New York.
Warren Co., S. D., Boston, Mass.
West Virginia Pulp and Paper Co., 200 Fifth ave., New York, and 732 Sherman, Chicago. (Bleached.)

SULPHATE FIBRE.

Aroostook Pulp & Paper Co., Van Buren, Me.
Atlantic Pulp & Paper Corp., Savannah, Ga.
Bogalusa Paper Co., Inc., Bogalusa, La.
Brown Co., Portland, Me.
Central Paper Co., Muskegon, Mich.
Chesapeake Pulp & Paper Co., West Point, Va.
Deerfield Pulp Co., Mountain Mills, Vt.
Eastern Mfg. Co., Bangor, Me.
E-Z Opener Bag Co., Taylorville, Ill.
Falls Mfg. Co., Oconto Falls, Wis.
Filer Fibre Co., Filer City, Mich.
Halifax Paper Corp., Roanoke Rapids, N. C.
Howland Pulp & Paper Corp., Boston, Mass.
Jaite, The, Co., Boston, Ohio.
Louisiana Fibre Board Co., Bogalusa, La.
Minnesota & Ontario Power Co., International Falls, Minn.
Nekoosa-Edwards Paper Co., Nekoosa, Wis.
New York and Pennsylvania Co., 200 Fifth av., New York.
Southern Fibre Co., Portsmouth, Va.
Southern Paper Co., Moss Point, Miss.
Stevens Point Pulp and Paper Co., Stevens Point, Wis.
Thilmany Pulp & Paper Co., Kaukauna, Wis.
Wausau Sulphate Fibre Co, Mosinee, Wis.
West Virginia Pulp Products Co., 200 Fifth ave., New York; 732 Sherman, Chicago.
Yellow Pine Paper Mills Co., Orange, Tex.

DIETZ TOILET PAPER MACHINES

For making toilet paper rolls, With or Without Perforations, as well as for making

SANITARY CREPE PAPER TOWELS

We also manufacture

AUTOMATIC TUBE MACHINES

For Making Wire Stitched Toilet and Towel Tubes Directly from Web or Sheets; also Rotary Card Cutting and Collating Machines, Slitting and Rewinding Machines, Photo Mount Beveling Machines, Side and Center Seam Merchandise Envelope Machines, Punch Presses for Playing Cards, Drop Roll Slitters, Candy Bag Machines, Etc.

Correspondence solicited.

DIETZ MACHINE WORKS, Mfrs., 126-128 Fontain Street, PHILADELPHIA, PA.
Corner Waterloo Street, Below Diamond Street, Between Front and Second Streets

---

THOMAS H. SAVERY, Jr.   1630 The Republic Building
CHICAGO, ILLINOIS

Special Machinery for Pulp and Paper Mills

JENNINGS Hydro-Turbine Dryer Exhaust Units
NASH Hydro-Turbine Air Compressor
NASH Hydro-Turbine Vacuum Pump

BIRD Inward Flow Rotary Screens

BIRD SAVE-ALL   WANDEL SCREEN

Westbye Centrifugal Screen   Farnham Suction Roll
Huband & Nash Deckle Supports   Puseyjones Steam Dryer Joints
Economy Oil Box

LINDSAY WIRES

ARE *THE* WIRES FOR AVERAGE LONG LIFE AND LARGE TONNAGE

ALL SIZES MADE BY

The Lindsay Wire Weaving Co.

Collinwood Station - - CLEVELAND, OHIO

Hall, Ward & Walker, Inc.
Successors to Hall Process Corporation
SHERMAN BUILDING, WATERTOWN, N. Y.

Specialists in the Manufacture of Mechanical Wood Pulp

Owners of U. S. and foreign patents covering the process of grinding mechanical wood pulp known as the Hall Process and the Burr used in connection therewith, all of which, whether straight or spiral, are made to feature the flat bottom and thin tooth, as shown in cut.

Both Process and Burr have passed the experimental stage, and are now in use in several of the most progressive mills in this country and Canada.

Terms pertaining to rights and cost of installation cheerfully furnished interested parties, and expert assistance given in solving pulp and paper-making problems at reasonable cost.

Style No. 125-A.

The Hall patent Burr is made exclusively in the shops of the International Burr Corporation, Watertown, N. Y., and the Roberts Manufacturing Company, Lockport, N. Y.

ARE SUPERIOR TO ALL OTHERS. ALL SIZES IN STOCK.
LOMBARD & CO., Importers & Manufacturers, 236 & 238 A Street, Boston.

Classified List—United States

SULPHITE FIBRE.

Aldrich Paper Co., Natural Dam, N. Y.
Analomink Paper Co., North Water Gap, Pa.
Arrowhead Mills, Inc., Fulton, N. Y.
Bayless Mfg. Corp., Austin, Pa.
Brown Co., Portland, Me.
Carolina Fibre Co., Hartsville, S. C.
Carthage Sulphite Pulp & Paper Co., Carthage, N. Y.
Carthage Tissue Paper Mills, Carthage, N. Y.
Central Paper Co., Muskegon, Mich.
Champion Fibre Co., Canton, N. C.
Champion-International Co., Lawrence, Mass.
Cherry River Paper Co., Richwood, W. Va.
Combined Locks Paper Co., Combined Locks, Wis.
Crown Willamette Paper Co., Alaska Commercial Bldg., San Francisco, Cal.
Cushnoc Paper Co., Augusta, Me.
De Grasse Paper Co., Pyrites, N. Y.
Dells Paper and Pulp Co., Eau Claire, Wis.
Detroit Sulphite Pulp and Paper Co., Detroit, Mich.
Dexter Sulphite Pulp and Paper Co., Dexter, N. Y.
Eastern Mfg. Co., Bangor, Me.
Falls Mfg. Co., Oconto Falls, Wis.
Fletcher Paper Co., Alpena, Mich.
Gould Paper Co., Lyons Falls, N. Y.
Great Northern Paper Co., 30 East 42d, New York. (Mitscherlich.)
Green Bay Paper and Fibre Co., Green Bay, Wis.
Hammermill Paper Co., Erie, Pa.
Hartje Paper Mfg. Co., Pittsburg, Pa.
Hawley Pulp & Paper Co., Oregon City, Ore.
Highland Paper Co., 200 Fifth ave., New York.
Hinckley Fibre Co., Hinckley, N. Y. (Bleached and Unbleached.)
Hoberg, The John, Co., Green Bay, Wis. (White.)
Hollingsworth & Whitney Co., Boston, Mass.
Howland Pulp & Paper Corp., Boston, Mass.
Inland Empire Paper Co., Spokane, Wash.
International Paper Co., 30 Broad, New York.
Interlake Pulp and Paper Co., Appleton, Wis.
Island Paper Co., Menasha, Wis.

Kaukauna Pulp Co., Kaukauna, Wis.
Kimberly-Clark Co., Neenah, Wis.
Malone Paper Co., Malone, N. Y.
Marathon Paper Mills Co., Wausau, Wis. (Mitscherlich.)
Marinette and Menominee Paper Co., Marinette, Wis.
Menasha Paper Co., Ladysmith, Wis. (Bleached.)
Menasha Printing & Carton Co., Menasha, Wis.
Minnesota & Ontario Power Co., International Falls, Minn.
Mt. Tom Sulphite Pulp Co., 50 State, Boston, Mass.
Munising Paper Co., Munising, Mich.
Nekoosa-Edwards Paper Co., Nekoosa, Wis.
Newton Falls Paper Co., Newton Falls, N. Y.
New York and Pennsylvania Co., 200 Fifth ave., New York.
Northern Michigan Pulp Co., Petoskey, Mich.
Northern Paper Mills, 298 Broadway, New York.
Northwest Paper Co., Colquet, Mich.
Odell Mfg. Co., Groveton, N. H.
Orono Pulp & Paper Co., Bangor, Me.
Oxford Paper Co., 200 Fifth av., New York.
Parker-Young Co., Lincoln, N. H.
Parsons Pulp and Lumber Co., Finance Bldg., Philadelphia, Pa.
Pejepscot Paper Co., 111 Broadway, New York.
Penobscot Chemical Fibre Co., Great Works, Me.
Port Edwards Fibre Co., Port Edwards, Wis.
Port Huron Sulphite & Paper Co., Port Huron, Mich.
Racquette River Paper Co., Potsdam, N. Y.
Remington Paper & Power Co., Watertown, N. Y.
Rhinelander Paper Co., Rhinelander, Wis.
Riverside Fibre and Paper Co., Appleton, Wis.
Rogers Co., J. & J., Ausable Forks, N. Y.
St. Croix Paper Co., Boston, Mass.
St. Regis Paper Co., Watertown, N. Y.
Sugar Cane By-Products Co., New Iberia, La.
Union Bag and Paper Corp., New York.
United Paperboard Co., New York.

E. J. KELLER CO., INC.
200 FIFTH AVENUE E.J.KELLER, Pres. NEW YORK
FOREIGN AND DOMESTIC
Rags and Wastes
Gunny Bagging, Burlap Bagging, Ropes, Flax, Hemp, Cotton Wastes, Paper Stock, Wood Pulp and Rag Pulp.

ENGINEERING FOR PULP, PAPER AND POWER PLANTS
JOSEPH H. WALLACE & CO.
INDUSTRIAL ENGINEERS
Temple Court Building, NEW YORK
71 Bay Street, TORONTO, CAN

Lombard's English Newcastle Pulp Stones

Classified List—United States

SULPHITE FIBRE.
(CONTINUED.)

Wausau Paper Mills Co., Brokaw, Wis.
West Virginia Pulp and Paper Co., 200 Fifth ave., New York, and 782 Sherman, Chicago. (Bleached.)
Wheat Paper Co., Petoskey, Mich.
Wolf River Paper and Fibre Co., Shawano, Wis.
York Haven Paper Co., 290 Broadway, New York.

WOOD FLOUR.

Du Pont de Nemours, E. I., Co., Wilmington, Del. (For Explosives and Linoleum.)
John C. Hornbeek's Sons, Napanoch, N. Y. (For Explosives.)

RAG AND JUTE PULP.

Srere Bros. & Co., Franklin, Ohio.
The Riverton Co., Riverton, Conn.

PRESS ROLLS — Maple and Gum White Wood Felt Rolls — J. W. HEWITT MACHINE CO. Neenah, Wis.

ARE SUPERIOR TO ALL OTHERS. ALL SIZES IN STOCK.
LOMBARD & CO., Importers & Manufacturers, 236 & 238 A Street, Boston.

LIST OF
Paper Mills of Canada
CLASSIFIED ACCORDING TO GOODS MADE, AS SHOWN BY MILL REPORTS

BAG.
Wilson, Ltd., J. C., 61 St. Alexander, Montreal, Can.

BINDERS' BOARD.
Bennett, Ltd., Chambly Canton, Que.
Eddy, The E. B., Co., Ltd., Hull, Que.

BOARD.
Bennett, Ltd., Chambly Canton, Que.
Booth, J. R., Ottawa, Can.
Canada Boxboard Co., Ltd., 182 Shearer, Montreal, Inc.
Eastern Paper Co., St. Basile Station, Portneuf Co., Que.
Eddy, The E. B., Co., Ltd., Hull, Que.
Hinde & Dauch Paper Co. of Canada, Ltd., Toronto, Ont.
Jonquieres Pulp Co., Ltd., Jonquieres, Que.
Laurentide Co., Ltd., Grand Mere, Quebec.
Miller Bros., Ltd., Glenn Miller, Ont.
Northumberland Paper & Electric Co., Campbellford, Ont.
St. Croix Paper Co., Ltd., Ellershouse, N. S.
Walker & Co., J. R., 35 Common st., Montreal.

BOND.
Kinleith Paper Mills, Ltd., St. Catharines, Ont.
Jonquieres Pulp Co., Ltd., Jonquieres, Que.
Rolland, The, Paper Co., 142 St. Paul, W., Montreal, Que.
Provincial Paper Mills Co., Ltd., Bell Tel. Bldg., Toronto.
Smith, Howard, Paper Mills, Ltd., 138 McGill, Montreal, Ont.
Toronto Paper Mfg. Co., Ltd., Cornwall, Ont.

BOOK.
Canada Paper Co., Ltd., Windsor Mills, Que.
Eddy Co., The E. B., Ltd., Hull, Que.
Kinleith Paper Co., St. Catharines, Ont.
Provincial Paper Mills Co., Ltd., Bell Tel. Bldg., Toronto.
Rolland, The, Paper Co., 142 St. Paul, W., Montreal, Que.
Toronto Paper Mfg. Co., Ltd., Cornwall, Ont.

BOTTLE WRAPPING.
Interlake Tissue Mills, Ltd., Merritton, Ont.

BOX BOARD.
Booth, J. R., Ottawa, Can. (Folding.)
Brompton Pulp & Paper Co., East Angus, Que.
Eddy, The E. B., Co., Ltd., Hull, Que.
Hinde & Dauch Paper Co. of Canada, Ltd., The, Toronto.
Jonquieres Pulp Co., Ltd., Jonquieres, Que. (Folding.)
Montreal Boxboard Co., Ltd., Montreal, Que.
Northumberland Paper & Electric Co., Campbellford, Ont. (Filled boards.)
St. Croix Paper Co., Ltd., Ellershouse, N. S.

M. GOTTESMAN & CO., Inc.
18 E. 41st STREET, NEW YORK. Cable Address "Namettug."
EUROPEAN OFFICES: Stockholm, Sweden

HIGHEST GRADE KRAFT PULPS

ENGINEERING FOR PULP, PAPER AND POWER PLANTS
JOSEPH H. WALLACE & CO.
INDUSTRIAL ENGINEERS
Temple Court Building, NEW YORK
71 Bay Street. TORONTO, CAN.

Lombard's English Newcastle Pulp Stones

Classified List—Canada

BRISTOL.

Don Valley Paper Co., Ltd., Todmorden, Ont. (White and Colored.)
Rolland Paper Co., The, St. Jerome, Que.

BROWN WRAPPING.

Dominion Paper Co., Montreal, Que.
Don Paper Mills Co., Todmorden, Ont.
McArthur, Alex., & Co., Montreal, Que.
Wilson, Ltd., J. C., 61 St. Alexander st., Montreal, Que.

BUILDING.

Bird & Son, Ltd., Hamilton, Ont.
McArthur, Alex., & Co., Montreal, Que.
Montreal Paper Co., Ltd., Portneuf Station, Portneuf Co., Que.
Northumberland Paper & Electric Co., Campbellford, Ont.
Riordon Pulp & Paper Co., Ltd., The, 1 Beaver Hall Sq., Montreal, Que.

BUILDING BOARD.

Bird & Son, Ltd., Hamilton, Ont.

BUTCHER'S.

Stutt, James, & Sons, West Flamboro, Ont.

CARDBOARD.

Eddy, The E. B., Co., Ltd., Hull, Que.
Jonquieres Pulp Co., Ltd., Jonquieres, Que.

CARD MIDDLES.

Eddy, The E. B., Co., Ltd., Hull, Que.
Ford, Joseph, & Co., Portneuf Station, Portneuf Co., Que.

CARPET LINING.

Bird & Son, Ltd., Hamilton, Ont.
Eastern Paper Co., Ltd., St. Basile Station, Portneuf Co., Que.
Ford, Rowland, & Son, Portneuf Station, Que.
Lazier Paper Mills, Ltd., Bellville, Ont.
Montreal Paper Co., Portneuf Station, Que.

CATALOGUE.

McArthur, Alex., & Co., Ltd., Montreal, Que.
Provincial Paper Mills Co., Ltd., Bell Tel. Bldg., Toronto.

CHIP BOARD.

Canada Boxboard Co., 182 Shearer, Montreal, Que.
Hinde & Dauch Paper Co. of Canada, Ltd., Toronto, Ont.
Northumberland Paper & Electric Co., Campbellford, Ont.

COATED PAPERS.

Provincial Paper Mills Co., Ltd., Bell Tel. Bldg., Toronto, Ont. (Book, Cover, Litho Blanks and Box Boards.)

COLORED.

Canada Paper Co., Windsor Mills, Que.
Eddy Co., The E. B., Ltd., Hull, Que.
McArthur & Co., Ltd., Alex., Montreal, Que.
Toronto Paper Mfg. Co., Cornwall, Ont.

CHIP CRUSHER — We make a specialty of GROUND WOOD PULP and SULPHITE FIBRE MACHINERY

Carthage Machine Co.
CARTHAGE, N. Y.

CONTAINER BOARD.
Hinde & Dauch Paper Co. of Canada, Ltd., Toronto, Ont.

CORRUGATED.
Hinde & Dauch Paper Co. of Canada, Ltd., Toronto, Ont.
Lazier Paper Mills, Ltd., Bellville Ont.

COUNTER BOARD.
Bennett, Ltd., Chambly Canton, Que.
Richard & Co., 161 Arago, Que.

COVER.
Don Valley Paper Co., Ltd., Toronto, Ont.
Eddy Co., The E. B., Ltd., Hull, Que.
Provincial Paper Mills Co., Ltd., Bell Tel. Bldg., Toronto.
Toronto Paper Mfg. Co., Ltd., Cornwall, Ont.

CREPE.
Interlake Tissue Mills, Ltd., Merritton, Ont.

CREPE TISSUE.
Interlake Tissue Mills, Ltd., Merritton, Ont.

DEADENING FELT.
Ford, Joseph & Co., Portneuf Station, Portneuf Co., Que.

DRUG.
Eddy, The E. B., Co., Ltd., Hull, Que.
Interlake Tissue Mills, Ltd., Merritton, Ont.

EGG CASES AND FILLERS.
Miller Bros. Co., Ltd., Glen Miller, Ont.

ENVELOPE.
Don Valley Paper Co., Toronto, Ont.
Provincial Paper Mills Co., Ltd., Bell Tel. Bldg., Toronto.
Rolland Paper Co., 142 St. Paul, W., Montreal, Que.
Toronto Paper Mfg. Co., Ltd., Cornwall, Ont. (White and Colored.)

FELTS.
Bird & Son, Ltd., Hamilton, Ont.
Eastern Paper Co., Ltd., St. Basile Station, Portneuf Co., Que. (Deadening and Insulating.)
Ford, Joseph, Portneuf Station, Portneuf Co., P. Q. (Roofing.)
Ford & Son, Rowland, Portneuf Station, Portneuf Co., Que.
McArthur & Co., Ltd., Alex., Montreal, Que.
Montreal Paper Co., Ltd., Portneuf Station, Que. (Saturating and Deadening.)
Stutt, James, & Sons, West Flamboro, Ont.

FIBRE.
Beaver Wood Fibre Co., Thorold, Ont.
Dominion Paper Co., Montreal, Que.
Laurentide Co., Grand Mere, Que.
Lincoln Paper Mills Co., Merritton, Ont.
McArthur, Alex., & Co., Montreal, Que.
Wilson, Ltd., J. C., 61 St. Alexander st., Montreal, Que.

FIBRE BOARD.
Bennett, Ltd., Chambly Canton, Que.
Hinde & Dauch Paper Co. of Canada, Ltd., Toronto, Ont.
Richard & Co., 161 Arago St., Quebec.
Walker, J. R., & Co., Ltd., 35 Common, Montreal, Que.

Lombard's English Newcastle Pulp Stones

Classified List—Canada

FILLED BOARD.
Northumberland Paper & Electric Co., Campbellford, Ont.

FLOUR SACK.
Eddy, The E. B., Co., Ltd., Hull, Que.

FOLDER.
McArthur & Co., Ltd., Alex., Montreal, Que.
St. Lawrence Paper Mills, Mille Roches, Ont.

FOLDING BOX BOARDS.
Booth, J. R., Ottawa, Ont.
Canada Boxboard Co., 182 Shearer, Montreal, Que.
Jonquieres Pulp Co., Ltd., Jonquieres, Que.
Montreal Boxboard Co., Ltd., Montreal, Que.
Northumberland Paper & Electric Co., Ltd., Campbellford, Ont.

FOLDING WOOD BOARDS.
Laurentide Co., Grand Mere, Que.

FRICTION BOARD.
Walker, J. R., & Co., Ltd., 35 Common, Montreal, Que.
Richard & Co., 161 Arago, Quebec.

FRUIT WRAPPING.
Interlake Tissue Mills, Ltd., Merritton, Ont.

GLASSINE.
Lincoln Paper Mills Co., Ltd., Merritton, Ont.

GREASEPROOF.
Lincoln Paper Mills Co., Ltd., Merritton, Ont.

HANGING.
Booth, J. R., Ottawa, Can.
Ford, Joseph, & Co., Portneuf Station, Portneuf Co., Que.
McArthur, Alex., & Co., Ltd., Montreal, Que.
Spanish River Pulp & Paper Mills. Ltd., Sault Ste. Marie, Ont.

HARDWARE.
Bird & Son, Ltd., Hamilton Ont.
Dominion Paper Co., Montreal, Que.
Fisher & Son, Ltd., John, Dundas, Ont.
McArthur, Alex., & Co., Ltd., Montreal, Que.

INSULATING.
Bird & Son, Ltd., Hamilton, Ont.
Eastern Paper Co., Ltd., St. Basile Station, Portneuf Co., Que.

JUTE.
Hinde & Dauch Paper Co. of Canada, Ltd., The, Toronto, Ont.
Lincoln Paper Mills Co., Merritton, Ont.

KRAFT.
Brompton Pulp & Paper Co., East Angus, P. Q.
Dominion Paper Co., Montreal.
Dryden Timber & Power Co., Ltd., Dryden, Ont. (Sheathing.)
Interlake Tissue Mills, Ltd., Merritton, Ont.
Lincoln Paper Mills Co., Ltd., Merritton, Ont.
McArthur, Alex., & Co., Ltd., Montreal, Que.
Pacific Mills, Vancouver, B. C.
Wayagamack Pulp & Paper Co. Three Rivers, P. Q.

HARDY S. FERGUSON
CONSULTING ENGINEER
200 FIFTH AVENUE
NEW YORK CITY

PAPER, PULP AND FIBRE MILLS
WATER POWER DEVELOPMENT
DAMS, STORAGE RESERVOIRS AND
OTHER HYDRAULIC STRUCTURES

PRESS ROLLS Maple and Gum White Wood Felt Rolls
J. W. HEWITT MACHINE CO. Neenah, Wis.

ARE SUPERIOR TO ALL OTHERS. ALL SIZES IN STOCK.
LOMBARD & CO., Importers & Manufacturers, 236 & 238 A Street, Boston.

Classified List—Canada 327

LABEL.
Provincial Paper Mills Co., Ltd., Bell Tel. Bldg., Toronto, Ont.

LEATHER BOARD.
Canadian Leatherboard Co., Ltd., Chambly Canton, Que.
Richard & Co., 161 Arago, Quebec.
Walker, J. R., & Co., 35 Common, Montreal, Que.

LEDGER.
Eddy, Ltd., Co., The, Hull, Que.
Rolland, The, Paper Co., 142 St. Paul, W., Montreal, Que.
Smith, Howard, Paper Mills, Ltd., 138 McGill, Montreal, Que.
Toronto Paper Mfg. Co., Ltd., Cornwall, Ont.

LINEN.
Rolland Paper Co., The, 142 St. Paul W., Montreal.

LINING.
Joseph Ford & Co., Portneuf Station, Portneuf, Que.

LITHOGRAPH.
Eddy Co., The E. B., Ltd., Hull, Que.
Kinleith Paper Mills, Ltd., St. Catharines, Ont.
McArthur & Co., Ltd., Alex., Montreal, Que.
Provincial Paper Mills Co., Ltd., Bell Tel. Bldg., Toronto, Ont.
Rolland Paper Co., 142 St. Paul, W., Montreal, Que.
Toronto Paper Mfg. Co., Ltd., Cornwall, Ont.

MANIFOLD.
Eddy, The E. B., Co., Ltd., Hull, Que.
Interlake Tissue Mills, Ltd., Merritton, Ont.

MANILA.
Brompton Pulp & Paper Co., East Angus, P. Q.
Canada Paper Co., Ltd., Windsor Mills, Que.
Dominion Paper Co., Montreal, Que.
Don Valley Paper Mills, Todmorden, Ont. (Sulphite.)
Eddy Co., The E. B., Ltd., Hull, Que.
Fisher, John, & Son, Ltd., Dundas, Ont.
Ford & Co., Joseph, Portneuf Station, Portneuf Co., Que.
Interlake Tissue Mills, Ltd., Merritton, Ont.
Jonquieres Pulp Co., Ltd., Jonquieres, Que.
Lincoln Paper Mills Co., Ltd., Merritton, Ont.
McArthur, Alex., & Co., Ltd., Montreal, Que.
St. Croix Paper Co., Ltd., Ellershouse, N. S.
Stutt, James, & Sons, West Flamboro, Ont.
Wilson, Ltd., J. C., 61 St. Alexander st., Montreal, Que.

MILL WRAPPERS.
Booth, J. R., Ottawa, Ont.
McArthur, Alex., & Co., Ltd., Montreal, Que.

NAPKIN PAPER.
Interlake Tissue Mills, Ltd., Merritton, Ont.

NEWS.
Abitibi Power & Paper Co., Ltd., Montreal.
Anglo-Newfoundland Development Co., Ltd., Grand Falls, N. F.
Belgo-Canadian Pulp and Paper Co., Shawinigan Falls, Que.
Booth, J. R., Ottawa, Ont.
Brompton Pulp & Paper Co., East Angus, Que.
Canada Paper Co., Ltd., Windsor Mills, Que.

DRY ROSIN SIZE

Brittle, easy soluble. Cheapest size out; cheaper than mill made size. Ask us about it. Also all other grades.

ARABOL M'F'G CO.
100 William St., New York

ENGINEERING FOR PULP, PAPER AND POWER PLANTS

JOSEPH H. WALLACE & CO.
INDUSTRIAL ENGINEERS
Temple Court Building, NEW YORK
71 Bay Street, TORONTO. C/

Lombard's English Newcastle Pulp Stones

Classified List—Canada

NEWS.
(CONTINUED.)

Donnacona Paper Co., Ltd., The, Donnacona, P. Q.
Eddy Co., The E. B., Ltd., Hull, Que.
Ford, Joseph, & Co., Portneuf Station, Portneuf Co., Que.
Fort Frances Pulp & Paper Co., Fort Frances, Ont.
Jonquieres Pulp Co., Ltd., Jonquieres, Que.
Lake Superior Paper Co., Ltd., Sales Office, Dayton, Ohio.
Laurentide Co., Grand Mere, Que.
McArthur, Alex., & Co., Ltd., Montreal, Que.
News Pulp & Paper Co., 275 Craig St., Montreal.
Ontario Paper Co., Ltd., Thorold, Ont.
Pacific Mills, Vancouver, B. C.
Powell River Co., Ltd. Offices at mill and 804 Standard Bk. Bldg., Vancouver, B. C., and Plymouth Bldg., Minneapolis, Minn.
Price Brothers & Co., Ltd., Jonquieres, Quebec, Can.
Spanish River Pulp & Paper Mills, Ltd., Sault Ste. Marie, Ont.
St. Croix Paper Co., Ltd., Ellershouse, N. S.
St. Maurice Paper Co., Cape Madeleine, Que.

NEWS BOARD.
Northumberland Paper & Electric Co., Campbellford, Ont.

POST CARD.
Don Valley Paper Co., Ltd., Toronto, Ont.

POSTER.
Don Valley Paper Co., Ltd., Toronto, Ont.
Eddy Co., The E. B., Ltd., Hull, Que.
McArthur, Alex., & Co., Ltd., Montreal, Que.
Provincial Paper Mills Co., Ltd., Bell Tel. Bldg., Toronto, Ont.

RAILROAD MANILA.
British, The, Canadian Wood Pulp & Paper Co., 313 Cordova, Vancouver, B. C.

ROOFING.
Bird & Son, Ltd., Hamilton, Ont.
Ford, Joseph, & Co., Portneuf Station, Portneuf Co., P. Q. (Felt.)
Ford, Rowland, & Son, Portneuf Station, Que. (Felt.)
McArthur, Alex., & Co., Ltd., Montreal, Que.
Walker, J. R., & Co., Ltd., 35 Common st., Montreal, Que.

ROPE MANILA.
Fisher, John, & Son, Ltd., Dundas, Ont.
Lincoln Paper Mills Co., Merritton, Ont.

SATURATING FELTS.
Ford, Joseph, & Co., Portneuf Station, Portneuf Co., Que.

SHEATHING.
Bird & Son, Ltd., Hamilton, Ont.
Dominion Paper Co., Montreal, Que.
Dryden Timber & Power Co., Ltd., (Kraft Sheathing.)
Eastern Paper Co., Ltd., St. Basile Station, Portneuf Co., Que. (Tarred.)
Ford & Son, Rowland, Portneuf Station, Portneuf Co., Que.
Ford, Joseph, & Co., Portneuf Station, Portneuf Co., Que.
Jonquieres Pulp Co., Ltd., Jonquieres, Que.
Laurentide Co., Ltd., Grand Mere, Que.
McArthur, Alex., & Co., Ltd., Montreal, Que.
Montreal Paper Co., Portneuf Station, Que. (Straw and Gray.)
St. Croix Paper Co., Ltd., Halifax, N. S.
Strathcona Paper Co., The, Strathcona, Ont.
Walker, J. R., & Co., Ltd., 35 Common, Montreal, Que.

DARMSTADT, SCOTT & COURTNEY, Inc. Importers, Exporters and Dealers in **PAPER MAKERS' SUPPLIES** Also Mfrs. of DEADENING and SATURATING FELTS
178 and 184 SOUTH STREET, NEW YORK

Ground Pulp & Sulphite Fibre Mill Machinery — OUR SPECIALTY
CARTHAGE MACHINE CO. CARTHAGE, N. Y.

SHOE BOARD.
Bennett, Ltd., Chambly Canton, Que.

SPECIALTIES.
Garden City Paper Mills Co., Ltd., St. Catherines, Ont. (Tissue.)
Hinde & Dauch Paper Co. of Canada, Ltd., Toronto, Ont. (Corrugated Papers.)
Interlake Tissue Mills, Ltd., Merritton, Can. (Crêpe.)
Northumberland Paper & Electric Co., Ltd., Campbellford, Ont.

STRAW BOARD.
Canada Boxboard Co., Ltd., 182 Shearen, Montreal, Que.
McArthur, Alex., & Co., Ltd., Montreal, Que.
Miller Bros. Co., Ltd., Glen Miller, Ont.
Northumberland Paper & Electric Co., Campbellford, Ont.

STRAW WRAPPING.
McArthur, Alex., & Co., Ltd., Montreal, Que.

TAG.
Booth, J. R., Ottawa, Ont.
Don Valley Paper Co., Toronto, Que.

TARRED.
Eastern Paper Co., Ltd., St. Basile Station, Portneuf Co., Que.
Eddy, The E. B., Co., Ltd., Hull, Que.

TEA.
Eddy Co., The E. B., Ltd., Hull, Que.

TEST BOARD.
Booth, J. R., Ottawa, Ont.

TISSUE.
Eddy, The E. B., Co., Ltd., Hull, Que. (Copying.)
Garden City Paper Mills, Ltd., St. Catherines, Ont.
Interlake Tissue Mills, Ltd., Merritton, Ont. (M. G.)
Wilson, Ltd., J. C., 61 St. Alexander, Montreal, Que.

TISSUE MANILA.
Eddy, The E. B., Co., Ltd., Hull, Que.
Interlake Tissue Mills, Ltd., Merritton, Ont.
Wilson, Ltd., J. C., 61 St. Alexander, Montreal, Que.

TISSUE, WHITE AND COLORED.
Interlake Tissue Mills, Ltd., Merritton, Ont.

TOBACCO.
Ford, Joseph, & Co., Portneuf Station, Portneuf Co., Que.

TOILET.
Eddy, The E. B., Co., Ltd., Hull, Que.
Garden City Paper Mills, Ltd., St. Catharines, Ont.
Interlake Tissue Mills, Ltd., Merritton, Ont. (Plain and Crepe.)

TOWELING.
Interlake Tissue Mills, Ltd., Merritton, Ont.

TRUNK BOARD.
Walker, J. R., & Co., Ltd., 35 Common, Montreal, Que.

WALL BOARD.
Hinde & Dauch Paper Co. of Canada, Ltd., Toronto, Ont.

Lombard's English Newcastle Pulp Stones

Classified List—Canada

WAXING.
Fisher, John, & Son, Ltd., Dundas, Ont.
Interlake Tissue Mills, Ltd., Merritton, Ont.

WEDDING.
Rolland Paper Co., The, 142 St. Paul St., Montreal.

WOOD PULP BOARD.
Beaver Wood Fibre Co., Thorold, Ont.
Booth, J. R., Ottawa, Ont.
Canada Boxboard Co., Ltd., 182 Shearer, Montreal, Que.
Eddy, The E. B., Co., Ltd., Hull, Que.
Fisher, John & Son, Dundas, Ont.
Laurentide Co., Ltd., Grand Mere, Que.
Miller Bros. Co., Ltd., Glen Miller, Ont.
Northumberland Paper & Electric Co., Ltd., Campbellford, Ont.
St. Croix Paper Co., Ltd., Halifax, N. S.

WRAPPING.
Bird & Son, Ltd., Hamilton, Ont.
Brompton Pulp & Paper Co., East Angus, Que.
Canada Paper Co., Ltd., Montreal, Que.
Dominion Paper Co., Montreal, Que.
Dryden Timber & Power Co., Ltd., Dryden, Ont.
Eastern Paper Co., Ltd., St. Basile Station, Portneuf, Que.
Eddy, The E. B., Co., Ltd., Hull, Que.
Fisher, John. & Son, Ltd., Dundas, Ont.
Ford, Joseph, Portneuf Station, Portneuf Co., Que.
Interlake Tissue Mills, Ltd., Merritton, Ont. (Light Weight.)
Lincoln Paper Mills Co., Ltd., Merritton, Ont.
McArthur, Alex., & Co., Ltd., Montreal, Que.
St. Croix Paper Co., Ltd., Halifax, N. S.
Wilson, Ltd., J. C., 61 St. Alexander st., Montreal, Que.
Wayagamack Pulp & Paper Co., Three Rivers, P. Q.

WRITING.
Canada Paper Co., Ltd., Windsor Mills, Que.
Eddy Co., The E. B., Ltd., Hull, Que.
Kinleith Paper Mills, Ltd., St. Catharines, Ont.
Provincial Paper Mills Co., Ltd., Bell Tel. Bld., Toronto, Ont.
Rolland Paper Co., 142 St. Paul, Montreal, Que.
Smith, Howard, Paper Mills, Ltd., 138 McGill, Montreal, Que.
Toronto Paper Mfg. Co., Ltd., Cornwall, Ont.

COLONY OF NEWFOUNDLAND
NEWS.
Anglo-Newfoundland Development Co., Ltd., Grand Falls

PLEASE
LET US HEAR FROM YOU IF YOU NEED A
MILL SLITTER

KIDDER PRESS CO. DOVER, N. H.

New York, 261 Broadway Boston, 184 Summer St.
Gibbs-Brower Co., Agents Toronto, 445 King St. West

PRESS ROLLS Maple and Gum White Wood Felt Rolls J. W. HEWITT MACHINE CO. Neenah, Wis.

ARE SUPERIOR TO ALL OTHERS. ALL SIZES IN STOCK.
LOMBARD & CO., Importers & Manufacturers, 236 & 238 A Street, Boston.

M. GOTTESMAN & CO., Inc.
14 E. 41st STREET, NEW YORK. Cable Address "Nammettoq"
EUROPEAN OFFICES: Stockholm, Sweden

Strong and Easy Bleaching SULPHITE PULP

LIST OF
PULP MILLS of CANADA

CLASSIFIED ACCORDING TO GOODS MADE

GROUND WOOD.

Abitibi Power & Paper Co., Ltd., Montreal.
Beaver Wood Fibre Co., Thorold, Ont.
Belgo-Canadian Pulp and Paper Co., Shawinigan Falls, Que.
Booth, J. R., Ottawa, Ont.
Bronson Company, The, Ottawa, P. Q.
Brompton Pulp & Paper Co., East Angus, P. Q.
Campbell Lumber Co., Ltd., Weymouth, N. S.
Canada Boxboard Co., Ltd., 182 Shearer, Montreal.
Canada Paper Co., Ltd., Windsor Mills, Que.
Chicoutimi Pulp Co., Chicoutimi, Que
Clyde River Pulp & Paper Co., Clyde River, N. S.
Compagne de Pulp de Chicoutimi, Chicoutimi, Que.
Dominion Paper Co., Montreal, Que.
Donnacona Paper Co., Ltd., The, Donnacona, P. Q.
Eddy Co., The E. B., Ltd., Hull, Que.
Fibre Products, Ltd., 95 King, E., Toronto.
Foley-Krieger Pulp and Paper Co., Thorold, Ont.
Fort Frances Pulp & Paper Co., Fort Frances, Ont.
Great Eastern Paper Co., Grand Falls, Madeleine River, Gaspe.
Gulf Pulp & Paper Co., 17 St. James, Que.
Hydro-Electric Power Commission Pulp Mill, Campbellford, Ont.
Jonquières Pulp Co., Ltd., Jonquières, Que.
La Have Pulp Co., Ltd., Bridgewater, N. S.
Lake Megantic Pulp Co., Lake Megantic, Que.
Lake Superior Paper Co., Ltd., Sales Office, Dayton, Ohio.
Lotbiniere Lumber Co., Nicolet Falls, Que.
Laurentide Co., Ltd., Grand Mere, Que.

Maclaren Co., Ltd., The James, Buckingham, Que.
MacLeod Pulp Co., Ltd., Liverpool, N. S.
Medway Pulp & Power Co., Mill Village, Que.
Metabetchouan Co., Quebec.
Nairn Falls Power & Pulp Co., Ltd., Murray Bay, P. Q.
News Pulp & Paper Co., 275 Craig St., Montreal.
Ontario Paper Co., Ltd., The, Thorold, Ont.
Pacific Mills, Ltd., Standard Bank Bldg., Vancouver.
Peerless Pulp Co., Ltd., Thorold, Ont.
Powell River Co., Ltd. Offices at mill and Standard Bank Bldg., Vancouver, B. C., and Plymouth Bldg., Minneapolis, Minn.
Price Bros. & Co., Ltd., Jonquières, P. Q.
Price-Porritt Pulp and Paper Co., Rimouski, Que.
Quebec & Saguanay Pulp Co., St. Amedee de Perribonka, Que.
Rainy River Pulp & Paper Co., Standard Bank Bldg., Vancouver, B. C.
Riordan Pulp & Paper Co., Ltd., 355 Beaver Hall sq., Montreal.
River-du-Loup Pulp Co., Ltd., Frazerville, Que.
Soucy, F. Florentine, Old Lake road. Que.
Spanish River Pulp and Paper Mills, Ltd., Sault Ste. Marie, Ont.
St. Croix Paper Co., Ltd., Ellershouse, N. S.
St. George Pulp and Paper Co., Norwalk, Conn., U. S. A.
St. Maurice Paper Co., Ltd., Cap Madeleine, Que.
Thorold Pulp Co., Ltd., Thorold. Ont.
Union Bag & Paper Corp., Woolworth Bldg., New York City.
Wilson, J. C., Ltd., 61 St. Alexander Montreal, Que.

ENGINEERING FOR PULP, PAPER AND POWER PLANTS

JOSEPH H. WALLACE & CO.
INDUSTRIAL ENGINEERS
Temple Court Building, NEW YORK
71 Bay Street,   TORONTO, CAN

Lombard's English Newcastle Pulp Stones

SODA FIBRE.

British Canadian Wood Pulp & Paper Co., Ltd., 711 Dominion Trust Bldg., Vancouver, B. C.
Canada Paper Co., Ltd., Windsor Mills, Que.

Bathurst Lumber Co., Ltd., Bathurst, N. B.
Brown Corporation, 404 Commercial, Portland, Me.
Brompton Pulp & Paper Co., East Angus, P. Q.
Dominion Paper Co., Montreal.
Dryden Timber & Power Co., Ltd., Dryden, Ont.

Abitibi Power & Paper Co., Montreal.
Bathurst Lumber Co., Ltd., Bathurst, N. B.
Belgo-Canadian Pulp & Paper Co., Ltd., Shawinigan Falls, Que.
Booth, J. R., Ottawa, Can.
Colonial Pulp & Paper Mills, Quatsino Sound, B. C.
Dominion Pulp Co., Ltd., Chatham, N. B.
Donnacona Paper Co., Ltd., The, Donnacona, P. Q.
Eddy Co., The E. B., Ltd., Hull, Que.
Fraser Companies, Edmundston, N. B.
Ha! Ha! Bay Sulphite Co., Ltd., Bogotville, Que.
Lake Superior Paper Co., Ltd., Sales Office, Dayton, Ohio.
Laurentide Co., Grand Mere, Que.
Mattagami Pulp & Paper Co., Bank of Hamilton Bldg., Toronto, Ont.
Nashwaak Pulp & Paper Co., St. John, N. B.

Dominion Paper Co., Montreal, Que.
Provincial Paper Mills Co., Ltd., Bell Tel. Bldg., Toronto.

SULPHATE.

New Brunswick Sulphate Fibre Co., Ltd., Millerton, N. B.
Pacific Mills, Ltd., Vancouver, B. C.
Rainy River Pulp & Paper Co., Standard Bank Bldg., Vancouver, B. C.
St. Maurice Paper Co., Ltd., Cap Madeleine, Que.
Wayagamack Pulp & Paper Co., Three Rivers, Que.

SULPHITE FIBRE.

Pacific Mills, Ltd., Vancouver, B. C.
Port Arthur Pulp & Paper Co., Ltd., Port Arthur, Ont.
Powell River Co., Ltd. Offices at mill and Standard Bk. Bldg., Vancouver, and Plymouth Bldg., Minneapolis, Minn.
Price Bros. & Co., Ltd., Jonquières P. Q.
Riordan Pulp & Paper Co., Ltd., No 355 Beaver Hall Square, Montreal Que.
Spanish River Pulp & Paper Mills, Ltd., Sault Ste. Marine, Ont.
St. Lawrence Pulp & Lumber Co. Chandler, P. Q.
St. Maurice Paper Co., Ltd., Cap Madeleine, Que.
Toronto Paper Mfg. Co., Ltd., Cornwall, Ont.
Western Canada Wood Pulp & Paper Co., Ltd., Victoria, B. C.
Whalen Pulp & Paper Mills, Ltd., Merchants' Bank Bldg., Vancouver, B. C.

COLONY OF NEWFOUNDLAND.

GROUND WOOD.

Anglo-Newfoundland Development Co., Grand Falls.
Horwood Lumber Co., Ltd., St. John.

Reed, Albert E., & Co., Bishops Falls.

SULPHITE.

Anglo-Newfoundland Development Co., Grand Falls.

CHIPPERS We make a specialty of GROUND WOOD PULP and SULPHITE FIBRE MACHINERY | **Carthage Machine Co.** CARTHAGE, N. Y.

ARE SUPERIOR TO ALL OTHERS. ALL SIZES IN STOCK.
LOMBARD & CO., Importers & Manufacturers, 236 & 238 A Street, Boston.

A CLASSIFIED LIST
OF SOME OF THE MAKERS OF
PAPER SPECIALTIES
IN THE
UNITED STATES

NOTE. The list which was published for the first time six years ago is intended to include the names and addresses of the concerns that convert paper to special uses not covered in the other lists to be found in the Directory. Although only six years old, this section of the book has been greatly extended. But even with the hundreds of new names the list is far from complete, as the task of gathering all these special converters of paper is a difficult one, many of them being small producers and having little connection with the paper trade beyond the fact that they depend on paper as their chief raw material. Because of the difficulty of collecting a list of makers of Paper Specialties, the publishers of Lockwood's Directory would be glad to hear from concerns whose product should be included in this department; they would, too, be thankful for information from members of the trade for suggestions that will disclose the names, addresses and product of any of these innumerable users of paper for special purposes.

The Classified List of Goods Made by the Mills should be consulted in connection with this list.

ABSORBENT PAPER COTTON.
Howard Co., The, Norwood, Pa.

ACID PROOF.
Impervious Paper Products Co., Scranton, Pa.
Ralston, W., & Co., Ltd., Niagara Falls, N. Y.

ADDING MACHINE.
Beck, Chas., Co., 607 Chestnut, Philadelphia, Pa.
Camden Paper Co., Inc., Utica, N. Y.
Colonial Company, Mechanic Falls, Me.
Dudley Paper Co., Lansing, Mich.
ELLIOTT, W. R., CO., Boston, Mass.
Gurney Bros. Co., 1404 W. 3d, Cleveland, Ohio.
Henry, A. J., Co., Camden, N. Y.
Irish, Geo., Paper Corp., Buffalo, N. Y.
Int. Roll Paper Co., No. Manchester, Ind.
Latimer, Jr., E., 321 Chestnut, Philadelphia, Pa.
Linde, J. E., & Co., 84 Beekman, N. Y.
Manhattan Paper Co., 68 Wooster, New York.
Menasha Printing Co., Menasha, Wis.
Michigan Paper Co., Plainwell, Mich.
New York & Brooklyn Paper Co., 321 Pearl, New York City, N. Y.
Paper Manufacturers Co., Inc., 526 Cherry, Philadelphia.
PERRY, C. E., & CO., INC., 77 Washington North, Boston, Mass.
Pomeroy Paper Co., 1320 Advertisers' Bldg., Chicago.
Ralston, W., & Co., Ltd., Niagara Falls, N. Y.
Rockwell-Barnes Co., Munn bldg., Chicago, Ill.
Tuttle Press Co., Appleton, Wis.
Union Paper & Twine Co., Cleveland, O.
Union Paper & Twine Co. (of Michigan), Detroit, Mich.
Vermont Card Co., Burlington, Vt.
Western Penn. Paper Co., Pittsburgh, Pa.
Wheat Paper Co., Elkhart, Ind.
Wright, Chas. H., & Son, Kalamazoo, Mich.

E. J. KELLER CO., INC.
200 FIFTH AVENUE E. J. KELLER Pres. NEW YORK
FOREIGN AND DOMESTIC
Rags AND Wastes
Gunny Bagging, Burlap Bagging, Ropes, Flax, Hemp, Cotton Wastes, Paper Stock, Wood Pulp and Rag Pulp.

ENGINEERING FOR
PULP, PAPER AND POWER PLANTS
JOSEPH H. WALLACE & CO.
INDUSTRIAL ENGINEERS
Temple Court Building, NEW YORK
71 Bay Street, TORONTO, CAN.

Lombard's English Newcastle Pulp Stones

Paper Specialties

ADDING MACHINE—DUPLICATE.
American Sales Book Co., Elmira, New York.

ARTIFICIAL LEATHER.

Armitage Leather Co., 87 Congress, Detroit, Mich.
Barge, M. H., & Sons Co., Niagara and 7th, Buffalo, N. Y
Boston Art Leather Co., Stamford, Conn.
Chase, L. C., & Co., 89 Franklin, Boston, Mass.
De Jonge, Louis, Co., Fitchburg, Mass.
Diamond State Fibre Co., Elsmere, Del.
Fibre Finishing Co., Worcester, Mass.
FABRIKOID DEPT., DuPont Powder Co., Wilmington, Del.
Gebhart Art Leather Co., 306 E. Water, Milwaukee, Wis.
Keratal Co., Newark, N. J.
Leatheroid Mfg. Co., Kunnebunk, Me.
Marokene Leather Co., 6 Fletcher, New York City, N. Y.
Nashua Spool & Bobbin Co., 262 Washington, Boston, Mass.
Neumann, R., & Co., 76 Worth, New York City, N. Y.
O'Bannen Corporation, West Barrington, R. I.
Pantasote Leather Co., Passaic. N. J.
Paper Specialty Co., Shelton, Conn.
Pope, A. W., Co., 108 Lincoln, Boston, Mass.
Rogers, S. B., Boston, Mass.
Sanford Mills, Sanford, Me.
Selser & Ballantyne, 232 E. Eighth, Cincinnati, Ohio.
Silcocks Miller Co., S. Orange, N. J.
Standard Oil Cloth Co., 320 Broadway, New York City, N. Y.
Textileather Co., 1182 Broadway, New York City, N. Y.
Weymuth Art Leather Co., E. Weymuth, Mass.

ARTISTS' ILLUSTRATION BOARDS.
Hurlock Bros. Co., Philadelphia, Pa.

AUTOMOBILE BAGS.

Keystone Roofing Mfg. Co., York Pa.
Angel, H. Reeve, & Co., Inc., 120 Liberty, New York.

AUTOMOBILE COVERS.

Herrlinger & Co., Cincinnati, Ohio.
Seinsheimer Paper Co., The, Cincinnati, Ohio.

AUTOMOBILE TIRE WRAP.

Angier Mills, Ashland, Mass.
Keystone Roofing Mfg. Co., York, Pa.
Paper Manufacturers Co., Inc., 507 Commerce, Philadelphia, Pa.
Ralston, W., & Co., Ltd., Niagara Falls, N. Y.
Roto-Photo Printing Co., New York.
SAFEPACK PAPER MILLS, Boston, Mass.

BAGS (SPECIAL).
CONTINENTAL PAPER BAG CO., 17 Battery pl., New York.

BANDAGES.
Howard Co., The, Norwood, Pa.

BARBERS' HEAD RESTS.

International Roll Paper Co., North Manchester, Ind.
Marvin, Gilbert E., Nekoosa, Wis.
Pomeroy Paper Co., 1320 Advertisers Bldg., Chicago.
Tuttle Press Co., Appleton, Wis.

BEER PLAQUES.
Cushman, John L., 280 Sip av., Jersey City, N. J.

HARDY S. FERGUSON, CONSULTING ENGINEER, 200 FIFTH AVENUE, NEW YORK CITY
PAPER, PULP AND FIBRE MILLS, WATER POWER DEVELOPMENT, DAMS, STORAGE RESERVOIRS AND OTHER HYDRAULIC STRUCTURES

PRESS ROLLS — Maple and Gum White Wood Felt Rolls — J. W. HEWITT MACHINE CO. Neenah, Wis.

Paper Specialties

BERRY BOXES.
Kalamazoo Fibre Package Co., Kalamazoo, Mich.
Sanitary Package Co., Kalamazoo, Mich.
STONE & FORSYTH CO., Boston.

BERRY PAILS.
Henderson Paper Co., Dayton, Ohio.

BLANKETS.
Flexible Paper Co., Shelton, Conn.
KALAMAZOO VEGETABLE PARCHMENT CO., Kalamazoo, Mich.
The Specialty Paper Co., Shelton, Conn.
STONE & FORSYTH CO., Boston.
Whitelaw Paper Blanket Co., Cincinnati, O.

BLANKS.
Lignistra Fibre Products Co., Barberton, Ohio.

BLASTING.
Megargee Bros., Scranton, Pa.
Nat'l Paper Co., Atlanta, Ga.
Paper Manufacturers Co., Inc., 507 Commerce, Philadelphia, Pa.
The Seinsheimer Paper Co., Cincinnati, Ohio.

BLUE PRINT.
Aloe, A. S., Co., St. Louis, Mo.
American Blue Print Paper Co., 294 Dearborn, Chicago, Ill.
Cole, H., Co., 82 N. High, Columbus, O.
Dietzgen, Eugene, Co., 181 Monroe, Chicago, Ill
Dietzgen, Eugene, Co., 119 W. 23d, New York.
Dietzgen, Eugene, Co., 14 1st, San Francisco, Cal.
Electric Blue Print Co., 1501 Sansom, Philadelphia.
Elliot, B. K., Co., 723 Liberty av., Pittsburg, Pa.
Indianapolis Blue Print & Supply Co., 154 N. Illinois, Indianapolis, Ind.
Keystone Blue Print Paper Co., 910 Filbert, Philadelphia, Pa.
Knickerbocker Blue Print Co., 2 E. 42d, New York.
Kolesch & Co., 138 Fulton, New York.
Keuffel & Esser Co., 127 Fulton, New York.
Makeplace, B. L., 387 Washington, Boston.
Mathias, A. H., & Co., Pittsburgh, Pa.
Moss, Chas. E., 38 Broad, Boston, Mass.
New York Blue Print Paper Co., 58 Reade, New York.
New York Multi-Color Copying Co., 25 Pearl, New York.
Post, Frederick, Co., 218 S. Clark, Chicago, Ill.
Soltman, E. G., 134 W. 29th, New York.
Spaulding Print Paper Co., 44 Federal, Boston, Mass.
United States Blue Print Paper Co., 319 La Salle, Chicago, Ill.
Weber, F., & Co., 1125 Chestnut Philadelphia, Pa.
Weber, F., & Co., 709 Locust, St. Louis, Mo.
Weber, F., & Co., 5 N. Charles, Baltimore, Md.
Weil, J. H., & Co., 13th and Arch Philadelphia, Pa.
Williams, Brown & Earle, 918 Chestnut, Philadelphia, Pa.

BOARDS (EMBOSSED).
Lignistra Fibre Products Co., Barberton, Ohio.

BON BON CUPS.
Dragon Paper Mfg. Co., 48 E. 15th, New York.
Howard Co., The, Norwood, Pa.

BOOK WRAPPERS.
Thompson & Norris Co., Brooklyn, N. Y.

Lombard's English Newcastle Pulp Stones

Paper Specialties

BOTTLE CAPS.

Boyd, John, 45 Lake, Chicago, Ill.
Chic Mfg. Co., Rochester, N. Y.
Creamery Supply Mfg. Co., Clinton Junction, Wis.
Cresco Creamery Supply Co., 189 E. Kinzie, Chicago, Ill.
Iron Clad Mfg. Co., Varet, Brooklyn, N. Y.
San-Lac Bottle Cap Co., 830 Broadway, N. Y.
Rayl, J. S., & Co., Marion, Ohio.
Sayford Paper Specialty Co., Vineland, N. J.
Smith-Lee Co., Oneida, N. Y.
Standard Cap Co., 739 King, Baltimore, Md.
Thatcher Mfg. Co., Kane, Pa.

BOTTLE PACKING.

Hinde & Dauche Paper Co., The, Sandusky, O.
Sefton Mfg. Co., The, Chicago, Ill.

BOTTLES.

American Paper Bottle Co., 227 N. 3d, Philadelphia, Pa.
Dayton Paper Bottle Co., Dayton, O.
Fonda Container Co., Inc., Fonda, N. Y.
Greenfield Paper Bottle Co., 8 W. 40th, New York.
Hygienic Liquid Package Co., 179 Lake, Chicago, Ill.
Mono-Service Bottle Co., Verona av. and Oraton, Newark, N. J.
Paper Products Co., 49-51 Terminal Way, S. S., Pittsburgh, Pa.
Purity Paper Bottle Co., Washington, D. C.
Purity Paper Bottle Co., New Orleans, La.
Robinson, Thos., Fonda, N. Y.
Single Service Corporation of America, New York City, N. Y.
Universal Paper Milk Bottle Co., 39 Cortlandt, N. Y. City.
Weis Mfg. Co., Monroe, Mich.

BOTTLE WRAPPERS.

Lawrence Paper Mfg. Co., Lawrence, Kan.
Nat'l Paper Co., Atlanta, Ga.

BOX AND BARREL LAYERS

Dixie Paper Mills, Inc., Richmond, Va.

BOX STAY.

IDEAL COATED PAPER CO., Brookfield, Mass.

BREAD WRAPPERS—(PRINTED).

California Tissue Mills, Los Angeles, Cal.
Central Waxed Paper Co., Central and Taylor, Chicago.
CONTINENTAL PAPER BAG CO., 17 Battery pl., New York.
Johnson, Geo. T., Co., Boston, Mass.
KALAMAZOO VEGETABLE PARCHMENT CO., Kalamazoo, Mich.
National Paper Co., Atlanta, Ga.
Ralston, W., & Co., Ltd., Niagara Falls, N. Y.
ROBERTSON PAPER CO., Bellows Falls, Vt.
The Seinsheimer Paper Co., Cincinnati, Ohio.
Waxide Paper Co., Kansas City, Mo.

BUILDING—WATERPROOF.

Angier Mills, Ashland, Mass.
Bird & Son, Inc., East Walpole, Mass.
Barber Asphalt Paving Co., Philadelphia.
Howard Co., The, Norwood, Pa.
Keystone Roofing Mfg. Co., York, Pa.
SAFEPACK PAPER MILLS, Boston, Mass.

BURLAP LINE PAPER.

Auer & Twitchell, Chestnut and 9th, Philadelphia.
Ralston, W., & Co., Niagara Falls, N. Y.

DARMSTADT, SCOTT & COURTNEY, Inc., 178 and 184 SOUTH STREET, NEW YORK
Importers, Exporters and Dealers in PAPER MAKERS' SUPPLIES
Also Mfrs. of DEADENING and SATURATING FELTS

Ground Pulp & Sulphite Fibre Mill Machinery OUR SPECIALTY — CARTHAGE MACHINE CO. CARTHAGE, N. Y.

BUTTER CARTONS.
Campbell Paper Box Co., South Bend, Ind.

BUTTER DISHES.
Bloomer Bros. Co., Newark, N. Y.
Consolidated Paper & Box Mfg. Co., Richmond, Va. (Waxed lined.)
Mullen Bros. Paper Co., St. Joseph, Mich.
Nat'l Paper Co., Atlanta, Ga.
Webb Folding Box Co., Bogota, N. J.
Wolfson Paper Co., Columbus, Ga.

BUTTER AND LARD WRAPS (PRINTED).
Glen Mills, 1005 Stephen Girard bldg., Philadelphia, Pa.
KALAMAZOO PARCHMENT PAPER COMPANY, Kalamazoo, Mich.
Patterson Parchment Paper Company, Passaic, N. J.
West Carrollton Parchment Co., West Carrollton, Ohio.

CAKE BOARDS.
Bleyer, Alfred, & Co., 229 West, New York.

CAKE BOXES.
Bloomer Bros., Newark, N. Y.

CAKE CIRCLES.
Bleyer, Alfred & Co., 229 West, New York City, N. Y.
Dragon Paper Mfg. Co., Inc., 48 W. 15th, New York.
KALAMAZOO VEGETABLE PARCHMENT CO., Kalamazoo, Mich.

CORRUGATED CAKE CIRCLES.
Bleyer, Alfred, & Co., 229 West, New York.

CALENDAR AND PHOTO MOUNT STOCK
Hurlock Bros. Co., Philadelphia, Pa.
Ragenstein-Veedor Co., 1336 Halsted, Chicago.

CANDY PAILS.
Western Seamless Pail Co., Chicago.

CANISTERS.
Paper Canister Co., 3009 Chestnut, Philadelphia, Pa.

CANS.
American Can Co., 447 W. 14th, New York City, N. Y.
American Mono-Service Co., Bourse, Philadelphia, Pa.
Cadby & Son, Albany, N. Y.
Chicago Mailing Tube Co., 425 S. Hoyne, Chicago, Ill.
Chicago Paper Tube & Can Co., 168 N. May, Chicago, Ill.
Diamond State Fibre Co., Bridgeport, Pa.
Kemlweld Can Co., Detroit, Mich.
Levin, David R., 444 W. 31st, Chicago, Ill.
Portland Paper Box Co., Portland, Ore.
Ritchie, W. C., & Co., Van Buren and Green, Chicago, Ill.
St. Louis Paper Can & Tube Co., St. Louis, Mo.
Union Paper Co., 844 Washington, New York.
Wright, Edgar S., Bourse, Philadelphia, Pa.
Zellerbach Paper Co., San Francisco, Cal.

CAPS FOR HAYCOCKS.
Gair, Robt., Co., Brooklyn, N. Y.
Thompson & Norris Co., The, Brooklyn, N. Y.

Lombard's English Newcastle Pulp Stones

Paper Specialties

CARBON COPYING, DUPLICATING AND TRANSFER PAPERS.

Able & Willing Mfg. Co., 3715 Springfield, Philadelphia.
Allen, John & Co., 480 Pearl, New York.
American Ribbon & Carbon Co., Rochester, N. Y.
American Sales Book Co., Elmira, N. Y.
Apter Bros. Mfg. Co., 410-412 S. Fifth av., Chicago.
Ault & Wiborg Co., Seventh & Culbert, Cincinnati.
Bestwall Mfg. Co., 38 S. Dearborn, Chicago.
Black Diamond Ribbon & Carbon Co., Rochester, N. Y.
Blur Knot Carbon Co., 17 Montrose, Rochester, N. Y.
Brecher, E. A., & Co., 119 Lafayette, New York.
Buckeye Ribbon & Carbon Co., 311 St. Clair, Cleveland.
Carbonized Paper Co., Indianapolis, Noblesville, Ind.
Carter Ink Co., Cambridge, Mass.
Clark & Zugalla, 411 Warren, New York.
Columbus Carbon Co., Dayton, Ohio.
Columbia Carbon Paper Mfg. Co., Portland, Ore.
Columbia Ribbon & Carbon Co., 69 Wooster, New York.
Cooke, Douglas H., 18 Beaver, New York.
Consumers Mfg. Co., Earlville, N. Y.
Consumers Paper Co., Shicksbinny, Pa.
Copy Paper Co., Attleboro, Mass.
Corona Supply Co. Rochester, N. Y.
Crown Ribbon & Carbon Mfg. Co., Rochester, N. Y.
De Fl Mfg. Co., 150 Nassau, New York.
Detroit Coin Wrapper Co., 370 Harper av., Detroit, Mich.
Dodge Company, Syracuse, N. Y.
Downes & Co., 102 Fulton, New York.
Eastern Sales Book Co., Long Island City, N. Y.
Elliot, B. K., Co., 108 6th av., Pittsburgh, Pa.
Foyer, Chas. A., 1120 Prospect av., Cleveland, Ohio.
General Manifold Co., Franklin, Pa
Gerber, Hy., Co., 114 William, New York.
Heale, J. A., 96 John, New York.
Holyoke Carbon Paper Co., Holyoke, Mass.
Imperial Mfg. Co., 297 Washington, Newark, N. J.
International Carbon Co., 206 Broadway, New York.
Kee Lox Mfg. Co., Rochester, N. Y.
Keystone Carbon Paper Mfg. Co., Franklin, Pa.
King, John F., Co., N. Walpole, N. H.
Kruse Phillips Ink Co., 437 Pearl, New York.
Lakeside Specialty Co., 225 Dearborn, Chicago.
Lelvienthal & Co., 269 Dearborn, Chicago.
Little, A. P., Rochester, N. Y.
Linfoot Mfg. Co., 1708 Ludlow, Philadelphia, Pa.
Manifold Supplies Co., 188 3d av., Brooklyn, N. Y.
Mann, Wm., & Co., 529 Market, Philadelphia, Pa.
Miller, Bryant, Pierce, Aurora, Ill.
Mittag & Volger, Park Ridge, N. J.
Monarch Carbon Paper Co., Rochester, N. Y.
National Carbon & Paper Co., 220 Broadway, New York.
National Carbon Coated Paper Co., Sturgis, Mich.
New England Carbon Mfg. Co., 220 Devonshire, Boston, Mass.
New Era Mfg. Co., Covington, Ky.
Neidich Process Co., Burlington, N. J.
Neutric Chemical Co., 1319 Ridge av., Philadelphia, Pa.
Newton-Rotherick Mfg. Co., 32 S. Clinton, Chicago.
Non-Smut Carbon Mfg. Co., Rochester, N. Y.
Ohashi H., & Co., 395 Broadway, New York.
Pen Carbon Manifold Co., New Brunswick, N. J.
Pilot Ribbon & Carbon Co., Rochester, N. Y.
Premo Process Co., New Brunswick, N. J.
Rogers Manifold & Carbon Co., 3 Sullivan, New York.
Rothschild, M. N., 711 S. Dearborn, Chicago, Ill.
Royal Ribbon & Carbon Co., 14 Barclay, New York.
SMITH PAPER CO., Lee, Mass.
Snelling & Son, 225 34th, Brooklyn, N. Y.
Soltman, E. G., 136 W. 29th, New York.

PRESS ROLLS Maple and Gum White Wood Felt Rolls — J. W. HEWITT MACHINE CO. Neenah, Wis.

ARE SUPERIOR TO ALL OTHERS. ALL SIZES IN STOCK.
LOMBARD & CO., Importers & Manufacturers, 236 & 238 A Street, Boston.

Paper Specialties 339

CARBON COPYING, DUPLICATING AND TRANSFER PAPERS.
(CONTINUED.)

Stafford, S. S., 603 Washington, New York.
Storms, H. M., 11 Vanderwater, New York.
Straus, Hiram, & Co., 411 Frankfort av., Cleveland, Ohio.
Strip Carbon Co., Aurora, Ill.
Tempest, D. M., Co., Rochester, N. Y.
Thompson Carbon Co., Buffalo, N. Y.
Underwood, John, & Co., 30 Vesey, New York.
Union Ribbon & Carbon Co., 67 Laurel, Philadelphia.
U. S. Typewriter Ribbon Co., 806 Walnut, Philadelphia.
Vacuo Static Carbon Co., Rochester, N. Y.
Webster, F. S., & Co., 334 Congress, Boston, Mass.
Whitefield Paper Works, 33 Sullivan, New York.
Wood, Chas. H., & Co., 304 Randolph, Chicago.

CARNIVAL NOVELTIES.

Shackman B., & Co., 906 B'way, New York.
Zellerbach Paper Co., San Francisco, Cal.

CARPET LINING.

Angier Mills, Ashland, Mass.
SAFEPACK PAPER MILLS, Boston, Mass.
Thompson & Norris Co., Brooklyn, N. Y.

CARPETS.

Harvey Fibre Carpet Co., Janney and E. Allegheny av., Philadelphia, Pa.
Hodges, The, Fibre Carpet Co., 25 Madison, New York City, N. Y.

CARTONS.

American Paper Products Co., St. Louis.
Collins, H. L., Co., St. Paul, Minn. Folding.
National Folding Box & Paper Co., 132 Franklin, New York City, N. Y. Wine and Liquor.
National Paper Co., Atlanta, Ga.
Paper Products Co., Inc., Quincy, Ill.
Portland Paper Package Co., Portland, Ore.
St. Louis Paper Can & Tube Co., 3100 N. Broadway, St. Louis, Mo.
STONE & FORSYTH CO., Boston.
Sutherland Paper Co., Kalamazoo, Mich.
Thompson & Norris Co., The, Brooklyn, N. Y. (Corrugated.)
Union Paper Co., 844 Washington st., New York.

CASE LINING (WATERPROOF).

Angier Mills, Ashland, Mass.
Bird & Son, Inc., East Walpole, Mass.
Herrlinger & Co., Cincinnati, Ohio.
Keystone Roofing Mfg. Co., York, Pa.
Mansfield Co., Boston, Mass.
NATIONAL WATERPROOFING CO., 2129 Land Title Bldg., Philadelphia, Pa.
Ralston, W., & Co., Ltd., Niagara Falls, N. Y.
SAFEPACK PAPER MILLS, Boston, Mass.

CASH REGISTER.

"A. P. W." Paper Co., Albany, N. Y.
Burnham, Asa C., Camden, N. Y.
Eddy Paper Co., Three Rivers, Mich.
ELLIOTT, W. R., CO., Boston, Mass.
Henry, A. J., Co., Camden, N. Y.
International Roll Paper Co., No. Manchester, Ind.
New York & Brooklyn Paper Co., 321 Pearl, New York City, N. Y.
Paper Manufacturers Co., Inc., 526 Cherry, Philadelphia, Pa.
PERRY, C. E., CO., INC., 77 Washington North, Boston, Mass.
Rockwell-Barnes Co., Munn bldg., Chicago, Ill.
Standard Cash Register Co., No. Manchester, Ind.
Vermont Card Co., Burlington, Vt.
Western Penna. Paper Co., Pittsburgh, Pa.
Whitaker Paper Co., Cincinnati, O.
Wilson & Towne Paper Co., 22 N Moore, New York City, N. Y.

ENGINEERING FOR PULP, PAPER AND POWER PLANTS

JOSEPH H. WALLACE & CO.
INDUSTRIAL ENGINEERS
Temple Court Building, NEW YORK
71 Bay Street, TORONTO, CAN.

M. GOTTESMAN & CO., Inc.
18 E. 41st STREET, NEW YORK. Cable Address "Namectog"
EUROPEAN OFFICES: Stockholm, Sweden
BLEACHED and UNBLEACHED
WOOD PULP OF ALL KINDS

Paper Specialties

CASH SALES PADS.
Reichard Bros., 13-17 Crosby, New York.

CELLOPHANE.
Franz Euler & Co., 73 Warren st., New York. (Imptrs.)

CHAIR SEATS.
Lignistra Fibre Products Co., Barberton, Ohio.
Lockport Leather Board Co., Lockport, New York City, N. Y.
Pemble, Wm., & Sons, Stillwater, N. Y.
The International Chair Seat Co., Scranton, Pa.

CHARLOTTE RUSSE CUPS.
Bloomer Bros. Co., Newark, N. Y.
Cushman, John L., 280 Sip av., Jersey City, N. J.
Dragon Paper Mfg. Co., 48 W. 15th, New York.
National Folding Box & Paper Co., The, New Haven, Conn.
STONE & FORSYTH CO., Boston.

CHECKS FOR KEY REGISTERS.
International Roll Paper Co., North Manchester, Ind.

CHEST PROTECTORS.
Specialty Paper Co., The, Shelton, Conn.

CHOCOLATE DIVIDERS.
Dragon Paper Mfg. Co., 48 W. 15th, New York.

CHOCOLATE LAYER BOARD.
Dragon Paper Mfg. Co., 48 W. 15th, New York.

CIGAR BOXES.
Cedarold Co., Buffalo, N. Y.

CIGAR HOLDERS.
Kalamazoo Label Co., Chicago, Ill.

CLOTH LINED.
Angier Mills, Ashland, Mass. (Waterproof.)
Gummed Products Co., Troy, Ohio.
IDEAL COATED PAPER CO., Brookfield, Mass.
Keystone Roofing Mfg. Co., York, Pa.
Ralston, W., & Co., Ltd., Niagara Falls, N. Y.
NASHUA CARD, GUMMED & COATED PAPER CO., Nashua, N. H.
Reversible Collar Co., The, Cambridge, Mass.
SAFEPACK PAPER MILLS. Boston, Mass. (Waterproof.)
United Mfg. Co., Springfield, Mass.

COATED PAPER AND BOARD.
(See Glazed, Coated Paper & Board Mnfrs.)

COIN CARDS AND WRAPPERS.
Acorn Card Co., Albany, N. Y.
Bodoni Press, North Tonawanda, N. Y.
Detroit Coin Wrapper Co., Detroit, Mich.
Dorton, J. H., Co., Camden, N. J.
Ideal Coin Container Co., White Plains, N. Y.
Spies, John, Watertown, N. Y.
Winthrop Press, 141 E. 25th, New York.

COLLARS.
United Mfg. Co., 7 Waverly pl., New York City, N. Y.
Ward Mfg. Co., 88 Spring, New York City, N. Y.

Paper Specialties

COMBS.
Scott Paper Co., 7th and Glenwood av., Philadelphia, Pa.

CONES AND SHELLS.
Lowell Paper Tube Corp., Lowell, Mass.
Nat'l Paper Co., Atlanta, Ga.

CONFECTIONERS' PAPER SPECIALTIES.
Dragon Paper Mfg. Co., Inc., 48 W. 15th, New York.

CONFETTI.
Dennison Mfg. Co., Boston, Mass.
Gottlieb, A., & Sons Co., 54 S. 2d, Brooklyn, N. Y.
Zellerbach Paper Co., San Francisco, Cal.

CONTAINER BOARD LINED WITH GREASE PROOF
Rhode Island Card Board Co., Pawtucket, R. I.

CONTAINERS (SANITARY).
American Paper Products Co., St. Louis.
Penn Package Co., Harrisburg, Pa.
Fonda Container Co., Inc., Fonda, N. Y.

COOKERY BAGS.
CONTINENTAL PAPER BAG CO., 17 Battery pl., New York.
Union Bag & Paper Corp., Woolworth Bldg., New York.

CORES.
Climax Tube Co., 114 State, Boston, Mass.
ELIXMAN PAPER CORE CO., Corinth, N. Y.
Lowell Paper Tube Corp., Lowell, Mass.

CORK LINED.
Thompson & Norris Co., The, Brooklyn, N. Y.

CORRUGATED (ARTICLES).
American Corrugated Paper Co., 515 W. 26th, New York City, N. Y.
American Paper Products Co., St. Louis.
Corrugated Paper Products Co., 221 W. 26th, New York.
Detroit Corrugating Co., Detroit, Mich.
Fenton Fibre Box Co., N. Tonawanda, N. Y.
Fort Wayne Corrugated Paper Co., Fort Wayne, Ind.
Gair, Robert, Co., Washington cor. Plymouth, Brooklyn, N. Y.
Globe Paper Co., Evansville, Ind. Boxes.
Hinde & Dauch Paper Co., Sandusky, O.
Hummel & Dowling, Milwaukee, Wis.
Illinois Glass Co., Alton, Ill.
Lawrence Paper Mfg. Co., Lawrence, Kan.
National Corrugated Box Co., 590 W. 152d, New York City, N. Y.
N. Y. Tube & Corrugated Paper Co., 59 W. 10th, New York City, N. Y.
Park Novelty Co., 1211 Noble, Philadelphia, Pa.
Phillips, Thos., Co., Akron, O.
Portland Paper Package Co., Portland, Ore.
Richmond Corrugated Paper Co., Richmond, Va. Boards and boxes.
Sefton Mfg. Co., Chicago, Ill., and Bush Terminal, Brooklyn, N. Y.
Schmidt & Ault Paper Co., York, Pa.
Thompson & Norris Co., The, Prince and Concord, Brooklyn, N. Y.
Turner Bros. Co., Terre Haute, Ind.
Warner & Childs Co., Medford, Mass.

CORRUGATED BOARD SHIPPING CONTAINERS.
American Paper Products Co., St. Louis.
Thompson & Norris Co., The, Brooklyn, N. Y.

Paper Specialties

CORRUGATED FIBRE CASES.
Indiana Fibre Products Co., Marion, Ind.

CREAM CUPS.
Mono-Service Bottle Co., 89 Cortlandt, New York City, N. Y.

CREPE PAPER.
American Novelty Paper Co., 54 Murray st., New York.
Badger Tissue Mills, Kaukauna, Wis.
Bainbridge's, Chas. T., Sons, Brooklyn, N. Y.
Consumers Paper Mills, 15 Beekman, New York City.
Dennison Mfg. Co., Framingham, Mass.
Erving Mills, Erving, Mass.
Kaukauna Paper Novelty Co., Kaukauna, Wis.
Neben Mfg. Co., 137 Beekman, New York.
Papyrus, The, Co., Kenilworth, N. J.
Perseverance Paper Mills, Produce Exch. Bldg., New York.
Robertson & Co., W. F., Hinsdale, N. H.
Tuttle Press Co., Appleton, Wis. Plain and decorated.

CRIMPED BON BON CUPS.
Dragon Paper Mfg. Co., 48 W. 15th, New York.

CRINKLED.
Carthage Tissue Paper Mills, Carthage, N. Y.
Consumers' Paper Mills, 15 Beekman, New York City.
Erving Mills, Erving, Mass.
National Paper Supply Co., 132 Nassau, New York City.
Papyrus, The, Co., Kenilworth, N. J.
Perseverance Paper Mills, Produce Exch. Bldg., New York.
Schmidt & Ault Paper Co., York, Pa.
Scott Paper Co., 7th and Glenwood av., Philadelphia, Pa.

CURRENCY STRAPS.
Bodoni Press, North Tonawanda, N. Y.
Gaylord Bros., Syracuse, N. Y.

CUSPIDORS.
Howard Co., The, Norwood, Pa.
National Paper Co., Atlanta, Ga.
STONE & FORSYTH CO., Boston, Mass.
Schofield, F. E., Mt. Vernon, N. Y.
Wolfson Paper Co., Columbus, Ga.

DECALCOMANIA.
Brown-Sinraium Co., St. James Bldg., New York, N. Y.
Rose & Frank Co., 136 W. 21st, New York.

DENTAL HEAD RESTS.
Lehigh Paper Mills, Inc., Raubsville, Pa.

DENTAL SANITARY PAPERS.
Lehigh Paper Mills, Inc., Raubsville, Pa.

DIAPERS.
Consumers' Paper Mills, 15 Beekman, New York City.
Lehigh Paper Mills, Inc., Raubsville, Pa.
Neben Mfg. Co., 137 Beekman, New York.

DIE CUT CARDS.
Otten Brothers Co., 24-26 Richmond av., Detroit, Mich.

DIE WIPING.
Paper Manufacturing Co., Inc., 507 Commerce, Philadelphia, Pa.

Paper Specialties

DISCS (FIBRE).

American Vulcanized Fibre Co., Wilmington, Del.
Continental Fibre Co., Newark Centre, Del.
Delaware Hard Fibre Co., Wilmington, Del.
Diamond State Fibre Co., Elsmere, Del.
Lignistra Fibre Products Co., Barberton, Ohio.
Parker, J. C., & Sons Co., New Castle, Del.
Wilmington Fibre Specialty Co., Wilmington, Del.

DISCS (PAPER).

Carborundum Co., Niagara Falls, N. Y.
KALAMAZOO VEGETABLE PARCHMENT CO., Kalamazoo, Mich. (Parchment.)
New York & Brooklyn Paper Co., 321 Pearl, New York City, N. Y.

DISH CLOTHS (PARCHMENT).

KALAMAZOO VEGETABLE PARCHMENT CO., Kalamazoo, Mich.

DISHES.

Atlas Mfg. Co., New Haven, Conn.
Aull Bros. Paper & Box Co., Dayton, O.
Bleyer, Alfred, & Co., 229 West. New York City, N. Y. Pie Plates.
Bloomer Brothers Co., Newark, N. Y.
Consolidated Paper & Box Mfg. Co., Richmond, Va.
Cupples, Samuel, Wooden Ware Co., St. Louis, Mo.
Dayton Paper Novelty Co., Dayton, O.
Dennison Mfg. Co., 26 Franklin, Boston, Mass.
Empire Paper & Wooden Ware Co., 162 N. Desplaines, Chicago, Ill.
Gair, Robert, Co., Brooklyn, N. Y.
Grasberger, B. A., & Co., Richmond, Va.
Hygienic Cup & Specialties Co., 122 S. Michigan av., Chicago, Ill.
International Folding Paper Box Co., 291 Monroe, N. Y. City, N. Y.
Keyes Fibre Co., Old Colony Bldg., Chicago, Ill.
Kinnard Mfg. Co., Dayton, O.
Mullen Bros. Paper Co., St. Joseph, Mich.
National Paper Co., Atlanta, Ga.
No-Leak Paper Butter Dish Co., Wheeling, W. Va.
Northern Bag & Plate Co., Carthage, N. Y.
Star Paper Dish Co., 11 N. 13th, Richmond, Va.
STONE & FORSYTH CO., Boston, Mass.
Webb Folding Box Co., Bogota, N. J.
Wolfson Tray Co., Columbus, Ga.

DOILIES.

Dennison Mfg. Co., Boston, Mass.
Japanese Tissue Mills, Holyoke, Mass.
Milwaukee Lace Paper Co., Milwaukee, Wis.
Western Engraving & Embossing Co., Chicago.

DRAWING PAPER.

Angel, H. Reeve, & Co., Inc., 120 Liberty, New York.

DRINKING CUPS.

American Blank Book Co., 150 Lafayette, New York City, N. Y.
American Paper Goods Co., Kensington, Conn.
American Water Supply Co., 215 Causeway, Boston, Mass.
Brown Bag Filling Machine Co., Fitchburg, Mass.
Burnitol Mfg. Co., Binford, Boston, Mass.
Chicago Oyster Pail Co. (Monarch Sanitary), Chicago, Ill.
Consumers' Paper Mills, 15 Beekman, New York City.
Cleveland Akron Sign Co., Cleveland, O. (Collapsible.)
Crystal Paper Drinking Cup Co., 3528 Lake av., Chicago, Ill.
Dennison Mfg. Co., 26 Franklin, Boston, Mass.

Lombard's English Newcastle Pulp Stones

Paper Specialties

DRINKING CUPS.
(CONTINUED.)

Dewar Drinking Cups (Weeks), 60 John, New York City, N. Y.
Howard Co., The, Norwood, Pa.
Hygienic Cup & Specialties Co., 122 S. Michigan av., Chicago, Ill.
Individual Drinking Cup Co., 220 W. 19th, New York City, N. Y.
Mansell, Hunt, Catty & Co., 22 Reade, New York City, N. Y.
Public Service Co., Harrisburg, Pa.
Public Service Cup Co., Bush Terminal, Brooklyn, N. Y.
Robertson, J. A., 2 Commercial, Newark, N. J.
Sanitary Drinking Cup Co., 339 S. Wabash av., Chicago, Ill.
Sanitary Paper Cup Co., 97 Oliver, Boston, Mass.
Sanitary Paper Products Co., 100 S. 4th, Philadelphia, Pa.
SHERMAN ENVELOPE CO., Worcester, Mass.
Spangler, E. J., 1245 N. Howard, Philadelphia, Pa.
Standard Single Service Co., East Pepperell, Mass.
STONE & FORSYTH CO., Boston.
The Sanitary Fountain and Vending Machine Co., Fulton Bldg., Pittsburgh, Pa.
U. S. Engraving Co., Worcester, Mass.
Wayne Paper Goods Co., Fort Wayne, Ind.
Wolf Bros., 12th and Callowhill, Philadelphia.

EGG CARRIERS.
(See also Oyster Pail & Egg Boxes).

American Paper Products Co., St. Louis.
Bloomer Bros., Newark, N. Y.
Chic Manufacturing Co., Rochester, N. Y.
CONTINENTAL PAPER BAG CO., 17 Battery pl., New York City.
United States Egg Carrier Co., Inc., Newark, N. Y.

EGG CARTONS.

American Paper Products Co., St. Louis.
Bloomer Bros. Co., Newark, N. Y.
CONTINENTAL PAPER BAG CO., 17 Battery pl., New York.
Keystone Egg Box & Filler Co., Railroad, York County, Pa.
Portland Paper Package Co., Portland, Ore.
Schurman, W. A., & Co., 365 E. Illinois, Chicago, and 257 Diamond, Philadelphia.
Self-Locking Carton Co., 507 S. Clinton, Chicago, Ill.

ELECTRICAL CABLE.

Endura Mfg. Co., Philadelphia, Pa.
Ralston, W., & Co., Ltd., Niagara Falls, N. Y.
Specialty Paper Co., The, Shelton, Conn.

ELECTRICAL CONDUIT TWINES.
Gates Paper Twine Co., Inc., Pleasantville, N. Y.

EMBOSSING.
Manhattan Paper Co., 68 Wooster, New York.
Wright, The Charles H., Paper Co., Middletown, Ohio.

EMBOSSED SEALS.
Dragon Paper Mfg. Co., 48 W. 15th, New York.

FABRICS.
The Le Clere Co., Philadelphia, Pa.

FIBRE SHIPPING CONTAINERS.

American Paper Products Co., St. Louis.
Bird & Son, Inc., East Walpole, Mass.
Boehme & Rauch Co., The, Monroe, Mich.
Gair, Robert, Co., Brooklyn, N. Y.
Portland Paper Package Co., Portland, Ore.

DARMSTADT, SCOTT & COURTNEY, Inc., Importers, Exporters and Dealers in PAPER MAKERS' SUPPLIES
Also Mfrs. of DEADENING and SATURATING FELTS
178 and 184 SOUTH STREET, NEW YORK

Ground Pulp & Sulphite Fibre Mill Machinery — OUR SPECIALTY
CARTHAGE MACHINE CO. CARTHAGE, N. Y.

Paper Specialties

FILE BACKS.
American Box & File Co., Atlanta, Ga.

FILES—Paperoid.
Alvah Bushnell Co., Philadelphia, Pa.

FILTER.
Angel, H. Reeve, & Co., Inc., 120 Liberty, New York.
Baker, J. T., Chemical Co., Phillipsburg, N. J.
Baker & Adamson Chemical Co., Easton, Pa.
Bausch & Lomb Optical Co., Rochester, N. Y.
Berge, J. & H., 95 John, New York City, N. Y.
Diamond State Fibre Co., Bridgeport, Pa.
Eimer & Amend, 3d av. and 18th, New York City, N. Y.
Hewitt, C. B., & Bros., 49 Beekman, New York City, N. Y.
Rose & Frank Co., 136 W. 21st, New York.
Sargent, E. H., & Co., 143 Lake, Chicago, Ill.
Scientific Materials Co., Pittsburgh, Pa.

FINGER BOWLS.
Sayford Paper Specialty Co., Vineland, N. J.

FINISHED PAPERS.
(Papers, Bristol Boards, Etc., Finished To Suit Any Needs).

Fibre Finishing Co., The, Greendale, Mass. C. D. Brown & Co., Boston, Mass., Selling Agents.
Wright, Charles H., Middletown, Ohio.

FLEXIBLE PAPER.
Endura Mfg. Co., Philadelphia, Pa.
Howard Co., The, Norwood, Pa.
Rose & Frank Co., 136 W. 21st, New York.
Specialty Paper Co., The, Shelton. Conn.

FLEXOLOID.
Franz Euler & Co., 73 Warren, New York.

FLINT, EMERY AND SAND PAPER.
American Glue Co., Boston, Mass.
Armour Sand Paper Co., Chicago, Ill.
Baeder, Adamson & Co., Philadelphia, Pa.
Barton, H. H., & Sons Co., Inc., Philadelphia, Pa.
Behr, Herman, & Co., 75 Beekman, New York City, N. Y.
Carborundum Co., Niagara Falls, N. Y.
Manning Sand Paper Co., Troy, N. Y.
Minnesota Mining Mfg. Co., St. Paul, Minn.
U. S. Sand Paper Co., Williamsport, Pa.
Wausau Sandpaper Co., Wausau, Wis.

FLORISTS SHIPPING BOXES.
Thompson & Norris Co., Brooklyn, N. Y.

FLOWERS.
Kern Commercial Co., 114 Liberty, New York City, N. Y. Light weights for artificial flowers.

FLY PAPER.
Grand Rapids Sticky Fly Paper Co., Grand Rapids, Mich.
I X L Fly Paper Co., Rochester, N.Y.
Maumee Paper Co. (Porous), Maumee, Ohio.
Richardson Paper Co., Lockland, O.
Thum, O. W., & Co., Grand Rapids, Mich.

Paper Specialties

FOOD CONTAINERS.
Ahdawagam Paper Products Co., Grand Rapids, Wis.

FOOT PROTECTORS.
KALAMAZOO VEGETABLE PARCHMENT CO., Kalamazoo, Mich.

FRUIT WRAPPERS.
Crown Paper Co., Sanford, Fla.

GARMENT CONTAINERS.
CONTINENTAL PAPER BAG CO., 17 Battery pl., New York City.

GASOLINE PROOF PAPER.
Fibre Finishing Co., Worcester, Mass.

GELATINE SHEETS.
Arlington Co., 725 Broadway, New York.
Gelatine Products Co., 217 East Baltimore, Baltimore, Md.
Rose & Frank Co., 136 W. 21st, New York.

GIFT BOXES.
Dennison Mfg. Co., 26 Franklin, Boston, Mass.
The Tuttle Press Co., Appleton, Wis.

GLASSELOID.
Franz Euler & Co., 73 Warren, New York.

GLASSINE.
Diamond State Fibre Co., Bridgeport, Pa.
HARTFORD CITY PAPER CO., Hartford City, Ind.
Herrlinger & Co., Cincinnati, Ohio.
Rose & Frank Co., 136 W. 21st, New York.
Transatlantic Paper Co., Inc., 50 Franklin, New York.
Warren Mfg. Co., Woolworth Bldg., New York, N. Y.
Westfield River Paper Co., Westfield, Mass.

GLAZE COATED AND BOARD MANUFACTURERS.
(See Table of Contents for Location of this Department)

GOLD SEAL PAPERS.
Ideal Coated Paper Co., Brookfield, Mass.

GOLD WRAPS.
Rose & Frank Co., 136 W. 21st, New York.

GRANITE WRITING AND ENVELOPES.
Manhattan Paper Co., 68 Wooster, New York.

GREASE-PROOF PAPERS.
American Writing Paper Co., Holyoke, Mass.
Card Board Co., Pawtucket, R. I.
Diamond State Fibre Co., Bridgeport, Pa.
Fibre Finishing Co., Worcester, Mass.
McDowell Paper Mills, Manayunk, Pa.
Philadelphia Wax Paper Co., Swarthmore, Pa.
Rhinlander Paper Co., Rhinlander, Wis.
Robertson, J. A., 2 Commercial, Newark, N. J.
Transatlantic Paper Co., Inc., 50 Franklin, New York.
West Carrollton Parchment Co., West Carrollton, Ohio.

ARE SUPERIOR TO ALL OTHERS. · ALL SIZES IN STOCK.
LOMBARD & CO., Importers & Manufacturers, 236 & 238 A Street, Boston.

Paper Specialties 347

GUMMED.

Dennison Mfg. Co., 26 Franklin, Boston, Mass.
Gummed Products Co., Troy, Ohio.
IDEAL COATED PAPER CO., Brookfield, Mass.
Jones, Saml., & Co., Waverly Park, Newark, N. J.
Lang & Gross Mfg. Co., Brooklyn, N. Y.
Liberty Paper Co., 52 Vanderbilt av., New York.
NASHUA GUMMED & COATED PAPER CO., Nashua, N. H.
Page, Fred M., & Co., West Lynn, Mass.
Peters Company, 33 35th, Brooklyn, N. Y.
Standard Paper Co., Bellows Falls, Vt.
Thomas Mfg. Co., Springfield, Ohio.

GUMMED TAPE CORNERS.

Workmall Products Co., Cohasset, Mass.

GUMMED SEALING TAPES, PAPER AND CLOTH.

Anderson, W. J., & Co., 341 Broadway, New York, N. Y.
Bird & Son, Inc., Walpole, Mass.
Blanch & Co., World Bldg., New York.
Brown Bros. Co., 817 N. 17th., St. Louis, Mo. (Printed & Unprinted).
Dennison Mfg. Co., South Framington, Mass.
Eisler, Anthony, & Co., New York City, N. Y.
Fox Paper Company, Lockland, Ohio.
Gummed Products Co., Troy, Ohio.
Gummed Products Printing Co., Bush Terminal No. 19, Brooklyn, N. Y.
IDEAL COATED PAPER CO., Brookfield, Mass.
Jones, M., & Co., 3 Hancock pl., New York.
Jones, Samuel & Co., Waverly Park, Newark, N. J.
Knowlton, M. D., Co., Rochester, N. Y.
Lang-Gros Mfg. Co., Bush Terminal, Brooklyn, N. Y.
Liberty Paper Co., 52 Vanderbilt av., New York.
Mid-West Box Co., Chicago, Ill.
NASHUA GUMMED & COATED PAPER CO., Nashua, N. H.
National Binding Machine Co., 260 West st., New York.
Page, Fred M., Co., West Lynn, Mass.
Peters Co., 33 35th, Brooklyn, N. Y.
Pomeroy Paper Co., 1320 Advertisers Bldg., Chicago.
Reliable Gum Tape Co., New York City, N. Y.
Rexford Gummed Tape Co., Milwaukee, Wis.
Standard Paper Co., Bellows Falls, Vt.
Staty, Thos., Mfg. Co., Springfield, Ohio.
Thomas Mfg. Co., Springfield, Ohio.

GUN WADDING.

Wolsteneroft Felt Mfg. Co., Philadelphia, Pa.

HARD PAPER CONTAINERS

Hard Paper Products Co. of America, Lytton Bldg., Chicago.

HOLLY WRAPPING PAPER.

Dennison Mfg. Co., Framingham, Mass.
The Liberty Paper Co., 52 Vanderbilt av., New York.
Rose & Frank Co., 136 W. 21st, New York.
The Tuttle Press Co., Appleton, Wis.

HOUSES.

Keyes Products Co., 23d and 6th av., New York City, N. Y.

HYGIENIC PAPER SPECIALTIES.

Howard Co., The, Norwood, Pa.
Lehigh Paper Mills, Inc., Raubsville, Pa.
Rose & Frank Co., 136 W. 21st, New York.
STONE & FORSYTH CO., Boston, Mass.

M. GOTTESMAN & CO., Inc.
18 E. 41st STREET, NEW YORK. Cable Address "Namsettog"
EUROPEAN OFFICES: Stockholm, Sweden
BLEACHED and UNBLEACHED GROUND WOOD PULP

ENGINEERING FOR PULP, PAPER AND POWER PLANTS
JOSEPH H. WALLACE & CO.
INDUSTRIAL ENGINEERS
Temple Court Building, NEW YORK
71 Bay Street, TORONTO, CAN.

Lombard's English Newcastle Pulp Stones

Paper Specialties

ICE BLANKETS.
KALAMAZOO VEGETABLE PARCHMENT CO., Kalamazoo, Mich.
Schmidt & Ault Paper Co., York, Pa.
Tokio Mfg. Co., 116 Nassau st., New York.

ICE CREAM BOXES.
Bloomer Bros. Co., Newark, N. Y.
Chicago Oyster Pail Co., Chicago.
Gair, Robert, Co., Brooklyn, N. Y. (Collapsible style.)
Henderson Paper Co., Dayton, Ohio
Menasha Carton Co., Menasha, Wis.
STONE & FORSYTH CO., Boston.
Weis Mfg. Co., Monroe, Mich.

ICE CREAM PLATES.
Bleyer, Alfred, & Co., 229 West, New York.

ICE CREAM SPOONS.
Atlas Mfg. Co., New Haven, Conn.
STONE & FORSYTH CO., Boston.

IMPERVIOUS.
Fibre Finishing Co., Worcester, Mass.
Howard Co., The, Norwood, Pa.
Impervious Paper Co., Scranton, Pa.
Keystone Roofing Mfg. Co., York, Pa.
Rose & Frank Co., 136 W. 21st, New York.

JELLY PROTECTORS.
KALAMAZOO VEGETABLE PARCHMENT CO., Kalamazoo, Mich.

KRAFT—WATERPROOF.
Angier Mills, Ashland, Mass.
Keystone Roofing Mfg. Co., York, Pa.
NATIONAL WATERPROOFING CO., Philadelphia, Pa.
Ralston, W., & Co., Ltd., Niagara Falls, N. Y.
Rose & Frank Co., 136 W. 21st, New York.
SAFEPACK PAPER MILLS, Boston, Mass.

LACE PAPER.
Gair, Robt., Co., Brooklyn, N. Y.
Milwaukee Lace Paper Co., Milwaukee, Wis.
Royal Lace Paper Works, The, 846 Lorimer, Brooklyn, N. Y.
U. S. Lace Paper Works, 473 W. Broadway, New York.

LAMINATED STRAW, NEWS AND CHIP BOARD.
Lignistra Fibre Products Co., Barberton, Ohio.

LAUNDRY ENVELOPES.
Paper Products Co., Inc., Quincy, Ill.

LEAD PENCILS—PAPER
Blaisdell Pencil Co., Philadelphia, Pa.
Gordon Brown, Inc., Jersey City, N. J.

LEATHER.
Paper Specialty Co., Shelton, Conn. (For coating in making imitation leather.)

LETTER FILES.
American Box & File Co., Atlanta, Ga.
Globe-Wernicke Co., Cincinnati, Ohio.
Yawman & Erbe Mfg. Co., Rochester, N. Y.

LINED PAPER PLATES.
Bleyer, Alfred, & Co., 229 West, New York.

CHIP CRUSHER We make a specialty of GROUND WOOD PULP and SULPHITE FIBRE MACHINERY **Carthage Machine Co.** CARTHAGE, N. Y.

Paper Specialties 349

LINING (FANCY).
Lignistra Fibre Products Co., Barberton, Ohio.

LINING PAPER.
Commercial Ptg. & Litho Co., Akron, Ohio.

LUNCH SETS.
Dennison Mfg. Co., 26 Franklin, Boston, Mass.
Kuhmarker Mfg. Co., 260 West, N. Y.

MAILING CASES.
American Box & File Co., Atlanta, Ga.
Climax Tube Co., 148 State, Boston, Mass.
Thompson & Norris Co., The, Brooklyn, N. Y.
Union Paper Co., 844 Washington st., New York.
Zellerbach Paper Co., San Francisco, Cal.

MAILING DEVICES.
The Thompson & Norris Co., Concord and Prince, Brooklyn, N. Y. (Photo-mailer.)

MAILING TUBES.
American Box & File Co., Atlanta, Ga.
Brown, James, Jr., 4365 Main, Philadelphia, Pa.
Cadby & Son, Albany, N. Y.
Chicago Mailing Tube Co., 425 S. Hoyne, Chicago, Ill.
Chicago Paper Tube & Can Co., 168 N. May, Chicago, Ill.
Climax Tube Co., 148 State, Boston, Mass.
Cumberland Valley Box Co., Hagerstown, Md.
Empire Paper Tube & Box Co., 445 West, New York City, N. Y.
Hagerstown Bookbinding & Printing Co., Hagerstown, Md.
Hoffman, J. C., 609 Bergen av., New York City, N. Y.
Hoyt Mfg. Co., 73 Clymer st., Brooklyn, N. Y.
Improved Mailing Case Co., 192 W. Broadway, New York City, N. Y.
Kalamazoo Paper Box Co., Kalamazoo, Mich.
Kern & Son, 257-259 William, New York City, N. Y.
Levin, David R., 444 W. 31st, Chicago, Ill.
Lowell Paper Tube Corp., Lowell, Mass.
Lukens-Carroll Paper Tube Co., 459 N. Orianna, Philadelphia, Pa.
Mail Wrapper-Tube Co., 162 E. 118th, New York City, N. Y.
Melville, F. L., 83 Water, New York City, N. Y.
N. Y. Tube & Corrugated Paper Co., 59 W. 10th, New York City, N. Y.
St. Louis Paper Can & Tube Co., St. Louis, Mo.
Thames River Specialties Co., Uncasville, Conn. Also cones.
Thompson & Norris Co., The, Brooklyn, N. Y.
Union Paper Co., 844 Washington, New York City, N. Y.
U. S. Mailing Tube Co., 844 Washington, New York City, N. Y.
Ware Co., 60 Lispenard, New York City, N. Y.
Wilson, T. E., 1151 N. 3d, Philadelphia, Pa.
Zellerbach Paper Co., San Francisco, Cal.

MANIFOLD BOOKS.
American Sales Book Co., Elmira, N. Y.
Reichard Bros., 13-17 Crosby, New York.

MARBLE PAPER.
Anderson Marble Paper Co., Washington, cor. W. 13th, New York City, N. Y.
Commercial Ptg. & Litho. Co., Akron, Ohio.
Neben Mfg. Co., 137 Beekman, New York.

Lombard's English Newcastle Pulp Stones

Paper Specialties

OYSTER PAIL AND EGG BOXES (Sectional Only).

American Box & Pail Co., Dayton, Ohio.
Aull Bros. Paper & Box Co., Dayton, Ohio.
Dayton Paper Novelty Co., Dayton, Ohio.
Gem City Box Co., Dayton, Ohio.
Kinnard Mfg. Co., Dayton, Ohio. (Oyster Pails Only).
Rike Folding Box Co., Dayton, Ohio.

PACKING AGAINST OIL AND WATER.

Endura Mfg. Co., Philadelphia, Pa.
Fibre Finishing Co., Worcester, Mass.
Ralston, W., & Co., Ltd., Niagara Falls, N. Y.
Rose & Frank Co., 136 W. 21st, New York.

PAILS.

Cordley & Hayes, 7 Leonard, New York.
Fibre Corporation, Lockport, N. Y.
Fibre Pail & Package Co., Toledo.

PAPER CABLE FILLING.

Gates Paper Twine Co., Inc., Pleasantville, N. Y.

PAPER TWINE.

American Core Twine Co., Fulda, Roxbury, Mass.
Auer & Twitchell, 41 So. Fourth, Philadelphia.
Gates Paper Twine Co., Inc., Pleasantville, N. Y.
Gottlieb & Sons, Inc., A., 57 S. 2d, Brooklyn, N. Y.
Hayner, Geo. M., 541 W. 36th, New York.
Wortendyke Mfg. Co., Richmond, Pa.

PAPER YARNS.

Gates Paper Twine Co., Inc., Pleasantville, N. Y.
National Fibre Textile Co., Neenah, Wis.

PAPIER MACHE.

Decorative Supply Co., Archer and Leo, Chicago, Ill.
De Planque, F. R., 1849 Ridge av., Philadelphia, Pa.
Dini, Geo. L., 483 Baltic av., Brooklyn, N. Y.
Emmel, Chas. & Rose, Co., 383 Albany, Boston, Mass.
Hermann, F. S., 7225 State rds., Philadelphia, Pa.
Klee, Thomson, Co., 329 E. 40th, New York City, N. Y.
Lombard, A. P., 101 Bristol, Boston, Mass.
Milner & Pride, 43 Bristol, Boston, Mass.
Old King Cole Papier Maché Co., Canton, Ohio.
Plaster Relief Mfg. Co., 298 N. Halsted, Chicago, Ill.
Pride, Willis A., 43 Bristol, Boston, Mass.
Sinnott, Jas. M., & Co., 168 Atlantic av., Brooklyn, N. Y.
Tognarelli & Voigt, 2310 Chestnut, Philadelphia, Pa.
Van Malderen, F., Ann and Jumonville, Pittsburgh, Pa.
Verpellier, H. E., & Co., 288 Washington, Newark, N. J.

PARCHMENT.

(See Table of Contents for location of this Department.)

PARCHMENT LINEN BOARD.

Lignistra Fibre Products Co., Barberton, Ohio.

PARCHMOID

Diamond State Fibre Co., Bridgeport, Pa.

LINTON and SCOTT
New York—Chicago

Toilet Paper

Paper Towels

Paper Napkins

BRANCH OFFICES
ST. LOUIS, MO.   ST. PAUL, MINN.
KANSAS CITY, MO.   PORTLAND, ORE.

We Solicit Jobbers Business Only

MOSINEE KRAFT

The Standard No. 1 Uniform Kraft

Every roll and bundle bears this guarantee label

One Grade—One Finish—One Shade

Wausau Sulphate Fibre Co.
Mosinee, Wisconsin

Chicago Sales Office—1625 Conway Building

PARCHMYN.

Kern Commercial Co., 114 Liberty, New York City, N. Y.
Rose & Frank Co., 136 W. 21st, New York. (Embossed.)
Transatlantic Paper Co., Inc., 50 Franklin, New York.

PASSE PARTOUT.

Dennison Mfg. Co., Framingham, Mass.

PASTING.

Regenstein-Veedor Co., 1336 Halsted, Chicago, Ill.
Wright, The Charles H., Paper Co., Middletown, Ohio.

PHONOGRAPH RECORD ENVELOPES.

Cohoes Envelope Co., Inc., Cohoes, N. Y.
Sherman Envelope Co., Worcester, Mass.
U. S. Envelope Co., Springfield, Mass.

PHOTOGRAPHIC.

American Photographic Paper Co., Boston, Mass.
Artex Photo Paper Co., Columbus, O.
Rose & Frank Co., 136 W. 21st, New York.

PHOTO MOUNTS.

Harcourt & Co., Louisville, Ky.
Hurlock Bros. Co., Philadelphia, Pa.
Lignistra Fibre Products Co., Barberton, Ohio.
National Card, Mat & Board Co., 216 W. Superior, Chicago, Ill.
Regenstein-Veedor Co., 1336 Halsted, Chicago.

PICTURE BACKING BOARDS.

Hurlock Bros. Co., Philadelphia, Pa.

PICTURE FRAME CORNER PROTECTORS.

Hurlock Bros. Co., Philadelphia, Pa.

PIE BAGS.

CONTINENTAL PAPER BAG CO., 17 Battery pl., New York.

PLATES. (PULP.)

Bleyer, Alfred, & Co., 229 West, New York City, N. Y.
Bloomer Bros. Co., Newark, N. Y.
Economy Butter & Pie Plate Co., Marion, Ind.
Indiana Pie Plate Co., Marion, Ind.
Keyes Fibre Co., Old Colony Bldg., Chicago, Ill.
Northern Bag & Plate Co., Carthage, N. Y.
STONE & FORSYTH CO., Boston.
Webb Folding Box Co., Bogota, N. J.

PLATING.

Wright, The Charles H., Paper Co., Middletown, Ohio.

PLAYING CARDS.

Dougherty, Andrew, 432 4th av., New York City, N. Y.
Kalamazoo Playing Card Co., Kalamazoo, Mich., and 200 5th av., New York.
New York Consolidated Card Co., 4th and Webster aves., Long Island City, N. Y.
Perfection Playing Card Co., 10 W. 4th, New York City, N. Y.
Russell Playing Card Co., 200 5th av., New York.
Standard Playing Card Mfg. Co., 31 E. Indiana, Chicago, Ill.
United States Playing Card Company, Cincinnati, Ohio, and 432 4th av., New York City, N. Y.

PLUGS.

Shartle & Bevis Machine Co., Franklin, Ohio. Paper plugs.

Lombard's English Newcastle Pulp Stones

Paper Specialties

PRINTED FRUIT WRAPS.

Crown Paper Co., Sanford, Fla.
Hawley Pulp & Paper, Oregon City, Oregon.
Crown-Willamette Paper Co., Oregon City, Oregon.

PRINTED GUMMED TAPE.

King Specialty Co., Detroit, Mich.
Reliable Gummed Tape Co., Inc., 90 Cypress av., New York City.

PRINTED GUMMED TAPE FOR ADVERTISING.

King Specialty Co., Detroit, Mich.
Liberty Paper Co., 52 Vanderbilt av., New York.

PRINTED TISSUE.

Dennison Mfg. Co., Framingham, Mass.
Dunning, S. W., 182 Nassau, New York.
ROBERTSON PAPER CO., Bellows Falls, Vt.
The Tuttle Press Co., Appleton, Wis.
Crown-Willamette Paper Co., Oregon City, Oregon.

PULP BARRELS.

George H. Rosenblatt, 180 Broadway, New York City.

RIBBON BLOCKS.

Hagerstown Bookbinding & Printing Co., Hagerstown, Md.
Lowell Paper Tube Corp., Lowell, Mass.

RIBBON PAPER.

Cumberland Valley Box Co., Hagerstown, Md.
Fischer & Bond, Inc., Paterson, N. J.
Hagerstown Bookbinding & Printing Co., Hagerstown, Md.

ROOFING PAPER MANUFACTURERS.

(See Table of Contents for Location of this Department).

SAFETY PAPER.

Hammermill Paper Co., Erie, Pa.
La Monte, George, & Son, New York City.
Paramount Safety Paper Co., 77 Washington, North Boston, Mass.
Perfect Safety Paper Co., The, Holyoke, Mass.
Phelps Safety Paper Co., Holyoke, Mass.
Specialty Paper Co., Shelton, Conn. (Safety shipping paper.)

SALES BOOKS.

American Sales Book Co., Elmira, N. Y.
Boorum & Pease Co., 109 Leonard, New York City, N. Y.
Carter-Crume Co., Niagara Falls, N. Y.
Columbia Ptg. & Sales Check Co., 85 Frankfort, N. Y. City, N. Y.
Consumers Paper Co., Shickshinny, Pa.
N. Y. Cash Sales Book Co., 524 W. Broadway, New York City, N. Y.
Rapid Systems Co., Hawthorne, Cal.
Wirth Sales Book Co., 4440 N. Knox av., Chicago, Ill.

PRESS ROLLS Maple and Gum White Wood Felt Rolls — J. W. HEWITT MACHINE CO. Neenah, Wis.

ARE SUPERIOR TO ALL OTHERS. ALL SIZES IN STOCK.
LOMBARD & CO., Importers & Manufacturers, 236 & 238 A Street, Boston.

Paper Specialties

SAND (ALSO FLINT AND EMERY).

American Glue Co., Boston, Mass.
Armour Sand Paper Co., Chicago, Ill.
Baeder, Adamson & Co., Richmond and Allegheny av., Philadelphia, Pa.
Barton, H. H., & Son Co., Inc., 109 S. 3d, Philadelphia, Pa.
Behr, Herman, & Co., 75 Beekman, New York City, N. Y.
Carborundum Co., Niagara Falls, N. Y.
Manning Sand Paper Co., Troy, N. Y.
Minnesota Mining & Mfg. Co., St. Paul, Minn.
U. S. Sandpaper Co., Williamsport, Pa.
Wausau Sand Paper Co., Wausau, Wis.
West Jersey Paper Mfg. Co., Camden, N. J. Sand.

SANITARY PAPER TOILET SEAT.
Minnelli, F. P., Delaware, Ohio.

SEALING CLOTHS.
Gummed Products Co., Troy, Ohio.
The Liberty Paper Co., 52 Vanderbilt av., New York.

SERPENTINE.
Dennison Mfg. Co., Framingham, Mass.
Zellerbach Paper Co., San Francisco, Cal.

SHEATHING—WATERPROOF.
Angier Mills, Ashland, Mass.
Barber Asphalt Paving Co., Philadelphia.
Bird & Son, Inc., East Walpole, Mass.
Howard Co., The, Norwood, Pa.
Keystone Roofing Mfg. Co., York, Pa.
SAFEPACK PAPER MILLS, Boston, Mass.

SHEETING PAPERS.
Manhattan Paper Co., 68 Wooster, New York.

SHELF PAPER.
Gottlieb, A., & Sons Co., 54 S. 2d, Brooklyn, N. Y.
KALAMAZOO VEGETABLE PARCHMENT CO., Kalamazoo, Mich.
Tuttle Press, The, Appleton, Wis.

SHELLS AND CONES.
Lowell Paper Tube Corp., Lowell, Mass.

SHIPPING CASES.
American Paper Products Co., St. Louis, Mo.
Portland Paper Package Co., Portland, Ore.
Sefton Mfg. Co., Chicago, Ill.
Thompson & Norris Co., Brooklyn, N. Y.

SHIRT PROTECTORS.
Herrlinger & Co., Cincinnati, Ohio.
Seinsheimer Paper Co., The, Cincinnati, O.

SHOE COVER.
Endura Mfg. Co., Philadelphia, Pa.
Fibre Finishing Co., Worcester, Mass.
Howard Co., The, Norwood, Pa.
Keystone Shoe Paper Co., 910 Filbert, Philadelphia, Pa.
Shoe Mfrs. Supply Co., Newark, N. J.
Specialty Paper Co., The, Shelton, Conn.
STONE & FORSYTH CO., Boston.

SHOPPING BAGS.
CONTINENTAL PAPER BAG CO., 17 Battery pl., New York.

M. GOTTESMAN & CO., Inc.
18 E. 41st STREET, NEW YORK. Cable Address "Namsettog"
EUROPEAN OFFICES: Stockholm, Sweden

Finest Mitscherlich Sulphite

ENGINEERING FOR
PULP, PAPER AND POWER PLANTS

JOSEPH H. WALLACE & CO.
INDUSTRIAL ENGINEERS
Temple Court Building, NEW YORK
71 Bay Street, TORONTO, CAN.

Paper Specialties

TOWELS.
(CONTINUED)

National Paper Products Co., Carthage, N. Y.
National Paper Products Co., San Francisco, Cal.
NORTHERN PAPER MILLS, Green Bay, Wis.
Paper Mills Specialty Co., Inc., Chicago.
Paper Products Mfg. Co., New Orleans, La.
Paper Service Co., Inc., Hinsdale, N. H.
Peerless Paper Products Co., Menasha, Wis.
Perseverance Paper Mills, Lambertville, N. J.
Regal Paper Company, Pulaski, N. Y.
Robertson & Co., W. F., Hinsdale, N. H.
Sauquoit Toilet Paper Co., New Hartford, N. Y.
Scott Paper Co., Philadelphia, Pa.
Specialty Paper Co., The, Shelton, Conn.
STONE & FORSYTH CO., Boston, Mass.
Tuttle Press Co., Appleton, Wis.
Wayne Paper Goods Co., Wayne, Ind.
Zellerbach Paper Co., San Francisco, Cal.

TRACING PAPER.
Angel, H. Reeve, & Co., Inc., 120 Liberty, New York.

TRADE WORK DESIGNS.
The Liberty Paper Co., 52 Vanderbilt av., New York.

TRANSFER CASES.
American Box & File Co., Atlanta, Ga.

TRAYS.
Bleyer, Alfred, & Co., 229 West, New York.

TRUNK FIBRE.
Lignistra Fibre Products Co., Barberton, Ohio.

TUBES (CAP AND TAPER).
Adhawagam Paper Products Co., Grand Rapids, Wis.
Auer & Twitchell, Chestnut and 9th, Philadelphia.
Consolidated Paper Tube Co., Philadelphia.
Lowell Paper Tube Corp., Lowell, Mass.
Nat'l Paper Co., Atlanta, Ga.

VEGETABLE PARCHMENT PAPER MANUFACTURERS.
(For Location of this Department, See Table of Contents).

VERTICAL FILE POCKETS.
Alvah Bushnell Co., Philadelphia, Pa.
National Fiberstock Envelope Co., Philadelphia, Pa.
Weis Mfg. Co., Monroe, Mich.
Yawman & Erbe Mfg. Co., Rochester, N. Y.

VESTS.
Specialty Paper Co., The, Shelton, Conn.

WALL OR BUILDERS' BOARD, ARTIFICIAL LUMBER.
INDICATING MARKS.
*Make head lining for street and steam railroad cars as well as building boards.
†Make asbestos building boards.

*Agasote Board Co., The, Trenton, N. J.
American Paper Products Co., St. Louis.
Androscoggin Board Co., 50 State, Boston, Mass.
Beaver Board Companies, The, Beaver rd., Buffalo, N. Y.
Beaver Triangle, Toronto, Ont.
Bird & Son, Inc., East Walpole, Mass.
*Composite Board Co., Niagara Falls, N. Y.

WALL OR BUILDERS' BOARD, ARTIFICIAL LUMBER.
(CONTINUED)

*Gardner Artificial Lumber Co., 50 Church, New York City, N. Y.
Fibre Products, Ltd., Toronto, Can.
Heppes-Nelson Roofing Co., The, Chicago, Ill.
Hurlock Bros. Co., Philadelphia, Pa.
*Indestructible Fibre Co., Massena, N. Y.
†Johns-Manville, H. W., Co., 41st and Madison av., N. Y. City, N. Y.
†Keasby-Matteson, Ambler, Pa.
Lignistra Fibre Products Co., Barberton, Ohio.
Mac Sim Bar Paper Co., Otsego, Mich.
Mastic Wall Board & Roofing Co., The, 862 Este av., Cincinnati, O.
National Card, Mat & Board Co., 216 W. Superior, Chicago, Ill.
Northwestern Compo Board Co., 5778 Syndale av., Minneapolis, Minn.
Philadelphia Paper Mfg. Co., Philadelphia, Pa. Manayunk.
Philip Carey Mfg. Co., Cincinnati, O.
Plastergon Company, The, Tonawanda, N. Y.
Roberds Mfg. Co., The, 102 Railroad, Marion, Ind.
Rockford Paper Box Board Co., Rockford, Ill.
Sackett Plaster Board Co., 17 Battery pl., New York City, N. Y.
Schmidt & Ault Paper Co., York, Pa.
Upson Company, The, Lockport, N. Y.
Van Dyck Panel Co., 50 Church, New York City, N. Y.
Van Dyke Panel Co., East Rutherford, N. J.

WALLETS.

Bushnell, Alvah, Co., 10th and Market, Philadelphia, Pa. Paperoid.
Diemer, John F., Co., 67 Cortlandt, N. Y.
Yawman & Erbe Mfg. Co., Rochester, N. Y.

WASTE BASKETS.
American Vulcanised Fibre Co., Wilmington, Del.

WATERCLOSET SEATS.
Keyes Products Co., 23d and 6th av., New York City, N. Y. Seamless.

WATER PROOF PAPERS.
Heppes-Nelson Roofing Co., 4500 Fillmore, Chicago.
Keystone Roofing Mfg. Co., York, Pa.
Lebon Co., Chicago.

WATER PROOF SPECIALTIES.
Howard Co., The, Norwood, Pa.
Keystone Roofing Mfg. Co., York, Pa.

WATER PROOF WRAPPINGS.
Angier Mills, Ashland, Mass.
Bird & Son, Inc., East Walpole, Mass.
Elk Coated Paper Co., Jersey City, N. J.
Fibre Finishing Co., Worcester, Mass.
Howard Co., The, Norwood, Pa.
Keystone Roofing Mfg. Co., York, Pa.
Mansfield Co., Boston, Mass.
NATIONAL WATERPROOFING CO., Philadelphia, Pa.
Ralston, W., & Co., Ltd., Niagara Falls, N. Y.
SAFEPACK PAPER MILLS, Boston, Mass.
The Impervious Paper Products Co., Scranton, Pa.
Vellumoid Paper Co., Worcester, Mass.

WAXED PAPER MANUFACTURERS.
(For Location of this Department See Table of Contents.)

WINDOWPHANIE.
N. W. Malz, 19 E. 14th, New York.

WIRE WRAP—WATER PROOF.
Keystone Roofing Mfg. Co., York, Pa.

Parchment, Waxed, Toilet and Roofing Paper Manufacturers

VEGETABLE PARCHMENT PAPER MANUFACTURERS.

Diamond State Fibre Co., Bridgeport, Pa.
Glen Mills Paper Co., 1005 Stephen Girard st., Philadelphia, Pa.
KALAMAZOO VEGETABLE PARCHMENT CO., Kalamazoo, Mich.
Paterson Parchment Paper Co., Passaic, N. J.
Sutherland Paper Co., Kalamazoo, Mich.
West Carrollton Parchment Co., Dayton, Ohio.

WAXED PAPER MANUFACTURERS.

Amherst Waxed Paper Mills, Amherst, Mass., and Woolworth Bldg., New York.
BENNINGTON WAX PAPER CO., Bennington, Vt.
California Tissue Mills, Inc., Los Angeles.
Central Waxed Paper Co., Central and Taylor, Chicago, Ill.
Crystal Paper Co., Middletown, O.
Diem & Wing Paper Co., Cincinnati, O.
Hammerschlag Mfg. Co., 232 Greenwich, New York, and Garfield, N. J.
Henle Waxed Paper Mfg. Co., 535 E. 79th, New York.
KALAMAZOO VEGETABLE PARCHMENT CO., Kalamazoo, Mich.
Kuhmarker Mfg. Co., 149-155 W. 24th, New York.
Menasha Printing & Carton Co., Menasha, Wis.
NASHUA GUMMED & COATED PAPER CO., Nashua, N. H.
National Wax & Paper Mfg. Co., 203 37th, Brooklyn, N. Y.
National Wrapping Paper Co., Nashua, N. H.
NEWARK PARAFFIN PARCHMENT PAPER CO., Newark, N. J., and 82 W. Broadway, New York.
Ohio Wax Paper Co., Columbus, O.
PAPER MILLS SPECIALTY CO., Chicago, Ill.
Paraffin Paper Co., Otsego, Mich.
ROBERTSON PAPER CO., Bellows Falls, Vt.
Sani-Wax Paper Co., Kalamazoo, Mich.
Shawmut Waxed Paper Co., Holliston, Mass.
Sterling Wax Paper Mfg. Co., Newark, N. J.
Sutherland Paper Co., Kalamazoo, Mich.
UNION WAXED & PARCHMENT PAPER CO., Hamburg, N. J., and 45 Cedar, New York.
Waterproof Paper & Board Co., Cincinnati, O.
Waxide Paper Co., Kansas City, Mo.
West Carrollton Parchment Co., Dayton, Ohio.

WAXED PAPER CONCERNS IN CANADA.

MERRITTON
Garden City Paper Mills Co., Ltd.

MONTREAL.
Bradshaws Limited.
McNairn, J. H.

TORONTO.
Appleford Counter & Check Co.
British American Wax Paper Co., Ltd.

TOILET PAPER, ROLL AND PACKAGE.

Adams Paper Co., Wells River, Vt.
Albany Perforated Wrapping Paper Co., Albany, N. Y.
Atlas Mills, Boston, Mass.
Badger Tissue Mills, Kaukauna, Wis.
Carthage Tissue Paper Co., Carthage, N. Y.
W. A. Cole Paper Co., Putney, Vt.
CONTINENTAL PAPER BAG CO., 17 Battery pl., New York.
Crown Willamette Paper Co., San Francisco, Cal.
Crunden Martin Mfg. Co., St. Louis.
Deutsch Bros. Mfg. Co., 843 Greenwich st., New York.

Samuel M. Langston Company
CAMDEN, N. J., U. S. A.

Manufacturers of

Paper Can Machinery

Complete Sets of machinery for making cans such as are used for packing oats, coffee, baking powder, tobacco, snuff and cleansing powders.

Corrugated Paper Shipping Case Machinery

We build all the machinery necessary to make paper shipping boxes or cases such as are now replacing wooden boxes in the United States.

Paper Slitting and Rewinding Machines

Machines for cutting and rewinding rolls of paper. We build all width machines to handle any weight or thickness paper and any size rolls.

The Canadian Fairbanks-Morse Co., Ltd., Agents
Toronto and Montreal

The World's Cleanest Paper Mill

where cool, spotless, food-saving, "K.V.P." vegetable parchment paper and pure "K.V.P." waxed paper are produced in enormous quantities to help save food supplies and prevent waste.

WRITE FOR SAMPLES

Are you receiving the "Parchment Prattler" monthly?

Kalamazoo Vegetable Parchment Company
KALAMAZOO, MICHIGAN

NORTHERN PAPER MILLS
GREEN BAY, WIS.

MANUFACTURERS OF

Towels, Toilet Papers and Specialties

Solicits Patronage of Bona-fide Jobbers

TOILET PAPER, ROLL AND PACKAGE.
(CONTINUED.)

Dixie Paper & Box Co., Atlanta, Ga.
Fillmore & Slade, N. Bennington, Vt.
Fisk Paper Co., Hinsdale, N. H. (Packages only.)
Foley Paper Co., Springfield, Mass.
Garden City Paper Mills Co., St. Catherines, Ont.
Hoberg, John, Co., Green Bay, Wis.
HOFFMAN, R. S., Baldwinsville, N. Y.
Interlake Tissue Mills, Ltd., Merritton, Ont.
Irish, Geo., Paper Co., Buffalo, N. Y.
Jerome Paper Co., 314 W. 53d, New York.
Johnson, Geo. T., Co., Boston, Mass.
Lehigh Paper Mills, Inc., Raubsville, Pa.
LINTON & SCOTT, 110 W. 40th, New York.
Merlin-Keilholz Paper Co., 298 B'way, New York.
Meyer Bros. Paper Co., Cincinnati, O.
Morgan Envelope Co., Div. U. S. Envelope Co., Springfield, Mass.
Mt. Holyoke Tissue Mills, Holyoke, Mass.
Mumford Paper Mills, Inc., Mumford, N. Y.
National Paper Products Co., Carthage, N. Y.
National Paper Products Co., San Francisco, Cal.
NORTHERN PAPER MILLS, Green Bay, Wis.
H. NORWOOD EWING CO., Woolworth Bldg., New York.

Oswego River Paper Mills, Phoenix, N. Y.
Paper Mills Specialty Co., Inc., Chicago.
Paper Products Co., New Orleans, La.
Paper Service Co., Hinsdale, N. H.
Peerless Mfg. Co., Norristown, Pa.
Peerless Paper Products Co., Menasha, Wis.
Perseverance Paper Mills, Lambertville, N. J.
Phoenix Toilet and Paper Mfg. Co., Phoenix, N. Y.
Regal Paper Co., Pulaski, N. Y.
Rushmore Paper Co., Long Island City, New York.
Sauquoit Toilet Paper Co., New Hartford, N. Y.
Scott Paper Co., Philadelphia, Pa.
Stone & Forsyth Co., 67 Kingston Street, Boston, Mass.
Three Rivers Paper Co., Phoenix, N. Y.
Tissue Co., Saugerties, N. Y.
Tuttle Press Co., Appleton, Wis.
Victoria Paper Mills Co., Fulton.
Walton, D. S., & Co., 182 Franklin, New York.
Weston Paper Mfg. Co., Dayton, O. (Packages only.)
White-Washburn Co., 100 Hudson, New York. Br. of Kaukauna, Wis., and Hinsdale, N. H.
Wortendyke Mfg. Co., Richmond, Va.

TOILET PAPER CONCERNS IN CANADA

Eddy, E. B., Co., Hull, Que.

Wilson, J. C., Paper Co., Montreal, Inc.

ROOFING PAPER MANUFACTURERS

Acme Roofing Co., Walkerville, Ont.
Amalgamated Roofing Co., Clearing, Ill.
American Tar Products Co., 208 South La Salle st., Chicago.
Asphalt Ready Roofing Co., 9 Church St., New York City, N. Y.
Baltimore Roofing & Asbestos Mfg. Co., Asbestos, Md.
Barber Asphalt Paving, New York. (Asphalt Ready Roofings and Saturated Felts.)

Barrett Co., 17 Battery pl., New York, and Chicago, Boston, Philadelphia, and other large cities. (Saturators, Smooth Coated and Coal Tar.)
Bird & Son, Inc., East Walpole, Mass. (Saturators, Smooth Conted and Coal Tar.)
Carey, Philip, Mfg. Co., Lockland, Ohio. (Saturators, Smooth Coated and Coal Tar.)
Certain-teed Products Corp., St. Louis, Mo.

ENGINEERING FOR
PULP, PAPER AND POWER PLANTS

JOSEPH H. WALLACE & CO.
INDUSTRIAL ENGINEERS
Temple Court Building, NEW YORK
71 Bay Street, TORONTO, CAN.

ROOFING PAPER MANUFACTURERS
(CONTINUED.)

Chapman & Soden, Atlantic av., Boston, Mass. (Tarred Felt for Roofing.)
Chatfield Mfg. Co., Cincinnati, Ohio.
Elaborated Ready Roofing Co., 419 Wentworth av., Chicago.
Flintkote Mfg. Co., Rutherford, N. J. (Asphalt Roll and Slate Surfaced.)
Ford Mfg. Co., Chicago, Ill. (Saturators, Smooth Coated and Coal Tar.)
H. W. Johns-Manville Co., Madison av. and 41st st., New York.
Heppes Co., Chicago, Ill. (Saturators, Smooth Coated and Coal Tar.)
Hydrex Felt & Engineering Co., Office, 120 Liberty, New York.
Keystone Roofing Mfg. Co., York, Pa.
Lehon, The, Company, W. 44th and Oakley Ave., Chicago. (Asphalt.)
Lewis, F. J., Mfg. Co., Moline, Ill. (Saturators, Smooth Coated and Coal Tar.)
McHenry, Millhouse Mfg. Co., South Bend, Ind.
Moore, J. W., Co., Providence, R. I.
National Roofing Co., Tonawanda, N. Y. (Saturated, Mineral Surfaced and Smooth Coated Roofing.)
National Roofing Mfg. Co., York, Pa.
New England Felt Roofing Works, 18 Post Office Square, Boston, Mass. (Smooth Coated and Coal Tar Roofing.)
Pacific Refining & Roofing Co., San Francisco, Cal.
Paraffine Paint Co., San Francisco, Cal.
Patent Vulcanite Roofing Co., 49th and Oakley av., Chicago, Ill. (Smooth and Slate Coated.)
Pioneer Paper Co., Los Angeles, Cal. (Saturators, Smooth Coated and Coal Tar.)
Providence Slate & Gravel Roofing Co., Providence, R. I.
Reynolds Mfg. Co., H. M., Grand Rapids, Mich. (Mineral Surfaced Roll Roofing.)
Sall Mountain Asbestos Mfg. Co., Chicago, Ill. (Saturators, Smooth Coated and Slate Surfaced.)
Sidney Roofing Co., Sidney, B. C.
Standard Paint Co., Bound Brook, N. J.
Standard Vulcanite Co. (subsidiary of Standard Paint Co.), Woolworth Bldg., New York.
Stowell Mfg. Co., 244-280 Culver Ave., Jersey City, N. J.
Usona Mfg. Co., Aurora, Ill. (Saturators, Smooth Coated and Prepared Asphalt.)
Warren Chemical & Mfg. Co., Dept. of the Barrett Co., 17 Battery pl., New York.
Watson Co., H. F., Erie, Pa.
White Co., Ltd., A. H., New Orleans, La. (Saturators, Smooth Coated and Surfaced Roofing.)

PRESS ROLLS Maple and Gum White Wood Felt Rolls J. W. HEWITT MACHINE CO. Neenah, Wis.

Holyoke Card & Paper Co.

Manufacturers of Brightwood Brands

Cardboard, plain and coated, for high grade printing in all branches, and for photo mounts and folders, tickets, tags, signs, advertising novelties, playing cards, etc. Coated Cover Papers, glazed and plated, Box and Label Papers. Embossed and Waterproof Cover Papers.

SPRINGFIELD - - - - MASS.

FRED. M. TEMPLE, Pres. and Gen'l Mgr.　　CHAS. D. THOMPSON, Treas.

MERRIMAC PAPER CO.
LAWRENCE, MASS.

MANUFACTURERS OF

Coated Lithograph Papers

Especially adapted for two and three color Aluminum Press

OFFSET PAPER COATED AND UNCOATED

COATED POST CARD STOCK
ENAMELED BOOK AND LABEL
MACHINE DRIED WRITINGS

National Coated Paper Corporation
Pawtucket, Rhode Island

MANUFACTURERS OF

White and Colored Friction Glazed, Plate and Label Papers, Embossed Papers.

OFFICE AND FACTORY, YORK AVENUE

NEWTON PAPER CO. HOLYOKE MASS.

MANUFACTURERS OF

Sheathing, Wrapping, Manila Duplex Felt Papers and Specialties

ALSO

"Medal Brand" Corrugated Carpet Lining

FRANKLIN PAPER CO. HOLYOKE, MASS.

...Manufacturers of...

Jefferson Index Bristols, White and Colored Franklin Bristols, Victor and Special White Blanks, Sample Card Bristol, National Post Card Bristol, American Bristol.

Safepack

Waterproof Stormproof dampproof rustproof dirtproof airtight Wrap-stuff and case-lining Made by Safepack Paper Mills Boston Massachusetts

HAMPDEN GLAZED PAPER & CARD CO.

Glazed, Flinted, Waterproof Coated, Embossed and Printed Papers of all descriptions for Paper Box Makers' uses, Fancy Box Makers' Paper, Enameled Blotter, Litho. Papers, Cardboard, Photographic Mounts and Folders (Plain, Rippled and Embossed). Embossed Tissues, Bristols, etc. Leatherettes and Leathern Memo. Covers, SUNBURST COVERS, Rippled Finish; ALGONKIN and KWASIND COVERS (Antique and Embossed Finish).

Write For Samples.

HOLYOKE - - - MASSACHUSETTS

Whitmore Manufacturing Co.

Finest Coated Lithographic
and Three Color Plate.
Enameled and Glazed Papers.

HOLYOKE, MASSACHUSETTS

C. RIORDON, President   F. B. WHITTET, Secy. & Treas.
CARL RIORDON, V. Pres. & Mng. Director   THOS. E. WARREN, Manager
W. J. WILSON, Sales Manager

TICONDEROGA PULP & PAPER COMPANY

ESTABLISHED 1882

Paper Sales Department: 200 Fifth Avenue, New York City

MANUFACTURERS OF

Book Papers and Soda Fibre

MILLS AND PRINCIPAL OFFICE AT TICONDEROGA, N. Y.

IDEAL COATED PAPER CO.

MANUFACTURERS OF

GUARANTEED FLAT GUMMED PAPERS for labels. GUMMED SPECIALTIES of all kinds. All kinds of GUMMED and UNGUMMED Staying Materials, GUMMED CLOTH, CLOTH LINED papers. Gold Papers, GUMMED and UNGUMMED.

150 Nassau Street   600 Provident Bank Bldg.   2162-3 Transportation Bldg.
NEW YORK CITY   CINCINNATI, OHIO   CHICAGO, ILL.

Factory and Main Office, Brookfield, Mass.

NORMAN HARROWER

Linton Bros. & Co.

Fitchburg, Mass.

MAKERS

WHITE AND COLORED BRISTOLS

CARD INDEX BRISTOLS

AND

WHITE BLANKS

Established 1844
LOWELL EMERSON, Pres.

Incorporated 1886
LOWELL PIERCE EMERSON, Treas.

THE RHODE ISLAND CARD BOARD CO.

163 EXCHANGE STREET - - - PAWTUCKET, R. I.

MANUFACTURERS OF

PLAIN AND COATED CARDBOARDS
For Lithograph Printing, Half-Tone Process Plate Printing

PLAIN AND EMBOSSED SURFACE BOARDS
For Calendar and Photograph Mounts

SPECIAL SURFACES IN BRISTOLS OR CARDBOARDS
For Offset Printing and Gelatine Plate Printing

VEGETABLE PARCHMENT OR GREASE PROOF LINED
CARDBOARDS for Containers of Every Description

TAG STOCKS, BAGGAGE CHECKS AND TICKET STOCK
either paper or coated surface in sheets or rolls of any width.

SELECTED LISTS OF
Glazed, Coated Paper and Board Manufacturers
IN THE
UNITED STATES AND CANADA

With some data in regard to equipment of plants, products, capacity, etc

---

ALBANY CARD & PAPER MFG. CO., Albany, N. Y.

  Photo Mounts, Cardboard, etc.

AMERICAN COATED PAPER CO., Pawtucket, R. I.

  Glazed.

AMERICAN COATING MILLS, Elkhart, Ind.

  Five Single Coaters: one 36-inch, one 46-inch and three 60-inch. Calenders, Cutters and Platers to suit width of Coaters. Cardboard, Boxboard, Cover and Heavy Litho. Blanks.

APPLETON COATED PAPER CO., Appleton, Wis.

  Four Coating Machines. Two Single Coaters handle paper 50½ inches wide—one Single Coater handles paper 75 inches wide. One Double coater handles paper 60 inches wide. Supercalender widths up to 74 inches. Grades manufactured—Coated One Side Lithograph, Enamel Book, Embossing Cover, Enamel Cover and Ledger Index Bristol.

ARKELL & SMITHS, Canajoharie, N. Y.

  Three Flat Bed Coating Machines, loft drying. Average run 54 hours per week, one shift. Capacity, average 15,000 lbs. 24 hours. Product used entirely by the firm.

BARDEEN PAPER CO., COATING DIV., Otsego, Mich.

  Ten Single Coaters: Three, widest sheet, 45½ inches; one, widest sheet, 61½ inches; three, widest sheet, 54½ inches; two, widest sheet, 46½ inches; one, widest sheet, 60½ inches. Post Card, Blanks, Translucents, Book Papers, Offset Blanks, Dull Finish Enamel, Plate, Cover and Litho.

BLACKSTONE GLAZED PAPER CO., Pawtucket, R. I.

  Glazed. Ten Single Coating Machines and twelve Friction Calenders.

BRYANT PAPER Co. (Imperial Division), Kalamazoo, Mich.

  Twenty-eight Single Coaters: Three Machines which handle paper 56½ inches wide; four Machines which handle paper 42½ inches wide; three Machines which handle paper 46½ inches wide; two Machines which handle paper 36½ inches wide; eight Machines which handle paper 50½ inches wide; three Machines which handle paper 64½ inches wide. (See Mill Report for Products made.)

CANTINE COMPANY, MARTIN, Saugerties, N. Y.

  Five Single and Ten Double Coaters. Width of Sheets: Single Coaters, up to 53 inches; Double Coaters, from 48 to 53 inches. Lithograph, Plate and Enamel Book. Capacity 65 tons daily.

CASHIN F. D., GLAZED PAPER CO., West Haven, Conn.

  Glazed, Plated and Coated.

CHAMPION COATED PAPER COMPANY, Hamilton, Ohio.

  Sixteen Double Coaters; ten Single Coaters; all Widths up to 56 inches. Ten Paper Machines, widths up to 151 inches. Coated Paper, Cardboard and High Grade Book Papers.

CHAMPION-INTERNATIONAL CO., Lawrence, Mass.

  See Mill Report for Products of the company.

M. GOTTESMAN & CO., Inc.
18 E. 41st STREET, NEW YORK. Cable Address "Kammertop"
EUROPEAN OFFICES: Stockholm, Sweden

HIGHEST GRADE KRAFT PULPS

ENGINEERING FOR PULP, PAPER AND POWER PLANTS

JOSEPH H. WALLACE & CO.
INDUSTRIAL ENGINEERS
Temple Court Building, NEW YORK
71 Bay Street, TORONTO, CAN.

Glazed, Coated Paper and Board Manufacturers

COLLINS MFG. CO., A. M., 226-240 Columbia avenue, Philadelphia.
Six Single Coaters; four Calenders. Width of sheet, up to 42 inches. Book and Cardboard.

DE JONGE & CO., LOUIS, 71 Duane street, New York.
Factories on Staten Island, New York City, and Fitchburg, Mass. Surface Coated Papers. Fifteen Coaters, ranging from 48 to 58 inches, at Fitchburg, and seventeen Coaters, ranging from 25 to 40 inches, at Staten Island.

DILL & COLLINS CO., 140 N. Sixth street, Philadelphia.
Twenty Single Coaters; nine Super-Calenders. Width of sheet: up to 54 inches. See Mill Report for Products.

DOTY AND SCRIMGEOUR CO., Reading, Pa.
Surface Coated Papers, Friction Glazed, Flint Glazed and Plated in White and Colors. Non-Curling Papers for Automatic Press Work, Waterproof Coatings, etc.

FALULAH PAPER COMPANY, Fitchburg, Mass.
Five Single Coaters 36 to 48-inch paper. Coated Mill Blanks. See Mill Report.

FRANKLIN COATED PAPER CO., THE, Franklin, Ohio.
One Single and three Double Coaters. Widest Single Coated Sheet 66 inches; widest Double Coated Sheet 56 inches. Capacity 150 tons per week. Book Litho., Cover and Special Folding Enamels.

GEORGE, S., CO., Wellsburg, W. Va.
One 42-inch Coating Machine. Coated flour bag paper, 10,000 lbs. daily.

HAMPDEN GLAZED PAPER & CARD CO., Holyoke, Mass.
Glazed, Flinted, Waterproof Coated and Fancy Box Makers' Papers, Enameled Blotter, Litho. Papers, and Cardboard. Photographic Mounts and Folders. Embossed Tissues, Bristols and Leatherettes. Leathern Memorandum Book, Sunburst, Kuasind and Algonkin Covers, etc.

HOLYOKE CARD & PAPER CO., Springfield, Mass.
Photo Mounts, Cardboard, Coated Cover, Surface Coated, Glazed and Plated.

HOPE PAPER COMPANY, INC., THE, 296 Brook st., Pawtucket, R. I.
Glazed and Label Papers. White Shoe Glazed a Specialty.

IDEAL COATED PAPER CO., Brookfield, Mass., and 150 Nassau st., New York.
"Nontarno" Gold Seal Papers Gummed and Ungummed for Embossed Seals, etc., and Nontarno Gold Edging Papers.

INTERNATIONAL PAPER CO., 30 Broad st., New York. (Fall Mountain Mill, Bellows Falls, Vt.)
Two Single Coaters, 44 and 60 inches wide; two Super Calenders, one 44 and one 54 inches wide. Coated Box Board, Tag, Blanks, Bristol, Cardboard and Bond Stock.

KALAMAZOO PAPER CO., Kalamazoo, Mich.
Mill No. 4—Eighteen Single Coaters, maximum trim 58 inches. Coated Book, Lithograph, Cover, Brush Finish, Friction Glazed, Flint Glazed and Embossed Papers; Coated Blanks, Translucents and Post Card stock. Capacity, 50 tons daily.
Mill No. 5—Four 54-inch and two 64-inch Coaters. Three Super Calenders.

KING PAPER COMPANY, KALAMAZOO, Mich.
Nine Single Coaters: Two 44-inch, five 52-inch and two 62-inch Machines.

KUPFER BROS. CO., 112-114 Wooster st., New York. (Factory at Northbridge, Mass.)
All kinds of Surface Coated Papers, Plain and Embossed; also Gold and Silver Papers. Imitation Tin Foil —"Stannyn." In rolls and sheets.

LOCKE, E. G., Camden, N. J.
Surface Coated, Glazed, Plated, Enameled, Waterproof and Fancy Papers.

LOWE PAPER COMPANY, Ridgefield, N. J.
Six Single Coaters, Super Calenders, Rotary Cutters, Straight Knife Cutters and Slitters. Maximum width 64 inches. Clay Coated Blanks, Railroads, Tough Checks, Tag, Band Stock, Solid and Filled Folding Box Board, White, Colors and Waterproofed. Coated and Waterproofed Specialties; sheets and rolls from 2 inches in width to 54 inches in width; basis of weight from 22 x 28 —80 to 22 x 28—600 pounds to the 500 sheets. Capacity, 75,000 lbs.

MAINE COATED PAPER COMPANY, Rumford, Me.
L. M. Bickford, Pres.; H. S. Coke, Vice-Pres. and Mill Manager; F. E. Tufts, Treas.; J. H. Drummond, clerk. Six Single Coaters; two Double Coaters; five Calenders; maximum width, 64 inches. All grades of Single and Double Coated Book; all grades of Coated One Side Lithograph and Cover.

LOMBARD'S ENGLISH NEWCASTLE PULP STONES
ARE SUPERIOR TO ALL OTHERS. ALL SIZES IN STOCK.
LOMBARD & CO., Importers & Manufacturers, 226 & 228 A Street, Boston.

CHIP CRUSHER We make a specialty of GROUND WOOD PULP and SULPHITE FIBRE MACHINERY ‖ **Carthage Machine Co.** CARTHAGE, N. Y.

Glazed, Coated Paper and Board Manufacturers

MERRIMAC PAPER CO., Lawrence, Mass.
Five Single Coaters: Two 54, one 48 and two 43 inches; two Double Coaters, 54 inches. Enameled Book and Lithographic Papers. See Mill Section.

MONARCH PAPER COMPANY, Kalamazoo, Mich.
Fifteen Coating Machines.

NASHUA GUMMED & COATED PAPER Co., Nashua, N. H.
Coating Department: Nineteen Single Coaters; coating widths, 26 to 62 inches; principal products, Lithograph and Box Covering. Daily output, 30 tons. Gumming Department: Nine Gummers; gumming widths, 40 to 90 inches. Daily output, 25 tons. Wax Paper Department: Nine Wax Machines; waxing widths 60 to 76 inches. Daily output, 40 tons.

NATIONAL COATED PAPER CORPORATION, Pawtucket, R. I.
White and Colored Friction Glazed, Plate and Label Papers, Embossed Papers.

NEW ENGLAND CARD & PAPER CO., D. L. Swan's Sons, Proprietors, Springfield, Mass.
Coated Plate, Friction Glazed, Flint Glazed and Embossed Papers.

NEW JERSEY COATED PAPER CO., Montclair, N. J.
Ten Coaters; six Calenders; eight Rotary Cutters and four Straight Knife Cutters. Surface Coated, Litho., Label and Glazed Papers, Cardboard, Box Board, etc.

PAWTUCKET GLAZED PAPER Co., INC., Rear 171 N. Bend street, Pawtucket, R. I.
Six Coating Machines; seven Calenders. Can handle 24, 26, 28, 30 and 31-inch on all Machines.

PEPPERELL CARD & PAPER Co., East Pepperell, Mass.
Six Single and four Double Coaters; seven Calenders, widths from 44 to 52 inches; seven Cutters. Capacity 90,000 pounds 24 hours. Enameled Book, Litho, and Label Papers, Coated Manila, Translucent and Brush Enamel.

PHILIPS, THOMAS, Co., Akron, Ohio.
One Coating Machine; widest trimmed sheet, 37 inches. Capacity 8,000 lbs. 10 hours. Coat flour sack paper for own use.

READING PAPER MILLS, Reading, Pa.
Three Single Coating Machines: One for 32-inch, one for 36-inch and one for 58-inch paper. See Mill Report in Mill Section.

REX PAPER COMPANY, Kalamazoo, Mich.
Six Single Coaters: Four 54-inch and two 62-inch Coaters.

RHODE ISLAND CARD BOARD CO., Pawtucket, R. I.
Five 48-inch Single Coaters, 46-inch finish. Nine Pasting Machines. Cardboard. Special Surfaces in Bristols or Cardboard for Offset Printing and Gelatine Plate Printing, Bristols, Tag, Baggage and Ticket Stock, Coated Lithographic Stock, Photo Mounts, etc.

RICHMOND PAPER MFG. CO., Richmond, Va.
Four Single Coaters. Maximum width of sheet 44 inches. Principal product, Coated Blotting. The company also coats Board, Card and Litho. Label in White and Colors.

SHEA BROTHERS, Springfield, Mass.
Glazed.

SPRINGFIELD GLAZED PAPER Co., Springfield, Mass.
Eight Single Coaters. Plated, Friction and Flinted Papers; Embossed, Waterproof, etc.

STANDARD PAPER MFG. CO., Richmond, Va.
Two 32-inch and two 45-inch Single Coaters. Specialties: Colored and Waterproof Coatings, Coated Blotting, Coated Post Card, Litho. Label in White and Colors, and other Coated Specialties.

TAGGART BROS. CO., Watertown, N. Y.
One 60-inch Coating Machine. Bag paper for own use.

WABASH COATING MILLS, Wabash, Ind.
Seven Coaters: One 32½-inch, one 34-inch, two 42-inch, two 44½-inch and one 51-inch Machines; three Platers and five Stacks of Super Calenders. Blanks, Rawhide Leatherettes, Post Card, Car Sign, Railroads, Tough Check, Thick China, Check Book and Memo Cover, Photo Mounts, Label Paper, Embossed Cover Stock, Campaign Bristols, Linen Tag, and all grades of Enameled Folding Box Boards. Capacity, 25 tons per day.

WALTHER & Co., 72 Duane st., New York.
Surface Coated Papers and Specialties.

WARE COATED PAPER Co., Ware, Mass.
All kinds of Surface Coated Papers, Single and Double Coated. High class Litho. and Brush Enameled Papers, Single and Double Coated.

Glazed, Coated Paper and Board Manufacturers

WARREN Co., S. D., 120 Franklin street, Boston, Mass.
See Mill Report.

WATERVLIET PAPER Co., Watervliet, Mich.
Five 54-inch and two 64-inch Single Coaters; one 54-inch Cylinder Coater; two 56-inch and two 66-inch Calenders. See Mill Report in Mill Section.

WEST VIRGINIA PULP & PAPER CO., 200 Fifth ave., New York, and 732 Sherman st., Chicago, Ill.
See Mill Report—Luke, Md.
One Single Coater, widest sheet, 50 inches; two Double Coaters, widest sheet, 50 inches; three Double Coaters, widest sheet, 60 inches.

WHITMORE MFG. Co., Holyoke, Mass.
Fine Coated Lithographic Enameled and Plated Papers, Post Cards and Playing Cards.

WYOMISSING GLAZED PAPER CO., Reading, Pa.
Complete line Surface Coated Papers, Single and Double Coated; Flint Glazed, Friction Glazed and Plated Papers; white and colors, in sheets and rolls.

COATING PLANTS IN CANADA.

PROVINCIAL PAPER MILLS Co., LTD., Barber Division, Georgetown, Ont. Head office, 76 Adelaide St., Toronto, Ont.

GEORGETOWN COATED PAPER MILLS, Georgetown, Ont.

NATIONAL PAPER Co., LTD., Valleyfield, P. Q.
One 51-inch Double Coater; one 42-inch and one 56-inch Single Coaters.

RITCHIE & RAMSAY, LIMITED, Toronto.

Falulah Paper Company
FITCHBURG, MASS.
MANUFACTURERS OF
COATED CARDBOARDS
AND
SPECIALTIES

POST CARD   RAILROADS

CAR SIGN BOARD

Regular sizes and weights carried in stock ready for immediate shipment. As we manufacture the body stock required for our blanks we can give prompt service on orders for special sizes and thicknesses. Your inquiries solicited.

New York Sales Office: WOOLWORTH BUILDING

SPAULDING & TEWKSBURY CO.

FIBRE BOARD Specialties

PAPER and PAPER BOX BOARDS

232 Summer St. **BOSTON** Opp. South Station

ALVAH MILLER　　　　　TOM T. WALLER
JOHN A. DAVIS　　　　　NATHANIEL L. MILLER

H. G. CRAIG & CO.

Paper Merchants

52 VANDERBILT AVE., NEW YORK

NEWS HANGING COLORS
SPECIALTIES

J. Andersen & Company

FREDK. BERTUCH, Special Partner

Successors to

Frederick Bertuch & Company

21 East Fortieth Street, New York

Importers of Foreign Pulps

BLEACHED AND UNBLEACHED SULPHITE
KRAFT PULP AND GROUND WOOD

A SELECTED LIST OF
General Paper Dealers
IN THE
UNITED STATES

WHAT THE INDICATING LETTERS MEAN:
br. Those Concerns that are Branches of Houses located elsewhere. * General Paper Dealers who maintain Stores, *s* Dealers who sell from Storage, Warehouse or from Mill direct, *s. l.* Merchants in ther lines who carry paper as a side line, *w* Paper Dealers who sell principally from wagons.

ALABAMA
Ordway-Newell Co., Anniston.
*Alabama Paper & Printing Co., Birmingham.
*Birmingham Paper Co., Birmingham.
*City Paper Co., Birmingham.
Whitaker Paper Co., Birmingham. *br.*
L. Wind & Co., Huntsville. *s. l.*
Davis, A. D., Pkg. Co., Mobile. *s. l.*
Mobile Broom Co., Mobile. *s. l.*
Mobile Stationery Co., Mobile. *s. l.*
Partin, Malcom, Mobile. *s. l.*
Southern Paper Co., Mobile.
*Mercantile Paper Co., Montgomery.
A. Roemer, Montgomery. *s. l.*
*Montgomery Paper and Woodenware Co., Montgomery.

ARKANSAS
Calvert-McBride Ptg. Co., Ft. Smith.
*Ft. Smith Paper Co., Ft. Smith.
Weldon, Williams & Lick, Ft. Smith.
Fulton-Wassell Paper Co., Little Rock. *s.*
*Tunnah & Pittard Co., Little Rock.
*Western Newspaper Union, Little Rock.
*Turner Paper Co., Inc., Texarkana.

ARIZONA
The Arizona Hardware Co., Phœnix. *s. l.* (Wrapping, Paper Bags, Twine.)
Blake, Moffitt & Towne. *br.* Phoenix.
*The McNeil Co., Phœnix.
*Pilchen, B. A., Tucson.

CALIFORNIA
*Blake, Moffitt & Towne, Los Angeles.
General Paper Co., Los Angeles.

CALIFORNIA—Continued
*Kubler-Weaver Co., Los Angeles.
*Paper Warehouse Co., Los Angeles.
*Pioneer Paper Co., Inc., Los Angeles.
*Sierra Paper Co., Los Angeles.
Standard Woodenware Co., Los Angeles. *s. l.*
Stetson-Barrett Co., Los Angeles. *s. l.*
*Zellerbach Paper Co., Los Angeles.
Brand, Charles, Oakland.
*H. N. Gard & Co., Oakland.
Mackay, Walter S., Oakland.
Monahan, James T., Oakland.
Noffsinger, A. B., Oakland.
Pacific Wooden Ware & Paper Co., Oakland.
*Sunset Paper Co., Oakland.
*Zellerbach Paper Co., Oakland. *br.*
A. S. Hopkins Co., Sacramento. *s. l.*
*Richardson-Case Paper Co., Sacramento.
Blake, Moffitt & Towne, San Diego. *br.*
Klauber-Wagenheim Co., San Diego. *s. l.*
Wandry, Bangs & Ward Co., San Diego. *s. l.*
*Zellerbach Paper Co., San Diego. *br.*

SAN FRANCISCO
Paper Dealers.
Barry, Edward, Co. *s. l.*
*Blake, Moffitt & Towne, 37 First.
*Bonestell & Co., 118 First.
Brown, Ernest V.
California Card Mfg. Co., Potrero av. and Mariposa.
*Crocker, H. S., Co., 565 Market and 230 Brannan. *s. l.*

ENGINEERING FOR **PULP, PAPER AND POWER PLANTS**

JOSEPH H. WALLACE & CO.
INDUSTRIAL ENGINEERS
Temple Court Building, NEW YORK
71 Bay Street, TORONTO, CAN.

General Paper Dealers

SAN FRANCISCO—*Continued.*
Fischer, F. E., 112 Market.
Friedman, J., 1024 McAllister. *s. l.*
General Paper Co., 525 Market.
Kaas Paper Co., Hearst Bldg. *s.*
Lebanon Paper Co.
Maldonado & Co., 37 California. (Export.)
s Marsh & Kidd Co., 617 Mission.
Olcovich, Herman & Son, 625 Market.
Robb Bros., 1134 Valencia.
Schudel, Emil.
Taylor Paper Co.
Weinmann, Wm. L., & Co., 268 Market.
s Williar, H. R., Newhall bldg.
*Zellerbach Paper Co., 534 Battery.

CALIFORNIA—*Continued.*
Delmas, J. A. & A. J., San Jose.
San Jose Paper Co., San Jose.
Eastman-Gibbens Co., Stockton. *s. l.*
Villaron Paper Co., Stockton.

COLORADO.
*Carter, Rice & Carpenter Paper Co., Denver.
*Graham Paper Co., Denver. *br.*
*Peters Paper Co., Denver.
Post, H. H., & Co., Denver. *s. l.*
Western Paper Co., Denver. *br.*
Western Paper Co., Omaha.
*Hyde Paper Co., Pueblo. *br.*

CONNECTICUT.
Bridgeport Paper Co., 618 Water, Bridgeport.
s Gledhill & Co., Bridgeport.
Phelps & Lasher Paper Co., Bridgeport.
s R. M. Houston & Son, Bridgeport.
Smith-Comstock, The, Co., Bridgeport.
Gerry, E., Co., Danbury.
Capitol Paper Co., Hartford.
Chatfield Paper Co., Hartford.
Ginewaky, Julius, Hartford.
Hartford Paper Co., Hartford.
Judd Paper Co., Hartford. *br.*
*P. Garvan (Inc.), Hartford.
Plimpton Mfg. Co., Hartford. *s. l.*
*Rourke-Eno Paper Co., Hartford.
*Russell Hall Co., Meriden.
*Broatch, J. A., Middletown.
L. R. Hazen, Middletown.
*H. H. Corbin & Son, New Britain.
Lehrer, Barney, New Britain.
*The Chatfield Paper Co., New Haven.
Elm City Mfg. Co., New Haven. *s. l.*

CONNECTICUT—*Continued.*
Fowler, Frank E., New Haven.
*Ives, C. W., New Haven.
Kilborn Bros., New Haven. *s. l.*
*New Haven Paper Co., New Haven.
*Ellis, S. N., New London.
Humphrey Cornell Co., New London. *s. l.*
Solomon, Jacob, New London.
Stoddard & Gilbert, New London. *s. l.*
*Utley, H. D., New London.
L. A. Gallup Co., Norwich. *s. l.*
Lee & Osgood Co., Norwich. *s. l.*
Stoddard, Gilbert & Co., Norwich. *s. l.*
Hudson Paper Co., Stamford.
*Stamford Paper Co., Stamford.
Dalken, H. T., Paper Co., Waterbury.
Hotchkiss, Winfred E., Waterbury.
Ideal Wholesale Confectionery Co., Waterbury. *s. l.*
Mattatuck Press, Inc., Waterbury. *s. l.*
*Standard Paper Co., Waterbury.
White Wells Co., The, Waterbury. *s. l.*
Winsted Paper Co., Winsted.

DELAWARE.
Fulton, Harry K., Wilmington.
*Heid & Co., Wilmington.

DISTRICT OF COLUMBIA.
*Andrews, R. P., Paper Co., Inc.
Baum Paper & Stationery Co.
*Bond, B. F., Paper Co. *br.*
Cauthorne, R. A., Paper Co. *br.*
Creecy, W. B., Paper Co., Inc. *w.*
Freedman, S., & Sons. *w.*
*Mathers-Lamm Paper Co.
Morrison Paper Co., E.
Oriental Bag & Paper Co.
Smith, Dixon Co. *br. div.* Whitaker Paper Co.
*Stott, Charles G., & Co., Inc.
Washington Paper Co.
Wolpe & Son, S. R.

FLORIDA.
Antietam Paper Co., Jacksonville. *br.*
*The H. & W. B. Drew Co., Jacksonville.
*Bean & Son Co., E., Jacksonville.
*Florida Paper Co., Jacksonville.
Jacksonville Ptg. Co., Jacksonville. *s. l.*
Soundstrom, A. B., Jacksonville.
s Bear & Co., L., Pensacola.
s Consolidated Grocery Co., Pensacola.

General Paper Dealers

FLORIDA—*Continued.*

s Pensacola Grocery Co., Pensacola.
Peninsular Paper Co., Tampa.
*Roesch Paper Co., Tampa.

GEORGIA.

*American Mills Co., Atlanta.
*Atlanta Paper Co., Atlanta.
Atlanta Wooden Ware Co., Atlanta. s. l.
Dixie Paper & Box Co., Atlanta.
Gershon Bros. Co., Atlanta. s. l.
s Hirshberg Co., Atlanta.
Montag Bros., Inc., Atlanta. s. l.
*National Paper Co., Atlanta.
*Sloan Paper Co., Atlanta.
*S. P. Richards Co., Atlanta.
s United Paper Co., Atlanta.
Whitaker Paper Co., Atlanta. br.
Augusta Grocery Co., Augusta. s. l.
C. T. Pund & Co., Augusta. s. l.
Georgia, Carolina Paper Co., Augusta.
Lyon & Merritt, Augusta. s. l.
Southern Grocery Co., Augusta. s. l.
*Wolfson Paper Co., Columbus.
The J. W. Burke Co., Macon. s. l.
*Jacob Hirsch, Macon.
Macon Paper Co., Macon.
*American Specialty & Import Co., Savannah.
*Byck, M. S. & D. A., Co., Savannah.
Dixie Paper & Box Co., Savannah. br.
*Ehrenreich, I., Sons, Savannah.
Robison Stationery Co., Thomasville.
Valdosta Paper Co., Valdosta.

HAWAIIAN ISLANDS.

Hawaiian News Co., Honolulu, T. H.
*Patten Co., Ltd., Honolulu.

ILLINOIS.

*Erlenborn & Co., A. J., Aurora.

CHICAGO.

General Paper Dealers.

Acme Paper & Supply Co., 4044 Ogden.
Advance Bag Co., 344 N. Canal.
Advance Paper Co., 1002 N. Branch.
*Albany Perforated Wrapping Paper Co., 80 W. Austin.
s ALLEN, A. C., PAPER CO., 122 S. Michigan.
American Paper Goods Co., 126 N. Union.
American Paper Products Co., 130 N. Wells.
Badger Bag & Paper Co., W. Kinzie.

CHICAGO—*Continued.*

*Barton-Hobart Paper Co., 608 S. Dearborn.
Berkshire Co., The, 626 Federal.
Bermingham & Prosser Co., Otis bldg.
*Blohm, Richard, 3816 Ogden av.
Blunden-Lyon Co., 108 W. Harrison.
s Bowman, John R., 538 S. Clark.
Brocklebank, J. C., Conway Bldg.
Bruns, C. H., & Co., 30 N. La Salle.
Burgess, Frank A., & Co., Old Colony bldg.
s Burhop, Henry, Jr., 23 W. Austin av.
*Butler Paper Co., J. W., 212-218 Monroe.
s CADY, E. J., & CO., 336 W. Madison.
Casey, Robt. E., & Co., 340 N. Dearborn.
*Chicago Paper Co., 5th av. and Polk.
Chukerman, J., 2117 W. 12th.
Clarke, F. & J. Mfg. Co., 3438 W. Lake.
Cline, J. S., & Co., 19 S. La Salle.
Corby, S. B., 35 N. Dearborn.
*Cupples Woodenware Co., Samuel, St. Clair and Illinois.
Daily Bros., 20 W. Austin.
*DeJonge, Louis, & Co., 538 S. Clark.
*Diehl & Schroeder, 1381 W. Grand av.
*Duboc Paper Co., 712 Federal.
*Dwight Bros. Paper Co., 626-36 S. Clark.
*Eastern Paper Co., 11 N. Green.
*Empire Paper Co., 725 S. Fifth av.
Federal Paper Co., 224-230 W. Huron.
Flonacher, Henry, Co., 1229 S. Wabash.
s Forsythe Paper Co., 208 S. La Salle.
Fowler, W. A., Paper Co., 343 S. Dearborn.
Fried & Bell, 1617 W. 12th.
Garfield Paper Co., 2725 W. Madison.
Gilman, I., & Co., 1701 Fisher Bldg.
Goldstein, Jos. & Sons, 709 S. Dearborn.
Graham Paper Co., 1136 S. Wabash. br.
Grulee, Frank J., Monadnock Bldg.
*Hanchett Paper Co., 1002 N. Branch.
Hazen, Frederick B., 701 S. La Salle.
Henry, Willard J., 344 N. Canal.

ENGINEERING FOR **PULP, PAPER AND POWER PLANTS**

JOSEPH H. WALLACE & CO.
INDUSTRIAL ENGINEERS
Temple Court Building, NEW YORK
71 Bay Street, TORONTO, CAN.

General Paper Dealers

CHICAGO—Continued.
*Hollis & Duncan, 782 W. Lake.
Holmes, E. T., 112 W. Adams.
Holmes, Marc S., 161 W. Harrison.
Humboldt Paper Co., 2543 W. Division.
Immerwahr, M. E., 335 S. Market.
s Import Paper Co., 335 S. Market.
*Inlander, S., & Co., 5210 S. Ashland av., 11 N. Green and 9216 Burley av.
*Inlander & Steindler, 9216 Burley av.
Jansen Paper Co., 852 W. 103d.
Johnson, Geo. T. Co., 400 S. Clinton
Kalamazoo Stationery Mfg. Co., 209 S. State.
*Kirchheimer Bros Co., Ohio and Kingsbury.
*Knox & Wolcott Paper Co., 626 Federal.
*Kupfer Bros., 28 W. Illinois.
La Boiteaux, C. L., Co., 608 S. Dearborn.
La Salle Paper Co., 187 N. Dearborn.
s Lee Paper Co., 701 S. La Salle.
*Levin Bros., 1840 Carroll av.
s Lloyd, E. E., Paper Co., 208 S. La Salle.
s Luneschloss, J. S., 326 W. Madison.
MANUFACTURERS PAPER CO., 209 S. La Salle.
McENERY PAPER CO., 112 W. Adams.
*McGregor Paper Co., 536 S. Clark.
McNulty Paper & Twine Co., 18 W. Kinzie.
Megargee-Hare Paper Co., 327 S. La Salle.
*Messinger, W. D., & Co., 180 W. Randolph.
*Midland Paper Co., 322 W. Washington.
MID-STATES GUMMED PAPER CO., 312 Union Pk. Ct.
Mid-West Paper Co., 732 Federal.
Milwaukee Lace Paper Co., 115 S. Dearborn. (Branch.)
*Moser Paper Co., 621-31 Plymouth ct.
National Card, Mat & Board Co., 218 W. Superior.
National Paper Products Co., 224-230 W. Huron.
National Safety Paper Co., 38 S. Dearborn.
Newton, L., 527 S. Jefferson.
Niagara Bag & Paper Co., 1701 Fisher Bldg.
Opila & Biedka, 2012 S. Ashland av.
*Paper Mills Co., 517 S. 5th av.

CHICAGO—Continued.
Paper Mills Specialty Co., Inc., 222 W. Kinzie.
Paper Sales Co., 224 W. Huron.
Parke-McCauley Co., Inc., 1223 S. Wabash.
*Parker-Thomas-Tucker Paper Co., 537 S. Franklin.
Peck, D. F. Paper Co., 343 S. Dearborn.
Peerless Paper Co., Inc., 612 W. Randolph.
*Phillips, R. E., & Bro., 337 W. Madison.
*Pilcher-Hamilton Co., 330 N. Dearborn.
Pomeroy Paper Co., Conway bldg.
Pull-the-String Mailing Wrapper Co., 228 W. Superior.
Randolph Paper Co., 622 W. Randolph.
Rapp Co., The, Arthur R., Conway Bldg.
*Rauth Bros., 727 W. Lake.
Regenstein-Veeder Co., N. Halsted and Rees.
Reinhard, Abraham, 412 S. Wells.
*Rentz, Fred, Paper Co., 173 N. Green.
*Rockwell-Barnes Co., 823 S. Wabash av.
Rosenberg Paper Co., 3623 Jasper pl.
Royal Lace Paper Works, 1902 S. Albany.
Sanitary Cup & Service Co., 180 N. Market.
Schermerhorn Bros. Co., 5 N. La Salle.
s Schwarz, S. L., & Co., 1430 S. Canal.
Scott Paper Co., 113 E. Austin.
s SEAMAN PAPER CO., 208 S. La Salle.
Singer Paper Co., 815 W. Congress.
Sippel-Tress Co., 733 Eagle.
Smith, H. P., Paper Co., 1130 W. 37th.
*Smith, Bradner & Co., 175 W. Monroe.
Southworth Co., 35 S. Wabash.
Springfield Glazed Paper Co., 29 La Salle.
Stewart, A. G., Paper Co., 110 S. Dearborn.
Sutherland Paper Co., 110 S. Dearborn.
*Swigart Paper Co., 653 S. 5th av.
Tarentum Paper Mills, 1229 S. Wabash.
Taylor, A. E., & Co., 343 S. Dearborn.

PRESS ROLLS Maple and Gum White Wood Felt Rolls J. W. HEWITT MACHINE CO. Neenah, Wis.

General Paper Dealers

CHICAGO—*Continued.*
*Thoms Bros. Co., 216 N. Sangamon.
*Traver, F. C., Paper Co., 358 W. Ontario.
Tuttle Press Co., 326 W. Madison.
Watson, H. F., Co., 319 Wells.
*Well, Joseph, 1423 S. Halsted.
*Weir Bros. Paper Co., 564 W. Lake.
Whitaker Paper Co., Cont. & Corn Bk. Bldg. *br.*
*White, Jas., Paper Co., 219 W. Monroe.
Williams, Chas. W., & Co., 538 S. Clark.
*Williams Wrapper Co., 226 W. Superior.
Witkowsky, Leon, 335 S. Market.
*Wolf, Frank J., 1635 Blue Island av.
*Wray, Douglas, Paper Co., 732 Sherman.
Wright, Wm. E., 189 W. Madison.
Wrigley, C. A., 130 N. Wells.
s Wroe, W. E., & Co., 208 E. Illinois av.

Board Dealers.
ALTON BOX BOARD & PAPER CO., 11 S. La Salle.
Chicago Coated Board, 11 S. La Salle.
Cline, J. S., & Co., 19 S. La Salle.
Holmes, E. T., 112 West Adams.
La Boiteaux, C. L., Co., Transportation bldg.
MANUFACTURERS' PAPER CO., 209 S. La Salle.
United Paperboard Co., 111 West Monroe.

Building Papers.
Bird & Son, Inc., Monadnock Block.
Cabot, Sam'l, Inc., 24 W. Kinzie.
Ford Mfg. Co., 2389 La Salle.
Johns-Manville, S. W., Co., 1737 S. Michigan.
Hopkins, H. H., Co., 111 W. Lake.
Union Insulating Co., 1613 Great Northern bldg.
Watson, H. F., Co., 319 Wells.

Brokers' and Manufacturers' Agents.
s ALLEN, A. C., PAPER CO., 122 S. Michigan.
Blunden-Lyon Co., 108 W. Harrison.
Brocklebank, J. C., Conway Bldg.
Bowman, J. R., 14 E. Jackson.
Bruns, C. H., & Co., 10 S. La Salle.
Burgess, Frank A., & Co., Old Colony bldg.
Burhop, Henry, Jr., 23 W. Austin.
Casey, Robert E., & Co., 340 N. Dearborn.

CHICAGO—*Continued.*
Cline & Co., J. S., 19 S. La Salle.
Corby, S. B., 85 N. Dearborn.
Flight, W. N., 326 W. Madison.
Fox, Edwin V., 209 S. La Salle.
Haines, Jeremiah, 914 First National Bank Bldg.
Hanchett, Jr., L. J., 813 W. 22d.
Henry, Willard J., 344 N. Canal.
Johnson Co., Geo. T., 400 S. Clinton.
La Boiteaux, C. L., Co., 608 S. Dearborn.
Luneschloss, J. S., 326 W. Madison.
Mansell, Hunt, Catty & Co., 130 N. Dearborn.
McENERY PAPER CO., 112 W. Adams.
Miner, H. J., 5 N. La Salle.
Moody, F. K., & Co., 326 W. Madison.
Parke-McCauley Co., 1223 S. Wabash.
Phillips, Wm., 337 W. Madison.
Rosenberg Paper Co., 3623 Jasper pl.
Shuart, Irving J., 29 S. La Salle.
Taylor, A. E., & Co., 343 S. Dearborn.
Wilson, Chas. R., 209 S. La Salle.
Wright, Wm. E., 707 Security bldg.
Wrigley, C. A., 130 N. 5th av.

ILLINOIS—*Continued.*
West Paper Co., Decatur.
*Root, W. A., Elgin.
*Robert Pilcher, Joliet.
Blair Paper Co., Peoria.
Streibich, John C., Company, Peoria.
*Irwin Paper Co., Quincy.
Paper Products & Envelope Co., Quincy.
*Schocker Paper Co., Rock Island.
*Springfield Paper Co., Springfield.

INDIANA.
Elkhart Stationery Co., Elkhart.
*Evansville Paper & Woodenware Co., Evansville.
*Ferdinand Funke's Sons, Evansville.
*Smith Paper Co., Evansville.
Andrews, H. J., Co., Fort Wayne.
*Becker Paper Co., Fort Wayne.
*Fisher Brothers Paper Co., Fort Wayne.
*Rothschild Bros., Fort Wayne.
Smick, M. M., & Co., Fort Wayne.
Tapajna Gary Paper Co., Gary.
*Inlander & Steindler, Hammond. *br.*
*Atlas Paper Co., Indianapolis.
*Capital Paper Co., Indianapolis.

M. GOTTESMAN & CO., Inc.
13 E. 41st STREET, NEW YORK. Cable Address "Namettop"
EUROPEAN OFFICES: Stockholm, Sweden

Strong and Easy Bleaching SULPHITE PULP

ENGINEERING FOR PULP, PAPER AND POWER PLANTS

JOSEPH H. WALLACE & CO.
INDUSTRIAL ENGINEERS
Temple Court Building, NEW YORK
71 Bay Street, TORONTO, CAN.

INDIANA—*Continued.*
Central Ohio Paper Co., 1101 State Life bldg., Indianapolis. *br.*
*Crescent Paper Co., Indianapolis.
*Indiana Paper Co., Indianapolis.
Johnson, D. J., Hotel Service.
*O. P. Lesh Paper Co., Indianapolis.
*Standard Paper Co., Indianapolis.
Whitaker Paper Co., Bd. of Trade Bldg., Indianapolis. *br.*
Central Supply House, Lafayette. *s. l.*
Osborn Paper Co., 1119-21-23 S. Washington, Marion.
Guthrie Bros., New Albany.
Wiest, John, Richmond. *s.*
*Jacobson-Peterson Co., South Bend. *s.*
Bement-Rea Co., Terre Haute.
Hulman & Co., Terre Haute. *s. l.*
Levin Bros., Terre Haute. *s. l.*
S. Locke & Co., Terre Haute.
Standard Paper Co., Terre Haute.

IOWA.
*Burlington Paper Co., Burlington.
*Baker Paper Co., Cedar Rapids.
*Martin Klein, Cedar Rapids.
*Mullin, Geo. A., Co., Cedar Rapids.
*Davenport Bag and Paper Co., Davenport.
*H. A. Morrow Co., Davenport.
*Thomson & Ahrensdorf, Davenport.
*Carpenter Paper Co., Des Moines.
*Langan Bros. Co., Des Moines.
*Percival Co., C. L., Des Moines.
*Pratt Paper Co., Des Moines.
*Western Newspaper Union, Des Moines.
*Dubuque Paper & Supply Co., Dubuque.
*Standard Paper Co., Dubuque.
*McFarland Paper Co., Keokuk.
Gripper, D. W., Co., Mason City.
*Niemeyer Bros., Ottumwa.
Western Newspaper Union, Sioux City. *s. l.*
*Pill Bros. Paper Co., Sioux City.
*Sioux City Paper Co., Sioux City.
*Adams Paper Co., Waterloo.
McCartney, W. J., Waterloo.
*Waterloo Paper Co., Waterloo.

KANSAS.
*Leavenworth Bag Co., Leavenworth.
*Central-Topeka Paper Co., Topeka.
Gates Bros. Paper Co., Wichita.
*Western Newspaper Union, Wichita. *br.*
*Whitney Paper Co., Wichita.

KENTUCKY.
Faulconer, G. Z., Co., Lexington. *s. l.*
Lexington Paper Co., Lexington.
Whitaker Paper Co., Fayette Bank Bldg., Lexington. *br.*
Chatfield & Woods Co., The, Louisville. *br.*
Cincinnati Cordage & Paper Co., Louisville. *br.*
Diem & Wing Paper Co., Louisville. *br.*
E. B. Dye, Louisville.
L. Gould, Levy Co., Louisville. *s. l.*
Graham Paper Co., Louisville. *br.*
*Louisville Paper Co., Louisville.
Myer-Bridges Co., Louisville. *s. l.*
Paper Makers Co., Louisville.
*J. C. Parker Paper Co., Louisville.
*Southeastern Paper Co., Louisville.
*Weinberg, N. I., Louisville. *w.*
Whitaker Paper Co., Louisville. *br.*
*Schwer, W. J., Paper Goods, Newport.

LOUISIANA.
Cupples, Samuel, Woodenware Co., New Orleans. *br. s.*
*Diamond Paper Co., New Orleans.
*Graham Paper Co., New Orleans (branch).
Jos. Levy & Bros. Co., New Orleans. *s. l.*
Louapre, E. J., Co., New Orleans. *s. l.*
*Julius Meyer, New Orleans.
Morris Co., J. C., Ltd., New Orleans. *s. l.*
*E. C. Palmer & Co., Ltd., New Orleans.
*Southern Paper Co., Ltd., New Orleans.
*Standard Paper Co., New Orleans.
Wolbrette, Jules. *s.*
*Louisiana Paper Co., Shreveport.

MAINE.
Wardwell & Co., R. L., Augusta.
*Berry Paper Co., Lewiston.
Geo. W. Raymond, Lewiston.
*Palmer, Herbert L., Pittsfield.
*C. M. Rice Paper Co., Portland.
*Chas. H. Robinson Co., Portland.
Cobb, Francis, Co., Rockland.
St. Clair & Allen, Rockland.

MARYLAND.
BALTIMORE.
Baltimore Paper Co., Inc., 36 S. Hanover.
Barton, Duer & Koch Paper Co., 113 S. Gay.
*Beers & Co., Chas. W., 7 E. Lombard.

General Paper Dealers

MARYLAND—*Continued.*

*Bond Paper Co., B. F., 33 S. Hanover.
*Bradley-Reese Co., 308 W. Pratt.
Buccheri, Thomas, Baltimore. *w.*
Columbia Paper Bag Co., 921 E. Fort av.
*DOBLER & MUDGE, 113 Hopkins pl.
*Fenton, M. C., 18 W. Pratt.
Fine, A. J., & Sons, Baltimore.
*Frank, S., & Son, 502 W. Lexington.
*Harlem Paper Co., 4 E. Lombard.
*Hock, J. Francis, & Co., Inc., 30 S. Charles.
*Hubbs & Corning Co., 404 S. Eutaw.
Lengrick, H. A., Baltimore.
*Lindemeyr, Philip, Pratt & Charles, 2 W. Pratt.
Mallinckrodt, L. K., 122 S. Calvert.
Maryland Paper Co., 503 Forest.
Moore, W. H., Jr., Paper Co., 210 Guilford av.
*Mentzel, Henry D., & Co., 34 Light.
Mentzel-Fergusson Paper Co., 106 S. Charles.
Paper Products Co., 2405 to 2411 W. Franklin.
* *s* Reese & Reese, Calvert & German
Richards Paper Co., 124 S. Calvert.
*Robins Paper Co., 116 S. Eutaw.
* *s* Smith, Dixon, Co., Div. Whitaker Paper Co., Guilford av.
*Stevens, C. E. Bros., 124 Hopkins pl.
Walterboefer, Harry C., 122 N. Greene.
*Warner, O. F. H., & Co.
Younghemim, Charles, Paper Co., Baltimore.

CUMBERLAND.

*Tri-State Paper Co.

HAGERSTOWN.

Antietam Paper Co.
Hagerstown Bookbinding & Ptg. Co. *s, l.*

MASSACHUSETTS.
BOSTON.
General Paper Dealers.

A. P. W. Paper Co., 79 Milk.
s Albertine Paper Co., 914 Exchange Bldg.
s Alexander Paper Co., 184 Summer.
American Paper Co., 44 Cross.
*ANDREWS PAPER CO., 54 India.
*ARNOLD-ROBERTS CO., 180 Congress.
*BAIRD & BARTLETT CO., 63 High.
Bay State Paper Co., 327-333 Summer.

BOSTON—*Continued.*

s Blackstone Paper Co., 10 Marshall.
*Boston Paper Board Co., 161 Albany.
*Botsford, C. B., & Co., 127 Kingston.
s Bridge, Chas., 170 Summer.
BROWN, CHAS. D., & CO., 185 Devonshire.
s Burr, A. N., 10 High.
s Carrecabe, J. M., 78 High. Paper, Twine.
*CARTER, JOHN, & CO., 100-102 Federal.
*CARTER, RICE & CO., 240 Devonshire.
*Casey, Bigley & Co., 11 Otis, Winthrop Square.
s Chandler, L. W., Hancock Bldg.
*Cheever, John S., Co., 44 Farnsworth.
s Churchill, Asaph, Hancock Bldg.
*CLAFLIN, W. H., & CO., INC., 332-340 Summer.
*Cook-Vivian Co., 183 Congress.
s Curtis, Nelson, 2304 Washington.
s Denison-Pratt Paper Co., 67 Milk.
*Dill & Collins Co., 161 Pearl.
*Dodge, W. C., Paper Co., 75 High.
Eaton, Albert M., Paper Co., 839 Albany.
s Eastern Paper Co., 683 Atlantic.
*ELLIOTT, W. R., CO., 7 Sears.
Esty Paper Co., Chas., 81 Milk. *br.*
s Faneuil Hall Paper Co., 23 Merchants row.
*Fort Hill Paper Co., 143 High.
*Ginsburg Bros., 14 Minot.
s Ginsburg, I., 130 Commercial.
s Globe Paper Co., 110 Fulton.
s Greene, R. L., Paper Co., 170 Summer. *br.*
s Guild, H. R., 223 Hancock bldg.
s Hall, H. K. W., 16 Kingston.
s Hall, John E., 79 Milk.
*Hallett Bros. Co., 35 Sleeper.
*Johnson, G. T., Co., 75 Batterymarch.
s Jordan Card & Paper Co., 170 Summer.
Japan Paper Co., 453 Washington.
*LINDENMEYR, HENRY, & SONS, 86 Federal. *br.*
s Lindsay, E. P., 291 Congress.
*Lovejoy, L. H., & Co., 40 Gibson, Dorchester. (Paper Bags.)
s Macomber, F. E., 261 Franklin.
s Marr, Llewellyn A., 176 Federal.
Marshall, L. C., & Co., 114 State.
s Munro & Church Co., 10 High.
*MUNROE, D. F., CO., 299 Congress.

General Paper Dealers

BOSTON—*Continued.*

s Ogden, Ira B., 201 Devonshire.
s Paper House of N. E., 516 Atlantic av. *br.*
s Perry, J. E., Co., 10 High.
*Proctor Paper Co., Chas. S., 228 Congress.
*Riordan, John, 197 High.
s Rosenbloom, Eli, 8 Minot. (Wrapping Paper.)
s Sexton, Ralph E., 161 Devonshire. (Wax.)
Seymour Co., 176 Federal. *br.*
*Smith, Jr., H. G., Paper Goods Co., 200 Devonshire.
*SPAULDING & TEWKSBURY, 232 Summer.
s Spencer & Co., 184 Tremont.
*STIMPSON & CO., 65 Chatham.
*STONE & ANDREW, 280 Devonshire.
*STONE & FORSYTH CO., 67 Kingston.
*STORRS, A., & BEMENT CO., 138 and 150 Federal.
s Swain, Otis W., 118 Commercial.
s Teele, E. W., 627 John, Hancock bldg.
*Tileston & Livermore, 514 Atlantic av.
*Tyler Paper Co., 128 Pearl.
*VON OLKER-SNELL PAPER CO., 112 Pearl.
s Warner & Childs Co., Medford. (Corrugated Paper.)
Whitaker Paper Co., 327 Summer. *br.*
*Whitney Bros., Inc., 29-31 Fansworth.
s Wilkinson Bros. & Co., 131 State. *br.*
*Winchenbaugh, L. P., 98 Federal.
s Wise, Jr., George W., 86 Federal.

Paper Box Board Dealers.

*BAIRD & BARTLETT CO., 43 High.
Boston Paper Board Co., 161 Albany.
s BROWN, C. D., & CO., 185 Devonshire.
s Eastern Paper Co., 683 Atlantic av.
s. Munro & Church Co., 10 High.
s Perry Co., J. E., 10 High.
*SPAULDING & TEWKSBURY CO., 232 Summer.
s White Son Co., 530-540 Atlantic av.

Leather Board Dealers and Manufacturers.

Boston Leather & Fibre Co., 7 Sherman.

BOSTON—*Continued.*

Carrecabe, John M., 78 High.
Groton Leather Board Co., 16 State.
Gurney, D. B., 51 Lincoln.
Leatheroid Mfg. Co., 124 Beach.
National Fibre Board Co., 124 Beach.
Spaulding, J., & Sons Co., 89 Beach.
SPAULDING & TEWKSBURY, 232 Summer.

Twine and Cordage Dealers.

American Net & Twine Co., 575 Atlantic av.
ANDREWS PAPER CO., 54 India.
Botsford & Co., C. B., 127 Kingston.
CARTER, RICE & CO., 246 Devonshire.
Casey, Bigley Co., 11 Otis, Winthrop Square.
Cheever, John S., Co., 44 Farnsworth.
Columbian Rope Co., 131 Beverly. *br.*
Connor & Co., P. L., 1000 Harrison av.
Davis & Co., T. L., 110 State.
Graham, James J., & Co., 25 India sq.
Harrington, King & Co., 79 Commercial.
Hoffman-Corr Mfg. Co., 136 Federal.
Ludlow Mfg. Associates, 111 Devonshire.
Mullane, D. J., Chelsea.
MUNROE CO., D. F., 299 Congress.
Plymouth Cordage Co., 126 State.
Riordan, John, 197 High.
Sampson Cordage Works, 88 Broad.
STIMPSON & CO., 65 Chatham.
STONE & FORSYTH, 67 Kingston.
STORRS, A., & BEMENT CO., 138-150 Federal.

MASSACHUSETTS—*Continued.*

Atwood Paper Co., Brockton.
*M. F. Ellis & Co., Brockton.
Mullane Bros., Chelsea. *w.*
Spencer & Co., Everett.
Michael Cox, Fall River.
Roy Paper Co., Fall River.
Fitchburg Paper and Bag Co., 12 North Fitchburg.
H. E. Remington & Co., Fitchburg. *s. l.*
*F. H. Brown & Co., Greenfield.
*Noyes Paper Co., Inc., Haverhill.
s Garvan, P., Inc., Holyoke. *br.*
*Judd Paper Co., Holyoke.
*Judge, M. J., Holyoke.

HARDY S. FERGUSON
CONSULTING ENGINEER
200 FIFTH AVENUE
NEW YORK CITY

PAPER, PULP AND FIBRE MILLS
WATER POWER DEVELOPMENT
DAMS, STORAGE RESERVOIRS AND
OTHER HYDRAULIC STRUCTURES

PRESS ROLLS — Maple and Gum White Wood Felt Rolls — **J. W. HEWITT MACHINE CO.** Neenah, Wis.

General Paper Dealers 375

MASSACHUSETTS—*Continued.*
*O'Connell-Quirk Paper Co., Holyoke.
*Plymouth Paper Co., Holyoke.
Sabin-Robins Paper Co., Holyoke. *br.*
s Stedman, Wm. S., Holyoke.
Woodruff, J. B., Holyoke.
James R. Bailey, Lawrence.
s Berger, H., Lawrence.
George H. Hadley & Co., Lawrence.
s R. A. Davis, Lowell.
*F. J. Flemings, Lowell.
*Proctor Paper Co., Lowell.
Wight, M. G., & Co., Lowell.
Copeland, Leroy H., Lynn. *w.*
Essex Paper & Bag Co., Lynn.
H. O. Newhall, Lynn. *w.*
L. P. Purington, Lynn.
*Vincent Co., Frank E., Lynn.
*Curtis-Draper Co., Milford.
F. S. Brightman Co., New Bedford.
Kennedy & Kirwin, New Bedford.
Roy Paper Co., New Bedford.
Sales, W. B., Co., New Bedford.
Moulton Company, The, Newburyport.
S. H. Thurlow & Co., Newburyport.
A. R. Bloch, North Attleboro.
C. C. Blain, Pittsfield.
Brigham, C. T., & Co., Pittsfield.
*Central Paper Co., Salem.
L. B. Moody, Salem. *s. l.*
*Philbrick, L. B., Salem.
s S. H. Abbott, Somerville.
*H. W. Carter Paper Co., Springfield.
*Eastern Paper and Supply Co., Springfield.
Frank Bros. Paper Co., Springfield.
s Joseph Freedman, Springfield.
s New England Card & Paper Co., Springfield.
Standard Paper & Merchandise Co., Springfield.
*Thacker-Craig Co., Springfield.
*The Paper House of New England, Springfield.
*Thomas & Co., C. H., Springfield.
Gallivan, James P., Co., Taunton.
H. A. Dickerman & Son, Taunton.
*A. M. Eaton Paper Co., Waltham.
Bryan Hardware Co., Westfield. *s. l.*
J. R. Gladwin, Westfield. *s. l.*
s F. O. Davis, Worcester.
*Esty, Chas. A., Paper Co., Burgess-Lang bldg., Worcester.
Gaffney, J. H., representing Whitney Bros., Inc., Worcester.
Judd Paper Co., Worcester. *br.*
Paper House of New England, Worcester.

MASSACHUSETTS—*Continued.*
*Perkins & Butler, Worcester.
*H. B. Stone & Co., Worcester.
Worcester Woodenware & Paper Co., Worcester.

MICHIGAN.
Adrian Paper Co., Adrian.
Moreland, S. L., Bros. & Crane, Adrian.
J. F. Halladay & Son, Battle Creek. *s. l.*
Godsmark, Durand & Co., Battle Creek. *s. l.*
*Redner & Courtright, Battle Creek.
Carroll, D. J., Bay City. *s. l.*
Hurley Bros., Bay City.
Kavanagh & Madden, Bay City. *s. l.*
Kirchman Bros., Bay City. *s. l.*
s A. Robachek, Bay City.
Lockway, Stouck & Ludwig Co., Benton Harbor. *s.*
Ed. M. Lieblein, Calumet.
Beecher, Peck & Lewis, Detroit.
Central Ohio Paper Co., 1823 Ford bldg., Detroit. *br.*
Chope-Stevens Paper Co., Detroit.
*Gebhard Paper Co., Detroit.
*National Paper Co., Detroit.
Printers & Publishers Paper Co., Detroit.
Seaman-Patrick Paper Co., Detroit.
*Union Paper & Twine Co., Detroit.
*Welt & Sons Paper Co., Detroit.
Whitaker Paper Co., Detroit. *br.*
*C. E. Brandt & Co., Flint.
Symons-Moffet Co., Flint. *s. l.*
*Central Michigan Paper Co., Grand Rapids.
*Dwight Bros. Paper Co., Grand Rapids. (Fine papers.)
*Grand Rapids Paper Co., Grand Rapids. (Coarse papers.)
Judson Grocer Co., Grand Rapids. (Wrapping.) *s. l.*
Lee Paper Co., E. R., Grand Rapids. (Fine Papers.)
Mills, C. W., Paper Co., Grand Rapids.
National Grocer Co., Grand Rapids. (Wrapping.) *s. l., br.*
Radamaker-Dooge Co., Grand Rapids. (Wrapping.) *s. l.*
Silbar & Co., Grand Rapids. (Wrapping.)
Worden Grocery Co., Grand Rapids. (Wrapping.) *s. l.*
Lieblein, Ed. M., Hancock.
*The Crown Paper and Bag Co., Jackson.

ENGINEERING FOR
'ULP, PAPER AND POWER PLANTS

JOSEPH H. WALLACE & CO.
INDUSTRIAL ENGINEERS
Temple Court Building, NEW YORK
71 Bay Street,   TORONTO, CAN.

General Paper Dealers

MICHIGAN—*Continued.*
*Bermingham & Prosser Co., Kalamazoo.
*Johnson Paper and Supply Co., Kalamazoo.
*Star Paper Co., Kalamazoo.
Wright, Chas. H., & Son, Kalamazoo.
s Dudley, The, Paper Co., Lansing.
Moulton Grocer Co., Muskegon. *s. l.*
Hume Grocery Co., Muskegon. *s. l.*
*Steindler, S., Muskegon.
*Saginaw Paper Co., Saginaw.
Saginaw Woodenware Co., Saginaw. *s. l.*
Swinton & Co., Saginaw.

MINNESOTA.
Schleuder Paper Co., Austin.
*Duluth Paper and Stationery Co., Duluth.
*McClellan Paper Co., Duluth *br.*
Minneapolis Paper Co., Duluth. *br.*
*Peyton Paper Co., Duluth.
*Courtney, C. A., Minneapolis.
Falk, M. F., Paper Co., Minneapolis.
Falk Paper Co., Minneapolis. *br.*
*John Leslie Paper Co., Minneapolis.
*McClellan Paper Co., Minneapolis.
*Minneapolis Paper Co., Minneapolis.
Seaman Paper Co., Minneapolis. *s, br.*
*The Paper Supply Co., Minneapolis.
Wright, Barrett & Stilwell Co., Minneapolis. *br.*
s Inter-City Paper Co., Minnesota Transfer.
s Troendle, V. H., Minnesota Transfer.
s Cupples, Samuel, Woodenware Co., St. Paul. *br.*
Falk Paper Co., M. F., St. Paul.
*M. F. Kerwin Paper Co., St. Paul.
*Leslie-Donahower Co., St. Paul.
*Melady Paper Co., Inc., St. Paul.
*Nassau Paper Co., St. Paul.
*Price, Robbins & Newton, St. Paul.
*Stilwell, E. J., Co., St. Paul.
St. Paul Paper Co., St. Paul.
s Troendle, V. H., St. Paul.
*Wright, Barrett & Stilwell Co., St. Paul.

MISSOURI.
*Osborne Paper Co., Joplin.
*Benedict Paper Co., Kansas City.
*Berlau Paper House, Kansas City.
Cole, H. C., & Co., Kansas City.
*Cupples, W. W., Co., Samuel, Kansas City.

MISSOURI—*Continued.*
*Graham Paper Co., Kansas City. *br.*
*Kansas City Paper House, Kansas City.
*Missouri-Interstate Paper Co., Kansas City.
s A. U. Morse & Co., Kansas City.
s J. G. Schermerhorn Twine and Paper Co., Kansas City.
Schwarz, S. L., Paper Co., Kansas City.
Standard Paper & Woodenware Co., Kansas City.
Thompson Paper & Specialty Co., Kansas City.
St. Joseph Paper Co., St. Joseph.
*Sheridan Clayton Paper Co., St. Joseph.
*Springfield Paper and Supply Co., Springfield.

ST. LOUIS.
Acme Paper Co., 113-19 S. 8th.
American Paper Products Paper Co., 2d and Bremen av.
*Beacon Paper Co., 301 N. Second.
Bermingham & Seaman Co., 410 S. Fourth. *br.*
s Brooks Paper Co., Security bldg.
*Brown Paper Co., 1700 Franklin av.
Bulls, J. C., Mfg. Co., Inc., 1122 S. 12th. *s. l.*
*T. P. Chapman Paper Co., N. E. cor. Olive and Second.
Cree-Obear Paper Co., 525 N. 2d.
*Crescent Paper Co., 413 N. 2d.
Cruden-Martin, W. W., Co., Second and Gratiot. *s. l.*
*Cupples, W. W., Co., Samuel, 7th and Spruce.
Diem & Wing Paper Co., Rialto bldg. *br.*
*Evertz-Etz Paper Co., 1542 S. 7th.
Fitzwilliam Co., J. J., 208 Pierce Bldg.
*Graham Paper Co., 11th and Spruce. Branches at Nashville, Tenn., Kansas City, Mo., Denver, Colo., New Orleans, La., Chicago, Ills.
Hemple Paper Co., 1801 Biddle. *w.*
Jones Woodenware & Paper Co., 806 Spruce. *s. l.*
*Knoliman Paper Co., 2329 Dodier.
La Monte, Geo., & Son, 3d National Bank Bldg. *s.*
*Libby & Williams Paper Co., 419-421 N. 2d.
*Mack-Elliott Paper Co., 309 Valentine.
Mississippi Valley Paper Co., 215 N. 2d.

General Paper Dealers 377

ST. LOUIS—*Continued*.
*National Paper Co., Main and Brooklyn.
Robins Paper Co., Sabin, 218 Walnut. br.
Robinson Paper Co., 4804a Moffit av. w.
*Rosenthal Paper Co., 618 N. 2d.
Royal Paper Co., 4165 Grove. s.
Sabin Robins Paper Co., Boatman's Bank Bldg.
s St. Louis Box Board Co., Inc., Pierce Bldg.
*St. Louis Paper Co., 500-502 N. 3d.
Scott Paper Co., 420 N. 3d.
Security Safety Paper Co., Inc., 2086 Morgan.

MONTANA.
Standard Publishing Co., Anaconda. s. l.
*Butte Paper Co., Butte.
Calkins, B. E., Co., Butte.
*Great Falls Paper Co., Great Falls, Mont.
s Lindsay & Co., Ltd., Helena.
s Minneapolis Paper Co., Helena. br.

NEBRASKA.
*Lincoln Paper Co., Lincoln.
*Schwarz Paper Co., Lincoln.
Western Newspaper Union, Lincoln. br.
Bemis Omaha Bag Co., Omaha.
*Brinn & Jensen Co., Omaha.
*Carpenter Paper Co., Omaha.
*Field, Hamilton, Smith Co., Omaha.
Ribbel Paper & Woodenware Co., Omaha. s. l.
*The Marshall Paper Co., Omaha.
Western Newspaper Union, Omaha.
*The Western Paper Co., Omaha.

NEW HAMPSHIRE.
Carter & Co., John, Concord. br.
Forsaith, D. J., representing Whitney Bros., Inc., Manchester.
Varick, John B., Co., Manchester.

NEW JERSEY.
Winans Co., C. G., Asbury Park. br.
Burnett, J. Y., Bayonne.
Eisenberg Bros., Camden. s. l.
Feldman, A., & Son, Camden. s. l.
Hill, Geo., Camden.
Hersh, L. F., & Bro., Elizabeth, s. l.
Oderman, David H., Elizabeth.
Gatti-McQuade Co., Inc., Hoboken.
Kirschbroum, Max, Hoboken.
Liberman, J., & Co., Jersey City.
Maxwell, Chas., Jersey City.

NEW JERSEY—*Continued*.
s Wolgast, L., Jersey City.
Bishop, Charles H., Newark.
Bloom, Samuel, Newark.
Commerce Paper Co., Newark.
*Jacob Freudenthal, Newark.
Galowitz & Son, B., 280 Ferry, Newark.
S. Greenberg & Co., Newark.
HENRY LINDENMEYR & SONS, 32 Clinton, Newark. br.
Hersh & Bro., L. F., Newark.
Industrial Paper Co., Newark.
*J. E. Linde Paper Co., 48 Lafayette, Newark. br.
Miller, The, Bros. Co., Newark.
Mooney, H. G., Co., Newark.
Pagano, Angelo, Newark.
*M. Plum, Newark.
Ribbans, Charles, Newark.
Ringel Bros., Newark.
H. Sobo & Son, Newark.
S. Warschawsky & Son, Newark.
Vernon Bros. & Co. br.
Winans, C. G., Co., Newark.
Zinberg, B., & Son, Newark.
Bergen, J. S., New Brunswick.
Fertig, A. H., New Brunswick.
New Brunswick Paper Co., New Brunswick.
New York & New Jersey Paper Co., New Brunswick.
Samuel Berlin, Passaic.
Jewett, E. W., Passaic.
Malcolm, John, Passaic.
Fogelman, I., Passaic.
Roth, Robt., Passaic.
Tobin, J., Passaic.
J. W. Cleveland Hardware Co., Paterson. s. l.
Federbush, S., Paterson.
*Fischer & Bond, Inc., Paterson.
Goldberg, M., Paterson.
Hart & Co., Paterson. s. l.
Inglis Stationery Co., Paterson.
Muxxy Bros., Paterson. s. l.
Ribbon & Ticker Paper Co., Paterson.
Carp, Soloman, Perth Amboy.
Samuel Baum, Perth Amboy.
Neer, Frank, Perth Amboy.
Hersh & Bro., L. F., Plainfield.
Mancuso, Tony, Rahway.
Turner, M. E., & Co., Inc., Sewaren.
Winans, C. G., Co., Trenton. br.
New Jersey Paper Co., West Hoboken.

NEW YORK.
*Fischel Paper Co., Albany.
*Wm. H. Frazier, Albany.
*Hudson Valley Paper Co., Albany.
*Pullman Co., O. S., Albany.

ENGINEERING FOR
PULP, PAPER AND POWER PLANTS

JOSEPH H. WALLACE & CO.
INDUSTRIAL ENGINEERS
Temple Court Building, NEW YORK
71 Bay Street, TORONTO, CAN.

General Paper Dealers

NEW YORK—Continued.
*Scott Paper Mills, Albany.
*Auburn Paper Co., Auburn.
Central N. Y. Paper Co., Auburn.
*Cossum & Johnson, Auburn.
Johnson, F. W., Paper Co., Auburn.
W. E. Jones, Auburn.
Dunlap Paper Co., Inc., Batavia.
Jameson & Boyce, Binghamton. s. l.
Miller, W. R., & Co., Binghamton.
Mills, Ely, Co., Binghamton. s. l.
Newell & Truesdell, Binghamton. s. l.
*Stephens & Co., Binghamton.
Yager, W. H., & Co., Binghamton. s. l.
*Alling & Cory Co., The, Buffalo.
Crescent Paper Co., Buffalo.
Dishers Paper Co., Buffalo.
*Gebhard Paper Co., Buffalo.
*Holland Paper Co., Buffalo.
Hubbs & Howe, The, Co., Buffalo.
*George Irish Paper Co., Buffalo.
Johnson & Eggleston, Buffalo. w.
Mead Paper Co., Buffalo.
*Mugler & Umlauf, Buffalo.
*R. H. Thompson Co., Buffalo.
Union Paper & Twine Co., Buffalo. br.
*Wagner & Prince, Buffalo.
Carthage Supply Co., Carthage.
J. T. Baillargeon, Cohoes. w.
Weiss, Jacob, Cohoes.
Heyniger, Pitt & Co., Corning. s. l.
J. B. Maltby, Inc., Corning. s. l.
Robert S. Drewe & Co., Dunkirk. s. l
Henry G. Wagner, Dunkirk. s. l.

NEW YORK—Continued.
*Horwitz Bros., Elmira.
Walter, A. A., Elmira.
r Fulton Bag Co., Fulton.
*Geneva Mercantile Co., Geneva.
R. S. Batcheller & Co., Gloversville. s. l.
Cowles & Oasler, Gloversville. s. l.
E. L. Durkee & Co., Gloversville. s. l.
Seba Foy, Gloversville. s. l.
*Newton G. Snow, Gloversville.
Doscher, John H., Inc., Hollis.
*Hudson Falls Paper Co., 55 John, Hudson Falls.
*Miller, T. G., & Sons, Paper Co., Ithaca.
*George Irish Paper Co., Jamestown. br.
*Forsyth & Davis, Inc., Kingston.
Murphy, J. E., Lackawanna.
Newell, J. R., Little Falls. s.
Lockport Candy Co., Lockport. s. l.
Murphy Paper Co., Lockport. s. l.
Singleton, Wm. B., & Son, Lockport. s. l.
Snyder-Fancher Co., Middletown. s. l.
*Tichenor, Edmund L., Co., Middletown.
Briggs Paper Co., F. A., Natural Dam.
S. M. Bull, Newburgh. s. l.
Hilton, Gibson & Muller, Newburgh. s. l.
G. E. Howard & Co., Newburgh. s. l.
Matthews, J. W., Inc., Newburgh. s. l.
Monell Paper Co., Inc., Newburgh. s.
Brennan, T. J., New Hamburg.

NEW YORK CITY.

(NOTE—In New York City a number of the smaller dealers who, as a rule, do not buy from the mills are designated with an r, which means that they are considered as retailers of paper.)

INDICATION MARKS.
*Wholesale paper dealers maintaining stores.

s Wholesale paper dealers who sell from storage, warehouse or mill direct.

r Retail paper dealers.

s. l. Merchants who sell paper as a side line.

ABBREVIATIONS.
W.—Wrapping paper.
B.—Broker.
B.B.—Boxboard.
Br.—Branch.
C.B.—Cardboard.
Bg.—Paper bags.
Cig.—Cigarette paper.
S.—Strawboard.
W.W.—Woodenware.
T.—Twine.
X.—Tissue.

Borough of Brooklyn.
Paper Dealers.
Aetna Paper Co., 1011 Gates' av.
Agar Mfg. Co., 167 41st. (Corrugated.)
Baslaw, Max, 261 Atlantic av. r.
Bernstein Bros., 91 Moore.

Borough of Brooklyn—Continued.
Blum Folding Box Co., A., 64 Washington av.
Bradley, A. J., Mfg. Co., 11th. (Oil Paper.)
Brooklyn Standard Paper Co., 60 Washington av.

PRESS ROLLS Maple and Gum White Wood Felt Rolls J. W. HEWITT MACHINE CO. Neenah, Wis.

General Paper Dealers 379

Borough of Brooklyn—*Continued.*

Columbia Paper & Woodenware Co., 241-243 Floyd. *r.*
Conner Bros., 266 Johnson av.
Diamond, Wm., 538 Grand. *s. l.*
Droge, E. C., 226-228 Market av.
Finkel & Korenvoes, 614 Grand.
Hoyt Mfg. Co., 78 Clymer. *r.*
Hudson Bag Co., 77 Washington.
Jonas, Alfred, 602 Myrtle av.
Karlsruhe Bros., Inc., 884 Quincy. (W., Bg., T.)
Lauricella, Emanuel, 380 Court. *r.*
MacAdam, A. E., Inc., 97 Lexington av.
Miller, Valentine, Linden.
Muller Paper Goods Co., Linden.
Nors, Otto, 1914 Harmon.
Paulsen, John J., 220 Flushing av. *r.*
Pinsker, S., Sons, Surf av.
Pollack, Harris, 186 Osborn. (Bg.)
Price, A., 61 Whipple. *s.*
Reich & Spiegel, 61 Greenpoint av.
Reliable Bag & Paper Co., 1269 39th. *r.*
*Schrier Bros., 1124 Wallabout Market.
Schrier, H., Sons, 982 Flushing av. *r.*
*Shedlock & Hanlon Co., Inc., 169 Atlantic av.
Silfen, Benj., 200 Franklin. *r.*
Tiedemann, M. W., 101 Grove.
*Tompkins & Tuthill, 15 Fulton.
Warshawsky, Jacob, 80 Osborn.

Boroughs of Manhattan and The Bronx.
General Paper Dealers.

Abramowitz & Jacovitz, 629 E. 6th. (Laundry Supplies.) *r.*
Abramson, S., 1675 Madison av.
*Albere, J. H., 70 Duane. (C. B.)
*Alexander-Holden Paper Co., 20 W. 22d.
*Allan & Gray, 54 Beekman.
American Dry Goods Co., 105 Grand. *s. l.*
*American Envelope & Paper Co., 45 Lafayette.
s American Paper & Supply Co., 79 Chambers. (C. B.)
American Paper Co., 200 5th av. (Br. of Seattle, Wash.)
Amsterdam Grocery Co., 120 Morningside av. (W.)
Amsterdam Paper Co., Inc., 2143 Amsterdam av.
*Anderson, F. W., & Co., Inc., 34 Beekman

Boroughs of Manhattan and The Bronx—*Continued.*

*Anderson, O. H., & Co., 38 Park row.
*Andrews, H. P., Paper Co., Inc., 104 Worth.
Angel, H. Reeve, & Co., Inc., 120 Liberty.
Archibald, A. J., Co., 38 Park row.
s Armstrong Paper Co., Inc., W. A., 5 Beekman.
Atlantic Paper Co., 1878 Lexington av.
Atlas Card & Paper Co., 28-30 Waverly pl.
Atlas Paper & Twine Co., 142 West 17th.
Bacigalupo, J., & Son, 466½ Pearl.
*Baehm, Geo. A., 220 Fulton. (Bg.) *r.*
*Bahrenburg & Co., 401 Lafayette.
Bakal, S., & Son, 55 E. 8th. (T., *r.*)
Baker Trading Co., 39 E. 42d.
*BANKER, JNO. W., 17 White.
Barberie & Co., 70 Murray.
Barnet, Mark, 21 Park row. (Paper, Tar Roofings, Sheathing.)
*Barrett, Thos., & Son, 500 Broome.
s Barry, N. T., 309 Broadway.
*Bauer, Richard, 310 Church.
Bay State Paper Co., 501 5th av. (Br.)
*Beekman Paper & Card Co., 318 W. 39th.
s Belden, Frank M., 302 B'way. (W.W.)
Bendix Paper Co., 67 Irving pl. (Imptr.)
s Benedict, R. G., 299 B'way. (Manufacturers' agent.)
Benedict & Highet, 66 Dey. (W., T., X.)
Bennet's, Wm. J., Son, 49 Lispenard.
*Bergen, John S., & Son, 188 Franklin.
Berkowitz, I., & Son, 179 Wooster. *r.* Berlin & Jones Envelope Co., Inc., 136 William and 547 W. 27th.
s Bermingham & Prosser Co., 501 Fifth av.
Biller, Joseph, 81 E. 4th.
Birn & Wachenheim, 17 Jay. (Importers.)
Bishop Paper Co., 541 Pearl.
Blake, McFall & Co., 200 5th av.
Blake, Moffitt & Towne, 200 5th av. (Br. of San Francisco.)
*Blauvelt-Wiley Paper Mfg. Co., Inc., 129 Charlton. (W.)
Bleiden Paper Co., Inc., 128 Bleecker. (Paper & Twine.)

M. GOTTESMAN & CO., Inc.
18 E. 41st STREET, NEW YORK. Cable Address "Namestog"
EUROPEAN OFFICES: Stockholm, Sweden
BLEACHED and UNBLEACHED WOOD PULP OF ALL KINDS

ENGINEERING FOR PULP, PAPER AND POWER PLANTS

JOSEPH H. WALLACE & CO.
INDUSTRIAL ENGINEERS
Temple Court Building, NEW YORK
71 Bay Street, TORONTO, CAN.

General Paper Dealers

Boroughs of Manhattan and The Bronx—Continued.

*Bleyer, Alfred, & Co., 229-230 West. (W., Bg., W.W.)
Bleyer, Louis, 312 E. 23d. (Paper & Twine.)
Borough Paper Co., Inc., 151 Spring. (Also Twine.)
*Box Board & Lining Co., Inc., 12 Grand. (Box Boards, etc.)
BOYLE, LUKE, 390 W. B'way. (B.B.)
Bradley, A. J., Mfg. Co., 101 Beekman. (Stencil oil paper.)
s Briggs, T. G., 41 Park row.
Brockway-Fitzhugh-Stewart, 105 Hudson.
Bronx County Paper Co., 798 E. 161st.
s Browning, H. P., Paper Co., 33 W. 42d.
Bruning, Chas., 102 Reade. (Blue Print.)
*Brunner, Harry K., 45 Harrison. (Wrap. & Twine.)
Bubis, Harry H., 215 E. 4th. (Paper and Twine.)
*Bulkley, Dunton & Co., 75 Duane.
Butler, J. W., Paper Co., 25 Howard. (Br.)
Butterfield, Barry Co., Inc., The, 79 Crosby. (B.B., C.B., S.) s.
Campbell, Chas., 186 W. 21st.
*Canfield Paper Co., Inc., 62 Duane.
*CARTER, RICE & CO., CORP., 291 B'way. (Br. Boston.)
Catty, H. D., Co., 109 Worth.
*Central Card & Paper Co., 263 Greene.
Central Paper Co., 777 Westchester av. (W.)
r Charnas & Meyers, 40 Wooster. (W.)
Chaus, Benj., 337 E. 101st.
Cimberg, Jacob, 314 E. Houston.
s Clark & Co., 225 5th av.
Claussen, M., 94 Warren.
*Clement & Stockwell, Inc., 30 Beekman.
Cohen, M. M., 451 Washington.
Colabello, M., & Bros., 181 South.
Cole, O. V. Paper Co., 261 B'way.
Colonial Bag & Paper Co., 105 Hudson.
s Columbia Paper Co., 533 W. Broadway. (W.)
Commercial Paper & Card Co., 25 Howard.
Connecticut Valley Paper & Envelope Co., 60 Beekman.
*Conrow Bros., Inc., 114 Worth.

Boroughs of Manhattan and The Bronx—Continued.

Continental Supply Co., 449 E. 144th. (T.)
Cordano Bros., 73 Sullivan. (Bg)
Corenman, A., 105 Hudson. (Bags and Paper.)
Corrugated Box & Paper Co., 37 Barclay.
s Corwin, Jos. W., 299 Broadway.
*Coy, Hunt & Co., Inc., Lafayette and E. 4th.
s CRAIG, H. G., & CO., 52 Vanderbilt av.
*Crosby Paper Co., 120 W. 18th. (Also T.)
Cupples, Sam'l, Wooden Ware Co., 1 Hudson. s. l.
Davidson Bros., 2690 3d av. (W.)
DeAlessandro, Jos., 20 Spring.
*DeJonge, Louis, & Co., 78 Duane. (Fancy.)
Derowich, I., 424 E. 152d. (Paper Specialties.)
Deutsch Bros. Mfg. Co., Inc., 343 Greenwich. (Toilet.)
s Dillon & Barnes, 52 Vanderbilt av. (News.)
Direct Sales Co., 395 Broadway. (Gummed and Specialties.)
*DOMESTIC MILLS PAPER CO., 96-98 Reade. (W., B.B., C.B., T., X.)
Doty & Scrimgeour Sales Co., Inc., 74 Duane.
Duane Paper Co., 41 Union sq.
Dunning, S. W., 132 Nassau. (Manufacturers' agent. (X. W.)
*Elish, M. M., Co., 29 Beekman and 126 Norfolk.
Elsinore Paper Co., 131 W. 24th.
*Empire Card & Paper Co., 97 Greene.
Engel, David L., 10 W. 22d.
Engelberg-Weidmann & Co., 68 Thomas. (W. & T.)
s Etherington, Wm. F., & Co., Inc., 341 5th av.
s Eureka Paper Co., 265 W. B'way. (W., Bg., T., X.)
Federal Paper & Supply Co., 61 E. 11th.
Felch, Frank W., 200 5th av. (B.)
Fenigstein, M., 3943 3d av. (Paper Bags and Twine.)
Fey, F. W., Paper Co., Inc., 9 Jones. (B.B. & W.)
Fick & Warnecke, 172 Reade.
Fink, Geo. A., Co., Inc., 343 E. 104th. (W.W. & Bg., T.)
Fischel Paper Co., 82 Duane.

General Paper Dealers 381

Boroughs of Manhattan and The Bronx—*Continued.*

r Fischman, M., 119 Ludlow. (Also T.)
Fishman, H., 156 E. 106th. (Bags.)
Flanagan, E. A., Woolworth Bldg.
*Flinn, F. A., Inc., 32 Beekman.
*Forbes Paper Co., Inc., 32 Laight. (W.)
Fortgang, Morris B., 844 1st av. (W.W. & Bg.)
Foster, John W., 1835 Park av.
Freeman, Chas., 775 Westchester av.
s Fuchs, Hy., & Son, 280 E. Houston.
Fulling, Henry F., 120 W. 18th.
*Gade, Henry, Corp., 349 Broome. (W. & T.)
Garfield Paper Co., 320 B'way. Warehouse at 54 Beach.
General Paper Job Co., 43 Mercer.
Gensen, W. F., Paper Co., 184 Hudson.
s Germania Importing Co., Inc., 41 Union sq. (W.)
*Gilbert Paper Co., 177 Wooster. (W., B.B., X., T.)
*Gilman, I., & Co., 86 Hudson (W. & Bg.)
Gilman, K., & Sons, E. 102d.
s Gladwin, S. M., & Co., 82 Duane.
Glickman, L., & Co., 365 E. 3d. (Also T.)
Globe Paper & Cardboard Co., 122 Norfolk.
Gluckman, M., 62 Gansevoort. (Clg.)
Gluckman & Son, Inc., 21 Bond. (Clg.)
Gonser, Jacob J., 691 Eagle av.
*Grace, W. R., & Co. (W., B.B., C. B., Bg., Clg., S., X., T.)
GRADY, JOS. L., INC., 31 Beekman. (C. B.)
Graham, John S., 145 Nassau.
s Graham Paper Co., 33 W. 42d. br.
Green, H., 123 Bleecker. (Paper and Twine.)
Greenfield, D., 9 Little W. 12th (W.W.)
r Grover, Albert, 74 Suffolk.
Guiterman, Rosenfeld & Co., 35 S. William. (B.)
Gulf Pulp & Paper Co., 33 W. 42d.
s Hall Paper & Specialties Co., Inc., The, 105 Chambers.
s Hagenbacher, Karl, 253 B'way.
s Hallahan Paper Co., 115 Worth.
Hamilton & Hansell, 13-21 Park Row. (Export.)
*Harlem Card & Paper Co., 155 E. 128th.

Boroughs of Manhattan and The Bronx—*Continued.*

Harris-Wheeler Co., 100 Hudson.
*Harper Paper Co., Inc., 540 Pearl.
Harper, W. D., Inc., 74 Madison av.
Harris, Jno. B., Co., 100 N. Moore. (W.)
*Harris Paper Co., 31 E. 10th.
Hartig, Jas., 419 W. 42d.
s Hayward, Jos. A., 61 Beekman. (B.)
*Heffernan Paper Co., Jas. P., Inc., 25 Water. (W., Bg., Clg., S., X.)
s Heller, H., & Co., 78 Greene (W. & T.)
r Herman, S. J., 129 E. B'way. (also T.)
*Herrmann Paper Co., Inc., 115 Worth.
Herzog, C. F., 105 Hudson.
*HEWITT, C. B., & BROS., INC., 48 Beekman.
HILLS, GEO. F., CO., INC., 106 Cliff.
Hinrich Fred W., 404 E. 77th. (W. & Bg.)
Holden & Hawley, 24 Beekman.
Hollywood Paper Co., Inc., 48 E. 10th.
Howell, W. H., 47 Leonard.
*Hubbs, Chas. F., & Co., Inc., 383 Lafayette and 36 Beekman. (Also T.)
Hudson Packing & Paper Co., Inc., Woolworth Bldg.
Hudson Paper Mills, 93 Greene.
Hudson Trading Co., Inc., 18 E. 41st. (W., X, News, Export.)
Hudson Valley Paper Co., 70 5th av.
Hygrade Paper & Twine Co., 436 W. B'way.
*Hyman, L., & Son, 121 Spring. (W., T., X.)
Industrial Paper Co., 462 Broome.
Inter-City Paper & Supply Co., Inc., 61 E. 11th.
Jacobs, Louis, 199 Wooster. (B.B.)
Jacobus Bros., 163 W. 27th.
*Jaeger, Geo. A., 132 Mulberry.
*Japan Paper Co., Inc., 109 E. 31st.
s Jerome Paper Co., 314 W. 53d. (br)
Johnstone, M. P., Paper Co., 35 Warren.
*Jonas, J. W. W., 22 Spruce.
Jones, M., & Co., 683 B'way. (Gummed Tape.)
*Jones, Wm. L., 96 Prince.
Jones & Skinner, 66 Dey. (W., T., X.)
Judd Paper Co., 150 Nassau. (Br. of Holyoke.)

ENGINEERING FOR **PULP, PAPER AND POWER PLANTS**

JOSEPH H. WALLACE & CO.
INDUSTRIAL ENGINEERS
Temple Court Building, NEW YORK
71 Bay Street,   TORONTO, CAN.

General Paper Dealers

Boroughs of Manhattan and The Bronx—Continued

r Junger Paper Co., 30 Bond.
s Jupp, William C., 21 Park row. (B.)
s Kahlen, Cornelius, 349 B'way. (Importer and Exporter.)
*Kastner, R. C., Paper Co., Inc., 109-111 Worth.
Keefer, Jas. J., 41 Park row.
Keith Products Co., 417 Lafayette.
s Kennelly Paper Co., 200 5th av.
Kent Paper Co., B'way and 30th.
Kern Commercial Co., Inc., 114 Liberty. (Importer and Exporter.)
Keystone Paper Co., 162 W. 18th. (W.&T.)
King Bros., 60 West 37th.
Klein, Sam., 2058 2d av. (Paper and Twine.)
Kornahrens, Herman, Inc., 111 Murray. (W.W.)
Kornbluth, I., Paper Co., 135 W. 27th.
Kuhn, A., & Co., 447 W. 50th.
Kupetz Bros., 2349 1st av. (W.W.)
*Kupfer Bros. Co., Inc., 112 Wooster. (Coated.) (Br.)
Kupfer, Emil, 116 Nassau.
s Lane, Albert A., 73 Warren. (W.&T.)
Larschan, J., & Co., 1590 2d av.
*Lasher & Lathrop, Inc., 29-33 Lafayette.
r Laurencelle, L. A., 196 Greenwich.
r Lauricelli, John, 220 W. 14th. (Bg.)
Lawrence Paper Co., 151 Spring.
Lehman Paper Company, 39 W. 17th.
Levy, Frank, Inc., 9 E. B'way.
*Lewerth & Culbertson, Inc., 72 Duane.
*Linde, J. E., Paper Co., 84 Beekman, and 150 E. 129th.
*LINDENMEYR, H., & SONS, 32 Bleecker.
*Loesch, Richard C., Co., Inc., 76 Beekman.
s Luneschloss, J. S., Inc., 115 Worth.
Madden, R. S., 33 W. 42d.
Madison Paper Stock Co., Inc., 40 Commerce.
MAIN PAPER STOCK CO., 29 Peck slip.
Majestic Mills Paper Co., 462-4 Broome.
Majestic Paper & Twine Co., 43 E. 8th.
Maldonado & Co., Inc., 116 Broad. (Export.)
*Manhattan Card & Paper Co., Inc., 25-27 Beekman.

Boroughs of Manhattan and The Bronx—Continued

s Manhattan Paper Co., 72 Wooster. (W.&T.)
s MANUFACTURERS PAPER CO., INC., 30 E. 42d.
Marquardt, F. G., Inc., 320 Broadway.
Marwell Bros., 216 Franklin. (Paper and Twine.)
Mattes, S., Paper Co., 13-21 Park Row.
s McHugh, John, 200 5th av.
Mehrtens, D. H., 505 W. 52d. (W.)
*Melnick, I., 274 E. Houston. (Also T.)
Merchants Importing Co., Inc., 320 B'way. (Paper and Board Specialties.)
*Merchants' Grocery and Paper Co., 625-27 E. 5th.
s Merlin-Keilholz Paper Co., Inc., 296 B'way.
*Merriam Paper Co., Inc., 150 Lafayette.
Metzeler, Theo., 46 Vesey.
s Meyers, Harry, 121 Spring.
Meyerson, S., Paper Co., Inc., 321 Greenwich.
*Millar, Geo. W., & Co., 284 Lafayette.
Miller, David, 1994 2d av. (Also T.)
Miller, Jos. & Co., 41 W. 21st. (Also T.)
*Miller & Wright Paper Co., Inc., 65 Duane.
Milton Paper Co., 146 Greene.
s Morand, C. M., 200 5th av.
Morkin Paper Co., 309 B'way.
Muehsam Paper Co., Inc., 73 W. Houston. (W.&T.)
s Murray, Chas., & Son, 58 Ann. (W.&T.)
*Mutual Paper Co., 185 Canal. (W., T., X.)
Myers, W. E., Paper Co., Pulitzer Bldg.
National Binding Machine Co., Inc., 260 West. (Gummed.)
National Contracting Co., 105 Hudson.
National Holly Wrapping & Wax Paper Co., Inc., 621 B'way.
National Paper & Type Co., 32-38 Burling sl. (Export.)
National Paper Supply Co., 132 Nassau.
Nat'l Paper Trade Exch., 33 W. 42d.
*Nawrath, J. P., & Co., Inc., 109 Wooster. (Also T.)
Neiman, Jos. B., 150 Ludlow. (W.)

General Paper Dealers 383

Boroughs of Manhattan and The Bronx—Continued.

New York Paper Co., 120 W. 18th.
*New York Roll Wrapping Paper Co., 84 Beekman.
New York & Brooklyn Paper Co., Inc., 245-247.
New York & New Jersey Paper Co., Inc., 45 Lafayette.
s Nilsen, Rantoul Co., 30 E. 42d. (Import.)
O'Keefe, Thos. A. & E. J., 48 Duane. (Toilet.)
*O'Meara, Maurice Co., Inc., 448 Pearl.
Orbach, B., 216 E. 5th. (Paper and Twine.)
Pac-Rite Co., Inc., 280 Pearl. (Specialties.)
Palmer Paper Co., 153-155 Hudson.
Paper Manufacturers' Selling Co., 38 Park row.
Paper Mill Distributing Co., 151 Spring.
s PARSONS TRADING CO., 17 Battery pl. (Also Exporters.)
Parsons, Wm. H., & Co., Inc., 111 B'way.
s Parsons & Whittemore, Inc., 174 Fulton.
Perkins & Squier Co., Inc., 100 Hudson.
*Perkins-Goodwin Co., Inc., 33 W. 42d. (Also Import.)
Pernas & Callado, 130 Pearl. (Gen'l Exporters.)
*Phoenix Card & Paper Co., 47 Beekman.
Phoenix Paper Co., Ltd., 200 5th av.
Posner, Samuel, 1198 3d av. (Bg.)
s Post, John F., 38 Park row.
*Powell, Stephen A., Inc., 334 Hudson.
Pringle, W. M., & Co., Inc., 27 Howard.
Proudfoot-Jenks Paper Co., 82 Duane.
s Pulp & Paper Trading Co., 21 E. 40th.
s Rantoul, C. W., Co., Inc., 30 E. 42d.
Read, D. P., & Son, 54 Barclay.
Read, G. P., Inc., 199 Duane. (W. & Bg.)
Redelsheimer, Charles, 116-120 W. 32d.
Reich, Sam, 170 E. 107th. (W.&T.)
Reliable Paper Co., Inc., 81 Greene.
Reliance Bag and Paper Co., 42 Cooper sq.

Boroughs of Manhattan and The Bronx—Continued.

s Republic Bag Co., Inc., 200 5th av. (W., Bg., X.)
Restaurateur's Supply Co., 128 7th av.
Rhineland Import Paper Co., Inc., 60 E. 11th.
Rice, M., 535 B'way.
*Richardson Bros., 51 Franklin.
Richardson Co., The, 320 Broadway.
Rider, Chas. W., & Co., Inc., 104 Wooster.
s Riegel & Co., Inc., 302 B'way. (Br. Phila., Pa.)
Rod, C. H., 1627 Park av.
r Rosen Paper Co., 467 B'way. (W. & T.) s. l.
Rosenberg Bros., 644 German pl. (Gro. Spec.)
Roshke Bros., 871 Canal. (Also T.)
Rothschild, M., 195 Canal.
*Royal Card & Paper Co., Inc., 100-102 Duane.
Rudolph Bros., 105 Hudson.
Rutkovsky, L., 4 Allen.
s Ryan, J. F., & Co., 52 Vanderbilt.
s Ryan Paper Co., S. A., Inc., 10 Bridge.
Salwen Paper Co., 193 Greene.
Sanders-Rehders & Co., Inc., 1 State. (Exptrs. & Imptrs.)
Saratoga Paper & Laundry Supply Co., 629 E. 6th.
*Sarle, John F., Co., Inc., 85 John.
s Sawyer, Oliver H., 97 Warren. (B.)
Sayford Paper Specialty Co., 200 5th av.
*Scarborough, E. W., Co., Inc., 28 Beekman.
Schachnow, Max, & Co., 29 W. 38th. (Imptrs.)
*Schlosser, M. & F., 130 W. 24th.
s Schniewind, H. Z., 261 B'way. (Importer.)
s Schoeller & Hoesch Co., 17 Battery pl. (Import. Cig. & India.)
Schroeder, Henry, 408 E. 89th.
Schulman, Louis, 101 Greene. (Imptr.)
Schweitzer, Peter J., 109 Broad. (Importers Cig.)
Seaboard Pulp & Paper Co., 21 Park row.
Seaman Paper Co., 200 5th av. (Br. of Chgo.)
*Seymour Co., Inc., 245 7th av.
Shannon, S. A., 41 Park row.
Shea, Sturm Co., 35 Warren.
Shuttleworth, Keller & Co., Inc., 474 W. Broadway. (Bg.)

ENGINEERING FOR PULP, PAPER AND POWER PLANTS

JOSEPH H. WALLACE & CO.
INDUSTRIAL ENGINEERS
Temple Court Building, NEW YORK
71 Bay Street, TORONTO, CAN.

General Paper Dealers

Boroughs of Manhattan and The Bronx—*Continued.*

r Shuttleworth, W. E., & Co., Inc., 248 Greenwich. (Also T.)
Sill, Walter G., 200 5th av. (Imptr.)
Silverstein, A. M., 12 W. 18th.
Sincoff, Jacob, 125 Greene. (W., X., T.)
Singer, E., & Sons, 78 Sheriff.
Singer, Jos. J., 1810 Park av. (Also T.)
*Skinner & Benedict, 66 Dey. (W., T., X.)
s Smith, Augustine J., Co., Woolworth Bldg.
Smith, Harold S., 175 5th.
s Smith, Orin F., 38 Park row. (B.)
Smith, S. J., 69 Warren.
r Sohl, Arthur H., 147 W. 42d. (W.)
Sonnenshein, J., 309 Rivington.
s Squier, Frank, Paper Co., 200 5th av.
*Standard Card & Paper Co., 8 Spruce.
r Star Paper & Twine Co., 11 East 7th.
Steinfeld, Eugene A., 49-51 W. 24th. (W., T.)
Steinman, O. M., Inc., 22 Reade. (Imptrs.)
s Stevens, R. L., Jr., 233 B'way. (Also T.)
Stretton, Geo. W., 564 3d av.
Strype, Fred C., 320 B'way. (Export.)
Superior Paper Trading Co., 140 Cedar.
Sutherland Paper Co., 366 B'way.
*Sutphin Paper Co., Inc., 439 Lafayette.
Syrkin & Back, Inc., 9 Bond.
Tamm & Co., 66 Duane.
*Textile Paper Co., 13-21 Park row. Warehouse, 303-309 Monroe.
s Thorpe, Dawson K., 41 Park row.
Tissue Co., 395 Broadway.
Transatlantic Paper Co., 50 Franklin.
Trinity Bag & Paper Co., 105 Hudson.
*Union Card & Paper Co., Inc., 45 Beekman.
United Mfg. Co., Inc., 53-55 5th av. (Br.) (Glazed and Cloth Lined.)
United States Gummed Tapes Co., Inc., 136 Liberty.
United States Lace Paper Works, Inc., 472 W. B'way. (Imptrs.)
*United States Paper Co., Inc., 184 W. 17th. (W.)
United States Paper Export Assn., Inc., 80 Broad. (Export.)

Boroughs of Manhattan and The Bronx—*Continued.*

Universal Trading Co., 171 B'way. (W. & T.)
*Vernon Bros. & Co., 66 Duane.
*VERNON, PAUL E., & CO., 22 Reade.
Vogelius, Chas. F., 133 Nassau.
s Von Ullrich, F. H., Paper Co., 41 Park row. (Import.)
s Walker Paper Co., 261 Broadway.
Walther & Co., 72 Duane. (Br.) (Coated.)
*Walton, D. S., & Co., 132 Franklin.
Wang, J., 2010 1st av. (W.W.)
Wang, Simon, 334 E. 100th.
Weberman, Abr., 314 E. Houston.
Weill, A. J., Paper Co., 783 B'way. (W.)
Weill, H. Co., 100 William.
Weinstock, J., 218 E. 70th. (W.)
Weinstock & Son, Inc., 32 W. 21st. (Also T.)
Westchester Paper Co., Inc., 450 Westchester av. (W., T. & W.W.)
West Shore Paper Co., 505 E. 12th.
s Whitaker Paper Co., 501 5th av. br.
s White-Burbank Paper Co., 23 Beekman.
White-Washburn Co., Inc., 100 Hudson.
s Whitehead & Alliger Co., Inc., 8 Thomas.
*Whiting-Patterson Co., 536 Pearl. (Br. of Phila.)
Wilhelm, B., & Co., 83 Norfolk. (W. & T.)
*Wilkinson Bros. & Co., Inc., 419 Broome. (W., B.B., C.B., Cig., S.)
*Williams, Chas. W., & Co., 309 Lafayette. (T., X.)
*Willmann, Wm. G., 51 Beekman.
Wisser, E., & Co., 175 Prince.
*Wisser, Wm. R., 93 Prince. (Also T.)
Wittcoff & Levy, Inc., 7 Gt. Jones. (Also T.)
r Wolf, A. & L., 256 E. 138th. (Imptr.)
Wolf, Samuel, 1340 Park av.
s Wood, Joseph H., 150 Nassau.
York Paper Co., 949 Broadway.
Yorkville Paper Co., Inc., 437 E. 77th. (W. & T.)
Z. & Z. Paper Co., 12 Bleecker.

Paper Dealers (Fancy).

American Novelty Paper Co., 54 Franklin.
Catty Co., H., D., 109 Worth.
DeJonge, Louis, & Co., 71 Duane.

General Paper Dealers

Boroughs of Manhattan and The Bronx—*Continued.*

Dennison Mfg. Co., 15 John.
DOMESTIC MILLS PAPER CO., 96 Reade.
Doty & Scrimgeour Sales Co., Inc., 74 Duane.
Germania Importing Co., 41 Union Square.
Gladwin, S. M., & Co., 82 Duane.
Jacobs, Chas. D., 41 Park row. (Special Watermarked.)
Japan Paper Co., 109 E. 31st.
Kupfer Bros., 305 E. 118th.
Manhattan Paper Co., 70 Wooster.
Merchants' Importing Co., 320 B'way.
Milwaukee Lace Paper Co., 54 Barclay. (Br.)

Box Board Dealers.

American Strawboard Co., Broadway and 42d.
Box Board and Lining Co., 10 Grand.
BOYLE, LUKE, 390 W. B'way.
Butterfield-Barry Co., 79 Crosby.
De Alessandro, Jos., 20 Spring.
Gosling & Farr, 141 Wooster.
Harris-Wheeler Co., 100 Hudson.
Hewitt, C. B., & Bros., Inc., 48 Beekman.
Jaeger, G. A., 132-138 Mulberry.
LINDENMEYR, HENRY, & SONS, 34 Bleecker and 20 Beekman.
Walther & Co., 72 Duane.

Paper Importers.

Baker Trading Co., 32 Union sq.
Germania Importing Co., 41 Union sq. (W.)
Herrmann Paper Co., 115 Worth. (Also Export.)
Japan Paper Co., 109 E. 31st.
Kahlen, Cornelius, 349 Broadway.
Kraft, G. J., 86 Chambers.
Lips, Herman, 55 John.
Merchants Importing Co., 320 B'way.
Nilsen, Rantoul Co., 30 E. 42d.
Perkins-Goodwin Co., Inc., 33 W. 42d.
Pulp & Paper Trading Co., Inc., 21 E. 40th.
Rhineland Import Paper Co., 60 E. 11th.
Rose & Frank Co., 150 W. 22d.
Schachnow, Max, & Co., 878 B'way.
Schulman, Louis, 101 Greene.
Sill, Walter G., 200 5th av.
Standard Card & Paper Co., 8 Spruce.
Syrkin & Back, 9 Bond.
Thorpe, Dawson K., 41 Park row.

Boroughs of Manhattan and The Bronx—*Continued.*

Transatlantic Paper Co., Inc., 50 Franklin.
U. S. Lace Paper Works, Inc., 472 W. B'way.
Vernon Bros. & Co., 66 Duane.
VERNON, PAUL E., & CO., 22 Reade.
Von Ullrich, F. H., Paper Co., 41 Park row.
Walton, D. S., & Co., 132 Franklin.
Williams, Chas. W., & Co., 309 Lafayette.
Wilson & Towne Paper Co., Inc., 153 Hudson.
Wolf, A. & L., 256 E. 138th.
Yorkville Paper Co., 437 E. 77th. (W. & T.)

Twine Dealers.

Amer Mills Co., 200 Fifth av.
BANKER, JOHN W., 17-19 White.
Bauer, Richard, 310 Church.
Bernholz, Edw. J., 280 Madison av.
Buchman, Julius, 112 Prince.
Cable Flax Mills, 50 Leonard.
Columbian Rope Co., 3-35 Burling sl.
Coy, Hunt & Co.,(Lafayette and E. 4th.
Frank Alfred, 150 West 22d.
Gade, Henry, Corp., 349 Broome.
Grady, M. J., Co., 110 Reade.
Harris-Wheeler Co., 100 Hudson.
Jameson, John, 123 Liberty.
Johnstone, M. P., Paper Co., 213 W. 40th.
Kelley, Henry C., Co., 35, 37, 39 Worth.
King Bros., 60 West 37th.
Kornbluth, The I., Paper Co., 135 West 27th.
Lees Mfg. Co., 320 Broadway.
Lees, W. Sherman, 50 Leonard.
Lewis, G. W., Co., 45 Greene.
National Package Sealer Co., 260 West.
National Rope Company, 106 Wall.
Peerless Twine & Cordage Co., 225 West Broadway.
Purple, A. E., Co., 20 Broad.
Regan, John F., Co., 90 West Broadway.
Reliance Bag & Twine Co., 42 Cooper sq.
Reid, Alex. F., & Sons, 18 White.
Seaman, H. D., Co., 320 Broadway.
Shea, Sturm Co., 35 Warren.
Shuttleworth Keiller & Co., 474 West Broadway.
Sterling Twine & Cordage Co., 128 Chambers.
Thompson, Jas., & Co., 112 Prince.

ENGINEERING FOR PULP, PAPER AND POWER PLANTS

JOSEPH H. WALLACE & CO.
INDUSTRIAL ENGINEERS
Temple Court Building, NEW YORK
71 Bay Street, TORONTO, CAN.

General Paper Dealers

Boroughs of Manhattan and The Bronx—*Continued.*

Travers Twine & Cordage Co., 81 Warren.
Travers, J. R., & Sons, 46 Beekman.
Van Pelt, Wm. J., 33 Union sq.
Wahlers, J. H., 71 Cooper sq.
Wahlers, John H., 117 West 90th.
Winne, D. P., Co., 105 Worth.
Wolff, J. D., 474 West Broadway.
York Paper Co., 30 West 21st.

Borough of Queens.
Bohnhoff, Chas., Jr., Maspeth.

Borough of Richmond.
Baron & Goldfarb, Port Richmond.

NEW YORK STATE—*Continued.*
Ogdensburgh Merc. Co., Inc., Ogdensburgh. *s. l.*
Tallman Ptg. Corp., Ogdensburg. *s. l.*
*Oneonta Press, The, Oneonta.
Davis, I., Portchester.
Adirondack Paper Co., Potsdam.
*Forsyth & Davis, Inc., Poughkeepsie.
*The Alling & Cory Co., Rochester.
Berman Bros. Co., Inc., Rochester.
*Clark Paper and Mfg. Co., Rochester.
*Cramer-Force Co., Rochester.
*Daly & Ferguson, Rochester.
*Hubbs & Hastings Paper Co., Rochester.
*Fred. D. Morgan & Co., Rochester.
*R. M. Myers & Co., Rochester.
Robfogel Paper Co., Rochester.
s T. W. Shannon, Rochester.
*G. F. Blackmer & Son, Inc., Saratoga Springs.
Levi & Co., J., Schenectady. *s. l.*
Morris, S., & Son, Schenectady. *s. l.*
Schenectady Paper Co., Schenectady. *s. l.*
Stanton & Ouderkirk, Schenectady. *s. l.*
*J. & F. B. Garrett Co., Syracuse.
*National Paper Co., Syracuse.
*John Single Paper Co., Syracuse.
*Miller Paper Co., Syracuse.
Bull, Guy, Troy. *w.*
*Mann, Herbert R., Troy.
*Troy Paper Co., Troy.
Bowes Bros., Inc., Utica.
*Hobbie & Baker, Utica.
*J. G. Rosenwald, Utica.
*Utica Paper Co., Utica.
*Black River Paper and Mfg. Co., Watertown.
*Mack, Clarence A., Watertown.
s Samuel Hayward, Yonkers.

NORTH CAROLINA.
Murrill Paper Co., Charlotte, N. C.
Chatfield & Woods Co., Greensboro. *br.*
*Old North State Paper Co., Greensboro.
Parker Paper & Twine Co., High Point.

NORTH DAKOTA.
*Wright, Barrett & Stilwell Co., Minot. *br.*

OHIO.
*Bachtel Paper Co., Akron.
*Ashtabula Paper & Twine Co., Ashtabula.
*The Hanlon Paper Co., Barnesville.
Walter Melchoir, Canton. *s. l.*
Fromm Printing Co., Chillicothe.
Horney & Chapman, Chillicothe.
Scholl Printing Co., Chillicothe.

CINCINNATI.
General Paper Dealers.

American Paper & Woodenware Co., 104 Pearl.
Anchor Paper Co., 2d and Walnut.
Brown & Stuart, The, Co., 503 Neave Bldg.
*Chatfield & Woods Co., The, 3d and Plum.
*Cincinnati Cordage and Paper Co., 535-537 E. 3d.
*Diem & Wing Paper Co., Gilbert & Viaduct.
Fishwick, Albert B., 528 Walnut.
*Herrlinger, A., Cordage & Paper Co., 220 Main.
Herrlinger & Co., 206 Walnut.
Huwe-Kamman Paper and Woodenware Co., Bader and Massachusetts.
Johnston-Albershart Co., 321 Sycamore.
s La Boiteaux, C. L., Co., First National Bank Bldg.
Laing Paper & Woodenware Co., 112 E. Pearl.
Meyers Bros. Paper Co., 1243 W. 6th.
National Paper Co., 217 Main.
Paper Makers Co., 516 First Nat. Bank bldg.
*Queen City Paper Co., 515 Eggleston av.
Seaman Paper Co., 422 Un. Cent. bldg.
*Seinsheimer Paper Co., York, McLean and Exeter.
*Standard Paper Co., 135 W. 6th.
U. S. Paper Goods Co., 1224 W. 8th.
*Waterproof Paper & Board Co., 427 E. 6th.
*Whitaker Paper Co., 6th and Lock sts. and Eggleston av.

PRESS ROLLS   Maple and Gum White Wood Felt Rolls   **J. W. HEWITT MACHINE CO.** Neenah, Wis.

OHIO—Continued.

*Central Ohio Paper Co., 1125 Oregon av., Cleveland. br.
Central Paper Co., Cleveland.
*Cleveland Paper Mfg. Co., Cleveland.
Diem & Wing Paper Co., Cleveland. br.
Gilliam, Chas. H., 2618 Franklin, Cleveland.
Globe Paper Co., Cleveland.
Hubbs & Howe, Cleveland. br.
*Kingsley Paper Co., Cleveland.
La Boiteaux, C. L., Co., Cleveland. br.
Merchants Paper Co., 589 E. 102d.
Northern Ohio Paper Co., Cleveland.
*Petrequin, The, Paper Co., 1250 W. 3d.
*The Union Paper and Twine Co., Cleveland.
*Trostler, A. L., & Co., Cleveland.
Whitaker Paper Co., Cleveland. br.
*Central Ohio Paper Co., 226 N. 5th.
Chatfield & Woods Co., Columbus. br.
Diem & Wing, Columbus. br.
Whitaker Paper Co., Columbus. br.
*Central Ohio Paper Co., 620 Reibold bldg., Dayton. br.
Chatfield & Woods Co., Dayton. br.
Dayton Branch, The Cincinnati Cordage & Paper Co., 535-537 E. 3d, Dayton.
Dayton Paper Novelty Co., Dayton.
Diem & Wing Paper Co., Dayton. br.
*Keogh & Rike, The, Paper Co., Dayton.
*Lotz, F. W., Paper Co., Dayton.
Meisner, A. C., 415 East 5th, Dayton.
Whitaker Paper Co., 300 Columbus Arcade Bldg., Dayton. br.
Riggs Co., East Liverpool.
Weaver, W. A., Co., East Liverpool. s. l.
Robbins Sabin, The, Paper Co., Middletown.
James Congelton, New Philadelphia. s. l.
Gilbert Grocery Co., Portsmouth.
Carson, The Jos. Co., Springfield. s. l.
Fox, D. Z., Co., Springfield. s. l.
Rhodes Paper Co., Springfield.
Springfield Paper and Mdse. Co., Springfield. s. l.
Starrett Paper Co., Springfield.
Steel, Hopkins & Meredith, Springfield. s. l.
*Blade Printing and Paper Co., Toledo. s. l.
*Buckeye Paper Co., Toledo.
*Central Ohio Paper Co., 126 Ontario, Toledo.

OHIO—Continued.

Chatfield & Woods Co., Toledo. br.
Chicago Paper Co., Toledo. br.
*Gelzer & Murphy Co., Toledo.
*Ohio & Michigan Paper Co., Toledo.
*Paddock Merchandise Co., Toledo.
Whitaker Paper Co., Toledo. br.
s H-F Paper Co., Youngstown.
Hanlon, Frank F., Zanesville.
State Paper Co., Zanesville. s. l.

OKLAHOMA.

*Kansas City Paper House, Oklahoma City.
Miller-Jackson Woodenware Co., Oklahoma City. s. l.
*Oklahoma Paper Co., Oklahoma.
Rosenthal Paper Co., Oklahoma City.
*Western Newspaper Union, Oklahoma. br.

OREGON.

Whitman, O. W., Astoria.
*Blake, McFall Co., Portland.
*Crescent Paper Co., Portland.
s General Paper Co., Portland.
*J. W. P. McFall, Portland.
*Pacific Paper Co., Portland.
*Rodgers Paper Co., Salem.

PENNSYLVANIA.

*J. A. Rupp Paper Co., Allentown.
*H. W. Schmid, Allentown.
Anderson Paper & Twine Co., Altoona.
Henry B. Gerlach, Bethlehem. s. l.
Lahn, A. L., Chester.
*Seth, W. T., Chester.
*S. H. Ehrhart, Easton.
Nevin, George, Easton.
Erie Paper Co., Erie.
Walker, John H., Co., Erie.
*Donaldson Paper Co., Harrisburg.
*Johnston Paper Co., Harrisburg.
Keystone Twine & Paper Co., Lancaster.
*Strohl, S. D., & Co., Lancaster.
*Shartle, E. H., Meadville.
*Howard, The, Co., Norwood.
*Moody, G. W., & Son, New Castle.
*Burnett, Edward L., Norristown.
Peerless Mfg. Co., Norristown.

PHILADELPHIA.
General Paper Dealers.

*Abrams, Nathan, 3902 Germantown av.
s Altemas, Casper B., 305 Race.
American Lace Paper Co., Land Title Bldg.
*American Standard Paper Co., 6418 Germantown av.
s Angier Mills, Bulletin bldg
s A. P. W. Paper Co., 48 N. Front.
*Aronowitz, H. J., 337 N. 2d.

General Paper Dealers

PHILADELPHIA—*Continued*.

s Auer & Twitchell, 9th and Chestnut. (Importers and Exporters.)
s Bankerd Paper Co., Drexel bldg.
*Bartlett, Chas. J., 213 S. American.
s Barton-Hobart Paper Co., Land Title bldg.
s Beaver, Wm. H., 127 N. 5th.
*Beck Co., Chas., 609 Chestnut.
s Canfield Paper Co., Lafayette Bldg.
Carson, Cyrus, 2353 E. York.
s Clinton, C. H., Paper Co., 615 Crozer Bldg.
s Considine, Norbert A., N. Am. Bldg.
*Curtis & Bros., 16 S. 5th.
*Datz, A. S., & Son, 16 S. Marshall.
De Jonge, Louis & Co., 116 N. 7th. *br.*
s Diamond Shelf Paper Co., 2353 E. York.
*Dobbins, W. H., & Co., 48 N. Front.
*Dyson Paper Board Co., 2d and Vine.
s Eastern Paper Co., 213 S. American
s Emerson, Ralph W., Witherspoon Bldg.
Enterprise Paper Co., 2029 Germantown av.
s Farrell, F. W., Co., 1008 Drexel bldg.
Fort Orange Paper Co., Commonwealth bldg.
*FRANKLIN PAPER CO., 718 Cherry.
Gallen, Jas. F., & Son, 118 N. 2d.
Gallen Paper Co., 2421 Aspen.
*Garrett-Buchanan Co., 18 S. Sixth.
*Garrett, C. S., & Son Co., 20-22 S. Marshall.
s Garrett, Edwin T., Co., 512 Arch.
*Garrett, Sylvester S., & Co., 259 S. 3d.
Gatti-McQuade Co., 1416 Wood.
s George, William H., 1011 Chestnut.
Giles, E. H., & Co., 1015 Master.
Greenbaum, H. M., 836 S. 3d.
Griffiths, Philip, 417 Locust.
s Hall, Jos., Co., 337 N. 2d.
*Hartung, A., & Co., 506-12 Race.
s Hinde & Dauch Paper Co., 308 Chestnut.
Hopper Paper Co., Heed Bldg.
s Hubbs, Charles F., & Co., 56 S. 3d.
s Huff Paper Co., Denckla bldg.
s Hygienic Telephone Disc Co., 239 S. Front.
Isen, Nathan D., 2029 Germantown.
Japan Paper Co., 829 Witherspoon bldg.
s Jones, Newton H., Paper Co., Real Estate Trust Bldg.
Judd Paper Co., 213 S. American.
Kardon Harris Paper Co., 114 S. 2d.

PHILADELPHIA—*Continued*.

Kardon, S., 207 Vine.
Kendig, H. Ewert, 614 Chestnut.
*Keystone Paper Co., 148 N. 3d.
Labor, Chas. A., Drexel Bldg.
Lafore, J. A., Bellevue Court Bldg.
Lamson, A. D., Co., Drexel Bldg.
Latimer, Jr., E., 231 Chestnut.
Levis, Chas. Megargee, 16 S. 5th.
*Levison, Ezra, 26 S. 5th.
*Lewis, Robert, 1004 S. 20th.
*Lindsay Bros., Inc., 804 Sansom.
s Lynch, Thos., 415 Cherry.
McNutt, Jas., 825 Walnut.
Mallinckrodt, L. K., 517 Bourse Bldg. *br.*
*Matthias & Freeman Paper Co., 117 N. 7th.
McGarity, Wm. J., 206 N. Delaware av.
*Megargee-Hare Paper Co., 12 S. 6th.
Merion Paper Co., Bellevue Court Bldg.
s Miller, Frank E., 1615 N. American.
Mohr, E. L., & Co., 93 Moore.
*Molten Paper Co., 25 S. 6th.
s NATIONAL WATER PROOFING CO., Drexel Bldg.
s New England Paper Goods Co., 1300 Arch.
s Osburn Paper Co., 301 The Bourse.
*Paper Manufacturers Co., Inc., 528 Cherry.
Penn Card & Paper Co., 28 N. 6th. *s. l.*
Phila. Card & Paper Co., 25 N. 6th.
Phila. Paper Co., 231 S. Front. *s. l.*
s Preston-McCormick, Otis Bldg.
*Price Co., The Thomas W., 505 Ludlow.
s Prichard-Lewis Co., 1004 S. 20th.
*Quaker City Paper Co., 13 N. 6th.
*Raiguel, M. O., Co., 305 Florist. *s. l.*
s Ramsey, J. Bradford, Jr., 810 Drexel Bldg.
Raymond-McNutt Co., 825 Walnut.
Reliance Shelf Paper Co., 1304 N. Howard.
*Riegel & Co., Inc., 16 S. 6th.
s Royal, T. M., & Co., 614 Chestnut.
Saxe Paper Co., 134 N. 7th.
Schrenck, Jas. B., 257 S. 52d.
s Scott Paper Co., Glenwood and Chester.
Seaman Paper Co., Land Title Bldg.
s Sensenbocker, H. J., & Co., 1908 W. Columbia av.
*SHRYOCK BROS., 928 Cherry.
Shuttleworth-Hogg & Mather, Inc., 118 N. 2d.
Smitheman, Geo. B., 1119 N. Front.

General Paper Dealers 389

PHILADELPHIA—Continued.
*Smythe Co., J. L. N., 61 Ranstead.
s States Paper Co., 720 Arch.
Uneeda Paper Co., 3712 Lancaster av.
*Walter, Simon, 321 Cherry.
*Ward, D. L., Co., 28 S. 6th.
*Whiting-Patterson Co., 314-322 N. 13th.
*Wilder Bros. & Co., 148 N. 5th.
*Wilson Paper Co., 114 N. 3d.

Paper Manufacturers' Agents and Brokers.
American Standard Paper Co., 6418 Germantown av.
Auer & Twitchell, N. E. cor. 9th & Chestnut.
Bankerd, A. J., Drexel Bldg.
Bartlett, C. J., 213 S. American.
Clinton, C. H., Paper Co., 615 Crozer bldg.
Cohen, E. E., Drexel Bldg.
Considine, N. A., No. American Bldg.
Economic Power & Products Co., Lafayette bldg.
Emerson, R. W., Witherspoon Bldg.
Farrell Co., F. W., Real Estate Trust Bldg.
George, Wm. H., 1011 Chestnut.
Holt, DeWitt, Real Estate Trust Bldg.
Jones, Newton H., R. E. Trust bldg.
Lattimer, E., 231 Chestnut.
Mason, A. C., Land Title Bldg.
Miller, Frank E., 1615 N. American Bldg.
Mohr, J. N., Bullitt Bldg.
National Waterproofing Co., Drexel bldg.
Newell, D. H., Bourse.
O'Neill, F. A., 525 Cherry.
Osburn Paper Co., 301 Bourse bldg.
Peerless Mfg. Co., 1214 Filbert.
Ramsay, J. B., Jr., 810 Drexel Bldg.
Royal, Thos. M., & Co., 614 Chestnut.
Safepack Paper Mills, Drexel Bldg.
Schroff, V. R., 1064 Real Estate Trust Bldg.
Wagner, Benj. I., Bulletin Bldg.
Walter, Simon, 821 Cherry.

PITTSBURGH.
Paper Dealers.
*Alling & Cory, The, Co., Alcor and River av., N. S.
Balter Paper Co., Overhill and Reed.
*Beeson Paper Co., 437 Liberty av.
s Briggs Selling Co., 2112 First National Bank Bldg.
*Central Ohio Paper Co., 1410 Keenan Bldg. br.

PITTSBURGH—Continued.
*Chatfield & Woods Co., 838 3d av. br
*General Paper & Cordage Co., 8 Federal.
*Hartje Paper Mfg. Co., 115 Wood.
s Huff, Barnes & Opie Co., 33 Terminal bldg.
*Inter-State Cordage & Paper Co., 14 4th av.
*Seager Bros., 331 Water.
*Western Pennsylvania Paper Co., 3d and Penn. av.
Whitaker Paper Co., 4148 Jenkins Arcade.

Paper Manufacturers.
Hartje Paper Mfg. Co., 115 Wood.
Tarentum Paper Mills, Second National Bank Bldg.
Bright, Geo., Hardware Co., Pottsville. s. l.
Hooven Merc. Co., Pottsville. s. l.
M. E. Miller, Pottsville. s. l.
Pottsville Supply Co., Pottsville. s. l.
Royal Wholesale Grocery Co., Pottsville. s. l.
Swaim Hardware Co., Pottsville. s. l.
Thompson, L. C., Pottsville. s. l.
Brown, Frank P., Reading. s. l.
*M. J. Earl, Reading.
*Van Reed Co., Reading.
*Megargee Bros., Scranton.
Scranton Paper & Twine Co., Scranton.
Stone, Hugh, Scranton.
*W. B. Haines, Sunbury.
Pippert, Fred, West Newton.
*H. A. Whiteman & Co., Wilkesbarre.
*Wilkesbarre Paper & Stationery Co., Wilkesbarre.
Williamsport Paper Co., Williamsport.

PHILIPPINE ISLANDS.
*Heilbronn, J. P., Co., Manila.

RHODE ISLAND.
National Wholesale Grocery Co., Newport. s. l.
*Newport Paper & Grocery Co., Newport.
Rex Mfg. & Supply Co., Newport. s. l.
*Adams Paper Co., Pawtucket.
s Bay State Paper Co., Providence. br.
s CARTER, JOHN, & CO., Providence. br.
s Coy, Hunt & Co., Providence. br.
*Greene, R. L., Paper Co., Providence.
s Judd Paper Co., Providence. br.
*Providence Paper Co., Providence.

ENGINEERING FOR PULP, PAPER AND POWER PLANTS || **JOSEPH H. WALLACE & CO.**
INDUSTRIAL ENGINEERS
Temple Court Building, NEW YORK
71 Bay Street, TORONTO, CAN.

General Paper Dealers

RHODE ISLAND—*Continued.*
*Royal Sales Co., Providence. *s. l.*
s STORRS & BEMENT CO., Providence. *br.*
w Turnell, J. T., Providence.
*Union Paper Co., Providence.
Whitaker Paper Co., 86 Weybosset. *br.*
Woonsocket Paper Co., Woonsocket.

SOUTH CAROLINA.
Brux Co., H. B., Charleston.
Dixon, Jr., I. G., Charleston.
Hollings, A. G., Charleston.
Trouche, P. E., Charleston.
*Columbia Paper Co., Columbia.
Walker Paper Co., Columbia.

SOUTH DAKOTA.
*Aberdeen Paper Co., Aberdeen.
Sioux Falls Fruit Co., Sioux Falls. *s. l.*
*Sioux Falls Paper Co., Sioux Falls.

TENNESSEE.
*Archer Paper Co., Chattanooga.
Louisville Paper Co., Knoxville. *br.*
Whitaker Paper Co., Knoxville. *br.*
*Memphis Paper Co., Memphis.
Seligstein Paper Co., Memphis.
*Tayloe Paper Co., Memphis.
*Tennessee Paper & Bag Co., Memphis.
Chatfield & Woods Co., Nashville. *br.*
*Clements Paper Co., Nashville.
*Graham Paper Co., Nashville. *br.*
*Morgan & Hamilton Co., Nashville.
Nashville Woodenware Co., Nashville. *s. l.*
Southern Woodenware Co., Nashville. *s. l.*
*Well Paper & Twine Co., Nashville.

TEXAS.
Advance Bag Co., Dallas. *br.*
Butler, J. W., Paper Co., Dallas. *br.*
*Dallas Paper Co., Dallas.
Fisher, John A., Dallas.
Hooper Co., Dallas.
*Southwestern Paper Co., Dallas.
*Texas Paper Co., Dallas.
*West-Cullum Paper Co., Dallas.
Hughes-Buie Co., El Paso.
Western Woodenware Co., El Paso. *s. l.*
Fort Worth Paper Co., Fort Worth.
Waples-Platter Grocery Co., Fort Worth. *s. l.*
W. D. Cleveland & Sons, Houston. *s. l.*
s Cupples, Samuel, Woodenware Co., Houston. *br.*
Flaxman Paper Co., Houston.
Hirsh Bros., Houston. *s. l.*

TEXAS—*Continued.*
Houston Wholesale Confectionery Co., Houston. *s. l.*
*Magnolia Paper Co., Houston.
Palmer, E. C., & Co., Houston. *br.*
*Southwestern Paper Co., Houston.
*Alling Paper Co., San Antonio.
R. L. Burnett Co., San Antonio.
*San Antonio Paper Co., San Antonio.
Standard Paper Co., San Antonio.
*Turner Paper Co., Texarkana.

UTAH.
*Earl & England Pub. Co., Logan.
*Scoville Paper Co., Ogden. *s. l.*
*Taylor Paper Co., Provo.
*Carpenter Paper Co. of Utah, Salt Lake City.
*Lambert Paper Co., Salt Lake City.
McMillen Paper & School Supply Co., Salt Lake City.
*Western Newspaper Union, Salt Lake City. *br.*
Utah Wholesale Grocery Co., Salt Lake City. . *s. l.*

VERMONT.
*Clapp & Jones, Brattleboro.
McAuliffe Paper Co., Burlington.
*H. J. Shanley & Co., Burlington.
*Argus & Patriot Co., Montpelier.
*H. A. Sawyer Co., Inc., Rutland.
*Tuttle, The, Company, Inc., Rutland.
*R. A. Brush, St. Albans.
H. B. Butler, St. Albans. *s. l.*
Windsor County Paper Co., Springfield.
White River Paper Co., White River Junction. *s. l.*
*Howard, The, Co., Norwood.
*Caskie-Dillard Co., Inc., Lynchburg.
*Andrews, R. P., Paper Co., Norfolk.

VIRGINIA.
*Cauthorne, R. A., Paper Co., Inc., Norfolk. *br.*
*Old Dominion Paper Co., Norfolk.
*Hampton Roads Paper Co., Norfolk.
*Anderson-Wilson Paper Co., Richmond.
Baughman Stationery Co., Richmond. *s. l.*
Cauthorne, R. A., Paper Co., Inc., Richmond.
*Consolidated Paper & Box Mfg. Co., Inc., Richmond.
*Eagle Paper Co., Richmond.
Epes Fitzgerald Paper Co., Richmond.

General Paper Dealers

VIRGINIA—*Continued.*
*Richmond Paper Co., Richmond.
Smith, Dixon Co., Richmond. *br.*
*Southern Paper Co., Richmond.
*United Paper Co., Richmond.
*Virginia Paper Co., Richmond.
Whitaker Paper Co., Richmond. *br.*
*Wilson, B. W., Paper Co., Richmond.
*Caldwell-Sites Co., Roanoke.
Roanoke Grocery & Specialty Co., Roanoke. *s. l.*

WASHINGTON.
*American Paper Co., Seattle.
*J. W. Fales Paper Co., Seattle.
*Mutual Paper Co., Seattle.
Normand, Neilson & Co., Seattle.
*Richmond Paper Co. Div., Zellerbach Paper Co., Seattle.
*Paper Bag and Supply Co., Seattle.
*Paper Warehouse Co., Seattle.
*Pioneer Paper Co., Seattle.
*Seattle Paper Co., Seattle.
American Type Founders Co., Spokane.
Ewing, B. G., Paper Co., Spokane.
*Graham, John W., & Co., Spokane.
*Spokane Paper & Stationery Co., Spokane.
*Tacoma Paper & Stationery Co., Tocoma. *br.*
Interior Grocery Co., Walla Walla. *s. l.*
Nichols-Snyder Paper Co., Walla Walla.
Wadham & Kerr Bros., Walla Walla. *br., s. l.*

WEST VIRGINIA.
Wilson Sons Co., R. D., Clarksburg.
Cincinnati Cordage & Twine Co., Wheeling. *br.*
*Clarke Paper Co., Wheeling.
*Olmstead Bros. Co., Wheeling.

WISCONSIN.
*Marshall Paper Co., Appleton.
*Woels Bros., Appleton.
*Badger Paper Co., Bristol.
Eau Claire Book and Stationery Co., Eau Claire. *s. l.*
*Eau Claire Paper Supply Co., Eau Claire. *so.*
Glasow Co., Fond du Lac.
*Astor Paper Specialty Co., Green Bay.
*I. Schilling & Sons, La Crosse.
General Paper & Supply Co., Madison.
Morris, T. S., Co., Madison.
*Plumb & Nelson Co., Manitowoc. *s. l.*
Theo. Schmidtman's Sons Co., Manitowoc. *s. l.*
Pomeroy Paper Co., Menasha. Specialties for Jobber.
*A. E. Sielaff Paper Co., Milwaukee.
Allmam-Christiansen Paper Co., Milwaukee.
Brandt, William C., Milwaukee.
Cantwell Paper Co., J. D., Milwaukee.
*Dever Bros. Paper Co., Milwaukee.
Dwight Bros. Paper Co., Milwaukee. *br.*
s E. A. Bouer Paper Co., Milwaukee.
*Frank G. Smith Co., Milwaukee.
Haferman Paper Co., Milwaukee.
Nackle, W. F., Paper Co., Milwaukee.
National Paper Co., Milwaukee.
Niedecken, H., Co., Milwaukee. *s. l.*
Seaman Paper Co., Milwaukee. *br.*
Banta, Geo., Paper Co., Neenah.
Gerbrick Paper Co., Neenah.
*Baker Paper Co., Oshkosh.
*James & Edwards Co., Oshkosh.
*Medberry-Findeisen Co., Oshkosh.
*W. H. Kranz, Racine.
Falk Paper Co., M. F., Superior. *br.*
*Twin Ports Paper Co., Superior.
Twohy-Elmon Merc. Co., Superior.

IT WILL PAY

TO WRITE US IF YOU NEED A SLITTER FOR MILL OR FINISHING ROOM

KIDDER PRESS CO. DOVER, N. H.
New York, 261 Broadway   Boston, 184 Summer St.
Gibbs-Brower Co., Agents   Toronto, 445 King St. West

ENGINEERING FOR
PULP, PAPER AND POWER PLANTS

JOSEPH H. WALLACE & CO.
INDUSTRIAL ENGINEERS
Temple Court Building, NEW YORK
71 Bay Street,   TORONTO, CAN.

A SELECTED LIST OF
PAPER DEALERS
IN CANADA

ALBERTA.
CALGARY.
Barber, Ellis Davis, Ltd.
Martin Paper Co., Ltd., John. *br.*
*Stanley Paper Co.

EDMONTON.
Parks, J. W., Paper Co., Ltd.

BRITISH COLUMBIA.
VANCOUVER.
Blake, Creedon Co., Ltd.
Columbia Paper Co., Ltd.
*Smith, Davidson & Wright.

VICTORIA.
Barber, Ellis, Ltd. *br.*
*Columbia Paper Co., Ltd. *br.*
Smith, Davidson & Wright, Ltd. *br.*
Wilson, J. C., Ltd. *br.*

MANITOBA.
WINNIPEG.
Barber-Ellis, Ltd., *br.*
Barkwell, Phillips Co.
Clark Bros. & Co., Ltd.
Gage, W. J., Co. *br.*
Hudson Paper Co., Ltd.
Kilgour Bros.
Martin, John, Paper Co., Ltd.
McAllister & Co.
Tees & Persse, Ltd.
J. C. Wilson Co., Ltd.
Walter Woods Co.

NEW BRUNSWICK.
ST. JOHN.
Brown & Co., D. F., Ltd.
Carritte-Patterson Mfg. Co., Ltd.
Emery Bros.
*Gunn Paper Co., Ltd.
Schofield Paper Co., Ltd.

NOVA SCOTIA.
HALIFAX.
Allen, T. C., & Co.
Mackinlay, A. & W., Ltd.
Richmond Ptg. Co.

PARRSBORO.
Berry, W. J.

SYDNEY.
Carritte-Patterson Mfg. Co., Ltd. *br.*
Moore, C. P. *s. l.*
Thompson & Sutherland, Ltd. *s. l.*

ONTARIO.
DUNDAS.
Fisher, John, & Son.

FORT WILLIAM.
Tees & Persse, Ltd. *br.*

GALT.
Freund, Chas.

GUELPH.
Guelph Paper Co.

HAMILTON.
*Buntin, Gillies & Co., Ltd.
McKichan, J. R.
Woods, W., & Co.

LONDON.
Reason, H. T., & Co.
Reid Bros. & Co.

OTTAWA.
s Barnard, W. R., 138 Bank.
s Federal Paper Co., 382 Wellington.
*Hastey, B. S., 14 Nicholas. *s. l.*
Hope, James, & Sons, 61 Sparks. *s. l.*
s Neville, I. F., 226 Albert. *s. l.*
*Whyte, James G., & Son., 60 Rideau.
Workman, A., & Co., Ltd., 300 Wellington. *s. l.*

PETERBORO.
Edgar, James.

TORONTO.
Barber-Ellis, Ltd., 3-71 Wellington, W.
Bell, W. J., 43 Richmond, E.
Bradshaws, Ltd., 109 Atlantic av.

DARMSTADT, SCOTT & COURTNEY, Inc., Importers, Exporters and Dealers in **PAPER MAKERS' SUPPLIES**
Also Mfrs. of DEADENING and SATURATING FELTS
178 and 184 SOUTH STREET, NEW YORK

TORONTO—Continued.

Brangs & Heinrich, 455, King, W.
British American Wax Paper Co., Wrigley bldg., Carlaw av.
Brown Bros., Ltd., 100 Simcoe.
Buntin-Reid Co., The, 18 Colborne.
Canada Paper Co., Ltd., 112 Bay.
Copp, Clark Co., Ltd., 517 Wellington, W.
Dominion Paper Co., 80 George.
Durnan Paper Co., 69 Jarvis.
Gage, W. J. Co., Ltd., 84 Spadina av.
Gain, J. H., 124 Richmond, W.
Garden City Paper Mills Co., Ltd., 439 Wellington, W.
Halls, Fred. W., Paper Co., Ltd., 250 Richmond, W.
Hodge-Sherriff Paper Co., 19 Melinda.
Howell Trading Co., The, 169 George.
Kilgour Bros., 21 Wellington, W.
Kinleith Paper Co., 82 Spadina av.
McGregor, O. P., Co., Ltd., 411 Spadina av.
McNairn, J. H., 5 Jarvis.
Monarch Paper Co., 79 Spadina.
National Paper Co., 28 Temperance.
Powley, Geo., & Co., 1311 Queen, W.
Ratcliff Paper Co., 44 York.
Ritchie & Ramsay, Ltd., 80 Bay.
Toronto Paper Mfg. Co., 108 Bay.
Scott Paper Co., 109 George.
Thorne, A. M., 38 Front, E.
Thorne, S. M., 38 Front E.
United Paper Mills, Ltd., 66 Temperance.
Victoria Paper & Twine Co., Ltd., 439 Wellington, W.
Weatherhead Paper Co., Ltd., 62 John.
Wilkins Smallware Co., 28 W. Market.
Williams, John H., 424 Wellington, W.
Wilson, Monroe, Co., 106 York.

QUEBEC.

LITTLE CASCAPEDIA.
Cascapedia Mfg. & Trading Co.

MONTREAL.
Bancroft Paper Bag Co.
Beveridge Paper Co., Ltd., 17 St. Therese.
*Buntin Gillies & Co., 63 St. Alexander.
Canada Paper Co., Ltd., 70 McGill.
Cole, E. A., & Co., 160 McGill.
Couvrette-Sauriol Ltee, 114 St. Paul, East.
Wm. V. Dawson, Ltd., 93 St. Urbain.
Dominion Paper Co., 345 St. James.
Federal Paper Co., 188 McGill.
Granger Freres, 158 St. Paul, West.
Little, T. B., & Co., 63 St. Alexander.
McArthur, Alex., & Co., Ltd., 82 McGill.
McFarlane Son & Hodgson, 14 St. Alexander.
MacGregor-Harkness, 70 Clark.
Marchand Freres La Cie, Ltee, 56 Amherst.
Munderloh & Co., Ltd., 57 Victoria sq.
National Paper Mfg. Co., Ltd., 45 St. Alexander.
Paper, Ltd., 46 Alexander.
Paterson Mfg. Co., Ltd., 2001 St. Hubert.
Pollak Bros. & Co., 45 St. Alexander.
Reid, C. de Wolf, 211 McGill.
Robertson & Parker, 301 St. Paul, West.
Victoria Paper & Twine Co., 52 Victoria sq.
Wilkens, John, & Co., 88 McGill.
Wilson, J. C., Paper Co., 61 St. Alexander.

QUEBEC CITY.
Frigon, Lucien.
Reid & Cie, Ltd.

Bring Us Your Dyestuff Problems

The application of the dyestuff to papers is as much an art as the production of the dyestuff.

Dyeing is a chemical, not a mechanical, process.

An intimate knowledge of the possibilities of every dyestuff is often necessary to meet the particular requirements of the consumer, and the variation of local conditions, due to differences in quality of water, steam and chemicals, makes the dyehouse problem an individual one.

Because of this individual factor, the technique of the application of dyes commands today, as it has done in the past, the best talent among those distributers who cater to the highest class of trade.

The technical department of this Company is manned by chemists who have been picked because of their exact knowledge, practical experience and demonstrated ability. Well-equipped laboratories are maintained at our different offices, for the service of our customers.

You are invited to submit your problems. Your questions are welcome. Our advice in answer involves no obligation on your part.

National Aniline & Chemical Company
Incorporated
21 Burling Slip, New York

Branches

Buffalo	Cincinnati	Milwaukee
Boston	Chicago	Minneapolis
Charlotte	Hartford	Philadelphia
	Kansas City	

A SELECTED LIST OF DEALERS IN
Rags, Paper Stock, Etc.
IN THE
UNITED STATES

Marks Indicating Stocks Handled.
r—Rags; p—Papers; r. p. Rags and Papers.
Importers marked with a *.
Where no marks are used the concerns handle a general line.

ALABAMA.
Harvey Bros., Mobile.
Metzger, Louis H., Mobile.
Sprague Bros., Mobile.

ARKANSAS.
Feenberg, L., & Co., Fort Smith.
Bennett, I., Little Rock. r. p.
Siesel, M. J., & Co., Little Rock.
Krumper, J., Pine Bluff.

CALIFORNIA.
A. B. C. Waste Paper Co., Los Angeles.
Senegram, Philip Co., Los Angeles.
Silverstein, A., Oakland.
Whitehead, I., Oakland.
Rosenberg & Son, Sacramento. r. p.
Harley, Chas., Co., San Francisco, 650 7th.
Levin, Max., Co., San Francisco.
Steinberg, S., & Co., San Francisco.

COLORADO.
Grimes & Friedsam, Denver.
Mulroy, R. F., Denver.

CONNECTICUT.
Clark Rubber & Metal Co., Bridgeport.
Gledhill & Co., Bridgeport.
Gordon, M., & Son, Corp., Bridgeport.
Garvan, P., Inc., Hartford.
Gross, E., & Co., Hartford.
Loveland, A. C., & Co., Hartford.
Lublin, B., & Son, Hartford.
Alderman Bros., New Haven.
Alpert, M., & Son, New Haven.
Hershman, Israel, New Haven.
Ives, C. W., New Haven.
Greenblatt & Gordon, New London.
New London Iron and Metal Co., New London.
Gordon, Max, & Son Corp., Norwich.
Gordon, Max, & Son Corp., Willimantic.

DELAWARE.
Caplan, Philip, Wilmington.
Central Iron Metal and Paper Co., Wilmington.
Lutz, Wm. J., Wilmington.
Norton, Wm. B., Est. of, Wilmington.
Raphaelson & Krigstein, Wilmington.
Sterleth, John, & Bro., Wilmington.

DISTRICT OF COLUMBIA.
Bensinger, Sylvan & Co., Washington.
Cook, Bernheimer & Co., Washington.
Hopfenmaier, L., Washington. p.
Mullin, Edw., Washington.

FLORIDA.
Tampa Bag Co., Tampa.

GEORGIA.
American Mills Co., Atlanta.
Kaplin, K., Atlanta.
Kaufman, N., & Son, Atlanta.
Stein Junk Co., Atlanta.
Knight, J. T., & Son, Columbus. r.
Du Bose, J. H., & Co., Macon.
American Specialty & Import Co., Savannah. p.

ILLINOIS.
Rubenstein Bros., Alton. r. p.
Hartman Bros., Alton. r. p.
Progressive Iron & Metal Co., Alton. r.
Kabacker, David, Est. of, Bloomington.
Tick, Morris, Bloomington.
Gudder & Co., Centralia.

CHICAGO.
Only the Wholesale Packers and Dealers are included in this list.

American Paper Co., 1501 S. Dearborn av.
Auto Paper Stock Co., 2173 N. California av.
Birkenstein, S., & Sons, 377 W. Ontario.
Chicago Coated Board Co., 420-468 E. North Water.
Chicago Paper Stock Co., 109 N. Sangamon.
Cohen, B., & Son, 1244 S. Union.
Cook Co. Paper Stock Co., 2321 S. La Salle.
Damato, Tony, 1134 Tilden av.
Dray, Philip, 1320 S. Albany.
Dry, M., & Sons, 724 N. Racine.
Felsenthal, D. F., 711 Christiana av.
Flett Paper Stock Co., 11 S. La Salle; 4801 S. Maplewood.
Goldberg, A. M., & Bros., 2139 Loomis.
Gumbinsky Bros. Co., 2261 S. Union av.
Heller, Jos., 614 W. Monroe.
Holmes, Marcus S., 161 W. Harrison.
Jaffe, Sam'l, 1510 S. Peoria.
Jameson, Robin & Jameson, 1510 Newberry av.
Kaufman, M., 347-55 N. Sheldon.
Kolb, David, 1903 Milwaukee.
Kraus & Golbus, 5833 Throop.
Krus, Chas. P., 613 W. Van Buren.
MEINCKE, A. M., 5 S. Dearborn.
MENDELSON BROS., 910 S. Michigan.
Mid West Box Co., 111 W. Washington.
National Paper Products Co., 39 S. La Salle.
Northern Paper Stock Co. (not inc.), 1421 Center.
Paper Mill Supply Co., 420 Federal.
Pioneer Paper Stock Co., 438-48 W. Ohio. p.
Rizzo, Rocco, 612 W. Taylor.
Sakanovsky, Harry, 1507 Milwaukee.
Schannes, John, 2173 N. California av.
Seaman Paper Co., 208 S. La Salle.
Superior Paper Stock Co., 729 S. Clinton.
U. S. Paper Supply Co., 140 S. Dearborn.
Western Paper Stock Co., 1452-1458 Indiana av.

CHICAGO—Continued.
Williams-Gray Co., Stock Exchange Bldg.

ILLINOIS (Continued)
Quinn, W. D., Marseilles.
Cinofsky, W., & Co., Peoria.
Reliable Iron and Metal Co., Peoria.
Heller, W., & Son, Peoria.
Rupp, Geo., & Bros., Quincy.
Goldman, D., Rockford.
Greenblatt, M., Rock Island. r.
Morris & Lewis, Rock Island. r. p.
Barker, A., Iron Co., Springfield.

INDIANA.
Goldburg, Jos., Crawfordsville. r. p.
Elkhart Junk Co., Elkhart.
Winer, Sam, & Co., Elkhart.
Coleman, D., Evansville.
Fligeltaub, Henry, Est. of, Evansville, Ind.
Loewenthal & Co., Inc., Evansville.
Greenberg, H., Hide and Junk Co., Evansville.
Trockman, J., & Sons, Evansville.
Fort Wayne Waste Paper Co., Fort Wayne.
Lonergan, W. J., & Co., Fort Wayne.
Strasburg's Sons Co., Ft. Wayne.
Weil Bros. & Co., Ft. Wayne.
Wunderlin, Wm., & Co., Fort Wayne.
Borinstein, A., Indianapolis.
National Paper Stock Co., Indianapolis.
Sagalowski, L., Indianapolis.
Atlass Produce Co., Lafayette. r. p
Cook, S. O., & Co., Logansport. r. p
Bernstein, H. J., Marion.
Goldreich Bros., Marion.
Jarodzki & Co., Mt. Vernon. r. p.
Feinburg, Abe., Muncie.
Joseph, R., New Albany. r. p.
Watson, Willard O., New Albany. r.p.
Holzapfel, Henry, Richmond.
Bergan, J., & Co., South Bend.
Ciralsky, Abraham, & Son, South Bend.
Gilbert, Meyer, South Bend. r. p.
Dresher, J. W., So. Bend. p.
Bogard, A., Terre Haute.
Terre Haute Scrap Material Co., Terre Haute. p.
Duncan, Kingsolver Co., Terre Haute.
Terre Haute Rag & Metal Co., Terre Haute.
Vincennes Iron & Metal Co., Vincennes.
Cook-Simon Co., Wabash.

IOWA.

Gross, H. S., Burlington.
Goldberg, S., & Co., Cedar Rapids. r. p.
Effron-Kushner & Co., Cedar Rapids.
Heend, A., & Son, Clinton.
Katelman, J., Council Bluffs.
Stein, J., Council Bluffs.
Whitebrook, Geo., Council Bluffs.
Raphael, J. H., & Sons, Davenport.
Cohen Bros., Des Moines.
Cohen, E. M., & Sons, Des Moines.
Iowa Iron & Metal Co., Des Moines.
Levy, L., & Sons, Des Moines.
Dubuque Hide & Fur Co., Dubuque.
Harris & Co., Dubuque.
Kassler & Son, M., Dubuque.
Magdal, H., Dubuque.
Robinson Bros., Ft. Dodge.
Resnick Bros., Ft. Madison. r. p.
Shultz, H. & I., Keokuk.
Sterne, Louis, Keokuk.
Friedman, J. M., Marshalltown.
Gervich, Max, Marshalltown.
Cohn Bros., Waterloo.
Fuoss, J. H., Waterloo.

KANSAS.

Feinberg-Wayne Iron, Metal & Paper Co., Kansas City.
Phillips, L., Leavenworth.
Dyal Bros. & Co., Topeka.
Dyal, S. E., & Bro., Wichita.
Kamenesky, J., & Bro., Wichita.

KENTUCKY.

Bruck, Charles, Covington.
Gleeson, T. M., Covington.
Misel, Michael, Covington.
Barnes, E. B., Lexington.
Byrns, E. J., Lexington.
Lexington Rag & Paper Co., Lexington.
London Traffic Co., Lexington.
Munich & Wides, Lexington.
Speyer & Sons, Lexington.
Hyman, E., Louisville.
Hyman, Jacob, Louisville.
Hyman, L. P., & Co., Louisville.
Hyman, Mose, Louisville.
Indianapolis Paper Stock Co., Louisville.
Louisville Scrap Material Co., Louisville. r. p.
Gotterdam, Philip, Louisville. r. p.
Levy, Philip, & Sons, Louisville.

LOUISIANA.

Glaser, M., New Orleans.
d'Hemecourt, Jules, & Sons, New Orleans. p

LOUISIANA—Continued.

Letellier-Phillips Co., New Orleans. r. p.

MAINE.

Miller, Isaac, & Co., Auburn.
Lampert, H., Auburn.
Roggle, Abram, Auburn.
O'Connor, Francis, Co., Augusta r. p.
Brown Bros., Bangor.
O'Connor, Chas. G., Bangor. r. p.
Davis, John, Bath.
Hart, L. N., Bath.
Dvilinsky, A., Belfast.
Gott, J. H., Belfast.
Shapiro, Louis, Biddeford.
Solmer, M. A., Biddeford. r. p.
Sawyer, W. E., Booth Bay Harbor.
Goldberg, Max, & Son, Gardiner. r. p.
Levine, Morris, Gardiner. r. p.
Alpert, M., & Co., Lewiston. r. p.
Main Mfgrs. Supply Co., Lewiston.
Gordon, Albert, Lewiston. r. p.
Miller, S., & Co., Lewiston.
Gutterson & Gould, Portland. r. p.
Gerber, Issac M., Portland.
Perry, Buxton, Doan & Co., Portland. r. f.
Sacknoff Bros., Portland. r. p.
Silverman, P., & Son, Portland.
Seiger, Samuel, Portland.
Shapero, Thomas, Rockland.
Towle, Thomas, Co., Portland.
Alperin, L. L., Rockland. r. p.
Perry, Buxton, Doan & Co., Waterville. r. p.

MARYLAND.
BALTIMORE.

Baker, N., & Son, 833 S. Sharp.
Bond, W. T., & Co., 1138 Penna. av.
Frank, N., & Sons, 1402-4 Mullikin.
GOLDSTEIN, R., & SON.
O'Connor, Thos. H., Co., 445 Guilford av.
Radford, Jno. T., 1018 Ashland av.

MARYLAND—Continued.

Cumberland Junk Co., Cumberland.
Knop, Philip, Cumberland.
Baumgartner, John, Est. of, Frederick.
Boyer & Heard, Hagerstown.
Gerber, J. H., Hagerstown.
Reliable Junk Co., Hagerstown.

MASSACHUSETTS.

Baker, Abraham, Athol.
Fiskel, Brandwein, Amesbury.
Reingold, M., Amesbury.
Silvesky, Jacob, Amesbury.

Rags and Paper Stock Dealers

MASSACHUSETTS—*Continued.*
Bernard, Albert, Beverly.
Arth, Robert, Beverly.
Flagler, Harris, Beverly.
Kransberg, Philip, Beverly.
Winn, Julius, Beverly.
McAdams, F. J., & Co., Beverly. r. p.
Zalinski, Nicholas, Beverly. r. p.

BOSTON.
Only the Wholesale Packers and Dealers are included in this list.

Aronson, H., 101 West 4th.
Brown, Chas. D., & Co., Inc., 185 Devonshire.
Butler, Thos., & Co., 15-23 Medford. r. p.
*Butterworth, Edwin, & Co., 160 Congress. r.
Collins, M. J., 215 A. r. p.
Collins, M. J., A, S. B.
De Stefano, D., Co., 32 Dannell, S. B.
De Vito, John A., & Co., 283 Commercial. r. p.
Dillingham, I. S., 127 Federal. r.
Driscoll, M. F., 210 Milk and 105 Central.
Ford, Alex. S., 165 A. r. p.
Graham, B., 19 Ellery. r.
Graham, James J., Otis, East Cambridge. r. p.
Graham, P. H., & Co., 12 Ewer. r. p.
Hodgkins, O., & Co., 14 Commercial.
*International Purchasing Co., 141 Milk. (Rope.)
Luca & Bro., 134 A. p.
MOREY & CO., E. Cambridge.
Miller, Harry, 49 Central Wharf.
Stockbridge, M. G., 49 Federal. r. p.
*Train, Smith Co., Equitable Bldg.
*True & McClelland, 165 A. r.

MASSACHUSETTS—*Continued.*
Brockton Junk and Metal Co., Brockton. r. p.
Butler-Green Co., Brockton. r. p.
Wilbur, F. R., Brockton, Mass.
Promboun & Son, L., Cambridge. r. p.
Abramsohn & Walk, 171 2d, Chelsea.
Bittel & Helfitz, Chelsea.
Cutler & Brickman, Chelsea.
Gillman & Bro., 110 5th, Chelsea.
Levin & Sons Co., Chelsea.
N. E. Mill Supply Co., 263 B'way, Chelsea.
Feinberg, B., & Sons, Chelsea. r. p.
Iaide, W.
Resnick & Goodman, Chelsea. r. p.
Rosenberg Bros., Chelsea.
Salter, M., & Sons, Chelsea. r. p.

MASSACHUSETTS—*Continued.*
Stein Bros., 213 2d, Chelsea. r. p.
Vinal & Co., S. S., Chelsea. r. p.
Dunn, W. J., Fall River.
Garnson & Banor, Fall River.
Massasoit Mfg. Co., Fall River. r.
Phelan, Jos. F., Fall River. r. p.
Roy Paper Co., Fall River. r. p.
Barrowsky, Jacob, Fitchburg. r. p.
Wallace, Rodney, Fitchburg. r. p.
Brophy, T. W., Gloucester. r. p.
Roberts, Alex., Co., Haverhill. r. p.
Seigle, M., Haverhill. r. p.
Barowski, D. H., & Co., Holyoke. r. p.
Belsky & Goldberg, Holyoke. r. p.
Garvan, P., Inc., Holyoke. r.
Woodruff, J. B., Inc., Holyoke.
American Woolen Co., Bag & Burlap Dept., Lawrence. r.
Franks Bros., Lawrence. r. p.
Gutterson & Gould, Lawrence. r.
Chase, E. T., & Son Co., Lowell. p.
Lowell Waste Co., Lowell. r. p.
Ansin, M., & Co., Lynn.
Glenn, Linde, & Co., Lynn. r. p.
Candia Iron & Metal Co., Lynn. r.
Michelson & Co., Lynn. r. p.
McCullough, John, New Bedford.
Barth, Isaac, & Son, Newburyport. r. p.
Brudno, Lazarus, Newburyport.
North Adams Paper Stock Co., North Adams.
Batchelder, Hy. C., Salem.
Myers, A., Salem.
Dexter & Bowles, Springfield. r.
*Castle, Gotthiel & Overton, Springfield. r. p.
Collins, E. F., & Son. Springfield. r.
Eastern Paper and Supply Co., Springfield. r.
Fisher & Kurnitsky, Springfield. r. p.
Freedman, Joseph, Springfield. r. p.
Goodman, H. A., Springfield.
Hunt, S. M., Springfield. r.
Shapiro, M. J., Springfield.
Corr, P. H., Taunton. r.
Berman Bros., Waltham.
Nadell, W. F., Weymouth. r. p.
Cotton, B. S., Worcester. r. p.
Edinberg, Harris & Co., Worcester. r. p.
General Supply Co., Worcester, Mass.
Glick, Harris, Worcester. r. p.

MICHIGAN.
Lansky, Wm., & Co., Ann Arbor.
Hirschfield, H., Bay City.
American Paper Stock Co., Detroit.

Rags and Paper Stock Dealers

MICHIGAN—*Continued.*
Detroit Paper Stock Co., Detroit. *p.*
Michigan Waste Paper Co., Detroit. *p.*
Monroe Paper Stock Co., Detroit.
Simon, A., & Co., Detroit. *p.*
Flint Scrap Iron & Metal Co., Flint.
Shear, George W., & Co., Flint. *r. p.*
Bommelje, Wm., & Son, Grand Rapids.
Brandy, M., & Sons, Grand Rapids.
Grand Rapids Salvage Co., Grand Rapids.
Morrison, A., & Co., Grand Rapids.
Acme Rag Co., Kalamazoo. *r.*
City Iron and Metal Co.
Graff & Sons, Kalamazoo.
Gumbinsky, Oscar, & Bros., Kalamazoo.
Michigan Sanitary Cloth Co., Kalamazoo.
Nielson, Jr., Charles F., Kalamazoo. *p.*
Sanitary Rag Co., Kalamazoo. *r.*
Monroe Iron & Metal Co., Monroe.
Muskegon Iron & Metal Co., Muskegon.
Feldman, J., Petosky.
Goldman Bros., Port Huron. *r. p.*
Clinkofstine, L., Saginaw.
Lenick, E., & Co., Saginaw.
Braucly, S., Sault Ste. Marie.
Jacobs, Louis, & Son, Sault Ste. Marie.
Lavine Bros., Sault Ste. Marie.

MINNESOTA.
Duluth Paper Stock Co., Duluth.
Acme Paper Stock Co., Minneapolis.
Minnesota Paper Stock Co., Minneapolis. *r. p.*
American Paper Stock Co., St. Paul. *p.*
Goldbarg, Gedal, St. Paul.
Paper, Calmenson & Co., St. Paul.

MISSOURI.
Rupp, Geo., Co., & Bros., Chillicothe. *r. p.*
Rupp, Geo., Co., & Bros., Hannibal. *r. p.*
Epstein, A., & Sons, Kansas City.
Kansas City Waste Paper Co., Kansas City. *p.*
Salvation Army, Kansas City. *p.*
Cohen, L. J., & Co., St. Louis. *r.*
FEDERAL PAPER STOCK CO., St. Louis. *r. p.*
GENERAL PAPER STOCK CO., St. Louis. *r. p.*
Klauber, A., & Sons, St. Louis. *r.*

MISSOURI—*Continued.*
Mathes, G., Co., St. Louis. *r.*
Missouri Paper Stock Co., St. Louis.
Standard Paper Stock Co., St. Louis.
Republic Metal & Rubber Co., St. Louis. *r.*

NEBRASKA.
Omaha Paper Stock Co., Omaha. *p.*

NEW HAMPSHIRE.
Addelson, Wm., Berlin. *r. p.*
Concord Iron & Metal Co., Concord. *r. p.*
Fisher, H. E., Concord. *r. p.*
Bennett, Martin, Dover.
New England Iron & Metal Co., Keene. *r. p.*
Manchester Iron & Metal Co., Manchester.
Portsmouth Iron & Metal Co., Portsmouth.

NEW JERSEY.
Acorn Iron & Metal Co., Atlantic City.
Atlantic City Waste Paper Co., Atlantic City. *p.*
Tarter Bros., Camden.
Dawe, J., & Son, Dover.
Trudgian, J. E., Dover.
Cardinelli, Peter, & Son, Hoboken, N. J.
Gatti-McQuade Co., Hoboken.
Marrone, John, Hoboken. *p.*
Carlo, John H., Newark.
Kelly & Co., Newark. *r. p.*
Leonardis, P., & Sons, Newark. *r. p*
Verrone, L., Newark. New rags.
New Brunswick Iron & Metal Co., New Brunswick.
Ellis, Herman, Perth Amboy.
Mancuso, Tony, Rahway.
Gilinsky, M., Trenton.
Milner, S., & Son, Trenton.
Trenton Paper Stock Co., Trenton. *r. p.*

NEW YORK.
Forman, J. T., Albion.
Becker, Charles W., Amsterdam. *r. p.*
Mohawk Valley Waste & Metal Co., Amsterdam. *r. p.*
Raphael, Meyer, Amsterdam. *r. p.*
Auburn Iron Co., Auburn.
Peniod, Geo. W., Auburn.
Binghamton Metal & Paper Co., Binghamton.
Buffalo Waste Paper Co., Buffalo.
Fox, Morris, & Son, Buffalo. *r.*

Rags and Paper Stock Dealers

NEW YORK—*Continued.*
Oppenheimer & Co., Buffalo. *r. p.*
Oppenheimer, Jesse. *r. p.*
Ullman's Sons, D., Buffalo. *r. p.*
Troy Waste Mfg. Co., Cohoes.
Hofeller-Loeser Co., Depew. *r. p.*
Dunkirk Rag & Metal Co., Dunkirk.
Baker, S., Elmira. *r. p.*
Fisher, H., Elmira. *r. p.*
Spiegel Bros., Elmira. *r. p.*
Sittinfield, J., Elmira. *r. p.*
Doxey, N. D., Elmira.
Elmira Iron & Metal Co., Elmira.
Spiegel, W. M., Elmira.
Godelle, O., Geneva.
Glens Falls Waste Co., Glens Falls. *r.*
Bernstein & Kaplan, Glens Falls. *r. p.*
Katzman & Son, A., Gouverneur.
Levine, Harris & Son, Hoosick Falls.
Hudson Iron & Storage Co., Hudson. *r. p.*
Ithaca Junk Co., Ithaca.
Davis, Samuel, Jamestown.
Katz, Aaron, Kingston.
Laughlin, John, Little Falls.
Modern Equipment Co., Lockport.
Koff Bros., Malone.
Malone Rag, Iron and Metal Co., Malone.
Hart, Patrick, Newburgh.
Newburgh Iron & Metal Co., Newburgh.

NEW YORK CITY.
Only the Wholesale Packers and Dealers are included in this list.

BROOKLYN BOROUGH.
Abbatemarco, Jas., 268 4th av. *p.*
Carrizzo, George, & Co., 200 6th. *r. p.*
Casella, Tony, & Co., 771 Metropolitan av. *p.*
Costarino, P., 110 Classon av. *r.*
De Angelis, A., Inc., 6 Park av.
Equity Trading Co., 139 N. 6th.
Flynn, Michael, 61 Congress and 56 Columbia. (Bagging, canvas, old rope.)
Garsat Co., 64 Frost.
Guagliardi, P., 404 Marcy av. *p.*
Hughes, Laurence, 235 Union av.
Hughes, Wm., Inc., 84 Metropolitan av.
International Mill Supply Co., 546 Eastern Parkway.
McGrath, John V., Leonard.
Parascand, Fred., & Bro., 16 Whitehall pl.
Plunkett, Peter, Sons, 432 Van Brunt. (Rope.)

Brooklyn Borough—*Continued.*
Shaw, Wm. C., 20 Bergen. (Waste fibres and jute.)
South Brooklyn Paper & Rag Co., 93-95 Prospect av. *r. p.*
Union Rag Co., 560 President. *r.*
Williamsburg Paper & Rag Co., 14 Steuben.

MANHATTAN BOROUGH.
Abenheimer, Louis H., 60 Wall.
Acme Mill Supply Co., 24 Grove. *p.*
American Woodpulp Corp., 347 Madison av.
Antoniello, R., 274 Lafayette.
*ATTERBURY BROS., INC., 38 Park row. *r. p.*
*Atterbury & McKelvey, Inc., 145 Nassau.
Banbino, J., & Co., 2371 1st av.
Bartley Mfg. Co., 261 South. (Burlap, bagging and *r.*)
Bartow, Theo., & Son, 33 W. 42d.
Berlowitz, P., 132 Nassau. *p.*
Blank, Robert, 140 Nassau. *r. p.*
Box Board & Lining Co., 10 Grand.
Bronstein, A., & Sons, 160 Greene. *r.*
*Butterworth, Edwin, & Co., 132 Nassau. *r. p.*
Campbell, Peter C., 1 New Bowery. *r.*
Campbell, T., 32 New Bowery.
CANTASANO, VITO G., BROS., 185 South.
Capo, T., & Co., 337 E. 107th.
Casella Bros., 177 South. *p.*
Castle, Gottheil & Overton, 200 5th av. *r. p.*
Chambers Paper Stock Co., 8 Wooster.
Chase & Norton, 277 Water. *p.*
Cotton, M., 132 Nassau.
Conwie Waste Co., 150 Nassau.
*DARMSTADT, SCOTT & COURTNEY, 178 South. *r. p.*
DeAlessandro, Joseph, 291 Hudson. *p.*
Delia, Nicola, & Co., 159 South.
Derrico, J., 338 E. 110th.
De Luca, G., & M. De Fina, 163 Crosby.
Dezego Bros., 307 Water. *p.*
Dorfman, I., & Sons, 269 South.
Esposito, T., 261 E. 140th.
Ferrando, James, & Son, 366 Water.
Galante, Thomas, 256 E. 149th.
Gallipoli, P., 200 W. Houston.
Gallipoli, P., & Co., 200 W. Houston.
Garvan, P., Inc., 200 5th av.
Goldman, Julius, 19 Cedar.
GOLDSTEIN, R., & SONS, 200 5th av.
Gotham Paper Stock Co., 31 Ferry.

Rags and Paper Stock Dealers

Manhattan Borough—*Continued.*
*GOTTESMAN & SON, M., 18 E. 41st. r. p.
Hicks, Daniel M., Inc., 140 Nassau. r. p.
HILLS, GEO. F., CO., 108 Cliff and 9 Hague. p.
Jaffe, Jacob M., 335 Cherry.
JAFFE & CO., 236 South. r.
Joseph & Miller, 449 Water. r.
Kaplan, B. D., & Co., 7 Vestry. r.
KELLER, E. J., CO., 200 5th av.
Lacorazza, John, & Co., 178 Prince r. p.
McGuire, Michael, 102 10th av. r.
Madison Paper Stock Co., 24 Grove.
Maier, Marx, 200 5th av.
MAIN PAPER STOCK CO., (INC.), 29 Peck sl. and 27 Front. r. p.
Manhattan Paper Stock Co., Produce Exchange.
Marquardt, F. G., 320 Broadway.
Mastronardi, N., & Co., 24 New Bowery. p.
Mazzie & Capozzolo, 247 E. 136th.
Mazzei, Nicholas & Co., 146-148 Lincoln av.
Melrose Paper Stock Co., 2862 Park av.
Messinas', B., Sons, 436 Canal.
Millar, Geo. W., & Co., 284 Lafayette. r. p.
Monteleone & Son, 2950 Park av.
Murphy, Dan'l I., 182 Nassau.
Mutnick Bros., 61 Crosby. r.
North Paper Stock Co., 230 W. 30th.
*O'MEARA, MAURICE, CO., 265 Front and 448 Pearl. r. p.
O'Neill, P. F., Paper Stock Co., 417 E. 124th.
PARSONS TRADING CO., 17 Battery pl. r. p.
Pascarella, Michael, 232 W. B'way. p.
Pearl Paper Stock Co., 51 Ann.
Quirk, E. M., 2 Carlisle.
Ragone, Gerard, & Son, 352 Water.
Rizzo, Antonio, & Son, 261 Front. p.
*SALOMON, A., INC., 15 Park row. r.
*Salomon Bros. & Co., 299 B'way. r.
Salvati, Bragio, Gerard av. and 138th.
*Sergeant, E. M., Co., Madison av. & 29th. r. p.
*Sergeant, J. V., & Co., 132 Nassau. r. p.
Shea Bros., 46 Ann.
Shoenfeld, L. B., & Co., 56 Beaver.
Smith, Thomas, & Son, 75 Pike sl. r. p.

Manhattan Borough—*Continued.*
Stramiello, Chas., 407 E. 123d. r. p.
Stramiello, Michael, 281 Front. p.
Taddonio, H., 403 E. 109th.
Thomas, E. B., & Co., 100 Hudson.
Tocci, Paul, 444 Water. p.
Troiano & Defina, 442 Pearl. r. p.
Tully, Joseph C., & Co., 313 West.
Tucker, J. J., 63 Prince. r. p.
Vincenzo, Antonio, 132 Nassau. r.
Viverito, G., 300 Pearl.
Vriono, A., & Co., 105 John.
Ward's, Owen, Sons, 448 W. 39th. r.
Waste Paper Stock Co., 210-212 W. 29th.
Wilkinson Bros., 419 Broome.

NEW YORK STATE—*Continued.*
Baker, L., Ogdensburg.
Dinberg, D., Ogdensburg.
Katzman, Max, Ogdensburg.
Moody & Gould Co., Oneonta.
Welner, B., & Son, Oswego.
Baker, Samuel, Plattsburg.
Kudon, Benj., Plattsburg.
Taylor, Nathan, Plattsburg.
Trombly, Otis, Plattsburg.
Braz, Louis, Rochester. r.
Cohen, Jacob, & Son, Rochester. r. p.
Cohen, Max, & Bro., Rochester. r. p.
Cohen, Moses, Rochester. r. p.
Eidelstern, J. B., Rochester. r.
Frankel Bros. & Co., Rochester. r.
Levi, M. A., Rochester. p.
Sarachan & Rosenthal, Rochester. r.
Cohen, I. L., Schenectady.
Schenectady Iron & Metal Co., Schenectady.
Barber, William, Syracuse.
Butin, Morris, Syracuse.
Davis Co., L. J., Syracuse.
Hurwitz Bros., Syracuse.
Parks, E. A., Syracuse.
Stolusky, J., & Son, Syracuse. p.
Bloch Iron & Metal Co., Troy.
Cohen & Symansky, Troy.
Goldstein, Herman, Troy.
Hedges, W. F., Troy.
Palowansky, Harris, Troy.
Symansky Bros., Troy.
Troy Waste Mfg. Co., Troy.
United Waste Mfg. Co., Troy.
Witham & Co., Troy. br.
Baxter, T. W. Co., Utica.
Horwitz, H., & Co.
Mettleman's, Jacob, Sons, Utica. r. p.
Watertown Paper Stock Co., Watertown.

NORTH CAROLINA.
Southern Waste Co., Newton.
King, J. E., & Co., Raleigh.

NORTH DAKOTA.
Gingsburg Bros., Grand Forks.
Redick Hide & Fur Co., Grand Forks.

OHIO.
Akron Scrap Iron Co., Akron.
American Scrap Iron Co., Akron.
Alliance Iron & Metal Co., Alliance. r. p.
Weizer, W., & Co., Bellaire.
Canton Junk Co., Canton.
Levie-Heller Company, Canton.

CINCINNATI.
Fettig, Joseph, 1910 Plum. r. p.
Queen City Rag & Paper Co., 122 E. Water. r. p.
Sutphin, The I. V., Co., Union Cent. Life Ins. Bldg. r. p.
Toenjes Co., C., 219 E. 2d. r.

OHIO—Continued.
Blee, J., Cleveland.
Cleveland Waste Paper Co., Cleveland.
Goldman, J., & Sons, Cleveland.
Koblitz-Kohn, The, Co., Cleveland.
Koblitz, R. C., & Son, Cleveland.
Silberman, S., & Co., Cleveland. r. p.
Weiskopf, J., & Son, Cleveland.
Columbus Waste Paper Co., Columbus. r. p.
Indianapolis Paper Stock Co., Columbus. br, p.
Mellman Bros., Columbus. r. p.
Silberstein, F., & Sons, Columbus.
Dayton Iron & Metal Co., Dayton.
Holz, Samuel, & Son, Dayton.
Slavin, L., & Sons, Dayton.
Slavin, S., & Co., Dayton.
Sheeter, John, Delphos.
Wernick, Selker & Co., Fostoria.
Srere Bros. & Co., Franklin.
Wolf & Co., Hamilton.
Bernstein, M., & Co., Lima.
Jackman, J. B., & Son, Lima.
Lima Paper Stock Co., Lima.
Appleman, C. D., Mansfield. r. p.
Cousins, Jacob, Mansfield. r. p.
Mehl, G., Middletown.
Kulke, Sam, Sandusky.
Ebner Son's, The, Co., Springfield. r. p.
Schadel, J., & Co., Springfield.
Spector, J., & Co., Springfield. r. p.
Springfield Iron & Metal Co., Springfield. r. p.

OHIO—Continued.
Berger, Joseph, Steubenville.
Tiffin Junk Co., Tiffin. r. p.
Gerson, I., & Son, Toledo.
Kasle Iron & Metal Co., Toledo.
Mostov, S., Toledo.
Rosen, Henry, Toledo. r. p.
Toledo Paper Stock Co., Toledo. r. p.
Rolland, J. W., & Son, Youngstown.

OKLAHOMA.
Kansas City Paper House, Oklahoma.
Oklahoma Paper Co., Oklahoma.
Western Newspaper Union, Oklahoma.

OREGON.
Chicago Junk Co., Portland.
Simon, J., & Bro., Portland.
Wolfman, A., Portland.

PENNSYLVANIA.
Isay, Herman, Allegheny.
Jones & Co., J. B., Allegheny.
Streng's Sons, Moritz, Allegheny.
Allentown Waste Material Co., Allentown.
Sofranscy, H., Co., Allentown.
Abelson, A., Altoona. r. p.
Goodman, Theo., & Co., Bradford.
Letzic, H., & Co., Carbondale.
Garrett, Edwin, Chester. r. p.
Smedley Bros., Chester.
Brodsky, A. J., Corry. r.
Sulkin, Louis, & Co., Easton.
Erie Iron & Steel Co., Erie.
Smith, Wm., East Stroudsburg.
Capitol City Junk Co., Harrisburg.
Williams & Freedman, Harrisburg. g.
Levy, A., & Co., Hazelton. r. p.
Cambria Junk Co., Johnstown.
Caples & Moore, Johnstown.
Miller, Isaac, Lancaster.
Caplan, J., & Co., Lebanon.
Claster, Ellis, & Co., Lock Haven.
Meadville Waste Co., Meadville.
Mintz, I. M., & Son, Oil City.

PHILADELPHIA.
Only the Wholesale Packers and Dealers are included in this list.
Bicking Paper Co., 113 N. 2d. p.
Caplan, Jacob L., Co., 234 Queen. r.
Castle, Gottheil & Overton, 126 Cuthbert. r. p.
Chaulk, J. J., Company, 508 S. Delaware. r.
Clapp, H. D. B., & Co., 824 American. r. p.

Rags and Paper Stock Dealers

PHILADELPHIA—*Continued.*
Coll, Leo J., 1205 Kenilworth. *p.*
*Corner, Edward, 1060 Beach. *r.*
Di Santi, Alexander, 1721 Carpenter. *p.*
Dougherty, John, & Son, 1422 N. 20th.
Feldman & Co., 615 Webster and 325 S. Water. *r.*
Gatti-McQuade & Co., 1416 Wood. *r. p.*
Glazer, Morris, 112 N. 6th. *p.*
Goldman, Chas., 335 N. American.
Hemingway Co., 243 Elbow Lane. *p.*
Infante Bros., 1131 Vine. *r. p.*
King, Alphonso, 149 S. Hancock. *p.*
Lenhart, J. I., 236 N. Delaware av. *r. p.*
*Linton, Josiah, & Co., 22 N. 4th. *r.*
Lynch, Thomas, 415 Cherry. *p.*
Matusow Bros., 454 N. 9th. *r. p.*
Minskey, I., 515 S. Randolph. *r.*
Monville, Gilles & Co., 127 Catharine. *r.*
Mullin Co., A. F., 1221 Bainbridge. *r.*
*Murphy, Daniel I., 39 N. Water. *r.*
O'Neill & Co., P., 408 S. 6th. *r.*
PENN. PAPER & STOCK CO., 206 N. Delaware av. *p.*
Philadelphia Wool Stock Co., Inc., 214 S. 5th. *r.*
*Ridsdale, John, & Co., 122 N. Front. *r.*
Raiguel, M. O., Co., 305 Florist. *p.*
Rose & Son, A., 1831 N. Warnock. *r. p.*
Schwab, F. A., Co., 16 N. Front. *r.*
Silverwood, Jos., Sons, 150 N. Front. *r. p.*
Simmons', John, Sons, 28-30 S. Marshall. *p.*
Southwestern Junk Co., 1705 Carpenter.
Specter & Matusow, 534 N. 3d. *p.*
Starley Paper Stock Co., 1125 Vine.
Strosier, F. William, 626 Cherry. *p.*
Sullivan, P., & Son, 218 Wood. *p.*
Well's, Morris, Sons, 837 N. 3d. *r. p.*
Woods & Hooker, 1740 N. Front. *r.*

PITTSBURGH.
Forst & Wolf Co. *r. p.*
Hausman & Wimmer Co. *r. p.*
PENNSYLVANIA PAPER STOCK CO. *r. p.*
Siefert Paper Co., 238 1st av.
Soracco, John J. *r. p.*
Streng's, J. J. M. Son's Co.
Wimmer, Wm. F. *r. p.*

PENNSYLVANIA—*Continued.*
Brenner & Weiner, Pottsville. *r. p.*
Krouse, Simon, Punxsutawney. *r. p.*
Grieshaber, W., Reading. *r. p.*
Mehlmann, A. M., Pottstown.
Luria Rag Co., York.
Luria Bros. & Co., Reading. *r. p.*
Moyer, L. A., Reading. *r. p.*
Pear & Isecovitz, Reading. *r. p.*
Shru, L., & Son, Reading.
Feld, Jacob, Scranton. *r.*
Grass, Alexander, Scranton. *r.*
Levin, H., Scranton. *r.*
Penn Waste Paper Co., Scranton. *p.*
Scranton Waste Paper Co., Scranton. *p.*
Wartowsky, Chas., Scranton. *r.*
Levine, Isaac, Shenandoah. *r. p.*
Steinferst, E., & Son, Titusville.
Epstein, Lewis, West Newton.
Adleson, Simon, & Son, Wilkes Barre.
Wilkes Barre Iron & Metal Co., Wilkes Barre.
Luria Rag Co., York. *r. p.*
Standard Rag & Paper Co., York. *r. p.*
Williams & Levine, York. *r. p.*
York Iron & Master Co., York. *r. p.*

RHODE ISLAND.
Horowitz, S., Newport. *r. p.*
Briggs, H. A., & Co., Pawtucket. *r. p.*
Union Bag & Burlap Co., Pawtucket. *r.*
Union Wading Co., Pawtucket. *r.*
Blanding, C. L., Mfg. Co., Providence.
Brooks, Geo. B., Providence. *r.*
Klein, S., & Sons, Providence.
Priest, Henry, Providence. *r. p.*
Rhode Island Paper Stock Co., Providence.
Ray, E. K., Est. of, Woonsocket. *r. p.*
Union Bag & Burlap Co., Woonsocket. *r.*

SOUTH DAKOTA.
Margulies, M., Sioux Falls.

TENNESSEE.
American Iron & Metal Co., Chattanooga.
Cassell, B., & Co., Chattanooga.
Consolidated Iron & Metal Co., Chattanooga. *r. p.*
De Vorkin Bros., Memphis.
Gabay, Samuel, Est. of, Memphis.
Cline & Bernheim, Nashville.
Hightower, W. T., Nashville.

Rags and Paper Stock Dealers

TENNESSEE—*Continued.*
Nashville Paper Stock Co., Nashville.
Papianus, B. S., & Co., Nashville.

TEXAS.
American Paper Stock Co., Dallas.
Lipshitz, Philip, Co., Dallas.
Texas Junk Co., Forth Worth.
Block, J., & Co., Galveston.
Phoenix Waste Mfg. Co., Galveston.
Houston Paper Stock Co., Houston. r. p.

UTAH.
Utah Junk Co., Salt Lake City.

VERMONT.
Burlington Paper Stock Co., Burlington. r. p.
Burlington Waste & Metal Co., Burlington. r. p.
Samelson, H., & Co., Burlington. r. p.
Granite City Paper Stock Co., Montpelier. r. p.
St. Albans Paper Stock Co., St. Albans. r. p.

VIRGINIA.
Dreifus & Son, Alexandria.
Eichelbaum, M., Lynchburg. r. p.
Lynchburg Iron & Metal Co., Lynchburg. r. p.
Cashin, M. T., Norfolk.
Imperial Bagging Co., Norfolk.
Woodman, J. W., Portsmouth.
Keville, John T., Portsmouth. r. p.
Cosly, Clarence, Richmond. r.
Hey, D. H., Richmond. p.
Nott, F. H., Richmond. r.
Rose, L., & Co., Richmond. r.
Smith, J. C., & Co., Richmond. r.
Portsmouth Hyde & Metal Co., Portsmouth. r. p.
Virginia Mfg. Co., Portsmouth. p. r.

WEST VIRGINIA.
Silverstein, A. P., & Son, Charleston. r. p.
Abrahams & Co., Huntington. r. p.
Wolf Pollack Co., Huntington.
Cohen, M., Huntington.
Parkersburg Junk Co., Parkersburg.

WISCONSIN.
Appleton Iron & Metal Co., Appleton.
Glicksman, W., Chippewa Falls.
Hudson, Henry, Eau Claire.
Wright Bros. Paper Box Co., Fond du Lac.
Rosenberg, A., & Sons, Green Bay.
La Crosse Scrap Iron & Metal Co., La Crosse. r. p.
Kassler-Lewis Co., La Crosse. r. p.
Natenshon, L., & Co., La Crosse. r. p.
Paley Bros., Madison.
Sinaiko Bros., Madison.
Manitowoc Iron & Metal Co., Manitowoc.
Miller Bros., Marsfield. r. p.
Franzen Paper Co., Milwaukee. p.
Milwaukee Scrap Iron Co., Milwaukee. r.
Ruplinger, M. P., Milwaukee.
Seeboth Bros. Co., Milwaukee. r.
Shafrin, Schmitz & Co., Milwaukee.
* Wishnefsky & Makler Co., Milwaukee. r.
Oshkosh Iron & Metal Co., Oshkosh.
Wisconsin Iron & Metal Co., Oshkosh.
Fox Pioneer Scrap Iron Co., Racine.
Balkonsky, J., & Sons, Sheboygan.

A SELECTED LIST OF
Dealers in Rags, Paper Stock, Etc., in CANADA

BRITISH COLUMBIA.
Franks, Z., Vancouver.
Aaronson, B., Victoria.

MANITOBA.
Black, Moses, Winnipeg.
Dominion Metal Exporting Co., Winnipeg.
Manitoba Junk Co., Winnipeg. r. p.
Owl Metal Co., Ltd., Winnipeg.
Red River Metal Co., Ltd., Winnipeg.
Shragge, The B., Iron & Metal Co., Winnipeg.
Soronow, Max, Winnipeg.
Winnipeg Bottle & Metal Exchange, Winnipeg.
Winnipeg Paper Co., Winnipeg. r. p.

NEW BRUNSWICK.
Cunningham, Nicholas, Chatham.
Rich, Chas., Chatham.
Rosenburg, S., Chatham.
Lavine, Louis, Fredericton.
Attis & Ross, Moncton.
Babb, Isaac, St. John.
Baig, Henry, St. John.
Canada Iron & Metal Co., St. John.
Dominion Metal Co., St. John.
Goldberg, I., & Co., St. John.
Lantalum, E., St. John.
McGoldrick, Jno. T., St. John.

NOVA SCOTIA.
Brister, Chas., & Son, Ltd., Halifax.
Donohue, Jas., Halifax.
Grant, Wm., Halifax.
McFatridge, Wm., Halifax.
Simon, J., Halifax.
Stairs Son, Wm., & Morrow, Ltd., Halifax.
Cann, Chas., North Sydney.
Stone, K., Westville, North Sydney.

ONTARIO.
Saxe, M., Acton.
Lipovitch, A., Barrie.
Rosenfeld & Levitt, Barrie.
Dominion Rag & Metal Co., Brantford.
Martin Bros., Brantford.
Martin, E. R., Brantford.
Montgomery, A. G., Brantford.

ONTARIO—*Continued.*
Montgomery, J. D., Brantford.
Ives, B., Belleville.
Springer, B., Belleville. r. p.
Safe, A., Belleville. r. p.
Brister, J., & Son, Brockville.
Steinberg, A., Chesley.
Caplan, L., Chatham.
Geller, S., Chatham.
Kovensky, S., Chatham.
Brown, D., Clinton.
Faith, M., Collingwood.
Viner, J., Collingwood.
Miller, J., & Son, Cornwall.
Parmos, M., Erin.
Rodenburg, N., Fort Erie.
Galt Rag & Metal Co., Galt.
Ontario Rag & Metal Co., Galt.
Brown, D., Goodrich.
Guelph Rag & Metal Co., Guelph.
Royal City Rag & Metal Co., Guelph
Cohen, M., Hamilton.
Frank, S., Hamilton.
Hamilton Rag & Metal Co., Hamilton.
Siderski, H., Hamilton.
Takefman, S., Hamilton.
Takefman & Goldblatt, Hamilton.
Grossberg, B., Kincardine.
Field, A. E., Kingston.
Kingston Rag & Metal Co., Kingston.
Kitchener Rag & Metal Co., Kitchener.
Steinberg, M., Kitchener.
Hoehn, M., London.
Hughes, I., London.
Leff, W., & Co., London.
Clouth, F., Newmarket.
Salit, M., Niagara Falls S.
Baker & Betcherman, Ottawa.
Florence, A. L., Ottawa.
L'Heureux, F. H., Ottawa.
Sachs Bros., Ottawa.
Addleman, M., Pembroke.
Florence, D., & Son, Peterboro.
Law, A., Peterboro.
Stevens, Chas., Peterboro.
Stevens, George, Peterboro.
Ottas, J. W., Picton.
Holmes, T. G., Port Hope.
Friedman, Wm., Renfrew.
Gunsberg, P., St. Catherines.

ONTARIO—*Continued.*

Canada Rag & Metal Co., St. Thomas. r. p.
St. Thomas Rag & Metal Co., St. Thomas. r. p.
Jacques & Son, Simcoe. r. p.
Cornblatt, M., Smiths Falls.
Gerofsky, J., Stratford.
Montgomery, R. B., Stratford.
Clay, M., Thorold.
Christie, John, Toronto.
Frankel Bros., Toronto.
Goldberg, Charles, Toronto.
Granatstein, M., & Sons, Toronto.
Levi's The, Toronto.
Helpert Bros., Toronto.
Howell Trading Co., Toronto.
Pullan, E., Toronto.
Brittle, John, Woodstock.
Stone, W., Woodstock.

QUEBEC.

Canada Waste Paper Co., 305 William, Montreal.
City Waste Paper Co., 1069 Craig, E., Montreal.
Diamond Metal Co., Ltd., 871 St. Paul, W., Montreal.
Kader Paper Stock Co., Inc., 332 William, Montreal.
Montreal Waste Paper Co., 79 Dorion, Montreal.
United Waste Paper & Metal Co., 113 St. Martin, Montreal.
Walker, J. R., Co., 35 Common, Montreal.
Wilson, J. C., & Co., Montreal.
Reid & Co., Ltd., Quebec.

ST. PIERRE ET MIQUELON.
Busnot, Constant.

NEWFOUNDLAND.
Joy, Samuel, St. Johns.

A SELECTED LIST OF
Paper Bag Manufacturers
IN THE
UNITED STATES AND CANADA

CALIFORNIA.
SAN FRANCISCO.
Crown Willamette Paper Co.
Taylor, The, Paper Co.
Cal. Bag & Paper Co.

CONNECTICUT.
HARTFORD.
CONTINENTAL PAPER BAG CO., 847 Main.
KENSINGTON.
American Paper Goods Co.

GEORGIA.
ATLANTA.
CONTINENTAL PAPER BAG CO.
Atlanta Paper Co.

ILLINOIS.
CHICAGO.
American Paper Goods Co., 126 N. Union. (Br. Kensington, Conn.)
Badger Bag & Paper Co., 222 W. Kinzie.
Chicago-Detroit Bag Co., 648 Marquette Bldg.
CONTINENTAL PAPER BAG CO., 346 N. Ada.
HOLLIS & DUNCAN, 724 W. Lake.
Kennedy Car Liner & Bag Co., 140 S. Dearborn.
Kirchheimer Bros., Ohio and Kingsbury.
Niagara Bag & Paper Co., 343 S. Dearborn.
STANDARD PAPER BAG CO., McCormick Bldg.
Tarentum Paper Mills, 1229 S. Wabash. (Branch Pittsburgh.) (Sacks.)
Union Bag & Paper Corp., 3737 S. Ashland.
DECATUR.
E-Z Opener Bag Co.

INDIANA.
INDIANAPOLIS.
Bemis Bros. Bag Co. (Sacks.)
CONTINENTAL PAPER BAG CO., 307 Commercial Club bldg.
GOSHEN.
Chicago-Detroit Bag Co., The.

LOUISIANA.
NEW ORLEANS.
CONTINENTAL PAPER BAG CO., 635 S. Peters.

MAINE.
RUMFORD.
CONTINENTAL PAPER BAG CO.
WOODLAND.
Grand Lake Co.

MARYLAND.
BALTIMORE.
Columbia Paper Bag Co.
CONTINENTAL PAPER BAG CO.
Stevens Bros., J. E., Inc.

MASSACHUSETTS.
BOSTON.
Advance Bag Company. (Br.)
Union Bag & Paper Corp., 185 Devonshire. (Br. of New York.)
SOMERVILLE.
Consolidated Paper Bag Co.
WALTHAM.
Waltham Paper & Bag Co.

MICHIGAN.
DETROIT.
CONTINENTAL PAPER BAG CO.
ST. JOSEPH.
Mullen Bros. Paper Co.

MINNESOTA.
MINNEAPOLIS.
Bemis Bro. Bag Co. (Sacks.)
CONTINENTAL PAPER BAG CO., 324 N. First.
Hardwood Mfg. Co. (Sacks.)

MISSOURI.
KANSAS CITY.
Bemis Bros. Bag Co. (Sacks.)
ST. LOUIS.
Bemis Bro. Bag Co. (Sacks.)
Chase, H. & L., Bag Co. (Sacks.)
CONTINENTAL PAPER BAG CO., 9th and Spruce.
Crunden Martin Mfg. Co.
Cupples Woodenware Co., Samuel.

Leading Paper Bag Manufacturers

NEBRASKA.
OMAHA.
Bemis Bro. Bag Co. (Sacks.)

NEW JERSEY.
JERSEY CITY.
Riegel Sack Co. (Flour Sacks.)
NEWARK.
National Paper Bag Co. (Flour Sacks.)
NEW BRUNSWICK.
Bergen, John S.

NEW YORK.
BUFFALO.
Buffalo Bag Co.
CANAJOHARIE.
Arkell & Smiths. (Sacks.)
DEXTER.
Howland Bag & Paper Corp
FULTON.
E-Z Opener Bag Co.
HUDSON FALLS.
Union Bag & Paper Corp.

NEW YORK CITY.
BROOKLYN BOROUGH.
Arkell Safety Bag Co., N. 11th, c. Wythe av. (Sacks.)
Fulton Bag & Cotton Mills (Sacks), Brooklyn.

MANHATTAN BOROUGH.
Bleyer, A., & Co., 229 West.
Clochessy, John, 82 Thomas.
CONTINENTAL PAPER BAG CO., 17 Battery pl. Local Sales Dept., 268 West Broadway.
Croce, D. F., 228 Washington. (Banana.)
Gilman, I., & Co., 86 Hudson.
Gilson Bros.
Grand Lake Co., 280 Madison av.
Miller & Tompkins Co., 485 Washington. (Sugar and Sacks.)
Republic Bag and Paper Co., 200 5th av.
Schorsch & Co., 508 East 133d.
Shuttleworth, Keiller & Co., 474 W. B'dway.
Terminal Paper Bag Co.
Union Bag and Paper Corp., Woolworth Bldg.

BOROUGH OF QUEENS.
LONG ISLAND CITY.
Columbia Paper Bag Co., 4th st. & Van Ness av.
BROOKLYN.
Hudson Bay Co.

NEW YORK STATE.
NORTH TONAWANDA.
Niagara Bag & Paper Co.

WATERTOWN.
Taggart Bros. Co. (Sacks.)

OHIO.
AKRON.
The Thomas Phillips Co. (Sacks.)
BOSTON.
The Jaite Co. (Sacks.)
CHAGRIN FALLS.
Adams Bag Co. (Sacks.)
CINCINNATI.
Chatfield & Woods Co., Central av. and 4th. (Sacks.)
CONTINENTAL PAPER BAG CO., 327 Lock.
Diem & Wing Paper Co.
Seinsheimer Paper Co., The.
U. S. Paper Goods Co.
CLEVELAND.
Adams Bag Co., 502 Euclid Bldg.
Cleveland-Akron Bag Co.
CONTINENTAL PAPER BAG CO., 1281 W. Ninth.
DAYTON
Henderson Paper Co.
MIDDLETOWN.
The Advance Bag Co.

OREGON.
OREGON CITY.
Crown Willamette Paper Co.

PENNSYLVANIA.
BRYN MAWR.
Thomas M. Royal & Co. (Fancy Coffee Bags.)
Harrisburg F. S. Mfg. Co., Harrisburg, Pa. (Sacks.)
NEW HOPE.
Universal Paper Bag Co.
PHILADELPHIA.
Boyer, Evans & Co. (Sacks.)
Albert Haverstick & Sons.
Sanderson, C. E.
PITTSBURGH.
Tarentum Paper Mills, Second National Bank Bldg. (Sacks.)
READING.
The Hercules Paper Bag Mills.
TARENTUM.
Rutherford Paper Co. (Sacks.)
Tarentum Paper Mills. (Sacks.)

TEXAS.
DALLAS.
Fulton Bag & Cotton Mills. (Sacks.)
HOUSTON.
CONTINENTAL PAPER BAG CO., cor. Baker and Pine.

Leading Paper Bag Manufacturers

ORANGE.
E-Z Opener Bag Co.

VIRGINIA.
RICHMOND.
Eagle Paper Co.
Wortendyke Mfg. Co.

WASHINGTON.
CAMAS.
Crown-Willamette Paper Co.

WEST VIRGINIA.
WELLSBURG.
S. George Co. (Sacks.)
George-Sherrard Paper Co. (Sacks.)

WISCONSIN.
KAUKAUNA.
Union Bag and Paper Corp.
MILWAUKEE.
Milwaukee Bag Co. (Sacks.)
WAUSAU.
Badger Bag & Paper Co.

COMPANIES MAKING IMPROVED AUTOMATIC OR SELF-OPENING PAPER BAGS IN THE UNITED STATES.

Advance Bag Co., Middletown, Ohio.
Atlanta Paper Co., Atlanta, Ga.
Badger Bag & Paper Co., Wausau, Wis.
California Bag & Paper Co., San Francisco, Cal.
Cleveland-Akron Bag Co., Cleveland, Ohio.
Clochessy, John, New York City.
Columbia Paper Bag Co., 4th and Van Ness av., Long Island City, N. Y.
Columbia Paper Bag Co., Baltimore, Md.
CONTINENTAL PAPER BAG CO., 17 Battery pl., New York.
Crown-Willamette Paper Co., Alaska Commercial bldg., San Francisco.

Crunden-MartinMfg.Co.,St.Louis,Mo.
Eagle Paper Co., Richmond, Va.
E-Z Opener Bag Co., Fulton, N. Y.
E-Z Opener Bag Co., Decatur, Ill., and Orange, Tex.
Grand Lake Co., 30 Broad, New York.
Mullen Bros. Paper Co., St. Joseph, Mich.
Schorsch & Co., 508 East 133d, New York.
Union Bag & Paper Corp., Woolworth Bldg., New York.
Universal Paper Bag Co., New Hope, Pa.
Wortendyke Mfg. Co., Richmond, Va.

Bag Manufacturers in Canada

AUTOMATIC.
CONTINENTAL BAG & PAPER CO., THE, Ottawa.
Quebec Paper Bag Co., Quebec City.
Kilgour Bros., Toronto.
Specialty Paper Bag Co., Toronto.

FLOUR SACK.
St. Lawrence Paper Bag Co., Quebec.
Eddy Co., E. B., Hull.
Kilgour Bros., Toronto.
Lincoln Paper Mills, Merritton, Ont.
Wilson Co., Ltd., J. C. Montreal.

CONTINENTAL PAPER BAG CO.
MANUFACTURERS OF
PAPER BAGS AND SACKS
WRAPPING, TOILET *and* TISSUE PAPERS, ENVELOPES, PAPER CANS, SAFETY EGG CARTONS *Etc.*

Distributing Points in Every Large City
Executive Offices: 17 Battery Place, New York City

An Innovation in Bags

Bags in Roll

Paper-Bags-on-Rolls

New bag holders in units. Units can be assembled or disassembled according to requirements

Standard Paper Bag Company
People's Gas Building, Chicago, Ill.

A SELECTED LIST OF
Paper Box Manufacturers
AND
Consumers of Boards
IN THE
UNITED STATES AND CANADA

NOTE—Names of Consumers in the Larger Cities are Omitted. Many of the Consumers named make boxes for their own use.

Indicating Marks: (*f*) folding boxes; (*s. f.*) stiff and folding boxes; (*cor.*) corrugated boxes. Where no letters are used, the concerns make stiff boxes.

ALABAMA.
Mobile Box & Paper Co. *s. f.*

ARKANSAS.
LITTLE ROCK.
Karcher, A., Candy Co. *s.*

CALIFORNIA.
LOS ANGELES.
Angelus Paper Box Co., N. Broadway. *s.*
Barker, T. J., N. Clarence. *s.*
Jones, T. T., & Co.
Los Angeles Paper Box Co. *s. f.*
Pridham, R. W., Co., Cor. *s. f.*
Renshaw, Jones & Sutton. *s. f.*

OAKLAND.
Independent Paper Box Co., 268 Market. *s. f.*
Paraffine Companies, Inc., Pridham Div., 900 high. *cor., s. f.*
Western Paper Box Company, 5th and Adeline. *s. f.*

SACRAMENTO.
Schmitt-Bachmann Co. *f.*

SAN FRANCISCO.
Briggs & Schmitt, 515 Folsom.
California Paper Box Co., 3179 17th. *f.*
Coast Folding Paper Box Co., 560 Mission.
Enterprise Paper Box Co., 73 Beal. *s.*

San Francisco—Continued.
Fleischbacker, A. & Co., 401-19 Second. *s. f.*
Independent Paper Box Co., 268 Market S.
Pacific Container Co., Rialto Bldg., Cor. and Solid Fibre Ship. Cases.
Pacific Folding Box Co., 350 Second.
Pridham, R. W., Co., 24 California.
Raisin & Zaruba, 986 Howard.
Schmidt Lithograph Co., Second & Bryant. *f.*
Stern, A. W., 515 Folsom.
Thiebaut Bros., 861 Folsom. *s.*
Union Paper Box Factory, 718 Mission st. *s.*
Wallace Egg Carrier Co., Anthony and Jessie.
Western Paper Box Co., 436 Market.
York-Bradford Co., 662 Howard.

SAN DIEGO.
San Diego Paper Box Co., San Diego, Cal. *s. f.*

COLORADO.
DENVER.
Deline Mfg. Co., 1079 Santa Fe. *s.*
Inland Paper Box Co., 1624 Blake. *s.* and *cor.*
Luby Paper Box Co., 3308 W. 38th. *s.*
Western Paper Box Co., 2133 Blake. *s. f.*

Leading Paper Box Manufacturers

CONNECTICUT.

ANSONIA.
Redshaw, Samuel G. *s.*

BETHEL.
Clark, Frank.
John Reid. *Hat.*

BERLIN.
American Paper Goods Co.

BRIDGEPORT.
Bonne Fldg. Box & Ptg. Co. *s. f.*
Compressed Paper Box Co.
Crown Paper Box Co.
Keeton, D. S.
Knapp, Geo. S.
Taylor, Thomas P.
Warner, The, Bros. Co. *s. f.*

BRISTOL.
American Folding Box Co. *s. f.*
Mills, H. J.

BURNSIDE.
Taylor-Atkins Paper Co.

CHESTER.
Doane, H. Z.
Watrous, C. H.

DANBURY.
I; Armstrong & Co. *Hat.*
The Clark Box Co. *Hat.*
Danbury Square Box Co. *Fibre.*
The Hines Box Co.

DEEP RIVER.
Kingsley, H. C.

DERBY.
Alling, A. H. & A. B.
Sterling Pin Co.

EASTHAMPTON.
L. S. Carpenter & Son.

EAST KILLINGLY.
Marcus Bros.

GLASTONBURY.
J. B. Williams Co.

HARTFORD.
Bokus, F. H.
Case, Lockwood & Brainard.
Hartford Paper Box Co.
Nichols Paper Box Co.
Plympton Mfg. Co.

MERIDEN.
E. J. Doolittle. *s.*
Miller & Co., Ed.
O. E. Schunack.

MIDDLETOWN.
Miller, W. S.

MILFORD.
Vanderhof & Co.

MONTVILLE.
Robertson, C. M., Co.

NAUGATUCK.
White & Wells Co.

NEW BRITAIN.
H. H. Corbin & Son. *s. f.*
Minor & Corbin. *s. f.*
New Britain Paper Box Co.
North & Judd Mfg. Co.
Stanley Works.

NEW HAVEN.
Candee Co., C.
Clogston, J. O., 30 E. Grand av.
Cronan, P. J., Paper Box Co.
National Folding Box and Paper Co., 325 Congress av.
New England Mfg. Co., 94 Temple.
Newman, I., & Sons.
Old Colony Mfg. Co.
Seamless Rubber Co.
Strouse, Adler & Co., 60 Court.
Winchester Repeating Arms Co.

NEW LONDON.
Bingham Paper Box Co.

NEW MILFORD.
New Milford Hat Co.

NORWALK.
Trowbridge, C. S., & Co.

NORWICH.
Atlantic Carbon Co. *f.*
Bliven, S. E., Norwich Paper Box Co. *s. f.*

PLAINVILLE.
Try-It Mfg. Co. *Lunch.*

PUTNAM.
Putnam Paper Box Corp.

SANDY HOOK.
Curtis, S., & Son.

SHELTON.
Blumenthal, Sidney & Co.
Radcliffe Bro.

LOMBARD'S ENGLISH NEWCASTLE PULP STONES ARE SUPERIOR TO ALL OTHERS. ALL SIZES IN STOCK. LOMBARD & CO., Importers & Manufacturers, 236 & 238 A Street, Boston.

SOUTH COVENTRY.
Kingsbury Box and Printing Co. *s.*

SOUTH MANCHESTER.
Cheney Bros.

SOUTH NORWALK.
Crofut & Knapp Co.
Norwalk Box Co.
Trowbridge, C. S., and Son.

STAMFORD.
American Box Co.
Harris Box Co.

UNIONVILLE.
H. W. Humphrey.

WALLINGFORD.
Backes, Inc., M., Sons.
Hodgetts, W. J., Paper Box Mfg. Co.
Judd Mfg. Co.

WATERBURY.
American Pin Co. *s.*
Scoville Mfg. Co.
Waterbury Button Co. (for own use.)
Waterbury Clock Co.
Waterbury Mfg. Co.
Waterbury Paper Box Co. *s. f.*
White & Wells Co. *s.*

WATERTOWN.
Heminway & Sons Silk Co.
Heminway & Bartlett Silk Co.

WILLIMANTIC.
S. C. L. Box Co.
Willimantic Linen Co.

WINDSOR LOCKS.
Medicott Co.

WINSTED.
Gilbert Clock Co.
New England Pin Co.
Strong Mfg. Co. *s.*

DELAWARE.
WILMINGTON.
Bancroft, Jos. S., & Sons Co.
Held & Co., Wilmington. *f. s.*
Wilmington Paper Box Co. *s.*

DISTRICT OF COLUMBIA.
WASHINGTON.
Columbia Specialty Paper Box Co., 54 Hanover, N. W. *s. f.*
Killian, Geo. P., Co., 452 Pennsylvania av., N. W. *s. f.*
Monahan & Co.

GEORGIA.
ATLANTA.
American Box File Co., Davis. *s.*
Atlanta Paper Co. *f. cor.*
Dixie Paper & Box Co. *f.*
Empire Printing & Box Co., Madison av. *s. f.*
National Paper Co. *f.*
Novelty Hat Mfg. Co. *s.*
Paragon Box Co. *s.*

CEDARTOWN.
Kuster Mfg. Co.

COLUMBUS.
Wolfson Paper Co.

NEWNAN.
Murray Mfg. Co. *f.*

ROSSVILLE.
Richmond Hosiery Mills.

ILLINOIS.
AURORA.
Pictorial Printing Co. *s. f.*

BLOOMINGTON.
Belch, Paul F., Co. *s.*

CENTRALIA.
Centralia Envelope Co.

CHICAGO.
A. & A. Paper Box Wks., 104 E. 13th.
Aaren Paper Box Co., 815 W. Congress.
Adelstein, J., 1111 Blue Is. Av.
Albany Paper Products Co., 647 N. Green.
Alderman, Fairchild & Co., 326 W. Madison.
American Carton Co., 552 W. Adams.
American Corrugated Fibre Box Co., 8 S. Dearborn.
American Paper Products Co., 130 N. Wells.
Armstrong, Harry, 1253 S. Michigan.
Arnold, A. A., Paper Box Co., 1302 W. Division.
Automatic Paper Box Works, 1011 S. California.
Bachmann Mfg. Co., 1011 S. California.

Leading Paper Box Manufacturers

Chicago—Continued.

Bauer & Broccolo, 913 W. Van Buren.
Brown, M. A., Paper Box Co., 830 W. Congress.
Burt, F. N., Co., Inc., 23 N. Franklin.
Chicago Carton Co., 4433 Ogden av.
Chicago Folding Box Co., 2555 Taylor. *s. f.* and *cor.*
Chicago Label and Box Co., 812 N. May.
Chicago Mailing Tube Co., 425 S. Hoyne av.
Chicago Mill & Lumber Co., 111 W. Washington. *cor.*
Chicago Oyster Pail Co., 504 S. Green.
Chicago Paper Tube and Can Co., 168 N. May.
Clark & Pfister, 14 N. May.
Climax Container Co., 53 W. Jackson blvd. and 318 W. 43d.
Couper, W. D., 8 S. Dearborn.
Crescent Paper Box Co., 442 W. Ontario.
Dunbar, H. C., 53 W. Jackson blvd.
Duro Paper Products Co., 729 S. Wabash.
Economy Metal Edge Box Co., 500 S. Peoria. *f.*
Ellegant, Jake, 2231 W. 12th.
Empire Board & Box Works, 171 W. Lake.
Evers Paper Box Co., 1302 W. Division.
Federal Folding Box Co., Congress and Loomis. *f.*
Ferguson-Lander Mfg. Co., 410-426 S. Clinton. (Formerly Lanzit Paper Pail Co.)
Ft. Wayne Corrugated Paper Co., 327 S. LaSalle.
Gair, Robert, Co., 336 W. Madison.
Globe Paper Box Co., 105-109 S. Jefferson.
Hauf & Co., R. C., 214 N. Clinton.
Henry, Ira L., Co., 6127 Indiana av.
Hertle-Roberts Box & Label Co., 552 W. Harrison.
Hinde & Dauch Paper Co., The, 826 River. *s.* and *cor.*
Hollis & Duncan, 782 W. Lake.
Hummel & Downing Co., Conway bldg.
Hunt-Crawford Co., The, 8 S. Dearborn. *s.* and *cor.*
Illinois Flower Box Co., 180 N. Dearborn.
Illinois Glass Co., 402 W. Randolph. *s.* and *cor.*

Chicago—Continued.

Illinois Paper Box Co., 1323 Carroll av.
Imperial Box Co., 1403 W. Congress.
Improved Mailing Case Co., 323 W. Randolph.
Keys, Benjamin, & Co., 554 W. Adams.
Kluefer, Julius, Paper Box Co., 220 Institute pl.
Kroeck, George J., & Co., 220 Institute pl.
Kroeck-Kluefer Paper Box Co., 216-220 Institute pl.
Lachmann, A. H., 817 Rees.
Lanzit Corrugated Box Co., 506 S. Jefferson.
Lawrence, C. J., & Bro., Inc., 2301 Archer av.
Leon, M., 411 S. Jefferson.
Lewis, A. L., 1419 Plum.
Madison Paper Box Co., 1214 W. Madison.
Marquardt, Julius, Co., 345 W. Austin.
Maynard, Y. C., 552 W. Adams.
McCracken, H. S., Box & Label Co., 923 W. 19th.
Menasha Printing & Carton Co., 111 W. Washington.
Mid-West Box Co., 111 W. Washington.
Miller's, John C., Sons, 209 W. Washington.
Milwaukee Paper Box Co., 6 E. Kinzie.
Morris Paper Mills, 111 W. Washington.
Munson Forbes, 333 S. Dearborn.
National Paper Box Co., 1253 S. Michigan.
Newton, Louis, 527 S. Jefferson.
Paragon Paper Box Factory, 2325 W. 12th.
Pharmacy Paper Box Co., 2334 Polk.
Pictorial Printing Co., 647 N. Green.
Pinkerton Folding Box Co., 900 W. Lake.
Randall, L. E., 23 N. Franklin.
Randolph Box & Label Co., 843 W. Van Buren.
Reliable Box Co., 820 N. Western av.
Rents Paper Box Co., Fred., 172 N. Green.
Ritchie & Co., W. C., W. Van Buren & Green and 18 Sloan, 89th & Erie av.
River Raisin Paper Co., 25 E. Washington.

Leading Paper Box Manufacturers

Chicago—Continued.
Runtz, Henry, Paper Box & Novelty Co., 56-62 W. Kinzie. *f.*
Schleicher, F. J., Paper Box Co., 808 W. Congress.
Schlutz, Chas., Co., 2373 Milwaukee.
Schultz, H., & Co., 517-31 W. Superior.
Schulz, A. Geo., Co., 352 W. Ohio.
Schurmann, W. A., & Co., 365 E. Illinois.
Schuster-Bohnsach Co., 1330 N. Halsted.
Sefton Mfg. Co., J. W., 1301-41 W. 35th. *f. s.* and *cor.*
Self-Locking Carton Co., 465 E. Illinois.
Shlutz, Harry, 1112 S. Jefferson.
Shoup, A. D., Co., Inc., 1545 W. 35th.
Simon, John P., 128 W. Kinzie.
Singer Paper Box Co., 815 W. Congress.
Single Service Package Corp., 551 Fulton.
Smith, L. W., Paper Box Co., 820 N. May.
Sode, E. B., Paper Box Co., 1113-17 Fry.
Standard Paper Box Co., 214 N. Clinton.
Stange-Bueschel Co., 125 N. Green.
Star Paper Box Co., 312 Union Pk. Ct.
Stayart, Albert C., 2011 Larrabee.
Universal Paper Products Co., Dearborn and N. Water.
Vavra & Co., E. H., 2541 S. 50th Av.
Wayne Paper Goods Co., 305 S. Wells.
Weinstein, S., & Co., 430 N. Oakley blvd.
Wells, C. A., 6525 S. Lincoln.
Western Paper Box Co., 172 N. Green. *f.*
Wheatley, Thos. N., 1214 W. Madison.
Wolff, O. F., & Sons, 155 W. Ohio.
Zorn, H. A., Co., 606-624 N. Oakley av.
Zwick, Joseph, 1253 S. Michigan.

DECATUR.
Keck, John A., Church and Wood.

FREEPORT.
Whiteside & Co. *s. f.*

JOLIET.
National Carton Co. *For Food Products.*

PEORIA.
Peoria Paper Box Co. *s. f.*
Streibich, John C., Company.

PONTIAC.
Pontiac Shoe Mfg. Co.

QUINCY.
Quincy Box & Printing Co. *s* and *candy.*
Sheer Co., H. M.
Stahl, Geo. H.

ROCKFORD.
Bennett, Paul P., Paper Box Co., 1008 Mulbery. *s.*
Zlock Paper Box Co. *s.*

INDIANA.

BROOKVILLE.
Thompson & Norris, The, Co., of Indiana. *cor.*

CRAWFORDSVILLE.
Indiana Match Corporation.

DECATUR.
Indiana Board & Filler Co.

ELKHART.
Barger Bros. *s.*
Dr. Miles Medical Co.

EVANSVILLE.
Herbert-Jour. Ptg. Co.
Horn, A. F., & Co.
Keller-Crescent Ptg. & Eng. Co.

FORT WAYNE.
Fisher Bros. Paper Co.
Fort Wayne Box Co., Calhoun and Superior. *s. f.*
Fort Wayne Corrugated Paper Co. *cor.*

GAS CITY.
Lindley Box & Paper Co. *s. f.*

INDIANAPOLIS.
Bee Hive Paper Box Co., 625 S. Delaware. *s. f.*
Harry B. Mahan Co.
International Printing Co. *f.*
U. S. Corrugated Fibre Box Co. Plant No. 1.

LAFAYETTE.
Jenks, Geo. E., 300 Vine.
Murphy-Bivins Co.

Leading Paper Box Manufacturers

MARION.
Indiana Fibre Products Co. *cor.*
Lindley Box & Paper Co. *s. f.*
Macbeth-Evans Glass Co.
Marion Paper Box Co. *s. f.*

MICHIGAN CITY.
Michigan City Paper Box Co. *s. f.*

MUNCIE.
Ball Bros. Glass Mfg. Co. *cor.*

RICHMOND.
Nicholson Printing and Mfg. Co. *s.*

SOUTH BEND.
Campbell Paper Box Co., Main. *s. f.*

TERRE HAUTE.
McWhinney, A. B. & Co.
Turner Bros. Co. *cor.*

IOWA.

BURLINGTON.
Tabor-Burns Co., Smith and Plane. *Fancy.*

CEDAR RAPIDS.
Cherry Co., J. G.
Enterprise Box Co.
Independent Bkg. Co.
Knostman & Peterson Furn. Co.

DAVENPORT.
Kerker, Geo. W., Paper Box Co., 315 E. 5th.

DES MOINES.
Chamberlain Med. Co. *For own use.*
Des Moines Paper Box Co., 430-434 E. Grand av. *s. f.*

DUBUQUE.
Dickinson, E. H.
Dubuque Paper Co.
Key City Paper Box Co., Garfield av.
Spahn, E. P., & Co.

KEOKUK.
Hough, C. R.
Hubinger, J. O., Co.

OTTUMWA.
Niemeyer Bros. *f.*

SIOUX CITY.
Sioux City Box Co. *s.*

KANSAS.

LAWRENCE.
Lawrence Paper Mfg. Co. *cor.*

WICHITA.
Ownes, E. Newell. *s.*

KENTUCKY.

FRANKFORT.
Hoge-Montgomery Co.

LOUISVILLE.
Bradley & Gilbert Co.
Brinkhaus & Block.
Kentucky Paper Box Co., Kentuck and Swan. *s. f.*
Mengel Box Co. *cor. f.*
Menne Paper Box Co., 514 E. Madison.
Meune, F. A., Box Co.
Myer Bridges Co.
Pilcher, J. V., Mfg. Co.

LOUISIANA.

NEW ORLEANS.
Crescent Paper Box Factory, Inc.
Huye Wid., George, Est. of, Steam Box Factory.
New Orleans Corrugated Fibre Box Factory.
Woody, N. A., Paper Box Co.

SHREVEPORT.
Excelsior Steam Laundry Co., Ltd.

MAINE.

AUBURN.
Auburn Paper Box Co.
H. Wesley Hutchins Co.
Manufacturers' Box Co.
Standard Box Co.

AUGUSTA.
Smith & Reid.

BATH.
Baxter Paper Box Co. *s.*

BELFAST.
Leonard & Barrows.

BREWER.
Bangor Box Co.

BRUNSWICK.
Baxter Paper Box Co. *s.*

FREEPORT.
Stanchwood & Wood. *s.*

GARDINER.
Alger Paper Box Co.

 **Paint and Chemical Company**
PAPER COLORS AND MILL PAINT SPECIALTIES
BOSTON   SPRINGFIELD, MASS.   NEW YORK

Leading Paper Box Manufacturers

LEWISTON.
Bates Street Shirt Co. *s.*
Maine Box & Paper Co.

PORTLAND.
Ayer, Houston & Co.
Bicknell, J. Carleton.
Burrowes, H. J., Co.
Casco Paper Box Co., 68 Cross.
Portland Paper Box Co., 40 Union.
Standard Box Co.
Wyman Paper Box Co., 131 Preble.

MARYLAND.
BALTIMORE.
H. M. Adler & Co., 305 S. Sharp. *s.*
Baltimore Paper Box Co.
Bartgis Bros. Co. *f.*
Bradley Reese Co.
Bromrell Brush & Wire Co.
Erlanger Underwear Co.
Geo. Franke, 112 S. Eutaw. *s. f.*
Gordon Paper Box Co.
L. Gordon & Son, 230 N. Front. *s.*
Hagerstown Book Bdg. Co.
Hagerstown Cap Co.
Hartel, J. M. *s.*
Levy & Son.
Levy & Sons, M. S.
Matthews Bros., Hopkins Pl. *s. f.*
Monumental Paper Box Co.
North Bros. & Straus.
Raffel, J. M., & Co., Heath & Clarkson.
Rogers Printing Co., 102 W. Pratt. *f.*
Smith, J. E., & Co. *s. f.*
Southern Label & Box Corp.
Taylor, C. J., & Co.
C. J. Youse & Co., 23 S. Gay. *s.*

HAGERSTOWN.
Cumberland Valley Box Co. *s.*
Hagerstown Bookbinding & Printing Co. *s.*

MASSACHUSETTS.
AMESBURY.
Merrimack Hat Co.
Parry, A. N., & Co.
Wing, Chas., & Co.

AMHERST.
Hills, The, Co.
Burnett, Geo. B., & Son.

ANDOVER.
Tyre Rubber Co.

ATHOL.
Cass, N. D., & Co. *s.*
Powers, O. J., & Son.

ATTLEBORO
Babcock, A. H., & Co.
Mason Box Co.
Rueckert Mfg. Co.
Sweet & Son, A. H. *s. f.*

BEVERLY.
Allen, George H.
Beverley Box Co.
Copp, A. W., Co.

BOSTON.
Abrahams, Albert, Dorchester.
Acme Paper & Paper Box Co., 92 Blackstone. *s. f.*
Alger Paper Box Co., 683 Atlantic av. *s. f.*
American Paper Box Co., 10 Mechanic. *s. f.*
Atlas Box Co., 46 Cornhill.
Baird Box Co., 28 Beach.
Barnes, Walter S., & Son, 33 Farnsworth.
Bergquist & Wheeler, 80 Broad. *s.*
Bicknell & Fuller Paper Box Co., 50 Chardon. *s. f.*
Bond & Bond Co., 45 Vale.
Cook, Herbert, Co., 463 Commercial.
Corrugated Paper Mills, 37 Wormwood.
Davis, W. B., 62 Sudbury.
Dickerman Maurland Box Co., 535 Albany.
Forbes Lithograph Manufacturing Co., 185 Summer. *s.*
Hill, Myrton & Co., 297 Congress.
Hinde & Dauch Paper Co., br. 185 Devonshire. *s. f.*
Horle, F. A., 95 Albany.
Hunt, F. E., 20 Chardon.
Improved Mailing Case Co., 137 Pearl.
Merchants' Box & Paper Co., 77 Bedford.
Morse-Brackett, 144 High. *s. f.*
Natick Box Co., 48 Summer.
National Folding Box and Paper Co., 76 Chauncey. *s. f.*
Paris Paper Box Mfg. Co., 53 Troy.
Plant, T. G., & Co., Roxbury. *s.*
Rochester Paper Box Co., 114 State. (Druggists.)
Royal Box Co., Cambridge.
Standard Package Co., 50 State.
STONE & FORSYTH CO., 67 Kingston. *s. f.*
Thompson & Norris Co., Allston.
F. B. Tilton & Co., 51 Beverly.
Wilkins Paper Box Co., 65 Beverly.

BRIDGEWATER.
White Shoe Co. *s.*

 **Roll Bar White** A lasting tough coating for iron work in beaters and washers

Leading Paper Box Manufacturers

BROCKTON.
Alger Paper Box Co.
Brigham, D. F.
Brockton Paper Box Co.
Low, E. M.
Montello Paper Box Co.
Nelson Paper Box Co.
Packard Carton Co.
Snow, Geo. H., Co.
Washburn Co., F. B.

CAMBRIDGE.
Babcock, C. W.
Boston Woven Hose Co.
Cambridge Paper Box Co.
Climax Paper Box Co.
Page, Geo. G., Box Co.
Page & Shaw.
Thompson Box Co.
University Paper Box Co.

CHELSEA.
Atlas Paper Box Co.
Bay State Candy Box Co.
Imperial Paper Box Co. *s.*
Russell Box Co.
Standard Box Co.
Walton, A. G., Co.

CHICOPEE FALLS.
Page Paper Box Co.

EVERETT.
Everett Paper Box Co. *s.*
Northern Box Co. *s.*
Stone & Forsyth Co. *s. f.*

FITCHBURG.
Eric H. Whittemore.

FRAMINGHAM.
Dennison Mfg. Co. *s. f.*
Williams & Bridges. *s.*

GREENFIELD.
Greenfield Paper Box Co.

HAVERHILL.
Ayer & Webster.
Chesley & Rugg Box Co. *s.*
Dalton, A., & Co.
H. D. Foss & Co.
Hayes, C. H., Corporation.
Hoyt, George H., & Son.
Owens, John, & Co.
Tapley, I. W.

HOLYOKE.
Skinners' Satin Co.
Taite & Marsh. *s.*
White Paper Box Co. *s. f.*
White Wyckoff Mfg. Co. *s.*

HUDSON.
Novelty Paper Box Co. *s.*
Sawyer, C. J. *s.*

LAWRENCE.
Brush Hat Mfg. Co., The.
Essex County Training School.
Poore, E. E.

LEOMINSTER.
Cluett-Peabody Co.
E. F. Dodge & Co.
Leominster Paper Box Co.
Whitney & Co. *s.*

LOWELL.
Ayer Co., J. C.
French, A. F., & Co.
Hatch, C. F., Co.
Shaw Stocking Co.

LYNN.
Allen, Geo. H.
Eaton & Hobbs.
Grover, B. E.
Littlefield & Moulton.
Lynn Box Co.
Potter, Albert G.
Sprague, Chas. E., Box Co.
Valpey Press.

MARBLEHEAD.
Metcalf, G. C., Wood and Paper Box Mfg. Co.

MARLBORO.
Rice & Hutchins.
Stevens, O. H., Mfg. Co.

MEDFORD.
Warner & Childs Co. *s. f.*

MEDWAY.
Medway Box Co.

MIDDLEBORO.
Alger Paper Box Co.

MILFORD.
Eastman, S. A., Co. *s. f.*

NATICK.
Natick Box Co.

NEEDHAM HEIGHTS.
Dailey, Edward E.

NEW BEDFORD.
Coffin Bros.
Pairpont Corporation.

 **Paint and Chemical Company**
PAPER COLORS AND MILL PAINT SPECIALTIES
BOSTON   SPRINGFIELD, MASS.   NEW YORK

Leading Paper Box Manufacturers

NEWBURYPORT.
Gurney, O. J.
Hale, E. A.
Tapley, I. W.

NORTH ADAMS.
Clark, H. W., Biscuit Co.
McMillin, E. A., & Co. *s.*

NORTH GRAFTON.
Story, Edwin B.

NORTHAMPTON.
Kingsbury Box and Printing Co.
Northampton Paper Box Co.

NORTON.
A. H. Sweet & Son.

PITTSFIELD.
Eaton Crane & Pike Co.
W. E. Tillotson Mfg. Co.

RANDOLPH.
Cliaff, M., & Sons, Inc. *s.*

ROCKLAND.
Packard Carton Co.

ROXBURY.
Alden, J. W.
Bond & Bond.
Farrington Mfg. Co.
Hovey-Woodbury Co.
Marston, I. G., & Co.

SALEM.
Central Paper Co. *f.*
Friend Box Co.
Irving Box Co.

SHELBURNE FALLS.
Shelburne Falls Paper Box Co. *s.*

SOMERVILLE.
Atlas Box Co.
Babcock, C. W., & Son, Inc.
Gilmore & Co., K. M.

SOUTHBRIDGE.
American Optical Co.

SOUTH WEYMOUTH.
Sherman Sons Co. *s.*

SPENCER.
Phenix Paper Box Co. *s.*
Spencer Paper Box Co. *s.*

SPRINGFIELD.
Bay State Corset Co.
Birnie Paper Co.
Brooks Bank Note Co.
Brown, L. W.
Kibbe Bros.
Murphy, J. A., Co.
Natl. Papeterie Co.
Powers Paper Co.
United Art Box Co.
U. S. Envelope Co.

STONEHAM.
W. P. Fletcher Box Co.

TAUNTON.
Taunton Paper Box Co. *s. f.*

WAKEFIELD.
Wakefield Paper Box Co.

WESTFIELD.
Bryant Box Co.

WEYMOUTH.
Pray & Kelly. *s.*

WHITMAN.
Kingsbury Box & Printing Co. *s.*

WORCESTER.
American Steel & Wire Co.
Hill, W. H., Envelope Co., Div. U. S. Envelope Co.
Logan, Swift & Brigham Envelope Co., Div. U. S. Envelope Co.
N. E. Envelope Co.
Royal Worcester Corset Co. *s.*
SHERMAN ENVELOPE CO.
Whitcomb Envelope Co., Div. U. S. Envelope Co.
Whitney Mfg. Co.
Geo. C. Whitney Co.
Williams & Bridges.
Worcester Envelope Co.
Worcester Paper Box Co.

MICHIGAN.

BATTLE CREEK.
Battle Creek Paper Co., Ltd. *s.*
Michigan Carton Co.

BELDING.
Grand Rapids Paper Box Co. *s.*

DETROIT.
Bagley, J. J., & Co.
Beecher, Peck & Lewis.
Chope-Stevens Paper Co.
Detroit Paper Tube & Can. Co.
Eagle Paper Box Co.

Rubercoat Elastic Carbon Paint
For your leaky gravel, paper, cloth and metal roofs.

Leading Paper Box Manufacturers

Detroit—Continued.
Gregory, Mayer & Thom Co.
Holliday Box Co.
Kurtz Paper Box Co.
Parke Davis & Co.
Richmond & Backus Co.
Stand Pat Easel Co.
Stearns, Fred, Co.
Stecker, H. J., Paper Box Co.
Union Paper & Twine Co.
Welt & Sons Paper Co.
Western Paper Box Co.

GRAND RAPIDS.
American Corrugating Co. cor.
American Paper Box Co. f.
Grand Rapids Paper Box Co. s. f.
Ideal Paper Box Co. s.

JACKSON.
Crown Paper & Bag Co.
Hahn, G. A., Paper Box Co. s.
Jackson Corset Co.

KALAMAZOO.
Doubleday Bros. & Co.
Ihling Bros. Everard Co.
Illinois Envelope Co.
Kalamazoo Paper Box Co., 233 Kalamazoo av. s.
Sutherland Paper Co.

MONROE.
Boehme & Rauch Co.
Monroe Corrugated Box Co.
River Raisin Paper Co.
Weis Mfg. Co.

SAGINAW.
American Paper Box Co. s. f.
Sommers Bro. Match Co.

ST. JOSEPH.
Williams Bros.

YPSILANTI.
Oak Knitting Co.
Scharf Tag & Label Co.

MINNESOTA.

DULUTH.
Duluth Paper Box Co.
Union Match Co.

MANKATO.
Anderson, Geo. s.

MINNEAPOLIS.
Cream of Wheat Co. For own use.
Fisher Paper Box Co. s. f.
Flour City Paper Box Co. s. f.
Heywood Mfg. Co.
Nelson Paper Box Co. s. f.
Standard Paper Box Co. f.

ST. PAUL.
Collins Co., H. L. f.
Kaplan, Shadur Co., 130 S. Wabash.
Mullory Paper Box Co. s. f.
Weinhagen, Chas., & Co., 476-484 Jackson. s. f.

STILLWATER.
Smithson Paper Box Factory. s. f.

MISSOURI.

HANNIBAL.
Helm Paper & Cigar Box Co. s.
International Shoe Co.

KANSAS CITY.
American Chicle Co.
Burd & Fletcher Prtg. Co. f.
Lechtman Printing Co. f.
National Paper Box Co. s. f.
Pearsons Paper Box Co. s.
Western Paper Box Co. s.

ST. JOSEPH.
Combe Printing Co. s.
St. Joseph Paper Box Co. s. f.
Wyatt & Green. s.

ST. LOUIS.
Advance Paper Box Co., 110 Pine.
All Paper Box Co.
American Paper Products Co. (Corrugated and Solid Fibre Board Shipping Cases.)
Brown-Engel & Olian, 1108 N. 3d.
Brown, M. A., Paper Box Co., 817 N. 17th.
Brown Shoe Co.
Bulls, J. C., Mfg. Co.
T. T. Chapman Paper Co., 328 N. 3d.
Crunden Martin Mfg. Co.
Ely & Walker Dry Goods Co.
Great Western Paper Box Co.
Holman Paper Box Co., 8th and Chouteau.
International Shoe Co., The.
Moser Cigar and Paper Box Co., 206 Elm.
Owens Paper Box Co., 520 N. Main.
St. Louis Paper, Can & Tube Co.
Schleicher Paper Box Co., 1311 Chouteau av.
Superior Folding Box Co., 214 S. 17th.

WASHINGTON.
Peerless Box & Lumber Co.

 **Paint and Chemical Company**
PAPER COLORS AND MILL PAINT SPECIALTIES
BOSTON   SPRINGFIELD, MASS.   NEW YORK

Leading Paper Box Manufacturers

NEBRASKA

OMAHA.
Carpenter Paper Co.
Eggerss & O'Flyng Co. *s. f.*
Lee & Co., Geo. H.
Marshall Paper Co.
Omaha Paper Box Co. *s.*
Omaha Fibre & Corrugated Box Co. *cor.*
Smith, M. E., & Co.

NEW HAMPSHIRE.

ANTRIM.
S. E. Robinson.

ASHLAND.
Ashland Knitting Mills.
Continental Paper Bag Co.

FARMINGTON.
Cloutman & Co., J. F.
Thayer-Osborne Shoe Co.

FRANKLIN.
Franklin Falls Paper Box Co. *s.*

LACONIA.
Tetley, E., & Co.

LEBANON.
Lebanon Paper Box Co.

MANCHESTER.
Brown Box Mfg. Co.
Dalton, A., Box Co.
McElwain Co., W. H. *s.*
Tilton Box Co.

NASHUA.
Nashua Paper Box Co. *s. f.*
Phillips, N. H.

ROCHESTER.
Trask, C. F., & Co.
Thayer, N. B., Shoe Co., E. Rochester.

NEW JERSEY.

BLOOMFIELD.
Nevins-Church Press. *f.*

BURLINGTON.
Turner & Co. *s.*

BUTLER.
J. A. Farrell. *s.*

CAMDEN.
American Macaroni Co. *f.*
Box Mfg. Corp.
Esterbrook Steel Pen Mfg. Co. *s.*
McCausland, Wm. J. *r.*
Pyne Poynt Ptg. & Paper Box Co.

HOBOKEN.
American Lead Pencil Co. *s.*
Grove Straw Hat Co. *r.*
Kemmet, G. & F. *s.*
Owens & Traeger. *s.*

JERSEY CITY.
Doscher, John, 114 Lincoln. *s.*
Kiernan-Hughes Co., 348 Ninth. *s. f.*
Leo, Jas., Co., 251 Varick. *s. f.*
  (Suit boxes a specialty).
Waldesk, E., & Co., 31 Oakland av. *s.*

NEWARK.
American Color Type Co.
A. F. Dieterle, 1 Ann.
Dougher & Mooney, 60 Union.
Gauch, Wm., & Son, 61 N. J. R. R. av.
Grane, Chas., Co.
Grover Bro.
Hartung, Lewis, 35 North Fifth.
Jones, S., & Co.
Maulhetsch & Whittemore.
Mennen Chemical Co.
Mooney & Mooney.
Mork, M. S., & Co., Ogden av.
Newark Embroidery Co.
New Jersey Paper Box Co., 80 Orange av.
Osborne Co.
Plum, Mathias.
Progressive Paper Box Co., 27 17th av.
Rauchbach & Goldsmith Co.
Savacool, G. H.
Schiffenhaus Bros., 4th and Dickerson.
Seeley Tube & Box Co.
Specialty Paper Box Co., Chestnut.
United Corrugating Paper Co.
W. B. Paper Box Co.

NEW BRUNSWICK.
Kalteissen, Peter. *s.*

ORANGE.
Riley, A. M., & Co., 34 William.

PASSAIC.
Garfield Paper Box Co., 351 Main.
Howe Paper Box Co., Park pl.
McLaughlin-Miller Co., Passaic.
Passaic Paper Box Co.
Passaic Print Wks.

 **Black Paste** Will not crock in the paper. Strongest, cleanest and most economical.

Leading Paper Box Manufacturers

PATERSON.
Blackburn, Robert.
Harding Box Co.
Harding Bro.
Martin, J. G.
Nicholson File Co.
Paterson Ribbon Block & Tube Co.
Union Box Co. *s. f.*
Van Ness Bros.

RIVERSIDE.
Holt, Wm., & Son. *s.*
Taubel, William F., Inc.

TRENTON.
Bayley, Ralph S.
Trent Folding Box Co. *f.*
Trenton Paper Box Co.
W. F. Yard Box Co. *s.*

VINELAND.
Kenyon, The, Co. *s.*

NEW YORK.
ALBANY.
Albany Card & Paper Co.
Bacon, Stickney & Co.
Cadby & Son, 50-4 Grand.
Eastern Tablet Co.
Embossing Co., The.
Simpson & Morehead.

AMSTERDAM.
Amsterdam Paper Box Co.
Blood Knitting Co. *s.*
Inman Mfg. Co. *s.*
Inman Paper Box Co.
Sanford, S., & Son.

AUBURN.
F. A. Benson.
Cossum-Johnston Paper Co.
Schicht, Robert, Box Mfg. Co.

BATAVIA.
W. T. Palmer (Est. of).

BINGHAMTON.
Ansco Co. *s.*
Binghamton Folding Box Co. *f.*
Dunn & McCarthy. *s.*
Noyes Comb Co. *s.*
Parlor City Paper Box Co. *s.*
Weed, Co., L. M. *s.*

BUFFALO.
Bison City Paper Box Works, 567 Washington.
Buffalo Box Fac. *cor.*
Buffalo Corrugated Container Co., 25 Imson.

Buffalo—Continued.
Buffalo Jewelry Case Co., 329-335 Broadway. *s.*
Buffalo Trunk Mfg. Co. *s.*
Burt, F. N., Co., cor Seneca and Hamburgh. *s. f.*
Cooper Paper Box Co., Sycamore and Mortimer. *s. f.*
Corona Paper Box Co. *s.*
Drescher, Charles A. *s.*
Electric City Box Co., 144 B'way. *s.*
Glasston & Allen, 45 N. Division. *s.*
Hecker, Jones, Jewell Milling Co. *s.*
Juengling, Henry E., 506 Genesee. *s.*
Larkin Soap Co. *s. f.*
Monarch Nusbaum Paper Box Co., Inc., 106 B'dway.
National Jewelry Case Co., 7 Ellicott.
Smith, J. F., Paper Box Co. *s. f.*
Springfels Mfg. Co., 68 E. Utica.

CASTLE-ON-HUDSON.
Parchment Paper Goods Co., Office, Steneck bldg., Hoboken, N. J. *f.*

CASTLETON.
Fort Orange Paper Co. *f.*

COHOES.
Enterprise Paper Box Fact'y, Inc. *s.*
Leggett, John, & Son.
Snyder, Wm. W., Mfg. Co.

DOLGEVILLE.
Thomas Box Co. *s.*

DUNKIRK.
The Marsh-Burgess Co. *s.*

ELMIRA.
Bartlett, Geo. H.
Howell, F. M., & Co. *s. f.*
Thatcher Mfg. Co.

FORT PLAIN.
Yordon, J. M.

GLENS FALLS.
Leggett, John, & Son. *s. f.*
Warren Box Co. *s. f.*

GLOVERSVILLE.
Allen, C. F.
H. D. Edwards. *s.*
J. K. Sammons. *s.*
Wurtzberger & Co. *f.*

HERKIMER.
Acme Paper Box Co.

 **Paint and Chemical Company**
PAPER COLORS AND MILL PAINT SPECIALTIES
BOSTON   SPRINGFIELD, MASS.   NEW YORK

Leading Paper Box Manufacturers   423

HOOSICK FALLS.
Shaw Bro. *s.*

JAMESTOWN.
Eastman Kodak Co.

JOHNSTOWN.
Johnson, George.
Robinson, F. M., & Co.
Trumbull, S. E.

KINGSTON.
Powell Paper Box Co. *s. f.*

LITTLE FALLS.
Little Falls Mfg. Co. *s. f.*

McGRAW.
Central Paper Box Co. *s.*

MATTEAWAN.
A. E. Mills.

MIDDLETOWN.
McIntyre, A. E., & Co.
Union Hat Co.

MOHAWK.
J. M. Bellinger.

NEWARK.
BLOOMER BROS. CO.

NEWBURGH.
Ferry Hat Co. (Round and Oval.)
Newburgh Paper Box Co. *s.*

NEW HARTFORD.
New Hartford Paper Co.

NEW YORK CITY.
Brooklyn Borough.
Albert Paper Box Co., Harrison pl. *s. f.*
Banner Paper Box Co., Inc., 219 36th.
Blum, A., Folding Paper Box Co., 64 Washington av.
Cohen, M., & Bro., 59 Liberty av.
Ebisch, Wm. A., 876 Jerome.
Franklin Paper Box Co., Inc., 782 Wythe av.
Fuehrer & Peter, Inc., 56 Scholes.
Gair, Robert, Co., Washington and Water. *s. f.*
Greenpoint Paper Box Co., 156 Withers.
Haedrich, Wm., & Sons, 311 Jay.
Housman, Moses, 101 18th.
Huschle's Sons, Wm., 429 S. 5th.
International Folding Box Co., Inc., 396 S. 2d.

Brooklyn Borough—Cont'd.
Johnston, Selden, 264 Greene av.
Jonas, Alfred, 1570 Fulton.
Just Mfg. Co., 137 Duffield.
Keator, E. W., 589 Park av.
Kings County Paper Box Co., Inc., 23 Gratton.
Knox Hat Co., 601 Grand av.
Koch, John W., 856 Driggs av.
Lawrence Paper Box Co., 1188 Fulton.
McLoughlin Bros., 46 S. 11th.
Minkboff & Co., 822 Lexington av.
Modern Cigarette Box Co., Inc., 377 Blake av.
Modern Paper Box Co., 87 3d av.
Muller Paper Goods Co., Inc., 2350 Linden av.
National Eagle Paper Box Co., 965 Flushing av.
Poppe, The, Co., 83 Prospect.
Progress Paper Box Co., 756 Glenmore av.
Royal Paper Box Co., 505 Sackman.
Schurman, Frederick A., 868 Willoughby av.
Standard Knitting Mills Co., Inc., Ralph and Grandview avs.
Thompson & Norris Co., Concord & Prince.
Trum, Edward J., 55 Third.
United Paper Box Co. of America, 33 34th.
White's, R. Tyson Sons, 320 Bridge.
Williamsburg Paper Box Co., 178 Hope.
Woerner, R., Co., 150 Skillman
Wohlgemuth Paper Box Co., Inc., 196 Hopkins.

Manhattan Borough
Acme Folding Box Co., 137 Wooster.
Adams, Henry P., Co., 200 Greene.
Advance Paper Box Co., Inc., 87 Bowery.
Albert, D., & Son, 567 W. Broadway. *s.*
Alderman, Fairchild Co., 220 B'way.
American Corrugated Paper Co., Inc., 516 W. 26th.
American Folding Box Co., Inc., 21 W. Fourth.
American Leader Paper Co., 131 Prince.
American Paper Box Co., 152 Wooster.
Andy Paper Box Co., 21 Wooster.
Arrow Paper Box Co., 58-62 W. 20th.
Atlantic Paper Box Co., 148 Wooster.

Ruling Colors — The best for Ruling Inks.

Leading Paper Box Manufacturers

Manhattan Borough—Cont'd.

Atlantic Paper Box Wrap. Co., 438 W. 37th.
A. & T. Box Co., 529 B'way.
Aubert, Henry, 405 W. 13th.
B. & M. Paper Box Co., 372 Broome.
Bacher & Kaplan, 79 Greene.
Baldwin, Eli & Son, Inc., 84 Wooster.
Bartlet, Orrin D., 263 9th av.
Baxter Paper Bag Co., 1 Mad. av.
Berlin & Jones Envelope Co., Inc., 136 William and 553 W. 27th.
Boehme & Rauch Co., 39 Cortlandt.
Bonime, R. Arkin, 71 Grand.
Borgadus, V. C., 140 Nassau.
Box & Bag Mart. of N. Y., 25 E. 54th.
Brick & Ballerstein, 126 6th av. s. cor.
Bricker & Dolinsky, 25 Mercer.
Broadway Paper Box Co., 27 E. 4th.
Bronx Paper Box Co., 972 Washington av.
Brooks & Porter, 406-426 W. 31st. *f.*
Brown & Bailey Co., 31 Union sq.
Buedingen, Wm., & Son, 233 B'way.
Butz, Fred L., 253 B'way.
Carlin, Wayland, 126 W. 23d.
Casselman, T. & E., Inc., 356 W. 18th.
Century Paper Box Co., 71 Greene.
Cheiken Paper Box Co., 209 Bowery.
City Central Paper Box Co., Inc., 310 Sixth av.
Cohen, C., & Co., Inc., 20 Commerce.
Columbia Corrugated Co., 50-02 W. 20th.
Columbus Paper Box Co., 526 W. B'way.
Corrugated Paper Products Co., 221 W. 26th.
Cosmopolitan Paper Box Co., 47 W. 34th.
Crawford, A. O., Co., 47 W. 34th.
Crescent Folding Box Co., 179 Wooster. *f.*
Crown Paper Box Co., 167 Wooster.
Crystal Box & Label Co., 43 Fulton.
Davis, Thomas, Inc., 261 Greenwich.
Dennison Mfg. Co., 15 John.
Densen, H., Co., Inc., 165 Mercer.
Densen, M., 129 W. 20th.
Diemer, John F., & Co., Inc., 67 Cortlandt.
Dix & Co., Fourth av., cor 12th.
Dolinsky, Jos., 25 Mercer.
Dominion Paper Box Co., 21 Bowery.
Dufft, Edw. W., 214 Sullivan.
Duschnes & Lieb, 83 Wooster.

Manhattan Borough—Cont'd.

Eagle Paper Box Co., 121 Greene.
Eagle Pencil Co., 703 E. 13th.
Edelson, S., 147 Wooster.
Ellman, M., 467 Grand.
Empire Paper Case Co., 149 Wooster. cor.
Empire Paper Tube and Box Co., 155 Bank.
Esterbrook Steel Pen Mfg. Co., 95 John.
Ettlinger, Louis, & Sons, 65 Nassau. (Jewelry.)
Falkin Paper Box Co., 146 Wooster.
Famous Paper Box Co., 145 Greene.
Farquhar Harrison & Co., 148 Wooster.
Favorite Paper Box Co., 79 Wooster.
Feinberg, Max, 91 Mercer.
Fenton Fibre Box Co., 29 B'way.
Fleischer, Chas., 303 Fifth av.
Fort Orange Paper Co., 200 Fifth av.
Fox Paper Box Co., 276 Ninth av.
Foy Folding Box Co., 313 Washington.
G. & Z. Paper Box Mfg. Co., 109 Greene.
Gebhart Folding Box Co., 24 E. 21st.
Gem Paper Box Co., Inc., 430 W. 14th.
General Paper Box Co., 47 W. 34th.
Gerbereux, Dufft & Kinder, Inc., 214 Sullivan.
Gilde & Feinberg, 136 W. 21st.
Globe Paper Box Co., 71 Mercer.
Gold, J., 109 Greene.
Goldenthal Bros., 118 Wooster.
Goldflam, J., Paper Box Co., 43 Mercer.
Goldflam, Jacob, 42 Bowery.
Goldstein & Bookspan Paper Box Co., 84 Forsyth.
Gotham Folding Box Co., 52 Elizabeth.
Grand Corrugated Paper Co., Inc., 30 Crosby.
Grand Union Folding Box Co., 21 East 4th.
Green Bros., 211 Wooster.
Grodsky, S., 165 Attorney.
Grossman, Benj., 111 Greene.
Hagenbuchle, H., 143 W. 19th.
Hall & Paneth, Inc., 108 W. 11th.
Hefter & Co., Inc., 342 W. 14th.
Helmus Paper Box Co., Inc., 99 Mott.
Hendon & Rappaport, 186 W. 4th.
Heppe, E. H., 396 Canal.

 **Paint and Chemical Company**
PAPER COLORS AND MILL PAINT SPECIALTIES
BOSTON   SPRINGFIELD, MASS.   NEW YORK

Leading Paper Box Manufacturers   425

Manhattan Borough—Cont'd.
Herman, William, & Co., Inc., 103 Wooster.
Hess, H. M., 129 W. 20th.
Hobbs Mfg. Co., 160 Wooster.
Hoffman, Joseph C., 10 Jones.
Hoffman & Itkin, 202 Canal.
Honigstock, Sandler, Co., 149 W. 24th.
Hughes, B. G., & Bro., 133 Mulberry.
Huhn, F., Inc., 82 Duane.
Imperial Paper Box Co., 157 W. 29th.
Independent Paper Box Co., 114 Greene.
Jacobson, Isaac J., 46 Greene.
Jaffe, M., & Bro., 235 Mercer.
Jefferson Paper Box Co., 98 Greene.
Kaye & Friedman, Inc., 97 Bank and 585-7 Hudson.
Kern & Son, 409 Pearl.
Keystone Paper Box Co., 162 W. 18th.
Koch Bros. & Co., 83 Greene.
Kovner Paper Box Co., Inc., 202 Greene.
Lakin Bros., 149 Wooster.
Landowne & Marantz, 50 West Houston.
Laski & Anchel, 222 Greene.
Lehmann, Ludwig, 72 Beekman. (Jewelry.)
Lemberger, H., 201 Wooster.
Lessem Paper Box Co., 51 Greene.
Levow, J., 213 W. 111th.
Levy & Rappaport, 141 Wooster.
Lewis, Phil. M., & Son, 39 W. 19th.
Lewitt, Aissak, Paper Box Co., Inc., 169 Wooster.
Livingston & Co., 114 E. 13th.
Loeb & Allmayer, 81 Crosby.
Lorscheider-Schang Co., 1133 B'way.
Mayer, Leopold, 83 Warren.
Mayer & Newman, 79 Wooster.
Metropolitan Paper Box Co., 133 Greene.
Meyer, Bernard, 47 Murray.
Meyer, Gustave A., 21 Cliff.
Myers, J. & P. B., Inc., 407 Broome.
National Folding Box and Paper Co., 132 Franklin. (See New Haven, Conn.)
National Label & Box Co., 129 Fulton.
National Paper Box Frame Co., 47 E. Houston.
Neff, Frederick, Inc., 115 King.
Nesmith, F. E., & Co., 142 W. 14th.
Nevins-Church Press, Inc., 135 William.

Manhattan Borough—Cont'd.
New England Box Co., Woolworth bldg.
Newitter, Gus, 319 Canal.
Newland Paper Box Co., Inc., 103 Greene.
N. Y. Amer. Paper Box Co., 276 Ninth av.
New York Label & Box Works, 510 E. 73d.
N. Y. Metal Edge Box Works, 212 Front.
N. Y. Paper Tube Co., 69 W. Houston.
Niagara Box Factory, Inc., 710 E. 13th.
Novelty Paper Box Co., 209 Sullivan.
Otis Manufacturing Co., Inc., 154 11th av.
Paradise Paper Box Co., 25-27 W. Houston.
Peerless Paper Box Co., 119 Wooster.
Perfect Patent Folding Box Co., Inc., 36 W. 24th s. cor.
Phoenix Paper Co., Inc., 200 Fifth av.
Port Morris Box Co., 82-88 Brown pl.
Rapid Paper Box Co., Inc., 163 Mercer.
Rebholz, Joseph, 46 Wooster.
Rector Paper Box Co., 127 Mercer.
Redler & Robbins, 17 Bowery.
Reissman, Charles, 214 Centre.
Reliable Paper Box Co., 36 W. 24th. s. f.
Renown Paper Box Co., Inc., 333 Bowery.
Rising Star Paper Box Co., 178 Suffolk.
Ritchie, W. C., & Co., 47 W. 34th.
Robinson & Freidheim, 142 Greene.
Rochester Folding Box Co., 1 Hudson.
Rogers, Edward H., Inc., 142 E. 32d.
Rosenberg, I., 65 Greene.
Rosenberg, Oscar, 131 Chrystie.
Rosenthal & Sobel, 28 W. Houston.
Rubin, Jos., & Son, 142 Greene.
Rudnick, F., Inc., 53 W. 14th.
Rudnick, H., 53 W. 14th.
Ruskin, M., 3 Rivington.
S. C. S. Box Co., 47 W. 34th.
S. & M. Paper Box Co., 207 Wooster.
Schenk & Schlichte, Inc., 22 Jones.
Schiffenhaus Bros., 213 W. 111th. cor.
Schinzel, Geo. P., & Son, Inc., 523 8th av. cor

 **Crucible Enamel** For hot or cold iron pipes, boiler fronts, etc.

Leading Paper Box Manufacturers

Manhattan Borough—Cont'd.
Schmidt, Henry, & Bro., 23 W. 31st.
Schmieder, John C., 392 W. B'way.
Schramm Paper Box Co., Inc., 231 Bowery.
Seligson & Marcus, 207 Wooster.
Sherwood-Beers Co., Inc., 536 W. 23d.
Siegel & Gabrelow, 276 9th av.
Sigal, Mary, 17 Lispenard.
Singer, J. B., & Co., 200 William. f.
Sonn, Jacob, 113 W. 17th.
Sonn, Leopold, & Bro., 229 W. 28th.
Spar, Harris, 147 Baxter.
Standard Paper Box Co., 132 Mulberry.
Star Corrugated Box Co., 372 South.
Star Paper Box & Tube Co., 478 Broome.
State Paper Box Co., 41 Greene.
Stelz Bookbinding Co., Inc., 85 E. 10th.
Stoehr, Geo., Inc., 356 W. 18th.
Stoll & Ward, 580 W. Broadway.
Sun Paper Box Co., Inc., 139 W. 19th.
Sykes & Seidman, 344 E. 23d.
Tabl, I., 319 Canal.
Taranto, T. S., 201 Wooster.
Tip-Top Paper Box Co., 41 Great Jones pl.
Travin, S., & Son, 191 Mercer.
Triest, J. S., 155 Spring.
Trum, E. J., 55-57 3d.
Union Paper Co., 844 Washington. s. f.
Unique Paper Box Co., 109 Spring.
Universal Circle Paper Box Co., 16 E. 12th.
Unterberg, I., & Co., 90 Franklin.
Un-X-L-D Paper Box Co., Inc., 106 Spring.
Usinger & Colgan Paper Box Co., Inc., 142 W. 14th.
Waterbury Paper Box Co., 253 B'way.
Weeks Carrier Co., 387 Washington.
Weinstein-Shufro Co., Inc., 303 E. 21st.
White Paper Box Co., Inc., 368 B'way.
Whiting Mfg. Co., 15 Malden Lane. (Jewelry.)
Whitney & Co., 303 Fifth av.
Wiemers, J. H., Inc., 155 Spring.
Wiltchik & Wiltchik, Inc., 192 Greene.
Wirth, Jno., 528 B'way.
Wolf, A. & L., 256 E. 138th.
Wuensch Paper Box Factory, 329 E. 153d.

Borough of Queens.
American Druggists Syndicate, Long Island City.
Columbia Paper Bag Co., Inc., 3d, cor. Van Alst av., L. I. City.
Lackner, John, Co., Inc., 306 7th av., L. I. City.
Trilsch Co., Oscar, Inc., Whitestone.

Borough of Richmond.
Ettlinger, Louis, & Son, Port Richmond.

NEW YORK STATE—Continued.
NIAGARA FALLS.
Hinds Paper Box Works, Inc.

NORTHVILLE.
Drake, Harry D.

ONEIDA.
Stanton, Elmer A. s. f.

ORISKANY FALLS.
Utica Knitting Co. s.

OSWEGO.
Benson, H. M., & Co. s.
Conde, Frederic. s.
Lastlong Underwear Co., Inc. s.

PALMYRA.
Drake, H. R., & Sons. s.

PEEKSKILL.
Peekskill Hat Mfg. Co.

PHILMONT.
High Rock Knitting Co. For own use.

PORT CHESTER.
Port Chester Paper Box Co.

POUGHKEEPSIE.
Osborne, Jas. B., & Son. s.

ROCHESTER.
Alderman, Fairchild Co., Inc., 29 Elizabeth.
American Paper Box Co., 197 State.
Bausch & Lomb Optical Co.
Bridges Mfg. Co.
Buedingen, W., & Son, 89 Allen.
Commercial Paper Box Co., Inc., Brown, cor. State.
Cowles, Arthur B., 25 S. Water.
Curtice Bros. Co.
Defender Photo Supply Co.
Diamond Paper Box Co., Brown.
Fairchild & Co., 367 Orchard.

 **Paint and Chemical Company**
PAPER COLORS AND MILL PAINT SPECIALTIES
BOSTON   SPRINGFIELD, MASS.   NEW YORK

Leading Paper Box Manufacturers

Rochester—Continued.
Flower City Specialty Co., Inc., 345 Maple.
Gillies, George J., 268 State.
Hunt, John F., 32 S. Paul.
Hunt, John K., 100 Mill.
Karle Lithographic Co., Inc., 444 Central av.
Kee Lox Mfg. Co.
Levis, John A., Co., Inc., 129 Andrews.
Little Giant Egg Carrier Co., 203 State.
Lorscheider-Schlang, The, Co., 57 Andrews.
MacMillan Litho. Co., Inc., 315 State.
McLean-Ward Fibre Case Co., Inc., 13 S. Water.
Munz, Theo., 65 Worth.
Neun, H. P., 135 N. Water.
Ott, A. W., Co., Inc., 121 Merrimac.
Rochester Fireworks Co.
Rochester Folding Box Co., foot of Commercial.
Star Egg Carrier & Tray Mfg. Co.
Stecher Lithographic Co., 272 N. Goodman. *f. For food and seed.*
Wagner, John A., & Son, 2 Benson.
Woodworth's C. B., Sons Co., 287 State.
Yawman & Erbe Mfg. Co.

ROME.
Edick, Anna E.

RONDOUT.
Powell, C. E.

SCHENECTADY.
Superior Ptg. & Box Co., Inc.

SYRACUSE.
Friedel, J. F., Paper Box Co.
Hotaling-Warner, The, Co.
Jordan, Charles L.
Oak Knitting Mills.
Schmeer's Paper Box Co.
Syracuse Paper Box Co.

TROY.
Albia Box and Paper Co.
Cluett, Peabody & Co.
Hall, Hartwell & Co.
Leggett, John, & Son.
Simpson & Moorehead.
West, A. E., Est.

UTICA.
Foster Box Board Co. *s.*
Mohawk Valley Cap Co. *s.*
Utica Paper Box. Co. *s.*

WARSAW.
Warsaw Paper Box Co.

NORTH CAROLINA.
ALBEMARLE.
Lillian Knitting Mills. *s.*
Wiscassett Mills Co. *s. For own use.*

DURHAM.
Durham Hosiery Mills. *s.*

HIGH POINT.
Parker Paper & Twine Co.

REIDSVILLE.
Reidsville Paper Box Co. *s.*

TRYON.
Tryon Paper Box Co.

WINSTON-SALEM.
Carolina Paper Box Co.

OHIO.
AKRON.
Goodrich, The B. F., Co.
Peterson, The A., Co., 31 Gardiner.

CANTON.
Wrigley Bros.

CINCINNATI.
American Trunk Co. *f.*
Boldt, Chas., Co. *cor.*
Cincinnati Mailing Device Co.
Cincinnati Paper Box Co., 1209 Sycamore. *s.*
Crane Paper Box Co., 307 Walnut. *s.*
Davenport Paper Box Co., 239 Main. *s.*
Dayton Folding Box Co., 2727 Spring Grove av. *f. cor.*
Duncan, J. H., Co., 8th and Broadway. *s.*
Enquirer Job Ptg. Co. *f.*
Globe Folding Box Co., Cherry. *f.*
Koehl, The Wm., Co., 1034 Hulbert av.
Miami Paper Novelty Co., 2409 Colerain av. *s.*
Neuman, Robert, 14th and Plum. *s.*
Nivison-Weiskopf Co., 317 E. 2d. *cor.*
Ohio Paper Box Co., Pugh bldg. *s.*
Peters Cartridge Co.
Quarry, W. J., Co. *f.*
Queen City Box Co.
Richardson Taylor Printing Co., Harrison av. and Patterson. *f.*
Rukin Paper Box Co., 230 N. 3d. *s.*
Schoepfel Paper Box Co., *s. f.*

 **Regal Wall Coating** A white cold water paint. Will not rub, scale or peel off.

Leading Paper Box Manufacturers

Cincinnati—Continued.
Smith, H. D., & Co., 206 to 210 Main. *s. f.*
Standard Folding Box Co., 122 W Pearl. *f.*
U. S. Paper Goods Co., 1224 W. 8th. *s. f.*
U. S. Playing Card Co.
U. S. Printing Co. (Norwood.) *f.*
Western Paper Goods Co. *f.*
Zumbiel, Chas. W., 122 W. Pearl. *s. f.*

CLEVELAND.
American Chicle Co.
American Steel & Wire Co.
Atlas Paper Box Co. *s.*
Crown Paper Box Co. *s.*
Grossman Paper Box Co., 1730 Superior av. *s. f.*
Ideal Paper Box Co., Lakeside av., E. 10th. *s.*
Ohio Boxboard Co., 1390 E. 30th. *s. f.*
Peerless Paper Box Mfg. Co., 1137 W. 6th. *s. f.*

COLUMBUS.
Frankenberg Bros., 37½ Front.
Herb Paper Box Co., 1596 S. High.

DAYTON.
Aull Bros. Paper Co., Detroit and Railroad. *f.*
Dayton Paper Novelty Co., 1126 E. Third. *f.*
Rike Folding Box Co.

LOCKLAND.
Carey, Philip, Mfg. Co.
Richardson Paper Co. *f.*

MANSFIELD.
Mansfield Paper Box Co., 184 W. 15th. *s. f.*

MIDDLETOWN.
Fairbanks Fibre Box Co.
Interstate Folding Box Co.
O K Paper Pail Co.

PIQUA.
Piqua Paper Box Co., College and Covington. *s.*

PORTSMOUTH.
Patterson, T. M., Paper Box Co. (Shoe.)

RAVENNA.
Johnson & Co. *Tubular and Stiff.*

SPRINGFIELD.
Rhoades Paper Box Co., St. John pl. *s.*

TOLEDO.
Ames-Bonner, The, Co.
Blade Printing and Paper Co., 318 to 324 St. Clair.
National Paper Box Co., 320 Monroe. *s. f.*
Smith, G. L., Co.
Union Paper Box Co. *s. f.*

ZANESVILLE.
Abel Box Co.

OKLAHOMA.
OKLAHOMA CITY.
Oklahoma Paper Co. *s. f.*

OREGON.
PORTLAND.
Columbia Paper Box Co. *f.*
Oregon Paper Box Co. *s.*
Portland Paper Box Co. *s. f.*
Portland Paper Package Co. *cor.*
Stettler, F. C., Mfg. *s. f.*

PENNSYLVANIA.
ALLENTOWN.
Allentown Paper Box Co. *s.*
Ryan, Wm. H., & Co. *s.*

BANGOR.
Bangor Paper Box Co.

BERLIN.
Engle, William.

CARLISLE.
Carlisle Paper Box Co.
Zang & Co.

CLEONA.
Cleona Paper Box Co.

EAST DOWNINGTOWN.
Downingtown Paper Box Co. *f.*

ERIE.
Griffin Mfg. Co.
Herald Paper Box Co. *s. f.*
McCrary Mfg. Co. (Round Boxes.)

FLEETWOOD.
Bickel, Thos. C.

HANOVER.
Brandstaedter, William.
Keystone Variety Works.

 **Paint and Chemical Company**
PAPER COLORS AND MILL PAINT SPECIALTIES
BOSTON   SPRINGFIELD, MASS.   NEW YORK

Leading Paper Box Manufacturers

HARRISBURG.
Ferriday, A. Reeder. *s.*
Kuhn Paper Box Co. *f.*
Harrisburg Bag & Box Co. *s.*

HAZLETON.
Saul & Zang, Inc.

HONESDALE.
W. G. Blakney.

HUNTINGDON.
J. C. Blair Co.

KURTZTOWN.
Boyer, Joseph K.

LANCASTER.
American Caramel Co.
Pennsylvania Soap Co.
Standard Caramel Co.
Wisner, Geo. E.

LEBANON.
Lebanon Paper Box Co. *s.*

LITITZ.
Ideal Chocolate Co.
Lititz Paper Box Co.

LYKENS.
Lehr, H. R., & Son. *s.*

MACUNGIE.
Wieder, J. F. *s.*

MOHRSVILLE.
Heffner & Stepp.

NAZARETH.
Nazareth Paper Box Co.

NORRISTOWN.
Norristown Box Co.
Lewis E. Taubel.

ORWIGSBURG.
Knipe, Oscar, & Co.
Orwigsburg Paper Box Co., Inc.

OXFORD.
Oxford Confectionery Co.

PALMYRA.
Palmyra Paper Box Co.

PHILADELPHIA.
Adelphia Paper Box Co., American and Jefferson. *s. f.*
American Paper Box Co., Dauphin and American. *s. f.*

Philadelphia—Continued.
Atlas Folding Box Co., 1666 Kinsey. Fkd. *f.*
Avart, Isaac, 2412 S. 6th. *s. f.*
Beggs & Graham, 204 Chancellor. *s. f.*
Berkowitz, Max E., 603 Chestnut. *s. f.*
Bischoff, Frank S., 1732 Blair. *s. f.*
Bisler, G. A., Inc., 245-255 N. 6th. *f.*
Boas, W. J., Co., 1427 Vine. *f.*
Brown & Bailey Co., Franklin and Willow. *f.*
Burt, F. N., Co., Ltd., Land Title Bldg. *s. f.*
Cigarette Paper Box Co., 452 York av.
Cohen, Chas. J., Co., 5th and Ludlow. *s. f.*
Crescent Corrugated Paper Products Co., 447 N. 5th. *cor.*
Crompton, John, Co., 828 N. Randolph. *s. f.*
Datz Co., 417 N. Orianna. *s. f.*
Deisroth, Wm. H., Co., 713 Spring Garden. *s. f.*
Donaldson, Harry S., 445 N. 3d. *s. f.*
Downes, Walter, 2022 S. 11th. *s. f.*
Dresden Box Co., 245 N. 6th. *s. f.*
Eichhorn, Albert, & Son, Palethorp and Turner. *s. f.*
Enterprise Paper Box Co., 452 York av. *s. f.*
Federal Paper Box Mfg. Co., 935 N. Orianna. *s. f.*
Franklin Co., 719 Samson. *s. f.*
Gair, Robert, Co., 1202 Pennsylvania bldg. *s. f.*
Garbell Mfg. Co., 1027 Ridge av.
Hahn, J. N., Co., Drexel Bldg. *s. f.*
Hauck, Philip, & Son, 1227 N. 4th. *s. f.*
Hoffman, H. B., 1710 Wylie.
Jones, Jesse, Paper Box Co., Inc., 615 Commerce. *s. f.*
Jones, Saml., & Sons. 2230 Hamilton. *s. f.*
Kaplan, W., 716 S. 11th. *s. f.*
Kardon, M., Paper Co., 220 Pine. *s. f.*
Keim, Edwin S., 307 Arch. *s. f.*
Kenyon Co., 503 Commerce. *s. f.*
Keystone Box Mfg. Co., 701 E. Girard av.
Kreeger & Connolly, 225 N. Lawrence. *s. f.*
Landow, A., & Co., 435 N. Broad. *s.*
Leckner, Chas., Co., 349 N. 2d. *s. f.*
Lee Paper Box Co.. 1608 N. Howard.
Leichner Bros., Montgomery av. and Howard. *s. f.*

 **Pulp Colors** For paper staining, surface coating and printing.

Leading Paper Box Manufacturers

Philadelphia—Continued.
Lockwood Folding Box Co., Ltd., 251 S. 3d *s. f.*
Loeb, Herman, & Co., 239 N. Lawrence. *s. f.*
Lovejoy, L. W., 2008 N. 2d. *s.*
Mayall, L. A., & Son, 743 S. Swanson. *s. f.*
Mendelsohn-Neil Co., American and Jefferson. *s. f.*
Metal Edge Paper Box Co., 1217 Callowhill. *s. f.*
Miller, Walter P., 452 York av. *s. f.*
National Folding Box and Paper Co., 212 Heed bldg. *f.*
National Metal Edge Box Co., 13th and Callowhill. *f.*
Nelson, S., 2412 S. 6th. *s.*
Novelty Paper Box Mfg. Co., 309 Arch. *s. f.*
Palmer Paper Box Co., Inc., 40 E. Wister, Gtn. *s. f.*
Peerless Paper Box Mfg. Co., Inc., 1423 N. Randolph. *s. f.*
Penna. Fibreform Co., 119 S. 4th. *s. f.*
Philadelphia Paper Box Co., 1706 Wylie. *s. f.*
Philpot, M. P., & Co., 412 Locust. *s. f.*
Plumly, Eugene K., Broad and Federal. *s. f.*
Plumly, Geo. W., Co., 218 N. 4th. *s. f.*
Progress Paper Box Co., 209 N. 2d. *s. f.*
Quaker City Folding Box Co., Richmond, nr. Brill. *f.*
Roggenburger's, I., Sons, 130 N. 3d. *s. f.*
Royal Pioneer Paper Box Mfg. Co., 944 N. 3d. *s. f.*
Schmidt, H., & Bro., 321 New. *s. f.*
Schoettle, Edwin J., Co., 533 N. 11th. *s. f.*
Schoettle, Ferdinand, 310 Florist. *s. f.*
Schoettle Paper Box Co., Front and Laurel. *s. f.*
Schott, H., 503 Commerce. *s. f.*
Schurmann, W. A., & Co., 17 South Water. *s f.*
Sefton Mfg. Co., 420 Drexel bldg., *s.*
Service Paper Box Co., 400 N. 12th. *s. f.*
Siler, A. K., 245 N. 6th. *s. f.*
Snyder, Geo. H., 3631 N. Smedley. *s. f.*
Souders, I. D., & Co., 1027 Ridge av. *s. f.*
Southwark Paper Box Co., 2412 S. 6th. *s.*

Philadelphia—Continued.
Sprowles, C. H., 1619 Ruan, Fkd. *s. f.*
Stanger, Wm. D., 1217 Callowhill. *s. f.*
Thaleg, E., 2218 Race. *s. f.*
Thompson & Norris Co., 486 The Bourse. *s. f. cor.*
Tioga Paper Box Co., Hancock and Westmoreland. *s. f.*
Tunick Bros. & Kaplan, 720 S. 11th. *s. f.*
United States Paper Box Co., 537 N. 3d. *s. f.*
Weber, David, & Co., 511 Locust. *s. f. cor.*
Weisman, A., 935 N. Orianna. *s.*
Whiting-Patterson Co., Inc., 11th and Race.
Whitwell, Geo. B., 206 Filbert. *s. f.*
Wilson, Wyle T., 1151 N. 3d. *s. f.*
Young & Keim, 307 Arch. *s. f.*

PHOENIXVILLE.
Phoenixville Paper Box Co.
Pierson, Edwin J.

PITTSBURGH.
Atlas Corrugated Box Co.
Keystone Box Co., 26th and Liberty av.
Kress, F. J., Box Co. *cor.*
Penn Paper Box Co., Ross and 3d av. *s. f.*
Pittsburgh Paper Box Co., 51st and Butler. *f.*
Pittsburgh Corrugated Box Co., 1416 Spring Garden av.
Rex, D. J., & Co., Locust and Boyd. *s. f.*
Sterling Paper Box Co., 1414 Spring Garden av. *s.*
Walker, A., Sons Co., Grant blvd. *s.*
Wasser, Jos., 1 Miller. *s.*
Woods, H. H., Paper Box Co., 1322 Sherman av. *s.*

PLYMOUTH.
Shawnee Paper Box Co.

POTTSTOWN.
Feroe, Robert A.
Pottstown Paper Box Co.

POTTSVILLE.
Morrison Box Factory. *s. f.*
Sterner, Allen W. *s. f.*

RAILROAD, YORK CO.
Keystone Egg Box & Filler Co.

 **Paint and Chemical Company**
PAPER COLORS AND MILL PAINT SPECIALTIES
BOSTON   SPRINGFIELD, MASS.   NEW YORK

Leading Paper Box Manufacturers

READING.
Advance Folding Box T Container Co.
Alexander, G. W., & Co.
Curtis & Jones Co.
Hendel Co., Chas. W.
Hendel, George, & Sons.
Hendel Hat Co.
Hendel's, John, Son.
Kachline, J. F.
Kessler, C. F., & Sons.
Luden & Co., W. H.
Meinig Co., E. Richard.
Miller Hat Co., Henry.
Nolde & Horst.
Penn Hardware Co.
Reading Hardware Co.
Reading Ribbon Badge Co.
Standard Paper Box Mfg. Co.
Werner & Sons, E. G.

SCHUYLKILL HAVEN.
Davis & Co.
Saul & Zang.
Stine, W. F.

SCRANTON.
Keystone Paper Box Mfg. Co.
Lackawanna Mills. *s.*
Original Picture Frame Mfg. Co.
Penn Baking Co. *s.*

SHOEMAKERSVILLE.
Acme Paper Box Co. *s.*

SOUTH BETHLEHEM.
Rankey Paper Box Co.

SPRING CITY.
American Paper Box Co.

WILKES BARRE.
Pfahler, Charles L. *f.*

WILLIAMSPORT.
Ertel Bros. *s.*
Eureka Paper Box Co. *f.*
Williamsport Paper Box & Printing Co. *s.*

YORK.
York Paper Box Co.

RHODE ISLAND.
PAWTUCKET.
Little, J. W., & Co.
Pawtucket Paper Box Co.
Standard Paper Box Corp. *s. f.*

PROVIDENCE.
Buffington, F. H.
Chester, F. E., Mfg. Co.
Elmwood Box Co.
Fox, C. J., The, Co., Inc.
Jencks Paper Box Co.
Poole, John T.
Rueckert, The, Mfg. Co.
Taylor Card & Box Co.
Young Bros.

WOONSOCKET.
Colwell, F. A. *s. f.*

SOUTH CAROLINA.
GREENVILLE.
Greenville Paper Box Co.

TENNESSEE.
CHATTANOOGA.
Andrews, O. B., Co. *s. f.*
Star Box & Printing Co. *s. f.*

KNOXVILLE.
Knoxville Paper Box Co. *s. f.*
Standard Knitting Mills Co.

MEMPHIS.
Memphis Paper Co. *f.*
Tri-State Paper Box Mfg. Co. *s. f.*

NASHVILLE.
Rock City Paper Box Co., Charlotte av. and 42d. *s. f.*

TEXAS.
DALLAS.
Pollock-Burt Paper Box Co. *s. f.*
Texas Paper Co. *s. f.*

HOUSTON.
Magnolia Paper Co. *s. f.*

SAN ANTONIO.
Burnett, R. L., Co. *s.*

UTAH.
SALT LAKE CITY.
Union Paper Box Co. *s. f.*

VERMONT.
BENNINGTON.
Bennington Paper Box Factory. *s.*
Cooper Mfg. Co. (For own use.)

BURLINGTON.
National Paper Tube & Box Co.

READSBORO.
National Metal Edge Box Co.

Hamilton **Canary Yellow** A true color. Makes bright tints and solid finishes.

A SELECTED LIST OF
Envelope Manufacturers
IN THE
UNITED STATES AND CANADA

Only concerns that operate machines included in this list.

CALIFORNIA.
LOS ANGELES.
Coast Envelope Co., 737-739 Wall.
SAN FRANCISCO.
Griffin Envelope Co., 156 Perry.
UNITED STATES ENV. CO., Pacific Coast Env. Co., Division.

CONNECTICUT.
HARTFORD.
UNITED STATES ENVELOPE CO., Plimpton Mfg. Co. Division.
KENSINGTON.
The American Paper Goods Co.
NEW HAVEN.
Moffat Paper Goods Co., 219 Water.
ROCKVILLE.
UNITED STATES ENVELOPE CO., White Corbin & Co. Division.

GEORGIA.
ATLANTA.
Atlanta Envelope Co.
Montag Bros.

ILLINOIS.
CENTRALIA.
Centralia Env. Co.
CHICAGO.
American Envelope Co., 817 W. Washington blvd.
American Paper Goods Co. (also at Kensington, Conn.)
Berkowitz Envelope Co.
Bright Envelope Mfg. Co.
Bourke-Rice Envelope Co., 511 W. Jackson blvd.
Chicago Envelope Co., 59 E. Madison.
Columbia Envelope Co., 349 W. Austin.
Cupples, Samuel, Envelope Co., 508 St. Clair.
Gaw-O'Hara Envelope Co., 725 S. Fifth av.
Garden City Envelope Co., S. Peoria.
Heco Envelope Co., 351 East Ohio.
Hogan Envelope Co.

Chicago—Continued.
Hoyler Envelope Co., 411 S. Jefferson.
Independent Envelope Co. of the U. S. A., 360 E. Grand av.
Luck, Chas. H., Envelope Co., 701 S. La Salle.
Outlook Envelope Co., 6 N. Michigan av.
Sewell-Clapp Mfg. Co., 28 N. Desplaines.
Taylor, Chas. E., & Co., 570 W. Randolph.
Transo Paper Co., 735 W. Division.
UNITED STATES ENV. CO., 10 So. Wabash av.
QUINCY.
American Papeterie & Envelope Co.
Paper Products Co.
ROADHOUSE.
Roadhouse Envelope Co.
WAUKEGAN.
UNITED STATES ENVELOPE CO., National Envelope Co. Division.

INDIANA.
INDIANAPOLIS.
Central States Envelope Co.
UNITED STATES ENV. CO., Central States Envelope Co. Division.
MARION.
Mid-West Paper & Envelope Co.

MAINE.
RUMFORD.
CONTINENTAL PAPER BAG CO.

MARYLAND.
Oles Envelope Co., Baltimore.

MASSACHUSETTS.
BOSTON.
Boston Envelope Co., 295 Franklin.
Ward, Samuel, Mfg. Co., 59 Franklin.
HOLYOKE.
UNITED STATES ENVELOPE CO.
PITTSFIELD.
Eaton, Crane & Pike Co.

ARE YOU LOOKING FOR QUALITY GRADES OF

TWINES AND CORDAGE

COTTON TWINES
LINEN FINISHED TWINES
FLAX TWINES
SISAL TWINES
AMERICAN HEMP TWINES
FINISHED INDIA TWINES
JUTE WRAPPING TWINES
BOX TWINES
SAIL TWINES

UNFINISHED INDIA
TUBE ROPE
FINE TUBE YARN
PAPER MAKERS'
MANILA ROPE
BALING ROPE
SEAMING CORD
TRANSMISSION ROPE
COLORED SPECIALTIES

We Sell the Well-Known Keystone Brands of Jute Cordage

REG. U. S. PATENT OFFICE

Manufactured by The Schlichter Jute Cordage Co.

WE MAKE A SPECIALTY OF THE REQUIREMENTS OF PAPER, BOARD AND PULP MANUFACTURERS

PAPER

WRAPPINGS	TISSUES	BOARDS	FINE PAPERS
KRAFT	WHITE	NEWS	WRITINGS
JUTE AND ROPE	MANILA	BINDERS'	BONDS
MANILA	JUTE	CHIP	LEDGER
FIBRE	ANTI-TARNISH	TAG	M.F. and LAID BOOK
LINING	PATTERN	STRAW	SUPER
TEXTILE	OILED and WAXED	TRUNK	COVER
OILED and WAXED	COLORS and	FRICTION	FOLIO
COLORS and	SPECIALTIES	BRISTOL	BIBLE
SPECIALTIES		MILL BLANKS	PRINT NEWS

WE HAVE UNUSUAL FACILITIES FOR OFFERING TIME CONTRACTS AND CARLOAD LOTS PROMPT DELIVERIES

ESTABLISHED 1898

JOHN W. BANKER

TELEPHONES, FRANKLIN { 4624 / 4625 / 4626 }

17-19 WHITE STREET
NEW YORK CITY

THE IMPROVED		THE
COLUMBIAN CLASP		**OUTLOOK**
Best and most satisfactory Mailing Envelope in the world.		The Time, Money and Trouble Saving Envelope

GOOD ENVELOPES
TRADE MARK

OF EVERY DESCRIPTION

AND

FINE STATIONERY
FROM

EMBLEMS OF REFINED TASTE AND COURTLY ELEGANCE

TO

THE NECESSITIES OF ORDINARY CORRESPONDENCE

AT ATTRACTIVE PRICES

TOILET PAPERS
OF EVERY GRADE

PAPETERIES

For Samples and Prices Address any of Our
DIVISIONS

Logan, Swift & Brigham Envelope Co., Worcester, Mass.
United States Envelope Co., Holyoke, Mass.
White, Corbin & Co., Rockville, Conn.
Plimpton Manufacturing Co., Hartford, Conn.
Morgan Envelope Co., Springfield, Mass.
National Envelope Co., Waukegan, Ill.
P. P. Kellogg & Co., Springfield, Mass.
Whitcomb Envelope Co., Worcester, Mass.
W. H. Hill Envelope Co., Worcester, Mass.
Pacific Coast Envelope Co., San Francisco, Cal.
Central States Envelope Co., Indianapolis, Ind.

 **Paint and Chemical Company**
PAPER COLORS AND MILL PAINT SPECIALTIES
BOSTON   SPRINGFIELD, MASS.   NEW YORK

Leading Envelope Manufacturers 435

SPRINGFIELD.
Birnie Paper Co.
Murphy, John A., Co.
National Papeterie Co.
Powers Paper Co.
UNITED STATES ENVELOPE CO.
 Main office, Springfield, Mass. Incorporated under the laws of the State of Maine, July, 1898.
 Authorized capital..... $5,000,000
 Divided as follows, viz.:
  Preferred Stock........ $4,000,000
  Common Stock........ 1,000,000
 OFFICERS—Chas. H. Hutchins, Pres.; James Logan, Ernest M. Whitcomb, Robert W. Day, Vice-Pres.; William O. Day, Treas.; W. M. Wharfield, Assistant Treas. & Sec'y.

LIST OF PROPERTIES OWNED BY THE COMPANY.

W. H. Hill Envelope Co., Worcester, Mass.
UNITED STATES ENVELOPE CO., Holyoke, Mass.
P. P. Kellogg & Co., Springfield, Mass.
Logan, Swift & Brigham Envelope Co., Worcester, Mass.
Morgan Envelope Co., Springfield, Mass.
National Envelope Co., Waukegan, Ill.
Plimpton Mfg. Co., Hartford, Conn.
Whitcomb Envelope Co., Worcester, Mass.
White, Corbin & Co., Rockville, Conn.
Pacific Coast Envelope Co., San Francisco, Cal.
Central States Envelope Co., Indianapolis, Ind.

WORCESTER.
Colonial Envelope Co.
New England Envelope Co.
SHERMAN ENVELOPE CO.
UNITED STATES ENVELOPE CO., W. H. Hill Envelope Co. Division.
UNITED STATES ENVELOPE CO., Logan, Swift & Brigham Envelope Co. Division.
UNITED STATES ENVELOPE CO., Whitcomb Envelope Co. Division.
Worcester Envelope Co.

MICHIGAN.
DETROIT.
Tullar Envelope Co., 45 Congress, W.
 KALAMAZOO.
ILLINOIS ENVELOPE CO.
 OSHKOSH.
Fox River Valley Envelope Co.

TRENTON.
Challenge Envelope Co.
MINNESOTA.
MINNEAPOLIS.
Gopher Env. Co.
Heywood Mfg. Co.
Security Envelope Co.
 ST. PAUL.
St. Paul Envelope Co.
MISSOURI.
KANSAS CITY.
Berkowitz Envelope Co.
Martin-Legg Envelope Co.
Mid-West Envelope Co.
Western Envelope Mfg. Co.
 ST. JOSEPH.
Western Tablet Co.
 ST. LOUIS.
Continental Paper Bag Co.
Cruden Martin Mfg Co.
Samuel Cupples Envelope Co., Sixth and Cerre.
Envelope Mfg. Co.
Hesse Envelope & Litho. Co., 501 N. First.
St Louis Envelope Co.
NEBRASKA.
OMAHA.
Burkley Envelope & Printing Co.
NEW YORK.
ALBANY.
American Papeterie Co.
 BUFFALO.
Alling & Cory Co., The.
Buffalo Envelope Co., 268 Michigan.
Niagara Envelope Manufactory, 567 Washington.
 COHOES.
Cohoes Envelope Co., Inc.
 NEW YORK CITY.
BROOKLYN BOROUGH.
Bainbridge's, Chas. T., Sons, 12 Cumberland.
Robert Gair Co.
Tension Envelope Co., Bush Terminal.
Thompson & Norris Co., 10-34 Prince.
General Paper Goods Manufacturing Co., 3 Bush Terminal, 219-253 36th, Brooklyn.
MANHATTAN BOROUGH.
American Envelope & Paper Co., 45 Lafayette.
American Paper Goods Co., 179 Duane.
Berlin & Jones Envelope Co., 547-553 W. 27th.
Birnie Paper Co., 389 B'way.

 **Permanent Reds** LIGHT ALKALI WATER } PROOF

Leading Envelope Manufacturers

Manhattan Borough—Cont'd.
C. & M. Envelope Co., 535 Pearl.
Clasp Envelope Co., 109 Leonard.
Cohoes Envelope Co., 150 Nassau.
Commercial Envelope & Box Co., Woolworth Bldg.
CONTINENTAL PAPER BAG CO., 17 Battery pl.
Samuel Cupples Envelope Co., 7 Laight.
Diemer, John F., Co., 67 Cortlandt.
Eastern Envelope Co., 35 Great Jones.
Goodbody, William, 505 W. Broadway.
Improved Mailing Case Co., 309 Broadway.
Jones, H. & A., 50 Beekman.
Jones, William C., 154 W. 18th.
Lion Envelope Co.
National Fibre Stock Envelope Co., 21 Park row.
Neostyle Envelope Co., 109 Leonard.
Parks Claspless Envelope Co., 133 E. 16th.
Powers Paper Co., 621 B'way.
Raynor & Perkins Envelope Co., 222 William.
SHERMAN ENVELOPE CO., 395 Broadway.
Transo Paper Co., 290 B'way.
UNITED STATES ENVELOPE CO., 261 Broadway.
Whiting, F., 38 Murray.
Whiting-Patterson Co., 261 Canal.

OHIO.
CINCINNATI.
UNITED STATES ENVELOPE CO., Cincinnati Env. Co. Division.
U. S. Paper Goods Co., The.
CLEVELAND.
Standard Envelope Mfg. Co.
The Wolf Envelope Co., Middle and High.
COLUMBUS.
Columbus Envelope Co.
DAYTON.
Mercantile Corporation.

WEST CARROLLTON.
American Envelope Co.

PENNSYLVANIA.
GREENSBURG.
Pittsburg Envelope Co.
HUNTINGDON.
J. C. Blair Co.
PHILADELPHIA.
Bushnell, Alvah, Co., 925 Filbert.
Cohen, Chas. J., Co.
Cupples, Samuel, Envelope Co., 2120 Land Title Bldg.
Griffiths, Phillip, Co.
Jewell & Co., Inc.
Morgan Envelope Co.
National Envelope Co.
National Fibrestock Envelope Co., 427 Moyer.
New England Envelope Co.
Penn Envelope Co.
Rossiter, A. D., & Sons Co.
Spangler, E. J., Co.
Standard Envelope Co.
Weaver Mailing Envelope & Box Co.
Whiting-Patterson Co.
Wolf Bros., 12th and Callowhill.
PITTSBURGH.
Schrock, M. P.
Steel City Envelope Co.
WEST CHESTER.
Commercial Envelope & Box Co.
WILKES-BARRE.
Pfahler, Charles L.

TEXAS.
DALLAS.
Hesse Envelope Co. of Texas.

VIRGINIA.
RICHMOND.
Union Envelope Co.

WISCONSIN.
MILWAUKEE.
Milwaukee Envelope Mfg. Co.
Western States Envelope Co.
OSHKOSH
Fox River Valley Envelope Co.

CANADA

BRANTFORD, ONT.
Barber-Ellis, Ltd.
HAMILTON, ONT.
National Envelope Co.
MONTREAL, QUE.
Canada Envelope Co.
Dawson, W. V., Ltd.
Rolland Paper Co.
Wilson, J. C., Ltd.

TORONTO, ONT.
Barber-Ellis, Ltd., Wellington, W.
Bouvier & Hutchinson.
Davis & Henderson.
Dominion Envelope Co., Ltd.
Gage, W. J., & Co.
Toronto Envelope Co.
WINNIPEG, MAN.
Barber-Ellis, Ltd.
Winnipeg Envelope Co.

 **Paint and Chemical Company**
PAPER COLORS AND MILL PAINT SPECIALTIES
BOSTON SPRINGFIELD, MASS. NEW YORK

A SELECTED LIST OF
Tablet & Pad Manufacturers
IN THE
UNITED STATES

KEY TO ABBREVIATIONS TO FIRMS IN OTHER LINES WHO ALSO MAKE TABLETS

B. S.   Booksellers, Stationers.
S.   Stationers.
W. S.   Wholesale Stationers.
W. P.   Wholesale Paper.
T. M.   Tablet Manufacturers.
L.   Lithographers.
P. S.   Printers, Stationers.
W. P. S. Wholesale Paper, Stationers.
Bb. S. Blank Books, Stationers.
P.   Printers.
B. B.   Blank Book Manufacturers, or Book Binders.

COLORADO.
DENVER.
Kistler, W. H., Stationery Co.—S

CONNECTICUT.
BURNSIDE.
Taylor-Atkins Paper Co.—TM

DISTRICT OF COLUMBIA.
WASHINGTON.
Andrews, R. P., Paper Co.—WPS

GEORGIA.
ATLANTA.
Montag Bros., Inc.—WS—TM

ILLINOIS.
BLOOMINGTON.
Pantagraph Printing and Stationery Co.—PS—BB

CHICAGO.
Interstate Tablet Co.—TM

DANVILLE.
Illinois Printing Co.—PS

INDIANA.
ELKHART.
Elkhart Stationery Co.

FORT WAYNE.
Fisher Bros. Paper Co—WPS

INDIANAPOLIS.
Central Paper & Tablet Co.—TM
Indiana Paper Co.—WPS
O. P. Lesh Paper Co.—WPS

LOGANPORT.
Longwell-Cummings Co.—PS

MARION.
Osborn Paper Co.—WP

KANSAS.
LEAVENWORTH.
J. C. Ketcheson—PS

MASSACHUSETTS.
BOSTON.
Adams, Cushing & Foster, Inc., 168 Devonshire—WS
J. L. McIntosh, 185 Franklin—Bb.S Paging and Numbering
Ward, Samuel, Mfg. Co., 59 Franklin—WP and Papeteries.

FITCHBURG.
H. E. Remington & Co.—WS

HOLYOKE.
Affleck Ruling and Stationery Co.—PS
American Pad and Paper Co.—TM
Essex Pad and Paper Co.—TM
Highland Mfg. Co.—WP and Ruling
Judd Paper Co.—WP
Smith Tablet Co., Inc.—TM
White & Wyckoff Mfg. Co.—TM and Papeteries.
Whiting & Cook, Inc.—Papeteries.
Whiting Paper Co.—Papeterie mfrs.—WS

PITTSFIELD.
Eaton, Crane & Pike Co.—Mfrs of Papeteries and TM

 **Cement Floor Coating** Makes concrete floors wet, oil and dust proof

Leading Tablet and Pad Manufacturers

SPRINGFIELD.
Powers Paper Co.—TM.
Birnie Paper Co.—TM

MICHIGAN.
KALAMAZOO.
Kalamazoo Stationery Co.—TM

MINNESOTA.
MINNEAPOLIS.
Leslie, The John, Paper Co.—WP
McClellan Paper Co.—WPS
Minneapolis Paper Co.—WP
Paper Supply Co.—WP
ST. CLOUD.
Northwest Tablet Co.
ST. PAUL.
Leslie-Donahower Co.—WP
Wright, Barrett & Stilwell Co.—WPS

MISSOURI.
ST. JOSEPH.
Western Tablet Co.—TM
ST. LOUIS.
Crunden-Martin Woodenware Co.—TM
Sam'l Cupples Envelope Co.—TM

NEW YORK.
ALBANY.
Eastern Tablet Co.—TM
BUFFALO.
Irish, Geo., Paper Co.
NEW YORK CITY.
BROOKLYN BOROUGH.
Marcus Ward, Inc.
MANHATTAN BOROUGH.
Am. Pad & Paper Co.—309 Broadway; same as Holyoke (Agency) TM
Boorum & Pease Co., 109 Leonard—BB—TM
Geo. B. Hurd & Co., 425 Broome.—Papeterie mfg.; tables small way.
S. E. & M. Vernon, 69 Duane—Blank Books.
Whiting Paper Co., 14th and 7th av.—Papeterie mfg. and WS
Wynne Paper Co., 318 W. 39th.
OSWEGO.
Schubert, John M., & Son—BB—BS
TROY.
Mann, H. R., & Co.—WS
Troy Paper Co.—WP

OHIO.
COLUMBUS.
The Central Tablet Mfg. Co.—TM
DAYTON.
Reynolds & Reynolds Co.—TM
MANSFIELD.
Ricketts & Nichols—BBP
TOLEDO.
Blade Printing & Paper Co.—WPS
Wendt & Rausch Co.—BB
WEST CARROLLTON.
Miami Tablet Co.—TM

PENNSYLVANIA
HUNTINGDON.
J. C. Blair Co.—TM
JOHNSONBURG.
Hopper Paper Co.—TM and Composition Books.
JOHNSTOWN.
W. H. Raab & Bro.—Bb
READING.
M. J. Earl—WP
ROARING SPRING.
Roaring Spring Blank Book Co.—Bb—TM
WILLIAMSPORT.
F. R. Miller Blank Book Co.—BB

VIRGINIA.
RICHMOND.
Baughman Stationery Co.—WS
Bell Book and Stationery Co.—WS
E. Waddey Co.—WS

WASHINGTON.
EVERETT.
Everett Pulp & Paper Co.

WISCONSIN.
APPLETON.
The Post Publishing Co.—P
EAU CLAIRE.
Eau Claire Book and Stationery Co. BS, BB, PS
Elwell & Fangen—BB
GREEN BAY.
American Tablet Co.—TM
MANITOWOC.
Schmidtmann, Theo., Sons Co.—WS
NEENAH.
Warner & Pickert—TM

 **Paint and Chemical Company**
PAPER COLORS AND MILL PAINT SPECIALTIES
BOSTON SPRINGFIELD, MASS. NEW YORK

A SELECTED LIST OF

TAG MANUFACTURERS

ILLINOIS.
American Tag Co., 6133-43 S. State, Chicago.
International Tag Co., Lake, Union and Eagle, Chicago.
Cupples, Samuel, Envelope Co., Illinois and St. Clair, Chicago.

INDIANA.
Tag Printing Co., Indianapolis.
Campbell Paper Box Co., South Bend.

MASSACHUSETTS.
American Tag Co. of New Jersey, 139 Federal, Boston.
Dennison Mfg. Co., 26 Franklin, Boston.
Security Tag Co., 70 Washington, North Boston, Mass.
Sandwich Card and Tag Co., Sandwich.

MICHIGAN.
American Mfg. Co., Battle Creek.
Michigan Tag Co., Grand Rapids.

NEW JERSEY.
American Tag Co. of New Jersey, Newark, N. J.

NEW YORK.
NEW YORK CITY.
American Tag Co. of New Jersey, 220 Broadway.
Denney, The, Tag Co., Inc., 1265 Broadway.
Dennison Mfg. Co., 5th av. and 26th, New York.

New York City—Continued.
Eisler, A., & Co., 221 Canal.
Keystone Tag Co., 150 Nassau.
Lehmicke Co., 621 Broadway.
Monarch Tag Co., 1269 Broadway.
Pan American Tag Co., 39 W. 8th.
Reyburn Mfg. Co., 115 Worth St.
Robinson Tag & Label Co., 142 W. 18th.
Salisbury Mfg. Co., 817 Broadway, New York.
Tag Envelope Co., 86 Walker.

OHIO.
Dancyger's Safety Pin Ticket Co., Cleveland.
Denney Tag Co., Inc., The, 303 Marshall, Cleveland.
Dennison Mfg. Co., 206 Andrews Bldg., Cincinnati; also 822 Guardian bldg., Cleveland.
National Tag Co., Dayton.
Thomas Stationery Mfg. Co., Springfield.

PENNSYLVANIA.
Dennison Mfg. Co., 1007 Chestnut street, Philadelphia; also 914 Farmers' Bank bldg., Pittsburgh.
Gifford, H. M., The, Mfg. Co., Philadelphia.
Spangler, E. J., & Co., Philadelphia
Denney Tag Co., West Chester.
Keystone Tag Co., West Chester.

RHODE ISLAND.
Dennison Mfg. Co., 402 E. A. Smith bldg., Providence.
Salisbury Mfg. Co., Providence.
Diamond Tag Co., Warren.

Hampden Pure Blues For paper staining, coating and ruling.

A SELECTED LIST OF

WALL PAPER PRINTERS

IN THE

United States and Canada

DELAWARE.
NEWARK.
Jacob Thomas Co.

WILMINGTON.
Joseph Thomas Co.

ILLINOIS.
CHICAGO.
The Aristo Co., 2909 Indiana av.
Art Wall Paper Mills, Western av. and 21st.
Audebert Wall Paper Mills, 1800 Foster av.
Commercial Wall Paper Mill, Ogden blvd. and Tallman av.
Sears, Roebuck & Co.

JOLIET.
Joliet Wall Paper Mills.
Star-Peerless Wall Paper Mills.

MASSACHUSETTS.
CHELSEA.
Thomas Strahan Co.

WORCESTER.
Allen-Higgins Wall Paper Co.

NEW JERSEY.
HACKENSACK.
Wm. Campbell Wall Paper Co.

HOBOKEN.
Hobbs Wall Paper Co., 18th and Willow av.

NEW BRUNSWICK.
Janeway & Carpender.

JERSEY CITY.
Robert Griffin Co., 151 West Side av.

SOMERVILLE.
Cott-a-lap Co.

PATERSON.
United States Varnished Tile Co., 245-251 Crooks av.

NEW YORK.
BUFFALO.
M. H. Birge & Sons Co.

GLENS FALLS.
Glens Falls Wall Paper Co.
Imperial Wall Paper Co.

CORTLAND.
Cortland Wall Paper Co.
Wallace Wall Paper Co.

HUDSON FALLS.
Standard Wall Paper Co.

SARATOGA.
Saratoga Wall Paper Co.

NEW YORK CITY.
BROOKLYN BOROUGH.
Baeck, E. C., Corporation, 34th and Third av.
Baeck Wall Paper Co., 237 37th.
Robert Graves Co., 929 Third av.

MANHATTAN BOROUGH.
Gledill Wall Paper Co., 541-545 W. 34th.
Robert Graves Co., 169 Madison Ave.
Walcutt Bros. Co., 141 E. 25th.

PLATTSBURG.
Plattsburg Wall Paper Co.

NIAGARA FALLS.
Niagara Wall Paper Co.

 **Paint and Chemical Company**
PAPER COLORS AND MILL PAINT SPECIALTIES
BOSTON SPRINGFIELD, MASS. NEW YORK

Leading Wall Paper Printers 441

SCHUYLERVILLE.
Standard Wall Paper Co.

OHIO.

CLEVELAND.
Bailey Wall Paper Co.
Schmitz-Horning Co.

STEUBENVILLE.
Chicago Wall Paper Mill.

PENNSYLVANIA.

HANOVER.
Haffelfinger, E. R., Co.

PHILADELPHIA.
Becker, Smith & Page, Inc., Snyder av. and Water.
Enterprise Wall Paper Co., 1020-1024 Nevada.

Philadelphia—Continued.
Furlong Wall Paper Mfg. Co., Leverington av. and Baker, Monayunk.
Premier Mfg. Co., Delaware av., Water and Morris.
Quaker City Wall Paper Co., Thompson and Westmoreland.
Vornhold Wall Paper Co., Garden and Kennedy, Bridesburg.

READING.
Sun Wall Mfg. Paper Co.

NEW BRIGHTON.
Pittsburg Wall Paper Co.

YORK.
Barnes, Rudolph & Co.
Gilbert Wall Paper Co.
York Card and Paper Co.
York Wall Paper Co.

WALL BURLAP MANUFACTURERS.
(Use Ground Wood for Backing and Filling.)

Holliston Mills, Norwood, Mass.
H. B. Wiggins Sons Co., Bloomfield, N. J.

Cott-a-Lap Co., Somerville, N. J.
Richter Mfg. Co., Tenafly, N. J.

CANADA

MONTREAL, QUEBEC.
McArthur, Colin & Co.
Watson, Foster Co., Ltd.

TORONTO, ONTARIO.
Boxer, Reg. N., Co., Ltd.
Stauntons, Limited.

Hampden Victoria Lake A perfect color for blending with Yellow to produce shades of Buff, Corn, etc.

A SELECTED LIST
OF
Twine Manufacturers
IN THE
UNITED STATES AND CANADA

COTTON

ALABAMA.
American Net and Twine Co., Blue Mountain.
Enterprise Cotton Mills, Enterprise.
West Huntsville Cotton Mills Co., Huntsville.
Montgomery Cordage Co., Montgomery.
Tallassee Falls Mfg. Co., Tallassee.

CALIFORNIA.
California Cotton Mills Co., Oakland.

CONNECTICUT.
Brownell & Co., Moodus.
Crawford Cotton Mills, Crawford.
Neptune Twine and Cord Mills, Moodus.
Purple, A. E., Moodus.
Mystic Twine Co., Mystic.
Turner & Stanton Co., Norwich.
Paul Ackerly, Vernon.
Lees Mfg. Co., Westport.

FLORIDA.
Palmetto Products Co., Jacksonville.

GEORGIA.
Fulton Bag and Cotton Mills, Atlanta.
Whittier Mills Co., Chattahoochee.
Crawford Cotton Mills, Crawford.
Forsyth Cotton Mills, Forsyth.
Bowen Jewell Co., Jewell.
Juliette Milling Co., Juliette.
Hillside Cotton Mills, La Grange.
Bibb Manufacturing Co., Macon.
Manchester Mfg. Co., Macon.
Georgia Duck & Cordage Mill, Scottdale.

ILLINOIS.
American Net & Twine Co., Chicago.

INDIANA.
Eagle Cotton Mills Co., Madson.

KENTUCKY.
Argonaut Cotton Mills Co., Covington.
Grahamton Mfg. Co., Grahamton.
January & Wood Co., Mayville.

LOUISIANA.
Kohlmann, C., Mill & Mfg. Co., New Orleans.
Maginnis Cotton Mills, New Orleans.

MAINE.
Lord, R. W. Co., Kennebunk.

MARYLAND.
Chesapeake Belting Co., Baltimore.
Hooper, Wm. E., & Sons Co., Baltimore.

MASSACHUSETTS.
American Core-Twine Co., Boston.
Tate Mfg. Co., Inc., Boston.
Tribble Cordage Mills, Inc., Boston.
American Net and Twine Co., East Cambridge.
Estes Mills, Fall River.
Holden, Jas., Fall River.
Lawrence Duck Co., Lawrence.
Toohey, M. J., & Co., Fall River.
New Bedford Textile Corpn., New Bedford.
Sampson Cordage Works, Shirley.
Central Mills Co., Southbridge.
Westport Mfg. Co., Westport.

MISSISSIPPI.
Yocona Mills, Water Valley.

MISSOURI.
Hoover & Allison Co., North Kansas City.
Missouri Cotton Yarn Mfg. Co., St. Louis.

NEW HAMPSHIRE.
Boscowen Mills, Penacock.

 **Paint and Chemical Company**
PAPER COLORS AND MILL PAINT SPECIALTIES
BOSTON SPRINGFIELD, MASS. NEW YORK

Leading Twine Manufacturers

COTTON.
(CONTINUED)

NEW JERSEY.
Nitram Mfg. Co., East Orange.

NEW YORK.
Auburn Converting Co., Auburn.
Cayuga Linen & Cotton Mills, Auburn.
Thompson & Co., James, Valley Falls.

NORTH CAROLINA.
Double Shoals Cotton Mills, Double Shoals.
Shuford, A. A., Mill Co., Hickory.
Oakdale Cotton Mills, Jamestown.
Cleveland Mill & Power Co., Lawndale.
Oxford Cotton Mills, Oxford.

OHIO.
Atkins & Pearce Mfg. Co., Cincinnati.
Jacob Cordage Co., Cincinnati.

OKLAHOMA.
Pioneer Cotton Mills, Guthrie.

PENNSYLVANIA.
Emory Mills, Hulmeville.
Fricke, J. E. Co., Chester.
Barrows Mfg. Co., Lansdale.
Hooper Sons Mfg. Co., Philalelphia.
Johnston & Co., Inc., Philadelphia.

PENNSYLVANIA—*Continued.*
McComesky, Thomas, Philadelphia.
Moore, O., & Co., Philadelphia.
Morice Twine Mills, Philadelphia.
Whitaker, Wm. D., Philadelphia.
Young, John B., Philadelphia.

RHODE ISLAND.
Union Twine Co., Canonchet.
Dexter Yarn Co., Pawtucket.
Greene & Daniels Co., Pawtucket.
Yawgo Line & Twine Co., Rockville.

SOUTH CAROLINA.
Townsend, H. C., Cotton Mill, Anderson.
Pendleton Mfg. Co., Autun.
Glencoe Cotton Mills, Columbia.
Orange Cotton Mills, Orangeburg.
Beaumont Manufacturing Co., Spartanburg.

TENNESSEE.
Tennessee Line & Twine Co., Elizabethtown.
Jonesboro Yarn Mills, Jonesboro.
Rockford Mfg. Co., Rockford.

VIRGINIA.
Twine Mill Corpn., Roanoke.
Wortendyke Mfg. Co., Richmond.

WISCONSIN.
Rock River Cotton Co., Janesville.

CANADA

ONTARIO.
Doon Twines, Ltd., Doon.
Hamilton Cotton Co., Hamilton.
Imperial Cotton Co., Hamilton.
Shurley & Derrett, Toronto.

QUEBEC.
Dominion Textile Co., Montreal.

NOVA SCOTIA.
Cosmos Cotton Co., Yarmouth.

NEWFOUNDLAND
Colonial Cordage Co., St. Johns.

 **Structural Paint** For the preservation of structural iron and steel

Leading Twine Manufacturers

JUTE, HEMP, ETC.

CALIFORNIA.
California Cotton Mills Co., Oakland. (Flax and Hemp.)
Tub Cordage Co., San Francisco.

DELAWARE.
Crichton, Alex. F., Wilmington. (Jute.)

GEORGIA.
Fulton Bag and Cotton Mills, Atlanta. (Flax, Jute, Linen and Hemp.)
Trio Mfg. Co., Forsythe.

ILLINOIS.
International Harvester Co., Chicago. (Sisal.)
Peoria Cordage Co., Peoria. (Sisal, Manila, etc.)

INDIANA.
Hoosier Twine Mills, Michigan City. (Sisal.)

KENTUCKY.
Eagle Cordage Mills, Covington. (Jute, Hemp & Flax.)
Kentucky River Mills, Frankfort. (Hemp.)

MASSACHUSETTS.
Smith & Dove Manufacturing Co., Andover. (Flax.)
American Net and Twine Co., East Cambridge. (Linen.)
Finlayson Flax Spinning Co., North Grafton. (Linen, Flax.)
Ludlow Mfg. Associates, Ludlow. (Jute, Flax and Hemp.)
Plymouth Cordage Co., North Plymouth. (Hemp, Manila and Sisal.)

MINNESOTA.
Minnesota States Prison, Stillwater. (Manila and Sisal.)

MISSOURI.
St. Louis Cordage Mills, St. Louis.

NEW JERSEY.
Wall Rope Works, Inc., Beverly. (Manila, Sisal, Russia, Italian and New Zealand.)
Nitram Mfg. Co., East Orange. (Hemp.)
Whitlock Cordage Co., Jersey City.
Shrewsbury Mills, Newark. (Linen, Hemp and Flax.)

NEW JERSEY—Continued.
Barbour Flax Spinning Co., Paterson. (Flax, Linen & Hemp.)
Barbour, J. E., Co., Paterson. (Flax.)
Dolphin Jute Mills, Paterson. (Jute.)
Sutherland & Edwards Co., Paterson. (Jute.)

NEW YORK.
Auburn Converting Co., Auburn. (Linen and Flax.)
Cayuga Linen & Cotton Mills, Auburn. (Linen.)
Columbian Rope Co., Auburn. (Flax, Jute and Hemp.)
International Harvester Co., Auburn. (Manila and Sisal.)
American Mfg. Co., Brooklyn. (Jute, Manila and Sisal.)
Cating Rope Works, Brooklyn. (Flax.)
Chelsea Fibre Mills, Brooklyn. (Jute.)
Cuppler Cordage Co., Brooklyn.
Waterbury Co., Brooklyn. (Sisal.)
Cable Flax Mills, Schaghticoke. (Jute, Hemp, Flax and Linen.)
James Thompson & Co., Valley Falls. (Linen, Flax and Hemp.)

OHIO.
Jacobs Cordage Co., Cincinnati. (Hemp, Jute, Flax, Etc.)
Hooven & Allison Co., Xenia. (Jute, Manila, Hemp and Sisal.)
Kelly Co., R. A. (Sisal), Xenia.

PENNSYLVANIA.
Allentown Spinning Co., Allentown. (Jute.)
Radcliffe & Shaw, Glen Rock. (Jute.)
Hanover Cordage Co., Hanover. (Jute and Hemp.)
John Barrows, Lansdale. (Linen.)
Bailey, J. T., Co., Philadelphia. (Jute.)
C. Moore & Co., Philadelphia. (Linen.)
Morice Twine Mills, Philadelphia. (Jute, Hemp and Flax.)
Schlicter Jute Cordage Co., Philadelphia. (Jute.)
Jackson, Thomas, & Son, Reading. (Manila, Sisal and Jute Cordage, Commercial Twines.)

 **Paint and Chemical Company**
PAPER COLORS AND MILL PAINT SPECIALTIES
BOSTON SPRINGFIELD, MASS. NEW YORK

JUTE, HEMP, ETC.
(CONTINUED.)

SOUTH DAKOTA.
State Penitentiary, Sioux Falls. (Manila and Sisal.)

WISCONSIN.
John Rauschenberger Co., Milwaukee. (Jute, Hemp, Flax and Sisal.)

CANADA

ONTARIO.
Canada Flax Fibre Co., Alma. (Flax.)
Doon Twine, Ltd., Kitchiner. (Flax, Hemp and Jute.)

Independent Cordage Co., Toronto. (Jute, Hemp, Sisal and Manila.)
Shurley & Derrett, Toronto. (Jute, Hemp and Flax.)

NEWFOUNDLAND

Colonial Cordage Co., St. Johns. (Manila, Italian and Russian Hemp and Flax.)

Hampden. Roll Bar White — A lasting tough coating for iron work in beaters and washers

A SELECTED LIST OF
Papeterie Manufacturers

CONNECTICUT.
Taylor-Atkins Paper Co., Burnside.

ILLINOIS.
American Papetrie & Envelope Co., Quincy.

INDIANA.
Mid-West Paper & Envelope Co., Marion.

MASSACHUSETTS.
Colonial Monogram Co., 55 Bedford, Boston.
Ward, Samuel, Mfg. Co., 229 Atlantic av., Boston.
Crane, Z. & W. M., Dalton.
White & Wyckoff Mfg. Co., Holyoke
Highland Mfg. Co., Holyoke.
Whiting & Cook, Inc., Holyoke.
Whiting Paper Co., Holyoke.
Rising, B. D., Paper Co., Housatonic.
Eaton, Crane & Pike Co., Pittsfield.
Hampshire Paper Co., So. Hadley Falls.
Birnie Paper Co., Springfield.
Morgan Envelope Co., Div., Springfield.
Murphy, John A., Co., Springfield.
National Papeterie Co., Springfield.
Powers Paper Co., Springfield.
Whitney Mfg. Co., Worcester.

MICHIGAN.
Kalamazoo Stationery Co., Kalamazoo.
Lee Paper Co., Vicksburg.

MISSOURI.
Western Tablet Co., St. Joseph.

NEW YORK.
American Papeterie Co., Albany.
Bainbridge's, Chas. T. Sons, 2-24 Cumberland, Brooklyn.
Ward Co., Marcus, Pearson and Creek, Long Island City.
Bell Paper Company, 35 6th av., New York.
B. & J. Envelope Co., 547 W. 27th, New York.
Coyle-Gilmore Co., Inc., 122 5th av., New York.
Eaton, Crane & Pike Co., 225 5th av., New York.
Hurd, George B., & Co., 425-427 Broome, New York.
Kent Paper Co., 440 4th av., New York.
Weyand, Charles E., & Co., 22 Howard, New York.
Whiting Paper Co., 7th av. and 14th, New York.
Wynne Paper Co., 318 W. 39th, New York.

PENNSYLVANIA.
Blair Co., J. C., Huntingdon.

WISCONSIN.
Bunde & Upmeyer Co., Milwaukee.

 **Paint and Chemical Company**
PAPER COLORS AND MILL PAINT SPECIALTIES
BOSTON   SPRINGFIELD, MASS.   NEW YORK

OFFICE ADDRESSES
OF
Mills and Mill Supply Houses
IN
A FEW OF THE LEADING CITIES
IN THE
UNITED STATES AND CANADA

CHICAGO

Paper and Pulp Manufacturers.

Alton Box Board & Paper Co., 11 S. La Salle.
American Bread Wrapping Co., 361 E. Ohio.
American Straw Board Co., 122 S. Michigan.
American Tar Products Co., 208 S. La Salle.
American Writing Paper Co., Otis Bldg.
Bedford Pulp & Paper Co., 1701 Fisher Bldg.
Brown Co., 110 S. Dearborn.
Brownville Paper Co., 208 S. La Salle.
Cantine, Martin Co., 208 S. La Salle.
Central Box Board Co., 43d and Racine av.
Central Paper Co., Rookery Bldg.
Central Waxed Paper Co., 5600 Fillmore.
Champion Coated Paper Co., 7 S. Dearborn.
Cheboygan Paper Co., 343 S. Dearborn.
Chicago Coated Board Co., 422 E. N. Water and 1520 Lumber Ex.
Cleveland-Akron Bag Co., 140 S. Dearborn.
Collins, A. M., Mfg. Co., 30 E. Randolph.
CONTINENTAL PAPER BAG CO., 346 N. Ada.
Cornell Wood Products Co., 13 W. Jackson.
Creamery Package Mfg. Co., 61 W. Kinzie.
Crocker-McElwaine Co., 208 S. La Salle.
Crystal Paper Co., 1701 Fisher Bldg.
De Jonge, Louis, Co., 503 S. La Salle.

CHICAGO—Continued.

Diamond State Fibre Co., 1556 Besley ct. G. H. Friend.
Dixie Paper Mills, Inc., 1701 Fisher Bldg.
EASTERN MFG. CO., Conway Bldg.
Eaton-Dikeman Co., 208 S. La Salle.
Fibre Conduit Co., Monadnock Bldg.
Flambeau Paper Co., Conway Bldg.
Ford Mfg. Co., 2339 S. La Salle.
Fort Frances Pulp & Paper Co., Lumber Exch. Bldg.
GILBERT, FRANK, PAPER CO., 208 S. La Salle.
Gilman, I., & Co., 1701 Fisher Bldg.
Gummed Products Co., 892 Rand-McNally Bldg.
Halifax Paper Corporation, 1701 Fisher Bldg.
Hammerschlag Mfg. Co., 8 S. Dearborn.
HAMPDEN GLAZED PAPER & CARD CO., 701 S. La Salle.
HARTFORD CITY PAPER CO., 618 First National Bank Bldg.
Hartje Paper Mfg. Co., 208 S. La Salle.
Hinde & Dauch Paper Co., 826 River.
HOLLINGSWORTH & WHITNEY CO., 111 W. Washington.
IDEAL COATED PAPER CO., 2162 Transportation Bldg.
International Paper Co., Conway bldg.
Island Paper Co., 1701 Fisher Bldg.
KALAMAZOO VEGETABLE PARCHMENT CO., Railway Exch. Bldg.
Kimberly-Clark Co., 208 S. La Salle.
La Monte & Son, Geo., 1st Nat. Bank bldg.
Lee Paper Co., 208 S. La Salle.

Hampden Rubercoat Elastic Carbon Paint
For your leaky gravel, paper, cloth and metal roofs.

Mills and Mill Supply Office Addresses

CHICAGO—*Continued.*

Louisiana Fibre Board Co., 76 W. Monroe.
Marathon Paper Mills Co., Conway Bldg.
Menasha Paper Co., Steger bldg.
Menasha Printing & Carton Co., 1132 Conway Bldg.
Mid-West Box Co., Conway Bldg.
Minnesota & Ontario Paper Co., Lumber Exch. Bldg.
Monadnock Paper Mills, 208 S. La Salle.
Morris Paper Mills, Conway Bldg.
Mountain Mill Paper Co., 208 S. La Salle.
Mullen Bros. Paper Co., 54 W. Kinzle.
NASHUA GUMMED & COATED PAPER CO., Conway Bldg.
National Safety Paper Co., 38 S. Dearborn.
NEW YORK-NEW ENGLAND CO., 208 S. La Salle.
Niagara Bag & Paper Co., 1701 Fisher Bldg.
Niagara Paper Mills, 175 Monroe.
Northern Paper Mills, 10 S. La Salle.
Oglesby Paper Co., 208 S. La Salle.
Penobscott Chemical Fibre Co., 112 West Adams.
Quaker Oats Co., Railway Exchange.
RISING, B. D., PAPER CO., 208 S. La Salle.
River Raisin Paper Co., Marshall Field Annex Bldg.
Sail Mountain Co., 230 S. La Salle.
Schmidt & Ault Paper Co., Conway Bldg.
Southworth Co., 35 S. Wabash.
Springfield Glazed Paper Co., 29 S. La Salle.
STANDARD PAPER BAG CO., 122 S. Michigan.
Tarentum Paper Mills, 1229 S. Wabash av.
United Paper Board Co., 111 W. Monroe.
Watson, H. F., Co., 319 Wells.
WAUSAU SULPHATE FIBRE CO., 1625 Conway Bldg., under direction of Geo. K. Gibson.
WEST VIRGINIA PULP & PAPER CO., 732 Sherman.
WHITING PAPER CO., 318 W. Washington.

BOSTON
Paper and Pulp Manufacturers.

American Photograph Co., 2304 Washington.

BOSTON—*Continued.*

Androscoggin Pulp Co., Agasota Bldg., 683 Atlantic av.
Claremont Paper Co., 299 Congress.
Crehore, C. F., & Son, 87 Milk.
Cushnoc Paper Co., 1148 Old South Bldg.
Dill & Collins Co. (br. of Philadelphia, Pa.), 161 Pearl.
Emerson Paper Co., John Hancock Bldg.
Fort Orange Paper Co., 6 Beacon.
General Fibre Board Co., 27 School.
Great Northern Paper Co., 60 Congress.
Groton Leatherboard Co., 10 State.
Hammerschlag Mfg. Co., 294 Washington.
HARTFORD CITY PAPER CO., 143 Federal.
Herkimer Fibre Co., 51 Lincoln.
HOLLINGSWORTH & VOSE CO., 141 Milk.
HOLLINGSWORTH & WHITNEY CO., 185 Devonshire.
International Paper Co., Inter-Nat'l Trust Co. Bldg., 45 Milk.
Monadnock Paper Mills, 201 Devonshire.
Mt. Holly Paper Co., 17 Tremont.
Mt. Tom Sulphate Co., 50 State.
MUNROE FELT AND PAPER CO., 79 Summer.
Niagara Paper Mills, 140 Federal.
Parker-Young Co., 131 State.
Penobscot Chemical Fibre Co., 49 Federal.
POLAND PAPER CO., 458 Hancock Bldg.
River Raisin Paper Co., 1122 Old Smith Bldg.
Rogens Fibre Co., 121 Beach.
St. Croix Paper Co., Globe Bldg.
Schmidt & Ault Paper Co., 201 Devonshire.
South Coventry Paper Co., 46 South.
Spalding, J., & Son Co., 203 Albany Bldg.
TILESTON & HOLLINGSWORTH CO., 49 Federal.
Warren, S. D., Co., 120 Franklin.
Watson, H. F., Co., 79 Milk.
Westfield River Paper Co., 51 State.
WEST VIRGINIA PULP & PAPER CO., 180 Congress.
Wheelwright, Geo. W., Paper Co., 95 Milk.

Paper Makers' Chemicals and Supplies.

ARNOLD, HOFFMAN & CO., 88 Broad.

 **Paint and Chemical Company**
PAPER COLORS AND MILL PAINT SPECIALTIES
BOSTON SPRINGFIELD, MASS. NEW YORK

Mills and Mill Supply Office Addresses

BOSTON—*Continued.*
Avery Chemical Co., 88 Broad.
Bartow Estate, H. T., Equitable Bldg.
Bird, J. A. & W., 88 Pearl.
Blanchard, J. Henry, 170 Summer.
BROWN, CHAS. D., & CO., INC., 185 Devonshire.
HELLER & MERZ CO., 247 Atlantic av.
International Purchasing Co., 141 Milk.
King, E. & F., & Co., 367 Atlantic av.
KLIPSTEIN, A., & CO., 283 Congress.
Marble, J. Russell, & Co., 75 Pearl.
MERRIMAC CHEMICAL CO., 148 State.
Miles, Geo. W., 88 Broad.
MOREY & CO., INC., 27 Commercial, Cambridge.
Richardson, John, Co., 201 Devonshire.
Train, Smith Co., Equitable Bldg.

NEW YORK
Paper and Pulp Mill Offices.
Abitibi Power & Paper Co., 30 Church.
Aetna Paper Co., 251 W. 92d.
Agasote Mill Board Co., 11 B'way.
ALBEMARLE PAPER MFG. CO., 41 Park row. Oscar Dikeman.
Am. Coating Mills, 501 5th av. Berton C. Hill.
American Paper Co., 26 Cortlandt.
American Straw Board Co., Times Bldg.
American Writing Paper Co., 41 Park row.
Amherst Waxed Paper Mills, Woolworth bldg.
Ancram Paper Mills, 150 W. 22d.
Andrews, John T., & Co., 160 5th av.
Bardeen Paper Co., 501 5th av. Berton C. Hill.
Barrett Mfg. Co., 17 Battery pl.
Bathurst Lumber Co., 30 E. 42d.
Bayless Mfg. Corporation, 527 5th av.
Bedford Pulp & Paper Co., 200 Fifth av.
Bergen Paper Co., 178 South.
Bermingham & Seamon Co., 200 5th av.
Beveridge Paper Co., 299 Broadway. R. G. Benedict.
Bird & Son, Inc., 200 Fifth av.
Canada Paper Co., 52 Vanderbilt av.
Carthage Sulphite Pulp & Paper Co., 132 Nassau.

NEW YORK—*Continued.*
Central Paper Co., 30 E. 42d.
Champion Coated Paper Co., 324 Pearl.
Compagnie de Pulpe de Chicoutimi, 32 Vanderbilt av.
CONTINENTAL PAPER BAG CO., 17 Battery pl.
Cornell Paper Mfg. Co., 131 W. 24th.
Crescent Paper & Machine Co., 41 Park row.
Cushnoc Paper Co., 132 Nassau.
De Grasse Paper Co., 200 5th.
Dexter & Sons, C. H., 132 Nassau.
Diamond Mills Paper Co., 44 Murray.
Diamond State Fibre Co., 41 Park row. Oscar Dikeman.
Dill & Collins Co., 419 Lafayette.
Donnocana Paper Co., Ltd., Concourse Bldg.
Dupont De Nemours, E. I., & Co., 725-727 Broadway.
EASTERN MFG. CO., 501 5th av.
EATON-DIKEMAN CO., 41 Park row.
Emerson Paper Co., 200 Fifth av.
Erving Paper Mills, 501 Fifth av.
FALULAH PAPER CO., Woolworth bldg.
Fibre Conduit Co., 101 Park av.
Field & White Co., 116 Nassau.
Fillmore & Slade, 85 Post av.
Fitzdale Paper Co., 86 Hudson.
Fletcher Paper Co., 5 Beekman.
Fort Miller Pulp & Paper Co., 200 5th av.
Fort Orange Paper Co., 200 5th av.
General Paper Co., 175 Fifth av.
GILBERT, FRANK, Paper Co., 501 Fifth av.
Gilbert Paper Co., 200 5th.
Gould Paper Co., 200 5th av.
Great Northern Paper Co., 30 E. 42d.
Ha! Ha! Bay Sulphite Co., Ltd., 52 Vanderbilt av.
Hadley Paper Corp., Woolworth Bldg.
Hammerschlag Mfg. Co., 234 Greenwich.
HAMMERMILL PAPER CO., 291 Broadway.
HAMPSHIRE PAPER CO., 22 Reade.
HARTFORD CITY PAPER CO., Woolworth Bldg.
Hartje Paper Mfg. Co., Woolworth Bldg.
High Falls Paper Co., 200 5th av.
Hinde & Dauch Paper Co., 100 Hudson.
HOLLINGSWORTH & WHITNEY CO., 299 Broadway.

 **Black Paste** Will not crock in the paper. Strongest, cleanest and most economical.

Mills and Mill Supply Office Addresses

NEW YORK—*Continued.*
HOWARD PAPER CO., 251 W. 92d.
Interlake Pulp & Paper Co., 14 Wall.
International Paper Co., 30 Broad.
Island Paper Co., 132 Nassau.
Japanese Tissue Mills, 233 B'way.
Jessup & Moore Paper Co., 50 E. 42d.
Johns-Manville Co., H. W., Madison av. and 41st.
Kalamazoo Paper Co., 299 B'way. R. G. Benedict.
KALAMAZOO VEGETABLE PARCHMENT CO., 200 Fifth av.
Kenyon Paper Corp., 347 Madison av.
Keyes Products Co., 120 B'way.
Kimberly-Clark Co., 51 Chambers.
La Monte, Geo., & Son, 61 B'way.
Laurentide Co., Ltd., 33 W. 42d.
Lee Paper Co., 299 Broadway. R. G. Benedict.
Lefevre, Edward Y., 52 Vanderbilt av.
Lehigh Paper Mills, 41 Park row.
MacAndrews & Forbes Co., 200 Fifth av.
MacLaren Co., Ltd., 33 W. 42d.
Malone Paper Co., 200 5th av.
Mann, Wm., Co., Inc., 105 Chambers.
Marathon Paper Mills Co., 320 Broadway.
Marcellus Paper Co., 132 Nassau.
Mars Paper Corp., 448 Pearl.
Mattagami Pulp & Paper Co., Ltd., 52 Vanderbilt av.
Menasha Printing & Carton Co., 200 Fifth av.
Midway Pulp & Paper Co., 1737 Grand Central Terminal Bldg.
Mohawk Valley Paper Co., 291 B'way.
Moyer & Pratt, 132 Nassau.
Munising Paper Co., 132 Nassau.
Nashua River Paper Co., Times bldg.
Nashwook Pulp & Paper Co., 200 Fifth av.
Newark Paraffine and Parchment Paper Co., 90 West.
New York and Pennsylvania Co., 200 Fifth av.
Niagara Paper Mills, 72 Duane.
Nixon Paper Co., Martin & Wm. H., 200 5th av.
North American Pulp & Paper Co., 33 W. 42d.
North End Paper Co., 132 Nassau.
NORTHERN PAPER MILLS, 296 B'way.
Odell Mfg. Co., 527 Fifth av.
ORONO PULP AND PAPER CO., 132 Nassau.

NEW YORK—*Continued.*
OXFORD PAPER CO., 200 5th av.
Parker & Son Co., Joseph, 150 Nassau.
Pejepscot Paper Co., 111 Broadway.
Perseverance Paper Mills, Produce Exch. Bldg.
Philadelphia Paper Mfg. Co., 320 Broadway.
Philadelphia Wax Paper Co., 14-16 Waverly pl.
Phoenix Paper Co., Ltd., 200 5th av.
Pioneer Paper Co., 52 Vanderbilt av.
POLAND PAPER CO., 200 Fifth av.
Port Huron Sulphite & Paper Co., 5 Beekman, paper division; 21 E. 40th, pulp division.
Price Bros. & Co., Ltd., 30 W. 42d.
Publisher's Paper Co., World Bldg.
Racquette River Paper Co., Grand Cent. Terml.
Rainbow Paper Mills, 239 B'way.
Rainy River Pulp & Paper Co., 52 B'dway.
River Raisin Paper Co., Woolworth Bldg.
ROBERTSON PAPER CO., 230 West.
Rogers Co., J. & J., 5 Beekman.
Roanoke Fibre Board Co., 174 Fulton.
Ryegate Paper Co., 75 Duane.
St. Croix Pulp & Paper Co., 200 5th av.
St. Regis Paper Co., 200 5th av.
Schmidt & Ault Paper Co., 122 Nassau and 153 Greene.
Smeallie & Vorhees, 1016 Flatiron.
SMITH PAPER CO., 132 Nassau.
Sorg Paper Co., P. A., 132 Nassau.
Southern Paper Co., 5 Beekman and 30 W. 42d.
STANDARD PAPER MFG. CO., 140 Nassau.
Stark Paper Co., 52 Vanderbilt av.
STRATHMORE PAPER CO., 200 5th av.
Taggarts Paper Co., 200 5th av.
Taylor-Atkins Paper Co., 377 B'dway.
TICONDEROGA PULP AND PAPER CO., 200 5th av.
Tidewater Paper Mills Co., 33 W. 42d.
Ulster Tissue Mills, 45 Cedar.
Union Bag and Paper Corp., Woolworth Bldg.
UNION WAXED AND PARCHMENT PAPER CO., 45 Cedar.

 **Paint and Chemical Company**
PAPER COLORS AND MILL PAINT SPECIALTIES
BOSTON　　　SPRINGFIELD, MASS.　　　NEW YORK

Mills and Mill Supply Office Addresses

NEW YORK—Continued.
United Paperboard Co., 171 Madison av.
Vinton, Wm. H., & Son, 439 Lafayette.
Waldhof Sulphite Pulp Co., 5 Beekman.
WANAQUE RIVER PAPER CO., 290 Broadway.
Warren, S. D., Co., 25 Madison av.
Warren Mfg. Co., Woolworth Bldg.
Watervliet Paper Co., 21 Park row.
West End Paper Co., 200 5th av.
WESTFIELD RIVER PAPER CO., Tribune Bldg.
WEST VIRGINIA PULP AND PAPER CO., 200 5th av.
Wheat Paper Co., 501 5th av. Berton C. Hill.
Wheelwright Paper Co., Geo. W., 200 Fifth av.
WHITING PAPER CO., 14th and Seventh av.
Wolverine Paper Co., 501 Fifth av. Berton C. Hill.
Wrenn Paper Co., 54 Franklin.
Wyoming Valley Paper Mill, 61 Beekman.
York Haven Paper Co., 290 Broadway.

Paper Makers' Chemicals and Supplies.
Abenheimer, Louis H., 60 Wall.
American Woodpulp Corp., 347 Madison av.
ANDERSON, J., & CO., 20 E. 40th.
ARABOL MFG. CO., 100 William.
ARNOLD, HOFFMAN & CO., 61 B'way.
ATTERBURY BROS. (Inc.) 145 Nassau.
Atterbury & McKelvey, Inc., 145 Nassau.
Bartow, Theo., & Sons, 33 W. 42d.
Beebe, Chas., 182 Nassau.
Beebe, Ira L., & Co., 132 Nassau.
Berlin Aniline Works, 213 Water.
Blank, Robert, 140 Nassau.
BREDT, F., & CO., 240 Water.
Bush, Beach & Gent, 80 Maiden la.
Butterworth, E., & Co., 132 Nassau.
CABBLE EXCELSIOR WIRE MFG. CO., WM., 88 Ainslie, Bkln.
Casein Mfg. Co., 11 Pine.
Casey, John A., Co., Commerce.
Castle, Gottheil & Overton, 200 5th av.
Chase & Norton, 277 Water.
Columbia Naval Stores Co., 17 Battery pl.
Corn Products Co., 17 Battery pl.
Coulston & Co., J. W., 80 Maiden la.

NEW YORK—Continued.
DARMSTADT, SCOTT & COURTNEY, 178 South.
Domestic Mills Paper Co., 96 Reade.
Duché & Sons, T. M., 376 Greenwich. (Casein.)
Fuerst Bros. & Co., 2 Stone.
Garvan, P., Inc., 200 Fifth av.
General Chemical Co., 25 Broad.
General Naval Stores Co., 90 West.
GOTTESMAN, M., & SON, 18 E. 41st.
Hammill & Gillespie, 240 Front.
HARRISONS, INC., 54 Fulton.
HELLER & MERZ CO., 506 Hudson.
Hewitt, C. B., & Bros., 48 Beekman.
Hicks, Daniel M., Inc., 140 Nassau.
Hilton Trading Co., 120 Liberty.
Hooker Electro Chemical Co., 40 Wall.
Howe, Chas. T., 299 B'dway.
Hudson Trading Co., 18 E. 41st.
Innis, Speiden & Co., 46 Cliff.
International Mill Supply Co., 546 Eastern Parkway, Brooklyn.
INTERNATIONAL PULP CO., 41 Park row.
Kalbfleisch, The, Corp., 31 Union sq.
KLIPSTEIN, A., & CO., 654 Greenwich.
KUTTROFF, PICKHARDT & CO., 126 Duane.
Landau, Marcus, 150 Nassau.
Maier, Marx, 200 5th av.
Main Belting Co., 2 Rector.
Manhattan Rubber Mfg. Co., 120 B'way.
MARQUARDT, F. G., INC., 320 Broadway.
McCoy, Thos. F., 194 Hester.
Moore & Munger, 29 B'dway.
New York Belting and Packing Co., 91 Chambers.
New York Continental Jewell Filtration Co., Flatiron Bldg.
Nilsen, Rantoul & Co., 30 E. 42d.
Non-Antem Sulphite Digester Co., 30 E. 42d.
Oakland Chemical Co., 10 Astor pl.
Parsons & Whittemore, 174 Fulton.
Patton, J. F., & Co., Inc., 33 W. 42d.
Peerless Rubber Mfg. Co., 50 Reade.
PENNSYLVANIA SALT MFG. CO., 41 Park row.
Perkins-Goodwin Co., 33 W. 42d.
Price & Pierce, Ltd., 30 E. 42d.
PULP & PAPER TRADING CO., 21 E. 40th.
Riker, J. L. & D. S., 19 Cedar.
Roessler & Hasslacher Chemical Co., 100 William.

 **Ruling Colors** The best for Ruling Inks.

Mills and Mill Supply Office Addresses

NEW YORK—*Continued.*
SALOMON, A., INC., 15 Park row.
Salomon Bros. & Co., 200 Fifth av.
Salomon, L. A., & Bro., 216 Pearl.
Sergeant, E. M., & Co., 95 Madison av.
Standard Mill Supply Co., 132 Nassau.
Thompson, R. A., & Co., 405 Lexington av.
ULTRAMARINE CO., 88 Park row.
Union Casein Co., B'way and 16th.
UNION SULPHUR CO., 17 Battery pl.
Union Talc Co., 132 Nassau.
United States Talc Co., 41 Park row.
Warehouse Mercantile Co., 24 State.
Wing & Evans, 22 William.

Wood Pulp Importers.
Abenheimer, Louis H., 60 Wall.
American Woodpulp Corp., 347 Madison av.
ANDERSEN, J., & CO., 21 E. 40th.
ATTERBURY BROS., 145 Nassau.
Atterbury & McKelvey, Inc., 145 Nassau.
Bache Trading Co., Inc., 5 Beekman.
Bartow, Theo., & Sons, 33 W. 42d.
Beebe & Co., Ira L., 132 Nassau.
Castle, Gotthell & Overton, 200 5th av.
GOTTESMAN, M., & SON, 18 E. 41st.
Hamilton & Hansell, Inc., 13-21 Park row.
Helwig, Rudolf, 541 Washington.
Hudson Trading Co., 18 E. 41st.
Interstate Pulp & Paper Co., Grand Central Terminal.
Lagerloef Trading Co., 18 E. 41st.
New York Over Sea Co., Inc., 17 Battery.
Nilsen, Rantoul & Co., 30 E. 42d.
Pagel, A. J., & Co., 347 Madison av.
Parsons & Whittemore, 174 Fulton.
Perkins-Goodwin Co., 33 W. 42d.
Price & Peirce, Ltd., 30 E. 42d.
Rantoul, C. W., Co., 30 E. 42d.
Salomon, A., Inc., 15 Park row.
SCANDINAVIAN - AMERICAN TRADING CO., Produce Exchange Bldg.
Slocum, Avram & Slocum Trading Co., 44 Whitehall.
Steffanson & Co., 30 E. 42d.
Stromborg, Oscar, 154 Nassau.
Wood Pulp Trading Co., Ltd., 30 E. 42d.

PHILADELPHIA
Paper and Pulp Manufacturers.
Albany Paper Co., 48 N. Front.
American Writing Paper Co., 506 Bourse.

PHILADELPHIA—*Continued*
Baeder-Adamson & Co., Allegheny av. and Richmond.
Barton-Hobart Paper Co., Land Title Bldg.
Bedford Pulp & Paper Co., 1615 N. American Bldg.
Champion Coated Paper Co., Drexel Bldg.
CHERRY RIVER PAPER CO., Pennsylvania Bldg.
Chester Paper Co., 7th st. and Glenwood av.
Curtis & Bro., Inc., 16 S. Fifth.
Dill & Collins Co., 6th and Cherry.
Endura Mfg. Co., 63d and Eastwick av.
Fort Orange Paper Co., 12th and Chestnut.
Glen Mills Paper Co., 1005 Stephen Girard Bldg.
Hammerschlag Mfg. Co., Widener Bldg.
Hamilton, W. C., & Son, Wm. Penn. P. O., Montgomery County.
Hinde & Dauch Paper Co., 113 Sansom.
Jessup & Moore Paper Co., 16 S. Broad.
Keystone Paper Mills Co., Upper Darby.
Lang Paper Co., John, 24th c. Vine
McDowell Paper Mills, Main, cor. Levering.
McEwan Bros., Orianna and Willow.
Merion Paper Co., Bellevue Ct. Bldg.
Moorhouse, R. T., Paper Co., 2055 Bridge, Bridesburg.
National Metal Edge Box Co., 13th and Callowhill.
Niagara Paper Mills, 18 S. Sixth.
Parsons Pulp and Lumber Co., Financial Bldg.
Philadelphia Paper Mfg. Co., Manayunk.
Philadelphia Wax Paper Co., Chestnut.
Reading Paper Mills, 308 Chestnut.
Scott Paper Co., Chester, Pa.
United Paperboard Co., Bourse Bldg.
Valley Paper Co., Drexel Bldg., 720 Arch.
WEST VIRGINIA PULP & PAPER CO., 804 Sansom.
WHITING PAPER CO., 619 Chestnut.
York Haven Paper Co., 906 Land Title bldg.

 **Paint and Chemical Company**
PAPER COLORS AND MILL PAINT SPECIALTIES
BOSTON   SPRINGFIELD, MASS.   NEW YORK

PAPER and PULP MILL OFFICES in CANADA

TORONTO.

Canada Boxboard Co., Ltd., 32 Front E.
Canada Paper Co., 112 Bay.
Dickinson, John, & Co., 76 Bay.
Don Valley Paper Co., Dominion Bank Bldg.
Eddy, The E. B., Co., Ltd., 73 Wellington, W.
Interlake Tissue Mills, 76 Adelaide, W.
Kinleith Paper Co., 82 Spadina.
Lincoln Paper Mills Co., 112 Bay.
Laurentide Co., Bank of Hamilton Bldg., Yonge.
Mattagami Pulp & Paper Co., 67 Yonge.
Miller Bros. Co., Ltd., 11 Colbourne.
Provincial Paper Mills Co., 76 Adelaide, W.
Riordan Pulp & Paper Co., Ltd., 106 Bay.
Rolland Paper Co., Ltd., 723 Traders' Bank Bldg.
Smith, Howard, Paper Mills, Ltd., 120 Bay.
Toronto Paper Mfg. Co., Mail Bldg., Bay.
Wayagamack Pulp & Paper Co., 19 Melinda.

MONTREAL.

Abitibi Power & Paper Co., Ltd., The, Dominion sq.
Barrett Co., Ltd., 2021 St. Hubert.

MONTREAL—Continued.

Belgo-Canadian Pulp & Paper Co., 51 St. James.
Beveridge Paper Co., Ltd., 17 St. Therese.
Canada Paper Co., Ltd., 70 McGill.
Canada Boxboard Co., Ltd., 182 Shearer.
Dominion Paper Co., 345 St. James.
Eddy, E. B., Co., Ltd., 70 St. Peter.
Howard Smith Paper Mills, Ltd., 138 McGill.
Hughes, Owens Co., Ltd., 237 Notre Dame, W.
Laurentide Co., Ltd., Sun Life Bldg.
McArthur, Alex., & Co., Ltd., 82 McGill.
Miller Bros. Co., Ltd., 38 Dowd.
National Paper Co., Ltd., The, 45 St. Alexander.
News Pulp & Paper Co., Ltd., 273 Craig W.
Provincial Paper Mills, Ltd., 507 McGill Bldg.
Riordon Pulp & Paper Co., 355 Beaver Hall sq.
Rolland Paper Co., Ltd., The, 142 St. Paul, W.
Smith, Howard, Paper Mills, Ltd., 138 McGill.
Walker, J. R., & Co., 35 Common.
Wilson, J. C., Ltd., 61 Alexander.

OTTAWA.

Booth, J. R., 82 Bridge.
Bronson Co., 150 Middle.

PUBLISHED ANNUALLY, 850 PAGES
Price 15/- net, or post free, 15/6 net   Demy 8vo, cloth bound

The Paper Makers' Directory of all Nations

Annuaire de la Papeterie de Toutes les Nations

**ALPHABETICALLY ARRANGED
PRINTED IN CLEAR TYPE**

CONTENTS INCLUDE:

Principal Paper, Pulp and Board Mills, etc., of the World (5,000), arranged alphabetically according to Countries (40). Giving Names, Addresses, Makes of Paper, Number and Width of Machines, Weekly Turnout, Power Used, Telegraphic Addresses, Agents, etc., etc.

Firms Classified in *one list* according to Principal Productions.

Paper Agents and Mill Representatives, with Addresses and Firms Represented.

Exporters of Paper and Wholesale Stationers, and other useful Lists.

Waste Paper, Rag and Paper Stock Dealers.

Enamelers, Varnishers, Surfacers and Stainers of Paper, etc., etc., etc.

China Clay Merchants, Cardboard and Paper Box Manufacturers, Paper Bag Makers, etc.

British Paper Trade Customs, Sizes and Folds of Papers, etc. Also Buyers' Guide.

PUBLISHED BY

DEAN & SON, Ltd.

160a, Fleet Street   LONDON, E. C.

 **Paint and Chemical Company**
PAPER COLORS AND MILL PAINT SPECIALTIES
BOSTON   SPRINGFIELD, MASS.   NEW YORK

A LIST OF
Wholesale & Retail Stationers
TOGETHER WITH BOOKSELLERS AND OTHER MERCHANTS DEALING IN STATIONERY THROUGHOUT THE UNITED STATES, CANADA, CUBA AND THE PHILIPPINES.

☞ Wholesale Stationers marked (*), Commercial Stationers marked (c), Office Supply Dealers marked (o s), Dealers Handling Social Stationery marked (s), Stationers also Selling Books marked (b), Druggists Selling Stationery marked (d), Department Stores Selling Stationery (g), Jewelers Selling Stationery (j), Figures after cities and towns indicate population.

ALABAMA.

ABBEVILLE, 1500.
City Drug Store (d).
Long, J. B. (d).

ALABAMA CITY, 4313.
Cross Drug Co. (d).
Martin Drug Co. (d).

ALBANY, 4437.
People's Drug Co.
Dillehay Bros. (d).
Hildreth, C. J., Co. (o. s.).
Thompson, S. M. (d).
Prewitt & Dillehay (d, b).

ALBERTVILLE, 1544.
City Drug Co. (d).
Graham's Pharmacy.
Marshall Drug Co. (d).

ALEXANDER CITY, 1710.
Coley, L. B. (d).
Lightfoot, R. H. (d).
Christian, T. S. (d).
Carlisle Drug Co. (d).

ANDALUSIA, 2500.
Berman, I.
Brown & Broughton (b, o. s.).
Campbell, T. M., & Co. (o. s.).
Lewis, P. (j).
McEachen & McGowan Drug Co. (o. s.).
Riley, A. M. (b, o. s.).

ANNISTON, 13,686.
Lloyd, W. E. (d).
Montgomery, H. F. (b).
Robinson Book Store.
Scarbrough-Landham Drug Co. (d).
Winkle, J. L., Drug Co. (d).

ATHENS, 1010.
Crutcher Bros. (d).
Gilbert Drug Co. (d).
Limestone Drug Co. (d).
McConnell, R. H., & Son (b).

AUBURN, 1672.
Burton, R. W. (b).
Toomer, S. L. (d).
Wright Bros., Inc. (b).
Wright & Co. (d).

BEATRICE.
Stallworth, W. A., & Son (d).

BESSEMER, 15,360.
Edmundson-Randle Drug Co. (d).
Fulton Bros. Drug Co. (d).
Howard, C. W. (d).
Lewis-Reed Drug Co. (b, d).
Pegram-Patton Drug Co. (d).
Taylor, W. D., & Co. (d).

BIRMINGHAM, 132,685.
Alabama Paper & Printing Co.
Averyt Drug Co. (d).
Bains Drug Co. (d).
Birmingham Office Supply Co.
*Birmingham Paper Co.
Bowen Seating & School Supply Co.
Burchfiel, E. G. (d).
Burris, J. B., & Son (b).
*City Paper Co.
Commercial Ptg. Co.
Dewberry & Montgomery Stationery Co.
Doster-Northington Drug Co. (d).
Drennen Co. Dept. Stores (g).
East Lake Drug Co. (d).
Faulkner, W. H. (post cards).

 **Regal Wall Coating** A white cold water paint. Will not rub, scale or peel off.

Wholesale and Retail Stationers

ALABAMA.

BIRMINGHAM—*Continued.*
Five Points Drug Co. (d).
Jacobs, Eugene, Drug Store.
Kress, S. H., & Co. (g).
Loveman, Joseph, & Loeb (g).
Martin, H. L., & Co. (d).
Office Outfitters' Co., Inc. (o. s.).
Parker, J. L. (d).
Remington Typewriter Co. (c).
Reynolds, J. M. (g).
Richardson Engraving Co. (s).
Roberts & Son, Inc.
*Rogers Stationery Co.
Sadler, J. R. (g).
Smith, Zac, Stationery Co. (c).
Webb Book Co. (b).
Weinstein, Sam (g).
Woolworth & Co., F. W. (g).
Yeilding Bros. Co. (g).

DECATUR, 8114.
Cartwright, O. B. (d).
Decatur Drug Co.
Graves, R. B., & Son (b).
Sterrs, W. E. (d).

DEMOPOLIS, 2417.
Bailey Drug Co. (d).
City Drug Co. (d).
*Mayer Bros. (g).
Simmons-Hobson Drug Co. (d).
Welch, Wm. H. (b).

DOTHAN, 8000.
Brown's Drug Store (d).
Cash Drug Store (d).
Dixie Drug Co.
Ellison Drug Co.
McCallum, N. H. (d).
Strickland Jewelry Co. (j).

ENSLEY, 9000.
Linwood Drug Co. (d).

ENTERPRISE, 3128.
Enterprise Drug Co.
Laney-Warren Drug Co.
Martin, R. B. (d).

EUFAULA, 4532.
Eufaula Drug Co.
Hill & Britt (d).
Schaub, Julius D., & Co. (b).

EUTAW, 1001.
Eatman Drug Co. (d).
Hafner, T. T.
Murphy Drug Co.
Grubbs, J. V. (j).

EVERGREEN, 2000.
City Drug Store.
Evergreen Pharmacy (d).
People's Drug Co. (d).
Powell & Son.

FLORALA, 2000.
Brown Drug Store (d).
Florala Pharmacy.

FLORENCE, 6689.
Cromwell, W. H. (d).
Milner, Joseph, & Sons (d).
Sommer, J. W. (j).
Southall, C. M. (d).
Stutts Drug Co.
Sullivan, C. A. (d).

GADSDEN, 10,557.
Bellinger, W. A. (d).
Cottle, F. M. (d).
Cross, C. F., & Bro. (j).
Cross, E. H. (d).
Journal Publishing Co.
Kress & Co., S. H. (g).
Vance Drug Co. (d).
Whorton Drug Co. (d).
Wright Ten Cent Store (g).

GREENSBORO, 2048.
Apsey & Co. (b and j).
Greensboro Drug Co.
Jay, L. W. (d).

GREENVILLE, 3162.
Dunklin-Blackwell Drug Co. (d).
Greenville Book & Stationery Co. (b, c).
C. B. Herbert & Son (d).
Herlong & Barnes (d).
T. W. Peagler (d).
Stewart Drug Co. (d).

HUNTSVILLE, 7611.
Anderson, C. C. (d).
Gilbert, T. H. (d).
Humphrey & Son, J. D. (d).
Karthaus's, Ernest, Sons (j).
Monroe Ptg. Co. Printing.
Typewriters (o. s.).
Murray, M. R. (g, b).
Terry Bros. (g).
Young, Ben Lee (d).

MARION, 2000.
Brannon Drug Co.
Marion Pharmacy (d).
Mickleboro, J. C. (j).
Shivers, W. O., & Co. (d).

 **Paint and Chemical Company**
PAPER COLORS AND MILL PAINT SPECIALTIES
BOSTON   SPRINGFIELD, MASS.   NEW YORK

Wholesale and Retail Stationers 457

ALABAMA.

MOBILE, 51,521.
Akridge, T. E. (d).
Albright & Woods (d).
Alexander Bloch Dry Goods Co. (g).
Bauer, David S. (d).
Bidgood Stationery Co. (o. s.).
Bienville Pharmacy.
Braswell, R. L. (d).
Burke, C., Co., Cigars and Tobacco.
Burkett, C. H. (d).
Central Pharmacy.
Emerald Co. (j).
Fisch, Theodore (b).
Hammel, L., Dry Goods Co.
*Mobile Drug Co. (d).
*Mobile Stationery Co. (o. s.).
Neville, John.
Pollock Dry Goods Co.
Sherman Stationery Co. (o. s.).
Van Antwerp Drug Corp. (d).

MONTGOMERY, 45,000.
Brown Printing Co.
Burkes, John D. (d).
Dixie Printing Co. (c).
*Fowler Co., Ed. C. (b).
Leonard Fitzpatrick & Mueller (g).
McGehees Bros. (d).
*Mercantile Paper Co. (b, c, o. s.).
Montgomery Fair (g).
Moore, J. J. (d).
Paragon Press.
Peagler, Geo. W. (d).
Wilson Printing Co. (c).

OPELIKA, 4245.
Austin, J. P.
City Drug Store.
Collier, A. P. (d).
Darden Drug Store.
Haynie, J. K. (d).
Hamilton-Brown Co. (d).
Thomason, J. H. (d).
Willingham-Homer Drug Co. (d).

OXFORD, 1090.
Privett, J. B., & Co. (d).

POLLAND, 700.
Scroggins, R. H. (d).

PRATT CITY, 3485.
Cale Drug Co. (d).
Garlington's Pharmacy.
Lacey Hardware Co.
Owen Drug Co. (d).

SELMA, 13,649.
*Atkins, V. B., Grocery & Commission Co.
Butler, Walter S. (g, o. s.).
Cawthon-Coleman Co. (d).
Harrell Drug Co. (d).
Kyser & Cammack (d).
*Selma Stationery Co. (b, o. s.).
Snider Drug Co. (d).
*Southern Clothing & Notion Co.
Swift, Geo. A. (d).

SHEFFIELD, 3333.
Blalock, J. B. (d).
Buller, R. W. (d).
Sheffield Drug Co.
Wohl, Dave (g).

TALLADEGA, 5854.
Henderson, S. H. (d).
Joiner Drug Co. (d).
Owl Drug Co. (d).

TROY, 4961.
Crouch, Arthur (d).
Dixie Central Co.
McLeod, Herbert, Pharmacy (d).
Sanders, J. M. (b).
Troy Book and Stationery Co.
Troy Drug Co. (d).
Williams, Sam A. (d).

TUSCALOOSA, 9817.
Bingham Drug Co. (s).
Central Drug Co. (s).
Cooper Drug Co.
Davis-Leach Drug Co.
Davis, Luther (d, c).
Faucett Drug Co.
Kress & Co., S. H.
Lustig's Book Store.
People's Drug Co.
Red Pharmacy.
Southside Drug Co.
Taylor, T. R. (d).
Tuscaloosa Drug Co.
Ward Drug Co. (d).
Woolworth, F. W., & Co.
Wright, G. B. (s).

TUSCUMBIA, 2248.
Cromwell Pharmacy.
Globe Drug Co. (d).
Hill & Young.
Hyde, R. E. (d).
Kohn, A. (g).
People's Drug Store.

UNION SPRINGS, 3500.
Allen, A. G. (d).
City Drug Store.
Franklin Drug Store.

 **Pulp Colors** For paper staining, surface coating and printing.

Wholesale and Retail Stationers

ALABAMA.

UNION SPRINGS—*Continued.*
 Hayes, H. H. (d).
 Lamars Pharmacy.
 Ravenscroft Drug Co. (d, b).
 Rosenstihl, Henry J. (j).

UNIONTOWN, 1600.
 City Drug Store.
 Uniontown Drug Co. (d).

WEST BLOCTON, 982.
 Davis, J. B.
 Harvey-Wright Drug Co.
 Pope, M. F. (d).

WETUMPKA, 1200.
 Cain Sedberry Drug Co.
 Robison, George D.

ALASKA.

CORDOVA, 1779.
 Cordova Drug Store.
 Northern Drug Store.
 Rosswog, Chas. M.

DOUGLAS, 1800.
 Guys Drug Store.
 Smith, E. E. (d).

FAIRBANKS, 7675.
 Dunham & Clark (d).
 McIntosh & Kuboy.

JUNEAU, 5854.
 Britt, Wm. (d).
 Butler Mauro Drug Co.
 Cartright, C. E. (b).
 Nelson, R. P. (b).

KETCHIKAN, 3520.
 Heckman, J. R., & Co.
 Hunt, F. J.
 Ketchikan Drug Co.
 Ryus Drug & Jewelry Co.
 Tongass Trading Co.

NOME, 1500.
 Lomen Bros. (b, d).

SKAGWAY, 1980.
 Britt, William E. (b, d).
 Harrison, L. A. (g).
 Keller Bros. (d).
 Richter, E. H., & Co.

VALDEZ, 4815.
 Blum, S., & Co., Inc.
 Valdez Drug Co. (d).

ARIZONA.

BISBEE, 15,000.
 Ball, James M. (d).
 Bisbee Drug Co. (d).
 Central Pharmacy (d).
 Phelps, Dodge, Merc. Co. (g).

DOUGLAS, 7000.
 Arizona Drug Co.
 Douglas Drug Co. (d).
 Ferguson Drug Co.
 Owl Drug Co.
 Phelps, Dodge Mercantile Co. (g).

FLAGSTAFF, 2000.
 J. C. Brown.

GLOBE, 8500.
 Ryan & Co. (d).
 Van Wagenen, G. S., & Co. (b).

JEROME, 2861.
 Carroll, E. W.
 Jerome Drug Co. (d, b).
 Meyers Drug Co. (d).

NOGALES, 4000.
 Almada Staty. Co.
 Escabosa Staty. Co.

PHOENIX, 18,000.
 Adams Pharmacy (d).
 Bear Drug Co. (d).
 Berryhill Co., The (b, o. s.).
 Bower Co.
 Busy Drug Store (d).
 Capital Drug Co. (d).
 Five Points Drug Co. (d).
 Hunter Drug Co. (d).
 Miller Sterling Co. (b).
 *McNeil Co., The (b, o. s.).
 Sun Drug Co. (d).

PRESCOTT.
 Acker's Book Store (b, c, s).
 Bashford-Burmister Co. (g).
 Brisley Drug Co. (d).
 Heil, Jr., Fred J. (d).
 Owl City Drug & Candy Co. (d).
 Robinson, A. W.
 Timmerhoff, W. H. (d).

SAFFORD, 2000.
 Best Drug Store (d).
 Cooper's Pharmacy (d).
 Safford Drug Co. (d, b).

 **Paint and Chemical Company**
PAPER COLORS AND MILL PAINT SPECIALTIES
BOSTON   SPRINGFIELD, MASS.   NEW YORK

Wholesale and Retail Stationers

ARIZONA.

TUCSON, 13,193.
Bell Drug Co.
Jacobs, J. M., & Son.
*Kimball, F. E. A. (b, o. s.).
Litt, J. Ed.
Martin Drug Co.
*Moore & O'Neall (b, o. s.).
Owl Drug Co.
*Steinfeld, A., & Co. (g).
WINSLOW.
Kelly Drug Co. (d).
Neithammer, T.
Winslow Drug Co. (d).

YUMA, 4000.
Brownstetter, H. (g).
Caruthers Commercial Co., E. G. (g).
Elliott, F. E. (g).
Kirkpatrick, E. S.
McCutcheon & Bailey (d).
Owl Drug Co. (d).
Sanguinetti, E. F., Co.
Shorey, W. H. (d).
Smith, J. H. (d).

ARKANSAS.

ARGENTA, 11,138.
Miller, H. J. (b).

ARKADELPHIA, 2744.
Clark, Sloan & Co. (d).
Heard-Townsend Drug Co. (d).
Thomas, E. W. (d).

BATESVILLE, 3500.
Casey Drug Co. (d).
Goodwin, E. R., Est. of (d).
*Hail Dry Goods Co. (g).
Hail, S. A., & Sons (g, b).
Terry Drug Co. (d).

BENTON, 2709.
Bush Drug & Jewelry Co. (j).
Steed-Searcy Drug Co. (d).
Stinson, E. Y. (j).

BLYTHEVILLE, 3849.
Elkins-Hicks (b, d, s).
Jackson Drug Store (d).
Levy, B. H. (d).
Parkhurst & Crockett (b, c, s).
Robinson Drug Store (d).

CAMDEN, 3995.
Levy, A. (d).
Morgan, A. L. (d).
Stinson & Berg (j, b).
Usrey, J. C. (d).

CLARENDON, 3500.
Bateman & Franklin (d).
Everett, W. E.
Foster, Thomas, Drug Co. (d).

CLARKSVILLE, 2500.
Clarksville Book Co. (b).
Palace Drug Store (d).

CONWAY, 3500.
Anderson, S. E. (b, o. s.).
Florence Drug Co. (d).
Greesan Drug Co. (d).
Terry Drug Co. (d).

DE QUEEN, 3000.
Brooke, B. (d).
Huskins Drug Co.
Leslie, R. E. (b).

EARLE, 3000.
Crittenden Drug Co. (d).

EUREKA SPRINGS, 3228.
Hawley & Co. (a, c).
McLaughlin, T. S. (s).
Morris Pharmacy.
Pendergrass, H. T. (s).

FAYETTEVILLE, 4471.
Buck's Drug Store.
Frisco Drug Store.
Hollve Novelty Co. (s, o. s.).
McAdams, A. C. (d, b).
Red Cross Drug Store.

FORREST CITY, 3484.
Landvolgt & Vadakin.

FORT SMITH, 23,975.
Berry-Beall Dry Goods Co. (g).
Boston Store Dry Goods Co. (g).
Caldwell, W. O. (d).
Carnahan Drug Co. (d).
Catrom & Godt (d).
Crescent Drug Store (d).
Davis Drug Co. (d).
Friend, Jos. (d).
*Morris-Morton Drug Co. (d).
Morrow, A. H. (b).
Palace Drug Co. (d).
Pape, W. B. (b).
Schaap, John, & Sons (d).
Sterling Drug Store (d).

 **Mill White** Will not turn yellow like the ordinary White Lead paint.

Wholesale and Retail Stationers

ARKANSAS.

HAMBURG, 2500.
Baird, S. L. (b).
Hamburg Drug Co.

HARRISBURG, 942.
Brown Drug Co.
Harrisburg Drug Co. (d).

HARTFORD, 2500.
Jones Drug Co. (d).

HELENA, 12,500.
Beilenson, J. (j).
Blackwood, H. S.
Cottem's, A.
Mevan-King Drug Co.
McRee's Model Pharmacy.
Nicholls, The, Ptg. Co.
Palace Drug Store

HOPE, 5000.
Briant, P. E. (d).
Crosnoe & Cox (d).
Gibson, John S., Drug Co.
Jack's News Stand (b).
Ward & Key (d).

HOT SPRINGS, 14,434.
Angle, J. W. (d).
Foley, D. J. (b).
Lower, R. H. (d).
Merrett Biggs.
*Morris Drug Co., R. G. (d).
Schneck Drug Co.
Steigler Bros. (b, o. s.).
Taylor Drug Co. (d).
*Weaver, C. H. (b, s, o. s.).
Wyatt, L. E. (b, s, o. s.).

JONESBORO, 7123.
Bell Pharmacy, The (d).
Central Drug Co. (d).
Chapin, C. J. (d).
City Drug Store (d).
Clapp, W. P. (d).
Globe Drug Store (d).
Kehl, B. T.
*Nash Bros. Drug Co.
Reid's Drug Store (d).
Royal Pharmacy (b).
Tatum, A. J. (d).

LITTLE ROCK, 45,941.
*Allsopp & Chapple (b).
Bond, Jno. B. (d).
*Democrat Prtg. & Litho. Co.
Jungkind Photo Supply Co.
Lincoln Co., The C. J. (d).
Parkin & Longley Co.
Pfeifer, Albert, & Co. (j).
Stifft, C. S.

MARIANNA, 5000.
Daggett, M. D. (d).
Harrington Bros. (d).
Turner, P. R., Drug Co. (d).

MENA, 5117.
Nall, C. B. (b).

MORRILLTON, 3500.
Humphrey, C. J. (d).
Irving Bros. (g).
Presley, W. L., & Co. (d).
Witt, P. E. (d).

NEWPORT, 4000.
Price, I. D. (b).

OSCEOLA, 1769.
Gaylord, C. H. (d).
Mitchell & Co., J. B. (d).

PARAGOULD, 5248.
City Drug Co.
Fisher Drug Co. (d).
Hardesty & Lackey.
Herrick Jewelry Co. (j).
Inman Drug Co. (d).
Thompson Drug Co. (d).

PINE BLUFF, 15,102.
Babbitt & Dancy.
Brasher Drug Co. (d).
Central Pharmacy (d).
*Dewoody, W. L., & Co. (b, d).
McCammson, Dr. & Son (d).
Mann's Pharmacy (d).
Mann-Tankersley Drug Co.
Mills, D. L. (d).
Pines Drug Store (d).
Rosenberg, S. A. (b).

ROGERS, 4000.
Applegate, J. E. (b, d, o. s.).
Daniels, A. S., & Co.
McGill Drug Co.
McHenry Drug Co. (d).
McNeil Pharmacy (d).
Morgan, T. P. (b).
Palace Drug Co. (d).

RUSSELLVILLE, 4000.
Hood, Louis (d).
Jenkins, R. L. (d).
Wilson, R. J., & Sons (b).

SEARCY, 2000.
Baugh, W. L. (d).
Headlee Drug Co. (d).
Kimbrough Book Store.
Robertson, P. A. (d).
Snipes, Emmett (d).

 **Paint and Chemical Company**
PAPER COLORS AND MILL PAINT SPECIALTIES
BOSTON   SPRINGFIELD, MASS.   NEW YORK

Wholesale and Retail Stationers

ARKANSAS.

SPRINGDALE, 3000.
Ownbey, W. G., Drug Co. (d).
Joyce Drug Co. (d).

STUTTGART, 4000.
Crowe Drug Co. (d).
Morphew, L. H., & Co. (d).
Webb & Son (d).
Williams Bargain Store.

TEXARKANA, 5655.
Phelps Hooks Drug Co. (d).

TEXARKANA—Continued.
Presbyterian Committee of Publication (o. s.).
Prince, C. N.
*Ragland, J. S. (b, o. s.).
Smith Drug Co.
Vincent Drug Co. (d).
Williams & Williams Drug Co. (d).

WALDRON.
Pinnell, E. E., Jlry. & Staty.

CALIFORNIA.

ALAMEDA, 26,320.
Anderson Bros. (g).
Hartley, Jessie M. (b).
Hoeck, F. P. (b).
Horst, W. (b).
James, Miss Margaret (b).
Muhlhausen, Fred (b).
Riley, Carrie L. (d).
Rountree & Co. (b).
Schneider, H. (b).

ANAHEIM, 5000.
Anaheim Music and Novelty Co.
Efker, H. J.
Heying, A. H. (d).
Mullinix, O. A. (d).
Myers, Wm. P. (b).
Weber, L. B. (b).

ARCATA, 1121.
A. Brisard, Inc. (g).
Hub, The.
Keller, Wm. (d).
Skinner-Duprey Drug Co. (d).
Smith, Miss M. M. (b).

AUBURN, 2376.
Gibson, J. T. (d).
Grannell, E. W. (d).
Perry, Frank (b, o. s.).
Stevens, H. C. —
Stevens, Fred (d).

BAKERSFIELD, 15,538.
Bakersfield Drug Co. (d).
Bakersfield News Co.
Cohen, A.
Gardner, L. Alois.
Globe Drug Store.
McDonald, Ronald.
Tailor's Bargain Store (g).

BENICIA, 2816.
Chisholm, J. R.
Harvey, Geo. C. (d, b).

BENICIA—Continued.
Hoffman, F. A. (d).
McConlogue, J. J. (b).
Pine, A. J.

BERKELEY, 60,000.
Arrasmith, C. C. (b).
Bonham & Bonham.
Bowman Drug Co. (d).
Breck, P. S. (b).
Caldecott, T. E. (d).
Crew, J. S., Jr. (b).
Crist, Clara.
Crowe, Wm.
Crowl, M. C.
Glessner, Morse & Geary, Inc.
Gluckman, Mrs. Fanny.
Hill, Jas. F.
Hink, J. F., & Son (g).
Knox, J. T. (b).
Levinson, Samuel.
Nolle, Henry (b).
Perrin, Miss R. M. (b).
Pierce, Edward H. (b).
Radston, Inc. (b, o. s.).
Sadler, Frank E. (o. s.).
Saylor Drug Co. (d).
Schlueter, A., & Co. (g).
Stock, Mrs. L. A.
Wightman, R. S. (b).
Wood, John R. (b).

BISHOP.
Bernard, C. W.

BURLINGAME.
Regan, Harry W.

CALEXICO, 800.
Calexico Stationery Co.

CALISTOGA, 751.
Armstrong, C. W. (d).
Hoover, C. M.
Hopkins, Peter, Jr.

Canary Yellow — A true color. Makes bright tints and solid finishes.

Wholesale and Retail Stationers

CALIFORNIA.

CENTERVILLE, 1000.
Hawes, F. T.

CHICO, 3750.
Auldt, Thos. Stationery & Art Store (c, s, o. s.).
Bartletts Drug Store.
Chico Book Store (b, o. s.).
Hastings, Ben. (d).
Lee Pharmacy.
Waterland, G. F. (b).

CLAREMONT, 1300.
Duvall, O. H.

COALINGA, 4300.
Ayers, E. N. (d).
May, A. P. (g).
McIntyre, J. M. (j).
Stepp, L. S. (g).

COLTON, 5000.
Cochran, C. H.
Riley, R. L. (d).
Wood Bros.

COLUSA, 1700.
Baum & Minasian (j).
Burrows, Miss Fannie.
Cajacob, J. R. (d).
Finch, Geo.
Pryor, Bennett A.

CORNING, 2100.
Lyon, G. W.
Thompson Drug Store.

CORONA, 3540.
Billings, R. S., Est. (d).
Corona Variety Store.
Crown City Drug Co.
Murray, F. W. (d).

CROCKETT, 1800.
Crockett Drug Co.
Davis Bros. (g).
Hedemark, D. C.
Paul, A. A. (d).

DUNSMUIR, 2000.
Du Bose & Kilborn.

EL CENTRO, 6300.
Davis, John E. (d).
Durham, Albert (c, b. s.).
Greenleaf & Clement (d).
McColloch Drug Co. (d).
Office Supply Co., (c, b).
Valley Drug Co. (d).
Valley School Supply Co. (c, b, o. s.).

ESCONDIDO, 1800.
Fream, Beecher (d, j).
Marikle, J. C. (b).
Rolfes, Herman (d).
Young, C. D. (b).

EUREKA, 3768.
Atkinson & Woods.
Fitzell, C. R. (d).
Lincoln, C. O., & Co. (b).
Mathews, J. E.
Moll, F. O. (b).
Schnier, J. V. (d).
Skinner-Duprey Drug Co. (d).
Speegle, W. N.

FAIRFIELD, 834.
Hunter, Walter M.

FERNDALE, 905.
Alford, W. B. (d).
Ring, J. H. (d).
Mills, Mrs. Mildred.

FORTUNA, 883.
Bowman's Drug Store (d).
Evèrs, Charles F.

FRESNO, 29,809.
Bowman Drug Co. (d, s).
Cearley, C. T. (b, o. s.).
Einstein's, Inc. (g).
Eshelman, Effie M.
Forsyth Stationery Co.
Gottschalk, E., & Co., (Inc.) (g).
Kutner-Goldstein Co. (g).
Reige, C. H., Co. (b, o. s.).
Staples, Clarence H. (b, o. s.).
*Valley Paper Co.
*Zellerbach Paper Co.

FULLERTON, 1725.
Giles, Chas. A.
Volkers, H. A.

GILROY, 2437.
Gilroy Book Store.
Hollingsworth Music & Variety Store.
Johnson, E. F. (d).
Meyer & Castleman.
Wentz, Geo. A.

GLENDALE, 2746.
Bott, C. H. (b).
Guernsey, Frank H.
Spencer, O. (b).

GONZALES, 1000.
Sarmento, Agnes.

 **Paint and Chemical Company**
PAPER COLORS AND MILL PAINT SPECIALTIES
BOSTON　　　SPRINGFIELD, MASS.　　　NEW YORK

Wholesale and Retail Stationers

CALIFORNIA.

GRASS VALLEY, 5000.
    Knapp, O. R. (d).
    Lindstrom, O. (b).
    Loutzenheiser, John G. (d).
    Phillips, T. T., Est. of (d).
    Sampson, Wm. (b).
    Stevens, Charles (d).
    Tresize Bros. (b).

GUERNEVILLE, 633.
    Cobb & Co., O. O. (g).

HANFORD, 5116.
    Childs, A. W.
    James, W. D. (j).
    Manning, Thos.

HAYWARDS, 2800.
    Allen, Charles.
    Carren, J. T. (b).
    Reid, R. (d).
    Gray, N. (d).
    Rodgers, R. (d).

HOLLISTER, 4500.
    Shaw, Leslie W.
    Williamson Stationery Co. (b).

HOLLYWOOD, 15,000.
    Leonard, F. G. (b).
    Hollywood Citizen (c, s).
    Wagner, D. W.

HOLTVILLE, 1900.
    Baker, John B.

JACKSON, 2500.
    Datson, Jos.
    Rubser, F. W. (d).

LEMOORE, 1000.
    Brownstone, Al. (b, d).
    Howells, M. (g).
    McKay, Albert S. (d).
    Sanborn, W. H. (g).
    Scalley, W. L. (g).
    Stepp, L. S., Inc. (g).
    Wilson, W. M. (b).

LIVERMORE, 2030.
    Lawless, E. J.
    McKown & Mess (b, d).

LODI, 2697.
    Robinson, H. E. (g).
    Siegfried, F. S. (b).

LONG BEACH, 40,000.
    Abrams, E. D.
    Hewitts Book Store.
    Lord, C. C., & Co.
    Mercantile Co. (g).

LONG BEACH—*Continued*.
    McCutchen & Jutson (b).
    Schinnerer, F. J., & Co.
    Wall Co. (g).

LOS ANGELES, 488,914.
    Adams, O. M.
    Apell, A. A.
    Barker Bros. (g).
    *Blake, Moffitt & Towne.
    Bluemel, Emil H., Co.
    Boswell & Noyes Drug Co. (d).
    Boyarsky, Joseph.
    Broadway Dept. Store (g).
    Brock & Co. (j).
    *Brunswick Drug Co., Inc. (d).
    Bullock Dept. Store (g).
    California Art Photo Co.
    Chambers Drug Co. (d).
    *Cahen-Strodthoff Co.
    Co-operative Sales Co.
    *Cunningham, Curtiss & Welch Co. (o, s).
    Davis, A.
    Duncan Vail Co. (o, s).
    Fowler Bros. (b).
    Fusenot Co., A. (g).
    Gibbes, J. A.
    *Grimes-Stassforth Stationery Co. (o, s).
    Holmes Book Co.
    Jones Book Store (Inc.)
    Kingsley, Mason & Collins Co.
    Lehman, Mrs. John A.
    Limae, G. C.
    Little Co., A. E.
    *Los Angeles News Co.
    Los Angeles Stationery Co.
    McKee, W. E., Printing & Staty. Co.
    Mercer, John D.
    Montgomery Bros. (j).
    Neuner Co.
    Nordlinger & Son, S. (j).
    Owl Drug Co.
    Robinson, J. W., Co. (g).
    Sackin, F. J.
    Salewski, Gus.
    Sawa, K.—
    Stratford & Green (b).
    Sun Drug Co. (d).
    Sutton, M.
    University Book Store.
    Webb, James Co.
    Webb, Torrey.
    Western Book & Stationery Co.
    Western Cabinet Co.
    West Coast Stationery & Ptg. Co.

 **Permanent Reds** LIGHT ALKALI WATER } PROOF

Wholesale and Retail Stationers

CALIFORNIA.

LOS ANGELES—Continued.
  Westlake Pharmacy (d).
  Wolcott, N. A., & Co.
  "Wolcott's," Inc.
  Woolworth Co., F. W.
  *Zellerbach Paper Co.

LOS BANOS.
  Place, J. E.
  Thicercof, E. W. (d).

LOS GATOS, 2232.
  Crall Co., H. J. (b).
  Green, Geo. A. (d).
  Rasmussen, Geo. P.
  Wulzen's Pharmacy (d).

MADERA, 2404.
  Hill, G. E. (j).
  Hunter, W. W. W. (d).
  Madera Drug Co.
  Preciado, C. F., Co.
  Rosenthal-Kutner Co. (g).

MARTINEZ, 2115.
  Contra Costa Drug Co.
  Martinez Drug Co.
  Reed, W. G.

MARYSVILLE, 5430.
  Bluett, J. C.
  Hall, G. W.

MERCED, 3102.
  Baer Drug Co.
  Cody, A. N. L.
  Farrar, J. W.
  Landram, Jno. Wm.
  Leake, Amelia, Miss (b).

MODESTO, 6327.
  Book Shop, The (b).
  Husband, J. W. (d).
  Morris, L. M., Co.

MONROVIA, 5000.
  Jewell, James H. (b).
  Levy, I. (b).
  Monrovia Book & Music Co.
  Neville, T. (d).

MONTEREY, 4923.
  Duckworth, J. E.

NAPA, 5791.
  Haas, Morrison M.
  Haas Stationery Co. (b, o. s.).
  Levinson, Joseph (d).

NEVADA CITY, 2689.
  Bennetts, R. J. (d).
  Dailey, D. A.
  Dickerman, H. (d).

NILES, 1500.
  Sneden, M. B.

OAKDALE, 1035.
  Byington, C. U.
  Hubbell, Clarence F.

OAKLAND, 183,002.
  *Barber, Edgar H., Co. (s, o. s.).
  Bercovich, Wm.
  Blake, Lillian.
  Bowman Drug Co.
  Capwell, H. C., & Co. (g).
  Coggins, H. S.
  Cooper & Co.
  Fuchiwake, I.
  Gard, H. N., & Co.
  Hardy's Book Store (b, o. s.).
  Hazelwood, P. J. (b).
  Holst, Mrs. A. L.
  Kahn Bros. (g).
  Leber, A. L. (d).
  Oakland High School Stationery Store.
  Osgood Bros. (d).
  Owl Drug Co., The (d).
  Schlueter, A., & Co. (b).
  Schmulawitz, Henry.
  Smith Bros., Inc. (o. s.).
  Taft & Penmoyer (g).
  Taylor, Ed. P. (b).
  Thompson, E. W.
  Tobriner, I. (d).
  Trenchard, Ida M.

OCEANSIDE, 850.
  Exton & Nicholas (d).
  McKay, Geo. P.

ONTARIO, 7500.
  Fredericksen, L. C. (b).
  Gilliland's Drug Store (d).
  Kendrick Drug Co. (d).

ORANGE, 2920.
  Dittmer, A., Co. (d).
  Orange Book Store (b).
  Spray Book Store (b).
  Watson, K. E., Co. (d).

ORLAND, 876.
  Green, T. J. (j).

OROVILLE, 3859.
  Bowers, J. H.
  Kusel, Carl E.

OXNARD, 2490.
  Poggi, I. M. (d).

 **Paint and Chemical Company**
PAPER COLORS AND MILL PAINT SPECIALTIES
BOSTON　　　　SPRINGFIELD, MASS.　　　　NEW YORK

Wholesale and Retail Stationers

CALIFORNIA.

PACIFIC GROVE, 2384.
　Beardsley, D. R. (b).
　Moyes, C. J.

PALO ALTO, 4486.
　Congdon & Crome.
　Hyde, E. L.
　Woerner, Chas. H. (b).

PASADENA, 42,000.
　Brown, H. F. (b, o. s.).
　Hall, Herbert J., Co. (j).
　Jarvis & Prinz (b, o. s.).
　Mather, T. W., Co. (g).
　Modern Pharmacy (d).
　Owl Drug Co. (d).
　Pasadena Staty. & Ptg. Co., Inc.
　Ryan, F. A., & Co.
　Sun Drug Co. (d).
　Taber's Pharmacy (d).
　Vroman, A. C., Inc. (b, o. s.).
　Webb, H. H. (d).

PASO ROBLES, 1740.
　Tolle, Mrs. Sarah A.
　Waite, D.

PETALUMA, 6080.
　Ayers & McAskell (b).
　Clark Drug Co. (d).
　Herald Drug Co. (d).
　Nelson, Harvey E. (b).
　Otte & Veale (b).
　Schoneigh, Jos. (b).

PLACERVILLE, 1914.
　Duffey & Reeg.

POINT ARENA, 497.
　Halliday, J. C., & Son.
　Lobree, Phil. (g).
　Point Arena Mercantile Co.
　Scott, M. S.
　Vallandigham, Miss May L.

POMONA, 12,202.
　Afflerbaugh & Edigner (d).
　Armour, E. E. (d).
　Ayres, R. O.
　Blackmore Pharmacy.
　Campbell & Pierce (d).
　Collings, I. W.
　Hufford, W. S. (d).
　Leader Department Store (g).
　Liddle's Book & Stationery Store (o. s.).
　Ludden, J. A. (d).
　McKendrick Bros. (b).

PORTERSVILLE, 4000.
　James, E. W.

RANDSBURG, 600.
　Gunderson, Daniel.

RED BLUFF, 3530.
　Bradley, J. H.
　Brooks, P. I. (d).
　Red Bluff Drug Store (d).
　Wolf & Snowdem (d).

REDDING, 3572.
　Eaton, J. P., Co. (d, b).
　Powell, W. C. (d).

REDLANDS, 12,856.
　Arthur, J. F.
　Dunn, A. P. (b).
　Redlands Book & Stationery Co. (b).
　Smith, Sydney T. (b).
　Tucker Book and Staty. Co. (b).

REDONDO BEACH, 2935.
　Erickson, J. P. (b).

REEDLEY, 3000.
　Green, C. H. (d).
　Howell, Clyde H.
　Reedley Drug Co. (d).

RICHMOND, 6802.
　Delley, Melvin.
　Ferguson, E. M. (d).
　Kennon, J. L.
　Lang, A. C. (d).
　Neill, J. A.

RIVERSIDE, 18,297.
　Craig, C. W. (b).
　Fry, William L. (b).
　Gardner, F. A., & Co. (d).
　Keystone Drug Co. (d).
　McCarty, G. A. (d).
　Neblett, W. E. (d).
　Reed Stationery Co. (b).
　Twogood, Fred. W. (Stat'y and Photo. Supplies).

SACRAMENTO, 62,717.
　*Crocker Co., H. S.
　Hale Bros. (g).
　*Hopkins, A. S., Co.
　Purnell, W. F. (b).
　Wahl Stationery Co.
　Wasserman, Gattmann Co. (g).
　Weinstock, Lubin & Co. (g).
　Yorozu (The) Co.

SALINAS, 3736.
　Hitchcock, F. N. (d).
　Hughes, Mrs. J. A. (b, c).

 Cement Floor Coating — Makes concrete floors water, oil and dust proof

Wholesale and Retail Stationers

CALIFORNIA.

SALINAS—*Continued.*
Hughes, Jesse M.
Krough, Annie E. (d).
Scott, J. B. (d).

SAN BERNARDINO, 15,608.
Bates, A. W.
*Barnum & Flagg Co. (b, c. s).
Cohen Strodthoff Co.

SAN DIEGO, 90,000.
Arey-Jones Co. (b, c).
Carpenter's Book Store (b, c).
Crain's Book Store.
Eagle Drug Co. (d).
Ernsting Co., The (j).
Ferris & Ferris (d).
Holzwasser, Inc. (g).
Jessop & Son (j).
*Klauber-Wangenheim Co.
Lutes, Harold E.
Marston Co., The (g).
Monarch Drug Co. (d).
Owl Drug Co. (d).
Packard's Book Store (b).
Robinson Drug Co.
Schneider's Dept. Store (g).
Stephens & Son (b).
*Wandrey-Bangs-Ward Co.
Whitney & Co.
*Zellerbach Paper Co.

SAN FRANCISCO, 448,502.
Althof & Bahls, Inc.
Aoki-Tasedo Co., 1601 Geary (b).
Arding, Walter A., 268 Market.
Babbino, Antonio, 1435 Grant Ave.
Bancroft-Whitney Co., 200 McAllister (b).
Bartow, Wolf & Hastings, Inc.
Bates, Mrs. A. E., 1591 Haight.
Baum, Herman R., 783 Bush (d).
Benas & Gilbooly, 509 Sansome.
Bender-Moss Co., 11 City Hall av.
Bertsch, Joseph, 610 Sixth av.
Biro, Adolph A.
Blake, Mrs. Margaret C., 1108 Valencia.
Burgheimer & Osvald, 1707 Haight.
Burns, Mrs. M. W., 4300 Judah (d).
*California Notion & Toy Co., 555 Market.
*Cardinell-Vincent Co., 579 Market.
*Carlisle, A., & Co., 251 Bush.
Cavalli, A., & Co., 263 Montgomery av. (b).
Cellini, Eola, 250 Columbus av.
Chosez, Max, 2121 Clement.
Cohn, Harry, 2101 Fillmore.
Cohn, Jos., 3011 Sixteenth.

SAN FRANCISCO—*Continued.*
Couchman, Walter, 851 Broadway.
Creightons, Mary L., 803 Valencia.
Crocker, H. S., Co., 565 Market.
Davis, Max, 692 McAllister.
Denman, E. E., 561 Hayes.
Dixon, Fish & Co., 205 California.
Dresser, Geo. H., 226 Powell.
Eissler, Martin, 3463 Sixteenth.
Elder, Paul, & Co., 239 Grant.
Ellis St. Printing & Stationery Co., 218 Ellis.
Emporium, Market and Fourth (g).
Ephraim, J. A., 1501 Fulton.
Fairbrother, Mary, 3031 24th.
Fat Ming & Co.
Fitzsimmons, F. J., 835 Broadway.
Frey, A. R., 1395 Haight.
Gabriel, Meyerfield Co., 311 Battery.
Getz, A. M., 2056 24th.
Gierisch, Jr., W., 3116 16th.
Gillen, John, 450 Courtland av.
Greeninger Staty. Co., 561 Hayes.
Haas & Sommer.
Hadley, C. R., Co., 681 Market.
Hall & Smith, 349 Market.
Halliday, W. A., 2508 Mission.
Hays, Ira O., 527 Clement.
Heath, Mrs. J., 121 Fillmore.
Heininger, C. P., & Co., 687 Guerrero.
Heinrich, R. E., 82 29th.
Hewlett, Esther A. (Mrs. H.).
Hyman Bros., 536 Kearny.
Ingrim Stationery Co., 415 Montgomery.
Janofsky, A. W., 3294 Mission.
Jorgenson, O. P., 121 Grattan.
Kalmuk, Louis, 2911 Sacramento.
Katz, Samuel, 442 Vicksburg.
King Book Store, 1716 Market.
Koblik, Harry, 976 McAllister.
Latham, W. K., 1515 Polk.
Lesser, Samuel, 3401 Sacramento.
Loewenberg, F., & Co., 2690 Mission.
Long, Chas., 1100 Powell.
Lowe, E. A., Co., Monadnock Bldg.
Luce, Geo. H., 1101 Divisadero.
Madison, Anna C., 786 Haight.
Marks & Finck, 918 Market.
McCreary, Miss A. E., 2237 Fillmore.
McGeeney's, 1415 Jackson.
McNeil Bros., 926 Fillmore.
McSwegan, Chas., 1138 Page.
Miller, C. A., 235 Columbus av.
Mission Photo Supply Co., 88 3d.
*Mitchell, E. H., 3363 Army.
Morrison, Mrs. A. E., 839 Clement.
Morrison, D. J., 146 6th.
Mosss, Oscar, 2741 Bush.

 **Paint and Chemical Company**
PAPER COLORS AND MILL PAINT SPECIALTIES
BOSTON SPRINGFIELD, MASS. NEW YORK

Wholesale and Retail Stationers 467

CALIFORNIA.

SAN FRANCISCO—*Continued.*
Mysell-Rollins Bank Note Co., 22 Clay.
Nathan Sisters.
O'Connell & Davis, 247 California.
O'Harro, J. J., 1623 Haight.
Ott, H. J., 1556 Stockton.
*Pacific Novelty Co., 579 Market.
Parent, Louis, 1186 Market.
Parents' Stationery Co., 829 Van Ness av.
Patrick & Co., 560 Market.
Payot, Stratford & Kerr, 429 Market.
Peacock, Fred, 1217 Turk.
Pemberton, W. S.
Pernau Publishing Co., 758 Market.
Pitts, Fred W., 771 Market.
Pitts, That Man, Inc.
Poesch, A. F., 1202 Railroad av.
Post, Abraham, 1368 Haight.
Post, Rudolph C., Co., 378 Mills Bldg.
Phillips & Lippsitz, 217 Kearny.
Rademacher, A. H., 1104½ Market.
Raisis, Jas., 290½ 3d.
Raymond, A., 4360 Mission.
Regent News Co., 490 Sutter.
Reynolds, Roger, 404 Sutter.
Richards, David, 1674 Geary.
Richardson & Alten, 1640 Union.
Rieger, R., 1097 Market.
Robertson, A. M., Stockton and Union sq.
Rust, F. M., 1156 Valencia.
Ryan, D. B., 915 Cole.
*Sanborn, Vail & Co., 755 Mission.
Saunders, Jas., 3111 24th.
Schenk, Gustav, 2007A Fillmore.
Schudell, Louise, 2216 Polk.
Schultz, Jr., W. A., 3254 22d.
*Schwabacher-Frey Co., 541 Market.
Shapro's, Inc., 1461 Polk.
Shreve & Co., Grant av. and Post (j).
Silver, Mrs. Clara, 2824 California.
Small, A. W., 1284 Union.
Smart & Wilton, 56 Kearny.
Spencer, Henrietta, 4102 19th.
Stappenbeck, Minnie M., 3438 Mission.
Stern & Stern, 1986 Sutter.
Story, J. H., 1702 Divisadero.
Sullivan, J. F., 814 Clement.
Sullivan, Mary, 1002 Golden Gate.
Szukalski, Peter.
Torok, Alex., 804 Larkin.
Tremayne, William, 2200 Fillmore.
Troyer, Roderick A., 2473 Mission.
Union Litho. Co., 741 Harrison.

SAN FRANCISCO—*Continued.*
Unti & Perasso, 346 Columbus av.
Upham, Isaac & Co., 104 Battery.
Upton Bros. & Delselle, 144 2d.
Vail, Edward G., 2213 Fillmore.
Von Tillow Bros., 833 Divisadero.
Vrachliottis Bazaar, 1508 Polk.
Waibel, F., 1467 Haight.
Walter, H. W., 1212 9th av.
Warren, Mrs. May, 1898 Hayes.
Warren, Mrs. Roberta R., 1306 Castro.
Weir, G. C., 2272 Market.
Wellendorf, J. J.
White & Farnsworth, 425 Montgomery.
Wilhelm, Carl C., 500 Haight.
Williamson, C. & D., 1464 Divisadero.
Wobber's, Inc., 774 Market.
Wood, Geo. H., & Co., 558 Market.
Wright, John H., 417 Montgomery.
Wyemann, Chas., 422 Presidio av.
Young, George W.

SAN JOSE, 37,086.
Hale, O. A., & Co. (g).
Hubbard, T. B.
Maynard, A. M. & F. X.
Maynard's Book Store.
Melvin Printing Co.
Millard Bros. (b).
Miller & Hubbard.
Roberts & Horwarth (b).
San Jose Paper Co.
Tellier, Peter.
Winch, S. G. (b).
Wright, P. R.

SAN LEANDRO, 3471.
Wallis, Wm. John.

SAN LUIS OBISPO, 5157.
Carpenter & Matthews (d).
Childs, Harry.
Greenleaf, T. A. (d).
Hill, L. W. (b).
Latimer, B. G.
Lawrence Drug Co. (d).
Lind, Mrs. C. C. (b).
People's Drug Store (d).

SAN RAFAEL, 5934.
Du Bois, Mrs. L. B.
Hock, Chas. T.
Kellner, H.
Webb Rogers (d).

SANTA ANA, 9919.
Hatzfeld & Parsons (d).
Mateer, E. T. (d).

 Pure Blues For paper staining, coating and ruling

CALIFORNIA.

SANTA ANA—*Continued.*
Rankin Dry Goods Store (g).
Rowley Drug Co.
Santa Ana Book Store.
Stein, B.
Woolworth, F. W., Co.
White Cross Drug Co.

SANTA BARBARA, 13,813.
Farnum, E. O. (o. s.).
Gift Shop.
Gutierrez Drug Co.
Nicholas, F. C.
Osborne, W. W. (b).
Pacific Coast Pub. Co. (c).
Prechel, John (b).
Red Cross Drug Store (d).
Santa Barbara Drug Store (d).
Walton, J. A. Co. (g).
Western Book & Toy Store (b).
Whitcomb, Mrs. Eva.

SANTA CLARA, 4348.
Alderman, Mrs. Bertha (b).
Madden, Wm. A. (d).
Oberdeeners Pharmacy (d).

SANTA CRUZ, 13,482.
Carr, A. B.
Howe, F. R.
Irish, H. E., Co. (c, s, o. s.).
*Miller, F. J., & Co.
Palmer Drug Co. (d).

SANTA MARIA, 3193.
Jones, P. W. (d).
Jones, T. A., & Son (d).

SANTA MONICA, 7847.
Abbott, W. A. (b).
Berkley, S. L. (d).
Busier, A. (o. s.).
Henderson, R. P. (d).
Jackson, A. E. (b).
Silvernale, R. C. (d).

SANTA PAULA.
Elliott, A. W.

SANTA ROSA, 7817.
Andrew & Kendall.
Baldwin Drug Co.
Belden & Upp (d).
Dont, John G.
Fair, The.
Farmer, E. C. (d).
Hahmann Drug Co. (d).
Hood, John, Co. (j).
Hosmer, S. (b).
Lutrell Drug Co. (d).
Santa Rosa Dept. Store.

SANTA ROSA—*Continued.*
St. Rose Drug Store (d).
Tomasco's Pharmacy (d).
*Wright, O. A., & Co. (b).

SAUSALITO, 2383.
Noyes, I. E.

ST. HELENA, 1582.
Galewsky, Joseph.
Smith's Pharmacy (d).

SEBASTOPOL, 2000.
Borba, W. S.
Pease, Geo.
Worth, T. R. (b).

SELMA, 2800.
Byfield, E. S.

SIERRA MADRE, 1700.
Doucett, M. C.

SONORA, 3200.
Lester, Jas. R.

SOUTH PASADENA, 4649.
Jones, T. R. (j).
Merritt, E. A. (j).

STANFORD UNIVERSITY, 700.
*Stanford, The, Bookstore.

STOCKTON, 25,702.
*Eastman-Gibbens Co.
Friedberger, M., & Co. (j).
Gall, Jr., Joseph.
Haas, Chas., & Son (j).
Holden Drug Co. (d).
Lester & Graebe.
*Morris Bros. (b, c).
Quinn, Wm. P. (b, c).
Stewart, E. C., Co. (b).
Stewart, J. A. (b).
Sudow, W. (b).
Treadway Bros. (b, c).

SUISUN CITY, 700.
Harrington, L. A. (b).
Whitby & Rutherford (d).

SUSANVILLE, 1500.
Bangham, F. H.

TAFT, 3000.
Connard, A. T. (j).

TRUCKEE, 1500.
Lewis, J. L.

TURLOCK, 2000.
Lee Bros.

 **Paint and Chemical Company**
PAPER COLORS AND MILL PAINT SPECIALTIES
BOSTON   SPRINGFIELD, MASS.   NEW YORK

Wholesale and Retail Stationers

CALIFORNIA.

VACAVILLE, 1177.
Edstrom, E.

VALLEJO, 11,340.
Ball & Kilpatrick (d).
Frey, H. G. (j).
Haggerty, Frank B., & Son.
Knott, A. A. (d).
Madigan, J. J., Co.
Rexall Store.
Smith & Co.
Stuart, Donald.
White, A., Inc. (j).
Walker & Rockwood.

VENTURA, 2945.
Bartlett Co. (j).
Jones & Son.
Macgregor Bros.

VISALIA, 4550.
Huffaker, F. E. (b).
Hunter, Lovelace & Gilmer (d).
Rouse's.
Smith, E. L. (d).

VISALIA—*Continued.*
Visalia Drug Co.
Ward, J. C. (b).
Young, Geo. W.

WATSONVILLE, 4446.
Ruppert, F. W.
Smith, H. B. (g).

WHITTIER, 4550.
Moore, C. F. (b).
Robbins & Pelton (d).

WILLOWS.
Wright, E. W. (j).

WOODLAKE.
Mixter & Schelling (d).

WOODLAND, 3187.
Corner Drug Store (d).
Laurence, J. F.
Leithold, J. V. (d).
Purkitt, T. T. (d).
Shelton, J. R. (d).

COLORADO.

ALAMOSA, 3000.
Grove, J. L. (d).
Mt. Blanca Drug Co. (d).
Shone, G. H. (b).

ASPEN, 3303.
Cooper Book & Stationery Co. (b).

BOULDER, 11,000.
Burgess Drug Co., The (d).
Fonda, G. F. (d).
Greenman Stores Co. (d, b, o, c, s).
Johnson, Phil. C., (d).
Jones Drug Co. (d).
Potter, W. W., & Co. (d).
Temple Drug Co. (d).
University Store (b, d).

BUENA VISTA, 1008.
De Bolt & Langdon (d).
Halsey, C. R. (d).
McGinnis, Harry L.

CANON CITY, 5162.
Corner Drug Store Co. (d).
Fink-Kiensle Drug Co. (d).
Frey & Collins (g).
Pallace Drug Store (d).
Palmer, H. (d).
Whipple, F. H. (b, o, s.).

COLORADO SPRINGS, 29,078.
Beeson, E. B., Stat'y & Curio Co.
Butcher, D. Y., Drug Co.
Davis, Roy A. (o. s.).
Gidding & Kirkwood (g).
Hardy, Cliff (b).
Hefley Drug Co.
Hibbard, C. A., & Co. (g).
Kaufman & Co. (g).
McCauley, H. O. D. (b).
Miller Stationery & Curio Co.
Murray Drug Co.
*Out West Ptg. & Sta. Co. (o. s.).
Pike's Peak Book & Sta. Co. (b, o. s.).
Robinson Drug Co. (d).
Straw Printing Co.
Whitney & Grimwood (b).

CRIPPLE CREEK, 5000.
Armstrong, W. D. (j).
Haas, A.
Lewis, G. R. (d).
Palace Pharmacy Co. (d).
Second Street Pharmacy.
Williams & Snyder.

DELTA, 2338.
Osborne & Williamson Drug Co.
Van Volkenburgh, J. D. (b).

 **Victoria Lake** A perfect color for blending with Yellow to produce shades of Buff, Corn, etc.

Wholesale and Retail Stationers

COLORADO.

DENVER, 213,381.
Aarons Stationery Co. (c).
Angell, F. B. (d).
Clayton, C. J. (d).
*Colorado News Co.
Daniels & Fisher Stores Co. (g).
Davis Bros. Drug Co. (d).
Davis, C. M., Printing Co.
Denver Dry Goods Co. (g).
Denver Stationery Co.
Frankel, H., Stationery Co.
Hartman-Bruderlin-Foster (The), Staty. Co.
Herrick Book & Stationery Co. (b).
Hoeckel Blank Book & Lithograph Co., C. F. (c).
Howard, C. C.
Irwin-Stepp Co.
Joslin Dry Goods Co. (g).
Kendrick-Bellamy Co. (c, s).
*Kistler Stationery Co., W. H. (c, s).
Lewis, A. T., & Son (g).
Littleton, H. B. (d).
Logan, S. S.
Merritt Printing & Stationery Co.
Oxford Drug Co. (d).
Pierce & Zahn Book Co. (b).
Pratt's Book Store.
Rock Mountain Bank Note Co.
Scholtz Drug Co. (d).
Three Rules Stores (g).

DURANGO, 4686.
Bowman, T. E.
Durango Drug Co. (d).
Parsons, J. L. (d).
Tiffany, Geo. E., Jr. (d).
United Stationery & Confectionery Co. (d).
Wall, S. G. (d).

FLORENCE, 3500.
Austin, Frank P.
Daniels, W. J. (d).
Stewart, J. D. (d).
Tanner, Jennie.
Yeltor, J. W.

FORT COLLINS, 3210.
Brock, Edward.
Miller, Frank E. (b).
Secord, C. R. (b).
Solomon, Abe.

GARY, 200.
McDowell, Thos. H. (g).

GEORGETOWN, 1418.
Wood, Mrs. F. J.

GLENWOOD SPRINGS, 2000.
City Drug Store.
Howard & Hubbard (d).
Korn's Book & Stationery Co. (b).
Parkison, W. S. (d).
Thorson, O. (b).

GOLDEN, 2500.
Robinson, Fred B. (b).

GRAND JUNCTION, 7754.
Hamilton, R. M.
Winfield, E. Frank (b).

GREELEY, 8179.
Clark & Faulkner (d).
Fezer, J. F. (d).
Gilbert Bros. (d).
Hallett & Henderson (d).
Horne, Geo. D. (b, o. s.).
Ramsey Dry Goods Co. (g).
Seastrand, Edward (b).
Williams, D. H., Co. (b).

IDAHO SPRINGS, 2300.
Deis, E. J.
Marchington, C.

LA JUNTA, 4154.
Coltman, Thos. C. (d).
Fisher, J. W. (b).
Potter, A. M.

LAMAR, 5000.
Potter, A. M. (b).

LAS ANIMAS, 2800.
Morgan, F. B. (g).

LEADVILLE, 7508.
City Drug Co. (d).
Davis Drug Co. (d).
Hart-Zaitz Mercantile Co. (g).
Jett, Henry, Book & Staty. Co. (b).
Whipple Printing, Stationery & Mercantile Co.
Woolworth, F. W., & Co.

LITTLETON, 2000.
Swanson, Robt. (b).

LONGMONT, 5000.
Longmont Drug Co.
Worley, E. C. (b).

LOVELAND, 5000.
Columbine Drug Co.
Means Book Store.
Skelley, L. H. (b, j).
Walton Drug Co.

 **Paint and Chemical Company**
PAPER COLORS AND MILL PAINT SPECIALTIES
BOSTON   SPRINGFIELD, MASS.   NEW YORK

Wholesale and Retail Stationers 471

COLORADO.

MONTROSE, 4200.
 Culver Variety Store.
 Warner, W. W. (g).
OURAY, 1400.
 Dunbar, A. F. (b).
PAGOSA SPRINGS, 1000.
 Laughlin, John M.
PUEBLO, 44,395.
 Bridgeford, B. (d).
 Broome Bros. (b). 2 stores (s).
 Colorado Supply Co. (b).
 Crews, Beggs Dry Goods Co. (g, s).
 Franklin Press Co.
 Glover Drug Co.
 Haines, W. H. (b, s).
 *Hyde Paper Co. (s).
 Kress, 5-10-25c. Store (g).
 Metropolitan Drug Co. (d).
 Miller-Hohl Drug Co. (d).
 Jones Drug Co. (d).
 Pearson & Davies (d).
 Pueblo Drug Co. (d, s).
 *Pueblo Store Co., The.
 Stroup Drug Co. (d).
 Taylor, Bertha.
 Winch-Slayden Stationery Co.
 Woolworth, F. W., & Co. (g).

SALIDA, 4425.
 Allan, W. J. (b).
 Crozer, Chas. P.
 Hunt, J. W. (b).
STERLING, 3100.
 Bauman, Chas. R. (d).
 Gilbert, Chas. T. (d).
TRINIDAD, 10,204.
 Robinson Wright Ptg. Co.
 Seymour Drug Co.
 Zimmerman Bros. (b).
VICTOR, 3000.
 Ovren, Mrs. E. M.
 Schriver, Frank (b).
 Victor Drug Co. (b, d).
WALSENBURG, 3000.
 City Pharmacy (d).
 Huerfano Drug Co. (d).
 Klein, Fred E.
 Star Drug Co. (d).
 Wycoff-Fawks Drug Co. (d).
 Krier Stores Co.
WESTCLIFFE, 350.
 Adams, Frank E. (d).

CONNECTICUT.

ANSONIA, 15,152.
 Bristol Drug Co.
 *Jordan, H. A. (b).
 McQuade, E. (d).
 Tuttle, Ernest L.
 Walsh Co., R. Q. (g).
BETHEL, 3041.
 Garvin Drug Co., Inc. (d).
 Perkins & Cole.
BRANFORD, 2560.
 Leshine News Co.
 Spalding, C. G., Co., The (d).
BRIDGEPORT, 102,054.
 Ballard, F. E. (d).
 Bridgeport News Co.
 Challenger, H. S.
 Chamberlain & Shropshire (c, o. s.).
 Connecticut Office & Library Supply Co. (c, o. s.).
 Fargo, Frank H. (c, o. s.).
 Hamilton, Jennie (d).
 Hayes & Belts (b).
 Howland Dry Goods Co. (g).
 Keith, Charles E., Co. (d).

BRIDGEPORT—*Continued.*
 *Lyon & Chase.
 Mullens Typewriter Exchange.
 Plumb, L. D. (b).
 Post Office News Co.
 Read, D. M., Co. (g).
 Sherwood & Morgan Co.
 Siksay, Stephen S. (b).
 Southworth, G. E., Inc.
 Wooster & Co., J. S. (g).
BRISTOL, 8963.
 Barnard, B. O. (c, o. s.).
 Cullen, John C.
 Evans, Geo. B. (Est. of)
 Judson, J. N. (c, o. s.).
 Murray, Jas. L.
DANBURY, 20,234.
 Begg, Margaret F. (b).
 Bristol, H. B. (b).
 Canfield, J. A.
 Cuff, James E. (b).
 Ising, L. F. (j).
 McLean Brothers.
 Paull, Max.
 Robertson, Sarah L. A.

 **Structural Paint** For the preservation of structural iron and steel

Wholesale and Retail Stationers

CONNECTICUT.

DANIELSON, 2934.
Dowe, Mrs. Helen S.

DARIEN, 3116.
Allen, S. M. (d).

DERBY, 8991.
Allis, George C. (j).
Gilbert, A., & Sons.
Harding, G. H. (d).
Rolston, E. H.
Yudkin, A. H.

EAST HARTFORD, 5100.
Lowry Drug Co. (d).—

ESSEX, 1700.
Knowles, Jos. E.

GREENWICH, 3886.
Marks, Philip.
Mead Stationery Co.

GROTON, 6495.
Davis, C. S. W. (d).

GUILFORD, 1606.
Dudley & Beckwith.

HARTFORD, 98,915.
Barlow, J. R. (b).
Beebe, Chas. E.
Brown Thompson Co. (g).
Carlson, Julius.
Case, Lockewood & Brainard Co.
Cleveland, Henry W.
Conroy, Mary A.
Curtis, A. B.
Doyle, Martin J.
Dow, Jean I.
*Fischer, Gustave, Co. (c, o. s.).
Fox, G., & Co. (g).
Hartford Office Supply Co.
Hills, C. S., Co. (g).
Jacobson & Boya.
Jennings, Erwin M.
Kohn & Son, H. (j).
Levine, S.
McDonough, W. J. (b).
Nordstrom, Andrew J.
Olsen, Eugene A.
Parker, T. M.
Plimpton Mfg. Co. (c, o. s.).
Sage Allen Co. (g).
Warfield, G. F., & Co. (b).
Wise & Smith Co. (g).

MERIDEN, 27,265.
Barber, W. N. (d).
Blair, Wm. V. (j).

MERIDEN—*Continued.*
Ives, P. T. (j).
Lange, August J.
Molloy, John F. (c, o. s.).
Pelton Pub. Co. (b).
Schmelzer, A., Co., The.
Sills, E. T. (b).

MIDDLETOWN, 20,749.
Bride Bros.
Broatch, J. Allison (b).
*Hazen's Book Store (b).
Mylchreest, John J.
Wesleyan Book Store.

MILFORD, 4172.
Hones, John T. (d).
Milford Citizen Pub. Co.
Milford News Co.
Southworth Engraving Shop.
Trefey's Drug Store (d).

MOOSUP, 2950.
Bellvance, Wm.

MYSTIC, 3571.
Kreitzer, Conrad.
Seamans, E. B. (b).

NAUGATUCK, 7848.
Birdsall, Wm. K.
Brennan, E. P. (d).
Hard, W. G., 5 & 10 Cent Store.
Judd, Frank H., & Co. (d).
McCarthy, Henry P.
Newman, James J.
Sweeney, E. J.

NEW BRITAIN, 55,000.
Adkins Printing Co.
Boston Store (g).
*Cadwell, G. A.
Chatfield, Mrs. E. H. (b).
Crowell, W. H. (d).
Dickinson Drug Co.
Hultgren, Chas. M. (d).
McMillan, D. (g).

NEW CANAAN, 1672.
Dickerman Store, Inc.

NEW HAVEN, 133,605.
Beaney, Winfield C.
Beebe & Philips, 193 Church.
Blue, The, Print Co.
Bradley & Scoville Co. (c, o. s.).
Bronson & Pelcher.
City Hall Pharmacy, 159 Church st. (d).
Danzigan & Berman, 173 Meadow (b, s).

 **Paint and Chemical Company**
PAPER COLORS AND MILL PAINT SPECIALTIES
BOSTON   SPRINGFIELD, MASS.   NEW YORK

Wholesale and Retail Stationers

CONNECTICUT.

NEW HAVEN—*Continued.*
Elm City Mfg. Co., 871 State.
Ford Co., 960 Chapel (j).
Gamble Desmond Co.
Judd Co., Edward P., 827 Chapel. (b).
Kilborne Bros., 58 Orange (c, o. s.).
Lee Co., Wilson H. (c, o. s.).
Libbey, Clara S., Elm.
Malley Co., The Ed., Chapel and Temple (g).
Mendel & Freeman, 772 Chapel (g).
Office Equipment Co.
Puklin, M. M., Co., 729 State.
Ratner, Joseph, Temple (b).
Rembert, John R., Co., 181 Church (c, o. s.).
Shartenberg & Robinson, 771 Chapel (g).
Tuttle, Morehouse & Taylor Co., The, 123 Temple (c, o. s.).
Whitlock Book Store, Inc.
Yale Co-operative Corp., 199 Elm, Yale University (b).

NEW LONDON, 19,659.
  Goldsmith Co., S. A. (g).
  Halpern, J. (b).
  Hislop & Co., James (g).
  Keeney, Edw., & Co. (b).
  Larkin, John L.
  Perry & Stone (j).
  *Solomon, J.
  Starr Bros. (d).
  Tannebaum, M. (b).
  *Utley, H. D. (b).

NEW MILFORD, 4804.
  Cassidy, P. M. (Est. of).
  Soule, F. E.

NORWALK, 6954.
  Beers, Wm. P. (b).
  Benedict News Co.
  *Boston Store (g).
  *Hotchkiss Co., The E. H.
  Tristam & Hyatt (g).
  Weinstock, Leon.
  Wilcox, Fred E.

NORWICH, 20,367.
  Bowen, William.
  *Cranston Co., The (b, s).
  Hertz Bros. (b).
  Porteus & Mitchell (g).
  Reid & Hughes Co. (g).
  Ring & Sisk (d).
  Treat, C. C. (d).

PUTNAM, 6637.
  Burt, H. L. (d).
  Dresser, Geo. E. (d).

PUTNAM—*Continued.*
  Putnam News Co.
  Shaw, Geo. E. (j, s).

RIDGEFIELD, 2626.
  Bissell, Harvey P.

ROCKVILLE, 7997.
  Randall, Francis A. (b).)
  Weber, A. M. (g).
  Wenheiser, Geo. P.
  Wilson, E. L. (d).

SEYMOUR, 4786.
  Rolston, Ernest H.
  Smith, Geo., & Son (d).

SHELTON, 4807.
  Mahoney, Wm. G. (d).

SOUTH MANCHESTER, 8000.
  Dewey, Albert T.
  Magnell News Co.

SOUTH NORWALK, 8968.
  Briggerman Bros. (c, s).
  Coleman, Fred B.
  Donnelly, Jr., James (c, s).
  Plasted, R. H. (d).
  Ponty, Fred H. (s).
  Silliman, Stanley G.

STAFFORD SPRINGS, 3059.
  Fitzpatrick, F. E.
  McLaughlin, Lewis.
  Whiton, Nettie M. (b).

STAMFORD, 25,138.
  Axebrod, Max.
  Embree, A. L. (d), 18 Park row.
  Estroff & Nelson.
  Gillespie Bros., The, Inc.
  Harriott, Miss K. M., 63 Atlantic.
  Jones, Wm. H., Est. of.
  *Morgan, O. B., 111 Atlantic.
  The Miller Store (g), 196 Atlantic.

SUFFIELD, 2931.
  Reid, Frank H.

THOMPSONVILLE, 5900.
  Hunter & Co.

TORRINGTON, 15,483.
  Doty, C. D.
  Dougal, O. H. (d).
  Goodale, C. D. (d).
  Mertz, W. W. (g).
  Nolan, Edward (d).
  Reynolds News & Stat'y Co. (b).
  Whelan & Cummings (b).

Hampden Roll Bar White — A lasting tough coating for iron work in beaters and washers

Wholesale and Retail Stationers

CONNECTICUT.

WALLINGFORD, 8690.
 Bullock, George H.
 Hull, A. W.
 Kennedy News Co.
 Office Supply Co.
 Sanders & Co. (o. s.).

WATERBURY, 73,141.
 Baumgartner Bros. (b).
 *City Book Binding Co.
 Cone, J. W. (d).
 Curran Dry Goods Co. (g).
 Davis & Nye (b, o. s.).
 Devereaux & Co., J. H. (b).
 Dumphy, William (d).
 Ebbs, J. B. (d).
 Gladding, S. J. (d).
 Grieve, Bissett & Holland (g).
 Jones Pharmacy (d).
 Mattatuck Press, Inc. (o. s.).
 McCarthy, M. A. (d).
 McLinden, H. P. (d).
 Miller & Peck Co. (g).
 Pickett, W. H., & Co. (d).
 Pierpoint Book Store.
 Reed, James V. (b).
 Reid & Hughes Dry Goods Co. (g).

WATERBURY—*Continued.*
 *Standard Paper Co.
 Upham, N. A. (d).

WESTPORT, 4017.
 O'Connor, J. J.
 Salmon, D., A. & Co. (g).
 Westport Drug Co., The (d).
 Westport Herald.

WILLIMANTIC, 12,000.
 Andrews, A. C. (The), Music Co.
 Chesbro, Samuel (d).
 Courtney, J. D. (d).
 Dunn, D. P.
 Murray, H. C., Co. (g, b).
 Sweeney, W. J. (b).
 Utley, Charles R. (b).

WINSTED, 7754.
 Bannon, Frank P. (d).
 Bovee, Irving S. (b).
 Bristol, C. E. (g).
 Buck, O. C. (d).
 Gage, Geo. W. (g).
 Moore, Darwin S.
 *Winsted Paper Co.

DELAWARE.

BRIDGEVILLE, 989.
 Cannon, W., & Co.
DELMAR, 2000.
 Whayland Drug Co. (d).
GEORGETOWN, 1609.
 Layton & Layton, Inc.
 Marshall & Chipman.
LEWES, 2158.
 Chambers, Wm. H. (d).
 Long, H. M. (d).
MIDDLETOWN, 1899.
 Price, Samuel R.
 Wood, William, Jr. (g).
NEWARK, 1913.
 Rhoads, Geo. W. (d).

NEW CASTLE, 3351.
 Challenger, Edward & Son.
 Chase, L. E.

SMYRNA, 2168.
 Clifton & Jones (d).
 Swain, Chas. B. (d).

WILMINGTON, 87,411.
 Bee Hive (The) Co.
 Butler, E. S. R., & Son (b, c, s).
 Bradford, C. W. K., Co.
 Lippincott & Co. (g).
 Robinson, J. B. (o. s.).
 Smith, Chas., Co. (o s).
 Wilson, William C.

DISTRICT OF COLUMBIA.

TAKOMA PARK, 1250.
 P. O. at Washington.
 Feldman, David.

WASHINGTON, 819,112.
 Abner, Theodore, 406 E. Capitol.
 *Andrews' Paper Co., R. P., 727-731 13th, N. W.

WASHINGTON—*Continued.*
 Alexander, W. W., 1342 N. Y. av. (c).
 Ballantyne, William, & Sons, 1409 F, N. W.
 Baum Paper & Stat. Co., 623 F, N. W.
 Bause, F. W., 1304 7th, N. W. (c).

 **Paint and Chemical Company**
PAPER COLORS AND MILL PAINT SPECIALTIES
BOSTON   SPRINGFIELD, MASS.   NEW YORK

Wholesale and Retail Stationers

DISTRICT OF COLUMBIA.

WASHINGTON—*Continued.*
Beach, Eliz. C., 2006 18th, N. W.
Berry & Whitmore Co., 11th and F, N. W. (j).
Bowie, Geo. R., 3400 14th, N. W.
Brentano's, 1200-1204 F, N. W. (b).
Brewer, W. J., 664 Penn. av., S. E.
Brewood, 519 13th, N. W. (s).
Brown, M. M., 718 R. I. av., N. W.
Copenhaver, William A., 1427 F, N. W. (s.).
Creecy, W. B., & Son, Inc., 1337 H, N. E. (c).
Ervin, Edw. J., 2906 14th, N. W.
Fernald & Co.
Fisher, Elmer E., 1703 Penn av., N. W. (b).
Galt & Bro., 1107 Penn. ave., N. W. (j).
Garrison, W. B., & Co., 416 10th, N. W.
Globe-Wernicke Co., 1228 F, N. W. (o. s.).
Goldenberg, M., 912 Seventh st., N. W. (g).
Gould, Clarence E., Colorado Bldg. (c).
Graham, Chas. H., 1250 Wisconsin av., N. W.
Harris, Sam'l T., 84 M, S. W. (w).
Hausler & Co., 720 17th, N. W.
James, Mary E., 1722 Fourteenth, N. W.
Jones, Amelia, 1341 7th, N. W.
Kann, S., & Sons Co., 8th and Penn. av., N. W. (g).
Krouse, W. Joseph, 906, G, N. W.
Law Reporter Printing Co., 518 Fifth, N. W. (c).
Lee, George, 1604 7th, N. W.

WASHINGTON—*Continued.*
Lincoln, F. S., Inc., 612 12th, N. W. (o. s.).
McPhee, Murdock & Co., 221 Penn. av., S. E. (b).
*Morrison Paper Co., E., 1009 Penn. av., N. W.
Morrison, P. D., Sta. Co., 1110 F, N. W.
Offenbacher, Adam P., 101 H, N. W.
Peck, Wm. D., 810 14th, N. W.
Phillips, Max, 1233 7th, N. W.
Powers, C. W., 1826 Fourteenth, N. W.
Pursell, C. C., 807 G, N. W. (b).
Pusey, John R., 1211 E, N. E.
Roberts, W. F., Co., Inc., 1514 H, N. W.
Schmidt, F. A., 719 13th, N. W.
*Schrot Bros., 611 Louisiana av., N. W.
Shaw & Brown Co., 1114 F, N. W. (j).
Smith, Mrs. M. E., 1618 7th, N. W.
*Stockett-Fiske Co., 413 Ninth, N.
*Stott, Chas. G., & Co., Inc., 1310 N. Y. av.
Typewriter & Office Supply Co., 722 13th, N. W.
Ulrich, Howard, 3036 14th.
Wagner, Richard, 1304 B, N. E.
Wallace, Roland, 928 9th, N. W.
Washington Loose Leaf Co., 1342 N. Y. av.
*Washington News Co., 318 6th, N. W. (b).
Wilcox, C. B.
Woodward & Lothrop, Eleventh & F, N. W. (g).
Yawman & Erbe Mfg. Co., 614 12th, N. W. (o. s.).

FLORIDA.

ARCADIA, 4300.
  Arcadia Drug Co., Inc. (d).
  Cross, Harry (d).
  De Sota County News (c).
  Gottlieb & Co. (s).
  Wey, Jake.
BARTOW, 4000.
  Bartow Drug Co.
  Corner Drug Store.
  Wilson Drug Store.
DAYTONA, 3082.
  Alford, A. M.
  Clark, A. P. (d).
  Daytona Book & Stationery Co.

DAYTONA—*Continued.*
  Hankins Drug Co.
  Lesesue, R. H.
DE LAND, 2812.
  Allen, W. A., & Co. (d).
  Fisher, G. W., Drug Co. (d).
  Reeve & Howard (j).
FERNANDINA, 3482.
  Corner Stat. Store, The.
GAINESVILLE, 10,000.
  Avera, W. W. (b).
  Bodiford, J. S., & Co.
  Miller, P.
  Vidal, John.

 **Rubercoat Elastic Carbon Paint**
For your leaky gravel, paper, cloth and metal roofs.

Wholesale and Retail Stationers

FLORIDA.

JACKSONVILLE, 57,699.
Covington & Co.
*Drew, The H. & W. B., Co. (o. s.).
E. Bean & Son Co.
*Groover Stewart Drug Co. (d).
Logan & White.
Southern Office Supply Co. (o s.).

KEY WEST, 22,000.
Key West Stationery Co.
Rahner, H. B.

LAKE CITY, 3422.
Parker Railway News Co.

LIVE OAK, 4500.
Humphreys, C. E.

MIAMI, 22,500.
*Douglas, E. B., Co.
*Hall Wright Co.
Miami Drug Co. (d).

MILTON, 1500.
Williams, T. D., & Co.

OCALA, 4498.
Antimonopoly Drug Store.
Book Shop, The.
Court Pharmacy (d).
Gerigs Drug Store
Masters, H. B., Co. (g).
Tydings & Co.

ORLANDO, 8972.
Branch, W. S. (c).
Brigham & Hill (b).
Curtis & O'Neal (b).

PALATKA, 3000.
*Ackerman-Stewart Drug Co. (d).
Cochran, The, Co. (b).
Rowton, Chas. E. (j).

PENSACOLA, 23,000.
Balckom, V. T., & Co. (d).

PENSACOLA—Continued.
Central Pharmacy (d).
Johnson, C. R. (b).
White, W. H., & Co. (d).

PLANT CITY, 2500.
Central Pharmacy (b, d).

SANFORD, 3570.
Bower, Roumillat (d).
Herald Printing Co.
Phillips, L. R., & Co. (d).

ST. AUGUSTINE, 5494.
Allen, F. S.
Paffee, H. C.
Segui, Chas. D.
Usina, H. J.

ST. PETERSBURG, 7000.
Advance Art Printing.
Budd, D. W., & Co. (d).
Kemp, C. E. (b).
Pearce-O'Brien Drug Co. (d).
Reliance Pharmacy.

TALLAHASSEE, 5018.
Clark, E. W.
Hill, J. F.
Kaufman, H. R.

TAMPA, 52,176.
Bentley-Gray Dry Goods Co. (g).
Jones, J. W.
Shaw Clayton Stationery Co.
*Tampa Book & News Co. (b).
*Tampa Drug Co. (d).
Ybor City Pharmacy (d).

TARPON SPRINGS, 2500.
Central Pharmacy (d).
Tarpon Springs Drug Store (d).
Webster, Mrs. C. D. (d).
West Drug Co. (d).

WEST PALM BEACH, 1743.
Smith, A. Eugene.
Speers Pharmacy.

GEORGIA.

ALBANY, 13,125.
Lonsberg Book and Music House (b, o. s.).

AMERICUS, 8063.
Hightower Book Store.
Hook's Pharmacy (d).
Howell's Pharmacy.
Murray's Pharmacy (d).
Windsor Pharmacy (d).

ATHENS, 20,000.
Citizen's Pharmacy (d).
Davison-Nicholson Co. (g).
Gardner, W. J. (o. s.).
*McGregor Co. (b, o. s.).
Michael Bros. Co. (g).
Palmer & Sons (d).
Price Ave. Pharmacy (d).
Royal Pharmacy (d).
Smith, W. J., & Bro. (d).

 **Paint and Chemical Company**
PAPER COLORS AND MILL PAINT SPECIALTIES
BOSTON　　　SPRINGFIELD, MASS.　　　NEW YORK

Wholesale and Retail Stationers

GEORGIA.

ATLANTA, 179,292.
Bayliss Office Equipment Co. (c, o. s.).
Bradley Co., Milton.
Chamberlin-Johnson-D u Bose Co. (g).
Davison-Paxon-Stokes (g).
Fielder & Allen Co. (c, o. s.).
Foote & Davies Co. (c).
High, J. M., Co. (g).
*Hirshberg Co.
Jacobs Pharmacy (d).
Lester Book and Stationery Co. (b, o. s.).
Miller's Book Store, Inc., 64 N. Broad.
*Montag Bros., Inc.
Rich, M., & Bro. (g).
*Richards Co., S. P.
Stevens Engraving Co., J. P.
Southern Book Concern, 71 Whitehall (b).

AUGUSTA, 47,786.
*Augusta Drug Co., Inc. (d).
*Davenport, J. B., & Co. (d).
Delquest Book Co. (b).
Farrar's, Inc. (c, s, o. s.).
How & McGowan.
Jowitt Stationery Co. (c, s, o. s.).
Murphy Stationery Co. (b, c, o. s.).

BAINBRIDGE, 6000.
Bainbridge Drug Co.
Mills Pharmacy.
Preston, F. A.
Willis Drug Co. (d).

BRUNSWICK, 10,182.
Bennett Bros. (b).
Bryant, H. H.
Vickers & Mann.

CARROLLTON, 2207.
Horton's Book Store.

CARTERSVILLE, 4067.
Wikle, H. (b).

CEDARTOWN, 3551.
Bradford, Edward (d).
Burbank, T. F.
Crabb, J. O., & Son (b).

CHAMBLEE.
Reese Bros.

CHIPLEY, 742.
Floyd & Hill (g).

COLUMBUS, 20,000.
Columbus Office Supply Co. (c, o. s.).
Gilbert Printing Co. (c).
Frank Bros. (c).
Roberts, T. S.
Smith's Pharmacy (d).
Walton Ptg. Co. (c).
White Co. (b).
*Wolfson Printing & Paper Co.

DALTON, 5824.
Fincher & Nichols.
Horan, George.
Showalter Co., A. J. (b).

DARIEN, 1391.
Vickers & Mann.

DAWSON, 2827.
Mize, C. L. (b).

ELBERTON, 6483.
Cleveland Drug Co.

FORSYTH, 2208.
Alexander Bros. (d).
Moore, J. M. (b).
Morse, O. W. (d).

GAINESVILLE, 5925.
*Brown, M. C.
Gainesville Book Co.
Imperial Pharmacy (d).
Law, De Lacy.
Parker Book Store.
Piedmont Drug Co. (d).

GRIFFIN, 7478.
Brooks, T. J. (d).
Carlisle & Ward (d).
Deane & Amoss (b, o. s.).
Evans Drug Co. (d).
Forbes Drug Co. (d).
Mills Printing Co. (c, o. s.).

JACKSON, 1862.
Carmichael Drug & Book Store.

JEFFERSON, 1207.
Bennett & Dickson (d).
McDonald Pharmacy (d).
Pendergrass, N. N.

LAGRANGE, 5587.
Bradfield Drug Co. (d).
Callaways Dept. Store (g).
Dozier Pharmacy.

LAWRENCEVILLE, 1518.
Craig's Pharmacy (d).
Ezzard-Montgomery Drug Store (d).
McGee's Dept. Store, J. H. (g).

 **Black Paste** Will not crock in the paper. Strongest, cleanest and most economical.

Wholesale and Retail Stationers

GEORGIA.

LITHONIA, 1428.
Johnson, J. C., & Son (g).
Lithonia Drug Co.
Tucker, Chas. J. (b, d).

MACON, 40,665.
Brown's Bookstore.
Burke, J. W., Co.
Lamar, Taylor & Riley Drug Co.
McClure Office Equipment Co.
McClure Ten Cent Co.
McEvoy Book and Stationery Co. (b, o s.).
Parker Railway News Co.
Taylor-Bayne Drug Co. (d).

MARIETTA, 5949.
Collins Bros. (d).
Hodges Drug Co. (d).
McClure Ten Cent Co. (g).
Poole Drug Co.
Sams, W. A., Drug Co. (d).
Stringer, E. L. (b).

MILLEDGEVILLE, 4385.
Barrett, C. T. (d).
Culver & Kidd, Inc. (d).
Jones Drug Co.
Red Cross Pharmacy (d).
Williams & Ritchie (j).
Wootten, R. H.

NASHVILLE, 1100.
Tygart, W. H.

NEWNAN, 5548.
Cates, J. R., Drug Co. (d).
Lee, J. F., Drug Co. (d).
Murray Drug & Book Co. (b, d).
Murray Mfg. Co.

ROME, 14,400.
*Curry-Arrington Co. (d).
*Rome Stationery Co. (c).

ROME—*Continued.*
Taylor & Norton (d).
*Wyatt Book Store (c).

SAVANNAH, 67,917.
Adler, Leopold (g).
Braid & Hutton, Inc. (c, o. s.).
*Byck Co., M. S. & D. A. (c, s).
Coleman, Nathan, Co.
*Columbia Drug Co. (d).
Connor, E. M. (Est. of) (b, s).
Gardner, J. (b).
Kennickell Printing Co.
Nichols, Wm. N.
Shuptrine Co. (d).
*Solomon's Drug Co. (d).

THOMASVILLE, 6727.
Red Cross Drug Co. (d).
Robison Stationery Co. (b).

THOMSON, 2152.
Gibson Drug Co. (d).

TOCCOA, 3120.
Newton, J. W. (b).
People's Drug Store (d).
Wilhite, J. O.

VALDOSTA, 15,000.
Barnes, C. W. (d).
Bondurant, C. S. (d).
Dunnaway, W. D. (d).
Ingram Drug Co. (d).
Smith Drug Co. (d).
*Southern Stationery & Printing Co. (o. s.).
Vinson, T. M. (b, d).

WAYCROSS, 14,485.
Cherokee Pharmacy (d).
Elliston, L. W. (d).
Gem Pharmacy (d).
Redding, Henry S. (d).

HAWAIIAN ISLANDS.

HILO, 19,000.
Chikuami, T.
Hawaii Printing Co.
Hilo Stationery Co. (c, s).
Machida, T. (b).
Moses Stationery Co.

HONOLULU, 52,183.
Hawaiian News Co. (b).
Office Supply Co., Ltd.
Patten Co.
Thrum, Thomas G. (b).
*Wall, Nichols Co., Ltd. (b).

 Paint and Chemical Company
PAPER COLORS AND MILL PAINT SPECIALTIES
BOSTON   SPRINGFIELD, MASS.   NEW YORK

Wholesale and Retail Stationers

IDAHO.

BLACKFOOT, 3588.
Dustin, Leslie B. (d).
Hayes, T. A.
Jones, Percy.

BOISE, 22,000.
Cunningham, Arch., & Co. (b).
Idaho Staty. & Ptg. Co.
Rawls-Case Co. (b).

CALDWELL, 3543.
Saratoga Stationery Store.

CAMBRIDGE, 500.
Shepherd, C. H. (j).

CUL DE SAC, 800.
Keller, W. D., & Son (d).

EMMETT, 1350.
Rees, S. J.

HAILEY, 1540.
Aukema Drug Co. (d).
Tracy, J. J. (d).

IDAHO FALLS, 8500.
Bistorious, G. A.
Joy Drug Store.
Marker, Alma (o. s.).
Palace Drug Store (d).
Scott, G. M. (o. s.).

LEWISTON, 6043.
Beach, R. C., Co. (g).
Butler, O. E. (d).
*Idaho Drug Co. (d).
Lewiston Mercantile Co.
Lewiston Stationery & Ptg. Co.
Moxley, F. M. (d).
Thatcher & Kling (b).
Wright, M. M. (d).

MONTPELIER, 1924.
Lewis, Mose (g).
Meyrs, J. J.

MONTPELIER—*Continued.*
Modern Drug Co. (d).
Riter Bros. Drug Co.

MOSCOW, 3670.
Hodgins, R. (b, d).
Sherfey, R. R. (b).

NAMPA, 4205.
Bow, R. L.
Fisher, C. A.

OAKLEY, 1000.
Halverson, M. Z. W.

POCATELLO, 9110.
Book Store Pharmacy (b, d).
Bower Wholesale Groc. Co.
Collins, H. A.
Comer Pharmacy.
Cook, Mrs. A. L. (d).
Ferguson & Jenkins (d).
Hilliard Drug Co.
North Main Pharmacy.
People's Store.
Peterson's Stationery Co.
Rourk's Books.
Slohoma Stationery.
Whittelsey, H. H. (d).

REXBURG, 2000.
Flamm, Hy., Co. (g).

TWIN FALLS, 5258.
Clos, L.

WALLACE, 3500.
Croskey, J. G. (d).
Tabor, J. W.
Wallace Drug Co. (d).

WEISER, 2600.
Cutting Drug Co. (d).
Daus, L. L. (d).
Ellingson Drug Co.
Stuart, Geo. (d).

ILLINOIS.

ALBION, 1281.
Michels, B. F., & Son (b, d).

ALTON, 17,528.
Alton Drug Co.
Mather, Hiram G.

AMBOY, 1786.
Aschenbrenner's Pharmacy (d).
Gunning, Geo. (b).
Kauffman, A. C. (b, d).

ANNA, 2809.
Wiley, W. D.

ARCOLA, 2100.
Engle's Drug Co.
Huddleston, A. E.
Magnuson, Al.

ASHLAND, 1200.
Brownback, Henry O. (o. s.).
Wilburn, J. H. (b).

ASHTON, 900.
Dean, R. J. (b).

ASSUMPTION, 1918.
Wallace, W. T. (b, j).

 **Ruling Colors** The best for Ruling Inks.

Wholesale and Retail Stationers

ILLINOIS.

ASTORIA, 2000.
 Mooney Bros. (b, d).
 Toler & Kost.

AURORA, 29,807.
 *Aurora Office Outfitters (o s).
 Benton (d, s).
 Bishop Pharmacy.
 Dorchester-Wilcox Co. (d, s).
 *Erlenborn, A. J., & Co. (c, o. s.).
 Hartz, P. G. Drug Co. (d, s).
 Holmes Bros. (d, s).
 Rollins & Rice (d, s).
 Sanders, T. W. (d, s).
 Schlickler & Miller (b, c).
 Sencenbaugh, S. S., Co. (g, s).
 Staudt Bros. (d, s).
 Wade, Leitz & Grometer (g, s).

BARRY, 1647.
 Ware, G. L.

BEARDSTOWN, 6017.
 Brocker, John (b and d).
 Denton Bros. (d).
 Doyle, J. W.

BELLEVILLE, 21,122.
 Weisman, Jos. (b, c, s).
 Winkler & Schirmer (b, o. s.).

BELVIDERE, 7253.
 Fisher, E. B., & Co.
 Longcor, John C. (d).
 Niemeyer, F. H. (d).
 Veaco, S. H. (d).
 Wyman, W. L. (d).

BENTON, 2675.
 Browning, J. L. (b, o. s.).
 Hart, J. O. (d).
 Webster, J. E. (d, s).

BLOOMINGTON, 25,768.
 Griffin & Marquis.
 Pantagraph Printing & Sta. Co.
 Paxton Typewriter Exchange (o. s.).
 *Read, W. B., & Co. (b, o. s.).

BUNKER HILL, 1046.
 Fahrenkrog, William.
 Jansen, Louis E. (g).

BUSHNELL, 2700.
 Campbell, J. M. (est. of) (b, j).
 Clarke, A. S., & Co. (d, b).
 Frisbee, W. J. (d).

CAIRO, 14,548.
 Brewer, J. B. (d, c).
 Coleman, James (b, c, o. s.).
 De Baun, A. T. (b).
 Fahr, Fred G., Printing & Stationery Co. (b, c, o. s.).
 Henckell's Drug Store (d, s).
 Levitt, John (d, c).
 *Schuh Drug Co.
 Schuh, H. O. (d, c.).
 Schuh, Paul G. (d, s).
 Williams, Thos. W. (b, c, o. s.)

CANTON, 12,000.
 White, Frank & Bro. (b).

CARBONDALE, 5411.
 Fox, B. (b, d).
 Goss, A. R. (d).
 Hewitt, F. M. (d).
 Porter, E. K. (d).
 Seibert, N. C. (d).
 Sheppard, Chas. A. (b, o. s.).
 Veach, R. (b).
 Weiler Jewelry Co. (j).

CARLINVILLE, 3616.
 Graham, F. W. (d, s).
 Loehr, T. C. (d, b, c, s).
 Steinmeyer, A. C. (d, s).

CARLYLE, 1874.
 Shade, J. R. (b).

CARMI, 2833.
 Ball, Wm. A. (b, d).

CARROLLTON, 2323.
 English & Lunneen (d).
 Gimmy, K. K. (d, b).
 Smith, E (b, d).

CARTERVILLE, 2921.
 Hampton, R. H. H. (d).
 Vick, S. S.
 Walker, Geo. Daniel (b).

CARTHAGE, 2500.
 Hoch, Ed. (b).
 Nichols, Mrs. Isabel Cochran (b).

CASEY, 2157.
 Sturdevant & Co. (j).

CHADWICK, 600.
 Appel, Ernest.
 Spealman, H. L. (b, d).

CHAMPAIGN, 12,421.
 Cunningham Bros. (d).
 Faulkner, W. (d).
 Lloyd, D. H. (b, o. s.).
 Robeson, F. K. (g).

 **Paint and Chemical Company**
PAPER COLORS AND MILL PAINT SPECIALTIES
BOSTON　　　　SPRINGFIELD, MASS.　　　　NEW YORK

Wholesale and Retail Stationers

ILLINOIS.

CHAMPAIGN—*Continued*.
Ross-Sim Drug Co.
Swannell, Henry, & Son (d).
Tucker, S. C. (d).
Twin City Printing Co.
U. of I. Supply Store (b).

CHARLESTON, 5884.
Hill & Son (g).
Payne, Frank D.
Rogers Drug Co. (d).
Stuart, R. C. (d).
White, J. D. (d, s).

CHICAGO.

(Population 2,425,000)

Wholesale Stationers marked (*), Office Supply Dealers marked (o. s.), Booksellers selling Stationery marked (b), Druggists selling Stationery marked (d), Druggists selling Books and Stationery marked (b, d), Department Stores selling Stationery marked (g), Jewelers selling Stationery marked (j).
Commercial Stationers are marked (c), Social Stationers marked (s).

Abingdon, The, Press, 734-740 Rush (b).
Ackerman, Martin R., 1720 N. Kedzie bl. (b).
Allen, D. A., & Co., 508 S. Dearborn (b).
Alquist, Mrs. Lina, 1036 W. 59th.
American Bible Society, 332 S. Michigan (b).
American Stationery Co., 113-25 N. Green (o. s.).
Antiquarian Book Store, 26 E. Van Buren (b).
Art & Craft Book Shop, 104 S. Michigan (b).
*Associated Stationers Supply Co., 27 N. Franklin.
Augustana Book Concern, 901 Belmont (b).
Baldwin, Fred B., 53 W. Jackson (o. s.).
Baldwin Printing & Stationery Co., 318 S. La Salle (c, o. s.).
Bankers' Stationery Supply Co., 140 S. Dearborn (c, o. s).
Banovetz, Mathew, 5416 Grace.
Barnes, C. M., Wilcox Co., 1018 S. Wabash av. (b).
Bee-Bee Office Supply Co., 19 S. Wells.
Bear, M. M., Co., 14 W. Washington (s).
Benton, C., 4436 Armitage av.
Benziger Bros., 214 W. Monroe (o. s.).
Berg, Geo. M., 1041 N. Wells.
Bergman, Max, 4360 Broadway.
Bernstein, Ann, 2932 N. Clark (b).
Black, Frank L., 2464 N. Clark.
Book & Art Exchange, 81 E. Madison (b).
Book Supply Co., 231 W. Monroe (b).

Boston Store, State and Madison (g, o. s.).
Brauns, Wm., & Co., 121 N. Wabash (b).
Bruck's Stationery Store, 1406 N. Clark.
Burgwaldt, Ernest J., 611 N. Lamon.
Burr-Vack Co., 511 S. Wabash av. (c, o. s.).
*Butler Bros., W. Randolph & Bridge. Mail order (o. s.).
*Cameron, Amberg & Co., 17 W. Lake (c, o. s.).
Carrington, Geo. S., Co., 2330 W. Vanburen.
Carrithers & Co., 116 S. Michigan (c).
*Carson, Pirie, Scott & Co., Adams, N. W. cor. Franklin (o. s.).
Carson, Pirie, Scott & Co., State, S. E. cor. Madison (g, o. s.).
Carter & Allen, 205 W. Monroe.
Century Book Shop, 4360 Broadway.
Chamberlin, E. W., 5865 Glenwood av.
Chandler, Geo. M., 75 E. Van Buren (b).
Chicago Medical Book Co., 29 E. Madison (b).
Chicago Stationery Shop, 157 Quincy (c, o. s.).
Childs, S. D., & Co., 136 S. Clark (c, o. s.).
Claussen, Geo. W., 4600 N. Clark.
Cole, Geo. E., & Co., 119 W. Washington (c, o. s.).
Commercial Stationery & Loose Leaf Co., 20 S. Clark (c, o. s.).
Congregational Sunday School and Publishing Society, 19 W. Jackson blvd. (b).

ILLINOIS.

CHICAGO—*Continued.*

Cotter, Wm. J., 4908 St. Lawrence av.
Counsell, J. T., 2330 W. Madison (c, o. s.).
Covenant Book Concern, 56 W. Washington.
Curry's Bookstore, 1133 Wilson av.
Cut Cost Co., 64 W. Randolph.
Deardoff, E. B., 5961 Ridge av.
De Lang, Coles & Co., 309 S. La Salle (c).
Doblas, Vaclav, 1206 W. 18th (b).
Downing, Geo. F., 320 W. 63d.
Dunwell & Ford, 114 S. Wabash av. (c, s).
Dusenbery, J. E., 4001 Bway.
Economy Book Shop, 33 S. Clark and 23 E. Vanburen.
Edwards & Clemens, 56 W. Washington.
Ehret, Jos., 4300 Lincoln av.
Engelhardt, Alb. J., 1637 Barry av.
Engineering Agency, Inc., 58 W. Jackson (b).
Englert, Aug., 1027 Wilson av.
Erler, Edward J., 1808 E. 55th.
Ernst, Max F., 6721 Stony Is. av.
Everybody's Book Shop, 1018 Wilson av.
Exline, The, Co., 155 N. Clark.
Fair, The, State, Adams and Dearborn (g, o. s.).
Faithorn Co., 236 S. La Salle (c, o. s.)
Farber, S., 940 N. State.
*Farwell, John V., Co., 102 S. Market (g, o. s.).
Fay, Daniel, 1202 Thorndale (b).
Fieberg, P. H., Co., 213 W. Austin av.
*Field, Marshall, & Co., State, Washington, Randolph and Wabash (g, o. s.).
Fish, Cora C, 250 W. 59th.
Fitzgerald Book Co., 180 N. Dearborn.
Freund, Wm., & Sons, 20 E. Randolph (s).
Gard Stationery Co., 3025 Colorado av.
Garvey, Ed. A., & Co., 8 S. Dearborn (o. s.).
Gilby, J. H., 5423 Blackstone av.
Goldman, Chas., & Co., 424 S. Dearborn (b).
Goldsmith, B. J., 2310 Potomac av.
Gossman, Frank, 5846 Glenwood.

CHICAGO—*Continued.*

Greek Book & Novelty Store, 602 Blue Is. av.
Greenwood's, 1953 W. Madison (b).
Hall & McCreary, 430 S. Wabash av. (b).
Hall, Mrs. Minnie, 1651 School.
Halley Book Co., 711 S. Dearborn (b).
Harden, L. R., 6414 Woodlawn.
Harrison, Frank A., 2142 W. Vanburen.
Harrison Technical Book Store, 2315 Marshall bl.
Heinz, Anton, 1935 Nebraska av.
Heirich, Mrs. Minnie, 1357 E. Marquette rd.
Heller, Louis, 650 W. 45th.
Henry, Patk. J., 952 Irving Pk.
Higgins, Miss Nellie, 502 E 31st.
Hildreth, Joseph H., 85 S. Dearborn.
Hill, Wm. R., 945 E. 47th (b).
Hill, Walter M., 22 E. Washington (b).
Hillman's, State and Washington (g, o. s.).
Hirsch, Felix, 2608 N. Clark.
Hoekstra, Albert J., Arcade bldg.
Horder's Stationery Stores, 108 N. La Salle, 10 N. Franklin, 324 S. Dearborn, 124 W. Adams, 60 E. Monroe (c, o. s.).
Hornstein, E. F., 6928 Normal av.
Howe, Noble, 20 E. Randolph.
Hutchinson, John W., 601 S. Dearborn (o. s.).
Hyman, Gustavus S., 938 E. 55th.
Ingleside, The, Press, 6233 Cottage Grove av.
Ioas & Brodack, 339 S. Wabash (o. s.).
Jackson, Dwight and M. H., 111 W. Monroe (c, o. s.).
Jennings, Albert, 1734 Armitage.
Jensen, Neils P., 2852 Broadway.
Johnson, Adolph, 11,313 Forest av.
Johnson, Nillis, 2224 W. Vanburen (b).
Keath, Earl W., 6224 Greenwood.
Kellner, Frank, 443 W. 63d (b, o. s).
Kendall Bros., 801 E. 63d.
Kendle, R. B., 803 E. 63d.
Koder, James J., 5314 N Clark (b).
Koelling-Brodack Co., 206 W. Randolph (c, o. s.).
Koelling & Klappenbach, 206 W. Randolph (foreign book sellers).
Kohl, P. J., & Co., 230 W. Huron.
Krause, H. C., & Co., 32 S. Clark (c).

 **Paint and Chemical Company**
PAPER COLORS AND MILL PAINT SPECIALTIES
BOSTON   SPRINGFIELD, MASS.   NEW YORK

Wholesale and Retail Stationers

ILLINOIS.

CHICAGO—*Continued.*
Kroch, A., & Co., 22 N. Michigan (b).
L.-M. Stationery Co., 506 S. Dearborn (c, o. s.).
Library Bureau, 6 N. Mich. (o. s.).
Liebl, Frank X., 1658 Cleveland av. (b).
Linka, Bohuslav, 3345 W. 26.
Little Book Shop, The, 1143 E. 55th (b).
Lively, Jos. T., 6223 Broadway.
Low Cost Tablet & Note Book Supply Co., 64 W. Randolph.
Low-Cost Co., 154 W. Randolph.
Lokost Co., 154 W. Randolph.
Lucas, W. M., 458 W. 63d.
Lund, L. H., 2818 W. North (b).
Lundberg, B., & Co., 176 N. Dearborn.
Magee, Ludlow & Co., 1102 S. Wabash av.
Mahr, Chas., 2205 Belmont.
Malcolm, Nathaniel D., 708 E. 63d.
Malloy, Anna, 154½ W. Jackson (b).
Mandel Bros., State and Madison (g, o. s.).
Manhattan Distributing Corporation, 608 S. Dearborn (b).
Marshall Book Store, 3211 Colorado av.
Marshall, Geo. E., & Co., 26 S. Clark (c, o. s.).
Marshall-Jackson Co., 26 S. Clark (c, o. s.).
Martin, A. J., & Co., 80 W. Washington.
Massenberg, Jessie, 3112 Broadway.
Mathieu, F. G., & Co., 7819 S. Halsted (b).
McAllister Art & Stationery Co., 3416 Lawrence.
*McClurg, A. C., & Co., 222 S. Wabash av. and 330 E. Ohio (b, c, o. s.).
McDonald, J. S., Co., 638 Federal (o. s.).
McGauley, Thos., 19 S. Halsted.
McGrath, Mrs. Della, 5442 W. Monroe.
McIntosh, F. W., Co., 5 S. Wabash.
Mead & Wheeler, 35 S. Wabash (o. s.).
Mengus, A., 4762 Lincoln av.
Merchants Litho. Co., 321 S. Sangamon.
Metcalf Stationery Co., 154 E. Erie (a, c).

CHICAGO—*Continued.*
Methodist Book Concern, 734-740 Rush (b).
Middleton, J. W., & Co., 35 S. Dearborn.
Mielzynski, Walenty, 1714 W. 48th.
Miesler, Wm. J., 1837 Sedgwick.
Miller, H. C., Co., 25 S. Market (c, o. s.).
Monarch Stationery Co., 128 N. La Salle (c, o. s.).
Monroe, Austin F., 312 S. Clark.
Montgomery, Ward & Co., Chicago av. and Halsted (o. s.).
Morgan Stationery Co., 3971 Cottage Grove av. (b).
Morris Book Shop, 24 N. Wabash (b).
Morris-Sidney & Co. (o. s.), 5 S. La Salle.
Most, Edward W., 1133 Wilson.
Mumford, E. G., 62 W. Madison.
Nabb, James A., 5085 Broadway.
Naber, F. A., 1361 E. 63d.
Nat'l Law Book Co., 105 N. Monroe.
Neuson, Theo., 313 W. North av. (b).
New Thought Book Shop, 5 S. Wabash.
Newton Shop, 1207 E. 63d.
Norton, Frank W., 1369 E. 57th (b).
Oberst, Dode G., & Co., 38 S. Dearborn (o. s.).
O'Dea, M. T., 521 N. State (b).
Open Court Pub. Co., 122 S. Michigan (b).
Orde, Chas. W., & Co., 108 S. La Salle.
Peacock, C. D., & Co., State cor. Adams (j).
Pearson, R. M., 5706 Stony Island av.
Perfection Legal Blank Co., 172 W. Washington.
Peterson, G. N., 1132 Thorndale av.
*Pettibone, P. F., Co., Inc., 18 S. La Salle and 27 N. Desplaines (c, o. s.).
Pieritz Bros., 358 N. Laramie.
Pilgrim Press, The, 19 W. Jackson (b).
Porter, J. B., & Co., 714 S. Dearborn.
Powner, Chas. T., Co., 37 N. Clark (b).
Practical Sunday School Supplies Co., 14 W. Washington.
Rex, Geo. P., & Co., 422 S. Dearborn.

 **Regal Wall Coating** A white cold water paint. Will not rub, scale or peel off.

Wholesale and Retail Stationers

ILLINOIS.

CHICAGO—*Continued.*
Reynolds, Mrs. Elizabeth, 1018 N. State.
Riddle & Wunderle Co., 62 W. Washington (c, o. s.).
Ridley, W. G., & Son, 170 W. Randolph (o. s.).
Roman, The, Book Shop, 154 W. Jackson.
Rothschild & Co., State, N. E. cor. Vanburen (g, o. s.).
Ruzicka, John, 1857 W. 21st.
Salisbury, Schulz & Co., 159 W. Randolph.
Sampson Note Book Co., 8 E. Austin.
Sapersten, Meyer, 307 S. Dearborn (b).
Schallerer, Jos. J., 350 E. 71st.
Schmidt, Emma A., 1157 N. State.
Schock Bros., 3234 W. Madison (o. s.).
Schon, Mrs. B., 1452 E. 63d.
Schwarz, Joseph, 1424 W. 51st. (b).
Sears, Roebuck Co., Homan av. and Harvard st. Mail orders. (o. s.).
Seffer, Adolph, 434 S. Wood (b).
Senn Store, The, 5865 Glenwood av.
*Shure, N., Co., 237 W. Madison (o. s.).
Sidney-Morris & Co., 5 S. La Salle (o. s.).
Simpson, Harry M., 533 W. 65th pl.
Singer & Brandy, Toys, 1429 S. Halsted.
*Smith, Shea & Co., 322 Federal (c, o. s.).
Smyth, John M., Co., mail order, 701 W. Madison (o. s.).
Spaulding & Co., 332 S. Michigan av. (j)
Speakman's, E., Sons, 435 Honore.
Speakman's Crane Book Store, school supplies, 2302 W. VanBuren (b).
Speakman's McKinley Book Store, school supplies, 2053 W. Adams (b).
Spencer, Addison G., 2004 Larrabee.
*Stationers' Supply Mfg. Co., 29 S. La Salle.
Stationery Mfg. Co., 732 Federal.
Stevens, Maloney & Co., 21 S. La Salle (c, o. s.).
Stranberg, Hokan C., 1054 E. 47th.
Stromberg, Allen & Co., 430 S. Clark (o. s.).
Swedish M. E. Book Concern, 351 W. Oak (b).
Swigart Paper Co., 653 S. 5th av.

CHICAGO—*Continued.*
Tablet & Note Book Supply Co., 64 W. Randolph.
Tallman, Robbins & Co., 314 W. Superior (o. s.).
Thayer & Jackson Stationery Co., 26 S. Clark (c, o. s.).
Theosophical Book Concern, 304 S. Wabash av. (b).
Thomas, W. E., 1351 E. 55th.
Thompson, P. D., 4090 Broadway.
Union Stationery Co., 192 N. Clark (o. s.).
Van Dort, G. Broes, Co., 19 W. Jackson (b).
Varley, Albert, 3628 Milwaukee av.
Vining, Ezra, 3901 Vincennes av.
Vogue Stationery Shop, 20 E. Jackson.
Wallen, C. L., 22 Quincy (b).
Wallerstein, Harry, 1022 W. 12th (b).
Ward Co., Montgomery, Chicago av. and River. Mail order. (o. s.).
Wardle, Thos. C., 7909 Exchange av.
Weber, J. A., 2920 Southport.
Wertz, Henry J., 2218 Osgood.
Western Book and Stationery Co., 425 S. Wabash av. (b).
*Western News Co., 25 E. Austin av.
Whitacre, E. J., 2602 Orchard (b, o. s.).
Wiley, William, 3506 Vincennes av. (b, o. s.).
Wolf, Thomas R., 1401 E. 55th.
Zaleski & Jankiewicz, 1410 W. Division (b).
Zerkle Bros., 362 E. 43d.

COLCHESTER, 1600.
Coplin, A. G. (b).

CREAL SPRINGS, 936.
Anderson, D. S. (d).

DANVILLE, 30,000.
Baum, W. F. (d).
Fischer & McKee (j).
Hacker, F. J. (g).
*Illinois Ptg. Co. (o. s.).
Johnson, F. A. (d).
Lyric Pharmacy (d).
Oetzel & Torrance (d).
Overman, U. J. (d).
Plaster Drug Co. (d).
Schultz Drug Co.
Senger Drug Co. (d).
Stallings' Pharmacy (d).
Woodbury Book Co. (b, o. s.).
Woodbury Drug Co. (d).

 **Paint and Chemical Company**
PAPER COLORS AND MILL PAINT SPECIALTIES
BOSTON   SPRINGFIELD, MASS.   NEW YORK

Wholesale and Retail Stationers

ILLINOIS.

DECATUR, 43,000.
  Armstrong, E. W. (d).
  Bell Drug Co. (d).
  Davis, A. T. (d).
  Decatur Drug Co. (d).
  Gebhart, H. S., & Co. (g).
  Gushard, Wm., Dry Goods Co. (g).
  Haines & Essick (b).
  Herald Ptg. & Staty. Co.
  Linn & Scruggs Dry Goods & Carpet Co. (g).
  Linxweiler Ptg. Co. (s, o. s.).
  Mac's News Stand.
  Morrow, C. A., Art Store.
  Quaker Drug Co.
  Review Ptg. & Staty. Co.
  Schuerman, L., & Sons, Art Store.
  *Wait-Cahill Co. Notions.
  Wallender & Wilder (s, o. s.).
  *West Paper Co.

DE KALB, 8204.
  Crescent Drug Co. (d).
  Kahn's Drug Store (d).
  Leslie, R. N. (g).
  Powell, C. E. (d).
  Pritchard & Dickerman (b).
  Quarrestrom, Chas. A. (g).
  Secor, H. E. (d).

DENVER, 200.
  Scott, J. V. (d).

DIXON, 8200.
  Edwards, L. E. (b).
  Kramer, A. W. (g).
  Public Drug & Book Co.
  Rowland Bros. (d).
  Sterling & Sterling (d).
  Sullivan, Thos.

DOWNERS GROVE, 3000.
  Gress, Mrs. Emma.

DUQUOIN, 5454.
  Angel, A. F. (d).
  Bianco, M. (d).
  Jones, H. B. (b, d).
  Parks, W. W. (d).

EAST ST. LOUIS, 58,547.
  Homberg, W. H.
  Miller, Wm. J.
  *Watson & Son, M. W. (b).

EDINBURG, 918.
  Eaton, W. B. (b, d).

EDWARDSVILLE, 5014.
  Ballweg & Take (b, d).
  Burroughs & Whiteside (b, d).

EFFINGHAM, 3998.
  Barber, O. C. (b).
  Barlage, John (b).

ELDORADO, 3866.
  People's Drug Store.
  Webber Bros (b, d).

ELGIN, 25,970.
  Ackemann Bros. (g, s).
  Andres, A. A. (d, s).
  Gartland, W. J. (d, s).
  Hall, Edwin (d, s).
  Kennell Bros.
  Peck, G. M. (g, s).
  *Root, W. A., Est. (c).
  Zook, H. L. (c).

ELMHURST, 3000.
  Freeman, C. B.

EUREKA, 1661.
  Stumpf, F. B. (b, d).

EVANSTON, 33,000.
  Battles, C. E. (d).
  Central Pharmacy. (d).
  Chandler, H. E., & Co. (b).
  Evanston Art & Stat. Co.
  Hazeltine, J. H. (b).
  Howe & Anderson.
  Knothe Pharmacy. (d).
  Leffingwell, R. L. (d).
  Leffingwell Tyler Co. (d).
  Lord, W. S. (b).
  University Drug Store. (d).

FOREST PARK, 6504.
  Brum, William.
  Fritz, Oscar A. (d).

FORRESTON, 870.
  Haller, Edw. E. (d).

FREEPORT, 17,567.
  Brown & Dollmeyer (b).
  Emmert Drug Co. (d).
  Fargher, L. T.
  Guenther, C. P., & Co. (d).
  Hill-Garrity Drug Co.
  Jungkuns, W. F. (d).
  Johnson, Chas. F. (d).
  Moogk & Meisenbach (d).
  Schwartz & Crawford (d).
  Wagner, Otto (b).
  Woolworth, F. W., & Co.

FULTON, 2174.
  Johnson, Edward.
  Williamson, A. C. (d).

ILLINOIS.

GALENA, 5005.
Kempter, E. W. (b, o. s.).

GALESBURG, 22,089.
Burt, O. H. (d).
Coad, F. L. (b).
Hoover & Co., J. W. (d).
Johnson Co., O. T. (g).
Lescher Drug Co.
Stromberg & Tenney (b, o. s.).
Temple & Carroll (b, o. s.).
West Drug Co. (d).

GALVA, 2498.
Dexter's Book Store.

GENESEO, 3199.
Lynd's, O. M. (d).
Stein's Book Store.

GIBSON CITY, 2500.
Bryant, W. C.
Lowry's, E., Sons (o. s.).

GIRARD, 1891.
Deck, L. C. (b, d).

GLENCOE, 2100.
Chandler, H. E., & Co.

GRAND TOWER, 873.
Crow, Louis M.

GRANITE CITY, 9903.
Seboumenoff, A.

GRAPE CREEK, 500.
Hay, C. M.

GREENVILLE, 2504.
Mulford & Monroe (b, d).
Watson, Frank E. (d).

HAMILTON, 2000.
Gordon, J. A. (b).

HARVARD, 3000.
Fernhols, Emil G. (d).
Lanning, Frank (g).
Phalen Bros. (d).
Richardson, W. I. (d).

HARVEY, 7227.
Purdy, John, & Co.

HAVANA, 3525.
Jones, J. M., Book Store (b).
Krelling Drug Store (d).
Pfetzing Drug Store (d).
Tarbell & Ermeling (b, d).

HERRIN, 8700.
Cline's Drug Store.
Holland Drug Co.
Mifflin, L. A. (b).

HUMBOLT, 356.
Elkins, G. T. (b).
Marshall-Moore (g).
Stewart, S. E. (d).

JACKSONVILLE, 15,326.
Atherton, A. H. (b).
Lane, B. L. (b).
Ye Book Shop (b).

JERSEYVILLE, 4113.
Ford, Thos. S.

JOLIET, 36,170.
Ducker, G. A., & Co. (g).
Eagle, The (g).
*Joliet Book & Stat'y Co. (o. s.).
Joliet Dry Goods Co. (g).
Joliet Republican Ptg. Co. (c).
Klep, R. P. (j).
New York Store (g).
Oesterle, Carl (j).
*Pilcher, Robert.
Plitt, L. (d).
Stillman, H. A. (d).

KANKAKEE, 17,167.
Kankakee Book Store.
Rondy, J. J. (b, c, s).

KEWANEE, 15,563.
Heimbeck & O'Connor (d).
Hill & Sons (d).
Hirschy Drug Co. (d).
Lyman-Lay Co. (g).
Jones, Gertrude (b).
Red Cross Drug Store.
Scott, Geo. G. (d).
Scott's Dept Store (g).

KIRKWOOD, 108.
Servatius, L. A. (d).

KNOXVILLE, 2080.
Gottrick, F. O. (d).
Nelson, N. O. (b, d).

LA GRANGE, 5282.
Hartronft, John.
Quinn, F. D. (d).
Schroeder, Otto A. (d).
Smith, H. P. (d).
Tholin, Rose (b).

LA HARPE, 1591.
Vedder, F. F. (d).

LAKE FOREST, 2349.
French, G. G. (d).
Krafft, Carl L. (d).
Werban, Frank J. (d).

 **Paint and Chemical Company**
PAPER COLORS AND MILL PAINT SPECIALTIES
BOSTON   SPRINGFIELD, MASS.   NEW YORK

Wholesale and Retail Stationers

ILLINOIS.

LA SALLE, 11,537.
 Clancy Drug Store, Inc. (b, d).
 Feurer, E. J. (b, d).
 Hermann, W. F. (b and d).
 Malone, James E. (b, d).
 Murray, John (b and d).

LE ROY, 1861.
 Peters, H. O. (d).
 Van Deventer, S. D. (b, d).

LERNA, 1252.
 Whitacre, Izatus (d).

LINCOLN, 10,892.
 Alvey, H. W. (d).
 Corwine & Craddock Co.
 Feurbacher, A. J. (d).
 Knochel, Geo. (d).
 Pfau, Frank.
 Purcell, Clyde (b).

LITCHFIELD, 5971.
 Hartwell, F., Jewelry Co.
 Holderread, W. (b-d).
 Hood & Son (b and d).
 Kunkel & Frain (b, d).
 Litchfield Drug Co. (b, d).
 Litchfield Printing & Stat'y Co.
 Woolworth, F. W., & Co.

LYONS, 1483.
 Yabusch, Emil.

McLEANSBORO, 1796.
 Robinson, F. W. (d).

MACOMB, 7000.
 McClellan, F. G. (b).
 Miner, W. C. (b, o. s.).

MARENGO, 2005.
 Richardson, H. W. (b-d).

MARION, 7098.
 Moore, G. N. (b-j).

MAROA, 1160.
 Smelz, Hobbs & Co. (b, d).

MARSHALL, 2500.
 City Drug Store (d).
 Duncan, E. M. (d).
 Kiefer Drug Co. (b and d).

MASCOUTAH, 1842.
 Winkler, John.

MASON CITY, 1890.
 McKinley, Clyde D. V. (b, d).

MATTOON, 11,456.
 Armentrout, J. C. (b).
 Christian Book Store.
 Ritter (b, d).

MAYWOOD, 8032.
 Gruschow, C. J.
 Schwanke, Louis.
 Swan, J. C. (d).

MEDORA, 444.
 Loomis, T. A. (b and d).

MELROSE PARK, 5000.
 Giles News Co.

MENDON, 627.
 Chant, Frank (d).
 French, Frank.

MENDOTA, 4000.
 Denison Drug Co. (d).

MEREDOSIA, 951.
 Field, Roscoe B. (d).

MOLINE, 24,199.
 *Carlson Bros. (b, o. s.).
 Fish & Loosely Co. (g).
 Sohrbeck, G. H. (d).

MONMOUTH, 9900.
 Johnson, A. E. (d).
 Johnson, Frank O. (d).
 McQuiston, W. H., & Son (b).
 Wirts Book Co. (b).

MONTICELLO, 1980.
 Donohue, J. H. (d).
 McMillen, Geo. E.
 Raycroft, Joseph.

MORRIS, 4563.
 Foxford & Naker Drug Co.
 Mack, Harry.
 Wagner, Walter S.
 Warren & Son.

MOUNT CARMEL, 6934.
 Baggs Bros. (b, d).
 Hadley, W. C. (b, d).
 Martin, C. A. (b and d).

MOUNT MORRIS, 1200.
 Dean, Fred J.
 Mishler, C. H. (b).

MOUNT STERLING, 2026.
 Brockman & Son (b).
 Brooks, R. S. (b).

MOUNT VERNON, 8007.
 King City Drug Store (d).
 Mammoth, The (g).
 Mount Vernon News Co. (b).
 Porter & Bond (d, b).
 Rackaway & Maxey (d, b).
 Sanford, J. L. (d).
 Webb, R. L. (b).

 **Mill White** Will not turn yellow like the ordinary White Lead paint.

Wholesale and Retail Stationers

ILLINOIS.

MURPHYSBORO, 7485
Hensen, C. E. (d).
Horsfield, Geo.
Neadstine Drug Store (d).
M. & O. Drug Store.
O. K. Drug Store.
Post, F. H (d).
Rathgeber, F. W., & Bros. (o. s.).
Shaw's Drug Store (d).
Werner Drug Store.

NAPERVILLE, 3449.
Nichols, J. L., & Co. (b).

NEOGA, 1074.
Wilson, A. F. (b, d).

NEWARK, 600.
Bibbins & Co.

NEW BERLIN, 690.
Foutch, Mrs. J. W.

NEWMAN, 1400.
Skinner, R. A. (b).

NOKOMIS, 1872.
Kempton, C. H. (b, d).
Schaper, George (b, d).

NORA, 212.
Miner, H. B.

NORMAL, 4500.
Coen, G. H. (b, d, o. s.).
McKnight & McKnight (o. s.).

OAK PARK, 19,801.
Bristow, Jos., & Co.
Card, C. I.
Dittman, F.
Oaks, W. W. (d).

OGLESBY, 3500.
Bent Bros. Co.
D. & S. Drug Co.

ONARGA, 1273.
Krause, Charles (d).

ONEIDA, 589.
Armstrong, Clara.
Shaffer, T. B.

OREGON, 2200.
Fischer, L. (b).
Jewett, T. A., & Sons (d).
Thorpe, R. W. (d).

OSWEGO, 600.
Cutler, Scott C. (b, d. s.).
Morse, W. J.

OTTAWA, 9535.
Duncan, W. D. (d).
Gapen, T. B., & Son (d).
Kneusal Bros. (b-d).
Kneusal, Frank (d).
Lutz, C. J. (d).
Mick, Carl, (d).
Weiss, Geo. W. (d).
Wheeler & Malo.

PANA, 6055.
Butts, Claude (d).
Coffman, C. B.
Grossmann, G. B. (d).
*Pana Grocery Co.
Sneider Bros.
Wittman & Marty (d).

PARIS, 8200.
Archer, N. Sam. (o. s.).
Crandall & Son (d).
Fitch Drug Co. (d).
Jones Dry Goods Store (g).
Kurtz, Geo. E. (d).
Schaeffer, A. L. (b, o. s.).

PAXTON, 3053.
Froyd's Book Store.

PEKIN, 9897.
Blenkiron Book Store.
Ehrlicher Bros. (d).
Harmel, J. W. (o. s.).
Ketterer, Emil (d).
Krager, Carl (d).

PEORIA, 66,950.
Barnhart, C. E. (d).
Bergner, P. A., & Co. (g).
Bloch & Kuhl (g).
Churchill Drug Co.
Dawson Drug Co. (d).
DeKroyft, F. M. (d).
Dufner, Wm. V. (d).
Durkin, J. E. (d).
Eichenberger, W. S.
Espenscheid, A.
Harsch, John (d).
Jacquin & Co. (b, c, s).
Kneer, Jr., John (d).
Kneer, Theo. F. (d).
McDougal, R. D. (d).
Modern System Sales Co.
Peoria News Stand.
Putnam, W. G., & Co. (g).
Reinhart, Joseph (d).
Rettberg, Anton (d).
Rettberg, John (d).
Roskoten, C. O. (d).
Schmid, E. A. (d).
Selby, James J. (d).

 **Paint and Chemical Company**
PAPER COLORS AND MILL PAINT SPECIALTIES
BOSTON   SPRINGFIELD, MASS.   NEW YORK

Wholesale and Retail Stationers

ILLINOIS.

PEORIA—*Continued.*
  Siegle, H. C. (d).
  Snider, D. S. (d).
  *Strelbich, J. C.
  Taylor, L. L. (d).
  *Tripp, D. H., & Son (b).
  Wagishauer, G. E. (b).
  Weisbruch Bros. (d).
  Wheeler, L. C. (d).
  Zagelmeyer, E. F. (d).
  Ziegler, Herman L. (d).

PEOTONE, 1250.
  Fletcher, J. H.
  Foster, A. J., & Co. (d).
  Laonkota, J. A. (d).

PETERSBURG, 2807.
  Finney, D. B. (d).
  Luthringer Bros. (d).
  Watkins, Sam L.

PITTSFIELD, 2095.
  Coley, L. A.
  Vertrees & Co.

POLO, 1869.
  Dingley, C. A. (b-d).
  Clothier, C. R. (b, d).
  Hunt, H. B. (b, d).

PONTIAC, 6099.
  Butler, F. J., Co. (d).

PRAIRIE CITY, 818.
  Fiske, E. D. (d).

PRINCETON, 4131.
  Case, Geo. E. (d).
  Cushing, C. G. (d).
  Dunbar, C. J., Co.
  Trulson & Rambo (d).

PROPHETSTOWN, 1250.
  Cleveland, Frank (d).
  Fenn, C. W. (d).

QUINCY, 36,587.
  Garrelts, Henry, & Sons.
  Heidbreder & Co. (d).
  *Irwin Paper Co.
  Jost & Kiefer Ptg. Co. (c).
  *Oenning Glass and Book Co.
  *Sommers-Aldo Drug Co.
  *Taylor, E. J., & Co. (b).
  White, Mrs. A. (b).

RANSOM, 400.
  Gaughan, P. J.
  Transau, J. W., & Co.
  Sulzburge, Mrs. M. (b).
  Whitmore, George J.
  Wright, J. C., & Son.

RANTOUL, 1500.
  Cox, R. M.

RAYMOND, 881.
  Seymour, W. L. (b).

RIVERSIDE, 1551.
  Opper, J. C. (b).

ROBINSON, 3863.
  Swarn, W. H. (b-j).

ROCKFORD, 45,401.
  Central Book Store (b).
  Croon & Co., J. A.
  Lundgren, A. G. (b).
  McFarland, H. D., & Co. (b).
  New Illinois Stationery Co.
  Rockford Office Supply House (b).
  Rockford Office Supply House, Inc.
  Shimmim, W. M. (b).
  Standard Book & Music Store (b).
  Stewart, D. J., & Co. (g).
  Swenson, N. E. (b).

ROCK ISLAND, 30,000.
  Augustana Book Concern.
  Harts & Bahnsen Co. (d).
  McCabe & Co., L. S. (g).
  Stationery Shop (c. s.).
  Valle, Jr., E. O. (o. s.).
  Young & McCombs (g).

RUSHVILLE, 2292.
  Phillips & Co., B. R. (d).

SALEM, 2669.
  Sweney Bros. Co. (b, d).

SANDWICH, 2557.
  Converse, Ira (d, b, s).
  Newton, F. J. (d).
  Resenstone, R. G. (d).

SHELBYVILLE, 3590.
  Beetle, Chas.
  Hopkins, E. M. (b, d).

SHELDON, 1236.
  Johnson Drug Co. (d).
  Kisner, A. S. (d).

SOUTH WILMINGTON, 4000.
  McNulty, R. (g).

SPARTA, 3051.
  Barker, A. M. (b, d).
  Gemmill, Anna.
  Grenslet, E. D.
  Skelly, O. J. (d).

 **Canary Yellow.** A true color. Makes bright tints and solid finishes.

Wholesale and Retail Stationers

ILLINOIS.

SPRINGFIELD, 51,678.
Barkers Art Store.
Bressmer Co., John (g).
*Capital City Paper Co.
Coe Bros. (o. s.).
Foutch-Kerns Supply Co. (b).
Goodpasture & Darneille.
Hartwell, J. F. (j).
Hulett, G. A.
Jefferson Printing Co. (o. s.).
Klaholt, J. C. (j).
Mitchell, A. S. (d).
Phillips, J. Robert (d).
Sell & Coe.
Simmons, Frank R. (b).
*Smith, Hal M.
*Springfield Notion Co.
*Springfield Paper Co.

STERLING, 6309.
Galt, H. M. (b.)

STEWARDSON, 720.
Penslar Store.

STREATOR, 15,000.
Barlow & Leroy.
Carew, W. H. (j).
Eggleson, John (d).
Gant & Co. (d).
Hattenbauer, W. (d).
Heenan, D., Mercantile Co. (g).
Herschey, D. A., Co. (d).
*The Independent-Times Printing Co. (b, c).
Murray, D. C., & Co. (g).
Theidoler, Walter (d).
Thompson, Poor (d).
Wooley, W. W. (d).

SULLIVAN, 3000.
Barber, E. E. (b-j).
Hall, Sam (b, d).

SUMNER, 1412.
Carter, E. H. (d).

SYCAMORE, 4500.
Lee, F. E., & Co. (b).

TAYLORVILLE, 5446.
Morton, Charles W. (b-d).

TISKILWA, 1000.
Kellogg, G. C. (b, d).
Wilkins, C. L. (d).

TRENTON, 1694.
Eickler, J. A. (g).

URBANA, 10,000.
Knowlton & Bennett (b, d).
Leslie, F. H. (b, d).
Oldham Bros. (b, d).
Sim Drug Co. (b, d).

VANDALIA, 2974.
Capps, Geo. B. (b, d).
Humphrey, F. C. (d, b).

VIRGINIA, 2000.
Coleman, Henry (b).
Gatton, C. B. (d).
Hubbard, C. M. (d).

WARSAW, 2254.
Brinkman, Louis (d).
Ferris & Raich (d).
Kirkpatrick, J. W. (j, o. s.).

WASHINGTON, 1601.
Brady, C. F., & Co. (d).
Zinser, Elmer F. (d).

WATERLOO, 2091.
Eilbracht, W. E. (d).
Hamacher, P. A. (b, d).
Voris, Hardy C.

WATSEKA, 2476.
Arnold, T. S., & Son (d).
Blake, F. E. (d).
Barnett Drug Co.
Foster, T. R. (b).

WAUKEGAN, 16,069.
Atterbury's Pharmacy.
Funk Book Shop (o. s.).
Globe Department Store (g).
Holstein, C. (d).
Jemison's Book Store (b).
Jewell, A. J. (d).
North Side Pharmacy.
Pierce, W. W. (d).
Rubins Dept. Store (g).
Wandel, W. F. (b).
Woolworth, F. W., & Co.

WAVERLY.
Wyle, F. A. (j).

WEST FRANKFORT, 2111.
Hill, Orlie (d).

WHITEHALL, 2854.
Rutschke, Oscar (b, d).
Winn, Harry L. (b).

WINCHESTER, 1689.
Danner, C. M.
Gaser, R. D. (d).
Higgins, M. E. & J. A.

 **Paint and Chemical Company**
PAPER COLORS AND MILL PAINT SPECIALTIES
BOSTON   SPRINGFIELD, MASS.   NEW YORK

Wholesale and Retail Stationers

ILLINOIS.

WOODSTOCK, 4500.
Hoy, L. T. (d).
Stone, E. E. (d, b).
Wright, A. S. (b, d).
Wicks & Copley.

YATES CITY, 586.
Lehman, W. G.

ZION CITY, 5000.
National Office Supply Co. (o. s.).

INDIANA.

ANDERSON, 31,296.
Anderson, The, News Co., (o. s.).
Brickley, E. T.
Cassell Bros. (d).
Central Pharmacy.
Decker Bros. Book Store (o. s.).
Harts City Drug Store (d).
Kimball, Hayse Drug Co.
McWilliams, N. E. (d, b).
Meyer Bros. Drug Co. (d).

ANGOLA, 3000.
Jackson, H. C. (d).
Kratz, H. E., & Son (o. s.).
Kolb Bros. (d).
Stoner, Geo. (b).

ATTICA, 3500.
Brady, J. A. (b).
Crigler, J. B. (d).
Crigler, F. B. (b, d).
De Selmo, O. C. (j).
Drake, F. O. (b).
McDermont, Frank J. (g).
Modern Pharmacy (d).
Robinson, C. F. (b, d).
Robinson, C. F., & Son, (d).
Schwartz, Harry G.

AUBURN, 5300.
Kettering, C. W. (d).
Staman, Ashton (d, b).

AURORA, 4410.
Leive, W., & Sons (j, c, s).
Riddell, J. A., & Co. (d, s).

BICKNELL, 3000.
Fox Bros. (d).

BLOOMINGTON, 8838.
Bowles Drug Store.
Bryant, R. J. (d).
City Book & Music Co.
O'Harrow, J. W. (d).
Penrod, T. J. (d).
Stout, W. A. (d).
Vermilya, J. C. (d).
Wiles Drug Co. (d).

BOSWELL, 814.
Scott Drug Co.
Simpkins Drug Co.

BOURBON, 1163.
Compton & Co., M. (j).
Fribley Dep't Store Co. (g).
Matchette Drug Store.
Martin Pharmacy Co. (d).

BRAZIL, 9340.
Brattin, Dudley W. (b).
Haggart, Alexander T. (b).

CAMBRIDGE CITY, 2237.
Carpenter, B. A. (d).
Danner Bros.

CARTHAGE, 1028.
Hill, Owen S. (b).

CHESTERTON, 1400.
Holst, Peter.

CLINTON, 6229.
Morgan Brown H. (g).

COLUMBIA CITY, 3800.
Chapman Bros.

COLUMBUS, 9000.
Cummins, Geo. H. (b).

CONNERSVILLE, 7738.
Ashworth Drug Store (d).
Green Bro. (d).
Roth, A. J. (g).
Young, L. B. (b).

CRAWFORDSVILLE, 9371.
Bischoff, L. (g).
Dick & Riley (d).
McNutt (d).
Myers, N. W. (d).
Nye & Booe (d).
Scharf (d).
Schultz & Schultz (b, c, s).

CROWN POINT, 2750.
Baker, Harry J. (j).

 **Permanent Reds** LIGHT ALKALI WATER } PROOF

Wholesale and Retail Stationers

INDIANA.

DANVILLE, 1802.
Hardy, J. B.
Hargraves, C. A.
Lochmiller, G. E.

DECATUR, 4471.
Callow & Kohne.
Enterprise Drug Co.
Smith, Yager & Falk.

EAST CHICAGO, 19,098.
Nassau & Thompson (b).
Schlieker, A. G. (d).

ELKHART, 19,282.
*Bell, J. A., Co. (b, o. s.).
Clark Drug Co. (d).
Clem Drug Co. (d).
Creech Drug Store (b, d).
*Elkhardt Stationery Co.
Houseworth Bros. (d).
Kuespert, Emil (j).
Nachtrieb, W. H. (d).
Timmins, F. S. (b, o).
Weiler, J. F. (d).

ELWOOD, 11,028.
Hinshaw, O. D. (d).
Kute & Conner (d).
Sneed, Bert E., & Co. (b, d).

EVANSVILLE, 69,647.
*Crescent News & Hotel Co. (g).
De Vry, Bernard.
Fowler, Dick & Walker, Inc. (g, b).
Geupel Bros. (b).
*Leich, Chas., & Co. (d).
Smith & Butterfield (b).

FAIRMOUNT, 3205.
Nolder, L. E.
O'Mara, P. H. (d).
Pioneer Drug Store.

FORT WAYNE, 83,250.
Baade Book & Office Supply Co.
*Becker Paper Co.
*Fisher Brothers Paper Co.
*Fort Wayne Drug Co. (d).
*Fort Wayne Ptg. Co.
Jocquel, L. (b).
Lehman Book & Stationery Co. (b).
Sanders, C. W. (b).
*Smick, M. M., & Son.
Wolf & Dessauer (g).

FOWLER, 1491.
Hinckley, W. A. (b).

FRANKFORT, 8634.
Ashman Drug Co. (b, d).
Bryant, Lena M. (b).
Campbell-Aughe Co.
*Grimes, B. H., Co.
McKown Drug Store (d).
Merritt, E. B. (d).
Norris, Fred L. (o. s.).
Norris Pharmacy (d).

FRANKLIN, 4005.
Wood, A. C., & Son.
Yager, Samuel O. (b).

GARRETT, 5000.
Betts, O. H.
Holter, A. F. (b).
Hunsell, Kal. (b).
Paterson, J. S. (b).
Stoehr, I. J. (b).

GARY, 36,000.
Hall Drug Store (d).
Tribe of K., Inc.

GAS CITY, 3622.
City Drug Co. (d).
Neely, P. O. (b).
Rothinghouse Bros. (d).

GOSHEN, 8514.
Central Drug Co.
Goshen Chemical Co.
Hawks, D. H. (d).
Himes, Grant.
MacDowell & Boylen (b, o. s.).
News Book Store (b, o. s.).
Owl Drug Store (d).
Rexall Drug Store.
Rule, G. W. (b, d).

GREENCASTLE, 3980.
Dunlavey Stoops Drug Co. (d).
Hamilton's Book Store.
Jones-Stevens Co. (d).
Langdon, J. K., & Co. (b).

GREENFIELD, 4448.
Lewis, W. M. (b).
Meyers, Walter.

GREENSBURG, 5420.
Batterton, J. H., & Sons (d, b).
Henry & Co. (d).
Magee, A. A., & Son (d).
Moss, J. S. (d).
St. John & Guthrie (d, b).
The Fair Store (g, b).

HAMMOND, 24,000.
Kaufman & Wolf (g).
Negele, Otto P. (d).

 **Paint and Chemical Company**
PAPER COLORS AND MILL PAINT SPECIALTIES
BOSTON   SPRINGFIELD, MASS.   NEW YORK

Wholesale and Retail Stationers

INDIANA.

HAMMOND—*Continued.*
Nelson, C. E. (d).
Norriss, W. (d, b).
Postlewaite, H. J. (o. s.).
Summers Pharmacy (d).
Weis, Joseph (d).
Weis, L. H. (d).

HARTFORD CITY, 6187.
Van Winkle, Theo. P. (b, d).

HUNTINGBURG, 2464.
Miller, A. H., Jr. (d).
Robinson, L. T. (d).
Schwartz, C. W. (d).

HUNTINGTON, 10,272.
Barnhart Book Store.
Beckstein, A. C. (b, d).
Bradley Brothers (d).
Lovett, Justin (d).

INDIANAPOLIS, 233,650.
Ayers, L. S., & Co., Washington and Meridian (g).
Block, Wm. H., & Co., Ills. and Market (g).
Burford, Wm. B., 38-40 So. Meridian (s, c).
*Central Paper & Tablet Mfg. Co., 304 Murphy Bldg.
*Crescent Paper Co., 211-217 W. Georgia.
*Dolmetsch, E. C., Co., 228 S. Meridian.
Hampton Printing Co., 117-121 W. Georgia (o. s.).
Hampton, W. W.
Hiller Office Supply Co., 35 S. Penna.
Hessel, Isidor (j).
Indianapolis Book & Staty. Co.
Kautz Stationery Co., 116 N. Penna (o. s.).
Kiefer, Stewart & Co., Georgia and Capital av. (d).
*Indiana Paper Co., 27 E. Maryland.
*Indianapolis Book and Stationery Co., 225 S. Meridian.
Levy Ptg. Co., Ohio and Senate avs. (c, o. s.).
Mayer, Chas., & Co. (b, s), 29 West Washington.
*Money, Mueller, Ward Co., 101 S. Meridian (d).
Pettis Dry Goods Co., 25-39 E. Washington (g).
Ratti, Joseph Printing Co., 123 W. Market (c, o. s.).

INDIANAPOLIS—*Continued.*
Silent Evangel Society (b), 522 Mass. av.
Stewart Co., W. K., 44 E. Washington (b, o. s.).
Thornton-Levey Co., 44 S. Penn and 36 E. Maryland (o. s.).
Wasson & Co., H. P., 6-8 W. Washington (g).

JASPER, 2500.
Block, Frances.
Sonderman, Francis (b).

JEFFERSONVILLE, 10,412.
Doherty, M. F. (d).
Doolittle, B. (d).
Graham Drug Co.
Parks, Floyd (d).
Pfau, W. C. (d).
Schimpff, Chas. A., & Son (b).

KENDALLVILLE, 5000.
Klinkenberg, Paul G. (b, d).
Otis, A. R. (d).
Snyder, James D. (d).

KNIGHTSTOWN, 2008.
Butler, J. T. (d, c).
Johnson, Harvey (d).
Jolly, Walter (d).
Reeves, N. W. (d).

KOKOMO, 17,010.
Mehlig-Crider Drug Co. (d, b).
Shumack, H. A. (b, d).

LAFAYETTE, 20,081.
City Book & Stationery Co.
*Curtis Son, S. C., & Co. (g).
Goodnight, Earl E. (d).
Hanks, Geo. C.
Haywood Pub. Co. (o. s.).
Hogan Drug Co. (d).
*Jaquee-Southworth Co.
Kimmel & Herbert (b).
Lafayette Book & Stationery Co.
Murphy-Bivins Co. (o. s.).
Schultz, M. (g).
Snoddy, R. C. (d).
Wells-Yeager (d).
Zinn, W. H., Co. (g).

LA PORTE, 10,525.
Canfield Pharmacy.
How Bros. (b, j).
La Porte Book & Stat'y Co.
Meissner, F. W. (d).
Red Cross Pharmacy (d).
The Boston Store (g).
Woolworth & Co. 5 & 10c. Store.

 Cement Floor Coating Makes concrete floors wat, oil and dust proof

Wholesale and Retail Stationers

INDIANA.

LAWRENCEBURG, 3930.
Decker, Carl B.
Oertling, E. G. (b).

LEBANON, 5474.
Jaques & Southworth Co.
Long & Davis (d).

LIBERTY, 1338.
Beard, H. F.
Bevis, M. J.
Husted, Frank B.
Richardson, H. G. (d).

LIGONIER, 2600.
Griffith & Goodall (d).
Hoffman, John H. (b, o. s.).
Hutchinson, H. F. (j).

LINTON, 5906.
Duncan's Pharmacy (d).
Haseman Drug Co. (b, d).

LOGANSPORT, 19,050.
*Longwell-Cummings Co. (o. s.).
Neff, E., & Co. (b).
Porter, W. H., & Co. (d, o. s.).
Seybold Dry Goods Co.
Smith Stationery Co.
Wiler & Wise (o. s.).

MADISON, 6934.
Harper, J. E. C., & Co. (d).
Peters, W. H. (d).
Rogers, W. G. (d).
Rousch, C. H., & Co. (b).
Steigerwald Co., The.
Todd, W. H. (j).

MARION, 19,359.
Boston Store (g).
Crawford & Seasholes (b).
Freel & Mason (b, d).
*Osborn Paper Co.
People's Drug Store (d).

MARTINSVILLE, 5000.
Carlton, J. M, (d).
Nutter, Huitt, H. (b).

MICHIGAN CITY, 19,024.
Congdon Drug Co.
Kloepfer, Otto (d, c).
Kramer, L. C. (d, c, s).
Moran, E. (d).
Office Equipment Co. (o. s.).
Ohming Drug Co. (d, s).

MILFORD, 853.
Sparklin, C. A., & Co.

MISHAWAKA, 13,220.
Mishawaka Pharmacy.
Pages Pharmacy (d).
Red Cross Pharmacy.
Went, E. C., & Co. (d).

MITCHELL, 3000.
Chastain & Jones.
Burton's, W. A., Sons (d, b).
Richardson, W. R.

MONON, 1184.
Richter, Wm. N.

MONROEVILLE, 980.
Heinfeldt & Niemeyer (g).
Peoples Drug Store.
Sweany, W. O.

MONTEZUMA, 1537.
Powell, A.

MONTPELIER, 3405.
Horton, J. P.

MUNCIE, 24,005.
Boyce, A. E. (s, o. s. c).
Campbell Bros. (d).
McNaughton Co., W. (g).
Nichol's, W. C., Drug Co., Inc. (d).
Penzel, C. A. (b).

NAPPANEE, 2560.
Dunhan & Love (d).
Johnson, C. W., & Son (d).
Walter & Walter (d).

NEW ALBANY, 20,629.
Baker's Ptg. House (o. s.).
Callahan, Chas. (d).
Conner's Drug Store (b, d).
Ewing & Zeller (b).
*Guthrie Bros.
Gwin, Wallace (d).
Knoefel, Bruno (d).
Knoefel, C. D. (d).
Kremer, A. E. (d).
Lawson, John A. (d).
McCulloch Pharmacy.
Miller, Frank (d).
Newberger & Co., S. W. (g).
Owens, Ollie.
Petery Hedden Ptg. Co. (o. s.).
Stalker Drug Co. (d).

NEWCASTLE, 9446.
Lynn, Chas. E. (d).
City News Stand.
Cooper, H. H. (b).
Mintch, H. M.

 **Paint and Chemical Company**
PAPER COLORS AND MILL PAINT SPECIALTIES
BOSTON   SPRINGFIELD, MASS.   NEW YORK

Wholesale and Retail Stationers   495

INDIANA.

NEWCASTLE—*Continued.*
Oak Pharmacy.
Ridge Pharmacy
Todd Drug Store.

NEWPORT, 610.
Carter, M. B.

NOBLESVILLE, 5073.
Axline, W. E. (b, d).
Gertler & Wall (b, d).
Haines & Glenn (d).
Weldy & Jump (d).

NORTH MANCHESTER, 2500.
Burdge, George (b, d).
Williams, J. B. (d).

NORTH VERNON, 2915.
Bacon, Frank E. (b).

PERU, 10,910.
Cassady, Roy (b).
Engelage, E. J. (b).
West & Stevens (b).

PLYMOUTH, 3838.
Rhodes, A. E. (g).
Roth's Art Studio.
Tanner, Lucius (b, d).

PORTLAND, 5130.
Hall, O. L. (b).

PRINCETON, 6448.
Biggs, F. J. (d).
Commercial Ptg. Co.
Ensley, E. E. (d).
May, H. G. (d).
Public Drug Store (d).
Shoptaugh Drug Co. (d).

RICHMOND, 22,324.
Adams & Co., J. L. (d).
Ballinger, Geo. O. (o. s.).
*Bartel, A. H., & Co. (o. s.).
Bartel & Robe (o. s.).
Boston Store (g).
Conkey, J. A. (d).
Dickinson Drug Store (d, b).
Fibe & Co., Leo H. (d).
Harrison Drug Store (d).
Hoosier Store (g).
Iliff & Co. (g).
Luken & Co., A. G. (d).
McDonald, T. F. (b).
Nicholson & Bro. (b, o. s.).
Nusbaum, Lee B. (g).
Quigley, M. J. (d, b).
Rail Road Store (g).
Richmond Art Store.

RICHMOND—*Continued.*
Ross, W. H., Drug Co. (d).
Sudhoff, W. H. (d).
Thistlewaite, Clem. (d).

ROCHESTER, 3364.
Beecher Sweet China Store.
Ross, G. T., & Co. (b).

RUSHVILLE, 6000.
Hargrove & Mullen (d).
Jones, The R. A., Co.
Johnson, F. B. & Co. (d).
Pitman & Wilson (d).
Wolcott, Frank (d).

SEYMOUR, 6305.
Bee Hive (g).
Carter, T. R. (b).
Cox, R. Alpha.
Fedderman Drug Co. (d).
Kraft Dept. Store (g).
Loertz, C. Ed.
Meyers, G. F. (d).
Miller, Leroy F. (b).

SHELBYVILLE, 9500.
Dorsey & Buxton.
Morrison & De Prez.
Nail, Oba W., & Co. (b).

SOUTH BEND, 65,000.
American Drug Co.
Applegate, Saml. T. (d, s).
Bastian, Otto O. (d, s).
Coonley & Co., Chas. (d).
Ellsworth Store (g).
*Jacobson-Peterson, Peltz & Kaufer.
Hans, V. C. (d).
Hardy, S. P., Co.
*Herr & Herr Co., (b, s, o. s.).
Kreidler, L. C. (d).
Liebelt, Anna.
Kuss, Ralph (d, s).
Landon Co., L. C.
*Marley-Johnson Co.
Mayo, F., & Sons (j).
Miller, H. S. (b, s).
Milton, R. P. (d).
*Model Ledger Co.
Public Drug Co.
Robertson Bros. (g).
*Rupel, E. B.
Spohn, Henry (d).
Tuttle Corp.

TERRE HAUTE, 64,601.
Buntin Drug Co. (d).
Craft, Isaac (b).

 Pure Blues For paper staining, coating and ruling.

Wholesale and Retail Stationers

INDIANA.

TERRE HAUTE—*Continued.*
 Herz, A. (g).
 Locke, S., & Co.
 *Marley-Johnson Co.
 Root Dry Goods Co. (g).
 Smith, L. D. (b).
 Vigueaney Co. (o. s.).

UNION CITY, 3800.
 Hook, Jr., Chas., & Co. (b, o. s.).

VALPARAISO, 6987.
 Bogarte, M. E., Book Co. (b).
 Brenner, B. L. (d).
 Heinemann & Sievers (d).
 Lowenstein, J., & Sons (g).
 Miner, A. C., & Co. (b).
 Thune & Meagher (d).

VEVAY, 1660.
 Golay, L. W. (b, d).
 Stevens, E. M. (b, d).

VINCENNES, 14,895.
 Duesterberg & Kramer (d).
 Liebermann, F. (c, s, o. s.).
 Miller, Chas. S., Drug and Stat'y Co. (d, c, s, o. s.).

WABASH, 8618.
 Bradley Bros. (d).
 Conner & Conner (b, j).
 Jones, W. P., & Son (o. s.).

WARSAW, 4430.
 Gilworth Stores (d).
 Gosbert, Oliver (c. s.).
 Lantz Drug Store.
 Thomas, W. R., 5 & 10c. Store.

WASHINGTON, 7854.
 Betts, W. C. (d).
 *Cabel & Kauffman Merc. Co. (g).
 Democrat Ptg. Co. (c).
 *Eskridge-Allen Co.
 Gazette & Herald (c).
 Godwin & Son, Geo. (g).
 Rickard, Mrs. Mollie B. (b).
 Sum, A. M. (d).

WILLIAMSPORT, 1850.
 Stephenson, J. H.

WINCHESTER, 4500.
 Britton, L. U. (d).
 Crass, H. R. (d).
 Reed, W. W., & Son (d).
 White, J. H. B. (d).

IOWA.

AKRON, 1130.
 Wintersteen, B. F.

ALBIA, 4969.
 Duncan, Mark W. (b).
 Fuller, L. B. (b).
 Lofland, M. R. (d).
 Miller, Geo. D. (d).

ALDEN, 699.
 Furry, C. L. (b, o. s.).

AMES, 4223.
 Ames News Stand.
 Bosworth & Co. (b, d).
 Cagin, J. E. b, d).
 Judisch Bros. (b, d).

ATLANTIC, 4560.
 Alexander, F. M.
 Frank Drug Co. (b, d).
 Lee, Arthur (b).
 Lewis & Harrison (b).
 Moore & Clark (b, d).

AUDUBON, 2084.
 Frick Drug Co. (d).
 Griffith, J. E. (d).
 Roberts, A. H. (b, d).

AVOCA, 1520.
 Barnes Jewelry Co. (j).
 Grulke, O. (d).
 Maxwell, W. J. (d).
 Wendt, C. C. (d).

BAXTER, 527.
 Downs Drug Co.

BOONE, 10,347.
 Boone Blank Book Co. (o. s.).
 Elliott-Wilson Drug Co. (d).
 Hewitt, Geo. F. (b).

BROOKLYN, 1236.
 Rainsburg, A. P., Drug Co. (d).

BURLINGTON, 24,324.
 *Acres, Blackmar & Co. (o. s.).
 Boesch, John, Dry Goods Co. (g).
 Burlington Book Co. (b, o. s.).
 *Burlington Paper Co.
 *Churchill Drug Co.
 Cooper, D. S. (o. s.).
 Gnahn, E. C. (o. s.).
 Henry's Drug Co. (d).
 Kaiser, W. O., Drug Co. (d).
 Robinson, E. H., Drug Co.
 Sutter & Ludman (d).

 **Paint and Chemical Company**
PAPER COLORS AND MILL PAINT SPECIALTIES
BOSTON   SPRINGFIELD, MASS.   NEW YORK

Wholesale and Retail Stationers

IOWA.

CARROLL, 3546.
Rellenmaier Bros. (d).
Sturges & Thurliman (d).
Tyndale, Geo. S. (d, j).

CEDAR FALLS, 5012.
Berg Drug Co. (d).
Cross & Co. (b).
Dilly's Vanity Store (g).
Green, S. E. (d).
Helber Drug Co. (d).
Pfeifer & Co. (d).
Watters Drug Co. (d).

CEDAR RAPIDS, 32,811.
Albright, J. W. (b).
*Churchill Drug Co. (d).
Denecke's (g).
Francis, J. W. (b).
Hanson-Holden Co. (b).
Keller, Walton A., Co.
Martin Dry Goods Co. (g).
*Mullin Co., Geo. A. (b).

CENTERVILLE, 6936.
Barlow, L. M. (b).
Beer, M. H. (d).
Standard Furniture Co. (o. s.).
Owl Drug Store (g).

CHARITON, 4500.
Fluke, C. E. (b).
Jones & Briles (d).

CHARLES CITY, 5892.
May Drug Co. (d).
Ruste Co. (g).

CHEROKEE, 4884.
Lamereau, Harry (d).
Martland, F. L., & Co. (d).
McWilliams, B. D. (d).
Parker News Co. (b).

CLEAR LAKE, 2014.
Etzel Drug Co. (o. s.).
Peterson, A. E.
Renz, E. N.
Thayer, M. L.

CLINTON, 25,577.
Allen Ptg. Co.
Henning, W. E. (d).
Hurd, C. D. (b).

COLFAX, 2524.
M. & M. Drug Co. (d).
Weirick, H. A., & Son (d).
Wood, H. W. (j).

COLUMBUS JUNCTION, 1200.
Sigafoos, Miss Frances (b).

CORNING, 1702.
Ankeny, W. B. (b, d).
Hilliard & McClelland (b, d).
Potter Drug Co. (d).
Shinn, A. F. (d).

CORYDON, 1550.
Bower, J. J. C. (b).

COUNCIL BLUFFS, 29,292.
Anderson, R. E. (d).
Brackett, Lewis C. (b).
Branson Drug Co.
Bushnell Book Store (o. s.).
Camp Bros. (d).
Clark Drug Co. (d).
Davis, Geo. S.
Fried, A. T. (d).
Geise Drug Co.
*Harle, Haas Drug Co. (d).
McCagor, H. A. (d).
Morgan, D. G. (d).
Morgan, F. H. (d).
Oard, A. W. (d).
Owl Drug Store.
Public Drug Co.
Wesner, Fred W.
Whaley, S. E. (d).

CRESTON, 6924.
Atkinson, G. H. (d).
Bartle, George J. (g).
Blair & Brennan (d, o. s.).
Book Shop, The.
Bowers, S. A. (b, s, j).
Foster & Co. (d).
Garrett Dep. Store (g).
Kraft Ten Cent Store (g).
Leach, J. W. (d).
Morrison Printing Co.
Newcomb, G. D. (d, o. s.).
Powers & York (d).
Spurgeon Merc. Co. (g).

DALLAS CENTER, 300.
Loring, J. O. (g).
Updegraff, S. L. (d).
Wise, Chas. J. (d).

DANBURY, 578.
Durst, Godfrey (d).

DAVENPORT, 43,028.
*Fidlar & Chambers.
Johnston-Session Co.
Harned & Von Maur (g).
Petersen's Sons, J. H. C. (g).
White, E. M. (b).
*Zoeckler, Pritchard Co.

 **Victoria Lake** A perfect color for blending with Yellow to produce shades of Buff, Corn, etc.

Wholesale and Retail Stationers

IOWA.

DECORAH, 4007.
Engbertson, R. A. (d).
Grahams (g).
Lutheran Pub. House (b).
Miller, R. H. (g).
Parman, E. J. (b, d).
Schimming, Jno. G. (d).
Schrubbe, Richard (b).
Sorenson, A. J. (d).
Vick, K. A. (j).
Wangler Bros. (d).
Wells, Mark D. (g).

DELTA, 700.
Burt, O. A. (b, d).

DES MOINES, 105,000.
Burzacott, Wm. (b).
*Des Moines Drug Co. (d).
Harris-Emery Co. (g).
Highland Park Drug & Supply Store.
Holley & Son, L. W. (c).
*Iowa Drug Co. (d).
Irwin Drug Co. (d).
Koch Bros. Printing Co.
*Langan Bros. Co.
McKay, F. P., Co. (d).
McNamara-Kenworthy Co. (s).
McNerney, John, Drug Co. (d).
Miller, H. Jesse (b).
Olsen, M. J. (d).
Plumb Jewelry Co. (j).
*Pratt Paper Co.
Swanson Co., B. F.
Wilkins Bros. Co. (g).
Younker Bros. (g).
Zaiser, W. H., Specialty Co. (c).

DE WITT, 1634.
Ginther, J. S. (d).
Kent & Co. (d).

DUBUQUE, 38,494.
*Buettell Bros. Co.
Clark, T. H. (d).
*Dubuque Paper & Supply Co.
Falkenhainer's West End Drug Store, Inc. (d).
Fitzpatrick, C. F., & Co. (b).
Fosselman, W. C. (d).
Haas, D. J. (d).
Hartig, A. J. (d).
Keating, E. O. (d).
Kresge Co.
Levi, Jas., & Co. (g).
Lorenz, A.
Peryon, E. P. (d).
Rosbek Bros. Co. (g).

DUBUQUE—Continued.
Stampfer, J. F., Co. (g).
Standard Supply Co.
Woolworth, F. W., Co.

DUNLAP, 1155.
Kavanagh, M. P. (d).
Lehan Drug Co.
Satterlee, E. S. (d).

EAGLE GROVE, 3387.
O'Toole & Parker (d).

EARLHAM, 749.
Brooker, C. B.
Scarr, E. L. (d).

FAIRFIELD, 4970.
Bell, Clyde (g).
Gammes Bros. (d).
Higley, D. G. (d, b).
Hub, The.
Jericho and Easton (d, b).
Jeries & Easton.
Leader, The.
Novelty Store.
Shriner & Johnson (d, b).
Wade & Bonfield (g).

FAYETTE, 1113.
Boyce, J. H. (j).
Davis, Frank J. (b, d).
Robinson, H. I. (j).
Walker, F. S. (b, d).

FONTANELLE, 789.
Block, B. R. (b, d, c. s.).
Stoll Drug Co. (b, d).

FORT DODGE, 15,543.
Boston Store (g).
Gillman, Geo. W.
Hine Thome Co. (d).
Merrile & Brown Drug Co.
Messenger Printing Co. (o. s.).
Oleson Drug Co. (b).
Sackett & Haire Drug Co.
Stevens, R. M., Co. (b).
Waldburger Drug Co. (d).
Welch's Pharmacy (d).

FORT MADISON, 8900.
Amborn, C., Jr., & Bro. (b, o. s.).
Axt Drug Co. (d).
Gott, Geo. (d).
Thomas, Camp (d).

GILMAN, 430.
Ward, W. J. & J. A. (d).

 **Paint and Chemical Company**
PAPER COLORS AND MILL PAINT SPECIALTIES
BOSTON   SPRINGFIELD, MASS.   NEW YORK

Wholesale and Retail Stationers

IOWA.

GLENWOOD, 4052.
Howe, A. J. (d).
Ironmonger, J. D. (g).
Robinson, L. S. (j).

GREENE, 1150.
Cole, J. L., & Son (d).

GRINNELL, 5036.
Mullen, W. R. (b, d).

HAMPTON, 2617.
Baldwin's Pharmacy (d).
Campbell, S. E. (b).
McMillan, Clare E. (b, o. s.).
Welty, O. H. (d).

HARLAN, 2570.
Harlan, C. L., & Co.
McPheeters, B. B. (d).
Norgaard Drug Co. (d).
Pexton, J. F. (d).

INDEPENDENCE, 3517.
Barnett, John T.
Bickenbach, H. H. (g).
McEven, C. A. (b, d).
Oliver, H. W.
Parker, May, Drug Co. (d).
Tabor, B. W. (b, d).

IOWA CITY, 10,091.
Craft and Book Shop.
Louis, Henry (d).
Ries, J. T. (b, o. s.).
Whetstone, J. H. (d).
Wienecke Arcade Book Store (b).
Whiting, N. (d).
University Book Store.

JEFFERSON, 2477.
Dick, O. L. (b).

KEOKUK, 14,008.
Ayers & Chapman (j).
Collier Stationery Co.
Rollins, C. H., & Co.

KNOXVILLE, 3190.
Dunlap Drug Co.
Power, J. H. (d).
Steele & Co. (b).

LAMONT, 600.
Abbott, W. A. (b, d).
Toole, Reed & Kleinsorge (g).

LANSING, 1542.
Metcalf, G. W.
Nachtwey, F. J.

LE MARS, 4157.
Sartori, The, Drug Co. (b, d).

LINEVILLE, 900.
Austin & Austin.

LYONS, 5799.
Dayton, Geo. (d).
Roff & Moeszinger (d).
Schenk, G. W. (d).

MANCHESTER, 2758.
Amsden, W. C. (d).
Grems, B. W. (d).
Meggenberg, D. J. (g).
Philipp, A. C. (d).

MARSHALLTOWN, 13,374.
Bowen Bros. (b, o. s.).
McBride & Will Drug Co. (d).
Miller, Hamlin B.
Marshall Printing Co. (o. s.).
Mayer, Henry S. (d).
Morgan, B. A. (d).
Pilgrim Drug Store.
Pinkerton, Frank M.
Simmons, J. B. (b, o. s.).

MASON CITY, 11,230.
Garman & Martin (d).
Globe Supply Store (o. s.).
Kilmer Drug Co. (d).
Le Mars Printing Co.
Letts, Spencer, Smith Co.
Mason City Book & Staty. Co.
Michael Drug Co.
Tiss Drug Co. (d).
Weed & Casey (d).

MISSOURI VALLEY, 3187.
Brown, J. D., & Son (d).
Shafer Drug Co.
Shiley, Geo. P., & Co. (d).

MOUNT PLEASANT, 3576.
Crane, F. B. (b, j).
Lines, Edw., & Co. (j).

MOUNT VERNON, 1532.
Bennett, Joe (d).
Cornell Drug Co.
Goldberg's Dept. Store.
Power & Bloom (b).

MUSCATINE, 16,178.
Gobble & Co.
Neidig, F. A. (b).
Umscheld & Astehalter (b).

NASHUA, 1102.
Woodbridge, McL. (d-b).

 **Structural Paint** For the preservation of structural iron and steel

Wholesale and Retail Stationers

IOWA.

NEVADA, 2188.
Murphy, Miss R. H.

NEWTON, 4616.
Foster, W. O.
Husband, C. E. (d).
Iowa Mercantile Co. (g).
McBride's Corner Drug Store (d).
Nollen, G. H. (d).
Stander Drug Co. (b, d).

OELWEIN, 6028.
Fox, R. S.

OSKALOOSA, 9466.
Blakeslee, John (d).
Central Book Store (b).
Green & Bently Drug Co. (d).
Pike, C. O. (d).
Ralston, C. H. (b, o. s.).
*Spencer, H. L. Co.
The Book Shop (o. s.).

OTTUMWA, 22,012.
Central Drug Co. (d).
Commercial Printing Co. (c).
Davis, D. B. (d).
Donelan, N. J., Co. (g).
*Edgerly, J. W., & Co.
Herrick & Downs (d).
Hoffman, F. P. (d).
Iowa Ave. Pharmacy (d).
Kidd, F. Z. (d).
Mynard Drug Co. (d).
Ottumwa Stamp Works (o. s.).
Parks, J. G. (d).
Sargent, W. L. (d).

PERRY, 5400.
Ainley Book Store.
Anderson, J. B.
Coakley, J. B. (d).
Dooley, E. P. (d).
Kerns Book Store.
Polonieus, Mrs. W. R.

ROCK RAPIDS, 2005.
Axlund, F. W. (b, d).
Brugmann, Conrad C. (d).
Roche, D. C. (b, d).
Vail, C. S. (j).

SAC CITY, 2201.
Brynteson, Chas. (d).
The Gordon Co.
Price Drug Co.
Van Way Variety Store.
Wilson Drug Co.

SEYMOUR, 2116.
Bateman Bros. (d).
Bonner, S. W. (d).
McCoy, J. R.

SHENANDOAH, 4976.
Gauss & Simmons (d).
Jay, Geo., & Co. (d).
Webster & Crone (d).

SIOUX CITY, 61,840.
Beck, W. H., Co. (j).
Becker, Todd Co. (d).
Book and Gift Shop (b).
College Book Store.
Curio Store.
Davidson Brothers Co. (g).
Davis, W. E. (o. s.).
Deitch & Lamar Co. (o. s.).
Fitzgibbon, G. (b).
Fitzgibbon, Maurice (b).
Graber's Dry Goods Co. (g).
*Hornick, Moore & Porterfield (b, d).
Hicks, Fuller, Pierson Co. (g).
Marshall Bros. (b).
Martin Dry Goods Co., T. S. (g).
Pelletier Dry Goods Co., The.
*Perkins Bros. Co.
Ruff, Oscar Co. (d).
Sioux City Stat'y Co., The (b).
Swan-Anderson Dry Goods Co. (g).
Woolworth, F. W., Co.

SPENCER, 3005.
Rasmussen, J. C. (b).

STORM LAKE, 2500.
McArthur Drug Co. (d).
Petersen, G. M. (d).
Triplett, G. M. (d).

TAMA, 2290.
Hixson, John.
Sheker & Todd (g).
Snyder, W. C. (b, d).
Soleman, T. A. (b, d).
Tama Drug Co. (b, d).

TOLEDO, 1626.
College Book Store.
Salzman, J. A. (g).
Toledo Drug Co. (d).

VALLEY JUNCTION, 2573.
Irwin-Askew, The, Drug Co.

VINTON, 3386.
Austin, Clyde (g).
Strong, Harry L. (d).

Paint and Chemical Company
PAPER COLORS AND MILL PAINT SPECIALTIES
BOSTON   SPRINGFIELD, MASS.   NEW YORK

Wholesale and Retail Stationers

IOWA.

WASHINGTON, 4489.
 Lemmon's Pharmacy (d).
 Nicola & Harmon (b).
 Phillips, T. R., Drug Co. (d).
 Sherman Bros. (d).

WATERLOO, 33,097.
 Ackerman, J. (d).
 *Adams Paper Co.
 Black, Jas., Dry Goods Co. (g).
 Hansen & Hansen (d).
 Henderson Drug Co. (b, d).
 Henderson, J. L. (d).
 Miller, C. J. (d).
 Parrott, Matt., & Sons Co.

WATERLOO—*Continued.*
 Taggert, H. W. (b, d).
 Warwick, W. T.
 Wangler Bros. Co. (d).
 Waterloo Office Supply Co.
 *Waterloo Paper Co.

WAVERLY, 3205.
 Brodie, H. H. (d).
 Meyers, E. H. (d).
 Staufer & Hartman (b, d).
 Taylor & McMurray (d).

WEST SIDE, 401.
 Kracht, C. R.

KANSAS.

ABILENE, 4800.
 Duckwall Bros.
 Gleisner, J. M., & Son (d).
 Hubbard, C. L. (b).
 Northcroft, C. E., & Co. (d).
 Reflector Publishing Co.

ARKANSAS CITY, 8300.
 Curtis & Ames (b).

ATCHISON, 16,429.
 Byrne, T. V. (d).
 Johnson, W. L. (b).
 Kaff, John (d).
 Kresge 5 and 10 Cent Store.
 Lockwood-Hazel Printing & Stationery Co. (o. s.).
 McGrath, J. M. (d).
 *Mount-Mize Drug Co.
 Noll, M. (d).
 Ramsey Bros. Dry Goods Co. (g).
 Ritner, T. J. (d).
 Stevens, A. W., & Co. (d).
 Walters & Behrnes (d).
 Woolworth's 5 and 10 Cent Store.

BELLEVILLE, 2200.
 Arbuthnot Drug Co. (b, d).
 Austin-Hollandsworth Mer. Co. (g).
 Dawson Book Store.
 Duckwall 5 and 10c. Store.
 Myers Drug Store (b, d).
 Reed & Sandford Pharmacy (b, d).

BELOIT, 3000.
 Mahaffa, R. (b).

BURLINGTON, 2200.
 Briggs, W. J. (d).
 Cowgill, H. E. (d).

BURLINGTON—*Continued.*
 W. W. Drug Co. (d).
 Whistler, Mrs. Jesse.

CANEY, 4691.
 Broome, H. H.
 Graves, H. H.

CHANUTE, 12,000.
 Brown, The, Pharmacy Co. (b, d).
 Chanute News Co. (b).

CHERRYVALE, 4936.
 Owl Drug Store (d).
 People's Drug Store (d).
 Rexall Drug Store.
 Veeder, L. C. (b).

CHETOPA, 1947.
 Dersham Drug and Book Store.
 Rich, L. W. (b).

CLAY CENTRE, 3800.
 Clay Centre Drug Co. (b, d).
 Held, A. (b).

COFFEYVILLE, 18,500.
 Central Drug Co.
 Columbia Drug Store (d).
 Jordan-Florea Drug Co. (d).
 Kane, E. W., & Co. (d).
 Lang, J. S., & Sons (d, j).
 McCrum Book Store.
 Owl Drug Co.
 Truby, F. M. (j).

COLBY, 1100.
 Donelan Bros.

COLUMBUS, 3800.
 Mitchell, Henry (b).

 **Roll Bar White** A lasting tough coating for iron work in beaters and washers

Wholesale and Retail Stationers

KANSAS.

CONCORDIA, 5113.
 Kerin, E. L. (b).
 Layton & Neilson (d).
 Sorgatz, F. F.

COUNCIL GROVE, 2670.
 Smith, Lester H. (b).

DODGE CITY, 5000.
 Bangs Jewelry Co.
 Mosher & Cochran (d).
 Palace Drug Co.
 Rath & Bainbridge (d).

ELDORADO, 4150.
 Miller, W. Y. (d).
 Selig, C. H.
 Thompson Brothers.

ELLSWORTH, 2000.
 Seitz & Truby (d).
 Sherriff, W. E. (d).
 Shock, Luke.

EMPORIA, 10,000.
 Booknook, The (b, o. s.).
 Eckdall-McCarty (b, o. s.).
 Irwin, W. R. (d).
 Leatherbery Drug Co. (d).
 Morris Drug Co.
 Normal Book Store.
 Red Cross Pharmacy (d).
 Sloan Office Supply & Bible Co.

FLORENCE, 1168.
 Coyne & Coyne.

FORT SCOTT, 1200.
 City Book Store.
 Carrhier, F. A. (b).
 Enrich, H. C.
 Kurtz, D. H.
 Pritchard-Blalchley (d).
 Smith, Geo. S.

GALENA, 7,000.
 Big Racket (g).
 Brumfield, J. P. (d).
 Dunegan, E.
 Gosh, D. L. (b).
 Haines, L. J. (d).
 Moore Drug Co.
 Ober, Mrs. M. E. (b).
 Shellock Drug Co., Inc.
 Wheeler, E. R.

GARDEN CITY, 4500.
 Baugh, L. A. (d).
 Harvey, Walter.
 Laughlin, T. C. (d).

GIRARD, 3000.
 Cushenberry, J. H., & Co.
 Montee, Walter (d).
 O'Riley, P. (d).

GREAT BEND, 5000.
 Barriclow Drug Co.
 Harper Drug Co.
 Wilcek, Leo.

GREELEY, 495.
 Pease, D. E.

HARPER, 1454.
 McDonald, H. C.

HAYS, 2150.
 Harkness, C. A. (b, d).
 King Bros. (d).
 Markwell, R. S. (b).

HILLSBORO, 1250.
 Harder Bros.

HILL CITY, 1000.
 Creighton, M. J.

HUMBOLDT, 2300.
 Gem Pharmacy (b, d).
 Hess Drug Co. (b, d).

HUTCHINSON, 16,364.
 A. & A. Drug Co. (d).
 Adams Drug Co. (d).
 Book & Art Co.
 Cash Drug Co. (d).
 Hutchinson Office Supply & Ptg. Co. (o. s.).
 Pegues, Wright D. G., Co. (g).
 Rorabaugh-Wiley D. G. Co. (g).

INDEPENDENCE, 10,500.
 Case, A. S. (b).
 Corner Pharmacy (d).
 Cramer, J. A. (d).
 Fair, E. Clate (d).
 Fowler, J. G. (d).
 Pratt, W. R. (o. s.).
 Robley, H. E.
 Stevens Bros. (d).
 Sunflower Pharmacy (d).
 Yeager, J. O. (o. s.).
 Yoe, Frank F. (d).

IOLA, 10,412.
 Brown's Drug Co. (d).
 Burrell, S. R. (d).
 Evans Bros. (b, o. s.).
 Mundis, J. D., & Co. (d).

JUNCTION CITY, 7000.
 Hay, Philip (b).
 Kibbey Drug Co. (d).

 **Paint and Chemical Company**
PAPER COLORS AND MILL PAINT SPECIALTIES
BOSTON   SPRINGFIELD, MASS.   NEW YORK

Wholesale and Retail Stationers

KANSAS.

JUNCTION CITY—*Continued.*
 Trott, O. H., & Bro. (b).
 Vols Drug Co. (d).

KANSAS CITY, 82,331.
 Foulks, C. A. (d).
 Lake, G. Q. (d).
 Lane Printing Co.
 Lilley, Thomas (d).
 Maunder & Dougherty (b).
 Melvin, Mrs. M. L. (b).
 Tibbs, Harry T. (b).

LARNED, 3000.
 Code Drug Co. (d).
 Duncan Drug Co. (b, d).
 Wickwire, E. G. (d, b).

LAWRENCE, 14,000.
 Carter, F. I. (b, o. s.).
 Gibb, Mrs. L. M. (b, o. s.).
 Keeler, John A. (b).
 *Poehler Mercantile Co.
 Rowland, R. J. (b).
 Wolf, G. O. (b, o. s.).

LEAVENWORTH, 19,363.
 Brennan, K. M.
 Fewing, E. (b).
 Ketcheson, John C. (Est. of).
 Kirkham, W. A. (j).
 Kiser, S. H. (b).
 Mehl & Schott (d).
 Wettig & Theel (o. s.).
 Wuerth, J. H., & Son (j).

LINDSBORG, 2300.
 F. Goodholm.

McPHERSON, 4500.
 Hultquist, Geo. G. (b).
 Miller, Richard (j).

MANHATTAN, 6899.
 Brewer, H. W. (b).
 Lofinck, R. E. (b).

MARYSVILLE, 2006.
 Barlow, M., Jr. (b).

MINNEAPOLIS, 2000.
 Hurley, T. E.

NEODESHA, 3500.
 Shipley, S. P. (b).

NEWTON, 7862.
 Anderson Book Store (b).
 Herbert, M. M.
 Reese, John (d).

OLATHE, 3500.
 Weir, Chas.

OSAGE CITY, 3010.
 Brown Drug Co.

OSAWATOMIE, 4046.
 Harker, D. C.
 Meeks Drug Store.

OTTAWA, 7650.
 Brombacker, H. B. (d).
 Dorsey Drug Co. (b, d).
 Hill, E. W. (d).
 Kaiser, F. G. (d).
 Lucas, S. H. (d).
 Thompson, E. H. (d).

PAOLA, 3800.
 Brandon, J. F. (b).
 Clifton, H. T. (d).
 Gsell, W. E. (d).
 Humphrey Drug Co. (b, d, o. s.).
 Ringer, W. H. (d).

PARSONS, 12,463.
 Bero, E., Jr.
 Fecea, W. E., & Co. (d).
 Holmes, W. O. (d).
 Hubbard & Lott (b).
 McKnight, M. J. (b).
 Talbot, W. P., Jr. (b).

PEABODY, 1600.
 Roberts, D. J.

PHILLIPSBURG, 2000.
 Charvat, J. (b).
 Greenstreet, E., Variety Store

PITTSBURG, 23,000.
 Evans, T. J. (Est. of) (b).
 Hogeboom, D. (d).

READING.
 Stratton, A. J. (d).

ROSEDALE, 5960.
 Kautz, J. E. (d).
 Leavengood, Clyde (d).
 Sawyer, Ray.

SALINA, 9688.
 American Drug Corporation.
 Ekstrand Drug and Book Co.
 *Lee, H. D., Mercantile Co.
 Montgomery Book & Stat'y Co.
 Porter & Co. (b).
 Salina Typewriter Co. (c).

 **Rubercoat Elastic Carbon Paint**
For your leaky gravel, paper, cloth and metal roofs.

Wholesale and Retail Stationers

KANSAS.

TOPEKA, 45,143.
*Arnold Drug Co.
Bair, H. H.
Crane & Co., Inc. (c).
Crosby & Co., Warren M. (s, g).
Crosby Bros. (s, g).
*Hall Stationery Co., The (b).
Hobart, F. (d, s).
Miller, W. S. (d, s).
Zercher Book & Stationery Co. (b, s).

WAMEGO, 1750.
Bignall, O. O.

WASHINGTON, 2000.
Cook, O. W.

WELLINGTON, 7034.
Crane, Stephen (b).

WICHITA, 52,450.
Allen Book & Office Supply Co.
Brown's Peerless (j).
Goldsmith Book & Stat. Co., The.

WICHITA—*Continued.*
Innes Dry Goods Co., Geo. (g).
Miller, George W.
Orr, G. F., & Co. (b).
*Potts Drug Co. (d).
Southwestern Drug Co. (d).
*Tanner, C. A., & Co. (b).
Western Litho and Office Supply Co.

WILSON, 1000.
Stimm, Wm.

WINFIELD, 6700.
Bird, R. B. (d).
Dyer Drug Co.
Friedenberg, M. W. (d).
Garver Bros. (b).
Olds, J. W. (d).
Pierce, E. H. (b).
Plagmann & Doane (d).
Snyder, A. K. (d).

YATES CENTRE, 2500.
White, E. H. (b).

KENTUCKY.

ASHLAND, 8688.
Tri-State Printing Co. (s, c).

BOWLING GREEN, 9173.
Alexander, H. L. (d).
Callis Bros. (d).
Carpenter, Dent & Sublett Co. (d).
Garvin, W. V. (b).
Grier, Wm. (d).
Kenne, Sr., Fred (d).
Munkle, C. A. (b).
Nahm Bros. (g).
Noell, L. P. (d).
Smith, T. J., & Co. (b).
Stowers, Harry (d).
Taylor & Motlock (d).

CATLETTSBURG, 3520.
Black, F. V. (d).
Gallup, G. F. (j).
Mahood, W. H. (d).
*Patton Bros. (d).

COVINGTON, 53,270.
Kyle Printing Co.
Mendenhall, Carrie S. (b).
Wieschoerster, Louisa (d).

DANVILLE, 5700.
Curry, T. P., & Son.
Spoonamore Drug Co.
Wells, John S. (d).

FRANKFORT, 10,465.
Barrett, Guy L. (b).

FULTON, 5500.
Coulter & Morehead (d)
Irby-Redfern Drug Co.
Owl Drug Co.
Paschall Bros. (d).

GEORGETOWN, 3823.
Arnold, C. H. (d).
Bell, T. C. & L. (b).
Golden-Parry (d).

GLASGOW, 2019.
Ellis & Ellison (d).

GREENVILLE, 2500.
Hale, J. Leslie (d).
Jarvis, R. F.

HOPKINSVILLE, 9419.
Anderson & Fowler Drug Co. (d, b).
Cook, J. O. (d).
Elgin, L. L. (d).
Higgin, E. H. (d).
Johnson, L. A., & Co. (d).
Kitchen, O. W.
Lawson, Faxon (d).
Martin & Boyd (d).

LEXINGTON, 35,099.
Barnes & Heau (d).
*Byrnes, J. M. (c, s).

 **Paint and Chemical Company**
PAPER COLORS AND MILL PAINT SPECIALTIES
BOSTON   SPRINGFIELD, MASS.   NEW YORK

Wholesale and Retail Stationers

KENTUCKY.

LEXINGTON—*Continued.*
  Caden Drug Co. (d).
  College Stationery Co. (b).
  Dunn Drug Co.
  Harting Drug Co. (d).
  McAdams & Morford (d, s).
  Purcell, J. D., Co., Inc. (g).
  Smith-Carroll Co. (b, s).
  Transylvania Printing Co. (s, c).
  University Book Store (b, s).
  Veach, E. D. (o. s.).
  Wrenn & King.

LOUISVILLE, 223,928.
  Bacon, J., & Son (g).
  Baptist Book Concern (b).
  *Bradley & Gilbert Co. (c).
  Esler & Goodman.
  Fetter, G. G., Co.
  Harcourt & Co.
  Hauber, A., & Son.
  Jenner Co., The, Inc. (c, s).
  Kaufman, Straus & Co. (g).
  Liebschutz, N. (b).
  *Morton, John P., & Co. (b).
  Office Equipment Co.
  *Peter-Neet-Richardson Co. (d).
  *Robinson Pettet Co. (g).
  Rogers Church Gds. Co.
  Stewart Dry Goods Co. (g).
  Stewart, W. K., Co. (b, o. s.).
  Tonini, Ferdinand (b).
  Ye Booke Stalle.

MADISONVILLE, 4966.
  Sisk, Ben.

MAYFIELD, 700.
  Morehead Bros. (b).

MAYSVILLE, 6141.
  Chanslor, Ike (d).
  *Kackley, Jas. T., Co. (b, o. s.).
  Merz Bros. (g).
  Pecor, J. C., Drug Co. (d, s).
  Swift, M. (d).
  Williams & Co., M. F. (d, s).
  Wood, J. J., & Son (d, s).

OWENSBORO, 16,011.
  Cox Co., The Geo. H. (b).
  Gant's Book Store (b).

OWENSBORO—*Continued.*
  Mills & Co. (d).
  Parrish Book Store (b).
  Pirtle, R. L., & Co. (d).
  Public Drug Co. (d).
  Smith & Bates (d).
  Weldon, R. L. (d).

OWINGSVILLE, 958.
  Daugherty, W. H.

PADUCAH, 22,760.
  Clements & Co., R. D. (b).
  *Kolb Bros. Drug Co.
  Duboir Son Co. (d).
  Gilbert, W. J. (d).
  Rieke, W. M., Co. (g).
  Rudy, J. A., & Son (j, s).
  Walker, R. W., Co. (d).
  Wilson, D. E. (o. s.).

PARIS, 5859.
  Brooks, W. T. (b, d).
  Paris Book Co. (b).

RICHMOND, 5340.
  *Arnold-Hamilton-Luxon.
  *Kellogg & Co.
  Madison Drug Co.
  Middelton, B. L. (d, b).
  Perry, H. L. (d, b).
  Richmond Drug Co.
  Stockton & Sons (d, b).

SCOTTSVILLE, 2000.
  Settle & Welch (j).

SHELBYVILLE, 4700.
  Deiss, W. F.

STANFORD, 1651.
  Coleman, E. R.

VANCEBURG, 1161.
  Elliott, Florence (b).

WINCHESTER, 7156.
  Corner Drug Store (b, d).
  Duty, W. S., Co. (b, d, s).
  Gilliam Drug Store (b, d).
  Strodes Drug Co. (d, b, s).

LOUISIANA.

ALEXANDRIA, 15,000.
  Baynard's Drug Store.
  Central Drug Co., Inc. (d).
  Central Ptg. Co.
  Chronicle Publishing Co., Ltd. (b, o. s.).

ALEXANDRIA—*Continued.*
  Ebert, J. H. (b).
  Phoenix Drug Store (d).
  *Rapides Drug Store, Ltd. (d).
  Rateau Drug Store.
  Sonlier's City Drug Store.

Hampden Black Paste — Will not crock in the paper. Strongest, cleanest and most economical.

Wholesale and Retail Stationers

LOUISIANA.

BATON ROUGE, 11,212.
  Anderson, J. A. (b).
  Dupuy, S. T. (d).
  Heroman, F. W. (b).
  Jolly, O. H. (d).
  McNeel Stationery Co. (o. s.).
  Paulsen, H. C. (d).
  Ramires-Jones Ptg. Co. (b).
  Straube Drug Co. (d).
  Waddill, H. (d).
  Woods, Van A. (d).

COLFAX, 2000.
  Jones, W. O. (Est. of) (d).

DONALDSVILLE, 4090.
  Duffel, V. L.

JEANERETTE, 2206.
  Frank, Leo (j).
  Jeanerette Drug Co.
  People's Drug Store.
  Tarleton Pharmacy.

LAFAYETTE, 8000.
  Moss Pharmacy.

LAKE CHARLES, 11,409.
  Gunn, Mrs. R. J., Est. of (b).
  Harrop, John W.
  Mathieu & Chronau (b).

MONROE, 10,209.
  Levi, F., Stationery Co., Ltd.

MORGAN CITY, 5477.
  Blum, Sam.

NEW IBERIA, 7499.
  Lee, C. H., Est. of.

NEW ORLEANS, 361,221.
Bennett Photo Supply Co.
Bohne & Wilt, 1328 Dryades (b).
Buckley, James, & Co., Ltd.
Bryant, J. W.
Dameron-Pierson Co., Ltd. (o. s.).
Dietzgen, Eugene, Co. Drawing materials.
Ecuyer, E. G.
*Finlay, Dicks & Co. (d).
Fitzwilliam, T., & Co., 824 Camp (o. s.).
Garcia Stationery Co., Ltd.
Gessner Co.
Grover, H. W.
Hansell, F. F., & Bro., Ltd. (b, o. s.).

NEW ORLEANS—*Continued.*
Hill, O. E. (b).
Holmes, D. H., Co., Ltd. (b, g)
Hyatt Stationery Mfg. Co., A. W.
Jones Robinson Co.
Kaufman, C. A., Co., Ltd. (g).
Laporte, B.
*Levy, Jos., & Bros. Co. (b, o. s.).
*Lyons, I. L, & Co. (b, d).
Maison Blanche Co., Ltd. (g).
Majors, J. A., Co. (b).
Meade & Sampsell.
*Meyer, Julius, 815 Magazine.
Moran, Thos. J.
*New Orleans News Co. (b).
O'Donnell Bros.
Palfrey-Rodd-Purcell Co., Ltd.
Parker, Blake & Co. (b-d).
Petetin & Co.
Perry & Buckly Co.
Reuter, Gus A., 824 Poydras (b).
Schumert-Warfield-Watson, Inc.

OPELOUSAS, 4623.
  Bodemuller, H. (c).
  Jacobs News Depot Co., Inc. (b).
  Shute's Drug Store (d).

SHREVEPORT, 42,000.
  Baird Co., Ltd. (g).
  *Bath, M. L., Co., Ltd.
  Bernstein Bros. (d).
  Carter, Allen, Jewelry Co. (j).
  *Castle Ptg. Co. (c).
  Dreyfuss Dry Goods Co. (g).
  *Dreyfus, S. G., Co. (g).
  *Florsheim Bros. Dry Goods Co.
  Hearne Dry Goods Co. (g).
  Hirsch & Leman Co. (b, c, s).
  Journal Job Ptg. Co. (c).
  Kress & Co., S. H. (g).
  *Louisiana Paper Co.
  Majestic Drug Co. (d).
  Meyer Drug Co. (d).
  *Morris & Dickson (d).
  Peyton Drug Co. (d).
  Quality Ptg. Co. (c).
  Renfro's Pharmacy (d).
  Saenger Bros. (d).
  Shreveport Drug Co. (d).
  Shreveport Ptg. Co. (c).
  Styron, J. A., Engraving Co.
  West End Drug Co. (d).
  Woolworth, F. W., Co. (g).

 **Paint and Chemical Company**
PAPER COLORS AND MILL PAINT SPECIALTIES
BOSTON   SPRINGFIELD, MASS.   NEW YORK

Wholesale and Retail Stationers   507

MAINE.

AUBURN, 15,064.
Bumpers & Getcheld (d).
Burnham, R. R. (d).
Foss, Geo. L.
Jones, O. W. (d).
Packard, Henry C. (d-b).
Pollister, S. A. (b).

AUGUSTA, 13,211.
Bither, B. E. (d).
Merrill, Geo. W.
Morse, W. W.
Patridge, Willis R. (d).
Pierce, J. Frank, Store.
Quimby, G. W. (b).
Swift & Turner Co.

BANGOR, 24,867.
*Adams Dry Goods Co. (g).
Bean, O. Crosby (b).
Cunningham, F. C. (b).
Dillingham, E. F. (b).
McKeen-Jellison Co.
Pfaff, Adolph (b).
Sullivan, Dan. T. (o. s.).

BAR HARBOR, 1181.
Bee, A. W.
Foster-Hinch, Mrs. Alice.
Sherman, W. H.

BATH, 9396.
Shaw, Fred. P. (b).
Smith & Son, W. H. (b).
Swett, L. B., Co. (d).

BELFAST, 4615.
Mixer, F. G. (b).
Read & Hills.
Woodcock, M. P., & Son (b).

BIDDEFORD, 17,079.
Cartier, Geo. H.
Dearborn, Lowell A.
Evans, T. L.
Kendall, N. W. (o. s.).
Marin Drug Co.
Seamman, C. G.
Streeter, W. L.

BRUNSWICK, 6806.
*Chandler & Son, F. W.
*Davis, J. E. Co.
Will Co., J. F. (g, b).

BUCKSPORT, 2329.
Emery, J. R. (b, j).
Page, A. F. (d).
Stover, R. B. (d).
Williams, C. A.

CALAIS, 6116.
Murchie & Lane, Inc. (b).
Ryan Bros.
St. Croix Book Store.

CAMDEN, 2835.
Bartlett, Miss M. E.
Clark, E. M. (j).
Dickens, D. J.
Village Shop.

CARIBOU, 4758.
Caribou Drug Co.
Pendell, L. J.

DAMARISCOTTA, 1012.
Adams Co.
Dodge, W. W.
Nash, E. W., Co.

EASTPORT, 5311.
Andrews, Byron N. (d).
Byram, Minnie W. (d).
Capen, W. F. (d).
Havey & Wilson (d).
Hutchison, J. P. (d).

ELLSWORTH, 4297.
Clark, Jr., W. J.
Leland, C. H.
Thompson, Miss J. A. (b).

FARMINGTON, 3288.
White, H. P., & Co. (b).

FORT FAIRFIELD, 4181.
Scates & Co. (d).

FREEPORT, 2339.
Merrill, F. E.
Mitchell, A. W.

GARDINER, 5311.
Bussell, F. Irving.
Eastman, H. W. (d).

HALLOWELL, 2714.
Randall's Book Store (b).
Spaulding, Calvin L. (b).
Spaulding, W. D. (d).
White, Guy K. (d).

HOULTON, 8000.
Smith, O. M. (b).

KENNEBUNK, 2500.
Bodge, E. A.
Bowdoin, J. W. (d).

LEWISTON, 26,247.
Bradbury & Marcotte (b).
Estes, N. D. (b).

 Ruling Colors The best for Ruling Inks.

Wholesale and Retail Stationers

MAINE.

LEWISTON—*Continued.*
  Grant Dept. Store Co. (g).
  Sacre, E. (b).
  White & Westall (b).

LIVERMORE FALLS, 2200.
  Waite, Leroy L.

MADISON, 3000.
  Gilman, F. A.
  Haines, H. H. (d).

NORWAY, 2902.
  Stone, F. P.

OLD TOWN, 6317.
  Burnham, H. M. (d).
  Fraser, Alex. (d).
  Mutty, C. (d).

ORONO, 3555.
  Nichols, Chas. F. (d).

PORTLAND, 58,571.
  Barber, C. T. (b).
  Barnett, W. B.
  Barrows, Chas. O., Co. (c, o. s.).
  Brickett & Rand (b).
  Bryant, F. M.
  Chisholm Bros. (b).
  *Cook, Everett & Pennell.
  Donnell, B. L. (b).
  *Eastern News Co.
  Eastman Bros. & Bancroft (g).
  Fessenden News Co. (b).
  *Goold, J. E., & Co. (d).
  Libby Co., The J. R. (g).
  *Loring, Short & Harmon (b).
  Owen, Moore & Co. (g).
  *Perkins & Co., J. W. (d).
  Peterson, J. W.
  Porteous, Mitchell & Braun (g).
  Roberts, William W. Co. (c, o. s.)
  *Robinson Co., The C. H.

PRESQUE ISLE, 5179.
  Larrabee, Geo. P. (d).
  Thompson, W. S., & Co. (d).
  Whitney, H. M. (d).

ROCKLAND, 8174.
  *Bird & Co., John.
  Carver, J. F. (b, o. s.).

ROCKLAND—*Continued.*
  Fuller & Cobb Co. (g).
  Green Bros. 5 & 10 Cent Store.
  Hewitt Co., W. O. (g).
  Hill's Drug Co. (d).
  *Huston-Tuttle Book Co. (b, o. s.).
  Kittridge, W. H. (d).
  Maine Music Co.
  New York 5 and 10 Cent Store.
  Sheldon's Drug Store.
  Siminton Dry Goods Co. (g).
  Woolworth & Co., F. W.

ROCKPORT, 2314.
  Rockport Ice Co. (g).

RUMFORD, 7000.
  Fitzgerald, W. M.
  Rendell, F. E.
  Rumford Drug Co. (b, d).

SACO, 6583.
  Kendrick, H. B., & Co. (b).

SANFORD, 6000.
  Averill Press, The (*, c, s).
  Clark, Geo. W. (g).
  Demers Bros. (d).
  Goodwin's Drug Store (d, b).

SOUTH BERWICK, 2935.
  Harrity, M. B.

THOMASTON, 2688.
  Robinson, G. I., Drug Co. (d).

WATERVILLE, 11,458.
  McAlary, Walter.
  Berry, S. L. (b).
  Berry, W. W., & Co. (b).
  Hawker, W. C., & Co. (d).
  Kelley, Herbert L. (b).
  Soper Co., L. H. (g).
  Wardwell Dry Goods Co.

WESTBROOK, 8281.
  Anderson, Frank D. (g).
  Brigham, J. D. (g).
  Payne, L. K. (d).
  Raymond, K. S. (d).
  Raymond & Marr (d).
  Vallee, Chas. A. (d).
  West End Drug Co.

 **Paint and Chemical Company**
PAPER COLORS AND MILL PAINT SPECIALTIES
BOSTON   SPRINGFIELD, MASS.   NEW YORK

Wholesale and Retail Stationers

MARYLAND.

ANNAPOLIS, 8609.
Cassidy, Ed. R. (b).
Davis, George J. (b).
Feldmeyer, C. G. (b).
Hohberger, Isaac.
Jones, Geo. W. (b).

BALTIMORE, 558,485.
Baltimore Office Supply Co., 641 Columbia av. (o. s.).
Baltimore Staty. Supply Co. (c).
*Beck, E. H., & Co., 21 S. Howard.
Biden, H. M., & Co., 112 W. Fayette (c).
Cann, Harry P., & Bro.
Commercial Ptg. & Staty. Co., 308 N. Charles.
Deetjen Bros., 510 E. Baltimore.
Downs, James H., 229 N. Charles.
Dulany-Vernay Co., 339-341 N. Charles (c. s).
Durkee, H. B.
Falconer Co., The, Gay and Water (c).
Geise Co., C. C., 207 N. Calvert.
Hadaway, Jas.
*Harlem Paper Co., 110 S. Charles.
*Harrison, W. E. C., & Sons, 214 E. Baltimore (b).
Henderson, H. F., & Co., 229 N. Howard.
Horswitz, Charles S.
Kennedy, J. W., & Co., 15 S. Gay (c).
Kohn & Pollock, Inc., 295 W. Baltimore (c).
Lanahan, J., 325 N. Howard.
Landragan, Jas. J., 426 W. Baltimore.
Leven, Isaac.
Lucas Bros., Inc., 221 E. Baltimore.
Lycett, 317 N. Charles (b).
Martin and Co., C. H., 109 S. Charles.
Medical & Standard Book Co., 301 N. Charles.
Methodist Protestant Book Concern, 316 N. Charles.
Meyer & Thalheimer, 10 and 12 N. Howard.
Newton, L. H., & Sons, 1400 W. Baltimore.
Norman-Remington Co., Charles and Mulberry.
O'Donovan Bros., 221 Park av.
*Ottenheimer, I. & M., 321 W. Baltimore (b).
Paul, The, Co., 510 Penna. av. (c).
Price Co., The, 23 S. Calvert (c).

BALTIMORE—Continued.
Richardson, J. E., & Co., 112 E. Baltimore (c).
Rittler & Co., 27 W. Fayette.
Royston, Campbell B., 7 E. German (c).
Saumenig, John H., & Co., 229 Park av. (s, c).
Scheffenacker, W., & Co., 504 E. Lombard (c).
Seibert, Daniel D.
Tall Brothers, 119 Light (c).
Tissenbaum, David, 826 E. Baltimore.
U. S. Engraving Co., 235 Park av.
*Wolf, M. W., Co., 105 W. German.
Young & Selden Co., 301 N. Calvert (c).

CAMBRIDGE, 6407.
Hoge & Holder (o. s.).
Hooper, M. Warren.

CUMBERLAND, 24,000.
*Cumberland Dry Goods & Notion Co.
Cumberland Office Supply Co. (c).
Earlougher, Chas. F. (c).
Fulton, J. A., & Co. (b, c, s).
Harbaugh, M. E. (b).
*Tri State Paper Co.
White & Ankeney (b, c, s).

EASTON, 3083.
Hancock & Stam.
Robson Bros.

FREDERICK, 10,411.
Poole, Georgia.

FROSTBURG, 6028.
Pearce, G. E., Drug Co. (d, b).
Thomas & Brown Co. (b).

HAGERSTOWN, 16,507.
*Hagerstown Bookbinding & Ptg. Co.
Hays, R. M., & Bros. (b).
Rowland, C. F.
Shaffer, Faber & Co.

HAVRE DE GRACE, 4212.
Robinson, M. V. (b).

MIDLAND, 1173.
Cavanaugh, John P.
Grant, E. R. (b).
Reid, S. W.

Hampden Crucible Enamel For hot or cold iron pipes, boiler fronts, etc.

Wholesale and Retail Stationers

MARYLAND.

OAKLAND, 1366.
Hamill, James D.

SALISBURY, 6690.
Collier, L. D. (d).
White & Leonard (b, d).

WESTMINSTER, 3295.
Boyle, Jos. B. (d).
Dieffenbach, F. A. (b).
Mather & Sons, T. W. (g).
Moore, C. W. (d).
Nusbaum & Jordan (g).
Rose, J. J. (d).

MASSACHUSETTS.

ADAMS, 12,485.
Snow, F. L.

AMESBURY, 9594.
Allen's Book Shop.

AMHERST, 3694.
Amherst Book Store.
Hastings, A. J.

ANDOVER, 7301.
Allen, W. A. (d).
Chase, H. F.
Cole, John F.

ARLINGTON, 11,187.
Grossmith, Chas W. (d).

ASHLAND, 2005.
Adams, W. A.

ATHOL, 8336.
Lee, Miss Ellen F. (b).
Longley & Oliver.

ATTLEBORO, 16,215.
Allen's Book & Stationery Store (b, c, s).
Ashley & Co. (d, s).
Clarke & Co., J. P. (d, s, c).
Collins, H. N. (d, s).
Mullaly, T. O. (d, s).
Reeves, E. (d, s).

BEVERLY, 20,000.
Beverly News Co.
King, Chas. A.

BILLERICA, 2321.
Lyons, Frank T.

BOSTON.

(Population 670,585)

Wholesale Stationers marked (*), Commercial Stationers marked (c), Office Supply Dealers marked (o. s.), Booksellers selling Stationery marked (b), Druggists selling Stationery marked (d), Druggists selling Books and Stationery marked (b, d), Department Stores selling Stationery marked (g), Jewelers selling Stationery marked (j).

*Adams, Cushing & Foster, Inc., 168-170 Devonshire and 19-21 Federal (o. s.).
Alger, Bertrand H., 358 B. Warren.
Allen Stationery Co., 104 Essex.
American Paper Co., 44 Cross.
Amstaco, Inc., 18 Washington.
Ames Stationery & Printing Co., 31 Milk, Room 313.
Andelman, Michael, 291 Tremont.
Archway Bookstore, 12 Franklin.
Atwell, George H., 670 Dudley (j).
Babb, E. E., & Co., 93 Federal (b).
Back Bay News Co., 230 Huntington.
Ball, T. H., Pemberton sq. (o. s.).
Barrows Co., C. M., 2 N. Market.

Barry, F. W., & Beale Co., 108 Washington and 14 Exchange pl. o. s.).
*Bennet, C. S., Corp., 107 Pearl.
Bennett, M., 7 Federal and 35 Exchange.
Bigelow-Kennard (j).
Bird, M. T., & Co., 5 West.
Bleck, Samuel, 77 Endicott.
Boutwell, Geo. W., 80 Cambridge.
Boyd, David G., 87 Pleasant.
Buckley, Neil, 81 Milk.
Butman & Stone Co., 34 Hawley.
Campbell, Peter J., 50 Howard av.
Carroll, Daniel J., 1072 Dorchester av.
Cohen, Sidney S., 185 Summer.

 **Paint and Chemical Company**
PAPER COLORS AND MILL PAINT SPECIALTIES
BOSTON   SPRINGFIELD, MASS.   NEW YORK

MASSACHUSETTS.

BOSTON—*Continued.*

*Comer, E. A., & Co., 12 Pearl.
Cook, Jos. F., 244 Milk.
Cotton & Gould, 24 Hawley.
*Crafts, Clinton W., 81 Milk.
Damon, G. E., Co., 7 Pemberton sq. (o. s.).
Dangel, H., & Co., 161 Devonshire.
Davis & Co., F. W., 36 West.
Dix & Co., H. E., 161 Devonshire.
Doane, Francis, & Co., 116 State.
Edwards, Leander M., 19 High.
Emerson Stationery Co., 21 Bromfield.
Estabrook, Fred B., & Co., 184 Summer.
Fairbanks, J. L., & Co., 12 Franklin.
Filene's, 416 Washington.
Fisher, Andrew, 1190 River, Hyde Park.
Fitzgerald & Co., J. F., 81 Milk.
Fletcher, David B., & Co., 150 Devonshire.
Flister, Jr., Herman, 81 Milk.
Gardenside Book Shop, Inc., 270 Boylston.
Gay, H. C., 797 Washington.
Gilchrist Co., 417 Washington.
Greenough, W. S., & Co., 169 Devonshire and 30 Arch (o. s.).
Groom, Thos., & Co., Inc., 105 State (o. s.).
Hallet, Clarence, 675 East B'way.
Hallett, Eben, 117 Dudley, Roxbury.
Hammond, Edward A., 294 Devonshire.
Harvey, Gertrude, 475 Columbus av.
Herrick, A. W., 294 Washington.
Hill, Smith & Co., 8 Milk (o. s.).
Hobbs & Warren Co., 34 Hawley (o. s.).
Houghton & Dutton, 55 Tremont (g).
James, Samuel D., 365 W. Broadway.
Jordan, Marsh & Co., 450 Washington (g).
Jordan, Mrs. Margaret A., 146 Dudley.
Kittredge & Co., H. R., 234 Milk.
Lane, A. C., 59 Charles.
Lawyers' Supply Co., 448 Tremont Bldg.
Libby, A. C., & Son, 32 Dock sq. and 4 Devonshire.
Maclachlan, A. D., 502 Boylston (o. s.).
May, Charles E., 185 Franklin.

BOSTON—*Continued.*

McAdams, Wm. M. L., 272 Devonshire (o. s.).
Marcus, Samuel, 16 Devonshire and 80 Washington.
Martell, A. E., Co., 159 Devonshire.
Mitchell Co., Guy T., 1 Hartford (accounting supplies).
Muran, L. E., 51 Franklin (o. s.).
*N. E. News Co., 93 Arch (b).
Ochs, C. A., 1781 Washington.
Poulson, Harper W., 284 Boylston (s).
Reynolds & Reynolds Co., 17 Milk (o. s.).
Robbins, I. D., 181 Cambridge.
Ruby, S., 137 Summer.
*Schrader, William O., & Co., 81 Milk.
Shepard, H. A., & Co., 52 Cornhill.
Safeguard Expense Book Co., 183 Essex.
Shepard, Norwell Co., 30 Winter (g).
Shreve, Crump & Lowe Co., 147 Tremont (j).
Simons, Arthur, 66 Huntington av.
Southwell, T. J., & Co., 1241 Commonwealth av., Allston.
Standard Stationery Co., 90 High.
Stearns Co., R. H., 140 Tremont (g).
Stone, Isaac A., 37 Chelsea, Charleston.
*Thorp & Martin Co., 64 Franklin (o. s.).
*United Stationery Co., 93 Leon, Roxbury.
United Stationers, Inc., 116 Bedford.
Walker & Co., 1311 Washington.
Ward, Sam'l, Mfg. Co., 299 Atlantic av.
Ward's, 59 Franklin (o. s.).
White Co., R. H., 518 Washington (g).
White, Walter H., 104 Dorchester.
Woodbine, Herbert J., 17 Milk.
Woodruff, J., 469 Tremont.

BRIDGEWATER, 8282.
Cole, O. B. (d).

BROCKTON, 68,000.
*Atwood Paper Co.
Burke & Kendrew (b).
Bailey, G. T., 42 Centre.
Chaplain, William A., Co. (d).
Edgar Co., James (g).
Holmes, This Is, Inc., 58 Main.
Hunter Stationery Co., 8 High (c).

 **Regal Wall Coating** A white cold water paint. Will not rub, scale or peel off.

Wholesale and Retail Stationers

MASSACHUSETTS.

BROCKTON—*Continued.*
Leighton, C. F., & Co., 3 Main.
Lemay, S. E., 357 N. Main.
Maguire Bros., 85 Centre (b).
Saxton, Bernard, 52 Main (s).
Thayer Bros., 1114 Main (b).
Thompson, E. M. (b).
Trudeau, James, 106 Pleasant.

BROOKLINE, 27,792.
Ayer, Anna C., 1338 Beacon.
Bowker, A. W. (d)
Dizer, Walter M., 55 Vernon.
Gammon Drug Co. (d).
Lyceum Hall Pharmacy (d).
Paine, Wm. D., 256 Washington (d).

CAMBRIDGE, 104,839.
Ames Bros., 1380 Massachusetts av. (b).
Beunke, Fred L. (b).
Corcoran, J. H., & Co. (g).
*Carroll, Daniel J., 528 Green.
Harvard Co-operative Society, 1322 Massachusetts av. (b).
*Hunnewell, James W., 2074 Massachusetts av.
Hunt, Edgar F., & Co., 575 Massachusetts av. (b).
Kent, Geo. H., 1354 Massachusetts av. (b).
Parker, Abbott (b).
Segresten, August, 454 Main av.
Woods, James H., 10 Brattle (b).

CANTON, 5010.
Loud, G. B.

CHELSEA, 32,452.
*Emerson, Fred. B.
Freeman, C. W. (d).
Perkins, W. A. (d).
Rice, M. E. (g).

CHESTER, 1273.
Harrington, James J.

CHICOPEE, 14,331.
Buckley (The) Co.

CHICOPEE FALLS, 9120.
Burzynski-Przybcien Co.
Beaudry, Euclide.

CLINTON, 13,075.
Finnerty, P. F. (b).
Gordon, L. S. (b).
McGrath, J. H. (d).
Morrill, F. W. (b).
O'Toole, J. E. (b).

DANVERS, 9814.
Suburban Quality Shop.

DEDHAM, 9284.
Wardle, H. L., Drug Co. (d).

EVERETT, 33,484.
Carver, W. Otis.
Driscoll, T., & Sons (c).
Haslem, A. (c).
Kimball & Co. (d).
Mitchell & Gaynor (d).
O'Donnell, Joseph V.
Philbrick & Co., J. W. (g).
Sargent, K. P., & Co. (d).

FAIR HAVEN, 6277.
Card, Henry L.

FALL RIVER, 125,000.
Adams, Robert (Est. of) (b).
Bamford, George E. (b).
Bouvier, Albert J. (b).
Brown Co., E. S. (g).
Charlton, Earle P. (g).
Forest, Mrs. F. A. (b).
Franklin, J. H., & Co.
McWhirr Co., R. A. (g).

FITCHBURG, 42,605.
Estabrook, Henry.
Fitchburg Drug Co. (d, b).
Nichols & Frost (g).
*Remington & Co., H. E. (b).
Rice, F. W., & Co. (j, s, c).

FLORENCE, 2479.
McCarthy, Michael J.

FOXBORO, 3555.
Alden, J. H.
Prew, C. H.

FRANKLIN, 6140.
Bachelor, J. W.
Dana, A. C., & Son.
Dio, John H.
Mason, Albert C.
Smith, Mrs., Alice E.

GARDNER, 16,376.
Dora Bros.

GEORGETOWN, 2058.
Andrews, F. P.

GREAT BARRINGTON, 3466.
Sturtevant, M. G.

GLOUCESTER, 25,989.
Brown, W. G., & Co. (g).
Butnam & French (g).

 **Paint and Chemical Company**
PAPER COLORS AND MILL PAINT SPECIALTIES
BOSTON   SPRINGFIELD, MASS.   NEW YORK

Wholesale and Retail Stationers

MASSACHUSETTS.

GLOUCESTER—*Continued.*
  Marshall, R. D., & Co.
  Shurtleff, F. M.

GREENFIELD, 10,427.
  *Brown, The F. H., Co.
  Demond, C. H., & Co. (o. s.).
  Greenfield Office Supply Co.
  Greenfield News Co. (b).
  Hovey Pharmacy (d).
  Jones, A. W.
  Logan, J. P. (g).
  Wilson, John, & Co. (g).

HAVERHILL, 44,115.
  *Chase Press, The.
  *How, W. E. (c, s, o. s.).
  Leslie Dry Goods Co. (g).
  Mitchell Dry Goods Co. (g).
  *Noyes Paper Co (o. s.).
  Parker, Marcellus E.
  Simonds & Adams (g).
  Tuck, W. O.

HOLBROOK, 2538.
  Megley, J. F.

HOLYOKE, 57,730.
  Curran Bros. (d).
  Desrocher, Napoleon.
  Elmwood Pharmacy (d).
  *Fitzgerald Book & Art Co. (b).
  Fringelin, Joseph C. (b).
  Glessman, A. F. (d).
  Herbert, Arthur (d).
  *Judge, Martin J.
  McAuslan & Wakelin (g).
  Millane Bros. (d).
  Nickerson Supply Co. (c, o. s.).
  *O'Connell-Quirk Paper Co.
  Quigley, John F. (d).
  Riker-Jaynes Co. (d).
  Roy Co., John T. (b).
  Steiger, A., & Co. (g).
  Wolski, K. J.

HUNTINGTON, 1290.
  Daugherty, C. W.

IPSWICH, 5777.
  Conley, Brainard J. (d).
  Measures, D. E.
  Prescott, W. N.
  Stone, L. E.

LAWRENCE, 85,892.
  Cole, A. L. (o. s.).
  Cross, Grace H. (b).
  Kellett, Ephraim (b).
  Morgan, Charles H., & Co.
  Reid & Hughes Co. (g).
  *Snow, George A.
  Ward, Prescott T. (b).

LENOX, 2467.
  Hughes, P. H.

LEOMINSTER, 16,280.
  Hosmer, Allen C. (b).

LOWELL, 106,294.
  Bon Marche Dry Goods Co. (g).
  Cryan, Edward J.
  Kittredge, H. C.
  Pollard & Co., A. G. (g).
  *Prince, G. C., & Son, Inc. (b, o. s.).
  *Rexford, John T.

LYNN, 95,000.
  Bauer, R. S., Co.
  Burke & Co., P. H. (d).
  Burrows & Sanborn (g, b).
  Davis, Chas. E., & Co.
  Emery & Taylor (d).
  Furbush, W. M.
  Goddard Bros. (g).
  Magrane, P. B. ().
  Newhall, F. W.
  Rogers Co., T. W. (g).
  Ropes Drug Co. (d).
  Small, J. B. (d).
  Sullivan, J. C. (g).
  Wilkens, Charles E. (d).

MALDEN, 44,404.
  Boyd, David G.
  Crocker, Austin F.
  Dean, J. Richmond (j).
  Hunt & Co., W. B.
  Joslin, F. N., & Co. (g, b).
  Keaney, J. J. (d).
  Sheldon, W. P. (d).

MANSFIELD, 3989.
  Stearn, W. L., & Son.

MARBLEHEAD, 7338.
  Goodwin, Elizabeth G.
  Tusker, N. Lewis.

MARLBORO, 7238.
  Barnard, Harry A. (d).
  Burke Drug Co. (d).
  Collins Bros.
  Morse, F. A. (d).
  Thomson, C. S.
  Wheeler & Stephenson (d).

MEDFIELD, 3548.
  Allan, Alex.

MEDFORD, 23,150.
  Morgan, John A. (Est. of) (d).
  Morse's Paper Store.

Hampden Pulp Colors — For paper staining, surface coating and printing.

Wholesale and Retail Stationers

MASSACHUSETTS.

METHUEN, 14,407.
  Ekhlin, W. K.

MIDDLEBORO, 7017.
  Hathaway, C. L., & Co.
  Sullivan, J. J.

MILFORD, 12,905.
  Cahills News Agency (c, s, o. s.).
  Ryan, J. M.
  Wheeler, Mrs. E. M.

MILTON, 6224.
  Means Bros.

MONSON, 4758.
  Chapman, F. S.

NANTUCKET, 2762.
  Jemegan, E. H.

NATICK, 9200.
  Dewitt, J. E., & Co.
  Fairbanks & Son.

NEEDHAM, 4321.
  Southworth, Geo. W.

NEW BEDFORD, 100,000.
  Berthiaume, E. P.
  Briggs, George L. (b).
  Brightman Co., F. S. (b).
  Browne Pharmacy (d).
  Higham, W. M. (d).
  Hutchinson & Son, R.
  Hutchinson, H. S., & Co. (o. s.).
  Keating, F. P., & Co. (d).
  La Forest, O. L.
  Lewin, Chas. (b).
  Lussier, C. M. (d).
  New Bedford Dry Goods Co. (g).
  Pease & Dandurand (d).
  Shurtleft, I. H. (d).
  Steiger Dudgeon Co. (g).
  White & Fairchild (d).

NEWBURYPORT, 14,675.
  Dow, Charles W.
  Eaton, E. W. (d, s).
  Fisher & Co. (g, b).
  Hoyt, Frank (d, s).
  Pearson, Geo. H., Est. (b).
  Plumer, G. H. (g).
  Sanders, P. K. (b, s).

NEWTON, 9555.
  Josselyn, C. E.

NEWTONVILLE.
  Hatchall, H. G.

NORTH ADAMS, 22,019.
  Brackley, John, & Co.
  George & Mitchell (s).
  Hastings, George A. (d, s).
  Hurd, A. J. (j, s).
  Martin, Frank Tilton, Inc. (b, c, s).
  *Sperry, W. H., & Co. (c, s).

NORTH ABINGTON, 2846.
  Sheehan, W. J.

NORTHAMPTON, 19,431.
  Bridgman & Lyman (b, c).
  Heffernan, J. W. (b, c).
  McCollum & Co., A. (g, c).
  Nequette, L. B., & Co. (d).
  Smith College Book Store.
  Wiswell, H. A. (d).

NORTH ATTLEBORO, 9562.
  *Block, A. R. (b).

NORTH BROOKFIELD, 2947.
  Clark, S. A.

ORANGE, 5082.
  Harrington, George P.

PITTSFIELD, 32,121.
  Berkshire News Co., The.
  Bence Pharmacy (d).
  Bencephey, Eli.
  Chamberlain Bros. (b).
  Cooney, Jr., T. (c).
  *Eaton, Crane & Pike Co.
  England Bros. (g).
  Hagyard, W. R. (d).
  Holden & Stone (g).
  Kennedy-MacInness Co. (g).
  Meyer, Harry M. (b).
  Nugent, Wm. (b).
  Riker & Hegeman Drug Co.
  Secor, Charles (b).
  Shandoff, W. H. (c).
  Union Drug Co.
  Wallace, Co., T. (g).

PLYMOUTH, 11,569.
  Burbank, A. S. (b, o. s.).
  Cooper Drug Co. (d).
  Moore Bros. (g).
  Smith, C. A. Estate of.

QUINCY, 32,642.
  Brown & Co.
  Shunk, Gilbert C.

ROCKLAND, 7074.
  Estes, J. J.
  Peterson, A. S.

Paint and Chemical Company
PAPER COLORS AND MILL PAINT SPECIALTIES
BOSTON SPRINGFIELD, MASS. NEW YORK

Wholesale and Retail Stationers

MASSACHUSETTS.

ROCKPORT, 3311.
Roffey, Mrs., M. L.
Savage, Sidney.

SALEM, 43,697.
Almy, Bigelow & Washburn (g).
Bauer, R. S. (c, o. s.).
Epstein, Jacob.
Kaplan, Henry.
Low & Co., Daniel (j).
Moody Co., The L. B. (b).
Patterson, Abraham.
Webber Co., W. G. (g).

SHELBURNE FALLS, 1329.
Sawyer, H. J.

SOMERVILLE, 77,236.
Brundage, A. H.
Rogers, Geo. E.
Stickel, W. C.
Vorce, Martin E.
Wentworth, Harry E.

SOUTHBRIDGE, 9525.
Dakin, E. F., Co.
Hartwell, G. H. (d).
Shepherd, G. C., Co. (d).
St. Onge, Theo. (d).
Small & Vinton.
Wald & Dowd.

SOUTH FRAMINGHAM, 7248.
Eber, J. F.

SPENCER, 6740.
Boulton, F. W. (d).
Collette, F. (d).

SPRINGFIELD, 88,926.
*Carter Paper Co., H. W.
Forbes & Wallace (g).
Goldsmith, Charles.
Huntting Co., Inc., H. R. (b).
Johnson's Bookstore (b).
Meekin, Pachard & Wheat (g).
Mitchell, F. D. (c, o. s.).
Newton, E. W. (s).
*Springfield News Co., The.
Springfield Office Supply Co.
Steiger, Albert (g).
*Thacker-Craig Paper Co.

STOCKBRIDGE, 1705.
Sullivan, David.

STONEHAM, 7090.
Emerson, Herman L. (d).
Woodhead, H. W. (b, c. s).

TAUNTON, 34,259.
Barker, A. J., Co., Inc. (d, b).
Coffin, A. P., Drug Co.
Davis, H. L., Co.

TAUNTON—*Continued.*
*Dickerman, Henry A., & Son (b).
Goldthwait, C. H. (d).
Guillo, F. W. (d).
Hanson & Co. (g).
Lewis, Jas. E.
People's Drug Store.
Ripley & Briggs (d).
Tisdale, E. D., & Son (j).
Whittenton Drug Co. (d).

TURNERS FALLS, 5229.
Bardwell & Haigis.
Carey, C. A.
Gulow, E. M., & Co.

VINEYARD HAVEN, 1275.
Vincent, Charles.

WAKEFIELD, 11,404.
Butler, Henry E.
Kelsey, A. M. (d).
Lucas Bros. (j).
McMaster, L. L.
Teague & Cobb.

WALTHAM, 27,834.
Ball, Mrs., E. S. (c).
Butman, E. E. (d).
Hall, Fred B. (b).
Hernandes, A. H., & Co. (b).
Hogan, Mrs., Mary A.
Towne, N. W. (b).

WARE, 8774.
Gates Book Store.
Person's Pharmacy.
Ware Drug Store.

WARREN, 3047.
Shumway, Alfred E.

WEBSTER, 12,500.
Banister, H. E. (d).
Hinchcliffe, Wm. H.
Larcher & Branch, Inc.
Mason Drug Co.

WELLESLEY.
Flagg, H. L., Co.
Haines, Wm. H. (b).

WESTFIELD, 16,044.
Blech, J. (b).
Conner, S. S. (b).
Dewey, T. J., Jr., & Co. (d).
Geekern, Joseph F.
Hall, P. N. (d).
Snow & Hayes.

 **Mill White** Will not turn yellow like the ordinary White Lead paint.

Wholesale and Retail Stationers

MASSACHUSETTS.

WEST NEWTON, 6870.
  Green, Joseph V.
WEYMOUTH, 3800.
  Harlow, C. D. (d).
  Kemple, Geo. R. (d).
  Smith, C. H.
  Watts, Edward (g).
WHITMAN, 7292.
  Blaisdell, Oscar A.
WILLIAMSTOWN, 3509.
  Muldowney, W. J.
  Smith, C. G. (b).
WINCHENDON, 4321.
  Merrill, C. A. (b).
  Parker, Alfred G.
WINCHESTER.
  Richardson, C. M., Co.
  Wilson, Jr., T. D.
WINTHROP, 12,758.
  Rising, Harold E.

WORCESTER, 145,986.
  Anderson Bros. (d).
  Barnard, Sumner & Putnam Co. (g).
  Browning, L. H.
  Davis & Banister (b).
  Denholm & McKay Co. (g, c).
  Frost Stamp & Stationery Co. (c. o. s.)
  Gordan Stationery Co.
  Jones Supply Co.
  Lundborg, A. P. (b).
  Morgan Co., Inc.
  Office Equipment Co.
  *Perkins & Butler.
  Sanford-Putnam Co. (c, o. s.).
  Sherer Co., C. T. (g).
  Stimson, Geo. E., Co. (c, o. s.).
  Van Hoosear & Co., W.
  Whalen Bros.
  Williams, J. I.
  *Worcester News Co.

MICHIGAN.

ADRIAN, 10,763.
  *Adrian Paper Co.
  Fisher Yellow Front Book Store (b, o. s.).
  Hart, Shaw & Millard (d).
  Shepard, E. J., & Co. (d).
  Swift, G. Roscoe (b, o. s.).
  Woolworth, F. W., Co.
ALANSON, 473.
  O'Reilly, R. I.
ALBION, 5833.
  Bullen, G. T. (g).
  Kinmont, B. F. (d).
  Ludwig, B. E.
  Moore, E. L. (d).
  Roberts, Chas.
  Smith, A. R.
  Van Gordon, L. C. (d).
ALMA, 2757.
  Look-Paterson Drug Co.
ALMONT, 718.
  Bowman, H. D., & Son (d).
  Hallock's Pharmacy.
ALPENA, 12,706.
  Adam's Book Store.
  La Londe, E. J. (d).
  Ludewig, Adam (b).
  Sepull Pharmacy.
  Spens, E. C., & Sons (d).
  Spens, Jas. A. (d).

ANN ARBOR, 14,817.
  Barthell, C. E.
  Brown, Fred W., Book Co. (b).
  Haarer, John (b).
  Mack & Co. (g).
  Mayer & Schairer Co. (o. s.).
  Sheehan & Co. (b).
  Slater, Myron (b).
  Tice, John (d).
  Wahr, George (b, o. s.).
BAD AXE, 1800.
  Cornell & Son (d).
  Lane, I. D. (d).
  Skinner, Misses (b).
BATTLE CREEK, 25,267.
  *Fisher, E. C., & Co. (b).
  Gage Ptg. Co. (c).
BAY CITY, 45,166.
  Crotty, H. (b).
  Gregory, C. & J. (o. s.).
  Fowley & Co., W. T. (d).
  Frantz, C. H. (d).
  Hawley Dry Goods Co. (g, b).
  *Hurley Bros. (b, o. s.).
  Layerer, Geo. S. (d).
  Manassa, Edw. E., & Co. (b).
  Martin, J. F. (d).
  Walthers Department Store. (g).
  Wendland, H. G., & Co. (g).
  Wilton & Mack (b, o. s.).

 **Paint and Chemical Company**
PAPER COLORS AND MILL PAINT SPECIALTIES
BOSTON   SPRINGFIELD, MASS.   NEW YORK

Wholesale and Retail Stationers

MICHIGAN.

BENTON HARBOR, 9185.
*Benton Harbor Paper Co.
Connell, Frank T. (d, b).
Public Drug Co.
Red Cross Drug Co.

BIG RAPIDS, 4519.
Bidwell, W. T. (b).

BOYNE CITY, 5218.
Bailey Drug Co., Inc. (d).
Bergy Bros. (g).
Hyslop, Wm. A. (d).
Watson Drug Co.

BUCHANAN, 1883.
Binns, Harry P. (b, J.).
Broderick, W. N. (d).
Santax Drug Co.

CADILLAC, 8375.
McCormick-McMullen Co.
Van Vranken, G. D. (d).

CALUMET, 25,991.
Laurium Pharmacy (d).
Martin Pharmacy.
Pine Street Pharmacy (d).
Vasbinder & Read (d).
Vertin Bros. & Co. (g).

CARO, 2272.
Moore, W. W. (b).

CHARLEVOIX, 2420.
Herman, B. A.

CHARLOTTE, 4886.
Beard, Frank E. (d, b).

CLARE, 1350.
Anderson, E. A.
Dunlop, J. W. (b, d).

COLDWATER, 5945.
Branch, J. B., & Co. (g).
Chapman, O. D. (j).
Clarke, E. R., & Co. (d).
Kingsley's Pharmacy (d).
Pennock, C. B., & Co. (g).
Reed, F. J. (b).
Roby, N. E. (d).
The Tribolet Store (g).

DECATUR, 1286.
St. Germain, C. R. (b, d).

DETROIT, 465,766.
*Beecher, Peck & Lewis, 134 Jefferson av.
Burnham, R. E., 116 Farmer.

DETROIT—*Continued.*
*Chope-Stevens Paper Co., 555 Fort W.
Crowley, Milner & Co., Farmer and Library.
Dennen's Book Shop (b).
*Detroit News Co., 86-90 Larned.
Detroit Pt. & Stationery Co., 30 Library.
Drake Co., G. A., 106 Woodward av. (o. s.).
Elliott, Taylor, Woolfenden & Co., Woodward and Henry (g).
Envelope Sales Co., 504 Sun Bldg.
General Polish Book & Printing Co.
German-American Book Store, 625 Gratial.
Gregory, Mayer & Thom Co., 19-25 Cadillac sq.
Hilton, Hart & Garrett Co., 193 Jefferson (o. s.).
Hudson, J. L., Co., Gratiot and Farmer (g).
Huser, Geo., 1763 Gratiot (b).
Krieg Bros., 197 Gratiot (b).
Macauley Bros., 78 Library.
McClure, Fred. H., Co., 239 Woodward.
Richmond & Backus Co., The, 111-113 Woodward av. (o. s.).
Richter, Frederick W.
Schwenk, Geo., 110 Gratiot (b).
Sheehan, John V., & Co., 260 Woodward.
Tucker, Richard B.
Wright, Kay & Co., 207 Woodward (j).

DURAND, 2315.
Beck, Geo. W. (Est. of) (d).
Durand Drug Store (b, d).
Nesbitt, F. O. (b, d).

EATON RAPIDS, 2095.
Birney, John D. (d).
Graham, F. A. (d).
Millbourn, John J. (d).

ELK RAPIDS, 1673.
Butts, M. E. (b, d).
Marriott, F. H.

ESCANABA, 13,194.
Ammerman, W. E.
Ellsworth, A.
Groos, P. J.

EVART, 1386.
Bruce, Geo. N.

Canary Yellow A true color. Makes bright tints and solid finishes.

Wholesale and Retail Stationers

MICHIGAN.

GARDEN, 465.
  Saladin, Herman J. (d).
FENTON, 2331.
  Cook, L. M. (d).
  Davis, Mrs. Carrie M.
  Enders, M. P. (d).
  Plumb, A. Frank (d).
FLINT, 85,000.
  *Brandt & Co., C. P.
  Bush-Catterfield Co.
  *Carlton, M. E., Co. (o. s.).
  Hill Bros. (g).
  Sanders Artz Co. (o. s.)
FLUSHING, 938.
  Sprague, Wesson G. (d).
GRAND HAVEN, 5856.
  *Reichardt Book Shop (b, o. c. s.).
GRAND RAPIDS, 140,000.
  Bixby Office Supply Co. (o. s.).
  Dickinson-Drueke Co.
  Dutmers, J. C., & Son (d).
  *Grand Rapids Novelty Co.
  Grand Rapids Paper Co.
  Greene, C. R. (d).
  *Hazeltine & Perkins Drug Co.
  *Heyboer Stationery Co.
  Higgins, E., & Co.
  Peterson, P. C.
  Raymer's Book Store (b).
  Riechel, Henry, Drug Co. (d).
  Schrouder's Drug Co.
  Senfling, The, Co., Ltd. (o. s.).
  Tisch-Hine, The, Co. (o. s.).
  Van Bochove, R. (d).
  West's (d).
GRAYLING, 2000.
  Lewis, A. M.
GREENVILLE, 4045.
  Edsall, P. D. (b, o. s.).
HANCOCK, 8981.
  City Drug Store (d).
  Finnish Lutheran Book Concern (c, s).
  Nichols, Geo. H. (d).
  Twin City Commercial College (o. s.).
HILLSDALE, 5001.
  *Hillsdale Grocery Co.
  Thatcher, C. L., & Son (b).
HOLLAND, 12,500.
  Brink, H. R. (b).
  Fris Book Store.

HOUGHTON, 5000.
  Atkin & Olson (d).
  Brook's, P. C.
  Kroll, F. W. (b, d).
  Pollock Book Store.
HOWELL, 2338.
  Barron & Wines (b, d).
IONIA, 5030.
  Hemens, S. (b).
  Smith, Smith & McSween (b).
IRON MOUNTAIN, 9216.
  Siebert Drug Store (d).
  Sim, E. (d).
  Uddenberg, A. (d).
IRONWOOD, 12,821.
  Bean, C. M. (j).
  City Drug Store.
  Ironwood Pharmacy.
  McCabe's Drug Store.
ISHPEMING, 12,448.
  Clement, L., Estate (d).
  Tillson, F. P., Drug Co. (d).
ITHACA, 1920.
  Cowdrey's Drug Store (b, d).
  Goodwin, Theron A. (d).
  Sprague, A. A. (b, d).
JACKSON, 31,433.
  Acorn Press (o. s.).
  Cook & Feldher Co. (g).
  Field, L. H., Co., Dry Goods (g).
  Foster, E. M. (b).
  Glasgow Bros. (g).
  Graver, A. B. (b, o. s.).
  Hyndman & Way (d).
  Kurtz Drug Co.
  Lockhart, Robert (j).
  Murray Drug Co.
  Security Drug Co.
  Week's Drug Co.
  Weinman & Mathews (d).
KALAMAZOO, 39,437.
  Beecher, Kymer, Patterson & Clarke (b).
  Caryl, Chas. H. (o. s.).
  City Drug Store (d).
  Clark Paper Co. (o. s.).
  Coleman Drug Co. (d).
  Doubleday Bros. & Co. (o. s.).
  Doubleday-Hunt-Dolan Co.
  Gilmore Bros. (g).
  Ihling Bros. Everard Co. (c. s).
  *Johnson Paper & Supply Co.

 **Paint and Chemical Company**
PAPER COLORS AND MILL PAINT SPECIALTIES
BOSTON   SPRINGFIELD, MASS.   NEW YORK

Wholesale and Retail Stationers

MICHIGAN.

KALAMAZOO—*Continued.*
  Jones' Sons, J. R., & Co. (g).
  *Star Paper Co.
  Van Avery, Ray (d).
KALKASKA, 1415.
  Colson, E. M. (b, d).
  Harroun.
  Stover, H. E. (b, d).
LANSING, 31,229.
  Allen & De Kline Co. (o.).
  Arbaugh, F. N., Co. (g).
  Benriter, George W.
  Butler Block Pharmacy (d).
  Crotty, John F.
  *Dudley Paper Co.
  Emery, A. M. (b, o. s.).
  Hammond Pub. Co.
  Hedges & Gibson (b, d).
  Hodson, M. J.
  Ivory Bros. Drug Store.
  Kimmick & Nesper (g).
  Knapp, J. W., & Co. (g).
  Knox & Co., S. H. (g).
  Robinson Drug Co.
LOWELL, 1761.
  Look, D. G. (d).
LUDINGTON, 9132.
  Andrew, F. W. (c, d).
  Magnussen, John (d).
  Sherman, John A. (b).
McBAIN.
  Koster, H., & Co. (j).
MANCELONA, 1200.
  Blakeley, C. E.
  Rodenbaugh & Stevens.
MANCHESTER, 1047.
  Haeussler, G. J., & Son (b, d).
MANISTEE, 12,381.
  Bailey Gift Shop.
  *Lyman, A. H., Co. (b, d).
  Piotrowski, J. & A. J. (d).
  Shults, J. H., Co. (c).
MANISTIQUE, 5000.
  Neville & Neveaux.
  Orr & Co., E. N.
  Putnam, A. S., & Co. (d).
MARQUETTE, 11,503.
  Pendell's Pharmacy.
  Stafford Drug Co.
MARSHALL, 4236.
  O'Keefe, Myron S., & Co. (b).

MENOMINEE, 10,507.
  Mullins, R. J. (b).
MIDLAND, 2800.
  Thompson, Geo. O. (b).
MILAN, 1355.
  Miller, Frank W. (d).
MONROE, 6893.
  Comstock's Pharmacy.
  Hagan's Drug Co.
  McMillan Ptg. Co., Inc. (o. s.).
  Meier, Fred. W. (b).
  Merz, G. C. (d).
  Mitchell, Andrew, & Son.
  *Mitchell, F. L. A.
  Peter's Drug Store (d).
MONTAGUE, 942.
  Ripley, L. G., & Co.
MOUNT CLEMENS, 7707.
  Bannow Drug Co. (d, s).
  Central Drug Store (d, s).
  Chambers & Stewart Co. (b, j).
  Dalby Drug Co. (d, s).
MUNISING, 2014.
  Farrell, Frank G. (d).
  Tredway, O. R. (d).
MUSKEGON, 24,062.
  Brundage, Fred. (Est.) (d).
  Central News Depot (b).
  Daniels Book Shop (b, o. s.).
  Hathaway, Frank E. (b).
  Kuizenga & Whipple (b).
  Leahy Co. (g).
  Shaw, Walker Co., The.
NEGAUNEE, 8460.
  Bice, A. J.
  Perkins, J. M. (d).
  Tompkins, F. E. (d).
NILES, 5156.
  Griffin, E. C. (d).
  Richter, H. T. (d).
OWOSSO, 9639.
  Johnson, J. C., & Son (d).
  Lawrence, C. A. (g).
  Sprague & Co. (g).
  Willoughby, T. B.
PETOSKEY, 4778.
  Fallas Drug Store.
PLAINWELL, 1498.
  Mesick, H. J. (d).
  Miller Drug Co. (d).
  Treat, O. B. (d).

 **Permanent Reds** LIGHT ALKALI WATER } PROOF

Wholesale and Retail Stationers

MICHIGAN.

PONTIAC, 14,532.
  Brown Bros.
PORT HURON, 25,000.
  Adams, H. M. (d).
  Hollis, Frank E. (d).
  Kresge & Wilson (d).
  Lohrslorfer, J., & Co. (d).
  MacTaggart, David, Co., Inc.
  Sylvester, Wilbur (d).
REED CITY, 1690.
  Norman, L. H. (b-j).
SAGINAW, 60,000.
  Anderson, J. E., Co. (o. s.).
  Arnold, H. B., Co. (c).
  Barie Dry Goods Co. (g).
  Connery-Palmer Co. (b).
  Kelsey & Son, F. J.
  *Saginaw Paper Co.
  *Saginaw Woodenware Co. (g).
  Seeman & Peters (o. s.).
  Swinton & Co. (b).
  Tanner, M. W., Co. (g).
SAULT STE. MARIE, 13,575.
  Conway & Hall (d).
  Haller, Eugene J. (b).
  Maltas, Joe (d).
  Pearce, R. W. (d).
  Price Drug Co. (d).
  Rudell Drug Co. (d).
  Zellar, S. (d).
SHERIDAN, 437.
  Wood, W. H. (d).
SOUTH HAVEN, 3577.
  Reusch, Henry (b, o. s.).
ST. JOSEPH, 5936.
  Dahlke, Wm. J.
ST. LOUIS, 2600.
  McIntyre Drug Co.
  Randolph, Henry.
  Raycroft, Glen.
STAMBAUGH, 1700.
  Anderson, M. A.

STURGIS, 2635.
  Cory, E. D. (b).
  Moore, A. E. (b).
TECUMSEH, 2332.
  Gaston & Son, Wm.
  Pulver, B. J. (b, d).
TRAVERSE CITY, 12,115.
  American Drug Co. (d).
  Coleman, G. E. (b, d).
  *Fitch, John, & Co.
  *Hannah & Lay Co
  Hobart Co. (o. s.).
  Johnson Drug Co. (d).
  McAllister Drug Store (d).
  *Musselman Grocery Co.
  Scott, John P. (d).
  Waite & Son, S. E. (d).
VICKSBURG, 1624.
  Dunning & Son, O. B. (b, d, s.).
VULCAN, 1500.
  Kearns, Patrick
WYANDOTTE, 10,000.
  Calahan Bros. Co. (d).
  Dorrance & Garrison (b, d).
  Thomas, C. W. (d).
YPSILANTI, 6230.
  Baker, R. O. C. (g).
  Dudley, C. S. (b).
  Haig's Pharmacy (d).
  Harnack, August (b).
  Hutchins Dept. Store (g).
  Killian, R. H. (d).
  Maegle, Jno. (g).
  McAllister Pharmacy (d).
  Nissly, F. H. (g).
  Peters, M. & M.
  Rowima, The, Co. (b).
  Smith Bros. (d).
  Smith, Frank (d).
  Weinmann & Matthews (b, d).
  Zwergel's (b).

MINNESOTA.

ALBERT LEA, 9150.
  Spicer & Dills (d).
  Takle-Dock-Hopperstad Co.
  Vanden Berg Shop, The.
AUSTIN, 9000.
  Earl Ptg. Co.
  McCulloch Ptg. Co. (b).
  Pooler Drug Co. (b, d).

AUSTIN—*Continued.*
  Schlender Paper Co. (b).
  Wold, K. O., Drug Co. (b, d).
BLACKDUCK, 942.
  Smith, E. N.
BLUE EARTH, 2319.
  Kamdar, J. W. (d).
  Scoles, Harry.

 **Paint and Chemical Company**
PAPER COLORS AND MILL PAINT SPECIALTIES
BOSTON   SPRINGFIELD, MASS.   NEW YOR

Wholesale and Retail Stationers 521

MINNESOTA.

CHATFIELD, 1228.
Anderson, Charles H. (j).

CLOQUET, 7031.
Companie's Store.
Johnson's E. M. (d).

CROOKSTON, 7559.
Crookston Times Ptg. Co. (o. s.)
Wallace, S. A., & Co. (d).

DULUTH, 78,466.
Bagley & Co. (j).
Beyer Bros. (d).
Chamberlain & Taylor (o. s.).
Christie Litho. & Ptg. Co. (o. s.).
*Duluth Paper & Stat'y Co. (o. s.).
Friemuth, J.
Glass Block Store.
Gray & Co., Geo. A.
Grochau, E. A. (d).
Lutz & Lund Co. (c).
*McClellan Paper Co.
*National Notion Co.
Nelson, J. W. (b).
Northern Drug Co. (d).
Ouellethe & Co. (o. s.).
*Peyton Paper Co. (o. s.).
Smith & Smith (d).
Steele, C. D., Co.
Stewart, McIntosh Co. (c).
Stone, Edward M. (b).
Tredway, E. M. (d).
*Tupper & Spiegel

FARIBAULT, 9001.
Mee, George H., (b).

FERGUS FALLS, 6887.
Smith, W. R. (b).
Westberg & Kissinger (d).

GRAND RAPIDS, 2055.
Bell, Roy R. (d).

HASTINGS, 3983.
Finch, F. W. (d).
Glendenning, H. A. (b, d).
Harms, E. P. J.
Sieben, J. G. (b, d).

JACKSON, 2000.
Ashley, O. M. (b, d).
Fiddes, A. I. (b, d).
Ganett, O. M. (g).

LAKE CITY, 3142.
Collins, M. L. (b, d).
Steele, R. C. (b, d).

LE SUEUR, 1755.
Rethwell, W. H. (d).

LITTLE FALLS, 6078.
Wetzel, M. V. (d).

LUVERNE, 2540.
Harroun, J. A. (b).

MANKATO, 10,365.
Clark, Loren (b).
Free Press Ptg. Co. (o. s.).
Laack Book & Stationery Co.
Laack Drug Co. (d).
Lamm, E. L. (d).
Lamm, John J. (d).
Steiner's Pharmacy (d).
Thomas, Frank (d).
Thompson, E. C. (d).
Thro, John C. (d).

MARSHALL, 2152.
Healy, Chas. (b).
Worman, A. M., & Co.

MINNEAPOLIS, 360,000.
Barker, Albert.
Beard Art & Stationery Co.
Bertelson Bros.
Burke's Stationery Store.
Cootey, The, Co.
Davies, Chas. W.
Donaldson, L. S., & Co. (g).
Dow, Louis F., Co.
Farnham Ptg. & Stat'y Co.
Jacobs & Co., S. (j).
Jeffrey & McPherson Co.
Kimball-Storer Co.
*Leslie Paper Co., John.
McCarthy, Nathaniel (b).
Miller-Davis Co.
Minneapolis Drug Co. (d).
Minneapolis Dry Goods Co. (g).
*Minneapolis Paper Co.
Minnesota Co-operative Co. (b).
Northwestern School Supply Co.
Patro Ptg. & Stat'y Co.
Preston, A. L., Co.
Thomas & Grayston Co.
Todd, J. S., & Co.
Williams, Edwin R., Stationery Co.
Williams, S. M.

NORTHFIELD, 3265.
Crary, Charles (d).

PIPESTONE, 2475.
Cook, J. W. (d).
Evans & Burgert Co. (g).
Menzel, Max (d).

 Cement Floor Coating — Makes concrete floors water, oil and dust proof

MINNESOTA.

ROCHESTER, 7844.
Adams, H. S. (b).
Eagle Drug Store (d).
Hargesheimer, Max (d).
Weber & Judd Co. (d).

SPRING VALLEY, 1817.
Huntley, B. W.
Lyman, W. L. (b).

ST. CLOUD, 15,000.
Atwood, E. W., & Co. (b).
Carter, B. F. (d).
Columbian Book Store (b).
Fritz-Cross Co., The
Henry, J. A. (d).
Molitor, Martin (d).
Security Blank Book & Printing Co.

ST. PAUL, 214,744.
Boyeson Co., H. C., 350 Minnesota.
Brown, Blodgett & Sperry Co., 379 Minnesota.
Dow, L. F., Co., 381 Jackson (o. s.).
Emporium, 7th and Robert (g).
Golden Rule (g).
*Leslie Donahower Co., 230 E. Ninth.
McClain & Hedman Co., 144 E. Fourth (c, o. s.).
*McGill-Warner Co., 9th and Sibley.
Mannheimer Bros., Sixth and Robert (g).
Maybell, R. J., Staty. Co., 150 E. 5th.
*Melady Paper Co., 316 Sibley.
*Minnesota News Co., 19 W. Third (b).
*Noyes Bros. & Cutler, Sixth and Sibley (d).
Schuneman & Evans, Sixth and Wabasha (g).
*Sommers, G., & Co., 6th and Wacouta.
*St. Paul Book and Stationery Co., 55 E. 6th.

ST. PAUL—*Continued.*
St. Paul Drug Co.
Wedelstaedt, Henry E., Co., 91 East Sixth (o. s.).
*Wright, Barrett & Stillwell Co., 220-226 University & Hampton.

STAPLES, 2558.
Waldrom, H. L. (j).

STILLWATER, 10,198.
Brenner Drug Co. (d).
King Bros. Drug Co. (d).
Murphy & Co. (g).
St. Croix Drug Co. (d).
*Stillwater Book & Stationery Co.
Stocking, T. C. (d).

TRACY, 2600.
Dodd, E. R. (d).
Gustafson & Co. (d).
Heine, P. H.
Searles & Kelley (b).

VIRGINIA, 10,473.
Tredway, E. M. (d).

WASECA, 3054.
Breen, Miss Alice (b).
Dedra O. (d).
Model Drug Store (d).
Stuckey, A. (d).

WILLMAR, 4135.
Carlson Bros. (d).

WINONA, 21,000.
Jones & Kroeger Co. (o. s.).
Inter State Merc. Co. (g).
Morgan, Allyn (j).
Taylor, O. L. (b, o. s.).

WORTHINGTON, 2385.
Herbert Drug Co. (b, d).
Morland, R. L. (d).

MISSISSIPPI.

BAY ST. LOUIS, 2888.
Fahey's Drug Store (d).
Welch, Miss Josie E.

BILOXI, 8149
Biloxi News Co.
Suter & Suter

BROOKHAVEN, 5293.
Brookhaven Drug Co.
Grafton Drug Co.
Hoffman Bros. (b).
Price Drug Co. (d).

CLARKDALE, 5000.
Cartwright, M. J.
Ellis Drug Co.
McGowan, R. C. (d).
Noah Drug Co.

COLUMBUS, 8988.
Divelbiss, L. B. (b).

CORINTH, 5020.
Corinth Drug Co. (d).
McAmis, H. M., Drug Co.
Walker, H. E., Drug Co.

 **Paint and Chemical Company**
PAPER COLORS AND MILL PAINT SPECIALTIES
BOSTON   SPRINGFIELD, MASS.   NEW YORK

Wholesale and Retail Stationers

MISSISSIPPI.

GREENVILLE, 9610.
Carter, Mrs. L. (b).
Johnson, W. A., & Co. (b).
Mayor, Julius (c).

GREENWOOD, 7100.
Stein Book Co.

GULFPORT, 6386.
Day Drug Co.
*Gulfport Grocery Co.
Jones Bros. Drug Co. (d).
Parlor Drug Co. (d).
*Southern News & Stationery Co.

HATTIESBURG, 11,733.
Love Drug Co.

HAZELHURST, 2500.
Burnley Drug Co.
Pitts Bros. (d).
White, J. O. (d).

JACKSON, 21,869.
Chambers Office Supply Co. (o. s.).
Eyrich & Co. (b).

KOSCIUSKO, 2078.
Boyd & Jackson (b, d).
Harvey, Wade.
Roby, E. W. (b).

MACON, 2057.
Ferris, Mrs. C. L. (Est. of).

MERIDIAN, 23,285.
Commercial Ptg. Co. (o. s.).
*Dement Printing Co. (o. s.).
Holt & Cook.
Lyde & Cheatham (d).
M'Corkle, J. W., & Son.
Princess Book Store (b).
*Standard Drug Co. (d).

NATCHEZ, 11,791.
Adams, W. A. (d).
Byrne, R. L. (b, d).
Geisenberger Bros. (d).
Grover & Co., Gus B. (d).

NATCHEZ—*Continued.*
Henderson, T. N. (b).
*Natchez Drug Co. (d).

OKOLONA, 3000.
Meridian Book Store.

OXFORD, 2350.
Bramlett & Sons
Carter's Drug Store.
Chillon, R. R. & Co.
Davidson & Wardlow (b).
Fraser, H. M.
Neilson, J. E., Co. (g).
Rowland Drug Co. (d).

PORT GIBSON, 2113.
Bock's Dept. Store (g).
Jacob, Joseph.
Shreve, John A. (d).

SENATOBIA, 1500.
Senatobia Blank Book & Staty. Co.

STARKVILLE, 2441.
Gill, J. J. (d).
Wier, R. K. & F. L. (b, d).

VICKSBURG, 20,814.
*Baer & Bro.
*Bock-Fischel
Block-Hazlip Drug Co. (d).
Clarke & Co. (b).
*Rose, Adolph, & Co. (g).
Woolworth, F. W., Co.

WATER VALLEY, 4275.
Knox, M. C.
Metcalf, W. S., & Co (d).
Nolen Bros.
Trusty, W. T.
Turnage-Atkinson Drug Co.

WEST POINT, 4864.
Paslay, Lindsay Drug Store (d).

WINONA, 5000.
Bachman Drug Co. (d, b).

YAZOO CITY, 6796.
Brown's Drug Store.

MISSOURI.

AURORA, 4400.
Hutchinson Bros. (b).

BELTON, 1107.
Sam & Meador.

BOONVILLE, 4252.
Hirlinger, Chas. E. (b).
Tompkins Drug Store (d).

BOWLING GREEN, 1585.
Dixon, G. W. (d).
Lee, George T. (d).
Purnell & McGee (b, d).
Summerkamp, W. F. (d).

BROOKFIELD, 5749.
Bunch, W. M.
Green's Drug Store (d).
Hallburton Dry Goods Co. (g).

 **Pure Blues** For paper staining, coating and ruling

MISSOURI.

BRUNSWICK, 1606.
  Bowen, C. W. (j).
  Defani, Geo.
  Mann, L. H.
  Rucker Sisters.

BUCKNER, 410.
  Martin, Lloyd.

BUTLER, 2900.
  Ludwick, J. F. (b, d).
  Smith, R. J. (b).

CANTON, 2218.
  Bradrick, O. A.

CAPE GIRARDEAU, 8475.
  Coervers Drug Store.
  Dalton Drug Co. (d).
  Finney's Drug Store (d).
  Gockel Pharmacy (d).
  Haman & Wichterich (d).
  Miller, I. Ben. (d).
  Miller & Kinder (d).
  Osterloh Book Store (b).
  St. Charles Pharmacy.
  Wasem's Drug Store (d).

CARTHAGE, 9483.
  Gallaway's Drug Store (d).
  Holbrook, N. T.
  Jackson, M. F., Drug Co.
  Ramsey Bros. Dry Goods Co. (g).
  Rose, R. H., Merc. Co. (g).
  Sweatt, R. M. (b).

CENTRALIA, 2116.
  Hope, R. L. (d).
  Wilson, O. G.

CHILLICOTHE, 6265.
  Clark, W. O. (b).
  Clark's Pharmacy (d).
  Hatcher Ptg. Co. (o. s.).
  Leeper House Pharmacy (d).
  Reynolds, F. T. (b).
  Ryburn's Pharmacy (d).
  Sauer Bros.' Book Store (b).
  Sailor, J. P., Book Store.

CLINTON, 5000.
  Armstrong, A. L. (d).
  Cohn, J. L. (b).
  McKee Book Store (b).
  Sams' L. C. & Son.
  Williams C. C., Drug Co. (d).

COLUMBIA, 9662.
  Co-op. Store (b).
  Mo. Store (b).
  Scott Bros. Book Shop.

DE SOTO, 4721.
  Buckley's Drug Store.
  Donnell, R. E. (d).
  Hinchy, Paul P.

EXCELSIOR SPRINGS, 4000.
  Sisk, W. C. (b).

EDINA, 1562.
  Brown, B. B. (d).
  Morris Drug Co. (d).
  Werner, A. C. (d).

FARMINGTON, 2613.
  City Drug Store.
  Pelty's Book Store.

FULTON, 5228.
  Baker, R. O. (c, s.).
  Bolton-Smith Drug Co.
  Moore's, R. A., Drug Store.
  Patton, C. A. (b).
  Pollard & Tucker.
  Wrights' Pharmacy.

GLASGOW, 1507.
  Digges Bros. (d).
  Henderson, Walter (b, d).

GLENWOOD, 375.
  Franklin, J. S.

HAMILTON, 1761.
  Thornton, J. O. (b, d).

HANNIBAL, 18,341.
  *Boughton Book and Stat'y Co.
  Brown Jewelry Store (j).
  DeGaris, Ed. (d).
  Kent, S. G. (b).
  Hoffman, Albert (d).
  Miller, Geo. P. (d).
  Richman, Dixie R.
  Standard Printing Co.
  Stewart, A. L. (d).
  Walker, Chas., & Son (d).

HOLDEN, 2250.
  Golladay, M. L. (b, d).
  Hibbs & Harmor (b, d).
  Mayhew, A. E. (b).
  Miller, Robert L. (b, d).

HOPKINS, 975.
  Hopkins Drug Co.
  Luce, R. B. (j).
  Martin & Bowman. (d).

INDEPENDENCE, 10,069.
  Mills, H. R., & Sons (b).
  Sturges Jewelry Co. (j).

 **Paint and Chemical Company**
PAPER COLORS AND MILL PAINT SPECIALTIES
BOSTON　　　SPRINGFIELD, MASS.　　　NEW YORK

Wholesale and Retail Stationers

MISSOURI.

JACKSON, 2105.
　Grant & Graef.
　Jackson Drug Co. (d).
　Jones, H. L., Sons.

JASPER, 900.
　Homer, F. Pitts (d).

JEFFERSON CITY, 16,000.
　Armstrong & Tolson (b, d).
　Bartlett, Claude (b).
　Brandenburger, A. (d).
　Bredeman, E. J. (d).
　Dallmeyer Dry Goods Co. (g).
　De Wyl, Henry (d).
　Hunt, Paul (o. s.).
　Ott, J. F. (d).
　Schell Music Co.
　South Side Drug Co.

JOPLIN, 40,000.
　Bullard, Bell Co.
　Christman's (g).
　Jackson Drug Co. (d).
　King, J. W. (b).
　Newman's (g).
　*Osborn Paper Co.
　Osterloh, T. W. (b).
　*Spring, C. M., Drug Co.
　Thornton Drug Co. (d).
　Wheeler & Liffin.

KANSAS CITY, 248,381.
　Anderson Co., H. F.
　Baird, Geo. E.
　Brown-Preuss Staty. Co. (b).
　Bryant & Douglass Book and Staty. Co.
　Burke Eng. Co.
　Burnap Stat'y & Print'g Co., F. P.
　*Burnham, Munger, Root Dry Goods Co. (g).
　Cady & Olmstead (j).
　Crowley, Robt. S.
　Dodsworth, S., Book Co.
　Evans-Smith Drug Co.
　Emery, Bird, Thayer & Co. (g).
　*Faxon & Gallagher (d).
　Federman Drug Co.
　Hall's Stationery & Engraving Co.
　Jaccard Jewelry Corporation.
　Jones Dry Goods Co. (g).
　Kansas City Sta. Co. (c).
　*Lee, H. D., Merc. Co., 20th and Wyandotte.
　*McClurg, A. C., & Co.
　*McPike Drug Co. (d).
　Maunder & Dougherty (c).
　*Maxwell-McClure-Fitts Dry Goods Co. (g).

KANSAS CITY—*Continued.*
　Miller, W. K. (o. s.).
　Missouri Embossing Co. (s).
　Peck, Geo. B., Dry Goods Co. (g).
　*Poindexter, H. T., Merc. Co.
　Schooley Staty. & Ptg. Co.
　Scotford Stamp and Stationery Co.
　Selp Printing Co.
　Shepard, H. H.
　*Smith, McCord, Townsend Dry Goods Co.
　*Southwest News Co.
　Stenographer's Supply Co. (c).
　Taylor, John, Dry Goods Co. (g).
　Tibbs, Harry T. (c).
　Van Noy Railroad News Co.

KIRKSVILLE, 6347.
　Henry, B. F. (d).
　Janish, J. F. (b, s, c).
　Journal Ptg. Co.
　Mook, L. C. (b, s, c).
　Normal Book Store.
　Sholly, Wm. F. (b).
　Students' Book Store.

KNOX CITY, 400.
　Kelley, G. L. (d).

LAMAR, 2600.
　Diamond Drug Co.
　Earp, J. M., & Sons (j).

LEXINGTON, 6000.
　Crenshaw & Young (d).
　Marshall, Luther (d).
　Weber, Chas. (j).
　Westerman, Barnett Drug Co.
　Young, B. R. (b).

LIBERTY, 3000.
　Barnes, Joe H. (d).
　Liberty Book Store.

LOUISIANA, 4454.
　Bray, J. W. (d).
　Howden, W. J. (b).
　Jocquin, W. J. (b).
　Stichler, Fred. D. (d).
　Teasdale, F. X. (d).

MACON, 3584.
　Patton, John W.
　Smith, J. D., & Son (d).

MARSHALL, 4869.
　Fisher, Thos. H.
　Franklin, P. H. (b, d).
　Scott, E. C.
　Vaughn, J. W.

 **Victoria Lake** A perfect color for blending with Yellow to produce shades of Buff, Corn, etc.

Wholesale and Retail Stationers

MISSOURI.

MARYVILLE, 6720.
Alderman-Yeble Dry Goods Co. (g).
Hotchkin, D. E. (o. s.).
Kuck Bros. (j).
Orear-Henry Drug Co. (d).

MEXICO, 5939.
McIntyre, G. W. (b).
Sallee, J. H. (b).

MOBERLY, 15,000.
McQuitty, J. E. (c).
*Robinson Book Store Co.
Priesmeyer, Fred (d).
Rucker Bros. (d).

MONETT, 5000.
Corner Pharmacy.
Hogler, E. L. (b, d).
Kingery, D. B. (b).
Sanders, J. W. (g).

MOUND CITY, 1681.
Harman Drug Co.
McRoberts Bros. (d).
Mitchell, J. A. (b).

MOUNT VERNON, 1161.
Marbut, W. N. (b, d).
Sloan, W. H. (d).

NEOSHO, 3680.
Arcularius, H. E. (b, d).
Guthrie & Guthrie (b, d).
Price Bros. (b, d).

NEVADA, 8000.
Ballagh's Drug Store (c).
Nave Book Store (b).
Voss Book Store Co. (b).
Young, H. M. (b).

PALMYRA, 2168.
Allen Pharmacy.
Bailey, Knott S. (b).
Spectator Print Co. (c).

PARIS, 1474.
English, J. (d).
Moss, Dr. F. M. (d).
Porter & McCann.
Shaw, Ruth Y.

PIERCE CITY, 2300.
Lucas, J. F. (b).

RICHMOND, 4958.
Sanderson, Francis.

ROLLA, 2261.
Faulkner, M. F. (d).
Scott, John W. (b, d).

SEDALIA, 17,882.
Scotten Drug Co. (b).
Scott's Book Shop.
Thomas Printing Co. (c).

SHELBINA, 2174.
Stalcup, Ethel (b).

SLATER, 3238.
Land, J. B. (d).
Smith, J. W. (d).

SPRINGFIELD, 35,201.
Barrett, John R. (d).
Brownie Book & Stat'y Co. (b).
Browne Bros. Book Shop (b).
Clements Jewelry Co., C. A. (j).
Crank Drug Co., J. W.
Dalrymple, C. H. (d).
Denton, C. E. (d).
Gardner Office Supply Co.
*Hall Drug Co.
Heer, Chas H., Dry Goods Co. (g).
Lisch, Robert (d).
Meyer & Meyer Drug Co. (d, b).
Moore & Houston (d).
Office Equipment Co.
Owl Drug Store (d).
Reed, W. A., & Son (d).
Reps Dry Goods Co. (g).
Rose, J. W. (b).
Ross, A. Y. (d).
Van Metre Drug Co. (d).

ST. CHARLES, 9437.
Ahmann, F. F.

ST. JOSEPH, 77,403.
*Brittan, J. S., Dry Goods Co.
Combe Printing Co. (c).
Manschreck, Sam.
Nelson Hanna Ptg. Co. (c).
Robidoux Ptg. Co.
*Richardson Dry Goods Co.
Schroeder, W. (b).
*Sheridan-Clayton Paper Co.
*Smith Drug Co. (d).
Smith, F. G. (b).
*St. Joseph Paper Co.
Tootle-Campbell D. G. Co.
*Van Natta Drug Co. (d).
Wheeler-Motter Merc. Co.

ST. LOUIS, 734,667.
Adams, S. G., Stamp & Staty. Co., 412 N. 6th.
American Baptist Pub. Society, 514 North Grand.
Barnard, Geo. D., Stationery Co, Laclede and Vandeventer av.

 **Paint and Chemical Company**
PAPER COLORS AND MILL PAINT SPECIALTIES
BOSTON SPRINGFIELD, MASS. NEW YORK

MISSOURI.

ST. LOUIS—*Continued.*
*Blackwell-Wielandy Book and Stationery Co., 16th and Locust.
*Buxton & Skinner Printing & Stationery Co., 306-308 N. Fourth.
Comfort Printing & Stationery Co., 804 Pine.
Dewer, A. B., Ptg. & Stat. Co. 804½ Pine.
Drosten Jewelry Co., 7th and Locust.
*Fabricus Merc. Co., 1823 Washington av.
Famous Barr Co., 6th and Olive (g).
Grand Ave. Staty. Co., 214 N. Grand av.
Grand Leader Dry Goods Co., 6th and Washington av. (g).
Hess & Culbertson, 7th and St. Charles (j).
Kennedy Stationery Co., W. J., 210-212 N. 4th.
Lambert-Deacon-Hull Printing Co., 21st and Locust.
Mermod, Jaccord & King Jewelry Co., 10th and Locust.
*Merrell Drug Co., 4th and Market (d).
*Meyer Bros. Drug Co. (d).
Meyerson, S. F., Printing Co., 32d and Chestnut.
*Monroe, Chas. M., Stationery Co., 406 N. Fourth.
Nugent & Bros., B., Broadway and Washington (g).
Reuter Ptg. Co., H. J., 318 Olive.
Roeder, P., 616 Locust (b).

ST. LOUIS—*Continued.*
Scruggs, Vandervoort & Barney, 10th and Olive (g).
Severson, Cooper S., Staty. Co., 111 N. Eighth.
Shallcross Ptg. & Stat'y Co., 419 N. Fourth.
Skinner & Kennedy Stationery Co., 416 N. 4th.
Spalding Stationery Co., 324 Olive.
Studley, R. P., Printing Co.
*St. Louis News Co., 1008 Locust
Universal Mfg. & Stat. Co., 722 Walnut.
Witter, O., 19 S. Broadway (b).
Woods, Wm. K., Stationery Co., 4th and Olive.
Woodward & Tiernan Printing Co., 309 N. Third.

TRENTON, 5656.
Kathan, E. G. (d).
Mallett, Elgin (d).
Pennell, W. E., Jewelry Co.

UNIONVILLE, 2000.
Hale & Elson (d).
Howard, L. H. (d).
Tatman, P. J. (d).
Timmons, Rollie (d).

WARRENSBURG, 4689.
Beazell, Wm. H. (b).

WASHINGTON, 3670.
Kamps Mercantile Co. (g).

WAYLAND.
Kearns, Roy A.

MONTANA.

ANACONDA, 10,134.
Copper City Com. Co. (g).
Fuller Drug Co. (d).
Greig, R. M. (b).
Minor, J. M.
Standard Drug Co. (d).

BILLINGS, 10,031.
McDowell Co. (b, o. s.).

BOULDER, 955.
Trutnan, August.

BOZEMAN, 5107.
Gall Drug Co.
Phillips, S. G. (b).
Rose Drug Co.
Wilson, Geo., Co.

BUTTE, 39,165.
*Butte Paper Co.
Calkins, B. E., Co.
Keefe Bros. (b).

DILLON, 1835.
City Drug Co.
Kupfer Drug Co. (d).
Potts, A. (d).
Thomas, C. P. (b, c).
Tribune Pub. Co. (b, c, s).

GREAT FALLS, 13,948.
La Peyre Bros. (d).
*McKee Stationery Co.
*Morris, Chas. E., Co., Inc
Tribune Ptg. Co.
Wiegand, W. A.

 **Structural Paint** For the preservation of structural iron and steel

Wholesale and Retail Stationers

MONTANA.

HAMILTON, 2240.
Hamilton Book Store Co.

HELENA, 12,515.
Budd Fisher Drug Co. (d).
Chatfield Drug Co.
*Curtin Book and Stationery Co., A. P.
Grainey, J. J.
Helena Drug Co.
Horsky, Jno., Jr. (d).
McFarland Drug Co.
*Moore Book and Stationery Co., W. A.
N. Y. Dry Goods Co. (g).
Parchen Drug Co. (d).
Starz, E. (d).
State Publishing Co.

KALISPELL, 5549.
Chester, T. E.
Fitch-Smithers Co. (b, d, c, s).

LIVINGSTON, 6000.
Brown, Arthur L.
Sax & Fryer.
Husted, George.
*Scheuber Drug Co.
Seaman, G. M. (d).
Shipton, James.

MISSOULA, 16,000.
*Batemen, H. H., & Co. (b, d).
Dunstan, T. H.
Griffin, Chas. T.
*Missoula Drug Co.
*Missoula Merc. Co.
Office Supply Co. (o. s.).
Peterson, G. F. (d).
Smith, D. C. (d).

VIRGINIA CITY, 467.
Rank, C. W., & Co. (d).

WHITEFISH, 1479.
Mathews, C. A.

NEBRASKA.

BEATRICE, 9356.
Beckwith, O. W. (b, d).
Harper, H. L. (d).
Walter, W. B. (d).

BLAIR, 2584.
Hailer, W. D. (d).

CENTRAL CITY, 2428.
Gray, D. R.
Hastings, M. L.
Hastings, M. L. (j).
Lock & Son (d).
Peregrine, E.
Tooley, R. (d).

COLUMBUS, 5014.
Butts, W. C. (d).
Columbus News & Stat'y Co.
Dack, C. H. (d).
Pollock & Co. (d).
*Spiece & Bower Co.
Teller, F. E. (b).

FALLS CITY, 3255.
Caverzagie, C. J.

FREMONT, 8718.
Brown-Frederickson Drug Co.
Chappel, R. H. (b).
Clarke Drug Co.
Devries Pharmacy.
Eddy Bros. (g).
Fidelity Pharmacy.

FREMONT—*Continued.*
Hammond Printing Co.
Hauser, John (b).
Hauser, Harry.
Pohl, Otto (d).
Rowe, S. C. (d).

FULLERTON, 1638.
Hoppock, F. R.

GERING.
Wood, A. B.

HARVARD, 1102.
Ketcham, C. E.

HEBRON, 1778.
Huntsman, Albert.

HOLDREDGE, 3030.
Norris & Co., W. P. (d).

HUMBOLDT, 1176.
Crane, E. L. (j).

KEARNEY, 6202.
Kearney News & Staty. Co.
Kyser, A.
Lautz, A. C. (d).

LINCOLN, 42,973.
College Book Store (s).
George Bros. (s).
Co-op. Book Store (c).
Gilbert, D. B.

 **Paint and Chemical Company**
PAPER COLORS AND MILL PAINT SPECIALTIES
BOSTON SPRINGFIELD, MASS. NEW YORK

Wholesale and Retail Stationers

NEBRASKA.

LINCOLN—*Continued.*
Hallett, E. (j).
Hargraves Drug Co. (d).
Harley Drug Co. (d).
Herpolsheimer & Co. (g).
Huffman Gen'l Supply Co. (c).
Lincoln Book Store (b).
*Lincoln Drug Co.
Lincoln Pharmacy (d).
Meier Drug Co. (d).
Miller & Paine (g).
Nebraska Bible House.
Nebraska Printing Co.
*Nebraska School Supply House.
Office Equipment & Supply Co.
Porter, Harry (c).
Rector, O. E. (d).
Rudge & Guenzel (g).
*Schwarz Paper Co.
State Journal Co. (s, c).
State Ptg. Co. (c).
University Book Store.

LOUP CITY, 1228.
Graefe, Wm. (d, b).

MADISON, 1708.
Brinckman, Paul (b, d).

McCOOK, 3765.
Woodworth, O. R.

NEBRASKA CITY, 5488.
Meyer, G. O. (b).

NORFOLK, 6025.
Huse Pub. Co., The (c, s).

NORTH PLATTE, 4793.
Gummere Dent. Drug Co.
Newton, O. M.
Troup, E. T., & Sons.

OMAHA, 124,096.
Barkalow Bros. (b).
Brandies & Sons, J. L. (g).
*Brinn & Jensen Co.
*Bruce, E. E., & Co.
Burgess-Nash Co. (g).
*Carpenter Paper Co., 9th & Harney.
Corey & McKenzie Ptg. Co., Inc. (o. s.).
Hayden Bros. (g).
Hixenbaugh, W. A., & Co. (b).
Kieser's Book Store (b).
Kilpatrick, Thos., & Co. (g), 1507 Douglas.
Klopp-Bartlett Ptg. Co., 10th and Douglass (o. s.).
*Marshall Paper Co., 1102 Douglas.

OMAHA—*Continued.*
Mathews, W. R. (b).
*McCord-Brady Co.
McLaughlin & Co.
*Megeath Stationery Co., 1611 Farnam (b).
Moyer, Charles E.
Moyer Staty. Co., 1614 Farnam.
*Omaha News Co., 1417 Davenport (b).
Omaha Printing Co., 134 Farnam (o. s.).
*Omaha School Supply Co.
Omaha Stationery Co. (b).
*Paxton & Gallagher Co.
*Richardson Drug Co.
Superior Ptg. Co.

RED CLOUD, 1686.
Cook, Henry (d).

SCHUYLER, 2152.
Chase, Chas.
Janecek, Chas. M. (d).
Roberts, J. P.

SOUTH SIDE STATION, OMAHA.
Anderson Drug Co.
Brown Park Pharmacy.
City Drug Store.
Clark, D. S. (d).
Dequoy, A. L. (d).
Forest & Meaney Drug Co. (d).
Highland Park Pharmacy.
Maple Av. Drug Co.
Melcher Drug Co. (d).
Munt Pharmacy.
Phillips Department Store (g).
Q Street Pharmacy.
Scarr Drug Co. (d).
Staneks Pharmacy (d).
*Superior Printing Co.
Tobins Pharmacy.
Vocek Department Store (g).

TECUMSEH, 1748.
Brundage, F. L. (b).
Defoe & Vanlaningham (d).
Hamel, M. O. (d).
Smith Drug Co.

WAYNE, 2140.
Felber, H. J. (d).
Jones, F. H. (b).

WYMORE, 2613.
Pennington, F. G.

YORK, 6235.
York Blank Book Co.

Hampden Roll Bar White — A lasting tough coating for iron work in beaters and washers

Wholesale and Retail Stationers

NEVADA.

AUSTIN, 700.
  Dalton, Thos H. (d).
ELKO, 1800.
  Elko Drug Co. (d).
  Elko Music & Stat'y Co. (b).
ELY, 2055.
  Knecht, Arthur W.
EUREKA, 750.
  Schneider, H. M., & Co. (d).
FALLON, 1200.
  Ferguson, Mrs. C. B.
GOLDFIELD, 4500.
  Polin Bros. (b).
MANHATTAN, 1200.
  North, Ferguson & Co.

RENO, 17,000.
  Carlisle, A., & Co.
  Mott Stationery Co.
  Reno News Agency.
  Reno Staty. Co.
SPARKS, 2500.
  Beemer, Chas. A. (c, s).
  King, F. A., Drug Co.
TONOPAH, 4000.
  Rotholtz Bros.
  Union Drug Co.
VIRGINIA CITY, 3045.
  Davis, Mrs. J. M.
WINNEMUCCA, 2200.
  Cooney, Mrs. Dora.

NEW HAMPSHIRE.

ALTON, 900.
  Morrell, H. E.
BENNINGTON, 690.
  Dodge, Edward I. (g).
BERLIN, 11,780.
  Cole, Owen S.
  Dresser, M. J.
BRISTOL, 1478.
  Musgrove, Mrs. Mary.
  Phipps, A. C.
CLAREMONT.
  Hough, F. L.
CONCORD, 17,947.
  Brown & Saltmarsh (b).
  Glick, E. L.
  Eastman, Edson C., Co. (b).
  Sullivan & Co. (d).
  The Gift Shop.
DERRY, 4540.
  Bartlett, Chas. (d).
  Benson, Harry L. (d).
DOVER, 13,247.
  Anderton, Mrs. W. (g).
  *Brewster, Chas. E. (d).
  Buckley's Drug Store.
  Cavanaugh Bros. (b).
  Cook, Geo. N. (b).
  Davis, H. G. (d).
  Gordan, A. S.
  Hopkins, H. C. (g).
  Kennard, B. F. (d).
  Lothrops-Pinkham Co. (b, d).

DOVER—*Continued*.
  Quimby, Edward H.
  Varney, Thos. (d).
  Vickery, W. H., & Son.
ENFIELD, 745.
  Abbott, W. A.
EXETER, 4897.
  Batchelder, James H. (b).
  Tilton & Co. (g).
FRANKLIN, 6132.
  Stewart, W. S. (b).
HANOVER, 2500.
  Storrs, E. P. (b).
HILLSBORO, 1520.
  Butler, C. F.
HINSDALE, 1678.
  Mann, M. S. (d).
KEENE, 10,068.
  Adams Co. (g).
  Bullard Co., T.
  Bullard & Shedd Co. (d).
  Central Pharmacy (d).
  Chamberlain Co., W. P. (g).
  Daniel, M. E. (d).
  Dodges Pharmacy (d).
  Farr, Norman E. (d).
  Spalter, W. H. (b).
  Tilden, G. H., & Co. (b).
LACONIA, 7000.
  Baker, Elmer G.
  Clark, Clarence A., Co.
  Maher, Fred C. (b).

NEW HAMPSHIRE.

LAKEPORT, 3183.
Collins, Geo. A. (d).

LANCASTER, 3054.
Smith, H. S. (b).

LEBANON, 5000.
Foster, C. W.

LITTLETON, 3059.
Green, F. E. (d).
Wallace, E. B.

MANCHESTER, 70,063.
Barton Co., The (g).
Big Six, The (g).
Cheney Book Shop.
Eames Drug Co. (d).
Fitts, Geo. D. (b).
Goodman, W. P. (b).
Hill Co., James W. (g).
Marshall, J. H. (d).
Smith, Dante (d).
*Temple & Farrington Co.
Williams, J. Arthur.

MILFORD, 3839.
Epps, Emma.

NASHUA, 26,005.
City Drug Store (d).
Cole, F. E., & Co.
Grover, Charles R., Co.
Hallisey Drug Co. (d).
Lovejoy, W. H., & Co. (b).
Morris, Phillip, Co.
Nelson, F. E. (g).
Rice, H. E., Co. (d).
Smith's Book Store (b).
Wingate, Frank H. (d).

NEWPORT, 3415.
Hurd & Bronson (b, d).
Lovell Drug Store.

NORTH CONWAY, 1500.
Ward, A. T.

PETERBORO, 1977.
Steele, J. Henry (b).

PLYMOUTH, 2200.
Avery, A. W.
Brown, Fred W. (b, d).

PORTSMOUTH, 11,269.
Acorn, The (b).
Boardman & Norton (d).
Borthwick, D. F. (g).
French Co., G. B. (g).
Grace, W. D. (d).
Green, Benj. (d).
Hoyt & Dow (c).
Mowry, Walter H. (b).
Philbrick, G. E. (d).
Portsmouth News Agency.
Staples, L. E., & Co. (g).

ROCHESTER, 7800.
Meader, Fred P.
Osgood, T. W.

SOMERSWORTH, 6704.
Carter & Son, A.
Desmarais, H. G.
Harmon, C. H.
Jeneau, A. B.
Morin, John B. (d).
Nutter, Geo. W. (d).
Somersworth Free Press.
Woolworth, F. W., & Co.

SUNCOOK, 2880.
Gordon, George E., & Co.

TILTON, 1500.
Morse, H. A.

WALPOLE, 800.
Davis, A. P. (d).
Weber, John A.

WINCHESTER, 1900.
Guernsey, W. H. (Est. of) (b).
Powers Co., J. A. (d).

WOLFSBORO, 1850.
Irish, J. H.

NEW JERSEY.

ARLINGTON, 12,000.
Beadell, W. W.
Davis, J.
Fleischer, David L.
Gould's, A. M., Pharmacy (d).
Horowitz, T.
Kaplan, I.
Pearl, Jos.
Spence, Wm. H.

ARLINGTON—*Continued.*
Thomson, J. B. (d).
Wolk, M.

ASBURY PARK, 14,000.
*Borden, H. A. (b).
Borden's Stationery Store.
Broome, Leonard.
Eidelsberg, E.
Gould, Harry.
Steinbach Co., Inc. (g).

 **Rubercoat Elastic Carbon Paint**
For your leaky gravel, paper, cloth and metal roofs.

Wholesale and Retail Stationers

NEW JERSEY.

ALTANTIC CITY, 53,952.
Ackerman, Annie E. (b).
*Beyer, Ernest.
Braunstein's (g).
Brooks & Idler.
Chapman, R. T. (b).
Clement, J. A. (b).
Galbreath Pharmacy (d).
*Haslett, Wm. M., Co.
Lee, Harry A.
Mellon, Sarah.
Mulvey & Son.
Park Stationery Store.
Patrick Pharmacy.
Potter, Wolf.
Shaner & Knauer.
Shreve, E. G., Co.
Vansant, Oscar J.
Woolworth, F. W., & Co.

ATLANTIC HIGHLANDS, 1480.
Snedeker, W. N.

BAYONNE, 55,545.
Basin, Max.
Brunda, John.
Dwyer, Bernard.
Reimers, Mary.
Stern, Geo. (b).
Thompson, F. E. (b).

BEACHHAVEN, 434.
Hopper, Eliza.

BELVIDERE, 1823.
Cornell, Arthur W.

BERNARDSVILLE, 1000.
Kronenberg, Jos. B.
Merkel, H. H.

BLOOMFIELD, 17,306.
Garlock & Mishell.

BOONTON, 3901.
Brown, J. H. (d).
Boonton Pharmacy (d).
Davis, Samuel (d).
Hitchcock, Herbert S. (j).
Parks, D.

BORDENTOWN, 4250.
Allen, Caleb.

BOUND BROOK, 3389.
Fetterly & Loree (d).
Huyzing, John H. (g).
Lloyd, E. H. (d).
Ross, D. H.

BRIDGETON, 14,209.
Bowen, S. E., & Co.
*Dare, C. F., & Son (b, d).
Davis, Ovid (d).
Jordan, H. A. (d).
Whipple, Geo. H., & Son. (d).

BURLINGTON, 8336.
Burlington News Agency.
Cameron, J. H. (d).
Ridgway, Willis N. (b).
Rigg, John (d).
Shaw, Mrs. James.
Warthman, Wm. B.
Williams, Geo. T. (d).

CAMDEN, 94,538.
Baker, Flick Co.
Barrett, Jerome V.
Bleakly Bros. (c, s).
Butler Drug Co. (d).
Carter, George R.
Eberhard, Alfred J.
Hibbs, W. W.
McAdams, E. (d).
Moon, J. R. (d).
Twelves, Richard (s).

CAPE MAY, 1000.
Warrington, M. Louise.

CLINTON, 830.
Bellis, L. B., & Son.

DOVER, 5938.
Havens, M. C.
Lowe, J. T.

EAST ORANGE, 34,371.
Brodie & Kolodin (b).
Davis Quality Shop (b, s).
Frankel & Nelson (c, s).
Menagh, C. E. (d).
Piggins, J. W.
Rosen, Benj. (c).
Sabloff's.
Yeager, Louis E., 549 Main.

EGG HARBOR CITY, 2416.
Goldsmith, Mary.
Rose, Louise.

ELIZABETH, 73,409.
Bollwage, W. C.
Chesney, W. L.
Elizabeth Novelty Co.
Fulton Specialty Co.
Gommel, Ernest G. (b).
Gordon, B.
Hearn, Edward L.
Hersh, C., & Sons (g).

 **Paint and Chemical Company**
PAPER COLORS AND MILL PAINT SPECIALTIES
BOSTON   SPRINGFIELD, MASS.   NEW YORK

Wholesale and Retail Stationers 533

NEW JERSEY.

ELIZABETH—*Continued.*
  Koestler, Morris.
  Kreielsheimer, A.
  Ludcking, Fred, Jr.
  Magnus, A.
  Mostwill, M.
  Norris, F. E., & Co. (b).
  Piehler, W. M.
  Rowland, H. E.

ENGLEWOOD, 9924.
  Ellerin, Sam'l.
  Livingston, Robert.
  Rockefeller, L. (d).

FLEMINGTON, 2745.
  Cooley, J. S. (d).
  Green, Frank (d).
  Vosseller Stores.

FREEHOLD, 3064.
  Yard's Stationery Store.

GLOUCESTER CITY, 10,000.
  Stetser, Jacob. (b).

HACKENSACK, 14,050.
  Ackerman, L. E.
  Commercial Stat'y Co.
  Fast, Max (b).
  Oken, Max.

HACKETTSTOWN, 2594.
  Nolan, Harry G.
  Rea, C. V. S. (d).

HADDONFIELD, 4142.
  Wright, W. L.

HARRISON, 10,596.
  Beebe, Winfield S.
  Clifton, Fred.
  Daly, John.
  Goodman, P. J.
  Sawelson, Jacob.

HIGHTSTOWN.
  Mount, Jonah D.

HOBOKEN, 70,324.
  Adelman, Emil M., 94 Hudson (c).
  Gent, A.
  Mallander, P., 121 Washington (b, s).
  *N. J. Merchandise Co.
  Reiner, Louis.

JERSEY CITY, 267,779.
  Amdur, Rubin, 174 Duncan av.
  Aronsohn, J., 335 Central av.
  Batchelar, E. J., 44 Montgomery.
  Blum, Christian, 78 Romaine av.

JERSEY CITY—*Continued.*
  Borrmann, Morris, 176 Jackson.
  Bramm, C. F., 613 Newark av.
  *Brenner, Morris, 69 Erie.
  Brenner, Saml., 603 Grove.
  Burch, N. A., 325 Summit av.
  Burkhardt, Wm. J., 165 Danforth av.
  Coesters, Henry F., 561 W. Side av.
  Datz, Albert Co., R.R. av.
  Edelsohn, Morris E., 373 Communipaw av.
  Ehnl, Joseph, 348 Jackson av.
  Eichbaum, Samuel, 745½ Jersey av.
  Feinstein, Jos., 119 York.
  Feigenson, Harris.
  Ferb, Kalman, 16 Erie.
  Ferber, Harry.
  Freed, John S., 510 Jersey av.
  Freese Bros., 538 Jersey av.
  Gold, Philip, 265 Grove.
  Goodman, Adolph, 197 Summit av.
  Gootzeit, Samuel, 292 Jackson av.
  Grinnalds, J. H., 60 Claremont.
  Handman, Carl, 188 Ocean av.
  Hansen, Lars P., 81 Montgomery.
  Harrison, J. W., 8 Exchange pl.
  Hoffman, William, 168 Grand.
  Hudson-Supply Co., Inc. (The).
  Johnson, Geo., Jr., 728 Bergen av.
  Kaplan, Samuel, 388 Jackson av.
  Karel, S. & A., 389 Ocean av.
  Klein, Louis, 258 Jackson av.
  Laub, Wm. J., 94 Bowers.
  Lawrence, Elenor, 623 Ocean av.
  McCloskey, Wm. H., 708 Communipaw av.
  Morrison, David, 214 Central av.
  Moskowitz, Hyman, 475 Jackson av.
  Nielson, Anders, 206 Pavonia av.
  Novick, Morris, 406 Pacific av.
  Nugent & Crocker, 428 Jackson av.
  Ostoroff, A., 440 Central.
  Petersen, Chas. H., 38 Beacon av.
  Porepp, G. F.
  Pottruck, Irving, 171 Danforth av.
  Prendergast, Edw.
  Raskin, Leo.
  Sachs, Louis H., 85 Jefferson av.
  Sanders Bros., 394 West Side av.
  Schmitt, Jacob, 524 Ocean av.
  *Schranz & Bieber Co., 364 Hoboken av.
  Seeman, Jacob, 454 Ocean av.
  Shapiro, Max, 413 West Side av.
  Shapiro, Samuel, 270 Jackson av.
  Sinai, Julius, 334 Jackson av.
  Sinowitz & Kaplan.
  Smith, James J., 734 Newark av.

Hampden Black Paste — Will not crock in the paper. Strongest, cleanest and most economical.

Wholesale and Retail Stationers

NEW JERSEY.

JERSEY CITY—*Continued.*
Soman, Isidore, 291 Central av.
Solt, Thos. F., 788 West Side av.
*Star Staty. Co.
Strobel, Albin, 520 Pat. Plank rd.
Taubkin, William, 127 Monticello av.

KEYPORT, 3385.
Petteys, Ellison D.

LAKEWOOD, 3000.
Finkelstein, E. (s).
Hurburt's, Geo. H., Co.
Mohr, Jos.
Simons, H. M. (b).

LAMBERTVILLE, 5016.
Cochran, S. W., & Co. (d).
Cooper, H. A.
Jarrett & Son (b).

LONG BRANCH, 13,298.
Alexander, Mrs. A. N.
Bennett, L. Bertha.
Bennett, W. Richard.
Britton, John D. (b).
Brokaw, Wm. J.
McGuire, J. A.
Seller, James (d).
Steinbach, Jacob (g).
*Werner, H.
Wert, P. M. (d).

MILLVILLE, 12,451.
*Fath, E. J., & Bros.
Mulford, Ludlam (d).

MONTCLAIR, 24,000.
Baldwin, D. H. (d).
Burner, Wm. S.
Cole, H. M. (g).
Fox, Jas. B., & Co. (g).
Goman, E. E.
Harris, Louis (g).
Hake's Pharmacy.
Hubley, John H.
Ketcham, J. B.
Madison, Edw., Co. (b).
Rudensey, Jacob.
Stammelman, Joseph.
Wrensch, Albert.
Wrensch, Henry, Jr. (d).

MOORESTOWN, 2800.
Hubbs, William.

MORRISTOWN, 11,267.
Lamberts, G. M. (b, c).
Muchmore, W. K. (b).
Naylor, Frank T. (b).
Stillwell, D. C., Stationery Co.

MOUNT HOLLY, 5750.
Asay, S. E., & Co.
Boyce, L. S.
Naylor, Nora W.

NEWARK, 347,469.
Ahr, Fred, Jr., 307 S. Orange av.
Baker Printing Co., 251 Market.
Bamberger, L., & Co., 147 Market (g).
Blumer, J. G., 212 Ferry.
Brant, R., 237 Market (b).
Buob Bros., 236 Springfield av. (b).
Greenwood, J. H., 913 Bergen.
Groebe, McGovern Co., 75 Clinton.
Grover Bros., 764 Broad.
Hahne & Co., 125 Broad (b, g).
Hall, Inc., 881 Broad (c).
Hogan, G. N., & Co.
Kilner, Harry.
Kish, Edward, 43 Clinton.
Kolodin, Morris (Est. of).
Loges Wiener Co., 161 Washington.
Longfelder, D., 293 Plane (c).
Luberg & Rosenstein, 93 Bellville av.
Migatz, Harry, 89 Springfield av.
Mulligan, P. F., 927 Broad (b).
Pierson, Amsi, & Co., 80 Clinton.
Plate, E., 221 Market (c).
Plaut, L. S., & Co., 715 Broad (g).
Shapiro, I.
Shlikerman, J.
Shurts Co., The W. H., 280 Plane.
Soltanoff, Samuel.
Tompkins & Christian, 28 Clinton (c).

NEW BRUNSWICK, 20,006.
Housell, Elmer (b).
Reed, W. R. (b).
Schneider Bros. (b).
Sieffert, Henry.

NEW EGYPT.
Chambers, William.

NEWTON, 4427.
Decker & Auble.
Sherred, William H.

OCEAN CITY, 1950.
Abbott, Wm. (b).
Broome, Leonard L. (b).
Gardner, William F.
Lee, James W. (b).

OCEAN GROVE, 3000.
Broome, L. & L. (b).

 **Paint and Chemical Company**
PAPER COLORS AND MILL PAINT SPECIALTIES
BOSTON   SPRINGFIELD, MASS.   NEW YORK

Wholesale and Retail Stationers

NEW JERSEY.

ORANGE, 29,630.
Beegle, S. L. (d).
Estell, John (b).
Lorton, Mrs. Francis D. (b).
McGuirk, F. E. (b).
*Schmidt, H. F., Inc. (b).

PASSAIC, 54,773.
Borig, A. F.
Jewett, E. W.
Malcolm, John.
Rochies, S.
Van Auken, W. J.

PATERSON, 135,000.
Braen-Heusser Ptg. & Stationery Co.
Compa, Wm.
Crabtree, A.
Dempsey, W. G.
Devine, Joseph.
Gilmore, Edw. J.
Gordon, Wm.
*Haywood, Henry B.
Inglis Stationery Co.
Kernochen, J. K.
Layton, Geo.
Quackenbush & Co. (g).
Rumler Bros. (c).
*Tier, Wm. F.
Voellmy, E., & Sons.
Weinstein, Joseph.

PERTH AMBOY, 32,121.
Barnekow & Petz (d).
Neer, Frank (b).
Seaman & Co. (d).

PHILLIPSBURG, 13,903.
Fisk, W. H. (b).
Yeisley, Geo. L. (b).

PLAINFIELD, 20,550.
Brower, J. L.
Estil, H. Mulford.
Laing, Ed. A. (b).
Olmstead, Wm. W.
Williams, Will.

PRINCETON, 6029.
Princeton University Store (b).
Sinclair, W. C.
Van Marter, E. J.

RAHWAY, 9337.
Doran, Timothy.
Kirstein, A. F.
Litt, Henry.
McCrory, J. C.
Minton Bros.

RAHWAY—*Continued.*
Moore, H. L.
Stutzlen, J. B.
Verneau, E. J.

RED BANK, 6263.
Elliott, C. F. & S. H.
Tetley, M. F.
Trubin Bros. & Co.

RIDGEFIELD PARK, 7000.
Schneider & Freidman.
Stroem, A. (Mrs. O. F.)

RIDGEWOOD, 5416.
Cannel, Louis.
Cobb, E. W.
Jackson & Wehrell.
Karlin, Bennett.
Simonson, J. F.

RUTHERFORD, 11,320.
Bergen Pharmacal Co. (d).
Goff, W. B. (d).
Lempert, Jacob.
McFarland, E. S.
Rutherford Drug Co. (d).
Siegel & Kaplan.
Siegel & Kaplan (c, s).
Silverman, S.
Waller, W. E. (g).

SALEM, 6614.
Andrews, Wm. H. (d).
Bowen, Clinton (b).
Dixon & Fogg (d).
Newkirk, Howard B.
Robinson, Albert C. (b).
Sparks, T. Warren (b).

SOMERVILLE, 4843.
Case, John D. (d).
Letson, W. N.
Morehead, Wm. H. (b).

SOUTH AMBOY, 7482.
Bergen, Christopher I.

SOUTH ORANGE, 4608.
Wallace, E. A.

SOUTH RIVER, 2792.
Whitehead, S. R.

SUMMIT, 7500.
Siegel, Alexander.

TOMS RIVER, 1800.
Robbins, Lula H.

TOWN OF UNION, 21,737.
Margolus, Abraham.

 **Ruling Colors** The best for Ruling Inks.

Wholesale and Retail Stationers

NEW JERSEY.

TRENTON, 96,815.
Capital Stationery.
Dwyer Bros. (c, s).
Fine, Horace E. (c, s).
Garside, K. W. (b).
Kaufman, S. E., Co. (g).
Siegle Bros.
Stenograph & Reporting Co. (c, s).
*Stoll Blank. Book & Stat'y Co. (c, s).
Traver, C. L. (b).

VINELAND, 4593.
Ellis, Albert (s).
Goodfellow, Chas. R. (d).
Kulp, Howard.
Michael, Grace A.
Pioneer Drug Store.
Red Cross Pharmacy.
Wilson, Geo. I. (d).
Winslow, John H (d).

WEEHAWKEN, 4500.
Nemirofsky, David.
Rinne, Ernest.

WEST HOBOKEN, 38,776.
Snowflack, F. W.

WESTFIELD, 8000.
Casey, James (d).
Francis, Harold.
Gale, Wm. (d).
Glasser, Louis.
Smith, Robt. M., Jr.
Wittke, O. F. W. (b).

WEST ORANGE, 6889.
Brandis, Augustus, Jr.

WOODBRIDGE, 12,183.
Concannon, John.
Fink, William.

NEW MEXICO.

ALAMOGORDO, 3500.
Rolland, D. F. C.
Warren, W. E., & Co. (d).

ALBUQUERQUE, 20,000.
Allright & Anderson.
Matson, O. A., & Co.
Strong's Book Store.

CARLSBAD, 1736.
Braden, Harry I.

DEMING, 5000.
Field's.

GALLUP, 2204.
Banner Drug Store (b, d).
Cregar, W. R.
Jenkins Drug Store (b, d).

LAS CRUCES, 3836.
Las Cruces Drug Co. (d).

LAS VEGAS, 8000.
Bailey, Mrs. C. L. Mann.
Murphy, E. G.

RATON, 4539.
Sandusky Stationery Co.

ROSWELL, 8000.
Leland Pharmacy (The).

SANTA FE, 6000.
Weltmer-Burrows Drug Co., Inc., The (b).
Zooks Pharmacy (d).

SILVER CITY, 3217.
Agee Drug Co.
Blackwell's Book Store (b).
Howell Drug Co.

NEW YORK.

ADDISON, 2027.
Sackett & Taber, Inc. (d).

ALBANY, 100,253.
Advertising Specialty Co., 25 Hamilton.
*Albany News Co., The, 506-510 Broadway and 27 James (b).

ALBANY—*Continued.*
Barbric, Mrs. W., North Allen and Kent.
Blichfeldt, A. G., 373 Madison av. (d).
Bradt, Frank, 656 Central av.
Brennan, T. J., 453 Washington av.
Capitol City News Co., 70 Washington av.

 **Paint and Chemical Company**
PAPER COLORS AND MILL PAINT SPECIALTIES
BOSTON　　　SPRINGFIELD, MASS.　　　NEW YORK

Wholesale and Retail Stationers 537

NEW YORK.

ALBANY—*Continued.*
Clapp, R. F., Jr., 70 N. Pearl (b).
Conkey, J. J., 215 Central av.
Coon, Chas. F., 25 Hamilton.
Cummings, J. A., 91 North Pearl.
Dearstyne, A. J., Lark and Spring.
Doyle, M. L., 1064 Madison av.
Fitzsimmons, A. V., 9 Central av.
Gibson-Snow Co., 649 Broadway.
Harper, G. W., 47 Maiden (o. s.).
Harrig, Geo. A., 338 S. Pearl (d).
Henzel, P. J., 49 Central av. (b).
Honikel, H. F., 159 Central av. (d).
*Hudson Valley Paper Co., 520-522 Broadway.
Hutman, E. C., 222 Hamilton (d).
Kattrein, John H., 45 Maiden lane.
Kimball Bros., 46 Columbia.
Knapp, W. G., 849 Madison av.
Leahy, T. J., 179 S. Pearl.
Leake, O. C., 78 Maiden la.
Mulligan, T. E., 356 Madison av. (o. s.).
Murray, John S., 22 Steuben (b).
Myers, John G., Co., 39-41 N. Pearl. (g).
Peters Print, The, 344 Broadway.
Phillip, B. F., 89 Dove.
Pierce & Scope Co., Inc.
*Pulman, O. S., Co., 38 Beaver.
Reuter, G. J., 299 S. Pearl (b).
Richter, D., 842 Delaware av.
Sargent, F. D., 16 James.
Scopes, John E., & Co., 53 Maiden lane (b).
Skinner (Estate of), John, 44 N. Pearl (b).
Spiegel, Charles, 119 Central av.
*Stetson, Fisk Co.
Thompson & Hare, 7 Clinton.
Watson, W. D., 51 State (o. s.).
Wechsler, Arthur, 269 S. Pearl.
Weinline, Edward.
Whitney, W. M., & Co., 273 S. Pearl (g).

AMSTERDAM, 31,267.
Adams, Frank S. (d).
*Conover, Seely Co. (c).
Schoeffler, F. E. (b).
Shelly, Katie (b).
Tucker's New Shop (b, s).
Wilson, Wm. J. (d).

ATHENS, 1925.
Harvey, Mary.
Perry, Le Roy.

AUBURN, 34,668.
Allen, F. G. (b).
Colwell, Irving S.

AUBURN—*Continued.*
Crosman, Wm., & Son (j).
Ferries, Geo. F. (d).
Hanlon, Miles L. (j).
Hislop, W. B., & Co. (g).
*Johnson, F. S., Paper Co.
Jones, W. E.
Sagar, Chas. (d).
*Schicht, Wm.
*Sperry, L. F.
Weld & Co. (d).
Whipple & Foreman (b).

BALDWINSVILLE, 2099.
Gardner & Davis (d).
Howard, Hiram, Co. (j).
Smith, A. T. (d).

BALLSTON SPA, 4138.
Feeney Bros. & Co.

BATAVIA, 13,340.
Chase, B.
Leadley Drug Co. (d).
McGreevey, Sleight, De Graff Co.
Vaughan & Rider.

BATH, 3695.
Harper, S. N. (b).

BINGHAMTON, 48,443.
Barkman Drug Store (d).
Berry, Joseph H.
Dalton, B. H. (b, d).
Dean's Pharmacy (d).
Dennis, F. B. (d).
Dixon, H. M. (d).
Douglas, R. D. (d).
Fowler, Dick & Walker (g).
Gaige, A. H. (d).
Hamlin, Lucius F. (d).
Hills, McLean & Haskins (g).
Liggett, L. K., Co. (d).
*Miller, Walter R., & Co.
Mottram, R. M. (d).
Olmstead, E. M. (d).
Ostrom, E. L. (d).
Perry, G. S., & Co. (b).
Roucke, Josef.
Russell, F. E. (d).
Smith, C. V. (b).
*Stephens & Co.
Strait, Mrs. Elizabeth.
Waldron Drug Co. (d).
Webster, W. D. (d).

BREWSTER, 1402.
Tuttle, Howard.

Hampden Crucible Enamel — For hot or cold iron pipes, boiler fronts, etc.

538 *Wholesale and Retail Stationers*

NEW YORK.

BUFFALO, 423,715.
Adam, J. N., & Co., 388 Main (g).
Adam, Meldrum & Anderson Co., 396 Main (g).
Adams & White Co., 94-96 Pearl.
*Bachman News Co., 155 Ellicott.
*Barnum, S. O., & Son (g), 365-367 Main and 274 Washington.
Beres, Marian L.
*Besser's, Inc., 544 Main (b).
Bleyler & Fisher, 204½ Pearl.
*Buffalo News Co., 56 E. Mohawk.
Case, Martha R.
*Clawson & Wilson Co. (g).
Dahlke Stat. & Mfg. Co., 610 Niagara.
Drewelow, Max F., 586 Main (c, o. s.).
Eaton Bros. Co., Inc., 331 Washington.
Engel, Bernhardt & Turner, 686 Main.
Evans, Penfold Co., 68-72 Court.
Flint & Kent, 544 Main (g).
Gillott, A. J., 1039 Main.
Hengerer Co., The Wm., 455 Main (g).
Lockwood, Millington, 207 to 209 Ellicott sq. (c, o. s.).
Meldrum Co., H. A., 460 Main (g).
Michalski, Wladyslaw.
Paul, Peter, & Son, 256 Delaware av. (d).
Person, Henry J.
Ryan & Williams, 84 Pearl (c).
Schallmo, Albert L.
*Ulbrich Co., Otto, 386 Main (b).
White, E. R., 1423 Main (j).
Whiting Stationery Co., Swan & Washington (c).
Williamson Co., David F., 200 Main.

CAMDEN, 2900.
Farnsworth, Almon N.
Fenton, Albert.
Maloney, A. H., & Son.
Stone, Benjamin H.

CANANDAIGUA, 7217.
McGreevey, Sleight, De Graff Co. (b).
McFarlane, W. J. (b).

CANISTEO, 1985.
Barker, Edwin C.

CANTON, 2701.
Dezell, Robert B.
Stevens, Bing S. (b).

CAPE VINCENT, 1178.
Laird, W. D.

CARTHAGE, 3295.
Schwartz Bros. (d).
Villars, Edward (d).
Westcott, Fred (d).

CASTLETON, 1396.
Sweet & Fitzgerald.

CATSKILL, 5294.
Magee, L. R.
Van Gorden & Co.

CEDARHURST, 700.
Hurwitz, Lazar.

CHATHAM, 2090.
Whyland, L. H.

CHESTER, 1280.
Wilson, G. L.

CLINTON, 1360.
Watson Drug Co.

COBLESKILL, 2158.
Loy, R. J. (b).

COHOES, 24,709.
McClintock, H. T. (b).
Steenburg, F. E. (b).

COPIAGUE, 546.
Crollus, Charles L.

CORNING, 13,730.
Cain & Bernkopf, Inc. (g).
Ecker Drug Co.
Goodridge, L. T., & Co. (b).
Kling, Wm. E. (b).
Lamb's Pharmacy (d).
Nichols Drug Co. (d).
Terbell Calkins Drug Co. (d).
Wing & Bostwick Co. (g).

CORNWALL ON THE HUDSON, 2240.
Engers, J. N. (Cigars).

CORTLAND, 11,504.
Fair Store, The (g).
McGraw & Elliott (d).
*McKinney & Doubleday (b).
Nye Drug Co. (d).
Sager & Hammond (d).
Walsh & Allen (d).
Watson, Geo. I. (d).
Mullen Wall Paper Co. (b).

 **Paint and Chemical Company**
PAPER COLORS AND MILL PAINT SPECIALTIES
BOSTON   SPRINGFIELD, MASS.   NEW YORK

Wholesale and Retail Stationers   539

NEW YORK

DANSVILLE, 3908.
  De Long, H. W. (b).
  Lieb, F. A. (b).

DELHI, 2000.
  Williams, Carlton D.

DEPOSIT, 1544.
  Brown, Chas K. (d).
  Smith, S. D. (d).

DOLGEVILLE, 3326.
  Yonker, F J.

DUNKIRK, 17,221.
  Donovan & Sons.
  Economy 5 and 10 Cent Store.
  Harper Drug Co.
  Jordan, Jr., Frank.
  Monroe Pharmacy (d).
  Pfleeger, C.
  *Roberts Drews Co.
  Rusch, E. J.
  Safe Store (g).
  Shinners News Co.
  West Drug Co. (b).

EAST RANDOLPH.
  Culver, R. J.

ELIZABETHTOWN.
  Richards, E. W.

ELLENVILLE, 2872.
  Booth, William.
  Hyman & Fisk.
  McMullen.
  Palmer, Ulster.
  Spock, Eugene.

ELMIRA, 37,176.
  *Baker Bros.
  Derby, Cora A. & Eva N.
  *Holmes, L. T. (g).
  Horwitz Bros., 325 Carroll.
  Issard Co., S. F. (g).
  McGreevey, Sleight, De Graff Co. (b).
  Plummer, Mrs. F. F. (b).
  Rubin Bros.
  Sheehan, Dean & Co. (j).
  Spillan, James R. (d).
  Sullivan, Florence (b).
  *Thompson, N. J., Co. (g).

ELMSFORD, 1380.
  Diskin, Morris.

ENDICOTT, 10,050.
  Pezzulla, V., & Son.

FONDA, 1120.
  Snell, Mary E.

FORT EDWARD, 3762.
  Blackall, E. J.
  Contryman & Donnell (d).

FORT PLAIN, 2596.
  Diefendorf, Fenton G., & Son.

FRANKFORT, 4206.
  Hardell, John G.

FREDONIA, 5148.
  Chatsey, Frank C. (d).
  Hart, Waldo R.
  Robinson, H. C. (b).

FREEPORT, 4705.
  Liberman, F. R., & Son.
  Michnoff, Meyer.

FULTON, 10,480.
  Conley Bros.
  Giesler, H. C. (d).
  Halstead, Clara T.
  Hargrave, M. B. (d).
  Katz, M., & Co. (g).
  Lasher, F. W. (b).
  Patterson, W. H. (g).
  Putnam, E. A. (d).

GENEVA, 12,446.
  Foster, James G.
  *Geneva Mercantile Co.
  Klopfer, Louis (b).
  Linden Pharmacy (d).
  Mulcahy, E. J. (b).
  Scott, B. W. (b).
  Seneca Drug Co. (d).
  Weld Drug Co. (d).

GLEN COVE, 7500.
  Breuer, Ph.
  Chittenden, S. K. (d).
  Croft, C. O., & Co. (d).
  Harrold, R. W.
  Jacques, Henry H.
  Ledewitz, Benjamin.
  Long Island Book Exchange.
  Rogers, James H.

GLENS FALLS, 15,243.
  Boston Store (g).
  Braley, P. P. (b).
  Collins, J. J.
  Empire Stationery Co.
  Fowler & Co., B. B. (g).
  Larkins & Davenport (d).
  Russell & Wait (b).
  Viele, F. C. (d).
  Wiley, Fred. W.

 **Regal Wall Coating** A white cold water paint. Will not rub, scale or peel off.

Wholesale and Retail Stationers

NEW YORK.

GLOVERSVILLE, 20,642.
Alvord & Smith Co.
Argensinger, The, Co. (g).
Cowles & Casler Co.
Martin & Naylor Co. (g).
Snow, Newton G.

GOSHEN, 3099.
Robinson, John W.

GOUVERNEUR, 4128.
Mead Drug Co.

GOWANDA, 2063.
Galley, Carl W.

GREENPONIT, 2817.
Fordham & Doyle.
Merrill Harry W.

GREENWOOD, 1082.
Hazen's Cash Store.

GROTON, 1188.
Atwater, F. C.

HAMBURG, 2134.
Hengerer, Robt.

HAMMONDSPORT, 1141.
Neff & Layton.
Smellie, James H. (d).

HARRISON, 1485.
Kunitz, Max.

HASTINGS, 3500.
Goodwin, T. J.

HAVERSTRAW, 6182.
Farley Bros.
Jenkins, Wm. H.
Smith, Clarence.

HEMPSTEAD, 4426.
Agneg, Henry (Est. of) (b).
Carman Lash Pharmacy (d).
Cohen, Louis, Dept. Store (g).
Ertell Pharmacy.
Geisler, W. L.
Levine, Morris.

HERKIMER, 7520.
Gallinger Drug Co.
Herkimer News Co.
Munger, H. G., & Co. (g).
Rasbach, Charles.
Sauer Drug Co.

HIGHLAND FALLS, 2518.
Dickey, Chas. H.
Hoffman, Nathan.

HOMER, 2878
Potter, C. W. (g).
Stevens, Chas., & Son.
Watson, Adaline.

HOOSICK FALLS, 5532.
Dooley, Alice.
Gaffney, Peter.
Kantz P. L.

HORNELL, 13,617.
Hollands, Geo., & Sons (d).
Hornell Drug Co. (d).
Pierson, Horace G. (d).
Van Winkle, A. S. (d).

HUDSON, 11,417.
Dowling, E. A. (b).
Downing, Jeremiah (b).
Gasler, Mr. & Mrs. Carl O.
Maloney, Frank M. (b).
Ziesenitz, W, H. (b).

HUDSON FALLS, 5189.
Mosher, A. C.
Smith, A. E. (b).

HUME, 385.
Sandford, F. E.

HUNTER, 525.
Iskin, Max.

HUNTINGTON, 6200.
Hanning, William H.

ILION, 10,000.
Bonn, L. A.
Bentley, B. H. (d).
Carney, G. M.
Getman, C. T. (d).
Powers, W. J.
Russell, B. H. (d).

INWOOD, 1925.
Sidel, Jos. P.

IRVINGTON, 2480.
Hoffman & Becker.

ISLIP, 2200.
Epstein, Isaac.

ITHACA, 15,510.
Andrus & Church (b).
College Book Shop.
Cornell Co-operative Society.
Corner Book Stores, The.
Larkin, Thomas J.
*Miller, Thomas G., & Sons Paper Co.
O'Daniel, H. L.

NEW YORK.

ITHACA—*Continued.*
Osborn, R. C., & Co. (b).
Rothschild Bros. (b, g).
Students Supply Store.
University Stationery Store.

JAMESTOWN, 31,297.
Abrahamson-Bigelow Co. (g).
City Drug Store.
Clark, F. M. (b, d).
Eckard's Drug Store.
Geer, C. M.
Hatch, Fred. E. (b, d).
Jones, G. E., & E. A.
Mason News Co. (b).
McCormick, F. J., News Co.
*Monarch Stationery & Paper Co.
Samuels Drug Co. (d).
Swanson, C. A., Drug Co. (d).

JOHNSTOWN, 10,447.
Dawes & Co. (g).
Dewitt, R. G., & Co.
Newton, B. B. (b, c).
Palmer, Frank (d).
Schwemmer, R. (b).
Smith & Lather.
Thyne's Drug Store.
Walwrath, J. R.

KINGSTON, 25,908.
*Forsyth & Davis (b).
Murphy, A. J.
O'Reilly, Wm.
Winters, E., Sons Co., Inc. (b).

LARCHMONT, 1760.
Zvirin's Stationery Shop.

LAWRENCE, 1500.
Hirsch, Joseph.

LE ROY, 4075.
Sutherland, The, Co.

LIBERTY, 2072.
Jacoby, Gertrude.
Steenrod, B. & M.

LINDENHURST, 2000.
Edelman, Louis.
Riehl, Charles.

LITTLE FALLS, 14,000.
*Chapman, B. E. (b).
Newell, J. R. (c).
Robinson, Geo. A. (s).
Wolf Bros. (g).

LOCKPORT, 17,970.
Bayliss & Sweet (d).
Croft (g).

LOCKPORT—*Continued.*
Cushman, R. M., Co.
Frank News Co.
Jenss Bros. (g).
Laux, A. J., & Co. (c).
*Lockport Candy Co.
Parsons Drug Co. (d).
*Richmond & Mathers.
Plaster News Co.
Stephanski, R. A.
Williams Bros. (g).
Wright, L. J. (Est. of) (b).

LONG LAKE, 1233.
Murray, A.

LOWVILLE, 3000.
Jackson, George D.
Murray, Mrs. Lucia.

LYONS, 4758.
Bourne, W. E. (g).
Calvin, W. P. (d).
Carpenter, W. E., & Co.
Getman's Drug Store.
Moore & Moore (b, d).

MALONE, 6475.
*Buttrick, Thos. T. (b).
Empsall, Wm. A., Co. (g).
Hyde Drug Co. (d).
McDonald, The, Book Store (b).
Rennie, L. G. (b).
Robbins, E. N.

MAMARONECK, 5090.
Cotter, Wm. J. (c, s).
Foshay, H. E.

MATTEAWAN, 6727.
White, Wellington C.

MECHANICVILLE, 6634.
Caldwell, M. B.
*Hughes, Chas. W. (b).
Wendell, N. P. (g).
Williams, A. R. (d).

MEDINA, 5683.
Hunt & James.
Mack, Chas. (b, d).
Mercer & Fassett (d, b).
O'Malley, Walter.
Wright & Ross Drug Co. (b, d).

MIDDLEBURG, 1059.
Bulson Bros. (g).
Vroman, Geo. W. (d).
Wells, Frank A.

MIDDLEPORT, 1358.
Hoyt, W. D., & Son.

Hampden Mill White — Will not turn yellow like the ordinary White Lead paint.

Wholesale and Retail Stationers

NEW YORK CITY.

Borough of Brooklyn—*Continued.*

Pearlman, I., 8307 Church av.
Pech, Harry, 857 Green av.
Penny, E. M., 566 Myrtle av.
Perlof, D., 1944 Coney Island av.
Pesselnick, C., 217 Ditmas av.
Pomerance, Harry, 114 Livingston.
Potekar, S., 425 Potter av.
Price & Rosenbaum, Inc., 1295 B'way. (g).
Prussin, Jacob, 219A 5th av. (b).
Ratner, I., 2669 Pitkin av.
Reuben, J., 882 7th av.
Richardson, H., 422 DeKalb av.
Robin, Lewis, 117 Saratoga av.
Rosenberg, H., 1769 B'way.
Rosenberg, M., 5418 New Utrecht av.
Rosenfeld, Sam'l, 2369 Myrtle av.
Rothbart, S., 358 Flushing av.
Rudner, B., 786 Nostrand av.
Sabloff & Pickard, 3331 Fulton.
Sadowsky, Max, 550 3d av.
Sanders, Wm., 1679 Nostrand av.
Sarokin Bros., 4917 12th av.
Sauer, Andrew, Jr., 13 Putnam av. and 794 Manhattan av.
Scharf, Jos., 8502 18th av.
Schulman, Max, 1577 Fulton.
Schwartz, Sam'l, 6830 3d av.
Seaver Bros., 5208 3d av. (g).
Seigel, Louis, 171 Ainsle.
Seyffarth, F., 435 Ralph.
Sforza, M. J., 6009 14th av.
Shapiro, Morris, 803 Halsey.
Shaplvo, S., 59 5th av.
Shniper, Isadore, 2953 Fulton.
Siegel, A., 1507 Ave. U.
Silverman, S., 4207 13th av., 4421 14th av.
Sink, Sam., 353 Myrtle av.
Siskind, S., 301a Halsey.
Sleplan, Harry, 5007 6th av.
Smith, G. A., 85 Main.
Solow, Sam'l, 5904 Ft. Hamilton.
Starke Bros., 233 Nostrand av. and 3122 Fulton.
Stein, F., 448 DeKalb av.
*Stein, B. & H., Co., Inc., 72 Graham av.
Stein Bros., 192 Wallabout Mkt. (g).
Stern, Max, 178 Hull.
Stevenson & Marsters, Inc., 373 Fulton.
Stone, Frank, 1486 Bushwick av.
Stores, Chas. Williams Co., 1 Main.
*Sukon, Nathan, Sons, Estate, 556 Grand.
Susman, Louis, 116 Albany av.
Tandy, Van Brunt, 413 Fulton.

Borough of Brooklyn—*Continued.*

Tauger, Max, 8335 Fulton.
Taxin, Morris, 46 Wyckoff av.
Thall, Ph., 646 Bedford av.
Tobin, Geo., 1842 Bath av.
Turner & Wild, 1214 Fulton.
Urquhart & Fitzgerald, 16 Court.
Urquhart, Colin K., 1120 Fulton.
Ventres, T. B. (Firm of), 286 Livingston.
Webster, A. A., & Co., 440 Fulton (j).
Webster, Frank C., 269 Central av.
Weinstein, B., 898 Myrtle av.
Weinstraub, D., 384 Liberty av.
*Wollman, A., 1708 E. N. Y. av.
Wollman, M., 562 Grand.
Wornov, Frank, 333 Albany av.
Zelmanowitz, P., 149 Franklin.

Boroughs of Manhattan and The Bronx.

Abt, Leo J., 621 B'way.
Acme Press, Inc., 18 W. 31st.
Adams-Flanigan Co., Inc., 410 Westchester av. (g).
Adams & Grace Co., Inc., 22 Thames.
Adler, G., 634 Prospect av.
Ahern & Randel, 150 E. 23d.
Aisenson Bros., 321 E. 166th.
Aitken Sons & Co., 417 5th av. (g).
Albert, Martin E., 30 Ferry.
Albertson, Rob't J., 149 Church.
Alexander, C., Co., Inc., 284 Pearl.
Allan, W. W., Inc., 116 Prince.
Allen, Williams & Co., Inc., 470 B'way.
*American News Co., 9 Park pl.
*American Tract Society, Inc., 101 Park av.
Applebaum, B., & Son, 326 Church.
Arcade Staty. & Prtg. Co., 1779 B'way.
Armbrust, F., 422 Amsterdam av.
Armstrong, R., 946 Amsterdam av.
Arnfeld, H., 856 9th av.
Arnold, Samuel, 1046 Westchester av.
Arthur, Mountain & Co., 111 Liberty.
Atlas Staty. Co., 52 Duane.
*Auerbach & Wilensky, 116 Ludlow. (Toys, etc.)
Babcock, J. S., Co., 56 Pine.
Bachrach, M., & Son, 2275 3d av.
*Bainbridge, Henry, & Co., 101 William.
Barsky, H. & S., 1435 3d av.
Bartel, Saml., 2388 Webster av.
Bartley, Wm. F., 21 Ann.

 **Paint and Chemical Company**
PAPER COLORS AND MILL PAINT SPECIALTIES
BOSTON   SPRINGFIELD, MASS.   NEW YORK

Wholesale and Retail Stationers   545

NEW YORK CITY.

Boroughs of Manhattan and The Bronx—*Continued.*

Batlin, Morris, 2800 3d av.
Beeken, Alfred D., 94 Chambers.
Belfer, Wm., 1267 5th av.
Bellows, Theo., 18 Spruce.
Benedicks, S., & Son, 29 E. 31st.
Benedict, G. S., 73 Murray.
Bennett, N. G., 102 Beekman.
Bennett, Raymond D., 66 Duane.
*Benson, B. D., & Sons, Inc., 11 Cliff.
Benzer, Louis, 643 3d av.
*Berg Bros., 480 B'way.
Bergmaier Bros., 77 E. 125th.
Bergman, Max, 2190 5th av.
Berndt, Chas., 540 8th av.
Bernstein, Henry, & Co., 487 B'way.
Bertine, J. H., & Co., Inc., 81 Fulton.
Biglow, L. H., & Co., 62 Broad.
Birnbaum, C., 34 St. Marks pl.
Bloch, M. H., 1205 Tinton av.
Bloomingdale Bros., 990 3d av. (g).
Blumberg, Julius, 262 Grand.
Bollong, Andrew, 129 La Fayette.
Borchardt, C., 794 E. 149th.
*Borgfelt, Geo., & Co., Inc., 119 E. 16th. (Notions.)
Borsig, Herman, Jr., 361 E. 138th.
Bosworth, J. G., 299 B'way.
Bowne & Co., Inc., 161 Maiden La.
Bracklow, Robt. L., 101 Maiden La.
Brandt, E., 905 E. Tremont av.
Brentano's, Inc., 5th av. and 27th.
Brewer, F. A., 352 St. Ann's av.
Brewer, H. K., & Co., 58 Liberty and 306 Madison av.
Bright, R. E., 166 W. 46th.
Brinberg, G., 2636 8th av.
Bristol & Bristol, Inc., 650 6th av.
Brokaw, Edward V., & Bro., 52 New.
Broun-Green Co., Inc., 48 John.
Brower Bros., 317 B'way.
Brown, Lent & Pett, Inc., 90 William.
Bulmer's, Ltd., 323 Canal and 225 5th av.
Burns, Catherine, 948 2d av.
Burns, M., 68 Columbus av.
Bushell, J., 1323 Prospect av.
Buskirk Co., 70 Fulton.
*Butler Bros., Inc., 495 B'way.
Butler, J. K., Co., Inc., 130 Pearl.
Caiati, A., & Co., 625 E. 187th.
*Calhoun, Robbins Co., 895 B'way.
Cameron & Bulkley, Inc., 18 E. 30th.
Capen's, A. M., Sons, 60 Pearl.
Cassel, Bernard, 150 W. 34th.
Cavanagh, John G., 30 E. 42d.

Boroughs of Manhattan and The Bronx—*Continued.*

Charney, Max, 381 E. 143d.
Chase, J. M., & Co., 99 Nassau.
Cheerful Store, 444 6th av.
Chief Pub. Co., Inc., 5 Beekman and 129 Fulton.
Chisholm Staty. Co., Inc., 63 Cliff.
Circle, John, Co., 30 Church.
*Claflin, H. B., Co., Inc., 224 Church. (g).
Clayton, C. H., & Co., Inc., 227 Pearl.
Clement, H. H., 168 Amsterdam av.
Climax Stationery Co., Inc., 33 Sullivan. (L. L. Ledgers.)
Cohen, Harry, 679 9th av.
Cohen, H., 954 Madison av.
*Cohen, Sam'l, 100 Orchard. (Toys, etc.)
Connolly, James E., 105 Chambers.
Cook, A. F., 1328 3d av.
Cook, John, 1537 Castle Hill av.
Cooper Union Supply Store, 7th and 4th av.
*Corlies, Macy & Co., Inc., 40 John.
Costa, T., & Co., 153 W. 28th.
Cowan, Elton T., Co., 133 W. 19th.
Cramer, Peter, 319 E. 136th.
Crown Printing Co., 83 Nassau.
Crown Stationery Co., 12 W. 17th.
Curtin, John J., 198 Greenwich.
Daly, John W., 1350 Ogden av.
Davidson Bros., 2690 3d av.
Davis, D., 416 Willis av.
Davison, H., 225 W. B'way.
Deatly, Arthur G., & Co., 24 Gold.
*Defiance Mfg. Co., 384 B'way.
Dempsey & Carroll, Inc., 431 5th av. (Plate Ptg. & Eng.)
Dennison, Robt. S., & Co., Inc., 75 Fulton.
*Dennison & Sons, Inc., 21 Cliff.
Dince, M., 980 Lexington av.
Dorfman, H., 1234 Lexington av.
Doushkess, Jacob, 21 Church.
Dresner Co., J., B'way and 42d.
Drimmer, E., 4 W. 3d.
Drimmer, Ed., 4 W. 3d (Cont. Ptr.)
Drucker, Leo, 208 Centre.
Dutton, E. P., & Co., Inc., 681 5th
Edgar Ptg. & Staty. Co., 68 W. 39th.
Ehrenberg, J. T., 2889 B'way.
Elliot, H. R., & Co., 13 Stone.
Elting, P. & L., 2177 3d av. (Toys.)
Endicott Staty. & Novelty Shop, 442 Columbus av.
*Enlow Co., Inc., 354 B'way.

Canary Yellow A true color. Makes bright tints and solid finishes.

Wholesale and Retail Stationers

NEW YORK CITY.

Boroughs of Manhattan and The Bronx—*Continued.*

Evans & Morford, 35 Warren. (Tprl. S'plies.)
Excelsior Stationery Co., 116 Nassau.
Farhi, I., 153 W. 32d.
Felgin, Sol., Co., Inc., 34 Houston.
Felginow, I. R., 881 6th av.
Feinstein, Jacob M., 423 Audubon av.
Feinstein, B., 1472 Amsterdam av.
Feldman, Morris, 174 W. B'way.
Fiedler & Hanau, Inc., 633 B'way.
Fillmore, W. C., Ptg. & S. Co., 108 Fulton.
Findler & Wibel, 115 Nassau.
Fischer, A., 1876 Clinton av.
Fishkin, D., 6 E. Fordham rd.
Fishman, W., 817 1st av.
Fitzpatrick, Julia, 378 W. 35th.
Flynn, Mary C., 48 E. 59th.
Fogelman, H., 160 Bowery.
Forstein, A., 1779 B'way.
Foster, M. P., Inc., 49 Liberty.
Fountain, J. H., 291 Pearl.
Frank & Tichenor, 39 E. 20th.
*Frankel, G., & Son, 550 B'way.
Frankel, J., 2182 Amsterdam av.
Frankel, Sol., 3754 White Plains av.
Freed, Keva, 508 Amsterdam av.
Freeman, Jacob, 106 10th av.
Frey, O., 2288 Beaumont av.
Friedland, Isaac, 3140 B'way.
Friedman, H., 600 3d av.
Fry, S. W., 101 Beekman. (Carbon Paper, etc.)
Ganz Bros., 21 W. 30th.
Gardner, DeWitt C., 179 Pearl.
Gerry & Murray, 75 Broad.
Gimbel Bros., B'way and 32d. (g)
Ginsburg, Isaac, 1094 Amsterdam.
Gluck, S. J., 539 2d av. (Toys.)
*Goldberg, C. H. & E. S., Inc., 114 Reade.
Goldberg, D., 840 St. Nicholas av.
Goldberg, M., 1516 Lexington av.
Golde, M. E., & Sons, 1005 6th av.
Golding, I., 436 W. 42d.
Goldman, M. L., 130 Fulton.
Goldmann, Chas., & Son, 80 W. B'way.
Goldshider, J. K., 465 Amsterdam av.
Goldsmith Bros., Inc., 77 Nassau.
Gordon Press, Inc., 727 Westchester av.
Gottesman, Jos., 2363 2d av.
*Gottlieb, L., & Sons, Inc., 263 E. 2d.

Boroughs of Manhattan and The Bronx—*Continued.*

Gould, W. Reid, 141 Nassau and 111 B'way. (Law.)
Graham-Chisholm Co., Inc., 9 Murray.
Graves Typewriter Co., Inc., 6 Church. (Tprl. S'plies.)
Greenwald, J., B'way and 96th.
Gregg, T. F., Co., Inc., 126 Maiden Ln.
Gross, Wm., 791 Jackson av.
Grossman, Maurice J., 41 Warren.
Haag, R. A., 98 Maiden la.
Halperin, H., 428 Mott av.
Halpern, R. H., 239 4th av.
Halsted, H. M., 226 William. (Cont. Ptr.)
Hamburger, S., 395 B'way.
Hanley, Wm., 157 Alexander av.
Harjes, Geo., Co., Inc., 141 W. 36th.
*Harlem Toy & Staty. House, 2332 2d av. (Notions.)
Harman Bros., 62 W. B'way. (Cont. Ptr.)
Harmann, S., & Son, 71 E. B'way.
Harris Bros., 36 Washington.
Hartmann, M. H., 39 E. 28th. (Art Mtls.)
Hasbrouck, R. S., & Co., 25 Cliff.
Head, Geo. W., 96 John.
Heinrichs, John, 50 Ave. A.
Hepp & Co., Albert, 22 Thames.
Heyman & Sons, R., 802 8th av.
Hitzelberger, Tietenberg & Co., 54 Franklin. (Cont. Ptr.)
Hodgens, H. C., 444 6th av.
Holder Bros., 261 Columbus av.
Holloway, John H., 66 Nassau.
Horowitz, J. L., 87 5th av. (Cont. Ptr.)
Houston, John C., 1 Platt.
Howard, Franklin, 71 Broad.
Howe, A. D., 89 Fulton.
*Hubner, A. W., & Co., 13 Chatham sq. (Fancy Gds.)
Hudson Staty. Co., 36 W. 28th.
Hulin, John S., 75 Franklin.
Hull & Deppisch, 108 Fulton.
Humbert, Edwd., 395 B'way.
Hunter, W. J., 58 Broad.
Huth, J. R., 61 Fulton. (Cont. Ptr. and Stat.)
*Hyman, L., & Son, 121 Spring.
*Industrial Supply Co., Inc., 41 Broad.
Inter-City Paper & Supply Co., Inc., 61 E. 11th.
*International News Co., 85 Duane.

 **Paint and Chemical Company**
PAPER COLORS AND MILL PAINT SPECIALTIES
BOSTON　　　　SPRINGFIELD, MASS.　　　　NEW YORK

Wholesale and Retail Stationers

NEW YORK CITY.

Boroughs of Manhattan and The Bronx—*Continued.*

*International Stationery Co., Inc., 50 Warren.
Irving Press, Inc., 121 E. 31st.
Isaacson, H., 1597 Lexington av.
Jackson Staty. Co., 1186 3d av.
Jacobson, John N., & Co., 212 Broadway.
Jacobstat, D., 385 Amsterdam av.
Jaffe, Morris, 1812 Amsterdam av.
Jansen, Hugo, 75 8th av.
Jaques & Co., Inc., 116 E. 41st.
Jerome, Frank D., 148 Chambers.
Johnson Co., Milton C., Inc., 78 Walker.
Jones & Leigh Mfg. Co., 58 Fulton.
Jordan, Mrs. E., 2185 Washington av.
Jordan Staty. & Ptg. Co., Inc., 3 Cedar.
Kahn, D., 330 1st av.
Kantrowitz, A., 19 W. 100th.
Kapelowitz, M., 622 E. 135th.
Kaplan, Morris, 1879 So. Boulevard.
Karow, R., 651 E. 138th.
Katz, M., 1330 Brook av.
Katzenberg, M., & Co., 424 Broome.
Kellman Staty. Co., 496 3d av.
Kelly & Wefer, Inc., 80 4th av.
Kempen, F. G., 1669 3d av.
Kendrick, John, 415 4th av.
Keogh, J. C., 3559 B'way. (d)
Kerr, Edwin J., 74 Beekman.
Ketcham, Chas. F., & Co., 41 Liberty.
*Kimpton, Edward Co., Inc., 60 John.
*Kimpton, Haupt & Co., 53 Beekman.
Kinne, Horace, 475 Amsterdam av.
Knapp, F. H., 146 Hamilton pl.
Knickerbocker Staty. Co., Inc., 49 E. 12th.
Knickerbocker Stenographic Offices, 60 B'way.
Koch, H. C. F., & Co., Inc., 132 W. 125th. (g)
Koch Sons & Co., 541 Pearl.
Kohn, Max, 1331 3d av.
Kopilovitz, A., 1629 Amsterdam av.
Kraft, T. V., & Co., 6 Warren.
Kraiman, Sam'l, 405 Amsterdam av.
Kress, S. H., & Co., 350 B'way. (5 & 10 Cent Gds.)
Krieger, David, 120 Prince.
Kushner, P., 1009 Westchester av.
Laks, B., 734 Melrose av.
Landsberg Bros., 86 Fulton.
Landsberg, J., 11 W. 27th.

Boroughs of Manhattan and The Bronx—*Continued.*

*Landsberg, Lewis, 162 Greenwich.
Lane, Miss M. M., 1046 Madison av.
Langstadter, A., 513 6th av.
Laurel Stationery Co., 41 Warren.
Laurier, Joseph, 56 University pl.
Lawrence, L. W., Inc., 40 Nassau.
Lazarus, H., 1939 So. Boulevard.
Lazarus, M. C., 17 W. 35th.
Leach, Jas., Estate of, 86 Nassau.
Lehrhaupt, Sam'l, 189 E. 2d.
Leibovitz, P., 872 Willis av.
Leifer, F. J., Co., 12 E. 13th. (Carbon Paper, etc.)
Lein, A., 925 Prospect av.
Levits & Mardfin, 125 5th av.
Levitz, Max, 1900 B'way.
*Levy, Frank, Inc., 483 Broadway
Levy, Jacob, 773 Amsterdam av.
Levy & Bros., Louis, 2275 B'way.
Liberty Staty. Co., 123 Liberty.
Libien, M., 904 8th av.
Licari, P. & Co., 414 Greenwich.
Lincoln Staty. Co., 288 Willis.
Lippman, A., 807 E. 152d.
Lipset Bros., 1017 6th av.
Livingston, Arthur, 35 Warren.
Lord & Taylor, 480 5th av. (g)
Loveman, Jos., & Loeb, Inc., 120 W. 32d.
Lubelsky, I., 1225 Madison av.
*Lusk, R. E., & Son, Inc., 27 Park pl.
Lustig, Morris Co. (Inc.), 45 Rose.
MacDonald-Greene Co., Inc., 26 Cortlandt. (Tprl. S'plies.)
MacDonald Staty. Co., 42 Nassau.
Machles, M., 108 4th av.
Macoy Pub. & Masonic Supply Co., Inc., 45 John.
Macy, R. H., & Co., B'way and 34th.
Mahler, Louis, 524 Grand.
Maisel, Max N., 424 Grand.
Malatzky, Max, 871 Columbus av.
Manes, Benj., 1628 3d av.
Mann, Wm., Co. Inc., 105 Chambers.
Marguiles, C., 568 Columbus av.
*Matzke, Sam'l, 25 Av. C. (Notions.)
May Department Stores Co., Inc., 37 W. 26th. (g)
McClunn & Co., 6 Stone.
McCreery, Jas., & Co., Inc., 5 W. 34th. (g)
McCutcheon, C. A., 424 Broome.
McGlynn, Jas. S., 708 Columbus av.
Mealy, A. S., 950 6th av.
Mellor, J. C., 900 6th av.
Melnik, M., 986 E. 167th.

 **Permanent Reds** LIGHT ALKALI WATER } PROOF

Wholesale and Retail Stationers

NEW YORK CITY.

Boroughs of Manhattan and The Bronx—*Continued.*

Mendelson, A., 806 6th av.
Mercantile Stationers, 101 W. 42d.
Merchants Stationery Co., 61 E. 11th.
Merritt & Hanfling, Inc., 461 8th av.
Merson, Abr., 362 E. 167th.
Messina, M., 196 Grand. (Cigars.)
Metcalf, N. R., 117 Liberty.
*Methodist Book Concern, Inc., 150 5th av.
Meyer, John E., 687 6th av.
Meyers, Jacob, 302 B'way.
Millard & Co., 23 W. 32d.
Miller, S., 2096 Webster av.
*Millet, Max, & Co., Inc., 151 Park row. (Toys.)
Mintzer, A., 942 Av. St. John.
Mirman, J., 1054 2d av.
Mishnum, Solomon, 2843 & 3849 B'way. (b).
Mitchell, Bosworth, & Co., Inc., 41 & 48 Warren.
Mitchell, S. J., 51 Maiden La. (Embossing.)
Mittelsberg, A., 699 Beck.
Modern Stationery Co., 62 W. B'way.
Mohle, Frederic, 51 Maiden la.
Montrose & Clarke Co., Inc., 12 Cliff.
Morgan, T., 1986 Webster av.
Morits, H., 1268 1st av.
Morrison, Geo. C., Co., Inc., 422 E. 53d.
Moskowitz & Cohen, 300 E. 101st.
Moskowitz, T., 282 E. Houston. (Peddlers' Supplies.)
Murphy, D. P., Jr., 14 Barclay. (b).
Murray, Charles, 75 Broad.
Naiman, O. & M., 2568 B'way.
Naiman & Siegel, 2045 B'way.
Nelkin & May, 201 E. 28th.
Netter, A., 837 7th av. (b).
*Neustadter Bros., 118 Ridge.
*Neustadter & Bro., Inc., 118 Ludlow. (Toys, etc.)
Newcomb, J. F., & Co., 35 B'way and 441 Pearl.
Newman, H., 907 So. Boulevard.
Newman, S., 182 9th av.
Ninger, C. J., 258 5th av.
Nolan, Thos., & Sons, Inc., 41 Liberty.
Novick Bros., 23 W. 24th.
Novick, S., & Son, 62 E. Houston.
*Oberly & Newell, 545 Pearl.
Office Systems & Supply Co., 45 Lafayette. (Cont. Ptr.)

Boroughs of Manhattan and The Bronx—*Continued.*

Oklander, M., 330 E. 9th.
Ostrowsky, J., 886 9th av.
Paul, Siewers & McKay, Inc., 441 Pearl.
Pearlman, Benj., 25 B'way.
Pearlman, Paul, Washington av. and 180th.
Peck, Jacob, 1940 & 2122 7th av. (b).
Peck & Durham, Inc., 165 William.
*Peckham, Little & Co., Inc., 57 E. 11th. (School S'plies.)
Peniston Ptg. Co., Inc., 36 Beaver.
Penn, Hyman, 913 Columbus av.
Penn, Isaac, 3363 B'way.
Penn, Jennie, 2711 B'way.
Penny, H. E., 95 Cliff.
Perlman, Max, 50 Norfolk.
Perlmuter, S., 1406 Prospect av.
Perrin, W. N., & Co., 15 Spruce.
Pertain, G. W., 18 Exchange pl.
Pesetzky Bros. & Moloshok, 3201 B'way. (Cigars.)
Pestiaux, M. Miss, 191 W. 102d.
Pikulin, Simon, 2006 Amsterdam av.
Plunkett, Geo. J., 110 John. (Cont. Ptr.)
Polhemus Ptg. Co., Inc., 121 Fulton.
Popper, Wm. C., & Co., Inc., 114 Worth.
Powell, Wm. H., 983 6th av. (Art Mtls.)
Powers, J. C. & W. E., (Inc.), 65 Duane. (B.B. Mfrs.)
*Prigosen, S., Staty. & Ptg. Co., 29 Beekman.
Provost, Franklin, 1115 Amsterdam av.
Provost, Humbert & Williams, 395 B'way.
*Pulvermacher, L., & Bro., 176 Park row.
*Putnam's, G. P., Sons (Inc.), 2 W. 45th.
Rabinovitch, M., 1715 Washington av.
Rabinowitz Bros. Co., 1133 B'way.
Rabinowitz, M., 108 5th av.
Radbridge Co., 144 Pearl.
Radinsky, H., 405 6th av.
Rankin, Jno. C., Co. (Inc.), 216 William.
Ratner, M., & Son, 857 Elsmere pl.
Reader & Sabloff, 1408 St. Nicholas av.
Real Stationery Shop, 66 W. 38th.
Regents Book Store, 30 Canal.
Rehbein, Charlotte, 512 W. 145th.

 **Paint and Chemical Company**
PAPER COLORS AND MILL PAINT SPECIALTIES
BOSTON   SPRINGFIELD, MASS.   NEW YORK

Wholesale and Retail Stationers

NEW YORK CITY.

Boroughs of Manhattan and The Bronx—*Continued.*

Reich, S., 875 E. 180th.
Reid, A., 424 Broome.
Reilly, Chas., & Co., 127 Fulton.
Reingold, D., 104 8th av.
Reisberg, A., 393 E. 198th.
Reliable Ptg. & Staty. Co., 312 Broome.
Reliable Stationery Shop, 144 5th av.
Richter, Sam'l H., 490 6th av.
Riker-Hegeman Co. (Inc.), 34th cor. 7th av. (d).
Rindner, H., 536 E. 168th.
Roberts & Bokee, 118 Pearl.
Rollnik, S., 1021 Prospect av.
Ronaldson, E. A., & Co., 129 Fulton.
*Rose, Lee, 154 E. Houston.
Rosenbaum, I., 826 Jackson av.
Rosenberg, A., 439 E. 145th.
Rosner, Edward, & Co., 94 Spring and 25 E. 20th.
Roth, Max J., 1495 3d av. (Toys.)
Rothenberg, J., 740 Jennings.
Rough, R. H., & Co., 228 Pearl.
*Rouss, Chas. Broadway, 549 B'way. (g).
Royal Stationery Co., 129 Fulton.
Rubenstein, B., 4216 3d av.
Rubin, Harry, 1 Madison av.
Rubinstein, D., 1813 So. Boulevard.
Ruggles, R. S., & Co. (Inc.), 165 William. (Cont. Printer.)
Ryskind, A., 3557 B'way.
Sackwitz, 1912 Webster av.
Saletan, H., 2157 B'way.
Saletan, H., 2163 B'way.
Salomon, Abram L., & Co., 345 B'way.
Sarlat Bros., 1123 B'way, 20 Murray. (Cont. Printers.)
Schapiro, J., 3414 3d av.
Scherer Bros., 88 E. 8th.
Schiller, Isaac, 2957 B'way.
Schmidt, Otto, & Son, 944 3d av.
Schrell & Brock, 29 E. 31st. (Drawing Mtls.)
Schulman, J., 64 E. 105th.
Schum Bros., 216 3d av.
Schumacher, Geo., 506 7th av.
Schwagerl Bros. (Inc.), 812 B'way.
*Scribner's, Chas., Sons, 597 5th av.
Scudder, Wm., E., Inc., 68 Pine.
Sennett, Benj., 150 Lafayette.
Seymour, C. W., 37 Malden la.
Shaffer, B., 651 Morris Park av.
Shapiro, M. & I., 1492 Vyse av.
Shea, Jas., 76 Nassau.

Boroughs of Manhattan and The Bronx—*Continued.*

Sherwood Co. (Inc.), 40 John.
Shipman Stationery Co., 447 E. Tremont av.
Shipman's, Asa. L., Sons, 100 Chambers.
Shnuer, L., 1227 1st av.
Shriner, Chas. A., 35 Warren.
*Shulman & Sons, 109 Ludlow. (Toys.)
Siegel, J., 454 9th av.
Siegert Bros., 72 Beaver.
*Siewers, Arthur, 441 Pearl.
Siewers, Wm. A., 78 Walker.
Silver Stationery Co. (Inc.), 70 Fulton.
Simon, L., & Son, 2876 B'way.
Simon, M., 234 E. 81st.
Sinsheimer, M., 547 So. Boulevard.
Smith, Edw. M., 67½ Pine.
Smith, J. Bradlee, 206 B'way.
Smith & Thomson, 58 Broad.
Sobel, M., 625 Fox av.
Sohl, Arthur H., 243 W. 42d.
Sonnenberg, L., & Co., 320 B'way.
Sorin, Joseph, 2166 8th av.
Speed, A. M., Co. (Inc.), 52 Dey.
Spiro, J., 503 Col. av.
Stearns & Beale (Inc.), 237 Lafayette.
Stein, Louis, 580 10th av.
Stein, Samuel, 78 3d av.
Steiner & Co., 51 E. 8th and 162 W. 23d. (Tags, etc.)
Stempel, Wm. P., 115 Nassau.
Stern Bros. (Inc.), 41 W. 42d. (g).
Stern & Greenberg, 876 Columbus.
*Stewart, Warren & Co. (Inc.), 129 Lafayette.
Stoll, Moses, 7 E. Broadway.
Stolle, Chas., 106 W. 125th.
Stores, Chas. William, Co., 49 E. 21st.
Storer, Eben, 39 Chambers.
Storm, M., & Co., 529 B'way.
Strathmore Press, 441 Pearl.
Sturman, Louis, 48 Nassau.
Styles & Cash (Inc.), 135 W. 14th.
Superior Stationery Co., 401 6th av.
Supply Bureau (Inc.), 108 Fulton. (Cont. Printer.)
Suritz, A., 3670 B'way.
Swastika Office Equipment Co. (Inc.), 42 B'way.
Swenarton Stationery Co. (Inc.), 461 8th av.
Taksen, Chas., 1545 1st av.
Taylor & Co., Douglas, 202 Centre.

 **Pure Blues** For paper staining, coating and ruling.

NEW YORK.

OGDENSBURG, 15,933.
McCarter, Herbert (j).
Ogdensburg Wholesale Mercantile Co., Inc.
Rose, W. H. (d).
Sears, A. J., & Son (d).
Smith, Mrs. E. (b).
Tallmann, Ralph (c).
Wholesale Merc. Co.
Williams Drug Co. (d).

OLEAN, 14,743.
Brothers, F. R., & Co. (b and d).
Bryant, W. A. (d).
Murphy, John V. (d).
Oakleaf, F. H., Co. (b).
Palmer, A. M., & Co. (d).
Piechota, Ignatius.
Smith, J. Edward (d).
Studholme Bros. (d).

ONEIDA, 8317.
Cary, T. H., & Co. (b).
Clark, Allen S.
Hernan, Frances B. (d).
Meyers Bros. Drug Co.

ONEONTA, 9491.
Breezee, F. H., & Son (g).
Dickson Bros. (d).
Hutson, Albert (d).
*Oneonta Press.
Reynolds, Geo., & Son (b).
Saunders, Henry (b).
Scatchard, E. E.
Slade, Geo. S. (d).
Tipple, A. H. (b).

OSSINING, 7185.
Griffin Drug Co. (d).
Rice Bros. (d).
Sherow, L. M. (d).
Terhune, Wm. (b).

OSWEGO, 23,368.
Butler Pharmacy (d).
Campbell, G. H., & Co. (g).
Casey, M. F. (b).
Schuler, J. M., & Son (b).
Sutton, Jas. (b).
Wallace, W. P. (b).
Woolworth, F. W., Co.

OVID, 577.
Horton, Seymour (d).

OWEGO, 4700.
Bowes, A. L., & Son.
Corey, W. H., Jr.

OXFORD, 1865.
Jones, Wm. A.
Quackenbush, G. W.

OYSTER BAY, 3692.
Bernstein, Sidney.
Kursman Bros.
Ledawitz Bros.
Simon, Jacob J.
Snouder, Andrew, & Son.

PATCHOGUE, 3706.
Conklin, H. S. (b).
Ketcham, Wm. A. (b).

PEARL RIVER, 1500.
Vaillequez, Elenore.

PEEKSKILL, 15,200.
Barker, A. R. (g).
Clinton Drug Co. (d).
Greenfest, D., Co., Inc. (s).
*Harth, Frank.
Seligman Co. (b).

PENN YAN, 4504.
Bennet, Harry O.
*Cornwell, Geo. R.
Metropolitan, The, of Penn Yan.

PERRY, 4500.
Baker & Roberts (d).
Owen, J. H. (d).
Severns, Ray E. (b).

PHELPS, 1352.
Hucthens, J. F.
Wisewell, F. H. (b, d).

PHILMONT, 2060.
Lockwood, G. A.

PIERMONT, 1481.
Leitner, J. H.

PINE PLAINS, 1500.
Kupperman, A.

PLATTSBURG, 11,138.
Goldwater, Alex. (d).
Hitchcock Pharmacy.
Jacques Drug Co.
Larkin, O. T. (d).
*Tuttle, J. W., & Co. (b).

PLEASANTVILLE, 2464.
Hacker, S. L.

PORT BYRON, 1128.
Blake, Wm., & Son. (b, d).

PORT CHESTER, 11,198.
Berenblum, Isaac.
Connolly, T. F. (b).
Hamill, Joseph (b).
Levene, H. J.
Silbereisen Bros. (b).
Smith, H. B., Co. (g).
Steiger-Schick Co. (g).

 **Paint and Chemical Company**
PAPER COLORS AND MILL PAINT SPECIALTIES
BOSTON SPRINGFIELD, MASS. NEW YORK

Wholesale and Retail Stationers 553

NEW YORK.

PORT JERVIS, 9314.
  Jones, L. M. (d).
  Laidley, E. T .(d).
  Mahoney, L. L.
  Mason, The, Drug Co.
  Pippit, Jeweler, The (j).
  Squires & Hoffman (d).
  Stevens, Whiting & Denton (g).
  Voight, Robert H.

PORT WASHINGTON, 3000.
  Jacobs, Benard.
  Raff, Meyer.
  Witt, W. O.

POTSDAM, 4036.
  Perrin & Co. (d).
  Van Ness, H.
  Weston, J. R. (b).

POUGHKEEPSIE, 27,936.
  Fitchett, J. H. (b).
  *Forsyth & Davis.
  Luckey Platt & Co. (g).
  Pierce-Ambler, The, Co.
  Wallace Co. (g).
  Wetmore, F. G.
  Wiggers, John.

RENSSELAER, 11,201.
  Hickey & Connelly.

RICHFIELD SPRINGS, 1684.
  Getman, Horace G. (b).

RINEBECK, 1,580.
  Latson, Frank.

RIVERHEAD, 2750.
  Bishop, John A.
  Harding, Sam.
  McCabe, Chas.

ROCHESTER, 241,518.
  Burke, Fitzsimons, Hone & Co. (g).
    122 E. Main.
  *Doell, Geo., & Co., 71-75 St. Paul.
  Duffy, Powers Co. (g).
  Edwards, W. C., Clinton av. (s).
  Edwards, E. W., & Son (g), 132 Main st. East.
  Goldstein Book & Stat'y Co. (b), 125 State and 105 Main.
  Guilford Drug Co., 3 North and 138 State.
  Harvey, R. & S.
  Hoffman, S. J.
  Lazarus, Isaac B. (b), Powers Bldg.
  Moore, John C., Corp., 67 Stone.
  Myers, R. M., & Co.
  O'Keefe, A. E.

ROCHESTER—*Continued.*
  Provenzano, Oscar, 463 State (b, s).
  Robinson, McCurdy & Robinson Co. (g).
  *Rochester News Co., 27 Church.
  *Scrantom, Wetmore & Co., State and Main (o. s.).
  *Sibley, Lindsay & Curr Co. (g), 237 Main st. East.
  Smith, C. W. (b), 44 East av.
  Stupp, Frank J., 92 Franklin.
  Trant, Esther, 10 Clinton (s).
  Williamson Law Book Co. (b), 41 State.

ROCKVILLE CENTRE, 2648.
  Griffin, Margaret M.
  Michnoff, Robert.

ROME, 23,000.
  Bacon & Co., F. E. (g).
  Hager & Co., F. J. (d).
  Hamlin, F. M., Co. (d).
  Jackson Co. (g).
  *Sturtevant-Wilson Co. (b).
  Wilson, J. H. (b).

ROSLYN, 2847.
  Simon, B., & Son.
  Clifton, C. H., Round Lake.

ROUSE'S POINT, 1783.
  Laundries Cash Bazaar.

RYE, 4076.
  Hartung, W.
  King, M. J.
  Trubin Bros. & Co\

SAG HARBOR, 3587.
  Cook, Wm. M.
  Klein, S., & Son.
  Lyn & Sherwood, The, Co.

ST. JOHNSVILLE, 2705.
  Dillenback, Ezra H.
  Handy, Erwin A.
  Walrath, Seward.

SALAMANCA, 8000.
  Krieger's Drug Store (b, d).
  Nies, Carl J. (d).

SARANAC LAKE, 3834.
  Gray, E. L., & Co. (c, s).
  Kollecker, W. F.
  Hushion, Katherine (b).
  Loomis, Fred (c, s).

SARATOGA SPRINGS, 12,693.
  *Blackmer, G. F., & Son, Inc.
  Brunner, Bernard (b).

 **Victoria Lake** A perfect color for blending with Yellow to produce shades of Buff, Corn, etc.

Wholesale and Retail Stationers

NEW YORK.

SARATOGA SPRINGS—Continued.
 Menges, Fred (d).
 Robson & Adee (b).
 Starbuck & Co., E. D. (g).
 Stroup, Walter M.

SAUGERTIES, 4300.
 Myer Bros. (d).
 Reed & Reed (d).
 Van Buskirk (d).
 Van Steenberg, N. H.

SAYVILLE, 3927.
 Nauert, Joseph A.

SCHENECTADY, 72,826.
 Barney, H. S., Co. (g).
 Baum's News Room.
 Boston Store (g).
 Carl Co. (g).
 Cherry, Fred.
 Frumkin, Max.
 Gapczynski, Chas.
 Gleason Book Co. (b).
 Johnson's Gift Shop.
 Joseph, W. B. (j).
 Lobel, Louis.
 Lyons, J. T. & D. B. (d).
 Moore & Caldwell (d).
 Riker-Hegeman (d).
 Robson & Adee (b).
 Union Book Co., Inc. (b).
 Walker Bros. (d).
 Wallace Co. (g).

SCOTIA, 3790.
 Grundhoeffer, Herman.
 Heitkamp, F. C.
 Magee, Samuel.

SEA CLIFF, 1846.
 Lowenberg, Isidor.
 Schmitt, John P.

SENECA FALLS, 6588.
 Hull, William E.
 Wayne, Robert C. (b).

SHERMAN, 797.
 Benjamin & Davenport.
 Myrick & Miles.

SIDNEY, 2507.
 Rushton, J. H.
 Wheeler, R. B. (b).

SILVER CREEK, 2073.
 Montgomery & Sons (d).

SINCLAIRVILLE, 542.
 Phillips, A. E. (d).

SOUTHAMPTON.
 Biggs, Francis E.
 Curtis, F. W., & Co.

SPARKILL, 550.
 G. T. Variety Store.

SPENCER, 618.
 Emmons, Cornelia H (d).

SPRING VALLEY, 2804.
 Paul, Harry H.
 Smith, Abe.
 Wicks, A. J.

SPRINGVILLE, 2246.
 Bargar, J. M. C. (d).

STAMFORD, 973.
 Lawrence, George W.

SUFFERN, 2665.
 Wassmer, F. J.

SYRACUSE, 137,249.
 Bailey's Book Store (b).
 *Bardeen, C. W. (b).
 *Chamberlain, W. H. H.
 Dey Bros. & Co. (g).
 Edwards, E. W., & Son (g).
 *Foote Co., William Y. (b).
 *Garrett Co., J. & F. B.
 Howe, H. J. (j).
 Hunter-Tuppen Co. (g).
 Kirtland, G. D., Co.
 Liggett, L. K., Co. (d).
 *Neal & Hyde (g, d).
 Nye, F. J.
 Stone, H. G. (g).
 Student's Supply Co.
 *Syracuse Dry Goods Co. (g).
 *Zenner Bros.

TARRYTOWN, 5370.
 Cohen, Dora.
 Flockhart, G. & M.
 Geiger & Newman.
 Levy, Morris.
 Scott, S., & Co.
 Weber, P. A.

TONAWANDA, 11,995.
 Fries, Arthur G. (d, s).
 Jacobs, Thos. H. (o. s.).
 Keer, Chas.

TROY, 76,813.
 Allen Book & Stat. Co. (b).
 Bloomfield, M. (b).
 Frear, Wm. H., & Co. (b, g).
 Gilbert, W. H.
 Griffin, T. L., & Co.

Paint and Chemical Company
PAPER COLORS AND MILL PAINT SPECIALTIES
BOSTON   SPRINGFIELD, MASS.   NEW YORK

Wholesale and Retail Stationers

NEW YORK.

TROY—*Continued.*
Haskins, C. G.
Lavender, J. A. (b).
McGrane, Wm. J.
*Mann, Herbert R.
*Northern News Co. (b).
Quackenbush, G. V. S., & Co. (g).
Shea, Daniel A.
*Troy Paper Co.
Werger, Chas., & Co.
Williams, M. L.

TRUXTON, 1186.
Wiegand, Est. J. C.

TUCKAHOE, 3559.
Freeman Sons.
Greenspan Sons.
Monahan, John.

UNADILLA, 1125.
Homan, Robt.
Palmer, G. A. (d).

UTICA, 74,419.
Barnes, Harry E. (o. s.).
*Bowes Bros.
Butler, Chas. M. (o. s.).
Fraser, R. (g).
Grant, John L. (o. s.).
*Hobbie & Baker (b).
Hunter, A. S. & T. (g).
Purvis, A. J. (b).
Rich & Dunning.
Roberts, John A., & Co. (g).
*Rosenwald, J. G.
Taylor, E. M. (b).
Utica Office Supply Co. (o. s.).
*Utica Paper Co.
Utica Sales & Specialty Co. (o. s.).
Vitullo & Ulisse (b).
Wells, Son & Co., J. B. (g).

VALATIE, 1410.
Liephutz, S., & Sons.

WALDEN, 3737.
Clark & McGowan (g).
Lustig, Carl (g).
Sohns, J. A. A.
Steer, Herbert (j).
Whitmore, Roscoe D.

WAPPINGERS FALLS, 3588.
Tibbs, F. V.

WATERFORD, 3245.
Davis, Isaac V.
Michon, S. N.

WATERLOO, 3931.
Baker, J. A.
Batsford, Jas. E., & Son (d).
Conant, Edward O.
Smith, F. G. (b, d).

WATERTOWN, 26,730.
Cooke, F. E.
Empsall, Frank A., & Co., Inc. (g).
Howe & Allen (o. s.).
Miller, D. S., Co. (c, s).
Robinson, E. E.
Sterling, John (b).

WATERVILLE, 1410.
Bissell's, W. J., Son (d).
Luke, John M.
White, J. P. (d).

WATERVLIET, 15,074.
Hulsapple, H. M.
Kane, C. J.

WELLSVILLE, 4355.
Barnes Bros.
Richart, F. E. (d).

WHITE PLAINS, 11,579.
Keating, J. J.
Plofsky Bros.
Shapiro, Samuel.
Warren & Warren.
White Plains Stationery Store.

YONKERS, 79,803.
Biber Bros., Inc.
Blatt, Jonas.
Caskey, A. W.
East, W. Palmer, Co.
Friedman, Herman.
*Lauterboch, Samuel.
Rosenberg, I. E., & Bro.
Schwartz, W. M.
*Wallin, Walter W.
Warburton Avenue Book & Art Co.
Yonkers News Co.

 **Structural Paint** For the preservation of structural iron and steel

NORTH CAROLINA.

ALBEMARLE.
Horton, W. P.

ASHEVILLE, 20,157.
Brown Book Co. (c, s).
Carmichael, W. C. (d).
Goode & Hage (d).
Grant's Pharmacy (d).
Pack Square Book Co. (c, s).
Powell & Nimock (d).
Rogers, H. Taylor (b).
*Smith Drug Store (d).

BESSEMER CITY, 1100.
Bessemer City Drug Co.
George, H. D.
Golden Rule Cash Store.

BURLINGTON, 4808.
Freeman Drug Co.
Neese, C. F. (b, j).
Ralff, Geo. L.

CHARLOTTE, 34,014.
Beatty, R. R. Co. (d).
Belk Bros. (g).
Blake, J. S., Drug Co.
Brockman & Co. (b).
*Burwell & Dunn Co.
Caton Drug Co. (d).
Ivey, J. B., & Co. (g).
Pound & Moore (c, o. s.).
Queen-City Printing & Paper Co.
*Scott, J. M., & Co.
Stone & Barringer Book Co. (b).
Stowe, J. P., & Co. (d).
Tryon Drug Co. (d).

CONCORD, 8715.
Park-Belk Co.
Ritz, H. G.
White-Morrison-Flower Co. (b).

DURHAM, 22,863.
Blacknall & Son (d).
*Durham Book & Stat'y Co., C. B.
Five Points Drug Co. (d).
Green & Poteat (b).
Haywood & Boone (d).
King, C. E., & Sons (d).
Mabry's Drug Store.
Main St. Pharmacy Co.
Rexall Pharmacy (d).
Woolworth, F. W., & Co.

FAYETTEVILLE, 4670.
Judge Printing Co.
Standard Stationery Store.

GASTONIA, 7000.
Atkins-Baber Book Co.
Hunter, John A.
Kennedy, J. H., & Co. (d).

GOLDSBORO, 6107.
Goldsboro Book Store.

GREENSBORO, 15,891.
Greensboro Book Co. (b).
Justice Drug Co. (d).
Proximity Merc. Co. (g).
*Scott, J. W., & Co.
*The Old North State Paper Co.
Wills Book & Staty. Co. (b).

GREENVILLE, 4101.
Bowar, W. A.

HENDERSON, 3746.
Henderson Book Co.

HICKORY, 6000.
Bowles, J. A.
Hickory Drug Co.
Lutz Drug Co.
Shuford, C. M. (s).
Van Dyke Shop (s).

HIGH POINT, 11,610.
Hart Drug Co. (d).
Jarrett Stationery Co.
Mann Drug Co. (d).
Moore, B. E. (b).
Ring Drug Co. (d).

KINSTON, 6995.
Hood's Book Store.
Hood, J. E., & Co. (d).
Hudson Drug Co.
Lenoir Drug Co. (d).
Marston Drug Co., E. B.
Pitman, A. J.

MONROE, 4500.
English Drug Co.
Rudge Co. (The), W. J. (b).
Simpson, C. N., Jr. (d).
Union Drug Co.

MORGANTON, 3000.
Gaither, B. S. (b).

MOUNT AIRY, 3844.
*Creed, J. W.
Hawks, Rathrock Drug Co.

NEWBERN, 9961.
Dunn, Owen G.
Whitehurst, M. E. (b).

 **Paint and Chemical Company**
PAPER COLORS AND MILL PAINT SPECIALTIES
BOSTON   SPRINGFIELD, MASS.   NEW YORK

Wholesale and Retail Stationers

NORTH CAROLINA.

RALEIGH, 19,218.
Brantley, J. C. (d).
Capital Drug Store (d).
Circle Pharmacy (d).
Commercial Ptg. Co.
*Edwards & Broughton Printing Co.
Galloway Drug Co.
Hicks, Henry T., Drug Co.
King Crowell Drug Co.
*King Drug Co., W. H.
Mitchell Printing Co. (d).
Pescud, E. F. (b).
Riggan & Chappell.
Saunder St. Phar.
Storr, H. S. (c).
Thiem, J. E. (o. s.).
Tucker Building Pharmacy.
Wake Drug Co.
Williams, Alfred, & Co. (b).

REIDSVILLE, 4828.
Smith Staty. & Printing Co.

ROCKINGHAM, 4000.
Stephenson-Belk Co.
Terry, E. B.

ROCKY MOUNT, 8051.
Hicks, H. L., Drug Co.
May & Gorham (s).
Rose, I. W., Drug Co.
Standard Drug Co.
Thomas Book & Staty. Co.

ROXBORO, 1425.
Lipshitz, A.
Raiff, Leo L.

SALISBURY, 7153.
Buerbaunn, Theo. (b).
Empire Drug Co.

SALISBURY—Continued.
Feldman, J., & Son.
Main Pharmacy.
People's Drug Co.
Smith Drug Co.

SHELBY, 5000.
Ebeltoft, T. W. (b).

STATESVILLE, 6000.
Allison, R. P.
Statesville Ptg. Co.

TARBORO, 2499.
Cook, R. E. L. (d).
Edgecombe Drug Co.
Mc Nair Drug Co. (b, d).

WADESBORO, 4000.
Liles, The, Co.

WASHINGTON, 8000.
Blount's Drug Store.
Latham's Book Store.
Worthy & Etheridge.

WILMINGTON, 29,892.
Northam's Book and Staty. Store.
*Yates, C. W., Co. (b).

WINSTON-SALEM, 29,034.
Jones, W. A. (d).
Goldstein, B.
*Marler-Dalton-Gilmer Co. (g).
Meyers, Westbrook Co. (g).
*Nading, H. A.
O'Hanlon, E. W. (d).
Owens Drug Co. (d).
Shaffner & Sandquist (d).
Welfare, Sam. E. (d).

NORTH DAKOTA.

BISMARCK, 7000.
Fifth St. Staty. Co.
Harris & Co.
Hoskins Stat'y Co.

CANDO, 1332.
Forest, Mary L.

CHASELEY, 150.
Heeren, H. B., & Co.

DEVIL'S LAKE, 5157.
Mills, C. D.

ELLENDALE, 1389.
Leiby, Ed N. (d).

FARGO, 22,618.
Christianson Drug Co.
Crusoe, Bruce (d).
Economy Drug Co.
Fargo Drug Co.
*Greenwood Stationery Co.
Ricker, A. E., Co. (g).
Walker Brothers, Inc.

GRAND FORKS, 15,739.
Arhart, E. A., & Co. (j).
*Colborn School Supply Co.
Dacotah Pharmacy.
*Grand Forks Herald Co.
*Griffith, R. B., Co. (g).

 **Roll Bar White** A lasting tough coating for iron work in beaters and washers

NORTH DAKOTA.

GRAND FORKS—Continued.
McGrath Pharmacy (d).
McKallor Co. (b).
Page Printerie.
Palmer, A. E., Co. (j).
*Rasmussen, Bemis & Co.
Trepanier, C. P. (d).
University Book Store.
Vanderhoef, W. R. (b).
Vold, J. H. (d).

JAMESTOWN, 5000.
Clemens Drug Co.
Smith, W. N.
White, H. E., Co. (b, d).
Wonnenberg & Avis (d).

MANDAN, 3873.
Hudson, F. S.

MINOT, 10,053.
McCoy Drug Co.
Minot Drug Co.

PARK RIVER, 1008.
Anderson, Henry.

VALLEY CITY, 4606.
Dakota Drug Co. (d).

WAHPETON, 2741.
*Globe-Gazette Ptg. Co.
Keen, J. J. (s).
Whiting Drug Co. (s).

WILLISTON, 6200.
Herald Co.

OHIO.

ADA, 2465.
Landon & Son (b, d).
Wilson, C. R., & Co. (b).

AKRON, 69,067.
*Akron Dry Goods Co. (g).
Brittian, J. A. (b).
Burch & Laraway Co.
Dutt Drug Co. (d).
Harper Drug Co. (d).
Kaufman Drug Co. (d).
Lemaster & Beard (d).
Long & Taylor Co. (b).
*Miller Merchandise Co.
National Blank Book & Supply Co.
O'Neil & Co., The M. (g, b).
Richardson, J. K. (b).
Warner & Bahler (d).
Wilson & Hawkins (b).
Yeager, C. H., Co.

ALLIANCE, 15,083.
Cassaday Drug Co., The (d).
Cassaday Furniture Co. (o. s.).
Diver Drug Store.
England Drug Co. (d).
Morris, E. J., Drug Co. (d).
Partner, C. C. (d).
Vale, B. E., Drug Store (d).
Valentine, F. C.

ASHLAND, 7400.
Sterling Shop (c, s).

ASHTABULA, 18,266.
Ashtabula Paper & Twine Co.
Brooks, John.

ASHTABULA—Continued.
Canfield, C. R. (d).
Cook & Co., A. B. (d, b).
*Kahne, Alfred.
Knowlton & Windling (d).
Knowlton, R. W. (d, b).
Konter, Eda.
Rust, B. S. (d).
Schafner, Chas. F. (d).
Shaffner Drug Store (d, b).
Wentling, O. O (d).

ATHENS, 5463.
Walker, Geo. R.

BARBERTON, 9410.
Woolsey & Blaser (d).

BARNESVILLE, 4233.
Graves Book Store.

BELLAIRE, 12,946.
Conner, M. G. (b).
Dankworth Bros. (d).
Darrah, D. H. (d).
Hoffman, M. (d).
McKelvey, C. N. (d).
Woolworth Five & Ten Cent Store.
Wyrick, C. M. (d).
Wyrick Drug Co., The (d, b).

BELLEFONTAINE, 8238.
Annat, H. M. (g).
Frazier, G. M., Co.
Cowman, Edward C. (b, d).
Guy, Geo. H.
Powell, Perry.

 **Paint and Chemical Company**
PAPER COLORS AND MILL PAINT SPECIALTIES
BOSTON   SPRINGFIELD, MASS.   NEW YORK

Wholesale and Retail Stationers 559

OHIO.

BELLEVUE, 5200.
Brinker, J. H. (b, d).
Hale & Son, Frank P. (d).

BOWLING GREEN, 5222.
Bolles Drug Store.
Butler, E. M. (b, d).
Lincoln & Dirlam (b, d).
Powell Bros. (d).
Rust Dept. Store.

BUCYRUS, 8122.
Birk Bros. (d).
Bucyrus Pharmacy.
Farquhar Bros. (b, d).
Graetz, W. H. (d).
Jesson, Thos.
Johnston Pharmacy (d).
Kern, J. E., & Bro. (d).
Turn Bros. (d).

CAMBRIDGE, 11,327.
McCleary, H. (d).

CANAL DOVER, 6621.
Holland & Henderson Drug Store.
Le Page Drug Store.
O'Donnell, H. B. (b).
Winkler, W. A. (d, b).

CANTON, 70,000.
Anthony, C. W. (d).
Baer's.
Deuble, Walter H. (j).
Eagle Drug Store (b).
Fielliez, Marie.
Kenny Bros. (g).
Miller Drug Co. (d).
News Exchange Co., The.
Roth & Hug Co. (b, d).
Schlabach, E. J. (b, d).
Sibila & Schmidt (d).
Stark Bindery Co. (c, s).
Union Drug Co. (d).
Zollinger, W. R., & Co. (g).

CELINA, 3493.
Baker, Perry.
Hight, W. W. (d).
Kendell, B. L. (d).
Puthoff, H. F. (d).

CHICAGO JUNCTION, 2960.
Berk, W. J. (d).
Christian, W. W.
Williams, R. K. (d).

CHILLICOTHE, 14,508.
Griesheimer, Rudolph (d).
Horney & Chapman (b).

CHILLICOTHE—*Continued.*
Howson, A. B. (d).
Howson, Harold (d).
Penny Store.
Sultzbacher, W. F. (d).
Stevenson-Clark & Stevens (d).
Toohy Drug Co.
Wissler, R. D.
Wolf Lee & Bros.

CINCINNATI, 416,119.
Alms & Doepke Co., Main and Canal (g).
Andrews, Loring Co., 117 E. 4th.
Armstrong Stationery Co., 419 Main.
Brand, Peter, 12 Green (b).
*Carpenter Co., The W. B., 422-428 Main.
*Chatfield & Woods Co.
*Cincinnati News Co., The, 127-129 Shillito place.
Dow Drug Co.
Eckert's New Dry Goods Store, 309 East Pearl.
Gibson & Perin Co., 121 W. 4th (c).
Hawley, J. R., News Co., 7 Arcade.
Jonap, H., & Co., 415 Race (g).
Kindel, R. E., & Co., 312 Plum (c).
Lederman, G., 115 E. Third (c).
Lotz Ptg. & Staty. Co., 2224 Spring Grove av. (c).
Macey-Hall Co., 548 Main (c).
McAlpin Co., 13 W. 4th (g).
Mills' Sons, J. R., 512 Main (c).
Motz, J. Louis Co.
Ohio Valley Co., rear of 323 Race.
Pogue Co., H. & S., 20 W. Fourth (g).
*Pounsford Stationery Co.
Schaefer, W. F., & Co., 323 W. Seventh (c).
Sellers, Davis & Co., 311 Walnut (c).
Shillito Co., John S., 7th and Race.
*Stanage, W. H., Co., 119 E. Sixth.
Stewart & Kidd Co., 121 E. Fifth (b).
The Fair, Sixth and Race (g).
*Vogeler, The Alfred, Drug Co.
Webb-Biddle, The, Co. (c).
Weil, Max, & Co. (c).
Western Methodist Book Concern (b).
Willenborg's Stat. Co., 319 Walnut (c).
*Woodrow Co., 726 Main (c).

CIRCLEVILLE, 6744.
Grand, Girard, Geo. F. (d).
Hoffman, Lyman (g).
Teegardin, G. A. (d).
Weldon, Lawrence.

 **Rubercoat Elastic Carbon Paint**
For your leaky gravel, paper, cloth and metal roofs.

Wholesale and Retail Stationers

OHIO.

CLEVELAND, 707,683.
Barker, S., & Sons, 2034 E. Fourth.
*Brooks Co., The, 715 Superior av. W.
Burrows Bros., The, Co., 633-635 Euclid av, N. E. (b).
*Cleveland News Co., 1552 W. 3d.
Cowell & Hubbard Co., 605 Euclid (j).
Forman-Bassett Co., 1431 W. 3d.
Halle Bros. Co., Euclid and Huron (g).
*Hall-Van Gorder Co., 1382 W. 9th (d).
Higbee Co., Euclid and 13th (g).
Kirkpatrick, J., 5507 Woodland av. (b).
Korner & Wood (The) Co., 737 Euclid av.
May Co., Euclid, Ontario and Prospect (g).
*Mutual Drug Co., 1200 W. 9th.
Office Supply & Ptg. Co., 811 Superior av. W.
Pushaw, James S., 5807 Euclid av.
Roberts, F. W., Co., 4th & Prospect.
Schroeder, Oliver C.
Schroeder, O. C., 213 Superior av., East (b).
Seckel, Frederick, 2820 Lorain av.
Straus, J. & F. Co.
Taylor, H. E., Co., 622 Vincent av. (c).
Taylor, Wm., Son & Co., 630 Euclid (g).
University Book Store, 10514 Euclid av.

CLYDE, 2815.
Letson, Frank E.

COLUMBUS, 204,567.
Bergener, A. H. (b).
Blosser, E. W., Paper Co.
*Central Ohio Paper Co.
*Central Tablet Mfg. Co.
Cole, H., Co.
College Book Store.
Columbus Blank Book Mfg. Co. (c).
Columbus Dry Goods Co. (g).
*Columbus Merchandise Co.
Cott, The, Printing & Indexing Co.
Diehl Office Equipment Co. (c).
Dobson, Evans Co., The (b).
Dunn, Taft & Co. (g).
*Green, Joyce & Co.
*Jones-Witter Co.

COLUMBUS—*Continued.*
*Kauffman-Lattimer Co.
Lazarus, The F. & R., Co. (g).
McClelland & Co. (b).
Mench, Milton J.
Morehouse-Martens Co., The (g).
*Nitschke Paper Co.
Noethlick, A. (b).
*Orr, Brown & Price.
State Office Supply Co.
Sell & Co., E. H. (c).
Shipley & Co.
Smythe, The Incorporated Co. (b).
*Tracy-Wells Co.
White Co., Z. L. (g).
Zaner & Bloser Co. (b).

CONNEAUT, 8319.
Conneaut Drug Co.
Guthrie, J. H. (d).
Hahn, Sig. (d).
Stines, Geo. (d).
West End Drug Store (d).
Whitmore, F. L. (d).

COSHOCTON, 9603.
Cash Store (g).
Frew, Edward (d, b, s).
Metler & Robertson (d, s).
Page & Lorenz (d, b, s).
Siegrist & Williams (d, s).
Smith Drug and Book Store.
Wimmer & Arnold (d, b).

CUYAHOGA FALLS, 4020.
Creque, E. A. (d).
Freeman News Co. (b).
Heath Drug Co. (d).
Owen, Walter (d).

DAMASCUS, 400.
Pim Aden & Son.

DAYTON, 116,577.
Buntell-Roth Co. (c).
*Dayton Blank Book & Ptg. Co.
Elder & Johnston (g).
*Everybody's Book Shop, The.
Gift Shop.
*Johnson & Watson.
*Miller, The, Staty. Co.
Newsalt, A. (j).
Oelman, W. F., & Co. (g).
Rike-Kumler Co. (g).
Todd, Frank P. (d).
*Wolf, Lee, & Bro. (b).

 **Paint and Chemical Company**
PAPER COLORS AND MILL PAINT SPECIALTIES
BOSTON   SPRINGFIELD, MASS.   NEW YORK

Wholesale and Retail Stationers

OHIO.

DEFIANCE, 7327.
Defiance Ptg. & Eng. Co.
Weisenburger, F. P., & Bro. (d).
Woodward, N. G. (d).

DELAWARE, 9076.
Hardin & Gallant.

DELPHOS, 5038.
Bush Bros. (b, d).
King Bros. (d).
King & Williams (d).
Swisler & Swisler (b, d).
Wahmhoff, J. H. (b, d).
Wahmhoff, F. S. (d).

EAST LIVERPOOL, 22,386.
Anderson, G. C. (d).
Ashbaugh, Reed (d).
Diamond Drug Store.
Flick, T. C. (d).
Hodson, John I. (d).
Larkins, Chas. T. (d).
Potter's Drug Store (d).
Wilson Stationery Co. (b).
Yates Novelty Co. (g).

ELYRIA, 14,825.
Central Book Store.
Loomis Book Store (b).

FINDLAY, 14,858.
Blackford & Creighton.
Central Drug Store.
Firmin, J. C. (b, d).
Jackson, C. F., Co. (g).
Marvin, O. B. (j).
Oak Pharmacy (d).
Rexall Drug Store.

FOSTORIA, 9957.
Book Shop (s).
Harbaugh & Mickey (d).
Rice Music Store (s).

FREMONT, 10,578.
Grund, H. C., Drug Co. (d).

GALION, 8174.
Baumgartner, Simon J.
Gelsanliter, J. E.
Seeman, E. W., & Co. (d).

GALLIPOLIS, 5560.
Kerr, C. D., Drug Co. (d).
Moore Co., S. A. (b).
Neal, D. D. (d).

GRANVILLE, 1394.
Ullman, W. P. (d).

GREENFIELD, 4228.
Galbraith, J. M. (d).
Gossett Co. (b).
Hurd, H. H. (d).

GREENVILLE, 6237.
Brodrick, Omer S. (b).
Kipp Drug Co. (d).
Wenger, R. E.

HAMILTON, 35,279.
Beeler Bros. (d).
Beeler, C. S. (d).
DuBois, Jos. (d).
*Forbes & Todd (b).
Harper Bros. (d).
Heck, F. M.
Lindenwald Drug Co. (d).
Mathes-Sohngen Co. (g).
Robinson-Schwenn Co. (g).
Radcliffe Drug Co. (d).
Wuebbold, H., & Co. (c).

HILLSBORO, 4296.
Bowles & Co. (b).

IRONTON, 13,147.
*Ball-Warfield Drug Co., The (d).
Brandt Bros. (b).
Hill, J. M., & Bro. (b).
Ironton Book Store (b).
Lucas Drug Co.
Murdock Art Co. (b).
Woolworth's 5 & 10 Cent Store (g).

JACKSON, 5468.
Alexander, John C. (b).

JAMESTOWN, 6153.
Harper, W. F.

JEFFERSON, 1461.
Case, Chas. H.

KENMORE, 1800.
Herald Publishing Co.

KENT, 4488.
Trory, A. J. (b).
Trory, Fred W. (d).

KENTON, 7185.
Furney, M. G., & Son (d).
Gilmore, Charles (j, b).
McCoy & Sons (d).
Roby Ptg. Co. (c).

LANCASTER, 13,093.
Brink, Henry W. (d).
Gillespie, H. E. (o. s.).

Black Paste — Will not crock in the paper. Strongest, cleanest and most economical.

Wholesale and Retail Stationers

OHIO.

LANCASTER—*Continued.*
Hickle, Geo. M. (g).
Lancaster Book Shop.
Scovell Decorating Co.

LEBANON, 2698.
Hamilton, Heber.

LEETONIA, 2665.
Holz, Ed. W.

LIMA, 45,000.
Burton, Don M., Co. (c).
Economy Art Store (c).
Heister (b, d).
Hunter, C. M. (b, d).
Lima Book & Bible Co.
*Price, The Emerson W., Co.
Schell, C. E. (b).

LISBON, 3084.
Galley, F. R. (b).
Hamilton's (d).
Morgan's Drug Store (d).
Nace, M. T. (d).
Ourant, C. W. (d).
Williams, T. C. (d).

LORAIN, 28,883.
Bretz, Geo. (g).
Craft, E. J. (d).
Eddy, E. H. (d).
Eldred & Co. (g).
Folkins, John (d).
Honeeker, Wm. (d).
Jameson, Jos., Jr. (d).
Krupp, Chas. (d).
Kutza, L. G. (d).
Tiffany, C. J. (d).
Willis, V. E. (j).

MANSFIELD, 20,768.
Barton, W. M. (d).
Black & Lautsbaugh (d).
*Caldwell & Bloor (d).
Lucas Bro. (d).
Ritter Co., Chas. (c, s).
Tawse Pharmacy (d).

MARIETTA, 12,939.
*Bailey Grocery Co.
Corner Drug Store (d).
Dyale & Co., J. W. (d).
Kelly's Book & News Co.
Marietta Book Store Co. (b, c, s).
National Drug Co. (d).
Richards, Albert (d).
Roby, V. R. (b).
Turner-Ebinger Co. (g).

MARION, 25,000.
*Bindley Grocery Co.
Dumble, M. L. (d).
Frank, D. A., & Co. (g).
Gem Pharmacy (d).
Henney & Cooper (d).
Liggett, L. M., & Co. (d).
Lower's Pharmacy (d).
*McKinnis, F. D., Co.
Strayer Bros. (d).
Tschanen Bros. (d).
Uhler, Phillips & Co. (g).
Waldorf Pharmacy, The (d).
Warner & Edwards Co. (g).
Wiant, Charles G. (b).

MARTIN'S FERRY, 9133.
Dougherty, P. (b).
Hoge, Ernest (b, d).
Ralston & Parker (d).
Selby & Reed (d).

MARYSVILLE, 3576.
Asman & Smith Pharmacy.
Central Drug Store.
*Hazen, L. W. (c, s).
Wolgamot, Wm. (d).

MASSILLON, 13,879.
*Bahney, E. F. (c, o).
Baltzley Co., The (d).
Craig, E. S. (d).
Eclipse Bargain Store (g).
Hughes, Sidney.
Kirchhoffer Drug Store (d).
Rider & Snyder (d).
Seaman, F. E. (d).

MEDINA, 2734.
Fuller, N. O.

MIAMISBURG, 4271.
Andrews & Heinfeld.
Stansby Drug Co.

MIDDLEPORT, 3194.
Calderwood, A. (b).
Davis, E., & Co. (d).
Stansburg Drug Co.

MIDDLETOWN, 13,152.
Johnson Co. (d).
Ohio Office Supply Co.
The Book Shop.

MINGO JUNCTION, 4049.
Long, Winifred (Mrs. Chris.).

MOUNT VERNON, 9087.
Arnold Merchandise Co.
Allen, Wm. F.
Book & Art Shop (b)

 **Paint and Chemical Company**
PAPER COLORS AND MILL PAINT SPECIALTIES
BOSTON SPRINGFIELD, MASS. NEW YORK

Wholesale and Retail Stationers

OHIO.

NAPOLEON, 4007.
  Morey & Myers (d).

NEWARK, 25,404.
  East, B. M. (d).
  *Edmiston, T. M. (b).
  Hall, Frank D. (d).
  Norton Co., A. L. (b).

NEW PHILADELPHIA, 8542.
  Marsh Ptg. Co. (o. s.).
  Opes, Apollo (b, d).
  Rea, Frank C. (d).
  Wilson, E. E. (d).
  Wyss, Walter H.

OBERLIN, 4800.
  Chennon, Irvin N.
  Comings, A. G., & Son (b).

OXFORD, 2017.
  Adams Drug Store.
  Gilliard Drug Store.
  Miami Co-operative Store.
  Oxford Drug Store.
  Snyder Art. Store.

PAINESVILLE, 5501.
  Austin's Pharmacy (d).
  Colby, Geo. S. (b).
  Gehring's Drug Store (d).
  Lightner, J. E. (b).
  Lord, George A., & Son (b).

PIQUA, 13,388.
  *Armstrong, W. H.
  Rankin & Zimmermann (b).

PORTSMOUTH, 23,481.
  Amann, Frank (d).
  Anderson Bros. Co. (g).
  Brandau Book & Staty. Co. (b).
  Corner Book Store (b).
  *Davis Drug Co. (d).
  Fisher & Streich (d).
  Flood & Blake (d).
  Marting Bros. (g).
  Nye, Winfield S. (d).
  Pressler, Albert E. (d).
  Pure Drug Co. (d).
  Red Cross Pharmacy.
  Reeg, Adam (d).
  Reilly, W. W., & Co. (b).
  Schloss, Samuel M.
  Stewart, I. H.
  Wurster Bros. (d).

RAVENNA, 5310.
  Case, W. A., & Co. (b).
  Hart's Drug Store (d).
  Lyon & Morgan.
  McGraw & Eckler (b).

RIPLEY, 1840.
  Newcomb, J. C. (c).
  Petry, Mrs. E. (b).

SABNIA, 1514.
  Wolf Lee & Bro.

SALEM, 8943.
  Campbell, D. & J. H. (b).
  McMillan, Mrs. J. (b).
  Trimble, Frank F. (d).

SANDUSKY, 19,989.
  Herb & Meyers Co., The (g).
  Windisch, G. F., & Co. (b).

SHAWNEE, 2280.
  Blaire, E. G. (j).
  Shore, Mrs. George.

SIDNEY, 6607.
  Borher, Henry.
  Briggs, C. J. (d).
  Christian, F. D. (d).
  Lohmire Drug Co.

SPRINGFIELD, 46,921.
  Buchholtz, C. F. (d).
  Coblentz, E. & S. (d).
  Fireoved & McCann.
  Garwood, F. A. (d).
  Higgins Drug Co. (d).
  Limbocker, H. S. (b)
  Morrow Drug Co. (d).
  Pierce & Co. (b).
  Roth & Livingston (d).
  *Springfield Paper & Mdse. Co.
  Troupe Drug Co., The (d).
  Wren Co., E. (g).

ST. MARYS, 5732.
  Dunathan Drug Co. (b, d).
  Meck, Frank (b, d).
  Siewert, Theo. E. (b, d).

STEUBENVILLE, 22,391.
  *Erwin, E. M. (b).

TIFFIN, 11,894.
  Bridinger, Frank (d).
  Comstock, Harry (d).
  Good, Will H. (o. s.).
  Hayden, Albert (d).
  Warner-Koller Co. (g).
  Weidling & Son (d).
  Youman & Son (d).

TOLEDO, 184,126.
  *Blade Printing and Paper Co., 820-324 St. Clair.
  *Brown, Eager & Hull Co., The, 608 Monroe.

 **Ruling Colors** The best for Ruling Inks.

Wholesale and Retail Stationers

OHIO.

TOLEDO—*Continued.*
Franklin Printing and Engraving Co. (c, o. s.), 321-325 Superior.
Freeman, J. J., Co., 307 Summit (j).
Lasalle & Koch Co., Adams and Huron.
Lion Dry Goods Co., 325 Summit (g).
McManus-Troup Co., The, 412 Huron (e).
Milner, W. L., & Co., Summit and Jefferson (g).
Newton, The N. B., Co., 222 Huron (c).
Thompson-Hudson Co., Summit and Adams (g).
*Toledo Merchandise Co., 31 S. Superior.
Wade, B. F., & Sons Co. 429 St. Clair (c).
Wendt & Rausch Co., 125 St. Clair (c).

TROY, 6122.
Bretland & Stephey (b).
Lefevre, C. W., & Son (b).
Rinehardt, H. M. (d).
Tobey, C. W. (d).

URBANA, 7739.
Banta, J. A., Jr. (b).
Todd, Lee H. (b).

WAPAKONETA, 5349.
Central Dry Goods Store.
Hamilton, M. W. (d).
Hunter & Son.
Kayser, Wm. (d).

WARREN, 11,081.
Byard & Volt (d).
Griswold, The, Co. (g).
Jenkins, S. J.
Kneeland Bros. (b).
McClure, J. E. (d).
Perry, F. W. (b).
Van Gorder Hapgood Drug Store.
Webb & Craig (d).

WASHINGTON COURT HOUSE, 7277.
Christopher, Frank (d).
Craig Bros. (g).
Rodecker, H. R. (b).
Smith, Jess M. (g).
Stutson, F. L. (g).
Tuttle, J. T. (b).

WELLSTON, 6875.
Kelly Bros. (d).
Palace Drug Store.
Wellston Book & News Co.

WELLSVILLE, 7769.
Brannan, C. N. (d).
Fuller, E. M. (b).

WILMINGTON, 4491.
Hildebrandt Book Store.

WOOSTER, 6136.
Alcock Stationery Store.
Burkholder, G. W.
City Book Store.
Figert Jewelry Store (j).
Proctor, E. J. (d).
*Tyler, The L. C., Co.

YOUNGSTOWN, 91,648.
Jonas, A., & Sons (j).
Krauter, C. H. (d).
*McKelvey Co., The G. M. (g).
McNally, J. A. (b).
*Pardee-Ellis, The, Co.
*Youngstown Dry Goods Co. (g).

ZANESVILLE, 28,026.
*Bailey Drug Co. (d).
Bailey, F. P. (d).
*Edmiston, J. D. (b).
*Fox, Geo. R. (b).
McCaddon & Co.
Ross' Book Store.
Sturtevant, H. H. (g).
Zimmer, C. E. (d).

OKLAHOMA.

ALVA, 5000.
Beegle Bros. (b, d).
Bradbury Bros. (b).
Montfort, J. W. (b).
Schuhmacker, L. (b, d).

ANADARKO, 3430.
Combs, L. V. (d).
Dinkler, J. A. (d).
Stephenson, O. C. (d).

ARDMORE, 11,675.
Bomar Drug Co. (d).
City Drug Store (d).
Frame Drug Co. (d).
Johnson Drug Co. (d).
Myers-Boyd Drug Co.
Ramsey, F. J. (d).
Ringer Drug Co.

 **Paint and Chemical Company**
PAPER COLORS AND MILL PAINT SPECIALTIES
BOSTON   SPRINGFIELD, MASS.   NEW YORK

Wholesale and Retail Stationers

OKLAHOMA.

BARTLESVILLE, 12,000.
Bartlesville Phar.
Condit, W. A. (b).
Eureka Drug Store.
Red Cross Drug Store.
Rexall Drug Store.
Star Drug Store.

CHECOTAH, 2200.
Kniseley, H. D. (d).

CHICKASHA, 10,320.
Adams Drug Co. (d).
Booth, S. (b).
Brownson's Pharmacy (d).
Gadd's Music & Book Store (c, s).
Owl Drug Store.
Palace Drug Store (d).
Wrenn Drug Co.

CLEVELAND, 3000.
Gilbert, O. A. (d).

DURANT, 5,100.
Reilly Book Store.

EDMOND, 2090.
Deveraux Drug Store (d).
Howard Drug Store (d).
Slack, P. O. (b).

ELK CITY, 3165.
Gambills Plain Price Store (g).
Hixon, H. O. (d).
Palace Drug Store (d).
Reid, R. L. (b, d).

EL RENO, 7872.
City Drug Store (b, d).
Hensley, T. F. (b).
Jones Drug Co.
Patterson Drug Co.
Randall, F. S., & Co. (b).

EUFAULA, 3000.
Morhart, The, Drug & Book Co. (b).

GUTHRIE, 11,654.
*Cooperative Publishing Co.
Owl Drug Store (b, d).
Post Office Drug Store (d).
Tyler, A. P.

KINGFISHER, 2588.
Lott Bros (b).

LAWTON, 7788.
Central Drug Store (d).
*Goodner Book & Stationery Co., Inc. (b).

LAWTON—*Continued.*
*Jones Bros (d).
Kerans, J. S.
Kress 5 and 10 Cent Store (g).
Lawton Drug Store (d).
Powell's Drug Store (g).

LEHIGH, 2188.
Adams, S. R. (d).

McALESTER, 14,766.
Daniel's Drug Store.
Edwards, W. R. (b).
Krone's Dept. Store (g).
White Bros. (d).

NEWKIRK, 1992.
Adams, C. F.

OKLAHOMA CITY, 103,000.
*Alexander Drug Co. (d).
Arcade Book Co.
Hartwell Jewelry Co. (j).
Manly Office Supply Co.
*Oklahoma Book Co.
Parkhurst Book Co.
Schiff-Mayer Co. (o. s.).
Stealey Book and Pub. Co.
Western Bank Supply Co.
Westfall Drug Co. (d).

OKMULGEE, 6000.
Moore, L. S. (b).

PAUL'S VALLEY, 2689.
Baker's Drug Co.

PAWNEE, 2500.
Jay & Jay (d).
Pawnee Drug Co. (d).
Peter Drug Co. (d).

PERRY, 3133.
Barton, J. W., Book Co. (b).
City Drug Co. (d).
Southside Pharmacy.

PONCA CITY, 3500.
McDowell & Castator (b, d).
Morrison, R. E., & Co. (b, d).
Panton, O. A. (b, d).

SHAWNEE, 12,474.
Proffit, E. R.

SAPULPA, 8302.
Udeir, Edgar A. (b).

TAHLEQUAH, 1916.
Hudson, Waddle (g).

TECUMSEH, 1626.
Hartoon, C. B. (b).

 **Crucible Enamel** For hot or cold iron pipes, boiler fronts, etc.

Wholesale and Retail Stationers

OKLAHOMA.

TULSA, 61,355.
Black Printing Co.
Boatwright Stationery Co.
Burkhart Printing & Stationery Co.
Henry, Geo. W.
Kendall Drug Co.
Palace Office Supply Co.
Quaker Drug Co.
Rexall Drug Co.
Sternberg Bros. (d).
Tulsa Book Store.
Vawter Office Supply Co.
Western Bank Supply Co.
Younkman Drug Co. (d).

VINITA, 4082.
Bero, J. (b).
Chapman's Drug Store (d).
Shanahan & Mitchell (d).
Wright Mercantile Co. (g).

WAGONER, 4500.
McGuire, R. E. (b).

WEATHERFORD, 2118.
Jansen, C. N. (b).
Owl Drug Store.
Weatherford Drug Co.

WELEETKA, 1239.
Lawley, Miss Clara.

OREGON.

ALBANY, 4275.
Dawson, Fred (d).
Foshay & Mason, Inc. (b, d).
Woodworth Drug Co.

ASTORIA, 9599.
Farr Drug Co.
Svenson, John (b).
Utzinger & Son.
*Whitman, O. W. (b, c, s).

BAKER, 6742.
Andrews, Wesley.
Blackman's Pharmacy (d).
Book Shop, The.
Grace & Bodinson Drug Co.
Levinger Drug Store.
Muegge, N. A. (d).
Rogers & Simmers (b).
*Ryder Bros. (c).

CORVALLIS, 4552.
Allen's Drug Store (d).
Berman's Drug Store (d).
Gerhardt's Book Store (b).
Graham & Wells (d).
Graham & Wortham (d).

DALLAS, 3000.
Hayter, J. C.

EUGENE, 12,000.
Allen's Drug Store.
Coe Stationery Co.
Church & School Pub. Co. (b).
Cressey, J. A.
Linn Drug Co.
Schwarzschild, E. (b).
University Pharmacy.

HOOD RIVER, 2831.
Slocum & Canfield (b).

INDEPENDENCE, 1160.
Craven & Walker.

LA GRANDE, 4843.
La Grande Pharmacy.
Levy Vogel Drug Co.
Newlin Book & Stationery Co.

McMINNVILLE, 3000.
Hembree & Jamison.
Rogers Bros. Drug Co.
Shirley-Parsons Co. (d).

MARSHFIELD, 4500.
Norton & Hansen Staty. Co.

MEDFORD, 8840.
Medford Book Store.

OREGON CITY, 4287.
Huntley Drug Co. (d, b).

PENDLETON, 4460.
Economy Drug Co. (d).
Frazier, L. G. (b).
Pendleton Drug Co.
Thompson Drug Co.

PORTLAND, 260,601.
Allen, A. W. (d).
Brochman Ptg. & Staty. Co.
*Blake, McFall Co.
Budelman News Co. (b).
Bushong & Co. (c).
Cole News Co.
Cunningham, P. D.
*Gill Co., The J. K. (b).
Glass & Prudhomme Co.
Helwig, Hibbard Co. (c).
Hyland Bros. (b).
Irwin-Hodson Co.
Johnson, M. (b).

 **Paint and Chemical Company**
PAPER COLORS AND MILL PAINT SPECIALTIES
BOSTON SPRINGFIELD, MASS. NEW YORK

Wholesale and Retail Stationers

OREGON

PORTLAND—*Continued.*
Kilham Stationery & Ptg. Co.
Kubli-Howell Co.
Lipman, Wolfe & Co. (g).
Meier & Frank Co. (g).
Olds, Wortman & King (g).
Owl Drug Store.
Pacific Stationery & Ptg. Co.
Perkins Hotel Pharmacy.
Pike & Martin (d).
Roberts Bros. (g).
Schmale, A. W., Co. (b).
Woodard, Clark & Co. (d).

SALEM, 14,094.
Commercial Book Store.
Crown Drug Store.
Fry, Daniel (d).
Myers, H. A. & M. L. (g).
*Patton Bros. (b).
Perry, J. C. (d).
Schaffer Drug Store (d).
Ward's Drug Store (d).

THE DALLES, 4880.
Crosby, A. B. (d).
Donnell, M. Z. (d).
Nickelsen, I. C. (b).

PENNSYLVANIA.

ALLEGHENY.
(See Pittsburgh.)

ALLENTOWN, 51,913.
Berkemeyer, Keck & Co.
Griesemer Staty. Co.
Hess Bros. (g, b).
Keller, E., & Sons (j).
*Leh, H., & Co. (g).
*Schmid, H. W.
Shafer's Book Store (b).
Zollinger-Harned Co. (b, g).

ALTOONA, 52,127.
Bartle, W. H. (b, c, s).
Boecking & Meredith (d, s).
Harris, W. K. G. (d, s).
Kline Bros. (g).
Leh, H., & Co. (g).
Turner Drug Co.
Welsh Bros. (d).

AMBLER, 1884.
Shepherd, Henry W.

ASHLAND, 6855.
Donahue, Wilfred.
Williams, S. F. (b).

BEAVER FALLS, 12,191.
Hummel & Hetzler (b).
Reeder, W. T.
Stucky's Pharmacy (d).

BELLEFONTE, 4145.
Index Book & Stationery Co.

BERWICK, 5357.
Chop, Andrew.

BETHLEHEM, 30,000.
Bush & Ball Co.
Koch, P. O.
Moravian Book Store.
Rau's Drug Store.
Weand, R. B.

BRADDOCK, 21,181.
Braddock Pharmacy (d).
Cassidy, M. J. (d).
Oyzewski, B. (d).
Edmunds Drug Store (d).
Herring, E. A. (d).
Hollander, S., & Co. (d).
Klein, Geo. B. (d).
Kulp, W. A. (d).
Kutscher, Geo. W., & Co. (d).
Miller Drug Co. (d).
Roderus & Klaban (b).
Straight, S. A.
Weyles, Chas. (d).
Weyles, W. J. (d).

BRADFORD, 14,544.
Auerhaim's (g).
Davis, Fred. G. (j).
Garbarshy, Barney (b).
Leonard's Drug Store.
Thompson & Wood (d).

BRISTOL, 9256.
Lerman, Jacob J.
Tracy & Baker.

BUTLER, 22,500.
Eyth's Book Store (b).
Lichty, J. L. (b).
Pollack, Chas. R.
Reed, J. M. (b).
Reiber, A. M., & Bro. (g).
Troutman & Sons, A. (g).

CARBONDALE, 17,040.
Clark, H. F. (d).
Connor, Jos. M. (d).
Gramer, F. E. (d).
Kelley, Frank (d).
Lunny, John A. (d).
Roberts, Wm. J.
Van Bergen, R. B. & N. (b).
Woolworth, F. W. (g).

Hampden Regal Wall Coating — A white cold water paint. Will not rub, scale or peel off.

Wholesale and Retail Stationers

PENNSYLVANIA.

CARLISLE, 10,303.
  Bowman & Co. (g).
  Central Book Store.
  Clarke, W. C.
  Cromlich, Foster G.
  Eckels, N. O. (b, d).
  Haverstick, S. W.
  Kunkle, W. G. (d).
  McClain, J. A.
  Ritchey, V. H. (g)
  Shearer, Wm. R. (d).
  Sipe, J. E. (d).
  Stephen's Drug Store.
  Trimmer, J. H.

CARNEGIE, 10,009.
  Cowen, A. J., Co. (g).
  Croushore, H. G. (d).
  Cruzan, G. G. (d).
  Gulth, Mrs. H. L. (d).
  Hardy, R. J. (d).
  McConaughy, James (g).
  Perrin, J. M. (d).

CHAMBERSBURG, 11,800.
  Banks Bros. (g).
  Haller Drug Store.
  Miller, Martha A. (d).
  Montgomery, John (d).
  Skinner, H. W. (d).
  Stauffer's Book Store.
  Shull's Drug Store (d).
  Yeager, Howard (b).

CHARLEROI, 9000.
  Might Book Store.

CHESTER, 38,537.
  Duncan, Walter.
  Simmonds, A. D. (b).
  Spencer Stationery Co.

CLEARFIELD, 8000.
  Dooley Drug Co.
  Kurtz Stationery Store.
  Stewart Drug Co.
  Woodward & McPherson Drug Co.

COATESVILLE, 11,084.
  Davy, G. W., & Son (d).
  Doan, Chester C. (d).
  Gibney & Bro. (d).
  *Speakman, C. N., & Sons.
  Steinfeldt, R., & Bro. (b).

COLUMBIA, 11,593.
  Richards & Ekman (b).

CONNELLSVILLE, 15,000.
  Artman & Work.

CONSHOHOCKEN, 7480.
  Graham & Johnson.

CORRY, 5991.
  *Ames, N. F., & Co. (d).
  Babbitt & Son, C. O. (b, d).
  Downey, Thomas (d).
  Durham Drug Co. (d).
  Lindsley, R. G., & Son (d).

CURWENSVILLE, 2700.
  Leib, J. L. (d).
  Way, T. & R. W.
  Wrigley, W. K. (d).

DANVILLE, 7517.
  Harris, A. G. (b).

DU BOIS, 15,000.
  Boyles, C. J. (d).
  Hay, Charles L. (d).
  Holland, A. P. (d).
  Humphreys, G. W. (d).
  Mathews Book Co.
  Schrum's Drug Store.

DUQUESNE, 15,727.
  Barozy, Steve.

EASTON, 28,523.
  Bush & Bull (g).
  Correl Staty. & Supply Co.
  Free Press Publishing Co. (s, c).
  Laubach, Wm., & Sons (g).
  Montague, Chas. J. (b).
  Nixon, Frank, Co. (b).
  Vogel, Ellsworth D. (b).

ELLWOOD CITY, 8000.
  Leedham, J. S. (j).

ERIE, 66,525.
  Ashby Printing Co. (c).
  Dispatch Printing & Eng. Co. (c, s).
  Dugan-Rider Co. (c, s).
  Erie Dry Goods Co. (g).
  *Erie Paper Co.
  Fredericks, P. (b).
  Himrod Engraving Co.
  Klein Bros. (d).
  Sell, W. J. (b).
  Stearns, J. M. (b).
  Trask, Prescott & Richardson Co. (g).
  *Walker, J. H.

ETNA, 5830.
  Eiszler, Charles F.

FRACKVILLE, 3118.
  Holt, W. P.

 **Paint and Chemical Company**
PAPER COLORS AND MILL PAINT SPECIALTIES
BOSTON   SPRINGFIELD, MASS.   NEW YORK

Wholesale and Retail Stationers

PENNSYLVANIA.

FRANKLIN, 9767.
  Griffin, O. L. (b).
  Smith, J. H. (b).

FREELAND, 6197.
  Alden, J. A.

GALETON, 4500.
  City Drug Store (d).

GREENSBURG, 20,000.
  Clements & Hill.
  T. & G. Bookshop (b).

GREENVILLE, 4814.
  Beatty, E. T. (b).
  Stinson, J. M. (b).

HAMBURG, 2301.
  Shomo, Allen L. (c).

HANOVER, 7057.
  Fischer, J. W., & Co.

HARRISBURG, 90,000.
  Althause, F. J. (d).
  Althause, H. B. (d).
  Capital City News Co.
  Central Book Store (b).
  Cotterel, John W. (d).
  Cotterel, D. W. (b).
  Dives, Pomeroy & Stewart (g).
  Ebner, Geo. F., Jr. (c).
  Ensminger, John T., Jr. (d).
  Evangelical Pub. Co (b).
  Garland, J. K. (d).
  Gorgas, G. A. (d).
  Hoffman, Wagner.
  Potts, G. C. (d).
  Pound, W. R. (d).
  *Roberts & Meck.
  Tunis, W. S.
  Willis Latimer.
  Zimmerman, Bessie L. (s).

HAZLETON, 30,147.
  Altmiller, Charles.
  *Brown, A. E. (b).
  Keiser, Charles W. (b).

HELLERTOWN, 2000.
  Laubach, John A.

HOBOKEN, 700.
  Eberhart, Fred L.

HOLLIDAYSBURG, 4000.
  Smith, Geo. M.

HOMESTEAD, 18,714.
  McConegly, Mrs. K.

HONESDALE, 8000.
  Green, Mrs. Theresa.

HOUTZDALE, 1482.
  Arnold, J. A.

HUNTINGDON, 8000.
  *Blair Co., J. C. (b).
  Henry, R. A. (d).
  Morningstar, L. A.
  Read, John, & Sons (d).
  Steel, H. E. (d).
  Tyson, W. S.

INDIANA, 8000.
  Foulman's Dept. Store (g).
  Hall, H. (b, s).
  Hetrick Bros. (d).
  Hildebrand, T. E. (d).
  Johnston's News Stand.

JOHNSTOWN, 55,482.
  Benshoff Ptg. & Stat. Co.
  Cohen, Arthur (d).
  Horan Book Store.
  Nathan & Bro., M. (g).
  Penn Traffic Co. (g).
  Ruth, James J.
  Waters & Bro., W. B. (b).
  Young, Chas. & Geo. E. (d).
  Zolner, W. J. (b).

KANE, 6626.
  Kane Drug Co. (d).
  Main Drug Store (d).
  Moberg's (g).
  Newcomer's Pharmacy.

KENNETT SQUARE, 1516.
  Voorhees, John H.

KINGSTON, 6449.
  Church, W. F. (d).
  Hershberger, H. A.
  Lehman, John (d).

KITTANNING, 8500.
  Brodhead, W. F. (d).
  Brown's Drug, Book and Music Co.
  *Furnee & Kennerdell (b).
  Sturgeon, W. J. (d).

KUTZTOWN, 2360.
  Christ, Alvin S. (b).

LANCASTER, 49,685.
  Buchanan & Brown (g).
  Donovan Co. (g).
  Fondersmith, G. L. (b).
  Garvin, M. T., & Co. (g).
  Hager & Bro. (g).

 Pulp Colors — For paper staining, surface coating and printing.

Wholesale and Retail Stationers

PENNSYLVANIA.

LANCASTER—Continued.
Herr, L. B., & Son (c, s).
Kurtz, Zook S. (j).
Landis, Frank B.
Leinbach & Co. (g).
Madigan, Walter D. (b).
Meekins, W. J. (b).
Miller, John Henry (d).
Nixdorf & Bard (c).
Ream, Chas. (b).
Steinfeldt, I. (b).
Watt & Shand (g).
Weber & Son, L. (j).

LANSDALE, 3100.
Freeman, E. J. (d).
Kuhns, E. J. (d).
Landis, A. H. (j).

LANSFORD, 7800.
Albert, Howard (d).
Reese, Thomas J. (s).

LEBANON, 22,500.
Atkins, Frank H. (d)
Boger, C. E. (d).
Bollman, K. S. (b).
*Dutweiler, Ira K. (b, c, s).
*Harpel, L. G. (c, s).
Hersh, A. O. (d).
Hoch, Chas. (d).
Kramer's Art Store (s).
Loehle, J. F. (d).
Mader, E. R. (d).
Turner, W. H. (d).

LEWISBURG, 3081.
Fegley, J. A.

LEWISTOWN, 8166.
Hoffman Novelty Store.
Raymer, P. G. (b).

LOCK HAVEN, 7772.
Burkett Bros.
Clark Ptg. and Mfg. Co. (c).
Frederick's Pharmacy (d).
Kinsloe & Sons, J. B. G. (b).
Smith & Winters (g).

LYKENS, 2943.
Wynn, Frank.

MAHANOY CITY, 15,936.
Jones, Harry L.
Madden, W. V. (b).

MAUCH CHUNK, 4029.
Luckenbach, Jennie M.

McKEESPORT, 42,694.
Finley Co. Dept. Store (g).
Forrester & Co., W. T.

McKEESPORT—Continued.
Galvin, J. B.
*Myers-Norton Co.
O'Neil, J. D., Co. (g).
Schmidt, Adolph (d).

MEADVILLE, 15,900.
Ballinger & Siggin (d).
Henrici, Jacob (b).
*Hotchkiss, J. S., & Bro. Co.
*Shartle, E. H.

MEDIA, 3075.
Media Staty. Co.

MERCERSBURG, 1410.
Phillips, D. Caleb.

MEYERSDALE, 4000.
Cook, W. B., & Son.
McCune, Mrs. W. A.

MILLVALE, 7861.
Farmerie, J. L. (g).

MILTON, 7460.
Buoy, John Y., Co.
Krebs, Clyde S.
Reed, W. A., Estate.

MINERSVILLE, 7240.
Bowman, Geo. F.
Coombe, L. A.
Jones, W. W. (b).

MONESSEN, 12,000.
Taylor, James F.

MONONGAHELA, 7508.
Kelly, W. P. (b).
Mackey, Robt. P.

MOUNT CARMEL, 17,532.
Watkins, M. K.

MOUNT PLEASANT, 6000.
Leonard, J. P.
Overholt, W. M.

MUNCY, 1934.
McCarty, J. R. (j).

NAZARETH, 4000.
Aswald, John (b).
Crawford, Walter (d).
Oswald, John L. (b).

NEW BRIGHTON, 8000.
Brubaker, E. S. (d).
Kenah, C. J. (d).
Kenah Bros.
Kramer, C. F.
Schweppe, H. L. (d).

 **Paint and Chemical Company**
PAPER COLORS AND MILL PAINT SPECIALTIES
BOSTON   SPRINGFIELD, MASS.   NEW YORK

Wholesale and Retail Stationers

PENNSYLVANIA.

NEW CASTLE, 36,280.
Burchfield, W. C. (d).
Clutton Drug Store, The (d).
Hainer, The, Drug Co. (d).
Love & Megown (d.)
Mahoning Pharmacy (d).
McCandless-Hamilton Co.
McKee, M. B. (d).
McKinley & Frantz (d).
*Metzler, Chas. T., Co. (b, c, s).
*Moody & Son, G. W.
Neely, J. F. (d).
*New Castle Notion Co.
New Castle Pharmacy (d).
Paisley, Scott (d).
Physicians Pharmacy (d).
Terminal Apothecary (d).
Woolworth, F. W., & Co. (g).
5 & 10 Cent Store.

NEW KENSINGTON, 8000.
Yoke, William G.

NEW WILMINGTON, 800.
Hutchison, William A.

NORRISTOWN, 27,875.
Hydeman, Marcus (g, b).
Kennedy Stationery Co. (c).
Sames, Thomas (b).

OIL CITY, 17,373.
Delahoyde & Muller (s).
Ormston, A. J. (b).

PARKERS' LANDING, 1500.
Needle, Jr., G. A.

PHILADELPHIA.

(Population 1,549,008).

Wholesale Stationers marked (*), Dealers in Office Supplies marked (o. s.), Booksellers selling Stationery marked (b), Druggists selling Stationery marked (d), Druggists selling Books and Stationery marked (b, d), Department Stores selling Stationery marked (g), Jewelers selling Stationery marked (j).

Commercial Stationers are marked (c), Social Stationers marked (s).

Altemus & Co., 33 S. Fourth (c, o. s.).
Amer. Ribbon & Carbon Co., 331 R. E. Trust Bldg. (o. s.).
Am. School Supply Co., 1110 Sansom.
Anderman, Albert, 705 Filbert (c, o. s.).
Anderson, John A., 5401 Girard av.
*Anderson, John, & Co., 142 S. Third.
Atkinson, Wm., 1507 Arch (c, s).
Automatic Ptg. & Staty. Co., 826 Arch.
Bachman, C. O., 1831 Frankford av.
Bailey, Banks & Biddle, 1218 Chestnut (j, s).
Baker, Frederick T., 311 S. 52d.
Baker, Geo. W., 2238 Frankford av.
Beckman, Thos. J., Company, 310 N. 11th (s).
Bedford, R. H., 3426 Germantown av.
Belmmer, Wm. H., 3315 G.
Bieregel, A., 6085 Germantown av.
Bingham, The, Co., 139-141 N. Juniper (c).
*Blackburn & Anderman, 705 Filbert.
Blaney, James, 109 Levering, Manayunk.
Born, Chas. W., 2318 Jasper (s, c).
*Bradley, John A., 14 S. 7th.
*Bradley, Milton, Co., 17th and Arch.
Brimmer, Wm. H., 3315 Germantown av.
Bunnell, O. S., 30 N. 7th.
Burger, Peter, 118 Vine.
Burgoyne, Sidney J., Widener Bldg. (s).
Carr, Wm., 201 E. Girard av.
Carson, T. D., 5520 Germantown av. (c, s, o. s.).
*Central News Co., 614 S. Washington sq.
Clark, John C., Company, 230 Dock and 1430 S. Penn sq.
Columbia Ribbon & Carbon Mfg. Co., 1305 Arch (o. s.).
Cooper, Henry, 2752 Germantown av.
Coryell, Maud M., 3940 Market.
Culbertson, J. W., 5641 Chester av.
Cunn. D. S., 446 E. Girard av.

Mill White — Will not turn yellow like the ordinary White Lead paint.

Wholesale and Retail Stationers

PENNSYLVANIA.

PHILADELPHIA—*Continued.*
Deitch, David, 359 N. 2d.
Dell, Albert G., 106 Grape, Myk.
Dennison & Son, 606 Sansom.
De Peters, B. Frank, 3041 Germantown av.
*Dixon, T. P. & H. H., 1001 Chestnut.
*Dobbins, W. H., & Co., 48 N. Front.
Dougherty, Mrs. Mary C., 5222 Vine (s, c).
Dreka Co., 1121 Chestnut (s).
Edmundson, Rhoda, 3221 N. Front.
Eiser, Mrs. W., G and Westmoreland.
*Elliot Co., Chas. H., 17th and Lehigh av.
Emmert, M. H., 4054½ Lancaster av.
Evans, Geo. B., Co. (d), 1106 Chestnut; 1012 Market; 17th and Chestnut.
Fish, Geo. B., Co., Mutual Life Bldg. (c).
Fleu & Fetterolf, 5954 Germantown av. (c, s, o. s.).
Flint, Wm., 1904 Columbia av.
Forderer, F. B., 2051 Germantown av.
Friedman, Inc., Jerome A., 113 S. 15th (c, o. s.).
Fry, Geo., Co., 119 S. 13th.
Galloway, Chas. W., 4075 Market.
Gans Bros., 1225 Sansom (c).
Getts, W. H., 401 S. 5th.
Getz, Leo A., 1543 Germantown av.
Getz, Max M., 1405 W. Columbia.
Gimbel Bros., 9th and Market (g).
Goldsmith, Mary, 1810 Columbia av.
Goldstein, Moses, 743 S. 3d.
Gordon, Wm. R., 420 Market (c, o. s.).
Grambo, C. H., 3307 Woodland av.
Gray, Irene, 2042 Frankford av.
Greir Typewriting Co., 1211 Arch (o. s.).
Groebeldinger, Peter, 1541 Germantown av. (c, s).
Gross, Harry A., & Co., 603 Sansom (c).
Guarantee Typewriter Co., 47 N. 10th (o. s.).
Gubler & Co., 118 S. 4th (c, o. s.).
Haberland, Oscar F., 6027 Market.
Hainer, Alice M., 4923 Germantown av.
Hall, Wm. O. F., 2322 N. Beechwood.
Harlow, C. P., 157 N. 12th (c, o. s.).
Haslett, Geo. U., 2128 N. 17th.
Hawthorne, J. W., 2458 Frankford av.

PHILADELPHIA—*Continued.*
Helb, Anna M., 2041 Ridge av.
Hildreth, F. Nelson, 321 S. 60th.
Hogan, The James, Co., 607 Chestnut (c, o. s.).
Hornberger, Mary C., 5033 Baltimore av.
Horr, A. G., 1715 Columbia av.
Hoskins, Wm. H., Co. (Inc.) 904-906 Chestnut (c, s, o. s.).
Index Visible, Inc., Stock Exchange Bldg. (o. s.).
Jacobs, G. W., & Co., 1628 Chestnut (b).
Jaisohn, Philip, & Co., 1537 Chestnut (c, o. s.).
Jaspan, Samuel, & Son, 846 S. 2d.
Jenkins, W. H., 140 N. 15th.
Ka Dis Paper Co., 34 S. 16th (o. s.).
Kalwaic, Martin, 4121 Germantown av.
Katz, Samuel, 804 S. 2d (s).
*Keating Co., S. E. Cor. 9th and Sansom (s).
Keenan, Mrs. M., 2933 E. Thompson.
Kemble, Katherine L., 3735 Lancaster av.
Kent, W. G., Co., 124 S. 8th.
Keystone Cabinet Co., 731 Arch (o. s.).
Kiesling, F., 2139 N. 6th.
Krouse, Daniel S., 2512 Germantown av.
Ladley, John N., 6200 Germantown.
Lakoff, Henry M., 316 Market.
Lamb Bros., 38 S. 6th (c, o. s.).
Landau, Max, 2422 Kensington av. (c, s).
Leek, J. C., 4801 Old York Road.
Levinson, Ezra, 26 S. 5th.
Levis, Harry B., 702 Arch (c, o. s.).
Levis, Seth Pancoast, 1621 Sansom (c).
Liberty Typewriter Co., 911 Walnut (o. s.).
Linfoot Mfg. Co., 1708 Ludlow (o. s).
Lincoln Business Bureau, 811 Arch (o. s.).
Lit Bros., 8th and Market (g).
Logan, A. L., & Co., 137 S. 10th.
*Loughead & Co., 512 Race.
Macey, Fred., Co., 811 Arch (o. s.).
Magee, Thomas, 44 S. Second.
Mann, Wm., Co., 529 Market (c, o. s.).
Marcus & Co., Inc., 6 N. 13th and 1303 Market (c, o. s.).

 **Paint and Chemical Company**
PAPER COLORS AND MILL PAINT SPECIALTIES
BOSTON   SPRINGFIELD, MASS.   NEW YORK

Wholesale and Retail Stationers

PENNSYLVANIA.

PHILADELPHIA—*Continued.*
*Matlack, E. L., 1024 Filbert.
McCausland Staty. Co., 4426 Frankford av. (c, o. s.)
*McConnell School Supply Co., 4437 Ludlow.
McIntire & Co., 1011 Chestnut (c, s).
*Mellor, S. S., Drexel bldg.
Moore, P. H., 6646 Germantown av.
*Mousley, Geo. E., 502 Ranstead.
Mullen, W. B., Magazine Agency, 4905 Frankford av.
Murphy, W. F., Sons Co., 509 Chestnut (c, o. s.).
Nonnamaker, Wm. M., 3535 Germantown av. (c, s).
North Eastern Spec. Co., 2220 Frankford.
Office Requirements Co., 1215 Filbert.
Office Specialty Co., Bourse Bldg. (o. s.).
O'Neil, Annie, 1409 N. 2d.
Owens, Wm. R., Heed Bldg.
*Penn Jobbing Co., 804 S. 2d.
Penton, W. A., & Bro., 400 Chestnut.
Pflueger, Mary A., 2637 Germantown av.
Phelps, Chas. A., 17th and Erie av.
Phila. Typewriter Exchange, 601 Chestnut (o. s.).
Phillips, Walter E., 5141 Germantown av.
Piper, E. A. S., 1916 Fairmont av.
Pomerantz, A. & Co., 1525 Chestnut.
Poore, Emma R., 1806 Susquehanna av.
Progressive Carbon Paper Co., 137 S. 10th (o. s.).
Prentice Mfg. Co., 212 N. 13th.
Rafferty, Matilda, 1806 Market.
Reinhart, J. E., 3435 Germantown.
Reuther, H. C., 250 N. 8th.
*Reynolds & Reynolds, 1527 Real Estate Trust bldg.
Robinowitz, Hannah, 634 South.
Rosenthal, David, 104 N. 2d.
Rovner, A., 520 South.
Schachterle, Edward, 7120 Germantown (s).
Schiff Bros., Inc., 336 Market.
Schmidt, H. W., 6531 Stenton av. (c, o. s.).
Schneider, H. A., 2977 Frankford.
Schramn, Andrew A., 1114 Sansom.
Shallcross, Harold, 5019 N. Broad.
*Shepherd & Spooner, 806 Cherry.
Shohat, Jacob, 528 Greenway.

PHILADELPHIA—*Continued.*
Sippel, Ida, 1447 N. 5th.
Smith, Thos. C., 2928 Kensington av. (b).
Snellenburg, N., & Co., 12th and Market (g).
Snyder, Meta A., 5539 Germantown av.
Spayd's Typewriter Co., Inc., 823 Walnut (o. s.).
Speier, Leon, 1020 Girard av.
Standard Office & T. W. Supply Co., 1339 R. E. Trust Bldg. (o. s.).
Standard Typewriter Exchange, 1022 Arch (o. s.).
Starr, A., & Son, 6 S. 2d.
Stationers Supply Mfg. Co., Penna bldg.
Stationery Spec. Co., Witherspoon Bldg.
Staton, R. W., 5439 Germantown av.
Steppacher, Henry, 2800 W. Lehigh av.
Strauss, Max, 337 Poplar.
Strawbridge & Clothier, 8th and Market (g).
Streano, Catello, 1235 S. 19th.
Strohm, R. C. H., 935 N. 2d.
*Stuart Bros. Co., 410 Market (c).
Teplitz, Louis, 1313 N. 10th.
Them, A. H., 3532 Longshore and Tacony.
Thomson, Thos. R., 252 N. Sixteenth.
Toub Bros. 532 South.
Tyler, J. E., 2826 Kingston av.
Typewriter Headquarters, 524 Walnut (o. s.).
Union Ribbon & Carbon Co., 67 Laurel (o. s.).
Unique Carbon Paper Co., 1211 Arch (o. s.).
United Printing Co., 411 S. 5th.
United Stationery Mfg. Co., 720 S. 11th.
U. S. Typewriter Ribbon Mfg. Co., 124 S. 8th (o. s.).
Ursprung, S. E., 12th and Ridge av.
Victor, Louis, 2017 Germantown av.
Voorsanger, Florence, 4083 Lancaster av.
Wagner, Katherine E., 210 Manheim.
Wambach, Charles, 1623 Germantown av.
Wanamaker, John, 13th and Market (g).
Warner, C. A., 638 York.
Warwick, J. E. & M. F., 262 S. Eleventh.

Canary Yellow — A true color. Makes bright tints and solid finishes.

Wholesale and Retail Stationers

PENNSYLVANIA.

PHILADELPHIA—*Continued.*
Waters, J. C., 3501 Longshore, Tacony.
Weatherby, Katherine, 1508 Columbia av.
Webster, S. S., Co., 908 Walnut (o. s.).
Weil, J. H., & Co., 1300 Arch (c).
Weiss, Herman, & Son, 511 South.
Werner, Emil O., & Co., 931 Dauphin (o. s.).
White, H. T., & Co., 127 S. 11th.
Wilkins Press, 522 N. American Bldg.
*Wilson, B. Y., 1024 Filbert (c).
Wonderly, Bella, 1607 Vine.
Wright, E. A., Banknote Co., Broad and Huntington (s).
Wright, Ed., 2235 N. Front.
Yeo & Lukens Company, 719 Walnut and 23 N. 13th.
Young, Joseph, Heed Bldg.

PHOENIXVILLE, 10,743.
Keely, H. D.
O'Neill, M. J., Jr.
Shaffer, R. G.

PITTSBURGH, 533,905.
Accountant Supply Co., Farmers' Bk. Bldg.
Alexander, Geo. H., Co., Inc., 410-412 Wood.
Baker Office Furniture Co., 813 Wood.
Boggs & Buhl, Federal, Allegheny (g).
Braun Co., The.
De Santis, A., & Co., 807 Webster.
Dietzgen, Eugene, Co., 805 Liberty av. Drawing materials.
Dyer, Samuel W., 413 Prospect.
Finn, Jacob, 127 W. Ohio.
Gibson, Chas., 1500 Beaver.
Gundlach, Chas. H., 4113 Butler.
Guthrie's Priscilla Book Shop, Union Arcade.
Hall, Homer D.
Hays Book & Art Store, 6126 Penn (b).
Herget, F. C., Smithfield (b).
Hellstern, R., 4718 Liberty av.
Hilger, Jos. W., 4205 Penn. av.
Horne, Jos., Co., 524 Penn. av. (g).
Ideal Office Supply Co., Jenkins Arcade.
Ignotas, John A.
Johnston, Wm. G., Co., 429 Wood.
Jones Book Shop, 437 Wood.

PITTSBURGH—*Continued.*
Kaufman Bros., Smithfield (g).
Kirkland, Norman, & Co., Bessemer Bldg.
Kurtz, Langbein & Swartz, 535 Wood.
Ludwig & Fuhr, 602 Homewood.
Luntz, John B., 1618 Clairn.
McCloy, A. W., Co., 642-644 Liberty av. (c).
McCreery & Co., Sixth & Wood (g).
McKnown-Carnes Co., 431 Wood.
*Marohnic, J., 1420 Ohio (b).
Meth, Harry, Jenkins Arcade.
Methodist Book Concern, 105 5th av.
Munhall, The, Co., 723 Liberty av.
Myers & Shinkle Co., 633 Liberty Pl. O., Co., 483 4th.
Nathan, Alfred, Union Arcade.
Pittsburgh Stat. Co., 128 Anderson.
Reed & Witting, 610 Wood.
Rehbeck, W. J., 106 W. Grant.
Roberts, C. D., & Co., 541 Wood.
Sattler, Henry.
Schafer, H. A., News Co., 309 3d (b).
Seefried, Louis B., 864 E. Ohio, Allegheny.
Smith, Josiah, 524 4th.
Steinsaper, Julius L., 336 4th.
*Stevenson & Foster Co., 947 Liberty.
Strassburger, A., & Co., 927 Fifth av.
Thumm, J. A., 1734 Fifth.
Weinberg, Benj., Jenkins Arcade.
*Weldin, J. R., Co., 413 Wood (b).

PITTSTON, 67,700.
*Andrews, C. R. (b).
Kane, James (d).
Peck, J. W. (d).

PLYMOUTH, 16,995.
Davenport, A. Livingstone (b).
Durbin, Geo. J. (d).
Groblewski, A. G. (d).
Howland, W. E. (b).
Roan, Patrick A. (d).
Williams, R. D. (d).

POTTSTOWN, 15,599.
Bentz, Chas. S. (d).
Dives, Pomeroy & Stewart (b, g).
Fink & Corbett.
Landis, F. B. (b).
*Gilbert & Guldin.
Porter, S. H. (d).
Sweeney, Edw. J. (d).

 **Paint and Chemical Company**
PAPER COLORS AND MILL PAINT SPECIALTIES
BOSTON   SPRINGFIELD, MASS.   NEW YORK

Wholesale and Retail Stationers

PENNSYLVANIA.

POTTSVILLE, 20,236.
Cowen, W. S. (d).
Dives, Pomeroy & Stewart (g).
Evening Chronicle.
Green's Son, R. C. (j).
Gregory, J. E. (d).
Miller, M. E. (b).
Mudey, F. A., & Co.
Zerbey, W. M., & Son (b).

PUNXSUTAWNEY, 11,000.
Beyer, J. M. (d).
Eberhart, J. B., & Co.
Feicht, C. M. (d).
*Nolph, J. G., & Co.
Spirit Pub. Co.

READING, 107,000.
*Breneiser Novelty Co.
Dives, Pomeroy & Stewart (b, g).
*Eagle Book Store.
*Earl, M. J. (b).
*Hintz, J. George (b).
Kincaid, Mrs. Wm.
Kline, Epplinner Co. (g).
Lord & Gage (g).
*Miller, James H. (b).
Reading News Agency, Inc.
Tenacity Mfg. Co.
Whitner, C. K., & Co. (g).

SAYRE, 8000.
Jump, H. D. (d).
Weber, P. J.

SCHUYLKILL HAVEN, 4747.
Pflueger, Susan L.
Quinter, Milton W.

SCOTTDALE, 6000.
Broadway Drug Co. (d).
Brooks Drug Store (d).
Lewellyn, F. M. (b).
Rutherford, T. H. (b).

SCRANTON, 129,867.
Deemer & Co.
Kadak, Paul K.
*Megargee Bros.
Prendergast, R. E.
Price, Thomas E.
Reisman Bros.
Reynolds Bros.

SHAMOKIN, 19,588.
Deibler, E. W. (g).
Lewis, The, Stationer.
Smink, W. H. R. (b).

SHARON, 8916.
Beck, A. L. (d, s).
Conner, M. C. (b).
Hartman, M. (d).
Herald Stationery Store (b).
Sayre, Charles A. (d).
Sharon Book Store.
Snyder & Hyde (d).
Rabinowitz, J. M.

SHEFFIELD, 15,000.
Skelton, Wm. O. (d).
Smith, C. H., Co.

SHENANDOAH, 25,774.
Burke Drug Co. (d).
Hooks, F. W. (b).
Jones, B. F.
Kuzunas, L. M. (d).
Mellet, Michael.
Woolworth & Co., F. W.

SLATINGTON, 4950.
*Art Wall Paper & Staty. Co.
Horn, Chas. W. (d).
Jones Bros.
Jones Bros. & Miller (g).

SOUTH BROWNSVILLE, 4500.
Robinson, D. Fred (d).

SPRING CITY, 2880.
Kimes Stationery Co.
Lewis, Harry L., Estate of.
National Supply Co.

ST. CLAIR, 6455.
Holmes, M. B. (b).

ST. MARY'S, 6346.
Miller, Chas. D. (b).

STEELTON, 14,246.
Wells, J. C.

SUNBURY, 13,770.
*Haines, W. B. (b).
Kelley, R. E.
Melick, C. F. (b).
Nicely, W. M. (b).
Yeager, B. F. (j).

SUSQUEHANNA, 4000.
Carrington, C. R.
Reddon, Frank.
Wagner, Charles.
Williams, Joseph M.

TAMAQUA, 11,687.
Aurand, A. B. (b).

PENNSYLVANIA.

TITUSVILLE, 8533.
Brown, Geo. B. W. (d).
Cohn & Oakleaf (b, g).
Gideon, Andrew A. (b).
O'Hare, Condra.
Thompson, E. K., & Son.

TOWANDA, 4663.
Boyle, George H. (b).
Swartwood, Edith (d).

TREVORTON, 1500.
Smith, John R (j).

UNION CITY, 3104.
Black, James (d).
Gates, Wm. (b, d).
Main, C. B. (d).
Wontenay, L. J. (b).

UNIONTOWN, 13,344.
Beeson, Harry (b).
Central Drug Store.
Fayette Drug Co.
Farwell, W. H., Co.
Penn Office Supply Co.
Robinson Office Furniture Co.

VANDERGRIFT, 45,000.
McGeary & McGeary.

WARREN, 11,080.
Harvey-Carey-Babcock Co. (d).
Hileman, H. H., News Co.
Newell Bros. (d).
Newell, John T. (c).
Schindler, H. J. (c).
Smith, C. H., Co. (g).
Warren News Co.
Wendelboe, N. K. (b).

WASHINGTON, 23,000.
Caldwell, A. B. (The), Co. (g).
Ecker, W. S.
Holbert's Drug Store (d).
Lewis Pharmacy.
Reed, C. M., & Co. (b).
Smith, T. J.
Vowell, L. S. (d).
Washington News Co.

WAYNESBORO, 7199.
Arco Drug Co.
Croft, Clarence (d).
Henderson, J. Munro.
Miller, D. L., & Co. (d).
Morrison, W. H.

WELLSBORO, 2954.
Smith & Smith.

WEST CHESTER, 11,767.
Brown, H. H. (d).
De Haven's Drug Store (d).
Fath, Peter (b).
Hall, Albert P.
Hammond, N. (d).
Henry, A.
Hickman, F. S.
Jones, H. A. (d).
Pierce, W. A. (d).
Rubenstein Bindery.
Stroud, J. Geary (d).

WHITE HAVEN, 1438.
Teel, Robt.

WILKES BARRE, 67,105.
Diemer & Co. (c).
Fowler, Dick & Walker (g).
Frank & Barber (d).
Geary Book & Office Supply Co.
Klipple, E. L. (b).
Long's Sons, Jonas (g).
Madden, J. C. (b).
Pauling, W. J. (d).
Penn Printery.
Puckey, Wm., & Bro. (b).
Shupp, H. G. (j).
*Whiteman, H. A., & Co.
*Wilkes Barre Stationery & Paper Co.

WILKINSBURG, 18,924.
Caldwell & Graham.
Pilgrim, F. J.
Rice, C. B. (b).

WILLIAMSPORT, 31,860.
Bush & Bull Co. (g).
Holmes, Harry W. (d).
Loan Book Store (b).
Meehan, M. J.
Millener Drug Co. (d).
Otto, Horace Y. (b).
Plankenhorn Staty. Co.
Scholl, Chas. E.
Siess Book Store.
Smith, E. W., & Co. (d).
Stearns, L. L., & Sons.
Wilhelm, John A. (b).
*Williamsport Paper Co.
Wolf, B. Geo.
Wood, Bert (b).

WILLIAMSTOWN, 2904.
Blanning, J. Roy.

PENNSYLVANIA.

YORK, 44,750.
Andrews Paper Co.
Barnhart, H. C. (b).
*Feder, Ziegler Co.
Grumbacher & Son (g).
Gross, L. P. (b).
Keller, E. H. (b).

YORK—Continued.
*Lau, B. H., & Co.
McLean, James, & Sons (g).
Regal Umbrella Co.
Shambaugh, M. J.
Wiest's Sons, P. (g).

PHILIPPINE ISLANDS.
MANILA.

Agencia Editorial, The, 50 Carriedo, Sta. Cruz.
Bren, R., 29 Magallanes, Walled City.
Fajardo, Juan, Rizal av.
*Frank & Co. (o. s.).
Heacock, H. E., & Co. (j).
*Heilbronn, J. P., Co.

Lambert Sales Co., Islade Romero.
La Viuda de Bota, 89 Escolta.
Manila Trading & Supply Co.
Martinez, J., 34 Plaza Motaga.
Nam Shing, 86 San Viente, Binondo.
Philippine Education Co., Inc.
Ton Chong Son, 103 San Vicente, Binondo.

RHODE ISLAND.

BLOCK ISLAND, 1314.
Dodge, Darius B. (d).

CENTERVILLE, 2700.
Shippee, F. E.

CENTRAL FALLS, 22,754.
Burns, J. H.

EAST GREENWICH, 3420.
Browning, W. A. (s).

EAST PROVIDENCE, 13,750.
Carpenter, Freemont (d).
Payne, G. W. (d).

NEWPORT, 27,149.
Carr, Geo. H. (Est. of) (b).
Chase & Chase (b).
Clark, W. P.
Hall & Lyon Co. (d).

PAWTUCKET, 51,622.
Capwell's Pharmacy.
Deahy Bros. (g).
Dimard Co. (g).
Fisk Drug Co. (d).
Freeman, E. L., Co. (c, o. s.).
Luther, C. E., & Co. (b).
Pawtucket News Co.
Shartenberg & Robinson (g).
Wood, Willard L. (d).

PROVIDENCE, 224,326.
Blanchard Young Co.
*Callender, McCusland & Troup Co. (g).
Dimond Co. (g).

PROVIDENCE—Continued.
*Freeman, E. L., Co., 109 Westminster (c, o. s.).
Gibson, J. Fred (d).
Hall & Lyons Co. (d).
Hayden, T. J., & Bro. (g).
Potter, Wm. K., 346 Westminster.
Preston & Rounds Co. (b).
*Rhode Island News Co., 57½ Weybosset and 21 to 23 Pine.
Shepard Co. (g).
Tilden-Thurber Co. (j).
*Young, Leonard & Harrall Co.

WARREN, 6585.
Bliss, Chas. C. (b).

WESTERLY, 8696.
Fisher Bros. (g).
Opie & Co., F. H. (g).
Rhode Island Drug Co. (d).
Stanton, C. H. (b, c, s).
Stillmann, Orville (b, c, s).
Var Bros. (c, o. s.).

WOONSOCKET, 38,125.
Daniels, L. L. (b, s).
Farrington, J. B. (j).
Fellman, H. (j).
*Flynn, J. F. (b).
Harris & Mowry Co. (g).
Lally, F. M. (b).
Marty & Addison (g).
McCarthy Dry Goods Co.
Preston, W. S. (b).
Rousseow & Brown (d).
*Woonsocket Paper Co.

TENNESSEE.

BRISTOL (TENN. AND VA.), 7148.
Bunting & Son (d).
Drosser Bros. (g).
Kemble, Cochran Co.
King, H. P., Co.
Minar's Drug Store.
Owl Drug Co.
Paramount Drug Co.
Taylors Dept. Store (g).
Turner Drug Co.
Wood-Nickels Co. (g).

CHATTANOOGA, 44,604.
*Archer Paper Co.
*Davenport Bros. (g).
Embrey, C. P. (d).
*Fritts & Wiehl Co. (d).
Kavanaugh Co. (b).
Live & Let Live Drug Co.
Loveman Co., D. B. (g).
*Miller Bros. Co. (g).
Morrison Drug Co. (d).
*Payne, T. H., & Co. (h).
Pettus, L. J. (d).
*Thomas & Moore Dry Goods Co. (g).
Voigt Bros. (d).

CLARKSVILLE, 3548.
Dickson-Sadler Co.

CLEVELAND, 5549.
Cooper, G. U.
Moon's Drug Store (d).
Philips Drug Co.
Steed, J. A. (d).

DYER, 1600.
Gladhill, E. W., Est. of (d).

DYERSBURG, 4149.
City Drug Co.
Jacobi Drug Co.
Parker, S. G. (j).
Reed, John H. (d).
Taylor Drug Co.

FAYETTEVILLE, 2708.
McKinfey, James D. (b, d).

JACKSON, 21,000.
McCowat-Mercer Printing Co.

JOHNSON CITY, 10,500.
Colon Drug Co.
Crouch, J. E. (b).
Ferguson Drug Co. (d).
Gregory Drug Co.
Jones-Vance Drug Co. (d).
Miller, H. C. (d).

JOHNSON CITY—Continued.
The Bee Hive (g).
Whitehouse Drug Co. (d).

KNOXVILLE, 80,000.
Bean, Warters & Co.
*Briscoe, Daniel, Co. (g).
*Chapman Drug Co. (d).
*Cowan McClung Co. (g).
*Deaver, Kennedy Co. (g).
Doll & Co. (b).
Gaut-Ogden Co.
Hackney Grocery Co. (g).
Hazen, Trent & Harrell (g).
Hope Bros. (j).
Howard, Monroe (b).
Kuhlman & Chambliss Co. (d).
Miller Store Co. (g).
Newcomer, M. M., Co. (g).
Newman, S. B., Co.
Rosenthal, D. A. (s).
*Sanford, Chamberlain & Albers (d).
Southern School Supply Co.
*Swan, Sullins, Brandau (g).

LEBANON, 1956.
Rogers, A. J. (g).

McKENZIE, 1800.
Cannon's, J. P., Sons (d).

MEMPHIS, 131,105.
Clarke, E. H., & Bro., 18 S. Main.
Corner Drug Store.
Ellis-Jones Drug Co., 159 Union av. (d).
Goldsmith, J., & Sons, 125 S. Main (g, s).
Hessig-Ellis Drug Co., Front and McCall (d).
Isaac, M. & S. L., 205 N. Main (b).
Memphis Paper Bag Co.
Tayloe Paper Co., 420 S. Front.
Taylor Co., A. R., 46 S. Main (b).
Van Vleet-Mansfield Drug Co., 52 S. Main (d).
Wilkerson, W. N., & Sons, 324 S. Front (d).

MORRISTOWN, 4007.
Corner Drug Store.
Freel's Drug Store.
Globe Book Co.
Roberts & Turner (d).

MURFREESBORO, 4679.
Blumenthal & Becker.
Gilbert & Richardson (d).
Home Journal Pub. Co.

TENNESSEE.

MURFREESBORO—Continued.
Kerr's Drug Store.
News Banner Pub. Co.
Price & Buchanan (d).
Smith, H. L., & Co. (d).
Vickers & Stickney (d).

NASHVILLE, 110,364.
Ambrose Printing C⁰. (c).
Baird, Ward Co. (c).
Benson Printing Co. (c).
*Berry Demoville & Co. (d).
Brandon Printing Co. (c, s).
Brandon - Craig - Dickerson Co. (c).
Castner-Knott Co. (g).
Coin-Sloan Co. (g).
DeMoville, Page, Sims Co. (d).
*Eskind, J., & Sons (g).
Foster & Parkes Co. (c, s).
*Harris Davis & Co. (g).
Jensen-Herzer & Teck (j).
Jeck (j).
Lebeck Bros. (g).
Marshall & Bruce Co. (c).
McQuiddy Printing Co. (c).
Methodist Pub. House (b).
Mills, R. M. (b, s, two stores).
*Neely Harwell & Co. (g).
Presbyterian Board of Publications (b).
Presbyterian Book Store (b).
*Reeves, J. S., & Co. (g).
Remy & Nance Ptg. Co. (c).
*Riddle, W. S., Notion Co. (g).
*Simon, H. D., & Co. (g).
*Spurlock-Neal Co. (d).
Stein Co. (g).
Stief Jewelry Co. (j).

NASHVILLE—Continued.
Warner Drug Co.
Williams Printing Co. (c).
Zibart Bros. (b, s).

NEWBERN, 2500.
Arnold Drug Co.
Westbrook, J. R., Co. (d).

PARIS, 6000.
Cooper Drug Co. (d).
Kirk Drug Store (d).
Parisian, The (c).
Warren & Murray (j).

PULASKI, 2838.
Lloyd Drug Co.
Reeves, W. P., & Son (d).

ROCKWOOD, 4000.
George, J. E. (d).

ROGERSVILLE, 1500.
Blakeley, W. H. (d).
Caldwell, S. & M. L. (b).
Ripley Drug Co.

SHELBYVILLE, 2236.
Brantley, S. K. (d).
McGrew Drug Co. (d).
Shapard's, H. C., Sons (d).

UNION CITY, 3407.
Burchard, Chas. (d).
Hester, Jr., J. D. (d).
Niles Drug Co.
Nyles, J. H.
Red Cross Drug Co. (d).
Caldwell, D. P.

WINCHESTER, 1500.
Simmons & Rowell (d).

TEXAS.

ABILENE, 12,806.
Abilene Drug Co.
City Drug Store.
Compton, R. B. (d).
Corner Drug Store.
McLemore-Bass Drug Co.
Montgomery Drug Co.

AUSTIN, 35,000.
City Book Store (b).
Everybody's Book Store (b).
Keller, John E. (c, s).
Lewis, S. H.
McFadden, P. W. (d).
*McKean, Eilers & Co. (g).
Scarbrough, E. M., & Sons.
Steck, E. L. (c, s).

AUSTIN—Continued.
Old Book Store, The (b).
*Tobin's Book Store (c, s).
University Co-operative Society.

BEAUMONT, 37,746.
Am. Printing Co.
Hicks, D. J., Book Store (b).
Keith Drug Co.
Service Drug Co.
*Szafir & Son, E. Co. (b).

BELTON, 5500.
Hunter Co. (b, d).
Freeman & Jackson.

BLOOMINGTON, 500.
Evans, J. J.

TEXAS.

BONHAM, 6600.
Peeler, J. W. (d).

BRENHAM, 4718.
Langraff, L.

BROWNWOOD, 6967.
Jones & Dublin (c, s).

BRYAN, 6500.
Emmel, A. W. (b).
James, M. H. (d).
Jenkins, E. J. (d).
Haswell, Tyler (b).

CLARKSVILLE, 3500.
Keeton, W. R. (g).

CLEBURNE, 14,797.
Crow, E. E.
Huzza, M. D.

COLUMBUS, 2000.
Tisinger, J. R., & Co. (d).
Zumwalt, O. A. (d).

COMANCHE, 35,000.
Reese Co., Wm. (b, d).

CORSICANA, 11,894.
Beaton & Bagly (d).
Collin Street Ptg. Co. (c).
Corsicana Printing Co.
Coulson Drug Co.
Griffin-Greig & Harper (d).
Johnson, E. A. (d).
McKinney, V. V. (d).
Rice Book Store.
William, H. E. (d).

CUERO, 4500.
Heaton Bros. (d).

DALLAS, 114,743.
Britton, T. J. (d).
*Butler Bros.
*Crowdus Drug Co., J. W.
*Dorsey Co., The.
Edwards Co.
Everts, A. A. (j).
Greiner-Kelly Drug Co.
Hargreaves Ptg. Co.
Linz, Jos., & Bro. (j).
*Sanger Bros. (g).
Stewart Office Supply Co.
*Texas Drug Co. (d).
Thornton & Bracey.
Titcher-Goettinger Co. (g).
Toole Ptg. & Stat. Co. (c).
*Van Winkle, J. D. (b).
Weichsel, E., & Co. (c).
Yeargan Stationery Co. (c).

DECATUR, 3000.
Decatur Drug Co. (d).
Gunn, C. B. (d).
Man & Simmons (d).

DENISON, 17,000.
B. & M. Co.
Hanna, E. H. (d).
Kingston Drug Store.
Reynolds Drug Store (d).
Sea & Noe (d).
Waldron Drug Store (d).
Yeidel & Son (b).

DENTON, 6300.
Curtis, O. M. (d).
Dyche, O. R. (d).
Garrison, R. H. (b, d).
Lipscomb Drug Store (d).
Minnis, J. A. (d).

EL PASO, 71,000.
Curran, P. H. (b).
*Ellis Bros. Ptg. Co.
El Paso Book Co. (c, s).
Hixon, W. T., Co. (j).
Ideal Book Co.
International Book & Stat'y Co.
McLean, Gifford Co. (b).
Typewriter and Office Supply Co.
Ward, Herbert (d).
Western Woodenware Co.

ENNIS, 5669.
Castellaw Drug Co. (b, d).
Glover & Guthrie Co. (d).

FARMERSVILLE, 1848.
Riker & Holloway (d).
Williams, P. C. (b).

FORT WORTH, 94,494.
Barnes, L. A. (c).
Brashear, J. P. (d).
Canton Pharmacy.
Conner, E. R., & Co. (c).
Covey & Martin Co.
Dillin Bros. (d).
Fair, The (g).
Gaither, F. Z. (d).
Grammer, N. E. (d).
Hassell-White Drug Co.
Pangburn, H. T., & Co. (d).
Reimers Co. (c).
Renfro Drug Co.
Smith & Wessons (o. s.).
Stripling, W. C. (g).

TEXAS.

GAINESVILLE, 10,500.
Cunningham Bros. (b, d).
Dickerman, Roy (d).
Field, R. M. (b, d).
Gould, J. S.
Killgore Co., Wm. (g).
Pugh & Morrison (d).
Siddall Drug Co. (d).
*Stark Drug Co.
Watts Bros. (d).

GALVESTON, 44,000.
Clarke & Courts (c).
Daferner, Charles (b).
Erhard, F. W., & Co. (c).
Hunter, Fred. F. (c).
Knapp Bros. (c).
Ohlendorf, F. (b).
Purdy Bros (b).
Springer, Oscar (c).

GATESVILLE, 1920.
Arnold, A. D., & Co. (d).
Honeycut, A. D., & Co. (b, d).
Torbett, J. S. (b).

GEORGETOWN, 3096.
Hodges Bros. (d).
Long, J. W. (d).
Richardson Book Store.
Wilcox Bros. (j, s).

GOLDTHWAITE, 1127.
Miller, L. E., & Son (j).

GRANBURY, 2000.
Cherry Drug Co.
Hannaford, E. A. (Est. of) (d).

GREENVILLE, 15,000.
Johnson, Mrs. L. L. (b).

HALLETTSVILLE, 1379.
Braunig, Henry J.
Saft, Albert.

HILLSBORO, 6115.
Bond, T. B. (d, j).

HOUSTON, 93,122.
Bottler Bros.
Cargill, The, Co. (c).
Cockrell, Abbott (d).
Coyle, W. H., & Co. (c).
Cummings & Son (c).
Dealy-Adey-Elgin Co. (c).
Foley Bros. Dry Goods Co. (g).
*Houston Drug Co. (d).
Levy Bros. Dry Goods Co. (g).
Lewis, M.
*Magnolia Paper Co.

HOUSTON—Continued.
Munn, W. C., Co. (g).
*Palmer & Co., E. C., Ltd.
Parrish Book Store (b, c).
Pillot, T., Co. (b, c, s).
Rouse Drug Store (d).
*Southern Drug Co. (d).
*Southwestern Paper Co.
Standard Ptg. and Litho. Co.
Swartz, R. H., Co. (c).
Teetshorn Co. (b).

HUNTSVILLE, 2072.
King, J. R. (b, d).
Nauer & Co., V. S. (d).
Rudolph & Ernst (j, s).

LA GRANGE, 1850.
Hermes, W., Jr. (d).
Meyenberg, J. (d).

LAREDO, 22,000.
City Drug Co.
Herrera's Pharmacy (d).
Horner, G. C.
Laredo Novelty Co.
Richter, Aug. C. (g).
Windrew Drug Co. (d).

LOCKHART, 2945.
McDannald & Co., C. E. (d)
Ploeger, C. A. (d).

MARSHALL, 11,452.
Fry-Hodge Drug Co. (d).

MEXIA, 4165.
Roller, H. C. (d).

MOUNT PLEASANT, 3500.
Stephens, Chas. S. (d).
Wallace Drug Store (b, j).

NEW BRAUNFELS, 4000.
Voelcker, B. E., & Son (b, d, s).

ORANGE, 5527.
Griggs, W. C. (b).

PALESTINE, 10,482.
City Drug Store.
Douthit, Leland (d).
Hamilton Bros. (c).
Palestine Ptg. Co.
Swift & Hombs.

PARIS, 11,269.
Alexander Book Co. (b)
*Bennett Printing Co.
Crook-Record Co. (g).
Greiner & Mohr (d).
Murphy, R. J. (d).

TEXAS.

PARIS—*Continued.*
　Palace Drug Co. (d).
　Williams-Coffee Drug Co.
PORT ARTHUR, 7663.
　Corner Drug Co.
　Harris Book Store.
ROCKDALE, 2073.
　Hill & Co. (b, j).
ROSEBUD, 1472.
　Monroe & Blasieuz.
　Rosebud Drug Store (d).
RUSK, 1588.
　Odom & Moseley (d).
SAN ANGELO, 10,321.
　Potter, J. E. (b).
SAN ANTONIO, 115,063.
　Acme Book & Cigar Co.
　*Alling Paper Co. (b).
　American Stationery Co. (c).
　Block's Book Store.
　Joske Bros. Co. (b, g).
　Louis Book & Cigar Co.
　*Maverick-Clarke Litho Co. (c).
　Moos, Henry A. (b).
　Roe, Geo. (b).
　*San Antonio Drug Co.
　San Antonio Ptg. Co.
　*Tengg, Nic. (b).
　Texas Blue Print Co.
　Wolff & Marx Co. (b, g).
SAN MARCOS, 4071.
　Glasscock Drug Co.
　Lewis, Mrs. F. (b).
SANTA ANNA, 1453.
　Phillips, S. H. (d).
SHERMAN, 17,943.
　Reynolds-Parker Co.
STEPHENVILLE, 4000.
　Cross Drug Store (d).
　Livingstone, A. D. (s).
　Perry Bros. (d).
　White Drug Co. (b, d).
SULPHUR SPRINGS, 5151.
　Long & Burns.

TAYLOR, 6000.
　Thames, J. J., Drug Co. (b, d).
TEMPLE, 16,500.
　Temple Book Concern.
TERRELL, 7050.
　Griffith & Co., L. R. (b, d).
TEXARKANA, 15,445.
　De Fee & Adams (d).
TYLER, 14,943.
　Bryans Book Store.
　Byrne Pub. Co.
VICTORIA, 3673.
　Cooke, W. E.
WACO, 35,573.
　Armstrong & Pfaeffle (j).
　*Behrens Drug Co.
　Carter's Drug Store.
　Colgin, W. E. (d).
　Craddock, C. Y. (b).
　Goldstein & Migel Co. (g).
　Hers Bros. (b).
　Hill Printing & Staty. Co.
　Jurney Drug Co. (d).
　Namans (j).
　Old Corner Drug Store (d).
　Power-Kelley Drug Co. (d).
　*Sanger Bros. (g).
　Smith, Norman H., & Co. (b).
　*Standard Ptg. Co.
　Stetler, O. K. (d).
　Waco Drug Co. (d).
　Wilkins & Foreman (d).
WICHITA FALLS, 10,769.
　Martin, J. H. (b).
　Miller's Drug Store (d).
　Palace Drug Store.
YOAKUM, 4657.
　Koerth Bros. (d).
　Palace Drug Store (d).
　Quality Pharmacy (d).
　Shropshire Co.
　Toland, Wm.
　Weyman Drug Co.
　Yoakum Book Store.
YORKTOWN, 1800.
　Riedel, M., & Son (d).

UTAH.

BINGHAM CANYON, 2881.
　Bingham Merc. Co. (g).
　Geffen, A. (j).
　James, M. L.
　Watson Drug Co. (d).

BINGHAM CANYON—*Continued.*
　Woodring Drug Co. (d).
BRIGHAM, 3685.
　Horsley, J. H., Book Co.

UTAH.

EPHRAIM, 2296.
Anderson, D. W., & Co.
Odell & Co.

LOGAN, 7522.
Agricultural College (b).
City Drug Co.
Coop Drug Co.
Earl & England Pub. Co.
Howell Cardon Co. (g).
Riter Bros. Drug Co.
Smith, J. P., & Sons (c).
Wilkinson & Son (b).

OGDEN, 35,000.
Bramwell Book & Stationery Co.
Carr, T. H. (d).
Cave, G. F.
Culley Drug Co.
De Witt Bros.
Ensign Drug Co.
Lowe Bros.
Marshall Drug Co.
McBride Drug Co.
McIntyre, A. R.
Ogden Book & Curio Co.
Spargo, James H. (b).
Tabernacle Pharmacy.
Wright, W. H., & Sons Co. (g).

PARK CITY, 2439.
Blyth, Fargo Co. (g).
Jefford, W. R. (b).
Welch, Driscoll & Buck (g).

PAYSON, 2397.
Modern Pharmacy.

PAYSON—Continued.
Ott, B. F.
Page, J. S., Jr. (b).

PROVO, 8925.
Columbia Music & Jewelry Co.
Dangerfield, J. W. (b).
Enterprise Music & Staty. Co.
Provo Drug Co.
Hedquist Drug Co.
*Taylor Paper Co.

SALT LAKE CITY, 110,000.
Arrow Press, The.
Callahan, D. A. (b).
Dayton Drug Co., W. H. (d).
Desert News Book Store (b).
Druehl & Franken (d).
Held Engraving Co.
Keith-O'Brien Co. (g).
Kelly Co.
*Lambert Paper Co.
*McMillen Paper & School Supplies.
Owl Drug Co. (d).
Pembroke Co. (c, s).
Schramm-Johnson (d).
Shield Stationery Co.
*Smith-Faus Drug Co.
Walker Bros. Dry Goods Co. (g).
*Western Newspaper Union.
*Zion's Co-operative Mercantile Institution.

SPRINGVILLE, 3356.
Jordan, E. N.

VERMONT.

BARRE, 10734.
Drown, E. A. (d).
Martin, Carroll W. (b).

BARTON, 1330.
*New England Paper Co.

BELLOWS FALLS, 4883.
Fuller, A. H. (d).
Winnewisser, F. C.

BENNINGTON, 6211.
Eddy, Almon (b).
Evans, Joseph A. (b).
Griswold, E. T. (b).

BETHEL, 1943.
Miller, G. M. (d).

BRANDON, 1606.
Leffinwell, W. C.
Ray, C. E. (s).

BRATTLEBORO, 6517.
Brattleboro News Co.
*Clapp & Jones (b).

BURLINGTON, 20,468.
Abernathy, F. D. (g).
Ahern, T. F.
Bellrose, J. G. (d).
Bessey, C. H. (b).
Churchhill, G. A. (d).
Clarkson, E. E., Co. (b, g).
Combination Cash Store Co. (g).
Free Press Printing Co.
*McAuliffe Paper Co. (c).
O'Sullivan, J. W. (d).
*Shanley, H. J., & Co. (b).
Stearns, R. B., & Co. (d).
Zottman, W. H., Co. (d).

CHELSEA, 1074.
Buck, Guy A. (d).

Wholesale and Retail Stationers.

VERMONT.

FAIR HAVEN, 2554.
  Hughes, Carl.
GRAFTON, 719.
  Hall, T. S.
LUDLOW, 1621.
  Agan, W. H.
  Coolidge, D. G.
MIDDLEBURY, 1866.
  Rich, C. F. (j).
MONTPELIER, 7856.
  Argus & Patriot Co.
  Buswell, C. F. (b).
  Sequin, E. T.
NEWPORT, 2548.
  Hildreth, D. W.
NORTHFIELD, 1918.
  Huntley, E., Co.
RUTLAND, 13,546.
  Chalmers, Geo. E. (b).
  *Sawyer, H. A., Co., Inc.
  *Tuttle, The, Co.
SPRINGFIELD, 3250.
  Wheeler W. H., & Son (d, j).

ST. ALBANS, 6381.
  Alexander, E. J. (d).
  Royce, E. H.
  Smith, Avery (d).
ST. JOHNSBURY, 6693.
  Caledonian Co., The.
  Cowles, The, Press.
  Eastman, W. B. (d).
  Flint Bros. (d).
  Randall & Whitcomb (j).
  Randall, E. N. (g).
  Stiles, Don C. (b).
  Taylor, Fred W. (b).
VERGENNES, 1483.
  Neville, T. (d).
WHITE RIVER JUNCTION, 2600.
  *White River Paper Co. (b).
WINDSOR, 1906.
  Ephlin, Chas. J. (b).
WINOOSKI, 4520.
  Crandell, E. R. (d).
  Siegel, Alex. (j).
WOODSTOCK, 1383.
  Clough, W. D. (d).

VIRGINIA.

ABINGDON, 1862.
  Barbee, M. A. (j).
ALEXANDRIA, 15,329.
  Bell, Robert, & Sons (c).
  Dienelt, J. A. (d).
  *Dyson, S. F., & Bro. (c. s).
  Gibson, Richard (d).
  Knight, R. E., & Son (b).
BEDFORD CITY, 2508.
  Heller, F. F.
  Lyle, W. L. (d).
BRISTOL (See under Tennessee).
  Bunting & Sons (d).
  Kemble-Cochran Co., Inc. (c).
  Minor Drug Co. (d).
  Turner Drug Co. (d).
CHARLOTTESVILLE, 6765.
  Anderson Bros. (b).
  Brechin, A. C., & Son (b).
  Jarman Book Co.
  Oliver, Geo. W. (b).
  University Book Store.

CHATHAM, 1200.
  Chatham Pharmacy.
  Hunt, Jno. P.
  Thompson Drug Co.
CLIFTON FORGE, 5748.
  City Book Store.
  Cliff Drug Co.
  Farrar, G. M. (d).
  Salles, J.
COVINGTON, 4234.
  Covington News & Music Co.
CULPEPER, 1795.
  Goldsborough, Chas. H. (d).
  Latham, J. F.
  Macoy, R. B. (d).
  *Merchants' Grocery Co., Inc.
DANVILLE, 29,750.
  Danville Book & Sta. Co.
  Parker, J. F. (b).
FREDERICKSBURG, 5874.
  Adams, J. W. (b).
  Bond, W. L. (d).
  Goslrick, K. N. (d).
  Kishpaugh, R. A. (b).

VIRGINIA.

FRONT ROYAL, 1133.
  Poulton, E. D. (b).

HAMPTON, 6650.
  Palmer, Chas. H., Jr.
  Standard Book & Staty. Co.

HARRISONBURG, 4879.
  Baugher, P. H.
  City 5 and 10c. Co.
  Ott Drug Co.
  Vendo 5 and 10c. Co.
  Williamson Drug Co.

LEESBURG, 1597.
  Jackson & Pleasants (b).

LEXINGTON, 2931.
  Boley's Book Store.
  McCrum Drug Co.

LYNCHBURG, 29,494.
  *Bell Co., The J. P. (b).
  Moore Staty. Co.
  Strother Drug Co. (d).

NEWPORT NEWS, 20,205.
  Burcher & Burcher (d).
  Epes Stationery Co., Inc.
  Klor, A. E. G. (d).
  Meyers Bros., Inc. (g).
  Morton, Alice W., Book Co., Inc., (c, s).

NORFOLK, 67,452.
  *Andrews, R. P., Paper Co.
  Atlantic Book Store (b).
  Broulette, P. H. (b).
  Freeman, Wm.
  *Hampton Roads Paper Co.
  Miller, Rhodes & Swarts (g).
  Norfolk Stationery Co.
  Nusbaum Book and Art Co. (b).
  *Old Dominion Paper Co.
  Shafer's Book & Stationery Store.
  Watt, Rettew & Clay (g).

PETERSBURG, 24,127.
  Armstrong, W. E., & Co. (d).
  Beckwith, T. S., & Co., Inc. (b).
  Burgess Paper Co.
  Franklin Press Co., Inc. (c).
  Frey, W. H. (d).
  Lum Bros. (d).
  Totty, R. R. (d).

PHOEBUS, 2094.
  Brown, F. M.
  Brown, L. M.

PORTSMOUTH, 65,000.
  Parker Railway News Co.
  Virginia Paper & Art Co., Inc.

RICHMOND, 153,500.
  Abbott, James T., & Son.
  *Baughman Stationery Co.
  *Bell Book & Stat'y Co., The (b).
  Cohen Co. (g).
  *Consolidated Paper & Box Mfg. Co.
  Cowardin, W. H., & Sons (j).
  Fourqurean-Temple Co. (g).
  Hunter & Co. (b).
  Miller & Rhodes, Inc. (g).
  Myer's Book Store (b).
  Owens & Minor Drug Co. (d).
  Powers-Taylor Co. (d).
  Presbyterian Committee Publication (b).
  Purdle, J. A., & Co. (b).
  Reinach & Schwartz, Inc.
  Southern Stamp & Staty. Co.
  Tragle Drug Co. (d).
  Vaughan-Robertson Drug Co. (d).
  Virginia School Supply Co.
  Virginia Stationery Co.
  Waddey, Everett Co.

ROANOKE, 34,874.
  *Caldwell-Sites Co., The (b).
  Heironimus, S. H., Co. (g).
  MacBain, Geo., Co. (g).
  Roanoke Book & Stationery Co.
  Van Lear Bros.

SALEM, 4849.
  Magee, C. H., & Co.

STAUNTON, 10,604.
  Bell, F. W., & Co. (d).
  *Beverly Book Co., Inc. (b, s, o. s.).
  Bratton & Bratton.
  Bryan, E. M., & Son.
  Hogshead, Thos. (d).
  Virginia Pharmacy.
  Wilson Bros.

UNIVERSITY OF VIRGINIA, 1000.
  University Book Store.

WINCHESTER, 5864.
  Baker, Frank, & Son (d).

WYTHEVILLE, 3003.
  Moore & Co. (b).
  Owens & Owens (d).

WASHINGTON.

ABERDEEN, 15,330.
Aberdeen Drug Co.
Beckenhauer Drug Co. (d).
Benson Office Supply Co.
Broadway Pharmacy (d).
Eaton & Swany (d).
Evans Drug Co. (d).
Liberty Drug Co.
Red Cross Pharmacy (d).

BELLINGHAM, 31,143.
Engberg's Pharmacy (d).
Graham Drug Co.
*Griggs Stationery & Printing Co., Inc. (c, s).
Mathes Book Co., E. T. (b).
Nattrass, J. C. (d).
Offerman, F. P. (d).
Sun Drug Co., Inc.
*Union Printing & Stationery Co. (c).

BLAINE, 2389.
Hawkins, J. Q. (b).

BREMERTON, 2993.
Bremerton Drug Co. (d).
Cork's Pioneer Pharmacy.
Diamond Pharmacy.
Fetterman's Drug Store.
King's Drug Store.
Ward's Book Store and Music House.

CENTRALIA, 7311.
Hackett, W. H. (d).
Shuler, E. E. (d).
Stahl Drug Co.
White & Gabel (b).
Young Drug Co. (d).

CHEHALIS, 4507.
Ellsworth Drug Store (d).
Lewellin's Pharmacy (d).
Marr, Herbert W. (d).
Prigmore & Sears (d).
Taylor, M. F., Co. (b, c, s).
White & Gabel (b, c, s).

COLFAX, 2783.
King's Book Store (s).

DAYTON, 2389.
Wall, W. L. (d).

ELLENBURG, 5000.
Ellwood, H. S. (d).
Perry Drug Store.
Risslers Pharmacy.
Wheeler & Craig (b).

EVERETT, 24,814.
Black & King (c).
Bridgham, M. H. (c, s).
Hawes, K. L., Inc. (c).
Quaker Drug & Book Store, The (b).

LEAVENWORTH, 2500.
Koerner, John (d).
Wheeler, E. G. (d).

MONTESANO, 2468.
Moffitt, Antonio.

MT. VERNON, 2381.
Hall, D. B. (d, s).
Hall, Frank A. (c).
Nailor, Elmer C. (d, s).
Ropes, W. B. (b).

NORTH YAKIMA, 14,082.
Beaumont, Jr., Geo. E. (s).
Bradbury (The) Co. (b).

OLYMPIA, 6996.
Bookstore, The (b, s).

POMEROY, 1608.
Kuykendall, C. E. (d).

PORT ANGELES, 3000.
Dale, Carl S.
Mathewson, W. J. (d).

PORT TOWNSEND, 4181.
Hill, N. D., & Sons (d).
Rutz Pharmacy, The (d).

PULLMAN, 2603.
Corner Drug Store.
Davis Drug & Stationery Co.
Students (The) Book Co.
Watts, G. H. (d).
White's Drug Store.

PUYALLUP, 4544.
Gray, S. P. (s).
Truedson Drug Co. (d, s, c).

REPUBLIC, 1200.
Basinski, Simon.

SEATTLE, 313,029.
Allen, Pliny L., Co.
*American Paper Co.
Bartell Drug Co. (d).
Bon Marche (g).
*Fales, J. W., Paper Co.
Fraser, Patterson Co. (g).
Frederick & Nelson (g).
Griffin, E. M., & Co. (o. s.).
Gillam & Bird Co. (c).

INVESTIGATIONS REPORTS INSPECTIONS
C. A. CHAPMAN, Inc.
14 E. JACKSON BLVD.　ENGINEERS　CHICAGO

Wholesale and Retail Stationers　589

WASHINGTON.

SEATTLE—*Continued.*
Guy, Geo. O. (d).
Justice Staty. Co. (c).
*Lowman & Hanford Co.
MacDougall & Southwick (g).
Morey Stationery Co.
*Mutual Paper Co. (c).
Owl Drug Co.
*Paper Warehouse Co.
*Puget Sound News Co. (b).
Rhodes Bros. (g).
*Richmond Paper Co.
*Seattle Paper Co.
Smith Drug Co. (d).
Society Staty. Shop.
Stanley, A. J. (s).
Trick & Murray, Inc. (c).
Wilson, F. B.
Wilson-McVay Co.
Wolter Stationery Co.

SPANGLE, 299.
Sullivan, Mrs. M. H.

SPOKANE, 104,402.
Coates-Hughes Printing Co.
Cubbertson-Grote-Rankin Co.
Demert Drug & Chemical Co.
Ewing, B. G., Co.
Feise, Henry (b).
*Graham, J. W., & Co. (b).
*Gray, Ewing & Co.
Kemp & Hebert (g).
Kershaw, F. L.
Murgittroyd's Drug Store.
Ritter's Drug Store.
Shaw & Borden Co. (c, s).
Spokane Dry Goods Co. (g).

SPOKANE—*Continued.*
*Spokane Drug Co. (d).
Spokane Office Supply Co.
The Palace (g).
Whitehouse Co. (g).

SUNNYSIDE, 1400.
Brown, F. W.
Miller, A.
Pioneer Pharmacy (d).

TACOMA, 103,418.
Berg, Walter, Stationery Co.
Cole-Martin Co.
Gibson, Chas. P.
Pioneer Bindery & Printing Co.
Pirret, P. K., & Co. (c).
Rhodes Bros., Inc. (g).
Rosenburg, Chas.
*Standard Paper Co.
Stone-Fisher Co. (g).
*Tacoma Paper & Stationery Co.

TOPPENISH, 2500.
Stephenson, Geo.

VANCOUVER, 13,180.
Vancouver Stationery Co.

WALLA WALLA, 19,364.
Book Nook, The.
Clark & Crecelius.
Crescent Drug Store.
Smalley, E. L. (d).
Thompson, F. B.

WENATCHEE, 5000.
Armstrong, C. H.

WEST VIRGINIA.

BELINGTON, 2000.
Graham, Grant (d).

BLUEFIELD, 11,188.
Central Art & Sta. Co. (b).
Curtis-Pearson Co. (b).
East End Pharmacy (d).
Kleiman, Philip (b).
White Pharmacy, The (d).

CHARLESTON, 22,996.
*Abney, Barnes & Co. (g).
Coffey, C. I. (b).
*Kanawha Drug Co.
Moore, The S. Spencer, Co. (b).

CHARLESTOWN, 2662.
Beard, O. N.

CLARKSBURG, 9201.
Arena, Antonio.
Bland, F. G. (d).
Burke, H. F. (d).
*Clarksburg Drug Co. (d).
Dent's Drug Store.
Farrell's Drug Store.
Harrison, Chas. R. (d).
Nusbaum, I., & Son.
Stone & Mercer (d).
Sturm & Wilson (d).
The James & Law Co. (b).
Waldo Drug Store (d).
Wells & Haymaker (d).

ELKINS, 5260.
Elder, J. H.

APPLETON MACHINE CO., APPLETON, WIS.
REFINING ENGINES, SCREENS, SAWING & SPLITTING MACHINERY
HIGH GRADE **CENTRIFUGAL PUMPS**

MINER EDGAR CO., Sole Agents
KEYSTONE CLAY & REDUCTION CO.
30 Church Street　　　New York
CLAY
PRECIPITATED REFINED
LIGHT GRAVITY SOFT TEXTURE
<K L M>
HIGH NATURAL COLOR, HIGH RETENTION

WISCONSIN.

KENOSHA—Continued.
  Ernst, C. H., & Co. (o. s.).
  Glerum Book Store.
  Pitts, J. A.
  Robinson, W. H.

LA CROSSE, 30,417.
  de Ranitz, S. J., & Co. (c, s).
  de Ranitz, Theo. (c, s).
  Doerflinger Co., Wm. (g).
  Hebbard & Co. (d).
  Hoeschler Bros. (b).
  Inland Printing Co. (c, s).
  La Crosse News Co. (b).
  Mariner, G. E. (d).
  Norlke, C. B. (s).
  Partridge, H. D., & Co. (d).
  *Spence-McCord Drug Co.
  Weis, Charles L. (b).

LAKE GENEVA, 3079.
  Arnold, R. B. (b, d).

LANCASTER, 2408.
  Bennett, J. T. (b, d).
  Hatch, J. D. (b, d).
  Wheeler, L. G. (b).

MADISON, 25,531.
  Menges, A. F. (d).
  *Morris, T. S., Co.
  Moseley Book Co.
  *Netherwood, H. C., Ptg. Co.
  Ott, H. S. (d).
  Sumner, Edwin, & Son (d).
  University Co-operative Co. (b).
  University Supply Assn.
  Williams, Ed. (d).

MANITOWOC, 13,027.
  Bigel & Son, J. (b).
  *Schmidtman's, Theo., Sons Co.

MARINETTE, 14,610.
  Krueger, E. B. (d).
  Lauerman Bros. Co. (g).
  Lundgren, V. A.
  McDonald, R. A. (d).
  Peterson, John S. (d).
  Schulz, Wm. F. (d).

MENASHA, 6081.
  Rosch, John (d).

MERRILL, 8659.
  Braun, Aug. (d).
  Mead, Fred L. (b, s, c).

MILWAUKEE, 378,857.
  Andreucetti, F., 519 Chestnut (b).
  Oneida (b).

MILWAUKEE—Continued.
  Biersach, Albert, 315 Third (b).
  Boston Store (g).
  Brown, H. W., & Co.
  Bunde & Uppmeyer Co. (j).
  Burghardt, Chas. A. & Sons, 59 Oneida
  Caspar, Carl N., Co., 454 E. Water (b).
  Chapman Co., T. A., 123 Wisconsin (g).
  Des Forges & Co., 108 Wisconsin (b).
  Gimbel Bros., 3 Grand av. (g).
  Gray Co., Ltd., T. S., 104 Wisconsin (b).
  Higgins, Edw., Co., 321 Grand av. (b).
  Koster, Albert, & Co., 123 Wisconsin.
  Kroeger Bros. Co., 421 National av. (g).
  Lingeman, F. J., Co., 62 Macon.
  Miller, H. C., Co., 342 Broadway (c).
  Milwaukee Drug Co., 141 Michigan (d).
  Moser & Maves, 312 B'way.
  *Niedecken, The H., Co., 387 E. Water.
  Northwestern Publishing House, 263 4th.
  Schuster, Ed., & Co., 3d and Harmon, 3d and Garfield (g).
  Siekert & Baum Stat'y Co., 381 E. Water (c).
  *Smith, F. G., & Co., 324 E. Water.
  South Side Book Store, 316 Grove.
  Sullivan, Henry, Eng. Co., 111 Wisconsin.
  Thielke Stationery House, 905 First National Bk. Bldg. (c).
  West, H. H., Co., 389 E. Water (c).
  *Wisconsin News Co., 306 E. Water.

MINERAL POINT, 3500.
  Hanscom, J. J., & Co. (b).

MOUNT HOREB, 364.
  Brager, J. H. (j).

NEENAH, 6134.
  Barnett, M. E., & Co. (d).
  Elwers, Fred. (d).
  Marsh Bros. (d).
  Shultz Bros. (d).

NEW LONDON, 3288.
  Trayser & Co. (d).

WISCONSIN.

OCONTO, 5629.
Ford, S. W. (d).
Luckenbach, Walter (d).
Young, L. M. (d).
White Cross Pharmacy.

OSHKOSH, 33,062.
*Baker Paper Co.
Bauman Co. (d).
Brennan, J. (d).
Church Bros. (g).
Coe, J. A. (d).
Henderson-Hoyt Co.
Horn, E. A. (d).
Huhn, J. (b).
*Medberry-Findeisen Co.
Mueller Drug Co. (d).
Ryckman, A. D. (b).

PLATTEVILLE, 4452.
Bishop, M. A. & Co. (b).
Gilmore, C. E. (b).

PORTAGE, 5440.
Graham, John (d).

RACINE, 38,002.
Christoffel, J. J. (b).
Ditmann, Wm., & Son (b).
Gieseler's Pharmacy.
Hansen & Son, L. P.
Heck Drug Co.
*Kranz, W. H., Co.
North Side Drug Store (d).
Pokorney Drug Store Co. (d).
Red Cross Drug Co., 5 stores (d).
Stokes City Drug Store (d).
White, Miss S. H. (b).
Wooster, Park (b).

REEDSBURG, 2615.
Mueller-Henry Drug Co. (d).

RHINELANDER, 5637.
Hinman & Co., F. L. (d).
Kretlow, Frank E. (d).
McRae, K. M.
Maxwell, C. R. (b, g).
Reardon, J. J. (d).
Reed, E. H.

RICHLAND CENTRE, 2670.
Burnham, J. W., & Son (b, d).
Luckey, Geo.

RIPON, 3511.
Burnside, E. J. (b, d).
Diedrich, W. F. (b, d).

RIVER FALLS, 1991.
Freeman, R. S., & Co. (d).
Gevers & Weld (b).
Taggart, C. R. (d).

SHEBOYGAN, 26,398.
Bock Drug Co. (d).
Bruhn Drug Co. (d).
Christiansen, C., & Co.
Hoppe, Fred (d).
Jung, J. & W., Co. (g).
Kuener, Adolph (b).
Northside Drug Co. (d).
Office Supply Co.
Prange Co., H. C. (g).
Roenitz Drug Co. (d).
Schraut, Oscar.
Thomas, I. C., & Co. (d).
Zimmerman, E. F. W. (b).
Zimmerman-Witt Co. (c).

SOUTH MILWAUKEE, 6092.
Bergmann, H. F. (d).
Whalen's Book & Stationery Store.

SPARTA, 8793.
Seidel, Geo. H. (d, b).
Williams, E. R. (b).

SPRING GREEN, 621.
Conell, W. G.

STEVENS POINT, 8692.
Christenson, O. H. (g).
French, Campbell & Co. (b).
Hannan & Bach (d).
Krembs, Jr., Alex., Drug Co., Inc. (d).
McCulloch, H. D., Co., Ltd. (b, d).
Taylor Bros. (d).

STOUGHTON, 4761.
Falk, F. N. (d).

SUPERIOR, 40,384.
*Chamberlain, J. F., & Co. (b).
Friis, C. (d).
Johnson & Co.
Lightbody & Wingate Co. (g).
Mast, R. C.
Opera House Drug Co. (d).
Priest, Floyd D. (d).
Roen, Thomas.
Roth Bros. Co. (g).
Russell Bros.
Ryan Pharmacy (d, s).
Scanlon, D.
*Twin Ports Paper Co.

FELTS AND JACKETS | Appleton Woolen Mills
APPLETON - - WIS.

Wholesale and Retail Stationers

WISCONSIN.

TOMAH, 3419.
  Palmer & Austin (b).
TWO RIVERS, 4550.
  Kirst, C. F. (d).
  Stephany, J. K. (d).
  Stockmeyer, O. C. (d).
WATERTOWN, 8829.
  Bittner & Tetzlaff (d).
  Eberle, H. T. (d).
  Gamm Corner Drug Store (d).
  Gehrke, Wm. (d).
  Gruetzmacher, W. F. (g).
  Heyn, Otto (b).
  Ryan's Book Store.
  Salick, Chas. J. (j).
  Schempf Bros. Co. (g).
  Sproesser Co., W. D. (j).
  Stapleton, E. M. (d).
WAUKESHA, 8740.
  Hoeveler Drug Co. (d).

WAUPUN, 3155.
  Hunter, M. M. (b, d).
  McConochie, H. B. (b).

WAUSAU, 16,650.
  Albers, W. W. (d).
  Collie, R. J. (b, c, s).
  Heinemann Dept. Store (g).
  *Kickbush Grocery Co.
  Ploss Drug Co. (d).
  Pradel, Geo. (d).
  Rohde, Julius (b, c, s).
  Schmidt, W. (d).
  Welchman Pharmacy.
  Winkleman Dept. Store.

WEST BEND, 2350.
  *Schowalter Book Store.

WHITEWATER, 3405.
  O'Connor, H. J. (d).

WYOMING.

CHEYENNE, 15,564.
  Barry, J. P.
  Klein's Stationery & Music Store.
  Logan, E. (s).
  Palace Pharmacy.
  Roedell, Andy E., Drug Co. (d).
  Roedell, Fred., Drug Co. (d).
  Sands Drug Co.
  Wyoming Book Store Co.
DOUGLAS, 2246.
  Barrow, Mrs. M. F.
EVANSTON, 4000.
  Cashin, Frank.
  Evanston Drug Co.
  Rex, A. G.

LARAMIE, 10,000.
  Eggleston Drug Co. (d).
  Sitter, Wm. G.

RAWLINS, 4256.
  Kelly, Fred.
  Rawlins Drug Co.

ROCK SPRINGS, 5778.
  Kellogg & Holmes.

SHERIDAN, 12,000.
  Brown Drug Co.
  Coffeen, H. A.
  Jackson Book & Stationery Co.

JAMES H. HARRISON
'ULPSTONE MANUFACTURER | GENUINE NEWCASTLE STONES
18 Killowen St., GATESHEAD-ON-TYNE

INVESTIGATIONS REPORTS INSPECTIONS
C. A. CHAPMAN, Inc.
26 E. JACKSON BLVD. ENGINEERS CHICAGO

DOMINION OF CANADA

ALBERTA.

ALIX, 267.
Shore, A. E.

ATHABASKA LANDING, 500.
Cull, H. F. (b, d).

BASSANO, 540.
Stiles, J. H. (b, d).

BLAIRMORE, 1187.
Blairmore Pharmacy.

CALGARY, 75,000.
*Barber-Ellis-Davis, Ltd.
Calgary Notion Co.
Hudson Bay Co., First, W.
Hughes, Robert H.
Linton Bros., 120 Eighth av., E.
*Martin Paper Co., Ltd., Ninth av., W.
McDermid Drug Co. (d).
McFarlane Drug Co. (d).
McEwen Drug Store.
Oliver Bros., Ltd. (d).
*Osborne, F. E., 112 Eighth av., W.
Palmer, J. A., 325 Eighth av.
Pearson, A. E., 216 Eighth av., E.
*Stanley Paper Co., Eighth, W.
West & Brown, Armstrong Bldg. (c).
Wilson Stat'y Co., Eighth, W. (c).
Wilson, L. C.
Young, D. J., & Co., Ltd., 715 First, W.

CAMROSE, 1550.
Camrose Drug Co.

CARMANGAY, 287.
Follis, E. O.

CLARESHOLM, 1250.
Reinecke, O. L. (d).

CONSORT, 125.
Consort Drug Store.

DAYSLAND, 500.
Burrows, J. H. (d).
Daysland Press.

DIDSBURY, 726.
Chambers, H. W. (d).

EDBERG, 50.
Young's (d).

EDMONTON, 70,000.
Archibald, A., 313 Jasper av., E. (d).
Armstrong, G. S., 435 Namayo av. (d).
Edmonton Law Stat's, Ltd.
Empire Book Store.
*Esche, H. H., & Co., Ltd., cor. Jasper av. and 4th.
Hudson Bay Co. (g).
Hutton, J. D., 40 Whyte av., W.
Kennedy, E. N., Co.
Ramsay & Co., James (g).
Revillon Wholesale Co., Ltd.
Robertson, The, Safe & Typewriter Co.
Smith, A. C., 744 First.
Willson Staty. Co., Ltd.

EDSON, 250.
Switzer, H. A., & Co. (d).

FORT SASKATCHEWAN, 900.
Southerland, A. M.

GADSBY, 213.
Hart, H. A. (d).

GAHERN.
Ahern, H. G. (s).

GLEICHEN, 588.
Yates, A. R.

HANNA, 300.
Red Cross Drug Store.
Johnston, C. P.

HIGH RIVER, 1182.
Eversfield & Blair (d.

MINER EDGAR CO., Sole Agents
KEYSTONE CLAY & REDUCTION CO.
30 Church Street - - New York
C L A Y
PRECIPITATED REFINED
LIGHT GRAVITY SOFT TEXTURE
<K L M>
HIGH NATURAL COLOR, HIGH RETENTI

FELTS AND JACKETS | Appleton Woolen Mills, APPLETON - - WIS.

Wholesale and Retail Stationers

ALBERTA.

INNISFREE.
  Bethune, A. W. (d).

LACOMBE, 1029.
  Creighton, A.
  McDermid Drug Co.

LETHBRIDGE, 8050.
  *Campbell, Wilson & Horne, Ltd.
  Everall & Franks.
  Hedley, Frank, Drug Co.
  Kenny & Allen.
  *Macdonald, A., & Co., Ltd.
  Printers & Stationers (o. s.).
  Red Cross Drug & Book Co., Ltd.
  Robertson, J. G., & Co.

MACLEOD, 1844.
  Barnes, R. B.
  McNay, R. D.

MAGRATH, 995.
  Fletcher, Ira. C. (d).
  Magrath Trading Co.

MEDICINE HAT, 1500.
  Alberta Book Co.
  Cawker, E. M.
  Pingle, Chas. S.
  Rainbow, C. W.
  Souch, Gordon P.

MORINVILLE, 400.
  Roper, Wright (d).

NANTON, 871.
  Nanton Drug Co.

PINCHER CREEK, 1027.
  McCrea, D. L.
  Tucker, S. A.

PONOKA, 642.
  Campbell Drug Co.

RAYMOND, 1465.
  Blair, Wm., & Co.

REDCLIFF, 1200.
  Blundell, J. P. (c, s).

RED DEER, 2118.
  Gaetz Cornett Drug & Book Co., Ltd.
  McVicar, John.
  Standard Drug Co.

RETLAW, 107.
  McNab, P. W. (d).

SEDGEWICK, 250.
  Purvis, H. S. (d).

STONY PLAIN, 265.
  Oatway, R. M.

STRATHMORE, 531.
  Lambert, E. W. R., & Co.

TABER, 1400.
  Taber Drug & Stationery Co., Ltd.
  Westake's Jewelry & Stationery Store.

VEGREVILLE, 1100.
  Lang, F. J. (d).
  Vegreville Drug & Book Co., The.
  Worth, I. D. (j, s).

VERMILION, 850.
  Brimacombe Bros.
  Hassard, H. C. (d).
  Long, F. C.

WAINWRIGHT, 1000.
  Lush, Frank (b).
  Red Cross Pharmacy.
  Wainwright Pharmacy.

WETASKIWIN, 2200.
  Enman, C. D. (b).
  Liversidge, A. H. (b).

YOUNGSTOWN, 500.
  Ramage, H. E. (d).

BRITISH COLUMBIA.

ABBOTSFORD, 500.
  Weir, E. T.

ARMSTRONG, 1000.
  Abbott, E. T. (d).
  Best, Herbert S.

ASHCROFT, 500.
  Huston, W. M.

CHILLIWACK, 3000.
  Barber, H. J.

CRANBROOK, 2090.
  Beattie, Murphy & Co., Ltd.
  Cranbrook Drug & Book Co., Ltd.

CRESTON, 400.
  Creston Drug & Book Co.

BLOTTING PAPERS STANDARD PAPER MFG. CO., Richmond, Va.
Largest Manufacturers

BRITISH COLUMBIA.

CUMBERLAND, 2000.
King, Mrs. Alex.
McLean, T. D.
Peacey, A. H.

DUNCANS, 1200.
Duncan Pharmacy.
Prevost, H. F. (b).

EBURNE, 800.
McGinness, J. W.
Wilson, H. R. (b, d).

ENDERBY, 700.
Reeves, A.

FERNIE, 2146.
Bleasdell, A. W. (b, d).
McLean Drug and Book, Ltd.
Suddaby, N. E. (b, d).

FORT FRASER.
Fort Fraser Drug Co.
Nechako Drug Co. (d).

GOLDEN, 1000.
Buckham, J. A.

GRAND FORKS, 1700.
Petrie, Robert F.
Woodland & Co. (b, d).

HAZELTON, 500.
Wrinch, Horace C.

HEDLEY, 200.
Baxter, R. E. (d).

KAMLOOPS, 4500.
Clements, J. H.
Cliffe, J. B., & Co.
Taylor, A. C., & Co.

KASLO, 500.
Abey, Frank T. (d).

KELOWNA, 2200.
Crawford & Co.
Trench, W. R., & Co. (b, d).
Willets, P. B., & Co. (b, d).

LADNER, 1000.
Fisher, S. W.

LADYSMITH, 2500.
Hughes & Hayes.
Knight, J. A.

MERRITT, 1500.
Rankine, A. F.

MISSION CITY, 1000.
Stephen, A.

NAKUSP, 400.
McLean, E. H. S. (d).

NANAIMO, 10,000.
Hodgins, The, J. B., Ltd. (d).
Jephson Bros.
Van Houton, A. C.

NELSON, 6000.
Canada Drug & Book Co., Ltd.
City Drug & Stat. Co.
Hickingbottom, R. L. (b).
Stanley, Mrs. E. J. (b).

NEW DENVER, 250.
Nelson, Chas. F.

NEW WESTMINSTER, 16,000.
Burr, The, Office Supplies and Blue Ptg. Co.
Fair, The (g).
Fawcett, A. E. (d).
Hill, Frederick T. (d).
Morey & Co. (d).

NORTH VANCOUVER, 9000.
Dawson, R. P., 1501 Lonsdale av.
Robertson's Drug Store, 1103 Lonsdale av.
Sale Stationery Co., 5 Lonsdale av.
Wyard, J. B., 38 Lonsdale av.

PENTICTON, 3600.
Chittenden & McKeen.
Main, Henry W.
Mitchell, Mrs. E.

PHOENIX, 1200.
Almstrom, Albin.

PORT ALBERNI, 1250.
Jackson, H. B.
Pineo & Truswell.

PORT MANN.
Campbell, W. S.

PRINCE GEORGE, 1250.
James, G. A.

PRINCE RUPERT, 6000.
*McRae Bros., Ltd.
Orme's, Limited.
Wrathall, W. W.

PRINCETON, 600.
Princeton Drug & Book Store.

REVELSTOKE, 3000.
Bews, Walter.
MacDonald, C. R.

BRITISH COLUMBIA.

ROSSLAND, 3000.
Stout, Thomas.
Wainman, W. H.

SALMON ARM, 600.
Bedford, A.

SMITHERS, 400.
Adams, J. M. (d).

TRAIL, 1500.
Haselwood, E. W.
Hunt Bros. & Kennedy.
Margeson, K. A. (d).
Warren, F. W., & Co.

VANCOUVER, 150,000.
Atkinson, Thos. H., 955 Nicola. (d).
Barber-Ellis, Ltd.
Campbell, W. S. (b).
Clarke & Stuart Co., Ltd., 320 Seymour (c).
*Columbia Paper Co.
Forsyth, G. S., & Co., 349 Hastings, W.
Galloway, E. J., 435 Granville.
Galloway, Walter, 307 Main.
Granville Staty. Co., 540 Granville.
Hanscome & Gehrke, Ltd.
Love, W. G. (d).
Mitchell, Foley, Ltd. (c).
*Smith, Davidson & Wright, Ltd.

VANCOUVER—Continued.
Spencer, David, Ltd., 515 Hastings, W.
Thurston, F.
Vancouver Stationers (c).
Webster, R. A.
Western Specialty Co., Ltd. (c, s).
*Wilson, J. C., Ltd.
Woodward Department Stores, Ltd., 101 Hastings, W.

VANDERHOOF, 200.
Nechako Drug Co. (d).

VERNON, 3200.
Berry, R. E.

VICTORIA, 45,000.
Acme Press, Ltd.
Clarke Ptg. Co.
*Columbia Paper Co.
Dick, James.
Diggan Ptg. Co.
Hibben, T. N., & Co., 1122 Government.
*Lucas, Jno.
Macey Office Equipment Co. (o. s.).
*Smith, Davidson & Wright, Ltd.
Spencer, David, Ltd., View Cor. Broad (g).
Sweeney & McConnell, Ltd.
Victoria Book & Staty. Co.

MANITOBA.

ALEXANDER, 325.
Walker, W. S. (d).

ALTONA, 400.
Dyck, P. J.

BALDUR, 400.
Cleghorn, I. M.

BELMONT, 300.
Belmont Pharmacy.
Tumoth, George.

BINSCARTH, 250.
Lanigan, A. O. (d).

BIRTLE, 550.
Birtle Drug Co.

BOISSEVAIN, 918.
Gamble, H. L. (d).
Johnston (d).

BRANDON, 17,000.
Christie, E. L.
Jorry, I. G.
Kennedy's Pharmacy.
Wheat City Pharmacy.

BROOKDALE, 125.
Brookdale Pharmacy.

CARBERRY, 878.
Haslam, G. S. (b).
Lawson, Alex. (d).
Spearin, H. D.

CARMAN, 1266.
Sanders, E. M. (d).
Watson, J. (b).

DAUPHIN, 3650.
McCormack, W. R.
Manby & Co.

MANITOBA.

DELORAINE, 808.
 Hasselfield, C. F.
 Hays, F. J.

ELKHORN, 574.
 Mooney, Jno.

FRANKLIN, 100.
 Coade, W. E. R.

GILBERT PLAINS, 542.
 Green, J. T. (d.)
 Porter, W. J. (j.)
 Whelan, B. R.

GRAND VIEW, 820.
 Lloyd, A. O.
 Prust, M. C.
 Shortreed, Dr. D. G. (d).

HAMIOTA, 565.
 Chambers Co. (g).
 Fraser, Flora.
 McNaught, R. R. (d).

HARTNEY, 628.
 Woodhull, F., & Co. (d).

HOLLAND, 480.
 Campbell, F. R.

KILLARNEY, 1010.
 Carson, W. J.
 Evans, P. D. (d).

MANITOU, 639.
 Parker, C. C.

MELITA, 690.
 Hewitt, J. W.

MIAMI, 350.
 Westaway, M.

MINNEDOSA, 1483.
 Butchart, R. T.
 McQuarrie, T. C.
 Minnedosa Pharmacy.

MORDEN, 1438.
 Collins, J. W., & Co.

MORRIS, 500.
 Collins, R. C. T.

NAPINKA, 326.
 Cosgrove, W. R. (d).

NEPAWA, 1854.
 McKay, J. L.

NEWDALE, 200.
 Rungay, L. B. (d).

PORTAGE LA PRAIRIE, 5085.
 Arnold, Major (b).
 Canniff, B. M. (d).
 Hill, J. K. (d).
 Sutton, H. O., & Co. (b).

RESTON, 600.
 Chapman, A. B.

RIVERS, 800.
 Offen, Thomas W.
 Rivers Drug Co.

ROBLIN, 450.
 Forfar, Mrs. A. M.

RUSSELL, 562.
 McIntyre, Jos.

ST. BONIFACE, 11,469.
 Keroack, M.
 McRuer, R. A.
 Waller, A. (d).

SELKIRK WEST, 3602.
 Gibbs, W. H. G.
 Gilhuly, R. H. (b, d).

SOURIS, 2198.
 MacPherson & Burnett.

STONEWALL, 1000.
 Leonard, A. R.

SWAN RIVER, 806.
 Agnew, H. H., & Co. (d).
 Hemming, W. W. (d).

TREHERNE, 585.
 Graham, George.

VIRDEN, 1550.
 Boggs, E. E. (b).
 Higginbotham & Son (d).
 Ross, J. F. (d).

WAWANESA, 350.
 Batty, Fred.

WINNIPEG, 203,255.
 Baird, C. A., Grosvenor & Stafford.
 Barber, Ellis, Ltd.
 Bardal, H. S., 892 Sherbrooke N Cor. Elgin.
 Blanchard Staty. Co.
 Brathwaite, W. F. C., 288 Main.
 Brooking, Arthur I., 116 Osborn.
 Brown, F. L., Pembine & Wardlaw.
 Brown, Jas. B., 823 Garry.
 Brown, J. K., 808 Nairn.

FELTS AND JACKETS | Appleton Woolen Mills
APPLETON - - WIS.

Wholesale and Retail Stationers

MANITOBA.

WINNIPEG—*Continued.*
  Campbell, Donald, Staty. Co.
  *Clark Bros. & Co., Ltd.
  Colcleugh & Co.
  Connell & Co., 474 Main.
  Consolidated Staty. & Fancy Goods Co.
  Eaton, T., & Co., Ltd. (g).
  Keroack, Malvina, 227 Main.
  Liggett, L. K., Co., Ltd.
  Manitoba Stationers.
  McAllister & Co.
  Modern Office Appliance Co.

WINNIPEG—*Continued.*
  Murphy Bros.
  Pioneer News and Novelty Co.
  Robinson & Co., Ltd., 398 Main.
  Richardson & Bishop, Ltd.
  Russell, Lang & Co., 298 Portage av.
  Sargent Pharmacy.
  Western News Agency, Ltd., 335 Portage av.
  Willson Staty. Co., Ltd., 222 McDermot.

NEW BRUNSWICK.

BATHURST, 2300.
  Johnson, Mrs. W. R.
  Smith, A. C., & Co.

CAMPBELLTON, 3516.
  Andrew, Miss Jane (s).
  Central Book Co. (c, s).

CHATHAM, 4666.
  Benson, Fred J. (b).

FREDERICTON, 7208.
  Hall, Chas. W. (b).
  McMurray Book Staty. Co., Ltd. (b).

MONCTON, 16,000.
  City Book Store.
  Colpitts, R. R., & Son (b, c, s).
  Gross, H. M. (b, c, s).
  Maritime Press, Ltd.
  Tweedle, Miss Hattie (b, c, s).

NEWCASTLE, 3945.
  Durick, Thos. J.
  Follansbee & Co. (b).
  McKay, H. H., & Co. (g).

PERTH, 200.
  Johnson, O. C. (d).
  *Wade Drug Co.

ST. JOHN, 60,000.
  Allan Pharmacy.
  Barnes & Co., Ltd., 84 Prince William.
  Dwyer, Mrs. J. J.
  Gray & Ritchie.
  Ingraham, E. R. W. (b, d).
  McArthur, A., 548 Main.
  McArthur, D., 84 King.
  McMillan, J. & A., 98 Prince William.
  Nelson, E. G., & Co., King.
  O'Neill's Pharmacy (b, d).
  Ryan, Mary A.
  *Schofield, The, Paper Co.
  Wasson, E. M. (b, d).

ST. STEPHEN, 2536.
  Wall, H. L.

SUSSEX, 1906.
  Fairweather, G. M. (d).

WOODSTOCK, 3856.
  Baird Co.
  Hanson, Guy L.
  Leighton, L. C., & Co.
  McDonough, Miss Kate.

NEWFOUNDLAND.

ST. JOHN'S, 29,594.
  Ayre & Sons, Ltd. (g).
  Bowring Bros., Ltd. (g).
  Byrne, Garrett.
  Dicks & Co., Ltd.
  Garland, S. E.
  Gray & Goodland.
  Johnson, Percie, Ltd.
  Knowling, Geo. (g).
  March, C. L., & Co., Ltd. (g).
  O'Mara, Peter (d).
  Royal Stores, Ltd. (g).
  Royal Store, Ltd. (g).
  Stafford & Sons.

BLOTTING PAPERS — "STANDARD," "IMPERIAL," "STERLING"
Royal Worcester and Defender Enameled
STANDARD PAPER MFG. CO., - - Richmond, Va.

INVESTIGATIONS   REPORTS   INSPECTIONS
C. A. CHAPMAN, Inc.
28 E. JACKSON BLVD.   ENGINEERS   CHICAGO

Wholesale and Retail Stationers   601

NOVA SCOTIA.

AMHERST, 8973.
  Barkers, The Two (g).
  Bent, Mrs. M. S. (b).
  Black, C. E., & Son.
  Campbell, W. T., & Co. (b).
  Rodd, M. E., & Co. (b).
  Smith, W. P., & Co. (b).

ANNAPOLIS ROYAL, 1019.
  Atlee, A. E. (d).
  Cunningham, W. R. (d).

ANTIGONISHE, 1787.
  Hart, Miss C. M.
  McDonald, C. J.

BRIDGEWATER, 2775.
  Cragg, E. B. (d).
  Herman, Maggie W.

GLACE BAY, 16,561.
  Gallant, Chas.
  Glace Bay Book Store.
  McArel Bros.
  MacLeod, C. & G.

HALIFAX, 60,000.
  Allen, T. C., & Co., 124 Granville.
  Book Room, The, 141 Granville.
  Canada Railway News Co., I. R. C. Depot, North.
  Connelly, Jno. L., 487 Barrington.
  Creighton & Marshall, 64 Upper Water.
  Davis, T. W.
  Davidson, L. C., & Co., 497 Barrington.
  Faulkner, P. B., 16 Spring Garden rd.
  Griffin, J. P.
  *MacKinlay, A. & W., Ltd., 135-137 Granville.
  Marshall, Henry H., 91 Gottingen.
  Penn Stationery & Loose Leaf Co., 44 Granville.
  Richmond Paper Co., 208 Hallis.
  Smith, C. H.

KENTVILLE, 2304.
  Clark, J. D.
  McDougall, Geo. C.
  Morton, C. C.
  Ross, W. J.

LIVERPOOL, 2109.
  Harlow, Allister.
  Madden's Drug Store (d).
  Mersey Drug Store (d).

NEW GLASGOW, 6383.
  Cochrane, T. H. (d).
  Fanjay's, Ltd.
  Faulkner Bros. (b).
  Grant Bros.
  McKenzie, E. S. (d).
  Tory's Book Store.
  White, George.

NORTH SYDNEY, 5418.
  Fry & Co. (d).
  Lovett, C. W., & Co.
  Rudderham, F. H. (d).
  Vooght Bros. (g).

OXFORD, 1500.
  MacKintosh, A. S. (b, d).
  Smith, A. E.

PARRSBORO, 2856.
  Berryman, Mrs. C. A.
  Davidson, Miss Harriet.

PICTOU, 3170.
  Ives, Wm. A.
  McLean, James, & Sons (b).

ST. PETERS, 1000.
  Morrison, R. C.

SPRING HILL, 5713.
  Davis, Frank E.
  McDonald, J. S.
  Roney, L.

STELLARTON, 3910.
  Faulkner Bros.

SYDNEY, 21,000.
  Andrews, James J. (Est. of).
  Davis, R. H., & Co., Ltd.
  Hall's Book Store.
  Iron City Pharmacy.
  McLeod, C. & G.
  Murphy's Book Store.

SYDNEY MINES, 7464.
  Francis, J. W. (b).
  Vooght Bros.

TRENTON, 100.
  McKay, Hugh.

TRURO, 5993.
  Crowe Bros. (b, d).
  Fulton, G. O., Ltd.
  *Pattillo, T. S., & Co., Ltd.
  Thomas, G. Y. (b).

WESTVILLE, 4526.
  Reid, W. A.

MINER EDGAR CO., Sole Agents
KEYSTONE CLAY & REDUCTION CO.
30 Church Street   - -   New York

CLAY

PRECIPITATED REFINED
LIGHT GRAVITY SOFT TEXTURE
<K L M>
HIGH NATURAL COLOR, HIGH RETENTION

APPLETON MACHINE CO.
APPLETON, WIS.
REFINING ENGINES,
SCREENS, SAVING & SPLITTING MACHINERY
HIGH GRADE CENTRIFUGAL PUMPS

Wholesale and Retail Stationers

NOVA SCOTIA.

WINDSOR, 3398.
  Book & Novelty Co.
  Knowles, E. J.

YARMOUTH, 6430.
  *Davis, R. H., & Co., Ltd.
  Gardiner, L. C., & Co. (d).
  McKinlay, H. (s).
  Vickery, E. J. (c, s).

ONTARIO.

ALEXANDRIA, 2323.
  Kerr, F.
  McLeister, J.
  Ostrom & Sons, B. (c, s).
  Simpson, W. J. (c, s).

ALLISTON, 1279.
  Edmonds, Leon (b, s).
  Hipwell, J. R. (d).
  Schell, E. B. (d).

ALVINSTON, 803.
  McDiarmid, P. A., & Son (d).
  Warner, J. E. (d).

ANGUS, 250.
  Patterson, A. E. (d).

ARTHUR, 1035.
  Buschlen, A. W.
  Henry, F. O.

ATHENS, 800.
  Knowlton, H. R.
  Lamb, J. P., & Son (d).

AURORA, 1901.
  Forsyth, M. (b).
  Willis, J. F. (d).
  York, F. E. (d).

AYLMER, 2102.
  Caughell, E. A. (d).

AYR, 823.
  McGeorge, Chas.
  Gillies, A. C.

BARRIE, 7750.
  Keenan, James (b).
  Patterson, A. E. (d).
  Robertson, Herbert G.
  Scott, Walter.
  Stone, Roy H.

BEAVERTON, 1015.
  Williamson, W.

BEETON, 564.
  Morrow, D. S.

BELLE RIVER, 520.
  La Charlate Bros.

BELLEVILLE, 9876.
  Geen, Albert L. (d).
  Jennings & Sherry.
  McIntosh Bros. (g).
  McKeon, J. S. (d).
  Sills, G. L. (b).
  Sulman, C. N. (g).

BLENHEIM, 1387.
  Christmas, Jno. D. (d).
  Johnston, A. M.

BLIND RIVER, 2000.
  Hewitt, O. H. (d, s).
  White, W. G.

BOBCAYGEON, 951.
  Woodland, E. J. (d).

BOTHWELL, 800.
  Adkin, J. F. (b, s).
  Graham, A. D.
  Haller, Thos.

BOWMANVILLE, 4000.
  Allen, W. T. (b).
  Trebilcock, P. (b).

BRACEBRIDGE, 2863.
  Elliott, J. H. (j).
  Thomas Co., The.

BRADFORD, 946.
  Campbell, W. L.
  Gardner, T. H. S.
  Wood, Wm.

BRAMPTON, 4000.
  Boyle's Drug Store (d).
  Copeland & Chatterson, Ltd.
  Hodgson, J. (d).
  Thauburn, Thos. (b).

BRANTFORD, 26,617.
  Barber & Ellis, Ltd.
  Levine, S.
  Linscott Publishing Co.
  Park & Co.
  Stedman Bros.
  Stedman's Book Store.
  Sutherland, Jas. L.
  Wainwright, H.

NEW MILLS-DESIGNED   POWER PLANTS   OLD MILLS REBUILT
C. A. CHAPMAN, Inc.
28 E. JACKSON BLVD.   ENGINEERS   CHICAGO

Wholesale and Retail Stationers

ONTARIO.

BRIGHTON, 1320.
Freeman, W. R. (d).
Lapp, O. T.
Marshall, Fred E. (d).
Porte, W. W. (j).

BROCKVILLE, 9372.
Copland, J. S. (b, c, s).
Currie, F. R. (d).
Fullerton, A. (d).
Greene, J., & Co. (b, c, s).
Stayner, G. F. (d).
Wright, Robert, Co. (g).

BRUSSELLS, 902.
Downing Bros.
Smith, Frank R.

BURKS FALLS, 976.
Hall, H.
Partridge, A. W.

BURLINGTON, 2500.
Jocelyn, T.
La Patourel, T. A.

CAMPBELLFORD, 3051.
Cairns, J. W.

CANNINGTON, 945.
Henderson's Drug Co. (d).
Hoyle, Geo. J. (d).

CHATHAM, 14,000.
Garen & Weir (b).
Gunn, C. H., & Co. (d).
McCall, I., & Co. (d).
Sulman & Son (b).
Turner, W. W. (d).

CHESLEY, 1956.
Davey, Samuel R.
Leitch, David G.

CLIFORD, 595.
Raitcheson, J.
Robb, Geo. E. (d).

CLINTON, 2254.
Cooper, A. T.

COBALT, 5635.
Black, T. H. (The), Co.
Devlin, R. D.
Moore, C. H., Drug Co.
Shaw, Fred.
Stadleman, L.

COBOURG, 5074.
Bowen, S.
Healey, Margaret H.
Nichols, J. G.
Semple, W. H. A.

COCHRANE, 2345.
Carter Drug & Staty. Co., Ltd.

COLDWATER, 649.
Martin, Harry.
Millard, C. G.

COLLINGWOOD, 7090.
Brown, E. S.
Connolly, Dr. E. L. (b, d).
Howard, F. (d).
Johnson, H. H. (d).

CORNWALL, 6598.
Kyte, C. W.
Weber & Co.

CREEMORE, 643.
Corbett, W. J., & Son.

DELTA, 500.
Phelps, W. W.

DESERONTO, 2300.
Frost, N. Maud.
Malley, W. J.

DRAYTON, 706.
Henderson, Richard.
Pollock, P. (b).

DRESDEN, 1700.
Jarvis, Thos. N.
McDonald & Bentley (d).

DUNGANNON, 300.
Stothers, Thomas.

DUNNVILLE, 2854.
Coleberry, W. A. (d).
Harrison, R. A. (d).
McKee, E. J. (d).
Smith, J. H. (b, d).

DURHAM, 1600.
Graham, Finlay.
McFarlane & Co.
Saunders, Robert.

DUTTON, 836.
Reekie, R. P. (b, d).
Roberts, A. E.

ELMIRA, 1732.
Klinck, Geo. (j).
Ludwig, W. D. (b).
Ruppel & Co.
Werner, A. (d).

ELMVALE, 900.
McGuire, W. J.

ELORA, 1216.
Capell, F. J.

603

APPLETON MACHINE CO., APPLETON, WIS.
REFINING ENGINES, SCREENS, SAWING & SPLITTING MACHINERY
HIGH GRADE CENTRIFUGAL PUMP

ONTARIO.

BRIN, 511.
  Gear, Henry.

ESSEX, 1353.
  Sadler, S. H. (d).
  Tweedale, T. B. S.

EXETER, 1555.
  Browning, J. W.
  Grigg Stat. Co.

FENELON FALLS, 1053.
  Vicars, G. F.

FERGUS, 1534.
  Phillips, R., & Son.

FLESHERTON, 437.
  Richardson, Wm. E., & Son.

FOREST, 1445.
  Crosby, R. B.
  Rawlings, S. J.

FORT FRANCIS, 2500.
  Bruce, A. D. (b, d).
  Fraleigh, W. E.
  Preston & Co. (b, d).

FORT WILLIAM, 16,498.
  Hill & Co.
  Neville, M. J.
  Rutledge, J. E.
  Stewart, A.

GALT, 10,299.
  Chapple, F. H.
  Coulthart & Co.
  Macdonald, R. F. (b).
  Meikleham, D. R.

GANANOQUE, 3804.
  Austin, W. E.
  Sine, Clifford.

GODERICH, 4522.
  Porter, Geo.

GORE BAY, 703.
  McRae, George R., & Co.

GRAVENHURST, 1734.
  McLeay, L. (b, d).
  Parritt, G. H. (d).

GUELPH, 16,799.
  Anderson, C., & Co.
  Guelph Paper Co.
  McKee, J. D.

HAILEYBURY, 3874.
  Jory, P. H., Ltd.
  Strong Drug Co., Ltd.

HAMILTON, 101,000.
  Bale, Walter, 109 King, E.
  Buntin, Gillies, & Co., Ltd., John and Jackson.
  Cloke & Son, 16 King, W.
  Dell, James.
  Duncan, R., & Co., 17 James, N.
  French, Thomas (d).
  *Hyslop, R., & Co., Ltd., 16 Macnab, S.
  Irvin Van Fleet Co., Ltd., 23 John's, S.
  Johnston, Benson & Co. (c).
  Mills, Stanley, & Co., Ltd. (g).
  Stuart, J. A. (b).
  Teeter, Harry P.
  Turnbull, A. C. (b).
  Ward, W. J. (b).
  Watkins, Thomas C., & Co., Ltd. (g).
  Wells, J. R. (b).

HANOVER, 2342.
  Ball, John.
  Clark, S. B.
  Taylor, Jno. (b).

HARRISTON, 1491.
  Brisbin, W. F.
  Dale, R. F.
  McKibbon & Co. (d).

HARROW, 700.
  Darby, E. F. (b, d).
  Rogers, Geo.

HEPWORTH, 650.
  Campbell, V. S.

HESPELER, 3086.
  Conway, J. D.

HUNTSVILLE, 2235.
  Booth, Henry M.
  Brand, W. N. (d).
  Wattson, C. A.

INGERSOLL, 4763.
  Murray, J. H.
  Thurtell, R. N. (d).
  Wood, Geo. W.

IROQUOIS, 849.
  Copeland, Est., C. C.
  Stone & Fisher.
  Tindale, James (b).

JARVIS, 510.
  Rogers, E.

KEEWATIN, 1242.
  Johnson's Pharmacy (b, d).

MILLS ELECTRICALLY EQUIPPED ECONOMIES IN STEAM PLANTS
C. A. CHAPMAN, Inc.
28 E. JACKSON BLVD.   ENGINEERS   CHICAGO

Wholesale and Retail Stationers 605

ONTARIO.

KINCARDINE, 2348.
Cook, J. C. (d).
Henry, Wm. J. (b).
Henry, E. A. (b).
Thompson, R. (d).

KINGSTON, 18,874.
Bucknell, Miss J. M.
College Book Store.
McAuley, Thos.
Mahood Bros. (j).
Mahood Drug Co.
Rogers, R. J. (s).
Uglow, R., & Co.

KINGSVILLE, 1427.
Layman, H. C.
Leggett, Chas. (b).
Pickard, R. H. (d).

KINMOUNT, 650.
Train, George.

KITCHENER, 19,056.
Bender, J. P.
Jaimet & Co., Ltd.
McCullum, J. J.
Moyer Press (The).

LAKEFIELD, 500.
Burgess, J. A., & Son.
Ridpath Bros. (b).
Tanner Drug Co. (b, d).

LANSDOWNE, 400.
Campbell, Dr. J. deL.
Deane, F. G.

LEAMINGTON, 2652.
Halliday, W. C.

LINDSAY, 6964.
Little, G. A.
Porter, R. S.

LISTOWEL, 2289.
Hacking, John A.
Livingstone, John, Jr.

LITTLE CURRENT, 1205.
Carruthers, Dr. J. (b, d).
Currie, Herman (b, d, s, c).

LONDON, 55,026.
Childs, H. J., 632 Dundas (d).
Ellwood, Mary (b).
Hay, John B., 173 Dundas (c).
Holmes & Popham (b, s).
Langford, A. A., Co., Ltd., 426 Richmond (c).
Lewson & Jones, Ltd.

LONDON—*Continued.*
McEwen, Ellen, 501½ Richmond (b).
Mills, Jno., Ltd., 398 Richmond (b).
Reason, H. T., & Co., 180 York (c).
Red Star News Co., 10 Market la. (b).
*Reid Bros. & Co.
Robertson, J. B., 531 Richmond (b).
Scott, John L., 417 Richmond (b).
Smith, C. R., & Co., 298 Richmond (c).
Wilson, Janet, 262 Dundas (b).

MARKDALE, 925.
Stephen, R. L.
Turner, W., & Co.

MARKHAM, 909.
Hellems, Clarence W.
Hicks, O. S.
Markham Drug Co.

MARMORA.
Sabine, Howard W.

MATHESON, 500.
Booth, Dorothy M.

MAXVILLE, 759.
Maxville Pharmacy.

MEAFORD.
Henderson, J. B.
Muxlow, F. G.
Stephen, W. W.

MERRITTON, 1670.
Daley, James (b).
Stuart, Robert (d).
Vanderburg, Dr. J. F.

MIDLAND, 6253.
Gerrie, George W.
Kinch, W. (b, s).
Macartney, H. E. (b, d).
Parker, J. (b, s).
Wray, W. (d).

MILDMAY, 1000.
Schurter, Rosina (Est. of).

MILTON, 1657.
Brown, Thos. J. (d).

MITCHELL, 2000.
Cameron, W. A. (j).
Hord, F. C. (b, s).
Smith, H. C. (j).

APPLETON MACHINE CO.
APPLETON, WIS.
REFINING ENGINES, SCREENS, SAWING & SPLITTING MACHINERY
CENTRIFUGAL PUMPS HIGH GRADE

MINER EDGAR CO., Sole Agents
EDGAR BROS. CO.
KEYSTONE CLAY & REDUCTION CO.
30 Church Street — — New York
CLAY
<E W> <K L M> <C M>
WASHED FLOATED REFINED
LARGEST CAPACITY AND STOCK IN AMERICA. PROMPT SHIPMENTS

FELTS AND JACKETS | Appleton Woolen Mills
APPLETON - - WIS.

Wholesale and Retail Stationers

ONTARIO.

MOUNT FOREST, 2200.
Penwarder, E. E. (d).
Skales, J. T., & Co.
Yeomans, H. E. (d).

NAPANEE, 2807.
Henry's Book Store.
McLaughlin, E. (c).

NEW HAMBURG, 1484.
Peine, Louis.

NEW LISKEARD, 2300.
Bevins, W. H. (b, s).
Wismer, C. A.

NIAGARA FALLS, 9245.
Booth, R. W.
Brant, G. W. (d).
Briggs, G. A. (b).
Buckley, Wright H.
McNally, E. C.
McPherson, Malcolm (b).
Thorburn, A. C.
Troup, Gordon (d).

NIAGARA-ON-THE-LAKE, 1318.
Connolly, James.

NORTH BAY, 9000.
Bazaar, The.
Campbell, H. S. (d).
Carruthers, G. T.
Fosdick, Fred, Co.
Lambertus, James A. (d).
Rorabeck, A. C. (d).
Smith, Cyril P. (d).
Thomas, The, Co. (j).

NORWOOD, 870.
Stewart, Robt.

OIL SPRINGS, 646.
Dewar, Albert W. (b, d).
Kerby, Geo. M.

OMEMEE, 505.
Mulligan, R. J.

ORANGEVILLE, 2340.
Jeffers, C. V. (d).
McGuire & McKittrick.
McWilliam, N. T.

ORILLIA, 7300.
Cook, H., & Co. (b, d).
Haffey, F. M. (d).
*Smith, R. O., Co., Ltd.

OSHAWA, 8235.
Hallitt, F. E.

OTTAWA, 87,062.
Allen & Cochrane, 37 Sparks.
Beattie's Drug Store.
Birks & Sons, 101 Sparks (j).
Borts, N., 191 Bank (b).
Capital Office Supply Co., Ltd., 587 Sussex.
Clarke, Miss Florence, 344 Elgin.
Crain Printers, Ltd.
Daly Co.
Godin, N. A., 261 Dalhousie.
Hope, Jas., & Sons, 61 Sparks.
Jarvis, A. H., 157 Bank.
Johnston, D. S., 580 Rideau (d).
Kilt, J. G., 28 Rideau.
Korn, S., 787 Bank.
Laflamme, Ellen, 420 Bank.
Laflamme, M. S., 314 Bank.
Lafontaine, M. R., 118 Rideau.
Larose, A. J., 162 Rideau.
O'Brien's Book Store, 141 Nicholas.
Popham, G., 124 Queen.
Reid, B., 182 Sparks.
Seguin, A., & Co., 167½ Somerset.
Serre & Co., 92 Rideau.
Whyte, J. G., & Son, Ltd., 60 Rideau.

OTTERVILLE, 750.
Downing, H. (d).
Fish, J. W.

PALMERSTON, 1700.
Greenwood, A. S.
Parish, W. M.

PARIS, 4500.
Fisher, J. H., & Son (s, c).
Shepherd, C. J. (b).

PARK HILL, 1289.
Benham, A. E.
Munro, T.

PARRY SOUND, 3429.
Badger, J. H.
Foot, W. R.

PEMBROKE, 5622.
Grigg Book & Stationery Co.
McGee, The Misses.
O'Gorman Co., Ltd., The.

PENETANGUISHENE, 3568.
McDonald, Dr. P. A. (d).
Mundy, T. J. (b, d).
Nettleton, C. A. (b, d).

**JAMES H. HARRISON
PULPSTONE MANUFACTURER** | **GENUINE NEWCASTLE STONES**
18 Killowen St., GATESHEAD-ON-TYNE, ENG.

Wholesale and Retail Stationers

ONTARIO.

PERTH, 3588.
Adams, J. Harry.
Girdwood, F. A. (d, s).
Hart, John (b, s).
Robertson, W. S.
Walker, Geo. (b, d).

PETERBORO, 20,653.
Graham, W. & N.
Routley, C. B.
Soden, R. J.
Treblicock Bros.

PETROLIA, 3518.
Fisher, F. C.
Lowery, J. A.

PICTON, 3700.
Allison, C. B.
Case, E. W.
Wright, W. A.

PORT ARTHUR, 11,216.
Crooks, J. W., & Co. (d).
Cooke, W. P. (j).
Lowery, S. M.
Marin & MacKenzie (c).
McEachern, W. T.

PORT HOPE, 5092.
Davison, W. J. B. (d).
Mitchell, H. W. (d).
Randall, L. B. (b).
Strong, Geo. V. (b).
Steen, J. T. (b).
Watson, T. G. (d).
Williamson & Son (b).

PORT McNICOLL, 800.
Beattie, P. H.

PORT PERRY, 1148.
Davis, A. J.
McGaw, W. H.

PRESCOTT, 2801.
Brown, W. S.
Miller, Morton.

RAINY RIVER, 1689.
Bourgeois, A.
Calvert, E. D.

RIDGETOWN, 1954.
Hiles, C.
Little, J. G. (c).
Mayhew Bros.

RODNEY, 676.
Thomson, W. H.
Wray, C. A.

ROSEVILLE, 150.
Kaiser, L. M.

RUNNYMEDE, 3000.
Begley, J. E.

ST. CATHARINES, 16,000.
Bixby, Mrs. C. B.
Fairfield, B. C., & Son.
Greenwood, R. S.
Keating, M. Y.
Robertson, W. J.

ST. JACOBS, 500.
Winkler, W. H.

ST. MARYS, 3388.
Reesor, L. H.
Willard, Jno.

ST. THOMAS, 17,000.
Curran, J. E. (b).
Gundy's Book Store, Ltd.
Manley, Agnes M.
McDonald & Co.
McLachlin, Robt.

SARNIA, 9947.
Fry, H. W.
Manley, Ltd.

SAULT STE. MARIE, 15,000.
Barnes Drug Co. (d).
Blaine, J. G. (d).
Broughton's Drug Store.
Cliffe's Book Store.
Hamill, H. S. (d).
Kenney, N. J. (d).
Lawrence, Ltd.
McDowell, P. W.
Smith, C. B., & Co.
Sault Stationers.

SEAFORTH, 1983.
Aberhart, Chas. (d).
Thompson, W. (b).
Williams, C. L. (b, d).

SIMCOE, 3227.
Wallace, W. Y.

SMITH'S FALLS, 6370.
Kerfoot, W. H. (b).
Wilson, L. A. (d).

STAYNER, 1039.
Watson, T. J.
West, Norman B.

STEELTON, 5000.
Kenny, N. J. (d).

FELTS AND JACKETS | Appleton Woolen Mills
APPLETON - - WIS.

Wholesale and Retail Stationers

ONTARIO.

STOUFFVILLE, 1084.
Boadway, J. (b, d).
Collard, Geo.

STRATFORD, 12,946.
Alexander, A. H.
Easson, R. . (d).
Gregory & Jury (d).
Kenner, J. H. (b).
Lightfoot, Geo. H. (b).
Nasmyth, C. E. (d).
Patterson's Book Store.
Ramore, J. W. (d).
Robertson, E. A. (d).

STRATHROY, 2823.
Dickenson, R.

SUDBURY, 8,000.
Jaworski, Wasyl.
McNaughton, F. D., & Co.

SUTTON WEST, 753.
Chapelle, Mrs. P.

TARA, 551.
Madill, E. J. (d).
Van Dusen, H. A., & Son (c, s).

THEDFORD, 559.
Clerke, Harney S. (d).

THOROLD, 4500.
Dunn, Mary C.

TILBURY, 962.
Johnston, Hugh.

TILLSONBURG, 3000.
Davis, E. F.
Maddock, G. O.

TIMMINS, 3000.
Burke, Frank A. (d).
Curtis Drug Co. (b, d).
Meyers Drug Store (b, d).
Peters Stationery Store.
Stadelman, The L., Co.

TORONTO, 470,000.
*American News Agency, 81 Queen, W.
Arnold, Joshua, 660 Lansdowne.
Bain, Thos, 1953 Queen, E.
Bain & Cubitt, 9 Wellington, E.
*Ballantine Bros., 672 College.
*Barber, Ellis, Ltd., 71 Wellington, W.
Barnes, Frank, 225 Roncesvalles.
*Beare, S. B., Ltd., 56 Wolseley.

TORONTO—*Continued.*
Bennett & Hall.
Birch, G. H., 110 Queen.
Blake, W. E., & Sons, Ltd., 123 Church (b).
Britnell, Albert, 263 Yonge (b).
Brown Bros., Ltd., 100 Simcoe.
Brown, L. H.
Brown & Stainton, 77 Bay.
*Buntin Reid Co., 13 Colborne.
Canada Law Book Co.
Canadian Office Appliance & Supply Co.
Canada Stat. Jobbers, 3178 King, W.
Capps, Alfred.
Claridge, Charles.
Copeland Chatterson Co., Ltd.
*Copp-Clark, Co., Ltd., 517 Wellington.
Davis & Henderson, Ltd., 578 King, W.
Dobson, James, 856 Yonge.
Doust, Joseph, 58 Adelaide, E.
Dye & Durham, 9 Toronto Arcade.
Eaton, T., Co., Ltd., 190 Yonge. (g).
Evans, W. H., 458 College.
Fletcher Cope Co., 906 Bloor.
*Gage, W. J., & Co., Ltd., 82 Spadina av.
Grand & Toy, Ltd., 14 Wellington, W.
*Hart, S. R., & Co., 40 Wellington, E.
Harwood, Harriett, Bloor W.
Hill, Richard J.
*Hustwitt, A. S., Co., 44 Adelaide, W.
Hyde, P. E.
Johnston, J.
Jones, Margaret, 448 Spadina av.
Legge, E. A., 831 College (d).
McEntee, Bernard, 28 Queen, E.
McKenna, J. P., 169 Yonge (b).
*Menzies & Co., Ltd., 439 King, W.
*Methodist Book & Pub. House, 299 Queen, W.
Musson, John G., Dundas.
Newsome & Gilbert, Ltd., 122 Richmond, W.
Newsome, W. B., & Co., 188 Adelaide.
Parsons, T. J., 3 Wellington, E.
Perrin, J. H., 940 Queen, W.
Rayson, Jas. A., 1426 Queen, W.

BLOTTING PAPERS — "STANDARD," "IMPERIAL," "STERLING"
Royal Worcester and Defender Enameled
STANDARD PAPER MFG. CO., - - Richmond, Va.

ONTARIO.

TORONTO—*Continued.*
  Robin, Elizabeth R.
  Rooke, Isaac.
  *Scheinman, L. J., 295 Queen, W.
  Simpson, Robt., Drug Co., Ltd., 176 Yonge, E.
  Stanton, O. B., & Wilson Co., Ltd., 54 Yonge.
  Thomson, Wm. W., 224 Wellesley.
  Tyrrell, Wm., & Co., 780 Yonge.
  *Warwick Bros. & Rutter, 401 King, W.
  Wianco Bros., 731 Yongest.
  Wilson, H. A.
  Wilson Staty. & Ptg. Co., 118 King, W.
  Withers, Herbert, 462 Yonge.

TOTTENHAM, 517.
  Weaver, O. A.

TRENTON, 7000.
  Dickey, J. H.
  Digby, Wm.
  Finger, S. J.
  Fraser, W. A. (d).
  German, S. A. (d).
  McLean, Nellie (b).
  Shurie, James (d).

TWEED, 1,868.
  Bartlett, F. A. (d).
  Newton, P. K. (d).

UXBRIDGE, 1483.
  Nichols, T. C. (d).
  Willis, R. F. (d).

WALKERTON, 3300.
  Hunter, H. G. (d).
  McCrum, R., & Co. (b, d).
  Sieveright, A. P. (d).

WALLACEBURG, 3427.
  Colwell, W.

WATERFORD, 1083.
  Coliver, H. R.
  York, L. E., & Co.

WATERLOO, 4359.
  Doersam, Katie.

WATFORD, 1300.
  Taylor & Son.
  McLaren, J. W.

WELLANDPORT, 253.
  Heaslip, J. L.

WELLINGTON, 785.
  Shurie, J. S.

WEST LORNE, 740.
  Brown, Loyal G. (j).

WESTON, 2200.
  Inch, Wm. J.

WESTPORT, 808.
  Castle, Geo. W.

WHITBY, 3400.
  Copp, Edwin (b).
  Odlum, E. L. (d).
  Whitfield, T. B. (d).

WIARTON, 2266.
  Manley, W. J. (b, d).
  Paterson, Jas. (d).
  Sawyer, Raymond W. (b, d).
  Wigla, E. R. (d).

WINCHESTER, 1500.
  Challis, J. G.

WINDSOR, 25,000.
  Copeland, Geo. E. (b).
  Laing, F. H. (d).
  Lansbery, C. A. (d).
  Marentette, Victor E., & Son. (b).
  Pond, W. A. (d).
  Whyte, J. F. (b).

WINGHAM, 2288.
  Mason, Geo., & Son (b).
  McKibbon, J. W. (d).

WOODSTOCK, 9321.
  Coles & Co.
  Goodeve, Agnes (b).
  Shanley, Mrs.
  Sheddon Co.
  *Sutherland, J. & J.

PRINCE EDWARD ISLAND.

CHARLOTTETOWN, 12,080.
  Brace, R. K. (b).
  *Carter & Co., Ltd.
  Maritime Stationers.
  McDonald, C. A.

SUMMERSIDE, 2678.
  Gourlies, Ltd.
  Jardine, J. C. (b).
  McLellan, M. J. (b).

Wholesale and Retail Stationers

QUEBEC

ANCIENNE LORETTE, 2740.
Drolet, J. A.

ARTHABASKA, 689.
Librairie, La, De L'Union.

BEDFORD, 1482.
Saunders, F. C. (d)

BERTHIERVILLE, 1335.
Paquette, J. P.

COATICOOK, 3165.
McNamara, M. J.

EAST DRUMMONDVILLE, 6000.
Brillon, Jos. R.

FARNHAM, 3560.
Comeau, E. J.

FRASERVILLE, 7572.
Mercier, J. E.

GRAND MERE, 4783.
Chamberland, W. E., & Cie.
Colin, Dr. J. E.
Daplez, Misses (b).
Leduc, I. A.
Lemay, W. E.

HEMMINGFORD, 313.
Lacasse, Ovila (j).

HULL, 20,000.
Groulx, Hildage.

JOLIETTE, 8400.
Archambault, J. D.
Gervais, Albert (b, d).
Lafortune, L. A. (b, d).
Page, J. O. (b, d).
Rivest, Conrad L. (d).

KNOWLTON, 865.
Bedee, M. H. (j).
Davies, W. M. b, d).
Smith, H. F., Ptg. Co.

LA TUQUE, 3500.
Bellemare, Geo. Pierre.

LENNOXVILLE, 1211.
McKindsey, W. J. H.

L'EPIPHAINE, 1675.
Vian, Albert M.

LEVIS, 7448.
Guenette, George (j, c, s).

L'EPIPHAINE, 1675.
Vian, Albert M.

LITTLE CASCAPEDIA, 400.
Campbell, James.

LOUISVILLE, 1765.
Siguerre, J. A., & Co.

MAGOG, 4200.
Samson, J. D. (c).
Smith, E. D. & A. E. (g).
West, J. R. (b, d).
Wilcox, J. R. (s).

MARIEVILLE, 1587.
Gendreau, Alphé (b).
Leduc, L. P.
Prefontaine, C. E. (b).

MONTREAL, 757,996.
Almy's, Ltd., St. Catherine, W. (g).
Arseneault, A., 124 Park av.
Barwick, O. W., 155 Notre Dame, W.
Birks, Hy. & Son, 9 Phillips, S., (j).
Black, W. G., 401 St. Denis.
Bogue Bros. & Henry, 178 St. James (c).
Boyd, J. N., 340 St. James.
Brown-Foster Co., Ltd., 472 St. Catherine, W.
*Buntin, Gillies & Co., 68 St Alexander.
Century Stamp Co., 258 Beaver Hall Hill.
Chapman's Book Store, Ltd., 190 Peel.
Chatham, W., 230 Sherbrooke, W.
Chaumont, A., 2994 St. Lawrence bvd. (b).
Clarke, G. W., & Co., 370 St. Catherine, W.
Cole, E. A., & Co., 9 St. Peter.
Crites & Riddell, 20 St. Nicholas.
Crozier, C. A., 363 Craig, W.
Dawson Bros., 14 St. John.
Dawson, C. F., Ltd., 239 Notre Dame, W.
*Dawson, W. V., Ltd., 93 St. Urbain.
Dawson, Wm., 3186 St. Adele av.
Dowlers Drug Store, 300 St. Catherine, W. (d).
Fortier, Jos., Ltd., 210 Notre Dame, W.
Fry, S., 381 Victoria av. (b).

QUEBEC

MONTREAL—Continued.
- Gareau, J. O., Ltd., 1 Mount Royal av. (g).
- Goodwins, Ltd., St. Catherine, W. (g).
- Grafton, F. E., & Son, 227 Notre Dame.
- *Granger Freres, 43 Notre Dame, W.
- Guay, J. Alf (La Cie), 5 Notre Dame, E. (b).
- Hall, W. M., & Co., 221 Notre Dame, W.
- *Hodgson Sumner Co., 87. St. Paul, W.
- Imperial News Co., 254 Lagauchetiere, W.
- King, J. L., 27 Bleury av. (b).
- Latter Bros., 18 Hospital.
- Librairie Notre Dame, 35 Notre Dame, W.
- Librarie J. J. A. Derome, Ltd., 36 Notre Dame, W.
- Library Bureau of Canada, 20 St. Nicholas.
- McAran, James, 28 Chaboillez.
- Malo, U., 69 Prince Arthur, E. (s).
- Manning, O. H., 20 St. Nicholas (c).
- Melrose Book Store, 5722 Sher.
- *McFarlane Son & Hodgson, Ltd., 14 St. Alexander.
- Milloys Book Store, 241 St. Catherine, W. (b).
- Montreal Book Room, 33 McGill College av. (b).
- Morgan, Henry, & Co., Ltd., Phillips sq. (g).
- Morton, Phillips & Co., 115 Notre Dame, W.
- Ogilvy, James A., St. Catherine, W. (g).
- Phelan, F. E., 437 St. Catherine, W.
- Pineault, J. O., 280 Rachel, E. (b).
- Poole, Miss M., 45 McGill College av. (b).
- Rennick, J. E., 42 St. Sacramento.
- Renouf Pubg. Co., 25 McGill College av. (b).
- *Rolland, J. B., et Fils, La Cie, 6 to 53 St. Sulpice.
- Sadler, D. & J., & Co., 18 Notre Dame, W. (b).
- Walkinshaw, F., 207 St. James.
- Watters, Alex., 141 St. Peter.

MONTREAL—Continued.
- *Wilson, J. C., Ltd., 61 St. Alexander.
- Woolworth, F. W., Co., 395 St. Catherine, W. (g).

MONTREAL WEST, 1359.
- Jones, E. P., (d).

NICOLET, 2593.
- Smith & Smith (d).

QUEBEC, 78,190.
- Angus, J. R., 344 St. John.
- Brophy, T. J., 25 Buade.
- Dery, I. P., & Fils, 59 Dalhousie.
- Dumontier, Phillias, 351 St. Joseph.
- Evoy, P. J., 141 St. John.
- Garneau, J. P., 47 Buade.
- Gauvreau, P., 122 Mountain Hill.
- Hunt, Jos., 276 St. Jean.
- Kimball, H. F., 148½ St. John.
- Kirouac, J. A., & Co., 34 Fabrique.
- Moore, T. J., & Co., Ltd., 118-120 Mountain Hill.
- Mulroney, W. J. & G., 59 St. Peter.
- Pruneau, A. O., 60 St. Jean.
- Staton, Geo. W., 33 Sault Au Matelot.
- United Photographic Stores, Ltd., 21 Buade.
- Walsh, John E., 11 St. John.

RICHMOND, 2175.
- Bedard, A. J. (d).

ST. AGATHE DES MONTS, 4000.
- Grignon, Dr. E. (d).
- St. Amour (d).

STE. ANNE DE BELLEVUE, 1780.
- Vallee, J. S.

ST. BARTHELEMI, 600.
- Sylvestre, F. J.

ST. CESAIRE, 941.
- Grise, Henri.

ST. GABRIEL DE BRANDON, 1602.
- Provost, J. N.

ST. HYACINTHE, 9797.
- Charpentier, G. A.
- Solis, Emile.
- Richer, E. H., & Fils.

Wholesale and Retail Stationers

QUEBEC

ST. JACQUES, 2589.
Forest, J. O. E.

ST. JEROME, TERREBONNE, 3479.
Fournier, J. E.
Parent, Henri.
Prevost, J. E., Jr.

ST. JOHNS, 7035.
Boudreau, Jr., J.

ST. THOMAS DE JOLIETTE, 250.
Coutu, Hercule.

SHAWINIGAN FALLS, 9500.
Farley, J. N. (d).

SHAWVILLE, 715.
Klock, R. H.

SHERBROOKE, 16,405.
Ansell Drug Store.
Anthier, P. D.
Richard, Gustave (d).
Rosemary Gift Shop.
Spearing, R. J. (j).

SOREL, 8419.
Hardy, Gustave.
Morancy, Albert.

SUTTON, 986.
Sutton Printing Co.

THREE RIVERS, 22,000.
Ayotte, P. V.
Charbonneau, J. A. (c).
Dupaul, Jas.
Roy, W. E.
Vanasse, F. X.
Williams, R. W. (d).

VALCOURT, 1600.
Drainville, Eug.
Dupaul, Jas.
Fontaine, J. A.
Tandeau, Amedie.

VALLEYFIELD, 9447.
Leduc, L. N.
Solis, J. E. (j).

VICTORIAVILLE, 3025.
Larose, Dr.
Librarie St. Jean.
Welch, C. H.

VILLE MARIE, 850.
Aubin, A. J.

WATERLOO, 1886.
Welch, C. H.

WINDSOR MILLS, 2233.
Leonard, E.

YAMACHICHE, 965.
Beausheimer, Dr. C. N.
Bellemare, Dr. L. O. M.
Descoteaux, C. A.

ST. PIERRE ET MIQUELON
(FRENCH POSSESSION)

ST. PIERRE ET MIQUELON.
Brehier, A. M.

SASKATCHEWAN

ARCOLA, 794.
Donaldson, J. S. (b, d).

ASSINIBOIA, 1039.
Carter & Wright.
Stephen, H. D.

AVONLEA, 250.
Ferras, T. A. B.

BENGOUGH, 300.
McCuaig, G. A.

BRODERICK, 130.
Brough, James.

CANORA, 1200.
Robertson, J. D.

CARNDUFF, 469.
Elliott, J. H.
Lockhart, W. T.

CARON, 300.
Boylan, J. F. (d).

CEYLON, 150.
Sweet & Brown.

COLGATE, 150.
Watts, Wm. I., & Co.

SASKATCHEWAN

CRAIK, 530.
  Robertson, A. C.

DAVIDSON, 496.
  People's Drug & Book Store.

DELISLE, 450.
  Fear, F. J.

DUNDURN, 239.
  Black, D. R. (d).

ELBOW, 450.
  Coghlan, R. O.

EYEBROW, 400.
  Porter, A. A.

FILLMORE, 187.
  Cook, R. G.

FOAM LAKE, 185.
  Somers, W. E.

HERBERT, 1014.
  Herbert Drug Co.

INDIAN HEAD, 1595.
  Orchard, A. G.

KERROBERT, 850.
  McMullen, W. J. M.

LANGENBURG, 220.
  Denmark, A. G.

LLOYDMINSTER, 1000.
  Medical Hall Drug Co. (b, d).

MAPLE CREEK, 1600.
  Cousins Pharmacy (d).

MARENGO, 150.
  Mann, Jennie E.

MELFORT, 1522.
  Humphries, A. H. (j).
  Moore, Sidney G.

MIDALE, 156.
  Koch, H. E. (b, d).

MILESTONE, 436.
  Currie, J. J.
  Elliott, M. A.

MOOSE JAW, 18,000.
  Binnings Fair.
  Carruthers, E. B. (d).
  Davidson, H. A. (d).
  Fysh, L. (d).
  Hamilton, H. S. (d).
  Moose Jaw Drug & Staty. Co.

MOOSE JAW—Continued.
  Nixon, D. C., Ltd.
  Ostrander, T. C. (d).
  Willson Stationery Co.
  Young, R. S. (d).

MORTLACH, 550.
  Beacock, T. A.
  Bradley, T. W.

PRINCE ALBERT, 11,000.
  Merritt, J. N.
  Merritt, J. R.
  Mitchell, W. D.
  Rowe, W. H.

RADISSON, 535.
  Angley, F. B. (d).
  Clarke, Alfred H.

RADVILLE, 625.
  Koch, H. E.

REGINA, 30,000.
  Canada Drug & Book Co., Ltd.
  Regina Pharmacy, Ltd.
  *Sask. Wholesale Stationers, Ltd.
  United Typewriter Co.
  Wilson Stationery.

ROSTHERN, 1500.
  Fleury, R. S.

SASKATOON, 23,000.
  Argue, T. A., Ltd. (b, d).
  Cairns, J. F., Ltd. (g).
  Chown-MacMillan, Ltd. (d).
  Hazen Twiss, Ltd. (g).
  MacMillan, Ltd. (b).
  Parrott Stationery Co.
  Saskatoon Drug & Staty. Co.
  Stewart, C. H.
  Willson Staty. Co., Ltd.

STRASSBURG STATION, 811.
  Bierns, A. A. (d).
  Groh, Edith E.

SWIFT CURRENT, 6050.
  Cooper, W. W., Co. (g).
  Hutcheson, T. W.
  Rooney, J. P. (b, d).
  Swift Current Pharmacy.

WADENA, 763.
  Ellis, Walter.

SASKATCHEWAN.

WEYBURN, 5413.
Boylan Drug Co.
Kempton Bros. (b).
McKinnons, Ltd. (g).
Mitchell, O. S.

WHITEWOOD, 447.
Bird, J. R., & Co.
Ely, M. A. (b, d).
Patrick, R. A. (b, d).

YORKTON, 4500.
Eby, M. A.
Patrick, R. A.

YUKON TERRITORY.

DAWSON, 2000.
Cribbs, Wm. (d)
McHenry & Brennan.
Zaccarelli Book Store.

WHITE HORSE, 800.
MacPherson, H. G. (d).

SELECTED LIST OF
Stationers in Cuba

CAMAGUEY.
  Aguero, Carlos M., Estrada Palma 7.

CIENFUEGOS.
  Martin, L. F., D'Clouet 42.
  Vells, F. R., Sah Carlos 113 y 115.

GIBARA.
  Martin Bim.

HAVANA.
  *Barandiaran y Comp., Mercaderes 38.
  *Fernandez, Castro y Comp., Ricla 23.
  *Harris Bros. & Co., O'Reilly 104.
  *Lopez, Rodriguez Jose, Obispo 133.
  *Rambla & Bouza, Obispo 35.
  Robins, Frank Co., Obispo 69-71-73.
  Ruiz, y Ho., Obispo 22.
  Solana & Co., Mercaderes 22.

HAVANA—Continued.
  Solana, Hno., y Comp., Mercaderes 28.
  Suarez, Carasa, y Comp., Tte. Rey 12.
  Swan, H. E., Obispo 55.
  Veloso, Ricardo, Galiano 62.

HOLGUIN.
  Jose Betancourt.

MATANZAS.
  Carreno, Independencia 41.
  Paulino Solés, e hyos, Melanes 96.
  Viuda de Quiros & Estrada, Independencia 59.

NUEVITAS.
  Corrales & Co.
  Iriarte y Sobs.

SANTIAGO.
  Beltran Eduardo.
  Gutierres Hermanos.
  Mir y Blanco.

THE PAPER TRADE JOURNAL

ESTABLISHED IN 1872
PRICE $4.00 A YEAR

PUBLISHED EVERY THURSDAY

A WEEKLY JOURNAL for Paper Makers, Managers of Mills, Manufacturers of Mill Machinery, and Dealers in Paper and Paper Makers' Supplies. Practical information regarding Paper and Pulp Manufacture, the Chemistry of Paper Making, Illustrations of New Mechanical Appliances, and Technical Queries and Answers.

Fullest News Reports of what is going on in the Paper Trade at Home and Abroad. The World's Commercial Intelligence relating to Mill Construction and the Paper and Allied Trades.

Financial Notes on the Money Market and the Securities in which the trade is interested.

Dependable Market Reports, with Quotations of Wood Pulp, Rags, Chemicals and all Raw Materials used in Paper Making.

A Weekly Record of Imports at and Exports from United States Ports.

THE PAPER TRADE JOURNAL far surpasses any journal in the trade, either at home or abroad, in the following particulars: In the amount of reading matter it contains; in the number of illustrated articles on the mechanical and chemical features of the art of paper making; in the fullness and completeness with which it covers the home and foreign news of the trade.

PUBLISHED BY

The Lockwood Trade Journal Company, Inc.

Specimen Copy sent free to any address

10 East 39th Street, New York

The American Stationer and Office Outfitter

PUBLISHED EVERY SATURDAY

Established in 1874   **$2.00 a Year**   **40 to 48 Pages**

THE AMERICAN STATIONER AND OFFICE OUTFITTER is the oldest and by far the best publication in its field, with a circulation bigger than all the rest combined.

It tells all about the Standard Goods and about the Novelties in Stationery, Papeteries, Calendars, Christmas Cards, Valentines, Toys and Games, and Stationers' Specialties, Office Supplies and Kindred Lines.

It offers Practical Hints about Window Dressing, the Artistic Display of Goods, and the like.

PUBLISHED BY

The Lockwood Trade Journal Company, Inc.

Specimen Copy sent free to any address

10 East 39th Street, New York

MILLS ELECTRICALLY EQUIPPED — ECONOMIES IN STEAM PLANTS
C. A. CHAPMAN, Inc.
15 E. JACKSON BLVD. — **ENGINEERS** — **CHICAGO**

A LIST OF
WATERMARKS AND BRANDS
USED IN THE
American Paper Trade

(w) = watermark. (b) = brand.
Papers known by numbers will be found in a list that follows the alphabetical

This is a list of *owners* of Watermarks and Brands. It is restricted to papers of various kinds. Bags, envelopes and other paper products are excluded because of their multiplicity.

The publishers respectfully ask the co-operation of the trade with a view to the settlement of disputed questions of ownership and also solicit suggestions for the improvement of the list. Data for the next revision can be sent in at any time.

A

A in a diamond—(b)—flat—F. W. ANDERSON & CO., New York.
A in a diamond—(b)—book paper—RIEGEL & CO., INC., Philadelphia.
"A"—manila tag—(b)—COOK-VIVIAN CO., Boston.
"A"—(b)—plate and book—PAPER MILLS CO., Chicago.
"A"—(b)—tissue—ANCRAM PAPER MILL, Ancram, N. Y.
"A" Grade—(b)—blotting—DISTRICT OF COLUMBIA PAPER MANUFACTURING CO., Washington, D. C.
"A. & C."—(b)—kid finish bristol—THE ALLING & CORY CO., Rochester.
"A" Map Bond—(b)—HY. LINDENMEYR & SON, New York.
A. A. A. Extra Super Proofing—(b)—MINNEAPOLIS PAPER CO., Minneapolis, Minn.
A. A. A. Kraft—(b)—R. L. GREENE PAPER CO., Providence, R. I.
A1—(w)—flats—MOUNT HOLLY PAPER CO., Mount Holly Springs, Pa.
"A1" Grade—(b)—blotting—DISTRICT OF COLUMBIA PAPER MANUFACTURING CO., Washington.
"AA1" Grade—(b)—blotting—DISTRICT OF COLUMBIA PAPER MANUFACTURING CO., Washington.
A. B. C.—(b)—pattern boards—C. R. HEWITT & BROS., INC., New York.
A. B. C. No. 1—(b)—manila fibre and toilet paper—ALFRED BLEYER & CO., New York.
A. B. C. Silk Fibre—(b)—silver fibre packing—ALFRED BLEYER & CO., New York.

A. B. C.—(w and b)—bond, ledger, writing—NEENAH PAPER CO., Neenah, Wis.
"A" Lithe. Finish—(b)—F. W. ANDERSON & CO., New York.
Abbotsford—(w)—antique laid and wove book—LASHER & LATHROP, New York.
Abco—(b)—ADAMS BAG CO., Chagrin Falls, Ohio.
Aberdeen Super—(b)—book—MERRIAM PAPER CO., New York.
Abenaquis—(b)—HOLLINGSWORTH & WHITNEY CO., Boston.
Aberdeen—(b)—ALBANY PERFORATED WRAPPING PAPER CO., Albany, N. Y.
Aberdeen—(w)—AMERICAN WRITING PAPER CO., Holyoke, Mass.
Aberdeen—(b)—colored enameled book—PETERS PAPER CO., Denver.
Aberdeen Ledger—(w)—WHITING-PATTERSON CO., Philadelphia.
Absolute White—(b)—J. C. BLAIR CO., Huntingdon, Pa.
Absorbent Mimeograph—(b)—EATON, CRANE & PIKE CO., Pittsfield, Mass.
Absorber—(b)—blotting—PARSONS & WHITTEMORE, INC., New York.
Absorbit—(w)—blotting—PARSONS TRADING CO., New York.
Abstract Bond—(w)—UNION PAPER & TWINE CO., Detroit.
Abstract Linen—(w)—UNION PAPER & TWINE CO., Detroit.
Abstract Linen Ledger—(w)—UNION PAPER & TWINE CO., Detroit.

MINER EDGAR CO., Sole Agents
EDGAR BROS. CO.
KEYSTONE CLAY & REDUCTION CO.
30 Church Street - - New York

CLAY

<E W> <K L M> <C M>
WASHED FLOATED REFINED
LARGEST CAPACITY AND STOCK I
AMERICA. PROMPT SHIPMENTS

FELTS AND JACKETS | Appleton Woolen Mills
APPLETON - - WIS.

Watermarks and Brands

Academic Ant. Book—(b)—HY. LINDENMEYR, New York.
Acea — (b) —bond— SOUTHERN PAPER CO., Richmond, Va.
Accountants' Bond—(w)—TAYLOR-LOGAN CO. PAPERMAKERS, Holyoke.
Accountants' Linen Ledger—(w)—TAYLOR-LOGAN CO. PAPERMAKERS, Holyoke, Mass.
Account Linen Ledger—(w)—AMERICAN WRITING PAPER CO., Holyoke, Mass.
Achievement—(w and b)—bond, ledger, writing—NEENAH PAPER CO., Neenah, Wis.
Acme—(w)—flat—L E S L I E-D O N A-HOWER CO., St. Paul, Minn.
Acme—(b)—enamel—DWIGHT BROS. PAPER CO., Grand Rapids, Mich.
Acme—(b)—news—J. W. BUTLER PAPER CO., Chicago.
Acme — (b)— writing — CLEVELAND PAPER MFG. CO., Cleveland, Ohio.
Acme—(b)—book — PERKINS-GOODWIN CO., New York.
Acme—(b) — wax tissue — GRAHAM PAPER CO., St. Louis.
Acme Bond—(w)—BEECHER, PECK & LEWIS, Detroit, Mich.
Acme Chrome Plate—(b)—HENRY LINDENMEYR & SONS, New York.
Acme Hectograph — (b) — PETREQUIN PAPER CO., Cleveland, Ohio.
Acme Index Bristol—(b)—THE ALLING & CORY CO., Rochester, N. Y.
Acme Laid—(b)—antique laid book—PETERS PAPER CO., Denver, Col.
Acme Linen—(b)—E. H. THOMPSON CO., Buffalo, N. Y.
Acme Linen Ledger—(w)—CINCINNATI CORDAGE AND PAPER CO., Cincinnati, Ohio.
Acme Linen Ledger—(w)—SOUTHWORTH CO., Mittineague, Mass.
Acme Mimeograph—(b)—PETREQUIN PAPER CO., Cleveland, Ohio.
Acme Tinted—(b)—HUDSON VALLEY PAPER CO., Albany, N. Y.
Acorn—(b)—wrapping—LOUISVILLE PAPER CO., Louisville, Ky.
Acorn Bond—(w)—BLAKE, McFALL CO., Portland, Ore.
Acra—(b)—roll toilet—JEROME PAPER CO., New York.
Active Bond —(w)—COLLINS MFG. CO., N. Wilbraham, Mass.
Actuary—(b)—CROCKER-McELWAIN CO., Holyoke, Mass.
Actuary Linen Ledger—(w)—CROCKER-McELWAIN CO., Holyoke.
Adair—(b)—enameled book—J. C. PARKER PAPER CO., Louisville, Ky.
Adaman—(b)—binders' trunk and friction board—GRAHAM PAPER CO., St. Louis.
Adelia—(w)—ROLLAND PAPER CO., St. Jerome, Canada.
Adelia Superfine—(w)—ROLLAND PAPER CO., St. Jerome, Canada.

Adirondack—(b)—cover — STRATHMORE PAPER CO., Mittineague, Mass.
Adjustment Bond—(w)—COLLINS MFG. CO., N. Wilbraham, Mass.
Admiral—(b)—flats—B R A'D N E R SMITH & CO., Chicago.
Admiration Bond—(b) — HARLEM CARD & PAPER CO., New York.
Admiration Ledger—(b)—HARLEM CARD & PAPER CO., New York.
Adna—(b)—mimeograph — TROY PAPER CO., Troy, N. Y.
Adriatic Pasteboards—(b)—PARSONS TRADING CO., New York.
Advance—(b)—bristol — RIEGEL & CO., INC., Philadelphia.
Advance.,—(b)—news, sheathing — GRAHAM PAPER CO., St. Louis.
Advance—(w)—R.R. man.—DIEM & WING PAPER CO., Cincinnati, Ohio.
Advance—(b)—toilet—U N I T E D STATES ENVELOPE CO. (Morgan Envelope Co. Division), Springfield.
Advance Document Manila—(b)—bristol—C. P. LESH PAPER CO., Indianapolis.
Advance Ledger—L A S H E R & LATHROP, New York.
Advance Linen—(w)—PETREQUIN PAPER CO., Cleveland, Ohio.
Advance Linen Ledger—(w)—L. L. BROWN PAPER CO., Adams, Mass.
Advance Tag—(b)—C. P. LESH PAPER CO., Indianapolis, Ind.
Advertisers'—(b)—blotting, bristols and blanks—PAPER MILLS CO., Chicago.
Advertisers' Announcement—(b)—bristol—J. W. BUTLER PAPER CO., Chicago.
Advertisers' Bond—(w)—TAYLOR-LOGAN CO. PAPERMAKERS, Holyoke.
Advertisers' Cover—(b)—ADVERTISERS' PAPER MLLS, Holyoke.
Advertisers' Japan Vellum—(w)—ADVERTISERS' PAPER MILLS, Holyoke, Mass.
Advertisers' Text—(w)—book—ADVERTISERS PAPER MILLS, Holyoke, Mass.
Advertisers' Translucent—blotting—(w)—THE PAPER MILLS CO., Chicago.
Advocate Bond—(w)—E A T O N, CRANE & PIKE, Pittsfield, Mass.
Advocate—(w)—POWERS P A P E R COMPANY, Springfield, Mass.
Aeolian — (b) — cover — TAYLOR-LOGAN CO., Papermakers, Holyoke.
Aerial Book—(b)—D I S T R I C T OF COLUMBIA PAPER MFG. CO., Washington, D. C.
Aerial Covers—(b)—DISTRICT OF COLUMBIA PAPER MFG. CO., Washington, D. C.
Aerie Bond—(w)—DIEM & WING PAPER CO., Cincinnati, Ohio.
Aero—(b)—envelope—GRAHAM PAPER CO., St. Louis.

JAMES H. HARRISON ULPSTONE MANUFACTURER | **GENUINE NEWCASTLE STONES** 18 Killowen St., GATESHEAD-ON-TYNE, ENG.

Watermarks and Brands

Aerograph R. R.—(b)—writing—BEECHER, PECK & LEWIS, Detroit, Mich.
Aetna—(b)—cardboards and cards—GRAHAM PAPER CO., St. Louis.
Aetna—(b)—white wove—F. A. FLINN, New York.
Aetna No. 2—(b)—enamel cover—J. C. PARKER PAPER CO., Louisville.
Aetna Linen—(w)—AETNA PAPER CO., Dayton, Ohio.
Aetna Mills—(b)—EAST HARTFORD MANUFACTURING CO., Burnside, Conn.
Aetna Mimeograph—(b)—C. P. LESH PAPER CO., Indianapolis, Ind.
Aetna Standard—(w)—AETNA PAPER CO., Dayton, Ohio.
Afton Linen—(w)—CINCINNATI CORDAGE AND PAPER CO., Cincinnati, Ohio.
Agate—(w and b)—bond, ledger, cover and bristols—UNION CARD & PAPER CO., New York.
Agate—(b)—wrapping—LOUISVILLE PAPER CO., Louisville, Ky.
Agate Binding Board—(b)—GRAHAM PAPER CO., St. Louis.
Agate Bond—(w)—UNION CARD & PAPER CO., New York.
Agawam Bond—(w)—AMERICAN WRITING PAPER CO., Holyoke.
Agosota — (b) — AGOSOTA MILLBOARD CO., Trenton, N. J.
A.-H. Extra Strong Ledger—(w)—ALEXANDER-HOLDEN PAPER CO., New York.
Ailsa—(b)—J. C. BLAIR CO., Huntingdon, Pa.
Aircraft Bond—(w)—BARBER ELLIS, LTD., Toronto, Can.
Air Line—(b)—toilet—UNITED STATES ENVELOPE CO. (Morgan Envelope Co. Division), Springfield.
Airline—(b)—wrapping — GRAHAM PAPER CO., St. Louis.
Ajax—(b)—toilet—ALBANY PERFORATED WRAPPING PAPER CO., Albany, N. Y.
Ajax—(b)—box board — BRADNER SMITH & CO., Chicago.
Ajax—(b)—cordage—GRAHAM PAPER CO., St. Louis.
Ajax—(b)—rope tag — TROY PAPER CO., Troy, N. Y.
Ajax—(b)—tagboard—J. C. PARKER PAPER CO., Louisville, Ky.
Ajax—(b)—white envelope, fibre and folding bristol—DONALDSON PAPER CO., Harrisburg, Pa.
Ajax Fibre—(b)—butchers' waterproof—MARCELLUS PAPER CO., Syracuse, N. Y.
Ajax File Tag Board—(b)—OSBURN PAPER CO., Philadelphia.
Ajax Kraft—(b)—JOHN CARTER & CO., Boston.
Ajax Linen—(w)—writing—CAREW MANUFACTURING CO., South Hadley Falls, Mass.

Ajax Linen Ledger—(w)—DWIGHT BROS.' PAPER CO., Chicago.
Ajax Mills—(w)—CLEVELAND PAPER MANUFACTURING CO., Cleveland, Ohio.
Ajax Mills — (w) — writing — S T. LOUIS PAPER CO., St. Louis.
Ajax Parchment—(b)—drug bond—OLD DOMINION PAPER CO., Norfork, Va.
Ajax Parchment Wrapping—(b)—OLD DOMINION PAPER CO., Norfolk, Va.
Ajax R. C. Cards—(b)—BRADNER SMITH & CO., Chicago.
Ajax Tag—(b)—RICHMOND PAPER CO., Richmond, Va.
Ajax Writing—RICHMOND PAPER CO., Richmond, Va.
Alabaster—(b)—wrapping, sheathing—GRAHAM PAPER CO., St. Louis.
Alabaster—(b)—enamel and dull finish—DIEM & WING PAPER CO., Cincinnati, Ohio.
Alabaster Blanks—(b)—BRADNER SMITH & CO., Chicago.
Aladdin—(h)—toilet—H. NORWOOD EWING CO., New York.
Aladin—(b)—box cover and writing—STRATHMORE PAPER CO., Mittineague, Mass.
Alameda—(b)—ALBANY PERFORATED WRAPPING PAPER CO., Albany, N. Y.
Alamo Bond—(w)—MINNEAPOLIS PAPER CO., Minneapolis, Minn.
Alaska Index Bristol—(b)—COOKVIVIAN CO., Boston, Mass.
Alaska—(b)— cardboard — McCLELLAN PAPER CO., Minneapolis, Minn.
Alaska—(w)— writing — GRAHAM PAPER CO., St. Louis.
Alaska Linen—(w)—WHITAKER PAPER CO., Cincinnati, Ohio, and BAY STATE PAPER CO., Boston.
Alaska White Tag—(b)—bristol—C. P. LESH PAPER CO., Indianapolis.
Alba Linen—(w)—U. S. ENVELOPE CO., Worcester, Mass.
Alba Linen—(w)—WORCESTER ENVELOPE CO., Springfield, Mass.
Alban Bond—(w)—HUDSON VALLEY PAPER CO., Albany, N. Y.
Alban Tag—(h)—HUDSON VALLEY PAPER CO., Albany, N. Y.
Albany—(b)—toilet—ALBANY PERFORATED WRAPPING PAPER CO., Albany, N. Y.
Albany Eggshell Book—(b)—SEYMOUR CO., INC., New York.
Albany Parchment Manila—(b)—BRADNER SMITH & CO., Chicago.
Albany Railroad—(b)—THE UNION PAPER & TWINE CO., Detroit, Mich.
Albany—(b)—tough check—J. C. PARKER PAPER CO., Louisville, Ky.

FELTS AND JACKETS | Appleton Woolen Mills, APPLETON - - WIS.

Watermarks and Brands

Alba Rex—(b)—white manila—DWIGHT BROS. PAPER CO., Chicago.
Albeatem—(b)—ALBANY PERFORATED WRAPPING PAPER CO., Albany, N. Y.
Albemarle—(b)— toilet — ALBANY PERFORATED WRAPPING PAPER CO., Albany, N. Y.
"Albemarle Half Tone"—(b)—ALBEMARLE PAPER MFG. CO., Richmond, Va.
Albermarle Enameled—(b)—Blotting—ALBERMARLE PAPER CO., Richmond, Va.
Alberta Bond—(w)—W. G. WILLMANN, New York.
Alberta Bond—(w)—AMERICAN WRITING PAPER CO., Holyoke.
Alberta Bond — (w) — A. PRICE, Brooklyn, N. Y.
Albion Book—(b)—AMERICAN WRITING PAPER CO., Holyoke, Mass.
Albion Bristol — (b) — MATTHIAS PLUM, Newark, N. J.
Albion White Tag—(b)—MINNEAPOLIS PAPER CO., Minneapolis.
Alcazar—(b)—toilet—ALBANY PERFORATED WRAPPING PAPER CO., Albany, N. Y.
Alcor Enameled — (b) — blotting — THE ALLING & CORY CO., Rochester
"Alcor"—(w)—THE ALLING & CORY CO., Rochester, N. Y.
Alcor Embossing—(b)—cover—THE ALLING & CORY CO., Rochester
Alcor Enameled Book—(b)—THE ALLING & CORY CO., Rochester.
Alcor Linen—(b)—THE ALLING & CORY CO., Rochester, N. Y.
Alcor Manifold Copying—(b)—writing—THE ALLING & CORY CO., Rochester, N. Y.
Alcor Mills—(w)—THE ALLING & CORY CO., Rochester, N. Y.
Alcor No. 1 Index—(b)—bristol—THE ALLING & CORY CO., Rochester.
Alcor India Tint Enamel—(b)—book—THE ALLING & CORY CO., Rochester, N. Y.
Alcor Oiled Tympan—(b)—THE ALLING & CORY CO., Rochester.
Alcor Railroad Manila — (b) —writing—THE ALLING & CORY CO., Rochester, N. Y.
Alcor Souvenir Post Card—(b)—bristol—THE ALLING & CORY CO., Rochester, N. Y.
Alcor Translucent—(b)—bristols—THE ALLING & CORY CO., Rochester.
Alcyone Linen—(w)—ESLEECK MANUFACTURING CO., Turner's Falls, Mass.
Alcyone Linen Bond—(w)—KINGSLEY PAPER CO., Cleveland, Ohio.
Alden Ledger—(b)—O. H. ANDERSON & CO., New York.

Alderney—(b)—waxed butter wraps—THE CHATFIELD & WOODS CO., Cincinnati, Ohio.
Aldine Extra Super—(b)—MILLER & WRIGHT PAPER CO., INC., New York.
Aleutian—(w)—ledger—W. R. GRACE & CO., New York.
Aliamet Half Tone Writing—HY. LINDENMEYR & CO., New York.
Aldine—(b)—antique white wove text—LASHER & LATHROP, New York.
Aldine — (b) — MILLER & WRIGHT PAPER CO., New York.
Aldine—(b)—bristol — TROY PAPER CO., Troy, N. Y.
Aldine—(b)—railroad ticket—J. C. PARKER PAPER CO., Louisville, Ky.
Aldine—(w and b)—bond—J. E. LINDE PAPER CO., New York.
Aldine—(b)—toilet — UNITED STATES ENVELOPE CO. (Morgan Envelope Co. Division), Holyoke.
Aldine Bristol—(b)—TROY PAPER CO., Troy, N. Y.
Aldine Flats—(w)—writing—KINGSLEY PAPER CO., Cleveland, Ohio.
Aldine Mills—(b)—fine—KINGSLEY PAPER CO., Cleveland, Ohio.
Aldine Mills—(w)—writing — TROY PAPER CO., Troy, N. Y.
Aldine Text—(b)—India tint antique book—LASHER & LATHROP, New York.
Aldus Mills—(w)—white wove—KINGSLEY PAPER CO., Cleveland.
Alert—(b)—ALBANY PERFORATED WRAPPING PAPER CO., Albany.
Albert Mills—(b)—writing—CONROW BROS., New York.
Alexandra Brilliant — (w) — STRATHMORE PAPER CO., Mittineague, Mass.
Alexandra U. S. A.—(w)—book—STRATHMORE PAPER CO., Mittineague, Mass.
Alexandra Japan—(b)—STRATHMORE PAPER CO., Mittineague, Mass.
Alexandra Linen Bond—(w)—STRATHMORE PAPER CO., Mittineague, Mass.
Alexandra—(w)—deckle-edge book and cover—STRATHMORE PAPER CO., Mittineague, Mass.
Alexandra Vellum Cover—(b)—STRATHMORE PAPER CO., Mittineague, Mass.
Alexandria Wove—(b)—EATON, CRANE & PIKE CO., Pittsfield.
Alexis—(w)—bond, cover and folding bristol—STRATHMORE PAPER CO., Mittineague, Mass.
Alexis Bond—(w)—STRATHMORE PAPER CO., Mittineague, Mass.
Alexis Detail Paper—(b)—STRATHMORE PAPER CO., Mittineague, Mass.

BLOTTING PAPERS — STANDARD PAPER MFG. CO., Richmond, Va. Largest Manufacturers

NEW MILLS DESIGNED — POWER PLANTS — OLD MILLS REBUILT

C. A. CHAPMAN, Inc
28 E. JACKSON BLVD. — ENGINEERS — CHICAGO

Watermarks and Brands — 621

Alexis Folding Bristols—(b)—STRATHMORE PAPER CO., Mittineague, Mass.
Alexis Linen Ledger—(w)—STRATHMORE PAPER CO., Mittineague, Mass.
Algo—(b)—HOLLINGSWORTH & WHITNEY CO., Boston.
Algoma White Writing—(w)—ISLAND PAPER CO., Menasha, Wis.
Algonkin—(b)—cover—HAMPDEN GLAZED PAPER & CARD CO., Holyoke, Mass.
Algonquin—(b)—toilet—STONE & FORSYTH CO., Boston.
Alhambra—(w)—AMERICAN WRITING PAPER CO., Holyoke, Mass.
Alhambra—(b)—covers—KNOWLTON BROS., Watertown, N. Y., and RIEGEL & CO., INC., Philadelphia.
Alhambra Offset—(b)—WHITING-PLOVER PAPER CO., Stevens Point, Wis.
Alhambra Bristol—(b)—THE CHATFIELD & WOODS CO., Cincinnati, Ohio.
Allandale—(b)—M. F. book—HAGEN PAPER CO., St. Louis.
Alliance—(b)—news—GRAHAM PAPER CO., St. Louis.
Alliance—(w)—bond—SYRKIN & BACK, INC., New York.
Alliance Linen—(w)—JUDD PAPER CO., Holyoke, Mass.
Alligator—(b)—gummed—LOUISVILLE PAPER CO., Louisville, Ky.
All Rag Clearwater—(w)—book—GRAHAM PAPER CO., St. Louis.
All-Rag—(b)—ROBERTS & MECK'S, Harrisburg, Pa.
All-Rag Mounts—(b)—STRATHMORE PAPER CO., Mittineague, Mass.
All-Rag Deckle-Edge Writing—(b)—CARTER, RICE & CO., CORP., Boston.
All-Rag Linen Ledger—(w)—CARTER, RICE & CO., CORP., Boston.
Alma—(b)—blotting—UNION CARD & PAPER CO., New York.
Alpaca—(w)—ledger—MIDLAND PAPER CO., Chicago.
Alpenrose Linen—(w)—EATON, CRANE & PIKE CO., Pittsfield, Mass.
Alpha—(b)—filter—H. REEVE ANGEL & CO., INC., New York.
Alpha—(w)—mimeograph—MILLER & WRIGHT PAPER CO., INC., New York.
Alpha—(b)—writing—GRAHAM PAPER CO., St. Louis.
Alpha Bond—(b)—CHARLES H. WRIGHT, Kalamazoo, Mich.
Alpha Bond—(b)—PENINSULAR PAPER CO., Ypsilanti, Mich.
Alpha Coated Paper—(b)—HY. LINDENMEYR & SONS, New York.
Alpha Deckle Edge—(b)—WHITING PAPER CO., Holyoke, Mass.

Alpha Linen Ledger—(w)—WRIGHT, BARRETT & STILWELL CO., St. Paul, Minn.
Alpha Mimeograph Linen—(w)—MILLER & WRIGHT PAPER CO., New York.
Alpha Offset Bond—(w)—MIDLAND PAPER CO., Chicago.
Alpine—(b)—bond, ledger—ALEXANDER-HOLDEN PAPER CO., New York.
Alquin—(b)—HOLLINGSWORTH & WHITNEY CO., Boston.
Alriba—(w and b)—No. 1 Manila writing—A. R. BARNES & CO., Chicago.
Alsace Linen—(w)—EATON, CRANE & PIKE CO., Pittsfield, Mass.
Alstead—(b)—book—JUDD PAPER CO., Holyoke, Mass.
Alta Bond—(w)—LAMBERT PAPER CO., Salt Lake City, Utah.
Altha—(w and b)—cover and bond—CHARLES H. WRIGHT, Kalamazoo.
Alton Writing—(w)—SPRING GROVE PAPER CO., Spring Grove, Pa.
Altonia Bristol—(b)—REGENSTEIN-VEEDOR CO., Chicago.
Aluminum Bristol—(b)—F. A. FLINN, INC., New York.
Aluminum Parchment—HY. LINDENMEYR & SONS, New York.
Alva—(b)—news—LOUISVILLE PAPER CO., Louisville, Ky.
Alvan—(b)—translucent—TROY PAPER CO., Troy, N. Y.
Amazon—(b)—cover—LASHER & LATHROP, New York.
Amazon—(b)—toilet—SCOTT PAPER CO., Philadelphia.
Amazon—(w)—writing—MIDLAND PAPER CO., Chicago.
Amazon—(w)—white writing—MIDLAND PAPER CO., Chicago.
Amazon Blanks—(b)—DIEM & WING PAPER CO., Cincinnati, Ohio.
Amazon Book—(b)—DIEM & WING PAPER CO., Cincinnati, Ohio.
Amazon Mills—(w)—JOHN CARTER & CO., Boston.
Ambassador Bond—(w)—J. W. BUTLER PAPER CO., Chicago.
Amber—(b)—waxed and case lining—LOUISVILLE PAPER CO., Louisville, Ky.
Amboy Bristol—(b)—FARLEY PAPER CO., Farley, Mass.
America First—(w)—NEENAH PAPER CO., Neenah, Wis.
American—(b)—box covering—DISTRICT OF COLUMBIA PAPER CO., Washington, D. C.
American—(b)—tissue—GRAHAM PAPER CO., St. Louis.
American—(w)—AETNA PAPER CO., Dayton, Ohio.
American—(b)—bristol—JOHN CARTER & CO., Boston.

APPLETON MACHINE CO., APPLETON, WIS.
REFINING ENGINES, SCREENS, SAWING & SPLITTING MACHINERY
HIGH GRADE CENTRIFUGAL PUMPS

MINER EDGAR CO., Sole Agents
Edgar Bros. Co. 30 CHURCH STREET NEW YORK
C A — WASHED <E W> HIGH COLOR — GRITLESS <C M> HIGH RETENTION

Watermarks and Brands

American — (b) — pattern — THE CHATFIELD & WOODS CO., Cincinnati, Ohio.
American—(b)—enamel book— WHITAKER PAPER CO., Cincinnati, Ohio, and BAY STATE PAPER CO., Boston.
American —(b)— ready roofing — CHATFIELD & WOODS CO., Cincinnati, Ohio.
American—(b)—toilet — NORTHERN PAPER MILLS, Green Bay, Wis.
American (with a star)—(w)—MORGAN & HAMILTON CO., Nashville.
American—(b)—copying tissue— SMITH PAPER CO., Lee, Mass.
American Bank—(w)—MISSOURI PAPER HOUSE, Kansas City, Mo.
American Bank Bond—(w)—WHITING-PLOVER PAPER CO., Stevens Point, Wis.
American Beauty — (b) — toilet — NORTHERN PAPER MILLS, Green Bay, Wis.
American Beauty — (b) — toilet — SCOTT PAPER CO., Philadelphia.
American Bond—(w)—AMERICAN WRITING PAPER CO., Holyoke.
American Bristol—(b)—white— CHATFIELD & WOODS CO., Cincinnati, Ohio.
American Bristol—(b)—JOHN CARTER & CO., Boston.
American Buckram—(b)—bond and blotting—MERRIAM PAPER CO., New oYrk.
American Drawing—(b)— PARSONS PAPER CO., Holyoke, Mass.
American Esparto—(b)—book— ARNOLD-ROBERTS CO., Boston.
American Fabric—(w)—POWERS PAPER CO., Springfield, Mass.
American First—(w and b)—writing, bond, ledger—NEENAH PAPER CO., Neenah, Wis.
American Flag Bond—(w)—EMPIRE CARD & PAPER CO., New York.
American Flax Linen—AMERICAN WRITING PAPER CO., Holyoke.
American Ledger—(w)—VALLEY PAPER CO., Holyoke, Mass.
American Linen—(w)—AMERICAN WRITING PAPER CO., Holyoke.
American Linen Bond—(w)— AMERICAN WRITING PAPER CO., Holyoke, Mass.
American Linen Ledger—(w)— WORTHY PAPER CO., Mittineague, Mass.
American Linen Record—(w)—ledger—J. W. BUTLER PAPER CO., Chicago.
American Linen Record—(w)— ledger—WHITING-PATTERSON CO., Philadelphia.
American Mills—(w)—COOK-VIVIAN CO., Boston.
American Mills—(w)—AETNA PAPER CO., Dayton, Ohio.
American Prepared Roofing—(b) —CHATFIELD & WOODS CO., Cincinnati, Ohio.
American Resin Sized Sheathing —(b)—CHATFIELD & WOODS CO., Cincinnati, Ohio.
American Slaters' Felt—(b)— CHATFIELD & WOODS CO., Cincinnati, Ohio.
American Standard Bond—(w)— AMERICAN STANDARD PAPER CO., Philadelphia.
American Standard Linen—(w)— AMERICAN STANDARD PAPER CO., Philadelphia.
American Standard Linen Ledger —(w)—AMERICAN STANDARD PAPER CO., Philadelphia.
American Standard Superfine— (w)—AMERICAN STANDARD PAPER CO., Philadelphia.
American Star—AMERICAN WRITING PAPER CO., Holyoke, Mass.
American Superfine—(w)—VALLEY PAPER CO., Holyoke, Mass.
American Tag—(b)—THE UNION PAPER & TWINE CO., Detroit, Mich.
American Typewriter—(b)—tissue —SMITH PAPER CO., Lee, Mass.
American Vellum Wedding—(b) —JOHN CARTER & CO., Boston.
Americus—(b)—MARTIN & WM. H. NIXON PAPER CO., Manayunk, Philadelphia.
Americus Bond—(w)—STRATHMORE PAPER CO., Mittineague, Mass.
Americus Linen Ledger—(w)— STRATHMORE PAPER CO., Mittineague, Mass.
Americus Text—(w)—MARTIN & WILLIAM H. NIXON PAPER CO., Manayunk, Philadelphia.
Amesbury—(b)—ALBANY PERFORATED WRAPPING PAPER CO., Albany, N. Y.
Amfalula Fine—(w)—CROCKER-McELWAIN CO., Holyoke, Mass.
Amherst—(b)—catalog—GRAHAM PAPER CO., St. Louis.
Amherst—(b)—card board—MISSOURI PAPER HOUSE, Kansas City.
Amor—(w)—JAPAN PAPER CO., New York.
Amstel Linen—(w)—EATON, CRANE & PIKE CO., Pittsfield, Mass.
Amsterdam—(b)—bond — GRAHAM PAPER CO., St. Louis.
Analoston—(h)—box covering—DISTRICT OF COLUMBIA PAPER MFG. Co., Washington, D. C.
Anawanda Mills—(b)—folded ESSEX PAD & PAPER CO., Holyoke.
Anchor—(b)—writing and No. 1 manila—CHATFIELD & WOODS CO., Cincinnati, Ohio.
Anchor—(b)—toilet—ALBANY PERFORATED WRAPPING PAPER CO., Albany, N. Y.

Watermarks and Brands

Anchor—(b)—ribbon paper—WILSON & TOWNE PAPER CO., New York.
Anchor Enamel—(b)—book—LOUISVILLE PAPER CO., Louisville, Ky.
Anchor—(b)—souvenir post card—BRADNER SMITH & CO., Chicago.
Anchor—(b)—roofing—R. L. GREENE PAPER CO., Providence, R. I.
Anchor—(b)—ruled—JUDD PAPER CO., Holyoke, Mass.
Anchor Bond—(b)—linen finish—DWIGHT BROS. PAPER CO., Chicago.
Anchor Book—(b)—DIEM & WING PAPER CO., Cincinnati, Ohio.
Anchor Brand—JUDD PAPER CO., Holyoke, Mass.
Anchor Bristol—(b)—THE CHATFIELD & WOODS CO., Cincinnati.
Anchor Index—(b)—HUDSON VALLEY PAPER CO., Albany, N. Y.
Anchor Index Bristol—(b)—HUDSON VALLEY PAPER CO., Albany.
Anchor Linen—AMERICAN WRITING PAPER CO., Holyoke, Mass.
Anchor Linen—(w)—MINNEAPOLIS PAPER CO., Minneapolis, Minn.
Anchor Safety Paper—(b)—LAMONTE & SON, New York.
Andover Mills—(w)—A. STORRS & BEMENT CO., Boston.
Andstone Bond—(b)—STONE & ANDREW, Boston.
Angelo—(b)—blanks—LOUISVILLE PAPER CO., Louisville, Ky.
Angelo Art — (b) — bristol — BAY STATE PAPER CO., Boston.
Angier Mills — (b) — waterproof wrapping—ANGIER MILLS, Quincy, Mass.
Anglo-Saxon—(w)—wove and laid, antique and velvet book—JAMES WHITE PAPER CO., Chicago.
Anglo-Saxon Bond — (w) — J. C. PARKER PAPER CO., Louisville, Ky.
Anglo-Saxon Bond — (w)—HAMPSHIRE PAPER CO., South Hadley Falls, Mass.
Annuity—(w)—MT. HOLLY PAPER CO., MT. HOLLY MILLS, INC., Mt. Holly Springs, Pa.
Annuity Bond—(w)—MT. HOLLY PAPER MILLS, INC., Mt. Holly Springs, Pa.
A No. 1—(b) — toilet — ALBANY PERFORATED WRAPPING PAPER CO., Albany, N. Y.
A No. 1 Machine Finish Book—(b)—IRWIN N. MEGARGEE & CO., Philadelphia.
Antietam Extra Fine—(w)—ANTIETAM PAPER CO., Hagerstown, Md.
Antiquarian—(b)— cover — ADVERTISERS PAPER MILLS, Holyoke.
Antique Laid Club Writing—(b)—THE W. B. OGLESBY PAPER CO., Middletown, Ohio.
Antique Parchment—(w)—WHITING PAPER CO., Holyoke, Mass.

Antique Style—(w and b)—GEORGE B. HURD & CO., New York.
Antique Style Bond—(w and b)—GEORGE B. HURD & CO., New York.
Antrim Linen—(b)—BUNTIN, GILLIES & CO., Hamilton, Can.
Antwerp—(b) — cover — BUNTIN, GILLIES & CO., LTD., Hamilton, Ontario, Can.
A No. 1 Blanks—(b)—HY. LINDENMEYR & SONS, New York.
A. No. 1 White Bristol—(b)—HY. LINDENMEYR & SONS, New York.
Anvil—(b)—tag—W. H. CLAFLIN & CO., Boston.
Anvil—(b) — roofing — GRAHAM PAPER CO., St. Louis.
Anvil Blanks—(b)—TROY PAPER CO., Troy, N. Y.
Apache—(b)—toilet—ALBANY PERFORATED WRAPPING PAPER CO., Albany, N. Y
Apache Fabric — (b)—MISSOURI PAPER HOUSE, Kansas City, Mo.
Apex—(b)—envelope — THE CHATFIELD & WOODS CO., Cincinnati.
Apex Linen Ledger—(w)—GILBERT PAPER CO., Menasha, Wis.
Apex Linen — (w) — writing — CAREW MFG. CO., South Hadley Falls, Mass.
"A" Plate—(b)—book—S. & S. C. THE PAPER MILLS CO., Chicago.
A. P. W. Brand—roll and flat—ALBANY PERFORATED WRAPPING PAPER CO., Albany, N. Y.
A. P. L. Linen, U. S. A.—A. P. LITTLE, Rochester, N. Y.
Apollo Bond—(b)—HY. LINDENMEYR & SONS, New York.
Apollo Writing—(b)—HY. LINDENMEYR & SONS, New York.
Applewood—(b)—wrapping—LOUISVILLE PAPER CO., Louisville, Ky.
A. R. Fine—(b)—ARNOLD-ROBERTS CO., Boston.
Arabia—(b)—toilet — WHITING-PATTERSON CO., New York.
Arabian—(b)—toilet—UNITED STATES ENVELOPE CO. (Morgan Envelope Co. Division), Springfield.
Arabian—(b)—LOUISVILLE PAPER CO., Louisville, Ky.
Arabian Bond — (w) — MISSOURI PAPER HOUSE, Kansas City, Mo.
Aragon—(b)—bristol — STANDARD CARD & PAPER CO., New York.
Arapahoe Bond — (w) — THE PETERS PAPER CO., Denver, Col.
Arbest—(b)—toilet—SCOTT PAPER CO., Philadelphia.
Arbitration—(w and b)—bond, ledger, writing—NEENAH PAPER CO., Neenah, Wis.
Arbor Bond—(b)—PULP & PAPER TRADING CO., New York.
Arbutus—(b)—FOX RIVER PAPER CO., Appleton, Wis.
A. R. C. Linen Ledger — (w)—ARNOLD-ROBERTS CO., Boston.

FELTS AND JACKETS | Appleton Woolen Mills, APPLETON - - WIS.

Arcadia—(b)—ruled goods—R. L. GREENE PAPER CO., Providence, R. I.
Arcade Bond—(w)—AETNA PAPER CO., Dayton, Ohio.
Arcadia Bond — (w) — GRAHAM PAPER CO., St. Louis.
Arcadia Superfine—(w)—HAMMERMILL PAPER CO., Erie, Pa.
Archaic Ant. Wove Deckle Edge Book—(b)—HENRY LINDENMEYR & SONS, New York.
Archdale—(b)—ALBANY PERFORATED WRAPPING PAPER CO., Albany, N. Y.
Archer Bond—(w)—ARCHER PAPER CO., Chattanooga, Tenn.
Archer Fibre—(b)—fibre—ARCHER PAPER CO., Chattanooga, Tenn.
Archer Toilet Paper—(b)—toilet—ARCHER PAPER CO., Chattanooga.
Architect Cover—(b)—MINNEAPOLIS PAPER CO., Minneapolis, Minn.
Archive Bond—(w) — AMERICAN WRITING PAPER CO., Holyoke.
Archive Linen — (w)—AMERICAN WRITING PAPER CO., Holyoke.
Archive Linen Ledger — (w) — AMERICAN WRITING PAPER CO., Holyoke.
Archive Manila—(h)—B U N T I N, GILLIES & CO., LTD, Hamilton, Ontario, Can.
Arco Double Coated — (b)—book—ARNOLD-ROBERTS CO., Boston.
Arco Text Deckle Edge — (w) — book — ARNOLD-ROBERTS CO., Boston.
Arctic—(b) — blotting — C. P. LESH PAPER CO., Indianapolis, Ind.
Arctic—(b)—tag board—AMERICAN WOOD BOARD CO., Schuylerville, N. Y.
Arctic—(b)—tarred felt — GRAHAM PAPER CO., St. Louis.
Arctic—(h)—white fibre wrapping—WHITING-PATTERSON CO., New York.
Arctic White — (b)—STRATHMORE PAPER CO., Mittineague, Mass.
Arctic White Wedding Bristol—(b)—STRATHMORE PAPER CO., Mittineague, Mass.
Arcturus No. 1 Enamel — (w)—coated book—SWIGART PAPER CO., Chicago.
Arden—(b)—book—M E G A R G E E BROS., Scranton, Pa.
Ardmore — (b) — bond and linen—RIEGEL & CO., INC., Philadelphia.
Ardmore Bond—(b)—W O R T H Y PAPER CO., Mittineague, Mass.
Ardshire—(b)—white bristol—J. C. PARKER PAPER CO., Louisville, Ky.
Area Bond—(w)—CLARKE PAPER CO., Wheeling, W. Va.
Arena Bond—(w)—THE ALLING & CORY CO., Rochester, N. Y.
Are-And-Be — (w) — ledger—RICHMOND & BACKUS CO., Detroit, Mich.

Argentine—(b)—white fibre wrapping—WHITING-PATTERSON CO., New York.
Argentum Silver Tissue — (b) — HENRY LINDENMEYR & SONS, N. Y.
Argillite—(b)—roofing — GRAHAM PAPER CO., St. Louis.
Argosy Bond—(w)—ALEXANDER-HOLDEN PAPER CO., New York.
Argosy Bond—(w)—CROCKER-McELWAIN CO., Holyoke.
Argus—(b)—envelope—UNION CARD & PAPER CO., New York.
Argus—(b)—toilet—H. NORWOOD EWING CO., New York.
Argus Index Bristol—(b)—PARSONS TRADING CO., New York City.
Argus Writing — (b) — PARSONS TRADING CO., New York City.
Argyle —(w)— writing — CENTRAL OHIO PAPER CO., Columbus, Ohio.
Argyle—(b)—bristol boards—DONALDSON PAPER CO., Harrisburg, Pa.
Argyle—(b)—super-calendered book—THE PETERS PAPER CO., Denver.
Argyle — (b) — toilet — UNITED STATES ENVELOPE CO. (Morgan Envelope Co. Division), Springfield.
Argyle Linen—(w)—WHITING PAPER CO., Holyoke, Mass.
Arion — (b) — writing—MERRIAM PAPER CO., New York.
Aristo—(b)—half-tone book and folder—BRADNER SMITH & CO., Chicago.
Aristo Pasted Wedding—(b)—MINNEAPOLIS PAPER CO., Minneapolis
Aristocrat—(b)—coated — LEWERTH & CULBERTSON, New York.
Arizona—(b)—sheathing — GRAHAM PAPER CO., St. Louis.
Arizona—(w) — writing—MIDLAND PAPER CO., Chicago.
Arizona — (b) — wrapping — LOUISVILLE PAPER CO., Louisville, Ky.
Arizona Bond—(w)—THE McNEIL CO., Phoenix, Ariz.
Arkwright—(w) — COLLINS M F G. CO., N. Wilbraham, Mass.
Arlington—(b) — translucent cardboard — ARNOLD-ROBERTS CO., Boston.
Arlington — (b) — news—GRAHAM PAPER CO., St. Louis.
Arlington—(b)—shipping tags—R. P. ANDREWS PAPER CO., Washington, D. C.
Arlington—(b)—blotting — EATON-DIKEMAN CO., Lee, Mass.
Arlington Bond—(w)—R. P. ANDREWS PAPER CO., Washington, D. C.
Arlington Bristol—(b)—wedding—R. P. ANDREWS PAPER CO., Washington, D. C.
Arlington Cover—(b)—R. P. ANDREWS PAPER CO., Washington, D. C.
Arlington Dull Coated—(b)—book—R. P. ANDREWS PAPER CO., Washington, D. C.

BLOTTING PAPERS "STANDARD," "IMPERIAL," "STERLING" Royal Worcester and Defender Enameled
STANDARD PAPER MFG. CO., - - Richmond, Va.

Watermarks and Brands 625

Arlington Mills—(b)—writing—R. P. ANDREWS PAPER CO., Washington, D. C.
Arlington Ledger—(w)—R. P. ANDREWS PAPER CO., Washington, D. C.
Arlington Mills — (w)—writing—WHITING PAPER CO., Holyoke.
Arlington Mills — (w)—CARTER, RICE & CO., Boston.
Arlington Mimeograph—(b)—R. P. ANDREWS PAPER CO., Washington, D. C.
Arlington Post Card—(b)—R. P. ANDREWS PAPER CO., Washington, D. C.
Arlington Printers Cards—(b)—R. P. ANDREWS PAPER CO., Washington, D. C.
Armor Ledger — (w) — THOS. W. PRICE CO., Philadelphia.
Armory—(b)—enameled cover—JAS. WHITE PAPER CO., Chicago.
Armory Linen—(b)—double enameled cover—JAMES WHITE PAPER CO., Chicago.
Army Bond — (b)—BUNTIN, GILLIES & CO., Hamilton, Can.
Army Bristol—(b)—HARLEM CARD & PAPER CO., New York.
Arlington R. P. Cards—(b)—R. P. ANDREWS PAPER CO., Washington, D. C.
Army and Navy—(b)—toilet—ALBANY PERFORATED WRAPPING PAPER CO., Albany, N. Y.
Arnold Unbleached—(w) — JAPAN PAPER CO., New York.
Aroostook —(b)—HOLLINGSWORTH & WHITNEY CO., Boston.
Asrah Linen — (b)—cover—PAPER MILLS CO., Chicago.
Ariv Half Tone—(b)—AMERICAN WRITING PAPER CO., Holyoke.
Arrow — (b) — onion skin — LOUISVILLE PAPER CO., Louisville, Ky.
Arrow—(b) — envelopes—BRADNER SMITH & CO., Chicago.
Arrow—printing—W. H. PARSONS & CO., New York.
Arrow Bond — (b) — BRADNER SMITH & CO., Chicago.
Arrow Book — (b) — KINGSLEY PAPER CO., Cleveland, Ohio.
Art Book—(b)—DILL & COLLINS CO., Philadelphia.
Artcraft Antique Book—(b)—HY. LINDENMEYR & SONS, New York.
Artcraft Antique Cover—(b)—HY. LINDENMEYR & SONS, New York.
Art Finished Book—(b)—KIMBERLY-CLARK CO., Neenah, Wis.
Art Halftone Super Book—(b)—PETREQUIN PAPER CO., Cleveland.
Arthur Mountain & Co., Ledger—(w)—ARTHUR MOUNTAIN & CO., New York.
Art Relief Embossed Cover—(b)—CARTER, RICE & CO., CORP., Boston.

Artesian Bond — (w) — WHITING-PLOVER PAPER CO., Stevens Point, Wis.
Artillery—(b)—box covering — DISTRICT OF COLUMBIA PAPER CO., Washington, D. C.
Artillery Blotting—(b)—DISTRICT OF COLUMBIA PAPER MFG. CO., Washington, D. C.
Artillery Cover — (b)—DISTRICT OF COLUMBIA PAPER MFG. CO., Washington, D. C.
Artist—(b)—blanks—UNION CARD & PAPER CO., New York.
Artist Offset—(b)—E. E. LLOYD PAPER CO., Chicago.
Artist Pasted Bristol—(b)—BRADNER SMITH & CO., Chicago.
Artist Ripple Mounts—(b)—MINNEAPOLIS PAPER CO., Minneapolis.
Artistic Coated—(b)—dull finish white and colored book—THE ALLING & CORY CO., Rochester, N. Y.
Artistic Tints—(b)—EAST HARTFORD MANUFACTURING CO., Burnside, Conn.
Artistic Weddings — (b) — flats—EAST HARTFORD MANUFACTURING CO., Burnside, Conn.
Artistic Tints—(b)—EAST HARTFORD MFG. CO., Burnside, Conn.
Art Velvet Finish Book—(b)—PETREQUIN PAPER CO., Cleveland.
Artistic Weddings — (b)—flats—EAST HARTFORD MFG. CO., Burnside, Conn.
Artogravure—(b)—white and india tint, book (English surface for offset press)—S. D. WARREN CO., Boston.
Arvada—(w)—flat writing — THE PETERS PAPER CO., Denver, Col.
Arvey Offset Blanks—(b)—REGENSTEIN-VEEDOR CO., Chicago.
Arvey Offset Bristols —(b)— REGENSTEIN-VEEDOR CO., Chicago.
Arvey Photo Mount—(b)—REGENSTEIN-VEEDOR Co., Chicago.
A. S. & B. Linen Ledger—(w)—A. STORRS & BEMENT CO., Boston.
Ashco—(b) — CROWN COLUMBIA PAPER CO., San Francisco.
Ashcroft Mills—CARTER, RICE & CO., CORP., Boston.
Ashland—four leaf clover—(w)—BLAKE, MOFFITT & TOWNE, San Francisco and Los Angeles.
Ashmere— (b) — blotting—CONROW BROS., New York.
Ashmere — (w) — MOUNTAIN MILL PAPER CO., Lee, Mass.
Ashmere Ledger—(w)—B. D. RISING PAPER CO., Housatonic. Mass.
Ashmere Ledger — (w) — STRATHMORE PAPER CO., Mittineague, Mass.
Ashuelot—(b)—book—JUDD PAPER CO., Holyoke, Mass.
Assurance Bond—(w)—AMERICAN WRITING PAPER CO., Holyoke, Mass.

Watermarks and Brands

Assyrian Linen—(w)—A. STORRS & BEMENT CO., Boston.
Aster—(b)—toilet—ALBANY PERFORATED WRAPPING PAPER CO., Albany, N. Y.
Astor—(b)—toilet—GRAHAM PAPER CO., St. Louis.
Astor Bond—(w)—K A L A M A Z O O PAPER CO., Kalamazoo, Mich.
Astoria—(b)—toilet—SCOTT PAPER CO., Philadelphia.
Astra Manifold—(b)—B. F. BOND PAPER CO., Baltimore.
Astrakhan Bond — (w)—WHITING PATERSON CO., Philadelphia.
Astral — (b) — enamel book — SEYMOUR CO., New York.
Astral Featherweight—(b)—enamel book—SEYMOUR CO., New York.
Atalanta—(w)—FOX RIVER PAPER CO., Appleton, Wis.
Athenaeum Vellum—(w)—GEO. E. DAMON CO., Boston.
Athena Plate—(b)—English finish book — TILESTON & HOLLINGSWORTH CO., Boston.
Athena Bond—(w)—THE BLUNDEN LYON CO., Chicago.
Athens — (b) — bond — WHITING-PATTERSON CO., Philadelphia.
Athens—(b) — manifold unglazed — GRAHAM PAPER CO., St. Louis.
Atlanta — (w) — flat — FOX RIVER PAPER CO., Appleton, Wis.
Atlantic—(b) — flat—BASSETT & SUTPHIN, New York.
Atlantic — (b) — blotting—W. H. CLAFLIN & CO., Boston.
Atlantic—(b)—enamel — DIEM & WING PAPER CO., Cincinnati, O.
Atlantic—(b)—toilet—ALBANY PERFORATED WRAPPING PAPER CO., Albany, N. Y.
Atlantic—(b)—coated blotting—VON OLKER-SNELL PAPER CO., Boston.
Atlantic—(b)—writing—BASSETT & SUTPHIN, New York.
Atlantic Bond — (w)—EASTERN MANUFACTURING CO., Bangor, Me.
Atlantic Butchers — (b) — cordage —GRAHAM PAPER CO., St. Louis.
Atlantic Ledger — (w)—EASTERN MANUFACTURING CO., Bangor, Me.
Atlantic Linen—(b)—toilet—SCOTT PAPER CO., Philadelphia.
Atlantic Mills—(b)—fibre — W. H. CLAFLIN & CO., Boston.
Atlantic Mills—(b)—TILESTON & LIVERMORE, Boston.
Atlantic Mills—(b)—toilet—UNITED STATES ENVELOPE CO. (Morgan Envelope Co. Division), Springfield.
Atlantic Super — (b)—WESTERN PENNA. PAPER CO., Pittsburgh.
Atlantic Tinted Flats — (b) — WRIGHT, BARRETT & STILWELL CO., St. Paul, Minn.
Atlas—(b) — pattern — LOUISVILLE PAPER CO., Louisville, Ky.

Atlas—(b)—mimeograph — CLAFLIN & CO., Boston.
Atlas—(b)—news, cordage—GRAHAM PAPER CO., St. Louis.
Atlas—(b)—toilet — ALBANY PERFORATED WRAPPING PAPER CO., Albany, N. Y.
Atlas—(b)—roofing—R. L. GREENE PAPER CO., Providence, R. I.
Atlas—(b)—toilet—R. L. GREENE PAPER CO., Providence, R. I.
Atlas—(b)—tag—C. P. LESH PAPER CO., Indianapolis, Ind.
Atlas—(w) — POWERS PAPER COMPANY, Springfield, Mass.
Atlas All Jute—(b)—bristol—C. P. LESH PAPER CO., Indianapolis.
Atlas—(b)—envelope—PULP & PAPER TRADING CO., New York.
Atlas—(b)—fibre wrapping—MEGARGEE BROS., Scranton, Pa.
Atlas Bond—(w)—CHATFIELD & WOODS CO., Cincinnati, Ohio.
Atlas Bond—(w)—white bond only—R. C. KASTNER PAPER CO., N. Y.
Atlas Coated Bond—(b)—book—MILLER & WRIGHT PAPER CO., New York.
Atlas Coated Bond—(b)—MILLER & WRIGHT PAPER CO., INC., New York.
Atlas Book—(b)—KINGSLEY PAPER CO., Cleveland, Ohio.
Atlas Envelopes—(b)—A. STORRS & BEMENT CO., Boston.
Atlas Kraft—(b) — wrapping—O L D DOMINION PAPER CO., Norfolk, Va.
Atlas Linen Ledger—(w)—DWIGHT BROTHERS PAPER CO., Chicago.
Atlas Manila — (b) — wrapping — LOUISVILLE PAPER CO., Louisville, Ky.
Atlas M. F. Book—(b)—HARLEM CARD & PAPER CO., New York.
Atlas Mills — (w)—W. G. WILLMANN, New York.
Atlas Offset Bond — (b) — THE CHATFIELD & WOODS CO., Cincinnati, Ohio.
Atlas Oval — (b) — toilet—GEO. T. JOHNSON CO., Boston.
Atlas Super—(b)—HARLEM CARD & PAPER CO., New York.
Atlas Tag—(b)—ARNOLD-ROBERTS CO., Boston.
Attean—(b) — HOLLINGSWORTH & WHITNEY CO., Boston.
Auburn—(b)—enameled book — CINCINNATI CORDAGE AND PAPER CO., Cincinnati, Ohio.
Au Chat Noir—(b)—toilet—ALBANY PERFORATED WRAPPING PAPER CO., Albany, N. Y.
Audit Linen Ledger — (w)—THE CHATFIELD & WOODS CO., Cincinnati, Ohio.
Auditor—(b)—tag board — GRAHAM PAPER CO., St. Louis.
Auld Scotia Lynene—(w)—AMERICAN WRITING PAPER CO., Holyoke.

Watermarks and Brands

Aureola Coated Book—(b)—THE PAPER MILLS COMPANY, Chicago.
Aurora—(b)—bristol—LOUISVILLE PAPER CO., Louisville, Ky.
Aurora—(b)—FOX RIVER PAPER CO., Appleton, Wis.
Aurora—(b)—book and flat writing—MINNEAPOLIS PAPER CO., Minneapolis.
Aurora—(b)—toilet—H. NORWOOD EWING CO., New York.
Aurora Bank Folio—(b)—HY. LINDENMEYR & SONS, New York.
Aurora Enameled—(b)—MILLER & WRIGHT PAPER CO., INC., New York.
Aurora Enameled Tints—(b)—book—MILLER & WRIGHT PAPER CO., New York.
Aurora Fine—(w)—writing—PARSONS TRADING CO., New York.
Ausable—(b)—manila—PULP & PAPER TRADING CO., New York.
Australian Mail—GEO. B. HURD & CO., New York.
Austrian—(w)—WHITAKER PAPER COMPANY, Cincinnati, Ohio.
Authors'—(b)—book—MILLER & WRIGHT PAPER CO., New York.
Authors' Linen—(w)—AMERICAN WRITING PAPER CO., Holyoke.
Auto—(b)—flats—BRADNER SMITH & CO., Chicago.
Autumn—(b)—bristol—LOUISVILLE PAPER CO., Louisville, Ky.
Autumnal Cover—(b)—HY. LINDENMEYR & SONS, New York.
Autocopy Bond—(b)—THE UNION PAPER & TWINE CO., Detroit.
Autocrat Linen—(w)—WHITE & WYCKOFF MFG. CO., Holyoke, Mass.
Avalon—(b)—writing—BAY STATE PAPER CO., Boston.
Avelra—(b)—PEERLESS MFG. CO., Norristown, Pa.
Aviator S. & S. C—(b)—MINNEAPOLIS PAPER CO., Minneapolis, Minn.
Avon—(b)—cover—THE CHATFIELD & WOODS CO., Cincinnati, Ohio.
Avon Bond—(w)—McCLELLAN PAPER CO., Minneapolis, Minn.
Avondale—(b)—ALBANY PERFORATED WRAPPING PAPER COMPANY, N. Y.
Avondale—(b)—envelope—GRAHAM PAPER CO., St. Louis.
Avondale Mills—(w)—STRATHMORE PAPER CO., Mittineague, Mass.
Avon Linen—cream laid—THE ALLING & CORY CO., Rochester, N. Y.
Avon Mills—(b)—writing—J. H. WALKER, New York.
Aymore—(w)—bond, ledger—W. R. GRACE & CO., New York.
Ayr—(b)—J. C. BLAIR CO., Huntingdon, Pa.
Ayre—(b)—all rag writing—FOX RIVER PAPER CO., Appleton, Wis.

Azo—(b)—Kraft wrapping—HORWITZ BROS., Elmira, N. Y.
Azev—(b)—toilet—ALBANY PERFORATED WRAPPING PAPER CO., Albany, N. Y.
Aztec—(b)—sheathing—GRAHAM PAPER CO., St. Louis.
Aztec Bond—(w)—THE McNEIL CO., Phoenix, Ariz.
Azure White Vellum—(w)—GEORGE B. HURD & CO., New York.

B

B—(b)—blanks—I. N. MEGARGEE & CO., Philadelphia.
"B"—(b)—HY. LINDENMEYR & SONS, New York.
B & B Mimeograph—(b)—McCLELLAN PAPER CO., Minneapolis, Minn.
Badge Bond—(w)—SWIGART PAPER CO., Chicago.
Badger Blue—(w)—manilas—SWIGART PAPER CO., Chicago.
B. E. Fibre—(b)—R. L. GREENE PAPER CO., Providence, R. I.
B. Fibre—(b)—R. L. GREENE PAPER CO., Providence, R. I.
B. Tissue—(b)—R. L. GREENE PAPER CO., Providence, R. I.
Badger Index Bristol—(b)—KINGSLEY PAPER CO., Cleveland.
Badger Parchment—(b)—manilas—SWIGART PAPER CO., Chicago.
Badger Pink—(b)—manilas—SWIGART PAPER CO., Chicago.
Badger Railroad Manila—(b)—SWIGART PAPER CO., Chicago.
Bainbridge—(w)—writing—C. T. BAINBRIDGE'S SONS, Brooklyn.
Balbriggan—(b)—extra superfine—J. C. BLAIR CO., Huntington, Pa.
Baldric Bristol—(b)—C. P. LESH PAPER CO., Indianapolis, Ind.
Balkan Kraft—(b)—MICHIGAN BAG & PAPER CO., Jackson, Mich.
Balkan M. F.—(b)—book—SPRINGFIELD PAPER & SUPPLY CO., Springfield, Mo.
Balmoral—(b)—UNITED STATES ENVELOPE CO. (Morgan [Env.] Co. Division), Springfield, Mass.
Balmoral—(w)—UNITED STATES ENVELOPE CO. (Morgan Division), Springfield, Mass.
Balsam Fir—(b)—toilet—NORTHERN PAPER MILLS, Milwaukee, Wis.
Balsam Sanitissue—(b)—toilet—SCOTT PAPER CO., Philadelphia.
Balsamic—(b)—toilet—SCOTT PAPER CO., Philadelphia.
Baltic—(b)—No. 1 Manila—WHITING-PATTERSON CO., New York.
Baltic—(b)—writing and book—GRAHAM PAPER CO., St. Louis.
Baltic Bond—(b)—PARSONS TRADING CO., New York.
Baltic Bristol—(b)—PARSONS TRADING CO., New York.

FELTS AND JACKETS | Appleton Woolen Mills, APPLETON - - WIS

Watermarks and Brands

Baltic Ledger—(w)—CRITCHLEY & WHITE, N. Y.
Baltic Mills—(b)—flats—DONALDSON PAPER CO., Harrisburg, Pa.
Baltland—(w)—ledger and writing—J. FRANCIS HOCK & CO., Baltimore.
Balsac Deckle Edge Fine Laid Book—(b)—HY. LINDENMEYR & SONS, New York.
Bamboo Bond—(b)—DREW'S WHOLESALE PAPER HOUSE, Jacksonville, Fla.
Bamboo—(b)—toilet—UNITED STATES ENVELOPE CO. (Morgan Envelope Co. Division), Springfield.
Bamboo—(w)—J. C. BLAIR. CO., Huntingdon, Pa.
Bamboo Fibre—(b)—D. S. WALTON & CO., New York.
Bancroft—(b)—translucent cardboard—ARNOLD-ROBERTS CO., Boston.
Bank Check—(w)—W. E. Wroe & Co., Chicago.
Bangalore—(b)—PERKINS, GOODWIN CO., New York.
Bangkok—(b)—index—WHITING-PATTERSON CO., Philadelphia.
Bank Bond—(w)—R. H. THOMPSON CO., Buffalo, N. Y.
Bank Bond—(w)—writing—CAREW MANUFACTURING CO., South Hadley Falls, Mass.
Bank Book—(w)—ledger—DAVID L. ENGLE, New York.
Bank Index—(b)—bristol—THE ALLING & CORY CO., Rochester, N. Y.
Bank Linen—(b)—bond—RIEGEL & CO., INC., Philadelphia.
Bank Superfine—(w)—LEE PAPER CO., Vicksburg, Mich.
Bank Record Ledger—(w)—AMERICAN WRITING PAPER CO., Holyoke, Mass.
Bankers—(b)—bristol—UNION CARD & PAPER CO., New York.
Banker's—(b)—coated blotting—GARRETT-BUCHANAN CO., Philadelphia.
Bankers' Ledger—(w)—LASHER & LATHROP, New York.
Bankers' & Merchants' Ledger—(w)—BRADNER SMITH & CO., Chicago.
Bankers' Board—(b)—BRADNER SMITH & CO., Chicago.
Bankers' Bond—(w)—AMERICAN WRITING PAPER CO., Holyoke, Mass.
Bankers' Bond—(w)—VERNON BROS. & CO., New York.
Bankers' Fine—(b)—writing—RIEGEL & CO., INC., Philadelphia.
Bankers' Ledger—(w)—STRATHMORE PAPER CO., Mittineague, Mass.
"Bankers' Ledger"—(w)—SAUGERTIES MFG. CO., Saugerties, N. Y.
Bankers' Ledger—(w)—AMERICAN WRITING PAPER CO., Holyoke, Mass.
Bankers' Linen—(w)—SOUTHWORTH CO., Mittineague, Mass.
Bankers' Linen—(w)—SOUTHWORTH CO., Mittineague, Mass.
Bankers' Linen Bond—(w)—SOUTHWORTH CO., Mittineague, Mass.
Bankers' Linen Finish—(b)—blotting—STANDARD PAPER MANUFACTURING CO., Richmond, Va.
Bankers' Linen Ledger—(w)—SOUTHWORTH CO., Mittineague, Mass.
Bankers' Onion Skin Bond—(b)—CARTER, RICE & CO., CORP., Boston.
Bankers' Safety—(b)—GEO. LA MONTE & SONS, New York.
Bankers Super—(b)—writing—O. F. H. WARNER & CO., Baltimore.
Bankers' Woven Fabrics—(b)—E. E. LLOYD PAPER CO., Chicago, Ill.
Bankers' Writing—(w)—THE CHATFIELD & WOODS CO., Cincinnati, Ohio.
Bank Exchange—(w)—W. G. WILLMANN, New York.
Bank Exchange Linen—(w)—W. G. WILLMANN, New York.
Bank Ledger—SOUTHWORTH CO., Mittineague, Mass.
Bank Note Bond—(w and b)—GEO. B. HURD & CO., New York.
Bank of England—(w)—bond—Kansas City Paper Co., Kansas City.
Bank Parchment—PAYOT, UPHAM & CO., San Francisco, Cal.
Bank Parchment—(w)—EAST HARTFORD MANUFACTURING CO., Burnside, Conn.
Bank Record Ledger—AMERICAN WRITING PAPER CO., Holyoke, Mass.
Bank Superfine—(w)—writing—LEE PAPER CO., Vicksburg, Mich.
Banner—(b)—toilet, cordage—GRAHAM PAPER CO., St. Louis.
Banner—(b)—photo mounts—UNION CARD & PAPER CO., New York.
Banner—(b)—SOUTHERN PAPER CO., Richmond, Va.
Banner—(b)—sheathing and toilet and adding machine—LOUISVILLE PAPER CO., Louisville.
Banner Blanks—(b)—HY. LINDENMEYR & SONS, New York.
Banner Book—(b)—KINGSLEY PAPER CO., Cleveland, Ohio.
Banner Linen—(w)—SOUTHWORTH CO., Mittineague, Mass.
Banner Writing—(w)—HARLEM CARD & PAPER CO., New York.
Bannockburn Cover—(b)—STRATHMORE PAPER CO., Mittineague, Mass.
Banque Bond—RICHMOND PAPER CO., Richmond, Va.
Bantam Weight Bond—(b)—manifold—MEGARGEE BROS., Scranton, Pa.

BLOTTING PAPERS STANDARD PAPER MFG. CO., Richmond, Va. Largest Manufacturers

Watermarks and Brands

Banzai Ledger—(w and b)—THE PAPER MILLS CO., Chicago.
Ba Pa Co. Bond—(w)—BAKER PAPER., Oshkosh, Wis.
Ba Pa Co. Mills—(w)—BAKER PAPER CO., Oshkosh, Wis.
Ba Pa Co. Mimeograph—(b)—BAKER PAPER CO., Oshkosh, Wis.
Bardeen—(w)—BARDEEN PAPER CO., Otsego, Mich.
Bar Design—(w)—MARATHON PAPER MILLS, Wausau, Wis.
Baronet—(w)—INLAND EMPIRE PAPER CO., Millwood, Wash.
Baronial Bond—(b)—GEORGE B. HURD & CO., New York.
Barrington Bond—(w)—B. D. RISING PAPER CO., Housatonic, Mass.
Barrington Ledger—(w)—B. D. RISING PAPER CO., Housatonic, Mass.
Barrington Linen—(w)—B. D. RISING PAPER CO., Housatonic, Mass.
Barrington Wedding Bristol—B. D. RISING PAPER CO., Housatonic, Mass.
Bartlett Bond—(w)—A. PRICE, Brooklyn, N. Y.
Barristers' Bond—(w)—A. R. ANDREWS, Boston.
Bartholdi—(w)—white wove—EASTERN PAPER AND SUPPLY CO., Springfield, Mass.
Battery Bond—(b)—HENRY LINDENMEYR & SONS, New York.
Basket Weave—(b)—Z. & W. M. CRANE, Dalton, Mass.
Bassett & Sutphin Extra Fine—(w)—wove—BASSETT & SUTPHIN, New York.
Bassphin—(b)—BASSETT & SUTPHIN, New York.
Battalion Bond—(w)—PARSONS TRADING CO., New York.
Battery—(b)—blotting—PARSONS TRADING CO., New York.
Battery Bond—Made in U. S. A.—(w)—PARSONS TRADING CO., New York.
Battery Ledger—(w)—(laid)—(woven)—PARSONS TRADING CO., New York.
Battery Manifold Paper—(b)—PARSONS TRADING CO., New York.
Battery Pencil Carbon Paper—(b)—PARSONS TRADING CO., New York.
Battery Laid Writing—(b)—PARSONS TRADING CO., New York.
Battery Ledger—(b)—WHITAKER PAPER CO., Cincinnati, Ohio.
Battery Wove Writing—(b)—PARSONS TRADING CO., New York.
Battle Ship—(w)—bond and ledger—FOX RIVER PAPER CO., Appleton, Wis.
Baunog—(w)—white and colored bond—J. ERNEST HAMMOND, 129 Dyer St., Providence, R. I.

Bavarian Parchment—(b)—BRADNER SMITH & CO., Chicago.
Baxter—(b)—news—GRAHAM PAPER CO., St. Louis.
Bay Bond—(w)—ARCHER PAPER CO., Chattanooga, Tenn.
Bay Path Cockle Finish—(w)—bond—STRATHMORE PAPER CO., Mittineague, Mass.
Bay Path Cover—(b)—STRATHMORE PAPER CO., Mittineague, Mass.
Bay Path Multi Copy Bond—(w)—STRATHMORE PAPER CO., Mittineague, Mass.
Bay Path Wedding—(b)—STRATHMORE PAPER CO., Mittineague, Mass.
Bay State—(b)—blotting—BAY STATE PAPER CO., Boston.
Bay State—(b)—ledger—BAY STATE PAPER CO., Boston.
Bay State Folding Bristol—(b)—JOHN CARTER & CO., Boston.
Bay State Index Bristol—(b)—BAY STATE PAPER CO., Boston.
Bay State Linen Finish—(b)—bristol—BAY STATE PAPER CO., Boston.
Bazaar—(b)—toilet—ALBANY PERFORATED WRAPPING PAPER CO., Albany, N. Y.
B.C.W. (Bond Circular Wedding)—(w)—MILLER & WRIGHT PAPER CO., INC., New York.
Beach—(b)—translucent cardboard—ARNOLD-ROBERTS CO., Boston.
Beacon Book—(b)—JOHN CARTER & CO., Inc., Boston.
Beacon—(b)—translucent cardboard—ARNOLD-ROBERTS CO., Boston.
Beacon—(b)—news—WHITAKER PAPER CO., Cincinnati, Ohio.
Beacon—(b)—toilet—UNITED STATES ENVELOPE CO. (Morgan Envelope Co. Division), Springfield.
Beacon—(b)—No. 2 manila—STONE & FORSYTH CO., Boston.
Beacon Bond—(w and b)—also in writing—PAPER MILLS CO., Chicago.
Beacon Hill Bond—(w)—GEO. E. DAMON CO., Boston.
Beacon Hill Linen—(w)—GEO. E. DAMON CO., Boston.
Beacon Mills—(b)—A. STORRS & BEMENT CO., Boston.
Beacon Souvenir Post Card—(b)—BRADNER SMITH & CO., Chicago.
Beau Brummel—(b)—cover—WILKINSON BROS. & CO., Phila.
Beaufort Antique—(b)—laid book—HY. LINDENMEYR & SONS, New York.
Beaufort Colored Laid—(b)—flat writing—MERRIAM PAPER CO., New York.
Beaulieu Antique—(b)—wove book—HY. LINDENMEYR & SONS, New York.

FELTS AND JACKETS | Appleton Woolen Mills
APPLETON - - WIS.

Watermarks and Brands

Beaver—(b)—manila—STONE & FORSYTH CO., Boston.
Beaver Board—(b)—BRADNER SMITH & CO., Chicago.
Beaver Brand Boards—(b)—boards—J. P. LEWIS CO., Beaver Falls, New York.
Beaver Dam—(w)—BUNTIN, GILLIES & CO., Hamilton, Ontario, Can
Beaver Mills—(b)—ledger writing—CANFIELD PAPER CO., THE, New York.
Beckett Bond—(w)—BECKETT PAPER CO., Hamilton, Ohio.
Bedford—(b)—toilet—ALBANY PERFORATED WRAPPING PAPER CO., Albany, N. Y.
Bedford Mills—(b)—toilet—UNITED STATES ENVELOPE CO. (Morgan Envelope Co. Division), Springfield.
Bed Rock—(b)—colored bristol—KANSAS PAPER HOUSE, Kansas City, Mo.
Bed Rock Flats—(b)—BRADNER SMITH & CO., Chicago.
Bedford Bond—(b)—HY. LINDENMEYR & SONS, New York.
Bee—(b)—writing—ANTIETAM PAPER CO., Hagerstown, Md.
Beechmore Mills—(w)—flats—LOUISVILLE PAPER CO., Louisville, Ky.
Beechnut—(b)—wrapping—LOUISVILLE PAPER CO., Louisville, Ky.
Beechwood—(w)—AMERICAN WRITING PAPER CO., Holyoke.
Beechwood—(b)—bristol—JUDD PAPER CO., Holyoke, Mass.
Beechwood—(w)—A. STORRS & BEMENT CO., Boston.
Bee Gee Blanks—(b)—BUNTIN, GILLIES & CO., LTD., Hamilton, Ontario, Can.
Beekman—(b)—bristol—UNION CARD & PAPER CO., New York.
Beekman Blotting—(b)—HY. LINDENMEYR & SONS, New York.
Beekman Bond—(w)—LEHMAIER & BROTHER, New York.
Beekman Colored Bristol—(b)—F. A. FLINN, INC., New York.
Beekman Mills—HOOPER, LEWIS & CO., Boston.
Beekman Toilet Tissue—(b)—HY. LINDENMEYR & SONS, New York.
Bee Line—(b)—toilet—UNITED STATES ENVELOPE CO. (Morgan Envelope Co. Division), Springfield.
Beeswing Opaque—(b)—catalogue—BEECHER, PECK & LEWIS, Detroit, Mich.
Belfast—(b)—book—KANSAS CITY PAPER HOUSE, Kansas City, Mo.
Belfast Barnet Linen—(w)—UNITED STATES ENVELOPE CO. (Whitcomb Envelope Co. Division), Worcester, Mass.
Belfast Crash Linen Lawn—(b)—OLD DOMINION PAPER CO., Norfolk, Va.

Belfast Fabric—(b)—J. C. PARKER PAPER CO., Louisville, Ky.
Belfast Bristol—(b)—BRADNER SMITH & CO., Chicago.
Belfast Ledger—(w)—HAGEN PAPER CO., St. Louis.
Belfast—(b)—index bristol—WHITING-PATTERSON CO., Philadelphia.
Belfast Linen—(b)—linen—STANDARD CARD & PAPER CO., New York.
Belfast Linen Bond—(w)—BERKSHIRE HILLS PAPER CO., Adams, Mass.
Belfast Linen Bond—(w)—C. S. PROCTOR PAPER CO., Boston.
Belfast Linen Ledger—(w)—PETREQUIN PAPER CO., Cleveland.
Belfield Bond—(w)—RIEGEL & CO., INC., Philadelphia.
Belfield Mills—(w)—DONALDSON PAPER CO., Harrisburg, Pa.
Belford Linen—(w)—UNION CARD AND PAPER CO., New York.
Belford Parchment—(w)—EAST HARTFORD MANUFACTURING CO., Burnside, Conn.
Belgian Bond—(w)—EASTERN MFG. CO., Bangor, Me.
Belgian Ledger—(w)—EASTERN MFG. CO., Bangor, Me.
Belgian Linen—(w)—EASTERN MFG. CO., Bangor, Me.
Belgrade Cover—(b)—HY. LINDENMEYR & SONS, New York.
Bellcourt—(w)—UNION CARD AND PAPER CO., New York.
Belleview Mills—(w)—writing—GARRETT-BUCHANAN CO., Philadelphia.
Bellevue—(b)—toilet—E. L. GREENE PAPER CO., Providence, R. I.
Bellfast Bond—(w)—HOWARD SMITH PAPER MILLS, LTD., Montreal, Can.
Belmere Linen—(w)—EATON, CRANE & PIKE CO., Pittsfield, Mass.
Belmont—(b)—CHATFIELD & WOODS CO., Cincinnati, Ohio.
Belmont Mills—(b)—JOHN CARTER & CO., INC., Boston.
Belmore Bond—(w)—A. PRICE, Brooklyn, N. Y.
Belvedere—(b)—cover—GRAHAM PAPER CO., St. Louis.
Belvedere—(b)—toilet—ALBANY PERFORATED WRAPPING PAPER CO., Albany, N. Y.
Belwood—(b)—envelope—UNION CARD & PAPER CO., New York.
Bemis Ledger—(w)—McCLELLAN PAPER CO., Minneapolis, Minn.
Ben Day Cover—(b)—DILL & COLLINS CO., Philadelphia.
Ben Franklin—(b)—enamel book—THE CHATFIELD & WOODS CO., Cincinnati, Ohio.
Ben Franklin—(b)—enamel—UNION PAPER & TWINE CO., Detroit, Mich.
Ben Franklin Bond—(w)—B. F BOND PAPER CO., Baltimore.

JAMES H. HARRISON
PULPSTONE MANUFACTURER

GENUINE NEWCASTLE STONES
16 KBowen St., GATESHEAD-ON-TYNE, ENG.

Watermarks and Brands

Ben Franklin Bond—(w)—B. D. RISING PAPER CO., Housatonic, Mass.
Ben Franklin Text—(b)—India book—F. A. FLINN, INC., New York.
Bengal—(b)—s. and s. c. book—J. W. BUTLER PAPER CO., Chicago.
Bengal—(b)—toilet—WHITING-PATTERSON CO., New York.
Bennington — (b) — tag—JUDD PAPER CO., Holyoke, Mass.
Bennington Bible—(b)—unglazed—CANFIELD PAPER CO., New York.
Bennington Ledger—(w)—LASHER & LATHROP, New York.
Berkeley—(w)—extra fine—THOMAS W. PRICE CO., Philadelphia.
Berkeley Linen Ledger—(b)—CONROW BROTHERS, New York.
Berkeley Mills Linen Ledger—(w)—CONROW BROTHERS, New York.
Berkett — (b) — book — BRADNER SMITH & CO., Chicago.
Berkeley Bristol—(b)—A. STORRS & BEMENT CO., Boston.
Berkshire—(b)—blotting — EATON, DIKEMAN & CO., Lee, Mass.
Berkshire—(b) — copying tissue — SMITH PAPER CO., Lee, Mass.
Berkshire Bond Fabric — (w)—EATON, CRANE & PIKE CO., Pittsfield, Mass.
Berkshire Hills First Class Ledger—(w)—BERKSHIRE HILLS PAPER CO., Adams, Mass.
Berkshire Linen Fabric — (w)—EATON, CRANE & PIKE CO., Pittsfield, Mass.
Berkshire Bond U. S. A.—(w and b)—typewriter—EATON, CRANE & PIKE CO., Pittsfield, Mass.
Berkshire Bristol — (b) — WHITAKER PAPER CO., Cincinnati, O.
Berkshire Duplicate Copy Paper—(b)—typewriter—EATON, CRANE & PIKE CO., Pittsfield, Mass.
Berkshire Hills Loose Leaf Ledger—(w)—BERKSHIRE HILLS PAPER CO., Adams, Mass.
Berkshire Hills Linen — (w) — BERKSHIRE HILLS PAPER CO., Adams, Mass.
Berkshire Hills Index Bristol—(b)—BERKSHIRE HILLS PAPER CO., Adams, Mass.
Berkshire Litho Bond—(b)—BERKSHIRE HILLS PAPER CO., Adams, Mass.
Berkshire Hills Extra Angora Wedding — (b) — BERKSHIRE HILLS PAPER CO., Adams, Mass.
Berkshire Hills Superfine Wedding—(b)—BERKSHIRE HILLS PAPER CO., Adams, Mass.
Berkshire Hills Superior Typewriter Paper—(b)—BERKSHIRE HILLS PAPER CO., Adams, Mass.
Berkshire Hills Two-tone—(b)—BERKSHIRE HILLS PAPER CO., Adams, Mass.

Berkshire Hills Loose Leaf—(b)—book—LASHER & LATHROP, N. Y.
Berkshire Linen — (w)—ledger—J. W. BUTLER PAPER CO., Chicago.
Berkshire Linen U. S. A.—(w and b)—typewriter—EATON, CRANE & PIKE CO., Pittsfield, Mass.
Berkshire Linen Parchment—(b)—typewriter—EATON, CRANE & PIKE CO., Pittsfield, Mass.
Berkshire Manuscript Cover U. S. A.—(w)—typewriter—EATON, CRANE & PIKE CO., Pittsfield, Mass.
Berkshire Parchment Linen U. S. A. — (w) — typewriter — EATON, CRANE & PIKE CO., Pittsfield, Mass.
Berkshire Satin Finish — (b)—EATON, CRANE & PIKE CO., Pittsfield, Mass.
Berkshire Souvenir Bond U. S. A.—typewriter — EATON, CRANE & PIKE CO., Pittsfield, Mass.
Berkshire Text — (w)—AMERICAN WRITING PAPER CO., Holyoke.
Berkshire Tinted Bristol—(b)—W. G. WILLMANN, New York.
Berkshire Typewriter Paper U. S. A. — (w) — typewriter—EATON, CRANE & PIKE CO., Pittsfield.
Berkshire Vesper Linen U. S. A.—(w)—typewriter—EATON, CRANE & PIKE CO., Pittsfield, Mass.
Berkshire Valley—(w and b)—TAYLOR-ATKINS PAPER CO., Hartford, Conn.
Berkshire Vellum—(b)—EATON, CRANE & PIKE CO., Pittsfield.
Berkshire Vellum Bond U. S. A.—(w)—typewriter—EATON, CRANE & PIKE CO., Pittsfield, Mass.
Berlin —(b)— writing — WHITING-PATTERSON CO., Philadelphia.
Berlin—(b) — colored bristol—W. H. CLAFLIN & CO., Boston.
Berlin Linen—(b)—BASSETT & SUTPHIN, New York.
Berlin Mills—(w)—bond—BERLIN & JONES ENVELOPE CO., New York.
Berlin—(b)—ALBANY PERFORATED WRAPPING PAPER CO., Albany.
Bermico Sheathing Paper—(b)—BERLIN MILLS CO., Portland, Me.
Bermuda Onion Skin Folio—(b)—BRADNER SMITH & CO., Chicago.
Berne Ledger—(w and b)—WHITING-PATTERSON CO., Philadelphia.
Berthcill—(b)—litho. blanks, bond. book—BURTON C. HILL, New York.
Berwick—(b and w)—ledger—F. W. ANDERSON & CO., New York.
Berwick—(b)—H. REEVE ANGEL & CO., INC., New York.
Berwick Linen—(w)—VALLEY PAPER CO., Holyoke, Mass.
Berwick Mills—(b)—folded—POWERS PAPER CO., Springfield, Mass.
Bessemer—(b)— cover — SEYMOUR CO., New York.
Best Linen — (b) — HY. LINDENMEYR & SONS, New York.

FELTS AND JACKETS | Appleton Woolen Mills, APPLETON - - WIS.

Watermarks and Brands

Bestever Bond—(w)—MERRIAM PAPER CO., New York.
Bestok—(b)—toilet—SCOTT PAPER CO., Philadelphia.
Best-Value—(w)—bond, ledger—BAKER-VAWTER CO., Benton Harbor, Mich.
Bestyet Fibre—(b)—OLD DOMINION PAPER CO., Norfolk, Va.
Beverly Bond—(w)—PAUL E. VERNON & CO., New York.
Beverwyck—(b)—toilet—ALBANY PERFORATED WRAPPING PAPER CO., Albany, N. Y.
Bible Paper—(b)—B R A D N E R SMITH & CO., Chicago.
Bifold Enamel—(b)—bristol—J. W. BUTLER PAPER CO., Chicago.
Bigelow—(b)—book—CINCINNATI CORDAGE AND PAPER CO., Cincinnati, Ohio.
Big Five—(b)—toilet—R. M. MYERS & CO., Rochester, N. Y.
Big Four R.R. Manila—(b)—KINGSLEY PAPER CO., Cleveland.
Big Hit—(b)—toilet—THE SEINSHEIMER PAPER CO., Cincinnati.
Big Lick—(b)—toilet—NORTHERN PAPER MILLS, Green Bay, Wis.
Big Value—(b)—roll toilet—THE CHATFIELD & WOODS CO., Cincinnati, Ohio.
Bill—(b)—tag board—AMERICAN WOOD BOARD CO., Schuylerville, N. Y.
Billiken—(b)—No. 1 manila and toilet—THE SEINSHEIMER PAPER CO., Cincinnati, Ohio.
Bill of Lading Manila—(b)—BRADNER SMITH & CO., Chicago.
Biplane Bond—(w)—C E N T R A L OHIO PAPER CO., Columbus, Ohio.
Birch Bark—(w and b)—GEO. B. HURD & CO., New York.
Birchwood Superfine—(w)—CARTER, RICE & CO., CORP., Boston.
Birchwood Text—(b)—JUDD PAPER CO., Holyoke, Mass.
Bird Bond—(w)—HAMMERMILL PAPER CO., Erie, Pa.
Birchbark—(b)—wrapping—LOUISVILLE PAPER CO., Louisville, Ky.
Birchmont Linen—(w)—POWERS PAPER COMPANY, Springfield, Mass.
Bird's-Eye Maple—(b)—GEO. B. HURD & CO., New York.
Birmingham—(b)—ledger—WHITING-PATTERSON CO., Philadelphia.
Bismarck Bond—(w)—WRIGHT, BARRETT & STILWELL CO., St. Paul, Minn.
Bison—(b)—toilet—ALBANY PERFORATED WRAPPING PAPER CO., Albany, N. Y.
Bison—(b)—wrapping—LOUISVILLE PAPER CO., Louisville, Ky.
Black and White—(b)—surface coated—DILL & COLLINS CO., Philadelphia.

Black and White—(b)—duplex—WHITING-PATTERSON CO., Philadelphia.
Black Bass—(b)—gummed—LOUISVILLE PAPER CO., Louisville, Ky.
Blackbird—(w)—SMITH BLANK BOOK CO., INC., New York.
Blackbird Bond—(w)—SMITH BLANK BOOK CO., INC., New York.
Blackbird Ledger—(w)—SMITH BLANK BOOK CO., INC., New York.
Blackbird Linen—(w)—SMITH BLANK BOOK CO., INC., New York.
Black Diamond—(b)—tarred felt—ALEX. McARTHUR & CO., Montreal, Canada.
Black Letter Text—(w)—book—ADVERTISERS' PAPER MILLS, Holyoke, Mass.
Black Hawk—(b)—toilet—ALBANY PERFORATED WRAPPING PAPER CO., Albany, N. Y.
Blackstone—(w)—AETNA PAPER CO., Dayton, Ohio.
Blackstone—(b)—toilet—UNITED STATES ENVELOPE CO. (Morgan Envelope Co. Division), Springfield.
Blackstone—(b)—manifold—WHITING-PATTERSON CO., Philadelphia.
Blackstone Law Book—(b)—WHITAKER PAPER CO., Cincinnati.
Blackstone Mills—(w)—AETNA PAPER CO., Dayton, Ohio.
Blade Manifold—(lightweight)—(b)—BLADE PTG. & PAPER CO., Toledo, Ohio.
Blair's Keystone—(w)—J. C. BLAIR CO., Huntingdon, Pa.
Blandford Bond—(w)—STRATHMORE PAPER CO., Mittineague, Mass.
Blandford Book—(w)—STRATHMORE PAPER CO., Mittineague, Mass.
Blandford Cover—(b)—STRATHMORE PAPER CO., Mittineague, Mass.
Blanford Ledger—(w)—STRATHMORE PAPER CO., Mittineague, Mass.
Blank Book Ledger—(w)—GRAHAM PAPER CO., St. Louis.
Bleecker Bond—(w)—HY. LINDENMEYR & SONS, New York.
Bleecker Ledger—(b)—HY. LINDENMEYR & SONS, New York.
Bleecker Linen Laid—(b)—HY. LINDENMEYR & SONS, New York.
Blue Bells—(b)—toilet—ALBANY PERFORATED WRAPPING PAPER CO., Albany, N. Y.
Blue Bird—(w)—COYLE & GILMORE CO., INC., New York.
Blue Cross—(b)—toilet—NORTHERN PAPER MILLS, Green Bay, Wis.
Blue Grass—(b and w)—bristol—J. C. PARKER PAPER CO., Louisville.
Blue Grass Book—(b)—DIEM & WING PAPER CO., Cincinnati, Ohio.
Blue Hill Text—(w and b)—TILESTON & HOLLINGSWORTH CO., Boston, Mass.

BLOTTING PAPERS "STANDARD," "IMPERIAL," "STERLING" Royal Worcester and Defender Enameled STANDARD PAPER MFG. CO., - - Richmond, Va.

NEW MILLS DESIGNED   POWER PLANTS   OLD MILLS REBUILT

C. A. CHAPMAN, Inc.
8 E. JACKSON BLVD.   ENGINEERS   CHICAGO

Watermarks and Brands — 633

Blue Jacket Kraft—(b)—wrapping—LOUISVILLE PAPER CO., Louisville, Ky.
Blue Jay Bond—(w)—KANSAS CITY PAPER HOUSE, Kansas City.
Blue Label Blotting—(b)—PAUL F. VERNON & CO., New York.
Blue Linden Wove Writings—(b)—HENRY LINDENMEYR & SONS, New York.
Blue Ribbon—(b)—white writing—J. ERNEST HAMMOND, 129 Dyer St., Providence, R. I.
Blue Ribbon Brand—(b)—manila wrapping, roofing and sheathing—SCHMIDT & AULT PAPER CO., York, Pa.
Blue Ridge—(b)—bleached soda fibre—COLUMBIAN PAPER CO., Bristol, Va.
Blue Ridge Bond—(w)—ANTIETAM PAPER CO., Hagerstown, Md.
Blue Ridge Record—(w)—ANTIETAM PAPER CO., Hagerstown, Md.
Blue Ridge Linen Ledger—ANTIETAM PAPER CO., Hagerstown, Md.
Blue Seal—(b)—toilet—NORTHERN PAPER MILLS, Milwaukee, Wis.
Blue Seal—(b)—KANSAS CITY PAPER CO., Kansas City, Mo.
Blue Seal Blasting Paper—(b)—SEINSHEIMER PAPER CO., Cincinnati, Ohio.
Blue Seal Tarred Building Paper—(b)—SEINSHEIMER PAPER CO., Cincinnati, Ohio.
Blueskin Flour Sacks—(b)—LINCOLN PAPER MILLS CO., LTD., Merritton, Ont.
Blue Stone Mills—(w)—writing—GRAHAM PAPER CO., St. Louis.
Blue White—(b)—wedding—MOUNTAIN MILL PAPER CO., Lee, Mass.
Bluewhite—(b)—wedding bristol—B. D. RISING PAPER CO., Housatonic, Mass.
Blyco Bond—(w)—BLUNDEN-LYON CO., Chicago.
B. M.—(b)—book—J. W. BUTLER PAPER CO., Chicago.
Board of Education—(w)—HOPPER PAPER CO., Johnsonburg, Pa.
Board of Trade Bond—(w)—ELSINORE PAPER CO., INC., New York.
Board of Trade Bond—(w)—MT. HOLLY PAPER MILLS, INC., Mt. Holly Springs, Pa.
Bobolink—(b)—bond—LOUISVILLE PAPER CO., Louisville, Ky.
Bob White—roll, flat—(b)—ALBANY PERFORATED WRAPPING PAPER CO., Albany, N. Y.
Bogus—(b)—bristol—J. W. BUTLER PAPER CO., Chicago.
Bohemian—(b)—LOUISVILLE PAPER CO., Louisville, Ky.
Bohemian Vellum—(b)—EASTERN MFG. CO., Bangor, Me.

Bokhara—(b)—cover—SEYMOUR CO., New York.
Bolton—(b)—colored bristol—B. F. BOND PAPER CO., Baltimore.
Bombay—(b)—butchers' manila and wrapping—GRAHAM PAPER CO., St. Louis.
Bombay Blotting—(b)—WHITING-PATTERSON CO., Philadelphia.
Bombay Ledger—(b)—F. A. FLINN, INC., New York.
Bona Fide—(b)—linen—J. C. BLAIR CO., Huntingdon, Pa.
Bona Fide Superfine—(w)—B. F. BOND PAPER CO., Baltimore.
Bonanza—(b)—blank and flat writing—JOHN CARTER & CO., Boston.
Bonanza—(b)—manila—BRADNER SMITH & CO., Chicago.
Bond Circular Wedding—(b)—bond—MILLER & WRIGHT PAPER CO., New York.
Bo[F]nd—(b)—F. A. FLINN, INC., New York.
Bond of Republic—(w)—bond—TAYLOR-ATKINS PAPER CO., Hartford, Conn.
Bond No. XVI—(w)—GEORGE B. HURD & CO., New York.
Bond No. XXI—(w)—GEO. B. HURD & CO., New York.
Bond No. XXV—(w)—GEO. B. HURD & CO., New York.
Bond No. XXIX—(w)—GEO. B. HURD & CO., New York.
Bonita—(b)—writing—BASSETT & SUTPHIN, New York.
Bonita—(w)—flat—DIEM & WING PAPER CO., Cincinnati, Ohio.
Bonita Writing—(b)—SUTPHEN PAPER CO., INC., New York.
Bonnybrook—(b)—HY. LINDENMEYR & SONS, New York.
Bonnybrook Linen—(b)—MARCUS WARD CO., Brooklyn, N. Y.
Bon Ton—(b)—toilet—ALBANY PERFORATED WRAPPING PAPER CO., Albany, N. Y.
Bon Ton—(w)—white and canary writing—B. F. BOND PAPER CO., Baltimore.
Bonus Bond—(b)—LEWERTH & CULBERTSON, New York.
Bookkeepers' Linen Ledger—(w)—CARTER RICE & CO., CORP., Boston.
Booklet—(w and b)—book—PAPER MILLS CO., Chicago.
Booklovers' Text—(w)—book—ADVERTISERS' PAPER MILLS, Holyoke, Mass.
Booster—(b)—envelope—GRAHAM PAPER CO., St. Louis.
Bopaco Bond—(w)—B. F. BOND PAPER CO., Baltimore.
Bordeaux—(b)—cover—AMERICAN WRITING PAPER CO., Holyoke, Mass.
Boss—(b)—paper and paper bags—ATLANTA PAPER CO., Atlanta, Ga.
Boston—(b)—ALBANY PERFORATED WRAPPING PAPER CO., Albany.

APPLETON MACHINE CO., APPLETON, WIS. — REFINING ENGINES, SCREENS, SAWING & SPLITTING MACHINERY — HIGH GRADE CENTRIFUGAL PUMPS

IINER EDGAR CO., Sole Agents   CLA   WASHED   GRITLESS
Isaac Rees Co. 30 CHURCH STREET   <E W>   <C M>
    HIGH COLOR   HIGH RETENTION

Watermarks and Brands

Assyrian Linen—(w) — A. STORRS & BEMENT CO., Boston.
Aster—(b) — toilet — ALBANY PERFORATED WRAPPING PAPER CO., Albany, N. Y.
Astor—(b)—toilet—GRAHAM PAPER CO., St. Louis.
Astor Bond—(w)—K A L A M A Z O O PAPER CO., Kalamazoo, Mich.
Asteria—(b)—toilet—SCOTT PAPER CO., Philadelphia.
Astra Manifold—(b)—B. F. BOND PAPER CO., Baltimore.
Astrakhan Bond — (w) —WHITING PATERSON CO., Philadelphia.
Astral — (b) — enamel book — SEYMOUR CO., New York.
Astral Featherweight—(b)—enamel book—SEYMOUR CO., New York.
Atalanta—(w)—FOX RIVER PAPER CO., Appleton, Wis.
Athenaeum Vellum—(w)—GEO. E. DAMON CO., Boston.
Athena Plate—(b)—English finish book — TILESTON & HOLLINGSWORTH CO., Boston.
Athena Bond—(w)—THE BLUNDEN LYON CO., Chicago.
Athens — (b) — bond — WHITING-PATERSON CO., Philadelphia.
Athens—(b) — manifold unglazed — GRAHAM PAPER CO., St. Louis.
Atlanta — (w) — flat — FOX RIVER PAPER CO., Appleton, Wis.
Atlantic—(b) — flat—BASSETT & SUTPHIN, New York.
Atlantic — (b) — blotting—W. H. CLAFLIN & CO., Boston.
Atlantic—(b)—enamel — DIEM & WING PAPER CO., Cincinnati, O.
Atlantic—(b)—toilet—ALBANY PERFORATED WRAPPING PAPER CO., Albany, N. Y.
Atlantic—(b)—coated blotting—VON OLKER-SNELL PAPER CO., Boston.
Atlantic—(b)—writing—BASSETT & SUTPHIN, New York.
Atlantic Bond — (w)—EASTERN MANUFACTURING CO., Bangor, Me.
Atlantic Butchers — (b) — cordage —GRAHAM PAPER CO., St. Louis.
Atlantic Ledger — (w)—EASTERN MANUFACTURING CO., Bangor, Me.
Atlantic Linen—(b)—toilet—SCOTT PAPER CO., Philadelphia.
Atlantic Mills—(b)—fibre — W. H. CLAFLIN & CO., Boston.
Atlantic Mills—(b)—TILESTON & LIVERMORE, Boston.
Atlantic Mills—(b)—toilet—UNITED STATES ENVELOPE CO. (Morgan Envelope Co. Division), Springfield.
Atlantic Super — (b)—WESTERN PENNA. PAPER CO., Pittsburgh.
Atlantic Tinted Flats — (b) — WRIGHT, BARRETT & STILWELL CO., St. Paul, Minn.
Atlas—(b) — pattern — LOUISVILLE PAPER CO., Louisville, Ky.
Atlas—(b)—mimeograph — CLAFLIN & CO., Boston.
Atlas—(b)—news, cordage—GRAHAM PAPER CO., St. Louis.
Atlas—(b)—toilet — ALBANY PERFORATED WRAPPING PAPER CO., Albany, N. Y.
Atlas—(b)—roofing—R. L. GREENE PAPER CO., Providence, R. I.
Atlas—(b)—toilet—R. L. GREENE PAPER CO., Providence, R. I.
Atlas—(b)—tag—C. P. LESH PAPER CO., Indianapolis, Ind.
Atlas—(w) — POWERS PAPER COMPANY, Springfield, Mass.
Atlas All Jute—(b)—bristol—C. P. LESH PAPER CO., Indianapolis.
Atlas—(b)—envelope—PULP & PAPER TRADING CO., New York.
Atlas—(b)—fibre wrapping—MEGARGEE BROS., Scranton, Pa.
Atlas Bond—(w)—CHATFIELD & WOODS CO., Cincinnati, O.
Atlas Bond—(w)—white bond only—R. C. KASTNER PAPER CO., N. Y.
Atlas Coated Bond—(b)—book—MILLER & WRIGHT PAPER CO., New York.
Atlas Coated Bond—(b)—MILLER & WRIGHT PAPER CO., INC., New York.
Atlas Book—(b)—KINGSLEY PAPER CO., Cleveland, Ohio.
Atlas Envelopes—(b)—A. STORRS & BEMENT CO., Boston.
Atlas Kraft—(b) — wrapping—O L D DOMINION PAPER CO., Norfolk, Va.
Atlas Linen Ledger—(w)—DWIGHT BROTHERS PAPER CO., Chicago.
Atlas Manila — (b) — wrapping — LOUISVILLE PAPER CO., Louisville, Ky.
Atlas M. F. Book—(b)—HARLEM CARD & PAPER CO., New York.
Atlas Mills — (w)—W. G. WILLMANN, New York.
Atlas Offset Bond — (b) — THE CHATFIELD & WOODS CO., Cincinnati, Ohio.
Atlas Oval — (b) — toilet—GEO. T. JOHNSON CO., Boston.
Atlas Super—(b)—HARLEM CARD & PAPER CO., New York.
Atlas Tag—(b)—ARNOLD-ROBERTS CO., Boston.
Attean—(b) — HOLLINGSWORTH & WHITNEY CO., Boston.
Auburn—(b)—enameled book — CINCINNATI CORDAGE AND PAPER CO., Cincinnati, Ohio.
Au Chat Noir—(b)—toilet—ALBANY PERFORATED WRAPPING PAPER CO., Albany, N. Y.
Audit Linen Ledger — (w)—THE CHATFIELD & WOODS CO., Cincinnati, Ohio.
Auditor—(b)—tag board — GRAHAM PAPER CO., St. Louis.
Auld Scotia Lynene—(w)—AMERICAN WRITING PAPER CO., Holyoke.

Watermarks and Brands

Aureola Coated Book—(b)—THE PAPER MILLS COMPANY, Chicago.
Aurora—(b)—bristol—LOUISVILLE PAPER CO., Louisville, Ky.
Aurora—(b)—FOX RIVER PAPER CO., Appleton, Wis.
Aurora—(b)—book and flat writing—MINNEAPOLIS PAPER CO., Minneapolis.
Aurora—(b)—toilet—H. NORWOOD EWING CO., New York.
Aurora Bank Folio—(b)—HY. LINDENMEYR & SONS, New York.
Aurora Enameled—(b)—MILLER & WRIGHT PAPER CO., INC., New York.
Aurora Enameled Tints—(b)—book—MILLER & WRIGHT PAPER CO., New York.
Aurora Fine—(w)—writing—PARSONS TRADING CO., New York.
Ausable—(b)—manila—PULP & PAPER TRADING CO., New York.
Australian Mail—GEO. B. HURD & CO., New York.
Austrian—(w)—WHITAKER PAPER COMPANY, Cincinnati, Ohio.
Authors—(b)—book—MILLER & WRIGHT PAPER CO., New York.
Authors' Linen—(w)—AMERICAN WRITING PAPER CO., Holyoke.
Auto—(b)—flats—BRADNER SMITH & CO., Chicago.
Autumn—(b)—bristol—LOUISVILLE PAPER CO., Louisville, Ky.
Autumnal Cover—(b)—HY. LINDENMEYR & SONS, New York.
Autocopy Bond—(b)—THE UNION PAPER & TWINE CO., Detroit.
Autocrat Linen—(w)—WHITE & WYCKOFF MFG. CO., Holyoke, Mass.
Avalon—(b)—writing—BAY STATE PAPER CO., Boston.
Avelra—(b)—PEERLESS MFG. CO., Norristown, Pa.
Aviator S. & S. C.—(b)—MINNEAPOLIS PAPER CO., Minneapolis, Minn.
Avon—(b)—cover—THE CHATFIELD & WOODS CO., Cincinnati, Ohio.
Avon Bond—(w)—McCLELLAN PAPER CO., Minneapolis, Minn.
Avondale—(b)—ALBANY PERFORATED WRAPPING PAPER COMPANY, N. Y.
Avondale—(b)—envelope—GRAHAM PAPER CO., St. Louis.
Avondale Mills—(w)—STRATHMORE PAPER CO., Mittineague, Mass.
Avon Linen—cream laid—THE ALLING & CORY CO., Rochester, N. Y.
Avon Mills—(b)—writing—J. H. WALKER, New York.
Aymore—(w)—bond, ledger—W. R. GRACE & CO., New York.
Ayr—(b)—J. C. BLAIR CO., Huntingdon, Pa.
Ayro—(b)—all rag writing—FOX RIVER PAPER CO., Appleton, Wis.

Azo—(b)—Kraft wrapping—HORWITZ BROS., Elmira, N. Y.
Asev—(b)—toilet—ALBANY PERFORATED WRAPPING PAPER CO., Albany, N. Y.
Aztec—(b)—sheathing—GRAHAM PAPER CO., St. Louis.
Aztec Bond—(w)—THE McNEIL CO., Phœnix, Ariz.
Azure White Vellum—(w)—GEORGE B. HURD & CO., New York.

B

B—(b)—blanks—I. N. MEGARGEE & CO., Philadelphia.
"B"—(b)—HY. LINDENMEYR & SONS, New York.
B & B Mimeograph—(b)—McCLELLAN PAPER CO., Minneapolis, Minn.
Badge Bond—(w)—SWIGART PAPER CO., Chicago.
Badger Blue—(w)—manilas—SWIGART PAPER CO., Chicago.
B. E. Fibre—(b)—R. L. GREENE PAPER CO., Providence, R. I.
B. Fibre—(b)—R. L. GREENE PAPER CO., Providence, R. I.
B. Tissue—(b)—R. L. GREENE PAPER CO., Providence, R. I.
Badger Index Bristol—(b)—KINGSLEY PAPER CO., Cleveland.
Badger Parchment—(b)—manilas—SWIGART PAPER CO., Chicago.
Badger Pink—(b)—manilas—SWIGART PAPER CO., Chicago.
Badger Railroad Manila—(b)—SWIGART PAPER CO., Chicago.
Bainbridge—(w)—writing—C. T. BAINBRIDGE'S SONS, Brooklyn.
Balbriggan—(b)—extra superfine—J. C. BLAIR CO., Huntingdon, Pa.
Baldric Bristol—(b)—C. P. LESH PAPER CO., Indianapolis, Ind.
Balkan Kraft—(b)—MICHIGAN BAG & PAPER CO., Jackson, Mich.
Balkan M. F.—(b)—book—SPRINGFIELD PAPER & SUPPLY CO., Springfield, Mo.
Balmoral—(b)—UNITED STATES ENVELOPE CO. (Morgan [Env.] Co. Division), Springfield, Mass.
Balmoral—(w)—UNITED STATES ENVELOPE CO. (Morgan Division), Springfield, Mass.
Balsam Fir—(b)—toilet—NORTHERN PAPER MILLS, Milwaukee, Wis.
Balsam Sanitissue—(b)—toilet—SCOTT PAPER CO., Philadelphia.
Balsamic—(b)—toilet—SCOTT PAPER CO., Philadelphia.
Baltic—(b)—No. 1 Manila—WHITING-PATTERSON CO., New York.
Baltic—(b)—writing and book—GRAHAM PAPER CO., St. Louis.
Baltic Bond—(b)—PARSONS TRADING CO., New York.
Baltic Bristol—(b)—PARSONS TRADING CO., New York.

Watermarks and Brands

Baltic Ledger—(w)—CRITCHLEY & WHITE, N. Y.
Baltic Mills—(b)—flats—DONALDSON PAPER CO., Harrisburg, Pa.
Baltland—(w)—ledger and writing—J. FRANCIS HOCK & CO., Baltimore.
Balsac Deckle Edge Fine Laid Book—(b)—HY. LINDENMEYR & SONS, New York.
Bamboo Bond—(b)—DREW'S WHOLESALE PAPER HOUSE, Jacksonville, Fla.
Bamboo—(b)—toilet—UNITED STATES ENVELOPE CO. (Morgan Envelope Co. Division), Springfield.
Bamboo—(w)—J. C. BLAIR. CO., Huntingdon, Pa.
Bamboo Fibre—(b)—D. S. WALTON & CO., New York.
Bancroft—(b)—translucent cardboard—ARNOLD-ROBERTS CO., Boston.
Bank Check—(w)—W. E. Wroe & Co., Chicago.
Bangalore—(b)—PERKINS, GOODWIN CO., New York.
Bangkok—(b)—index—WHITING-PATTERSON CO., Philadelphia.
Bank Bond—(w)—R. H. THOMPSON CO., Buffalo, N. Y.
Bank Bond—(w)—writing—CAREW MANUFACTURING CO., South Hadley Falls, Mass.
Bank Book—(w)—ledger—DAVID L. ENGLE, New York.
Bank Index—(b)—bristol—THE ALLING & CORY CO., Rochester, N. Y.
Bank Linen—(b)—bond—RIEGEL & CO., INC., Philadelphia.
Bank Superfine—(w)—LEE PAPER CO., Vicksburg, Mich.
Bank Record Ledger—(w)—AMERICAN WRITING PAPER CO., Holyoke, Mass.
Bankers—(b)—bristol—UNION CARD & PAPER CO., New York.
Banker's—(b)—coated blotting—GARRETT-BUCHANAN CO., Philadelphia.
Bankers' Ledger—(w)—LASHER & LATHROP, New York.
Bankers' & Merchants' Ledger—(w)—BRADNER SMITH & CO., Chicago.
Bankers' Board—(b)—BRADNER SMITH & CO., Chicago.
Bankers' Bond—(w)—AMERICAN WRITING PAPER CO., Holyoke, Mass.
Bankers' Bond—(w)—VERNON BROS. & CO., New York.
Bankers' Fine—(b)—writing—RIEGEL & CO., INC., Philadelphia.
Bankers' Ledger—(w)—STRATHMORE PAPER CO., Mittineague, Mass.
"Bankers' Ledger"—(w)—SAUGERTIES MFG. CO., Saugerties, N. Y.
Bankers' Ledger—(w)—AMERICAN WRITING PAPER CO., Holyoke, Mass.
Bankers' Linen—(w)—SOUTHWORTH CO., Mittineague, Mass.
Bankers' Linen—(w)—SOUTHWORTH CO., Mittineague, Mass.
Bankers' Linen Bond—(w)—SOUTHWORTH CO., Mittineague, Mass.
Bankers' Linen Finish—(b)—blotting—STANDARD PAPER MANUFACTURING CO., Richmond, Va.
Bankers' Linen Ledger—(w)—SOUTHWORTH CO., Mittineague, Mass.
Bankers' Onion Skin Bond—(b)—CARTER, RICE & CO., CORP., Boston.
Bankers' Safety—(b)—GEO. LA MONTE & SONS, New York.
Bankers Super—(b)—writing—O. F. H. WARNER & CO., Baltimore.
Bankers' Woven Fabrics—(b)—E. E. LLOYD PAPER CO., Chicago, Ill.
Bankers' Writing—(w)—THE CHATFIELD & WOODS CO., Cincinnati, Ohio.
Bank Exchange—(w)—W. G. WILLMANN, New York.
Bank Exchange Linen—(w)—W. G. WILLMANN, New York.
Bank Ledger—SOUTHWORTH CO., Mittineague, Mass.
Bank Note Bond—(w and b)—GEO. B. HURD & CO., New York.
Bank of England—(w)—bond—Kansas City Paper Co., Kansas City.
Bank Parchment—PAYOT, UPHAM & CO., San Francisco, Cal.
Bank Parchment—(w)—EAST HARTFORD MANUFACTURING CO., Burnside, Conn.
Bank Record Ledger—AMERICAN WRITING PAPER CO., Holyoke, Mass.
Bank Superfine—(w)—writing—LEE PAPER CO., Vicksburg, Mich.
Banner—(b)—toilet, cordage—GRAHAM PAPER CO., St. Louis.
Banner—(b)—photo mounts—UNION CARD & PAPER CO., New York.
Banner—(b)—SOUTHERN PAPER CO., Richmond, Va.
Banner—(b)—sheathing and toilet and adding machine—LOUISVILLE PAPER CO., Louisville.
Banner Blanks—(b)—HY. LINDENMEYR & SONS, New York.
Banner Book—(b)—KINGSLEY PAPER CO., Cleveland, Ohio.
Banner Linen—(w)—SOUTHWORTH CO., Mittineague, Mass.
Banner Writing—(w)—HARLEM CARD & PAPER CO., New York.
Bannockburn Cover—(b)—STRATHMORE PAPER CO., Mittineague, Mass.
Banque Bond—RICHMOND PAPER CO., Richmond, Va.
Bantam Weight Bond—(b)—manifold—MEGARGEE BROS., Scranton, Pa.

MILLS ELECTRICALLY EQUIPPED   ECONOMIES IN STEAM PLANTS

C. A. CHAPMAN, Inc.
28 E. JACKSON BLVD.   ENGINEERS   CHICAGO

Watermarks and Brands   629

Banzai Ledger—(w and b)—THE PAPER MILLS CO., Chicago.
Ba Pa Co. Bond—(w)—BAKER PAPER., Oshkosh, Wis.
Ba Pa Co. Mills—(w)—BAKER PAPER CO., Oshkosh, Wis.
Ba Pa Co. Mimeograph—(b)—BAKER PAPER CO., Oshkosh, Wis.
Bardeen—(w)—BARDEEN PAPER CO., Otsego, Mich.
Bar Design—(w)—MARATHON PAPER MILLS, Wausau, Wis.
Baronet—(w)—INLAND EMPIRE PAPER CO., Millwood, Wash.
Baronial Bond—(b)—GEORGE B. HURD & CO., New York.
Barrington Bond—(w)—B. D. RISING PAPER CO., Housatonic, Mass.
Barrington Ledger—(w)—B. D. RISING PAPER CO., Housatonic, Mass.
Barrington Linen—(w)—B. D. RISING PAPER CO., Housatonic, Mass.
Barrington Wedding Bristol—(b)—B. D. RISING PAPER CO., Housatonic, Mass.
Bartlett Bond—(w)—A. PRICE. Brooklyn, N. Y.
Barristers' Bond—(w)—A. R. ANDREWS, Boston.
Bartholdi—(w)—white wove—EASTERN PAPER AND SUPPLY CO., Springfield, Mass.
Battery Bond—(b)—HENRY LINDENMEYR & SONS, New York.
Basket Weave—(b)—Z. & W. M. CRANE, Dalton, Mass.
Bassett & Sutphin Extra Fine—(w)—wove—BASSETT & SUTPHIN, New York.
Basephin—(b)—BASSETT & SUTPHIN, New York.
Battalion Bond—(w)—PARSONS TRADING CO., New York.
Battery—(b)— blotting — PARSONS TRADING CO., New York.
Battery Bond—Made in U. S. A.—(w)—PARSONS TRADING CO., New York.
Battery Ledger—(w)—(laid)—(woven)—PARSONS TRADING CO., New York.
Battery Manifold Paper—(b)—PARSONS TRADING CO., New York.
Battery Pencil Carbon Paper—(b)—PARSONS TRADING CO., New York.
Battery Laid Writing—(b)—PARSONS TRADING CO., New York.
Battery Ledger—(b)—WHITAKER PAPER CO., Cincinnati, Ohio.
Battery Wove Writing—(b)—PARSONS TRADING CO., New York.
Battle Ship—(w)—bond and ledger—FOX RIVER PAPER CO., Appleton, Wis.
Baunog—(w)—white and colored bond—J. ERNEST HAMMOND, 129 Dyer St., Providence, R. I.

Bavarian Parchment—(b)—BRADNER SMITH & CO., Chicago.
Baxter—(b)—news—GRAHAM PAPER CO., St. Louis.
Bay Bond—(w)—ARCHER PAPER CO., Chattanooga, Tenn.
Bay Path Cockle Finish—(w)—bond—STRATHMORE PAPER CO., Mittineague, Mass.
Bay Path Cover—(b)—STRATHMORE PAPER CO., Mittineague, Mass.
Bay Path Multi Copy Bond—(w)—STRATHMORE PAPER CO., Mittineague, Mass.
Bay Path Wedding—(b)—STRATHMORE PAPER CO., Mittineague, Mass.
Bay State — (b) — blotting — BAY STATE PAPER CO., Boston.
Bay State—(b)—ledger—BAY STATE PAPER CO., Boston.
Bay State Folding Bristol—(b)—JOHN CARTER & CO., Boston.
Bay State Index Bristol—(b)—BAY STATE PAPER CO., Boston.
Bay State Linen Finish — (b) — bristol — BAY STATE PAPER CO., Boston.
Bazar—(b)—toilet — ALBANY PERFORATED WRAPPING PAPER CO., Albany, N. Y.
B.C.W.(Bond Circular Wedding)—(w)—MILLER & WRIGHT PAPER CO., INC., New York.
Beach—(b)—translucent cardboard—ARNOLD-ROBERTS CO., Boston.
Beacon Book—(b)—JOHN CARTER & CO., Inc., Boston.
Beacon—(b)—translucent cardboard—ARNOLD-ROBERTS CO., Boston.
Beacon—(b) — news — WHITAKER PAPER CO., Cincinnati, Ohio.
Beacon—(b) — toilet — UNITED STATES ENVELOPE CO. (Morgan Envelope Co. Division), Springfield.
Beacon—(b)—No. 2 manila—STONE & FORSYTH CO., Boston.
Beacon Bond—(w and b)—also in writing—PAPER MILLS CO., Chicago.
Beacon Hill Bond—(w)—GEO. E. DAMON CO., Boston.
Beacon Hill Linen—(w)—GEO. E. DAMON CO., Boston.
Beacon Mills—(b) — A. STORRS & BEMENT CO., Boston.
Beacon Souvenir Post Card—(b)—BRADNER SMITH & CO., Chicago.
Beau Brummel — (b) — cover — WILKINSON BROS. & CO., Phila.
Beaufort Antique—(b)—laid book—HY. LINDENMEYR & SONS, New York.
Beaufort Colored Laid—(b)—flat writing—MERRIAM PAPER CO., New York.
Beaulieu Antique—(b)—wove book—HY. LINDENMEYR & SONS, New York.

APPLETON MACHINE CO., APPLETON, WIS.
REFINING ENGINES, SCREENS, SAWING & SPLITTING MACHINERY
HIGH GRADE CENTRIFUGAL PUMPS

MINER EDGAR CO., Sole Agents
EDGAR BROS. CO.
KEYSTONE CLAY & REDUCTION CO.
10 Church Street - - New York

CLAY

<E W> <K L M> <C M>
WASHED FLOATED REFINED
LARGEST CAPACITY AND STOCK IN AMERICA. PROMPT SHIPMENTS

I-FELTS AND JACKETS | Appleton Woolen Mills, APPLETON - - WIS.

Watermarks and Brands

Beaver—(b)—manila—STONE & FORSYTH CO., Boston.
Beaver Board—(b)—BRADNER SMITH & CO., Chicago.
Beaver Brand Boards—(b)—boards—J. P. LEWIS CO., Beaver Falls, New York.
Beaver Dam—(w)—BUNTIN, GILLIES & CO., Hamilton, Ontario, Can
Beaver Mills—(b)—ledger writing—CANFIELD PAPER CO., THE, New York.
Beckett Bond—(w)—BECKETT PAPER CO., Hamilton, Ohio.
Bedford—(b)—toilet—ALBANY PERFORATED WRAPPING PAPER CO., Albany, N. Y.
Bedford Mills—(b)—toilet—UNITED STATES ENVELOPE CO. (Morgan Envelope Co. Division), Springfield.
Bed Rock—(b)—colored bristol—KANSAS PAPER HOUSE, Kansas City, Mo.
Bed Rock Flats—(b)—BRADNER SMITH & CO., Chicago.
Bedford Bond—(b)—HY. LINDENMEYR & SONS, New York.
Bee—(b)—writing—ANTIETAM PAPER CO., Hagerstown, Md.
Beechmore Mills—(w)—flats—LOUISVILLE PAPER CO., Louisville, Ky.
Beechnut—(b)—wrapping—LOUISVILLE PAPER CO., Louisville, Ky.
Beechwood—(w)—AMERICAN WRITING PAPER CO., Holyoke.
Beechwood—(b)—bristol—JUDD PAPER CO., Holyoke, Mass.
Beechwood—(w)—A. STORRS & BEMENT CO., Boston.
Bee Gee Blanks—(b)—BUNTIN, GILLIES & CO., LTD., Hamilton, Ontario, Can.
Beekman—(b)—bristol—UNION CARD & PAPER CO., New York.
Beekman Blotting—(b)—HY. LINDENMEYR & SONS, New York.
Beekman Bond—(w)—LEHMAIER & BROTHER, New York.
Beekman Colored Bristol—(b)—F. A. FLINN, INC., New York.
Beekman Mills—HOOPER, LEWIS & CO., Boston.
Beekman Toilet Tissue—(b)—HY. LINDENMEYR & SONS, New York.
Bee Line—(b)—toilet—UNITED STATES ENVELOPE CO. (Morgan Envelope Co. Division), Springfield.
Beeswing Opaque—(b)—catalogue—BEECHER, PECK & LEWIS, Detroit, Mich.
Belfast—(b)—book—KANSAS CITY PAPER HOUSE, Kansas City, Mo.
Belfast Barnet Linen—(w)—UNITED STATES ENVELOPE CO. (Whitcomb Envelope Co. Division), Worcester, Mass.
Belfast Crash Linen Lawn—(b)—OLD DOMINION PAPER CO., Norfolk, Va.

Belfast Fabric—(b)—J. C. PARKER PAPER CO., Louisville, Ky.
Belfast Bristol—(b)—BRADNER SMITH & CO., Chicago.
Belfast Ledger—(w)—HAGEN PAPER CO., St. Louis.
Belfast—(b)—index bristol—WHITING-PATTERSON CO., Philadelphia.
Belfast Linen—(b)—linen—STANDARD CARD & PAPER CO., New York.
Belfast Linen Bond—(w)—BERKSHIRE HILLS PAPER CO., Adams, Mass.
Belfast Linen Bond—(w)—C. S. PROCTOR PAPER CO., Boston.
Belfast Linen Ledger—(w)—PETREQUIN PAPER CO., Cleveland.
Belfield Bond—(w)—RIEGEL & CO., INC., Philadelphia.
Belfield Mills—(w)—DONALDSON PAPER CO., Harrisburg, Pa.
Belford Linen—(w)—UNION CARD AND PAPER CO., New York.
Belford Parchment—(w)—EAST HARTFORD MANUFACTURING CO., Burnside, Conn.
Belgian Bond—(w)—EASTERN MFG. CO., Bangor, Me.
Belgian Ledger—(w)—EASTERN MFG. CO., Bangor, Me.
Belgian Linen—(w)—EASTERN MFG. CO., Bangor, Me.
Belgrade Cover—(b)—HY. LINDENMEYR & SONS, New York.
Bellcourt—(w)—UNION CARD AND PAPER CO., New York.
Belleview Mills—(w)—writing—GARRETT-BUCHANAN CO., Philadelphia.
Bellevue—(b)—toilet—R. L. GREENE PAPER CO., Providence, R. I.
Bellfast Bond—(w)—HOWARD SMITH PAPER MILLS, LTD., Montreal, Can.
Belmere Linen—(w)—EATON, CRANE & PIKE CO., Pittsfield, Mass.
Belmont—(b)—CHATFIELD & WOODS CO., Cincinnati, Ohio.
Belmont Mills—(b)—JOHN CARTER & CO., INC., Boston.
Belmore Bond—(w)—A. PRICE, Brooklyn, N. Y.
Belvedere—(b)—cover—GRAHAM PAPER CO., St. Louis.
Belvedere—(b)—toilet—ALBANY PERFORATED WRAPPING PAPER CO., Albany, N. Y.
Belwood—(b)—envelope—UNION CARD & PAPER CO., New York.
Bemis Ledger—(w)—McCLELLAN PAPER CO., Minneapolis, Minn.
Ben Day Cover—(b)—DILL & COLLINS CO., Philadelphia.
Ben Franklin—(b)—enamel book—THE CHATFIELD & WOODS CO., Cincinnati, Ohio.
Ben Franklin—(b)—enamel—UNION PAPER & TWINE CO., Detroit, Mich.
Ben Franklin Bond—(w)—B. F. BOND PAPER CO., Baltimore.

JAMES H. HARRISON PULPSTONE MANUFACTURER | **GENUINE NEWCASTLE STONES** 16 Killowen St., GATESHEAD-ON-TYNE, ENG.

Watermarks and Brands

Ben Franklin Bond—(w)—B. D. RISING PAPER CO., Housatonic, Mass.
Ben Franklin Text — (b) — India book—F. A. FLINN, INC., New York.
Bengal—(b)—s. and s. c. book—J. W. BUTLER PAPER CO., Chicago.
Bengal—(b)— toilet—WHITING-PATTERSON CO., New York.
Bennington — (b) — tag—JUDD PAPER CO., Holyoke, Mass.
Bennington Bible—(b)—unglased—CANFIELD PAPER CO., New York.
Bennington Ledger—(w)—LASHER & LATHROP, New York.
Berkeley—(w)—extra fine—THOMAS W. PRICE CO., Philadelphia.
Berkeley Linen Ledger—(b)—CONROW BROTHERS, New York.
Berkeley Mills Linen Ledger—(w)—CONROW BROTHERS, New York.
Berkett — (b) — book — BRADNER SMITH & CO., Chicago.
Berkeley Bristol—(b)—A. STORRS & BEMENT CO., Boston.
Berkshire—(b)—blotting — EATON, DIKEMAN & CO., Lee, Mass.
Berkshire—(b) — copying tissue — SMITH PAPER CO., Lee, Mass.
Berkshire Bond Fabric — (w)—EATON, CRANE & PIKE CO., Pittsfield, Mass.
Berkshire Hills First Class Ledger —(w)—BERKSHIRE HILLS PAPER CO., Adams, Mass.
Berkshire Linen Fabric — (w)—EATON, CRANE & PIKE CO., Pittsfield, Mass.
Berkshire Bond U. S. A.—(w and b)—typewriter—EATON, CRANE & PIKE CO., Pittsfield, Mass.
Berkshire Bristol — (b) — WHITAKER PAPER CO., Cincinnati, O.
Berkshire Duplicate Copy Paper—(b)—typewriter—EATON, CRANE & PIKE CO., Pittsfield, Mass.
Berkshire Hills Loose Leaf Ledger —(w)—BERKSHIRE HILLS PAPER CO., Adams, Mass.
Berkshire Hills Linen — (w)—BERKSHIRE HILLS PAPER CO., Adams, Mass.
Berkshire Hills Index Bristol—(b)—BERKSHIRE HILLS PAPER CO., Adams, Mass.
Berkshire Litho Bond—(b)—BERKSHIRE HILLS PAPER CO., Adams, Mass.
Berkshire Hills Extra Angora Wedding — (b) — BERKSHIRE HILLS PAPER CO., Adams, Mass.
Berkshire Hills Superfine Wedding—(b)—BERKSHIRE HILLS PAPER CO., Adams, Mass.
Berkshire Hills Superior Typewriter Paper—(b)—BERKSHIRE HILLS PAPER CO., Adams, Mass.
Berkshire Hills Two-tone—(b)—BERKSHIRE HILLS PAPER CO., Adams, Mass.

Berkshire Hills Loose Leaf—(b)—book—LASHER & LATHROP, N. Y.
Berkshire Linen — (w)—ledger—J. W. BUTLER PAPER CO., Chicago.
Berkshire Linen U. S. A.—(w and b)—typewriter—EATON, CRANE & PIKE CO., Pittsfield, Mass.
Berkshire Linen Parchment—(b)—typewriter—EATON, CRANE & PIKE CO., Pittsfield, Mass.
Berkshire Manuscript Cover U. S. A.—(w)—typewriter—EATON, CRANE & PIKE CO., Pittsfield, Mass.
Berkshire Parchment Linen U. S. A. — (w) — typewriter — EATON, CRANE & PIKE CO., Pittsfield, Mass.
Berkshire Satin Finish — (b)—EATON, CRANE & PIKE CO., Pittsfield, Mass.
Berkshire Souvenir Bond U. S. A. —typewriter — EATON, CRANE & PIKE CO., Pittsfield, Mass.
Berkshire Text — (w)—AMERICAN WRITING PAPER CO., Holyoke.
Berkshire Tinted Bristol—(b)—W. G. WILLMANN, New York.
Berkshire Typewriter Paper U. S. A. — (w) — typewriter—EATON, CRANE & PIKE CO., Pittsfield.
Berkshire Vesper Linen U. S. A.—(w)—typewriter—EATON, CRANE & PIKE CO., Pittsfield, Mass.
Berkshire Valley—(w and b)—TAYLOR-ATKINS PAPER CO., Hartford, Conn.
Berkshire Vellum—(b)—EATON, CRANE & PIKE CO., Pittsfield.
Berkshire Vellum Bond U. S. A.—(w)—typewriter—EATON, CRANE & PIKE CO., Pittsfield, Mass.
Berlin — (b) — writing — WHITING-PATTERSON CO., Philadelphia.
Berlin—(b)— colored bristol—W. H. CLAFLIN & CO., Boston.
Berlin Linen—(b)—BASSETT & SUTPHIN, New York.
Berlin Mills—(w)—bond—BERLIN & JONES ENVELOPE CO., New York.
Berlin—(b)—ALBANY PERFORATED WRAPPING PAPER CO., Albany.
Bermico Sheathing Paper—(b)—BERLIN MILLS CO., Portland, Me.
Bermuda Onion Skin Folio—(b)—BRADNER SMITH & CO., Chicago.
Berne Ledger—(w and b)—WHITING-PATTERSON CO., Philadelphia.
Bertheill—(b)—litho. blanks, bond, book—BURTON C. HILL, New York.
Berwick—(b and w)—ledger—F. W. ANDERSON & CO., New York.
Berwick—(b)—H. REEVE ANGEL & CO., INC., New York.
Berwick Linen—(w)—VALLEY PAPER CO., Holyoke, Mass.
Berwick Mills—(b)—folded—POWERS PAPER CO., Springfield, Mass.
Bessemer—(b)— cover — SEYMOUR CO., New York.
Best Linen — (b) — HY. LINDENMEYR & SONS, New York.

Watermarks and Brands

Beaver—(b)—manila — STONE & FORSYTH CO., Boston.
Beaver Board — (b) — BRADNER SMITH & CO., Chicago.
Beaver Brand Boards—(b)—boards—J. P. LEWIS CO., Beaver Falls, New York.
Beaver Dam—(w) — BUNTIN, GILLIES & CO., Hamilton, Ontario, Can
Beaver Mills—(b)—ledger writing—CANFIELD PAPER CO., THE, New York.
Beckett Bond — (w) — BECKETT PAPER CO., Hamilton, Ohio.
Bedford—(b)—toilet—ALBANY PERFORATED WRAPPING PAPER CO., Albany, N. Y.
Bedford Mills—(b)—toilet—UNITED STATES ENVELOPE CO. (Morgan Envelope Co. Division), Springfield.
Bed Rock — (b) — colored bristol—KANSAS PAPER HOUSE, Kansas City, Mo.
Bed Rock Flats — (b)—BRADNER SMITH & CO., Chicago.
Bedford Bond—(b)—HY. LINDENMEYR & SONS, New York.
Bee—(b) — writing — ANTIETAM PAPER CO., Hagerstown, Md.
Beechmore Mills — (w) — flats — LOUISVILLE PAPER CO., Louisville, Ky.
Beechnut — (b) — wrapping — LOUISVILLE PAPER CO., Louisville, Ky.
Beechwood — (w) — AMERICAN WRITING PAPER CO., Holyoke.
Beechwood — (b) — bristol — JUDD PAPER CO., Holyoke, Mass.
Beechwood—(w) — A. STORRS & BEMENT CO., Boston.
Bee Gee Blanks—(b)—BUNTIN, GILLIES & CO., LTD., Hamilton, Ontario, Can.
Beekman—(b) — bristol — UNION CARD & PAPER CO., New York.
Beekman Blotting—(b)—HY. LINDENMEYR & SONS, New York.
Beekman Bond — (w)—LEHMAIER & BROTHER, New York.
Beekman Colored Bristol—(b)—F. A. FLINN, INC., New York.
Beekman Mills—HOOPER, LEWIS & CO., Boston.
Beekman Toilet Tissue—(b)—HY. LINDENMEYR & SONS, New York.
Bee Line — (b) — toilet—UNITED STATES ENVELOPE CO. (Morgan Envelope Co. Division), Springfield.
Beeswing Opaque—(b)—catalogue—BEECHER, PECK & LEWIS, Detroit, Mich.
Belfast—(b)—book—KANSAS CITY PAPER HOUSE, Kansas City, Mo.
Belfast Barnet Linen — (w) — UNITED STATES ENVELOPE CO. (Whitcomb Envelope Co. Division), Worcester, Mass.
Belfast Crash Linen Lawn—(b)—OLD DOMINION PAPER CO., Norfolk, Va.
Belfast Fabric—(b)—J. C. PARKER PAPER CO., Louisville, Ky.
Belfast Bristol — (b)—BRADNER SMITH & CO., Chicago.
Belfast Ledger — (w) — HAGEN PAPER CO., St. Louis.
Belfast—(b)—index bristol—WHITING-PATTERSON CO., Philadelphia.
Belfast Linen—(b)—linen—STANDARD CARD & PAPER CO., New York.
Belfast Linen Bond—(w)—BERKSHIRE HILLS PAPER CO., Adams, Mass.
Belfast Linen Bond—(w)—C. S. PROCTOR PAPER CO., Boston.
Belfast Linen Ledger — (w) — PETREQUIN PAPER CO., Cleveland.
Belfield Bond—(w)—RIEGEL & CO., INC., Philadelphia.
Belfield Mills—(w) — DONALDSON PAPER CO., Harrisburg, Pa.
Belford Linen—(w)—UNION CARD AND PAPER CO., New York.
Belford Parchment — (w)—EAST HARTFORD MANUFACTURING CO., Burnside, Conn.
Belgian Bond—(w)—EASTERN MFG. CO., Bangor, Me.
Belgian Ledger—(w)—EASTERN MFG. CO., Bangor, Me.
Belgian Linen—(w)—EASTERN MFG. CO., Bangor, Me.
Belgrade Cover—(b)—HY. LINDENMEYR & SONS, New York.
Bellcourt—(w)—UNION CARD AND PAPER CO., New York.
Belleview Mills — (w) — writing —GARRETT-BUCHANAN CO., Philadelphia.
Bellevue—(b)—toilet—R. L. GREENE PAPER CO., Providence, R. I.
Bellfast Bond — (w) — HOWARD SMITH PAPER MILLS, LTD., Montreal, Can.
Belmere Linen — (w) — EATON, CRANE & PIKE CO., Pittsfield, Mass.
Belmont — (b) — CHATFIELD & WOODS CO., Cincinnati, Ohio.
Belmont Mills—(b)—JOHN CARTER & CO., INC., Boston.
Belmore Bond—(w)—A. PRICE, Brooklyn, N. Y.
Belvedere—(b)—cover — GRAHAM PAPER CO., St. Louis.
Belvedere—(b)—toilet — ALBANY PERFORATED WRAPPING PAPER CO., Albany, N. Y.
Belwood—(b) — envelope — UNION CARD & PAPER CO., New York.
Bemis Ledger—(w) — McCLELLAN PAPER CO., Minneapolis, Minn.
Ben Day Cover—(b)—DILL & COLLINS CO., Philadelphia.
Ben Franklin—(b)—enamel book—THE CHATFIELD & WOODS CO., Cincinnati, Ohio.
Ben Franklin—(b)—enamel—UNION PAPER & TWINE CO., Detroit, Mich.
Ben Franklin Bond — (w) — B. F BOND PAPER CO., Baltimore.

Watermarks and Brands

Chief Tough Check—(b)—WABASH COATING MILLS, Wabash, Ind.
Chiffon Vellum and Bond—(w)— GEO. B. HURD & CO., New York.
Chilcoot—(b)—wrapping and toilet— STANDARD PAPER CO., Tacoma.
Chilton Lawn — (w) — POWERS PAPER CO., Springfield, Mass.
Chief Tag—(b)—R. P. ANDREW PAPER CO., Washington, D. C.
Chieftain—(w and b)—bond, writing, ledger—NEENAH PAPER CO., Neenah, Wis.
Chilton Linen—(b)—EATON, CRANE & PIKE CO., Pittsfield, Mass.
China—(b)—white bristols—STRATHMORE PAPER CO., Mittineague, Mass.
China White—(b) — STRATHMORE PAPER CO., Mittineague, Mass.
Chin Chin—(b)—toilet—H. NORWOOD EWING CO., New York.
Chinese—(b)—wrapping — GRAHAM PAPER CO., St. Louis.
Chinese Bond — (w) — BRADNER SMITH & CO., Chicago.
Chinese—(b)—bristol— C. P. LESH PAPER CO., Indianapolis, Ind.
Chinese Express — (b)—wrapping— GRAHAM PAPER CO., St. Louis.
Chinese Linen Bond — (w) — CARTER, RICE & CO., CORP., Boston.
Chinook—(b)—toilet—H. M. RICHMOND PAPER CO., Seattle, Wash.
Chippendale Cover — (b)—ADVERTISERS' PAPER MILLS, Holyoke.
Chippendale Text — (w) — book — ADVERTISERS' PAPER MILLS, Holyoke, Mass.
Chippewa—(b)—toilet — ALBANY PERFORATED WRAPPING PAPER CO., Albany, N. Y.
Chippewa Bond — (b) — WHITING PLOVER PAPER CO., Menasha, Wis.
Chippewa Linen Ledger—(w)— WHITING-PLOVER PAPER CO., Stevens Point, Wis.
Chiswick Eggshell—(b)—MILLER & WRIGHT PAPER CO., INC., New York.
Circuit Bond—(w)—WESTERN PENNA. PAPER CO., Pittsburgh, Pa.
Circular Writing—(b)—EASTERN MFG. CO., Bangor, Me.
Cirrus Covers—(b)—DISTRICT OF COLUMBIA PAPER MFG. CO., Washington, D. C.
Citizen Mills — (w) — INDIANA PAPER CO., Indianapolis.
Citizens' Bond — (w) — PAUL E. VERNON & CO., New York.
City—(w)—bond—F. W. ANDERSON & CO., New York.
City—(b) — writing and bristol — UNION CARD AND PAPER CO., N. Y.
City Bank Bond—(w)—SOUTHERN PAPER COMPANY, Richmond, Va.
City Bond — (b) — GARRETT-BUCHANAN CO., Philadelphia.

City Ledger—(w)—BRADNER SMITH & CO., Chicago.
City Mills — (b)—writing—UNION CARD AND PAPER CO., New York
City of Scranton Bond—(w)—MEGARGEE BROS., Scranton, Pa.
Civic—(w)—bond, linen and writings —UNION CARD & PAPER CO., N. Y.
Civic Bond — (w)—UNION CARD AND PAPER CO., New York.
Civic Ledger—(w and b) — UNION CARD & PAPER CO., New York.
Claiborne Bristol—(b)—HY. LINDENMEYR & SONS, New York.
Claremont—(b)—wrapping— STONE & FORSYTH CO., Boston.
Claremont Bond — (b) — HARLEM CARD & PAPER CO., New York.
Clarendon—(b)—toilet — ALBANY PERFORATED WRAPPING PAPER CO., Albany, N. Y.
Clarion—(b)—enamel book — THE CHATFIELD & WOODS CO., Cincinnati, Ohio.
Clarion Linen Bond — (w)—C. P. LESH PAPER CO., Indianapolis. Ind.
Clarion Flats — (b)—McCLELLAN PAPER CO., Minneapolis, Minn.
Clarion Mills—(w)—writing — ST. LOUIS PAPER CO., St. Louis.
Classic—(b)—PERKINS GOODWIN CO., New York.
Classic Bond—(w)—CAREW MFG. CO., South Hadley Falls, Mass.
Classic Eggshell—(b)—book—J. W. BUTLER PAPER CO., Chicago.
Classic Enamel—(w)—coated book— SWIGART PAPER CO., Chicago.
Classic Linen—(w)—STRATHMORE PAPER CO., Mittineague, Mass.
Classic Music—(b)— GRAHAM PAPER CO., St. Louis.
Clayco Blanks — (trade mark) — WABASH COATING MILLS, Wabash. Ind.
Clayton—(b)—toilet—UNITED STATES ENVELOPE CO. (Morgan Envelope Co. Division), Springfield.
Clear View—(b) — J. W. BUTLER PAPER CO., Chicago.
Clearwater — (w) — AMERICAN WRITING PAPER CO., Holyoke, Mass.
Clearwater Bond—(w)—GARRETT-BUCHANAN CO., Philadelphia.
Clear-Water Bond—(w)—KINGSLEY PAPER CO., Cleveland, Ohio.
Clear White Coated Book — (b)— WILLIAM H. GEORGE, Philadelphia.
Clearing House Bond — (w)—INLAND PAPER CO., Chicago.
Cleaver—(b)—wrapping—E. B. EDDY CO., Hull, Canada.
Clement Writing—(b)—CLEMENT & STOCKWELL, New York.
Cleveland—(w) — writing — PARSONS TRADING CO., New York.
Cliffdale—(w)—writing — HAMMERMILL PAPER CO., Erie, Pa.

I-FELTS AND JACKETS | Appleton Woolen Mills
APPLETON · · WIS.

Watermarks and Brands

Beaver—(b)—manila—STONE & FORSYTH CO., Boston.
Beaver Board—(b)—BRADNER SMITH & CO., Chicago.
Beaver Brand Boards—(b)—boards—J. P. LEWIS CO., Beaver Falls, New York.
Beaver Dam—(w)—BUNTIN, GILLIES & CO., Hamilton, Ontario, Can.
Beaver Mills—(b)—ledger writing—CANFIELD PAPER CO., THE, New York.
Beckett Bond—(w)—BECKETT PAPER CO., Hamilton, Ohio.
Bedford—(b)—toilet—ALBANY PERFORATED WRAPPING PAPER CO., Albany, N. Y.
Bedford Mills—(b)—toilet—UNITED STATES ENVELOPE CO. (Morgan Envelope Co. Division), Springfield.
Bed Rock—(b)—colored bristol—KANSAS PAPER HOUSE, Kansas City, Mo.
Bed Rock Flats—(b)—BRADNER SMITH & CO., Chicago.
Bedford Bond—(b)—HY. LINDENMEYR & SONS, New York.
Bee—(b)—writing—ANTIETAM PAPER CO., Hagerstown, Md.
Beechmore Mills—(w)—flats—LOUISVILLE PAPER CO., Louisville, Ky.
Beechnut—(b)—wrapping—LOUISVILLE PAPER CO., Louisville, Ky.
Beechwood—(w)—AMERICAN WRITING PAPER CO., Holyoke.
Beechwood—(b)—bristol—JUDD PAPER CO., Holyoke, Mass.
Beechwood—(w)—A. STORRS & BEMENT CO., Boston.
Bee Gee Blanks—(b)—BUNTIN, GILLIES & CO., LTD., Hamilton, Ontario, Can.
Beekman—(b)—bristol—UNION CARD & PAPER CO., New York.
Beekman Blotting—(b)—HY. LINDENMEYR & SONS, New York.
Beekman Bond—(w)—LEHMAIER & BROTHER, New York.
Beekman Colored Bristol—(b)—F. A. FLINN, INC., New York.
Beekman Mills—HOOPER, LEWIS & CO., Boston.
Beekman Toilet Tissue—(b)—HY. LINDENMEYR & SONS, New York.
Bee Line—(b)—toilet—UNITED STATES ENVELOPE CO. (Morgan Envelope Co. Division), Springfield.
Beeswing Opaque—(b)—catalogue—BEECHER, PECK & LEWIS, Detroit, Mich.
Belfast—(b)—book—KANSAS CITY PAPER HOUSE, Kansas City, Mo.
Belfast Barnet Linen—(w)—UNITED STATES ENVELOPE CO. (Whitcomb Envelope Co. Division), Worcester, Mass.
Belfast Crash Linen Lawn—(b)—OLD DOMINION PAPER CO., Norfolk, Va.
Belfast Fabric—(b)—J. C. PARKER PAPER CO., Louisville, Ky.
Belfast Bristol—(b)—BRADNER SMITH & CO., Chicago.
Belfast Ledger—(w)—HAGEN PAPER CO., St. Louis.
Belfast—(b)—index bristol—WHITING-PATTERSON CO., Philadelphia.
Belfast Linen—(b)—linen—STANDARD CARD & PAPER CO., New York.
Belfast Linen Bond—(w)—BERKSHIRE HILLS PAPER CO., Adams, Mass.
Belfast Linen Bond—(w)—C. S. PROCTOR PAPER CO., Boston.
Belfast Linen Ledger—(w)—PETREQUIN PAPER CO., Cleveland.
Belfield Bond—(w)—RIEGEL & CO., INC., Philadelphia.
Belfield Mills—(w)—DONALDSON PAPER CO., Harrisburg, Pa.
Belford Linen—(w)—UNION CARD AND PAPER CO., New York.
Belford Parchment—(w)—EAST HARTFORD MANUFACTURING CO., Burnside, Conn.
Belgian Bond—(w)—EASTERN MFG. CO., Bangor, Me.
Belgian Ledger—(w)—EASTERN MFG. CO., Bangor, Me.
Belgian Linen—(w)—EASTERN MFG. CO., Bangor, Me.
Belgrade Cover—(b)—HY. LINDENMEYR & SONS, New York.
Bellcourt—(w)—UNION CARD AND PAPER CO., New York.
Belleview Mills—(w)—writing—GARRETT-BUCHANAN CO., Philadelphia.
Bellevue—(b)—toilet—B. L. GREENE PAPER CO., Providence, R. I.
Belfast Bond—(w)—HOWARD SMITH PAPER MILLS, LTD., Montreal, Can.
Belmere Linen—(w)—EATON, CRANE & PIKE CO., Pittsfield, Mass.
Belmont—(b)—CHATFIELD & WOODS CO., Cincinnati, Ohio.
Belmont Mills—(b)—JOHN CARTER & CO., INC., Boston.
Belmore Bond—(w)—A. PRICE, Brooklyn, N. Y.
Belvedere—(b)—cover—GRAHAM PAPER CO., St. Louis.
Belvedere—(b)—toilet—ALBANY PERFORATED WRAPPING PAPER CO., Albany, N. Y.
Belwood—(b)—envelope—UNION CARD & PAPER CO., New York.
Bemis Ledger—(w)—McCLELLAN PAPER CO., Minneapolis, Minn.
Ben Day Cover—(b)—DILL & COLLINS CO., Philadelphia.
Ben Franklin—(b)—enamel book—THE CHATFIELD & WOODS CO., Cincinnati, Ohio.
Ben Franklin—(b)—enamel—UNION PAPER & TWINE CO., Detroit, Mich.
Ben Franklin Bond—(w)—B. F BOND PAPER CO., Baltimore.

JAMES H. HARRISON PULPSTONE MANUFACTURER | **GENUINE NEWCASTLE STONES** 18 Killowen St., GATESHEAD-ON-TYNE, ENG.

INVESTIGATIONS   REPORTS   INSPECTIONS
C. A. CHAPMAN, Inc.
19 E. JACKSON BLVD.   ENGINEERS   CHICAGO

Watermarks and Brands   631

Ben Franklin Bond—(w)—B. D. RISING PAPER CO., Housatonic, Mass.
Ben Franklin Text— (b) — India book—F. A. FLINN, INC., New York.
Bengal—(b)—s. and s. c. book—J. W. BUTLER PAPER CO., Chicago.
Bengal—(b)— toilet—WHITING-PATTERSON CO., New York.
Bennington — (b) — tag—JUDD PAPER CO., Holyoke, Mass.
Bennington Bible—(b)—unglazed—CANFIELD PAPER CO., New York.
Bennington Ledger—(w)—LASHER & LATHROP, New York.
Berkeley—(w)—extra fine—THOMAS W. PRICE CO., Philadelphia.
Berkeley Linen Ledger—(b)—CONROW BROTHERS, New York.
Berkeley Mills Linen Ledger—(w)—CONROW BROTHERS, New York.
Berkett — (b) — book — BRADNER SMITH & CO., Chicago.
Berkeley Bristol—(b)—A. STORRS & BEMENT CO., Boston.
Berkshire—(b)—blotting — EATON, DIKEMAN & CO., Lee, Mass.
Berkshire—(b) — copying tissue — SMITH PAPER CO., Lee, Mass.
Berkshire Bond Fabric — (w)—EATON, CRANE & PIKE CO., Pittsfield, Mass.
Berkshire Hills First Class Ledger—(w)—BERKSHIRE HILLS PAPER CO., Adams, Mass.
Berkshire Linen Fabric — (w)—EATON, CRANE & PIKE CO., Pittsfield, Mass.
Berkshire Bond U. S. A.—(w and b)—typewriter—EATON, CRANE & PIKE CO., Pittsfield, Mass.
Berkshire Bristol — (b) — WHITAKER PAPER CO., Cincinnati, O.
Berkshire Duplicate Copy Paper—(b)—typewriter—EATON, CRANE & PIKE CO., Pittsfield, Mass.
Berkshire Hills Loose Leaf Ledger—(w)—BERKSHIRE HILLS PAPER CO., Adams, Mass.
Berkshire Hills Linen — (w)—BERKSHIRE HILLS PAPER CO., Adams, Mass.
Berkshire Hills Index Bristol—(b)—BERKSHIRE HILLS PAPER CO., Adams, Mass.
Berkshire Hills Litho Bond—(b)—BERKSHIRE HILLS PAPER CO., Adams, Mass.
Berkshire Hills Extra Angora Wedding — (b) — BERKSHIRE HILLS PAPER CO., Adams, Mass.
Berkshire Hills Superfine Wedding—(b)—BERKSHIRE HILLS PAPER CO., Adams, Mass.
Berkshire Hills Superior Typewriter Paper—(b)—BERKSHIRE HILLS PAPER CO., Adams, Mass.
Berkshire Hills Two-tone—(b)—BERKSHIRE HILLS PAPER CO., Adams, Mass.

Berkshire Hills Loose Leaf—(b)—book—LASHER & LATHROP, N. Y.
Berkshire Linen — (w)—ledger—J. W. BUTLER PAPER CO., Chicago.
Berkshire Linen U. S. A.—(w and b)—typewriter—EATON, CRANE & PIKE CO., Pittsfield, Mass.
Berkshire Linen Parchment—(b)—typewriter—EATON, CRANE & PIKE CO., Pittsfield, Mass.
Berkshire Manuscript Cover U. S. A.—(w)—typewriter—EATON, CRANE & PIKE CO., Pittsfield, Mass.
Berkshire Parchment Linen U. S. A. — (w) — typewriter — EATON, CRANE & PIKE CO., Pittsfield, Mass.
Berkshire Satin Finish — (b)—EATON, CRANE & PIKE CO., Pittsfield, Mass.
Berkshire Souvenir Bond U. S. A.—typewriter — EATON, CRANE & PIKE CO., Pittsfield, Mass.
Berkshire Text — (w)—AMERICAN WRITING PAPER CO., Holyoke.
Berkshire Tinted Bristol—(b)—W. G. WILLMANN, New York.
Berkshire Typewriter Paper U. S. A. — (w) — typewriter—EATON, CRANE & PIKE CO., Pittsfield.
Berkshire Vesper Linen U. S. A.—(w)—typewriter—EATON, CRANE & PIKE CO., Pittsfield, Mass.
Berkshire Valley—(w and b)—TAYLOR-ATKINS PAPER CO., Hartford, Conn.
Berkshire Vellum—(b)—E A T O N, CRANE & PIKE CO., Pittsfield.
Berkshire Vellum Bond U. S. A.—(w)—typewriter—EATON, CRANE & PIKE CO., Pittsfield, Mass.
Berlin —(b)— writing — WHITING-PATTERSON CO., Philadelphia.
Berlin—(b)— colored bristol—W. H. CLAFLIN & CO., Boston.
Berlin Linen—(b)—BASSETT & SUTPHIN, New York.
Berlin Mills—(w)—bond—BERLIN & JONES ENVELOPE CO., New York.
Berlin—(b)—ALBANY PERFORATED WRAPPING PAPER CO., Albany.
Bermico Sheathing Paper—(b)—BERLIN MILLS CO., Portland, Me.
Bermuda Onion Skin Folio—(b)—BRADNER SMITH & CO., Chicago.
Berne Ledger—(w and b)—WHITING-PATTERSON CO., Philadelphia.
Bertheill—(b)—litho. blanks, bond, book—BURTON C. HILL, New York.
Berwick—(b and w)—ledger—F. W. ANDERSON & CO., New York.
Berwick—(b)—H. REEVE ANGEL & CO., INC., New York.
Berwick Linen—(w)—V A L L E Y PAPER CO., Holyoke, Mass.
Berwick Mills—(b)—folded—POWERS PAPER CO., Springfield, Mass.
Bessemer—(b)— cover — SEYMOUR CO., New York.
Best Linen — (b) — HY. LINDENMEYR & SONS, New York.

APPLETON MACHINE CO.
APPLETON, WIS.
REFINING ENGINES, SCREENS, SAWING & SPLITTING MACHINERY
HIGH GRADE CENTRIFUGAL PUMPS

MINER EDGAR CO., Sole Agents
KEYSTONE CLAY & REDUCTION CO.
30 Church Street - - - New York
CLAY
PRECIPITATED REFINED
LIGHT GRAVITY SOFT TEXTURE
<K L M>
HIGH NATURAL COLOR, HIGH RETENTION

Watermarks and Brands

Columbian—(b)—bristol board—BUNTIN, GILLIES & CO., Hamilton, Ontario, Canada.
Columbian—(w and b)—blotting—EATON, DIKEMAN & CO., Lee, Mass.
Columbian—(b)—toilet—STONE & FORSYTH CO., Boston.
Columbian Bond — (w) — writing — CAREW MANUFACTURING CO., South Hadley Falls, Mass.
Columbian Bond —(w)— STRATHMORE PAPER CO., Mittineague, Mass.
Columbian Bond—(w)—BROWN, TREACY & SPERRY CO., St. Paul.
Columbian Bond—(w)—GILBERT PAPER CO., Menasha, Wis.
Columbian Bristol—(b)—BUNTIN, GILLIES & CO., LTD., Hamilton, Ontario, Can.
Columbian Japan Plate—(b)—HY. LINDENMEYR & SONS, New York.
Columbian Ledger—(w)—AMERICAN WRITING PAPER CO., Holyoke.
Columbian Ledger—(w)—BROWN, TREACY & SPERRY CO., St. Paul.
Columbian Ledger—(w)—PARSONS TRADING CO., New York.
Columbine Parchment—(w)—bond—GRAHAM PAPER CO., St. Louis.
Columbus — (w) —fine — CENTRAL OHIO PAPER CO., Columbus, Ohio.
Comanche—(b)—sheathing—GRAHAM PAPER CO., St. Louis.
Combination—(b)—toilet—ALBANY PERFORATED WRAPPING PAPER CO., Albany, N. Y.
Comet —(b)— covers — KNOWLTON BROS., Watertown, N. Y., and BIEGEL & CO., INC., Philadelphia.
Comet—cover—(b)—LASHER & LATHROP, New York.
Comet Bond—(w)—BRADNER SMITH & CO., Chicago.
Comet Flats—(b)— HY. LINDENMEYR & SONS, New York.
Commander Bond—(w)— LEE PAPER CO., Vicksburg, Mich.
Commerce—(b)—railroad manila—GRAHAM PAPER CO., St. Louis.
Commerce—(b)—flat writing — MINNEAPOLIS PAPER CO., Minn.
Commerce Bond—(b)—MILLER & WRIGHT PAPER CO., New York.
Commerce Bond—(w)—PACIFIC PAPER CO., Portland, Ore.
Commerce Bond—(w)—E. E. LLOYD PAPER CO., Chicago, Ill.
Commerce Ledger—(w)—COOK-VIVIAN CO., Boston.
Commerce Linen — (w) — H. K. BREWER & CO., New York.
Commerce Linen — (w) — WM. G. JOHNSTON & CO., Pittsburg, Pa.
Commerce Manila—(b)—HY. LINDENMEYR & SONS. New York.
Commercial—(b)—pasted cardboard—J. W. BUTLER PAPER CO., Chicago.
Commercial—(b)—blotting—JOSEPH PARKER & SON CO., New Haven.
Commercial—(b)—pasted wedding bristol—J. W. BUTLER PAPER CO., Chicago.
Commercial — (b) — roofing —L. J. DODD CO., INC., Elmira, N. Y.
Commercial — (w) — UNITED STATES ENVELOPE CO., Holyoke
Commercial Bond—(w)—VALLEY PAPER CO., Holyoke, Mass.
Commercial Bond—(b)—O. F. H. WARNER & CO., Baltimore.
Commercial Bristol—(b)—CHATFIELD & WOODS CO., Cincinnati.
Commercial Fine—(w)—GARRETT-BUCHANAN CO., Philadelphia.
Commercial Fine—(w)—VALLEY PAPER CO., Holyoke, Mass.
Commercial Index—(b)—BEECHER, PECK & LEWIS, Detroit, Mich.
Commercial Index Bristol—(b)—MACK-ELLIOTT PAPER CO., St. Louis.
Commercial Ledger—(w)—C. S. PROCTOR PAPER CO., Boston.
Commercial Linen—(w)—VALLEY PAPER CO., Holyoke, Mass.
Commercial Linen—(b)—toilet—UNITED STATES ENVELOPE CO. (Morgan Envelope Co. Division), Springfield, Mass.
Commercial Linen Bond — (w) — VALLEY PAPER CO., Holyoke, Mass.
Commercial Linen Ledger—(w)—VALLEY PAPER CO., Holyoke, Mass.
Commercial Manifold — (b) — GRAHAM PAPER CO., St. Louis.
Commercial Mills—(b)—R. P. MOLTEN & CO., Philadelphia.
Commercial Superfine—(w)—FOX RIVER PAPER CO., Appleton, Wis.
Commodity Bond—(w)—SMITH, DAVIDSON & WRIGHT, LTD., Vancouver, B. C.
Commonwealth—(b)—toilet — GEO. T. JOHNSON CO., Boston.
Commonwealth Bond—(w)—PLYMOUTH PAPER CO., Holyoke, Mass.
Commonwealth Linen—(w)—GEO. E. DAMON CO., Boston.
Commonwealth Linen—(w)—THOMAS W. PRICE CO., Philadelphia.
Community —(b)— CROCKER-McELWAIN CO., Holyoke, Mass.
Community Bond—(w)—CROCKER-McELWAIN CO., Holyoke, Mass.
Como—(b)—book and writing—WHITE & LEONARD, St. Paul, Minn.
Compass—(b)—envelope — GRAHAM PAPER CO., St. Louis.
Competition Half Tone—(b)—blotting—WRENN PAPER CO., Middletown, Ohio.
Competition—(b)— toilet — SCOTT PAPER CO., Philadelphia.
Competition Bond—(b)—R. P. ANDREWS PAPER CO., Washington, D. C.

Watermarks and Brands

Competition Bond—(b)—CARTER, RICE & CO., CORP., Boston.
Competition Ledger — (b) — R. P. ANDREWS PAPER CO., Washington, D. C.
Competition Manifold — (b) — GRAHAM PAPER CO., St. Louis.
Comptoir Bond—(b)—typewriter—EATON, CRANE & PIKE CO., Pittsfield, Mass.
Concord—(b)—news—CHATFIELD & WOODS CO., Cincinnati, Ohio.
Concord—(w)—colored laid—VON OLKER-SNELL PAPER CO., Boston.
Concord Bond—(b)—JUDD PAPER CO., Holyoke, Mass.
Concord Ledger — (b) — JUDD PAPER CO., Holyoke, Mass.
Concord Manila—(b)—C. S. PROCTOR PAPER CO., Boston.
Concrete—(w)—CHATFIELD & WOODS CO., Cincinnati, Ohio.
Concrete Bond—(w)—UNION PAPER & TWINE CO., Detroit, Mich.
Concrete Bond—(w)—JOHN LESLIE PAPER CO., Minneapolis.
Condor — (b) — writing — W. M. PRINGLE & CO., INC., New York.
Condor Bond—(b)—W. M. PRINGLE & CO., INC., New York.
Conference—(w and b)—writing, ledger, bond—NEENAH PAPER CO., Neenah, Wis.
Conference Linen Ledger—(w)—NEENAH PAPER CO., Neenah, Wis.
Congress—(b)—half tone blotting—W. H. CLAFLIN & CO., Boston.
Congress—(b)—book and label—GRAHAM PAPER CO., St. Louis.
Congress—(b)—coated book—W. H. CLAFLIN & CO., Boston.
Congress—(w)—bond—MERRIAM PAPER CO., New York.
Congress—(b)—box covering—DISTRICT OF COLUMBIA PAPER MFG. CO., Washington, D. C.
Congress Blanks—(b)—JOHN CARTER & CO., Boston.
Congress Blotting—(b)—DISTRICT OF COLUMBIA PAPER MFG. CO., Washington, D. C.
Congress Bond—(w)—MERRIAM PAPER CO., New York.
Congress Covers—(b)—DISTRICT OF COLUMBIA PAPER MFG. CO., Washington, D. C.
Congress Fine—(b)—NITSCHKE PAPER CO., Columbus, Ohio.
Congress Index Bristol—(b)—HARLEM CARD & PAPER CO., New York.
Congress Linen—(w)—VALLEY PAPER CO., Holyoke, Mass.
Congress Linen Ledger—(w)—VALLEY PAPER CO., Holyoke, Mass.
Congress Mills—(b)—toilet—C. H. DEXTER & SON, INC., Windsor Locks, Conn.
Congress Mills — (w) — writing—J. FRANCIS HOCK & CO., Baltimore.

Congress Text—(w)—DISTRICT OF COLUMBIA PAPER CO., Washington, D. C.
Congress, Valley Congress Linen Bond—(w)—VALLEY PAPER CO., Holyoke, Mass.
Congressional Mills—(w)—JOHN CARTER & CO., Boston.
Connecticut Valley Mills—(w)—extra superfine folded—POWERS PAPER CO., Springfield, Mass.
Conniston Laid—(b)—colored writing—HAGEN PAPER CO., St. Louis.
Connoisseur Cover Brand—(b)—cover—RIEGEL & CO., INC., Philadelphia.
Conongue—(b)—roofing—L. J. DODD CO., INC., Elmira, N. Y.
Conqueror—(b)— ledger — WILKINSON BROS. & CO., INC., Philadelphia.
Conqueror — (w) — writing — MERRIAM PAPER CO., New York.
Conqueror — (b)— covers — KNOWLTON BROS., Watertown, N. Y., and RIEGEL & CO., INC., Philadelphia.
Conqueror Bond — (w) — DAVID L. ENGLE, New York.
Conquest Bond—(w)—LOUISVILLE PAPER CO., Louisville, Ky.
Conquest Linen Ledger — (w)—NEENAH PAPER CO., Neenah, Wis.
Conrow's Antique Laid—(b)—book—CONROW BROS., New York.
Conrow's Coated—(b)—CONROW BROS., New York.
Conrow's '99 Half Tone—(b)—CONROW BROTHERS, New York.
Conservation—(w and b)—writing, ledger, bond—NEENAH PAPER CO., Neenah, Wis.
Conservation Linen Ledger—(w)—NEENAH PAPER CO., Neenah, Wis.
Consols Bond — (w) — AMERICAN WRITING PAPER CO., Holyoke, Mass.
Constitution — (b) — book — GRAHAM PAPER CO., St. Louis.
Constitution Bond—(w)—BERKSHIRE PAPER CO., Adams, Mass.
Constitution Ledger—(w)—SWIGART PAPER CO., Chicago.
Constitution Ledger—(w)—BERKSHIRE PAPER CO., Adams, Mass.
Constitution Ledger—(w)—BERKSHIRE PAPER CO., Adams, Mass.
Constitution Linen —(w)— BERKSHIRE PAPER CO., Adams, Mass.
Construction Bond—(w)—W. E. WROE & CO., Chicago.
Construction Laid Antique—(w)—W. E. WROE & CO., Chicago.
Consumers' Bond—(w)—KALAMAZOO PAPER CO., Kalamazoo, Mich.
Consumers' Bond—(b)—THOS. W. PRICE CO., Philadelphia.
Contest Parchment—(w)—LOUISVILLE PAPER CO., Louisville, Ky.
Continental — (b) — blotting — GRAHAM PAPER CO., St. Louis.
Continental—(b)—roll toilet—STONE & FORSYTH CO., Boston.

Continental Bond—(w)—FOX RIVER PAPER CO., Appleton, Wis.
Continental Bond—(w)—WESTERN PAPER COMPANY, Omaha, Neb.
Continental Cover—(b)—THE UNION PAPER & TWINE CO., Detroit, Mich.
Continental Ledger—(w)—WESTERN PAPER CO., Omaha, Neb.
Continental Linen Fabric—(b)—EATON, CRANE & PIKE CO., Pittsfield, Mass.
Continental Mills—(b)—SCOTT PAPER CO., Philadelphia.
Contract Bond—(w)—AMERICAN WRITING PAPER CO., Holyoke, Mass.
Convention—(b)—cover—KANSAS CITY PAPER HOUSE, Kansas City.
Convertible Bond—(w)—COLLINS MFG. CO., N. Wilbraham, Mass.
Conway—(b)—white writing—B. F. BOND PAPER CO., Baltimore.
Copake—(b)—toilet—ALBANY PERFORATED WRAPPING PAPER CO., Albany, N. Y.
Copake—(b)—toilet—MEGARGEE BROS., Scranton, Pa.
Copco Bond—(w)—CENTRAL OHIO PAPER CO., Columbus, Ohio.
Copperfield Superfine—(b)—coated book—JAMES WHITE PAPER CO., Chicago.
Copperoid—(b)—red rope—CHAS. J. COHEN, Philadelphia.
Copy Papers—(b)—A. S. LANDSBERG, New York.
Copying Bond—(b)—WESTERN PENNA. PAPER CO., Pittsburgh, Pa.
Copywell—(b)—SCRANTOM, WETMORE & CO., Rochester, N. Y.
Coquille—(b)—GEO. B. HURD & CO., New York.
Coral Mills—(b)—white writing—THE ALLING & CORY CO., Rochester, N. Y.
Cordova—(w)—superfine—J. C. BLAIR & CO., Huntingdon, Pa.
Cordovan—(b)—bristols—DETROIT SULPHITE PULP & PAPER CO., Detroit, Mich.
Corduette—(b)—GEO. B. HURD & CO., New York.
Corduroy Bond—(w)—THE W. B. OGLESBY PAPER CO., Middletown, Ohio.
Corduroy Cover—LASHER & LATHROP, New York.
Corduroy Ledger—(w)—W. B. OGLESBY PAPER CO., Middletown, O.
Corinthian Bond—(w)—LEE PAPER CO., Vicksburg, Mich.
Corliss Bond—(w)—BECKETT PAPER CO., Hamilton, Ohio.
Cornelia Mills—(w)—flat writing—MEGARGEE BROS., Scranton, Pa.
Cornell—(b)—catalog—GRAHAM PAPER CO., St. Louis.
Cornell—(b)—toilet—UNITED STATES ENVELOPE CO. (Morgan Envelope Co. Division), Springfield.

Cornell—(b)—writing—THE WHITAKER PAPER CO., New York.
Cornish—(b)—book—LOUISVILLE PAPER CO., Louisville, Ky.
Corno Bond—(b)—CONROW BROS., New York.
Cornwall Bond—(w)—DONALDSON PAPER CO., Harrisburg, Pa.
Cornwall Bond—(w)—CORNWALL PAPER CO., Cornwall-on-Hudson, N. Y.
Corona—(b)—cardboards and cards—GRAHAM PAPER CO., St. Louis.
Corona Mills—(w)—UNION PAPER & TWINE CO., Detroit, Mich.
Corona Wedding Bristol—(b)—HARLEM CARD & PAPER CO., New York.
Coronation—(b)—W. E. WROE & CO., Chicago.
Coronation Covers—(b)—HENRY LINDENMEYR & SONS, New York.
Coronation Linen—(w)—JOHN WANAMAKER, Philadelphia.
Coronet—(w)—laid and wove—AMERICAN WRITING PAPER CO., Holyoke, Mass.
Coronet—(w)—STATE JOURNAL CO., Lincoln, Neb.
Coronet Bristol—(b)—UNION PAPER & TWINE CO., Detroit, Mich.
Coronet Cold Pressed—(w)—WRIGHT, BARRETT & STILWELL CO., St. Paul, Minn.
Coronet Enameled White—(b)—book—MILLER & WRIGHT PAPER CO., New York.
Corona—(w)—linen—J. E. LINDE PAPER CO., New York.
Corporation Bond—(w)—J. E. LINDE PAPER CO., New York.
Corporation Ledger—(b)—SCRANTOM, WETMORE & CO., Rochester.
Correct Bond—(w)—AETNA PAPER CO., Dayton, Ohio.
Correspondence Bond—(b)—McCLELLAN PAPER CO., Minneapolis.
Coruscan Coated Book—(b)—PAPER MILLS COMPANY, Chicago.
Coruscan Cover—(b)—PAPER MILLS COMPANY, Chicago.
Coruscan Post Card—PAPER MILLS COMPANY, Chicago.
Cosmic—(w)—bond and ledger—UNION CARD & PAPER CO., N. Y.
Cosmo—(b)—toilet—ALBANY PERFORATED WRAPPING PAPER CO., Albany, N. Y.
Cosmos—(b)—J. C. PARKER PAPER CO., Louisville, Ky.
Cossack—(w and b)—writing, ledger, bond—NEENAH PAPER CO., Neenah, Wis.
Cottage—(b)—SCOTT PAPER CO., Philadelphia.
Cotton Blossom—(b)—toilet—NORTHERN PAPER MILLS, Milwaukee, Wis.
Cottonette—(b)—toilet—MEGARGEE BROS., Scranton, Pa.

NVESTIGATIONS — **REPORTS** — **INSPECTIONS**

C. A. CHAPMAN, Inc.

8 E. JACKSON BLVD. — **ENGINEERS** — **CHICAGO**

Watermarks and Brands 649

Counselors' Law—(b)—book—MILLER & WRIGHT PAPER CO., N. Y.
Countess—(b)—UNITED STATES ENVELOPE CO. (Morgan Division), Springfield, Mass.
Countess Bristol—(b)—VON OLKER-SNELL PAPER CO., Boston.
Counting House—(w)—SAUGERTIES MFG. CO., Saugerties, N. Y.
Counting House Linen—(w)—J. S. LINDE PAPER CO., New York.
Country Club—(b)—toilet—LOUISVILLE PAPER CO., Louisville, Ky.
Country Club—(b)—toilet—THE SEINSHEIMER PAPER CO., Cincinnati, Ohio.
County Bond—(w)—PLYMOUTH PAPER CO., Holyoke, Mass.
County Ledger—(w)—CENTRAL OHIO PAPER CO., Columbus, Ohio.
Coupon—(b)—bristol—J. W. BUTLER PAPER CO., Chicago.
Coupon Bond—(w)—AMERICAN WRITING PAPER CO., Holyoke, Mass.
Coupon Safety—(b)—GEO. LA MONTE & SON, New York.
Coupon Toilet Tissue—(b)—HY. LINDENMEYR & SONS, New York.
Courier—(b)—bristol—cut cards—THE PAPER MILLS CO., Chicago.
Court—(b)—document manila—J. W. BUTLER PAPER CO., Chicago.
Court—(w)—ledger—J. FRANCIS HOCK CO., Baltimore.
Court Bond—(w)—EASTERN PAPER AND SUPPLY CO., Springfield.
Court Document—(b)—J. W. BUTLER PAPER CO., Chicago.
Court House—(b)—blotter—MINNEAPOLIS PAPER CO., Minneapolis, Minn.
Court Index Bristol—JOHN CARTER & CO., INC., Boston.
Court Ledger—(w)—ST. LOUIS PAPER CO., St. Louis.
Court Linen Ledger—(w)—C. S. PROCTOR PAPER CO., Boston.
Courtland—(b)—book—GRAHAM PAPER CO., St. Louis.
Court of Empire—(b)—EATON, CRANE & PIKE CO., Pittsfield, Mass.
Court of England—(w)—EATON, CRANE & PIKE CO., Pittsfield, Mass.
Court of Netherlands—(w)—EATON, CRANE & PIKE CO., Pittsfield, Mass.
Court of Russia—(w)—EATON, CRANE & PIKE CO., Pittsfield, Mass.
Court Tag—(b)—J. W. BUTLER PAPER CO., Chicago.
Court Vellum—(w)—MARCUS WARD CO., Brooklyn, N. Y.
Covenant—(b)—cover—PENINSULAR PAPER CO., Ypsilanti, Mich.
Coventry—(b)—book—J. W. BUTLER PAPER CO., Chicago.
Cowboy—(b)—wrapping—GRAHAM PAPER CO., St. Louis.
Cowhide—(b)—UNION BAG & PAPER CORP., New York.

Cowhide Wrapping—(b)—OLD DOMINION PAPER CO., Norfolk, Va.
Cowskin—(b)—wrapping—OLD DOMINION PAPER CO., Norfolk, Va.
Coymore—(w)—writing—COYLE & GILMORE CO., INC., New York.
C. P. A.—(w)—ledger—LEWERTH & CULBERTSON, New York.
C. P. R. Superfine Linen—(w)—Monogram—ROLLAND PARKER CO., St. Jerome, Canada.
Craftsman—(w and b)—linen ledgers, covers, deckled edge book, bristol, envelopes, blanks, parchment, writing, blotting, coated manila—MEGARGEE-HARE PAPER CO., Philadelphia.
Craigmere Damask—(b)—MACK-ELLIOTT PAPER CO., St. Louis.
Craigsmoor—(w)—writing and bond—W. R. GRACE & CO., New York.
Crane's All Linen—(w)—Crane on shield with date—CRANE BROS., Westfield, Mass.
Crane's Distaff Linen—(w)—Z. & W. M. CRANE, Dalton, Mass.
Crane & Co. Bond No. 16—(w)—CRANE & CO., Dalton, Mass.
Crane & Co. Bond No. 18—(w)—CRANE & CO., Dalton, Mass.
Crane & Co. Bond No. 21—(w)—CRANE & CO., Dalton, Mass.
Crane & Co. Bond No. 25—(w)—CRANE & CO., Dalton, Mass.
Crane & Co. Bond No. 29—(w)—CRANE & CO., Dalton, Mass.
Crane & Co. Bond No. 31—(w)—CRANE & CO., Dalton, Mass.
Crane & Co. Bond No. 36—(w)—CRANE & CO., Dalton, Mass.
Crane & Co. Bond No. 37—(w)—CRANE & CO., Dalton, Mass.
Crane & Co. Bond No. 43—(w)—CRANE & CO., Dalton, Mass.
Crane & Co. Bond No. 44—(w)—CRANE & CO., Dalton, Mass.
Crane & Co. Bond No. 55—(w)—CRANE & CO., Dalton, Mass.
Crane's Doeskin—(w)—Z & W. M. CRANE, Dalton, Mass.
Crane's Early English—(w)—Z. & W. M. CRANE, Dalton, Mass.
Crane's Floral Design—(w)—Z. & W. M. CRANE, Dalton, Mass.
Crane's Grecian Antique—(w)—Z & W. M. CRANE, Dalton, Mass.
Crane's Japanese Linen—(w)—Crane and date—CRANE BROS., Westfield, Mass.
Crane's Kid Finish—(w)—Z. & W. M. CRANE, Dalton, Mass.
Crane's Old Style—(w)—Z. & W. M. CRANE, Dalton, Mass.
Crane's Parchment Vellum—(w)—Z. & W. M. CRANE, Dalton, Mass.
Crane's Twilled Flax—(w)—Z. & W. M. CRANE, Dalton, Mass.
Crane's Underglaze—(w)—Z. & W. M. CRANE, Dalton, Mass.
Cranford—(b)—fine—MERRIAM PAPER CO., New York.
Cranford Ledger—(w)—MERRIAM PAPER CO., New York.

APPLETON MACHINE CO., APPLETON, WIS.
REFINING ENGINES, SCREENS, SAVING & SPLITTING MACHINERY
HIGH GRADE **CENTRIFUGAL PUMPS**

MINER EDGAR CO., Sole Agents
KEYSTONE CLAY & REDUCTION CO.
10 Church Street - - New York

<C L A Y>
PRECIPITATED REFINED
LIGHT GRAVITY SOFT TEXTURE
<K L M>
HIGH NATURAL COLOR, HIGH RETENTION

FELTS AND JACKETS | Appleton Woolen Mills
APPLETON - - WIS.

Watermarks and Brands

C. R. C. Linen Ledger — (w)— CARTER, RICE & CO., Boston.
Crash Fabric—(b)—GEO. B. HURD & CO., New York.
Cravenette Fibre — (b)—butchers' waterproof — THE SEINSHEIMER PAPER CO., Cincinnati, Ohio.
Cream Kraft—(b)—ORONO PULP & PAPER CO., Orono, Me.
Cream Manila Paper — (b) — extra grade No. 2 manila—THE SEINSHEIMER PAPER CO., Cincinnati, O.
Credential Bond—(w)—SOUTHWORTH CO., Mittineague, Mass.
Creme Bond—(w) — WOLF BROTHERS, Philadelphia.
Crepon—(w and b) — bond, writing, cover and bristol—UNION CARD & PAPER CO., New York.
Crescent—(b) — ALBANY PERFORATED WRAPPING PAPER CO., Albany, N. Y.
Crescent — (b) — tissue—BRADNER SMITH & CO., Chicago.
Crescent—(b)—document manila — J. W. BUTLER PAPER CO., Chicago.
Crescent—(b)—bristol —CHATFIELD & WOODS CO., Cincinnati, Ohio.
Crescent—(b)—crêpe paper and napkins—ERVING MILLS, Erving, Mass.
Crescent—(b)—crêpe tissue — ERVING MILLS, Erving, Mass.
Crescent—(b)—cardboards and cards —GRAHAM PAPER CO., St. Louis.
Crescent—(b)—toilet—HERBERT R. MANN, Troy, N. Y.
Crescent—(b)—toilet—UNITED STATES ENVELOPE CO. (Morgan Envelope Co. Division), Springfield.
Crescent Bond—CHAPIN & GOULD PAPER CO., Springfield, Mass.
Crescent Bond—(w)—LASHER & LATHROP, New York.
Crescent Bristol — (b) — COOKVIVIAN CO., Boston.
Crescent Fine — (b)—NITSCHKE PAPER CO., Columbus, Ohio.
Crescent Mills — (w) — bond and ledger—CHAPIN & GOULD PAPER CO., Springfield, Mass.
Crescent Mills Selena—CHAPIN & GOULD PAPER CO., Springfield.
Crescent Pasted Bristol — (b) — ARNOLD-ROBERTS CO., Boston.
Crescent Selena Writing—(w)— HY. LINDENMEYR & SONS, N. Y.
Crescent Superfine—(b) — CHAPIN & GOULD PAPER CO., Springfield.
Crescent Wove Writing—(b)—HY. LINDENMEYR & SONS, New York.
Cresco Halftone — (b) — book—C. P. LESH PAPER CO., Indianapolis.
Crescens—(b)—toilet—Northern Paper Mills, Green Bay, Wis.
Crest—(b)—WHITAKER PAPER CO., Cincinnati, Ohio.
Crestline Bond—(b)—PAPER MILLS COMPANY, Chicago.
Cretone Bond — (b) — E A T O N , CRANE & PIKE CO., Pittsfield, Mass.

Cretonne — (b) — decorative papers— NEBEN MFG. CO., New York.
Cretonne Bond — (w)—CHEMICAL PAPER MFG. CO., Holyoke, Mass.
Cretonne Bond—(w)—UNION CARD & PAPER CO., New York.
Cricket — (b)—CROWN COLUMBIA PAPER CO., San Francisco.
Crimean Bond — (w) — MOUNT HOLLY PAPER CO., Mount Holly Springs, Pa.
Crisis—(b)—toilet—UNITED STATES ENVELOPE CO. (Morgan Envelope Co. Division), Springfield, Mass.
Criterion Bond—(w)—BERKSHIRE HILLS PAPER CO., Adams, Mass.
Criterion Linen—(w)—W. G. WILLMANN, New York.
Critique—(b)—toilet — NORTHERN PAPER MILLS, Green Bay, Wis.
Crocker—(b)—cover — AMERICAN WRITING PAPER CO., Holyoke.
Crocker's E. G. H.—(w)—AMERICAN WRITING PAPER CO., Holyoke, Mass.
C r o c k e t t Onion Skin — (b) — GRAHAM PAPER CO., St. Louis.
Crofton — (b)—book—C. P. LESH PAPER CO., Indianapolis, Ind.
Crofton—(w)—book and cover—GRAHAM PAPER CO., St. Louis.
Cromwell — (b) — toilet—UNITED STATES ENVELOPE CO. (Morgan Envelope Co. Division), Springfield.
Crosscut—(b)—toilet—ALBANY PERFORATED WRAPPING PAPER CO., Albany, New York.
Crown—(b) — SMITH PAPER CO., Lee, Mass.
Crown — (b) — book—CINCINNATI CORDAGE AND PAPER CO., Cincinnati, Ohio.
Crown — (b) — toilet — NORTHERN PAPER MILLS, Green Bay, Wis.
Crown—(w) — BLADE PRINTING AND PAPER CO., Toledo, Ohio.
Crown—(b)—coated one side—F. A. FLINN, INC., New York.
Crown—(b) — envelopes and toilet— UNITED STATES ENVELOPE CO. (Morgan Envelope Co. Division), Springfield, Mass.
Crown—(b)—package, toilet—CHATFIELD & WOODS CO., Cincinnati, O.
Crown Blotting—(b)—HY. LINDENMEYR & SONS, New York.
Crown Bond—(w)—AETNA PAPER CO., Dayton, Ohio.
Crown Bond—(w)—FOX RIVER PAPER CO., Appleton, Wis.
Crown Bristol—(b)—PETERS PAPER CO., Denver, Col.
Crown Bristol—(b)—A. STORRS & BEMENT CO., Boston.
Crown Cover—(b) — BUNTIN, GILLIES & CO., LTD., Hamilton, Ontario, Can.
Crown Imperial Mills — (w)— CARTER, RICE & CO., CORP., Boston.

JAMES H. HARRISON
OILSTONE MANUFACTURER

GENUINE NEWCASTLE STONES
18 K____ St., GATESHEAD-ON-TYNE, ENG.

Crown Index Bristol—(b)—THE ALLING & CORY CO., Rochester.
Crown Kraft—(b)—D. S. WALTON & CO., New York.
Crown Label—(b)—JERSEY CITY PAPER CO., Jersey City, N. J.
Crown Ledger — (w)—AMERICAN WRITING PAPER CO., Holyoke.
Crown Leghorn Linen — (w)— AMERICAN WRITING PAPER CO., Holyoke, Mass.
Crown Leghorn Linen Bond—(w) —AMERICAN WRITING PAPER CO., Holyoke, Mass.
Crown Linen — (w)—C. W. WILLIAMS & CO., New York.
Crown Linen — (w) — ROLLAND PAPER CO., St. Jerome, Canada.
Crown Onion Skin — (b)—folio— BRADNER SMITH & CO., Chicago.
Crown Record Writing (w)—RICHMOND PAPER CO., Richmond, Va.
Crown Royal—(w)—extra fine writing—CENTRAL OHIO PAPER CO., Columbus, Ohio.
Crown Royal Linen—(w)—AMERICAN WRITING PAPER CO., Holyoke.
Crown Tissue — (b) — STRATFORD PAPER CO., Jersey City, N. J.
Crown Typewriter Papers—(b)— STRATFORD PAPER CO., Jersey City, N. J.
Crown Victoria—(w)—BARBER-ELLIS LTD., Toronto, Can.
Crusader—(b)—LOUISVILLE PAPER CO., Louisville, Ky.
Crusader—(w and b)—writing, ledger, bond—NEENAH PAPER CO., Neenah, Wis.
Crushed Linear—(w)—GEO. B. HURD & CO., New York.
Crushed Snow Flake—(b)—UNION CARD & PAPER CO., New York.
Crushed Vellum White—(w)—bond —MERRIAM PAPER CO., New York.
Crystal—(b)—bristol — C. P. LESH PAPER CO., Indianapolis, Ind.
Crystal—(b)—D. S. WALTON & CO., New York.
Crystal—(b)—dry finish butchers' fibre —CHATFIELD & WOODS CO., Cincinnati, Ohio.
Crystal—(b)—flat — DIEM & WING PAPER CO., Cincinnati, Ohio.
Crystal—(b) — waxed and bristol — LOUISVILLE PAPER CO., Louisville, Ky.
Crystal—(b)—roll toilet—THE CHATFIELD & WOODS CO., Cincinnati, O.
Crystal—(b)—toilet—W. A. STOWE PAPER CO., Grand Rapids, Mich.
Crystal—(w)—BUNTIN, GILLIES & CO., Hamilton, Can.
Crystal Blanks—(b)—coated blanks —SWIGART PAPER CO., Chicago.
Crystal Bond—(w)—THE BLUNDEN-LYON CO., Chicago.
Crystal Bristol—(b)—BUNTIN, GILLIES & CO., LTD., Hamilton, Ontario, Can.

Crystal Coated—(b)—LASHER & LATHROP, New York.
Crystal Coated Champion Superfine — writing — L A S H E R & LATHROP, New York.
Crystal Coated Blanks—(b)—RICHMOND PAPER CO., Richmond, Va.
Crystal Coated Blotting — (b) — HARLEM CARD & PAPER CO., New York.
Crystal Coated Book — (b) — HARLEM CARD & PAPER CO., New York.
Crystal Glassine—(b)—McDOWELL PAPER MILLS, Philadelphia.
Crystal Gummed—(b)—B U N T I N, GILLIES & CO., LTD., Hamilton, Ontario, Can.
Crystal Lake Mills—(b)—extra fine folded — POWERS PAPER CO., Springfield, Mass.
Crystal Ledger — (b) —PAUL E. VERNON & CO., New York.
Crystal Litho Coated—(b)—HARLEM CARD & PAPER CO., New York.
Crystal Manifold—(b) — McCLELLAN PAPER CO., Minneapolis, Minn.
Crystal Parchment — (b)—BRADNER SMITH & CO., Chicago.
Crystal Postcard — (b) — HARLEM CARD & PAPER CO., New York.
Crystal Super — (b) — TILESTON & HOLLINGSWORTH CO., Boston, Mass.
Crystal Translucent — (b) — HARLEM CARD & PAPER CO., New York.
Crystal White — (b)—folded—EAST HARTFORD MANUFACTURING CO., Burnside, Conn.
Crystal White — (b) — bristol—C. S. PROCTOR PAPER CO., Boston.
Crystal Wove—(w)—BUNTIN, GILLIES & CO., Hamilton, Ontario, Can.
Crystal Wove—(b)—M. G. wrapping —R. A. CAUTHORNE PAPER CO., Richmond, Va.
Crystalite—(w and b)—writing, ledger, bond—NEENAH PAPER CO., Neenah, Wis.
C. S. P. Ledger—(w)—C. S. PROCTOR PAPER CO., Boston.
C. S. P. Superfine — (w)—C. S. PROCTOR PAPER CO., Boston.
Cuban Bond—(w)—AETNA PAPER CO., Dayton, Ohio.
Cuban Bond—(w) — COOK-VIVIAN CO., Boston.
Cuban Crash Cover—(b)—THE ALLING & CORY, Rochester, N. Y.
Culebra Bond — (w) — OSBORN PAPER CO., Philadelphia.
Culebra Linen Ledger—(w)—OSBORN PAPER CO., Philadelphia.
Cumberland — (b)—enameled book— CINCINNATI C O R D A G E AND PAPER CO., Cincinnati, Ohio.
Cumberland—(b)—toilet — UNITED STATES ENVELOPE CO. (Morgan Envelope Co. Div.), Springfield, Mass.

Cumberland—(b)—coated book, regular coated surface—S. D. WARREN & CO., Boston.
Cumberland Linen Ledger—(w)—LASHER & LATHROP, New York.
Cumberland Mills — (b)—whitewriting—JOHNSTON PARKER CO., Harrisburg, Pa.
Cumberland Super—(b)—book, white SP. and MF.—S. D. WARREN & CO., Boston.
Cupid Bond—(w)—W. B. OGLESBY PAPER CO., Middletown, Ohio.
Cupid Pasted Bristol—(b)—V O N OLKER-SNELL PAPER CO., Boston.
Cupid Superfine — (w)—THE W. B. OGLESBY PAPER CO., Middletown, Ohio.
Curl—Cure—(b)—blotting — STANDARD PAPER MFG. CO., Richmond.
Currency Bond — (w)—DIEM & WING PAPER CO., Cincinnati, Ohio.
Currency Bristol—(b)—MINNEAPOLIS PAPER CO., Minneapolis Minn.
Currency Linen — (w)—($)—JOHN B. WATKINS, New York.
Currency Linen Ledger—(w)—C. P. LESH PAPER CO., Indianapolis.
Current Bond — (b)—LOUISVILLE PAPER CO., Louisville, Ky.
Custer—(b)—book and label—GRAHAM PAPER CO., St. Louis.
Custer Post Card—(b)—GRAHAM PAPER CO., St. Louis.
Custom House—(w)—bond - ANDERSON & CO., New York.
Customs Bond—(w)—HAMPSHIRE PAPER CO., South Hadley Falls, Mass.
Cuyahoga Bond—(w)—PETREQUIN PAPER CO., Cleveland, Ohio.
C.-V. Co. Ledger — (w) — COOK-VIVIAN CO., Boston.
Cyclone—(b)—ALEX. McARTHUR & CO., LTD., Montreal, Canada.
Cyclone—(b) — ruled and folded—BRADNER SMITH & CO., Chicago.
Cyclone Bristol—(b) — BRADNER SMITH & CO., Chicago.
Cyclone Mills — (b) — BRADNER SMITH & CO., Chicago.
Cylinder—(b)—anti-tarnish tissue — GRAHAM PAPER CO., St. Louis.
Cylinder—(b)—silver tissue—GRAHAM PAPER CO., St. Louis.
Cypress—(b)—enamel—C. P. LESH PAPER CO., Indianapolis, Ind.
Csar—(b) — enamel — DONALDSON PAPER CO., Harrisburg, Pa.
Csar Bond—(b)—McCLELLAN PAPER CO., Minneapolis, Minn.
Csar Mills—(b)—flat—J. W. BUTLER PAPER CO., Chicago.

D

"D" — (b) — HY. LINDENMEYR & SONS, New York.
"D"—(b)—S. & S. C. and M. F.—book—MAGARGE & GREEN, Philadelphia.
D in a Diamond—(b)—coated and super book—registered trade mark—DILL & COLLINS CO., Philadelphia.
D in a Diamond—(w)—linen ledger—DWIGHT BROS. PAPER CO., Chicago.
D. & W. English Art Finish—(b) —DIEM & WING PAPER CO., Cincinnati, Ohio.
D. & W. Linen Ledger—(w)—DIEM & WING PAPER CO., Cincinnati, Ohio.
"D. P. Co." Brand—(b)—postcard stock—DONALDSON PAPER CO., Harrisburg, Pa.
Daffodil—(b)—cover—GRAHAM PAPER CO., St. Louis.
Daffodil—(b)—toilet—ALBANY PERFORATED WRAPPING PAPER CO., Albany, N. Y.
Dagmar Linen — (b)—E A T O N, CRANE & PIKE CO., Pittsfield, Mass.
Dalsee — (b) — cordage—GRAHAM PAPER CO., St. Louis.
Daisy—(b)—tissue — A. M. EATON, Waltham and Boston.
Dakota Bond—(w)—LASHER & LATHROP, New York.
Dakota—(w)—flats—WRIGHT, BARRETT & STILWELL CO., St. Paul.
Dalkeith Bond — LOUISVILLE PAPER CO., Louisville, Ky.
Dalton—(b)—super calendered book—WHITAKER PAPER CO., Cincinnati, Ohio, and BAY STATE PAPER CO., Boston.
Dalton Ledger — (w) — GRAHAM PAPER CO., St. Louis.
Damascus—(b) — bond — WHITING-PATTERSON CO., Philadelphia.
Damascus—(b)—ledger — WHITING-PATTERSON CO., Philadelphia.
Damascus—(b)—No. 1 Manila—WHITING-PATTERSON CO., Philadelphia.
Damascus—(b)—tarred felt—GRAHAM PAPER CO., St. Louis.
Damascus—(b)—writing — WHITING-PATTERSON CO., Philadelphia.
Damascus Bond—(w)—BRADNER SMITH & CO., Chicago.
Damascus Bristol—(b)—BRADNER SMITH & CO., Chicago.
Damask—(b)—GEO. B. HURD & CO., New York.
Damask — (b)— toilet — GEO. T. JOHNSON CO., Providence, R. I.
Damask Bristol — (b) — STRATHMORE PAPER CO., Mittineague, Mass.
Damask Linen — (w) — COLUMBIA PAPER CO., Victoria, B. C.
Damask Linene—(w)—EAST HARTFORD MANUFACTURING CO., Burnside, Conn.
Damask Manuscript Cover—(b)—STRATHMORE PAPER CO., Mittineague, Mass.
Dameron — (b) — book—GRAHAM PAPER CO., St. Louis.

Watermarks and Brands

Damsel — (b) — music—GRAHAM PAPER CO., St. Louis.
Dana Mills — (w) —flat writing—WHITAKER PAPER CO., Cincinnati, Ohio, and BAY STATE PAPER CO., Boston.
Dana Mills—(b)—writing—R. C. KASTNER PAPER CO., New York.
Dandee—(b)—wrapping — ANDREWS PAPER CO., Boston.
Dandy—(b)—toilet—SCOTT PAPER CO., Philadelphia.
Dandy Bristol—(b)—MINNEAPOLIS PAPER CO., Minneapolis, Minn.
Dandy Bond—(b)—CLEVELAND PAPER MFG. CO., Cleveland, Ohio.
Danish Bond—(w)—B. D. RISING PAPER CO., Housatonic, Mass.
Danish Ledger—(w)—B. D. RISING PAPER CO., Housatonic, Mass.
Danish Linen—(w)—B. D. RISING PAPER CO., Housatonic, Mass.
Danish Parchment — (w) — B. D. RISING PAPER CO., Housatonic, Mass.
Danish Pasted Bristol—(b)—B. D. RISING PAPER CO., Housatonic, Mass.
Danish Typewriter—(b)—B. D. RISING PAPER CO., Housatonic, Mass.
Danube—(b)—toilet—A. M. EATON, Waltham and Boston.
Dardenelle—(b)— book — GRAHAM PAPER CO., St. Louis.
Dartford Linen—(w)—writing—CAREW MANUFACTURING CO., South Hadley Falls, Mass.
Dartmouth—(w)—superfine—CAREW MFG. CO., South Hadley Falls, Mass.
Dartmouth—(b)—catalog—GRAHAM PAPER CO., St. Louis.
Dartmouth Bond — (w) — MILLERS FALLS PAPER COMPANY, Millers Falls, Mass.
Dauphin—(b)—book—GRAHAM PAPER CO., St. Louis.
Dauphin—(b)—JOHNSTON PAPER CO., Harrisburg, Pa.
Dauphin Mills—(b)—white writing—JOHNSTON PAPER CO., Harrisburg, Pa.
Davenport — (b) — litho. coated — LOUISVILLE PAPER CO., Louisville, Ky.
Davenport—(b)—book—G R A H A M PAPER CO., St. Louis.
Dawn Fibre—(b)—wrapping— GRAHAM PAPER CO., St. Louis.
Daytona Bond — (w) — AETNA PAPER CO., Dayton, Ohio.
Daytona—(b)—blotting—HAGEN PAPER CO., St. Louis.
Deacon—(b)—book—GRAHAM PAPER CO., St. Louis.
Dealers Bond — (b) — MEGARGEE BROS., Scranton, Pa.
De-and-Se Tints—(b)—DILL & COLLINS CO., Philadelphia.
Deanoid—(b)—roofing—L. J. DODD, INC., Elmira, N. Y.

Dearham Bond—(w)—HAGEN PAPER CO., St. Louis.
Debenture Bond—(w)—AMERICAN WRITING PAPER CO., Holyoke, Mass.
Decatur Bond — (w) — GARRETT-BUCHANAN CO., Philadelphia.
Decatur Mills—(b)—R. P. MOLTEN & CO., Philadelphia.
Deerhide Manila — (b) — OSBURN PAPER CO., Philadelphia.
Deerlake—(w and b)—writing, book and wedding bristol—UNION CARD & PAPER CO., New York.
Deerlake Deckle Edge — (b) — UNION CARD & PAPER CO., N. Y.
Deerpark—(b)— writing — GRAHAM PAPER CO., St. Louis.
Deerskin Parchment—(b)—writing—WEST VIRGINIA PULP & PAPER CO., New York.
Deerslayer — (b) — w r a p p i n g — GRAHAM PAPER CO., St. Louis.
Deeside—(w)—BUNTIN, GILLIES & CO., LTD., Hamilton, Ontario, Can.
Deeside—(b)—coated—BUNTIN, GILLIES & CO., LTD., Hamilton, Ontario, Canada.
Defender—(w)—AETNA PAPER CO., Dayton, Ohio.
Defender—(w)—CHATFIELD & WOODS CO., Cincinnati, Ohio.
Defender—(b)—folded—ESSEX PAD AND PAPER CO., Holyoke, Mass.
Defender—(b)—enameled book—PETERS PAPER CO., Denver, Col.
Defender—(b)—blotting—RIEGEL & CO., INC., Philadelphia.
Defender—(b)—WHITAKER PAPER CO., Cincinnati, Ohio.
Defender—(w)—flats—W R I G H T, BARRETT & STILWELL CO., St. Paul, Minn.
Defender—(w)—fine—W R I G H T, BARRETT & STILWELL CO., St. Paul, Minn.
Defender— (b) —tag board—T R O Y PAPER CO., Troy, N. Y.
Defender Blanks — (b) — WABASH COATING MILLS, Wabash, Ind.
Defender Bond—(w)—FOX RIVER PAPER CO., Appleton, Wis.
Defender Bond — (w) — COLUMBIA PAPER CO., Victoria, B. C.
Defender Bond—(b)—SUTPHIN PAPER CO., INC., New York.
Defender Enamel—(b)—blotting—STANDARD PAPER MFG. CO., Richmond, Va.
Defender Parchment — (b) — waterproof sheathing—GRAHAM PAPER CO., St. Louis.
Defender Souvenir Post Cards—(b)—BRADNER SMITH & CO., Chicago.
Defendum Linen Ledger—(w)—PARSONS PAPER CO., Holyoke, Mass.
Defiance—(b)—waterproof lining paper—JUDD PAPER CO., Holyoke.
Defiance—(b)—bristol — MEGARGEE-HARE PAPER CO., Philadelphia.

Watermarks and Brands

Defiance—AMERICAN WRITING PAPER CO., Holyoke, Mass.
Defiance—(b)—book—BRADNER SMITH & CO., Chicago.
Defiance—(b)—enameled book—CHATFIELD & WOODS CO., Cincinnati, Ohio.
Defiance—(b)—bristol—C. P. LESH PAPER CO., Indianapolis, Ind.
Defiance — (b)—toilet—NORTHERN PAPER MILLS, Green Bay, Wis.
Defiance—(b)—toilet—WILSON & TOWNE PAPER CO., New York.
Defiance—(b)—glazed silk fibre—WHITING-PATTERSON CO., New York.
Defiance—(w)—white wove—E. W. SCARBOROUGH, New York.
Defiance Bond—(w)—BYRON WESTON CO., Dalton, Mass.
Defiance Bristol—(b)—A. STORRS & BEMENT CO., Boston.
Defiance Coated Book—(b)—R. L. GREENE PAPER CO., Providence, R.I.
Defiance Linen Ledger—(w)—BYRON WESTON CO., Dalton, Mass.
Defiance—(b)—rag envelope—MINNEAPOLIS PAPER CO., Minneapolis.
Defiance Mills—(b)—ledger—BYRON WESTON CO., Dalton, Mass.
Defiance Paper Works—(w)—BYRON WESTON CO., Dalton, Mass.
Defiance Tag—(b)—C. P. LESH PAPER CO., Indianapolis, Ind.
De Kalb Mills—UNITED STATES ENVELOPE CO., Springfield, Mass.
Delavan Linen Ledger—(w)—CONROW BROTHERS, New York.
Delavan Linen Ledger—(w)—CONROW BROS., New York.
Delaware—(b)—BUNTIN, GILLIES & CO., Hamilton, Canada.
Delaware—(b)—ALBANY PERFORATED WRAPPING PAPER CO., Albany, N. Y.
Delaware—(b)—bond—GRAHAM PAPER CO., St. Louis.
Delaware Bristol—(b)—McCLELLAN PAPER CO., Minneapolis, Minn.
Delaware—(b)—white bristol—J. C. PARKER PAPER CO., Louisville, Ky.
Delaware Mills—(b)—fine—LASHER & LATHROP, New York.
Delaware—(w)—MISSOURI PAPER HOUSE, Kansas City, Mo.
Delford—(b)—book—JUDD PAPER CO., Holyoke, Mass.
Delft Linen—(w)—EATON, CRANE & PIKE CO., Pittsfield, Mass.
Delhi—(b)—cover—F. A. FLINN, INC., New York.
Delmar—(b)—box board—GRAHAM PAPER CO., St. Louis.
Delmar Bond—(w)—UNITED STATES ENVELOPE CO. (The White, Corbin & Co. Division), Rockville. Conn.
Delphi—(b)—LOUISVILLE PAPER CO., Louisville, Ky.
Delphi—(b) — bond — WHITING-PATTERSON CO., Philadelphia.
Delta Mills—(w)—AMERICAN WRITING PAPER CO., Holyoke, Mass.
De Luxe—(b)—bristol—J. W. BUTLER PAPER CO., Chicago.
De Luxe Bond — (w) — SOUTHWORTH CO., Mittineague, Mass.
De Luxe Pasting Machine Ledger—(w)—E. E. LLOYD PAPER CO., Chicago.
Demand Ledger—(w)—AETNA PAPER CO., Dayton, Ohio.
Demand Bond—(w)—DWIGHT BROS. PAPER CO., Chicago.
Denmark—(b)—book — LOUISVILLE PAPER CO., Louisville, Ky.
Densmore Bond—(w)—HAGEN PAPER CO., St. Louis.
Denton—(b)—book—GRAHAM PAPER CO., St. Louis.
Department—(b)—manifold—HAGEN PAPER CO., St. Louis.
Department Blotting — (b) — MEGARGEE BROS., Scranton, Pa.
Department Bond—(b)—C. P. LESH PAPER CO., Indianapolis.
Department Bond—(b and w)—BASSETT & SUTPHIN, New York.
Department Bond — (b)—SUTPHIN PAPER CO., INC., New York.
Department Linen Ledger —(w)—R. P. ANDREWS PAPER CO., Washington, D. C.
Dependence Linen Ledger—(w)—CAREW MFG. CO., South Hadley Falls, Mass.
Dependence — (w) — ledgers—J. R. LINDE PAPER CO., New York.
Dependence — (w) — ledger — J. FRANCIS HOCK & CO., Baltimore.
De Pere Bond—(w)—AMERICAN WRITING PAPER CO., Holyoke, Mass.
De Pere Linen—(w)—AMERICAN WRITING PAPER CO., Holyoke, Mass.
De Pere Mills — (w) — superfine—AMERICAN WRITING PAPER CO., Holyoke, Mass.
De Pere Mills Ledger—(w)—AMERICAN WRITING PAPER CO., Holyoke, Mass.
De Pere Mills Superfine—(w)—AMERICAN WRITING PAPER CO., Holyoke, Mass.
De Pere Oriental Linen—(w)—AMERICAN WRITING PAPER CO., Holyoke, Mass.
De Pere Superfine—(w)—AMERICAN WRITING PAPER CO., Holyoke.
Deposit Bond—(w)—ST. LOUIS PAPER CO., St. Louis.
Derby—(b)—bristol—J. W. BUTLER PAPER CO., Chicago.
Derby—(b)—bristol—UNION CARD AND PAPER CO., New York.
Derby—(w)—writing—ST. LOUIS PAPER CO., St. Louis.
Derby Bond—(w)—AMERICAN WRITING PAPER CO., Holyoke, Mass.

Watermarks and Brands

Derby Royal Linen—(w)—AMERICAN WRITING PAPER CO., Holyoke, Mass.
De Soto Bond—(w)—white bond and white writing—H. & W. B. DREW CO., Jacksonville, Fla.
De Soto Mills—POWERS PAPER CO., Springfield, Mass.
De Soto Colored Laid—(b)—flats and colored writings—SWIGART PAPER CO., Chicago.
De Soto Mills Superfine—(w)—H. & W. B. DREW CO., Jacksonville, Fla.
Despatch—(b)—R.R. writing—HAGEN PAPER CO., St. Louis.
Despatch—(b)—writing manila—CHEMICAL PAPER MFG. CO., Holyoke, Mass.
Despatch Manila—(w)—BUNTIN, GILLIES & CO., LTD., Hamilton, Ontario, Can.
Detail—(b)—drafting—CHATFIELD & WOODS CO., Cincinnati.
Detroit Cover—(b)—UNION PAPER & TWINE CO., Detroit, Mich.
Devon—(b)—bristol—RIEGEL & CO., INC., Philadelphia.
Devon Mills—(b)—TILESTON & LIVERMORE, Boston.
Devonshire—(b)—toilet—STONE & FORSYTH CO., Boston.
Devonshire Linen—(b)—GEO. B. HURD & CO., New York.
Devonshire Weve Satin—(b)—EATON, CRANE & PIKE CO., Pittsfield, Mass.
Dexter Mills—(w)—fine—W. E. WROE & CO., Chicago.
Diadem—(b)—bristol—TILESTON & LIVERMORE, Boston.
Diadem Mills—(w)—CLEVELAND PAPER MANUFACTURING CO., Cleveland, Ohio.
Diagonal Plaid—(b)—GEO. B. HURD & CO., New York.
Diamond—(b)—toilet—GRAHAM PAPER CO., St. Louis.
Diamond—(b)—blotting—MISSOURI PAPER HOUSE, Kansas City, Mo.
Diamond—(b)—cardboard—McCLELLAN PAPER CO., Minneapolis, Minn.
Diamond—(b)—No. 2 manila—CHATFIELD & WOODS CO., Cincinnati.
Diamond—(b)—onion skin—R. L. GREENE PAPER CO., Providence.
Diamond Bond—(b)—WHITING PAPER CO., Holyoke, Mass.
Diamond F.—(b)—onion skin—JOHN F. SARLES CO., INC., New York.
Diamond Ledger—(w)—AETNA PAPER CO., Dayton, Ohio.
Diamond Ledger—(w)—DWIGHT BROS. PAPER CO., Grand Rapids, Mich.
Diamond Mills—(b)—wrapping—STONE & FORSYTH CO., Boston.
Diamond A Factory—(b)—toilet—ALBANY PERFORATED WRAPPING PAPER CO., Albany, N. Y.
Diamond A Hotel—(b)—toilet—ALBANY PERFORATED WRAPPING PAPER CO., Albany, N. Y.
Diamond A Standard—(b)—toilet—ALBANY PERFORATED WRAPPING PAPER CO., Albany, N. Y.
Diamond A Textile—(b)—toilet—ALBANY PERFORATED WRAPPING PAPER CO., Albany, N. Y.
Diamond B Factory—(b)—toilet—ALBANY PERFORATED WRAPPING PAPER CO., Albany, N. Y.
Diamond B Hotel—(b)—toilet—ALBANY PERFORATED WRAPPING PAPER CO., Albany, N. Y.
Diamond B Standard—(b)—toilet—ALBANY PERFORATED WRAPPING PAPER CO., Albany, N. Y.
Diamond B Sterling—(b)—toilet—ALBANY PERFORATED WRAPPING PAPER CO., Albany, N. Y.
Diamond B Textile—(b)—toilet—ALBANY PERFORATED WRAPPING PAPER CO., Albany, N. Y.
Diamond C—(b)—coated book—JOHN CARTER & CO., Boston.
Diamond Onion Skin—(b)—R. L. GREENE PAPER CO., Providence, R. I.
Diamond "K" Flats—(w)—KINGSLEY PAPER CO., Cleveland, Ohio.
Diamond—(b)—manila tag—WILKINSON BROS. & CO., INC., Philadelphia.
Diamond Onion Skin—(b)—PAUL E. VERNON & CO., New York.
Diana—(b)—toilet—ALBANY PERFORATED WRAPPING PAPER CO., Albany, N. Y.
Diana—(w)—bond—GRAHAM PAPER CO., St. Louis.
Diana—(b)—toilet—H. NORWOOD EWING, New York.
Diana—(w)—HY. LINDENMEYR & SONS, New York.
Diana—(b)—machine finished book—WHITAKER PAPER CO., Cincinnati, Ohio, and BAY STATE PAPER CO., Boston.
Diana—(b)—toilet—GRAHAM PAPER CO., St. Louis.
Diana Mills—(w)—fine—JOHN LESLIE PAPER CO., Minneapolis, Minn.
Dictate—(b)—second sheets—GRAHAM PAPER CO., St. Louis.
Dilcol—(b)—DILL & COLLINS CO., Philadelphia.
Dillen—(b)—book—GRAHAM PAPER CO., St. Louis.
Dimity—(w)—BUNTIN, GILLIES & CO., LTD., Hamilton, Canada.
Diploma Bond—(b)—B R A D N E R SMITH & CO., Chicago.
Diplomatique—(b)—GEO. B. HURD & CO., New York.
Diplomat Linen—(w)—POWERS PAPER COMPANY, Springfield, Mass.
Directoire—(b)—THE ALBEMARLE PAPER MFG. CO., Richmond, Va.

FELTS AND JACKETS | Appleton Woolen Mills
APPLETON - - WIS.

Watermarks and Brands

Directors' Ledger—(w)—SMITH, DAVIDSON & WRIGHT, LTD., Vancouver, B. C.
Directory — (w) — cover — JAMES WHITE PAPER CO., Chicago.
Dirigo—(b)—book—JOHN CARTER & CO., Boston.
Dirigo Extra Fine—(w)—writing—EASTERN MFG. CO., Bangor, Me.
Disfico—(b)—insulating — DIAMOND STATE FIBRE CO., Bridgeport, Pa.
Dispatch—(b)—manila writing—BAY STATE PAPER CO., Boston.
Distaff—(w)—Z. & W. M. CRANE, Dalton, Mass.
Dividend Ledger—(w)— GRAHAM PAPER CO., St. Louis.
Dividend Bond—(w)— WESTERN PAPER CO., Omaha, Neb.
Dividend Writing Manila—QUAKER CITY PAPER CO., Philadelphia.
Dividend Bond — (b) — W. M. PRINGLE & CO., INC., New York.
Dixie — (b) — writing—BALTIMORE BARGAIN HOUSE, Baltimore.
Dixie Cotton Sampling—(b)—wrapping—GRAHAM PAPER CO., St. Louis.
Dixie Envelope—(w)—WHITAKER PAPER CO., Cincinnati, Ohio.
Dixie Mills—(w)—superfine—HAMMERMILL PAPER CO., Erie Pa.
Dixie Mills—(b)—folded—AMERICAN NEWS CO., New York.
Dixie Parchment—(b)—sulphite—R. A. CAUTHORNE PAPER CO., Richmond, Va.
Document—(w)—No. 1 bond—DONALDSON PAPER CO., Harrisburg, Pa.
Document Bond—(w)—DONALDSON PAPER CO., Harrisburg, Pa.
Document Bond—(w)—white and colored—R. C. KASTER PAPER CO., New York.
Document Bond—(w)—ST. LOUIS PAPER CO., St. Louis.
Document Postcard—(b) — PAPER MILLS COMPANY, Chicago.
Doeskin Fibre — (b) — wrapping — LOUISVILLE PAPER CO., Louisville, Ky.
Doe Skin—(w)—Z. & W. M. CRANE, Dalton, Mass.
Doeskin—(b)—toilet—OLD DOMINION PAPER CO., Norfolk, Va.
Doeskin Die Wiping—(b)—WHITAKER PAPER CO., Cincinnati, Ohio.
Dolphin—(b)—figure of dolphin—fibre—CHATFIELD PAPER CO., New Haven, Conn.
Dolphin—(b)—white bristol — B. F. BOND PAPER CO., Baltimore.
Dolphin Mills—(b)—HY. LINDENMEYR & SONS, New York.
Dominant Bond — (w) — HARVARD PAPER CO., Urbana, Ohio.
Dominant Ledger—(w)—BLUNDENLYON CO., Chicago.
Dominion — (b) — bristol—W. H. CLAFLIN & CO., Boston.

Dominion—(b)—bristol—STANDARD CARD & PAPER CO., New York.
Dominion Antique Globe—(w)—VALLEY PAPER CO., Holyoke, Mass.
Dominion Bond — (w)—BUNTIN, GILLIES & CO., Hamilton, Ontario.
Dominion Book—(b)—GRAHAM PAPER CO., St. Louis.
Dominion Bristol — (b) — BUNTIN, GILLIES & CO., LTD., Hamilton, Ontario, Can.
Domino—(w)—VALLEY PAPER CO., Holyoke, Mass.
Donnaconda — (w) — ROLLAND PAPER CO., St. Jerome, Can.
Do-Pa-Co—(b)—special lines — DOMESTIC MILLS PAPER CO., N. Y.
Dorcas—(b)—toilet — U. S. ENVELOPE CO., Springfield, Mass.
Dore Drafting—(b)—HY. LINDENMEYR & SONS, New York.
Doreshire Linen—(b) — CONBOW BROTHERS, New York.
Doric—(w)—bond and ledger—UNION CARD & PAPER CO., New York.
Doric—(b)—bristol—UNION CARD & PAPER CO., New York.
Doric Bristol—(b)—C. P. LESH PAPER CO., Indianapolis, Ind.
Dorset—(b)—M. F. and super—CANFIELD PAPER CO., New York.
Dorset Linen—(b)—EASTERN MFG. CO., Bangor, Me.
Double Antique — (w) — CURTIS & BROTHER, Newark, Del.
Douglas—(b)—engine sized writing—MIDLAND PAPER CO., Chicago.
Douglas Wedding Covers—(b)—HY. LINDENMEYR & SONS, New York.
Dover—(b) — M. F. colored book—HAGEN PAPER CO., St. Louis.
Dover Ledger—(w)—F. W. ANDERSON & CO., N. Y.
Dragon Fibre — (b) — wrapping—GRAHAM PAPER CO., St. Louis.
Dragon—(b) — LOUISVILLE PAPER CO., Louisville, Ky.
Dragon—(w) — Canary writing — MEGARGEE BROS., Scranton, Pa.
Dragon Bond—(w)—HY. LINDENMEYR & SONS, New York.
Drashmere—(w)—writing — HAGEN PAPER CO., St. Louis.
D. Reg.—(b) — boards — INGALLS & CO., Castleton, N. Y.
Dresden—(b)—embossing cover and bristol—THE ALLING & CORY CO., Rochester, N. Y.
Dresden—(b) — coated book—F. A. FLINN, INC., New York.
Dresden—(w)—ledger—J. FRANCIS HOCK & CO., Baltimore.
Dresden — (b) — writing—McCLELLAN PAPER CO., Minneapolis, Minn.
Dresden—sub enamel book—(b)—WHITAKER PAPER CO., Cincinnati, and BAY STATE PAPER CO., Boston.

BLOTTING PAPERS "STANDARD," "IMPERIAL," "STERLING"
Royal Worcester and Defender Enameled
STANDARD PAPER MFG. CO., - -

EW MILLS DESIGNED   POWER PLANTS   OLD MILLS REBUILT

C. A. CHAPMAN, Inc.
) E. JACKSON BLVD.   ENGINEERS   CHICAGO

Watermarks and Brands   657

APPLETON MACHINE CO. APPLETON, WIS. REFINING ENGINES, SCREENS, SAWING & SPLITTING MACHINERY — HIGH GRADE CENTRIFUGAL PUMPS

Dresden—(b)—book, label and envelope — GRAHAM PAPER CO., St. Louis.
Dresden—(b) — envelope — GRAHAM PAPER CO., St. Louis.
Dresden—(b) — onion skin — LOUISVILLE PAPER CO., Louisville, Ky.
Dresden Bond — (w) — WHITING-PATTERSON CO., Philadelphia.
Dresden Lawn — (b) — MARCUS WARD CO., Brooklyn, N. Y.
Dresden Ledger — (w) — DIEM & WING PAPER CO., Cincinnati, O.
Dresden Linen—(w and b)—GEO. B. HURD & CO., New York.
Dresden Linen Fabric — (w) — EATON, CRANE & PIKE CO., Pittsfield, Mass.
Dresden Linen Ledger—(w)—R. C. KASTNER PAPER CO., New York.
Dresden Pamphlet—(w) — book—J. W. BUTLER PAPER CO., Chicago.
Drug Bond—(w)—wrapping and bond,—McDOWELL PAPER MILLS, Manayunk, Pa.
Drug Bond — (b) — wrapping and specialties — McDOWELL PAPER MILLS, Manayunk, Pa.
Druid—(b)—toilet tissue — W. H. CLAFLIN & CO., Boston.
Druid—(b)—onion skin—LOUISVILLE PAPER CO., Louisville, Ky.
Druid Oak Bond—(w)—O. F. H. WARNER & CO., Baltimore.
Drummer — (b) — toilet—GRAHAM PAPER CO., St. Louis.
Dry Proof — 25x38 — (b)—F. A. FLINN, INC., New York.
Dry Proofing — (b) — BRADNER SMITH & CO., Chicago.
Duane—(b)—cover —SEYMOUR CO., New York.
Duane Bond — (w) — WHITAKER PAPER CO., Cincinnati, Ohio, and BAY STATE PAPER CO., Boston.
Duane Cover—(b)—SEYMOUR CO., INC., New York.
Duane Ledger — (w)—MILLER & WRIGHT PAPER CO., New York.
Duane Standard Linen — (w)— HAMMERMILL PAPER CO., Erie, Pa.
Duane Standard Linen — (w) — BOORUM & PEASE CO., New York.
Duane Super—(b)—SEYMOUR CO., INC., New York.
Dublin Canvas —(b)— E A T O N, CRANE & PIKE CO., Pittsfield, Mass.
Dublin Coated—(b)—cover — PAPER MILLS CO., Chicago.
Dublin Extra Fine — (w)—WHITING-PATTERSON CO., Philadelphia.
Dublin Linen — (w) — AMERICAN WRITING PAPER CO., Holyoke.
Dubuque — (b) — book—GRAHAM PAPER CO., St. Louis.
Duchess—(b)—DILL & COLLINS CO., Philadelphia.
Duchesse—(b)—super book — CHATFIELD & WOODS CO., Cincinnati, O.

Duck Fibre—(b)—GRAHAM PAPER CO., St. Louis.
Duke—(b) — mimeograph—GRAHAM PAPER CO., St. Louis.
Dukes—(b)—bristol — BAY STATE PAPER CO., Boston.
Dunbar Superfine — (w)—KEITH PAPER CO., Turners Falls, Mass.
Dundee —(b)—BUNTIN, GILLIES & CO., Hamilton, Can.
Dundee—(b)—book and bond—GRAHAM PAPER CO., St. Louis.
Dundee — (b) — bristol — machine finished book—PETERS PAPER CO., Denver, Col.
Dundee—(b)— toilet — UNITED STATES ENVELOPE CO. (Morgan Envelope Co. Division), Springfield.
Dundee — (b) — enamel book—WHITAKER PAPER CO., Cincinnati, Ohio, and BAY STATE PAPER CO., Boston.
Dundee Bond — (w)—AMERICAN WRITING PAPER CO., Holyoke.
Dundee Bristol—(b)—BUNTIN, GILLIES & CO., LTD, Hamilton, Ontario, Can.
Dundee Record — (w) — AMERICAN WRITING PAPER CO., Holyoke.
Dundee Record Ledger — (w)— AMERICAN WRITING PAPER CO., Holyoke, Mass.
Dunkeld Linen — (w) — MOSER PAPER CO., Chicago.
Dunkirk Linen L e d g e r—(w) LOUISVILLE PAPER CO., Louisville.
Duo Coated Book—(b) — WILLIAM H. GEORGE, Philadelphia.
Duo-Tone—(b)—boards and bristols—UNION CARD & PAPER CO., N. Y.
Duplex — (b) — toilet — UNITED STATES ENVELOPE CO. (Morgan Envelope Co. Division), Springfield.
Duplicate Bond — (b)—BRADNER SMITH & CO., Chicago.
Duplicate Bond—(b)—CHATFIELD & WOODS CO., Cincinnati, O.
Duplicator Bond — (b)—EATON, CRANE & PIKE CO., Pittsfield, Mass.
Duplicator Coated Bond — (b)— HUDSON VALLEY PAPER CO., Albany, New York.
Duplicator Coated Bond — (b) — HUDSON VALLEY PAPER CO., New York.
Duplico —(b) — mimeograph — PENINSULAR PAPER CO., Ypsilanti, Mich.
Duquesne Bond—(w) — WESTERN PENNA. PAPER CO., Pittsburgh, Pa.
Durable Bond—(b)—PAUL E. VERNON & CO., New York.
Durham Cover—(b)—HY. LINDENMEYR & SONS, New York.
Durham Mills—(w) — writing — MEGARGEE BROS., Scranton, Pa.
Duro White Index — (b) — RICHMOND PAPER CO., Richmond, Va.
Duryea Bond—(b)—W. H. CLAFLIN & CO., INC., Boston.

IINER EDGAR CO., Sole Agents   CLAY   WASHED <E W> HIGH COLOR   GRITLESS <C M> HIGH RETENTION
lgar Bros. Co., 30 CHURCH STREET NEW YORK

FELTS AND JACKETS | Appleton Woolen Mills
APPLETON - - WIS.

Watermarks and Brands

Dustless Millinery — (b)—tissue—GRAHAM PAPER CO., St. Louis.
Dutch Fabrik—(w)—BUNTIN, GILLIES & CO., LTD., Hamilton, Can.
Dutch Fabric—(w)—BUNTIN, GILLIES & CO., LTD., Hamilton, Ontario, Can.
Dutch Linen—(w)—laid—FOX RIVER PAPER CO., Appleton, Wis.
D. & W. Ledger—(w)—DIEM & WING PAPER CO., Cincinnati.
Dwight Mills—(b)—DWIGHT BROS. PAPER CO., Chicago.
Dwight Superfine — (b) — tinted wove—DWIGHT BROS. PAPER CO., Chicago.
Dynamite—(b)—all sulphite—manila—W. H. CLAFLIN & CO., Boston.
Dynamo—(w) — J. B. WATKINS, New York.

E

"E" in a Diamond—(w)—No. 3 fine—N. Y. & UTAH PAPER CO., Salt Lake City, Utah.
"E" Manila—(b)—EASTERN MANUFACTURING CO., Bangor, Me.
Eagle—(b)—tissue—SMITH PAPER CO., Lee, Mass.
Eagle—(b)—tag—W. H. CLAFLIN & CO., Boston.
Eagle "A"—(w)—letter A with outline of eagle used on all watermarked papers made by the AMERICAN WRITING PAPER CO., Holyoke.
Eagle Blanks—(b)—JOHN CARTER & CO., INC., Boston.
Eagle Blanks—(b)—HY. LINDENMEYR & SONS, New York.
Eagle Bond — (w)—CHATFIELD & WOODS CO., Cincinnati, Ohio.
Eagle Bristol—(b)—DIEM & WING PAPER CO., Cincinnati, Ohio.
Eagle Coated Blanks—(b)—BRADNER SMITH & CO., Chicago.
Eagle Cover—(b)—HARLEM CARD & PAPER CO., New York.
Eagle Document Manila — (b)—BRADNER SMITH & CO., Chicago.
Eagle Drug Bond—(b)—McDOWELL PAPER MILLS, Manayunk, Pa.
Eagle Ledger—(w)—HY. LINDENMEYR & SONS, New York.
Eagle Mills—(b) — toilet — W. A. COLE PAPER CO., Putney, Vt.
Eagle Tag—(b) — DIEM & WING PAPER CO., Cincinnati, Ohio.
Eagle Tinted Bristol — (b)—DIEM & WING PAPER CO., Cincinnati, O.
Earl Duplex—(b)—wrapping—M. J. EARL, Reading, Pa.
Earloid—(b)—roofing—M. J. EARLE, Reading, Pa.
Earlton—(b)—cover—M. J. EARLE, Reading, Pa.
Early English — (w) — Z. & W. M. CRANE, Dalton, Mass.

Early Georgian—(b)—Z. & W. M. CRANE, Dalton, Mass.
Early Saxon—(w and b)—GEO. B. HURD & CO., New York.
Earnscliffe Linen Bond — (w) — ROLLAND PAPER CO., St. Jerome, Canada.
Earnscliffe Linen Ledger — (w)—ROLLAND PAPER CO., St. Jerome, Canada.
East Lake Bond—(w)—INDIANA PAPER CO., Indianapolis.
East Lake Linen—(w)—INDIANA PAPER CO., Indianapolis.
Eastern Bond — (w) — EASTERN MANUFACTURING CO., Bangor, Me.
Eastern Canary Writing — (b) — RICHMOND PAPER CO., Richmond, Va.
Eastern Extra Fine—(w)—EASTERN PAPER AND SUPPLY CO., Springfield, Mass.
Eastern Ledger—(w) — EASTERN MANUFACTURING CO., Bangor, Me.
Eastern Linen — (w) — ledger and bond—W. R. GRACE & CO., New York.
Eastern Superfine—(w)—EASTERN MFG. CO., Bangor, Me.
Eastern Tag—(b)—CHATFIELD & WOODS CO., Cincinnati, Ohio.
East Hartford's Genuine Irish Linen—(b) — EAST HARTFORD MANUFACTURING CO., Burnside, Conn.
East Hartford Ledger—(w)—EAST HARTFORD MANUFACTURING CO., Burnside, Conn.
East Hartford Linen—(w)—EAST HARTFORD MANUFACTURING CO., Burnside, Conn.
East Hartford Motre — (b)—fancy papers — EAST HARTFORD MFG. CO., Burnside, Conn.
East India—(b)—tissue—GRAHAM PAPER CO., St. Louis.
Eastern Offset — (b) — EASTERN MFG. CO., Bangor, Me.
Eastlack Superfine—(w)—ANTIETAM PAPER CO., Hagerstown, Md.
Eaton's Berkshire Bond — (w)—EATON, CRANE & PIKE CO., Pittsfield, Mass.
Easton Ledger —(w)— MERRIAM PAPER CO., New York.
Eaton — (b)—catalog—GRAHAM PAPER CO., St. Louis.
Easton Ledger—(w)—ledger — MERRIAM PAPER CO., New York.
Eaton Linen Ledger—(w)—C. P. LESH PAPER CO., Indianapolis.
Ebony Waterproof — (b)—UNION CARD AND PAPER CO., New York.
Ecalaso—(b)—toilet—WORTENDYKE MFG. CO., Richmond, Va.
Echo—(b)—news—LOUISVILLE PAPER CO., Louisville, Ky.
Ecke—(b)—toilet—H. NORWOOD EWING CO., New York.
Echo Bond—(w)—J. P. HEILBRONN CO., Manila, P. I.

JAMES H. HARRISON
PULPSTONE MANUFACTURER

GENUINE NEWCASTLE STONES
16 Killowen St., GATESHEAD-ON-TYNE, ENG.

MILLS ELECTRICALLY EQUIPPED — ECONOMIES IN STEAM PLANT

C. A. CHAPMAN, Inc.

26 E. JACKSON BLVD. — ENGINEERS — CHICAGO

Watermarks and Brands 659

Echo Bristol—(b)—C. P. LESH PAPER CO., Indianapolis.
Echo Fibre—(b)—white butchers' paper—SEINSHEIMER PAPER CO., Cincinnati, Ohio.
Eclipse Litho—(b)—LEWERTH & CULBERTSON.
Echo Tag—(b)—WHITAKER PAPER CO., Cincinnati, Ohio.
Eclipse—(b)—toilet—CHATFIELD PAPER CO., New Haven, Conn.
Eclipse—(b)—news—MINNEAPOLIS PAPER CO., Minneapolis, Minn.
Eclipse—(b)—toilet—NORTHERN PAPER MILLS, Green Bay, Wis.
Eclipse Bristol—(b)—C. P. LESH PAPER CO., Indianapolis.
Eclipse Bond—(w)—EASTERN PAPER AND SUPPLY CO., Springfield.
Eclipse Book—(b)—DIEM & WING PAPER CO., Cincinnati, Ohio.
Eclipse Enamel Book—(b)—PETREQUIN PAPER CO., Cleveland.
Eclipse Ledger—(w)—CENTRAL OHIO PAPER CO., Columbus, Ohio.
Eclipse Mills—(w)—writing—R. M. MYERS & CO., Rochester, New York
Eclipse Print—(b)—book—MINNEAPOLIS PAPER CO., Minneapolis.
Eclipse Superfine—(w)—CLEMENTS PAPER CO., Nashville, Tenn.
Econo Book—(b)—BRADNER SMITH & CO., Chicago.
Economic Bond—(b)—CLEMENT & STOCKWELL, INC., New York.
Economic Ledger—(w)—CROCKER-McELWAIN CO., Holyoke.
Economy—(b)—bristol—J. W. BUTLER PAPER CO., Chicago.
Economy—(w and b)—writing, bond, ledger—NEENAH PAPER CO., Neenah, Wis.
Economy—(b)—cardboards and cards—GRAHAM PAPER CO., St. Louis.
Economy—(w)—HAMMERMILL PAPER CO., Erie, Pa.
Economy—(b)—package toilet—CHATFIELD & WOODS CO., Cincinnati, Ohio.
Economy—(b)—plain and coated blanks—W. H. CLAFLIN & CO., Boston.
Economy—(b)—toilet—ALBANY PERFORATED WRAPPING PAPER CO., Albany, N. Y.
Economy—(b)—bread wrappers—GRAHAM PAPER CO., St. Louis.
Economy—(b)—adding machine—LOUISVILLE PAPER CO., Louisville, Ky.
Economy Bond—(w)—J. W. W. JONAS, New York.
Economy Linen Ledger—(w)—JOHN CARTER & CO., INC., Boston.
Eden—(b)—news—GRAHAM PAPER CO., St. Louis.
Edgewater Bond—(w)—JOHN F. SARLE, New York.
Edgewick Linen Ledger—(w)—BRADLEY-REESE CO., Baltimore.

Edgewood Superfine—(b)—writing—GRAHAM PAPER CO., St. Louis.
Edgewood Superfine—(w)—GRAHAM PAPER CO., St. Louis.
Edinburg—(b)—book—GRAHAM PAPER CO., St. Louis.
Edinburgh—(b)—bond—WHITING-PATTERSON CO., Philadelphia.
Edinburgh Ledger—(w)—WORTHY PAPER CO., Mittineague, Mass.
Edinburgh Linen—(w)—WHITING PAPER CO., Holyoke, Mass.
Edison Mimeograph—(w)—CLEMENTS PAPER CO., Nashville, Tenn.
Educator—(w and b)—writing, ledger, bond—NEENAH PAPER CO., Neenah, Wis.
Eelskin Wrapping—(b)—HY. LINDENMEYR & SONS, New York.
Efficiency—(w and b)—bond, ledger—NEENAH PAPER CO., Neenah, Wis.
Efficiency Bristol—(b)—RICHMOND PAPER CO., Richmond, Va.
Efficiency Linen Ledger—(w)—WESTERN PENNA. PAPER CO., Pittsburgh, Pa.
Efficiency Writing—(b)—RICHMOND PAPER CO., Richmond, Va.
Eggshell—(b)—cover and book—J. W. BUTLER PAPER CO., Chicago.
Egyptian—(b)—toilet—UNITED STATES ENVELOPE CO. (Morgan Envelope Co. Div.). Springfield, Mass.
Egyptian—(w)—J. W. BUTLER PAPER CO., Chicago.
Egyptian Black—(b)—pattern—LOUISVILLE PAPER CO., Louisville, Ky.
Egyptian Bond—(w)—MEGARGEE-HARE PAPER CO., Philadelphia.
Egyptian Bond—(b)—EATON, CRANE & PIKE CO., Pittsfield, Mass.
Egyptian—(b)—enamel—C. P. LESH PAPER CO., Indianapolis, Ind.
Egyptian Fibre—(b)—indented backing—GRAHAM PAPER CO., St. Louis.
Egyptian Linen—(w)—GEORGE B. HURD & CO., New York.
Egyptian Linen Ledger—(w)—IRWIN N. MEGARGEE & CO., Philadelphia.
Egyptian Parchment—HAMMERMILL PAPER CO., Erie, Pa.
Eiderdown Book—(b)—PAPER MILLS CO., Chicago.
Elba Bond—(b)—white and colors—RICHMOND PAPER CO., Richmond, Va.
El Capitan Enamel—(b)—WHITAKER PAPER CO., Cincinnati, Ohio.
El Cid Bristols—(b)—PARSONS TRADING CO., New York.
Eldorado—(b)—ALBEMARLE PAPER MFG. CO., Richmond, Va.
Eldorado—(w)—writing—J. W. BUTLER PAPER CO., Chicago.
El Dorado Bond—(w)—EATON, CRANE & PIKE, Pittsfield, Mass.

MINER EDGAR CO., Sole Agents
EDGAR BROS. CO.
KEYSTONE CLAY & REDUCTION CO.
30 Church Street - - New York

C L A Y

<E W> <K L M> <C M>
WASHED FLOATED REFINED
LARGEST CAPACITY AND STOCK
AMERICA. PROMPT SHIPMENTS

Electra—(b)—enamel book—CHATFIELD & WOODS CO., Cincinnati, O.
Electra Mills—(w)—WESTERN PENNA. PAPER CO., Pittsburgh, Pa.
Electric—(b)—blotting—H. S. CROCKER CO., San Francisco.
Electric—(b)—fine—THOMAS W. PRICE CO., Philadelphia.
Electric — (b) — writing manila — MEGARGEE-HARE PAPER CO., Philadelphia.
Electric—(w)—J. B. WATKINS, N. Y.
Electric—(b)—mimeograph — LOUISVILLE PAPER CO., Louisville, Ky.
Electric Bond—(w)—VON OLKERSNELL PAPER CO., Boston.
Electric City Manifold—(b)—MEGARGEE BROS., Scranton, Pa.
Electric Colored Bristol—(b)—MEGARGEE BROS., Scranton, Pa.
Electric Linen Ledger—with lamp—(w)—J. B. WATKINS, New York.
Electric Linen—with lamp—(w)—J. B. WATKINS, New York.
Electric Mimeograph — (w) — OSBURN PAPER CO., Philadelphia.
Electric Writing Manila—(w)—MEGARGEE-HARE PAPER CO., Philadelphia.
Elephant Brand—(b)—sheathing—NEWTON PAPER CO., Holyoke, Mass.
Elgin Rag—(b)—wrapping — GRAHAM PAPER CO., St. Louis.
Elite—(b)—cover—AMERICAN WRITING PAPER CO., Holyoke, Mass.
Elite Bond — (w) — SOUTHWORTH CO., Mittineague, Mass.
Elizabeth Bristol — (b) — OLD DOMINION PAPER CO., Norfolk, Va.
Elizabeth Linen—(b)—THE JENNER CO., Louisville, Ky.
Elizabeth River Manila Wrapping—(b)—OLD DOMINION PAPER CO., Norfolk, Va.
Elk Bond—(w)—MILLER-BRYANT-PIERCE CO., Aurora, Ill.
Elk Fibre—(b)—OLD DOMINION PAPER CO., Norfolk, Va.
Elk Fibre—(b)—No. 1 express—SEINSHEIMER PAPER CO., Cincinnati.
Elk Linen—(w)—MILLER-BRYANT-PIERCE CO., Aurora, Ill.
Elkhorn Mills—(w)—BRYANT PAPER CO., Kalamazoo, Mich.
Elko—(b)—toilet—ALBANY PERFORATED WRAPPING PAPER CO., Albany, N. Y.
Elkridge Bond—(b)—linen finish—O. F. H. WARNER & CO., Baltimore.
Elliott Linette—(w)—THE CHAS. H. ELLIOTT CO., North Philadelphia.
Elm City—(b)—toilet—sheathing and tarred roofing—CHATFIELD PAPER CO., New Haven, Conn.
Elm Embossing—(b)—cover—ARNOLD-ROBERTS CO., Boston.
Elmhurst — (b)— toilet — R. L. GREENE PAPER CO., Providence, R. I.

Elmore Linen Ledger—(b)—CONROW BROS., New York.
Elmwood Bond—(b)—F. W. ANDERSON & CO., New York.
Elmwood Bond—(w)—INLAND PAPER CO., Chicago.
Elmwood Wedding—(b)—JUDD PAPER CO., Holyoke, Mass.
Elmoto Bond—(b)—typewriter—EATON, CRANE & PIKE CO., Pittsfield, Mass.
Elras Bond—(w)—JOHN F. SARLE, New York.
Elseca Super—(b)—book — CLARKE & CO., New York.
Elsinore—(w)—fancy book — CHATFIELD & WOODS CO., Cincinnati, O.
Elsinore—(b)—glazed onion skin No. 1—ELSINORE PAPER CO., New York.
Elsinore—(b)—unglazed onion skin No. 1—ELSINORE PAPER CO., New York.
Elsinore Bond—(w)—fabric finish—ELSINORE PAPER CO., New York.
Elsinore Bond — (w) — ELSINORE PAPER CO., New York.
Elsinore Linen — (w) — ELSINORE PAPER CO., New York.
Elsinore Manifold — (b) — ELSINORE PAPER CO., New York.
Elsinore Manifold Linen—(b)—ELSINORE PAPER CO., New York.
Elsinore Manifold Parchment—(b)—ELSINORE PAPER CO., New York.
Elsinore Manila Writing—(b)—A. S. LANDSBERG, New York.
Elsinore Mimeograph—(b)—ELSINORE PAPER CO., New York.
Elsinore Parchment—(b)—imported—ELSINORE PAPER CO., New York.
Elsinore Semi Glazed Onion Skin—ELSINORE PAPER CO., New York.
Elsinore Typewriter Papers—ELSINORE PAPER CO., New York.
Elston—(b)—book—C. P. LESH PAPER CO., Indianapolis, Ind.
Elswick—(b)—drawing — H. REEVE ANGEL & CO., INC., New York.
Elwood Bond—(b)—F. W. ANDERSON & CO., INC., New York.
Embassador —(b)— envelope — GRAHAM PAPER CO., St. Louis.
Embassy Bond—(w)—F. E. LLOYD PAPER CO., Chicago, Ill.
Emblem Bond—(w)—LEWERTH & CULBERTSON, New York.
Embossed Flora Blotting—(b)—DISTRICT OF COLUMBIA PAPER MFG. CO., Washington, D. C.
Embossed Pique—CAREW MANUFACTURING CO., South Hadley Falls, Mass.
Embossed Transparent — (b) — parchment—BRADNER SMITH & CO., Chicago.
Embossing—(b)— bristol — UNION CARD & PAPER CO., New York.

Watermarks and Brands

Embossing Art Pasted—(b)—LOUISVILLE PAPER CO., Louisville.
Embossing Enamel—(b)—WEST VIRGINIA PULP & PAPER CO., New York.
Emco Onion Skin—(b)—ESLEECK MFG. CO., Turners Falls, Mass.
Emerald—(w)—flats—KANSAS CITY PAPER HOUSE, Kansas City, Mo.
Emerald Green—(b)—E A T O N, CRANE & PIKE CO., Pittsfield, Mass.
Emergency—(w)—LESLIE-DONAHOWER CO., St. Paul.
Emergency—(b)—bond—GRAHAM PAPER CO., St. Louis.
Emergency Bond—(b)—PAUL E. VERNON & CO., New York.
Empeco—(b)—blanks, index, leather cover, non-curling gummed, post office cover, oiled tympan, poster boards, enamel, passbook cover and mat boards—MINNEAPOLIS PAPER CO., Minneapolis, Minn.
Empeco Bond—(b)—MERRIAM PAPER CO., New York.
Empeco Bond—(w)—MINNEAPOLIS PAPER CO., Minneapolis, Minn.
Emperor—(b)—envelope and bristol boards—DONALDSON PAPER CO., Harrisburg, Pa.
Emperor—(b)—toilet—REGAL PAPER CO., Pulaski, N. Y.
Emperor Bond—(b)—McCLELLAN PAPER CO., Minneapolis, Minn.
Empire—(b)—colored laid—F. A. FLINN, INC., New York.
Empire—(b)—blanks—LOUISVILLE PAPER CO., Louisville, Ky.
Empire—(b)—book—CINCINNATI CORDAGE AND PAPER CO., Cincinnati, Ohio.
Empire—(b)—toilet—UNITED STATES ENVELOPE CO. (Morgan Envelope Co. Div.), Springfield, Mass.
Empire—(b)—toilet—ALBANY PERFORATED WRAPPING PAPER CO., Albany, N. Y.
Empire Bond—(monogram)—(w)—STATE JOURNAL CO., Lincoln, Neb.
Empire Bond—(w)—COOK-VIVIAN CO., Boston.
Empire Bond—(w)—CAREW MANUFACTURING CO., South Hadley Falls, Mass.
Empire Bond—(w)—W. G. WILLMANN, New York.
Empire Bond—(w)—GARRETT-BUCHANAN CO., Philadelphia.
Empire Bristol—(b)—DIEM & WING PAPER CO., Cincinnati, Ohio.
Empire Bristol—(b)—R. P. ANDREWS PAPER CO., Washington.
Empire Colored Enamel—(b)—THE UNION PAPER & TWINE CO., Detroit, Mich.
Empire Deckle-Edge Book—(b)—IRWIN N. MEGARGEE & CO., Philadelphia, Pa.

Empire Express—(b)—toilet—UNITED STATES ENVELOPE CO. (Morgan Envelope Co. Div.), Springfield, Mass.
Empire Laid Linen—(b)—THE UNION PAPER & TWINE CO., Detroit, Mich.
Empire Linen—(w)—AMERICAN WRITING PAPER CO., Holyoke, Mass.
Empire Linen Bond—(w)—ROLLAND PAPER CO., St. Jerome, Que., Can.
Empire Linen Ledger—(w)—CAREW MFG. CO., South Hadley Falls, Mass.
Empire Linen Ledger—(w)—SAUGERTIES MFG. CO., Saugerties, N. Y.
Empire Mills—(w)—THE ALLING & CORY CO., Rochester, N. Y.
Empire Mills—(b)—book—CINCINNATI CORDAGE & PAPER CO., Cincinnati, Ohio.
Empire Red—(b)—EATON, CRANE & PIKE CO., Pittsfield, Mass.
Empire Silver Lawn—(w)—PARSONS TRADING CO., New York.
Empire State—(b)—D. S. WALTON & CO., New York.
Empire State—(b)—writing—HUDSON VALLEY PAPER CO., Albany, N. Y.
Empire State Ledger—(w)—HUDSON VALLEY PAPER CO., New York.
Empress—(b)—asbestos felt—GRAHAM PAPER CO., St. Louis.
Empress—(b)—cover—J. W. BUTLER PAPER CO., Chicago.
Empress—(b)—enameled blotting—JOHN CARTER & CO., Boston.
Empress—(b)—mount boards—WILKINSON BROS. & CO., INC., Philadelphia.
Empress Bond—(w)—MISSOURI PAPER HOUSE, Kansas City, Mo.
Empress Book—(b)—KINGSLEY PAPER CO., Cleveland, Ohio.
Empress Linen—(w)—E A T O N, CRANE & PIKE CO., Pittsfield, Mass.
Enameloid—(b)—RITCHIE & RAMSAY, Toronto, Canada.
Endowment Bond—(w)—STRATHMORE PAPER CO., Mittineague, Mass.
Endurance—(b)—envelope—GRAHAM PAPER CO., St. Louis.
Endurance Bond—(w)—GRAHAM PAPER CO., St. Louis.
Enfield—(b)—book—SEYMOUR CO., New York.
Englewood Plate—(b)—book—SEYMOUR CO., New York.
English Antique Linen—(w)—R. C. KASTNER PAPER CO., New York.
English Bible—(b)—PAPER MILLS COMPANY, Chicago.
English Bond—(w)—FOX RIVER PAPER CO., Appleton, Wis.

Watermarks and Brands

English Cloth Blotting—(b)—SABIN ROBBINS PAPER CO., Middletown, Ohio.
English Finish Book—(b)—F. A. FLINN, INC., New York.
English Lawn—(w)—MARCUS WARD CO., Brooklyn, N. Y.
English Oak—(w)—GEO. B. HURD & CO., New York.
English Onion Skin Bond—(b)—CARTER, RICE & CO., CORP., Boston.
English Repp—(b)—GEO. B. HURD & CO. New York.
English Repp—(w)—CAREW MANUFACTURING CO., South Hadley Falls, Mass.
Engravers'—(b)—wedding paper and bristols—UNION CARD & PAPER CO., New York.
Engravers' Art Pasted—(b)—bristol—J. W. BUTLER PAPER CO., Chicago.
Engravers' Vellumplate—(b)—EATON, CRANE & PIKE CO., Pittsfield, Mass.
Engravers' (with C in a diamond)—(b)—proving plate—W. H. CLAFLIN & CO., Boston.
Engravers Crystal—(b)—white wedding cardboard and cards—GRAHAM PAPER CO., St. Louis.
Enfield Book—(w)—SEYMOUR CO., INC., New York.
Enfield Cover—(b)—SEYMOUR CO., INC., New York.
Ensign—(b)—BUNTIN, GILLIES & CO., Hamilton, Canada.
Ensign—(b)—toilet—NORTHERN PAPER MILLS, Green Bay, Wis.
Ensign Bond—(w)—WRIGHT, BARRETT & STILWELL CO., St. Paul.
Ensign Bond—(w)—LAMBERT PAPER CO., Salt Lake City, Utah.
Ensign Book—(b)—BUNTIN, GILLIES & CO., LTD., Hamilton, Ontario, Can.
Ensign Mills—(b)—TILESTON & LIVERMORE, Boston.
Enterprise Bristol—(b)—A. STORRS & BEMENT CO., Boston.
Envelope Manila—(b)—CHATFIELD & WOODS CO., Cincinnati.
Epoch Bond—(w)—WHITAKER PAPER CO., Cincinnati, Ohio.
Epsom—(b)—toilet—UNITED STATES ENVELOPE CO. (Morgan Envelope Co. Division), Springfield, Mass.
Equality—(w and b)—writing, bond, ledger—NEENAH PAPER CO., Neenah, Wis.
Equator—(w)—No. 2 Fine—THE W. B. OGLESBY PAPER CO., Middletown, Ohio.
Equator Offset—(b)—THE W. B. OGLESBY PAPER CO., Middletown, Ohio.
Equipment Bond—(w)—COLLINS MFG. CO., N. Wilbraham, Mass.

Equitable—(b)—toilet—SCOTT PAPER CO., Philadelphia.
Equitable Linen—(w)—B. D. RISING PAPER CO., Housatonic, Mass.
Equity Manuscript—(b)—LOUISVILLE PAPER CO., Louisville, Ky.
Era—(b)—toilet—ALBANY PERFORATED WRAPPING PAPER CO., Albany, N. Y.
Erie—(b)—tarred felt—GRAHAM PAPER CO., St. Louis.
Erie—(b)—J. W. BUTLER PAPER CO., Chicago.
Erie—(b)—toilet—ALBANY PERFORATED WRAPPING PAPER CO., Albany, N. Y.
Erie—(b)—white wove—F. A. FLINN, INC., New York.
Erie Bond—(w)—R. H. THOMPSON CO., Buffalo, N. Y.
Erie Bristol—(b)—BEECHER, PECK & LEWIS, Detroit, Mich.
Erie Flats—(w)—writing—KINGSLEY PAPER CO., Cleveland, Ohio.
Erie Mills—(b)—white wove—KINGSLEY PAPER CO., Cleveland.
Erie Writing—(w)—KINGSLEY PAPER CO., Cleveland, Ohio.
Eria Green—(b)—pattern—LOUISVILLE PAPER CO., Louisville, Ky.
Escolite Onion Skin—(b)—ESLEECK MFG. CO., Turners Falls, Mass.
Esenapaj Bond—(w)—H. & W. B. DREW CO., Jacksonville, Fla.
Essex—(b)—M. F. & S. & S. C.—W. H. CLAFLIN & CO., Boston.
Essex—(b)—colored poster—HAGEN PAPER CO., St. Louis.
Essex—(b)—toilet—ALBANY PERFORATED WRAPPING PAPER CO., Albany, N. Y.
Essex—(b)—ruled—CHATFIELD & WOODS CO., Cincinnati, Ohio.
Essex—(b)—No. 2 fine—WRIGHT, BARRETT & STILWELL CO., St. Paul, Minn.
Essex Bond—(w)—LASHER & LATHROP, New York.
Essex Bristols—(b)—HY. LINDENMEYR & SONS, New York.
Essex Extra Fine—(w)—white flat—J. C. PARKER PAPER CO., Louisville, Ky.
Essex Fibre—(b)—hardware—HENRY LINDENMEYR & SONS, New York.
Essex Fine Writing—(b)—CANFIELD PAPER CO., THE, New York.
Essex Flats—(b)—WRIGHT, BARRETT & STILWELL CO., St. Paul.
Essex Mills—(w)—writing—HUDSON VALLEY PAPER CO., Albany.
Essex Mills—(b)—folded and ruled—CHATFIELD & WOODS CO., Cincinnati, Ohio.
Essex Mills—(b)—folded—ESSEX PAD AND PAPER CO., Holyoke.
Essex Mills—(b)—white flat—J. C. PARKER PAPER CO., Louisville, Ky.

Essex Mills—(b)—ledger—CANFIELD PAPER CO., New York.
Essex Railroad Manila—(b)—writing—C. P. LESH PAPER CO., Indianapolis.
Essex Wrapping—(b)—HY. LINDENMEYR & SONS, New York.
Estimate Bond—(w)—CLEMENT & STOCKWELL, INC., New York.
Etching—(w)—Z. & W. M. CRANE, Dalton, Mass.
Etching Surface—(b)—book—THE PAPER MILLS CO., Chicago.
Eton Linen Ledger—(w)—C. P. LESH PAPER CO., Indianapolis, Ind.
Euclid Drafting — (b) — HY. LINDENMEYR & SONS, New York.
Euclid Mills — (w) — PETREQUIN PAPER CO., Cleveland, Ohio.
Eureka— (b) —coated blanks — TROY PAPER CO., Troy, N. Y.
Eureka—(b)—envelopes, litho. blanks and cards—DONALDSON PAPER CO., Harrisburg, Pa.
Eureka — (b) —tag board — LOUISVILLE PAPER CO., Louisville, Ky.
Eureka — (b) — white wove — F. A. FLINN, New York.
Eureka—(b)—toilet—R. M. MYERS & CO., Rochester, N. Y.
Eureka—(w and b)—writing—CUNNINGHAM, CURTISS & WELCH, Oakland, Cal.
Eureka Bond—(w)—EASTERN PAPER AND SUPPLY CO., Springfield.
Eureka Bond—(w)—white and tinted—CENTRAL OHIO PAPER CO., Columbus, Ohio.
Eureka Bond—(w)—STRATHMORE PAPER CO., Mittineague, Mass.
Eureka Blanks—(b)—HY. LINDENMEYR & SONS, New York.
Eureka Half Tone—(b)—TROY PAPER CO., Troy, N. Y.
Eureka Ledger—(b)—MILLER & WRIGHT PAPER CO., New York.
Eureka Linen—(b)—tissue—SMITH PAPER CO., Lee, Mass.
Eureka Linen Ledger — (w) — STRATHMORE PAPER CO., Mittineague, Mass.
Eureka Litho. Blanks—(b)—TROY PAPER CO., Troy, N. Y.
Eureka Tag—(b)—McCLELLAN PAPER CO., Minneapolis, Minn.
Evadne—WHITING PAPER CO., Holyoke, Mass.
Everett Linen—CAREW MANUFACTURING CO., South Hadley Falls, Mass.
Everglade—(b)—fine—H. & W. B. DREW CO., Jacksonville, Fla.
Everlast — (b) — toilet — GEO. T. JOHNSON CO., Boston.
Everybody's Bond — (b) — F. A. FLINN, INC., New York.
Excel Bond—(w)—PAUL E. VERNON & CO., New York.
Excel Coated—(b)—PAUL E. VERNON & CO., New York.
Excel Ledger—(b)—THOS. W. PRICE, Philadelphia.
Excello—(b)—roofing—GRAHAM PAPER CO., St. Louis.
Excello Bristol—(b)—C. P. LESH PAPER CO., Indianapolis, Ind.
Excello Ledger—(w) — DAVID L. ENGLE, New York.
Excello Mills — (w) — AMERICAN WRITING PAPER CO., Holyoke, Mass.
Excello Mimeograph—(b)—J. C. PARKER PAPER CO., Louisville, Ky.
Excelso Semi Dull Coated—(b)—MILLER & WRIGHT PAPER CO., INC., New York.
Excello Tag—(b)—WHITAKER PAPER CO., Cincinnati, Ohio.
Excelsior—(b)—toilet—UNITED STATES ENVELOPE CO. (Morgan Envelope Co. Div.), Springfield, Mass.
Excelsior Wedding and Bristol—(b)—WORTHY PAPER CO., Mittineague, Mass.
Excelsior—(w)—folded writing—C. M. BARNES CO., Chicago.
Excelsior Blanks—(b)—KINGSLEY PAPER CO., Cleveland, Ohio.
Excelsior Express — (b)— wrapping —GRAHAM PAPER CO., St. Louis.
Excelsior Laid Book—(b)—CINCINNATI CORDAGE AND PAPER CO., Cincinnati, Ohio.
Excelsior Ledger — (w) — CHASE BROS., Haverhill, Mass.
Excelsior Linen Ledger—(w)—STRATHMORE PAPER CO., Mittineague, Mass.
Excelsior Mills—(w)—A. STORRS & BEMENT CO., Boston.
Excelsior Mimeograph — (b) — BRADNER SMITH & CO., Chicago.
Excelsior Onion Skin Bond—(b)—CARTER, RICE & CO., CORP., Boston.
Excelsior Wedding—(b)—WORTHY PAPER CO., Mittineague, Mass.
Excelso Dull Coated—(b)—book—MILLER & WRIGHT PAPER CO., New York.
Exchange Bank Bond—(w)—C. P. LESH PAPER CO., Indianapolis, Ind.
Exchange Bond — (w) — CONROW BROTHERS, New York.
Exchange Linen—(w)—CONROW BROTHERS, New York.
Exchequer Bond—(w)—SMITH, DAVIDSON & WRIGHT, LTD., Vancouver, B. C.
Excise Linen—QUAKER CITY PAPER CO., Philadelphia.
Exclusive—(b)—J. C. BLAIR CO., Huntingdon, Pa.
Executive—(b)—cover and book—RIEGEL & CO., INC., Philadelphia.
Executive Blotting — (b) — DISTRICT OF COLUMBIA PAPER MFG. CO., Washington, D. C.
Executive Bond—(w)—R. P. ANDREWS PAPER CO., Washington, D. C.

FELTS AND JACKETS | Appleton Woolen Mills, APPLETON, WIS.

Watermarks and Brands

Executive—(b)—box covering — DISTRICT OF COLUMBIA PAPER MFG. CO., Washington, D. C.
Executive Cover and Text—(b)—typewriter—EATON, CRANE & PIKE CO., Pittsfield, Mass.
Executive Onion Skin—(b)—OSBURN PAPER CO., Philadelphia.
Executive Text — (w) — DISTRICT OF COLUMBIA PAPER MFG. CO., Washington, D. C.
Executive Text Bristol Duplex—(b)—DISTRICT OF COLUMBIA PAPER CO., Washington, D. C.
Executive Blotting — (b) — DISTRICT OF COLUMBIA PAPER MFG. CO., Washington, D. C.
Exemplar Bond — (w) — JOHN F. SARLES CO., INC., New York.
Exeter—(w)—book—SEYMOUR CO., New York.
Exeter—(b)—bristol — COOK-VIVIAN CO., Boston.
Exeter—(b) — envelope — WHITING-PATTERSON CO., Philadelphia.
Exeter Colored Bristol—(b)—C. P. LESH PAPER CO., Indianapolis, Ind.
Exeter Mills—(b)—A. STORRS & BEMENT CO., Boston.
Exeter Tag—(b)—KINGSLEY PAPER CO., Cleveland, Ohio.
Exmoor—(b)—book—J. W. BUTLER PAPER CO., Chicago.
Exora Steel Plate—(b)—HY. LINDENMEYR & SONS, New York.
Export—(b)—bristol—W. H. CLAFLIN & CO., Boston.
Export—(w)—bond and linen—THOS. W. PRICE CO., Philadelphia.
Export Kraft — (b) — S. S. GARRETT & CO., Philadelphia.
Export Waterproof Lining Paper—(b)—BRADNER SMITH & CO., Chicago.
Exposition Bond—(w)—WHITING PAPER CO., Holyoke, Mass.
Express—(b)—coated blotting—JOHN CARTER & CO., Boston.
Express—(b)—toilet—ALBANY PERFORATED WRAPPING PAPER CO., Albany, N. Y.
Express—(b)—toilet—CHATFIELD & WOODS CO., Cincinnati, Ohio.
Express—(w)—writing manila—E. B. EDDY CO., Hull, Canada.
Express—(b)—manila writing—J. W. BUTLER PAPER CO., Chicago.
Express—(w and b)—writing, bond, ledger—NEENAH PAPER CO., Neenah, Wis.
Express — (b) — shipping tags — OLD DOMINION PAPER CO., Norfolk, Va.
Express Bond—(w)—AETNA PAPER CO., Dayton, Ohio.
Express Bristol—(b)—CHATFIELD & WOODS CO., Cincinnati, Ohio.
Express Onion Skin—(b)—BRADNER SMITH & CO., Chicago.
Exter Bond—(b)—J. C. PARKER PAPER CO., Louisville, Ky.

Extra Bond—(w)—F. W. ANDERSON & CO., INC., New York.
Extra Bond—(w)—JOHN F. SARLES CO., INC., New York.
Extracoat—(b)—tinted enameled book—HAGEN PAPER CO., St. Louis.
Extra Ledger Index Bristol—(b)—COOK-VIVIAN CO., Boston.
Extra "E"—(b)—M. F. and S. & Sc. book—THE ALLING & CORY CO., Rochester, N. Y.
Extra Eggshell—(b)—white and india book—THE ALLING & CORY CO., Rochester, N. Y.
Extra Envelope — (b) — manila — CHATFIELD & WOODS CO., Cincinnati, Ohio.
Extra Fine—(b)—BASSETT & SUTPHIN, New York.
Extra Fine—(w)—fine—ARCHER PAPER CO., Chattanooga, Tenn.
Extra Fine—(b)—bristol—ARCHER PAPER CO., Chattanooga, Tenn.
Extra Fine—(w)—flat—FOX RIVER PAPER CO., Appleton, Wis.
Extra Fine Linen Wove—(w)—GEO. B. HURD & CO., New York.
Extra Fine Writing—(w)—THE UNION PAPER & TWINE CO., Detroit, Mich.
Extra Fine Writing—(b)—EASTERN MFG. CO., Bangor, Me.
Extra Folding Bristol—(b)—VON OLKER-SNELL PAPER CO., Boston.
Extra Half Tone—(b)—book—J. W. BUTLER PAPER CO., Chicago.
Extra Ivory Translucent—(b)—bristols—SWIGART PAPER CO., Chicago.
Extra Linen Bond—(b)—HARPER PAPER CO., New York.
Extra No. 1 Linen Bond—(w)—HY. LINDENMEYR & SONS, New York.
Extra Linen Ledger—(w)—HARPER PAPER CO., New York.
Extra No. 1 Manila Writing—(b)—HY. LINDENMEYR & SONS, New York.
Extra No. 1 Pasted Bristol—(b)—HY. LINDENMEYR & SONS, New York.
Extra No. 1 Music—(b)—book—CHATFIELD & WOODS CO., Cincinnati, Ohio.
Extra No. 1 Onion Skin—(b)—bond—UNION CARD & PAPER CO., New York.
Extra No. 1 Railroad Manila—(b)—writing — THE ALLING & CORY CO., Rochester, N. Y.
Extra No. 2 Writing—(b)—R. E. LLOYD PAPER CO., Chicago, Ill.
Extra Printers' Blank—(b)—JOHN CARTER & CO., Boston.
Extra Strong—(w)—bond and ledger—W. R. GRACE & CO., New York.
Extra Strong C. B.—(w)—CONROW BROTHERS, New York.
Extra Strong Coated—(b)—PAUL E. VERNON & CO., New York.

BLOTTING PAPERS — "STANDARD," "IMPERIAL," "STERLING" Royal Worcester and Defender Enameled
STANDARD PAPER MFG. CO., - - Richmond, Va.

Extra Strong Colored Folding Enamel—(b)—book—THE ALLING & CORY CO., Rochester, N. Y.
Extra Strong Tinted Enamel—(w)—cover—DILL & COLLINS CO., Philadelphia.
Extra Strong Tag — (b) — A. STORRS & BEMENT CO., Boston.
Extra Strong Unwatermarked—(b)—ledger — MERRIAM PAPER CO., New York.
Extra Super—(b)—SOUTHWORTH CO., Mittineague, Mass.
Extra Superfine—(b)—SOUTHWORTH CO., Mittineague, Mass.
Extra Superfine—(w and b)—GEO. B. HURD & CO., New York.
Extra S. & S. C.—(b)—litho.—J. W. BUTLER PAPER CO., Chicago.
Extra Super—(b) — SOUTHWORTH CO., Mittineague, Mass.
Extra Super Laid—(w)—AMERICAN WRITING PAPER CO., Holyoke.
Extra Super Wove—(w)—AMERICAN WRITING PAPER CO., Holyoke.
Extra Thick Plated—(b)—bristol—THE PAPER MILLS CO., Chicago.
Extra Value—(b)—envelope—GRAHAM PAPER CO., St. Louis.
Extra Velvet Finish—(b)—toilet tissue—W. H. CLAFLIN & CO., Boston.
Extra Wedding Plate — (b) — EATON, CRANE & PIKE CO., Pittsfield, Mass.
Extra White—(b)—news—A. M. EATON, Waltham and Boston.
Extra White Laid—(b)—book—THE ALLING & COBY CO., Rochester.
Eye Saving Green Pattern—(b)—C. H. DEXTER & SONS, INC., Windsor Locks, Conn.
E. Z.—(b)—carpet lining—GRAHAM PAPER CO., St. Louis.
E. Z. Y.—(b)—carpet lining—GRAHAM PAPER CO., St. Louis.

F

F. A. F. Manifold—(b)—F. A. FLINN, INC., New York.
F. O. C.—(b)—tissue—ANCRAM PAPER MILL, Ancram, N. Y.
Fabric Bond—(w)—AMERICAN WRITING PAPER CO., Holyoke, Mass.
Fabrikli Ka—(b)—toweling napkins, etc.—NEBEN MFG. CO., New York.
Factory—(b)—toilet—ALBANY PERFORATED WRAPPING PAPER CO., Albany, N. Y.
Faflian Ledger—(b)—F. A. FLINN, INC., New York.
Fairchild Cover—(b)—LASHER & LATHROP, New York.
Fairchild Parchment—(b)—LASHER & LATHROP, New York.
Fairdale Post Card—(b)—HY. LINDENMEYR & SONS, New York.
Fairfax—(b)—THOMAS W. PRICE CO., Philadelphia.

Fairfield—(b)—cover—STRATHMORE PAPER CO., Mittineague, Mass.
Fairfield Bristol—(b)—STRATHMORE PAPER CO., Mittineague, Mass.
Fairfield Deckle Edge—(b)—STRATHMORE PAPER CO., Mittineague, Mass.
Fairfield Fine—(w)—STRATHMORE PAPER CO., Mittineague, Mass.
Fairfield First Quality—(w)—laid linen—STRATHMORE PAPER CO., Mittineague, Mass.
Fairfield First Quality—(w)—wove bond—STRATHMORE PAPER CO., Mittineague, Mass.
Fairfield Japan—(b)—STRATHMORE PAPER CO., Mittineague, Mass.
Fairfield Linen Ledger—(w)—wove—STRATHMORE PAPER CO., Mittineague, Mass.
Fairfield Offset—(w)—wove book—STRATHMORE PAPER CO., Mittineague, Mass.
Fairfield Parchment—(w)—wove bond—STRATHMORE PAPER CO., Mittineague, Mass.
Fairmount — (b) — book — W. H. GEORGE, Philadelphia.
Fairmont—(b)—bristol—JUDD PAPER CO., Holyoke, Mass.
Fairmount Coated—(b)—ARNOLD-ROBERTS CO., Boston.
Fairview—(b and w)—AMERICAN WRITING PAPER CO., Holyoke, Mass.
Fairy—(w and b)—bond and writing—THE PAPER MILLS CO., Chicago.
Fairy — (b) — toilet — NORTHERN PAPER MILLS, Green Bay, Wis.
Falcon—(w)—JAPAN PAPER CO., New York.
Falcon Bond—(w)—PLYMOUTH PAPER CO., Holyoke, Mass.
Falcon Manila—(b)—THE ALLING & CORY CO., Rochester, N. Y.
Falcon Writing—(w)—THE UNION PAPER & TWINE CO., Detroit, Mich.
Falls — (b) — binders' board — C. B. HEWITT & BROS., INC., New York.
Falls City—(b)—white book—J. C. PARKER PAPER CO., Louisville, Ky.
Falls Linen—(b)—CHATFIELD & WOODS CO., Cincinnati, Ohio.
Falstaff—(b) — cover — LOUISVILLE PAPER CO., Louisville, Ky.
Falstaf—(b)—toilet—H. NORWOOD EWING CO., New York.
Family — (b) — toilet — NORTHERN PAPER MILLS, Green Bay, Wis.
Famous Bristol—(b)—UNION PAPER & TWINE CO., Detroit, Mich.
Famous Faultless—(b)—ready roofing—CHATFIELD & WOODS CO., Cincinnati, Ohio.
Fancy Lined Bond—(b)—GEO. B. HURD & CO., New York.
Faneuil — (w) — AMERICAN WRITING PAPER CO., Holyoke, Mass.
Fan-Tan Parchment — (b) — wrapping—LOUISVILLE PAPER CO., Louisville, Ky.

FELTS AND JACKETS | Appleton Woolen Mills
APPLETON - - WIS.

Watermarks and Brands

Fantana—(b)—toilet—H. NORWOOD-EWING CO., New York.
Far Mill—(b)—roll toilet—JEROME PAPER CO., New York.
Fargo Translucent — (b) — COOK-VIVIAN CO., Boston.
Faro—(w)—bond, writing and wrapping—W. R. GRACE & CO., New York.
Fast Mail—(b)—mailing and cover—GRAHAM PAPER CO., St. Louis.
Fast Mail Bond—(w)—TAYLOR-LOGAN CO. PAPERMAKERS, Holyoke, Mass.
Fast Mail Envelope—(w)—envelope paper—TAYLOR-LOGAN CO. PAPERMAKERS, Holyoke.
Father Pitt Antique Laid—WESTERN PENNA. PAPER CO., Pittsburg.
Faultless Prepared Roofing—(b)—CHATFIELD & WOODS CO., Cincinnati, Ohio.
Faust—(w)—flats—B R A D N E R SMITH & CO., Chicago.
Faust Bristol—(b)—B R A D N E R SMITH & CO., Chicago.
Favorite—(b)—toilet — NORTHERN PAPER MILLS, Green Bay, Wis.
Favorite Bond—BURGESS & WRAY PAPER CO., Chicago.
Favorite Coated—(b)—book—HUDSON VALLEY PAPER CO., Albany, N. Y.
Fawnskin—(b)—tissue and wrapping—GRAHAM PAPER CO., St. Louis.
Fayette Mills—(b)—colored laid—CONROW BROS., New York.
Fayette Onion Skin — (b) — GRAHAM PAPER CO., St. Louis.
Fearless Kraft—(b)—R. L. GREENE PAPER CO., Providence, R. I.
Feathercoat Enamel Book — (b) — BERMINGHAM & PROSSER CO., Kalamazoo, Mich.
Featheredge Writings—(w)—ADVERTISERS' PAPER MILLS, Holyoke, Mass.
Feather Edge—(b)—UNION CARD & PAPER CO., New York.
Featherfine Enamel — (b) — book — BEECHER, PECK & LEWIS, Detroit, Mich.
Featherweight—(b)—bond and linen —J. C. BLAIR CO., Huntingdon, Pa.
Featherweight—(b)—cover—J A S. WHITE & CO., Chicago.
Featherweight Bond — (b) — bond and onion skin—GRAHAM PAPER CO., St. Louis.
Featherweight Bond—(b)—O. F. H. WARNER & CO., Baltimore.
Featherweight Folio—(b)—BRADNER SMITH & CO., Chicago.
Featherweight Onion Skin Bond—(b)—CARTER, RICE & CO., CORP., Boston.
Federal — (w) — writing—COYLE & GILMORE CO., INC., New York.

Federal—(w and b)—ledger, bond, cover, blotting and bristol—UNION CARD & PAPER CO., New York.
Federal—(b)—ALBANY P E R F O-RATED WRAPPING PAPER CO., Albany, N. Y.
Federal Bank Bond—(b)—INDIANA PAPER CO., Indianapolis, Ind.
Federal Bank Bond—(w)—W. M. PRINGLE & CO., INC., New York.
Federal Bond — (w) — AMERICAN WRITING PAPER CO., Holyoke, Mass.
Federal Book—(b)—M. F. & S. & S. C.—THE ALLING & CORY CO., Rochester, N. Y.
Federal Index Bristol—(b)—HARLEM CARD & PAPER CO., New York.
Federal Linen Finish — (b) — A. STORRS & BEMENT CO., Boston.
Federal Manuscript Cover—(b)—UNION CARD & PAPER CO., N. Y.
Federal Mills—(w)—C. P. LESH PAPER CO., Indianapolis, Ind.
Federal Reserve Bond—(w)—bond —FOX RIVER PAPER CO., Appleton, Wis.
Federal Pure White Coated—(b)—A. STORRS & BEMENT CO., Boston.
Federal—(b)—railway manila—ROLLAND PAPER CO., St. Jerome, Can.
Fern Green—(b)—pattern — LOUISVILLE PAPER CO., Louisville, Ky.
Ferndale—(w)—flat writing—T H E PETERS PAPER CO., Denver, Col.
Fernside—(w)—AMERICAN WRITING PAPER CO., Holyoke, Mass.
Fernside — (w) —BUNTIN, GILLIES & CO., LTD., Hamilton, Ontario, Can.
Fernwood — (w) — writing — J. E. LINDE PAPER CO., New York.
Fernwood—(b)—bristol—JUDD PAPER CO., Holyoke, Mass.
Fez — (b) — bristol — WHITING-PATTERSON CO., Philadelphia.
F. F.—(b)—toilet—ALBANY PERFORATED WRAPPING PAPER CO., Albany, N. Y.
Fiberlic — (b) — board—McANDREWS & FORBES CO., Camden, N. J.
Fibre — (w) — linen — J. E. LINDE PAPER CO., New York.
Fibre—(b)—wrapping — LOUISVILLE PAPER CO., Louisville, Ky.
Fibrespun Bond — (b) — J. W. BUTLER PAPER CO., Chicago.
Fidelity—(b)—tag board—GRAHAM PAPER CO., St. Louis.
Fidelity—(b)—strong jute document —GRAHAM PAPER CO., St. Louis.
Fidelity — (b) — wrapping — LOUISVILLE PAPER CO., Louisville, Ky.
Fidelity Bond—(w)—BASSETT & SUTPHIN, New York.
Fidelity Bond—(w)—SUTPHIN PAPER CO., INC., New York.
Fidelity Coated — (b) — book — ARNOLD-ROBERTS CO., Boston.
Fidelity Ledger — (w) — KANSAS CITY PAPER CO., Kansas City, Mo.

JAMES H. HARRISON
PULPSTONE MANUFACTURER | **GENUINE NEWCASTLE STONES**
18 Killowen St., GATESHEAD-ON-TYNE, ENG.

Watermarks and Brands

Fidelity Linen Ledger—(w)—HAMMERMILL PAPER CO., Erie, Pa.
Fidelity Superfine—(w)—writing—WILKINSON BROS. & CO., INC., Philadelphia.
Fidelity Onion Skin—(b)—ESLEECK MFG. CO., Turners Falls, Mass.
Fifth Avenue Wedding—(b)—bristol and card—THE PAPER MILLS CO., Chicago.
Filecard Index Bristol—(b)—MEGARGEE BROS., Scranton, Pa.
Filing Index—(b)—bristol—STANDARD CARD & PAPER CO., New York.
Finance—(w)—bond—TROY PAPER CO., Troy, N. Y.
Finance Bond—(w)—DEARBORN PAPER CO., Chicago.
Finance Bond—(w)—B. D. RISING PAPER CO., Housatonic, Mass.
Finance Bond—(w)—FOX RIVER PAPER CO., Appleton, Wis.
Finance Ledger—(w)—B. D. RISING PAPER CO., Housatonic, Mass.
Finance Parchment—RICHMOND PAPER CO., Richmond, Va.
Finance Superfine—(w)—CLEMENTS PAPER CO., Nashville, Tenn.
Financial Bond—(w)—JOHN B. WATKINS CO., New York.
Financial—(w)—bond—MIDLAND PAPER CO., Chicago.
Fincastle Bond—(w)—LOUISVILLE PAPER CO., Louisville, Ky.
Finderne Ledger—(b)—MILLER & WRIGHT PAPER CO., New York.
Fine—(b)—bristol—MEGARGEE-HARE PAPER CO., Philadelphia.
Fine—(w)—writing—MEGARGEE-HARE PAPER CO., Philadelphia.
Fine Art Book—(b)—A. STORRS & BEMENT CO., Boston.
Fine Laid Linen—(b)—ESLEECK MFG. CO., Turners Falls, Mass.
Fine Line Linen—(w and b)—GEO B. HURD & CO., New York.
Fino—(b)—toilet—SCOTT PAPER CO., Philadelphia.
Finola—(b)—writing—GRAHAM PAPER CO., St. Louis.
First Class Bond—(w)—PARSONS PAPER CO., Holyoke, Mass.
First Class Ledger—(w)—VALLEY PAPER CO., Holyoke, Mass.
First Premium, double sized Fourdrinier, made by Byron Weston Co. Dalton, Mass.—(b)—BYRON WESTON CO., Dalton, Mass.
Fiscal Bond—(w)—B. D. RISING PAPER CO., Housatonic, Mass.
Fiscal Ledger—(w)—B. D. RISING PAPER CO., Housatonic, Mass.
Fish Brand—(b)—manila—STONE & FORSYTH CO., Boston.
Fiver—(b)—toilet—GEO T. JOHNSON CO., Boston.
Flake White Enamel Book—(b)—O. F. H. WARNER & CO., Baltimore.

Flambeau Fine—(b)—W. E. WROE & CO., Chicago.
Flamingo Linen—(b)—bond—LEE PAPER CO., Vicksburg, Mich.
Flat Rock English Finish—(b)—MARTIN & WM. H. NIXON PAPER CO., Manayunk, Philadelphia.
Flat Rock Envelope—(b)—MARTIN & WM. H. NIXON PAPER CO., Manayunk, Philadelphia.
Flat Rock Extra Bulk—(b)—MARTIN & WILLIAM H. NIXON PAPER CO., Manayunk, Philadelphia.
Flat Rock Machine Finish—(b)—MARTIN & WM. H. NIXON PAPER CO., Manayunk, Philadelphia.
Flat Rock Mimeograph—(b)—MARTIN & WM. H. NIXON PAPER CO., Manayunk, Philadelphia.
Flat Rock Offset—(b)—MARTIN & WM. H. NIXON PAPER CO., Manayunk, Philadelphia.
Flat Rock Rag Plate—(b)—MARTIN & WM. H. NIXON PAPER CO., Manayunk, Philadelphia.
Flat Rock Text—(w)—antique book—MARTIN & WM. H. NIXON PAPER CO., Manayunk, Philadelphia.
Flat Rock Super—(b)—MARTIN & WM. H. NIXON PAPER CO., Manayunk, Philadelphia.
Flax Bond—(w)—WOLF BROTHERS Philadelphia.
Flaxine—(b)—bond—TROY PAPER CO., Troy, N. Y.
Flax Linen—(w)—writing—KINLEITH PAPER CO., St. Catharines, Ontario, Canada.
Flax White—(b)—DILL & COLLINS CO., Philadelphia.
Flaxen Wove—(b)—MARCUS WARD CO., Brooklyn, N. Y.
Flaxon Bond—(w)—INDIANA PAPER CO., Indianapolis.
Fleetwood Bond—(w)—HY. LINDENMEYR & SONS, New York.
Flemish Book—(b and w)—antique, M. F. book—TILESTON & HOLLINGSWORTH CO., Boston.
Flemish Linen—(w)—AETNA PAPER CO., Dayton, Ohio.
Flemish Linen—(w)—SCRANTOM, WETMORE & CO., Rochester, N. Y.
Fleur-De-Lis—(b)—toilet—STONE & FORSYTH CO., Boston.
Fleur-De-Lis Linen—(w)—EATON, CRANE & PIKE CO., Pittsfield, Mass.
Flexible Cover—(b)—GRAHAM PAPER CO., St. Louis.
Flexible Loose Leaf Ledger—(w)—BYRON WESTON CO., Dalton, Mass.
Flex Kraft—(b)—wrapping—LOUISVILLE PAPER CO., Louisville, Ky.
Flexo Loose Leaf Ledger—(w)—BYRON WESTON CO., Dalton, Mass.
Flexofold Coated—(b)—MILLER & WRIGHT PAPER CO., INC., New York.
Flexoid Roofing—(w)—FISHER BROS. PAPER CO., Fort Wayne, Ind.

FELTS AND JACKETS | Appleton Woolen Mills, APPLETON - - WIS.

Watermarks and Brands

Flint—folding—(b)—LOUISVILLE PAPER CO., Louisville, Ky.
Flora—(b)—blotting—DISTRICT OF COLUMBIA PAPER MANUFACTURING CO., Washington, D. C.
Flora—(b)—M. F. colored book—BRADNER SMITH & CO., Chicago.
Flora—(b)—box covering—DISTRICT OF COLUMBIA MFG. CO., Washington, D. C.
Flora Cover—(b)—DISTRICT OF COLUMBIA PAPER MFG. CO., Washington, D. C.
Florence Wove—(w)—T. C. ALLEN & CO., Halifax, N. S.
Flora Tinted Bristol—(b)—V O N OLKER-SNELL PAPER CO., Boston.
Floradora Blank—(b)—A. STORRS & BEMENT CO., Boston.
Florence—(b)—bristol—J. W. BUTLER PAPER CO., Chicago.
Florence—(w)—cardboard, blotting and flat—J. W. BUTLER PAPER CO., Chicago.
Florence Enamel—(b)—book—HUDSON VALLEY PAPER CO., Albany, N. Y.
Florence Linen—(w)—UNITED STATES ENVELOPE CO. (The White, Corbin & Co. Division), Rockville, Conn.
Florence Superfine—(w)—BROWN, BLODGETT & SPERRY CO., St. Paul.
Florentine—(b)—book—MILLER & WRIGHT PAPER CO., New York.
Florentine—(b)—toilet—UNITED STATES ENVELOPE CO. (Morgan Envelope Co. Division), Springfield.
Florentine—(b)—cover—SEYMOUR CO., New York.
Florentine—(b)—cardboard & cards—GRAHAM PAPER CO., St. Louis.
Florentine Parchment—(w)—EATON, CRANE & PIKE CO., Pittsfield, Mass.
Flo-Roid—(b)—roofing—LOUISVILLE PAPER CO., Louisville, Ky.
Flour City Wood Envelope—(b)—MINNEAPOLIS PAPER CO., Minneapolis, Minn.
F. Manila—(b)—R. L. GREENE PAPER CO., Providence, R. I.
Folding Ivory Bristol—(b)—BRADNER SMITH & CO., Chicago.
Folding Translucent—(b)—bristols—UNION CARD & PAPER CO., N. Y.
Foldbert—(b)—enamel—DWIGHT BROS. PAPER CO., Grand Rapids, Mich.
Foldwell—(enameled)—(b)—CHICAGO PAPER CO., Chicago.
Foreign Correspondence—(b)—envelope—THE PAPER MILLS CO., Chicago.
Foreign Linen—(b)—MEGARGEE-HARE PAPER CO., Philadelphia.
Foreign Mail—(b)—bond and onion skin—GRAHAM PAPER CO., St. Louis.

Foreign Mail Fabric—(w and b)—GEO. B. HURD & CO., New York.
Foreign Mail Glazed—(b)—EATON, CRANE & PIKE CO., Pittsfield, Mass.
Foreign Mail Unglazed—(b)—EATON, CRANE & PIKE CO., Pittsfield, Mass.
Forensic Bond—(b)—PARSONS TRADING CO., New York.
Forest City Ledger—(w)—KINGSLEY PAPER CO., Cleveland, Ohio.
Forest Grove Mills—J. E. LINDE PAPER CO., New York.
Forest Rope—(b)—D. S. WALTON & CO., New York.
"Forpaco"—(b)—Sakura Japanese crepe toilet—FORBES PAPER CO., 32 Laight St., New York.
Fort Dearborn—(b)—enameled I. S. cover—JAMES WHITE PAPER CO., Chicago.
Fort Orange—(b)—ALBANY PERFORATED WRAPPING PAPER CO., Albany, New York.
Fort Pitt—(w)—superfine white writing—THE ALLING & CORY CO., Pittsburgh, Pa.
Fortuna—(w)—J. C. BLAIR CO., Huntingdon, Pa.
Fortuna Bond—(w)—MOSER PAPER CO., Chicago.
Forty-Five—(b)—envelope—UNION CARD & PAPER CO., New York.
Foru—(b)—toilet—SCOTT PAPER CO., Philadelphia.
Forum—(b)—toilet—NORTHERN PAPER MILLS, Green Bay, Wis.
Forum Bond—(w)—G. P. HEILBRONN CO., Manila, P. I.
Foulard Fabric—(b)—GEO. B. HURD & CO., New York.
Four Hundred—(b)—wedding and bristol—STANDARD CARD & PAPER CO., New York.
Foxhail—(b)—writing—GRAHAM PAPER CO., St. Louis.
Foxhail—(b)—cardboard—McCLELLAN PAPER CO., Minneapolis, Minn.
Fox River Paper Co., Est. 1893—(w)—flat or bond—FOX RIVER PAPER CO., Appleton, Wis.
Fox River Paper Co. Superfine—(w)—flat—FOX RIVER PAPER CO., Appleton, Wis.
Foxstraw—(b)—corrugating paper—W. H. FOX & SONS, Penn Yan, N. Y.
Franchise Bond—(w)—COLUMBIA PAPER CO., Victoria, B. C.
Francis Mills—(w)—writing—MEGARGEE BROS., Scranton, Pa.
Franconia—(b)—mat boards—WILKINSON BROS. & CO., INC., Philadelphia.
Franconia Mills—(b)—folded—CONROW BROS., New York.
Franklin—(b)—blotting—RIEGEL & CO., INC., Philadelphia.
Franklin—(b)—news—THE PETERS PAPER CO., Denver, Col.

BLOTTING PAPERS STANDARD PAPER MFG. CO., Richmond, Va. Largest Manufacturers

NEW MILLS DESIGNED   POWER PLANTS   OLD MILLS REBUILT
C. A. CHAPMAN, Inc.
28 E. JACKSON BLVD.   ENGINEERS   CHICAGO

Watermarks and Brands   669

Franklin — (b)—book—LASHER & LATHROP, New York.
Franklin—(b)—(colored M.F. book) cover—JAMES WHITE PAPER CO., Chicago.
Franklin—(b)—colored—THOMAS W. PRICE CO., Philadelphia.
Franklin—(b)—enameled book—VON OLKER-SNELL PAPER CO., Boston.
Franklin—(b) — white laid book—LASHER & LATHROP, New York.
Franklin — (b)—BUNTIN, GILLIES & CO., Hamilton, Can.
Franklin—(w) — fine writing—CENTRAL OHIO PAPER CO., Columbus
Franklin—(w)—bond — PENINSULAR PAPER CO., Ypsilanti, Mich.
Franklin Blotting—(b) — blotting—SWIGART PAPER CO., Chicago.
Franklin Bond—J. & F. B. GARRETT, Syracuse, New York.
Franklin Bond—(b)—PENINSULAR PAPER CO., Ypsilanti, Mich.
Franklin Bond—(w)—VON OLKER-SNELL PAPER CO., Boston.
Franklin Book—(b)—BUNTIN, GILLIES & CO., LTD., Hamilton, Ontario, Can.
Franklin Bristol—(b)—A. STORRS & BEMENT CO., Boston.
Franklin Extra Fine Writing—(w)—O. F. H. WARNER & CO., Baltimore.
Franklin Extra Strong—(w)—PARSONS TRADING CO., New York.
Franklin Linen Ledger—(w)—No. 2 ledger, white and buff — R. C. KASTNER PAPER CO., New York.
Franklin Mills — (b) — CONROW BROS., New York.
Franklin Mills — (b) — colored—THOS W. PRICE CO., Philadelphia.
Franklin Mills Superfine—(w)—A. STORRS & BEMENT CO., Boston.
Fraternity—(b)—bond — PENINSULAR PAPER CO., Ypsilanti, Mich.
Fraternity—(w)—laid book—GEO. A. WHITING PAPER CO., Menasha, Wis.
Fredricshire Ledger—(b)—CONROW BROS., New York.
Free Lance — (w) — SAUGERTIES MFG. CO., Saugerties, New York.
French Antique Bristol—(b)—W. G. WILLMANN, New York.
French Cambric — (w) — JOHN WANAMAKER, Philadelphia.
French Folio—(b)—A. S. LANDSBERG, New York.
French Ledger—(w)—VALLEY PAPER CO., Holyoke, Mass.
French Lily Linen—(w)—UNITED STATES ENVELOPE CO. (Whitcomb Envelope Co. Division), Worcester.
French Linen—(w)—VALLEY PAPER CO., Holyoke, Mass.
French Linear Fabric — (w) — GEORGE B. HURD & CO., New York.
French Linen Bond—(w)—VALLEY PAPER CO., Holyoke, Mass.

French Madras Bond — (w) — EATON, CRANE & PIKE CO., Pittsfield, Mass.
French Nainsook—(b) — GEO. B. HURD & CO., New York.
French Percale—(w and b)—GEO. B. HURD & CO., New York.
French Poplin — (b) — EATON, CRANE & PIKE CO., Pittsfield, Mass.
French Quadrille — (b)—EATON, CRANE & PIKE CO., Pittsfield, Mass.
Frontenac—(w) — DIEM & WING PAPER CO., Cincinnati, Ohio.
Frontenac Eggshell — (b) — CANFIELD PAPER CO., New York.
F. S. F.—(b)—trunk and friction boards—C. B. HEWITT & BROS., INC., New York.
F. S. Webster Co. Bond—(w)—typewriter—F. S. WEBSTER CO., Boston.
F. S. Webster Co. Linen — (w)—typewriter—F. S. WEBSTER CO., Boston.
Fujiyama— (b) —toilet—H. NORWOOD EWING CO., New York.
Full Moon—(b)—ALBANY PERFORATED WRAPPING PAPER CO., Albany, New York.
Fullworth Mills — (w) — ESSEX PAD AND PAPER CO., Holyoke.
Fulton—(b)—M. F. colored book—CHATFIELD & WOODS CO., Cincinnati, Ohio.
Fulton Bond — (w)—LASHER & LATHROP, New York.
Fulton Ledger—(w)—LEHMAIER & BROTHERS, New York.
Fulton Mills—(b)—writing—STANDARD CARD & PAPER CO., New York.
Fulton R. R. Manila—(b)—PETREQUIN PAPER CO., Cleveland, Ohio.

G

Gainsborough Cover — (b) — HY. LINDENMEYR & SONS, New York.
Gainsborough Mat—(b)—HY. LINDENMEYR & SONS, New York.
Galaxy Linen — (w)—ST. LOUIS PAPER CO., St. Louis.
Galvanite—(b)—FORD MFG. CO., Chicago.
Gal-Va-Nite Roofing—(b)—UNION ROOFING & MFG. CO., Clinton, Ia.
Galway Linen — (b) — EATON, CRANE & PIKE CO., Pittsfield, Mass.
Gambria Book — (b) — enameled — DIEM & WING PAPER CO., Cincinnati, Ohio.
Garden City — (b) — toilet—J. W. BUTLER PAPER CO., Chicago.
Garfield—(b)—book and news—GRAHAM PAPER CO., St. Louis.
Gasconade—(w)—writing—GRAHAM PAPER CO., St. Louis.
Gator Bond—(b)—DREW'S WHOLESALE PAPER HOUSE, Jacksonville, Fla.

APPLETON MACHINE CO., APPLETON, WIS.   REFINING ENGINES, SCREENS, SAWING & SPLITTING MACHINERY   HIGH GRADE CENTRIFUGAL PUMPS

MINER EDGAR CO., Sole Agents   Edgar Bros. Co. 30 CHURCH STREET NEW YORK   CLAV   WASHED <E W> HIGH COLOR   GRITLESS <C M> HIGH RETENTION

FELTS AND JACKETS | Appleton Woolen Mills APPLETON - - WIS.

Watermarks and Brands

Gauze—(b)—typewriter — BRADNER SMITH & CO., Chicago.
"G. C." Cover—(b)—HY. LINDENMEYR & SONS, New York.
Gebo—(b)—bond—TROY PAPER CO., Troy, N. Y.
Gem—(b)—toilet — NORTHERN PAPER MILLS, Green Bay, Wis.
Gem—(b)—grease proof parchment—GRAHAM PAPER CO., St. Louis.
Gem—(b)—toilet — GRAHAM PAPER CO., St. Louis.
Gem Bond — (w)—DIEM & WING PAPER CO., Cincinnati, Ohio.
Gem Bristol — (b)—VON OLKERSNELL PAPER CO., Boston.
General Bond—(w)—COLLINS MFG. CO., N. Wilbraham, Mass.
General Ledger — (w) — J. W. BUTLER PAPER CO., Chicago.
Genesee—(b)—toilet—ALBANY PERFORATED WRAPPING PAPER CO., Albany, N. Y.
Genesee Linen—(w)—THE ALLING & CORY CO., Rochester, New York.
Genesee—(b)—embossing translucent bristol—THE ALLING & CORY CO., Rochester, N. Y.
Genessee Superfine— (b) — Enamel book—THE ALLING & CORY CO., Rochester, N. Y.
Genessee Tinted Blanks—(b)—THE ALLING & CORY CO., Rochester.
Geneva Blotting—(b)—HY. LINDENMEYR & SONS, New York.
Geneva Bond — (w) — BROWN, TREACY & SPERRY CO., St. Paul.
Geneva Ledger — (w) — BROWN, BLODGETT & SPERRY CO., St. Paul.
Geneva Linen—(w) — VALLEY PAPER CO., Holyoke, Mass.
Geneva Linen — (b) — MATTHIAS PLUM, Newark, New Jersey.
Geneva Onion Skin — (b) — WHITING-PATTERSON CO., Philadelphia.
Geneva Onion Skin — (b) — CANFIELD PAPER CO., New York.
Geneva Superfine — (b) — enamel book—WHITAKER PAPER CO., Cincinnati, Ohio, and BAY STATE PAPER CO., Boston.
Genoa—(b)—cardboards and cards—GRAHAM PAPER CO., St. Louis.
Genoa Bond— (w)—WHITING-PATTERSON CO., Philadelphia.
Genoa Bond — (w) — HOWARD SMITH PAPER MILLS, LTD., Montreal, Can.
Gentry—(b)—toilet—NORTHERN PAPER MILLS, Green Bay, Wis.
Genuine Bond — (b) — R. P. ANDREWS PAPER CO., Washington.
Genuine Irish Linen—(w)—AMERICAN WRITING PAPER CO., Holyoke.
Genuine Linen Ledger—(w)—HARPER PAPER CO., New York.
German Pasted Bristol—(b)—W. G. WILLMANN, New York.

Germania—(b)—toilet—UNITED STATES ENVELOPE CO. (Morgan Envelope Co. Division), Springfield.
Germania — (b)—white wove—F. A. FLINN, New York.
Germanic—(w)—flat — BRADNER SMITH & CO., Chicago.
Germanic Ledger—(w)—BRADNER SMITH & CO., Chicago.
Giant — (b) — toilet — NORTHERN PAPER MILLS, Green Bay, Wis.
Giant Bond—(w) — MOSER PAPER CO., Chicago.
Giant Express—(b)—No. 1 screening—THE SEINSHEIMER PAPER CO., Cincinnati, Ohio.
Giant Jute Tag—(b)—VON OLKERSNELL PAPER CO., Boston.
Gibraltar—(b) — cover — PENINSULAR PAPER CO., Ypsilanti, Mich.
Gibraltar — (b) — kraft wrapping — GRAHAM PAPER CO., St. Louis.
Gibraltar Bond — (w) —ANTIETAM PAPER CO., Hagerstown, Md.
Gibraltar Cover — (b) — PENINSULAR PAPER CO., Ypsilanti, Mich.
Gibraltar Fibre — (b)— wrapping — VON OLKER-SNELL PAPER CO., Boston.
Gibralta No. 1 Jute Tag—(b)—OLD DOMINION PAPER CO., Norfolk, Va.
Gibralta Shipping Tags—(b)—OLD DOMINION PAPER CO., Norfolk, Va.
Gilbert Superfine — (w) — GILBERT PAPER CO., Menasha, Wis.
Gibraltar Tag Board—(b)— OLD DOMINION PAPER CO., Norfolk, Va.
Gilbert's Superfine—(w)—GILBERT PAPER CO., Menasha, Wis.
Gillian—(b) — book and news—GRAHAM PAPER CO., St. Louis.
Glace—(b)—book—MERRIAM PAPER CO., New York.
Glacier Enamel Book—(b)—BERMINGHAM & PROSSER CO., Kalamazoo, Mich.
Gladiator Bond—(w) — ST. LOUIS PAPER CO., St. Louis.
Gladiolus—(b)—ALBANY PERFORATED WRAPPING PAPER CO., Albany, N. Y.
Gladstone—(b)—book— McCLELLAN PAPER CO., Minneapolis.
Gladstone Linen Ledger — (w)— extra No. 2 ledger—JOHN CARTER & CO., Boston.
Gladstone Linen Ledger—(w)— JOHN CARTER & CO., Boston.
Gladwyne—(b)—bristol and writing —MEGARGEE-HARE PAPER CO., Philadelphia.
Glasgow—(b)—laid book—J. C. PARKER PAPER CO., Louisville, Ky.
Glasgow Flats—(b)—McCLELLAN PAPER CO., Minneapolis, Minn.
Glasgow Linen —(w)—CAREW MFG. CO., South Hadley Falls, Mass.
Glasgow Linen—(w)—WRIGHT, BARRETT & STILWELL CO., St. Paul, Minn.

JAMES H. HARRISON PULPSTONE MANUFACTURER | **GENUINE NEWCASTLE STONES** 18 K... St., GAT......... NE, ENG.

Watermarks and Brands

Glasgow Linen—(w)—E. W. SCARBOROUGH, New York.
Glasgow Linen Antique—(w)—WRIGHT, BARRETT & STILWELL CO., St. Paul, Minn.
Glencoe Bond—(w)—BLUNDEN-LYON CO., Chicago.
Glencoe Linen Ledger—(w)—J. C. PARKER PAPER CO., Louisville, Ky.
Glendale — (b) — binder's board — LOUISVILLE PAPER CO., Louisville, Ky.
Glendale — (b) — book and cover — JUDD PAPER CO., Holyoke, Mass.
Glendale—(w)—superfines—AMERICAN WRITING PAPER CO., Holyoke.
Glendale — (b) — bristol — R. L. GREENE PAPER CO., Providence, R. I.
Glendale Bond—(b)—R. L. GREENE PAPER CO., Providence, R. I.
Glendale Bristol — (b) — R. L. GREENE PAPER CO., Providence, R. I.
Glendale Mills — (b) — toilet—SCOTT PAPER CO., Philadelphia.
Glendeane—(b)—white bristol—J. C. PARKER PAPER CO., Louisville, Ky.
Glendon Bond — (w) — HAMMERMILL PAPER CO., Erie, Pa.
Glendora Mills—(w)—C. P. LESH PAPER CO., Indianapolis, Ind.
Gleneida Mills—J. E. LINDE PAPER CO., New York.
Glengarry—(w)—LOUISVILLE PAPER CO., Louisville, Ky.
Glenhurst—(w)—writings — UNION CARD AND PAPER CO., New York.
Glen Mills — (b) — toilet — G. W THOMPSON, New York.
Glen Mills—(b)—white writing—W. H. CLAFLIN & CO., Boston.
Glenmere Linen—(w)—MILLER & WRIGHT PAPER CO., New York.
Glenraven—(b)—book—LOUISVILLE PAPER CO., Louisville, Ky.
Glenrose—(b)—poster—GRAHAM PAPER CO., St. Louis.
Glenwood Superfine—(b)—writing—GRAHAM PAPER CO., St. Louis.
Glenwood—(b)—book — MISSOURI PAPER HOUSE, Kansas City, Mo.
Glenwood—(b)—toilet—UNITED STATES ENVELOPE CO. (Morgan Envelope Co. Div.), Springfield, Mass.
Glenwood—(b)—STATE JOURNAL CO., Lincoln, Neb.
Glenwood—(b)—THOMAS W. PRICE CO., Philadelphia.
Glenwood—(b)—bristol and onion skin—JUDD PAPER CO., Holyoke, Mass.
Glenwood—(b)—bristol onion skin—JUDD PAPER CO., Holyoke, Mass.
Glenwood Avenue —(b)— toilet—SCOTT PAPER CO., Philadelphia.
Glenwood Bond—(w)—JUDD PAPER CO., Holyoke, Mass.
Glenwood—(b)—bristol—JUDD PAPER CO., Holyoke, Mass.

Glenwood Superfine —(w)—GRAHAM PAPER CO., St. Louis.
Glenwood Superfine — (b) — McCLELLAN PAPER CO., Minneapolis.
Globe—(b)—cardboards and cards—GRAHAM PAPER CO., St. Louis.
Globe Blanks—(b)—KINGSLEY PAPER CO., Cleveland, Ohio.
Globe Bond — (w) — CINCINNATI CORDAGE AND PAPER CO., Cincinnati, Ohio.
Globe Bond—(w)—SWIGART PAPER CO., Chicago.
Globe Bristol—(b)—TROY PAPER CO., Troy, N. Y.
Globe Index Bristol—(b)—WILKINSON BROS. & CO., INC., Philadelphia.
Globe Linen Bond—(w)—BRYANT PAPER CO., Kalamazoo, Mich.
Globe Linen Fabric—(w)—AMERICAN WRITING PAPER CO., Holyoke.
Globe Linen Ledger—(w)—BOORUM & PEASE CO., New York.
Gloria — (b) — cover — KNOWLTON BROS., Watertown, N. Y.
Gloria—(b)—M. F.—C. S. PROCTOR PAPER CO., Boston.
Gloria—(b)—S. S. & C.—C. S. PROCTOR PAPER CO., Boston.
Gloria Antique Laid—(b)—C. S. PROCTOR PAPER CO., Boston.
Gloria Bond—(w)—AMERICAN WRITING PAPER CO., Holyoke, Mass.
Gloria Linen U. S. A.—(w)—typewriter—EATON, CRANE & PIKE CO., Pittsfield, Mass.
Glorious—(b)—toilet tissue—W. H. CLAFLIN & CO., Boston.
Gloucester Ledger—(w)—HY. LINDENMEYR & SONS, New York.
Gobelin—(b)—cover—SEYMOUR CO., New York.
Gold Bond—(w)—BASSETT & SUTPHIN, New York.
Gold Bond—(w)—SUTPHIN PAPER CO., INC., New York.
Gold Medal—(b)—toilet tissue—W. H. CLAFLIN & CO., Boston.
Gold Medal Superfine Writing—(w)—BAY STATE PAPER CO., Boston.
"Golden"—(b)—SCRANTOM WETMORE & COMPANY, Rochester, N. Y.
Golden Gate—(w and b)—writing—CUNNINGHAM, CURTISS & WELCH, Oakland, Cal.
Golden Gate—(b)—CROWN COLUMBIA PAPER CO., San Francisco.
Golden Glow—(b)—COLUMBIA PAPER BAG CO., New York.
Golden Rod Straw—(b)—wrapping—GRAHAM PAPER CO., St. Louis.
Gold Leaf—(b)—wrapping—W. H. FOX & SON, Penn Yan, N. Y.
Gold Mailing—(b)—mailing and cover—GRAHAM PAPER CO., St. Louis.
Gold Medal—(b)—half tone—MINNEAPOLIS PAPER CO., Minneapolis.

FELTS AND JACKETS | Appleton Woolen Mills
APPLETON - - WIS.

Watermarks and Brands

Gold Medal Bond—(w)—NEW YORK & NEW JERSEY PAPER CO., New Brunswick, N. J.
Gold Medal Linen—SAUGERTIES MFG. CO., Saugerties, N. Y.
Gold Medal Superfine—(w)—flat writing—WHITAKER PAPER CO., Cincinnati, Ohio, and BAY STATE PAPER CO., Boston.
Gold Seal—(b)—onion skin—MINNEAPOLIS PAPER CO., Minneapolis, Minn.
Gold Seal Envelope—(b)—A. STORRS & BEMENT CO., Boston.
Gold Standard—(b)—S. S. and C. book—SOUTHERN PAPER CO., Richmond, Va.
Goodenuf—(b)—toilet—GEO. T. JOHNSON CO., Boston.
Gopher Bond—(w)—MINNEAPOLIS PAPER CO., Minneapolis, Minn.
Gopher Flats—(b)—McCLELLAN PAPER CO., Minneapolis, Minn.
Gordon—(b)—news—GRAHAM PAPER CO., St. Louis.
Gordon—(b)—toilet—NORTHERN PAPER MILLS, Green Bay, Wis.
Goshen Linen—(b)—CONROW BROTHERS, New York.
Goalin's—(b)—toilet—UNITED STATES ENVELOPE CO. (Morgan Envelope Co. Div.), Springfield, Mass.
Gossamer Typewriting Paper—(b)—BRADNER SMITH & CO., Chicago.
Gotham Bond—(w)—KEITH PAPER CO., Turners Falls, Mass.
Gotham Vellum—(w)—wedding—ALLAN & GRAY, New York.
Gothic—(b)—drafting manila—HENRY LINDENMEYR & SONS, New York.
Gothic Fine—(b)—NEENAH PAPER CO., Neenah, Wis.
Gothic—(b)—tinted lines and pasted bristols—PAPER MILLS CO., Chicago.
Gothic Linen—(w and b)—cover—THE PAPER MILLS CO., Chicago.
Government Bond—(w)—AMERICAN WRITING PAPER CO., Holyoke.
Government Bond—(w)—COOK-VIVIAN CO., Boston.
Government Cover—(b)—GRAHAM PAPER CO., St. Louis.
Government Linen—(w)—AMERICAN WRITING PAPER CO., Holyoke.
Government Map Bond—(b)—F. A. FLINN, INC., New York.
Government Parchment Bond—(w)—NEW YORK & NEW JERSEY PAPER CO., New Brunswick, N. J.
Government Post Card—(b)—cardboard and tag—GRAHAM PAPER CO., St. Louis.
Government Record Ledger—(w)—AMERICAN WRITING PAPER CO., Holyoke, Mass.
Government Wove—(w)—writing—T. C. ALLEN & CO., Halifax, N. S.

Grafton—(b)—blue wove—MILLER & WRIGHT PAPER CO., New York.
Grafton—(b)—ALBANY PERFORATED WRAPPING PAPER CO., Albany, N. Y.
Grafton Colored Wove—(b)—MILLER & WRIGHT PAPER CO., INC., New York.
Graham's Extra Dry—(b)—tarred felt—GRAHAM PAPER CO., St. Louis.
Graham's Linen—(b)—cover—GRAHAM PAPER CO., St. Louis.
Grailstone Linen Ledger—(w)—CARTER, RICE & CO., CORP., Boston.
Gramercy—(b)—MILLER & WRIGHT PAPER CO., New York.
Grampion Wove—(b)—EATON, CRANE & PIKE CO., Pittsfield, Mass.
Granada—(b)—cover—CHATFIELD & WOODS CO., Cincinnati, Ohio.
Granada—(b)—KNOWLTON BROS., Watertown, N. Y.
Grand Circle—(b)—toilet—SCOTT PAPER CO., Philadelphia.
Grand Duchess Old Style Vellum—(b)—R. P. ANDREWS PAPER CO., Washington, D. C.
Grand Duke—(b)—toilet—SCOTT PAPER CO., Philadelphia.
Grand Quadrille—(w)—GEO. B. HURD & CO., New York.
Grand Rapids—(w)—bond—DWIGHT BROS. PAPER CO., Grand Rapids, Mich.
Granilite Wedding—(b)—HENRY LINDENMEYR & SONS, New York.
Granite—(b)—bag, carpet lining—GRAHAM PAPER CO., St. Louis.
Granite State Bond—(w)—C. P. LESH PAPER CO., Indianapolis, Ind.
Grant Tag—(b)—BEECHER, PECK & LEWIS, Detroit, Mich.
Granville Bond—(w)—T. C. ALLEN & CO., Halifax, N. S.
Graphic—(b)—cover—PENINSULAR PAPER CO., Ypsilanti, Mich.
Graphic Ledger—(w)—W. E. WROE & CO., Chicago.
Graphite—(b)—friction boards—INGALLS & CO., Castleton, N. Y.
Gray White Wedding Bristol—(b)—STRATHMORE PAPER CO., Mittineague, Mass.
Graylawn—(w)—GEO. B. HURD & CO., New York.
Greater New York Bristol—(b)—W. G. WILLMANN, New York.
Great West Bond—(w)—BARBER-ELLIS, LTD., Toronto, Can.
Grecian—(b)—cover—SEYMOUR CO., New York.
Grecian Antique—(w)—Z. & W. M. CRANE, Dalton, Mass.
Grecian Bond—(w)—WHITING PAPER CO., Holyoke, Mass.
Grecian Wove—(b)—EATON, CRANE & PIKE CO., Pittsfield, Mass.

BLOTTING PAPERS "STANDARD," "IMPERIAL," "STERLING" Royal Worcester and Defender Enameled
STANDARD PAPER MFG. CO., - - Richmond, Va.

INVESTIGATIONS REPORTS INSPECTIONS
C. A. CHAPMAN, Inc.
25 E. JACKSON BLVD. ENGINEERS CHICAGO

Watermarks and Brands 673

Greeley—(b)—bristol—STANDARD CARD & PAPER CO., New York.
Green Band Fibre—(b)—YORK HAVEN PAPER CO., York Haven, Pa.
Greenock—(b)—coated blotting—EATON-DIKEMAN CO., Lee, Mass.
Greenock—(b)—wedding and bristol—MOUNTAIN MILL PAPER CO., Lee, Mass.
Greenock Linen Ledger — (w) — HARPER PAPER CO., New York.
Greenock Linen Ledger—(w)—MOUNTAIN MILL PAPER CO., Lee, Mass.
Greenwich Fine—(w)—CROCKER-McELWAIN CO., Holyoke, Mass.
Greenwood—(b)—flat—F. W. ANDERSON & CO., New York.
Greenwood Mills—(w)—ledger—MOUNTAIN MILL PAPER CO., Lee, Mass.
Grenada—(b)—toilet—ALBANY PERFORATED WRAPPING PAPER CO., Albany, N. Y.
Grenada Linen Ledger — (w) — AMERICAN WRITING PAPER CO., Holyoke, Mass.
Grenada Mills—(b)—white flat—J. C. PARKER PAPER CO., Louisville.
Grenadier —(b)— toilet — ALBANY PERFORATED WRAPPING PAPER CO., Albany, N. Y.
Grey Lawn—(b)—Z. & W. M. CRANE, Dalton, Mass.
Greylock—(b)—tissue—SMITH PAPER CO., Lee, Mass.
Greylock Linen Ledger—(w)—L. L. BROWN PAPER CO., Adams, Mass.
Greystone—(b)—carpet lining—GRAHAM PAPER CO., St. Louis.
Grinnell —(b)— catalog — GRAHAM PAPER CO., St. Louis.
Grolier—(w)—book—MILLER & WRIGHT PAPER CO., New York.
Gros Grain—(b)— cover — STRATHMORE PAPER CO., Mittineague, Mass.
Ground Arms Bond—(w and b)—writing, bond, ledger—NEENAH PAPER CO., Neenah, Wis.
Ground Arms Ledger—(w)—NEENAH PAPER CO., Neenah, Wis.
Grover Bond—(w)—A. GROVER, New York.
Guam—(b)—toilet—ALBANY PERFORATED WRAPPING PAPER CO., Albany, N. Y.
Guarantee Bond—(w)—DWIGHT BROTHERS PAPER CO., Chicago.
Guaranty Bond—(w)—MILLER & WRIGHT PAPER CO., New York.
Gudenuff Blotting—(b)—MERRIAM PAPER CO., New York.
Gudstok—(b)—toilet—SCOTT PAPER CO., Philadelphia.
Gulliver—(b)—toilet—H. NORWOOD EWING CO., New York.

Gurdian Bond—(w)—LEWERTH & CULBERTHSON, New York.
Gurney's Star Security—(b)—colored writing—CONROW BROS., New York.
Gypsy—(b) — toilet — LOUISVILLE PAPER CO., Louisville, Ky.

H

"H" Manila—(b)—ORONO PULP & PAPER CO., Orono, Me.
H. and W.—(b)—HOLLINGSWORTH & WHITNEY CO., Boston.
Halbert Band—(w)—GENERAL PAPER CO., New York.
Half Moon—(b)—manila—E. B. EDDY CO., Hull, Canada.
Half Tone Enamel—(b)—KANSAS CITY PAPER CO., Kansas City, Mo.
Half Tone Superfine—(w)—W. E. WROE & CO., Chicago.
Half Tone Super Number Forty-Nine—(b)—PAUL E. VERNON & CO., New York.
Half Tone Writing—MOSER PAPER CO., Chicago.
Halifax Bond—(w)—BRADNER SMITH & CO., Chicago.
Hallbrooke Linen—(b)—EATON, CRANE & PIKE CO., Pittsfield, Mass.
Halpine Linen—(b)—EATON, CRANE & PIKE CO., Pittsfield, Mass.
Hamasote — (b) — AGOSATE MILLBOARD CO., Trenton, N. J.
Hamburg Mills—(b)—grease proof parchment—W. H. CLAFLIN & CO., Boston.
Hamburg Onion Skin—(b)—WHITING-PATTERSON CO., Philadelphia.
Hamilton Bond — (w) — HAMILTON CARD & PAPER HOUSE, INC., New York.
Hamilton Mills — (b) — AMERICAN NEWS CO., New York.
Hammermill—(w)— ledger — writing and superfine—HAMMERMILL PAPER CO., Erie, Pa.
Hammermill Bond — (w) — HAMMERMILL PAPER CO., Erie Pa.
Hammett's Bond—(w)—J. L. HAMMETT CO., Boston.
Hammett's Crown Regent—(w)—J. L. HAMMETT CO., Boston.
Hammett's Linen Ledger—(w)—J. L. HAMMETT CO., Boston.
Hammett's Standard—(w)—J. L. HAMMETT CO., Boston.
Hampden—(b)— cover — AMERICAN WRITING PAPER CO., Holyoke, Mass.
Hamper Linen Ledger—(w)—LESLIE-DONAHOWER CO., St. Paul.
Hampshire—(b)—bristol—BAY STATE PAPER CO., Boston.
Hampton Court Superfine — (w) — CROCKER-McELWAIN CO., Holyoke.
Hampton Mills—(w)—CINCINNATI CORDAGE AND PAPER CO., Cincinnati, Ohio.

APPLETON MACHINE CO.
APPLETON, WIS.
REFINING ENGINES,
SCREENS, SAWING & SPLITTING MACHINERY
HIGH GRADE **CENTRIFUGAL PUMPS**

MINER EDGAR CO., Sole Agents
KEYSTONE CLAY & REDUCTION CO.
30 Church Street - - New York

CLAY

PRECIPITATED REFINED
LIGHT GRAVITY SOFT TEXTURE
<K L M>
HIGH NATURAL COLOR, HIGH RETENTION

FELTS AND JACKETS | Appleton Woolen Mills, APPLETON - - WIS.

Watermarks and Brands

Hampton Roads—(w)—No. 1 fine—OLD DOMINION PAPER CO., Norfolk, Va.
Hancock—(b) — dull finish coated book—STONE & ANDREW, Boston.
Hand Craft Cover—(b)—A. STORRS & BEMENT CO., Boston.
Hand Made—(w)—GEO B. HURD & CO., New York.
Handspun Linen — (w)—MARCUS WARD CO., Brooklyn, N. Y.
Hanover — (b)—writing—GRAHAM PAPER CO., St. Louis.
Hanover—(b)— Kraft — WHITING-PATTERSON CO., Philadelphia.
Hanover Blank—(b)—C. S. PROCTOR PAPER CO., Boston
Hanover Duplex — (b) — envelope — WHITING-PATTERSON CO., Philadelphia.
Hanover Embossing Cover — MACK-ELLIOTT PAPER CO., St. Louis.
Hanover Mills — (w) — writing—WHITAKER PAPER CO., Cincinnati, Ohio, and BAY STATE PAPER CO., Boston.
Hanover Superfine—(w)—flat writing—THE PETERS PAPER CO., Denver, Col.
Hanover Tag — (b)—TILESTON & LIVERMORE, Boston.
Hanover Wove and Laid—(b)—envelope—WHITING-PATTERSON CO., Philadelphia.
Hapaco—(w)—bond—HAGEN PAPER CO., St. Louis.
Harco—(b)—writing—HARPER PAPER CO., New York.
Harcourt Bond—(w)—HARCOURT & CO., Louisville, Ky.
Harcourt's Queens Lawn—(w)—HARCOURT & CO., Louisville, Ky.
Hard Pan Bond — (b)—CARTER, RICE & CO., CORP., Boston.
Harding Linen Record-Ledger—(w)—AMERICAN WRITING PAPER CO., Holyoke, Mass.
Harding Paper Co., Superfine—(w)—AMERICAN WRITING PAPER CO., Holyoke, Mass.
Hare Express — (b)—wrapping—GRAHAM PAPER CO., St. Louis.
Harlem — (b)— writing—GRAHAM PAPER CO., St. Louis.
Harlem Bristol—(b)—B. F. BOND PAPER CO., Baltimore.
Harlem Wedding Bristol — (b) — HARLEM CARD & PAPER CO., New York.
Harmony Mills — (b) — toilet—UNITED STATES ENVELOPE CO., (Morgan Envelope Co. Division), Springfield, Mass.
Harrison Mills — (b)—RAYNOR & PERKINS ENVELOPE CO., N. Y.
Harrison —(b)— writing — HARPER PAPER CO., New York.
Hartford—(b)—CHATFIELD & WOODS CO., Cincinnati, Ohio.

Hartford Fire Ins. Co.—(w)—writing—HARTFORD FIRE INSURANCE CO., Hartford, Conn.
Harvard — (b)—catalog—GRAHAM PAPER CO., St. Louis.
Harvard—(b)—card board — MISSOURI PAPER HOUSE, Kansas City.
Harvard—(b)—book—JOHN CARTER & CO., Boston.
Harvard Bond—(w) — DONALDSON PAPER CO., Harrisburg, Pa.
Harvard Linen — (w)—AETNA PAPER CO., Dayton, Ohio.
Harvard Linen—(w) — PLYMOUTH PAPER CO., Holyoke, Mass.
Harvard Linen—(w and b)—JORDAN MARSH & CO., Boston.
Harvard Super — (w)—WHITAKER PAPER CO., Cincinnati, Ohio.
Harvard Tag—(b)—THE UNION PAPER & TWINE CO., Detroit, Mich.
Harvard Translucent—(b)—COOK-VIVIAN, Boston.
Harvest Mills — (b)—white wove—KINGSLEY PAPER CO., Cleveland.
Harwood—(b)— writing — HARPER PAPER CO., New York.
Harwood Bristol—(b)—B. F. BOND PAPER CO., Baltimore.
Hasbrook —(b)—writing — HARPER PAPER CO., New York.
Havana — (b) — manila writing — WHITING-PATTERSON CO., Philadelphia.
Havana Bond — (b)—CLEMENTS PAPER CO., Nashville, Tenn.
Havana — (b) — manila writing — WHITING-PATTERSON CO., Philadelphia.
Haviland — (b) — book—GRAHAM PAPER CO., St. Louis.
Havilock—(w)—DEARBORN PAPER CO., Chicago.
Havorole — (b)—toilet—SCOTT PAPER CO., Philadelphia.
Hawkeye—(b)—toilet — NORTHERN PAPER MILLS, Green Bay, Wis.
Hawkeye Bond — (w)—WESTERN PAPER CO., Omaha, Neb.
Hawkeye Bond—(b) — HAMMER-MILL PAPER CO., Erie, Pa.
Hawkeye Rag — (b)—wrapping—GRAHAM PAPER CO., St. Louis.
Hawthorne — (b) — book — LOUISVILLE PAPER CO., Louisville, Ky.
Hawthorne — (w) — AMERICAN WRITING PAPER CO., Holyoke.
Hawthorne—(w)—parchment bond—DWIGHT BROS. PAPER CO., Grand Rapids, Mich.
Hawthorne Linen Ledger—(w)—W. G. WILLMANN, New York.
Hawthorne Print — (b)—McCLELLAN PAPER CO., Minneapolis, Minn.
Hazel Blanks—(b)—C. P. LESH PAPER CO., Indianapolis, Ind.
Hazelhurst—(b)—book — GRAHAM PAPER CO., St. Louis.
Hazelton—(w)—PLYMOUTH PAPER CO., Holyoke, Mass.

JAMES H. HARRISON PULPSTONE MANUFACTURER | **GENUINE NEWCASTLE STONES** 18 Kittowen St., GATES-ON-TYNE, ENG.

NEW MILLS DESIGNED   POWER PLANTS   OLD MILLS REBUILT
C. A. CHAPMAN, Inc.
28 E. JACKSON BLVD.   ENGINEERS   CHICAGO

Watermarks and Brands — 675

Headlight—(w and b) — writings—THE PAPER MILLS CO., Chicago.
Heart of Trade Bond—(w)—INDIANA PAPER CO., Indianapolis.
Hearthside Linen — (b)—EATON, CRANE & PIKE CO., Pittsfield, Mass.
Heath—(b) — bristol—TILESTON & LIVERMORE, Boston.
Heather Bond — (b) — EATON, CRANE & PIKE CO., Pittsfield, Mass.
Heather Bond—(b)—HARPER PAPER CO., New York.
Heather Linen — (b) — EATON, CRANE & PIKE CO., Pittsfield, Mass.
Hebron—(b) — ALBANY PERFORATED WRAPPING PAPER CO., Albany, New York.
Hector Manila — (b) — wrapping—VON OLKER-SNELL PAPER CO., Boston.
Hector Offset—(b)—CLARKE & CO., New York.
Heilgar Linen — (b) — EATON, CRANE & PIKE CO., Pittsfield, Mass.
Hekla Flats — (b) — HY. LINDENMEYR & SONS, New York.
Helena—(b)—bond — GRAHAM PAPER CO., St. Louis.
Helios—(b)—drawing — KEUFFEL & ESSER CO., New York.
Heliotrope — (b) — toilet—W. A. STOWE PAPER CO., Grand Rapids, Mich.
Helmar Bristol — (b) — HARLEM CARD & PAPER CO., New York.
Helmet—(b) — cover—LOUISVILLE PAPER CO., Louisville, Ky.
Hel-Tela—(b)—wrapping—JAMES P. HEFFERNAN PAPER CO., New York.
Hemlock—(b)—wrapping—GRAHAM PAPER CO., St. Louis.
Hennepin Blanks — (b)—McCLELLAN PAPER CO., Minneapolis, Minn.
Herald—(b) — English Finish—THE PAPER MILLS CO., Chicago.
Herald Bond — (b) — writings and envelopes—THE PAPER MILLS CO., Chicago.
Herald Book—(w)—TAYLOR-LOGAN CO. PAPERMAKERS, Holyoke, Mass.
Herald Covers — (b)—ADVERTISERS' PAPER MILLS, Holyoke.
Herald M. F.—(b) — THE PAPER MILLS CO., Chicago.
Herald Text — (w)—book—ADVERTISERS' PAPER MILLS, Holyoke.
Herald Wedding — (b) — bristol, blanks and cards — THE PAPER MILLS CO., Chicago.
Heraldic Drawing—(b)—HENRY LINDENMEYR & SONS, New York.
Herbertshire—(b) — white ivory—CONROW BROS., New York.
Herculean —(b)—cover—AMERICAN WRITING PAPER CO., Holyoke.
Hercules—(b) — document manila—BRADNER SMITH & CO., Chicago.

Hercules — (b)—jute and writing manila—CHEMICAL PAPER MFG. CO., Holyoke, Mass.
Hercules—(b)—rope manila — JOHN CARTER & CO., Boston.
Hercules—(b)—wrapping — STONE & FORSYTH CO., Boston.
Hercules Blanks — (b)—DIEM & WING PAPER CO., Cincinnati, Ohio.
Hercules Bond—(w)—BARBER-ELLIS, LTD, Toronto, Can.
Hercules Bond—(w and b)—wrappings, bonds and specialties—McDOWELL PAPER MILLS, Manayunk, Pa.
Hercules Bond—(w)—FOX RIVER PAPER CO., Appleton, Wis.
Hercules Bristol—(b)—W. G. WILLMANN, New York.
Hercules Cover—(b)—HY. LINDENMEYR & SONS, New York.
Hercules Die Wiping — (b) — GRAHAM PAPER CO., St. Louis.
Hercules Embossing—(b)—cover—CHATFIELD & WOODS CO., Cincinnati, Ohio.
Hercules Fibre—(w)—wrapping and bond—McDOWELL PAPER MILLS, Manayunk, Philadelphia.
Hercules Fibre—(w and b)—wrappings, bonds and specialties — McDOWELL PAPER MILLS, Manayunk, Philadelphia.
Hercules Glassine —(b)— McDOWELL PAPER MILLS, Philadelphia.
Hercules Ledger — (w) — CHATFIELD & WOODS CO., Cincinnati.
Hercules Linen — (w)—MERRIAM PAPER CO., New York.
Hercules Linen—(w)—THE UNION PAPER & TWINE CO., Detroit, Mich.
Hercules Linen — (w)—ST. LOUIS PAPER CO., St. Louis.
Hercules Linen Record — (w)—CHATFIELD & WOODS CO., Cincinnati, Ohio.
Hercules Manila — (b) — tympan)—LOUISVILLE PAPER CO., Louisville, Ky.
Hercules Mills—(w and b)—wrappings, bonds and specialties — McDOWELL PAPER MILLS, Manayunk, Philadelphia.
Hercules Rope Manila — (b) — JOHN CARTER & CO., INC., Boston.
Hercules Tag—(b)—HUDSON VALLEY PAPER CO., Albany, N. Y.
Hercules Tag Board—(b)—OSBORN PAPER CO., Philadelphia.
Hercules Tough Check — (b) — KINGSLEY PAPER CO., Cleveland, Ohio.
Hercules Tracing — (b) — McDOWELL PAPER MILLS, Philadelphia.
Hercules Typewriter — (w)—McDOWELL PAPER MILLS, Manayunk, Philadelphia.
Hercules Wrappings — (b) —wrapping specialties—McDOWELL PAPER MILLS, Manayunk, Philadelphia.

APPLETON MACHINE CO., APPLETON, WIS.
REFINING ENGINES, SCREENS, SAWING & SPLITTING MACHINERY
HIGH GRADE CENTRIFUGAL PUMPS

MINER EDGAR CO., Sole Agents   WASHED <E W>   GRITLESS <C M>

FELTS AND JACKETS | Appleton Woolen Mills APPLETON - - WIS.

Watermarks and Brands

Hercules Wrappings — (w)—wrapping and bond—McDOWELL PAPER MILLS, Manayunk, Philadelphia.
Heritage Bond—(w) — WHITAKER PAPER CO., Cincinnati, Ohio, and BAY STATE PAPER CO., Boston.
Hermanos — (b) — writing — W. M. PRINGLE & CO., INC., New York.
Hermes Book—(b)—CLARKE & CO., New York.
Hermes Coated Ledger—(b)—HY. LINDENMEYR & SONS, New York.
Hermit—(w)—POWER PAPER COMPANY, Springfield, Mass.
Hero—(b)—blank—JOHN CARTER & CO., Boston.
Hero—(b)—blanks—CHATFIELD & WOODS CO., Cincinnati, Ohio.
Herring Bone—(w and b)—GEO. B. HURD & CO., New York.
Herringbone Kraft — (b) — MISSOURI PAPER HOUSE, Kansas City, Mo.
Hetchfield Flax — (b) — EATON, CRANE & PIKE CO., Pittsfield, Mass.
Heveetowl—(w)—UNITED STATES PAPER MILLS, INC., Chambersburg, Pa.
Hiawatha—(b)—S. & S. C. colored book—JAMES WHITE PAPER CO., Chicago.
Hiawatha Bond—(w)—HAMILTON CARD & PAPER HOUSE, INC., New York.
Hibulk—(b)—book—WEST VIRGINIA PULP & PAPER CO., New York.
Hickory — (b)—tag — JUDD PAPER CO., Holyoke.
Hickory—(b) — tag board — LOUISVILLE PAPER CO., Louisville, Ky.
Hickory—(b)—fibre—KANSAS CITY PAPER HOUSE, Kansas City, Mo.
Hickory—(b)—kraft—GRAHAM PAPER CO., St. Louis.
Hickory Bond—(w) — AMERICAN WRITING PAPER CO., Holyoke.
Hickory Fibre —(b)— wrapping — WILKINSON BROS. & CO., INC., Philadelphia.
Hickory Fibre — (b) — wrapping — LOUISVILLE PAPER CO., Louisville, Ky.
Hickory Ledger—(w) —AMERICAN WRITING PAPER CO., Holyoke.
High Art, H. F.—(b)—CHATFIELD & WOODS CO., Cincinnati, Ohio.
High Art Book—(b)—A. STORRS & BEMENT CO., Boston.
High Grade — (b)—roofing—M. J. EARL, Reading, Pa.
High Grade — (w)—SAUGERTIES MFG. CO., Saugerties, N. Y.
Highland—(b)—blotting— THE ALLING & CORY CO., Rochester, N. Y.
Highland—(b)—cardboard and cards —GRAHAM PAPER CO., St. Louis.
Highland—(w)—fine—JUDD PAPER CO., Holyoke, Mass.
Highland Blotting—(b)—THE ALLING & CORY CO., Rochester, N. Y.

Highland Ledger—(b) — GRAHAM PAPER CO., St. Louis.
Highland Linen — (b)—hand made style—EATON, CRANE & PIKE CO., Pittsfield, Mass.
Highland Linen—(b)—JUDD PAPER CO., Holyoke, Mass.
Highland Linen Bond — (w)— EATON, CRANE & PIKE CO., Pittsfield, Mass.
Highland Linen Parchment—(w) —EATON, CRANE & PIKE CO., Pittsfield, Mass.
Highland Linen—(b)—JUDD PAPER CO., Holyoke, Mass.
Highland Mills—(b)—fine — JUDD PAPER CO., Holyoke, Mass.
Highlight—(b) — cover—PENINSULAR PAPER CO., Ypsilanti, Mich.
Highlight—(w and b)—bond, writing and cover—THE PAPER MILLS CO., Chicago.
High White—(b)—coated book—THE PAPER MILLS CO., Chicago.
Hi-grade Mimeograph—RICHMOND PAPER CO.; Richmond, Va.
Hillcrest Bond—(w)—BERKSHIRE HILLS PAPER CO., Adams, Mass.
Hillcrest Ledger — (w) — BERKSHIRE HILLS PAPER CO., Adams, Mass.
Hillcrest Linen—(w)—BERKSHIRE HILLS PAPER CO., Adams, Mass.
Hillcrest Superfine — (w)—C. S. PROCTOR PAPER CO., Boston.
Hillsborough Booklet — (w) — WORTHY PAPER CO., Mittineague, Mass.
Hindo India Tint — (b)—book— BRADNER SMITH & CO., Chicago.
Hindoo—(b)—fibre— MINNEAPOLIS PAPER CO., Minneapolis, Minn.
Hindoo Onion Skin—(b)—OSBORN PAPER CO., Philadelphia.
Historical Bond — (w)—HAMMERMILL PAPER CO., Erie, Pa.
"H. L."—(b)—HY. LINDENMEYR & SONS, New York.
H. L. Litho.—(b)—HY. LINDENMEYR & SONS, New York.
H. L. & S. Coated Book—(b)—HY. LINDENMEYR & SONS, New York.
H. L. & S. Best Rope Tag—(b)— HY. LINDENMEYR & SONS, New York.
Hoffman — (b)—toilet—NORTHERN PAPER MILLS, Green Bay, Wis.
Holdfast—(b)—kraft—GRAHAM PAPER CO., St. Louis.
Holland Bond —(w)—HAMPSHIRE PAPER CO., South Hadley Falls, Mass.
Holland Bond — (w) — HAMILTON CARD & PAPER HOUSE, INC., New York.
Holland Fibre — (w)—WHITE & WYCKOFF MFG. CO., Holyoke, Mass
Holland Linen — (w) — GEO. B. HURD & CO., New York.

BLOTTING PAPERS STANDARD PAPER MFG. CO., Richmond, Va

Watermarks and Brands

Holland Linen — (w) — SWIGART PAPER CO., Chicago.
Holland Linen—(b)—toilet — NORTHERN PAPER MILLS, Green Bay, Wis.
Holland Linen Bond—(w and b)—GEO B. HURD & CO., New York.
Holland Linen Ledger — (w)—CAREW MANUFACTURING CO., South Hadley Falls, Mass.
Holland Text — (w)—McCLELLAN PAPER CO., Minneapolis, Minn.
Holly—(b) — writing—GRAHAM PAPER CO., St. Louis.
Hollywood—(b)—vegetable parchment —LOUISVILLE PAPER CO., Louisville, Pa.
Hollywood—(b)—blotting—A L B EMARLE PAPER MANUFACTURING CO., Richmond, Va.
Holyoke—(b)—cardboards and cards —GRAHAM PAPER CO., St. Louis.
Holyoke—(w) — white wove flats—MINNEAPOLIS PAPER CO., Minneapolis, Minn.
Holyoke Bond—(b)—OLD DOMINION PAPER CO., Norfolk, Va.
Holyoke Covers—(b)—ADVERTISERS' PAPER MILLS, Holyoke.
Holyoke Document—(b)—jute manila—CHEMICAL PAPER MFG. CO., Holyoke, Mass.
Holyoke Index Bristol — (b)—KINGSLEY PAPER CO., Cleveland, O.
Holyoke Linen Bond—(w) — TAYLOR-LOGAN CO., Papermakers, Holyoke, Mass.
Holyoke Linen Ledger — (w)—NATIONAL BLANK BOOK CO., Holyoke, Mass.
Holyoke Paper Co.—(w)—AMERICAN WRITING PAPER CO., Holyoke.
Holyoke Paper Co.'s Ledger—(w) —AMERICAN WRITING PAPER CO., Holyoke, Mass.
Holyoke Record—NATIONAL BOOK CO., Holyoke, Mass.
Holyoke Superfine Linen — (w)—TAYLOR-LOGAN CO., Papermakers, Holyoke, Mass.
Holyoke Superfine Vellum—(w)—TAYLOR-LOGAN CO., Papermakers, Holyoke, Mass.
Holyoke Text—(w)—book —ADVERTISERS' PAPER MILLS, Holyoke.
Homebound—(b)—wax paper—GRAHAM PAPER CO., St. Louis.
Home-Made Linen—(b)—BASSETT & SUTPHIN, New York.
Homer—(b)—bond—GRAHAM PAPER CO., St. Louis.
Homespun—(b)—bristol board—DONALDSON PAPER CO., Harrisburg, Pa.
Homespun—(b)—cover — NIAGARA PAPER MILLS, Lockport, N. Y.
Homespun Fabric—(b)—GEO. B. HURD & CO., New York.
Homespun Linen—(w)—HAMMERMILL PAPER CO., Erie, Pa.
Homestead—(b)—toilet—NORTHERN PAPER MILLS, Green Bay, Wis.
Homestead—(b)—railroad writing—GRAHAM PAPER CO., St. Louis.
Homuse—(b)—toilet—SCOTT PAPER CO., Philadelphia.
Honest Count—(b)—roll toilet—JEROME PAPER CO., New York.
Honest Linen — (w) — AMERICAN WRITING PAPER CO., Holyoke, Mass.
Honor — (w) — bond — ELSINOR PAPER CO., New York.
Hoosac Bond — (w) — BERKSHIRE HILLS PAPER CO., Adams, Mass.
Hoosac Ledger—(w)—BERKSHIRE HILLS PAPER CO., Adams, Mass.
Hoosac Linen —(w)— BERKSHIRE HILLS PAPER CO., Adams, Mass.
Hoosick—(b)—toilet—ALBANY PERFORATED WRAPPING PAPER CO., Albany, N. Y.
Hope—(b)—J. C. HALL CO., Providence, R. I.
Horatius—(b)—toilet—H. NORWOOD EWING CO., New York.
Horicon Mills Superfine—(w)—F. A. FLINN, INC., New York.
Hornet—(b)—gummed—LOUISVILLE PAPER CO., Louisville, Ky.
Hornet—(b)—news—C. P. LESH PAPER CO., Indianapolis, Ind.
Hornet Linen — (w) — AMERICAN WRITING PAPER CO., Holyoke, Mass.
Horseshoe—(b)—toilet—NORTHERN PAPER MILLS, Green Bay, Wis.
Horseshoe Bond—(w)—FOX RIVER PAPER CO., Appleton, Wis.
Horseshoe Bristol—(b)—KINGSLEY PAPER CO., Cleveland, Ohio.
Hot Pressed Vellum—(w)—EATON, CRANE & PIKE CO., Pittsfield, Mass.
Hotel—(b)—toilet—ALBANY PERFORATED WRAPPING PAPER CO., Albany, N. Y.
Hotel — (b) — blotting — BRADNER SMITH & CO., Chicago.
Hotel Special—(b)—toilet—JOHNSTON PAPER CO., Harrisburg, Pa.
Housatonic—(b)—blotting — EATON-DIKEMAN CO., Lee, Mass.
Housatonic—(b)—desk pad—EATON-DIKEMAN CO., Lee, Mass.
Housatonic Bond—(w)—B. D. RISING PAPER CO., Housatonic, Mass.
Housatonic Engravers' Bristol—(b)—pasted bristol—B. D. RISING PAPER CO., Housatonic, Mass.
Housatonic Ledger—(w)—B. D. RISING PAPER CO., Housatonic, Mass.
Housatonic Linen—(w)—B. D. RISING PAPER CO., Housatonic, Mass.
Housatonic Superfine—(w)—B. D. RISING PAPER CO., Housatonic, Mass.
Household—(b)—toilet—SCOTT PAPER CO., Philadelphia.
Houston Toilet Tissue—(b)—HY. LINDENMEYR & SONS, New York.

FELTS AND JACKETS | Appleton Woolen Mills, APPLETON - - WIS.

Watermarks and Brands

Howard—(b)—white wove—F. A. FLINN, INC., New York.
Howard Bond—(w)—HOWARD PAPER CO., Urbana, O.
Howard Ledger—(w)—HOWARD PAPER CO., Urbana, O.
Howard Ledger—(w)—HARLEM CARD & PAPER CO., New York.
Howard Mills—(b)—folded—WORTHY PAPER CO., Mittineague, Mass.
H. P. Suede Offset—(b)—MILLER & WRIGHT PAPER CO., INC., New York.
H. S. P. Board Laid—(w)—HOWARD SMITH PAPER MILLS CO., LTD., Montreal, Can.
H. S. P. Narrow Laid—(w)—HOWARD SMITH PAPER MILLS CO., LTD., Montreal, Can.
Hub—(b)—bristol—JOHN CARTER & CO., Boston.
Hub—(b)—No. 1 manila—W. H. CLAFLIN & CO., Boston.
Hub Blank—(b)—A. STORRS & BEMENT CO., Boston.
Hudson—(b)—BUNTIN, GILLIES & CO., Hamilton, Canada.
Hudson—(b)—cover—WHITAKER PAPER CO. Cincinnati, Ohio, and BAY STATE PAPER CO., Boston.
Hudson—(b)—M. F. book—CHATFIELD & WOODS CO., Cincinnati, O.
Hudson—(b)—toilet—ALBANY PERFORATED WRAPPING PAPER CO., Albany, N. Y.
Hudson Antique Wove—(b)—HUDSON VALLEY PAPER CO., Albany, N. Y.
Hudson Blank—HUDSON VALLEY PAPER CO., Albany, N. Y.
Hudson Bond—(b)—PAUL E. VERNON & CO., New York.
Hudson Bond—(b)—HUDSON VALLEY PAPER CO. Albany, N. Y.
Hudson Bond—(w)—GILBERT PAPER CO., Menasha, Wis
Hudson Bristol—(b)—HUDSON VALLEY PAPER CO, Albany, N. Y.
Hudson Cover—(b)—BAY STATE PAPER CO., Boston.
Hudson Eggshell Book—(b)—HUDSON VALLEY PAPER CO., Albany, N. Y.
Hudson Ledger—(b)—O. H. ANDERSON & CO., New York.
Hudson Mills—J. E. LINDE PAPER CO., New York.
Hudson White—(b)—JERSEY CITY PAPER CO., Jersey City, N. J.
Hudson Writing Manila—(b)—F. A. FLINN, INC., New York.
Hudtraco—(b)—kraft, manila, tissue, book, bond, writing—HUDSON TRADING CO., New York.
Hulda—(b)—white bristol—MEGARGEE BROS., Scranton, Pa.
Humanity First—(w and b)—ledger, writing, bond—NEENAH PAPER CO., Neenah, Wis.

Humboldt—(b)—bond—GRAHAM PAPER CO., St. Louis.
Hammer—(b)—LOUISVILLE PAPER CO., Louisville, Ky.
Humpty Dumpty—(b)—toilet—ALBANY PERFORATED WRAPPING PAPER CO., Albany, N. Y.
Hunter's Red Levant Morocco—(b)—EATON, CRANE & PIKE CO., Pittsfield, Mass.
Huntingdon—(w)—bond and linen—J. C. BLAIR CO., Huntingdon, Pa.
Huntress—(b)—book and label—GRAHAM PAPER CO., St. Louis.
Hurd's Irish Linen—(w)—GEO. B. HURD & CO., New York.
Huron—(b)—CHATFIELD & WOODS CO., Cincinnati, Ohio.
Huron—(b)—plaster board—GRAHAM PAPER CO., St. Louis.
Huron—(b)—toilet—ALBANY PERFORATED WRAPPING PAPER CO., Albany, N. Y.
Huron—(b)—cover—PENINSULAR PAPER CO., Ypsilanti. Mich.
Huron—(b)—flat manila—F. A. FLINN, INC., New York.
Huron Bond—(w)—bond—PENINSULAR PAPER CO., Ypsilanti, Mich.
Huron Book—(b)—KINGSLEY PAPER CO., Cleveland, Ohio.
Huron Bristol—(b)—BEECHER, PECK & LEWIS, Detroit, Mich.
Huron Manila—(b)—F. A. FLINN, INC., New York.
Huron Mills—(b)—EAST HARTFORD MANUFACTURING CO., Burnside, Conn.
Hussar—(b)—toilet—NORTHERN PAPER MILLS, Green Bay, Wis.
Hyde Park—(b)—white M. F. book and super—TILESTON & HOLLINGSWORTH CO., Boston.
Hygienic—(b)—toilet—STONE & FORSYTH CO., Boston.
Hygienic—(b)—PEERLESS MFG. CO., Morristown, Pa.
Hygrade—(b)—translucent—UNION CARD & PAPER CO., New York.
Hypatia Mills—superfine—(w)—JOHN CARTER & CO., Boston.
Hyperion Ledger—(b)—MILLER & WRIGHT PAPER CO., New York.
Hyperion Linen—(w)—MERRIAM PAPER CO., New York.
Hyloplate Post Card—(b)—MINNEAPOLIS PAPER CO., Minneapolis, Minn.
Hytone—(b)—toilet—SCOTT PAPER CO., Philadelphia.

I

I. B. L. (Investors' Bond Letter)—(w)—MILLER & WRIGHT PAPER CO., New York.
Icicle—(b)—coated—LEWERTH & CULBERTSON, New York.

JAMES H. HARRISON
ULPSTONE MANUFACTURER | GENUINE NEWCASTLE STONES
18 Killowen St., GATESHEAD-ON-TYNE, ENG.

Watermarks and Brands

Ideal—(b)—blotting—GRAHAM PAPER CO., St. Louis.
Ideal—(b)—No. 2 white manila—CHATFIELD & WOODS CO., Cincinnati, Ohio.
Ideal Bond—(w)—MOSER PAPER CO., Chicago.
Ideal Bond—(w)—DAVID L. ENGLE, New York.
Ideal Bristol White—RICHMOND PAPER CO., Richmond, Va.
Ideal Flax—(w)—JOHN WANAMAKER, Philadelphia.
Ideal Litho—(b)—coated—WEST VIRGINIA PULP & PAPER CO., New York.
Ideal Mills—(b)—headings—ESSEX PAD AND PAPER CO., Holyoke, Mass.
Ideal S & C—(b)—folder—MINNEAPOLIS PAPER CO., Minneapolis.
Ideal Typewriter Papers—(b)—CARTER, RICE & CO., CORP., Boston.
Ima Heluva Site the Best Paper—THE SEINSHEIMER PAPER CO., Cincinnati, Ohio.
Imperial—(w)—CAREW MFG. CO., South Hadley Falls, Mass.
Imperial—(b)—bristol—R. L. GREENE PAPER CO., Providence.
Imperial—(b)—copying tissue—SMITH PAPER CO., Lee, Mass.
Imperial—(b)—drawing, insulating, cardboard and cards—GRAHAM PAPER CO., St. Louis.
Imperial—(b)—blotting—STANDARD PAPER MANUFACTURING CO., Richmond, Va.
Imperial—(b)—cover—HENRY LINDENMEYR & SONS, New York.
Imperial—(b)—superfine—SOUTHERN PAPER CO., Richmond, Va.
Imperial—(b)—toilet and sheathing—LOUISVILLE PAPER CO., Louisville, Ky.
Imperial—(w)—writing—WHITING PAPER CO., Holyoke, Mass.
Imperial—(b)—enameled book and toilet—CHATFIELD & WOODS CO., Cincinnati, Ohio.
Imperial—(b)—toilet—UNITED STATES ENVELOPE CO., Springfield, Mass.
Imperial—(w)—writing—CAREW MANUFACTURING CO., South Hadley Falls, Mass.
Imperial—(w)—writing—BEECHER, PECK & LEWIS, Detroit, Mich.
Imperial—(b)—colored bristol—MEARGEE BROS., Scranton, Pa.
Imperial Bond—(w)—AMERICAN WRITING PAPER CO., Holyoke, Mass.
Imperial Bond—(w)—COLUMBIA PAPER CO., Victoria, B. C.
Imperial Bristol—(b)—DIEM & WING PAPER CO., Cincinnati, Ohio.
Imperial Bristol—(b)—THE ALLING & CORY CO., Rochester, N. Y.

Imperial Bristol—(b)—R. L. GREENE PAPER CO., Providence, R. I.
Imperial Bristol—(b)—OLD DOMINION PAPER CO., Norfolk, Va.
Imperial Coated—(b)—BEECHER, PECK & LEWIS, Detroit, Mich.
Imperial Fibre—(b)—R. L. GREENE PAPER CO., Providence, R. I.
Imperial Fibre—(b)—wrapping—LOUISVILLE PAPER CO., Louisville, Ky.
Imperial Folding Bristol—(b)—A. STORRS & BEMENT CO., Boston.
Imperial Irish Linen—(w)—RAYNOR & PERKINS ENVELOPE CO., New York.
Imperial Laid—(w)—DILL & COLLINS CO., Philadelphia.
Imperial Ledger—(w)—GEO. B. HURD & CO., New York.
Imperial Linen—(w)—AMERICAN WRITING PAPER CO., Holyoke, Mass.
Imperial Linen—(w)—RAYNOR & PERKINS ENVELOPE CO., N. Y.
Imperial Linen Ledger—(w)—writing—CAREW MANUFACTURING CO., South Hadley Falls, Mass.
Imperial Parchment—(w)—ruled and flat—H. S. CROCKER CO., San Francisco.
Imperial Superfine—(w)—writing—CAREW MANUFACTURING CO., South Hadley Falls, Mass.
Imperial Translucent—(b)—bristol—JOHN CARTER & CO., Boston.
Imperial Treaty Bond—(w)—writing—PARSONS TRADING CO., N. Y.
Imperial Vellum—(b)—EATON, CRANE & PIKE CO., Pittsfield, Mass.
Imperial Vellum—(w)—AMERICAN WRITING PAPER CO., Holyoke, Mass.
Imperial Writing—(w)—HAMMERMILL PAPER CO., Erie, Pa.
Imported Linen—(b)—tissue—GRAHAM PAPER CO., St. Louis.
Imported Linen—(b)—tissue—SMITH PAPER CO., Lee, Mass.
Imported Onion Skin—(b)—F. A. FLINN, INC., New York.
Imported White—(b)—glazed and unglazed, F. A. FLINN, INC., N. Y.
Imported Onion Skin—(b)—J. W. BUTLER PAPER CO., Chicago.
Impression Typewriter—(b)—writing—J. W. BUTLER PAPER CO., Chicago.
Improved India Bible—(b)—F. A. FLINN, INC., New York.
Indenture Bond—(w)—AMERICAN WRITING PAPER CO., Holyoke, Mass.
Independence—(w)—bonds—J. E. LINDE PAPER CO., New York.
Independence Bond—(b)—C. W. WILLIAMS & CO., New York.
Independence Ledger—(w)—C. S. PROCTOR PAPER CO., Boston.
Independence Linen—watermarked, RIEGEL & CO., INC., Philadelphia.

Watermarks and Brands

Independence Mills—(b)—No. 2 fine—C. W. WILLIAMS & CO., N. Y.
Indestructo Bond—(w)—SOUTHWORTH CO., Mittineague, Mass.
Index—(b)—linen ledger—RIEGEL & CO., INC., Philadelphia.
Index—(w and b)—writing, ledger, bond—NEENAH PAPER CO., Neenah, Wis.
Index Record—(w)—index ledger—PARSONS PAPER CO., Holyoke.
Index Record Bristol—(b)—W. G. WILLMANN, New York.
India—(b)—cover—LOUISVILLE PAPER CO., Louisville, Ky.
India Bond—(w)—INDIANA PAPER CO., Indianapolis.
India Fabric—(b)—wrapping—GRAHAM PAPER CO., St. Louis.
India Fibre—(b)—sulphite express—THE SEINSHEIMER PAPER CO., Cincinnati, Ohio.
India Linen—(b)—bond—GRAHAM PAPER CO., St. Louis.
India Linen—(w)—GRAHAM PAPER CO., St. Louis.
India Mail—(b)—GEO. B. HURD & CO., New York.
India Mills—(b)—wrapping—LOUISVILLE PAPER CO., Louisville, Ky.
India Mull—(w and b)—GEO. B. HURD & CO., New York.
India Parchment—(b)—wrapping—ANDREWS PAPER CO., Boston.
India Pongee—(b)—writing—UNION CARD & PAPER CO., New York.
India Tint Coated on India Tint—(b)—PAUL E. VERNON & CO., New York.
Indian Bond—(w)—HOWARD PAPER CO., Urbana, O.
Indian Brand—(b)—no-curl gummed paper—NASHUA GUMMED & COATED PAPER CO., Nashua, N. H.
Indian Pongee—(b)—UNION CARD & PAPER CO., New York.
Indiana Bond—(w)—INDIANA PAPER CO., Indianapolis.
Indiana Mills—(w)—INDIANA PAPER CO., Indianapolis.
Industrial—(w)—bond—GRAHAM PAPER CO., St. Louis.
Ingerslide—(w)—fine—EASTERN PAPER AND SUPPLY CO., Springfield, Mass.
Ingleside Colored Laid Writing—RICHMOND PAPER CO., Richmond, Va.
Ingormar—(b)—bristols—PLYMOUTH PAPER CO., Holyoke, Mass.
Inland—(b)—onion skin—JOHN F. SARLES CO., INC., New York.
Inland Linen Ledger—(w)—INLAND PAPER CO., Chicago.
Innercoat—(b)—ANGIER MILLS, Quincy, Mass.
Insurance Blotting—(b)—HY. LINDENMEYR & SONS, New York.

Insurance—(w and b)—writing, ledger, bond—NEENAH PAPER CO., Neenah, Wis.
Insurance Packing—(b)—W. P. and case lining—INSURANCE PACKING CO., Brockton, Mass.
Integrity Bond—(w)—NEW YORK & NEW JERSEY PAPER CO., New York.
Inter-City Bond—(w)—INTER-CITY PAPER CO., Minnesota Transfer, Minn.
Intercost Book—(b)—McCLELLAN PAPER CO., Minneapolis, Minn.
Interest Bond—(w)—CHARLES J. COHEN & SON, Philadelphia.
Interknit Fibre—QUAKER CITY PAPER CO., Philadelphia.
Interlake Bond—(w)—OSBURN PAPER CO., INC., Philadelphia.
International—(b)—folded—OLD BERKSHIRE MILLS CO., Dalton, Mass.
International Bond—(w)—WHITING-PLOVER PAPER CO., Stevens Point, Wis.
International Bond—(w)—W. M. PRINGLE & CO., INC., New York.
Interstate—(b)—onion skin—GRAHAM PAPER CO., St. Louis.
Interstate Bond—(w)—CENTRAL OHIO PAPER CO., Columbus, Ohio.
Interstate Parchment—(w)—R. C. OSBURN PAPER CO., Philadelphia.
Interstate R.R. Manila—(w)—OSBURN PAPER CO., Philadelphia.
Inter-State Way Bill Writing—(b)—MINNEAPOLIS PAPER CO., Minneapolis, Minn.
Interstate White Writing—(w)—R. C. OSBURN PAPER CO., Philadelphia.
Intervale—(b)—cover and coated book—JUDD PAPER CO., Holyoke.
Intervale—(w)—W. H. CLAFLIN & CO., INC., Boston.
Interwoven Cover—(b)—CONROW BROS., New York.
Invader—(w)—POWERS PAPER COMPANY, Springfield, Mass.
Inventory Bond—(b)—CLEMENT & STOCKWELL, INC., New York.
Inverness—(b)—EATON, CRANE & PIKE CO., Pittsfield, Mass.
Investment Bond—(w)—HUDSON VALLEY PAPER CO., Albany, N. Y.
Investors' Bond—(w)—CENTRAL-TOPEKA PAPER CO., Topeka, Kan.
Invicta Extra Strong—(w)—bond—W. R. GRACE & CO., New York.
Invictus Fibre—(b)—CANADA PAPER CO., LTD., Windsor Mills, Can.
Invincible—(b)—COLUMBIA PAPER BAG CO., New York.
Invincible—(b)—toilet—NORTHERN PAPER MILLS, Green Bay, Wis.
Invincible—(w)—typewriting paper—AMERICAN WRITING MACHINE CO., 345 Broadway, New York.

NEW MILLS DESIGNED POWER PLANTS OLD MILLS REBUILT

C. A. CHAPMAN, Inc.
28 E. JACKSON BLVD. ENGINEERS CHICAGO

Watermarks and Brands 681

Invincible Ledger—(w)—HAMPSHIRE PAPER CO., South Hadley Falls, Mass.
Invincible Linen—(w)—AMERICAN WRITING PAPER CO., Holyoke.
Invincible Linen Ledger—(w)—HAMPSHIRE PAPER CO., South Hadley Falls, Mass.
Invincible Onion Skin Bond—(b)—CARTER, RICE & CO., CORP., Boston.
Invincible Type Writing Paper—(b)—AMERICAN WRITING MACHINE CO., 345 Broadway, N. Y.
Invitation Wedding Bristol—(b)—B. D. RISING PAPER CO., Housatonic, Mass.
Invoice Bond—(b)—BRADNER SMITH & CO., Chicago.
Ionia Mills—(w)—C. P. LESH PAPER CO., Indianapolis, Ind.
Ionian Bond—(w)—HAMPSHIRE PAPER CO., South Hadley Falls, Mass.
Ionian Ledger—(b)—R. L. GREENE PAPER CO., Providence, R. I.
Ionic—(b and w)—folded writing papers—UNITED STATES ENVELOPE CO. (Plimpton Mfg. Co. Division), Hartford, Conn.
Iosco—(b)—toilet—ALBANY PERFORATED WRAPPING PAPER CO., Albany, N. Y.
I-Rest—(b)—ROBERTS & MECK, Harrisburg, Pa.
Iris—(b)—bond—J. C. HALL CO., Providence, R. I.
Iris Linen—(b)—EASTERN MFG. CO., Bangor, Me.
Iris Translucent—(b)—white bristol—J. C. PARKER CO., Louisville, Ky.
Irish—(b)—bristol—HAGEN PAPER CO., St. Louis.
Irish Bond—(w)—THE UNION PAPER & TWINE CO., Detroit, Mich.
Irish Linen—(b)—UNITED STATES ENVELOPE CO. (Whitcomb Envelope Co. Division), Worcester, Mass.
Irish Linen—(b)—toilet—NORTHERN PAPER MILLS, Green Bay, Wis.
Irish Linene—(w)—EATON, CRANE & PIKE CO., Pittsfield, Mass.
Irish Linen Bond—(w)—DIEM & WING PAPER CO., Cincinnati, Ohio.
Irish Linen—(b)—bristol—J. W. BUTLER PAPER CO., Chicago.
Irish Linen Fabric—(w)—AMERICAN WRITING PAPER CO., Holyoke.
Irish Linen Ledger—(w)—GRAHAM PAPER CO., St. Louis.
Irish Linen Ledger—(w)—AMERICAN WRITING PAPER CO., Holyoke.
Irish Poplin—(w)—MARCUS WARD CO., Brooklyn, N. Y.
Ironclad—(b)—JOHN LESLIE PAPER CO., Minneapolis, Minn.
Iron Fibre—QUAKER CITY PAPER CO., Philadelphia.
Iron Tag—(b)—HOLLINGSWORTH & VOSE CO., Boston, Mass.

Ironwood—(b)—tag board—LOUISVILLE PAPER CO., Louisville, Ky.
Iroquois—(b)—toilet—ALBANY PERFORATED WRAPPING PAPER CO., Albany, N. Y.
Iroquois—(b)—toilet—NORTHERN PAPER MILLS, Green Bay, Wis.
Iroquois—(b)—EATON, CRANE & PIKE CO., Pittsfield, Mass.
Iroquois—(w)—fine—CENTRAL OHIO PAPER CO., Columbus, Ohio.
Iroquois Bond—(w)—LASHER & LATHROP, New York.
Iroquois Kraft—(b)—MISSOURI PAPER HOUSE, Kansas City, Mo.
Iroquois Linen—(w)—LASHER & LATHROP, New York.
Iroquois Linen Ledger—(w)—JUDD PAPER CO., Holyoke, Mass.
Irquo—(b)—HOLLINGSWORTH & WHITNEY CO., Boston.
Irving Book—(w)—TAYLOR-LOGAN CO., PAPERMAKERS, Holyoke, Mass.
Irving Mill—(b)—RAYNOR & PERKINS ENVELOPE CO., New York.
Irving S. & S. C.—(b)—book—SWIGART PAPER CO., Chicago.
Irving Text—(w)—book—ADVERTISERS' PAPER MILLS, Holyoke.
Irvington—(w)—flat writing—MERRIAM PAPER CO., New York.
Irvington Writing—(w)—MERRIAM PAPER CO., New York.
Irwin's Quincy—IRWIN PAPER CO., Quincy, Ill.
Isabella—(w)—flats—BRADNER SMITH & CO., Chicago.
Isanti Ledger—(w)—MINNEAPOLIS PAPER CO., Minneapolis, Minn.
Island City Mills—(b)—AMERICAN NEWS CO., New York.
Island Mills—(b)—news—KANSAS CITY PAPER HOUSE, Kansas City, Mo.
Islington Superfine—(w)—AMERICAN WRITING PAPER CO., Holyoke.
Italia—(b)—cover—NIAGARA PAPER MILLS, Lockport, N. Y.
Italian Chiffon—(b)—EATON, CRANE & PIKE CO., Pittsfield, Mass.
Itasca—(b)—superfine—HAMPSHIRE PAPER CO., South Hadley Falls, Mass.
Itasca Bond—(w)—HAMPSHIRE PAPER CO., South Hadley Falls, Mass.
Ithaca—(w)—flat—BECKETT PAPER CO., THE, Hamilton, Ohio.
Ito—(b)—toilet—H. NORWOOD EWING CO., New York.
Itsuitsus—(b)—toilet—GEO. T. JOHNSON CO., Boston.
Ivanhoe—(w)—writing—EASTERN MFG. CO., Bangor, Me.
Ivanhoe Writing—MACK-ELLIOTT PAPER CO., St. Louis.
Ivanhoe—(b)—cover—SEYMOUR CO., New York.
Ivanhoe—(b)—fine—SOUTHERN PAPER CO., Richmond, Va.

APPLETON MACHINE CO., APPLETON, WIS.
REFINING ENGINES, SCREENS, SAWING & SPLITTING MACHINERY
HIGH GRADE CENTRIFUGAL PUMPS

MINER EDGAR CO., Sole Agents
Edgar Bros. Co. 30 CHURCH STREET NEW YORK

CLAY

WASHED
<E W>
HIGH COLOR

GRITLESS
<C M>
HIGH RETENTION

FELTS AND JACKETS | Appleton Woolen Mills, APPLETON - - WIS.

Watermarks and Brands

Ivanhoe—(b)—manila tag—ARNOLD-ROBERTS CO., Boston.
Ivanhoe Linen—(w)—JUDD PAPER CO., Holyoke, Mass.
Ivanhoe Linen—(w)—VERNON BROS. & CO., New York.
Ivanhoe Writing—(w)—MACK-ELLIOTT PAPER CO., St. Louis.
Ivorine—(w)—AMERICAN WRITING PAPER CO., Holyoke, Mass.
Ivorine—(b)—round-cornered cards—UNION CARD & PAPER CO., N. Y.
Ivorine Enameled Blotting—(b)—MINNEAPOLIS PAPER CO., Minneapolis, Minn.
Ivoroid—(b)—book—MERRIAM PAPER CO., New York.
Ivory—(b)—blotting, cardboards and cards—GRAHAM PAPER CO., St. Louis.
Ivory—(b)—enameled book—J. W. BUTLER PAPER CO., Chicago.
Ivory—(b)—flat—UNION PAPER & TWINE CO., Detroit, Mich.
Ivory—(b)—M. F. and Super—CANFIELD PAPER CO., New York.
Ivory Blanks—(b)—McCLELLAN PAPER CO., Minneapolis, Minn.
Ivory Bristol—(b)—BRADNER SMITH & CO., Chicago.
Ivory Enameled—(b)—blotting—CONROW BROS., New York.
Ivory Envelopes—(b)—WHITAKER PAPER CO., Cincinnati, Ohio.
Ivory Fine Blank—(b)—BUNTIN, GILLIES & CO., LTD., Hamilton, Ontario, Can.
Ivory Finish Book—(b)—PAUL E. VERNON & CO., New York.
Ivory Mills—(w)—flat—BUNTIN, GILLIES & CO., LTD., Hamilton, Ontario, Canada.
Ivory Tint—(b)—translucent—UNION CARD & PAPER CO., N. Y.
Ivory White Blanks—(b)—J. C. PARKER PAPER CO., Louisville, Ky.
Ivy—(b)—bristols—UNION CARD & PAPER CO., New York.
Ivy Leaf—(b)—cards, envelopes and wedding stationery—MINNEAPOLIS PAPER CO., Minneapolis, Minn.
Ivy Mills—(w)—CINCINNATI CORDAGE AND PAPER CO., Cincinnati.
I.X.L. Bond—(w)—SOUTHWORTH CO., Mittineague, Mass.
I. X. L. Linen—(w)—AETNA PAPER CO., Dayton, Ohio.
IXL Linen—(b)—WRIGHT, BARRETT & STILWELL CO., St Paul.
IXL Linen—(w)—DWIGHT BROS. PAPER CO., Chicago.
I X L Linen—(w)—BEECHER, PECK & LEWIS, Detroit, Mich.
I. X. L. Onion Skin—(b)—KINGSLEY PAPER CO., Cleveland, Ohio.

J

J. B. W. Insurance Special—(w)—JOHN B. WATKINS, New York.
Jack Frost—(b)—coated—LEWERTH & CULBERTSON, New York.
Jack Rose—(b)—toilet—W. A. STOWE PAPER CO., Grand Rapids.
Jack Rose Mills—(b)—folded writing—BRADNER SMITH & CO., Chicago.
Jackson—(w)—writing—WEST VIRGINIA PULP AND PAPER CO., N. Y.
Jackson Ledger—(w)—BRADNER SMITH & CO., Chicago.
Jackson Mills—(w)—MISSOURI PAPER HOUSE, Kansas City, Mo.
James River Superfine—RICHMOND PAPER CO., Richmond, Va.
January—(b)—wedding and bristol—MOUNTAIN MILL PAPER CO., Lee, Mass.
Janus—(b)—toilet—H. NORWOOD EWING CO., New York.
Jap—(b)—toilet—NORTHERN PAPER MILLS, Green Bay, Wis.
Japan Bond—(b)—RIEGEL & CO., INC., Philadelphia.
Japan Bond—(w)—AMERICAN WRITING PAPER CO., Holyoke, Mass.
Japan Bond—(w)—RIEGEL & CO., INC., Philadelphia.
Japan Cover—(b)—PAUL E. VERNON & CO., New York.
Japan Linen Bond—(w) BUNTIN, GILLIES & CO., LTD., Hamilton, Ontario, Can.
Japan Parchment—(b)—GEO. B. HURD & CO., New York.
Japanin—(b)—HY. LINDENMEYR & SONS, New York.
Japanese—(b)—toilet—NORTHERN PAPER MILLS, Green Bay, Wis.
Japanese Fibre—(b)—BRADNER SMITH & CO., Chicago.
Japanese Linen—(w)—CRANE BROTHERS, Westfield, Mass.
Japanese Parchment—(b)—book—LASHER & LATHROP, New York.
Japanese Parchment—(b)—M. G. wrapping—OLD DOMINION PAPER CO., Norfolk, Va.
Japatisu—(b)—toilet—GEO. T. JOHNSON CO., Boston.
Jasper—(b)—MATTHIAS PLUM, Newark, N. J.
Jefferson—(b)—colored bristol—J. C. PARKER PAPER CO., Louisville, Ky.
Jefferson—(b)—white wove—F. A. FLINN, INC., New York.
Jefferson—(w)—extra superfine—GARRETT-BUCHANAN CO., Philadelphia.
Jefferson Bond—(w)—GARRETT-BUCHANAN CO., Philadelphia.
Jefferson Linen Ledger—(w)—GARRETT-BUCHANAN CO., Philadelphia.
Jenson—(b)—MILLER & WRIGHT PAPER CO., New York.

JAMES H. HARRISON PULPSTONE MANUFACTURER | **GENUINE NEWCASTLE STONES** 18 Killowen St., GATESHEAD-ON-TYNE, ENG.

Watermarks and Brands

Jersey Bond—(w)—CARPENTER PAPER CO., Omaha, Neb.
Jewel—(b)—toilet—GRAHAM PAPER CO., St. Louis.
Jewel—(b)—toilet—NORTHERN PAPER MILLS, Green Bay, Wis.
Jewell M. F.—(b)—book—SPRINGFIELD PAPER & SUPPLY CO., Springfield, Mo.
Jewt—(b)—toilet—SCOTT PAPER CO., Philadelphia.
Jim Crow—(b)—toilet—NORTHERN PAPER MILLS, Green Bay, Wis.
Jingo—(b)—toilet—H. NORWOOD EWING CO., New York.
Job Roll—(b)—toilet—UNITED STATES ENVELOPE CO. (Morgan Envelope Co. Div.), Springfield, Mass.
John Hancock—(b)—BYRON WESTON CO., Dalton, Mass.
Joliette—(b)—ALEX. McARTHUR & CO., Montreal, Canada.
Journal Book—(b)—DIEM & WING PAPER CO., Cincinnati, Ohio.
Journal Index — (b) — bristol — STANDARD CORD & PAPER CO., New York.
J. P. Co. Fine—(w)—JOHNSTON PAPER CO., Harrisburg, Pa.
Jubilee Wedding Bristol—(b).—BEECHER, PECK & LEWIS, Detroit, Mich.
Judicial Linen Bond—(w)—CONROW BROTHERS, New York.
Julian—(w)—toilet, wrapping—W. R. GRACE & CO., New York.
Juliet—(b)—toilet—H. NORWOOD EWING CO., New York.
Juliette—(w)—bond—W. R. GRACE & CO., New York.
June—(b)—wedding and bristol—MOUNTAIN MILL PAPER CO., Lee, Mass.
Juniata—(w)—DEARBORN PAPER CO., Chicago.
Juniata—(b)—writing—WEST VIRGINIA PULP AND PAPER CO., N. Y.
Juniata Half Tone Plate—(b)—DIEM & WING PAPER CO., Cincinnati, Ohio.
Junior—(b)—toilet—NORTHERN PAPER MILLS, Green Bay, Wis.
Junior — (b) — toilet — MEGARGEE BROS., Scranton, Pa.
Juno—(b)—flats — HENRY LINDENMEYR & SONS, New York.
Jupiter—(b)—J. F. WALL & SON, Norfolk, Mass.
Jupiter—(b)—book and linen—GRAHAM PAPER CO., St. Louis.
Jupiter — (b) — flats — LOUISVILLE PAPER CO., Louisville, Ky.
Jupiter Fibre—(b)—wrapping—D. S. WALTON & CO., New York.
Jupiter Linen—(b)—HENRY LINDENMEYR & SONS, New York.
Jupiter Litho Blanks—(b)—HY. LINDENMEYR & SONS, New York.
Jupiter Rope—(b)—wrapping—VON OLKER-SNELL PAPER CO., Boston.

Jupiter Wove Writing—(b)—HY. LINDENMEYR & SONS, New York.
Justice Linen Bond—(w)—W. M. PRINGLE & CO., INC., New York.
Justice Linen Ledger — (w) — BEECHER, PECK & LEWIS, Detroit.
Justice Linen Ledger—(w)—W. M. PRINGLE & CO., INC., New York.
Justrite — (b) — toilet — GEO. T. JOHNSON CO., Boston.
Just-Tear-It Linen—(b)—UNITED STATES ENVELOPE CO. (Whitcomb Envelope Co. Div.), Worcester, Mass.
Jute Document Tag—(b)—CHATFIELD & WOODS CO., Cincinnati, O.

K

"K" in a Diamond—(w)—1 and 2 fines—N. Y. & UTAH PAPER CO., Salt Lake City, Utah.
K and "High Grade" in a diamond —(b)—KINLEITH PAPER CO., St. Catharines, Ont.
"K" Ledger—(b)—white ledger paper—R. C. KASTNER PAPER CO., New York.
K. O. S. H. T.—(b)—insulated papers—BIRD & SON, Walpole, Mass.
K. P. C. Linen Ledger—(w)—KINGSLEY PAPER CO., Cleveland.
K. P. C. Onion Skin—(b)—KINGSLEY PAPER CO., Cleveland, Ohio.
K. Translucent Bristol — (b) — KINGSLEY PAPER CO., Cleveland.
Kadesh Bond —(b)— typewriter — EATON, CRANE & PIKE CO., Pittsfield, Mass.
Kadesh Linen — (b) — typewriter — EATON, CRANE & PIKE CO., Pittsfield, Mass.
Kahoka—(b)—toilet—ALBANY PERFORATED WRAPPING PAPER CO., Albany, N. Y.
Kaiser—(b)—cover—BAY STATE PAPER CO., Boston.
Kaiser Brown—(b)—wrappings and specialties—McDOWELL PAPER MILLS, Philadelphia.
Kaiser Cover—(b)—WHITING-PATTERSON CO., Philadelphia.
Kadjo—(b) — HOLLINGSWORTH & WHITNEY CO., Boston.
Kalma—(w and b)—bond, book, bristol and cover—CHAS. H. WRIGHT, Kalamazoo, Mich.
Kamargo—(b)—flats — KNOWLTON BROS., Watertown, N. Y.
Kamargo Text—(b)—book paper — KNOWLTON BROS., Watertown, N. Y.
Kanawha Envelope — (b)—WEST VIRGINIA PULP AND PAPER CO., New York.
Kanesaw—(b)—colored rope cover—BRADNER SMITH & CO., Chicago.
Kangaroo Linen — (w) — L. W. LAWRENCE, New York.
Kansas—(b) — bristols — KANSAS CITY PAPER HOUSE, Kansas City,

FELTS AND JACKETS | Appleton Woolen Mills
APPLETON - - WIS.

Watermarks and Brands

Hercules Wrappings — (w)—wrapping and bond—McDOWELL PAPER MILLS, Manayunk, Philadelphia.
Heritage Bond—(w) — WHITAKER PAPER CO., Cincinnati, Ohio, and BAY STATE PAPER CO., Boston.
Hermanos — (b) — writing — W. M. PRINGLE & CO., INC., New York.
Hermes Book—(b)—CLARKE & CO., New York.
Hermes Coated Ledger—(b)—HY. LINDENMEYR & SONS, New York.
Hermit—(w)—POWER PAPER COMPANY, Springfield, Mass.
Hero—(b)—blank—JOHN CARTER & CO., Boston.
Hero—(b)—blanks—CHATFIELD & WOODS CO., Cincinnati, Ohio.
Herring Bone—(w and b)—GEO. B. HURD & CO., New York.
Herringbone Kraft — (b) — MISSOURI PAPER HOUSE, Kansas City, Mo.
Hetchfield Flax — (b) — EATON, CRANE & PIKE CO., Pittsfield, Mass.
Heveetowl—(w)—UNITED STATES PAPER MILLS, INC., Chambersburg, Pa.
Hiawatha—(b)—S. & S. C. colored book—JAMES WHITE PAPER CO., Chicago.
Hiawatha Bond—(w)—HAMILTON CARD & PAPER HOUSE, INC., New York.
Hibulk—(b)—book—WEST VIRGINIA PULP & PAPER CO., New York.
Hickory — (b)—tag — JUDD PAPER CO., Holyoke.
Hickory—(b) — tag board — LOUISVILLE PAPER CO., Louisville, Ky.
Hickory—(b)—fibre—KANSAS CITY PAPER HOUSE, Kansas City, Mo.
Hickory—(b)—kraft—GRAHAM PAPER CO., St. Louis.
Hickory Bond—(w) — AMERICAN WRITING PAPER CO., Holyoke.
Hickory Fibre—(b)— wrapping — WILKINSON BROS. & CO., INC., Philadelphia.
Hickory Fibre — (b) — wrapping — LOUISVILLE PAPER CO., Louisville, Ky.
Hickory Ledger—(w) —AMERICAN WRITING PAPER CO., Holyoke.
High Art, H. F.—(b)—CHATFIELD & WOODS CO., Cincinnati, Ohio.
High Art Book—(b)—A. STORRS & BEMENT CO., Boston.
High Grade — (b) —roofing—M. J. EARL, Reading, Pa.
High Grade — (w)—SAUGERTIES MFG. CO., Saugerties, N. Y.
Highland—(b)—blotting — THE ALLING & CORY CO., Rochester, N. Y.
Highland—(b)—cardboard and cards —GRAHAM PAPER CO., St. Louis.
Highland—(w)—fine—JUDD PAPER CO., Holyoke, Mass.
Highland Blotting—(b)—THE ALLING & CORY CO., Rochester, N. Y.

Highland Ledger—(b) — GRAHAM PAPER CO., St. Louis.
Highland Linen — (b)—hand made style—EATON, CRANE & PIKE CO., Pittsfield, Mass.
Highland Linen—(b)—JUDD PAPER CO., Holyoke, Mass.
Highland Linen Bond — (w)— EATON, CRANE & PIKE CO., Pittsfield, Mass.
Highland Linen Parchment—(w) —EATON, CRANE & PIKE CO., Pittsfield, Mass.
Highland Linen—(b)—JUDD PAPER CO., Holyoke, Mass.
Highland Mills—(b)—fine — JUDD PAPER CO., Holyoke, Mass.
Highlight—(b) — cover—PENINSULAR PAPER CO., Ypsilanti, Mich.
Highlight—(w and b)—bond, writing and cover—THE PAPER MILLS CO., Chicago.
High White—(b)—coated book—THE PAPER MILLS CO., Chicago.
Hi-grade Mimeograph—RICHMOND PAPER CO.; Richmond, Va.
Hillcrest Bond—(w)—BERKSHIRE HILLS PAPER CO., Adams, Mass.
Hillcrest Ledger — (w) — BERKSHIRE HILLS PAPER CO., Adams, Mass.
Hillcrest Linen—(w)—BERKSHIRE HILLS PAPER CO., Adams, Mass.
Hillcrest Superfine — (w)—C. S. PROCTOR PAPER CO., Boston.
Hillsborough Booklet — (w) — WORTHY PAPER CO., Mittineague, Mass.
Hindo India Tint — (b)—book— BRADNER SMITH & CO., Chicago.
Hindoo—(b)—fibre— MINNEAPOLIS PAPER CO., Minneapolis, Minn.
Hindoo Onion Skin—(b)—OSBORN PAPER CO., Philadelphia.
Historical Bond — (w)—HAMMERMILL PAPER CO., Erie, Pa.
"H. L."—(b)—HY. LINDENMEYR & SONS, New York.
H. L. Litho.—(b)—HY. LINDENMEYR & SONS, New York.
H. L. & S. Coated Book—(b)—HY. LINDENMEYR & SONS, New York.
H. L. & S. Best Rope Tag—(b)— HY. LINDENMEYR & SONS, New York.
Hoffman — (b)—toilet—NORTHERN PAPER MILLS, Green Bay, Wis.
Holdfast—(b)—kraft—GRAHAM PAPER CO., St. Louis.
Holland Bond —(w)—HAMPSHIRE PAPER CO., South Hadley Falls, Mass.
Holland Bond — (w) — HAMILTON CARD & PAPER HOUSE, INC., New York.
Holland Fibre — (w)—WHITE & WYCKOFF MFG. CO., Holyoke, Mass.
Holland Linen — (w) — GEO. B. HURD & CO., New York.

BLOTTING PAPERS STANDARD PAPER MFG CO Richmond, Va.

Watermarks and Brands

Holland Linen — (w) — SWIGART PAPER CO., Chicago.
Holland Linen—(b)—toilet — NORTHERN PAPER MILLS, Green Bay, Wis.
Holland Linen Bond—(w and b)— GEO B. HURD & CO., New York.
Holland Linen Ledger — (w)— CAREW MANUFACTURING CO., South Hadley Falls, Mass.
Holland Text — (w)—McCLELLAN PAPER CO., Minneapolis, Minn.
Holly—(b) — writing—GRAHAM PAPER CO., St. Louis.
Hollywood—(b)—vegetable parchment —LOUISVILLE PAPER CO., Louisville, Pa.
Hollywood—(b)—blotting—ALBEMARLE PAPER MANUFACTURING CO., Richmond, Va.
Holyoke—(b)—cardboards and cards —GRAHAM PAPER CO., St. Louis.
Holyoke—(w)— white wove flats— MINNEAPOLIS PAPER CO., Minneapolis, Minn.
Holyoke Bond—(b)—OLD DOMINION PAPER CO., Norfolk, Va.
Holyoke Covers —(b)—ADVERTISERS' PAPER MILLS, Holyoke.
Holyoke Document—(b)—jute manila—CHEMICAL PAPER MFG. CO., Holyoke, Mass.
Holyoke Index Bristol — (b)— KINGSLEY PAPER CO., Cleveland, O.
Holyoke Linen Bond—(w) — TAYLOR-LOGAN CO., Papermakers, Holyoke, Mass.
Holyoke Linen Ledger — (w)— NATIONAL BLANK BOOK CO., Holyoke, Mass.
Holyoke Paper Co.—(w)—AMERICAN WRITING PAPER CO., Holyoke.
Holyoke Paper Co.'s Ledger—(w) —AMERICAN WRITING PAPER CO., Holyoke, Mass.
Holyoke Record—NATIONAL BOOK CO., Holyoke, Mass.
Holyoke Superfine Linen — (w)— TAYLOR-LOGAN CO., Papermakers, Holyoke, Mass.
Holyoke Superfine Vellum—(w)— TAYLOR-LOGAN CO., Papermakers, Holyoke, Mass.
Holyoke Text—(w)—book —ADVERTISERS' PAPER MILLS, Holyoke.
Homebound—(b)—wax paper—GRAHAM PAPER CO., St. Louis.
Home-Made Linen—(b)—BASSETT & SUTPHIN, New York.
Homer—(b)—bond—GRAHAM PAPER CO., St. Louis.
Homespun—(b)—bristol board— DONALDSON PAPER CO., Harrisburg, Pa.
Homespun—(b)— cover — NIAGARA PAPER MILLS, Lockport, N. Y.
Homespun Fabric—(b)—GEO. B. HURD & CO., New York.
Homespun Linen—(w)—HAMMERMILL PAPER CO., Erie, Pa.

Homestead—(b)—toilet—NORTHERN PAPER MILLS, Green Bay, Wis.
Homestead — (b) —railroad writing — GRAHAM PAPER CO., St. Louis.
Homuse—(b)—toilet—SCOTT PAPER CO., Philadelphia.
Honest Count—(b)—roll toilet—JEROME PAPER CO., New York.
Honest Linen — (w) — AMERICAN WRITING PAPER CO., Holyoke, Mass.
Honor — (w) — bond — ELSINOR PAPER CO., New York.
Hoosac Bond — (w) — BERKSHIRE HILLS PAPER CO., Adams, Mass.
Hoosac Ledger—(w)—BERKSHIRE HILLS PAPER CO., Adams, Mass.
Hoosac Linen —(w)— BERKSHIRE HILLS PAPER CO., Adams, Mass.
Hoosick—(b)—toilet—ALBANY PERFORATED WRAPPING PAPER CO., Albany, N. Y.
Hope—(b)—J. C. HALL CO., Providence, R. I.
Horatius—(b)—toilet—H. NORWOOD EWING CO., New York.
Horicon Mills Superfine—(w)—F. A. FLINN, INC., New York.
Hornet—(b)—gummed—LOUISVILLE PAPER CO., Louisville, Ky.
Hornet—(b)—news—C. P. LESH PAPER CO., Indianapolis, Ind.
Hornet Linen — (w) — AMERICAN WRITING PAPER CO., Holyoke, Mass.
Horseshoe—(b)—toilet—NORTHERN PAPER MILLS, Green Bay, Wis.
Horseshoe Bond—(w)—FOX RIVER PAPER CO., Appleton, Wis.
Horseshoe Bristol—(b)—KINGSLEY PAPER CO., Cleveland, Ohio.
Hot Pressed Vellum—(w)—EATON, CRANE & PIKE CO., Pittsfield, Mass.
Hotel—(b)—toilet—ALBANY PERFORATED WRAPPING PAPER CO., Albany, N. Y.
Hotel — (b) — blotting — BRADNER SMITH & CO., Chicago.
Hotel Special—(b)—toilet—JOHNSTON PAPER CO., Harrisburg, Pa.
Housatonic—(b)—blotting — EATON-DIKEMAN CO., Lee, Mass.
Housatonic—(b)—desk pad—EATON-DIKEMAN CO., Lee, Mass.
Housatonic Bond—(b)—B. D. RISING PAPER CO., Housatonic, Mass.
Housatonic Engravers' Bristol— (b)—pasted bristol—B. D. RISING PAPER CO., Housatonic, Mass.
Housatonic Ledger — (w) — B. D. RISING PAPER CO., Housatonic, Mass.
Housatonic Linen—(w)—B. D. RISING PAPER CO., Housatonic, Mass.
Housatonic Superfine—(w)—B. D. RISING PAPER CO., Housatonic, Mass.
Household—(b)—toilet—SCOTT PAPER CO., Philadelphia.
Houston Toilet Tissue—(b)—HY. LINDENMEYR & SONS, New York.

Watermarks and Brands

Howard—(b)—white wove—F. A. FLINN, INC., New York.
Howard Bond—(w)—HOWARD PAPER CO., Urbana, O.
Howard Ledger—(w)—HOWARD PAPER CO., Urbana, O.
Howard Ledger—(w)—HARLEM CARD & PAPER CO., New York.
Howard Mills—(b)—folded—WORTHY PAPER CO., Mittineague, Mass.
H. P. Suede Offset—(b)—MILLER & WRIGHT PAPER CO., INC., New York.
H. S. P. Board Laid—(w)—HOWARD SMITH PAPER MILLS CO., LTD., Montreal, Can.
H. S. P. Narrow Laid—(w)—HOWARD SMITH PAPER MILLS CO., LTD., Montreal, Can.
Hub—(b)—bristol—JOHN CARTER & CO., Boston.
Hub—(b)—No. 1 manila—W. H. CLAFLIN & CO., Boston.
Hub Blank—(b)—A. STORRS & BEMENT CO., Boston.
Hudson—(b)—BUNTIN, GILLIES & CO., Hamilton, Canada.
Hudson—(b)—cover—WHITAKER PAPER CO. Cincinnati, Ohio, and BAY STATE PAPER CO., Boston.
Hudson—(b)—M. F. book—CHATFIELD & WOODS CO., Cincinnati, O.
Hudson—(b)—toilet—ALBANY PERFORATED WRAPPING PAPER CO., Albany, N. Y.
Hudson Antique Wove—(b)—HUDSON VALLEY PAPER CO., Albany, N. Y.
Hudson Blank—HUDSON VALLEY PAPER CO., Albany, N. Y.
Hudson Bond—(b)—PAUL E. VERNON & CO., New York.
Hudson Bond—(b)—HUDSON VALLEY PAPER CO. Albany, N. Y.
Hudson Bond—(w)—GILBERT PAPER CO., Menasha, Wis
Hudson Bristol—(b)—HUDSON VALLEY PAPER CO, Albany, N. Y.
Hudson Cover—(b)—BAY STATE PAPER CO., Boston.
Hudson Eggshell Book—(b)—HUDSON VALLEY PAPER CO., Albany, N. Y.
Hudson Ledger—(b)—O. H. ANDERSON & CO., New York.
Hudson Mills—J. E. LINDE PAPER CO., New York.
Hudson White—(b)—JERSEY CITY PAPER CO., Jersey City, N. J.
Hudson Writing Manila—(b)—F. A. FLINN, INC., New York.
Hudtraco—(b)—kraft, manila, tissue, book, bond, writing—HUDSON TRADING CO., New York.
Hulda—(b)—white bristol—MEGARGEE BROS., Scranton, Pa.
Humanity First—(w and b)—ledger, writing, bond—NEENAH PAPER CO., Neenah, Wis.

Humboldt—(b)—bond—GRAHAM PAPER CO., St. Louis.
Hummer—(b)—LOUISVILLE PAPER CO., Louisville, Ky.
Humpty Dumpty—(b)—toilet—ALBANY PERFORATED WRAPPING PAPER CO., Albany, N. Y.
Hunter's Red Levant Morocco—(b)—EATON, CRANE & PIKE CO., Pittsfield, Mass.
Huntingdon—(w)—bond and linen—J. C. BLAIR CO., Huntingdon, Pa.
Huntress—(b)—book and label—GRAHAM PAPER CO., St. Louis.
Hurd's Irish Linen—(w)—GEO. B. HURD & CO., New York.
Huron—(b)—CHATFIELD & WOODS CO., Cincinnati, Ohio.
Huron—(b)—plaster board—GRAHAM PAPER CO., St. Louis.
Huron—(b)—toilet—ALBANY PERFORATED WRAPPING PAPER CO., Albany, N. Y.
Huron—(b)—cover—PENINSULAR PAPER CO., Ypsilanti, Mich.
Huron—(b)—flat manila—F. A. FLINN, INC., New York.
Huron Bond—(w)—bond—PENINSULAR PAPER CO., Ypsilanti, Mich.
Huron Book—(b)—KINGSLEY PAPER CO., Cleveland, Ohio.
Huron Bristol—(b)—BEECHER, PECK & LEWIS, Detroit, Mich.
Huron Manila—(b)—F. A. FLINN, INC., New York.
Huron Mills—(b)—EAST HARTFORD MANUFACTURING CO., Burnside, Conn.
Hussar—(b)—toilet—NORTHERN PAPER MILLS, Green Bay, Wis.
Hyde Park—(b)—white M. F. book and super—TILESTON & HOLLINGSWORTH CO., Boston.
Hygienic—(b)—toilet—STONE & FORSYTH CO., Boston.
Hygienic—(b)—PEERLESS MFG. CO., Morristown, Pa.
Hygrade—(b)—translucent—UNION CARD & PAPER CO., New York.
Hypatia Mills—superfine—(w)—JOHN CARTER & CO., Boston.
Hyperion Ledger—(b)—MILLER & WRIGHT PAPER CO., New York.
Hyperion Linen—(w)—MERRIAM PAPER CO., New York.
Hyloplate Post Card—(b)—MINNEAPOLIS PAPER CO., Minneapolis, Minn.
Hytone—(b)—toilet—SCOTT PAPER CO., Philadelphia.

I

I. B. L. (Investors' Bond Letter)—(w)—MILLER & WRIGHT PAPER CO., New York.
Icicle—(b)—coated—LEWERTH & CULBERTSON, New York.

Watermarks and Brands

Ideal—(b)—blotting—GRAHAM PAPER CO., St. Louis.
Ideal—(b)—No. 2 white manila—CHATFIELD & WOODS CO., Cincinnati, Ohio.
Ideal Bond—(w)—MOSER PAPER CO., Chicago.
Ideal Bond—(w)—DAVID L. ENGLE, New York.
Ideal Bristol White—RICHMOND PAPER CO., Richmond, Va.
Ideal Flax—(w)—JOHN WANAMAKER, Philadelphia.
Ideal Litho—(b)—coated—WEST VIRGINIA PULP & PAPER CO., New York.
Ideal Mills—(b)—headings—ESSEX PAD AND PAPER CO., Holyoke, Mass.
Ideal S & C—(b)—folder—MINNEAPOLIS PAPER CO., Minneapolis.
Ideal Typewriter Papers—(b)—CARTER, RICE & CO., CORP., Boston.
Ima Heluva Site the Best Paper—THE SEINSHEIMER PAPER CO., Cincinnati, Ohio.
Imperial—(w)—CAREW MFG. CO., South Hadley Falls, Mass.
Imperial—(b)—bristol—R. L. GREENE PAPER CO., Providence.
Imperial—(b)—copying tissue—SMITH PAPER CO., Lee, Mass.
Imperial—(b)—drawing, insulating, cardboard and cards—GRAHAM PAPER CO., St. Louis.
Imperial—(b)—blotting—STANDARD PAPER MANUFACTURING CO., Richmond, Va.
Imperial—(b)—cover—HENRY LINDENMEYR & SONS, New York.
Imperial—(b)—superfine—SOUTHERN PAPER CO., Richmond, Va.
Imperial—(b)—toilet and sheathing—LOUISVILLE PAPER CO., Louisville, Ky.
Imperial—(w)—writing—WHITING PAPER CO., Holyoke, Mass.
Imperial—(b)—enameled book and toilet—CHATFIELD & WOODS CO., Cincinnati, Ohio.
Imperial—(b)—toilet—UNITED STATES ENVELOPE CO., Springfield, Mass.
Imperial—(w)—writing—CAREW MANUFACTURING CO., South Hadley Falls, Mass.
Imperial—(w)—writing—BEECHER, PECK & LEWIS, Detroit, Mich.
Imperial—(b)—colored bristol—MEARGEE BROS., Scranton, Pa.
Imperial Bond—(w)—AMERICAN WRITING PAPER CO., Holyoke, Mass.
Imperial Bond—(w)—COLUMBIA PAPER CO., Victoria, B. C.
Imperial Bristol—(b)—DIEM & WING PAPER CO., Cincinnati, Ohio.
Imperial Bristol—(b)—THE ALLING & CORY CO., Rochester, N. Y.
Imperial Bristol—(b)—R. L. GREENE PAPER CO., Providence, R. I.
Imperial Bristol—(b)—OLD DOMINION PAPER CO., Norfolk, Va.
Imperial Coated—(b)—BEECHER, PECK & LEWIS, Detroit, Mich.
Imperial Fibre—(b)—R. L. GREENE PAPER CO., Providence, R. I.
Imperial Fibre—(b)—wrapping—LOUISVILLE PAPER CO., Louisville, Ky.
Imperial Folding Bristol—(b)—A. STORRS & BEMENT CO., Boston.
Imperial Irish Linen—(w)—RAYNOR & PERKINS ENVELOPE CO., New York.
Imperial Laid—(w)—DILL & COLLINS CO., Philadelphia.
Imperial Ledger—(w)—GEO. B. HURD & CO., New York.
Imperial Linen—(w)—AMERICAN WRITING PAPER CO., Holyoke, Mass.
Imperial Linen—(w)—RAYNOR & PERKINS ENVELOPE CO., N. Y.
Imperial Linen Ledger—(w)—writing—CAREW MANUFACTURING CO., South Hadley Falls, Mass.
Imperial Parchment—(w)—ruled and flat—H. S. CROCKER CO., San Francisco.
Imperial Superfine—(w)—writing—CAREW MANUFACTURING CO., South Hadley Falls, Mass.
Imperial Translucent—(b)—bristol—JOHN CARTER & CO., Boston.
Imperial Treaty Bond—(w)—writing—PARSONS TRADING CO., N. Y.
Imperial Vellum—(b)—EATON, CRANE & PIKE CO., Pittsfield, Mass.
Imperial Vellum—(w)—AMERICAN WRITING PAPER CO., Holyoke, Mass.
Imperial Writing—(w)—HAMMERMILL PAPER CO., Erie, Pa.
Imported Linen—(b)—tissue—GRAHAM PAPER CO., St. Louis.
Imported Linen—(b)—tissue—SMITH PAPER CO., Lee, Mass.
Imported Onion Skin—(b)—F. A. FLINN, INC., New York.
Imported White—(b)—glazed and unglazed, F. A. FLINN, INC., N. Y.
Imported Onion Skin—(b)—J. W. BUTLER PAPER CO., Chicago.
Impression Typewriter—(b)—writing—J. W. BUTLER PAPER CO., Chicago.
Improved India Bible—(b)—F. A. FLINN, INC., New York.
Indenture Bond—(w)—AMERICAN WRITING PAPER CO., Holyoke, Mass.
Independence—(w)—bonds—J. E. LINDE PAPER CO., New York.
Independence Bond—(h)—C. W. WILLIAMS & CO., New York.
Independence Ledger—(w)—C. S. PROCTOR PAPER CO., Boston.
Independence Linen—watermarked, RIEGEL & CO., INC., Philadelphia.

Watermarks and Brands

Independence Mills—(b)—No. 2 fine—C. W. WILLIAMS & CO., N. Y.
Indestructo Bond—(w)—SOUTHWORTH CO., Mittineague, Mass.
Index—(b)—linen ledger—RIEGEL & CO., INC., Philadelphia.
Index—(w and b)—writing, ledger, bond—NEENAH PAPER CO., Neenah, Wis.
Index Record—(w)—index ledger—PARSONS PAPER CO., Holyoke.
Index Record Bristol—(b)—W. G. WILLMANN, New York.
India—(b)—cover—LOUISVILLE PAPER CO., Louisville, Ky.
India Bond—(w)—INDIANA PAPER CO., Indianapolis.
India Fabric—(b)—wrapping—GRAHAM PAPER CO., St. Louis.
India Fibre—(b)—sulphite express—THE SEINSHEIMER PAPER CO., Cincinnati, Ohio.
India Linen—(b)—bond—GRAHAM PAPER CO., St. Louis.
India Linen—(w)—GRAHAM PAPER CO., St. Louis.
India Mail—(b)—GEO. B. HURD & CO., New York.
India Mills—(b)—wrapping—LOUISVILLE PAPER CO., Louisville, Ky.
India Mull—(w and b)—GEO. B. HURD & CO., New York.
India Parchment—(b)—wrapping—ANDREWS PAPER CO., Boston.
India Pongee—(b)—writing—UNION CARD & PAPER CO., New York.
India Tint Coated on India Tint—(b)—PAUL E. VERNON & CO., New York.
Indian Bond—(w)—HOWARD PAPER CO., Urbana, O.
Indian Brand—(b)—no-curl gummed paper—NASHUA GUMMED & COATED PAPER CO., Nashua, N. H.
Indian Pongee—(b)—UNION CARD & PAPER CO., New York.
Indiana Bond—(w)—INDIANA PAPER CO., Indianapolis.
Indiana Mills—(w)—INDIANA PAPER CO., Indianapolis.
Industrial—(w)—bond—GRAHAM PAPER CO., St. Louis.
Ingerslide—(w)—fine—EASTERN PAPER AND SUPPLY CO., Springfield, Mass.
Ingleside Colored Laid Writing—RICHMOND PAPER CO., Richmond, Va.
Ingormar—(b)—bristols—PLYMOUTH PAPER CO., Holyoke, Mass.
Inland—(b)—onion skin—JOHN F. SARLES CO., INC., New York.
Inland Linen Ledger—(w)—INLAND PAPER CO., Chicago.
Innercoat—(b)—ANGIER MILLS, Quincy, Mass.
Insurance Blotting—(b)—HY. LINDENMEYR & SONS, New York.
Insurance—(w and b)—writing, ledger, bond—NEENAH PAPER CO., Neenah, Wis.
Insurance Packing—(b)—W. P. and case lining—INSURANCE PACKING CO., Brockton, Mass.
Integrity Bond—(w)—NEW YORK & NEW JERSEY PAPER CO., New York.
Inter-City Bond—(w)—INTER-CITY PAPER CO., Minnesota Transfer, Minn.
Intercoat Book—(b)—McCLELLAN PAPER CO., Minneapolis, Minn.
Interest Bond—(w)—CHARLES J. COHEN & SON, Philadelphia.
Interknit Fibre—QUAKER CITY PAPER CO., Philadelphia.
Interlake Bond—(w)—OSBURN PAPER CO., INC., Philadelphia.
International—(b)—folded—OLD BERKSHIRE MILLS CO., Dalton, Mass.
International Bond—(w)—WHITING-PLOVER PAPER CO., Stevens Point, Wis.
International Bond—(w)—W. M. PRINGLE & CO., INC., New York.
Interstate—(b)—onion skin—GRAHAM PAPER CO., St. Louis.
Interstate Bond—(w)—CENTRAL OHIO PAPER CO., Columbus, Ohio.
Interstate Parchment—(w)—R. C. OSBURN PAPER CO., Philadelphia.
Interstate R.R. Manila—(w)—OSBURN PAPER CO., Philadelphia.
Inter-State Way Bill Writing—(b)—MINNEAPOLIS PAPER CO., Minneapolis, Minn.
Interstate White Writing—(w)—R. C. OSBURN PAPER CO., Philadelphia.
Intervale—(b)—cover and coated book—JUDD PAPER CO., Holyoke.
Intervale—(w)—W. H. CLAFLIN & CO., INC., Boston.
Interwoven Cover—(b)—CONROW BROS., New York.
Invader—(w)—POWERS PAPER COMPANY, Springfield, Mass.
Inventory Bond—(b)—CLEMENT & STOCKWELL, INC., New York.
Inverness—(b)—EATON, CRANE & PIKE CO., Pittsfield, Mass.
Investment Bond—(w)—HUDSON VALLEY PAPER CO., Albany, N. Y.
Investors' Bond—(w)—CENTRAL-TOPEKA PAPER CO., Topeka, Kan.
Invicta Extra Strong—(w)—bond—W. R. GRACE & CO., New York.
Invictus Fibre—(b)—CANADA PAPER CO., LTD., Windsor Mills, Can.
Invincible—(b)—COLUMBIA PAPER BAG CO., New York.
Invincible—(b)—toilet—NORTHERN PAPER MILLS, Green Bay, Wis.
Invincible—(w)—typewriting paper—AMERICAN WRITING MACHINE CO., 845 Broadway, New York.

NEW MILLS DESIGNED   POWER PLANTS   OLD MILLS REBUILT

C. A. CHAPMAN, Inc.

28 E. JACKSON BLVD.   ENGINEERS   CHICAGO

Watermarks and Brands   681

Invincible Ledger—(w)—HAMPSHIRE PAPER CO., South Hadley Falls, Mass.
Invincible Linen—(w)—AMERICAN WRITING PAPER CO., Holyoke.
Invincible Linen Ledger—(w)—HAMPSHIRE PAPER CO., South Hadley Falls, Mass.
Invincible Onion Skin Bond—(b)—CARTER, RICE & CO., CORP., Boston.
Invincible Type Writing Paper—(b)—AMERICAN WRITING MACHINE CO., 345 Broadway, N. Y.
Invitation Wedding Bristol—(b)—B. D. RISING PAPER CO., Housatonic, Mass.
Invoice Bond—(b)—B R A D N E R SMITH & CO., Chicago.
Ionia Mills—(w)—C. P. LESH PAPER CO., Indianapolis, Ind.
Ionian Bond—(w)—HAMPSHIRE PAPER CO., South Hadley Falls, Mass.
Ionian Ledger—(b)—R. L. GREENE PAPER CO., Providence, R. I.
Ionic—(b and w)—folded writing papers—UNITED STATES ENVELOPE CO. (Plimpton Mfg. Co. Division), Hartford, Conn.
Iosco—(b)—toilet—ALBANY PERFORATED WRAPPING PAPER CO., Albany, N. Y.
I-Rest—(b)—ROBERTS & MECK, Harrisburg, Pa.
Iris—(b)—bond—J. C. HALL CO., Providence, R. I.
Iris Linen—(b)—EASTERN MFG. CO., Bangor, Me.
Iris Translucent—(b)—white bristol—J. C. PARKER CO., Louisville, Ky.
Irish—(b)—bristol—HAGEN PAPER CO., St. Louis.
Irish Bond—(w)—THE UNION PAPER & TWINE CO., Detroit, Mich.
Irish Linen—(b)—UNITED STATES ENVELOPE CO. (Whitcomb Envelope Co. Division), Worcester, Mass.
Irish Linen—(b)—toilet—NORTHERN PAPER MILLS, Green Bay, Wis.
Irish Linene—(w)—EATON, CRANE & PIKE CO., Pittsfield, Mass.
Irish Linen Bond—(w)—DIEM & WING PAPER CO., Cincinnati, Ohio.
Irish Linen—(b)—bristol—J. W. BUTLER PAPER CO., Chicago.
Irish Linen Fabric—(w)—AMERICAN WRITING PAPER CO., Holyoke.
Irish Linen Ledger—(w)—GRAHAM PAPER CO., St. Louis.
Irish Linen Ledger—(w)—AMERICAN WRITING PAPER CO., Holyoke.
Irish Poplin—(w)—MARCUS WARD CO., Brooklyn, N. Y.
Ironclad—(b)—JOHN LESLIE PAPER CO., Minneapolis, Minn.
Iron Fibre—QUAKER CITY PAPER CO., Philadelphia.
Iron Tag—(b)—HOLLINGSWORTH & VOSE CO., Boston, Mass.
Ironwood—(b)—tag board—LOUISVILLE PAPER CO., Louisville, Ky.
Iroquois—(b)—toilet—ALBANY PERFORATED WRAPPING PAPER CO., Albany, N. Y.
Iroquois—(b)—toilet—NORTHERN PAPER MILLS, Green Bay, Wis.
Iroquois—(b)—EATON, CRANE & PIKE CO., Pittsfield, Mass.
Iroquois—(w)—fine—C E N T R A L OHIO PAPER CO., Columbus, Ohio.
Iroquois Bond—(w)—LASHER & LATHROP, New York.
Iroquois Kraft—(b)—MISSOURI PAPER HOUSE, Kansas City, Mo.
Iroquois Linen—(w)—LASHER & LATHROP, New York.
Iroquois Linen Ledger—(w)—JUDD PAPER CO., Holyoke, Mass.
Irquo—(b)—HOLLINGSWORTH & WHITNEY CO., Boston.
Irving Book—(w)—TAYLOR-LOGAN CO., PAPERMAKERS, Holyoke, Mass.
Irving Mill—(b)—RAYNOR & PERKINS ENVELOPE CO., New York.
Irving S. & S. C.—(b)—book—SWIGART PAPER CO., Chicago.
Irving Text—(w)—book—ADVERTISERS' PAPER MILLS, Holyoke.
Irvington—(w)—flat writing—MERRIAM PAPER CO., New York.
Irvington Writing—(w)—MERRIAM PAPER CO., New York.
Irwin's Quincy—IRWIN P A P E R CO., Quincy, Ill.
Isabella—(w)—flats—B R A D N E R SMITH & CO., Chicago.
Isanti Ledger—(w)—MINNEAPOLIS PAPER CO., Minneapolis, Minn.
Island City Mills—(b)—AMERICAN NEWS CO., New York.
Island Mills—(b)—news—KANSAS CITY PAPER HOUSE, Kansas City, Mo.
Islington Superfine—(w)—AMERICAN WRITING PAPER CO., Holyoke.
Italia—(b)—cover—NIAGARA PAPER MILLS, Lockport, N. Y.
Italian Chiffon—(b)—E A T O N, CRANE & PIKE CO., Pittsfield, Mass.
Itasca—(b)—superfine—HAMPSHIRE PAPER CO., South Hadley Falls, Mass.
Itasca Bond—(w)—HAMPSHIRE PAPER CO., South Hadley Falls, Mass.
Ithaca—(w)—flat—BECKETT PAPER CO., THE, Hamilton, Ohio.
Ito—(b)—toilet—H. N O R W O O D EWING CO., New York.
Itsuitsus—(b)—toilet—GEO. T. JOHNSON CO., Boston.
Ivanhoe—(w)—writing—EASTERN MFG. CO., Bangor, Me.
Ivanhoe Writing—MACK-ELLIOTT PAPER CO., St. Louis.
Ivanhoe—(b)—cover—SEYMOUR CO., New York.
Ivanhoe—(b)—fine—SOUTHERN PAPER CO., Richmond, Va.

MINER EDGAR CO., Sole Agents   CLAY   WASHED <E W> HIGH COLOR   GRITLESS <C M> HIGH RETENTIC
Edgar Bros. Co. 30 CHURCH STREET NEW YORK

FELTS AND JACKETS | Appleton Woolen Mills, APPLETON - - WIS.

Watermarks and Brands

Ivanhoe—(b)—manila tag—ARNOLD-ROBERTS CO., Boston.
Ivanhoe Linen—(w)—JUDD PAPER CO., Holyoke, Mass.
Ivanhoe Linen—(w)—VERNON BROS. & CO., New York.
Ivanhoe Writing—(w)—MACK-ELLIOTT PAPER CO., St. Louis.
Iverine—(w)—AMERICAN WRITING PAPER CO., Holyoke, Mass.
Iverine—(b)—round-cornered cards—UNION CARD & PAPER CO., N. Y.
Iverine Enameled Blotting—(b)—MINNEAPOLIS PAPER CO., Minneapolis, Minn.
Ivoroid—(b) — book—MERRIAM PAPER CO., New York.
Ivory—(b)—blotting, cardboards and cards—GRAHAM PAPER CO., St. Louis.
Ivory—(b)—enameled book—J. W. BUTLER PAPER CO., Chicago.
Ivory—(b)—flat — UNION PAPER & TWINE CO., Detroit, Mich.
Ivory—(b)—M. F. and Super—CANFIELD PAPER CO., New York.
Ivory Blanks — (b) — McCLELLAN PAPER CO., Minneapolis, Minn.
Ivory Bristol—(b)—BRADNER SMITH & CO., Chicago.
Ivory Enameled — (b) — blotting — CONROW BROS., New York.
Ivory Envelopes—(b)—WHITAKER PAPER CO., Cincinnati, Ohio.
Ivory Fine Blank— (b) —BUNTIN, GILLIES & CO., LTD., Hamilton, Ontario, Can.
Ivory Finish Book—(b)—PAUL E. VERNON & CO., New York.
Ivory Mills —(w)— flat — BUNTIN GILLIES & CO., LTD., Hamilton, Ontario, Canada.
Ivory Tint — (b) — translucent — UNION CARD & PAPER CO., N. Y.
Ivory White Blanks—(b)—J. C. PARKER PAPER CO., Louisville, Ky.
Ivy—(b)—bristols—UNION CARD & PAPER CO., New York.
Ivy Leaf—(b)—cards, envelopes and wedding stationery—MINNEAPOLIS PAPER CO., Minneapolis, Minn.
Ivy Mills—(w)—CINCINNATI CORDAGE AND PAPER CO., Cincinnati.
I.X.L. Bond—(w)—SOUTHWORTH CO., Mittineague, Mass.
I. X. L. Linen—(w)—AETNA PAPER CO., Dayton, Ohio.
IXL Linen—(b)—WRIGHT, BARRETT & STILWELL CO., St Paul.
IXL Linen—(w)—DWIGHT BROS. PAPER CO., Chicago.
I X L Linen—(w)—BEECHER, PECK & LEWIS, Detroit, Mich.
I. X. L. Onion Skin—(b)—KINGSLEY PAPER CO., Cleveland, Ohio.

J

J. B. W. Insurance Special—(w)—JOHN B. WATKINS, New York.
Jack Frost—(b)—coated—LEWERTH & CULBERTSON, New York.
Jack Rose — (b) — toilet — W. A. STOWE PAPER CO., Grand Rapids.
Jack Rose Mills—(b)—folded writing—BRADNER SMITH & CO., Chicago.
Jackson—(w)—writing—WEST VIRGINIA PULP AND PAPER CO., N. Y.
Jackson Ledger —(w)— BRADNER SMITH & CO., Chicago.
Jackson Mills—(w)—MISSOURI PAPER HOUSE, Kansas City, Mo.
James River Superfine—RICHMOND PAPER CO., Richmond, Va.
January—(b)—wedding and bristol—MOUNTAIN MILL PAPER CO., Lee, Mass.
Janus—(b)—toilet—H. NORWOOD EWING CO., New York.
Jap—(b)—toilet—NORTHERN PAPER MILLS, Green Bay, Wis.
Japan Bond—(b)—RIEGEL & CO., INC., Philadelphia.
Japan Bond—(w)—AMERICAN WRITING PAPER CO., Holyoke, Mass.
Japan Bond—(w)—RIEGEL & CO., INC., Philadelphia.
Japan Cover—(b)—PAUL E. VERNON & CO., New York.
Japan Linen Bond—(w) BUNTIN, GILLIES & CO., LTD., Hamilton, Ontario, Can.
Japan Parchment—(b)—GEO. B. HURD & CO., New York.
Japanin—(b)—HY. LINDENMEYR & SONS, New York.
Japanese—(b)—toilet — NORTHERN PAPER MILLS, Green Bay, Wis.
Japanese Fibre — (b) — BRADNER SMITH & CO., Chicago.
Japanese Linen—(w)—CRANE BROTHERS, Westfield, Mass.
Japanese Parchment—(b)—book—LASHER & LATHROP, New York.
Japanese Parchment—(b)—M. G. wrapping—OLD DOMINION PAPER CO., Norfolk, Va.
Japatisu — (b) — toilet — GEO. T. JOHNSON CO., Boston.
Jasper—(b)—MATTHIAS PLUM, Newark, N. J.
Jefferson—(b)—colored bristol—J. C. PARKER PAPER CO., Louisville, Ky.
Jefferson—(b)—white wove—F. A. FLINN, INC., New York.
Jefferson — (w) — extra superfine—GARRETT-BUCHANAN CO., Philadelphia.
Jefferson Bond—(w)—GARRETT-BUCHANAN CO., Philadelphia.
Jefferson Linen Ledger—(w)—GARRETT-BUCHANAN CO., Philadelphia.
Jenson—(b)—MILLER & WRIGHT PAPER CO., New York.

JAMES H. HARRISON PULPSTONE MANUFACTURER | **GENUINE NEWCASTLE STONES** 18 Killowen St., GATESHEAD-ON-TYNE, ENG.

Watermarks and Brands

Jersey Bond—(w)—CARPENTER PAPER CO., Omaha, Neb.
Jewel—(b)—toilet—GRAHAM PAPER CO., St. Louis.
Jewel—(b)—toilet—NORTHERN PAPER MILLS, Green Bay, Wis.
Jewell M. F.—(b)—book—SPRINGFIELD PAPER & SUPPLY CO., Springfield, Mo.
Jewt—(b)—toilet—SCOTT PAPER CO., Philadelphia.
Jim Crow—(b)—toilet—NORTHERN PAPER MILLS, Green Bay, Wis.
Jingo—(b)—toilet—H. NORWOOD EWING CO., New York.
Job Roll—(b)—toilet—UNITED STATES ENVELOPE CO. (Morgan Envelope Co. Div.), Springfield, Mass.
John Hancock—(b)—BYRON WESTON CO., Dalton, Mass.
Joliette—(b)—ALEX. McARTHUR & CO., Montreal, Canada.
Journal Book—(b)—DIEM & WING PAPER CO., Cincinnati, Ohio.
Journal Index—(b)—bristol—STANDARD CORD & PAPER CO., New York.
J. P. Co. Fine—(w)—JOHNSTON PAPER CO., Harrisburg, Pa.
Jubilee Wedding Bristol—(b)—BEECHER, PECK & LEWIS, Detroit, Mich.
Judicial Linen Bond—(w)—CONROW BROTHERS, New York.
Julian—(w)—toilet, wrapping—W. R. GRACE & CO., New York.
Juliet—(b)—toilet—H. NORWOOD EWING CO., New York.
Juliette—(w)—bond—W. R. GRACE & CO., New York.
June—(b)—wedding and bristol—MOUNTAIN MILL PAPER CO., Lee, Mass.
Juniata—(w)—DEARBORN PAPER CO., Chicago.
Juniata—(b)—writing—WEST VIRGINIA PULP AND PAPER CO., N. Y.
Juniata Half Tone Plate—(b)—DIEM & WING PAPER CO., Cincinnati, Ohio.
Junior—(b)—toilet—NORTHERN PAPER MILLS, Green Bay, Wis.
Junior—(b)—toilet—MEGARGEE BROS., Scranton, Pa.
Juno—(b)—flats—HENRY LINDENMEYR & SONS, New York.
Jupiter—(b)—J. F. WALL & SON, Norfolk, Mass.
Jupiter—(b)—book and linen—GRAHAM PAPER CO., St. Louis.
Jupiter—(b)—flats—LOUISVILLE PAPER CO., Louisville, Ky.
Jupiter Fibre—(b)—wrapping—D. S. WALTON & CO., New York.
Jupiter Linen—(b)—HENRY LINDENMEYR & SONS, New York.
Jupiter Litho Blanks—(b)—HY. LINDENMEYR & SONS, New York.
Jupiter Rope—(b)—wrapping—VON OLKER-SNELL PAPER CO., Boston.

Jupiter Wove Writing—(b)—HY. LINDENMEYR & SONS, New York.
Justice Linen Bond—(w)—W. M. PRINGLE & CO., INC., New York.
Justice Linen Ledger—(w)—BEECHER, PECK & LEWIS, Detroit.
Justice Linen Ledger—(w)—W. M. PRINGLE & CO., INC., New York.
Justrite—(b)—toilet—GEO. T. JOHNSON CO., Boston.
Just-Tear-It Linen—(b)—UNITED STATES ENVELOPE CO. (Whitcomb Envelope Co. Div.), Worcester, Mass.
Jute Document Tag—(b)—CHATFIELD & WOODS CO., Cincinnati, O.

K

"K" in a Diamond—(w)—1 and 2 fines—N. Y. & UTAH PAPER CO., Salt Lake City, Utah.
K and "High Grade" in a diamond—(b)—KINLEITH PAPER CO., St. Catharines, Ont.
"K" Ledger—(b)—white ledger paper—R. C. KASTNER PAPER CO., New York.
K. O. S. H. T.—(b)—insulated papers—BIRD & SON, Walpole, Mass.
K. P. C. Linen Ledger—(w)—KINGSLEY PAPER CO., Cleveland.
K. P. C. Onion Skin—(b)—KINGSLEY PAPER CO., Cleveland, Ohio.
K. Translucent Bristol—(b)—KINGSLEY PAPER CO., Cleveland.
Kadesh Bond—(b)—typewriter—EATON, CRANE & PIKE CO., Pittsfield, Mass.
Kadesh Linen—(b)—typewriter—EATON, CRANE & PIKE CO., Pittsfield, Mass.
Kahoka—(b)—toilet—ALBANY PERFORATED WRAPPING PAPER CO., Albany, N. Y.
Kaiser—(b)—cover—BAY STATE PAPER CO., Boston.
Kaiser Brown—(b)—wrappings and specialties—McDOWELL PAPER MILLS, Philadelphia.
Kaiser Cover—(b)—WHITING-PATTERSON CO., Philadelphia.
Kadjo—(b)—HOLLINGSWORTH & WHITNEY CO., Boston.
Kalma—(w and b)—bond, book, bristol and cover—CHAS. H. WRIGHT, Kalamazoo, Mich.
Kamargo—(b)—flats—KNOWLTON BROS., Watertown, N. Y.
Kamargo Text—(b)—book paper—KNOWLTON BROS., Watertown, N. Y.
Kanawha Envelope—(w)—WEST VIRGINIA PULP AND PAPER CO., New York.
Kanesaw—(b)—colored rope cover—BRADNER SMITH & CO., Chicago.
Kangaroo Linen—(w)—L. W. LAWRENCE, New York.
Kansas—(b)—bristols—KANSAS CITY PAPER HOUSE, Kansas City

Kara—(b)—enamel book—HAGEN PAPER CO., St. Louis.
Kara Antique Laid — (b)—UNION CARD & PAPER CO., New York.
Kara Linen—(b)—EATON, CRANE & PIKE CO., Pittsfield, Mass.
Kara M. F. — (b)—book—UNION CARD & PAPER CO., New York.
Kara Linen Bond — (b)—EATON, CRANE & PIKE CO., Pittsfield, Mass.
Karat Brand—(b)—cards, envelopes, and wedding stationery—MINNEAPOLIS PAPER CO., Minneapolis, Minn.
Karbon Kopy Bond — KINGSLEY PAPER CO., Cleveland, Ohio.
Karnak—(b)—cover—JAMES WHITE PAPER CO., Chicago.
Karhak Bond — (w)—WHITAKER PAPER CO., Cincinnati, Ohio.
Karnat — (b)—cover—BAY STATE PAPER CO., Boston.
Kashmir Bond—(w)—INDIANA PAPER CO., Indianapolis.
Kashmir Correspondence—(w)—B. D. RISING PAPER CO., Housatonic, Mass.
Kashmir Covers — (b) — MACKELLIOTT PAPER CO., St. Louis.
Kasota—(w)—white wove flats—MINNEAPOLIS PAPER CO., Minneapolis.
Katahdin Bond — (b) — EASTERN MFG. CO., Bangor, Me.
Keep Dry—(b)—waterproof wrapping—ANGIER MILLS, Ashland, Mass.
Keith—(w) — crossed words—KEITH PAPER CO., Turner's Falls, Mass.
Keith Bond —(w)— KEITH PAPER CO., Turner's Falls, Mass.
Keith Linen—(w)—KEITH PAPER CO., Turner's Falls, Mass.
Keith Linen Ledger—(w)—KEITH PAPER CO., Turner's Falls, Mass.
Keith Linen Wove — (w)—KEITH PAPER CO., Turner's Falls, Mass.
Keith Parchment Bond — (w)— KEITH PAPER CO., Turner's Falls, Mass.
Keith Superfine Laid—(w)—KEITH PAPER CO., Turner's Falls, Mass.
Keith Superfine Tints Laid—(w)— KEITH PAPER CO., Turner's Falls, Mass.
Keith Superfine Tint Wove—(b)— KEITH PAPER CO., Turner's Falls, Mass.
Keith Superfine Wove — (w)— KEITH PAPER CO., Turner's Falls, Mass.
Keith's No. 1 Bridal White Wedding Paper and Bristols—(b)— KEITH PAPER CO., Turner's Falls, Mass.
Keith's Deckle Edge Parchment Cover—(b) — KEITH PAPER CO., Turner's Falls, Mass.
Keith's Sheepskin Parchment—(b) —KEITH PAPER CO., Turner's Falls, Mass.
Keith's Superfine Wedding Paper and Bristols—(b)—KEITH PAPER CO., Turner's Falls, Mass.
Keith's Superior Wedding Paper and Bristols—(b)—KEITH PAPER CO., Turner's Falls, Mass.
Kelso Bond—(b)—EATON, CRANE & PIKE CO., Pittsfield, Mass.
Kempton—(b)—translucent cardboard —ARNOLD-ROBERTS CO., Boston.
Kenawha—(b)—writing—O. F. H. WARNER, Baltimore.
Kenbrook Bond — (w) — INDIANA PAPER CO., Indianapolis.
Kenebis—(b)—HOLLINGSWORTH & WHITNEY CO., Boston.
Kendall—(b)—litho. coated—LOUISVILLE PAPER CO., Louisville, Ky.
Kenesaw—(w)— flats — BRADNER SMITH & CO., Chicago.
Kenesaw—(b)—colored rope bristol— BRADNER SMITH & CO., Chicago.
Kenilworth—(w)—extra fine—GRAHAM PAPER CO., St. Louis.
Kenilworth Wove Satin — (b)— EATON, CRANE & PIKE CO., Pittsfield, Mass.
Kenmare Linen — (w) — SMITH, DAVIDSON & WRIGHT, LTD., Vancouver, B. C.
Kenmare Linen Fabric — (b) — SMITH, DAVIDSON & WRIGHT, LTD., Vancouver, B. C.
Kenmore—(b)—NATIONAL BLANK BOOK CO., Holyoke, Mass.
Kenmore—(w)—NATIONAL BLANK BOOK CO., Holyoke, Mass.
Kenmore — (b) — toilet—ALBANY PERFORATED WRAPPING PAPER CO., Albany, N. Y.
Kenmore—(b)—M. F. book—HAGEN PAPER CO., St. Louis.
Kenmore—(w)—W. D. MESSINGER & CO., Chicago.
Kenmore Deckled Edge—(w)—book —KENMORE PULP & PAPER CO., Philadelphia.
Kenmore Linen—(w)—FOX RIVER PAPER CO., Appleton, Wis.
Kenmore Mills — (w) — book—MEGARGEE-HARE PAPER CO., Philadelphia.
Kenmore Parchment—(b)—cover— CAREW MANUFACTURING CO., South Hadley Falls, Mass.
Kennebago—(b)—ruled goods—R. L. GREENE PAPER CO., Providence, R. I.
Kennebago Ledger — (w) — R. L. GREENE PAPER CO., Providence, R. I.
Kennebec—(b)—THOMAS W. PRICE CO., Philadelphia.
Kennebec — (b)—toilet—ALBANY PERFORATED WRAPPING PAPER CO., Albany, N. Y.
Kennebec—(b)—R. R. man—DIEM & WING PAPER CO., Cincinnati, O.
Kennebec—(b)—book—GRAHAM PAPER CO., St. Louis.
Kennebec Bond—(w)—C. P. LESH PAPER CO., Indianapolis, Ind.
Kennebec Ledger—(w)—flats—R. L. GREENE PAPER CO., Providence.

INVESTIGATIONS — REPORTS — INSPECTIONS
C. A. CHAPMAN, Inc.
28 E. JACKSON BLVD. — ENGINEERS — CHICAGO

Watermarks and Brands 685

Kennebec Mills — (w) — writing — STANDARD CARD & PAPER CO., New York.
Keno — (b) — toilet — NORTHERN PAPER MILLS, Green Bay, Wis.
Kenosha Linen Ledger — (w) — FOX RIVER PAPER CO., Appleton, Wis.
Kenosha Mills — (w) — DWIGHT BROS. PAPER CO., Chicago.
Kensington — (b) — writing — GRAHAM PAPER CO., St. Louis.
Kensington — (b) — WHITAKER PAPER CO., Cincinnati, Ohio.
Kensington Linen — (w) — AMERICAN PAPER GOODS CO., Kensington, Conn.
Kensington Mills — (w and b) — AMERICAN PAPER GOODS CO., Kensington, Conn.
Kent Brief — (b) — C. P. LESH PAPER CO., Indianapolis, Ind.
Kent Mills — (w) — CHARLES J. COHEN, Philadelphia.
Kent Mills — (w) — flat — CINCINNATI CORDAGE AND PAPER CO., Cincinnati, Ohio.
Kent Super — (b) — book — UNION CARD & PAPER CO., New York.
Kentish Mills — (w) — WESTERN PENNA. PAPER CO., Pittsburgh, Pa.
Kenton — (b) — toilet — LOUISVILLE PAPER CO., Louisville, Ky.
Kenwood — (w) — ledgers — J. E. LINDE PAPER CO., New York.
Kenwood — (b) — toilet — ALBANY PERFORATED WRAPPING PAPER CO., Albany, New York.
Kenwood — (b) — coated blank — ARNOLD-ROBERTS CO., Boston.
Kenwood — (b) — MEGARGEE-HARE PAPER CO., Philadelphia.
Kenwood Bond — (b) — BLUNLEN-LYON CO., Chicago.
Kenwood Pasted — (b) — bristol — SWIGART PAPER CO., Chicago.
Kenyon — (b) — manila — UNITED RAILWAY AND TRADING CO., LTD., New Orleans, La.
Kermes — (b) — cover — J. W. BUTLER PAPER CO., Chicago.
Keswick — (b) — super and cover — CLARKE & CO., New York.
Keuka — (b) — toilet — ALBANY PERFORATED WRAPPING PAPER CO., Albany, N. Y.
Keystone — (b) — M. F. white book — THE ALLING & COBY CO., Rochester.
Keystone — (b) — toilet — J. W. BUTLER PAPER CO., Chicago.
Keystone — (b) — toilet — ALBANY PERFORATED WRAPPING PAPER CO., Albany, New York.
Keystone — (b) — book — CINCINNATI CORDAGE AND PAPER CO., Cincinnati, Ohio.
Keystone — (b) — flats — DIEM & WING PAPER CO., Cincinnati, Ohio.
Keystone — (b) — translucent cardboard — ARNOLD-ROBERTS CO., Boston.
Keystone — (w) — enclosing letters M. B. — MEGARGEE BROS., Scranton, Pa.
Keystone Bond — (w) — MERRIAM PAPER CO., New York.
Keystone Bristol — (b) — HARLEM CARD & PAPER CO., New York.
Keystone Cover — (b) — THE ALLING & COBY CO., Rochester, New York.
Keystone Crash White — (w) — bond — MERRIAM PAPER CO., New York.
Keystone Ferro-Satine — (w) — blue print — KEYSTONE BLUE PRINT PAPER CO., Philadelphia.
Keystone Fibre Wrapping — (b) — MEGARGEE BROS., Scranton, Pa.
Keystone Linen Ledger — (w) — R. P. MOLTEN & CO., Philadelphia.
Keystone Linen Ledger — (w) — MEGARGEE BROS., Scranton, Pa.
Keystone Mills — (b) — book — CINCINNATI CORDAGE AND PAPER CO., Cincinnati, Ohio.
Keystone Satin Folding — (b) — bristols in colors — SWIGART PAPER CO., Chicago.
Keystone S. D. & W. — (w) — SMITH, DAVIDSON & WRIGHT, LTD., Vancouver, B. C.
Keystone-Superfine — (w) — (the two words used to form a design) — SMITH, DAVIDSON & WRIGHT, LTD., Vancouver, B. C.
Keystone Typewriter Paper — (b) — SMITH, DAVIDSON & WRIGHT, LTD., Vancouver, B. C.
Keystone White — (w) — bond — MERRIAM PAPER CO., New York.
Kid Bristol — (b) — R. F. BOND PAPER CO., Baltimore.
Kid Finish — (w) — Z. & W. M. CRANE, Dalton, Mass.
Kildare Linen — (w) — BUNTIN, GILLIES & CO., LTD., Hamilton, Canada.
Kildare Linen — (w) — MOSER PAPER CO., Chicago.
Kildare Linen — (w) — BUNTIN, GILLIES & CO., LTD., Hamilton, Can.
Kimberly — (w and b) — design — bond, ledger, writing — NEENAH PAPER CO., Neenah, Wis.
Kimona — (b) — cover — AMERICAN WRITING PAPER CO., Holyoke.
Kineo — (b) — HOLLINGSWORTH & WHITNEY CO., Boston.
Kineo — (b) — writing — EASTERN MANUFACTURING CO., Bangor, Me.
King — (b) — sheathing — CHATFIELD PAPER CO., New Haven, Conn.
King — (b) — sulphate kraft — W. H. CLAFLIN & CO., Boston.
King — (b) — enamel book — DONALDSON PAPER CO., Harrisburg, Pa.
King — (b) — toilet — UNITED STATES ENVELOPE CO., (Morgan Envelope Co. Division), Springfield, Mass.
King Alfred — (b) — toilet tissue — W. H. CLAFLIN & CO., Boston.

MINER EDGAR CO., Sole Agents
KEYSTONE CLAY & REDUCTION CO.
30 Church Street - - New York

C L A Y

PRECIPITATED REFINED
LIGHT GRAVITY SOFT TEXTURE
<K L M>
HIGH NATURAL COLOR, HIGH RETENTION

APPLETON MACHINE CO., APPLETON, WIS.
REFINING ENGINES, SCREENS, SAWING & SPLITTING MACHINERY
HIGH GRADE CENTRIFUGAL PUMPS

Watermarks and Brands

King Atlas—(b)—toilet—H. NORWOOD EWING, New York.
King Dodo—(w and b)—book—PAPER MILLS CO., Chicago.
King's Dependable Offset Paper—(b)—KING PAPER CO., Kalamazoo, Mich.
King Durable Folder Enamel—(b)—coated papers—KING PAPER CO., Kalamazoo, Mich.
King Superior Enamel—(b)—coated papers—KING PAPER CO., Kalamazoo, Mich.
King Superba Enamel—(b)—coated papers—KING PAPER CO., Kalamazoo, Mich.
King Superfine Enamel—(b)—coated papers—KING PAPER CO., Kalamazoo, Mich.
King Fibre Manila—(b)—express fibre—SEINSHEIMER PAPER CO., Cincinnati, Ohio.
King Flats—(w)—writing—KINGSLEY PAPER CO., Cleveland, Ohio.
King Mills—(b)—white wove—KINGSLEY PAPER CO., Cleveland.
King Mills—(b)—wrapping—CHASE BROS., Haverhill, Mass.
King-of-All—(b)—kraft—CHATFIELD & WOODS CO., Cincinnati, O.
King Philip—(b)—envelope—R. L. GREENE PAPER CO., Providence, R. I.
King Philip Ledger—(w)—R. L. GREENE PAPER CO., Providence.
King Tough Check—(b)—KINGSLEY PAPER CO., Cleveland, Ohio.
Kingscourt—(w)—writing—UNION CARD & PAPER CO., New York.
Kings Court—(b)—toilet—LOUISVILLE PAPER CO., Louisville, Ky.
King's Mills—(w)—writing—GRAHAM PAPER CO., St. Louis.
Kingsland—(w)—GEO. LA MONTE & SON, New York.
Kingston—(b)—toilet—STONE & FORSYTH CO., Boston.
Kingston—(b)—binders' trunk and friction board—GRAHAM PAPER CO., St. Louis.
Kingston Linen—(w)—AMERICAN WRITING PAPER CO., Holyoke.
Kingston Linen Ledger—(w)—CARTER, RICE & CO., CORP., Boston.
Kinleith Bond—(w)—KINLEITH PAPER CO., LTD., St. Catharines, Ontario.
Kinloch Book—(b)—GRAHAM PAPER CO., St. Louis.
Kinloch Linen Ledger—(w)—GRAHAM PAPER CO., St. Louis.
Kipling—(b)—book—LOUISVILLE PAPER CO., Louisville, Ky.
Kismet Bond—(w)—PARSONS TRADING COMPANY, New York.
Kleentowl—(w)—UNITED STATES PAPER MILLS, INC., Chambersburg, Pa.

Kier Kut—(w)—carbon and typewriter—S. D. CHILDS & CO., Chicago.
Klik Bond—(w)—SAUGERTIES MFG. CO., Saugerties, New York.
Kling Kraft—(b)—wrapping—LOUISVILLE PAPER CO., Louisville, Ky.
Klondike—(b)—colored laid writing—BASSETT & SUTPHIN, New York.
Klondike—(b)—tarred felt—GRAHAM PAPER CO., St. Louis.
Klondike Paper Cutters—(b)—CHATFIELD & WOODS CO., Cincinnati, Ohio.
Knickerbocker—(b)—toilet—SCOTT PAPER CO., Philadelphia.
Knickerbocker Bond—(w)—HUDSON VALLEY PAPER CO., Albany, New York.
Knickerbocker Ledger—(w)—LASHER & LATHROP, New York.
Knickerbocker Mills—(w)—GEORGE B. HURD & CO., N. Y.
Knockabout—(b)—bristol—LOUISVILLE PAPER CO., Louisville, Ky.
Knollwood—(b)—wove writing—MILLER & WRIGHT PAPER CO., New York.
Koatine—(b)—WHITAKER PAPER CO., Cincinnati, Ohio.
Kobe-Jap Parchment—(w)—CHATFIELD & WOODS CO., Cincinnati, O.
Kobi Writing—(b)—WHITING-PATTERSON CO., Philadelphia.
Kodak Post Card—(b)—CLEMENTS PAPER CO., Nashville, Tenn.
Kohinoor Cover—(b)—MINNEAPOLIS PAPER CO., Minneapolis, Minn.
Kohinoor Text—(b)—MINNEAPOLIS PAPER CO., Minneapolis, Minn.
Ko Ko—(b)—toilet—H. NORWOOD EWING CO., New York.
Kokomo—(b)—boards—AMERICAN STRAW BOARD CO., Chicago.
Kongo—(b)—C. P. LESH PAPER CO., Indianapolis, Ind.
Kenite—(b)—SCRANTOM, WETMORE & CO., Rochester, New York.
Korean—(b)—cover—SEYMOUR CO., New York.
Koshi Mills Writing—(w)—CHATFIELD & WOODS CO., Cincinnati, O.
Kosmos Kraft—(b)—MOORE & THOMPSON CO., Bellows Falls, Vt.
Kowntil—(b)—toilet—SCOTT PAPER CO., Philadelphia.
Kraft Brown—(b)—wrappings and specialties—McDOWELL PAPER MILLS, Philadelphia.
Krag Bond—(w)—WHITAKER PAPER CO., Cincinnati, Ohio.
Kraftspun Wrapping—(b)—GRAHAM PAPER CO., St. Louis.
Krect—(b)—toilet—SCOTT PAPER CO., Philadelphia.
Kremlin—(b)—cover—J. W. BUTLER PAPER CO., Chicago.
Krepko—(b)—Kraft wrapping—HORWITZ BROS., Elmira, N. Y.

Krypton Linen Laid—(w)—HOWARD SMITH PAPER MILLS, LTD., Montreal, Can.
Krypton Parchment—(w)—HOWARD SMITH PAPER MILLS, LTD., Montreal, Can.
Kwasind Cover—(b)—HAMPDEN GLAZED PAPER & CARD CO., Holyoke, Mass.

L

"L"—(b)—White coated blanks—THE PAPER MILLS CO., Chicago.
"L" (in a Diamond) Writing—(b)—HY. LINDENMEYR & SONS, New York.
L. Fibre—(b)—R. L. GREENE PAPER CO., Providence, R. I.
L. & L.—(b)—blue wove—LASHER & LATHROP, New York.
L. & L. Superior Strength—(w)—ledger—LASHER & LATHROP, N. Y.
L. P. Fibre—(b)—R. L. GREENE PAPER CO., Providence, R. I.
Labelet—(b)—book and label—GRAHAM PAPER CO., St. Louis.
La Belle France Linen—(w)—UNITED STATES ENVELOPE CO. (Logan, Swift & Bridgham Envelope Co. Division), Worcester, Mass.
La Capital—(b)—toilet—NORTHERN PAPER MILLS, Green Bay, Wis.
Lackawanna—(b)—toilet—MEGARGEE BROS., Scranton, Pa.
Lackawanna Linen Ledger—(w)—MEGARGEE BROS., Scranton, Pa.
La Clede—(b)—carpet lining—GRAHAM PAPER CO., St. Louis.
Laclede—(w)—writing—HAGEN PAPER CO., St. Louis.
Laconia—(b)—white wove—F. A. FLINN, INC., New York.
Lady Washington Linen—(w)—POWERS PAPER COMPANY, Springfield, Mass.
Lafayette Bond—(w)—COY HUNT & CO., New York.
Lafayette Blotting—(b)—GEO. W. MILLAR & CO., New York.
Lafayette Ledger—JOHN F. SARLE, New York.
Lafayette Linen Ledger—(w)—JOHN F. SARLES CO., INC., New York.
Lahaina Linen—(w)—HARTFORD FIRE INSURANCE CO., Hartford, Conn.
Laitonia Bank—(w)—PARSONS TRADING CO., New York.
Lake—(b)—news—C. P. LESH PAPER CO., Indianapolis, Ind.
Lake—(b)—toilet—THE SEINSHEIMER PAPER CO., Cincinnati, Ohio.
Lake Front—(b)—toilet—NORTHERN PAPER MILLS, Green Bay, Wis.
Lake George—(b)—cardboard and cards—GRAHAM PAPER CO., St. Louis.
Lake Shore—(b)—J. W. BUTLER PAPER CO., Chicago.

Lakeside—(b)—tinted wove writing—CHATFIELD & WOODS CO., Cincinnati, Ohio.
Lakeside—(b)—S. & S. C. book—BRADNER SMITH & CO., Chicago.
Lakeside Bond—(b)—J. E. LINDE PAPER CO., New York.
Lakeside Bond—(w)—BRADNER SMITH & CO., Chicago.
Lakeside Mills—(b)—writing—CLEVELAND PAPER MFG. CO., Cleveland, Ohio.
Lakeside Mills—(w)—fine writing—LEE PAPER CO., Vicksburg, Mich.
Lakeside Tinted Bristol—(b)—BRADNER SMITH & CO., Chicago.
Lake View—(b)—flat—R. H. THOMPSON CO., Buffalo, N. Y.
Lake View Tinted Wove—(b)—THE UNION PAPER & TWINE CO., Detroit, Mich.
Lakewood—(b)—wedding paper and bristols—UNION CARD & PAPER CO., New York.
Lakewood Mills—(b)—PLYMOUTH PAPER CO., Holyoke, Mass.
Lakewood Wedding—(b)—UNION CARD & PAPER CO., New York.
Lakewood—(w)—writing—SYRKIN & BACK, New York.
La Monte—(w)—GEORGE LA MONTE & SON, New York.
La Monte Bond—(w and b)—GEO. LA. MONTE & SON, New York.
La Monte Quadrille—(w)—GEO. B. HURD & CO., New York.
La Monte Quadrille—(b)—GEO. LA MONTE & SON, New York.
Lancashire Bond—(w)—CENTRAL PAPER CO., Columbus, Ohio.
Lancaster—(b)—eggshell book—CHATFIELD & WOODS CO., Cincinnati, Ohio.
Lancaster—(b)—rag stock—GRAHAM PAPER CO., St. Louis.
Lanciers—(b)—Z. & W. M. CRANE, Dalton, Mass.
Landseer Felt Mounts—(b)—BRADNER SMITH & CO., Chicago.
Landseer Linen—(w)—GRAHAM PAPER CO., St. Louis.
Landseer Mills—(w)—GRAHAM PAPER CO., St. Louis.
Lane—(b)—book and folder—GRAHAM PAPER CO., St. Louis.
Lansdown—(b)—velvet finish book and music paper—MINNEAPOLIS PAPER CO., Minneapolis, Minn.
Lansdowne—(b)—book and envelope—GRAHAM PAPER CO., St. Louis.
Lansing—(b)—book—GRAHAM PAPER CO., St. Louis.
Lantana—(b)—book—GRAHAM PAPER CO., St. Louis.
Lantic Bond—(b)—CLEVELAND PAPER MFG. CO., Cleveland, Ohio.
Lapland-Randight—(b)—fibre—MINNEAPOLIS PAPER CO., Minneapolis.

King Atlas—(b)—toilet—H. NORWOOD EWING, New York.
King Dodo—(w and b)—book—PAPER MILLS CO., Chicago.
King's Dependable Offset Paper—(b)—KING PAPER CO., Kalamazoo, Mich.
King Durable Folder Enamel—(b)—coated papers—KING PAPER CO., Kalamazoo, Mich.
King Superior Enamel—(b)—coated papers—KING PAPER CO., Kalamazoo, Mich.
King Superba Enamel—(b)—coated papers—KING PAPER CO., Kalamazoo, Mich.
King Superfine Enamel—(b)—coated papers — KING PAPER CO., Kalamazoo, Mich.
King Fibre Manila — (b) — express fibre — SEINSHEIMER PAPER CO., Cincinnati, Ohio.
King Flats — (w)—writing—KINGSLEY PAPER CO., Cleveland, Ohio.
King Mills—(b) — white wove — KINGSLEY PAPER CO., Cleveland.
King Mills—(b)—wrapping—CHASE BROS., Haverhill, Mass.
King-of-All—(b)—kraft—CHATFIELD & WOODS CO., Cincinnati, O.
King Philip —(b)— envelope—R. L. GREENE PAPER CO., Providence, R. I.
King Philip Ledger—(w)—R. L. GREENE PAPER CO., Providence.
King Tough Check—(b)—KINGSLEY PAPER CO., Cleveland, Ohio.
Kingscourt—(w)—writing — UNION CARD & PAPER CO., New York.
Kings Court — (b) — toilet — LOUISVILLE PAPER CO., Louisville, Ky.
King's Mills—(w)—writing — GRAHAM PAPER CO., St. Louis.

Kier Kut — (w)—carbon and typewriter—S. D. CHILDS & CO., Chicago.
Klik Bond — (w) — SAUGERTIES MFG. CO., Saugerties, New York.
Kling Kraft—(b)—wrapping—LOUISVILLE PAPER CO., Louisville, Ky.
Klondike—(b)—colored laid writing—BASSETT & SUTPHIN, New York.
Klondike—(b)—tarred felt — GRAHAM PAPER CO., St. Louis.
Klondike Paper Cutters — (b)—CHATFIELD & WOODS CO., Cincinnati, Ohio.
Knickerbocker—(b)—toilet—SCOTT PAPER CO., Philadelphia.
Knickerbocker Bond — (w) — HUDSON VALLEY PAPER CO., Albany, New York.
Knickerbocker Ledger — (w) — LASHER & LATHROP, New York.
Knickerbocker Mills — (w) — GEORGE B. HURD & CO., N. Y.
Knockabout — (b)—bristol — LOUISVILLE PAPER CO., Louisville, Ky.
Knollwood—(b) — wove writing—MILLER & WRIGHT PAPER CO., New York.
Koatfne—(b)—WHITAKER PAPER CO., Cincinnati, Ohio.
Kobe-Jap Parchment—(w)—CHATFIELD & WOODS CO., Cincinnati, O.
Kobi Writing—(b)—WHITING-PATTERSON CO., Philadelphia.
Kodak Post Card—(b)—CLEMENTS PAPER CO., Nashville, Tenn.
Kohinoor Cover — (b) — MINNEAPOLIS PAPER CO., Minneapolis, Minn.
Kohinoor Text—(b)—MINNEAPOLIS PAPER CO., Minneapolis, Minn.
Ko Ko—(b)—toilet—H. NORWOOD EWING CO., New York.
Kokomo—(b)—boards — AMERICAN

Krypton Linen Laid—(w)—HOWARD SMITH PAPER MILLS, LTD., Montreal, Can.
Krypton Parchment—(w)—HOWARD SMITH PAPER MILLS, LTD., Montreal, Can.
Kwasind Cover—(b)—HAMPDEN GLAZED PAPER & CARD CO., Holyoke, Mass.

L

"L"—(b)—White coated blanks—THE PAPER MILLS CO., Chicago.
"L" (in a Diamond) Writing—(b)—HY. LINDENMEYR & SONS, New York.
L. Fibre—(b)—R. L. GREENE PAPER CO., Providence, R. I.
L. & L.—(b)—blue wove—LASHER & LATHROP, New York.
L. & L. Superior Strength—(w)—ledger—LASHER & LATHROP, N. Y.
L. P. Fibre—(b)—R. L. GREENE PAPER CO., Providence, R. I.
Labelet—(b)—book and label—GRAHAM PAPER CO., St. Louis.
La Belle France Linen—(w)—UNITED STATES ENVELOPE CO. (Logan, Swift & Bridgham Envelope Co. Division), Worcester, Mass.
La Capital—(b)—toilet—NORTHERN PAPER MILLS, Green Bay, Wis.
Lackawanna—(b)—toilet—MEGARGEE BROS., Scranton, Pa.
Lackawanna Linen Ledger—(w)—MEGARGEE BROS., Scranton, Pa.

Lakeside—(b)—tinted wove writing—CHATFIELD & WOODS CO., Cincinnati, Ohio.
Lakeside—(b)—S. & S. C. book—BRADNER SMITH & CO., Chicago.
Lakeside Bond—(b)—J. E. LINDE PAPER CO., New York.
Lakeside Bond—(w)—BRADNER SMITH & CO., Chicago.
Lakeside Mills—(b)—writing—CLEVELAND PAPER MFG. CO., Cleveland, Ohio.
Lakeside Mills—(w)—fine writing—LEE PAPER CO., Vicksburg, Mich.
Lakeside Tinted Bristol—(b)—BRADNER SMITH & CO., Chicago.
Lake View—(b)—flat—R. H. THOMPSON CO., Buffalo, N. Y.
Lake View Tinted Wove—(b)—THE UNION PAPER & TWINE CO., Detroit, Mich.
Lakewood—(b)—wedding paper and bristols—UNION CARD & PAPER CO., New York.
Lakewood Mills—(w)—PLYMOUTH PAPER CO., Holyoke, Mass.
Lakewood Wedding—(b)—UNION CARD & PAPER CO., New York.
Lakewood—(w)—writing—BYRKIT & BACK, New York.
La Monte—(w)—GEORGE LA MONTE & SON, New York.
La Monte Bond—(w and b)—GEO. LA MONTE & SON, New York.
La Monte Quadrille—(w)—GEO. B. HURD & CO., New York.
La Monte Quadrille—(b)—GEO. LA MONTE & SON, New York.
Lancashire Bond—(w)—CENTRAL PAPER CO., Columbus, Ohio.
Lancaster—(b)—eggshell book—CHATFIELD & WOODS CO., Cincinnati, Ohio.
Lancaster—(b)—rag stock—GRAHAM PAPER CO., St. Louis.
Lanstone—(b)—Z. & W. M. CRANE, Dalton, Mass.

FELTS AND JACKETS | Appleton Woolen Mills
APPLETON - - WIS.

Watermarks and Brands

La Precieuse—(b)—toilet—ALBANY PERFORATED WRAPPING PAPER CO., Albany, N. Y.
Larchmont—(w)—J. G. SHAW BLANK BOOK CO., New York.
Laredo—(b)—book—GRAHAM PAPER CO., St. Louis.
Larkhall Parchment—(w)—bond—LOUISVILLE PAPER CO., Louisville, Ky.
La Salle—(b)—FOX RIVER PAPER CO., Appleton, Wis.
La Salle India Tint Enameled—(b)—book—BRADNER SMITH & CO., Chicago.
La Salle Bond—(w)—BRADNER SMITH & CO., Chicago.
Latin—(b)—drawing—GRAHAM PAPER CO., St. Louis.
Laundry Bond—(w)—HAMMERMILL PAPER CO., Erie, Pa.
Laurel Bond—(b)—C. S. PROCTOR PAPER CO., Boston.
Laurel Mills—(w)—extra fine—DWIGHT BROTHERS PAPER CO., Cincinnati, Chicago.
Laurel Mills—(b)—writing—M. J. EARL, Reading, Pa.
Lawn Finish—(w and b)—GEO. B. HURD & CO., New York.
Lawnette—(w)—GEO. B. HURD & CO., New York.
Lawton—(b)—book—GRAHAM PAPER CO., St. Louis.
L. C.—(b)—toilet—ALBANY PERFORATED WRAPPING PAPER CO., Albany, N. Y.
Leader—(w)—bond—DONALDSON PAPER CO., Harrisburg, Pa.
Leader—(w)—bond—PENINSULAR PAPER CO., Ypsilanti, Mich.
Leader—(b)—sheathing—LOUISVILLE PAPER CO., Louisville, Ky.
Leader—(b)—toilet—THE SEINSHEIMER PAPER CO., Cincinnati.
Leader—(b)—writing—JUDD PAPER CO., Holyoke, Mass.
Leader Gummed Paper—(b)—BRADNER SMITH & CO., Chicago.
Leader Writing—(b)—IRWIN PAPER CO., Quincy, Ill.
Leather—(b)—COLUMBIA PAPER BAG CO., New York.
Leather Finish—(b)—GEO. B. HURD & CO., New York.
Leatherette Fibre—(b)—KANSAS CITY PAPER CO., Kansas City, Mo.
Leatherette Kraft—(b)—R. A. CANTHORNE PAPER CO., Richmond, Va.
Leclede—(w)—flats—HAGEN PAPER CO., St. Louis.
Ledger—(b)—writing—RIEGEL & CO., INC., Philadelphia.
Ledger Bond—(w)—WM. G. JOHNSTON & CO., Pittsburgh, Pa.
Ledger Index—(b)—bristol—BRADNER SMITH & CO., Chicago.
Ledger Fine—(w)—R. P. MOLTEN, Philadelphia.
Ledger Index Bristol—(b)—MILLERS FALLS PAPER CO., Millers Falls, Mass.
Ledger Index Bristol—(b)—MEGARGEE BROS., Scranton, Pa.
Ledger Mills—(w)—J. W. BUTLER PAPER CO., Chicago.
Lee Paper Co. Superfine—(w)—superfine writing—LEE PAPER CO., Vicksburg, Mich.
Leeds—(b)—onion skin—WHITING-PATTERSON CO., Philadelphia.
Leeds Linen Ledger—(w)—LEE PAPER CO., Vicksburg, Mich.
Leeds Manifold—(b)—WHITING-PATTERSON CO., Philadelphia.
Leffingwell—(b)—cardboard and tag—GRAHAM PAPER CO., St. Louis.
Legal Bond—(w)—KINGSLEY PAPER CO., Cleveland, Ohio.
Legal Bond—(w)—RIEGEL & CO. INC., Philadelphia.
Legal Ledger—(w)—AETNA PAPER CO., Dayton, Ohio.
Legal Ledger—(w)—CHATFIELD & WOODS CO., Cincinnati, Ohio.
Legal Linen Ledger—(w)—AMERICAN WRITING PAPER CO., Holyoke.
Legend Linen Ledger—(w)—AMERICAN WRITING PAPER CO., Holyoke, Mass.
Leghorn Bond—(w)—MEGARGEE-HARE PAPER CO., Philadelphia.
Leghorn Book Eggshell—(b)—PAUL E. VERNON & CO., New York.
Leghorn Ledger—(w)—MEGARGEE-HARE PAPER CO., Philadelphia.
Leghorn Mimeograph—(b)—WHITING-PATTERSON CO., Philadelphia.
Leland—(b)—book—GRAHAM PAPER CO., St. Louis.
Leland—(w)—ledger—MIDLAND PAPER CO., Chicago.
Lemaire Mills—(b)—colored laid—CONROW BROS., New York.
Lenore Writing—(b)—IRWIN PAPER CO., Quincy, Ill.
Lenox—(b)—tissue—SMITH PAPER CO., Lee, Mass.
Lenox—(b)—writing—GRAHAM PAPER CO., St. Louis.
Lenox—(b)—blotting—EATON, DIKEMAN CO., Lee, Mass.
Lenox Bond—(w)—writing—CAREW MANUFACTURING CO., South Hadley Falls, Mass.
Lenox Brands—fibre—ALFRED BLEYER & CO., New York.
Lenox Extra Super—(w)—AMERICAN WRITING PAPER CO., Holyoke.
Lenox Linen Finish—(w)—bond—LASHER & LATHROP, New York.
Lenox Pasted Bristol—(b)—BRADNER SMITH & CO., Chicago.
Lenox Superfine—(w)—AMERICAN WRITING PAPER CO., Holyoke, Mass.
Lenox Wedding Bristol—(b)—HARLEM CARD & PAPER CO., New York.
Leonard—(b)—book and envelope—GRAHAM PAPER CO., St. Louis.

BLOTTING PAPERS "STANDARD," "IMPERIAL," "STERLING"
Royal Worcester and Defender Enameled
STANDARD PAPER MFG. CO., - - Richmond, Va.

Watermarks and Brands

Lepaco Linen Bond—(w)—bond—LEE PAPER CO., Vicksburg, Mich.
Le Page—(b)—cardboard and tag—GRAHAM PAPER CO., St. Louis.
Lesdon—(w)—bond—LESLIE-DONAHOWER CO., St. Paul.
Lesdon Halftone—(w)—flat—LESLIE-DONAHOWER CO., St. Paul.
Leslie's Bond—(w)—JOHN LESLIE PAPER CO., Minneapolis, Minn.
Leslie's Linen Ledger—(w)—JOHN LESLIE PAPER CO., Minneapolis.
Letter File Manila—(b)—BRADNER SMITH & CO., Chicago.
Levant—(b)—cover—C. H. DEXTER & SONS, INC., Windsor Locks, Conn.
Levant Parchment—(b)—GEO. B. HURD & CO., New York.
Lexington—(b)—flat—JOHN CARTER & CO., Boston.
Lexington—(w)—fine writing—VON OLKER-SNELL PAPER CO., Boston.
Lexington Bond—(w)—F. A. FLINN, INC., New York.
Lexington Ledger—(w)—F. A. FLINN, INC., New York.
Lexington Linen—(w)—AMERICAN WRITING PAPER CO., Holyoke, Mass.
Leyden Mills—(w)—colored laid—CONROW BROS., New York.
L. Fibre—(b)—R. L. GREENE PAPER CO., Providence, R. I.
Liberty—(b)—covers—KNOWLTON BROS., Watertown, N. Y., and RIEGEL & CO., INC., Philadelphia.
Liberty—(b)—H. K. BREWER & CO., New York.
Liberty—(b)—news—GRAHAM PAPER CO., St. Louis.
Liberty—(b)—toilet—UNITED STATES ENVELOPE CO. (Morgan Envelope Co. Div.), Springfield, Mass.
Liberty Bell—(b)—toilet—SCOTT PAPER CO., Philadelphia.
Liberty Bond—(w)—HOWARD PAPER CO., Urbana, O.
Liberty Bond—(b)—MINNEAPOLIS PAPER CO., Minneapolis, Minn.
Liberty Bristol—(b)—JOHN CARTER & CO., Boston.
Liberty Ledger (Liberty Bell)—(w)—F. A. FLINN, INC., New York.
Liberty Linen—(w)—STRATHMORE PAPER CO., Mittineague, Mass.
Liberty Linen Pure Fibre—(w)—STRATHMORE PAPER CO., Mittineague, Mass.
Liberty Loan Bond—(b and w)—REESE & REESE, Baltimore, Md.
Liberty Loan Bond—(w)—HOWARD PAPER CO., Urbana, Ohio.
Liberty Manifold Tissue—(b)—ELSINORE PAPER CO., New York.
Liberty Mills—(b)—No. 3 fine—C. W. WILLIAMS & CO., New York.
Liberty Parchment—(b)—wrapping M. J. EARL, Reading, Pa.
Liberty Parchment—(b)—specialty wrapping—R. A. CAUTHORNE PAPER CO., Richmond, Va.
Liberty Wedding Bristol—(b)—RICHMOND PAPER CO., Richmond, Va.
Library—(b)—cover—TAYLOR-LOGAN CO., Papermakers, Holyoke.
Library Bond—(w)—HAMMERMILL PAPER CO., Erie, Pa.
Library Bristol—(b)—JOHN CARTER & CO., Boston.
Library Covers—(b)—ADVERTISERS' PAPER MILLS, Holyoke, Mass.
Library Text—(w)—book—ADVERTISERS' PAPER MILLS, Holyoke.
Library Text—(b)—book (English finish)—S. D. WARREN & CO., Boston.
Liege Linen Finish Bond—(w)—C. P. LESH PAPER CO., Indianapolis.
Lightholder—(b)—book—GRAHAM PAPER CO., St. Louis.
Lighthouse—(w)—bond, writing and wrapping—W. R. GRACE & CO., New York.
Lignine—(b)—detail board—C. B. HEWITT & BROS., INC., New York.
Lilies of France—(b)—toilet—SCOTT PAPER CO., Philadelphia.
Lilies of the Valley—(b)—toilet—SCOTT PAPER CO., Philadelphia.
Lily Bond—(w)—HOWARD PAPER CO., Urbana, O.
Lily Parchment—(b)—A. M. EATON, Waltham and Boston.
Limerick—(w)—BUNTIN, GILLIES & CO., LTD., Hamilton, Ontario, Can.
Limerick Linen—(w)—MEGARGEE BROS., Scranton, Pa.
Limoges Enameled Blotting—(b)—HY. LINDENMEYR & SONS, New York.
Linbrook Mills—(b)—CONROW BROS., New York.
Lincoln Bond—(w)—FOX RIVER PAPER CO., Appleton, Wis.
Lincoln Bond—(w)—HARLEM CARD & PAPER CO., New York.
Lincoln Ledger—(w)—FOX RIVER PAPER CO., Appleton, Wis.
Lincoln Ledger—(w)—GARRETT-BUCHANAN CO., Philadelphia.
Lincoln Linen Ledger—(w)—J. C. & W. E. POWERS, New York.
Lincoln Mills—(b)—RAYNOR & PERKINS ENVELOPE CO., New York.
Lincoln No. 1—(b)—coated—JAMES WHITE PAPER CO., Chicago.
Lincoln Mills—(b)—HY. LINDENMEYR & SONS, New York.
Linear Cambric—(w)—GEORGE B. HURD & CO., New York.
Lindell—(b)—book and envelope—GRAHAM PAPER CO., St. Louis.
Lindell Writing—(b)—MACK-ELLIOTT PAPER CO., St. Louis.
Linden—(b)—blue wove writing—HENRY LINDENMEYR & SONS, N. Y.

FELTS AND JACKETS | Appleton Woolen Mills, APPLETON - - WIS.

Watermarks and Brands

Linden Extra Superfine—(w)—AMERICAN WRITING PAPER CO., Holyoke, Mass.
Linden Linen—(w)—AMERICAN WRITING PAPER CO., Holyoke, Mass.
Linden Linen Ledger—(w)—AMERICAN WRITING PAPER CO., Holyoke, Mass.
Linden Paper Co. Bond—(w)—AMERICAN WRITING PAPER CO., Holyoke, Mass.
Lindenmeyr's Parchment Bristol—(b)—HY. LINDENMEYR & SONS, New York.
Lindhurst—(w)—J. E. LINDE PAPER CO., New York.
Lineal Linen—(w)—MARCUS WARD CO., Brooklyn, N. Y.
Linen Cloth Embossed—(w)—GEO. B. HURD & CO., New York.
Linen Fabric—(w)—WHITING PAPER CO., Holyoke, Mass.
Linen Fabric—(b)—GEO. B. HURD & CO., New York.
Linen Fibre—(w)—J. E. LINDE PAPER CO., New York.
Linen Finish Photo Blotting—(b)—SABIN ROBBINS PAPER CO., Middletown, Ohio.
Linen Finish Wedding—(b)—square-cornered card—THE PAPER MILLS CO., Chicago.
Linen Finish Weddings—(b)—MOUNTAIN MILL PAPER CO., Lee, Mass.
Linen Folding—(b)—bristol—J. W. BUTLER PAPER CO., Chicago.
Linen Grenadine—(w)—GEO. B. HURD & CO., New York.
Linen Index—(b)—folding bristol—THE ALLING & CORY CO., Rochester, N. Y.
Linen Lawn—(b)—Z. & W. M. CRANE, Dalton, Mass.
Linen Ledger—(w)—WHITING-PLOVER PAPER CO., Stevens Point, Wis.
Linen Ledger—(w)—AMERICAN WRITING PAPER CO., Holyoke, Mass.
Linen Ledger—(w)—HAMMERMILL PAPER CO., Erie, Pa.
Linen Ledger—(w)—LEE PAPER CO., Vicksburg, Mich.
Linen Ledger—(w)—MERRIAM PAPER CO., New York.
Linen Ledger—(w)—FOX PAPER CO., Appleton, Wis.
Linen Ledger—(w)—writing—CAREW MANUFACTURING CO., South Hadley Falls, Mass.
Linen Ledger—(w)—wove and laid—VALLEY PAPER CO., Holyoke, Mass.
Linen Ledger—(w)—ROLLAND PAPER CO., St. Jerome, Canada.
Linen Ledger—(w)—EASTERN MFG. CO., Bangor, Me.
Linen Ledger Index—(b)—bristol—J. W. BUTLER PAPER CO., Chicago.
Linen Parchment—(w and b)—GEO. B. HURD & CO., New York.

Linen Record—(w)—AMERICAN WRITING PAPER CO., Holyoke, Mass.
Linen Surface—(b)—cover—CONROW BROS., New York.
Linen Texture—(w)—book—GRAHAM PAPER CO., St. Louis, Mo.
Linen Typewriter—(b)—tissue—SMITH PAPER CO., Lee, Mass.
Linen Typewriter—(w)—A. P. LITTLE, Rochester, N. Y.
Linen Vellum—(w)—SOUTHWORTH CO., Mittineague, Mass.
Linene—(w and b)—THE PAPER MILLS CO., Chicago.
Linene Bond—(w)—CARTER, RICE & CO., CORP., Boston, Mass.
Linmar—(b)—writing—GRAHAM PAPER CO., St. Louis, Mo.
Linolin—(w)—bond and bristols—UNION CARD & PAPER CO., N. Y.
Linolin Bristol—(b)—UNION CARD & PAPER CO., New York.
Linwell—(b)—writing—GRAHAM PAPER CO., St. Louis.
Linwood—(b)—toilet—UNITED STATES ENVELOPE CO. (Morgan Envelope Co. Div.), Springfield, Mass.
Linwood Mills—(w and b)—R. P. MOLTEN & CO., Philadelphia.
Lion—(b)—toilet—UNITED STATES ENVELOPE CO. (Morgan Envelope Co. Division), Springfield, Mass.
Lion—(b)—manila tag—UNION CARD & PAPER CO., New York.
Lion—(b)—filter—H. REEVE ANGEL & CO., INC., New York.
Lion Brand Folding Satin—(b)—HOLYOKE CARD & PAPER CO., Holyoke, Mass.
Lion Half-Tone—(b)—flats—BRADNER SMITH & CO., Chicago.
Lion Linen Bond—(w)—KINGSLEY PAPER CO., Cleveland, Ohio.
Lion Parchment—(b)—OSBURN PAPER CO., Philadelphia.
Lion R.R. Manila—(b)—OSBURN PAPER CO., Philadelphia.
Lion White Writing—(b)—OSBURN PAPER CO., Philadelphia.
Lisbon Bond—(w)—PARSONS TRADING CO., New York.
Lisbon Extra Strong—(w)—PARSONS TRADING CO., New York.
Lisbon Ivory Laid—Made in U. S. A.—(w)—writing—PARSONS TRADING CO., New York.
Lisbon Ivory Wove—(w)—PARSONS TRADING CO., New York.
Lisbon Ledger—(w)—wove and laid—PARSONS TRADING CO., N. Y.
Lisbon Linen—(b)—WHITING-PATTERSON CO., Philadelphia.
Lisbon Superfine—(w)—PARSONS TRADING CO., New York.
Lisle Linen Ledger—(w)—KALAMAZOO PAPER CO., Kalamazoo, Mich.
Lisle Parchment Bond—(w)—EAST HARTFORD MFG. CO., Burnside, Conn.

JAMES H. HARRISON PULPSTONE MANUFACTURER | **GENUINE NEWCASTLE STONES** 18 Killowen St., GATESHEAD-ON-TYNE, ENG.

C. A. CHAPMAN, Inc.
ENGINEERS — REPORTS — INVESTIGATIONS — INSPECTIONS
E. JACKSON BLVD. — CHICAGO

Watermarks and Brands

Lisle Parchment Bond — (w) — HARTFORD FIRE INSURANCE CO., Hartford, Conn.
Litchfield — (b) — writing — GRAHAM PAPER CO., St. Louis.
Litho — (w and b) — bond — superfine, fine, laid, ledger and linen — GUGLER LITHOGRAPHIC CO., Milwaukee.
Litho — (b) — post cards — UNION CARD & PAPER CO., New York.
Litho Duplex — (b) — blanks — UNION CARD & PAPER CO., New York.
Litho Mills — (w) — extra superfine — JUDD PAPER CO., Holyoke, Mass.
Litho Post Card — (b) — UNION CARD & PAPER CO., New York.
Litho Rotary Bond — (b) — THE GUGLER LITHOGRAPHIC CO., Milwaukee, Wis.
Little Jewel — (b) — ALBANY PERFORATED WRAPPING PAPER CO., Albany, New York.
Livingston — (b) — book and envelope — GRAHAM PAPER CO., St. Louis.
L. L. Brown Paper Co. Fine — (w) — L. L. BROWN PAPER CO., Adams, Mass.
L. L. Brown Paper Co. Linen Ledger — (w) — L. L. BROWN PAPER CO., Adams, Mass.
L. L. Colored Coated — (b) — L. L. BROWN PAPER CO., Adams, Mass.
Lloyd's Monetised Safety Paper — (w) — E. E. LLOYD PAPER CO., Chicago.
Lochiel Record — (b) — ledger — JOHNSTON PAPER CO., Harrisburg, Pa.
Lockland — (w) — fine — GRAHAM PAPER CO., St. Louis.
Lockland Special Kraft — (b) — FOX PAPER CO., Lockland, Ohio.
Locksley — (b) — flats — LOUISVILLE PAPER CO., Louisville, Ky.
Locust — (b) — ruled goods — R. L. GREENE PAPER CO., Providence, R. I.
Locust Bond — (w) — flats — R. L. GREENE, Providence, R. I.
Locust Bond — (b) — envelopes — R. L. GREENE PAPER CO., Providence, R. I.
Locust Coated Book — (b) — R. L. GREENE PAPER CO., Providence, R. I.
Locust Jute Tag — (b) — R. L. GREENE PAPER CO., Providence, R. I.
Lodore — (b) — super book — HAGEN PAPER CO., St. Louis.
Logan — (b) — bond — GRAHAM PAPER CO., St. Louis.
Lois Linen — (w) — BROWN, LENT & PETT, New York.
Lombard — (b) — blanks and blotting — B. F. BOND PAPER CO., Baltimore.
Lombardy — (b) — envelope — WHITING-PATTERSON CO., Philadelphia.
Lombard Mills — (b) — JOHN A. DUSHANE & CO., Baltimore.

Lombard R. R. Manila — (b) — O. F. H. WARNER & CO., Baltimore.
London — (b) — book — BRADNER SMITH & CO., Chicago.
London Bond — (w) — PARSONS PAPER CO., Holyoke, Mass.
London Bristol — (b) — BRADNER SMITH & CO., Chicago.
London Cloth — (b) — BUNTIN, GILLIES & CO., LTD., Hamilton, Ontario, Can.
London Club Vellum — (w) — JOHN WANAMAKER, Philadelphia.
London Court Linen — (w) — CHAS. T. BAINBRIDGE'S SONS, INC., Brooklyn, New York.
London Court Parchment Vellum — (w) — CHAS. T. BAINBRIDGE'S SONS, INC., Brooklyn, New York.
London Court Perfection — (w) — CHAS. T. BAINBRIDGE'S SONS, INC., Brooklyn, New York.
London Court Stationery — (b) — CHAS. T. BAINBRIDGE'S SONS, INC., Brooklyn, New York.
London Linen Ledger — (w) — THOMAS W. PRICE CO., Philadelphia.
London Manila — (b) — BUNTIN, GILLIES & CO., LTD., Hamilton, Ontario, Can.
London Mills — (w) — WHITING PAPER CO., Holyoke, Mass.
London Mimeograph — (b) — BRADNER SMITH & CO., Chicago.
London Whipcord — (b) — BERLIN & JONES ENVELOPE CO., New York
Lone Star — (b) — ALBANY PERFORATED WRAPPING PAPER CO., Albany, New York.
Lone Star — (b) — roofing — JOHN G. FLEMING & SONS, Oak Cliff, Texas.
Long Acre — (b) — roll toilet — JEROME PAPER CO., New York.
Longfellow Linen — (w) — WHITING PAPER CO., Holyoke, Mass.
Long Fibre Bond — (w) — CARTER, RICE & CO., CORP., Boston.
Longwood Mills — (b) — TILESTON & LIVERMORE, Boston.
Lonsdale Bond — (b) — EATON, CRANE & PIKE CO., Pittsfield, Mass.
Lonsdale Fabric — (b) — GEO. B. HURD & CO., New York.
Lord — (b) — mimeograph — GRAHAM PAPER CO., St. Louis.
Loring — (b) — writing — UNION CARD & PAPER CO., New York.
Loring, Short & Harmon Portland — (w) — LORING, SHORT & HARMON, Portland, Me.
Lorna Doone — (w) — CENTRAL OHIO PAPER CO., Columbus, Ohio.
Lorraine — (b) — writing — GRAHAM PAPER CO., St. Louis.
Lorraine Bond — (b) — (duplex) — LOUISVILLE PAPER CO., Louisville, Ky.
Lorraine — (b) — proofing — LOUISVILLE PAPER CO., Louisville, Ky.

APPLETON MACHINE CO.
APPLETON, WIS.
REFINING ENGINES, SCREENS, SAVING & SPLITTING MACHINERY
HIGH GRADE **CENTRIFUGAL PUMPS**

—INER EDGAR CO., Sole Agents
EYSTONE CLAY & REDUCTION CO.
Church Street - - New York

CLAY
PRECIPITATED REFINED
LIGHT GRAVITY SOFT TEXTURE
<K L M>
HIGH NATURAL COLOR, HIGH RETENTION

Lorraine Bond — (w) — DAVID L. ENGLE, New York.
Lotus Bible—(b)—C. P. LESH PAPER CO., Indianapolis, Ind.
Lotus Bond — (w) — MINNEAPOLIS PAPER CO., Minneapolis, Minn.
Lotus Lawn—(w)—GEO. B. HURD & CO., New York.
Lotus Linen — (w) — AMERICAN WRITING PAPER CO., Holyoke.
Lotus Linen—(b)—EASTERN MFG. CO., Bangor, Me.
Louisiana Purchase—(b)—writing—GRAHAM PAPER CO., St. Louis.
Louisiana Purchase—(w)—writing—GRAHAM PAPER CO., St. Louis.
Louisiana 1803 Purchase — (w)—GRAHAM PAPER CO., St. Louis.
Louisine—(b) — EATON, CRANE & PIKE CO., Pittsfield, Mass.
Lowell — (b) — M. F. Book—BAY STATE PAPER CO., Boston.
Lowell Bond—(b)—C. S. PROCTOR PAPER CO., Boston.
Lowell Ledger—(b) — C. S. PROCTOR PAPER CO., Boston.
Lowest Jute Bag— (b) — R. L. GREENE PAPER CO., Providence.
Loyal—(w and b)—writing, ledger, bond—NEENAH PAPER CO., Neenah, Wis.
Loyal Legion—(w and b)—writing, ledger, bond—NEENAH PAPER CO., Neenah, Wis.
Lucerne—(b)—book — GRAHAM PAPER CO., St. Louis.
Ludington Bond—(w and b)—A. R. BARNES & CO., Chicago.
Ludington Linen Ledger—(w and b)—A. R. BARNES & CO., Chicago.
Ludlow—(b)—fine—THOS. W. PRICE CO., Philadelphia.
Ludlow—(b)—news — GRAHAM PAPER CO., St. Louis.
Lugano Linen—(w)—laid and wove —STRATHMORE PAPER CO., Mittineague, Mass.
Luna—(w)—bond — UNION CARD & PAPER CO., New York.
Lustro—(b)—enameled book — J. W. BUTLER PAPER CO., Chicago.
Lustro—(b)—coated book—S. D. WARREN & CO., Boston.
Luther—(b) — book — GRAHAM PAPER CO., St. Louis.
Luxacoated Porcelain — (b) — RITCHIE & RAMSAY, Toronto, Can.
Luxenberg—(b)—toilet tissue—W. H. CLAFLIN & CO., Boston.
Lux Fibre —(b)—C. S. PROCTOR PAPER CO., Boston.
Luxor Ledger—(w)—SWIGART PAPER CO., Chicago.
Luxuma—(b)—toilet—GEO. T. JOHNSON CO., Boston.
Luxury Linen—TOWER MFG. & NOVELTY CO., New York.
Luxway—(b) — toilet tissue—W. H. CLAFLIN CO., Boston.

Lus—(b)—wrapping—D. S. WALTON & CO., New York.
Lusan — (b) — bristol — J. P. HEILBRONN CO., Manila, P. I.
Luserne Writing—(b)—MEGARGEE BROS., Scranton, Pa.
Lus Fibre—D. S. WALTON & CO., New York.
Lusoid—(b)—wrapping—D. S. WALTON & CO., New York.
Luson—(b)—D. S. WALTON & CO., New York.
Luson—(b)—toilet — ALBANY PERFORATED WRAPPING PAPER CO., Albany, New York.
Luson—(b)—WHITING-PATTERSON CO., New York.
Luson Bristol—(b)—C. P. LESH PAPER CO., Indianapolis, Ind.
Luson Linen — (w) — AMERICAN WRITING PAPER CO., Holyoke.
Lyceum—(b) — book—GRAHAM PAPER CO., St. Louis.
Ly-Ka-Kloth—(b)—towel and dental paper — LEHIGH PAPER MILLS, INC., Raubsville, Pa.
Lyloe Bond—(b)—W. H. H. CHAMBERLAIN, Syracuse, N. Y.
Lynbrook Mills — (b)—CONROW BROTHERS, New York.
Lynnhaven Fine—(b)—OLD DOMINION PAPER CO., Norfolk, Va.
Lynhurst Antique Laid Book—(w) —KINGSLEY PAPER CO., Cleveland.
Lynhurst Eggshell Book — (b)—KINGSLEY PAPER CO., Cleveland, O.
Lynhurst R. R. Manila—(b)—KINGSLEY PAPER CO., Cleveland, Ohio.
Lynhurst Writing —(w) — KINGSLEY PAPER CO., Cleveland, Ohio.
Lynn—(b)—book—GRAHAM PAPER CO., St. Louis.
Lyons English Finish Book—(b) —HY. LINDENMEYR & SONS, New York.
Lyric—(b)—book and music—GRAHAM PAPER CO., St. Louis.

M

M in a Diamond—(w)—typewriter—MEGARGEE-HARE PAPER CO., Philadelphia.
M. & W. P. Co.'s Special—(b)—writing— MILLER & WRIGHT PAPER CO., New York.
Macinac Mimeograph — (b) —CANFIELD PAPER CO., New York.
Mackinac Bond—(w)—LEE PAPER CO., Vicksburg, Mich.
Mackinac Linen — (w) —linen—LEE PAPER CO., Vicksburg, Mich.
Macon Index—(b)—bristol—UNION CARD & PAPER CO., New York.
Madam Butterfly—(b) —H. NORWOOD EWING CO., New York.

Watermarks and Brands

Made in America—(w)—bond and ledger — JOHN B. WATKINS CO., New York.
Made for You in Kalamazoo Bond —(w)—BERMINGHAM & PROSSER CO., Kalamazoo, Mich.
Madeline Mills—(b)—proof—LOUISVILLE PAPER CO., Louisville, Ky.
Madison Bond—(w)—SWIGART PAPER CO., Chicago.
Madison Mills — (b) — JOHN F. SARLE, New York.
Madras—(b)—deckel-edged cover — C. H. DEXTER & SONS, INC., Windsor Locks, Conn.
Madrid Linen—(b)—WHITING-PATTERSON CO., Philadelphia.
Magazine Extra Strong — (b) — coated—WEST VIRGINIA PULP & PAPER CO., New York.
Magazine Text — (b) — MILLER & WRIGHT PAPER CO., INC., New York.
Magic — (b) — writing — STANDARD CARD & PAPER CO., New York.
Magic Blotting — (b) — CLEMENTS PAPER CO., Nashville, Tenn.
Magic City—(w)—STATE JOURNAL CO., Lincoln, Neb.
Magic Mills — (b)—CINCINNATI CORDAGE AND PAPER CO., Cincinnati, Ohio.
Magna Charta Bond—(w)—AMERICAN WRITING PAPER CO., Holyoke.
Magnet—(b)—news — GRAHAM PAPER CO., St. Louis.
Magnet—(w and b) — blotting — EATON, DIKEMAN & CO., Lee, Mass.
Magnet Coated—(b) — C. S. PROCTOR PAPER CO., Boston.
Magnet Index—(b)—B. F. BOND PAPER CO., Baltimore.
Magnet Mimeograph—(w)—linens—SWIGART PAPER CO., Chicago.
Magnolia—(b)—writing — GRAHAM PAPER CO., St. Louis.
Magnolia Bond—(w)—H. & W. B. DREW CO., Jacksonville, Fla.
Magnolia Coated—(b)—C. S. PROCTOR PAPER CO., Boston.
Magnolia M. F. — (b) — book - SWIGART PAPER CO., Chicago.
Magnolia Mills Writing — (w)— CHATFIELD & WOODS CO., Cincinnati, Ohio.
Magnolia Writing — (w) — THE UNION PAPER & TWINE CO., Detroit, Mich.
Mail Order—(b)—catalogue—HAGEN PAPER CO., St. Louis.
Mail Order Bond—(w)—TAYLOR-LOGAN CO. PAPERMAKERS, Holyoke.
Mail Order Envelope—(w)—envelope. paper—TAYLOR-LOGAN CO. PAPERMAKERS, Holyoke, Mass.
Mail Order Linen—(w) — TAYLOR-LOGAN CO., PAPERMAKERS, Holyoke, Mass.

Majestic—(b)—book — CINCINNATI CORDAGE AND PAPER CO., Cincinnati, Ohio.
Majestic—(b)—cut cards—MISSOURI PAPER HOUSE, Kansas City, Mo.
Majestic—(b)—book — GRAHAM PAPER CO., St. Louis.
Majestic—(b)—toilet — NORTHERN PAPER MILLS, Green Bay, Wis.
Majestic—(b)—toilet — SCOTT PAPER CO., Philadelphia.
Majestic — (w) — bond — SYRKIN & BACK, INC., New York.
Majestic Bond—(w) — B. F. BOND PAPER CO., Baltimore.
Majestic Bond — (b)—CHEMICAL PAPER MFG. CO., Holyoke, Mass.
Majestic Bond — (w) — EASTERN MFG. CO., Bangor, Me.
Majestic Kraft—(b)—OLD DOMINION PAPER CO., Norfolk, Va.
Majestic Linen—(w)—STRATHMORE PAPER CO., Mittineague, Mass.
Majestic Pasted — (b) — pasted — LOUISVILLE PAPER CO., Louisville, Ky.
Majesty Bond — (w)—A. PRICE, Brooklyn, New York.
Malapardis—(b)—box boards — MATTHIAS PLUM, Newark, N. J.
Malden — (b) — ALBANY PERFORATED WRAPPING PAPER CO., Albany, New York.
Malta Linen—(w)—CARTER, RICE & CO., CORP., Boston.
Maltese Kraft—(b)—CHATFIELD & WOODS CO., Cincinnati, Ohio.
Maltese Linen—(w) — AMERICAN WRITING PAPER CO., Holyoke.
Maltha—(b) — roof paint — GRAHAM PAPER CO., St. Louis.
Malvern Colored Laid — (b) — CANFIELD PAPER CO., New York.
Manchester—(b)—coated book—F. A. FLINN, INC., New York.
Manchester Bond — (w)—PETREQUIN PAPER CO., Cleveland, Ohio.
Manchester Linen — (w) — SAUGERTIES MFG. CO., Saugerties, N. Y.
Manchester—(b)—catalog—GRAHAM PAPER CO., St. Louis.
Manhattan—(b)—white wove—F. A. FLINN, INC., New York.
Manhattan — (b) — bristol — MINNEAPOLIS PAPER CO., Minneapolis, Minn.
Manhattan Grass Bleached—(b)—JERSEY CITY PAPER CO., Jersey City, N. J.
Manhattan Ledger — (b)—F. A. FLINN, INC., New York.
Manhattan Ledger—(w)—BOORUM & PEASE CO., New York.
Manhattan Mills — (w)—GEO. B. HURD & CO., New York.
Manheim—(b)—book and cover—WM. H. GEORGE, Philadelphia.
Manicopy Bond—(b)—WHITING-PLOVER PAPER CO., Stevens Point, Wis.

FELTS AND JACKETS | **Appleton Woolen Mills**, APPLETON - - WIS.

Watermarks and Brands

Manicopy Bond — RIEGEL & CO., INC., Philadelphia.
Manifest Bond — (w) — EASTERN MFG. CO., Bangor, Me.
Manifest Ledger—(w)—EASTERN MFG. CO., Bangor, Me.
Manifest Linen Ledger — (w) — HARLEM CARD & PAPER CO., New York.
Manifold—(b) — onion skin—CHATFIELD & WOODS CO., Cincinnati, O.
Manifold Bond — (b)—UNION PAPER & TWINE CO., Detroit, Mich.
Manifold Colored — (b) — F. A. FLINN, INC., New York.
Manila Writing—(b)—A. S. LANDSBERG, New York.
Manila Writing No. 1 — (b)— J. E. LINDE PAPER CO., New York.
Manitoba — (b) — toilet — GRAHAM PAPER CO., St. Louis.
Manitou White Wove Flats—(b)— MINNEAPOLIS PAPER CO., Minneapolis, Minn.
Manor Mills—(b)—CONROW BROS., New York.
Mansfield Bristol—(b)—A. STORRS & BEMENT CO., Boston.
Manufacturers Bond —(b)—CHAS. H. WRIGHT, Kalamazoo, Mich.
Manuscript — (b) — F. A. FLINN, INC., New York.
Manuscript Bond — (b) — J. W. BUTLER PAPER CO., Chicago.
Manuscript Bond—(w)—FOX RIVER PAPER CO., Appleton, Wis.
Manuscript Cover—(b and w)—ELSINORE PAPER CO., New York.
Map Bond—(b)—CANFIELD PAPER CO., New York.
Maple Leaf Bond — (w)—HAMPSHIRE PAPER CO., South Hadley Falls, Mass.
Maple Mills—(w) — ROLLAND PAPER CO., St. Jerome, Canada.
Maple Valley—(w)—STATE JOURNAL CO., Lincoln, Neb.
Marathon—(b)—envelope— GRAHAM PAPER CO., St. Louis.
Marathon Bond — (w)—CROCKERMcELWAIN CO., Holyoke, Mass.
Marathon Mills—(w)—A. STORRS & BEMENT CO., Boston.
Marble — (b) — bristol — LOUISVILLE PAPER CO., Louisville, Ky.
Marble — (b) — case lining — LOUISVILLE PAPER CO., Louisville, Ky.
Marble City Mills—(b)—THE TUTTLE & CO., Rutland, Vt.
Marble Finish—(b)—enamel book— W. H. GEORGE, Philadelphia.
Marble Parchment—(b)— wrapping —LOUISVILLE PAPER CO., Louisville, Ky.
Marcellus Linen — (w) — JOHN CARTER & CO., Boston.
Marco Ledger—(b)—MERRIAM PAPER CO., New York.
Marcus Ward's Monarch Bond— (w)—MARCUS WARD CO., Brooklyn.
Marcus Ward's Superfine — (w)— MARCUS WARD CO., Brooklyn, N. Y.
Marengo Bond—(b)—JENNER CO., THE, Louisville, Ky.
Marguerite Linen — (w)—AMERICAN WRITING PAPER CO., Holyoke.
Marigold—(b)—toilet—W. A. STOWE PAPER CO., Grand Rapids.
Marigold Bond—(w)—FOX RIVER PAPER CO., Appleton, Wis.
Marine — (b) — news—GRAHAM PAPER CO., St. Louis.
Marine—(b)—waterproof case lining— GRAHAM PAPER CO., St. Louis.
Marion Bond—(w)—ELSINORE PAPER CO., New York.
Marion Mills—(w)—WORTHY PAPER CO., Mittineague, Mass.
Marion Superfine — (b)—flats and writings — SWIGART PAPER CO., Chicago.
Maritime Mills—(w)—BROMPTON PULP & PAPER MILLS, East Angus, Canada.
Market—(w) — flat writing—MIDLAND PAPER CO., Chicago.
Marketplace—(w)—TAYLOR-LOGAN CO., PAPERMAKERS, Holyoke, Mass.
Marlboro—(b)—book—JUDD PAPER CO., Holyoke, Mass.
Marlboro—(b)—cardboard—McCLELLAN PAPER CO., Minneapolis, Minn.
Marlborough—(b)—toilet— UNITED STATES ENVELOPE CO. (Morgan Envelope Co. Div.), Springfield, Mass.
Marlborough Bond—(w)—THOS. W. PRICE CO., Philadelphia.
Marlowe — (b) — WORTHY PAPER CO., Mittineague, Mass.
Marquette Bond—(w)—FOX RIVER PAPER CO., Appleton, Wis.
Marquette Bond — (w) — SWIGART PAPER CO., Chicago.
Marquette Enamel — (b) — WEST VIRGINIA PULP & PAPER CO., New York.
Marquette Linen Ledger—(w)— SWIGART PAPER CO., Chicago.
Marseille Linen—(w)—AMERICAN WRITING PAPER CO., Holyoke, Mass.
Marseille Linen—(w)—H. S. CROCKER COMPANY, San Francisco.
Marseille Linen—(w)—UNITED STATES ENVELOPE CO. (P. P. Kellogg & Co. Div.), Springfield, Mass.
Martial—(w and b)—bond, ledger, writing—NEENAH PAPER CO., Neenah, Wis.
Maryland — (b) — mimeograph — GRAHAM PAPER CO., St. Louis.
Maryland Bond—(w)—JOHN A. DUSHANE & CO., Baltimore.
Maryland Mills—(w)—JOHN A. DUSHANE & CO., Baltimore.
Maryland Mills—(b)—C. P. LESH PAPER CO., Indianapolis.
Mascot—(b)—BASSETT & SUTPHIN, New York.

JAMES H. HARRISON | **GENUINE NEWCASTLE STONES**
ULPSTONE MANUFACTURER | 18 Killowen St., GATESHEAD-ON-TYNE, ENG.

MILLS ELECTRICALLY EQUIPPED   ECONOMIES IN STEAM PLANTS

C. A. CHAPMAN, Inc.
28 E. JACKSON BLVD.   ENGINEERS   CHICAGO

Watermarks and Brands   695

Mascot—(w)—flat—J. W. BUTLER PAPER CO., Chicago.
Mascot—(b)—litho. blanks—MINNEAPOLIS PAPER CO., Minneapolis, Minn.
Massachusetts Bond—(w)—CARTER, RICE & CO., CORP., Boston.
Massachusetts Linen—(w)—CARTER RICE & CO., CORP., Boston.
Massasoit Ledger—(w)—C O O K-VIVIAN CO., Boston.
Masterfold Enamel—(b)—book—BEECHER, PECK & LEWIS, Detroit, Mich.
Matchless—(w)—VALLEY PAPER CO., Holyoke, Mass.
Matchless R.R. Manila—(b)—PETREQUIN PAPER CO., Cleveland.
Mattapan—(b)—white M. F. book—TILESTON & HOLLINGSWORTH CO., Boston.
Matthias Plum—(w)—a plum—MATTHIAS PLUM, Newark, N. J.
Maud Muller—(b)—toilet—H. NORWOOD EWING CO., New York.
Mauretania Bond—(w)—POLAND PAPER CO., Mechanic Falls, Me.
Maverick-Clarke Linen Ledger—(w)—San Antonio, Tex.
Maxim Wireless—(b)—PERKINS, GOODWIN CO., New York.
Max Mills—(w)—writing—MEGARGEE-HARE PAPER CO., Philadelphia.
Maxwell Bond—(w)—HOWARD PAPER CO., Urbana, Ohio.
Mayfair—(b)—book—TILESTON & LIVERMORE, Boston.
Mayfield Linen—(b)—MEGARGEE BROS., Scranton, Pa.
Mayflower—(b)—toilet—ALBANY PERFORATED WRAPPING PAPER CO., Albany, N. Y.
Mayflower—(b)—wove antique book—W. H. CLAFLIN & CO., Boston.
Mayflower—(b)—wedding and bristol—MOUNTAIN PAPER CO., Lee, Mass.
Mayflower—(w)—egg-shell book—CENTRAL OHIO PAPER CO., Columbus, Ohio.
Mayon—(b)—M. F. book—J. P. HEILBRONN CO., Manila, P. I.
Mayville—(b)—offset, duplex tympan, die wiping, non-fading hand-painting poster, silver tissue and bond—GEO. W. MILLAR & CO., New York.
Mayville Perfecting Surface Offset—(b)—GEO. W. MILLAR & CO., New York.
Maseppa—(b)—toilet—H. NORWOOD EWING CO., New York.
Masurka—(b)—bond—JUDD PAPER CO., Holyoke, Mass.
Masurka Bond—(b)—JUDD PAPER CO., Holyoke, Mass.
McDowell's Mills—(w)—McDOWELL PAPER MILLS, Philadelphia.

McDowell's No. 1 Standard—(b)—tissue and silk goods wraps—McDOWELL PAPER MILLS, Philadelphia.
McDowell's No. 1—(b)—jute and rope bag, manila and white for coating—McDOWELL PAPER MILLS, Philadelphia.
Meadow—(b)—wax butter wrappers—GRAHAM PAPER CO., St. Louis.
Meadowdale—(b)—ALBANY PERFORATED WRAPPING PAPER CO., Albany, N. Y.
Meadow Mills—(w)—KALAMAZOO PAPER CO., Kalamazoo, Mich.
Medal Brand—(b)—carpet lining—NEWTON PAPER CO., Holyoke, Mass.
Medallion—(b)—toilet—NORTHERN PAPER MILLS, Green Bay, Wis.
Medallion Mills—(b)—t o i l e t—SCOTT PAPER CO., Philadelphia.
Media—(b)—toilet—GRAHAM PAPER CO., St. Louis.
Medical—(b)—toilet—A. M. EATON PAPER CO., Waltham and Boston.
Medicatus—(b)—toilet—J. T. MOORE, Bellows Falls, Vt.
Medina—(w)—fine—GRAHAM PAPER CO., St. Louis.
Medio Bond—(w)—THE ALLING & CORY CO., Rochester, N. Y.
Medium—(b)—sheathing—GRAHAM PAPER CO., St. Louis.
Mefisto—(b)—toilet—H. NORWOOD EWING CO., New York.
Megargee's Special Coated—(b)—MEGARGEE-HARE PAPER CO., Philadelphia.
Melba Bristol—(b)—WHITAKER PAPER CO., Cincinnati, Ohio.
Melbourne—(b)—kraft—WHITING-PATTERSON CO., Philadelphia.
Melbourne Wove and Laid—(b)—envelope—WHITING-PATTERSON CO., Philadelphia.
Mellocoated Colored—(b)—book—THE PAPER MILLS CO., Chicago.
Melrose—(b)—ALBANY PERFORATED WRAPPING PAPER CO., Albany.
Melrose—(w)—IRWIN PAPER CO., Quincy, Ill.
Melrose Bristol—(b)—C. P. LESH PAPER CO., Indianapolis, Ind.
Melrose Bristol—(b)—HUDSON VALLEY PAPER CO., Albany, N. Y.
Melton Art—(b)—photo mounts—J. W. BUTLER PAPER CO., Chicago.
Melton Mills—(w)—AMERICAN WRITING PAPER CO., Holyoke, Mass.
Melton Mills—(w)—flats and colored writings—SWIGART PAPER CO., Chicago.
Memoir Super—(b)—CLARKE & CO., New York.
Memorandum—(b)—tag cover—GRAHAM PAPER CO., St. Louis.
Menlo Litho. Blanks—(b)—C. P. LESH PAPER CO., Indianapolis, Ind.

APPLETON MACHINE CO., APPLETON, WIS.
REFINING ENGINES, SCREENS, SAWING & SPLITTING MACHINERY
HIGH GRADE **CENTRIFUGAL PUMPS**

MINER EDGAR CO., Sole Agents
EDGAR BROS. CO.
KEYSTONE CLAY & REDUCTION CO.
30 Church Street - - New York

C L A Y

<E W> <K L M> <C M>
WASHED FLOATED REFINED
LARGEST CAPACITY AND STOCK IN AMERICA. PROMPT SHIPMENTS

FELTS AND JACKETS | Appleton Woolen Mills, APPLETON - - WIS.

Watermarks and Brands

Mispah Wedding Bristol — (b)— BEECHER, PECK & LEWIS, Detroit, Mich.
Mobile Bond—(w)—B. F. BOND PAPER CO., Baltimore.
Model — (b) — plain blanks — HAGEN PAPER CO., St. Louis.
Model Enamel — (b) —MEGARGEE-HARE PAPER CO., Philadelphia.
Modena—(b)—news—GRAHAM PAPER CO., St. Louis.
Modern Bond—(b)—KINGSLEY PAPER CO., Cleveland, Ohio.
Modern Cover—(b)—DISTRICT OF COLUMBIA PAPER MFG. CO., Washington, D. C.
Mohawk—(b)—news—GRAHAM PAPER CO., St. Louis.
Mohawk—(b)—toilet—ALBANY PERFORATED WRAPPING PAPER CO., Albany, New York.
Mohawk—(w) — white wove—F. A. FLINN, INC., New York.
Mohawk Bond — (w) — WHITING-PLOVER PAPER CO., Stevens Point, Wis.
Mohawk Flats—(b)—WRIGHT BARRETT & STILWELL CO., St. Paul.
Mohawk Souvenir Post Card—(b) —BRADNER SMITH & CO., Chicago.
Mohegan—(b)—insulating—GRAHAM PAPER CO., St. Louis.
Mohican—(b)—toilet—ALBANY PERFORATED WRAPPING PAPER CO., Albany, New York.
Mohican Extra Linen — (w) — AMERICAN WRITING PAPER CO., Holyoke, Mass.
Mojave—(b)—toilet — ALBANY PERFORATED WRAPPING PAPER CO., Albany, New York.
Monarch—(w)—linen—J. E. LINDE PAPER CO., New York.
Monarch—(b)—bristol boards, colored M. F., envelope, fibre and typewriting paper — DONALDSON PAPER CO., Harrisburg, Pa.
Monarch—(b)—blotting—C. W. WILLIAMS & CO., New York.
Monarch—(b)—book — GRAHAM PAPER CO., St. Louis.
Monarch — (b) — kraft — HAGEN PAPER CO., St. Louis.
Monarch — (b) — sheathing—LOUISVILLE PAPER CO., Louisville, Ky.
Monarch—(b)—grass-bleached tissue—SMITH PAPER CO., Lee, Mass.
Monarch—(b)—toilet—ALBANY PERFORATED WRAPPING PAPER CO., Albany, New York.
Monarch — (b) — envelopes —R. L. GREENE CO., Providence, R. I.
Monarch—(b)—toilet — WILSON & TOWNE PAPER CO., New York.
Monarch Bond — (w) — MARCUS WARD CO., Brooklyn, N. Y.
Monarch Bristols — (b)—WABASH COATING MILLS, Wabash, Ind.
Monarch Linen Ledger — (w) — PLYMOUTH PAPER CO., Holyoke.

Monarch Manila Tag—(b)—R. L. GREENE PAPER CO., Providence, R. I.
Monarch Mills—(b)—CHARLES W. WILLIAMS & CO., New York.
Monarch Mills—(b)—white wove—KINGSLEY PAPER CO., Cleveland.
Monarch Rope Tag—(b)—GREENE PAPER CO., Providence, R. I.
Monarch Translucent — (b)—WABASH COATING MILLS, Wabash, Ind.
Monitor Fibre—(b)—CHATFIELD & WOODS CO., Cincinnati, Ohio.
Monitor Tinted — (b) — MINNEAPOLIS PAPER CO., Minneapolis.
Monmouth Linen Ledger — (w)—writing—CAREW MANUFACTURING CO., South Hadley Falls, Mass.
Monogram—(w)—BASSETT & SUTPHIN, New York.
Monogram—(w)—ROLLAND PAPER CO., St. Jerome, Canada.
Monogram—(b) — toilet—ALBANY PERFORATED WRAPPING PAPER CO., Albany, N. Y.
Monogram—(b)—wove and laid writing—BASSETT & SUTPHIN, N. Y.
Monogram Bond—(w)—SPRINGFIELD PAPER SUPPLY CO., Springfield, Mo.
Monogram Bristol — (b) — MINNEAPOLIS PAPER CO., Minneapolis.
Monogram Eggshell — (b) — book—BEECHER, PECK & LEWIS, Detroit, Mich.
Monogram Index—(b)—index bristol —SPRINGFIELD PAPER & SUPPLY CO., Springfield, Mo.
Monogram Linen—(w) — WHITING PAPER CO., Holyoke, Mass.
Monogram Linen —(w)— CINCINNATI CORDAGE AND PAPER CO., Cincinnati, Ohio.
Monogram Tariff — (w)—manila—MINNEAPOLIS PAPER CO., Minneapolis, Minn.
Monogram Vellum—(w)—wedding—ALLAN & GRAY, New York.
Monon—(b)—news — GRAHAM PAPER CO., St. Louis.
Monon—(b)—mimeograph — GRAHAM PAPER CO., St. Louis.
Monon Bond—(w)—THE BLUNDEN-LYON CO., Chicago.
Monona—(w)—flat—writing — MIDLAND PAPER CO., Chicago.
Monona Linen Fabric — (w) — AMERICAN WRITING PAPER CO., Holyoke, Mass.
Monoplane Bond — (w) — JOHN CARTER & CO., Boston.
Monroe—(b) — document manila—MISSOURI PAPER HOUSE, Kansas City, Mo.
Monroe—(w)—document —SWIGART PAPER CO., Chicago.
Monroe Bond—(w)—GEO. B. HURD & CO., New York.

JAMES H. HARRISON 'ULPSTONE MANUFACTURER | GENUINE NEWCASTLE STONES 18 KHowen St., GATESHEAD-ON-TYNE, ENG.

Watermarks and Brands

Monroe Bond—(b)—MOSER PAPER CO., Chicago.
Monroe Ledger—(w)—E. W. SCARBOROUGH, New York.
Monroe Linen—(w)—J. W. BUTLER PAPER CO., Chicago.
Monroe Linen Ledger — (w)— AMERICAN WRITING PAPER CO., Holyoke, Mass.
Monroe Tinted Bristol—(b)—THE ALLING & CORY CO., Rochester.
Montana—(w)—McCLELLAN PAPER CO., Minneapolis, Minn.
Montauk—(w)—ledgers—J. E. LINDE PAPER CO., New York.
Montauk Bond — (w) — HAMILTON CARD & PAPER HOUSE, INC., New York.
Montauk Linen—(w) — LASHER & LATHROP, New York.
Montauk Linen Ledger—(w)—J. E. LINDE PAPER CO., New York.
Montauk Mills — (w)—flat—F. W. ANDERSON & CO., New York.
Monte Carlo—(b) — toilet—NORTHERN PAPER MILLS, Green Bay, Wis.
Montour Mills—(b)—R. P. MOLTEN & CO., Philadelphia.
Montrose—(b) — binders' trunk and friction board — GRAHAM PAPER CO., St. Louis.
Montrose—(b)—flats — MOSER PAPER CO., Chicago.
Montrose Linen—(w) — AMERICAN WRITING PAPER CO., Holyoke.
Montrose Linen—(w) — MILLER & WRIGHT PAPER CO., New York.
Montrose Mills—(b)—CINCINNATI CORDAGE AND PAPER CO., Cincinnati, Ohio.
Montrose Mills—(b)—J. E. LINDE PAPER CO., New York.
Mont Royal Bond—(w)—ROLLAND PAPER CO., St. Jerome, Canada.
Moonstone Translucent Bristol—(b) — MINNEAPOLIS PAPER CO., Minneapolis, Minn.
Moonstone — (b) — cover — LOUISVILLE PAPER CO., Louisville, Ky.
Moorish—(b)—book—C. P. LESH PAPER CO., Indianapolis, Ind.
Moorish Deckle Edge Cover—(b) —HY. LINDENMEYR & SONS, New York.
Moorish Linen — (w) — writing— C A R E W MANUFACTURING CO., South Hadley Falls, Mass.
Moorish Linen Finish—(b)— feather edge book—HY. LINDENMEYR & SONS, New York.
Moose Skin—(b)—wrapping—M. J. EARL, Reading, Pa.
Moose Skin—(b)—wrapping — M. J. EARL, Reading, Pa.
Moosup—(b)—toilet — ALBANY PERFORATED WRAPPING PAPER CO., Albany, N. Y.
Mopaco Bond—(w)—MOSER PAPER COMPANY, Chicago.

Moquin—(b) — HOLLINGSWORTH & WHITNEY CO., Boston.
Morgan's Artistic Linen — (b)— UNITED STATES ENVELOPE CO., Springfield, Mass.
Morning Glory—(b)—toilet—W. A. STOWE PAPER CO., Grand Rapids, Mich.
Morocco Bond — (w) — WHITING-PATTERSON CO., INC., Philadelphia.
Morris Book—(b)—THE UNION PAPER & TWINE CO., Detroit, Mich.
Morris Extra Superfine — (b) — WORTHY PAPER CO., Mittineague, Mass.
Mosaic—(b)—blotting—WRENN PAPER COMPANY, Middletown, Ohio.
Mosaic Enamel—(b)—book — LOUISVILLE PAPER CO., Louisville, Ky.
Moscow Bond—(w)—J. W. BUTLER PAPER CO., Chicago.
Motor Bond—(b)—B. F. BOND PAPER CO., Baltimore.
Motor Bond—(b)—PAUL E. VERNON & CO., New York.
Mottled Bond—(b)—W. E. WROE & CO., Chicago.
Mountain Mill Snowdrift—(w)— MOUNTAIN MILL PAPER CO., Lee, Mass.
Mountain Spring Bond — (w) — CHAS. H. WRIGHT, Kalamazoo, Mich.
Mount Baker — (b)—toilet—H. M. RICHMOND PAPER CO., Seattle, Wash.
Mount Clair—(b)—TOWER MANUFACTURING AND NOVELTY CO., New York.
Mount Hope—(b)—envelope — R. L. GREENE PAPER CO., Providence, R. I.
Mount Hope—(b)—ruled goods—R. L. GREENE PAPER CO., Providence, R. I.
Mount Hope — (b) — toilet — R. L. GREENE PAPER CO., Providence, R. I.
Mount Hope Ledger—(w)—flats—R. L. GREENE PAPER CO., Providence, Rhode Island.
Mount Hood Superfine—(w)—J. K. GILL & CO., Portland, Ore.
Mount Kineo — (w) — superfine— EASTERN PAPER AND SUPPLY CO., Springfield, Mass.
Mount Penn— (b) — toilet — M. J. EARL, Reading, Pa.
Mount Pleasant Mills—(w)—fine— R. P. ANDREWS PAPER CO., Washington, D. C.
Mount Pleasant Mills—(w)—writing—J. & F. B. GARRETT, Syracuse, New York.
Mount Royal Bond—(b) — ROLLAND PAPER CO., LTD., St. Jerome, Canada.
Mount Royal Linen Ledger—(w)— ledger—LEE PAPER CO., Vicksburg, Mich.

FELTS AND JACKETS | Appleton Woolen Mills
APPLETON - - WIS.

Watermarks and Brands

Mount State — (w) — writing — CLARKE PAPER CO., Wheeling, W. Va.
Mount Vernon—(b)—straw board—GRAHAM PAPER CO., St. Louis.
Mount Vernon Bond—(w)—PAUL E. VERNON & CO., New York.
Mousseline—(b)—EATON, CRANE & PIKE CO., Pittsfield, Mass.
Mousseline de Paris—(b)—EATON, CRANE & PIKE CO., Pittsfield, Mass.
Mozart Music—(b)—F. A. FLINN, INC., New York.
M. P. Climax Mills—(w)—fine—MEMPHIS PAPER CO., Memphis.
M. P. CO. AMERICAN STAR—(w) MEMPHIS PAPER CO., Memphis.
Mt. Pocono — (b) — announcements—MEGARGEE BROS., Scranton, Pa.
Mt. Royal White—(w)—MERRIAM PAPER CO., New York.
Multifold Enamel Book—(b)—BERMINGHAM & PROSSER CO., Kalamazoo, Mich.
Multiform Manifolding — (b) — onion skin—GRAHAM PAPER CO., St. Louis.
Multiple — (w) — onion skin — ESLEECK MFG. CO., Turners Falls, Mass.
Multiplex—(w)—bond — MIDLAND PAPER CO., Chicago.
Multiplex—(w)—onion skin—MILLER & WRIGHT PAPER CO., INC., New York.
Multnomah Vellum—PACIFIC PAPER CO., Portland, Ore.
Multykolar—(b)—DILL & COLLINS CO., Philadelphia.
Munich Wedding—(b)—WHITING-PATTERSON CO., Philadelphia.
Municipal Bond — (w) — JOHN CARTER & CO., Boston.
Municipal Ledger—(w)—A. STORRS & BEMENT CO., Boston.
Municipal Linen Ledger—(w)—HARPER PAPER CO., New York.
Municipal Superfine — (w) — JORDAN CARD & PAPER CO., Boston.
Munising Bond—(w)—MUNISING PAPER CO., Munising, Mich.
Munson Parchment Bond—(w)—typewriter—EATON, CRANE & PIKE CO., Pittsfield, Mass.
Munson Parchment Linen—(w)—typewriter—EATON, CRANE & PIKE CO., Pittsfield, Mass.
Munson Superior Bond—(w)—typewriter—EATON, CRANE & PIKE CO., Pittsfield, Mass.
Munson Superior Linen — (w) — typewriter—EATON, CRANE & PIKE CO., Pittsfield, Mass.
Mustave—(b)—toilet—SCOTT PAPER CO., Philadelphia.
Mutual Bond—(w)—WESTERN PAPER CO., Omaha, Neb.
Mutual Bond—(w)—W. M. PRINGLE & CO., INC., New York.

Mutual Linen Ledger—(w)—HAMMERMILL PAPER CO., Erie, Pa.
Mutual Linen Ledger — (w) — DOBLER & MUDGE, Baltimore.
Mystic Mills—(w)—INDIANA PAPER CO., Indianapolis.
M. & W. Special—(b)—MILLER & WRIGHT PAPER CO., INC., New York.
Mystic—(w)—MOSER PAPER CO., Chicago.

N

Nakoma—(w)—writing—TAYLOR-ATKINS PAPER CO., Burnside, Conn.
Namelo — (b) — book — LOUISVILLE PAPER CO., Louisville, Ky.
Naneda—(b) — MORGAN & HAMILTON CO., Nashville, Tenn.
Napier Bond—(w)—WM. G. JOHNSTON CO., Pittsburgh, Pa.
Napier Bond—(w)—MOSER PAPER CO., Chicago.
Naples—(b) — bond — WHITING-PATTERSON CO., Philadelphia.
Naples Bond—(b)—KEITH PAPER CO., Turners Falls, Mass.
Naples Linen—(w)—KEITH PAPER CO., Turners Falls, Mass.
Napoleon—(w) — bond—MIDLAND PAPER CO., Chicago.
Napoleon Bond—(b)—WORCESTER ENVELOPE CO., Worcester, Mass.
Narragansett—(b)—Manila — R. L. GREENE PAPER CO., Providence.
Nashtenn — (b) — writing—GRAHAM PAPER CO., St. Louis.
Nassau—(b) — colored laid writing—W. H. CLAFLIN & CO., Boston.
Nassau — (b) — ALBANY PERFORATED WRAPPING PAPER CO., Albany, N. Y.
Nassau Bond — (w) — LASHER & LATHROP, New York.
Nassau Bristol—(b)—F. A. FLINN, INC., New York.
Nassau Ledger—(w)—H. K. BREWER & CO., New York.
Nassau Mills — (w) — flat writing—FOX RIVER PAPER CO., Appleton, Wis.
Nassau Mills—(w)—LESLIE-DONAHOWER CO., St. Paul.
Natches—(b)—toilet—ALBANY PERFORATED WRAPPING PAPER CO., Albany, New York.
National — (b) — box coverings—DISTRICT OF COLUMBIA PAPER MFG. CO., Washington, D. C.
National — (b) — enameled book—BAY STATE PAPER CO., Boston.
National—(w)—linen—J. E. LINDE PAPER CO., New York.
National—(w) — bond and ledger—UNION CARD & PAPER CO., N. Y.
National Flats—(b) — McCLELLAN PAPER CO., Minneapolis, Minn.
National—(b)—No. 1 manila—GRAHAM PAPER CO., St. Louis.

BLOTTING PAPERS   STANDARD PAPER MFG. CO., Richmond, Va.
Largest Manufacturers

Watermarks and Brands

National—(b) — toilet — ALBANY PERFORATED WRAPPING PAPER CO., Albany, New York.
National Bank—(w)—W. G. WILLMANN, New York.
National Bank Bond—(w)—J. W. BUTLER PAPER CO., Chicago.
National Bank Linen Ledger—(w)—W. G. WILLMANN, New York.
National Blanks—(b)—TILESTON & LIVERMORE CO., Boston.
National Blotting—(b)—DISTRICT OF COLUMBIA PAPER MFG. CO., Washington, D. C.
National Bond—(w)—UNION CARD AND PAPER CO., New York.
National Book Paper—(b)—DISTRICT OF COLUMBIA PAPER MFG. CO., Washington, D. C.
National Bristol — (b)—DIEM & WING PAPER CO., Cincinnati, O.
National Bristol—(b)—JOHN CARTER & CO., Boston.
National Bristol—(b)—W. G. WILLMANN, New York.
National Brown—(b) — wrappings and specialties — McDOWELL PAPER MILLS, Philadelphia.
National Capital Bond—(w)—R. P. ANDREWS, Washington, D. C.
National Cover—(b)—DISTRICT OF COLUMBIA PAPER MFG. CO., Washington, D. C.
National Defense—(w and b)—writing, bond, ledger—NEENAH PAPER CO., Neenah, Wis.
National Emblem Bond (figure of eagle)—(w)— F. W. ANDERSON & CO., New York.
National Embossing Cover—(b)— THE UNION PAPER & TWINE CO., Detroit, Mich.
National Ledger — (w) — UNION CARD AND PAPER CO., New York.
National Linen — (w)—AMERICAN WRITING PAPER CO., Holyoke.
National Linen—(w)—E. W. SCARBOROUGH, New York.
National Manila — (b) — GRAHAM PAPER CO., St. Louis.
National Record Ledger — (w)— GRAHAM PAPER CO., St. Louis.
National Safety Bond—(w and b)—GEO. LA MONTE & SON, New York.
National Safety Paper—(b)—GEO. LA MONTE & SON, New York.
National Safety Ticket Paper—GEO. LA MONTE & SON, New York.
National Security League—(w and b)—ledger, bond, writing—NEENAH PAPER CO., Neenah, Wis.
National Tinted Bristol — (b)—DIEM & WING PAPER CO., Cincinnati, Ohio.
National Writing Paper — (b)—GEORGE B. HURD & CO., N. Y.
Natural Brown—(b)—wrapping and specialties — McDOWELL PAPER MILL, Manayunk, Pa.

Navajo—(b)—cover — WORTHY PAPER CO., Mittineague, Mass.
Navajo Souvenir Post Card—(b)—BRADNER SMITH & CO., Chicago.
Navarre—(b)—cover—MERRIAM PAPER CO., New York.
Navarre — (b)—flats — LOUISVILLE PAPER CO., Louisville, Ky.
Navilius—(b) — super half tone—MARTIN & WM. H. NIXON PAPER CO., Manayunk, Philadelphia.
Navy — (b)—ALEX. McARTHUR & CO., LTD., Montreal, Canada.
Navy—(w)—bond and ledger—UNION CARD & PAPER CO., New York.
Navy—(b) — blotting and bristol—UNION CARD AND PAPER CO., New York.
Navy Blue Fibre—(b)—wrapping—GRAHAM PAPER CO., St. Louis.
Navy Bond—(w) — BUNTIN, GILLIES & CO., LTD., Hamilton, Can.
Nay Aug—(b)—toilet — MEGARGEE BROS., Scranton, Pa.
Neapolitan—(w)—GEO. B. HURD & CO., New York.
Neapolitan Cover—(b)—PENINSULAR PAPER CO., Ypsilanti, Mich.
N e b e n—(b)—Specialties—N E B E N MFG. CO., New York.
Neenah—(w and b)—design, ledger, bond, writing—NEENAH PAPER CO., Neenah, Wis.
Nehantic Mills—EAST HARTFORD MANUFACTURING CO., Burnside, Conn.
Nemesis (w. and b.)—bond, super—W. R. GRACE & CO., New York.
Nemo Mills—(w)—BLAKE, McFALL CO., Portland, Ore.
Neostyle Bond — (w)—NEOSTYLE ENVELOPE CO., New York.
Neostyle Linen — (w) — NEOSTYLE ENVELOPE CO., New York.
Neostyle Writing — (w) — NEOSTYLE ENVELOPE CO., New York.
Ne Plus Ultra—(w)—BUNTIN, GILLIES & CO., Hamilton, Ontario, Can.
Ne Plus Ultra—(b)—typewriter—AMERICAN WRITING PAPER CO., Holyoke, Mass.
Neponset Black — (b)—builders' papers—BIRD & SON, East Walpole, Mass.
Neponset Florian—(b)—BIRD & SON, East Walpole, Mass.
Neponset Paroid — (b)—insulating papers—BIRD & SON, East Walpole, Mass.
Neponset Proslate—(b)—BIRD & SON, East Walpole, Mass.
Neponset Red Rope—(b)—roofing—BIRD & SON, East Walpole, Mass.
Neponset Waterdyke—(b)—BIRD & SON, East Walpole, Mass.
Neptune—(b)—toilet—SCOTT PAPER CO., Philadelphia.
Neptune Mills—(w)—HY. LINDENMEYR & SONS, New York.

Watermarks and Brands

Neptune — (b) — gummed — LOUISVILLE PAPER CO., Louisville, Ky.
Nequo — (b) — HOLLINGSWORTH & WHITNEY CO., Boston.
Nereid Mills — (w) — TROY PAPER CO., Troy, New York.
Nero — (b) — book — C. P. LESH PAPER CO., Indianapolis, Ind.
Nesco Bristol — (b) — WHITAKER PAPER CO., Cincinnati, Ohio.
Nestor — (b) — M. F. book — HAGEN PAPER CO., St. Louis.
Nestor Linen — (b) — typewriter — EATON, CRANE & PIKE CO., Pittsfield, Mass.
Netherland — (b) — toilet — LOUISVILLE PAPER CO., Louisville, Ky.
Netherlands Bond — (w) — CONROW BROS., New York.
Nettunia — (w) — JAPAN PAPER CO., New York.
Nevatu — (b) — toilet — GEO. T. JOHNSON CO., Boston.
Nevatu Almoeslinen — (b) — towel — GEO. T. JOHNSON CO., Boston.
Nevatu Special — (b) — towel — GEO. T. JOHNSON CO., Boston.
Nevelee Mills — (b) — flat writing — CONROW BROS., New York.
Neverburst — (b) — ADAMS BAG CO., Chagrin Falls, Ohio.
Never Leak — (b) — rubber roofing — WHITING-PATTERSON CO., New York.
Neverwett — (b) — roofing — LOUISVILLE PAPER CO., Louisville, Ky.
New Century Bond — (w) — C. P. LESH PAPER CO., Indianapolis, Ind.
New England Bond — (w) — JUDD PAPER CO., Holyoke, Mass.
New England Cover — (w) — JUDD PAPER CO., Holyoke, Mass.
New England Ledger — (w) — JUDD PAPER CO., Holyoke, Mass.
New England Mills Blue Superfine — (w) — JOHN F. SARLE, New York.
New England Pasted — (b) — bristol — BAY STATE PAPER CO., Boston.
New Hemisphere — (b) — wrapping — GRAHAM PAPER CO., St. Louis.
New Hub Mills — (b) — writing — BAY STATE PAPER CO., Boston.
New Koat — (b) — white super book — HAGEN PAPER CO., St. Louis.
New Narcissus — (w) — fine — B. F. BOND PAPER CO., Baltimore.
New O. Tag — (b) — MEGARGEE-HARE PAPER CO., Philadelphia.
Newport — (b) — toilet — R. L. GREENE PAPER CO., Providence, R. I.
Newport Ledger — (w) — COLLINS MFG. CO., N. Wilbraham, Mass.
Newtex — (b) — toilet — SCOTT PAPER CO., Philadelphia.
Newton Cream Drawing — (b) — A. STORRS & BEMENT CO., Boston.
Newton Index Bristol — (b) — JOHN CARTER & CO., Boston.

New York Bond — (w) — F. W. ANDERSON & CO., New York.
New York Ledger — (w) — F. W. ANDERSON & CO., INC., New York.
New York Linen — (w) — EATON, CRANE & PIKE CO., Pittsfield, Mass.
New York Mills — (w) — EATON, CRANE & PIKE CO., Pittsfield, Mass.
New York Mimeograph — (b) — THE UNION PAPER AND TWINE CO., Detroit, Mich.
New York Standard Linen — (w) — VERNON BROS. & CO., New York.
New York Superfine — (b) — VERNON BROS. & CO., New York.
New York White Bristol — (b) — pasted bristol — B. D. RISING PAPER CO., Housatonic, Mass.
New York Wove — (w) — WHITING PAPER CO., Holyoke, Mass.
Niagara — (b) — blotting — THE ALLING & CORY CO., Rochester, N. Y.
Niagara — (b) — enameled book — HAGEN PAPER CO., St. Louis.
Niagara — (b) — SMITH PAPER CO., Lee, Mass.
Niagara — (w) — flat — R. H. THOMPSON CO., Buffalo, New York.
Niagara — (b) — roll toilet — STONE & FORSYTH CO., Boston.
Niagara — (b) — M. F. book — BRADNER SMITH & CO., Chicago.
Niagara — (b) — BUNTIN, GILLIES & CO., Hamilton, Canada.
Niagara — (b) — blotting — THE PAPER MILLS CO., Chicago.
Niagara Bond — (w) — AETNA PAPER CO., Dayton, Ohio.
Niagara Bond — (b) — DWIGHT BROS. PAPER CO., Grand Rapids, Mich.
Niantic — (w) — bristol — B. F. BOND PAPER CO., Baltimore.
Nibroe Kraft — (b) — BERLIN MILLS CO., Portland, Me.
Niobe — (w) — bond — PENINSULAR PAPER CO., Ypsilanti, Mich.
Niobe Bond — (w) — A. STORRS & BEMENT CO., Boston.
Niobe — (b) — bond — LOUISVILLE PAPER CO., Louisville, Ky.
Nippon Vellum — (b) — SEYMOUR CO., INC., New York.
N. M. Fine Bond — (b) — ROLLAND PAPER CO., LTD., St. Jerome, Can.
No Damp — (b) — insulating — GRAHAM PAPER CO., St. Louis.
Noiseless — (b) — carpet lining — GRAHAM PAPER CO., St. Louis.
No1 French Folio — (b) — HARLEM CARD & PAPER CO., New York.
No-lint Express — (b) — wrapping — LOUISVILLE PAPER CO., Louisville, Ky.
No1 Onion Skin — (b) — HARLEM CARD & PAPER CO., New York.
Nomarch Bristols — (b) — WABASH COATING MILLS, Wabash, Ind.
Non-Addressing — (b) — bond — WHITING-PATTERSON CO., Philadelphia.

Watermarks and Brands

Nonantum Mills — (w) — writing — CURTIS & BRO., Newark, Del.
No Name — (b) — toilet —R. L. GREENE PAPER CO., Providence, R. I.
Non-Curl Bond — (w) — NEENAH PAPER COMPANY, Neenah, Wis.
Non-Curling—(w and b)—bond, ledger, writing—NEENAH PAPER CO., Neenah, Wis.
None Such — (b) — toilet—GRAHAM PAPER CO., St. Louis.
Nonotuck — (b) — sermon paper — UNITED STATES ENVELOPE CO. (Morgan Envelope Co. Division), Springfield, Mass.
Nonotuck — (b) — toilet—UNITED STATES ENVELOPE CO. (Morgan Envelope Co. Div.), Springfield, Mass.
Nonotuck White Manila — (b) — SWIGART PAPER CO., Chicago.
Nonpareil—(w)—AMERICAN PAPER CO., Holyoke, Mass.
Nonpareil Flats—(b)—McCLELLAN PAPER CO., Minneapolis, Minn.
Nonpareil Superfine — (b)—fine— JOHN F. SARLE, New York.
Nonpareil — (b)—writing — JOHN F. SARLES CO., INC., New York.
Nonpareil Coated Book—(b)—MINNEAPOLIS PAPER CO., Minneapolis, Minn.
Nonsook Linen—(w)—TROY PAPER CO., Troy, N. Y.
Non-Transparent Bond — (w) — GEO. B. HURD & CO., New York.
No Protest Bond—(w)—CHEMICAL PAPER MFG. CO., Holyoke, Mass.
No Protest Bond— (w) — ALEXANDER-HOLDEN PAPER CO., New York.
Nordeling — (b)—hand-made book— HY. LINDENMEYR & SONS, N. Y.
Nordica Mills—(w)—JORDAN CARD & PAPER CO. Boston.
Norfolk Crepe—(b)—t o i l e t—OLD DOMINION PAPER CO., Norfolk, Va.
Norfolk Fibre—(b)—OLD DOMINION PAPER CO., Norfolk, Va.
Norfolk Mills—(b)—A. STORRS & BEMENT CO., Boston.
Norka Bond—(w)—W. B. OGLESBY PAPER CO., Middletown, Ohio.
Norka Ledger—(w)—W. B. OGLESBY PAPER CO., Middletown, Ohio.
Norman—(b)—envelope—THE PAPER MILLS CO., Chicago.
Norman—(b) — book — GRAHAM PAPER CO., St. Louis.
Norman Bond — (w)—AMERICAN WRITING PAPER CO., Holyoke.
Normandie—(b)—writing— GRAHAM PAPER CO., St. Louis.
Normandie—(w)—GRAHAM PAPER CO., St. Louis.
Normandy Linen — (b)—EATON, CRANE & PIKE CO., Pittsfield, Mass.
Normandy Vellum—(b)—STONE & ANDREWS, Boston.

Normil—(b) — toilet — NORTHERN PAPER MILLS, Green Bay, Wis.
Norse Bond—(w)—THE UNION PAPER AND TWINE CO., Detroit.
Norseman Bond — (b) — EATON, CRANE & PIKE CO., Pittsfield, Mass.
Northern Bee—(b)—toilet—NORTHERN PAPER MILLS, Green Bay, Wis.
Northern Bond—(b) — ROLLAND PAPER CO., LTD., St. Jerome, Can.
Northern Bond—(b)—HARPER PAPER CO., New York.
Northern Commercial—(b)—toilet —NORTHERN PAPER MILLS, Green Bay, Wis.
Northern Extra — (b)—NORTHERN PAPER MILLS, Green Bay, Wis.
Northern Extra — (b) — t o i l e t — NORTHERN PAPER MILLS, Green Bay, Wis.
Northern Mills Co.— (w) — ROLLAND PAPER CO., St. Jerome, Can.
Northern Mills Monogram—(w)— ROLLAND PAPER CO., LTD., Green Bay, Wis.
Northern Oval—(b)—toilet—NORTHERN PAPER MILLS, Green Bay, Wis.
Northern Roll—(b)—toilet—NORTHERN PAPER MILLS, Green Bay, Wis.
North Star — (b)—folded—DIEM & WING PAPER CO., Cincinnati, Ohio.
North Star — (b) — cardboard—McCLELLAN PAPER CO., Minneapolis.
Norwalk—(b)—tinted, bristol — THE PAPER MILLS CO., Chicago.
Norway—(b)—book—C. P. LESH PAPER CO, Indianapolis, Ind.
Norway—(b)—white bond wrapping— WHITING-PATTERSON CO., New York.
Norway Writing — (b) — HY. LINDENMEYR & SONS, New York.
Northwestern Bond—(w)—MINNEAPOLIS PAPER CO., Minneapolis.
Northwestern Ledger — (w)—MINNEAPOLIS PAPER CO., Minneapolis.
Norwich—(w)—bond and linen—ELSINORE PAPER CO., New York.
Norwood — (b) — coated blank — ARNOLD-ROBERTS CO., Boston.
Norwood — (b)—cover—LASHER & LATHROP, New York.
Notary Mills — (b)—TROY PAPER CO., Troy, New York.
Nottingham Enamel—(b) — book — LOUISVILLE PAPER CO., Louisville, Ky.
Novelty Bond Manifold—(b)—CONROW BROS., New York.
Novelty Mills—(b)—ruled—CONROW BROS., New York.
Novel Tint — (b) — book—J. W. BUTLER PAPER CO., Chicago.
Noxall—(b)— round corner card— BRADNER SMITH & CO., Chicago.
Noxall—(b)—toilet—GRAHAM PAPER CO., St. Louis.
Nuggett Bond—(w)—F. A. FLINN, INC., New York.

FELTS AND JACKETS | Appleton Woolen Mills
APPLETON - - WIS.

704 Watermarks and Brands

Nuoval—(b)—toilet—GEO. T. JOHNSON CO., Boston.
N. Y. Express—(b)—colored screening—MARCELLUS PAPER CO., Syracuse, New York.
N. Y. Mills—(b)—package toilet—JEROME PAPER CO., New York.
Nyack Bristol — (b)—THE UNION PAPER & TWINE CO., Detroit, Mich.
Nyasset—(b)—coated book—CONROW BROS., New York.

O

O. P. S. Bond — (w)—EVERETT PULP & PAPER CO., Everett, Wash.
O. P. S. Railroad—(w)—writing—EVERETT PULP & PAPER CO., Everett, Wash.
Oak Bond—(w) — PACIFIC PAPER CO., Portland, Ore.
Oakdale—(b) — ALBANY PERFORATED WRAPPING PAPER CO., Albany, New York.
Oakdale—(b)—envelope — GRAHAM PAPER CO., St. Louis.
Oakdale Toilet—(b)—HY. LINDENMEYR & SONS, New York.
Oakenrealm—(w and b)—fine writing—PAPER MILLS CO., Chicago.
Oakland—(b)—flat—J. W. BUTLER PAPER CO., Chicago.
Oakland — (b) — WORTHY PAPER CO., Mittineague, Mass.
Oakland Translucent—(b)—C. S. PROCTOR PAPER CO., Boston.
Oakleaf Linen — (w)—AMERICAN WRITING PAPER CO., Holyoke.
Oakleaf Linen — (w)—BRADNER SMITH & CO., Chicago.
Oak Mills—(b)—writing—LASHER & LATHROP, New York.
Oakwood—(b)—cover—LASHER & LATHROP, New York.
Oakwood—(w)—UNION CARD & PAPER CO., New York.
Oakwood—(w) — writing— UNION CARD & PAPER CO., New York.
Oakwood Folding Bristol—(b)—JOHN CARTER & CO., Boston.
Oakwood Mills—(b)—headings—ESSEX PAD AND PAPER CO., Holyoke.
Observo —(w)— book—PENINSULAR PAPER CO., Ypsilanti, Mich.
Occidental—(b)—cover—J. W. BUTLER PAPER CO., Chicago.
Ocean Mills—(w)—WESTERN PENNA. PAPER CO., Pittsburgh, Pa.
Oceanic Linen Laid—(b)—PARSONS TRADING CO., New York.
Oceanic Bond—Made in U. S. A.—(w)—PARSONS TRADING CO., New York.
Oceanic Paste Boards—(w)—PARSONS TRADING CO., New York.
Octagon Colored Laid—(b)—flats—CLEMENTS PAPER CO., Nashville.
October—(b)—wedding and bristol—MOUNTAIN MILL PAPER CO., Lee, Mass.

Odin—(w)—BOORUM & PEASE CO., New York.
Odpaco Ledger Index Bristol—(b)—OLD DOMINION PAPER CO., Norfolk, Va.
Office Blotting—(b)—O. W. BRADLEY, St. Louis.
Office Bond—(w)—UNION CARD & PAPER CO., New York.
Office Bond, E. A. W.—(w)—E. A. WRIGHT, Philadelphia.
Office Index Bristol—(b)—MEGARGEE BROS., Scranton, Pa.
Office Ledger—(w and b)—CUNNINGHAM, CURTISS & WELCH, Los Angeles, Cal.
Office Linen, E. A. W.—(w)—E. A. WRIGHT, Philadelphia.
Office Special—(b)—JOHNSTON PAPER CO., Harrisburg, Pa.
Official Blotting—(b)—DISTRICT OF COLUMBIA PAPER MFG. CO., Washington, D. C.
Official Bond—(w)—white bond only—R. C. KASTNER PAPER CO., N. Y.
Official Bond, Extra Strong—(w)—PARSONS TRADING COMPANY, New York.
Official Linen—(w)—No. 1 cream laid linen—R. C. KASTNER PAPER CO., New York.
Official Record Ledger—(w)—white ledger paper—R. C. KASTNER PAPER CO., New York.
Ogden —(b)—blanks — DONALDSON PAPER CO., Harrisburg, Pa.
Ogden Bond—(w)—INLAND PAPER CO., Chicago.
Oglesby Linen 1851—(w)—THE W. B. OGLESBY PAPER CO., Middletown, Ohio.
Ogonts—(b)—cover—MEGARGEE-HARE PAPER CO., Philadelphia.
Ohaco—(b)—bond, ledger, writing—O. H. ANDERSON & CO., New York.
Ohio Blanks—(b)—McCLELLAN PAPER CO., Minneapolis, Minn.
Ohio Bond—(w)—white—CENTRAL OHIO PAPER CO., Columbus, Ohio.
Ohio Bristol—(b)—WHITAKER PAPER CO., Cincinnati, Ohio.
Ohio Ledger—(w)—NITSCHKE PAPER CO., Columbus, Ohio.
Ohio Railroad Manila—(b)—WESTERN PENNA. PAPER CO., Pittsburgh, Pa.
Okay Book—(b)—writing — BEECHER, PECK & LEWIS, Detroit, Mich.
Okayed—(b)—toilet—SCOTT PAPER CO., Philadelphia.
Okeden Linen—(w)—JOHN WANAMAKER, Philadelphia.
O. K. Extra Rag News—(b)—BRADNER SMITH & CO., Chicago.
O. K. Mills—(b)—DWIGHT BROS. PAPER CO., Chicago.
Old Alcalde Superfine—(w)—flat—FOX RIVER PAPER CO., Appleton, Wis.

BLOTTING PAPERS
"STANDARD," "IMPERIAL," "STERLING"
Royal Worcester and Defender Enameled
STANDARD PAPER MFG. CO., - - Richmond, Va.

Old Arabian Linen Bond—(w)—SMITH, DAVIDSON & WRIGHT, LTD., Vancouver, B. C.
Old Arabian Linen Ledger—(w)—SMITH, DAVIDSON & WRIGHT, LTD., Vancouver, B. C.
Old Athens Bond — (w) — INDIANA PAPER CO., Indianapolis.
Old Badger Bond—(w)—FOX RIVER PAPER CO., Appleton, Wis.
Old Badger Ledger — (w) — FOX RIVER PAPER CO., Appleton, Wis.
Old Bank Bond—(w)—AETNA PAPER CO., Dayton, Ohio.
Old Barry—(w)—writing—ST. LOUIS PAPER CO., St. Louis.
Old Bay State Mills—(w)—AMERICAN WRITING PAPER CO., Holyoke.
Old Berkshire—(w)—writing—J. W. BUTLER PAPER CO., Chicago.
Old Berkshire Mills—(w)—OLD BERKSHIRE MILLS CO., Dalton, Mass.
Old Berkshire Mills — (b) — pasted bristols — OLD BERKSHIRE MILLS CO., Dalton, Mass.
Old Berwick Mills—(w)—DIEM & WING PAPER CO., Cincinnati.
Old Brittany Parchment—(b)—EATON, CRANE & PIKE CO., Pittsfield, Mass.
Old Cabot Bond—(w)—CROCKER-McELWAIN CO., Holyoke, Mass.
Old Cabot Extra Fine—(w)—CROCKER-McELWAIN CO., Holyoke, Mass.
Old Cabot Fine—(w)—CROCKER-McELWAIN CO., Holyoke, Mass.
Old Cabot Mills—(w)—CROCKER-McELWAIN CO., Holyoke, Mass.
Old Cabot Superfine—(w)—CROCKER-McELWAIN CO., Holyoke, Mass.
Old Canterbury — (w) — bond — J. FRANCIS HOCK & CO., Baltimore.
Old Canterbury Bond—(w)—CORNWALL PAPER MFG. CO., Cornwall-on-Hudson, N. Y.
Old Canterbury Bond—(w)—GARRET-BUCHANAN, Philadelphia.
Old Chelsea Bond—(w)—THE PETERS PAPER CO., Denver, Col.
Old Cheshire Mills—(w)—AMERICAN WRITING PAPER CO., Holyoke.
Old Chester Mills—(w)—AMERICAN WRITING PAPER CO., Holyoke.
Old Cloister—(b)—cover—STRATHMORE PAPER CO., Mittineague, Mass.
Old Cloister—(w)—book—STRATHMORE PAPER CO., Mittineague, Mass.
Old Colonial Linen Ledger—(w)—CARTER, RICE & CO., CORP., Boston, Mass.
Old Colony—(b)—fine—JOHN F. SARLE, New York.
Old Colony—(b)—blotting—VON OLKER-SNELL PAPER CO., Boston.
Old Colony Bond—(w)—WORTHY PAPER CO., Mittineague, Mass.
Old Colony Ledger—(w)—KINGSLEY PAPER CO., Cleveland, Ohio.
Old Colony Ledger—(w)—WORTHY PAPER CO., Mittineague, Mass.
Old Colony Linen—(w)—WORTHY PAPER CO., Mittineague, Mass.
Old Colony Superfine — (w) — WORTHY PAPER CO., Mittineague, Mass.
Old Council Tree—(w and b)—writing, ledger, bond—NEENAH PAPER CO., Neenah, Wis.
Old Crow—(b)—ALBANY PERFORATED PAPER CO., Albany, N. Y.
Old Crown—(w)—linen—UNION CARD AND PAPER CO., New York.
Old Deerfield—(w and b)—TAYLOR-ATKINS PAPER CO., Hartford.
Old Deerfield Bond—(w)—MILLERS FALLS PAPER CO., Millers Falls, Mass.
Old Devon— (w) —BARBER-ELLIS, LTD., Toronto, Can.
Old Devonshire Linen—(w)—A. STORRS & BEMENT CO., Boston.
Old Devonshire Linen Ledger— (w)—A. STORRS & BEMENT CO., Boston.
Old Devonshire Mills—(w)—A. STORRS & BEMENT CO., Boston.
Old Dominion—(b)—toilet—ALBANY PERFORATED WRAPPING PAPER CO., Albany, N. Y.
Old Dominion Bond — (w) — HOWARD SMITH PAPER MILLS, LTD., Montreal, Can.
Old Dominion Ledger—(w)—BASSETT & SUTPHIN, New York.
Old Downshire—(w)—(deckle edge) book—JAMES WHITE PAPER CO., Chicago.
Old Downshire — (w) — book — STRATHMORE PAPER CO., Mittineague, Mass.
Old Dresden Bond—(w)—KINGSLEY PAPER CO., Cleveland, Ohio.
Old Dutch Bond—(w)—CROCKER-McELWAIN CO., Holyoke, Mass.
Old Dutch Linen—(w and b)—GEO. B. HURD & CO., New York.
Old Dutch Linen Bond—(b)—GEO. B. HURD & CO., New York.
Old Eastern Mills—(w)—extra superfine—VALLEY PAPER CO., Holyoke, Mass.
Old English—(b)—bristols and cover —PAPER MILLS CO., Chicago.
Old English—(b)—laid antique book — W. H. CLAFLIN & CO., Boston.
Old English All Rag—(b)—book— C. P. LESH PAPER CO., Indianapolis.
Old English Bond—(w)—VALLEY PAPER CO., Holyoke, Mass.
Old English Ledger—(w)—VALLEY PAPER CO., Holyoke, Mass.
Old English Linen—(w)—VALLEY PAPER CO., Holyoke, Mass.
Old Faithful Bond—(w)—FOX RIVER PAPER CO., Appleton, Wis.

Old-Fashioned Linen—(w)—BERLIN & JONES ENVELOPE CO., N. Y.
Old Hamilton Bond—(w)—BANKERS SUPPLY CO., Denver and Chicago.
Old Hampden Bond—(w)—PARSONS PAPER CO., Holyoke, Mass.
Old Hampshire Bond—(w)—HAMPSHIRE PAPER CO., South Hadley Falls, Mass.
Old Hampshire Lawn — (w) — HAMPSHIRE PAPER CO., South Hadley Falls, Mass.
Old Hampshire Linen Record—(w)—HAMPSHIRE PAPER CO., South Hadley Falls, Mass.
Old Hampshire Vellum — (w) — HAMPSHIRE PAPER CO., South Hadley Falls, Mass.
Old Hempstead—(b)— bond — RIEGEL & CO., INC., Philadelphia.
Old Hempstead Bond—(w)—AMERICAN WRITING PAPER CO., Holyoke, Mass.
Old Hickory—(b)—cover—LASHER & LATHROP, New York.
Old Holyoke Bond—(w)—CHEMICAL PAPER MFG. CO., Holyoke.
Old Homestead—(b)—toilet—WILSON & TOWNE PAPER CO., N. Y.
Old Honesty Linen—(w)—AETNA PAPER CO., Dayton, Ohio.
Old Irish Linen—(b)—NORTHERN PAPER MILLS, Green Bay, Wis.
Old Italian Parchment—(b)—MACK-ELLIOTT PAPER CO., St. Louis.
Old Ivanshire — (w) — AMERICAN WRITING PAPER CO., Holyoke, Mass.
Old Ivory—(b)—DILL & COLLINS CO., Philadelphia.
Old Kent Bond—(w)—BUNTIN, GILLIES & CO., Hamilton, Ontario, Canada.
Old Mill—(w)—flat writing—LOUISVILLE PAPER CO., Louisville, Ky.
Old Mill Bond—(w)—INLAND PAPER CO., Chicago, Ill.
Old Mission Book Paper—(b)—BRADNER SMITH & CO., Chicago.
Old Nantucket Bond—(w)—B. D. RISING PAPER CO., Housatonic, Mass.
Old Oaken Bucket Linen—(w)—UNITED STATES ENVELOPE CO. (Whitcomb Envelope Co. Division), Worcester, Mass.
Old Parchment Bond—(w)—AMERICAN WRITING PAPER CO., Holyoke, Mass.
Old Reliable Bond—(w)—WHITING-PLOVER PAPER CO., Stevens Point, Wis.
Old Scotch Bond—(w)—KINGSLEY PAPER CO., Cleveland, Ohio.
Old Scotch Vellum—(w and b)—TAYLOR-ATKINS PAPER CO., Hartford, Conn.
Old Scotland Mills—(w)—flat writing—EAST HARTFORD MANUFACTURING CO., Burnside, Conn.
Old Shelburne Bond—(w)—MOUNTAIN MILL PAPER CO., Lee, Mass.
Old Stamford Bond—(w)—LEE PAPER CO., Vicksburg, Mich.
Old Stratford—(b)—book and parchment cover—STRATHMORE PAPER CO., Mittineague, Mass.
Old Stratford U. S. A.—(w)—STRATHMORE PAPER CO., Mittineague, Mass.
Old Style—(w)—Z. & W. M. CRANE, Dalton, Mass.
Old Style—(w)—egg-shell finish—S. D. WARREN & CO., Boston.
Old Suffolk Mills—(w)—JOHN CARTER & CO., Boston.
Old Tabard Bond—(w)—white bond only—R. C. KASTNER PAPER CO., New York.
Old Time—(w)—laid—FOX RIVER PAPER CO., Appleton, Wis.
Old Time Linen—(w)—J. W. BUTLER PAPER CO., Chicago.
Old Valley Mills Superfine—(w)—VALLEY PAPER CO., Holyoke, Mass.
Old Valley Mills Typewriter Bond—(w)—VALLEY PAPER CO., Holyoke, Mass.
Old Valley Mills Typewriter Linen—(w)—VALLEY PAPER CO., Holyoke, Mass.
Old Veda—(b)—bond—RIEGEL & CO., INC., Philadelphia.
Old Veda Bond—(w)—MILLERS FALLS PAPER CO., Millers Falls, Mass.
Old Veda Bristol—(b)—ADVERTISERS' PAPER MILLS, Holyoke, Mass.
Old Veda Cover—(b)—ADVERTISERS' PAPER MILLS, Holyoke, Mass.
Old Veda Text—(w)—book—ADVERTISERS' PAPER MILLS, Holyoke.
Old Vermont—(w)—bond and linen—UNION CARD AND PAPER CO., New York.
Old Vienna Bond—(w)—EATON, CRANE & PIKE CO., Pittsfield, Mass.
Old Yorkshire—(w)—C A R T E R. RICE & CO., Boston.
Old Yorkshire Bond—(w)—MOSER PAPER CO., Chicago.
Olde Style—(b)—book, white and India tint (egg-shell finish)—S. D. WARREN CO., Boston, Mass.
Olde Tyme Book—(b)—MERRIAM PAPER CO., New York.
Olive—(b)—news—GRAHAM PAPER CO., St. Louis.
Oliver Superfine—(w)—HAMMERMILL PAPER CO., Erie, Pa.
Olympia—(b)— writing — ARNOLD ROBERTS CO., Boston.
Olympia—(b)—white wove and colored writing—HENRY LINDENMEYR & SONS, New York.
Olympia — (b) — cover — J A M E S WHITE & CO., Chicago.

Watermarks and Brands

Olympia—(b)—toilet—UNITED STATES ENVELOPE CO. (Morgan Envelope Co. Div.), Springfield, Mass.
Olympia—(b)—toilet—H. M. RICHMOND PAPER CO., Tacoma, Wash.
Olympia—(w)—bond—GRAHAM PAPER CO., St. Louis.
Olympia Bond—(w)—C. W. WILLIAMS & CO., New York.
Olympia Ledger—(w)—AMERICAN WRITING PAPER CO., Holyoke, Mass.
Olympia Linen — (w) — C. W. WILLIAMS & CO., New York.
Olympia Manila—(b)—flat writing—MERRIAM PAPER CO., New York.
Olympia Print—(b)—THE UNION PAPER & TWINE CO., Detroit, Mich.
Olympia Writing—(b)—MERRIAM PAPER CO., New York.
Olympic—(b)—enameled cover and envelopes—CHATFIELD & WOODS CO., Cincinnati, Ohio.
Olympic—(b)—toilet—ALBANY PERFORATED WRAPPING PAPER CO., Albany, N. Y.
Olympic Bond—(w)—EASTERN MFG. CO., Bangor, Me.
Olympus Mills—(w)—writing—TROY PAPER CO., Troy, N. Y.
Omodaka Japan—(b)—japan, cover, bristol—UNION CARD & PAPER CO., New York.
Onandago Bond—J. & F. B. GARRETT, Syracuse, N. Y.
Ondawa—(b)—ALBANY PERFORATED WRAPPING PAPER CO., Albany, N. Y.
Oneida—(b)—toilet—ALBANY PERFORATED WRAPPING PAPER CO., Albany, N. Y.
Oneida Bond—(b)—WHITING-PLOVER PAPER CO., Menasha, Wis.
Oneida Bristol—(b)—O. W. BRADLEY, St. Louis.
Oneida Ledger—(w)—LASHER & LATHROP, New York.
Oneonta—(w)—flat—PACIFIC PAPER CO., Portland, Ore.
Onimbo Cover—(b)—PENINSULAR PAPER CO., Ypsilanti, Mich.
Onion Skin—(b)—folio Bermuda plate finish—BRADNER SMITH & CO., Chicago.
Onion Skin—(b)—KEITH PAPER CO., Turner's Falls, Mass.
Onion Skin—(b)—GEO. B. HURD & CO., New York.
Onion Skin Typewriter—(b)—SMITH PAPER CO., Lee, Mass.
Onito Mills—(b)—CONROW BROS., New York.
Onliwon No. 1—(b)—ALBANY PERFORATED WRAPPING PAPER CO., Albany, New York.
Onliwon No. 2—(b)—ALBANY PERFORATED WRAPPING PAPER CO., Albany, New York.
Onondaga — (b) — toilet—ALBANY PERFORATED WRAPPING PAPER CO., Albany, New York.

Onota Bond—(w)—MOUNTAIN MILL PAPER CO., Lee, Mass.
Ontario—(b)—felt roofing and sheeting—ALLING & CORY CO., Rochester.
Ontario—(b) — BUNTIN, GILLES & CO., Hamilton, Canada.
Ontario—(b)—tarred felt — GRAHAM PAPER CO., St. Louis.
Ontario Bond — (w)—F. A. FLINN, INC., New York.
Ontario Bristol—(b)—THE ALLING & CORY CO., Rochester, N. Y.
Ontario Bristol — (b) — BEECHER, PECK & LEWIS, Detroit, Mich.
Onyx—(b) — double coated cover—BRADNER SMITH & CO., Chicago.
Onyx—(b)—bonds, covers and bristol—KEITH PAPER CO., Turner's Falls, Mass.
Onyx—(b)—waxed—LOUISVILLE PAPER CO., Louisville, Ky.
Onyx Parchment Announcement—UNION CARD & PAPER CO., N. Y.
Ooze—(b)—DILL & COLLINS CO., Philadelphia.
O. P. S.—(w)—amber laid writing—EVERETT PULP & PAPER CO., Everett, Wash.
Opal Opaque Catalog — (b) — GRAHAM PAPER CO., St. Louis.
Opaque — (b) — MISSOURI PAPER HOUSE, Kansas City, Mo.
Opaque—(b) — toilet — NORTHERN PAPER MILLS, Green Bay, Wis.
Opaque Bond—(w) — CAREW MFG. CO., South Hadley Falls, Mass.
Ophir—(b)—cover — JAMES WHITE PAPER CO., Chicago.
Option Bond — (w) — AMERICAN WRITING PAPER CO., Holyoke.
Opportunity — (b) — envelope — GRAHAM PAPER CO., St. Louis.
Order Bond — (b)—CHATFIELD & WOODS CO., Cincinnati, Ohio.
Organdie Linen Finish — (w) — HOWARD SMITH PAPER MILLS, LTD., Montreal, Can.
Old Organdie Parchment Finish—(w) — HOWARD SMITH PAPER MILLS, LTD., Montreal, Can.
Organdie—(w and b)—bond, writing and bristol—UNION CARD AND PAPER CO., New York.
Organdie Parchment—(w)—HOWARD SMITH PAPER MILL CO., LTD., Montreal, Can.
Orkid Cover — (b) — PENINSULAR PAPER CO., Ypsilanti, Mich.
Orient—(b) — THOMAS W. PRICE, Philadelphia.
Orient—(b) — enamel — C. P. LESH PAPER CO., Indianapolis, Ind.
Orient Bristol—(b)—COOK-VIVIAN CO., Boston.
Orient Linen Ledger — (w)—VON OLKER-SNELL PAPER CO., Boston.
Orient Mills—(w)—PACIFIC PAPER CO., Portland, Ore.
Oriental—(b) — waxed tissue—W. H. CLAFLIN & CO., Boston.

Oriental—(b)—tissue—GRAHAM PAPER CO., St. Louis.
Oriental—(b) — colored wove—J. E. LINDE PAPER CO., New York.
Oriental Colored Enamel Book—(b) — PETREQUIN PAPER CO., Cleveland, Ohio.
Oriental Cover—(b)—HY. LINDENMEYR & SONS, New York.
Oriental Gray Kraft — (b) — ORONO PULP & PAPER CO., Orono, Maine.
Oriental Linen Parchment—(w)— AMERICAN WRITING PAPER CO., Holyoke, Mass.
Oriental Manifold—(b)—GARRETT BUCHANAN CO., Philadelphia.
Oriental Wedding Bristol—(b)—C. P. LESH PAPER CO., Indianapolis.
Origa — (b) — writing—WEST VIRGINIA PULP & PAPER CO., New York.
Original County Record — (w)— AMERICAN WRITING PAPER CO., Holyoke, Mass.
Original County Record Ledger—(w)—AMERICAN WRITING PAPER CO., Holyoke, Mass.
Original Lafayette—(w)—laid—writing—PARSONS TRADING CO., New York.
Original Owen Bond—(w)—B. D. RISING PAPER CO., Housatonic, Mass.
Original Turkey Linen — (w) — WHITING PAPER CO., Holyoke.
Orinoco Ledger — (w) — PIONEER PRESS, St. Paul, Minn.
Orinoque—(b)—roll toilet—JEROME PAPER CO., New York.
Oriole—(b)—HUBBS & CORNING CO., Baltimore.
Oriole Bond—(w) — MERRIAM PAPER CO., New York.
Oriole Linen—(w)—bond and onion skin — GRAHAM PAPER CO., St. Louis.
Oriole White—(w)—bond—MERRIAM PAPER CO., New York.
Orion—(b)—C. P. LESH PAPER CO., Indianapolis, Ind.
Orkid—(b) — cover — PENINSULAR PAPER CO., Ypsilanti, Mich.
Orkid Linen—(w)—laid flats—MINNEAPOLIS PAPER CO., Minneapolis.
Orleans—(b)—toilet—ALBANY PERFORATED WRAPPING PAPER CO., Albany, New York.
Ormond—(b) — envelope — UNION CARD AND PAPER CO., New York.
Ornithoid—(b)—cover — PENINSULAR PAPER CO., Ypsilanti, Mich.
Oronoko—(b)—detail board—C. B. HEWITT & BROS., INC., New York.
Orthodox Bible—(b)—TILESTON & HOLLINGSWORTH CO., Boston.
Orthodox Plate—(b)—English finish book — TILESTON & HOLLINGSWORTH CO., Boston.

Osage—(b)—toilet — ALBANY PERFORATED WRAPPING PAPER CO., Albany, New York.
Osceola—(b)—poster—GRAHAM PAPER CO., St. Louis.
Osceolia Bond — (b) — DREW'S WHOLESALE PAPER HOUSE, Jacksonville, Fla.
Oshkosh Bond— (w) —BAKER PAPER CO., Oshkosh, Wis.
Oshkosh Mills — (w) — BAKER PAPER CO., Oshkosh, Wis.
Ostrich—(b)—cover—JAMES WHITE PAPER CO., Chicago.
Oswego—(b)—toilet—ALBANY PERFORATED WRAPPING PAPER CO., Albany, New York.
Otsego Blanks—(b)—coated — BARDEEN PAPER CO., Otsego, Mich.
Otsego Superfine—(w)—STANDARD CARD AND PAPER CO., New York.
Ottawa Manila Tag—(b)—OLD DOMINION PAPER CO., Norfolk, Va.
Otter—(b)—CROWN COLUMBIA PAPER CO., San Francisco.
Ottoman—(w)—GEO. B. HURD & CO., New York.
Our Favorite Ledger—(b)—JOHN F. SARLE, New York.
Our Favorite Ledger—(w) — JOHN F. SARLES CO., INC., New York.
Our Ledger—(w)—VALLEY PAPER CO., Holyoke, Mass.
Our Special — (b)— envelopes—R. L. GREENE PAPER CO., Providence, R. I.
Our Own—(b)—ruled goods—R. L. GREENE PAPER CO., Providence, R. I.
Our Own Extra Fine—(w)—flats—R. L. GREENE PAPER CO., Providence, R. I.
Our Own Linen—(w)—FOX RIVER PAPER CO., Appleton, Wis.
Our Own Mills—(b)—A. STORRS & BEMENT CO., Boston.
Our Special—(b)—envelope — R. L. GREENE PAPER CO., Providence, R. I.
Our Special—(b)—THE JENNER CO., Louisville, Ky.
Our Special—(b)—UNITED STATES ENVELOPE CO. (Whitcomb Envelope Co. Division), Worcester, Mass.
Oval King — (b)—toilet—UNITED STATES ENVELOPE CO. (Morgan Envelope Co. Division), Springfield.
Overland—(b)—envelope — GRAHAM PAPER CO., St. Louis.
Overland—(w)—ledger — MIDLAND PAPER CO., Chicago.
Overland—(w and b) — GEO. B. HURD & CO., New York.
Overland — (w and b) — writing—RIEGEL & CO., INC., Philadelphia.
Overland — (b)—post card — LOUISVILLE PAPER CO., Louisville, Ky.
Overland Bond — (w)—WESTERN PAPER CO., Omaha, Neb.

Watermarks and Brands

Overland Book — (b) — MINNEAPOLIS PAPER CO., Minneapolis, Minn.
Overland Bristol—(b)—MILLER & WRIGHT PAPER CO., INC., New York.
Overland Mail — (b) — EATON, CRANE & PIKE CO., Pittsfield.
Overland Mail — (w) — MARCUS WARD CO., Brooklyn, N. Y.
Overlay — (b) — CHATFIELD & WOODS CO., Cincinnati, Ohio.
Oversea Bond — (w) — HAMPSHIRE PAPER CO., South Hadley Falls, Mass.
Overton Linen Bond—(w)—KINGSLEY PAPER CO., Cleveland, Ohio.
Overton Mills — (w)—laid linen—KINGSLEY PAPER CO., Cleveland.
Owen Linen — (w) — B. D. RISING PAPER CO., Housatonic, Mass.
Owen Linen Ledger—(w)—B. D. RISING PAPER CO., Housatonic, Mass.
Owen Superfine—(w)—B. D. RISING PAPER CO., Housatonic, Mass.
Owl — (b) — HOLLINGSWORTH & WHITNEY CO., Boston.
Oxford—(b) — bristol, onion skin, canary writing and coated book—JUDD PAPER CO., Holyoke.
Oxford—(b) — roll toilet — DONALDSON PAPER CO., Harrisburg, Pa.
Oxford—(b) — enamel — DIEM & WING PAPER CO., Cincinnati, Ohio.
Oxford—(w)—fine — SOUTHERN PAPER CO., Richmond, Va.
Oxford Bond—(w)—JUDD PAPER CO., Holyoke, Mass.
Oxford Antique—(b)—book — C. P. LESH PAPER CO., Indianapolis.
Oxford Binders' Board — (b) — BRADNER SMITH & CO., Chicago.
Oxford Bond—(w) — JUDD PAPER CO., Holyoke, Mass.
Oxford Bristol—(b)—COOK-VIVIAN CO., Boston.
Oxford Bristol—(b)—JUDD PAPER CO., Holyoke, Mass.
Oxford Cards—(b)—BUNTIN, GILLIES & CO., LTD., Hamilton, Ontario, Can.
Oxford F i b r e— (b) — screenings—CHATFIELD & WOODS CO., Cincinnati, Ohio.
Oxford Fine Writing—(w) — VAN OLKER-SNELL PAPER CO., Boston.
Oxford Halftone Writing — (b) — KINGSLEY PAPER CO., Cleveland, O.
Oxford Laid Book—(w)—MEGARGEE-HARE PAPER CO., Philadelphia.
Oxford Laid, M. & G. Co.—(w)—MEGARGEE-HARE PAPER CO., Philadelphia.
Oxford Linen—(b)—EATON, CRANE & PIKE CO., Pittsfield, Mass.
Oxford Linen—(w) — HAMPSHIRE PAPER CO., South Hadley Falls, Mass.

Oxford Linen—(w) — VALLEY PAPER CO., Holyoke, Mass.
Oxford Manifold—(b)—JUDD PAPER CO., Holyoke, Mass.
Oxford Manifold Bond—(b)—JUDD PAPER CO., Holyoke, Mass.
Oxford Mills — (w)—No. 2 fine—PLYMOUTH PAPER CO., Holyoke.
Oxford Onion Skin—(b)—JUDD PAPER CO., Holyoke, Mass.
Oxford Superfine—(b)—tinted wove—BRADNER SMITH & CO., Chicago.
Oxford Wedding — (b) — UNION CARD & PAPER CO., New York.
Oxford Wove and Laid—(b)—envelope—WHITING-PATTERSON CO., Philadelphia.
O. Y.—(b)—railroad copying — RAINBOW PAPER MILLS, Rainbow, Conn.
Ozark — (b) — flat — SPRINGFIELD PAPER & SUPPLY CO., Springfield, Mo.
Ozark—(b)—strong jute — GRAHAM PAPER CO., St. Louis.
Ozark M. F.—(b)—book—SPRINGFIELD PAPER & SUPPLY CO., Springfield, Mo.
Ozark F l a t — (w) — SPRINGFIELD PAPER SUPPLY CO., Springfield, Mo.
Ozark Mills — (b) — writing—GRAHAM PAPER CO., St. Louis.

P

Pacific—(b)—fibre—W. H. CLAFLIN & CO., Boston.
Pacific—(b)—news and toilet—GRAHAM PAPER CO., St. Louis, Mo.
Pacific — (b) — ALBANY PERFORATED WRAPPING PAPER CO., Albany, New York.
Pacific—(w and b)—CUNNINGHAM, CURTISS & WELCH, Los Angeles.
Pacific—(b)—flats—B R A D N E R SMITH & CO., Chicago.
Pacific—(b)—writing—GRAHAM PAPER CO., St. Louis.
Pacific Bond—(w)—ELSINORE PAPER CO., New York.
Pacific Bond—(w)—PACIFIC PAPER CO., Portland, Ore.
Pacific Coast—(w)—J. W. BUTLER PAPER CO., Chicago.
Pacific Extra Superfine — (w) — PACIFIC PAPER CO., Portland, Ore.
Pacific Linen—(w)—ELSINORE PAPER CO., New York.
Pacific Parchment — (b)—manila—WRIGHT, BARRETT & STILWELL CO., St. Paul, Minn.
Pacific Railroad — (b)—manila—WRIGHT, BARRETT & STILWELL CO., St. Paul, Minn.
Padlock Safety—(b)—safety paper—PERFECT SAFETY PAPER CO., Holyoke, Mass.
Pagoda—(b)—cover—STANDARD PAPER CO., Kalamazoo, Mich.
Palace—(b)—toilet — A. M. EATON PAPER CO., Waltham, Mass.

Palatine Enamel Book—(b)—BAR-DEEN PAPER CO., Otsego, Mich.
Palatine Parchment Bond—(w)—W. M. PRINGLE & CO., INC., New York.
Palm Superfine Guaranteed British Mftre.—(w and b)—PARSONS TRADING CO., New York.
Palmetto — (b) — toilet—ALBANY PERFORATED WRAPPING PAPER CO., Albany, N. Y.
Palmetto Fibre—(b)—H. & W. B. DREW CO., Jacksonville, Fla.
Palmetto Parchment Wrapping—(b)—OSBORN PAPER CO., Philadelphia.
Pamlico—(b) — blanks and bristols—THE PAPER MILLS CO., Chicago.
Pampas—(b)—flats—MOSER PAPER CO., Chicago.
Panama Bond—(w)—WHITING PAPER CO., Holyoke, Mass.
Panama Lawn — (b) — MARCUS WARD CO., Brooklyn, N. Y.
Panama Linen—(w)—WHITING PAPER CO., Holyoke, Mass.
Panama Manila—(b)—OSBORN PAPER CO., Philadelphia.
Panama Wedding—(b)—bristols—THE ALLING & CORY CO., Rochester.
Pandora—(b)—toilet—H. NORWOOD EWING CO., New York.
Pansy — (b) — toilet — STONE & FORSYTH CO., Boston, Mass.
Pansy Mills—(b)—colored fine—R. P. ANDREWS PAPER CO., Washington, D. C.
Pantagraph Bond — (w)—PANTAGRAPH PRINTING AND STATIONERY CO., Bloomington, Ill.
Pantagraph Extra Superfine—(w)—PANTAGRAPH PRINTING & STATIONERY CO., Bloomington, Ill.
Paperoid—(b)—ALVAH BUSHNELL CO., Philadelphia.
Papier De Luxe—(b)—book—MERRIAM PAPER CO., New York.
Papyrus Bond — (b)—CHATFIELD & WOODS CO., Cincinnati, Ohio.
Papyrus Parchment—(b)—pergamyn—GRAHAM PAPER CO., St. Louis.
Para White Flats — (b) — J. C. PARKER PAPER CO., Louisville, Ky.
Paradox—(b)—cover — AMERICAN WRITING PAPER CO., Holyoke.
Paradox—(b)—cover—J. W. BUTLER PAPER CO., Chicago.
Paradox—(b)—SEYMOUR CO., N. Y.
Paragon—(b)—blotting—C. P. LESH PAPER CO., Indianapolis, Ind.
Paragon—(b)—blotting—WRENN PAPER CO., Middletown, Ohio.
Paragon—(w) — CARTER, RICE & CO., CORP., New York.
Paragon—(w)—flat—H. S. CROCKER CO., San Francisco.
Paragon Blanks—(b)—TROY PAPER CO., Troy, New York.
Paragon Bond — (w) — STRATHMORE PAPER CO., Mittineague, Mass.

Paragon Enamel—(b)—MEGARGEE-HARE PAPER CO., Philadelphia.
Paragon Linen — (b)—WYCKOFF, SEAMANS & BENEDICT, N. Y.
Paragon Linen Ledger — (w) — STRATHMORE PAPER CO., Mittineague, Mass.
Paragon Mills — (b) — flats — DONALDSON PAPER CO., Harrisburg, Pa.
Paragon Onion Skin—(b)—C. S. PROCTOR PAPER CO., Boston.
Paragraph Cover and Text—(b)—LEWERTH & CULBERTSON, New York.
Parallel—(b)—news — GRAHAM PAPER CO., St. Louis.
Paramount Stationery—(w and b)—PAPER MILLS CO., Chicago.
Parasian —(b)— wrapping — LOUISVILLE PAPER CO., Louisville, Ky.
Parcel Post Bond—(b)—ELSINORE PAPER CO., New York.
Parcels Post Card—(b)—bristol—J. W. BUTLER PAPER CO., Chicago.
Parcel Post Kraft—(b)—MUNROE FELT & PAPER CO., Lawrence, Mass.
Parchment—(b)—copying — SMITH PAPER CO., Lee, Mass.
Parchment Bond—(w)—AMERICAN WRITING PAPER CO., Holyoke.
Parchment Bristol—(b)—PARSONS PAPER CO., Holyoke, Mass.
Parchment Cloth—(w) — CAREW MANUFACTURING CO., South Hadley Falls, Mass.
Parchment Cover — (b)—WABASH COATING MILLS, Wabash, Ind.
Parchment Deed—(w)—typewriter—SOUTHWORTH CO., Mittineague, Mass.
Parchment Ledger—(w) — AMERICAN WRITING PAPER CO., Holyoke.
Parchment Ledger—(b)—WORTHY PAPER CO., Mittineague, Mass.
Parchment Linen—(b)—cardboards and cards — GRAHAM PAPER CO., St. Louis.
Parchment Lithograph—(b) — WABASH COATING MILLS, Wabash, Ind.
Parchment Record—(w) — ledger, bond — HUDSON VALLEY PAPER CO., Albany, N. Y.
Parchment Vellum—(w)—Z. & W. M. CRANE, Dalton, Mass.
Parchment Vellum—(w)—RAYNOR & PERKINS ENVELOPE CO., N. Y.
Parchment Wedding—(b)—PAPER MILLS CO., Chicago.
Parian—(b)—bristol—W. H. CLAFLIN & CO., Boston.
Parian—(b)—book—GRAHAM PAPER CO., St. Louis.
Parian—(b)—MATTHIAS PLUM, Newark, N. J.
Parian Tag—(b)—DIEM & WING PAPER CO., Cincinnati, Ohio.
Parisian Fiber—(b)—LOUISVILLE PAPER CO., Louisville, Ky.

Paris Post Card—(b)—F. A. FLINN, INC., New York.
Paris—(b)—toilet—GRAHAM PAPER CO., St. Louis.
Parisian French Folio—(b)—MERRIAM PAPER CO., New York.
Park Colored Bristol—(b)—HY. LINDENMEYR & SONS, New York.
Park Mills—(w)—COOK-VIVIAN CO., Boston.
Parliament Bond—(w)—J. E. LINDE PAPER CO., New York.
Parliament Bond—(w)—THOMAS W. PRICE CO., Philadelphia.
Parnell Linen—(w)—UNITED STATES ENVELOPE CO. (The White, Corbin & Co. Div.), Rockville, Conn.
Parquetry Covers—(b)—STRATHMORE PAPER CO., Mittineague, Mass.
Parsons American Drawing—(b)—PARSONS PAPER CO., Holyoke.
Parsons Bond—(w)—PARSONS PAPER CO., Holyoke, Mass.
Parsons Defendum Linen Ledger—(w)—PARSONS PAPER CO., Holyoke, Mass.
Parsons Extra Superfine—(w)—laid and wove—CONROW BROS., New York.
Parsons Extra Superfine—(w)—AMERICAN WRITING PAPER CO., Holyoke, Mass.
Parsons' Gothic Bond—(w)—PARSONS PAPER CO., Holyoke, Mass.
Parsons' Mercantile Record—(w)—PARSONS PAPER CO., Holyoke, Mass.
Parsons Linen—(w)—PARSONS PAPER CO., Holyoke, Mass.
Parsons Paper Co.—(w)—superfines and flats—AMERICAN WRITING PAPER CO., Holyoke, Mass.
Parsons Paper Co., Extra Fines—(w)—AMERICAN WRITING PAPER CO., Holyoke, Mass.
Parsons Paper Co., Holyoke, Mass. (and date)—(w)—No. 1 bond—PARSONS PAPER CO., Holyoke, Mass.
Parsons Paper Co., Holyoke, Mass.—(w)—PARSONS PAPER CO., Holyoke, Mass.
Parsons Tinted Writing—(w)—superfine—AMERICAN WRITING PAPER CO., Holyoke, Mass.
Participating—(w and b)—bond, ledger—NEENAH PAPER CO., Neenah, Wis.
Passaic—(b)—flats—BRADNER SMITH & CO., Chicago.
Passport—(b)—manila writing—J. W. BUTLER PAPER CO., Chicago.
Pasted Wedding Bristol Boards—(b)—STRATHMORE PAPER CO., Mittineague, Mass.
Pathfinder—(b)—news—GRAHAM PAPER CO., St. Louis.
Patrician—(b)—ledger—W. H. CLAFLIN & CO., Boston.

Patrician—(b)—PENINSULAR PAPER CO., Ypsilanti, Mich.
Patriot Covers—(b)—JOHN CARTER & CO., Boston.
Patriot—(b and w)—bond, linen and ledger—NEENAH PAPER CO., Neenah, Wis.
Patriotic Ledger—(b)—F. A. FLINN, INC., New York.
Patroon—(b)—toilet—ALBANY PERFORATED WRAPPING PAPER CO., Albany, N. Y.
Paul Jones Bond—(w)—BRADNER SMITH & CO., Chicago, Ill.
Pawtucket Parchment—(b)—manila—SWIGART PAPER CO., Chicago.
Paxtang Linen—(b)—JOHNSTON PAPER CO., Harrisburg, Pa.
"P. B. 671"—(w)—writing—PARSONS TRADING CO., New York.
P. B. M. Bond—(w)—typewriter—H. H. WEST CO., Milwaukee, Wis.
Peacock Enamel—(b)—book—BEECHER, PECK & LEWIS, Detroit, Mich.
Peacock Fabric—(b)—KANSAS CITY PAPER CO., Kansas City, Mo.
Peacock Fibre—(w)—MARATHON PAPER MILLS CO., Wausau, Wis.
Peacock Linen—(w)—BEECHER, PECK & LEWIS, Detroit.
Pearl—(w)—MATTHIAS PLUM, Newark, N. J.
Pearl Bond—(w)—SOUTHWORTH CO., Mittineague, Mass.
Pearl Extra Superfine—(b)—folded—WORTHY PAPER CO., Mittineague, Mass.
Pearl Fibre Paper—(b)—No. 2 express—THE SEINSHEIMER PAPER CO., Cincinnati, Ohio.
Pearl Hill—(b)—ruled—CHATFIELD & WOODS CO., Cincinnati, Ohio.
Pearl Hill Mills—(b)—folded and ruled—CHATFIELD & WOODS CO., Cincinnati, Ohio.
Pearl Mills—(b)—C. S. PROCTOR PAPER CO., Boston.
Pearl Mills—(b)—MATTHIAS PLUM, Newark, N. J.
Pearl Spring—(w)—VALLEY PAPER CO., Holyoke, Mass.
Pebble Embossed—(b)—GEO. B. HURD & CO., New York.
Pebbled Parchment—(w)—(Special)—WHITING-PLOVER PAPER CO., Stevens Point, Wis.
Peconic—(b)—bristol, writing—UNION CARD AND PAPER CO., New York.
Pedro—(b)—toilet—NORTHERN PAPER MILLS, Milwaukee, Wis.
Peerless—(b)—M. F. white and colored book—THE ALLING & CORY CO., Rochester, N. Y.
Peerless—(b)—rag envelope—MINNEAPOLIS PAPER CO., Minneapolis.
Peerless—(b)—cover—GRAHAM PAPER CO., St. Louis.

Peerless—(w)—ledger—J. G. SHAW BLANK BOOK CO., New York.
Peerless—(b)—wedding paper and bristol—UNION CARD AND PAPER CO., New York.
Peerless—(b)—bristol—J. W. BUTLER PAPER CO., Chicago.
Peerless—(b)—fibre—W. H. CLAFLIN & CO., Boston.
Peerless—(b)—book and music—KANSAS CITY PAPER HOUSE, Kansas City, Mo.
Peerless—(b)—card board—McCLELLAN PAPER CO., Minneapolis, Minn.
Peerless—(b)—mimeograph—TROY PAPER CO., Troy, N. Y.
Peerless—(b)—toilet—PEERLESS MANUFACTURING CO., Philadelphia.
Peerless—(b)—pasted blanks—MEGARGEE-HARE PAPER CO., Philadelphia.
Peerless—(b)—toilet—NORTHERN PAPER MILLS, Green Bay, Wis.
Peerless—(w)—flat—J. W. BUTLER PAPER CO., Chicago.
Peerless—(w)—writing—R. M. MYERS & CO., Rochester, N. Y.
Peerless—(w)—writing—BEECHER, PECK & LEWIS, Detroit, Mich.
Peerless—(b)—adding machine—GRAHAM PAPER CO., St. Louis.
Peerless Blanks—(b)—BEECHER, PECK & LEWIS, Detroit, Mich.
Peerless Book—(b)—DIEM & WING PAPER CO., Cincinnati, Ohio.
Peerless Book—(b)—THE ALLING & CORY CO., Rochester, N. Y.
Peerless Book—(b)—THE UNION PAPER & TWINE CO., Detroit, Mich.
Peerless Bristol—(b)—C. P. LESH PAPER CO., Indianapolis, Ind.
Peerless Coated Book—(b)—MINNEAPOLIS PAPER CO., Minneapolis, Minn.
Peerless Jute Manila—(b)—CHATFIELD & WOODS CO., Cincinnati.
Peerless Label—(b)—coated book—SWIGART PAPER CO., Chicago.
Peerless Linen—(w)—RAYNOR & PERKINS ENVELOPE CO., N. Y.
Peerless Manifold—(b)—WHITAKER PAPER CO., Cincinnati, Ohio.
Peerless Mimeograph—(b)—BRADNER SMITH & CO., Chicago.
Peerless Mills—(w)—writing—R. M. MYERS & CO., Rochester, N. Y.
Peerless Mimeograph—(b)—AMERICAN WRITING PAPER CO., Holyoke, Mass.
Peerless Tag—(b)—CHATFIELD & WOOD CO., Cincinnati, Ohio.
Peerless Tag—(b)—BEECHER, PECK & LEWIS, Detroit, Mich.
Perfection—(b)—pasted bristol—TROY PAPER CO., Troy, N. Y.
Pelican—(b)—HY. LINDENMEYR & SONS, New York.
Pelican Linen—(w)—wove—CLEMENTS PAPER CO., Nashville, Tenn.
Pelican Linen—(w)—ARTHUR MOUNTAIN & CO., New York.
Pembroke Ledger—(w)—F. A. FLINN, INC., New York.
Pembroke Ledger—(w)—MILLER & WRIGHT PAPER CO., New York.
Pencil Safety—(b)—GEORGE LA MONTE & SON, New York.
Pencoyd Fibre—(w)—wrappings and bonds—(b)—wrappings and specialties—McDOWELL PAPER MILLS, Philadelphia.
Pendennis—(b)—toilet—LOUISVILLE PAPER CO., Louisville, Ky.
Penelope—(w)—linen—J. E. LINDE PAPER CO., New York.
Penfield Bond—(b)—HUDSON VALLEY PAPER CO., New York.
Peninsular—(w)—bond—PENINSULAR PAPER CO., Ypsilanti, Mich.
Peninsular Bond—(b)—PENINSULAR PAPER CO., Ypsilanti, Mich.
Peninsular Enamel Book—(b)—BARDEEN PAPER CO., Otsego, Mich.
Penman Ledger—(w)—JOHNSTON PAPER CO., Harrisburg, Pa.
Penman Ledger—(w)—LOUISVILLE PAPER CO., Louisville, Ky.
Penman's Linen—(w)—EAST HARTFORD MANUFACTURING CO., Burnside, Conn.
Penmans Linen Ledger—(w)—W. M. PRINGLE & CO., INC., New York.
Pen-Mar—(w)—fine—ANTIETAM PAPER CO., Hagerstown, Md.
Penn—(b)—J. C. BLAIR CO., Huntingdon, Pa.
Penna-Fibre—(b)—wrappings and specialties—McDOWELL PAPER MILLS, Manayunk, Philadelphia.
Penna-State—(b)—ROBERTS & MEEKS, Harrisburg, Pa.
Pennant Bond—(w)—W. E. WROB & CO., Chicago.
Pennant—(b)—gum paper—GRAHAM PAPER CO., St. Louis.
Pennant—(b)—white blanks—MEGARGEE BROS., Scranton, Pa.
Pennant Mills—(b)—poster—LOUISVILLE PAPER CO., Louisville, Ky.
Penn Cover—(b)—M. J. EARL, Reading, Pa.
Penn Mills—(b)—colored flats—WILKINSON BROS. & CO., Philadelphia.
Penn's Treaty—(w)—J. C. BLAIR CO., Huntingdon, Pa.
Pennsylvania Fibre—(b)—McDOWELL PAPER MILLS, Manayunk, Pa.
Penobscot—(b)—laid linen—CLAFLIN & CO., Boston.
Penobscot—(b)—PENOBSCOT CHEMICAL FIBRE CO., Boston.
Penokee—(b)—toilet—ALBANY PERFORATED WRAPPING PAPER CO., Albany, N. Y.
Penrod—(b)—napkins—F. E. SCHOFIELD, Mt. Vernon, N. Y.
Penwriter—(on pen)—(w)—WALKER, EVANS & COGSWELL CO., Charleston, S. C.

Pen-y-Bryn— (b) — MEGARGEE-HARE PAPER CO., Philadelphia.
People's Linen—(w)—CONBOW BROTHERS, New York
Pequot Bond—(w)—EAST HARTFORD MANUFACTURING CO., Burnside, Conn.
Pequod Mills—(b)—book—W. H. GEORGE, Philadelphia.
Pequod Mills—(b)—HY. LINDENMEYR & SONS, New York.
Pequot Mills—(b)—folded—EAST HARTFORD MANUFACTURING CO., Burnside, Conn.
Perfect—(b)—mimeograph paper—EASTERN MANUFACTURING CO., Bangor, Me.
Perfection—(b)—tag board—LOUISVILLE PAPER CO., Louisville, Ky.
Perfection English Finish Book—(b)—RICHMOND PAPER CO., Richmond, Va.
Perfection Ledger—(b)—RICHMOND PAPER CO., Richmond, Va.
Perfect M. F.—(b)—WESTERN PENNA. PAPER CO., Pittsburg, Pa.
Perfect Mimeograph—(b)—MOSER PAPER CO., Chicago.
Perfect Parchment—(w)—MAVERICK-CLARK, San Antonio, Tex.
Perfect Post Card—(b)—bristol—J. W. BUTLER PAPER CO., Chicago.
Perfect Safety—(b)—PERFECT SAFETY PAPER CO., Holyoke, Mass.
Perfect Safety Ticket—(b)—PERFECT SAFETY PAPER CO., Holyoke.
Perfect Tints—(b)—bristol—RIEGEL & CO., INC., Philadelphia.
Perfection—(b)—A. M. EATON PAPER CO., Waltham, Mass.
Perfection—(b)—wedding and bristols—UNION CARD & PAPER CO., New York.
Perfection—(b)—coated blank and onion skin—VON OLKER-SNELL PAPER CO., Boston.
Perfection—(b)—enameled book—CHATFIELD & WOODS CO., Cincinnati, Ohio.
Perfection—(b)—pasted bristol—MEGARGEE-HARE PAPER CO., Philadelphia.
Perfection—(b)—laid book—MERRIAM PAPER CO., New York.
Perfection—(w)—flats—MOSER PAPER CO., Chicago.
Perfection Catalog—(b)—GRAHAM PAPER CO., St. Louis.
Perfection Enameled—(b)—blotting—RICHMOND PAPER MANUFACTURING CO., Richmond, Va.
Perfection Enamel Book—(b)—PETREQUIN PAPER CO., Cleveland.
Perfection Imperial—(w)—POWERS PAPER CO., Holyoke, Mass.
Perfection Index Cards—(b)—GRAHAM PAPER CO., St. Louis.
Perfection Irish Linen—(w)—WHITING PAPER CO., Holyoke, Mass.

Perfection Laid Book—(b)—CINCINNATI CORDAGE AND PAPER CO., Cincinnati, Ohio.
Perfection Linen—(w)—POWERS PAPER CO., Holyoke, Mass.
Perfection Linen—(w)—envelopes only—UNITED STATES ENVELOPE CO. (Plimpton Mfg. Co. Division), Hartford, Conn.
Perfection Linen Ledger—(w and b)—A. R. BARNES & CO., Chicago.
Perfection Lithograph—(b)—BRADNER SMITH & CO., Chicago.
Perfection Wedding Announcements—(b)—UNION CARD & PAPER CO., New York.
Perfection Wedding Bristol—UNION CARD & PAPER CO., N. Y.
Perfection Wedding Paper—UNION CARD & PAPER CO., N. Y.
Perfection White Coated—(b)—A. STORRS & BEMENT CO., Boston.
Perfection Wove—(w)—AMERICAN WRITING PAPER CO., Holyoke, Mass.
Perfecto—(b)—check—J. C. PARKER PAPER CO., Louisville, Ky.
Perfecto Engraving Mts.—(b)—WHITAKER PAPER CO., Cincinnati.
Perfektowl—(w)—UNITED STATES PAPER MILLS, INC., Chambersburg, Pa.
Permanent Record—(w)—typewriter—SOUTHWORTH CO., Mittineague, Mass.
Perry's Bond (Brownie Policeman)—(w)—C. E. PERRY & CO., Boston.
Perry Superfine Writing—(b)—KINGSLEY PAPER CO., Cleveland.
Persian—(b)—cover—GRAHAM PAPER CO., St. Louis.
Persian—(b)—cover—HOLYOKE CARD & PAPER CO., Holyoke, Mass.
Persian—(b)—cover—HY. LINDENMEYR & SONS, New York.
Persian Bond—(w)—AMERICAN WRITING PAPER CO., Holyoke, Mass.
Persian Lawn Tints—(b)—EAST HARTFORD MANUFACTURING CO., Burnside, Conn.
Persian Ledger—(w)—AMERICAN WRITING PAPER CO., Holyoke, Mass.
Persian Linen—(w)—AMERICAN WRITING PAPER CO., Holyoke, Mass.
Perusia—(w)—JAPAN PAPER CO., New York.
Perth Linen Ledger—(w)—R. H. THOMPSON CO., Buffalo, N. Y.
Peter Pan—(b)—toilet—H. NORWOOD EWING CO., New York.
Petite—(b)—toilet—NORTHERN PAPER MILLS, Green Bay, Wis.
P. E. V. Translucent—(b)—PAUL E. VERNON & CO., New York.
Phelps Protective—(b)—PERFECT SAFETY PAPER CO., Holyoke, Mass.
Pheon Bond—(w)—W. E. WROE & CO., Chicago.
Philadelphia Bond—(w)—JOHN WANAMAKER, Philadelphia.

Philippine—(b)—cover—J. W. BUTLER PAPER CO., Chicago.
Philippine—(b)—manila—WHITING-PATTERSON CO., Philadelphia.
Philippine Fibre — (b) — CHATFIELD & WOODS CO., Cincinnati.
Phoenix—(w)—POWERS PAPER COMPANY, Springfield, Mass.
Phoenix—(b)—cardboards and cards—GRAHAM PAPER CO., St. Louis.
Phoenix—(b)—blanks—DONALDSON PAPER CO., Harrisburg, Pa.
Phoenix—(b)—colored super book—HAGEN PAPER CO., St. Louis.
Phoenix Coated Book—(b)—HY. LINDENMEYR & SONS, New York.
Phoenix Rope Tag—(b)—KINGSLEY PAPER CO., Cleveland, Ohio.
Photographer's—(b)—blotting — J. W. BUTLER PAPER CO., Chicago.
Photogravure Bristol No. 1—(b)—E. E. LLOYD PAPER CO., Chicago.
Photone—(b)—writing—J. W. BUTLER PAPER CO., Chicago.
Photo Super Book—(b)—MEGARGEE-HARE PAPER CO., Philadelphia.
P. H. Litho Finish—(b)—THE PAPER MILLS CO., Chicago.
Phynest—(b)—toilet—SCOTT PAPER CO., Philadelphia.
Piccadilly Deckle Edge—(b)—GEO. B. HURD & CO., New York.
Pickwick Bond — (w) — WRIGHT, BARRETT & STILWELL & CO., St. Paul, Minn.
Pickwick Linen—(b)—EATON, CRANE & PIKE CO., Pittsfield, Mass.
Pictorial Enamel—(b)—blotting—J. W. BUTLER PAPER CO., Chicago.
Piedmont Bond—(w)—MERRIAM PAPER CO., New York.
Pierce Bond—(w)—HAMMERMILL PAPER CO., Erie, Pa.
Pilgrim—(b)—toilet—ALBANY PERFORATED WRAPPING PAPER CO., Albany, N. Y.
Pilgrim—(b)—toilet — UNITED STATES ENVELOPE CO. (Morgan Envelope Co. Div.), Springfield, Mass.
Pilgrim Bond—(w)—EASTERN MFG. CO., Bangor, Me.
Pilgrim Laid—(b)—writing, colored—BAY STATE PAPER CO., Boston.
Pilgrim Ledger—(w) — EASTERN MANUFACTURING CO., Bangor, Me.
Pilgrim Mills—(w) —KALAMAZOO PAPER CO., Kalamazoo, Mich.
Pilgrim Mills — (w) — PETREQUIN PAPER CO., Cleveland, Ohio.
Pilgrim Offset Bristol—(b)—BRADNER SMITH & CO., Chicago.
Pilot—(b)—blanks—UNION CARD & PAPER CO., New York.
Pilot—(w)—bond and ledger—UNION CARD & PAPER CO., New York.
Pilot—(b)—toilet—ALBANY PERFORATED WRAPPING PAPER CO., Albany, N. Y.

Pin Ticket—(b)—board or tag—BRADNER SMITH & CO., Chicago.
Pink Railroad Manila — (b) — BRADNER SMITH & CO., Chicago.
Pink White Wedding Bristol—(b)—STRATHMORE PAPER CO., Mittineague, Mass.
Pinnacle Extra Strong — (b) — coated—WEST VIRGINIA PULP & PAPER CO., New York.
Pioneer—(b)—superfine—F. W. ANDERSON & CO., New York.
Pioneer—(b)—toilet tissue—W. H. CLAFLIN & CO., Boston.
Pioneer—(b)—super book — HAGEN PAPER CO., St. Louis.
Pioneer—(b)—wrapping—CHASE BROS., Haverhill, Mass.
Pioneer—(w)—flat writing—PETERS PAPER CO., Denver, Col.
Pioneer Bond—(w)—SWIGART PAPER CO., Chicago.
Pioneer Enamel Book—(b)—BERMINGHAM & PROSSER CO., Kalamazoo, Mich.
Pioneer Flats — (w) — writing — KINGSLEY PAPER CO., Cleveland.
Pioneer Ledger—(w)—PIONEER PRESS, St. Paul, Minn.
Pioneer Linen Ledger—(w)—F. W. ANDERSON & CO., New York.
Pioneer Mills — (b) — LOUISVILLE PAPER CO., Louisville, Ky.
Pioneer Mills—(w)—KINGSLEY PAPER CO., Cleveland, Ohio.
Pioneer Press Bond—(w)—PIONEER PRESS, St. Paul, Minn.
Pioneer Press Safety—(w)—PIONEER PRESS, St. Paul, Minn.
Pioneer Press Superfine—(w)—PIONEER PRESS, St. Paul, Minn.
Piqua—(b)—toilet—ALBANY PERFORATED WRAPPING PAPER CO., Albany, N. Y.
Piquet Embossed—(b)—GEO. B. HURD & CO., New York.
Pitchstuff—(b)—W. P.—wrapping and case lining—INSURANCE PACKING MILLS, Brockton, Mass.
Pittsburgh Bond—(w)—THE ALLING & CORY CO., Rochester, N. Y.
P. K.—(b)—linen and superfine—J. C. BLAIR CO., Huntingdon, Pa.
P. K. Blue—(b)—wrappings and specialties—McDOWELL PAPER MILLS, Manayunk, Philadelphia.
Plain Bond—(b)—SOUTHERN PAPER COMPANY, Richmond, Va.
Plain Linen Laid—(b)—BERKSHIRE HILLS PAPER CO., Adams, Mass.
Plain Roll—(b)—toilet—UNITED STATES ENVELOPE CO. (Morgan Envelope Co. Div.), Springfield, Mass.
Planet—(b)—news—GRAHAM PAPER CO., St. Louis.
Planet Blanks—(b)—HY. LINDENMEYR & SONS, New York.
Planet No. 1 Manila—(b)—D. S. WALTON & CO., New York.

Watermarks and Brands 715

Platine Tympan—(b)—DETROIT SULPHITE PULP & PAPER CO., Detroit, Mich.
Platner & Porter First Quality—(w)—AMERICAN WRITING PAPER CO., Holyoke, Mass.
Playing Card—(b)—bristol—J. W. BUTLER PAPER CO., Chicago.
Pleezu—(b)—toilet—SCOTT PAPER CO., Philadelphia.
Plover Bond—(w)—WHITING-PLOVER PAPER CO., Menasha, Wis.
Plum's Bank Ledger—(w)—MATTHIAS PLUM, Newark, N. J.
Plum's Linen Ledger—(w)—MATTHIAS PLUM, Newark, N. J.
Plutarch—(b)—toilet — NORTHERN PAPER MILLS, Green Bay, Wis.
Plymouth—(w)—PLYMOUTH PAPER CO., Holyoke, Mass.
Plymouth— (w)— laid book — CENTRAL OHIO PAPER CO., Columbus.
Plymouth—(b)—bristol— STANDARD CORD & PAPER CO., New York.
Plymouth Bond—(w)—DWIGHT BROTHERS' PAPER CO., Chicago.
Plymouth Book—(b)—WHITAKER PAPER CO., Cincinnati, Ohio.
Plymouth Bristol — (b) — CHATFIELD & WOODS CO., Cincinnati.
Plymouth Cover—(b)—PAUL E. VERNON & CO., New York.
Plymouth Egg-Shell—(b)—book—BRADNER SMITH & CO., Chicago.
Plymouth Laid—(b)—egg-shell book—BAY STATE PAPER CO., Boston.
Plymouth Ledger — (w) — PLYMOUTH PAPER CO., Holyoke, Mass.
Plymouth Pebbled Parchment—(b)—MOSER PAPER CO., Chicago.
Plymouth Wove—(b)—egg-shell book—BAY STATE PAPER CO., Boston.
P. Manila—(b)—R. L. GREENE PAPER CO., Providence, R. I.
P. L. S.—(w)—AMERICAN WRITING PAPER CO., Holyoke, Mass.
"P. M."—(b)—various lines—PAPER MILLS CO., Chicago.
P. M. Hand Made—(w)—PAPER MILLS CO., Chicago.
Pocahontas Bond—(w)—flats—R. L. GREENE PAPER CO., Providence.
Pochassic Bond — (w) — STRATHMORE PAPER CO., Mittineague, Mass.
Pocono Linen Ledger — (w) — MEGARGEE BROS., Scranton, Pa.
Pohono Mills — (w) — PACIFIC PAPER CO., Portland, Ore.
Polar Parchment—(b)—ANDREWS PAPER CO., Boston.
Polar White—(b)—wedding bristol—TILESTON & LIVERMORE, Boston.
Polaris—(b)—SABIN ROBBINS PAPER CO., Middletown, Ohio.
Pole Dried Superfine—(w)—SWIGART PAPER CO., Chicago.
Pole Dried Superfine—(w)—FOX RIVER PAPER CO., Appleton, Wis.
Policy Bond—(w)—J. W. BUTLER PAPER CO., Chicago.

Polychrome Special—(b)—coated—BARDEEN PAPER CO., Otsego, Mich.
Polygraphic Bond—(b)—THOS. W. PRICE CO., Philadelphia.
Pomeroy—(b)—book and news—GRAHAM PAPER CO., St. Louis.
Pomona Bond—(b)—HY. LINDENMEYR & SONS, New York.
Pompeian—(b)—cover—McCLELLAN PAPER CO., Minneapolis, Minn.
Pompeian Bond — (w) — HARLEM CORD & PAPER CO., New York.
Pompeian Linen—(w)—bond—GILBERT PAPER CO., Menasha, Wis.
Ponca—(b)—toilet—ALBANY PERFORATED WRAPPING PAPER CO., Albany, N. Y.
Ponemoh Mills—(b)—white wove—KINGSLEY PAPER CO., Cleveland.
Pongee—(w)—POWERS PAPER CO., Springfield, Mass.
Pongee Bond—(w)—MARCUS WARD CO., Brooklyn.
Pontiac—(w)—bonds—J. E. LINDE PAPER CO., New York.
Pontiac Linen—(w) — LASHER & LATHROP, New York.
Pony Express—(b)— toilet — SCOTT PAPER CO., Philadelphia.
Poplar Covers—(b)—C O N R O W BROS., New York.
Poplin—(w)—POWERS PAPER COMPANY, Springfield, Mass.
Poplin Berege—(b)—E A T O N. CRANE & PIKE CO., Pittsfield, Mass.
Popular—(b)—blank—B. F. BOND PAPER CO., Baltimore.
Popular Bond—(w)—J. W. BUTLER PAPER CO., Chicago.
Popular Music Book—(b)—CHATFIELD & WOODS CO., Cincinnati.
Popular Tinted Bristol—(b)—THE ALLING & CORY CO., Rochester.
Popular White and Colors—(b)—MERRIAM PAPER CO., New York.
Popwear Bond—(b)—MERRIAM PAPER CO., New York. (Con.)
Porcelain—(b)—envelope— GRAHAM PAPER CO., St. Louis.
Porcelain—(b)—blotting—MISSOURI PAPER HOUSE, Kansas City, Mo.
Porcelain—(b)—litho. car sign bristol—MINNEAPOLIS PAPER CO., Minneapolis.
Porcelain—(b)—half tone writing—MINNEAPOLIS PAPER CO., Minneapolis, Minn.
Porcelain—(b)—shelf — LOUISVILLE PAPER CO., Louisville, Ky.
Porcelain Coated — (b) — F. A. FLINN, INC., New York.
Porcelain Enamel Book — (b) — coated—BARDEEN PAPER CO., Otsego, Mich.
Porcelain Enameled — (b) — white book—THE ALLING & CORY CO., Rochester, N. Y.
Porcelain Enameled Blotting—(b)—HY. LINDENMEYR & SONS, New York.

Portland—(b)—news—GRAHAM PAPER CO., St. Louis.
Portland Bond—(w)—POLAND PAPER CO., Mechanic Falls, Me.
Portland Bond—(w)—EAST HARTFORD MANUFACTURING CO., Burnside, Conn.
Portland Bond—(w)—LORING, SHORT & HARMON, Portland, Me.
Portland Linen—(w)—POLAND PAPER CO., Mechanic Falls, Me.
Portobello Superfine—(w)—writing—PARSONS TRADING CO., N. Y.
Porto Rican Bond—(w)—ESLEECK MANUFACTURING CO., Turners Falls, Mass.
Portsmouth—(w)—superfine—R. C. KASTNER PAPER CO., New York.
Portsmouth Superfine—(b)—white wove writing—R. C. KASTNER PAPER CO., New York.
Postal—(b)—document manila—J. W. BUTLER PAPER CO., Chicago.
Postal — (w) — writing manila—MEGARGEE-HARE PAPER CO., Philadelphia.
Postal—(b)—tag board—AMERICAN WOOD BOARD CO., Schuylerville, N. Y.
Postal Bond—(w)—AMERICAN WRITING PAPER CO., Holyoke, Mass.
Postal Ledger — (w) — AMERICAN WRITING PAPER CO., Holyoke, Mass.
Postal Onion Skin—(b)—F. A. FLINN, INC., New York.
Postal Writing Manila—(w)—MEGARGEE-HARE PAPER CO., Philadelphia.
Postal Yellow—(b)—manila—BRADNER SMITH & CO., Chicago.
Post Board—(b)—W. G. WILLMANN, New York.
Post Card—(b)—dull-finished coated—S. D. WARREN & CO., Boston.
Postman—(b)—book and news—GRAHAM PAPER CO., St. Louis.
Post Office Bond—(w)—CARTER, RICE & CO., CORP., Boston.
Potomac—(w)—writing—WEST VIRGINIA PULP AND PAPER CO., N. Y.
Potomac—(b)—cover—DISTRICT OF COLUMBIA PAPER MANUFACTURING CO., Washington, D. C., and RIEGEL & CO., INC., Philadelphia.
Potomac Bond—(w)—DISTRICT OF COLUMBIA PAPER MFG. CO., Washington, D. C.
Potomac Half-Tone Blotting and No. 1 Photographic—(b)—DISTRICT OF COLUMBIA PAPER MFG. CO., Washington, D. C.
Power—(b)—tag board—LOUISVILLE PAPER CO., Louisville, Ky.
Power—(w)—bond—J. FRANCIS HOCK & CO., Baltimore.
Powers (J. C. & W. E.)—(b)—J. C. & W. E. POWERS, New York.
Powhatan Toilet — (b) — OLD DOMINION PAPER CO., Norfolk, Va.

Powhatan Mills — (b) — LOUISVILLE PAPER CO., Louisville, Ky.
Powhatan — (b) — toilet — OLD DOMINION PAPER CO., Norfolk, Va.
Powhatan Mills—(b)—pulp board—LOUISVILLE PAPER CO., Louisville, Ky.
Powndir—(b)—toilet—SCOTT PAPER CO., Philadelphia.
Practical—(w)—bond—GRAHAM PAPER CO., St. Louis.
Practice—(b)—drawing—CHATFIELD & WOODS CO., Cincinnati, Ohio.
Practical Cover—(b)—UNION PAPER & TWINE CO., Detroit, Mich.
Practical Cover—(b)—CHATFIELD & WOODS CO., Cincinnati, Ohio.
Prairie Queen—(b)—toilet—NORTHERN PAPER MILLS, Green Bay, Wis.
Pre-eminent Mills—(w)—LOUISVILLE PAPER CO., Louisville, Ky.
Preference Bond—(w)—BUNTIN, GILLIES & CO., Hamilton, Ontario, Canada.
Preferred Bond—(w)—AMERICAN WRITING PAPER CO., Holyoke, Mass.
Preferred Bond — (w) — A. PRICE, Brooklyn, N. Y.
Premier—(b)—matrix—BRADNER SMITH & CO., Chicago.
Premier Enameled — (b) — coated book—CHATFIELD & WOODS CO., Cincinnati, Ohio.
Premier Extra Strong Bond—(w)—HAMMERMILL PAPER CO., Erie, Pa.
Premier Linen Ledger—(w)—J. G. SHAW BLANK BOOK CO., New York.
Premium — (b) — adding machine — GRAHAM PAPER CO., St. Louis.
Premium Bond—(w)—CHARLES W. WILLIAMS & CO., New York
Premium Linen Ledger—(w)—C. W. WILLIAMS & CO., New York.
Premium Linen Record—(b)—BYRON WESTON CO., Dalton, Mass.
Premium Wedding Pasted Bristol (b)—GRAHAM PAPER CO., St. Louis.
Prescott Laid — (b) — WHITAKER PAPER CO., Cincinnati, Ohio.
Presden Mills Fine—(w)—flat writing—STANDARD PAPER CO., Tacoma, Wash.
Presidio—(b)—toilet—THE JOHN HOBERG CO., Green Bay, Wis.
Prestige Onion Skin — (b) — ESLEECK MFG. CO., Turners Falls, Mass.
Preston Superfine—(w)—flat writing—STANDARD PAPER CO., Tacoma, Wash.
Pretoria Wove and Laid—(b)—envelope—WHITING-PATTERSON CO., Philadelphia.
Primary Wedding Bristol—(b)—BEECHER, PECK & LEWIS, Detroit, Mich.
Primo—(b)—M. F. book—J. P. HEILBRONN CO., Manila, P. I.

Watermarks and Brands 717

Primordeal — (w) — bond — W. R. GRACE & CO., New York.
Primus Coated Book — (b) — R. L. GREENE PAPER CO., Providence, R. I.
Prince Bristol—(b)—KINGSLEY PAPER CO., Cleveland, Ohio.
Prince of Wales—(w and b)—GEO. B. HURD & CO., New York.
Prince Royal—(b)—BUTLER & KELLEY, New York.
Prince's Highland—(w)—superfine—G. C. PRINCE & SON, Lowell, Mass.
Princess—(b)—cover—C. H. DEXTER & SONS, INC., Windsor Locks, Conn.
Princess—(b)—blotting — CONROW BROS., New York.
Princess—(b)—bristol—VON OLKERSNELL PAPER CO., Boston.
Princess — (b) — enameled cover — JAMES WHITE & CO., Chicago.
Princess—(b)—railway manila and white writing — GARRETT-BUCHANAN CO., Philadelphia.
Princess—(b)—envelope—THE PAPER MILLS CO., Chicago.
Princess—(b)—flats—KANSAS CITY PAPER HOUSE, Kansas City, Mo.
Princess—(b)—laid book—DIEM & WING PAPER CO., Cincinnati, Ohio.
Princess Anne Blotting—(b)—OLD DOMINION PAPER CO., Norfolk, Va.
Princess Bond—(w)—PETREQUIN PAPER CO., Cleveland, Ohio.
Princess Book—(b)—KINGSLEY PAPER CO., Cleveland, Ohio.
Princess Bristol—(b)—OLD DOMINION PAPER CO., Norfolk, Va.
Princess Dull Coated Book—(b)—O. F. H. WARNER & CO., Baltimore.
Princess Mills—(b)—MATTHIAS PLUM, Newark, N. J.
Princess Mills—(w)—EAST HARTFORD MANUFACTURING CO., Burnside, Conn.
Princeton—(b)—super book—HAGEN PAPER CO., St. Louis.
Princeton—(b)—SCRANTOM, WETMORE & COMPANY, Rochester, N. Y.
Princeton—(w) — PLYMOUTH PAPER CO., Holyoke, Mass.
Princeton—(w)—THE J. G. SHAW BLANK BOOK CO., New York.
Princeton—(b)—book—GRAHAM PAPER CO., St. Louis.
Princeton Bond —(w)— HAMMERMILL PAPER CO., Erie, Pa.
Princeton Bristol—(b)— DIEM & WING PAPER CO., Cincinnati, Ohio.
Princeton Linen—(b)—MATTHIAS PLUM, Newark, N. J.
Princeton Parchment — (w) — writing—HAMMERMILL PAPER CO., Erie, Pa.
Princeton Parchment—(w)—HAMMERMILL PAPER CO., Erie, Pa.
Printcraft Bond—(b) — WHITAKER PAPER CO., Cincinnati, Ohio.

Printers—(b)—blanks—UNION CARD AND PAPER CO., New York.
Printers' Art—(b)—cover—LASHER & LATHROP, New York.
Printers' Blanks — (b) — UNION CARD & PAPER CO., New York.
Printers' Bond—Made in U. S. A.—(w)—PARSONS TRADING CO., New York.
Printone—(b)—book, imitation coated, glossy surface—S. D. WARREN & CO., Boston.
Priscilla—(b) — toilet — UNITED STATES ENVELOPE CO. (Morgan Envelope Co. Division), Springfield.
Priscilla — (w) — fine writing — LEE PAPER CO., Vicksburg, Mich.
Priscilla Pure Flax Bond—(w)—CARTER, RICE & CO., CORP., Boston.
Priscilla Pure Flax Linen—(w)—CARTER, RICE & CO., CORP., Boston.
Prismatic—(b)—blotting — STANDARD PAPER MFG. CO., Richmond.
Pristine Linen — (w)—AMERICAN WRITING PAPER CO., Holyoke.
Pristine Linen — (b) — UNITED STATES ENVELOPE CO. (Whitcomb Envelope Co. Division), Worcester, Mass.
Prize Medal—(b)—A. M. EATON PAPER CO., Waltham, Mass.
Prize Winner—(b)—toilet—NORTHERN PAPER MILLS, Green Bay, Wis.
Premier—(b)—toilet — NORTHERN PAPER MILLS, Green Bay, Wis.
Probate Bond — (b) — typewriter—EATON, CRANE & PIKE CO., Pittsfield, Mass.
Probate Ledger—(w)—PETERS PAPER CO., Denver, Col.
Probate Linen — (b) —typewriter—EATON, CRANE & PIKE CO., Pittsfield, Mass.
Process Plate—(b)—DILL & COLLINS CO., Philadelphia.
Producers Bond—(w)—W. E. WROE & CO., Chicago.
Profile Bond—(w)—MT. HOLLY PAPER MILLS, INC., Mt. Holly Springs, Pa.
Profile Ledger—(w)—MT. HOLLY PAPER MILLS, INC., Mt. Holly Springs, Pa.
Program—(b)—tag board — AMERICAN WOOD BOARD CO., Schuylerville, New York.
Progresso—(w)—writing — PARSONS TRADING CO., New York.
Progress—(b)—cardboards and cards—GRAHAM PAPER CO., St. Louis.
Progress — (b) — toilet—UNITED STATES ENVELOPE CO. (Morgan Envelope Co. Division), Springfield.
Progress—(w) — engine-sized—BOORUM & PEASE CO., New York.
Progress Bond—(w)—HOWARD SMITH PAPER MILLS, LTD., Montreal, Can.
Progress Index — (b) — colored — RICHMOND PAPER CO., Richmond, Va.

Watermarks and Brands

Progressive—(b)—white manila—McCLELLAN PAPER CO., Minneapolis.
Progressive Bond—(w) — PARSONS TRADING CO., New York.
Progressive Wove Writing—(w)—PARSONS TRADING CO., New York.
Prospect — (b and w) — bond, linen and ledger — NEENAH PAPER CO., Neenah, Wis.
Prosperity Bond —(w)— WHITING-PATTERSON CO., Philadelphia.
Protection—(b)—toilet — UNITED STATES ENVELOPE CO. (Morgan Envelope Co. Division), Springfield.
Protection Bond—(w)—FOX RIVER PAPER CO., Appleton, Wis.
Providence—(b)—toilet — UNITED STATES ENVELOPE CO. (Morgan Envelope Co. Division), Springfield.
Provincial Bond—(w) — ROLLAND PAPER CO., St. Jerome, Canada.
Providence Bond — (b) — R. L. GREENE PAPER CO., Providence, R. I.
Prudential Bond—(w) — PRUDENTIAL INSURANCE CO., Newark, N. J.
Prudential Bond — (w) — ALEXANDER-HOLDEN PAPER CO., New York.
Prussian —(b)— cover — LASHER & LATHROP, New York.
P. T. Co. No. 671—(w) — bond—PARSONS TRADING CO., New York.
Public Bond—(w)—EASTERN MFG. CO., Bangor, Maine.
Public Record Ledger — (w) — BERKSHIRE HILLS PAPER CO., Adams, Mass.
Public Record Ledger—(w)—C. S. PROCTOR PAPER CO., Boston.
Public Safety Bond—(w)—HARLEM CARD & PAPER CO., New York.
Publicity — (b) — car sign bristol—MINNEAPOLIS PAPER CO., Minneapolis, Minn.
Publicity—(b)—cover and blanks—ALEXANDER-HOLDEN PAPER CO., New York.
Publicity Enamel — (b)—blotting—BEECHER, PECK & LEWIS, Detroit, Mich.
Publicity Enamel Book—(b)—BARDEEN PAPER CO., Otsego, Mich.
Public Service Bond—(w) — THE TAYLOR-LOGAN CO. PAPERMAKERS, Holyoke, Mass.
Public Utility—(w and b)—bond, ledger—NEENAH PAPER CO., Neenah, Wis.
Public Welfare—(w and b)—bond, ledger—NEENAH PAPER CO., Neenah, Wis.
Publicity Halftone—(b)—flats—McCLELLAN PAPER CO., Minneapolis.
Publicity Print & Poster — (b)—WESTERN PENNA. PAPER CO., Pittsburgh, Pa.
Publishers' Cover — (b)—PAUL E. VERNON & CO., New York.

Pure Bond—(b) — drug wrapping—GRAHAM PAPER CO., St. Louis.
Pure Irish Linen—(w) — MARCUS WARD CO., New York.
Pure Jute—(b)—manila tag—UNION CARD AND PAPER CO., N. Y.
Pure Jute Tag—(b)—COOK-VIVIAN CO., Boston.
Pure Linen—(w)—PARSONS TRADING CO., New York.
Pure Linen — (w)—SOUTHWORTH CO., Mittineague, Mass.
Pure Linen—(w)—WHITING PAPER CO., Holyoke, Mass.
Pure Linen—with monogram — (w) —MINNEAPOLIS PAPER CO., Minneapolis, Minn.
Pure Linen Bond—(w)—BERLIN & JONES ENVELOPE CO., New York.
Pure Linen Ledger—(w)—MEGARGEE-HARE PAPER CO., Philadelphia.
Pure Linen Ledger—(w)—STRATHMORE PAPER CO., Mittineague.
Pure Linen Stock—(w) — AMERICAN WRITING PAPER CO., Holyoke.
Pure Rag Fibre—(w)—AMERICAN WRITING PAPER CO., Holyoke.
Pure Thistle Linen—(w)—UNITED STATES ENVELOPE CO., Holyoke.
Pure Tissue — (b)—toilet—ALBANY PERFORATED WRAPPING PAPER CO., Albany, New York.
Pure W. B. & S. Monogram Linen —(w) — WRIGHT, BARRETT & STILWELL, St. Paul.
Pure White—(b)—wedding bristol—MOUNTAIN MILL PAPER CO., Lee, Mass.
Pure White Coated Book—(w)—DILL & COLLINS CO., Philadelphia.
Pure White Vellum—(w)—GEO. B. HURD & CO., New York.
Puritan—(b) — ALBANY PERFORATED WRAPPING PAPER CO., Albany, New York.
Puritan—(b)—J. W. BUTLER PAPER CO., Chicago.
Puritan—(b)—book — GRAHAM PAPER CO., St. Louis.
Puritan—(b)—bristol — BAY STATE PAPER CO., Boston.
Puritan—(b) — laid book — JOHN CARTER & CO., Boston.
Puritan — (b) — toilet—UNITED STATES ENVELOPE CO., (Morgan Envelope Co. Division), Springfield.
Puritan—(b)—white enamel — C. P. LESH PAPER CO., Indianapolis.
Puritan Bristol — (b)—WHITAKER PAPER CO., Cincinnati, Ohio.
Puritan Egg Shell — (b)—CHATFIELD & WOODS CO., Cincinnati, O.
Puritan Enamel Book — (b) — PETREQUIN PAPER CO., Cleveland.
Puritan Fine Laid Book — (b)—JOHN CARTER & CO., Boston.
Puritan Half-Tone Book — (b) — THE UNION PAPER AND TWINE CO., Detroit, Mich.
Puritan Ledger — (w)—MERRIAM PAPER CO., New York.

Puritan Linen Ledger—(w)—MERRIAM PAPER CO., New York.
Puritan M. G.— (b) — wrapping — GRAHAM PAPER CO., St. Louis.
Puritan Mills—(b)—A. STORRS & BEMENT CO., Boston.
Puritan Pure Linen—(w) — G. P. PUTNAM'S SONS, New York.
Puritan Superfine—(w) — writing— CA' R E W MANUFACTURING CO., South Hadley Falls Mass.
Puriteen—(b)—toilet — SCOTT PAPER CO., Philadelphia.
Purity—roll and flat—(b)—ALBANY PERFORATED WRAPPING PAPER CO., Albany, New York.
Purity—(b)—waxed manila — W. H. CLAFLIN & CO., Boston.
Purity—(w)—MOUNTAIN MILL PAPER CO., Lee, Mass.
Purity — (w) — superfine — HAMMERMILL PAPER CO., Erie, Pa.
Purity—(b)—toilet — SCOTT PAPER CO., Philadelphia.
Purity —(b)— parchment — GRAHAM PAPER CO., St. Louis.
Purity Blotting — (b)—KINGSLEY PAPER CO., Cleveland, Ohio.
Purity Enamel—(b)—coated—BARDEEN PAPER CO., Otsego, Mich.
Putnam—b—bristol—CHATFIELD & WOODS CO., Cincinnati, Ohio.
Putnam—(b)—M. F. book—CHATFIELD & WOODS CO., Cincinnati, O.
Putnam Bond—(b)—EATON, CRANE & PIKE CO., Pittsfield, Mass.
Putnam—(w and b)—bond, ledger, writing—NEENAH PAPER CO., Neenah, Wis.
Pynchon Bond—(b)—No. 1 A. B. BARNES & CO., Chicago.
Pynetree—(b)—container board— PYNETREE PAPER CO., Gordon, Ga.
Pyramid — (b) — toilet — UNITED STATES ENVELOPE CO. (Morgan Envelope Co. Division), Springfield.
Pyramid Brand Tarred Felt— UNION ROOFING & MFG. CO., Clinton, Ia.

Q

Q.—(b) — super book — PERKINS GOODWIN CO., New York.
Q. T.—(b)—deadening felt—CHATFIELD & WOODS CO., Cincinnati, O.
Quadrette—(w)—GEO. B. HURD & CO., New York.
Quadroon—(b)—flat—KANSAS CITY PAPER HOUSE, Kansas City, Mo.
Quadroon Bond — (w)—A. PRICE, Brooklyn, New York.
Quaker — (b)—blotting—GARRETT-BUCHANAN CO., Philadelphia.
Quaker—(b) — white writing — W. H. CLAFLIN & CO., Boston.
Quaker—(b)—toilet—ALBANY PERFORATED WRAPPING PAPER CO., Albany, New York.

Quaker City Bleached Fibre— QUAKER CITY PAPER CO., Philadelphia.
Quaker City Linen — (w)—JOHN WANAMAKER, Philadelphia.
Quaker Finish—(b) — half tone— DILL & COLLINS CO., Philadelphia.
Quaker Ledger—(w)—HUDSON VALLEY PAPER CO., Albany, N. Y.
Quaker Linen — (w)—AMERICAN WRITING PAPER CO., Holyoke.
Quaker Vellum — (b) — EATON, CRANE & PIKE CO., Pittsfield, Mass.
Qualifine—(b)—toilet — SCOTT PAPER CO., Philadelphia.
Quality Blotting—(b)—OSBORN PAPER CO., Philadelphia.
Quality Bond — (w) — AMERICAN WRITING PAPER CO., Holyoke.
Quality Bond—(w) — ALEXANDER-HOLDEN PAPER CO., New York.
Quality Wrapping—(b)—fibre—dry finish—ANDREWS PAPER CO., Boston.
Queen—(b)—enamel book—DONALDSON PAPER CO., Harrisburg, Pa.
Queen—(w)—ledger — J. E. LINDE PAPER CO., New York.
Queen—(b)—linen — RIEGEL & CO., INC., Philadelphia.
Queen—(b)—toilet — ALBANY PERFORATED WRAPPING PAPER CO., Albany, New York.
Queen—(b) — tag — MINNEAPOLIS PAPER CO., Minneapolis, Minn.
Queen — (b)— cover—NIAGARA PAPER MILLS, Lockport, New York.
Queen Anne Bristol—(b)—BUNTIN, GILLIES & CO., LTD., Hamilton, Ontario, Can.
Queen Anne — (w) — BUNTIN, GILLIES & CO., LTD., Hamilton, Ontario, Can.
Queen Bee—(w)—flat — CENTRAL TOPEKA PAPER CO., Topeka, Kan.
Queen City — (b)—flat—DIEM & WING PAPER CO., Cincinnati, Ohio.
Queen City Bond — (w) — SPRINGFIELD PAPER SUPPLY CO., Springfield, Mo.
Queen Kraft — (b) — STONE & FORSYTH CO., Boston.
Queen Laid—(w)—DILL & COLLINS CO., Philadelphia.
Queen Linen—(w)—CONROW BROS., New York.
Queen Linen—(w)—cream laid linen —R. C. KASTNER PAPER CO., N. Y.
Queen's Bond — (w) — A. PRICE, Brooklyn, New York.
Queens Bond — (w) — A. PRICE, Brooklyn, N. Y.
Queenstown—(b)—envelope—WHITING-PATTERSON CO., Philadelphia.
Queen Wedding—(b) — STANDARD CARD & PAPER CO., New York.
Queen White—(w) — HARCOURT & CO., Louisville, Ky.

Quicksel —(b)— toilet—SCOTT PAPER CO., Philadelphia.
Quincy —(b)— toilet—ALBANY PERFORATED WRAPPING PAPER CO., Albany, New York.

R

"R" Bristol—(b)—ALLING & CORY CO., Rochester.
"R. C. K." Special—(b)—white wove writing—R. C. KASTNER PAPER CO., New York.
Racco Fibre—(b)—R. A. CANTHORN PAPER CO., Richmond, Va.
Racoon—(w)—flats—WESTERN PAPER CO., Omaha, Neb.
Radisson—(b)—flat writing—MINNEAPOLIS PAPER CO., Minneapolis.
Radium—(b)—toilet—SEINSHEIMER PAPER CO., Cincinnati, O.
Radium Bond — (w)—THE CHATFIELD & WOODS CO., Cincinnati, O.
Radium Bond—(w) — THE UNION PAPER AND TWINE CO., Detroit.
Rag Book—(b)—R. L. GREENE PAPER CO., Providence, R. I.
Rag Featherweight Wove Book—(b)—MEGARGEE-HARE PAPER CO., Philadelphia.
Ragstock Index Bristol—(b)—B. D. RISING PAPER CO., Housatonic, Mass.
Railroad—(b)—tag board — AMERICAN WOOD BOARD CO., Schuylerville, New York.
Railroad—(b)—roofing—L. J. DODD CO., INC, Elmira, N. Y.
Railroad Bond — (w)—MOSER PAPER CO., Chicago.
Railroad Ledger — (w)—THE ALLING & CORY CO., Rochester, N. Y.
Railroad Manila — (b) — UNION CARD & PAPER CO., New York.
Railroad Manila — (b)—writing—RIEGEL & CO., INC., Philadelphia
Railway Manila — (w) — CANADA PAPER CO., LTD., Windsor Mills, Can.
Rainbow — (b) — bristol — BAY STATE PAPER CO., Boston.
Rainbow—(b)—bristol—CHATFIELD & WOODS CO., Cincinnati, Ohio.
Rainbow—(b)—colored coated book—JAS. WHITE PAPER CO., Chicago.
Rainbow — (b) — MISSOURI PAPER HOUSE, Kansas City, Mo.
Rainbow — (b) — gummed — LOUISVILLE PAPER CO., Louisville, Ky.
Rainbow Bond—(w) — MEGARGEE BROS., Scranton, Pa.
Rainbow Colored M. F.—(b)—PAUL E. VERNON & CO., New York.
Rainbow M. F. Book—(b)—PAUL E. VERNON & CO., New York.
Rainbow Ticket Bristol — (b) — RICHMOND PAPER CO., Richmond, Va.
Rajah—(b) — sheathing — GRAHAM PAPER CO., St. Louis.
Rajah—(b)—bristol — THE PAPER MILLS CO., Chicago.
Rajah Bond — (w) — CHATFIELD & WOODS CO., Cincinnati, Ohio.
Rajah Bond—(w) — THE UNION PAPER & TWINE CO., Detroit.
Rajah Linen — (w) — UNITED STATES ENVELOPE CO. (The White, Corbin & Co. Division), Rockville, Conn.
Raleigh—(b) — book—F. A. FLINN, INC., New York.
Raleigh—(w)—flat writing— F O X RIVER PAPER CO., Appleton, Wis.
Raleigh—(w)—flat—FOX RIVER PAPER CO., Appleton, Wis.
Raleigh Bond—(w)—FOX RIVER PAPER CO., Appleton, Wis.
Raleigh Superfine—(w)—flat writing—STANDARD PAPER CO., Tacoma, Wash.
Ralston—(b)—toilet—SCOTT PAPER CO., Philadelphia.
Ramapo Bond—(w)—MERRIAM PAPER CO., New York.
Rameses Book—(b)—THE UNION PAPER & TWINE CO., Detroit, Mich.
Ramie Fibre—(b)—super book—J. W. BUTLER PAPER CO., Chicago.
Ramie Linen — (b)—EATON, CRANE & PIKE CO., Pittsfield, Mass.
Ramona—(w)—bond—GRAHAM PAPER CO., St. Louis.
Ramona—(w)—bond—GRAHAM PAPER CO., St. Louis.
Randolph Mills—(b)—extra fine—JUDD PAPER CO., Holyoke, Mass.
Ranier Offset—(b)—book—GRAHAM PAPER CO., St. Louis.
Raphael Text—(b)—LOUISVILLE PAPER CO., Louisville, Ky.
Rappahannock—(w)—cover— J A S. WHITE PAPER CO., Chicago.
Rattan—(b)—express—KANSAS CITY PAPER HOUSE, Kansas City, Mo.
Raylawn—(w)—COYLE & GILMORE CO., INC., New York.
Ravelstone Bond—(w)—KEITH PAPER CO., Turners Falls, Mass.
Ravelstone Extra Superfine—(w)—KEITH PAPER CO., Turners Falls, Mass.
Ravelstone Ledger — (w) — KEITH PAPER CO., Turners Falls, Mass.
Raven—(b)—toilet—ALBANY PERFORATED WRAPPING PAPER CO., Albany, N. Y.
Raven Black—(b)—pattern—LOUISVILLE PAPER CO., Louisville, Ky.
Ravenswood—(b)—white wove—F A. FLINN, New York.
Rawhide—(b) — boxboard — MUCKLE BROS. MFG. CO., Clearwater, Minn
Rawhide—(b)—waterproof roofing. sheathing and wrapping—C. S. GARRETT & SON CO., Philadelphia.
Rawhide — (b) — tympan manila — BRADNER SMITH & CO., Chicago.

Rawhide Manila—(b)—wrapping—LOUISVILLE PAPER CO., Louisville, Ky.
Rawhide Pattern—(b)—pattern—GRAHAM PAPER CO., St. Louis.
Reade Bond—(b)—PAUL E. VERNON & CO., New York.
Reading Mills—(b)—C A R T E R, RICE & CO., Boston.
Real Irish Linen—(w)—AMERICAN WRITING PAPER CO., Holyoke, Mass.
Realty L. D. Bond—(w)—TROY PAPER CO., Troy, N. Y.
Realty Bond—(w)—E. E. LLOYD PAPER CO., Chicago, Ill.
Reciprocity Bond—(b)—WHITAKER PAPER CO., Cincinnati, Ohio.
Record—(b)—bond—RIEGEL & CO., INC., Philadelphia.
Record—(b)—amber railroad manila—J. C. PARKER PAPER CO., Louisville, Ky.
Record—(w)—bond—J. E. LINDE PAPER CO., New York.
Record—(b)—white wove—MILLER & WRIGHT PAPER CO., New York.
Record Bond—(w)—AETNA PAPER CO., Dayton, Ohio.
Record Bond—(w)—DWIGHT BROS. PAPER CO., Grand Rapids, Mich.
Record Bond—(b)—NITSCHKE PAPER CO., Columbus, Ohio.
Record Bond—(w)—HAMMERMILL PAPER CO., Erie, Pa.
Record Bond No. 1—(w)—STRATHMORE PAPER CO., Mittineague, Mass.
Record Bond—(w)—PARSONS TRADING CO., New York.
Recorder—(b)—index bristol—MINNEAPOLIS PAPER CO., Minneapolis, Minn.
Recorder's Linen Ledger—(w)—ledger—STANDARD CARD & PAPER CO., New York.
Record Index—(b)—cardboards and cards—GRAHAM PAPER CO., St. Louis.
Record Index—(b)—bristols—UNION CARD AND PAPER CO., New York.
Record Linen Ledger—(w)—WHITING PAPER CO., Holyoke, Mass.
Record Mills—(b)—flats—CLEMENTS PAPER CO., Nashville, Tenn.
Recorder Bond—(w)—ESLEECK MFG. CO., Turners Falls, Mass.
Recorder's Irish Linen—(w)—GRAHAM PAPER CO., St. Louis.
Red Arrow—(b)—folding enamel—MINNEAPOLIS PAPER CO., Minneapolis, Minn.
Red Cloud—(b)—toilet—NORTHERN PAPER MILLS, Green Bay, Wis.
Red Clover—(b)—toilet—ALBANY PERFORATED WRAPPING PAPER CO., Albany, N. Y.
Red Cross—(b)—toilet—ALBANY PERFORATED WRAPPING PAPER CO., Albany, N. Y.
Red Cross Bond—(w)—HOWARD PAPER CO., Urbana, Ohio.
Red Diamond—(b)—waterproof lining paper—JUDD PAPER CO., Holyoke, Mass.
Red Feather Bond—(b)—LOUISVILLE PAPER CO., Louisville, Ky.
Red Fern Fine—(w)—BOORUM & PEASE CO., New York.
Red K Blotting—(b)—KINGSLEY PAPER CO., Cleveland, Ohio.
Red K Bond—(w)—KINGSLEY PAPER CO., Cleveland, Ohio.
Red Label—(b)—KANSAS CITY PAPER CO., Kansas City, Mo.
Red Leaf London—(w)—J O H N WANAMAKER, Philadelphia.
Red Linen Ledger—(w)—THE McNEIL CO., Phœnix, Ariz.
Red Lion—(b)—parchment—G L E N MILLS PAPER CO., Philadelphia.
Red Lion—(b)—toilet—CLARK-SAWYER CO., Worcester, Mass.
Red Mill—(w)—POWERS PAPER COMPANY, Springfield, Mass.
Red Robe—(b)—toilet—NORTHERN PAPER MILLS, Green Bay, Wis.
Red Rope—(b)—carpet lining—GRAHAM PAPER CO., St. Louis.
Red Seal—(b)—coated—RITCHIE & RAMSAY, Toronto, Canada.
Red Seal—(b)—flats—W E S T E R N PENNA. PAPER CO., Pittsburgh, Pa.
Red Seal—(b)—roll toilet—CHATFIELD & WOODS CO., Cincinnati, O.
Red Seal—(b)—toilet—NORTHERN PAPER MILLS, Milwaukee, Wis.
Red Seal Ledger—(w)—INDIANA PAPER CO., Indianapolis.
Red Seal Pasted Bristol—(b)—JOHN CARTER & CO., Boston.
Reference Ledger—(w)—GARRETT-BUCHANAN CO., Philadelphia.
Reference Linen Ledger—(w)—B. D. RISING PAPER CO., Housatonic, Mass.
Reflex Offset Bond—(b)—GRAHAM PAPER CO., St. Louis.
Reg—(b)—boards—INGALLS & CO., Castleton, N. Y.
Regal—(b)—waxed tissue—W. H. CLAFLIN & CO., Boston.
Regal—(b)—cover—B. F. BOND PAPER CO., Baltimore.
Regal—(b)—bristol—J. W. BUTLER PAPER CO., Chicago.
Regal—(b)—toilet—ALBANY PERFORATED WRAPPING PAPER CO., Albany, N. Y.
Regal—(b)—wrapping paper—ATLANTA PAPER CO., Atlanta, Ga.
Regal Antique—(w)—DILL & COLLINS CO., Philadelphia.
Regal Bond—(w)—BARBER-ELLIS, LTD., Toronto, Can.
Regal Bond—(w)—STRATHMORE PAPER CO., Mittineague, Mass.
Regal Bond—(w)—ST. LOUIS PAPER CO., St. Louis.

Regal Egg-Shell Book—(w)—BRADNER SMITH & CO., Chicago.
Regal Embossed Blotting—(b)—BRADNER SMITH & CO., Chicago.
Regal Embossing Cover—(b)—MINNEAPOLIS PAPER CO., Minneapolis, Minn.
Regal Linen—(w)—STRATHMORE PAPER CO., Mittineague, Mass.
Regal Linen Ledger—(w)—BERKSHIRE HILLS PAPER CO., Adams, Mass.
Regal Tinted Flats—(b)—SWIGART PAPER CO., Chicago.
Regal Wedding Bristol—(b)—BRADNER SMITH & CO., Chicago.
Regent—(b)—bristol—TILESTON & LIVERMORE CO., Boston.
Regent—(b)—toilet—UNITED STATES ENVELOPE CO. (Morgan Envelope Co. Div.), Springfield, Mass.
Regent—(w)—typewriter—WYCKOFF, SEAMANS & BENEDICT, N. Y.
Regent—(w)—writing—ST. LOUIS PAPER CO., St. Louis.
Regent—(b)—book—BRADNER SMITH & CO., Chicago.
Regent Folding—(b)—bristols—SWIGART PAPER CO., Chicago.
Regent Railroad Manila—(b)—MOORE & THOMPSON CO., Bellows Falls, Vt.
Reges Bond—(w and b)—A. R. BARNES & CO., Chicago.
Regional Bank Bond—(w)—WHITAKER PAPER CO., Cincinnati, O.
Regimental Gray—(w)—GEO. B. HURD & CO., New York.
Register—(b)—book—GRAHAM PAPER CO., St. Louis.
Register Bond—(w)—PARSONS TRADING CO., New York.
Regular Linen—(b)—MERRIAM PAPER CO., New York.
Regular Linen—(b)—BASSETT & SUTPHIN, New York.
Regular Linen—(b)—F. W. ANDERSON & CO., INC., New York.
Riegel's Jewel Brand—(b)—glassine—WARREN MFG. CO., Milford, N. J.
Relegud—(b)—toilet—SCOTT PAPER CO., Philadelphia.
Reliable Manifold Bond—(b)—MACK-ELLIOTT PAPER CO., St. Louis.
Reliable—(b)—blanks—ALEXANDER-HOLDEN PAPER CO., New York.
Reliance—(b)—tailor black pattern—STONE & FORSYTH CO., Boston.
Reliance—(b)—tag—JUDD PAPER CO., Holyoke, Mass.
Reliance—(b)—blotting—ALBEMARLE PAPER CO., Richmond, Va.
Reliance—(b)—colored flats—BRADNER SMITH & CO., Chicago.
Reliance—(b)—rope manila—BRADNER SMITH & CO., Chicago.
Reliance—(b)—toilet—R. L. GREENE PAPER CO., Providence, R. I.

Reliance—(b)—superfines—KANSAS CITY PAPER HOUSE, Kansas City.
Reliance—(w)—writing—WEST VIRGINIA PULP AND PAPER CO., N. Y.
Reliance Linen Bond—(w)—PETREQUIN PAPER CO., Cleveland.
Reliance Linen Ledger—(b)—E. P. MOLTEN & CO., Philadelphia.
Reliance Linen Ledger—(w)—AMERICAN WRITING PAPER CO., Holyoke, Mass.
Reliance Record—(w)—STATE JOURNAL CO., Lincoln, Neb.
Reliance Superfine—(w)—GRAHAM PAPER CO., St. Louis.
Rembrandt—(b)—cover—PAPER MILLS CO., Chicago.
Rembrandt—(b)—felt mounts—BRADNER SMITH & CO., Chicago.
Rembrandt Coated—(b)—PAUL H. VERNON & CO., New York.
Renfrew Bond—(w)—STRATHMORE PAPER CO., Mittineague, Mass.
Renier Bond—(w)—BROWN, Renowned—(b)—gum paper—GRAHAM PAPER CO., St. Louis.
BLODGETT & SPERRY CO., St. Paul.
Reorder Bond—(w)—LEE PAPER CO., Vicksburg, Mich.
Repoussé Bond Cover and Bristol—(b)—KEITH PAPER CO., Turners Falls, Mass.
Republic—(w)—white loose flats—MINNEAPOLIS PAPER CO., Minneapolis, Minn.
Republic Bond—(w)—BARTON HOBART PAPER CO., Chicago.
Republic Bond—(w)—extra fine writing—CENTRAL OHIO PAPER CO., Columbus, Ohio.
Republic Bristol—(b)—OLD DOMINION PAPER CO., Norfolk, Va.
Republican Pemana Ledger—(w)—PARSONS TRADING CO., New York.
Requisition—(w)—bond—GRAHAM PAPER CO., St. Louis.
Reserve Bank Bond—(b)—GRAHAM PAPER CO., St. Louis.
Resistance—(b)—waterproof lining—JUDD PAPER CO., Holyoke, Mass.
Resolute—(w and b)—bond, ledger, writing—NEENAH PAPER CO., Neenah, Wis.
Resolute Linen Ledger—(w)—NEENAH PAPER CO., Neenah, Wis.
Revelstone Bond—(h)—BRADNER SMITH & CO., Chicago.
Revenue Bond—(w)—AMERICAN WRITING PAPER CO., Holyoke, Mass.
Revenue Bond—(w)—A. PRICE, Brooklyn, N. Y.
Revenue Bristol—(b)—MINNEAPOLIS PAPER CO., Minneapolis, Minn.
Revenue Linen Ledger—(w)—INDIANA PAPER CO., Indianapolis.
Revere—(b)—cover—THE CHATFIELD & WOODS CO., Cincinnati.

Revere—(b)—translucent cardboard—ARNOLD-ROBERTS CO., Boston.
Revere—(b)—toilet—ALBANY PERFORATED WRAPPING PAPER CO., Albany, N. Y.
Revere—(b)—white wove writing—R. C. KASTNER PAPER CO., New York.
Revere Antique Book — (b) — HY. LINDENMEYR & SONS, New York.
Revere Linen Ledger—(b)—white ledger—R. C. KASTNER PAPER CO., New York.
Reveno—(b)—CONROW BROS., N. Y.
Reverco Mills—(b)—flat writing—CONROW BROS., New York.
Rex—(b)—fibre wrapping — DEXTER SULPHITE FIBRE AND PAPER CO., Dexter, N. Y.
Rex—(b)—bristol—R. L. GREENE PAPER CO., Providence, R. I.
Rex—(b) — toilet — NORTHERN PAPER MILLS, Green Bay, Wis.
Rex—(b)—toilet—REGAL PAPER CO., Pulaski, N. Y.
Rex Bond—(w)—BRYANT PAPER CO., Kalamazoo, Mich.
Rex Bond—(w)—CINCINNATI CORDAGE AND PAPER COMPANY, Cincinnati, Ohio.
Rex Flats—(b)—C. S. PROCTOR PAPER CO., Boston.
Rex India—(b)—coated book—BRADNER SMITH & CO., Chicago.
Rex Manilas—(b)—No. 1 manila—A. M. EATON, Waltham and Boston.
Rhododendron—(b)—cover, bristol, photo mounts, photo paper, announcements and box cover—STRATHMORE PAPER CO., Mittineague, Mass.
Rialto Mills—(w)—AMERICAN WRITING PAPER CO., Holyoke.
Ribbed Fabric—(b)—GEO. B. HURD & CO., New York.
Ribbed, Two Tone—(b)—box covers —DISTRICT OF COLUMBIA PAPER MFG. CO., Washington, D. C.
Ribbon Hinge Ledger — (w) — SOUTHWORTH CO., Mittineague, Mass.
Richelieu Covers—(b)—HY. LINDENMEYR & SONS, New York.
Richmond—(b)—super book—F. A. FLINN, New York.
Richmond—(b)—book — RICHMOND PAPER CO., Richmond, Va.
Richmond—(b)— book — MISSOURI PAPER HOUSE, Kansas City, Mo.
Richmond Eggshell Book—(b)—RICHMOND PAPER CO., Richmond, Va.
Richmond Extra Fine Writing—(w)—RICHMOND PAPER CO., Richmond, Va.
Richmond M. F. Book—(b)—RICHMOND PAPER CO., Richmond, Va.
Richmond Super—(b)—RICHMOND PAPER CO., Richmond, Va.
Rico Bond—(b)—RIEGEL & CO., INC., Philadelphia.

Ridgefield —(b)— toilet — ALBANY PERFORATED WRAPPING PAPER CO., Albany, N. Y.
Ridgeway Lining—(b)—corrugated packing—GRAHAM PAPER CO., St. Louis.
Riegel's Jewel Brand Parchmyn and Greaseproof—(b)—WARREN MFG. CO., 41 Park Row, New York.
Right-of-Way Bond — (w) — FOX RIVER PAPER CO., Appleton, Wis.
Rising Sun — (b)—toilet—UNITED STATES ENVELOPE CO., (Morgan Envelope Co. Division), Springfield.
Rittenhouse Bond—(w)—GILBERT PAPER CO., Menasha, Wis.
Ritual Linen — (b) — typewriter—EATON, CRANE & PIKE CO., Pittsfield, Mass.
Rival—(b) — toilet—ALBANY PERFORATED WRAPPING PAPER CO., Albany, New York.
Rival Bond — (w) — THOMAS W. PRICE CO., Philadelphia.
Rival Bond — (w) — AMERICAN WRITING PAPER CO., Holyoke.
Rival Fibre — (b) — R. L. GREENE PAPER CO., Providence, R. I.
Rival Linen — (w) — AMERICAN WRITING PAPER CO., Holyoke.
Rival Linen — (w)—THOMAS W PRICE CO., Philadelphia.
Rival Litho—(b) — coated blanks—UNION CARD AND PAPER CO., N. Y.
Rival Silver Tissue — (b) — R. L. GREENE PAPER CO., Providence, R. I.
Rivera Blanks—(b)—DIEM & WING PAPER CO., Cincinnati, Ohio.
Rivermont Bond — (b) — CASKIE-DILLARD CO., INC., Lynchburg, Va.
Riverside—(w)—NITSCHKE PAPER CO., Columbus, Ohio.
Riverside Bond — (b) — HARLEM CARD & PAPER CO., Nw York.
Riverside Coated Litho — (b) — ALLING & CORY CO., Rochester.
Riverside Fine — (b)—NITSCHKE PAPER CO., Columbus, Ohio.
Riverside Litho Blanks—(b)—THE ALLING & CORY CO., Rochester.
Riverview—(w)—ledger — HAGEN PAPER CO., St. Louis.
Rivington—(b)—cover — STONE & ANDREWS, Boston.
Risol — (b) — bristol — J. P. HEILBRONN CO., Manila, P. I.
R. L. G. Blotting — (b) — R. L. GREENE PAPER CO., Providence, R. I.
R. L. G. Sealing Wax—(b)—R. L. GREENE PAPER CO., Providence, R. I.
R. L. G. Manila Tag — (b) — R. L. GREENE PAPER CO., Providence, R. I.
Roanoke—(b)—book — C. P. LESH PAPER CO., Indianapolis, Ind.
Roanoke Bond — (w) — BRADNER SMITH & CO., Chicago.

Roanoke Linen — (b) — GEO. B. HURD & CO., New York.
Robin Hood — (b)—toilet—ALBANY PERFORATED WRAPPING PAPER CO., Albany, New York.
Robin Hood—(b)—toilet—H. NORWOOD EWING CO., New York.
Robinson Crusoe—(b)—t o i l e t—H. NORWOOD EWING CO., New York.
Rob Roy—(b)—toilet—ALBANY PERFORATED WRAPPING PAPER CO., Albany, New York.
Rob Roy Linen — (w) — writing — HAMPSHIRE PAPER CO., South Hadley Falls, Mass.
Rochester Bond—(w)—ALLING & CORY CO., Rochester.
Rock—(b)—tag board—TROY PAPER CO., Troy, N. Y.
Rockaway—(b) — roofing — LOUISVILLE PAPER CO., Louisville, Ky.
Rock-Barnes Linen Typewriting—(w)—ROCKWELL-BARNES CO., Chicago.
Rock-Barnes—(w and b)—various grades — ROCKWELL-BARNES CO., Chicago.
Rock City—(b)—MORGAN & HAMILTON CO., Nashville, Tenn.
Rockdale Mills — (b)—WHITAKER PAPER CO., Cincinnati, Ohio.
Rockbridge Bond—(w) — OLD DOMINION PAPER CO., Norfolk, Va.
Rockingham Bond—(b)—OLD DOMINION PAPER CO., Norfolk, Va.
Rock Springs—(b)—bond—GRAHAM PAPER CO., St. Louis.
Rockton Bond — (b) — BRADNER SMITH & CO., Chicago.
Rockton Index Bristol — (b) — BRADNER SMITH & CO., Chicago.
Rockwood Fines — (w) — GILBERT PAPER CO., Menasha, Wis.
Roland Linen Ledger—(w)—writing C A R E W MANUFACTURING CO., South Hadley Falls, Mass.
Rolland Parchment — (w)—ROLLAND PAPER CO., St. Jerome, Canada.
Rolland Superfine—(w)—ROLLAND PAPER CO., St. Jerome, Canada.
Rolleston Mills—(w) — AMERICAN WRITING PAPER CO., Holyoke.
Roll of Honor—(b)—toilet—NORTHERN PAPER MILLS, Green Bay, Wis.
Roma Bond—(w)—J. P. HEILBRONN CO., Manila, P. I.
Roman—(b)—translucent — W. H. CLAFLIN & CO., Boston.
Roman—(b)—cover—SEYMOUR CO., New York.
Roman—(w)—CARTER, RICE & CO., Boston.
Roman—(b)—wove and laid antique book—HAGEN PAPER CO., St. Louis
Roman Antique — (w) — WHITING PAPER CO., Holyoke, Mass.
Roman Bond — (w) — AMERICAN WRITING PAPER CO., Holyoke.

Roman Bristol — (b)—McCLELLAN PAPER CO., Minneapolis, Minn.
Roman Key—(w)—MARATHON PAPER MILLS CO., Wausau, Wis.
Roman Rag Envelope — (b) — WHITAKER PAPER CO., Cincinnati.
Roman Stripe—(b) — striped fibre—CHATFIELD & WOODS CO., Cincinnati, Ohio.
Romeo—(b)—toilet — H. NORWOOD EWING CO., New York.
Romona Mills—(b)—white flat—J. C. PARKER PAPER CO., Louisville, Ky.
Rookwood—(b)—pastel finish book—MINNEAPOLIS PAPER CO., Minneapolis, Minn.
Rope Fibre—(b) — A. M. EATON, Waltham and Boston, Mass.
Ropelet Kraft — (b) — wrapping—GRAHAM PAPER CO., St. Louis.
Ropeue — (b) — M. G. Kraft — CHAS. F. HUBBS & CO., New York.
Rope Tag—(b)—tag board — UNION CARD AND PAPER CO., New York.
Ropine — (b) — cover and bristol—UNION CARD AND PAPER CO., N. Y.
Roscoe—(b)—toilet—NORTHERN PAPER MILLS, Green Bay, Wis.
Rose—(b)—toilet — CHATFIELD PAPER CO., New Haven, Conn.
Rose Bud—(b)—vegetable parchment —LOUISVILLE PAPER CO., Louisville, Ky.
Rosedale Writing — (b) — MEGARGEE BROS., Scranton, Pa.
Rose Manila—(b)—envelope—UNION CARD AND PAPER CO., New York.
Rose White Bristol — (b)—pasted bristol—B. D. RISING PAPER CO., Housatonic, Mass.
Rose White Linen—(w)—PARSONS PAPER CO., Holyoke, Mass.
Roslin—(b) — flats—MOSER PAPER CO., Chicago.
Rowcon—(b) — No. 1 onion skin—CONROW BROS., New York.
Rowcon—(b) — No. 2 onion skin—CONROW BROS., New York.
Rowcon—(b) — special onion skin—CONROW BROS., New York.
Rowcon—(b) — colored onion skin—CONROW BROS., New York.
Rowcon—(b) — manifold typewriter, white wove and laid in colors—CONROW BROS., New York.
Rowcon—(b)—No. 1 laid linen—CONROW BROS., New York.
Rowcon—(b) — No. 1 wove linen—CONROW BROS, New York.
Rowcon—(b)—No. 20 laid typewriter —CONROW BROS., New York.
Rowcon—(b) — No. 22 laid typewriter —CONROW BROS., New York.
Rowcon—(b)—No. 24 wove typewriter —CONROW BROS., New York.
Rowcon—(b)—No. 29 laid typewriter —CONROW BROS., New York.
Rowcon—(b)—No. 31 laid typewriter —CONROW BROS., New York.

Roweon—(b)—No. 33 laid typewriter—CONROW BROS., New York.
Roweon—(b)—No. 51 wove typewriter—CONROW BROS., New York.
Roweon—(b)—No. 53 wove typewriter—CONROW BROS., New York.
Roweon—(b)—No. 1 French folio, in colors—CONROW BROS., New York.
Rowland Linen Ledger — (w)— CAREW MFG. CO., South Hadley Falls, Mass.
Roxboro Laid Antique — (b)— EATON, CRANE & PIKE CO., Pittsfield, Mass.
Roxboro Laid Satin—(b)—EATON, CRANE & PIKE CO., Pittsfield, Mass.
Roxburg—(w) — antique, plate and vellum—LASHER & LATHROP, N. Y.
Roxburge—(w) — WORTHY PAPER CO., Mittineague, Mass.
Roxbury—(b)—enamel book — W. H. GEORGE, Philadelphia.
Roxy—(b)—toilet, pure Manila toilet —SEINSHEIMER PAPER CO., Cincinnati, O.
Royal—(b)—envelope—GRAHAM PAPER CO., St. Louis.
Royal—(b) — document — document manila — SWIGART PAPER CO., Chicago.
Royal—(b)—toilet—NORTHERN PAPER MILLS, Green Bay, Wis.
Royal—(b)—book — KANSAS CITY PAPER HOUSE, Kansas City, Mo.
Royal—(b)—coated book — PAPER MILLS CO., Chicago.
Royal—(w)—ruled and flat — H. S. CROCKER CO., San Francisco.
Royal—(b)—tag—C. P. LESH PAPER CO., Indianapolis, Ind.
Royal Arms—(b)—colored wrapping —STONE & FORSYTH, Boston.
Royal Arms — (b)—toilet—NORTHERN PAPER MILLS, Green Bay, Wis.
Royal Bank — (w)—bond—UNION CARD AND PAPER CO., New York.
Royal Berkshire Linen — (w)— AMERICAN WRITING PAPER CO., Holyoke, Mass.
Royal Blue Leather Finish—(b)— GEO. B. HURD & CO., New York.
Royal Book—(b)—KINGSLEY PAPER CO., Cleveland, Ohio.
Royal Bond—(w)—PARSONS PAPER CO., Holyoke, Mass.
Royal Bristol—(b)—C. P. LESH PAPER CO., Indianapolis, Ind.
Royal Court Bond — (w) — EATON, CRANE & PIKE CO., Pittsfield, Mass.
Royal Court Linen—(w)—EATON, CRANE & PIKE CO., Pittsfield, Mass.
Royal Court Perfection — (w)— EATON, CRANE & PIKE CO., Pittsfield, Mass.
Royal Court Vellum—(w)—EATON, CRANE & PIKE CO., Pittsfield, Mass.
Royal Crown Bond — (w)—J. W. BUTLER PAPER CO., Chicago.
Royal Crown Linen — (w)—J. W. BUTLER PAPER CO., Chicago.
Royal Document Manila — (b) — bristol — C. P. LESH PAPER CO., Indianapolis.
Royal Dundee Bond — (w)—BASSETT & SUTPHIN, New York.
Royal Dundee Ledger—(w)—BASSETT & SUTPHIN, New York.
Royal Dundee Linen—(w)—BASSETT & SUTPHIN, New York.
Royal English Mail—(w and b)— GEO. B. HURD & CO., New York.
Royal Envelope Co. — (b)—JOHN LESLIE PAPER CO., Minneapolis.
Royal Exchange Bond — (w)— EATON, CRANE & PIKE CO., Pittsfield, Mass.
Royal Exeter Bond—(w)—EATON, CRANE & PIKE CO., Pittsfield, Mass.
Royal Finish — (w) — EATON, CRANE & PIKE CO., Pittsfield, Mass.
Royal Gray—(w and b)—GEO. B. HURD & CO., New York.
Royal Green Leather Finish—(b) —GEO. B. HURD & CO., New York.
Royal Highland Granite — (b)— EATON, CRANE & PIKE CO., Pittsfield, Mass.
Royal India Linen—(w)—CHARLES T. BAINBRIDGE'S SONS, Brooklyn.
Royal Irish Linen—(w)—MARCUS WARD CO., Brooklyn.
Royal Kraft—(b)—ORONO PULP & PAPER CO., Orono, Me.
Royal Laid Linen — (w) — BROMPTON PULP & PAPER MILLS, East Angus, Canada.
Royal League—(b)—toilet—GEO. T. JOHNSON CO., Boston.
Royal Linen Bond—(w)—BROMPTON PULP & PAPER MILLS, East Angus, Canada.
Royal Linen Ledger — (w)—PARSONS PAPER CO., Holyoke, Mass.
Royal Mail—(w)—bond—RIEGEL & CO., INC., Philadelphia.
Royal Mail Bond—(w) — TAYLOR-LOGAN CO. PAPERMAKERS, Holyoke.
Royal Melton—(b) — cover — NIAGARA PAPER MILLS, Lockport, New York.
Royal Mills—(b)—folded and ruled— CHATFIELD & WOODS CO., Cincinnati, Ohio.
Royal Mills — (w) — BROMPTON PULP & PAPER MILLS, East Angus, Canada.
Royal Mills Colored Laid—(b)—C. P. LESH PAPER CO., Indianapolis.
Royal Mills Superfine — (w) — BROMPTON PULP & PAPER MILLS, East Angus, Quebec.
Royal Offset—(b) — PAPER MILLS CO., Chicago.
Royal Post Card — (b) — PAPER MILLS CO., Chicago.
Royal Press Papers — (b) — RICHARDSON BROS., New York.

Royal Purple Velvet—(b)—toilet—GEO. T. JOHNSON CO., Boston.
Royal Quality Bond—(w)—GEO. B. HURD & CO., New York.
Royal Record Bond — (w) — HOWARD SMITH PAPER MILLS, LTD., Montreal, Can.
Royal Record Ledger—(w)—HOWARD SMITH PAPER MILLS, LTD., Montreal, Can.
Royal Red—(b)—leather finish—GEO. B. HURD & CO., New York.
Royal Scotch Linen—(b)—EATON, CRANE & PIKE CO., Pittsfield, Mass.
Royal Scotch Pure Fabric—(w)—AMERICAN WRITING PAPER CO., Holyoke, Mass.
Royal Scotch Plaid — (w)—JOHN WANAMAKER, Philadelphia.
Royal Seal—(b)—sheathing and toilet—LOUISVILLE PAPER CO., Louisville, Ky.
Royal Seal — (b) — sheathing and toilet—LOUISVILLE PAPER CO., Louisville, Ky.
Royal Seal Bond — (w)—writing—CAREW MANUFACTURING CO., South Hadley Falls, Mass.
Royal Seal Cover—(b) — ARNOLD-ROBERTS CO., Boston.
Royal Seal Kraft—(b)—A. STORRS & BEMENT CO., Boston.
Royal Vellum—(w and b)—GEO. B. HURD & CO., New York.
Royal Victoria Linen — (w) — TAYLOR-ATKINS PAPER CO., Burnside, Conn.
Royal White—(w and b)—GEO. B. HURD & CO., New York.
Royal White Linen—(b)—sulphite wrapping—W. H. CLAFLIN & CO., Boston.
Royal White Lithograph — (b)—PAPER MILLS CO., Chicago.
Royal Worcester — (w)—UNITED STATES ENVELOPE CO. (Whitcomb Envelope Co. Division), Worcester.
Royal Worcester — (b)—enameled blotting—STANDARD PAPER MANUFACTURING CO., Richmond, Va.
Royal Worcester Bond — (w)—SHERMAN ENVELOPE CO., Worcester, Mass.
Royal Worcester Linen — (w)—UNITED STATES ENVELOPE CO. (Whitcomb Envelope Co. Division), Worcester, Mass.
Royal Writing—(b) — KINGSLEY PAPER CO., Cleveland, Ohio.
Royal York Smooth—(b)—EATON, CRANE & PIKE CO., Pittsfield, Mass.
Royal York Vellum—(b)—EATON, CRANE & PIKE CO., Pittsfield, Mass.
Royalty Bond—(w)—AFFLECK RULING & STATIONERY CO., Holyoke, Mass.
Roycroft—(w)—bond—TROY PAPER CO., Troy, N. Y.
Roycroft—(b)—rag book — WHITAKER PAPER CO., Cincinnati, Ohio, and BAY STATE PAPER CO., Boston.
Roycroft Bond—(w) — HAMMERMILL PAPER CO., Erie, Pa.
Roycroft De Luxe—(w)—book—BAY STATE PAPER CO., Boston.
R. & P.—(b)—card and paper—RAYNOR & PERKINS ENVELOPE CO., New York.
R. & R. 1917 Bond—(b and w)—REESE & REESE, Baltimore, Md.
R. R. Parchment—(w)—HAMMERMILL PAPER CO., Erie, Pa.
R. R. Writing Manila—(b)—UNION CARD & PAPER CO., N. Y.
R. R. Yellow Copying Tissue—F. H. WHITTELSEY CO., Windsor Locks, Conn.
Ruby—(b)—card board—MISSOURI PAPER HOUSE, Kansas City, Mo.
Ruby—(b)—translucent, coated book—UNION CARD & PAPER CO., N. Y.
Rugby—(b)—bible—GRAHAM PAPER CO., St. Louis.
Ruby Blanks—(b)—BRADNER SMITH & CO., Chicago.
Rugby—(b)—coated blanks — TROY PAPER CO., Troy, N. Y.
Rugby—(b)—super calendered book—WHITAKER PAPER CO., Cincinnati.
Rugby Bond—(w)—EASTERN MFG. CO., Bangor, Me.
Rugby Coated Blanks—(b)—TROY PAPER CO., Troy, N. Y.
Rugby Wrapping—(b)—HY. LINDENMEYR & SONS, New York.
Runic Mills—(w)—TILESTON & LIVERMORE CO., Boston.
Runic Parchment—(b)—MOORE & THOMPSON CO., Bellows Falls, Vt.
Rushmore—(b) —toilet—MEGARGEE BROS., Scranton, Pa.
Ruskin Cover—(b)—HY. LINDENMEYR & SONS, New York.
Ruskin Bristols—(b)—HY. LINDENMEYR & SONS, New York.
Ruskin Photo Mounts—(b)—HY. LINDENMEYR & SONS, New York.
Ruskin Vellum—(b) — EATON, CRANE & PIKE CO., Pittsfield, Mass.
Russian—(b)—express—KANSAS CITY PAPER HOUSE, Kansas City.
Russian Linen Ledger—(w)—AMERICAN WRITING PAPER CO., Holyoke, Mass.
Rutland Bristol — (b)—MISSISQUOI PULP & PAPER CO., Sheldon Springs, Vt.
Rydall Mills—(b)—writing—W. H. GEORGE, Philadelphia.

S

S in a diamond—(b)—manila—SEINSHEIMER PAPER CO., Cincinnati, Ohio.
"S"—(b)—HY. LINDENMEYR & SONS, New York.
"S" Bristol—(b)—ALLING & CORY CO., Rochester.
S—(b)—super book—J. W. BUTLER PAPER CO., Chicago.

Sachem—(b)—UNION BAG & PAPER CORP., New York.
Saco—(b)—news—C. P. LESH PAPER CO., Indianapolis, Ind.
Saco—(b)—roll toilet—CHATFIELD & WOODS CO., Cincinnati, Ohio.
Saco Bristol—(b)—C. P. LESH PAPER CO., Indianapolis, Ind.
Safepack—(b)—waterproof wrapping and case lining—SAFEPACK PAPER MILLS, Boston, Mass.
Safety Check—(w)—writing—GEO. LA MONTE & SON, New York.
Safety Check Paper—(b)—GEO. LA MONTE & SON, New York.
Safety First—(w and b)—writing, ledger, bond—NEENAH PAPER CO., Neenah, Wis.
Safety First Ledger—(w)—NEENAH PAPER CO., Neenah, Wis.
Sahara—(b)—blotting—PARSONS PAPER CO., Holyoke, Mass.
Sahara—(b)—toilet—WHITING-PATTERSON CO., New York.
Ste. Claire Bond—(b)—PENINSULAR PAPER CO., Ypsilanti, Mich.
Salamanca—(b)—cover—JAS. WHITE PAPER CO., Chicago.
Salamander—(b)—toilet—H. NORWOOD EWING CO., New York.
Salambo—(b)—toilet—H. NORWOOD EWING CO., New York.
Salamo Asbestos—(b)—SALL MOUNTAIN PAPER CO., Chicago.
Salamo Millboard—(b)—SALL MOUNTAIN PAPER CO., Chicago.
Sales 12—(b)—bond—MERRIAM PAPER CO., New York.
Sales 14—(b)—flat writing—CONROW BROS., New York.
Sales 21—(b)—news—CONROW BROS., New York.
Sales 22—(b)—flat writing—CONROW BROS., New York.
Sales No. 60—(b)—supercalendered book—CONROW BROS., New York.
Sales No. 62—(b)—supercalendered book—CONROW BROS., New York.
Sales No. 76—(b)—machine-finished book—CONROW BROS., New York.
Sales 82—(b)—machine-finished book—CONROW BROS., New York.
Sales 122—(b)—flat writing—CONROW BROS., New York.
Sales Record Ledger—(b)—RIEGEL CO., INC., Philadelphia.
Sales Record Ledger—(w)—MILLERS FALLS PAPER CO., Millers Falls, Mass.
Salisbury—(b)—bible—PERKINS-GOODWIN CO., New York.
Samoa Bond—(b)—GRAHAM PAPER CO., St. Louis.
Samoa Bond—(w)—GRAHAM PAPER CO., St. Louis.
Sampson—(b)—die wiping and second sheets—GRAHAM PAPER CO., St. LOUIS.
Sampson—(b)—pure jute document—SWIGART PAPER CO., Chicago.

Sampson—(b)—tag—CHATFIELD & WOODS CO., Cincinnati, Ohio.
Sampson Cover—(b)—WORTHY PAPER CO., Mittineague, Mass.
Sampson Fibre—(b)—screenings express—MARCELLUS PAPER CO., Syracuse, N. Y.
Sampson Manila and Fibre Papers—(b)—S. S. GARRETT & CO., Philadelphia.
Samson—(b)—fibre—A. M. EATON, Waltham and Boston.
Samson—(b)—COLUMBIA PAPER BAG CO., New York.
Samson Bond—(b)—PAUL E. VERNON & CO., New York.
Samson Bond—(b)—PAUL E. VERNON & CO., New York.
Samson Bond—(b)—PARSONS & WHITTEMORE, New York.
Samson Extra Strong—(b)—PARSONS & WHITTEMORE, New York.
Samson Folding Bristol—(b)—BRADNER SMITH & CO., Chicago.
Samson Texture—(b)—ROSENTHAL PAPER CO., St. Louis.
Samurai—(b)—cover—AMERICAN WRITING PAPER CO., Holyoke, Mass.
Sandow—(b)—cover—J. W. BUTLER PAPER CO., Chicago.
Sandow—(b)—rope manila—STONE & FORSYTH CO., Boston.
Sandow Extra Strong—(w and b)—fine—MERRIAM PAPER CO., N. Y.
Sandow Tough Check—(b)—WABASH COATING MILLS, Wabash, Ind.
Sandow White and Colors—(w)—ledger—MERRIAM PAPER CO., New York.
Sanirap—(b)—FOX PAPER CO., Lockland, Ohio.
Sanital—(b)—specialties—HOWARD CO., Moores, Pa.
Sanitary—(b)—toilet—NORTHERN PAPER MILLS, Green Bay, Wis.
Sanitary—(b)—toilet—STONE & FORSYTH CO., Boston.
Sanitex Hotel and Laundry Shirt Protector—(b)—SEINSHEIMER PAPER CO., Cincinnati.
Sanitex Laundry Bags—(b)—THE SEINSHEIMER PAPER CO., Cincinnati.
Sanitex Toilet Paper—(b)—THE SEINSHEIMER PAPER CO., Cincinnati, Ohio.
San Marco—(w and b)—old style laid—PAPER MILLS CO., Chicago.
Santiago Red Express—(b)—BRADNER SMITH & CO., Chicago.
Sapho—(b)—blanks—LOUISVILLE PAPER CO., Louisville, Ky.
Sapphire Mills—(w)—OSBURN PAPER CO., Philadelphia.
Saranac—(b)—coated and super book, laid and egg-shell—F. A. FLINN, INC., New York.

Saranac—(b)—toilet—ALBANY PERFORATED WRAPPING PAPER CO., Albany, N. Y.
Saranac—(b)—No. 2 cream laid linen—DONALDSON PAPER CO., Harrisburg, Pa.
Saranac Bond—(w)—AMERICAN WRITING PAPER CO., Holyoke, Mass.
Saranac Linen—(w)—STRATHMORE PAPER CO., Mittineague, Mass.
Saratoga—(b)—tag board—AMERICAN WOOD BOARD CO., Schuylerville, N. Y.
Saratoga—(b)—writing—O. F. H. WARNER & CO., Baltimore.
Saratoga Bond—(w)—HAMMERMILL PAPER CO., Erie, Pa.
Sateen—(b)—coated book—JUDD PAPER CO., Holyoke, Mass.
Satin—(b)—white book—THE ALLING & CORY CO., Rochester, N. Y.
Satin Enameled Bristol—(b)—BRADNER SMITH & CO., Chicago.
Satin—(b)—coated blotting—W. H. CLAFLIN & CO., Boston.
Satin—(b)—cardboards and cards—GRAHAM PAPER CO., St. Louis.
Satin-Coat—(b)—bristol—J. W. BUTLER PAPER CO., Chicago.
Satin Enamel Book—(b)—PETREQUIN PAPER CO., Cleveland.
Satin Finish Pure Fibre—(b)—dry goods fibre—SEINSHEIMER PAPER CO., Cincinnati, Ohio.
Satin Flax—(w)—J. W. BUTLER PAPER CO., Chicago.
Satin Flax Linen—(w)—J. W. BUTLER PAPER CO., Chicago.
Satin Snow White Enameled Book—(b)—ALLING & CORY CO., Rochester.
Satin Surface—(b)—book—PAPER MILLS CO., Chicago.
Satintone—(b)—M. F. book—CHATFIELD & WOODS CO., Cincinnati, O.
Satin Wove—(w)—GEO. B. HURD & CO., New York.
Satinette—(b)—wrapping, shades, high grade—THE SEINSHEIMER PAPER CO., Cincinnati, Ohio.
Saturn Greaseproof—(b)—GRAHAM PAPER CO., St. Louis.
Sauquoit—(b)—writing—CHATFIELD & WOODS CO., Cincinnati.
Savaria—(b)—toilet—ALBANY PERFORATED WRAPPING PAPER CO., Albany, N. Y.
Savings Bank Bond—(w)—KANSAS CITY PAPER CO., Kansas City.
Savory—(b)—u. g. onion skin—WILKINSON BROS. & CO., INC., Philadelphia.
Savoy—(b)—enameled blotting—BAY STATE PAPER CO., Boston.
Savoy—(b)—toilet—STONE & FORSYTH CO., Boston.
Savoy—(b)—enameled colored book—BRADNER SMITH & CO., Chicago.
Savoy Blotter—(b)—WHITAKER PAPER CO., Cincinnati, Ohio.

Savoy Linen—(w)—E. W. SCARBOROUGH, New York.
Saxon—(b)—blotting and cover—UNION CARD & PAPER CO., N. Y.
Saxon—(b)—machine-finished book—WHITAKER PAPER CO., Cincinnati.
Saxon Bond—(w)—STRATHMORE PAPER CO., Mittineague, Mass.
Saxon Manuscript—(b)—cover—STRATHMORE PAPER CO., Mittineague, Mass.
Saxon Record—(w and b)—NATIONAL BLANK BOOK CO., Holyoke.
Saxon Superfine—(w)—GRAHAM PAPER CO., St. Louis.
Saxon Superfine—(b)—STRATHMORE PAPER CO., Mittineague, Mass.
Saxony Linen—(w)—AMERICAN WRITING PAPER CO., Holyoke, Mass.
Sceptre Bristol—(b)—TILESTON & LIVERMORE CO., Boston.
School Boy—(b)—drawing—GRAHAM PAPER CO., St. Louis.
Science—(w)—bond—NEENAH, PAPER CO., Neenah, Wis.
Science—(w)—ledger—NEENAH PAPER CO., Neenah, Wis.
Science—(w)—writing—NEENAH PAPER CO., Neenah, Wis.
Scioto Mills—(w)—No. 1 fine—CENTRAL OHIO PAPER CO., Columbus.
Scopaco—(b)—toilet—SCOTT PAPER CO., Philadelphia.
Scorpion—(b)—CROWN COLUMBIA PAPER CO., San Francisco.
Scotch Antique Mimeograph—(w)—flats—MINNEAPOLIS PAPER CO., Minneapolis, Minn.
Scotch Bond—(w)—NITSCHKE PAPER CO., Columbus, Ohio.
Scotch Bristol—(b)—HAGEN PAPER CO., St. Louis.
Scotch Granite—(b)—MARCUS WARD CO., Brooklyn, N. Y.
Scotch Granite—(w)—GEO. B. HURD & CO., New York.
Scotch Irish Bond—(w)—THE JENNER CO., Louisville, Ky.
Scotch Linen Ledger—(w)—PARSONS PAPER CO., Holyoke, Mass.
Scotch Raglan—(b)—EATON CRANE & PIKE CO., Pittsfield, Mass.
Scotia Bond—(w)—STRATHMORE PAPER CO., Mittineague, Mass.
Scotia Linen Ledger—(w)—STRATHMORE PAPER CO., Mittineague, Mass.
Scotland Laid—(b)—book—LOUISVILLE PAPER CO., Louisville, Ky.
Scottdale Mills—(w)—LEE PAPER CO., Vicksburg, Mich.
Scottish Crown—(w and b)—writing, ledger, bond—NEENAH PAPER CO., Neenah, Wis.
Scottish Union Bond—(w)—W. T. CHATTERLY, New York.
Scrantom, Wetmore & Co.—(w)—SCRANTOM, WETMORE & CO., Rochester, N. Y.

Scriptum—(w)—ledger—J. W. BUTLER PAPER CO., Chicago.
S. D. Childs & Co., Chicago, Ill.—(w)—typewriter—S. D. CHILDS & CO., Chicago.
Sea Glass Express—(b)—wrapping—LOUISVILLE PAPER CO., Louisville, Ky.
Seal—(b)—fibre—W. H. CLAFLIN & CO., Boston.
Seal—(b)—cardboards and cards—GRAHAM PAPER CO., St. Louis.
Seal Bond—(w)—AETNA PAPER CO., Dayton, Ohio.
Seal of Pittsburgh Bond—(b)—WESTERN PENNA. PAPER CO., Pittsburgh, Pa.
Seal Ledger—(w)—SUTPHIN PAPER CO., INC., New York.
Seal Linen Ledger—(w)—BASSETT & SUTPHIN, New York.
Sea Shell—(b)—toilet—GRAHAM PAPER CO., St. Louis.
Sea Shell—(b)—toilet—NORTHERN PAPER MILLS, Green Bay, Wis.
Sealskin—(b)—fibre—W. H. CLAFLIN & CO., Boston.
Searchlight—(w and b)—bond, writing—NEENAH PAPER CO., Neenah, Wis.
Sebago—(b)—toilet—ALBANY PERFORATED WRAPPING PAPER CO., Albany, N. Y.
Sebo — (b) — HOLLINGSWORTH & WHITNEY CO., Boston.
Security Manifold—(b)—McCLELLAN PAPER CO., Minneapolis, Minn.
Security—(b)—tag board—GRAHAM PAPER CO., St. Louis.
Security—(w)—writing — HAMMERMILL PAPER CO., Erie, Pa.
Security Blotting — (b) — SABIN, ROBBINS PAPER CO., Middletown. Ohio.
Security Bond—(w)—A. STORRS & BEMENT CO., Boston.
Security Bond—(w)—WESTERN PENNA. PAPER CO., Pittsburg, Pa.
Security Linen — (w) — STRATHMORE PAPER CO., Mittineague, Mass.
Security Linen Ledger — (w) — STRATHMORE PAPER CO., Mittineague, Mass.
Security Oiled Tympan—(b)—LOUISVILLE PAPER CO., Louisville, Ky.
Security Onion Skin—(b) — white and colors—RICHMOND PAPER CO., Richmond, Va.
Security Trust Bond—(w)—AMERICAN WRITING PAPER CO., Springfield, Mass.
Selkirk—(w and b)—writing, ledger, bond—NEENAH PAPER CO., Neenah, Wis.
Sellmore Bond—(b)—GRAHAM PAPER CO., St. Louis.
Selmer—(b)—toilet—SCOTT PAPER CO., Philadelphia.

Sels—(b)—toilet—SCOTT PAPER CO., Philadelphia.
Semaphore Bond— (w) —FOX RIVER PAPER CO., Appleton, Wis.
Semi-Antique—(b)—P E R K I N S, GOODWIN CO., New York.
Seminole Bond—(w)—white bond—H. & W. B. DREW CO., Jacksonville, Fla.
Semper Idem—(w)—linens and bonds—UNITED STATES ENVELOPE CO. (Morgan Envelope Co. Division), Springfield, Mass.
Senate—(b)—JOHNSTON PAPER CO., Harrisburg, Pa.
Senate Bond—(w)—JOHNSTON PAPER CO., Harrisburg, Pa.
Senate Index Bristol—(b)—HARLEM CARD & PAPER CO., New York.
Senate Onion Skin—(b)—OSBURN PAPER CO., Philadelphia.
Seneca—(b)—toilet—ALBANY PERFORATED WRAPPING PAPER CO., Albany, N. Y.
Seneca—(b)—NIAGARA COATED PAPER CO., Niagara Falls, N. Y.
Seneca Colored Laid—(b)—THE UNION PAPER & TWINE CO., Detroit, Mich.
Seneca Mills Superfine—(w)—writing—LASHER & LATHROP, N. Y.
Seneca News—(b)—C. P. LESH PAPER CO., Indianapolis, Ind.
Sentinel—(b) — toilet — NORTHERN PAPER MILLS, Green Bay, Wis.
Serake Blotting—(b) — UNION PAPER & TWINE CO., Detroit, Mich.
Seraph—(b)—pasted bristol — TROY PAPER CO., Troy, N. Y.
Servia Ledger—(w) — AMERICAN WRITING PAPER CO., Holyoke.
Service Blanks — (b) — RICHMOND PAPER CO., Richmond, Va.
Service Index Bristol — (b) — GRAHAM PAPER CO., St. Louis.
Service Writing—(b) — MEGARGEE BROS., Scranton, Pa.
Severn—(b)—B U N T I N, GILLIES & CO., LTD., Hamilton, Ontario, Can.
Seymour Specials — (b)—cover — SEYMOUR CO., New York.
Shagreen Vellum — (b) —MARCUS WARD & CO., Brooklyn, N. Y.
Shamrock—(b)—toilet— NORTHERN PAPER MILLS, Green Bay, Wis.
Shamrock—(b)—toilet — UNITED STATES ENVELOPE CO. (Morgan Envelope Co. Division), Springfield.
Shamrock Linen Laid — (w) — AMERICAN NEWS CO., New York.
Shawmut—(b) — ALBANY PERFORATED WRAPPING PAPER CO., Albany, New York.
Shawmut Bond—(w)—VON OLKERSNELL PAPER CO., Boston.
Shawnee—(b) — KANSAS CITY PAPER CO., Kansas City, Mo.
Shawmut Index—(b)—bristol—VON OLKER-SNELL PAPER CO., Boston.

Shawnee—(w) — flat — CENTRAL TOPEKA PAPER CO., Topeka, Kan.
Sheepskin—(b)—flat—J. W. BUTLER PAPER CO., Chicago.
Sheepskin Parchment—(w)—J. W. BUTLER PAPER CO., Chicago.
Sheffield — (b) — label — MINNEAPOLIS PAPER CO., Minneapolis.
Sheffield Bond—(w) — BRADNER SMITH & CO., Chicago.
Sheffield Ledger — (w)—WHITING-PATTERSON CO., Philadelphia.
Sheffield Parchment—(w) —MOSER PAPER CO., Chicago.
Shefield Plate—(b)—CANFIELD PAPER CO., New York.
Shellbark Wrapping — (b) — GRAHAM PAPER CO., St. Louis.
Sheik—(b)—toilet — ALBANY PERFORATED WRAPPING PAPER CO., Albany, New York.
Shepherd's Plaid—(w) — EATON, CRANE & PIKE CO., Pittsfield, Mass.
Sheraton—(b)—wove antique book— W. H. CLAFLIN & CO., Boston.
Sheridan—(w)—fine—W. E. WROE & CO., Chicago.
Sherman — (w)— flat—FOX RIVER PAPER CO., Appleton, Wis.
Sherman—(w)—flats and colored writings — SWIGART PAPER CO., Chicago.
Shetland Linen—(w)—POWERS PAPER COMPANY, Springfield, Mass.
Shield, Sword and Monogram R. S.—(w and b)—ROARING SPRING BLANK BOOK CO., Roaring Spring, Pa.
Shirley—(b) — white writing—B. F. BOND PAPER CO., Baltimore.
Shirley Linen—(b) — A. STORRS & BEMENT CO., Boston.
Shore—(b)—roofing — R. L. GREENE PAPER CO., Providence, R. I.
Shylock Bond—(w) — AMERICAN WRITING PAPER CO., Holyoke.
Siam—(b)—t o i l e t—WHITING-PATTERSON CO., New York.
Siberian Enamel—(b)—C. P. LESH PAPER CO., Indianapolis, Ind.
Signal Bond—(w)—FOX RIVER PAPER CO., Appleton, Wis.
Signet—(b)—roll toilet, manila and tissue—STONE & FORSYTH CO., Boston.
Signet Bond—(w)—paper—STANDARD PAPER CO., Tacoma, Wash.
Signet Bond—(w)—MILLERS FALLS PAPER CO., Millers Falls, Mass.
Silica — (b) — HY. LINDENMEYR & SONS, New York.
Silk Finish Opaque—(b)—M. F. and Super—CANFIELD PAPER CO., New York.
Silkote Dullo Enamel—(b)—book, white and India, regular coated surface—S. D. WARREN & CO., Boston.
Silk Parchment—(b) —tissue—GRAHAM PAPER CO., St. Louis.

Silk Surface — (b)—super book— TILESTON & HOLLINGSWORTH CO., Boston.
Silk Tissue — (b)—toilet — UNITED STATES ENVELOPE CO. (Plimpton Mfg. Co. Division), Hartford, Conn.
Silkirk Bond—(w)—COLUMBIA PAPER CO., Victoria, B. C.
Silver—(b)—fi b r e—CHATFIELD & WOODS CO., Cincinnati, Ohio.
Silverdale—(b)—toilet—OLD DOMINION PAPER CO., Norfolk, Va.
Silverdale — (b) —b o o k—PAPER MILLS CO., Chicago.
Silver Hemp — (b)—cordage—GRAHAM PAPER CO., St. Louis.
Silver Lake—(b)—M. F. book—F. A. FLINN, New York.
Silver Lake—(w)—POWERS PAPER COMPANY, Springfield, Mass.
Silver Lake Blanks—(b)—coated— BARDEEN PAPER CO., Otsego, Mich.
Silverlake Mills—(b)—fine folded— POWERS PAPER CO., Holyoke, Mass.
Silver Queen Onion Skin—(b)—OLD DOMINION PAPER CO., Norfolk, Va.
Silver State Ledger — (w)—THE PETERS PAPER CO., Denver, Col.
Silver Spring—(b)—ROLLAND PAPER CO., LTD., St. Jerome, Can.
Silver Super—(b)— book — PAPER MILLS CO., Chicago.
Silver Top—(b)—roofing — GRAHAM PAPER CO., St. Louis.
Silver Wedding Bristol—(b)—HARLEM CARD & PAPER CO., New York.
Simon Pure — (b) — J. C. B L A I R CO., Huntingdon, Pa.
Simpsic Linen — (w) — UNITED STATES ENVELOPE CO. (The White, Corbin & Co. Division), Rockville, Conn.
Sioux—(w)—bond—GRAHAM PAPER CO., St. Louis.
Sioux—(b)—ALBANY PERFORATED WRAPPING PAPER CO., Albany.
Sioux Bond — (w)—COOK-VIVIAN CO., Boston.
Sioux Linen — (w)—laid—MINNEAPOLIS PAPER CO., Minneapolis.
Sir Galahad — (b) — toilet—H. NORWOOD EWING CO., New York.
Sitka—(w)—AETNA PAPER CO., Dayton, Ohio.
Sitka Mills—(w)—C. P. LESH PAPER CO., Indianapolis, Ind.
Six Percent Bond—(w)—EASTERN MFG. CO., Bangor, Me.
Six Sixty—(b) — envelope—UNION CARD & PAPER CO., New York.
Sketch Book—(b) — drawing—GRAHAM PAPER CO., St. Louis.
Skyline Writing—(b) —WHITAKER PAPER CO., Cincinnati, Ohio.
Smooth Finish—(b)—DILL & COLLINS CO., Philadelphia.
Snapper—(b) —LOUISVILLE PAPER CO., Louisville, Ky.

Watermarks and Brands 731

Snipsic Linen—(w)—UNITED STATES ENVELOPE CO., Rockville, Conn.
Snoflake—(w and b)—specialties for dry goods purposes—THE SEINSHEIMER PAPER CO., Cincinnati.
Snoflake Bag—(b)—THE SEINSHEIMER PAPER CO., Cincinnati.
Snowbright—(b)—book and label—GRAHAM PAPER CO., St. Louis.
Snow Bond—(w)—O. H. ANDERSON & CO., New York.
Snow Bristol—(b)—F. A. FLINN, INC., New York.
Snow Case Lining—(b)—LOUISVILLE PAPER CO., Louisville, Ky.
Snow Drift — (b) — M. F. book—SOUTHERN PAPER CO., Richmond.
"Snowdrift" —(w)— bond — MOUNTAIN MILL PAPER CO., Lee, Mass.
Snowdrift—(w)—flat writing —MIDLAND PAPER CO., Chicago.
Snowdrift—(b)—translucent board—J. C. PARKER PAPER CO., Louisville, Ky.
Snowdrift—(b)—toilet—NORTHERN PAPER MILLS, Green Bay, Wis.
Snow-Drift—(b) — SOUTHERN PAPER COMPANY, Richmond, Va.
Snowdrift Featheredge—(w)—MOUNTAIN MILL PAPER CO., Lee, Mass.
Snow Drop—(b)—vegetable parchment—LOUISVILLE PAPER CO., Louisville, Ky.
Snow Flake—(b)—enameled book—J. W. BUTLER PAPER CO., Chicago.
Snowflake—(b)—tissue—SMITH PAPER CO., Lee, Mass.
Snow Flake — (b)—writing—J. H. WALKER, New York.
Snow Flake—(w and b)—writing—CUNNINGHAM, CURTISS & WELCH, Los Angeles.
Snow-Flake Fabric—(b)—wrapping—SEINSHEIMER PAPER CO., Cincinnati, O.
Snow Flake Ledger—(w)—McCLELLAN PAPER CO., Minneapolis.
Snow Flake Linen Bond—(w)—KINGSLEY PAPER CO., Cleveland.
Snow Flake Pure Linen—(w)—McCLELLAN PAPER CO., Minneapolis.
Snowhite Enameled—(b)—RICHMOND PAPER CO., Richmond, Va.
Snowhite Toilet—(b)—OLD DOMINION PAPER CO., Norfolk, Va.
Snow Waxed—(b)—LOUISVILLE PAPER CO., Louisville, Ky.
Snow White—(b)—ledger—STANDARD CORD & PAPER CO., New York.
Snow White—(b)—wedding bristol—MOUNTAIN MILL PAPER CO., Lee, Mass.
Snow White—S. & S. C.—(b)—MINNEAPOLIS PAPER CO., Minneneapolis, Minn.
Snowwhite—(w and b)—writings—THE PAPER MILLS CO., Chicago.

Snow White Bank—(b)—PARSONS TRADING CO., New York.
Snow-White Bond — (w) — THE NITSCHKE PAPER COMPANY, Columbus, Ohio.
Snow White Enamel—(b)—MEGARGEE-HARE PAPER CO., Philadelphia.
Snow-White Ledger—(w) — THE NITSCHKE PAPER COMPANY, Columbus, Ohio.
Snow-White Linen — (w) — THE NITSCHKE PAPER COMPANY, Columbus, Ohio.
Snow White Parchment—(b)—wrapping—OLD DOMINION PAPER CO., Norfolk, Va.
Snow-White Toilet—(b)—OLD DOMINION PAPER CO., Norfolk, Va.
Social Service—(w and b)—bond, writing, ledger—NEENAH PAPER CO., Neenah, Wis.
Social Service Ledger—(w)—NEENAH PAPER CO., Neenah, Wis.
Society Fabric—(b)—HAMPSHIRE PAPER CO., South Hadley Falls, Mass.
Solar Blanks — (b) — BRADNER SMITH & CO., Chicago.
Somerset—(b) — toilet — ALBANY PERFORATED WRAPPING PAPER CO., Albany, New York.
Somme Offset—(b)—book—BEECHER, PECK & LEWIS, Detroit, Mich.
Songo—(b) — HOLLINGSWORTH & WHITNEY CO., Boston.
Sorosis — (b) — toilet — UNITED STATES ENVELOPE CO. (Morgan Envelope Co. Division), Springfield.
Sorrento—(b)—colored laid writing—O. F. H. WARNER & CO., Baltimore.
Southdown Bond — (w)—WORTHY PAPER CO., Mittineague, Mass.
Southern Bond—(w)—O. F. H. WARNER & CO., Baltimore.
Southern Bond — (w)—SOUTHERN PAPER COMPANY, Richmond, Va.
Southern Cross Bond — (w) — TAYLOR-BURT CO., Holyoke.
Southern Cross Cover — (b) — ADVERTISERS PAPER MILLS, Holyoke.
Southern Cross Envelope — (w)—envelope paper—TAYLOR-LOGAN CO., PAPERMAKERS, Holyoke, Mass.
Southern Linen Vellum — (w) — SOUTHWORTH CO., Mittineague, Mass.
Southern Star—(b)—toilet—NORTHERN PAPER MILLS, Green Bay, Wis.
Southland Bond—(b)—CASKIE-DILLARD CO., INC., Lynchburg, Va.
Southwick Writing — (b)—MACKELLIOTT PAPER CO., St. Louis.
Southworth Ledger — (w)—SOUTHWORTH CO., Mittineague, Mass.
Southworth No. 1 Bond — (w) — SOUTHWORTH CO., Mittineague, Mass.

Southworth Linen Vellum—(w)—SOUTHWORTH CO., Mittineague, Mass.
Souvenir—(b) — post card—UNION CARD & PAPER CO., New York.
Souvenir Bond U. S. A. — (w)—EATON, CRANE & PIKE CO., Pittsfield, Mass.
Souvenir Plate — (b) — JOHN CARTER & CO., Boston.
Sovereign—(b) — coated cover—PAPER MILLS CO., Chicago.
Sovereign Bond —(w)— AMERICAN WRITING PAPER CO., Holyoke.
Sovereign Bristol — (b) — COOK-VIVIAN CO., Boston.
Sovereign Linen Ledger—(w)—C. W. WILLIAMS & CO., New York.
Sovereign Translucents — (b) — WILKINSON BROS. & CO., INC., Philadelphia.
Spanish Bond — (w)—PLYMOUTH PAPER CO., Holyoke, Mass.
Sparta — (b) — tag board — J. C. PARKER PAPER CO., Louisville, Ky.
Sparta—(b) — envelope — WHITING-PATTERSON CO., Philadelphia.
Sparta Document — (b)—manila—BRADNER SMITH & CO., Chicago.
Sparta Ledger — (w) — MACK-ELLIOTT PAPER CO., St. Louis.
Spartan—(b)—cover—JUDD PAPER CO., Holyoke, Mass.
Spartan — (w) — POWERS PAPER COMPANY, Springfield, Mass.
Spartan—(b)—cover—JUDD PAPER CO., Holyoke, Mass.
Spartan—(b)—kraft—HAGEN PAPER CO., St. Louis.
Spartan—(w and b)—flat—JUDD PAPER CO., Holyoke, Mass.
Spartan—(b)—super-calendered book—WHITAKER PAPER CO., Cincinnati.
Spartan Bond — (w)—AMERICAN WRITING PAPER CO., Holyoke.
Spartan Colored Bristol — (b) — HENRY LINDENMEYR & SONS, N. Y.
Spartan Mills — (b)—A. STORRS & BEMENT CO., Boston.
Special Check Wove—(b)—colored writing—CONROW BROS., New York.
Special No. 1 Pay Envelope—(b)—EASTERN MFG. CO., Bangor, Me.
Special—(b)—white gummed—BRADNER SMITH & CO., Chicago.
Special—(b)—M. F. book, news and onion skin—J. W. BUTLER PAPER CO., Chicago.
Special—(b)—blotting — RICHMOND PAPER MANUFACTURING CO., Richmond, Va.
Special M. G.—(b)—FOX PAPER CO., Lockland, Ohio.
Special No. 1 Writing—(b)—EASTERN MFG. CO., Bangor, Me.
Special—(w)—writing—MEGARGEE-HARE PAPER CO., Philadelphia.
Special Antique Wove—(b)—HY. LINDENMEYR & SONS, New York.

Special Blank—(b)—A. STORRS & BEMENT CO., Boston.
Special Bond—(b)—PAUL R. VERNON & CO., New York.
Special Bond — (w) — white and colored — R. C. KASTNER PAPER CO., New York.
Special Bristol — (b) — BRADNER SMITH & CO., Chicago.
Special Bristol—(b)—W. G. WILLMANN, New York.
Special Drive—(b)—envelopes—R. L. GREENE PAPER CO., Providence, R. I.
Special Drive — (b) — flat — R. L. GREENE PAPER CO., Providence, Rhode Island.
Special Fibre—(b)—A. M. EATON, Waltham and Boston, Mass.
Special Gummed Paper — (b) — BRADNER SMITH & CO., Chicago.
Special Half-Tone Book—(b)—MEGARGEE-HARE PAPER CO., Philadelphia.
Special Ledger—(w) — AMERICAN WRITING PAPER CO., Holyoke.
Special Linen—(b)—MEGARGEE-HARE PAPER CO., Philadelphia.
Special Linen Laid—(b)—MEGARGEE-HARE PAPER CO., Philadelphia.
Special Linen Ledger—(w)—WESTERN PENNA. PAPER CO., Pittsburg.
Special Linen Ledger — (w) — STRATHMORE PAPER CO., Mittineague, Mass.
Special Litho Bond — (b) — THE GUGLER LITHOGRAPHIC CO., Milwaukee, Wis.
Special Machine Finish Book — (b)—MEGARGEE-HARE PAPER CO., Philadelphia.
Special Mailing—(b) — mailing and cover — GRAHAM PAPER CO., St. Louis.
Special Manila Tag—(b)—THE ALLING & CORY CO., Rochester, N. Y.
Special Onion Skin—(b)—ESLEECK MFG. CO., Turners Falls, Mass.
Special Pay Envelope—(b)—EASTERN MFG. CO., Bangor, Me.
Special Super-Calendered Book—(b)—MEGARGEE-HARE PAPER CO., Philadelphia.
Special Wove Check—(b)—flat writing—CONROW BROS., New York.
Special Writing — (b)—MERRIAM PAPER CO., New York.
Special Pay Bond—(b)—EASTERN MFG. CO., Bangor, Me.
Speedway Bond — (b)—DIEM & WING PAPER CO., Cincinnati, O.
Speedwell —(b)— bond — PENINSULAR PAPER CO., Ypsilanti, Mich.
Sphinx—(b)—roll toilet—CHATFIELD & WOODS CO., Cincinnati, Ohio.
Sphinx—(b)—toilet—NORTHERN PAPER MILLS, Green Bay, Wis.
Sphinx—(w)—chemical—J. E. LINDE PAPER CO., New York.

Sphinx Bond—(w) — linen plated—CHEMICAL PAPER MFG. CO., Holyoke, Mass.
Sphinx Cover and Bristol—(b)—HY. LINDENMEYR & SONS, New York.
Spinning Wheel—(b)—linen—J. C. BLAIR CO., Huntingdon, Pa.
Springdale—(b)—book — GRAHAM PAPER CO., St. Louis.
Springfield—(b)—book — GRAHAM PAPER CO., St. Louis.
Springfield Bond — (w)—UNITED STATES ENVELOPE CO., Holyoke.
Springfield Oval — (b) — toilet—UNITED STATES ENVELOPE CO. (Morgan Envelope Co. Division), Springfield, Mass.
Springfield S. & S. C.—(b)—book—SPRINGFIELD PAPER & SUPPLY CO., Springfield, Mo.
Spring Grove Mills—(w) — P. H. GLATFELTER CO., Spring Forge, Pa.
Spring Lake—(b)—ruled — W. G. WILLMANN, New York.
Spring Lake Mills — (w)—W. G. WILLMANN, New York.
Springside Blanks—(b)—BUNTIN, GILLIES & CO., Hamilton, Can.
Spruce—(b)—wrapping — GRAHAM PAPER CO., St. Louis.
Spruce Manila Tag—(b)—PULP & PAPER TRADING CO., New York.
Spruce Mills—(w) — W. G. WILLMANN, New York.
Squadron—(b)—wrapping—GRAHAM PAPER CO., St. Louis.
Square Deal Bond—(w)—TAYLOR-LOGAN CO., PAPERMAKERS, Holyoke.
Square Deal Covers—(b)—ADVERTISERS PAPER MILLS, Holyoke.
Stag Bond—(w)—BLAKE, McFALL CO., Portland, Ore.
Stag Bristol—(b)—B R A D N E R SMITH & CO., Chicago.
Stalwart Bond—(w)—E A T O N, CRANE & PIKE CO., Pittsfield, Mass.
Standard—(b)—blotting—U N I O N CARD & PAPER CO., New York.
Standard—(b)—BUNTIN, GILLIES & CO., Hamilton, Canada.
Standard — (b) — cover— BEECHER, PECK & LEWIS, Detroit, Mich.
Standard—(b)—toilet—A L B A N Y PERFORATED WRAPPING PAPER CO., Albany, N. Y.
Standard—(b)— cover — AMERICAN WRITING PAPER CO., Holyoke, Mass.
Standard—(b)—back stay—S E I N-SHEIMER PAPER CO., Cincinnati.
Standard—(b)— manila — ANDREW PAPER CO., Boston.
Standard—(b)—enameled book and tinted cardboard—J. W. BUTLER PAPER CO., Chicago.
Standard — (b) — toilet — R. L. GREENE PAPER CO., Providence, R. I.
Standard—(b)—colored laid—J. C. PARKER PAPER CO., Louisville, Ky.
Standard—(w)—ruled and flat—H. S. CROCKER CO., San Francisco.
Standard—(w)—bond—L A S H E R & LATHROP, New York.
Standard—(b)—white litho. coated one side—W. H. CLAFLIN & CO., Boston.
Standard—(w and b)—blotting and matrix—STANDARD PAPER MANUFACTURING CO., Richmond, Va.
Standard—(b)—M. F. book—CHATFIELD & WOODS CO., Cincinnati, O.
Standard Banner — (w) — ledger — BOORUM & PEASE CO., New York.
Standard Blotting—(w)—fancy colors—SWIGART PAPER CO., Chicago.
Standard Bond — (w) — AMERICAN WRITING PAPER CO., Holyoke, Mass.
Standard Bristol—(b)—H U D S O N VALLEY PAPER CO., Albany, N. Y.
Standard Bristol—(b)—bristol board —PLYMOUTH PAPER CO., Holyoke.
Standard Coated Blank—(b)—HOLYOKE CARD & PAPER CO., Holyoke, Mass.
Standard Duane Linen—(w)—HAMMERMILL PAPER CO., Erie, Pa.
Standard Extra Fine—(w)—WM. G. JOHNSTON & CO., Pittsburgh, Pa.
Standard Extra Fine Flats—(w)—BRADNER SMITH & CO., Chicago.
Standard Half-tone Writing—(b) WORTHY PAPER CO., Mittineague, Mass.
Standard Index Bristol—(b)—CAREW MANUFACTURING CO., South Hadley Falls, Mass.
Standard Ledger—(w)—J. W. BUTLER PAPER CO., Chicago.
Standard Ledger — (w) — BOORUM & PEASE CO., New York.
Standard Ledger—(w)—THE ALLING & CORY CO., Rochester, N. Y.
Standard Linen — (w) — WHITING PAPER CO., Holyoke, Mass.
Standard Linen—(w)—BERLIN & JONES ENVELOPE CO., New York.
Standard Linen—(w)—U N I T E D STATES ENVELOPE CO. (Morgan Envelope Co. Div.), Springfield, Mass.
Standard Linen Bond — (w) — STANDARD PAPER CO., Tacoma.
Standard Mills — (b) — colored — STANDARD CARD & PAPER CO., New York.
Standard Mills—(w)—J. W. BUTLER PAPER CO., Chicago.
Standard Mills—(w)—flat—J. W. BUTLER PAPER CO., Chicago.
Standard Mimeograph—(b)—linen —RIEGEL & CO., INC., Philadelphia.
Standard New York Ledger—(w) —VERNON BROS. & CO., New York.
Standard of America — (w) — EATON, CRANE & PIKE CO., Pittsfield, Mass.
Standard Offset—(b)—P A P E R MILLS CO., Chicago.

Standard Pasted Bristol—(b)—JOHN CARTER & CO., Boston.
Standard Plated Bristol—(b)—A. STORRS & BEMENT CO., Boston.
Standard Pure Linen—(w)—ROLLAND PAPER CO., St. Jerome, Can.
Standard School Paper—(w)—WHITE & WYCKOFF MFG. CO., Holyoke, Mass.
Standard School Paper—(w)—THE McNEIL CO., Phoenix, Ariz.
Standard Super Cover—(b)—HARLEM CARD & PAPER CO., New York.
Standard Wove—(b)—GEO. B. HURD & CO., New York.
Standish — (b) — cover — ARNOLD-ROBERTS CO., Boston.
Standish Deckle Edge—(b)—book —ARNOLD-ROBERTS CO., Boston.
Standish Linen—(w)—(laid)—E. B. EDDY CO., Hull, Canada.
Stanhope Art Cover—(b)—CAREW MANUFACTURING CO., South Hadley Falls, Mass.
Stanton—(b)—bristol—RIEGEL & CO., INC., Philadelphia.
Staple Bond—(w)—WORTHY PAPER CO., Mittineague, Mass.
Star—(b)—toilet—STONE & FORSYTH CO., Boston.
Star—(b)—news—GRAHAM PAPER CO., St. Louis.
Star—(b)—manila tag—UNION CARD & PAPER CO., New York.
Star—(b)—toilet—ALBANY PERFORATED WRAPPING PAPER CO., Albany, N. Y.
Star—(b)—m. f. and s. & s. c. book—THE ALLING & CORY CO., Rochester.
Star—(b)—machine-finished book—J. W. BUTLER PAPER CO., Chicago.
Star—(b)—black pattern, rope patterns, manifold linen, tissues, bristol, onion skin, manifold and typewriter—C. H. DEXTER & SONS, INC., Windsor Locks, Conn.
Star—(b)—ribbon paper—WILSON & TOWNE PAPER CO., New York.
Star—(b)—blotting—RICHMOND PAPER MANUFACTURING CO., Richmond, Va.
Star—(b)—manifold—J. W. BUTLER PAPER CO., Chicago.
Star—(b)—toilet—E. L. GREENE PAPER CO., Providence, R. I.
Star — (b) — No. 2 fine — WRIGHT, BARRETT & STILWELL CO., St. Paul, Minn.
Star—(b)—toilet—GEO. T. JOHNSON CO., Boston.
Starbee—(b)—news—GRAHAM PAPER CO., St. Louis.
Star Blanks—(b)—WABASH COATING MILLS, Wabash, Ind.
Star Bond—(w)—FOX RIVER PAPER CO., Appleton, Wis.
Star Bristol—(b)—HUDSON VALLEY PAPER CO., Albany, N. Y.
Star Bristol—(b)—BRADNER SMITH & CO., Chicago.

Star C.—(b)—manila and fibre—CHATFIELD PAPER CO., New Haven, Conn.
Star Document — (b) — manila — BRADNER SMITH & CO., Chicago.
Star Drawing Roll—(b)—manila—BRADNER SMITH & CO., Chicago.
Star Drug Bond—(b)—wrapping—R. A. CAUTHORNE PAPER CO., Richmond, Va.
Star Eggshell Book—(b)—ALLING & CORY CO., Rochester.
Star Jute—(b)—WHITAKER PAPER CO., Cincinnati, Ohio.
Star Jute Manila—(b)—BRADNER SMITH & CO., Chicago.
Star Linen—(w)—F. A. FLINN, INC., New York.
Star Linen—(w)—UNITED STATES ENVELOPE CO., Holyoke, Mass.
Star Linen—(w)—WESTERN PENNA. PAPER CO., Pittsburgh, Pa.
Star Linen—(w)—MILLER & WRIGHT PAPER CO., New York.
Star Litho. Blanks—(b)—HARLEM CARD & PAPER CO., New York.
Star M. F. Book—(b)—ALLING & CORY CO., Rochester.
Star Manifold Linen—(b)—C. H. DEXTER & SONS, INC., Windsor Locks, Conn.
Star Manila—(b)—BRADNER SMITH & CO., Chicago.
Star Manila — (b) — RACQUETTE RIVER PAPER CO., Potsdam, N. Y.
Star Manila Tag—(b)—UNION CARD & PAPER CO., New York.
Star Manuscript Cover—(b)—C. H. DEXTER & SONS, INC., Windsor Locks, Conn.
Star Mills—(b)—silver, white and colored tissues and toilet—C. H. DEXTER & SONS, INC., Windsor Locks, Conn.
Star Mills—(w)—CARTER, RICE & CARPENTER PAPER CO., Omaha.
Star M Pure Fibre—(b)—MEGARGEE-HARE PAPER CO., Philadelphia.
Star S. & S. C. Book—(b)—ALLING & CORY CO., Rochester.
Stark—(b)—toilet—UNITED STATES ENVELOPE CO. (Morgan Envelope Co. Division), Springfield, Mass.
State—(b)—bristol—RIEGEL & CO., INC., Philadelphia.
State Bank Bond—(w)—C. P. LESH PAPER CO., Indianapolis, Ind.
State Bond—(w)—WHITING PAPER CO., Holyoke, Mass.
State Bristol—(b)—HARLEM CARD & PAPER CO., New York.
State Map — (b) — bond — UNION CARD & PAPER CO., New York.
State Mills—(w)—flat—J. E. LINDE PAPER CO., New York.
State Record Ledger—(w)—GRAHAM PAPER CO., St. Louis.
Stationers' Bond—(w)—HAMMERMILL PAPER CO., Erie, Pa.

Stationers' Linen Ledger—(w)—AMERICAN WRITING PAPER CO., Holyoke, Mass.
Stationers' Superfine Visiting Cards—(b)—BRADNER SMITH & CO., Chicago.
Statistic Linen Ledger—(w)—VON OLKER-SNELL PAPER CO., Boston.
Statute Bond—(w)—AMERICAN WRITING PAPER CO., Holyoke, Mass.
Steel Engravers—(b)—cardboard—J. W. BUTLER PAPER CO., Chicago.
Steel Plate Bristol—(b)—BRADNER SMITH & CO., Chicago.
Steel Plate Coated Paper—(b)—BRADNER SMITH & CO., Chicago.
Stella Mills Writing—(b)—HENRY LINDENMEYR & SONS, New York.
Steno.—(b)—manifold—HAGEN PAPER CO., St. Louis.
Sterling — (b) — book—LOUISVILLE PAPER CO., Louisville, Ky.
Sterling—(b)—grass-bleached tissue—SMITH PAPER CO., Lee, Mass.
Sterling—(b)—manila—CHASE BROS., Haverhill, Mass.
Sterling—(b)—SOUTHERN PAPER COMPANY, Richmond, Va.
Sterling—(b)—news—GRAHAM PAPER CO., St. Louis.
Sterling—(w)—blotting—STANDARD PAPER MANUFACTURING CO., Richmond, Va.
Sterling—(b)—toilet—NORTHERN PAPER MILLS, Green Bay, Wis.
Sterling—(w)—UNITED STATES ENVELOPE CO., Springfield, Mass.
"Sterling"—(w)—SAUGERTIES MFG. CO., Saugerties, N. Y.
Sterling—(b)—white wove—MILLER & WRIGHT PAPER CO., New York.
Sterling Enamel—(b)—WEST VIRGINIA PULP & PAPER CO., New York.
Sterling Blotting—(b)—SWIGART PAPER CO., Chicago.
Sterling Bond—(w)—WORTHY PAPER CO., Mittineague, Mass.
Sterling Bond—(w)—WRIGHT, BARRETT & STILWELL CO., St. Paul, Minn.
Sterling Bristol—(b)—W. G. WILLMANN, New York.
Sterling Bristol—(b)—MINNEAPOLIS PAPER CO., Minneapolis, Minn.
Sterling Cover—(b)—WORTHY PAPER CO., Mittineague, Mass.
Sterling Cover Craft—(b)—BRADNER SMITH & CO., Chicago.
Sterling Deckle Edge—(b)—book—LASHER & LATHROP, Philadelphia.
Sterling Deckle Edge — (w) — WORTHY PAPER CO., Mittineague, Mass.
Sterling Enamel — (b) — book — BEECHER, PECK & LEWIS, Detroit, Mich.
Sterling Half-Tone Writing—(b)—WORTHY PAPER CO., Mittineague, Mass.

Sterling Japanese Parchment—(b)—WORTHY PAPER CO., Mittineague, Mass.
Sterling Kraft—(b)—CHATFIELD & WOODS CO., Cincinnati, Ohio.
Sterling Ledger—(w)—WORTHY PAPER CO., Mittineague, Mass.
Sterling Linen—(w)—WORTHY PAPER CO., Mittineague, Mass.
Sterling Linen — (w) — PARSONS TRADING CO., New York.
Sterling Linen Ledger—(w)—WHITING PAPER CO., Holyoke, Mass.
Sterling Manifold—(b)—bond and linen—RIEGEL & CO., INC., Philadelphia.
Sterling Paper—(w)—WORTHY PAPER CO., Mittineague, Mass.
Sterling Superfine—(w)—WORTHY PAPER CO., Mittineague, Mass.
Sterling Superfine—(w)—writing—RIEGEL & CO., INC., Philadelphia.
Stockbridge—(b)—book and onion skin—JUDD PAPER CO., Holyoke.
Stockbridge Linen—(w)—AMERICAN WRITING PAPER CO., Holyoke.
Stock Exchange Bond—(w)—F. W. ANDERSON & CO., New York.
Stonewall—(b)—parchment wrapping—OLD DOMINION PAPER CO., Norfolk, Va.
Stonewall — (w and b) — writing, ledger, bond—NEENAH PAPER CO., Neenah, Wis.
Stonewall Shipping Tags—(b)—OLD DOMINION PAPER CO., Norfolk, Va.
Storm King Bond—(w)—CORNWALL PAPER MFG. CO., Cornwall-on-Hudson, N. Y.
Stormway—(b)—white book—J. C. PARKER PAPER CO., Louisville, Ky.
Stradivari — (b) — wrapping — W. R. GRACE & CO., New York.
Straight Cut—(b)—toilet—ALBANY PERFORATED WRAPPING PAPER CO., Albany, N. Y.
Strand Linen Cream Laid—(b)—HY. LINDENMEYR & SONS, New York.
Stratfield Bond—(w)—ALEXANDER HOLDEN PAPER CO., New York.
Stratford—(w)—STRATHMORE PAPER CO., Mittineague, Mass.
Stratford Bond—(w)—HAMPSHIRE PAPER CO., South Hadley Falls, Mass.
Stratford Linen—(w)—GARRETT-BUCHANAN CO., Philadelphia.
Stratford White Wove—(b)—writing—MILLER & WRIGHT PAPER CO., New York.
Stratford Writings—(b)—bond and linen mounts—STRATHMORE PAPER CO., Mittineague, Mass.
Stratford Writings—(b)—STRATHMORE PAPER CO., Mittineague, Mass.

Strathearn—(b)—art coated—BUNTIN, GILLIES & CO., LTD., Hamilton, Canada.
Strathearn Art Book— (b) —BUNTIN GILLIES & CO., LTD., Hamilton, Ontario, Can.
Strathlaid Booklet Covers—(b)—STRATHMORE PAPER CO., Mittineague, Mass.
Strathmore—(w)—bond, book, cover and drawing deed parchment—STRATHMORE PAPER CO., Mittineague, Mass.
Strathmore—(b)—bristols, announcements, typewriter, covers, marble and ripple mounts, parchment, artists' papers and boards—STRATHMORE PAPER CO., Mittineague, Mass.
Strathmore Bond—(w)—STRATHMORE PAPER CO., Mittineague, Mass.
Strathmore Booklet Papers—(b)—book and cover—STRATHMORE PAPER CO., Mittineague, Mass.
Strathmore Brochure — (b) — STRATHMORE PAPER CO., Mittineague, Mass.
Strathmore Cerulean—(b)—wedding and stationery papers and bristol board—STRATHMORE PAPER CO., Mittineague, Mass.
Strathmore Chameleon Cover—(b) —STRATHMORE PAPER CO., Mittineague, Mass.
Strathmore Deckle-Edge — (w)— book — STRATHMORE PAPER CO., Mittineague, Mass.
Strathmore De Luxe—(b)—book, cover, announcements and writing—STRATHMORE PAPER CO., Mittineague, Mass.
Strathmore Japan U. S. A.—(w)— STRATHMORE PAPER CO., Mittineague, Mass.
Strathmore Parchment — (w) — STRATHMORE PAPER CO., Mittineague, Mass.
Strathmore U. S. A. — (w) — STRATHMORE PAPER CO., Mittineague, Mass.
Strong Fibre — (w)—ledger—F. W. ANDERSON & CO., New York.
Strong Fold Enameled Book—(b) ALLING & CORY CO., Rochester.
Stronghold Linen Ledger—(w)— CLEMENT & STOCKWELL, INC., New York.
St. Andrews — (b) —cover—PAPER MILLS CO., Chicago.
St. Bernard Bond—(b)—RICHMOND PAPER CO., Richmond, Va.
St. Charles — (b) — bristol—J. W. BUTLER PAPER CO., Chicago.
St. Charles — (w) — flat—J. W. BUTLER PAPER CO., Chicago.
St. Clair—(b) — book—GRAHAM PAPER CO., St. Louis.
St. Clair—(b)—BLADE PRINTING & PAPER CO., Toledo, Ohio.
St. Claire—(w)—bond—PENINSULAR PAPER CO., Ypsilanti, Mich.
St. Clair Mills — (w)—CLEVELAND PAPER MANUFACTURING CO., Cleveland, Ohio.
St. Denis—(b)—toilet—LOUISVILLE PAPER CO., Louisville, Ky.
St. Denis — (b) — toilet—ALBANY PERFORATED WRAPPING PAPER CO., Albany, N. Y.
St. Elmo—(b)—MILLER & WRIGHT PAPER CO., New York.
St. George — (w) — superfine—EAU CLAIRE BOOK AND STATIONERY CO., Eau Claire, Wis.
St. Helene — (b) — toilet—H. M. RICHMOND PAPER CO., Seattle.
St. Ives—(w)—linen ledger—LOUISVILLE PAPER CO., Louisville, Ky.
St. Ives Linen Ledger — (w) — LOUISVILLE PAPER CO., Louisville, Ky.
St. James — (b) — toilet—ALBANY PERFORATED WRAPPING PAPER CO., Albany, New York.
St. James Antique Book—(b)—HY. LINDENMEYR & SONS, New York.
St. Julian — (b) — toilet—UNITED STATES ENVELOPE CO., (Morgan Envelope Co. Division), Springfield.
St. Lawrence—(b)—BUNTIN, GILLIES & CO., Hamilton, Canada.
St. Nicholas Ledger — (w) — WHITAKER PAPER CO., Cincinnati.
St. Nicholas Linen Bond — (w)— BAY STATE PAPER CO., Boston.
St. Nicholas Linen — (w)—WHITAKER PAPER CO., Cincinnati, Ohio, and BAY STATE PAPER CO., Boston.
St. Quintin—(b)—LOUISVILLE PAPER CO., Louisville, Ky.
St. Regis—(b)—cut cards—GRAHAM PAPER CO., St. Louis.
St. Regis — (b) — roll toilet—CHATFIELD & WOODS CO., Cincinnati, O.
Studio — (w and b)—bond, linen, cover, deckle-edge, bristol, envelopes, blanks, parchment writing, blotting, coated manila — MEGARGEE-HARE PAPER CO., Philadelphia.
Submarine Fibre—(b)—D. F. butchers — OLD DOMINION PAPER CO., Norfolk, Va.
Suburban—(w)—bond—GRAHAM PAPER CO., St. Louis.
Suburban Bond—BURGESS & WRAY PAPER CO., Chicago.
Success—(b) — LOUISVILLE PAPER CO., Louisville, Ky.
Success—(w and b)—writing, ledger, bond—NEENAH PAPER CO., Neenah, Wis.
Success Ledger — (w)—HUDSON VALLEY PAPER CO., Albany, N. Y.
Suede Finish—(w and b)—DILL & COLLINS CO., Philadelphia.
Suede Finish—(w)—DILL & COLLINS CO., Philadelphia.

Suffolk—(b) — ALBANY PERFORATED WRAPPING PAPER CO., Albany, New York.
Suitsall—(b)—toilet—GEO. T. JOHNSON CO., Boston.
Sulgrave—(b) — J. C. BLAIR CO., Huntingdon, Pa.
Sultag—(b)—tag board—HAGEN PAPER CO., St. Louis.
Sultan—(b)—cover — NIAGARA PAPER MILLS, Lockport, New York.
Sultan—(b)—writing—JUDD PAPER CO., Holyoke, Mass.
Summit— (b) — blanks—CHATFIELD FIELD & WOODS CO., Cincinnati.
Summit—(b)—writing—JUDD PAPER CO., Holyoke, Mass.
Summit Bond—(b)—ELSINORE PAPER CO., New York.
Summit Linen—(b)—ELSINORE PAPER CO., New York.
Sumurun—(b)—toilet—H. NORWOOD EWING, New York.
Sunburst Cover—(b) — HAMPDEN GLAZED PAPER & CARD CO., Holyoke, Mass.
Sundale—(w) — writing — UNION CARD & PAPER CO., New York.
Sunflower—(b)—ALBANY PERFORATED WRAPPING PAPER CO., Albany, New York.
Sunlight—(b)—book—GRAHAM PAPER CO., St. Louis.
Sunnyside Bond—(w) —KINLEITH PAPER CO., Canada.
Sun Proof—(b)—poster — BRADNER SMITH & CO., Chicago.
Sun Proof — (b) — poster—MINNEAPOLIS PAPER CO., Minneapolis.
Sunrise—(b)—cardboards and cards—GRAHAM PAPER CO., St. Louis.
Sunrise—(b)—ALEX. McARTHUR & CO., LTD., Montreal, Canada.
Sunrise—(w)—flats—MOSER PAPER CO., Chicago.
Sunrise—(b)—colored super — PAUL E. VERNON & CO., New York.
Sunrise Bond—(w)—THE ALLING & CORY CO., Rochester, New York.
Sunset—(b)—ruled headings and envelope—UNION CARD & PAPER CO., New York.
Sunset — (b) — toilet — STONE & FORSYTH, Boston.
Sunset Wedding Bristol — (b) — BEECHER, PECK & LEWIS, Detroit, Mich.
Sunshine Mills — (w) — S. BACHMANN & CO., Chicago.
Supatone — (b) — uncoated book—WANAQUE RIVER PAPER CO., Wanaque, N. J.
Superb—(b)—DILL & COLLINS CO., Philadelphia.
Superba—(b) — enamel book—J. C PARKER PAPER CO., Louisville, Ky.
Superba—(b)—writing—M. J. EARLE, Reading, Pa.
Superb Bond — (w) — WESTERN PENNA. PAPER CO., Pittsburg, Pa.

Superb Linen—(b) — typewriter — EATON, CRANE & PIKE CO., Pittsfield, Mass.
Superfine—(b)—blotting — EATON, DIKEMAN & CO., Lee, Mass.
Superfine—(b)—cover—UNION CARD & PAPER CO., New York.
Superfine—(b)—flats — LOUISVILLE PAPER CO., Louisville, Ky.
Superfine—(w and b) — GEO. B. HURD & CO., New York.
Superfine—(b) — blotting — RICHMOND PAPER MANUFACTURING CO., Richmond, Va.
Superfine—(b)—EATON, CRANE & PIKE CO., Pittsfield, Mass.
Superfine—(b) — wedding bristol—BRADNER SMITH & CO., Chicago.
Superfine Coated Blank — (b)—HOLYOKE CARD & PAPER CO., Holyoke, Mass.
Superfine Coated Book—(b)—DILL & COLLINS CO., Philadelphia.
Superfine Coated Book — (b) — (glossy surface)—S. D. WARREN & CO., Boston.
Superfine Half Tone—(b)—THOS. W. PRICE CO., Philadelphia.
Superfine Linen Record — (w)—ROLLAND PAPER CO., St. Jerome, Canada.
Superior—(b)—enameled book—JUDD PAPER CO., Holyoke, Mass.
Superior—(b)—ledger — RIEGEL & CO., INC., Philadelphia.
Superior — (b) — linen — MINNEAPOLIS PAPER CO., Minneapolis.
Superior—(b)—writing — GRAHAM PAPER CO., St. Louis.
Superior — (b) — colored bristol—DONALDSON PAPER CO., Harrisburg, Pa.
Superior—(b) — box boards, blanks, postal card, translucent, folding bristol and card boards—NIAGARA COATED PAPER COMPANY, Niagara Falls, New York.
Superior—(b)—typewriter — CAREW MANUFACTURING CO., South Hadley Falls, Mass.
Superior—(w)—bond—LESLIE-DONAHOWER CO., St. Paul.
Superior—(b)—bristol — MEGARGEE-HARE PAPER CO., Philadelphia.
Superior—(b) — cover and express wrapping—J. W. BUTLER PAPER CO., Chicago.
Superior Blanks — (b) — HARLEM CARD & PAPER CO., New York.
Superior Bond — (w) — DAVID L. ENGLE, New York.
Superior Bond—(w)—MIDLAND PAPER CO., Chicago.
Superior Bristol — (b) — BEECHER, PECK & LEWIS, Detroit, Mich.
Superior Bristol—(b)—bristol board —PLYMOUTH PAPER CO., Holyoke.
Superior Bristol — (b) — DIEM & WING PAPER CO., Cincinnati, Ohio.

Superior Colored S. & S. C.—(b)—ALLING & CORY CO., Rochester.
Superior Colored S. & S. C. Book—(b) — THE ALLING & CORY CO., Rochester, New York.
Superior Colored Superfine—(b)—ALLING & CORY CO., Rochester.
Superior Copyings — (b) — SMITH PAPER CO., Lawrence, Mass.
Superior Express—(b)—wrapping—GRAHAM PAPER CO., St. Louis.
Superior Halftone—(b) — writing—RIEGEL & CO., INC., Philadelphia.
Superior Index Bristol—(b)—OLD DOMINION PAPER CO., Norfolk, Va.
Superior Ledger—(b) — PAUL E. VERNON & CO., New York.
Superior Manifold — (b) — F. A. FLINN, INC., New York.
Superior Manifold—(b)—ESLEECK MFG. CO., Turners Falls, Mass.
Superior Manuscript Cover—(b)—CAREW MFG. CO., South Hadley Falls, Mass.
Superior Mills — (b) — writing — BEECHER, PECK & LEWIS, Detroit, Mich.
Superior Mills—(w)—writing—THE ALLING & CORY CO., Rochester.
Superior Mills — (b) — C. P. LESH PAPER CO., Indianapolis.
Superior Mills—(w) — loft dried—LOUISVILLE PAPER CO., Louisville.
Superior Pasted Bristol — (b)—C A R E W MANUFACTURING CO., South Hadley Falls, Mass.
Superior Powder Papers — (b)—SABIN ROBBINS PAPER CO., Middletown, Ohio.
Superior Print — (b)—BRADNER SMITH & CO., Chicago.
Superior Quality — (b)—UNITED STATES ENVELOPE CO. (Whitcomb Envelope Co. Division), Worcester, Mass.
Superior S. & S. C. Book—(b)—THE ALLING & CORY CO., Rochester, New York.
Superior Sign Card — (b)—SABIN ROBBINS PAPER CO., Middletown, Ohio.
Superior Slip Sheeting—(b)—HY. LINDENMEYR & SONS, New York.
Superior Superfine — (b) — colored writing—THE ALLING & CORY CO., Rochester, N. Y.
Superior Tag—(b)—F. A. FLINN, INC., New York.
Superior Typewriter Papers—(b)—CAREW MFG. CO., South Hadley Falls, Mass.
Super Kraft—(b)—COLUMBIA PAPER BAG CO., New York.
Superlative—(b)—book — GRAHAM PAPER CO., St. Louis.
Supernamel—(b)—book — THE PAPER MILLS CO., Chicago.
Super Wax—(b)—wrapping—WHITING-PATTERSON CO., New York.

Supreme—(b)—double coated book—JUDD PAPER CO., Holyoke, Mass.
Supreme — (b) — offset — MINNEAPOLIS PAPER CO., Minneapolis, Minn.
Supreme Bond—(w)—CLEMENT & STOCKWELL, INC., New York.
Supreme Bristol — (b) — HARLEM CARD & PAPER CO., New York.
Supremus Linen Ledger — (w)—CROCKER-McELWAIN CO., Holyoke.
Supreme Linen Ledger — (w) —CLEMENT & STOCKWELL, INC., New York.
Surah Silk—(b)—bond—J. C. BLAIR CO., Huntingdon, Pa.
Surety Bond — (w)—CROCKER-McELWAIN CO., Holyoke, Mass.
Surety—(b)—PEERLESS MFG. CO., Norristown, Pa.
Surety Offset—(b)—book—MILLER & WRIGHT PAPER CO., New York.
Surety Bond — (w) — ALEXANDER HOLDEN PAPER CO., New York.
Surprise—(b)—ALEX. McARTHUR & CO., LTD., Montreal, Canada.
Sussex—(w)—POWERS PAPER CO., Springfield, Mass.
Sussex Bristol — (b)—COOK-VIVIAN CO., Boston.
Sussex Bristol—(b)—HY. LINDENMEYR & SONS, New York.
Swallow—(b)—toilet—A. M. EATON, Waltham and Boston.
Swan—(b)—blotting—C. P. LESH PAPER CO., Indianapolis, Ind.
Swan—(b)—toilet — NORTHERN PAPER MILLS, Green Bay, Wis.
Swan—(b)—white manila—STONE & FORSYTH CO., Boston.
Swan Linen — (w)—white wove—CENTRAL OHIO PAPER CO., Columbus, Ohio.
Swan Linen—(w) — CANFIELD PAPER CO., New York.
"Swandee"—(b)—SCRANTOM, WETMORE & COMPANY, Rochester, N. Y.
Swandsdown—(b)—toilet— UNITED STATES ENVELOPE CO. (Morgan Envelope Co. Division), Springfield.
Swastika—(w and b)—GEO. B. HURD & CO., New York.
Swederope—(b) — natural or manila tag—DETROIT SULPHITE PULP & PAPER CO., Detroit, Mich.
Swederope—(b) — document — DETROIT SULPHITE PULP & PAPER CO., Detroit, Mich.
Swederope—(b) — envelope — DETROIT SULPHITE PULP & PAPER CO., Detroit, Mich.
Swedish Bond — (w) — CENTRAL OHIO PAPER CO., Columbus, Ohio.
Swedish Fibre—(b)—imported white kraft—THE SEINSHEIMER PAPER CO., Cincinnati, Ohio.
Sweet Pea—(b)—vegetable parchment —LOUISVILLE PAPER CO., Louisville, Ky.

Watermarks and Brands 739

Swift—(b)—carbon copy — BRADNER SMITH & CO., Chicago.
Swiss Fibre—(b)—wrapping—LOUISVILLE PAPER CO., Louisville, Pa.
Swiss Bond—(w) — CANFIELD PAPER CO., New York.
Swiss Chiffon—(b)—EATON, CRANE & PIKE, Pittsfield, Mass.
Swiss Ledger—(w)—CANFIELD PAPER CO., New York.
Swiss Linen—(b)—EATON, CRANE & PIKE CO., Pittsfield, Mass.
Swiss Linen—(b)—PAUL E. VERNON & CO., New York.
Swiss Twill Bond—(b)—EATON, CRANE & PIKE CO., Pittsfield, Mass.
Swiss Twill Linen—(b)—EATON, CRANE & PIKE CO., Pittsfield, Mass.
Sycamore Express — (b) — wrapping —LOUISVILLE PAPER CO., Louisville, Ky.
Sycamore Mills—(w)—writing—J. & F. B. GARRETT, Syracuse, New York.
Syca Kraft — (b)—CHATFIELD & WOODS CO., Cincinnati, Ohio.
Sylvan—(b)—cover — KALAMAZOO PAPER CO., Kalamazoo, Mich.
Sylvan—(b)—wedding and bristol—MOUNTAIN MILL PAPER CO., Lee, Mass.
Sylvania Bond—(w)—OSBURN PAPER CO., Philadelphia.
Sylvania Mills—(w)—in seven colors —OSBURN PAPER CO., Philadelphia.
Sylvania Parchment — (w) — OSBURN PAPER CO., Philadelphia.
Sylvania—railroad manila and white writing—OSBURN PAPER CO., Philadelphia.
Sylvanus Book — (b) — CLARKE & CO., New York.
Sylvia Linen Ledger—(b)—HENRY LINDENMEYR & SONS, New York.
Symphony—(b) — book — MINNEAPOLIS PAPER CO., Minneapolis.
Syndic Bond—(b)—PARSONS TRADING CO., New York.
Syndicate Bond—(w)—white only—R. C. KASTNER PAPER CO., N. Y.
System Index — (b) — BEECHER, PECK & LEWIS, Detroit, Mich.
System Index Bristol—(b)—MEGARGEE BROS., Scranton, Pa.
Systems Bond — (w) — EASTERN MFG. CO., South Brewer, Me.

T

Tacoma—(b)—toilet—ALBANY PERFORATED WRAPPING PAPER CO., Albany, New York.
Tacoma — (b) — water-finished fibre—TRINITY BAG & PAPER CO., New York.
Tacoma White Laid—(b) — F. A. FLINN, New York.
Tacoma Linen Ledger—(w)—W. D. MESSINGER & CO., Chicago.

Tacon No. 1 — (b) — HOLLINGSWORTH & WHITNEY CO., Boston.
Taconic Bond—(w) — AMERICAN WRITING PAPER CO., Holyoke.
Taconic Linen—(w) — AMERICAN WRITING PAPER CO., Holyoke.
Taconic Manila — (b)—BRADNER SMITH & CO., Chicago.
Taconnet—(b) — HOLLINGSWORTH & WHITNEY CO., New York.
Taffeta—(w)—GEO. B. HURD & CO., New York.
Taffeta—(b)—cover — NIAGARA PAPER MILLS, Lockport, New York.
Taffeta—(b) — Z. & W. M. CRANE, Dalton, Mass.
Tag Blank—(b)—BRADNER SMITH & CO., Chicago.
Taku—(b)—cover—C. P. LESH PAPER CO., Indianapolis, Ind.
Talbot—(b)—book—GRAHAM PAPER CO., St. Louis.
Talisman Linen—(w)—THE PAPER MILLS CO., Chicago.
Tally Ho — (b) — toilet—UNITED STATES ENVELOPE CO. (Morgan Envelope Co. Division), Springfield.
Tamarock—(b) — wrapping — GRAHAM PAPER CO., St. Louis.
Tam O'Shanter—(b)—toilet—H. NORWOOD EWING CO., New York.
Tampico—(b)—writing — GRAHAM PAPER CO., St. Louis.
Tampico—(b)—envelope — WHITING-PATTERSON CO., Philadelphia.
Tan Express—(b) — CHATFIELD & WOODS CO., Cincinnati, Ohio.
Tangier—(b)—cover — STANDARD PAPER CO., Kalamazoo, Mich.
Tangier Transparent Parchment — (b) — GRAHAM PAPER CO., St. Louis.
Tango Bond — (b) — MEGARGEE BROS., Scranton, Pa.
Tansey—(b)—book — GRAHAM PAPER CO., St. Louis.
Tapestry—(b) — cover — STRATHMORE PAPER CO., Mittineague, Mass.
Tapestry—(b)—cover and panel cards —STRATHMORE PAPER CO., Mittineague, Mass.
Tapestry Deckle Edge Book—(b) —STRATHMORE PAPER CO., Mittineague, Mass.
Target Bond—(b)—E. E. LLOYD PAPER CO., Chicago, Ill.
Tariff—(b)—flat—J. W. BUTLER PAPER CO., Chicago.
Tariff — (b) — SOUTHERN PAPER COMPANY, Richmond, Va.
Tariff Mimeograph—(w)—OSBURN PAPER CO., Philadelphia.
Tarine —(b)— moth paper — MANAHAN MOTH PAPER CO., New York.
Tarlton—(b) — sulphite kraft—W. H. CLAFLIN & CO., Boston.
Tartar Express — (b) — wrapping — GRAHAM PAPER CO., St. Louis.

Tatsu Linen—(w)—C. P. LESH PAPER CO., Indianapolis, Ind.
Taunton—(b)— book — McCLELLAN PAPER CO., Minneapolis, Minn.
Taurus — (b) — jute tag — MINNEAPOLIS PAPER CO., Minneapolis, Minn.
Taurus —(w)—ledger—CROCKER-McELWAIN CO., Holyoke, Mass.
Tavern—(b)—book—GRAHAM PAPER CO., St. Louis.
Tayla Tishu — (b) — toilet — LOUISVILLE PAPER CO., Louisville, Ky.
Tecumseh—(w)— bond — MIDLAND PAPER CO., Chicago.
Tee-Pee—(b)—roofing—LOUISVILLE PAPER CO., Louisville, Ky.
Tekoa — (b) — bristol and cover — STRATHMORE PAPER CO., Mittineague, Mass.
Tekoa Linen Bond—(w)—STRATHMORE PAPER CO., Mittineague, Mass.
Telanian Extra Super — (b) — STRATHMORE PAPER CO., Mittineague, Mass.
Telegraph—(b)—No. 2 manila writings—DONALDSON PAPER CO., Harrisburg, Pa.
Telegraph—(b)—railroad manila—MISSOURI PAPER HOUSE, Kansas City, Mo.
Telegraph—(b)—yellow manila copying—CHATFIELD & WOODS CO., Cincinnati, Ohio.
Telegraph Writing—(w)—CHATFIELD & WOODS CO., Cincinnati.
Telford White Wove—(b)—writing—MILLER & WRIGHT PAPER CO., New York.
Telulah Bond — (w) — KIMBERLY-CLARK CO., Neenah, Wis.
Temco Linen—(w)—TOWER MANUFACTURING & NOVELTY CO., N. Y.
Tempest Bond—(w)—LOUISVILLE PAPER CO., Louisville, Ky.
Temple Bond — (w) — WHITAKER PAPER CO., Cincinnati, Ohio, and BAY STATE PAPER CO., Boston.
Temple Text—(w)—book—ADVERTISERS PAPER MILLS, Holyoke.
Tensile Manila — (b) — writing — GRAHAM PAPER CO., St. Louis.
Tension — (b) — manifold unglazed—GRAHAM PAPER CO., St. Louis.
Tereve — (b) — EVERETT PULP & PAPER CO., Everett, Wash.
Terminal R.R. Manila—(b)—JOHN CARTER & CO., INC., Boston.
Terminal—(w)—bond—GRAHAM PAPER CO., St. Louis.
Terminal R.R. Manila—(b)—JOHN CARTER & CO., Boston.
Terrier Bond—(w)—HESSE ENVELOPE & LITHO. CO., St. Louis.
Testimony Papers—(b)—ELSINORE PAPER CO., New York.
Teton—(b)—toilet—ALBANY PERFORATED WRAPPING PAPER CO., Albany, N. Y.

Teutonic Linen Ledger—(w) — W. M. PRINGLE & CO., INC., New York.
Texas—(b)—bristols—KANSAS CITY PAPER HOUSE, Kansas City, Mo.
Texas Cover—(b)—KINGSLEY PAPER CO., Cleveland, Ohio.
Text — (b) — bristol—J. P. HEILBRONN, Manila, P. I.
Textan White Fibre—(b)—TRINITY BAG & PAPER CO., New York.
Textile—(b)—bristol—RIEGEL & CO., INC., Philadelphia.
Textile Bond—(w)—WHITING PAPER CO., Holyoke, Mass.
Textile Wrapping—(w and b—w—wrappings and bonds—b—wrappings and specialties)—McDOWELL PAPER MILL, Manayunk, Pa.
Texture—(b)—cover, bristol—UNION CARD AND PAPER CO., New York.
The Arlington—(b)—R. P. ANDREWS PAPER CO., Washington, D. C.
The Banner Linen—(w)—SOUTHWORTH CO., Mittineague, Mass.
"The Berkshire" Superior Typewriter Papers—(b)—BERKSHIRE HILLS PAPER CO., Adams, Mass.
The Berkshire Hills Criterion Bond — (w) — BERKSHIRE HILLS PAPER CO., Adams, Mass.
The Berkshire Hills Constitution Bond — (w) — BERKSHIRE HILLS PAPER CO., Adams, Mass.
The Berkshire Hills Belfast Linen Bond — (w) — BERKSHIRE HILLS PAPER CO., Adams, Mass.
The Berkshire Hills Public Record Ledger—(w)—BERKSHIRE HILLS PAPER CO., Adams, Mass.
The Berkshire Hills Constitution Ledger—(w)—BERKSHIRE HILLS PAPER CO., Adams, Mass.
The Berkshire Hills Hoosac Ledger—(w)—BERKSHIRE HILLS PAPER CO., Adams, Mass.
The Berkshire Hills Regal Linen Ledger—(w)—BERKSHIRE HILLS PAPER CO., Adams, Mass.
The Berkshire Hills No. 1 Index Bristol—(b)—BERKSHIRE HILLS PAPER CO., Adams, Mass.
The Berkshire Hills Typewriter Papers—(w and b)—BERKSHIRE HILLS PAPER CO., Adams, Mass.
The Best Paper (Wrapping)—(b)—THE SEINSHEIMER PAPER CO., Cincinnati, Ohio.
The Blue and the Gray—(w and b)—bond, ledger—NEENAH PAPER CO., Neenah, Wis.
The Boston Bond—(w)—SAMUEL WARD MFG. CO., Boston.
The Boston Linen—(w)—SAMUEL WARD MFG. CO., Boston.
The Century Linen—(w)—AMERICAN WRITING PAPER CO., Holyoke.
The Century Typewriter Paper—(w)—THORP & MARTIN CO., Boston.

The Imperial Bond—(w)—AMERICAN WRITING PAPER CO., Holyoke.
The King's Bond—(w)—JOHN WANAMAKER, Philadelphia.
The King's Vellum—(w)—JOHN WANAMAKER, Philadelphia.
The Norris—(b)—PEERLESS MANUFACTURING CO., Norristown, Pa.
The Official Bond—(w)—AMERICAN WRITING PAPER CO., Holyoke.
The P. M. Co. $1.00 Ledger—(w) —THE PAPER MILLS CO., Chicago.
The Quinsig—(b)—UNITED STATES ENVELOPE CO. (Whitcomb Envelope Co. Division), Worcester, Mass.
The Richmond & Backus Co., Detroit, Mich.—(w)—linen ledger— THE RICHMOND & BACKUS CO., Detroit, Mich.
The Roman Bond—(w)—THORP & MARTIN CO., Boston.
The Roycroft Bond—(w)—HAMMERMILL PAPER CO., Erie, Pa.
The R. & B. Co.'s Linen Ledger Paper—(w)—THE RICHMOND & BACKUS CO., Detroit, Mich.
The Standard Ledger—(w)—AMERICAN WRITING PAPER CO., Holyoke, Mass.
The Thos. W. Price Co.—(b)—extra fine—THOS. W. PRICE CO., Philadelphia.
Theatrical Poster — (b) — F. A. FLINN, INC., New York.
Thirty-Thirty "3030"—(b)—double-paper waterproof case-lining—SAFE-PACK PAPER MILLS, Brockton, Mass.
Thistle —(b)— book — LOUISVILLE PAPER CO., Louisville, Ky.
Thistle Linen—(w)—CARTER, RICE & CO., CORP., Boston.
Thistledown—(b)—book — KALAMAZOO PAPER CO., Kalamazoo, Mich.
Thorncliff Bond—(w)—WESTERN PAPER CO., Omaha, Neb.
Three Sixty—(b)—envelope—UNION CARD & PAPER CO., New York.
Thrift Bond—(w)—E. E. LLOYD PAPER CO., Chicago.
Thrift Bond—(b)—HOWARD PAPER CO., Urbana, Ohio.
Thro-away Diapers and Children's Bibs — (b) — LEHIGH PAPER MILLS, INC., Raubsville, Pa.
Throgg's Neck—(b)—package toilet —JEROME PAPER CO., New York.
Thrush Kraft — (b) — wrapping — LOUISVILLE PAPER CO., Louisville, Ky.
Thurso—(b)—white blanks—J. C. PARKER PAPER CO., Louisville, Ky.
Ticket Bristol—(b)—HARLEM CARD & PAPER CO., New York.
Tiffany — (b) — coated book — F. A. FLINN, INC., New York.
Tiger Coated Blanks— (b) —BUNTIN, GILLIES & CO., Hamilton, Can.
Tiger—(b)—onion skin—GRAHAM PAPER CO., St. Louis.

Tiger—(b)—white gummed—BRADNER SMITH & CO., Chicago.
Tiger Bond—(w)—DIEM & WING PAPER CO., Cincinnati, Ohio.
Tiger Brand—(b)—sheathing—NEWTON PAPER CO., Holyoke, Mass.
Tiger Bristol—(b)—B R A D N E R SMITH & CO., Chicago.
Tiger Fibre—(b)—A. STORRS & BEMENT CO., Boston.
Tiger Flats—(w)—BRADNER SMITH & CO., Chicago.
Tiger Leather Paper—(b)—CINCINNATI CORDAGE & PAPER CO., Cincinnati, Ohio.
Tiger Linen — (w) — CLEVELAND PAPER MANUFACTURING CO., Cleveland, Ohio.
Tinted Art Book—(b)—DILL & COLLINS CO., Philadelphia.
Tinted Check Wove—(b)—KEITH PAPER CO., Turners Falls, Mass.
Tinted Enamel—(b)—bristol—J. W. BUTLER PAPER CO., Chicago.
Tioga—(b)—cover—RIEGEL & CO., INC., Philadelphia.
Tioga Mills—(b)—colored writing—JOHNSTON PAPER CO., Harrisburg, Pa.
Tioga Mills—(w)—fine—JOHN LESLIE PAPER CO., Minneapolis, Minn.
Tipperary Linen — (w) — GILBERT PAPER CO., Menasha, Wis.
Tip Top — (b) — manila — TRINITY BAG & PAPER CO., New York.
Tirzah—(w)—bond—C. P. LESH PAPER CO., Indianapolis, Ind.
Tishu—(b)—toilet—SCOTT PAPER CO., Philadelphia.
Tisrite Bond—(w)—KEITH PAPER CO., Turners Falls, Mass.
Tisrite Ledger—(w)—KEITH PAPER CO., Turners Falls, Mass.
Tisrite Linen—(w)—KEITH PAPER CO., Turners Falls, Mass.
Tissue Bond — (b) — SOUTHWORTH CO., Mittineague, Mass.
Tissue Fibre—(b)—wrapping—GRAHAM PAPER CO., St. Louis.
Titan Bond—(w)—HAMPSHIRE PAPER CO., South Hadley Falls, Mass.
Titan Linen Ledger—(w)—HAMPSHIRE PAPER CO., South Hadley Falls, Mass.
Titanic Bond—(b)—PARSONS TRADING CO., New York.
Titanic Bond—(w)—PARSONS TRADING CO., New York.
Titanic Index Bristol—(b)—PARSONS TRADING CO., New York.
Title Bond—(w)—LOUISVILLE PAPER CO., Louisville, Ky.
Title Linen Ledger—(w)—WHITING PAPER CO., Holyoke, Mass.
Todd—(b)—book and label—GRAHAM PAPER CO., St. Louis.
Togo—(b)—toilet—H. NORWOOD EWING CO., New York.
Tokio — (b) — crepe napkins—WHITING-PATTERSON CO., New York.

Tokio Blanks—(b)—C. P. LESH PAPER CO., Indianapolis, Ind.
Tokyo Bond —(w)— CROCKER-McELWAIN CO., Holyoke, Mass.
Tokyo Index Bristol—(b)—COOK-VIVIAN CO., Boston.
Toned Practice Drawing—(b)—A. STORRS & BEMENT CO., Boston.
Top Notch—(b)—toilet—NORTHERN PAPER MILLS, Green Bay, Wis.
Torchon Bond—(w)—W. M. PRINGLE & CO., INC., New York.
Toro Bond—(w)—(colored) card—PARSONS TRADING CO., New York.
Tosa—(b)—toilet—GRAHAM PAPER CO., St. Louis.
Totem—(b)—HOLLINGSWORTH & WHITNEY CO., Boston.
Touchdown Bond—(w)—JOHN LESLIE PAPER CO., Minneapolis.
Touchstone Bond—(w)—STANDARD CARD & PAPER CO., New York.
Tough Check Tag—(b)—THE ALLING & CORY CO., Rochester, N. Y.
Town—(w)—bond and ledger—UNION CARD & PAPER CO., New York.
Town Index—(b)—bristols—UNION CARD & PAPER CO., New York.
Towner—(b)—book—GRAHAM PAPER CO., St. Louis.
Toxaway Bond—(w)—OSBURN PAPER CO., Philadelphia.
Toxaway Fine—(w)—OSBURN PAPER CO., Philadelphia.
Toxaway Linen Ledger—(w)—OSBURN PAPER CO., Philadelphia.
T. O. Y.—(b)—copying—RAINBOW PAPER MILLS, Rainbow, Conn.
Traction Ledger—(w)—MOSER PAPER CO., Chicago.
Trade Blank—(b)—KINGSLEY PAPER CO., Cleveland, Ohio.
Trade Blotting—(b)—QUAKER CITY PAPER CO., Philadelphia.
Trade Bond—(w)—WHITING PAPER CO., Holyoke, Mass.
Trade Bristol—(b)—W. G. WILLMANN, New York.
Trade Linen—(w)—WHITING PAPER CO., Holyoke, Mass.
Trade Linen Ledger—(w)—CINCINNATI CORDAGE AND PAPER CO., Cincinnati, Ohio.
Trade Mark —(w)— bond — J. E. LINDE PAPER CO., New York.
Traders—(b)—blanks—UNION CARD & PAPER CO., New York.
Traders—(b)— colored bristol — HAGEN PAPER CO., St. Louis.
Traders—(b)—flat—M. J. EARL, Reading, Pa.
Traders' Bond—(w)—AETNA PAPER CO., Dayton, Ohio.
Traders' Bond—(w)—GRAHAM PAPER CO., St. Louis.
Traders' Bond —(b)— bond — GRAHAM PAPER CO., St. Louis.
Tradesmen's Linen Cream Laid Writing—(w)—HENRY LINDENMEYR & SONS, New York.

Tradesmen's Linen Bond—(w)—HY. LINDENMEYR & SONS, New York.
Tradesmen's Linen Ledger—(w)—HENRY LINDENMEYR & SONS, N. Y.
Traffic—(b)—railroad manila and writing—GRAHAM PAPER CO., St. Louis.
Traffic Bond—(w)—W. E. WROE & CO., Chicago.
Traffic R. R.—(b)—writing—BEECHER, PECK & LEWIS, Detroit, Mich.
Traffic Writing—(b)—GARRETT-BUCHANAN CO., Philadelphia.
Trainmen's Oil—(b)—tissue—GRAHAM PAPER CO., St. Louis.
Transcript Bond—(w)—EASTERN MFG. CO., Bangor, Me.
Transcript Ledger—(w)—EASTERN MFG. CO., Bangor, Me.
Transcript—(w)—writing — HAMMERMILL PAPER CO., Erie, Pa.
Transfer Bond—flat writing—DOBLER & MUDGE, Baltimore.
Transfer Index— (b)—MILLER & WRIGHT PAPER CO., INC., New York.
Transit Railroad Folder—(b)—MINNEAPOLIS PAPER CO., Minneapolis, Minn.
Trans-Mississippi Parchment—(b)—CARPENTER PAPER CO., Omaha.
Transport—(b)—writing — GRAHAM PAPER CO., St. Louis.
Transvaal Ledger—(w)—HAMMERMILL PAPER CO., Erie, Pa.
Traveler—(b)—envelope and writing—GRAHAM PAPER CO., St. Louis.
Treasury—(b)—tag board—GRAHAM PAPER CO., St. Louis.
Treasury—(b)— blotting — JOSEPH PARKER & SON CO., New Haven.
Treasury Bond—(w)—writing—CAREW MANUFACTURING CO., South Hadley Falls, Mass.
Treasury Bond—(w)—O. H. ANDERSON & CO., New York.
Treasury Bristol—(b)—R. P. ANDREWS PAPER CO., Washington.
Treasury Ledger—(w)—AMERICAN WRITING PAPER CO., Holyoke, Mass.
Treasury Linen—(w)—AMERICAN WRITING PAPER CO., Holyoke, Mass.
Treasury Linen—(w)—wove and laid—VALLEY PAPER CO., Holyoke.
Treasury Linen — (w) — STRATHMORE PAPER CO., Mittineague, Mass.
Treasury Vellum—(w)—AMERICAN WRITING PAPER CO., Holyoke, Mass.
Tremont—(b)—toilet—ALBANY PERFORATED WRAPPING PAPER CO., Albany, N. Y.
Tremson — (b) — napkin — TRINITY BAG & PAPER CO., New York.
Triangle—(b)—toilet — UNITED STATES ENVELOPE CO. (Morgan Envelope Co. Div.), Springfield, Mass.
Triangle—(w and b)—bond, toilet—HERBERT R. MANN, Troy, N. Y.

Watermarks and Brands 743

Tribune Bond—(w)—R. P. MOLTEN & CO., Philadelphia.
Tribune Bond — (w) — HOWARD SMITH PAPER MILLS, LTD., Montreal, Can.
Tribune Bristol—(b)—TROY PAPER CO., Troy, N. Y.
Trichromatic—(b)—DILL & COLLINS CO., Philadelphia.
Trident—(b)—toilet—ALBANY PERFORATED WRAPPING PAPER CO., Albany, N. Y.
Trident Mills—(b)—TILESTON & LIVERMORE CO., Boston.
Trimount Cover—(b)—VON OLKERSNELL PAPER CO., Boston.
Trinidad—(b) — manila — WHITING-PATTERSON CO., Philadelphia.
Trinidad Greaseproof — (b) — GRAHAM PAPER CO., St. Louis.
Trinidad Silk—(b)—water finished fibre—TRINITY BAG & PAPER CO., New York.
Trinity—(b and w)—bond, linen and ledger — NEENAH PAPER CO., Neenah, Wis.
Triomphe—(w and b)—writing, coated book and card index—PAPER MILLS CO., Chicago.
Triplico Twelve Pound Bond—(w) —MILLER & WRIGHT PAPER CO., INC., New York.
Trissach Bond—(w)—J. C. PARKER PAPER CO., Louisville, Ky.
Tri-State—(b)—bristol—MINNEAPOLIS PAPER CO., Minneapolis, Minn.
Tri-State — (b) —ROBERTS & MECK'S, Harrisburg, Pa.
Triston Writing—(w)—ST. LOUIS PAPER CO., St. Louis.
Triton— (w) —bond—LESLIE-DONAHOWER CO., St. Paul.
Triton Bond — (w) — MIAMISBURG PAPER CO., Miamisburg, O.
Triton Linen Ledger—(w)—MIAMISBURG PAPER CO., Miamisburg, Ohio.
Triumph—(b)—blotting—W. B. OGLESBY PAPER CO., Middletown, Ohio.
Triumph—(b)—cover — McCLELLAN PAPER CO., Minneapolis, Minn.
Triumph —(b)— ruled goods — JUDD PAPER CO., Holyoke, Mass.
Triumph Bond—(w)—THE ALLING & CORY CO., Rochester, N. Y.
Triumph Linen—(w)—MINNEAPOLIS PAPER CO., Minneapolis, Minn.
Triumph Linen Ledger—(w)—MINNEAPOLIS PAPER CO., Minneapolis.
Triumph Mills—(b)—writing—JUDD PAPER CO., Holyoke, Mass.
Trojan—(b)—fibre — ANDREWS PAPER CO., Boston.
Trojan—(b)—toilet — ALBANY PERFORATED WRAPPING PAPER CO., Albany, New York.
Trojan—(b)—sheathing — GRAHAM PAPER CO., St. Louis.

Trojan Bond—(w)—ELSINORE PAPER CO., New York.
Trojan Bristol—(b)—TROY PAPER CO., Troy, New York.
Trojan Covers—(b)—SEYMOUR CO., INC., New York.
Trojan Glazed Onion Skin—(b)— imported No. 1—ELSINORE PAPER CO., New York.
Trojan Ledger—(w) — WHITAKER PAPER CO., Cincinnati, Ohio, and BAY STATE PAPER CO., Boston.
Trojan Linen—(w)—ELSINORE PAPER CO., New York.
Trojan Manifold Linen—(b) — in colors—ELSINORE PAPER CO., N. Y.
Trojan Mills—(w) — TROY PAPER CO., Troy, New York.
Trojan Unglazed Onion Skin—(b) —imported No. 1—ELSINORE PAPER CO., New York.
Trophy Bristol—(b)—TROY PAPER CO., Troy, New York.
Troutadem—(w and b)—bond, writing, ledger—NEENAH PAPER CO., Neenah, Wis.
Troy—(b)—writing—GRAHAM PAPER CO., St. Louis.
Trueworth — (b)—ledger—ALEXANDER-HOLDEN PAPER CO., New York.
Trust Bond—(w)—ST. LOUIS PAPER CO., St. Louis.
Trustee—(w and b)—bond, ledger— NEENAH PAPER CO., Neenah, Wis.
Truxton White Fibre—(b)—TRINITY BAG & PAPER CO., New York.
Tryme—(b)—toilet — SCOTT PAPER CO., Philadelphia.
T. S. Linen—(w)—laid—FOX RIVER PAPER CO., Appleton, Wis.
Tuck—(b)—manifold—TROY PAPER CO., Troy, N. Y.
Tudor Blotting — (b)—WHITAKER PAPER CO., Cincinnati, Ohio.
Tudor Mills—(b) — brown express— W. H. CLAFLIN & CO., Boston.
Tufenuf—(b)—cover — THE PAPER MILLS CO., Chicago.
Tuffenuff—(b) — cover — AMERICAN WRITING PAPER CO. (Windsor Locks Division), Holyoke, Mass.
Tuffold — (b) — book—LOUISVILLE PAPER CO., Louisville, Ky.
Tufiber—(b)—toilet — SCOTT PAPER CO., Philadelphia.
Tufrap—(b)—FOX PAPER CO., Lockland, Ohio.
Tuftex—(b)—toilet — SCOTT PAPER CO., Philadelphia.
Tulip — (b) — vegetable parchment — LOUISVILLE PAPER CO., Louisville, Ky.
Tulip Laid Linen — (w) — bond — LOUISVILLE PAPER CO., Louisville, Ky.
Tuna—(b)—Kraft—TRINITY BAG & PAPER CO., New York.
Tuniata Flats—(b) — DOBLER & MUDGE, Baltimore.

Tunica Bond—(b)—W. M. PRINGLE & CO., INC., New York.
Tunis —(b)— index bristol — WHITING-PATTERSON CO., Philadelphia.
Tunix Mills Linen Ledger—(w)— AMERICAN WRITING PAPER CO., Holyoke, Mass.
Turkey—(b) — fibre — STONE & FORSYTH CO., Boston.
Turkey Linen—(w)—wove and laid— CHATFIELD & WOODS CO., Cincinnati, Ohio.
Turkey Linen — (w)—THE UNION PAPER & TWINE CO., Detroit, Mich.
Tuscan—(b)—manila—TRINITY BAG & PAPER CO., New York.
Tuscan Text Book—(w) — J. C. PARKER PAPER CO., Louisville, Ky.
Tuscany Linen Deckle Edge—(b)— GEO. B. HURD & CO., New York.
Tutonic Bond — (w) — writing — PARSONS TRADING CO., New York.
"Tuxedo"—(b) — crêpe and waxed— SCRANTOM, WETMORE & COMPANY, Rochester, New York.
Tuxedo—(b) — W. G. WILLMANN, New York.
Tuxedo—(b)—J. W. BUTLER PAPER CO., Chicago.
Tuxedo—(b)—WORTHY PAPER CO., Mittineague, Mass.
Tuxedo Ivory—(w)—CAREW MANUFACTURING CO., South Hadley Falls, Mass.
Tuxy—(b) — toilet — NORTHERN PAPER MILLS, Green Bay, Wis.
Twentieth Century—(w)—flat and bond—FOX RIVER PAPER CO., Appleton, Wis.
Twentieth Century—(b) — KANSAS CITY PAPER CO., Kansas City, Mo.
Twentieth Century Bond—(w)—B. D. RISING PAPER CO., Housatonic, Mass.
Twentieth Century Ledger—(w)— B. D. RISING PAPER CO., Housatonic, Mass.
Twentieth Century Writing—(b)— GRAHAM PAPER CO., St. Louis.
Twenty Carat Linen—(w)—B. D. RISING PAPER CO., Housatonic, Mass.
Twildu—(b)—toilet — SCOTT PAPER CO., Philadelphia.
Twill Bond — (w) — PENINSULAR PAPER CO., Ypsilanti, Mich.
Twilled Flax—(w) — Z. & W. M. CRANE, Dalton, Mass.
Twilled Irish Linen—(b)—EATON, CRANE & PIKE CO., Pittsfield, Mass.
Twilled Irish Linen Bond—(b)— EATON, CRANE & PIKE—Pittsfield.
Twilled Pique—(w and b)—GEO. B. HURD & CO., New York.
Twin City Bond—(w) — WHITE & LEONARD, St. Paul, Minn.
Twin City Bond—(b)—OLD DOMINION PAPER CO., Norfolk, Va.
Twister—(b)—kraft—GRAHAM PAPER CO., St. Louis.

Twotone Linen — (w) — EATON, CRANE & PIKE CO., Pittsfield, Mass.
Tyler—(b) — book — GRAHAM PAPER CO., St. Louis.
Typewriter Bond — (b) — CHATFIELD & WOODS CO., Cincinnati.
Typewriter Bond—(b) — BRADNER SMITH & CO., Chicago.
Typewriter Bond— (w)—HAMMERMILL PAPER CO., Erie, Pa.
Typewriter Bond—(b)—GARRETT-BUCHANAN CO., Philadelphia.
Typewriter Onion Skin—(b)—J. W. BUTLER PAPER CO., Chicago.
Typic Bond—(b)—PARSONS TRADING CO., New York.
Typo—(w and b)—bond, onion skin and manifold—UNION CARD & PAPER CO., New York.
Typo Envelopes—(b)—HUDSON VALLEY PAPER CO., Albany, N. Y.
Typocount Linen Ledger—(w)— BYRON WESTON CO., Dalton, Mass.
Tyrone Linen—(w)—GRAHAM PAPER CO., St. Louis.
Tyronia—(b)—writing — WEST VIRGINIA PULP & PAPER CO., New York.

U

U. K. Ledger—(b)—CLEMENT & STOCKWELL, INC., New York.
Ulster — (b) — envelope — WHITING-PATTERSON CO., Philadelphia.
Ulster—(b)—cover — JAMES WHITE PAPER CO., Chicago.
Ulster Linen—(w)—MARCUS WARD CO., Brooklyn.
Ulster Linen— (w) —BUNTIN, GILLIES & CO., Hamilton, Can.
Umbria—(w)—GRAHAM PAPER CO., St. Louis.
Umbria—(b)—fine — MERRIAM PAPER CO., New York.
Unalloyed Grass Bleached — (b)— tissue — GRAHAM PAPER CO., St. Louis.
Uncas—(b)—ALBANY PERFORATED WRAPPING PAPER CO., Albany.
Uncle Sam Bond—(w)—ALLING & CORY CO., Rochester.
Uncle Sam Ledger—(w)—BRADNER SMITH & CO., Chicago.
Underglaze — (w) — Z. & W. M. CRANE, Dalton, Mass.
Underwriter Bond — (w) — CROCKER-McELWAIN CO., Holyoke.
Underwriter Linen Ledger—(w)— CROCKER-McELWAIN CO., Holyoke.
Undine Linen Ledger—(w)—GARRETT-BUCHANAN CO., Philadelphia.
Undressed Coated Book — (b) — BEECHER, PECK & LEWIS, Detroit, Mich.
Uneeda Blanks — (b) — BEECHER, PECK & LEWIS, Detroit, Mich.
Unglazed Linen — (w) — GEO. B. HURD & CO., New York.

Watermarks and Brands 745

Unicard Index—(b)—bristol—UNION CARD & PAPER CO., New York.
Unicorn—(b) — toilet — NORTHERN PAPER MILLS, Green Bay, Wis.
Unicorn Colored Bristols — (b)— HENRY LINDENMEYR & SONS, New York.
Uniform—(b)—RICHMOND PAPER CO., Richmond, Va.
Union—(b)—bristol board—DONALDSON PAPER CO., Harrisburg, Pa.
Union — (b) — bristol—J. P. HEILBRONN CO., Manila, P. I.
Union—(b)—bristol — UNION CARD AND PAPER CO., New York.
Union—(b)—manila—ANDREWS PAPER CO., Boston.
Union—(b)—toilet—GEO. T. JOHNSON CO., Boston.
Union—(b)— toilet — R. L. GREENE PAPER CO., Providence, R. I.
Union—(b)—toilet—NORTHERN PAPER MILLS, Green Bay, Wis.
Union — (b) — toilet—THE SEINSHEIMER PAPER CO., Cincinnati, O.
Union Bond—(w) — MERRIAM PAPER CO., New York.
Union Bond—(w)—white only—OLD DOMINION PAPER CO., Norfolk, Va.
Union Bond—(w) — WRIGHT, BARRETT & STILWELL CO., St. Paul.
Union Bristol—(b)—WM. G. WILLMANN, New York.
Union Crash White—(w)—bond— MERRIAM PAPER CO., New York.
Union Embossing—(b) — cover—J. W. BUTLER PAPER CO., Chicago.
Union Enameled Blank—(b)—THE UNION PAPER & TWINE CO., Detroit, Mich.
Union League—(b)—toilet—ALBANY PERFORATED WRAPPING PAPER CO., Albany, N. Y.
Union Linen — (w)—fine white—CENTRAL OHIO PAPER CO., Columbus, Ohio.
Union No. 1 Manila—(b)—D. S. WALTON & CO., New York.
Union Parchment Bond — (b) — WHITAKER PAPER CO., Cincinnati.
Union Rope—(b) -- PAPER MILLS CO., Chicago.
Union White—(w)—bond—MERRIAM PAPER CO., New York.
Unique — (b) — ALBANY PERFORATED WRAPPING PAPER CO., Albany, N. Y.
Unique—(b)—cover and bristol — C. H. DEXTER & SONS, INC., Windsor Locks, Conn.
Unique—(b)—cover—JAMES WHITE & CO., Chicago.
Unique Railroad — (b) — THE ALLING & CORY CO., Rochester, N. Y.
Unique Tough Check — (b) — THE ALLING & CORY CO., Rochester, N. Y.
United States—(b)—ALBANY PERFORATED WRAPPING PAPER CO., Albany, New York.

United States—(w and b)—blotting—STANDARD PAPER MANUFACTURING CO., Richmond, Va.
United States—(b)—cardboard—J. W. BUTLER PAPER CO., Chicago.
United States Bond—(w)—AMERICAN WRITING PAPER CO., Holyoke.
United States B o n d — (w) — CHARLES W. WILLIAMS & CO., New York.
United States Bristol—(b)—WM. G. WILLMANN, New York.
United States Linen—(w)—AMERICAN WRITING PAPER CO., Holyoke.
United States Linen Bond—(w)— AMERICAN WRITING PAPER CO., Holyoke.
United States Mills—(b)—VERNON BROS. & CO., New York.
United States Navy Linen—(w)— OLD DOMINION PAPER CO., Norfolk, Va.
United States Standard Linen—(w) —RAYNOR & PERKINS ENVELOPE CO., New York.
United States Standard Linen— (w) — DIEM & WING PAPER CO., Cincinnati, Ohio.
United States Title Bond—(w and b)—UNION CARD AND PAPER CO., New York.
United States Treasury Bond—(w) —GEO. E. DAMON CO., Boston.
Unity—(b)—bond — GRAHAM PAPER CO., St. Louis.
Unity—(b)—toilet—UNITED STATES ENVELOPE CO. (Morgan Envelope Co. Division), Springfield, Mass.
Unity Bond—(w) — HAMMERMILL PAPER CO., Erie, Pa.
Universal—(b)—ledger — RIEGEL & CO., INC., Philadelphia.
Universal—(b) — onion skin—GRAHAM PAPER CO., St. Louis.
Universal—(b) — coated blanks—HAGEN PAPER CO., St. Louis.
Universal—(b)—engine sized colored writings—SEYMOUR CO., New York.
Universal Army Service—(w and b)—bond, ledger, writing—NEENAH PAPER CO., Neenah, Wis.
Universal Carbon Paper—(b)— PARSONS TRADING CO., New York.
Universal Bond—(w) — AMERICAN WRITING PAPER CO., Holyoke.
Universal Bond—(w) — COLUMBIA PAPER CO., Victoria, B. C.
Universal Covers—(b) — SEYMOUR CO., INC., New York.
Universal Linen Record — (w) — GEORGE D. BARNARD & CO., St. Louis.
Universal Safety—(w and b)—bond, ledger, writing—NEENAH PAPER CO., Neenah, Wis.
University—(b)—writing— GRAHAM PAPER CO., St. Louis.
University—(w)—No. 1 linen ledger —DONALDSON PAPER CO., Harrisburg, Pa.

University — (w) — eggshell book— GEO. A. WHITING PAPER CO., Menasha, Wis.
University Bible—(b)—SMITH PAPER CO., Lawrence, Mass.
University Bond — (w)—FISHER BROS. PAPER CO., Fort Wayne, Ind.
University Bond—(w) — HAMMERMILL PAPER CO., Erie, Pa.
University Colored Laid — (b)— THE UNION PAPER & TWINE CO., Detroit, Mich.
University Ledger—(w)—DONALDSON PAPER CO., Harrisburg, Pa.
University Linen—(b)—HUDSON VALLEY PAPER CO., Albany, N. Y.
University Linen — (w)—VERNON BROTHERS & CO., New York.
University Linen Fabric — (b)— HUDSON VALLEY PAPER CO., Albany, New York.
University of Michigan Linen— (w)—BEECHER, PECK & LEWIS, Detroit, Mich.
University Text — (w)—book—ADVERTISERS PAPER MILLS, Holyoke, Mass.
Upton—(b)—ALBANY PERFORATED WRAPPING PAPER CO., Albany.
Up Top—(b) — COLUMBIA PAPER BAG CO., New York.
Urban—(b) — cards — THE PAPER MILLS CO., Chicago.
U. of M. Eggshell Book—(b)— MINNEAPOLIS PAPER CO., Minneapolis, Minn.
U. S.—(w)—bond—LESLIE-DONAHOWER CO., St. Paul.
U. S. A. Bond—(w) — BRADNER SMITH & CO., Chicago.
U. S. Blotting—(b) — THE UNION PAPER & TWINE CO., Detroit.
U. S. Bond—(w)—BASSETT & SUTPHIN, New York.
U. S. Bond—(w)—W. M. PRINGLE & CO., New York.
U. S. Coated Bond — (b) — C. P. LESH PAPER CO., Indianapolis.
U. S. Linen Ledger—(w)—STRATHMORE PAPER CO., Mittineague, Mass.
U. S. Postcard—(b)—HARLEM CARD & PAPER CO., New York.
U. S. Title—(b-w)—bond — UNION CARD & PAPER CO., New York.
Utilities R. R. Writing—(w)—SUTPHEN PAPER CO., New York.
Utility-Accord—(b)—NIAGARA PAPER MILLS, Lockport, New York.
Utility Book—(b)—PAUL E. VERNON & CO., New York.
Utility Ledger — (w)—C. P. LESH PAPER CO., Indianapolis, Ind.
Utility Wedding — (b)—PAPER MILLS CO., Chicago.
Utility Wedding Bristol — (b) — BEECHER, PECK & LEWIS, Detroit, Mich.
Utopia Cover—(b) — WORTHY PAPER CO., Mittineague, Mass.
Utopian—(b)— coated cover — JUDD PAPER CO., Holyoke, Mass.
Utopian Antique Laid Book—(w) —HY. LINDENMEYR & SONS, New York.
Utopian Superfine—(w)—writing— HAGEN PAPER CO., St. Louis.
Utopian Bond—(b) — JUDD PAPER CO., Holyoke, Mass.
Utopian Linen Ledger—(w)—JUDD PAPER CO., Holyoke, Mass.

V

Valcan Kraft — (b) — MICHIGAN BAG & PAPER CO., Jackson, Mich.
Valencia—(w)—linen—J. E. LINDE PAPER CO., New York.
Valencia Pasted Bristol — (b)— MACK-ELLIOTT PAPER CO., St. Louis.
Valentin — (b) — blue wove—F. A. FLINN, New York.
Valhalla—(w)—fine — LOUISVILLE PAPER CO., Louisville, Ky.
Valley Bond—(w)—FOX RIVER PAPER CO., Appleton, Wis.
Valley Congress Linen Bond— —(w)—VALLEY PAPER CO., Holyoke, Mass.
Valley Forge—(w)—flats—VALLEY PAPER CO., Holyoke, Mass.
Valley Forge — (b) — manila — BRADNER SMITH & CO., Chicago.
Valley Forge Ledger—(w)—GARRETT-BUCHANAN CO., Philadelphia.
Valley Library Linen—(w)—VALLEY PAPER CO., Holyoke, Mass.
Valley Litho—(b)—coated blanks— UNION CARD & PAPER CO., N. Y.
Valley Manila—(b)—tissue—SMITH PAPER CO., Lee, Mass.
Valley Paper Co. Linen Ledger— (w)—VALLEY PAPER CO., Holyoke.
Valley Paper Co. No. 1 Bond—(w) —VALLEY PAPER CO., Holyoke.
Valley Paper Co. Superfine—(w)— VALLEY PAPER CO., Holyoke.
Valley Paper Co. Typewriter Bond (w)—VALLEY PAPER CO., Holyoke.
Valley Paper Co. Typewriter Linen—(w)—VALLEY PAPER CO., Holyoke, Mass.
Valley Paper Co. U. S. A. Typewriter Bond—(w)—VALLEY PAPER CO., Holyoke, Mass.
Valley Paper Co. U. S. A. Typewriter Linen—(w)—VALLEY PAPER CO., Holyoke, Mass.
Valley Tissue—(b)—SMITH PAPER CO., Lee, Mass.
Valoir Bond—(w and b)—typewriter —EATON, CRANE & PIKE CO., Pittsfield, Mass.
Valoir Linen—(w and b)—typewriter —EATON, CRANE & PIKE CO., Pittsfield, Mass.
Valor Bond, Made in U. S. A.— PARSONS TRADING CO., New York.

Watermarks and Brands

Valour—(b)—DILL & COLLINS CO., Philadelphia.
Value Bond—(b)—PARSONS TRADING CO., New York.
Vanadium—(b) — folding bristol — UNION PAPER & TWINE CO., Detroit, Mich.
Vanadium Bond—(b)—LEWERTH & CULBERTSON, New York.
Vanaduum (Folding Bristol)—(b)—CHATFIELD & WOODS CO., Cincinnati, Ohio.
Vancouver White Wove—(w)—BARBER-ELLIS, Toronto, Can.
Vandyke—(b)—super half-tone book—JAMES WHITE PAPER CO., Chicago, Ill.
Van Dyke — (b) — felt mounts—BRADNER SMITH & CO., Chicago.
Vanity Bond —(w)— HOWARD PAPER CO., Urbana, O.
Varsity—(w)—bond—H. REEVE ANGEL & CO., INC., New York.
Vegetable Parchment Wrapping—(b)—GRAHAM PAPER CO., St. Louis.
Vehisote — (b) — AGOSOTA MILLBOARD CO., Trenton, N. J.
Velinian Bond — (w) — STRATHMORE PAPER CO., Mittineague, Mass.
Vellum—(b)—bristols—UNION CARD & PAPER CO., New York.
Vellum Mills—(w)—No. 1 fine—DONALDSON PAPER CO., Harrisburg, Pa.
Vellum Mounts — (b) — STRATHMORE PAPER CO., Mittineague, Mass.
Vellum Offset—(b) — TILESTON & HOLLINGSWORTH CO., Boston.
Vellum Surface — (b) — G E O. B. HURD & CO., New York.
Velutin—(b)—half tone and writing—UNION CARD & PAPER CO., N. Y.
Velveme—(b)—coated book—MEGARGEE BROS., Scranton, Pa.
Velvet—(b)—toilet, cardboards and cards—GRAHAM PAPER CO., St. Louis.
Velvet —(b)— toilet — U N I T E D STATES ENVELOPE CO. (Morgan Envelope Co. Div.), Springfield, Mass.
Velvet Antique Book—(b)—HARLEM CARD & PAPER CO., New York.
Velvet Blotting — (b) — HARLEM CARD & PAPER CO., New York.
Velvet Bristol—(b)—B R A D N E R SMITH & CO., Chicago.
Velvet Finish—(b)—GEO. B. HURD & CO., New York.
Velvet Finish—(b)—book and cardboard—J. W. BUTLER PAPER CO., Chicago.
Velvet Finish—(b)—blanks—MEGARGEE-HARE PAPER CO., Philadelphia.
Velvet Finish Book—(w)—CARTER, RICE & CO., CORP., Boston.
Velvet Tag Board — (b) — RICHMOND PAPER CO., Richmond, Va.

Velveteen—(b)—MISSOURI PAPER HOUSE, Kansas City, Mo.
Velveteen —(b)— book — D I E M & WING PAPER CO., Cincinnati, Ohio.
Velveteen Bristol—(b)—HOLYOKE CARD AND PAPER CO., Holyoke.
Velvet Granite—(b)—GEO. B. HURD & CO., New York.
Velvet Writing — (b) — white and canary — RICHMOND PAPER CO., Richmond, Va.
Velvetone Coated Book—(b)—MACK-ELLIOTT PAPER CO., St. Louis.
Velvety—(b)—book—GRAHAM PAPER CO., St. Louis.
Velvo Enamel — (b) — WEST VIRGINIA PULP & PAPER CO., New York.
Vencedor—(w)—bond, writing and wrapping—W. R. GRACE & CO., New York.
Vendome—(b)—colored bristol—W. H. CLAFLIN & CO., Boston.
Vendome Mills—(w)—COOK-VIVIAN CO., Boston.
Venetia—(w)—JAPAN PAPER CO., New York.
Venetian—(b)— cover — AMERICAN WRITING PAPER CO., Holyoke, Mass.
Venetian — (w) — CLEVELAND PAPER MANUFACTURING CO., Cleveland, Ohio.
Venetian Bond —(w)— AMERICAN WRITING PAPER CO., Holyoke, Mass.
Venetian Colored Coated—(b)—PAUL E. VERNON & CO., New York.
Venetian Repp—(b)—GEO. B. HURD & CO., New York.
Venetian Superfine Tinted Flat—(w)—MINNEAPOLIS PAPER CO., Minneapolis, Minn.
Venetian Vellum—(w)—POWERS PAPER COMPANY, Springfield, Mass.
Venesia—(w and b)—hand-made cover—PAPER MILLS CO., Chicago.
Venice—(b)—onion skin — WHITING-PATTERSON CO., Philadelphia.
Venus Transparent Parchment—(b)—GRAHAM PAPER CO., St. Louis.
Vera—(w)—bond—W. R. GRACE & CO., New York.
Vera Cruz — (b) — bond — WHITING-PATTERSON CO., Philadelphia.
Veritas Cover—(b)—JOHN CARTER & CO., Boston.
Vermont Bristol—(b)—MISSISQUOI PULP & PAPER CO., Sheldon Springs, Vt.
Vermont Linen Ledger—(b)—OLD DOMINION PAPER CO., Norfolk, Va.
Verndale—(b)—colored laid writing—PAUL E. VERNON & CO., New York.
Verno Catalog Book—(b)—PAUL E. VERNON & CO., New York.
Vernon—(b)—book—C. P. LESH PAPER CO., Louisville, Ky.
Vernon's Linen Ledger—(b)—PAUL E. VERNON & CO., New York.

Vernton Mills Extra Strong—(b) —colored, coated white and duplex— PAUL E. VERNON, New York.
Verona—(w)—LOUISVILLE PAPER CO., Louisville, Ky.
Verona Linen—(b)—PAUL E. VERNON & CO., New York.
Vertical — (b) — second sheets — GRAHAM PAPER CO., St. Louis.
V. Fine Writing—(b)—PAUL E. VERNON & CO., New York.
Veryfine Linen Laid—(w)—GEO. B. HURD & CO., New York.
Veryfine Linen Wove—(w)—GEO. B. HURD & CO., New York.
Vesper—(w)—bond—MIDLAND PAPER CO., Chicago.
Vesper Bond—(w)—W. M. PRINGLE & CO., INC., New York.
Vesper Manila—(b)—C. S. PROCTOR PAPER CO., Boston.
Vesta Colored Writing — (b) — HENRY LINDENMEYR & SONS, New York.
Vesta Fine—(w)—B O O R U M & PEASE CO., New York.
Vesta Linen Ledger—(w)—BOORUM & PEASE CO., New York.
Vesture Bond—(w)—GARRETT-BUCHANAN CO., Philadelphia.
Viceroy Blanks—(b)—TROY PAPER CO., Troy, N. Y.
Viceroy Bristol—(b)—THE UNION PAPER & TWINE CO., Detroit, Mich.
Vicksburg Bond—(w)—LEE PAPER CO., Vicksburg, Mich.
Victor—(b)— wrapping — GRAHAM PAPER CO., St. Louis.
Victor—(b)—blotting—GARRETT-BUCHANAN CO., Philadelphia.
Victor—(b)—b r i s t o l—MEGARGEE-HARE PAPER CO., Philadelphia.
Victor—(b)—enamel — ROBERTSON PAPER CO., Bellow Falls, Vt.
Victor—(b)—tag brand — C H A T-FIELD & WOODS CO., Cincinnati.
Victor—(b)—toilet—W I L S O N & TOWNE PAPER CO., New York.
Victor—(b)—toilet—ALBANY PERFORATED WRAPPING PAPER CO., Albany, N. Y.
Victor—(b)—flats—KANSAS C I T Y PAPER HOUSE, Kansas City, Mo.
Victor—(b)—rope manila—STONE & FORSYTH CO., Boston.
Victor—(b)—plain blanks — HAGEN PAPER CO., St. Louis.
Victor—(b)—folding bristol—McCLELLAN PAPER CO., Minneapolis.
Victor—(b)—half-tone—J. E. LINDE PAPER CO., New York.
Victor Blank—(b)—A. STORRS & BEMENT CO., Boston.
Victor Bond—(w)—white and tinted —CHATFIELD & WOODS CO., Cincinnati, Ohio.
Victor Bond—(w)—A M E R I C A N WRITING PAPER CO., Holyoke, Mass.

Victor Bond—(b)—CARTER, RICE & CO., CORP., Boston.
Victor Bristol—(b)—colored—CHATFIELD & WOODS CO., Cincinnati, O.
Victor Ivory Boards—(b)—PARSONS TRADING CO., New York.
Victor Manila—(b)—JOHN CARTER & CO., Boston.
Victor Manila—(w) — BRADNER SMITH & CO., Chicago.
Victor Mills—(b) — A. STORRS & BEMENT CO., Boston.
Victor Mills—(w)—writing—STANDARD CARD & PAPER CO., New York.
Victor Tag—(b) — CHATFIELD & WOODS CO., Cincinnati Ohio.
Victoria—(b) — pasted board—McCLELLAN PAPER CO., Minneapolis.
Victoria — (b) — second sheets — GRAHAM PAPER CO., St. Louis.
Victoria—(b)—toilet—OLD DOMINION PAPER CO., Norfolk, Va.
Victoria Bond—(w)—F. W. ANDERSON & CO., New York.
Victoria Bond — (w) — WM. G. JOHNSTON & CO., Pittsburgh, Pa.
Victoria Lawn—(w)—POWERS PAPER COMPANY, Springfield, Mass.
Victoria Linen—(b)—flat—DIEM & WING PAPER CO., Cincinnati, O.
Victoria Linen—(b)—O. F. H. WARNER & CO., Baltimore.
Victoria Linen—(w)—VALLEY PAPER CO., Holyoke, Mass.
Victoria Linen—(w and crown)—GARRETT-BUCHANAN CO., Philadelphia.
Victoria Linen Bond—(w)—VALLEY PAPER CO., Holyoke.
Victoria Linen Ledger—(w)—VALLEY PAPER CO., Holyoke, Mass.
Victoria Slaters—(b)—tarred felt—GRAHAM PAPER CO., St. Louis.
Victoria Vellum—(b) — GEO. B. HURD & CO., New York.
Victory Bond — (w) — HOWARD SMITH PAPER MILLS, LTD., Montreal, Que.
Victory Campaign—(b)—post card —LOUISVILLE PAPER CO., Louisville, Ky.
Vidalon—(w)—cover—C. D. BROWN & CO., Boston.
Vienna Bond — (w) — COOK-VIVIAN CO., Boston.
Vienna Cover—(b) —COOK-VIVIAN CO., Boston.
Vienna Crystal—(b) — BERLIN & JONES ENVELOPE CO., New York.
Vienna Index Bristol—(b)—COOK-VIVIAN CO., Boston.
Vienna Ledger—(w)—COOK-VIVIAN CO., Boston.
Vienna Linen—(b) — McCLELLAN PAPER CO., Minneapolis, Minn.
Vienna Linen — (w) — laid — FOX RIVER PAPER CO., Appleton, Wis.
Vienna Moire—(w)— ALBEMARLE PAPER MFG. CO., Richmond, Va.

Watermarks and Brands 749

Vienna Moire — (b) — blotting — W. H. CLAFLIN & CO., Boston.
Vigilant Bond — (w) — CAREW MANUFACTURING CO., South Hadley Falls, Mass.
Vignette—(b)—book—GRAHAM PAPER CO., St. Louis.
Vignette Half Tone Super—(b)— HENRY LINDENMEYR & S O N S. New York.
Viking—(b) — toilet—ALBANY PERFORATED WRAPPING PAPER CO., Albany, New York.
Viking Kraft—(w)—FISHER BROS. PAPER CO., Fort Wayne, Ind.
Viking Linen Cream Laid—(w)— HENRY LINDENMEYR & SONS, New York.
Vinco Mills—(b)—WHITAKER PAPER CO., Cincinnati, Ohio.
Vindex — (b)—toilet—M. J. EARL, Reading, Pa.
Vineta—(b)—photo mount — UNION CARD & PAPER CO., New York.
Violet—(w)—with design—writing—PARSONS TRADING CO., New York.
Violet—(b)—toilet—CHATFIELD PAPER CO., New Haven, Conn.
Violet Mills—(w)—CARTER, RICE & CO., CORP., Boston.
Violet Parchment — JOHN WANAMAKER, Philadelphia.
Vireo Bond — (w) — CINCINNATI CORDAGE AND PAPER CO., Cincinnati, Ohio.
Virgin White—(b) — coated book— W. H. CLAFLIN & CO., Boston.
Virginia—(b)—book — GRAHAM PAPER CO., St. Louis.
Virginia Antique Laid Book—(b) —KINGSLEY PAPER CO., Cleveland.
Vistula Bond—(w)—O. H. ANDERSON & CO., New York.
Vogue—(b)—cards — THE PAPER MILLS CO., Chicago.
Voile—(b) — POWERS PAPER CO., Springfield, Mass.
Voucher Bond—(w)—J. W. BUTLER PAPER CO., Chicago.
Vulcan—(w)—fine — EAU CLAIRE BOOK & STATIONERY CO., Eau Claire, Wis.
Vulcan—(b)—rope tag — ARNOLD-ROBERTS CO., Boston.
Vulcan Bond — CAREW MANUFACTURING CO., South Hadley Falls, Mass.
Vulcan Ledger — (w) — DIEM & WING PAPER CO., Cincinnati, Ohio.
Vulcan Linen — (b) — writing— CAREW MANUFACTURING CO., South Hadley Falls, Mass.
Vulcan Linen Ledger — (w)—writing—CAREW MANUFACTURING CO., South Hadley Falls, Mass.
Vulcan Mills—(b)—A. STORRS & BEMENT CO., Boston.
Vulcan Mills—(b)—colored laid flat — R. P. ANDREWS PAPER CO., Washington, D. C.

W

"W"—(b)—HY. L I N D E N M E Y R & SONS, New York.
Wabacoat—(b) — enamel book and cover, litho paper and blanks and folding bristol—WABASH COATING MILLS, Wabash, Ind.
Wabash Mills — (b) — THOS. W PRICE CO., Philadelphia.
Wabash Wove—(w)—WHITING PAPER CO., Holyoke, Mass.
Waconnah Mills—(w) — BYRON WESTON CO., Dalton, Mass.
Wadjo—(b) — HOLLINGSWORTH & WHITNEY CO., Boston.
Wafer Carbon Copy—(b) — BRADNER SMITH & CO., Chicago.
Wakefield—(b) — book — W. H. GEORGE, Philadelphia.
Waldo Mills—(b)—C. P. LESH PAPER CO., Indianapolis.
Waldo Mills—(b) — TROY PAPER CO., Troy, New York.
Waldorf—(b) — SCOTT PAPER CO., Philadelphia.
Waldorf Laid—(b)—book — LOUISVILLE PAPER CO., Louisville, Ky.
Wall Street Linen—(w) — F. W. ANDERSON & CO., New York.
Wallace — (b) — book—GRAHAM PAPER CO., St. Louis.
Walrus—(b)—ruled headings — CONROW BROS., New York.
Walton—(b)—PEERLESS MFG. CO., Norristown, Pa.
Walton—(b)—bristol — C. P. LESH PAPER CO., Indianapolis, Ind.
Wamesit Manila Tag—(b)—C. S. PROCTOR PAPER CO., Boston.
Wampum Linen—(b) — white laid— HENRY LINDENMEYR & SONS, New York.
Wang—(b)—toilet—H. N O R W O O D EWING CO., New York.
Wantaga—(b)—MORGAN & HAMILTON CO., Nashville, Tenn.
Ward's Boston Bond — (w)—SAMUEL WARD MFG. CO., Boston.
Ward's Boston Ledger — (w)— SAMUEL WARD MFG. CO., Boston.
Ward's Boston Linen — (w)—SAMUEL WARD MFG. CO., Boston.
Ward's Bunker Hill Bond—(w)— SAMUEL WARD MFG. CO., Boston.
Ward's Bunker Hill Ledger—(w) —SAMUEL WARD MFG. CO., Boston.
Ward's Bunker Hill Linen—(w)— SAMUEL WARD MFG. CO., Boston.
Ward's Elsmere Linen — (w)— SAMUEL WARD MFG. CO., Boston.
Ward's Swaco Linen — (w)—SAMUEL WARD MFG. CO., Boston.
Ward's Trimount Bond — (w)— SAMUEL WARD MFG. CO., Boston.
Ward's Wardwove Linen — (w)— SAMUEL WARD MFG. CO., Boston.

Watermarks and Brands

Warewell Enamel — (b) — book — LOUISVILLE PAPER CO., Louisville, Ky.
Warhawk—(b) — gummed — LOUIS- PER CO., Louisville, Ky.
Warp and Woof—(w)—extra superfine—J. C. BLAIR CO., Huntingdon, Pa.
Warrantee Bond — (b)—white and colored bond—R. C. KASTNER PAPER CO., New York.
Warranty—(b)—J. C. BLAIR CO., Huntingdon, Pa.
Warren's Art Gravure—(b) —book —J. W. BUTLER PAPER CO., Chicago.
Warren's Cameo Plate—(b)—writing—J. W. BUTLER PAPER CO., Chicago.
Warren's Cameo Plate Coated— (b)—book—J. W. BUTLER PAPER CO., Chicago.
Warren's Cumberland Coated — book—S. & S. C. and M. F.—J. W. BUTLER PAPER CO., Chicago.
Warren's Lustro Coated — (b)— book—J. W. BUTLER PAPER CO., Chicago.
Warren's Printone—(b)—book — J. W. BUTLER PAPER CO., Chicago.
Warren's Superfine Coated—(b)— book—J. W. BUTLER PAPER CO., Chicago.
Warrentown—(w)—regular book, eggshell and "Med" finish, white—S. D. WARREN & CO., Boston.
Warrington — (b) — b o o k —W. H. GEORGE, Philadelphia.
Warrior—(b)—bristol—LOUISVILLE PAPER CO., Louisville, Ky.
Warsaw Ledger—(w) — WHITING-PATTERSON CO., Philadelphia.
Warsaw Mills—(b)—colored—THOS. W. PRICE CO., Philadelphia.
Warwick— (w) — ledger—L E S L I E-DONAHOWER CO., St. Paul.
Warwick—(b)—LOUISVILLE PAPER CO., Louisville, Ky.
Warwick—(w)—flats—W E S T E R N PAPER CO., Omaha, Neb.
Warwick Ledger—(w)—FOX RIVER PAPER CO., Appleton, Wis.
Warwick Linen — (w)—STRATHMORE PAPER CO., Mittineague, Mass.
Warwick Plate—(b)—bristol—J. C. PARKER PAPER CO., Louisville, Ky.
Warwick Superfine—(w) — WHITING PAPER CO., Holyoke, Mass.
Warwick Wedding Bristol—(b)— UNION PAPER & TWINE CO., Detroit, Mich.
Waseda Bond—(w) — KALAMAZOO PAPER CO., Kalamazoo, Mich.
Washington— (b) —b o x covering— DISTRICT OF COLUMBIA PAPER MFG. CO., Washington, D. C
Washington—(b)—binders' trunk and friction board — GRAHAM PAPER CO., St. Louis.

Washington—(w) — writing — GRAHAM PAPER CO., St. Louis.
Washington Bond—(w)—LEE PAPER CO., Vicksburg, Mich.
Washington Brilliant — (b) — box coverings—DISTRICT OF COLUMBIA, Washington, D. C.
Washington C o v e r s — (b) —DISTRICT OF COLUMBIA PAPER MFG. CO., Washington, D. C.
Washington Mills—(b) — toilet— HALLETT BROS., Boston.
Washington Mills—(w) — HUDSON VALLEY PAPER CO., Albany, N. Y.
Washington Plate—(b)—SEYMOUR CO., New York.
Wateredge — (w)—bond—GRAHAM PAPER CO., St. Louis.
Watered Embossed—(b)—GEO. B. HURD & CO., New York.
Waterleaf—(b)—SOUTHERN PAPER COMPANY, Richmond, Va.
Waterleaf — (w) — mimeograph — GRAHAM PAPER CO., St. Louis.
Waterleaf—(b)—blotting — CHATFIELD & WOODS CO., Cincinnati.
Waterlite—(b)—vegetable parchment —MINNEAPOLIS PAPER CO., Minneapolis, Minn.
Waterways—(w)—writing — GRAHAM PAPER CO., St. Louis.
Waterways Bond—(w)—FOX RIVER PAPER CO., Appleton, Wis.
Waterways Bond — (w)—WRIGHT, BARRETT & STILWELL CO., St. Paul, Minn.
Watkins Press—Extra Quality— (w)—JOHN B. WATKINS CO., N. Y.
Waugumbang—(b)—bond — SOUTH COVENTRY PAPER CO., South Coventry, Conn.
Waukon Bond—(b) — C. P. LESH PAPER CO., Indianapolis, Ind.
Wavene Cover—(b)—PENINSULAR PAPER CO., Ypsilanti, Mich.
Waverly — (b) — book — BEECHER, PECK & LEWIS, Detroit, Mich.
Waverly — (b) — coated blotting— ARNOLD-ROBERTS CO., Boston.
Waverly—(w)—flats—KANSAS CITY PAPER HOUSE, Kansas City, Mo.
Waverly—(b)—blotting — KANSAS CITY PAPER HOUSE, Kansas City.
Waverly—(b)—news—GRAHAM PAPER CO., St. Louis.
Waverly Bond — (b) — C. P. LESH PAPER CO., Indianapolis.
Waverly Egg Shell — (b) — book —BRADNER SMITH & CO., Chicago.
Waverly Linen—(w) — MERRIAM PAPER CO., New York.
Waverly M i l l s—(w) —B Y R O N WESTON CO., Dalton, Mass.
Waverly Vellum — (b) — JOHN CARTER & CO., Boston.
Wawasa—(b)—flat, bristol and book— J. W. BUTLER PAPER CO., Chicago.
Waybill—(b)—writing — GRAHAM PAPER CO., St. Louis.

Wayne—(b)—super book—CHATFIELD & WOODS CO., Cincinnati, O.
Wayne Mills—(b)—J. E. LINDE PAPER CO., New York.
Wayne Mills—(b)—white writing—JOHNSTON PAPER CO., Harrisburg, Pa.
Wayside—(b) — writing — UNION CARD AND PAPER CO., New York.
Wayside—(w) — writing — UNION CARD AND PAPER CO., N. Y.
Webster—(w)—HAMMERMILL PAPER CO., Erie, Pa.
Webster—(b)—book—GRAHAM PAPER CO., St. Louis.
Webster— (b) — book—LOUISVILLE PAPER CO., Louisville, Pa.
Webster Bond—(w)—HOWARD PAPER CO.. Urbana. O.
Weeco Bond — (w) — WALKER, EVANS & COGSWELL CO., Charleston, S. C.
Weeco Superfine —(w)—WALKER, EVANS & COGSWELL CO., Charleston, S. C.
Wedgewood—(w) — white wove—UNITED STATES ENVELOPE CO. (Plimpton Mfg. Co. Division), Hartford, Conn.
Weldon Mills Fine—(w) — KEITH PAPER CO., Turners Falls, Mass.
Welfare Bond—(w and b)—bond, ledger—NEENAH PAPER CO., Neenah, Wis.
Welland Wove — (w)—writing—KINLEITH PAPER CO., LTD., St. Catharines, Ont.
Wellington—(w)—bond— MIDLAND PAPER CO., Chicago.
Wellington—(b) — writing — GRAHAM PAPER CO., St. Louis.
Wellington—(b)—toilet — UNITED STATES ENVELOPE CO. (Morgan Envelope Co. Division), Springfield.
Wellington — (b)—WHITAKER PAPER CO., Cincinnati, Ohio.
Wellington — (b) — flat—WHITING PAPER CO., Holyoke, Mass.
Wellington Check—(w)—writing — GRAHAM PAPER CO., St. Louis.
Wellington Colored Laid—(b) — J. E. LINDE PAPER CO., New York.
Wellington Wove — (w) — KINLEITH PAPER CO., Canada.
Wellmade Linen Ledger — (w) — HOWARD SMITH PAPER MILLS, LTD., Montreal, Can.
Wellworth— (b)—envelope—GRAHAM PAPER CO., St. Louis.
Welmaid—(b) — toilet — SCOTT PAPER CO., Philadelphia.
Wenlock Bond—(w)—ruled and flat —H. S. CROCKER CO., San Francisco.
Wenlock Linen—(w)—ruled and flat —H. S. CROCKER CO., San Francisco.
Wenlock Vellum — (w) — ruled and flat — H. S. CROCKER CO., San Francisco.
Wenonah Superfine — (w) — W. E. WROE & CO., Chicago.

Werner Bond—(w)—THE WERNER CO., Akron, Ohio.
Westend—(w)—flats—WESTERN PAPER CO., Omaha, Neb.
Westerly Writing—(b)—JUDD PAPER CO., Holyoke, Mass.
Western — (b)—toilet — NORTHERN PAPER MILLS, Green Bay, Wis.
Western King—(b) — ALEX. McARTHUR & CO., LTD., Montreal.
Western Blanks — (b) — McCLELLAN PAPER CO., Minneapolis, Minn.
Western Bond — (w) — KANSAS CITY PAPER CO., Kansas City, Mo.
Westfall—(b) — book and label — GRAHAM PAPER CO., St. Louis.
Westford Ledger—(b)—MILLER & WRIGHT PAPER CO., INC., New York.
Westgate Linen Ledger — (w)— BLUNDER-LYON CO., Chicago.
West Indian — (b) — cover—J. W. BUTLER PAPER CO., Chicago.
Westlaid Flats — (w) — WESTERN PAPER CO., Omaha, Neb.
Westlake—(w)—flats—WESTERN PAPER CO., Omaha, Neb.
Westlock Linen Record — (w)— KEITH PAPER CO., Turners Falls, Mass.
Westlock Superfine — (w)—KEITH PAPER CO., Turners Falls, Mass.
Westminster — (b)—cover—J. W. BUTLER PAPER CO., Chicago.
Westminster—(b)—GEO. T. JOHNSON CO., Boston.
Westminster, A. S. & B. Quality —(w)—A. STORRS & BEMENT CO., Boston.
Westminster Bond — (w)—flats—R. L. GREENE PAPER CO., Providence, R. I.
Westminster Linen—(w and b) — CUNNINGHAM, CURTISS & WELCH, Los Angeles.
Westminster Linen—(w) — CHAS. T. BAINBRIDGE'S SONS, INC., Brooklyn, New York.
Westmore—(w) — writing—BRYANT PAPER CO., Kalamazoo, Mich.
Westmont Enamel —(w) — WEST VIRGINIA PULP & PAPER CO., New York.
Weston—(b)—S. & S. C.—J. P. HEILBRONN CO., Manila, P. I.
Weston's Flexible Hinge Loose Leaf Ledger—(b)—BYRON WESTON CO., Dalton, Mass.
Weston's Linen Ledger and Record — (w) — BYRON WESTON CO., Dalton, Mass.
Westover—(b) — book — WM. H. GEORGE, Philadelphia.
Westover Mills — (b) — enamel— W. H. GEORGE, Philadelphia.
Westover Mills — (w) — No. 2 fine —OLD DOMINION PAPER CO., Norfolk, Va.
West Penna. Colored, Enameled, book—(b) — WESTERN PENNA. PAPER CO., Pittsburgh.

West Point—(b) — cover — JAS. WHITE PAPER CO., Chicago.
Westport—(w)—writing— M E G A R- GEE-HARE PAPER CO., Philadelphia.
West Rock Mills—(b) — blotting, matrix and cover—JOSEPH PARKER & SON CO., New Haven, Conn.
Westvaco—S. & S. C. and M. F.—(b) —book—WEST VIRGINIA PULP & PAPER CO., New York.
Wetherton Bond — (w) — HAGEN PAPER CO., St. Louis.
Wexford — (b) — ledger—MILLER & WRIGHT PAPER CO., New York.
Wexford Mills — (w) — ledger — J. G. SHAW BLANK BOOK CO., N. Y.
Wexford Mills—(b) — writing — GRAHAM PAPER CO., St. Louis.
Wexford Mills — (w) — GRAHAM PAPER CO., St. Louis.
Weymouth Bond—(w) — AFFLECK RULING & STATIONERY CO., INC., Holyoke, Mass.
Weymouth Superfine White—(w) —AFFLECK RULING & STATIONERY CO., INC., Holyoke, Mass.
What Cheer — (b) — manila — R. L. GREENE PAPER CO., Providence.
Whatman—(b)—filter, writing and ledger—H. REEVE ANGEL & CO., INC., New York.
W. H. H. Pure Linen — (w) — UNITED STATES ENVELOPE CO. (W. H. Hill Envelope Co. Division), Worcester, Mass.
White Bond Cover—(w)—JAMES WHITE PAPER CO., Chicago.
White Chinese Express Wrapping — (b) — GRAHAM PAPER CO., St. Louis.
White & Wyckoff Hand Spun— (w)—WHITE & WYCKOFF MFG. CO., Holyoke, Mass.
White Chief Jute — (b)—HOLLIS & DUNCAN, Chicago.
White Circular—(b) — BRADNER SMITH & CO., Chicago.
White Cloud—(b) — book and music —GRAHAM PAPER CO., St Louis.
White Drug—(b) — wrapping and specialties — McDOWELL PAPER MILL, Manayunk, Pa.
White Enameled Book—(b)—ME- GARGEE-HARE CO., Philadelphia.
White Exchange—(b) — KANSAS CITY PAPER HOUSE, Kansas City.
White Express — (b) — roll toilet —CHATFIELD & WOODS CO., Cincinnati, Ohio.
White Falls Dull Finish Butcher's Fibre—(b)—CHATFIELD & WOODS CO., Cincinnati, Ohio.
White Feather Bond — (w) — JOHN LESLIE PAPER CO., Minneapolis, Minn.
White Feather Bond—(w)—WHITING-PLOVER PAPER CO., Stevens Point, Wis.
Whitefriars—(b) — double enameled cover—JAMES WHITE PAPER CO., Chicago.

Whitehall—(w and b)—carbon, laid and woven writing, tags and boards— PARSONS TRADING CO., New York.
Whitehall—(b)—bristol and blotting —PARSONS TRADING CO., N. Y.
Whitehall—(w)—bond and ledger— PARSONS TRADING CO., N. Y.
White House—(b)—m. f. white book— THE ALLING & CORY CO., Rochester.
White House—(b)—s. & s. c. white book—THE ALLING & CORY CO., Rochester, N. Y.
White House—(b) — blotting—W. H. CLAFLIN & CO., Boston.
White House—(w and b)—GEO. B. HURD & CO., New York.
White House — (b) — white wove —F. A. FLINN, INC., New York.
White House Blotting — (b) — DISTRICT OF COLUMBIA PAPER MFG. CO., Washington, D. C.
White House Cover — (b)—DISTRICT OF COLUMBIA PAPER MFG. CO., Washington, D. C.
White House Cover—(b)—WHITING-PATTERSON CO., Philadelphia.
White Ivory Superfine Book—(b) —KINGSLEY PAPER CO., Cleveland.
White Kid—(b)—COLUMBIA PAPER BAG CO., New York.
White Lily—(b)—toilet — ALBANY PERFORATED WRAPPING PAPER CO., Albany, New York.
White Linen—(b) — M. F. white— A. M EATON, Waltham and Boston.
White Mountain—(b)—coated—BAY STATE PAPER CO., Boston.
White Mountain—(b)—deckle-edge cover—JAMES WHITE PAPER CO., Chicago.
White Mountain Enamel — (b)— WHITAKER PAPER CO., Cincinnati.
White Pacific Flats — (w) — BRADNER SMITH & CO., Chicago.
White Rapids Superfine—(b)—No. 1 writing—WHITING-PLOVER PAPER CO., Stevens Point, Wis.
White Rock Bond—(w)—THE W. B. OGLESBY PAPER CO., Middletown, Ohio.
White Rock Linen Ledger—(w)— THE W. B. OGLESBY PAPER CO., Middletown, Ohio.
White Satin — (b) — fibre—W. H. CLAFLIN & CO., Boston.
White Seal — (b) — toilet — NORTHERN PAPER MILLS, Green Bay, Wis.
Whiteside—(b) — writing — GRAHAM PAPER CO., St. Louis.
White Spruce — (b) — dry finish fibre—CHATFIELD & WOODS CO., Cincinnati, Ohio.
White Squadron — (b) — wrapping —GRAHAM PAPER CO., St. Louis.
White Star — (b) — fibre—W. H. CLAFLIN & CO., Boston.
White Star—(b)—cover—JAS. LEWIS PAPER CO., Chicago, Ill.
White's Bond Cover—(w) — JAS. WHITE PAPER CO., Chicago.

White Star—(b) — cover — JAMES WHITE PAPER CO., Chicago.
White Star—(w) — flats — HAGEN PAPER CO., St. Louis.
Whitestone — (w) — flat—DIEM & WING PAPER CO., Cincinnati.
Whitest White Enameled Book — (b)—THE UNION PAPER & TWINE CO., Detroit, Mich.
Whitewater — (w) — AMERICAN WRITING PAPER CO., Holyoke.
White Wove — (b) — CONROW BROS., New York.
White Wove Bond No. 1600—(b) UNITED STATES ENVELOPE CO., Springfield, Mass.
White Wove Bond No. 2100—(b) —UNITED STATES ENVELOPE CO., Springfield, Mass.
Whiting Paper Co.—(w)—superfine and colored writing—WHITING PAPER CO., Holyoke, Mass.
Whiting's Angora — (w)—WHITING PAPER CO., Holyoke, Mass.
Whiting's Bond—(w) — WHITING PAPER CO., Holyoke, Mass.
Whiting's Consulate Linen—(w) —WHITING PAPER CO., Holyoke.
Whiting's Edinburgh Linen—(w) —WHITING PAPER CO., Holyoke.
Whiting's Imperial Bond — (w)— WHITING PAPER CO., Holyoke.
Whiting's Irish Linen — (w) — WHITING PAPER CO., Holyoke.
Whiting's Linen Ledger—(w) — WHITING PAPER CO., Holyoke.
Whiting's Longfellow Linen—(w) —WHITING PAPER CO., Holyoke.
Whiting's No. 1—(w)—WHITING PAPER CO., Holyoke, Mass.
Whiting's Original Turkey Linen —(w)—WHITING PAPER CO., Holyoke, Mass.
Whiting's Parchment — (w) — WHITING PAPER CO., Holyoke.
Whiting's Pompeian—(w)—WHITING PAPER CO., Holyoke, Mass.
Whiting's Standard Ledger—(w) WHITING PAPER CO., Holyoke.
Whiting's Westminster Vellum— (w)—WHITING PAPER CO., Holyoke, Mass.
Whiting's Woven Linen — (w)— WHITING PAPER CO., Holyoke.
Whitover — (b) — book and label— GRAHAM PAPER CO., St. Louis.
Wicker—(b)— cover — ALEXANDER-HOLDEN PAPER CO., New York.
Wilbraham Ledger—(w)—COLLINS MFG. CO., N. Wilbraham, Mass.
Wild Grass—(b)—bond and bristol— UNION CARD & PAPER CO., N. Y.
Wild Grass—(b)—cover and bond— RIEGEL & CO., INC., Philadelphia.
Wild Grass Bond—(w)—with design —STRATHMORE PAPER CO., Mittineague, Mass.
Wild Grass Bristol—(w)—with design — STRATHMORE PAPER CO., Mittineague, Mass.

Wild Grass Cover—(w)—with design — STRATHMORE PAPER CO., Mittineague, Mass.
Wild Grass Duplex—(w)—with design—cover and mount — STRATHMORE PAPER CO., Mittineague, Mass.
Wildair—(b) — book — LOUISVILLE PAPER CO., Louisville, Ky.
Wildlawn—(b)—covers and bristol— —CHAS. H. WRIGHT, Kalamazoo.
Wildwood — (b)—covers and bristols —CHAS. H. WRIGHT, Kalamazoo.
Wilfred Bond — (w) — BLUNDEN-LYON CO., Chicago.
Wilfred Linen Ledger—(w)—BLUNDER-LYON CO., Chicago.
Wilgrad Bond—(b) — W. H. H. CHAMBERLAIN, Syracuse, N. Y.
Willamette Mills—(w) — PAYOT, UPHAM & CO., San Francisco.
William Esra Bond—(b)—THE JENNER CO., Louisville, Ky.
William Penn Bond—(w)—DONALDSON PAPER CO., Harrisburg, Pa.
Willkommen—(b)—toilet — NORTHERN PAPER MILLS, Green Bay, Wis.
Willow Bond — (w) — SWIGART PAPER CO., Chicago.
Willowdean Bond—(w) — LOUISVILLE PAPER CO, Louisville, Ky.
Wilsel—(b) — toilet—SCOTT PAPER CO., Philadelphia.
Wilton — (b) — book—MILLER & WRIGHT PAPER CO., New York.
Wimpus — (w) — WRIGHT, BARRETT & STILWELL CO., St. Paul.
Winchester — (b) — book—GRAHAM PAPER CO., St. Louis.
Windsor — (w and b) — cover — AMERICAN WRITING PAPER CO., Holyoke, Mass.
Windsor — (b) — writing — BASSETT & SUTPHIN, New York.
Windsor—(w) — McCLELLAN PAPER CO., Minneapolis, Minn.
Windsor — (b) — cover — SEYMOUR CO., New York.
Windsor Bristol — (b) —CHATFIELD & WOODS CO., Cincinnati.
Windsor Folding Bristol — (b) — KINGSLEY PAPER CO., Cleveland.
Windsor Mills — (w) — No. 8 fine— GRAY, EWING & CO., Spokane.
Windsor Offset Paper — (b) — BRADNER SMITH & CO., Chicago.
Windsor Tinted Superfine — (b) — C. P. LESH PAPER CO., Indianapolis.
Winfield—(b)—book—GRAHAM PAPER CO., St. Louis.
Wingate—(b)—book and label—GRAHAM PAPER CO., St. Louis.
Winnebago Bond—(b)—WHITING-PLOVER PAPER CO., Menasha, Wis.
Winnebago Flats—(w)—BRADNER SMITH & CO., Chicago.
Winner—(b)—KANSAS CITY PAPER CO., Kansas City, Mo.

Winner—(b)—toilet—ALBANY PERFORATED WRAPPING PAPER CO., Albany, N. Y.
Winner Bond—(w)—HOWARD PAPER CO., Urbana, O.
Winnetka —(b)—bristols—SWIGART PAPER CO., Chicago.
Winona—(b)—wrapping, book and label—GRAHAM PAPER CO., St. Louis.
Winona—(b)—white writing—CHATFIELD & WOODS CO., Cincinnati.
Winslow —(b)— HOLLINGSWORTH & WHITNEY CO., New York.
Winslow's—(b)—toilet—U N I T E D STATES ENVELOPE CO. (Morgan Envelope Co. Div.), Springfield, Mass.
Winston—(b)—half tone writing—C. P. LESH PAPER CO., Indianapolis.
Winter White Bristol—(b)—pasted bristol—B. D. RISING PAPER CO., Housatonic, Mass.
Winterset—(b)—book—GRAHAM PAPER CO., St. Louis.
Winthrop—(b)—coated blank—ARNOLD-ROBERTS CO., Boston.
Winthrop County Bond—(w)—PLYMOUTH PAPER CO., Holyoke.
Winthrop Ledger—(w)—MILLER & WRIGHT PAPER CO., New York.
Winthrop Onion Skin—(b)—JUDD PAPER CO., Holyoke, Mass.
Winthrop Superfine—(b)—writing—CAREW MANUFACTURING CO., South Hadley Falls, Mass.
Wm. G. Johnston & Co. Linen Ledger, Pittsburgh, Pa.—(w)—WM. G. JOHNSTON & CO., Pittsburgh, Pa.
Wm. G. J. & Co. Ledger Bond—(w)—WM. G. JOHNSTON & CO., Pittsburgh, Pa.
W. King—(w)—hand-made printing—C. D. BROWN & CO., Boston.
Wm. Penn Bond—(w)—DONALDSON PAPER CO., Harrisburg, Pa.
Wireless Bond—(w)—GILBERT PAPER CO., Menasha, Wis.
Wireless—(b)—PERKINS, GOODWIN CO., New York.
Wireless Bond—(w)—BUNTIN, GILLIES & CO., LTD., Hamilton, Can.
Wireless Onion Skin—(b)—F. A. FLINN, INC., New York.
Wirthmor—(b)—toilet—SCOTT PAPER CO., Philadelphia.
Wisconsin Bond—(w)—AMERICAN WRITING PAPER CO., Holyoke, Mass.
Wisdom—(b and w)—bond, linen and ledger — NEENAH PAPER CO., Neenah, Wis.
Wissahickon Carpet Lining—(b)—S. S. GARRETT & CO., Philadelphia.
Wissahickon Deadening Felt—(b)—S. S. GARRETT & CO., Philadelphia.
Wissahickon Gray Bogus — (b) — S. S. GARRETT & CO., Philadelphia.
Wissahickon Sheathing—(b)—S. S. GARRETT & CO., Philadelphia.

Wistaria—(w)—flat and bond—FOX RIVER PAPER CO., Appleton, Wis.
Wistaria Cold Pressed—(w)—flat—FOX RIVER PAPER CO., Appleton, Wis.
Wizard—(b)—cards—THE PAPER MILLS CO., Chicago.
Wizard—(b)—enamel—DWIGHT PAPER CO., Grand Rapids, Mich.
Wizard—(b) — toilet — NORTHERN PAPER MILLS, Green Bay, Wis.
Wizard Bond—(w)—D W I G H T BROS. PAPER CO., Chicago.
"Wo Bro" Bond — (w) — WOELZ BROS., Appleton, Wis.
Wolverine—(b)—cover — PENINSULAR PAPER CO., Ypsilanti, Mich.
Wolverine Blanks— (b) —coated—BARDEEN PAPER CO., Otsego, Mich.
Wolverine Bond — (w) — writing — CAREW MANUFACTURING CO., South Hadley Falls, Mass.
Wonder Bond—(b)—BERMINGHAM & PROSSER CO., Kalamazoo, Mich.
Woodbridge—(b)—book, bristol and writing—JUDD PAPER CO., Holyoke, Mass.
Woodbury Bond — (b) — BERMINGHAM & PROSSER CO., Kalamazoo, Mich.
Woodbury Bond —(w)— KALAMAZOO PAPER CO., Kalamazoo, Mich.
Woodlawn Mills — (w) — HARLEM CARD & PAPER CO., New York.
Woodsdale—(b)—colored laid writing—CHATFIELD & WOODS Co., Cincinnati, Ohio.
Woodstock Mill Bristol—(b)—MILLER & WRIGHT PAPER CO., INC., New York.
Worcester—(b)—book— McCLELLAN PAPER CO., Minneapolis, Minn.
Worco—(b)—bond—GRAHAM PAPER CO., St. Louis.
World —(w)— bond — GRAHAM PAPER CO., St. Louis.
World—(b)—kraft—HAGEN PAPER CO., St. Louis.
World —(w)—blotting—ALBEMARLE PAPER MANUFACTURING CO., Richmond, Va.
World Bond—(w)—GRAHAM PAPER CO., St. Louis.
World's Fair—(w)—flat—J. W. BUTLER PAPER CO., Chicago.
World's Fair—(b)—toilet—ALBANY PERFORATED WRAPPING PAPER CO., Albany, N. Y.
World's Standard Linen — (w) — ESLEECK MANUFACTURING CO., Turners Falls, Mass.
Wornoc —(b)— blotting — CONROW BROS., New York.
Wornoc Bond — (w) — CONROW BROS., New York.
Wornoc Linen—(b)—C O N R O W BROS., New York.
Wornoc Mills—(b)—writing and blotting—CONROW BROS., New York.

Wornoc Plate—(b)—C O N R O W BROTHERS, New York.
Woronoco—(b)—bristols — STRATHMORE PAPER CO., Mittineague, Mass.
Woronoco—(b)—cover — STRATHMORE PAPER CO., Mittineague, Mass.
Woronoco All Linen — (w) — STRATHMORE PAPER CO., Mittineague, Mass.
Woronoco Bond — (w) — STRATHMORE PAPER CO., . Mittineague, Mass.
Woronoco Damask—(w)—extra superfine—STRATHMORE PAPER CO., Mittineague, Mass.
Woronoco Extra Fine — (w) — STRATHMORE PAPER CO., Mittineague, Mass.
Woronoco Linen Ledger—(w)—STRATHMORE PAPER CO., Mittineague, Mass.
Woronoco Photo Mounts—(b)—STRATHMORE PAPER CO., Mittineague, Mass.
Woronoco Superfine—(w)—laid and wove—STRATHMORE PAPER CO., Mittineague, Mass.
Worsep Mills—(w)—writing—J. C. & W. E. POWERS, New York.
Worthmore—(b)—manifold—MINNEAPOLIS PAPER CO., Minneapolis, Minn.
Worthmore Bond —(w)— WHITAKER PAPER CO., Cincinnati, Ohio, and BAY STATE PAPER CO., Boston.
Worthmore Ledger—(w)—WHITAKER PAPER CO., Cincinnati, Ohio, and BAY STATE PAPER CO., Boston.
Worthy Linen Ledger — (w) — WORTHY PAPER CO., Mittineague, Mass.
Woven Linen—(w)—WHITING PAPER CO., Holyoke, Mass.
W. P. Co.—(w)—WHITING PAPER CO., Holyoke, Mass.
W. R. G. & Co.—(w)—W. R. GRACE & CO., New York.
Wrenn's Antlers —(b)— blotting — WRENN PAPER CO., Middletown, Ohio.
Wrenn's Basket Weave—(b)—blotting—WRENN PAPER CO., Middletown, Ohio.
Wrenn's Best — (b) — blotting — WRENN PAPER CO., Middletown, Ohio.
Wrenn's Lintless Photo—(b)—blotting—WRENN PAPER CO., Middletown, Ohio.
Wrenn's Mosaic — (b) — blotting — WRENN PAPER CO., Middletown, O.
Wrenn's No. 1 Cloth—(b)—blotting —WRENN PAPER CO., Middletown, Ohio.
Wrenn's Porcelain Photo—(b)—blotting—WRENN PAPER CO., Middletown, Ohio.
Wrenn's Record—(b)—blotting— WRENN PAPER CO., Middletown, Ohio.
Wrenn's Royal Colors—(b)—colored blotting—WRENN PAPER CO., Middletown, Ohio.
Writing Fine—(w)—WHITING PAPER CO., Holyoke, Mass.
Wryton Linen—(b)—E A T O N, CRANE & PIKE CO., Pittsfield, Mass.
Wyandotte—(w)—CENTRAL OHIO PAPER CO., Columbus, Ohio.
Wyandotte Linen Ledger—(w)— THE UNION PAPER & TWINE CO., Detroit, Mich.
Wynnetun Mills—(b)—writing—W. H. GEORGE, Philadelphia.
Wyoming—(b)—book—GRAHAM PAPER CO., St. Louis.
Wyoming Ledger—(b)—MEGARGEE BROS., Scranton, Pa.

X

Xenium—(b)—card — THE PAPER MILLS CO., Chicago.
XL — (b)—book—J. W. BUTLER PAPER CO., Chicago.
X. L.—(b)—sheathing—GRAHAM PAPER CO., St. Louis.
X. L. C. R. Butcher Fibre—(b)—CHATFIELD & WOODS CO., Cincinnati. Ohio.
X Manila—(b) ORONO PULP & PAPER CO., Orono, Me.
XX—(b)—toilet — UNITED STATES ENVELOPE CO., (Morgan Envelope Co. Division), Springfield, Mass.
XX Manila—(b)—ORONO PULP & PAPER CO., Orono, Me.
XX Tar Boards—(b)—INGALLS & CO., Castleton, New York.
XXth Century Wedding — (b) — bristol—THE ALLING & CORY CO., Rochester, N. Y.
XXX Buff Drawing Paper—(b)—THE W. B. OGLESBY PAPER CO., Middletown, Ohio.
XXX Coated Embossing Cover—(b)—CHAMPION COATED PAPER CO., Hamilton, Ohio.
XXX Ledger—(b)—W. M. PRINGLE & CO., INC., New York.

Y

Yale—(b)—cardboard—MISSOURI PAPER HOUSE, Kansas City, Mo.
Yale—(w) — colored wove writing — BAY STATE PAPER CO., Boston.
Yale Bond—(w) — HAMMERMILL PAPER CO., Erie, Pa.
Yale Ledger—(w)—WHITAKER PAPER CO., Cincinnati, Ohio.
Yale Manila—(w)—WHITAKER PAPER CO., Cincinnati. Ohio.
Yale Superfine Tinted—(b)—wove flats — BRADNER SMITH & CO., Chicago.

Vernton Mills Extra Strong—(b) —colored, coated white and duplex— PAUL E. VERNON, New York.
Verona—(w)—LOUISVILLE PAPER CO., Louisville, Ky.
Verona Linen—(b)—PAUL E. VERNON & CO., New York.
Vertical — (b) — second sheets — GRAHAM PAPER CO., St. Louis.
V. Fine Writing—(b)—PAUL E. VERNON & CO., New York.
Veryfine Linen Laid—(w)—GEO. B. HURD & CO., New York.
Veryfine Linen Wove—(w)—GEO. B. HURD & CO., New York.
Vesper—(w)—bond—MIDLAND PAPER CO., Chicago.
Vesper Bond—(w)—W. M. PRINGLE & CO., INC., New York.
Vesper Manila—(b)—C. S. PROCTOR PAPER CO., Boston.
Vesta Colored Writing— (b) — HENRY LINDENMEYR & SONS, New York.
Vesta Fine—(w)—BOORUM & PEASE CO., New York.
Vesta Linen Ledger—(w)—BOORUM & PEASE CO., New York.
Vesture Bond—(w)—GARRETT-BUCHANAN CO., Philadelphia.
Viceroy Blanks—(b)—TROY PAPER CO., Troy, N. Y.
Viceroy Bristol—(b)—THE UNION PAPER & TWINE CO., Detroit, Mich.
Vicksburg Bond—(w)—LEE PAPER CO., Vicksburg, Mich.
Victor—(b)— wrapping — GRAHAM PAPER CO., St. Louis.
Victor—(b)—blotting—GARRETT-BUCHANAN CO., Philadelphia.
Victor—(b)—bristol—MEGARGEE-HARE PAPER CO., Philadelphia.
Victor—(b)—enamel — ROBERTSON PAPER CO., Bellow Falls, Vt.
Victor—(b)—tag brand — CHATFIELD & WOODS CO., Cincinnati.
Victor—(b)—toilet—WILSON & TOWNE PAPER CO., New York.
Victor—(b)—toilet—ALBANY PERFORATED WRAPPING PAPER CO., Albany, N. Y.
Victor—(b)—flats—KANSAS CITY PAPER HOUSE, Kansas City, Mo.
Victor—(b)—rope manila—STONE & FORSYTH CO., Boston.
Victor—(b)—plain blanks — HAGEN PAPER CO., St. Louis.
Victor—(b)—folding bristol—McCLELLAN PAPER CO., Minneapolis.
Victor—(b)—half-tone—J. E. LINDE PAPER CO., New York.
Victor Blank—(b)—A. STORRS & BEMENT CO., Boston.
Victor Bond—(w)—white and tinted —CHATFIELD & WOODS CO., Cincinnati, Ohio.
Victor Bond—(w)—AMERICAN WRITING PAPER CO., Holyoke, Mass.
Victor Bond—(b)—CARTER, RICE & CO., CORP., Boston.
Victor Bristol—(b)—colored—CHATFIELD & WOODS CO., Cincinnati, O.
Victor Ivory Boards—(b)—PARSONS TRADING CO., New York.
Victor Manila—(b)—JOHN CARTER & CO., Boston.
Victor Manila—(w) — BRADNER SMITH & CO., Chicago.
Victor Mills—(b) — A. STORRS & BEMENT CO., Boston.
Victor Mills—(w)—writing—STANDARD CARD & PAPER CO., New York.
Victor Tag—(b) — CHATFIELD & WOODS CO., Cincinnati Ohio.
Victoria—(b) — pasted board—McCLELLAN PAPER CO., Minneapolis.
Victoria — (b) — second sheets — GRAHAM PAPER CO., St. Louis.
Victoria—(b)—toilet—OLD DOMINION PAPER CO., Norfolk, Va.
Victoria Bond—(w)—F. W. ANDERSON & CO., New York.
Victoria Bond — (w) — WM. G. JOHNSTON & CO., Pittsburgh, Pa.
Victoria Lawn—(w)—POWERS PAPER COMPANY, Springfield, Mass.
Victoria Linen—(b)—flat—DIEM & WING PAPER CO., Cincinnati, O.
Victoria Linen—(b)—O. F. H. WARNER & CO., Baltimore.
Victoria Linen—(b)—VALLEY PAPER CO., Holyoke, Mass.
Victoria Linen—(w and crown)—GARRETT-BUCHANAN CO., Philadelphia.
Victoria Linen Bond—(w)—VALLEY PAPER CO., Holyoke.
Victoria Linen Ledger—(w)—VALLEY PAPER CO., Holyoke, Mass.
Victoria Slaters—(b)—tarred felt—GRAHAM PAPER CO., St. Louis.
Victoria Vellum—(b) — GEO. B. HURD & CO., New York.
Victory Bond — (w) — HOWARD SMITH PAPER MILLS, LTD., Montreal, Que.
Victory Campaign—(b)—post card —LOUISVILLE PAPER CO., Louisville, Ky.
Vidalon—(w)—cover—C. D. BROWN & CO., Boston.
Vienna Bond — (w) — COOK-VIVIAN CO., Boston.
Vienna Cover—(b)—COOK-VIVIAN CO., Boston.
Vienna Crystal—(b) — BERLIN & JONES ENVELOPE CO., New York.
Vienna Index Bristol—(b)—COOK-VIVIAN CO., Boston.
Vienna Ledger—(w)—COOK-VIVIAN CO., Boston.
Vienna Linen— (b) — McCLELLAN PAPER CO., Minneapolis, Minn.
Vienna Linen — (w) — laid — FOX RIVER PAPER CO., Appleton, Wis.
Vienna Moire—(w)—ALBEMARLE PAPER MFG. CO., Richmond, Va.

Watermarks and Brands

Vienna Moire — (b) — blotting — W. H. CLAFLIN & CO., Boston.
Vigilant Bond — (w) — CAREW MANUFACTURING CO., South Hadley Falls, Mass.
Vignette—(b)—book—GRAHAM PAPER CO., St. Louis.
Vignette Half Tone Super—(b)— HENRY LINDENMEYR & SONS, New York.
Viking—(b) — toilet—ALBANY PERFORATED WRAPPING PAPER CO., Albany, New York.
Viking Kraft—(w)—FISHER BROS. PAPER CO., Fort Wayne, Ind.
Viking Linen Cream Laid—(w)— HENRY LINDENMEYR & SONS, New York.
Vinco Mills—(b)—WHITAKER PAPER CO., Cincinnati, Ohio.
Vindex — (b)—toilet—M. J. EARL, Reading, Pa.
Vineta—(b)—photo mount — UNION CARD & PAPER CO., New York.
Violet—(w)—with design—writing—PARSONS TRADING CO., New York.
Violet—(b)—toilet—CHATFIELD PAPER CO., New Haven, Conn.
Violet Mills—(w)—CARTER, RICE & CO., CORP., Boston.
Violet Parchment — JOHN WANAMAKER, Philadelphia.
Vireo Bond — (w) — CINCINNATI CORDAGE AND PAPER CO., Cincinnati, Ohio.
Virgin White—(b) — coated book—W. H. CLAFLIN & CO., Boston.
Virginia—(b)—book — GRAHAM PAPER CO., St. Louis.
Virginia Antique Laid Book—(b) —KINGSLEY PAPER CO., Cleveland.
Vistula Bond—(w)—O. H. ANDERSON & CO., New York.
Vogue—(b)—cards — THE PAPER MILLS CO., Chicago.
Voile—(b) — POWERS PAPER CO., Springfield, Mass.
Voucher Bond—(w)—J. W. BUTLER PAPER CO., Chicago.
Vulcan—(w)—fine — EAU CLAIRE BOOK & STATIONERY CO., Eau Claire, Wis.
Vulcan—(b)—rope tag — ARNOLD-ROBERTS CO., Boston.
Vulcan Bond — CAREW MANUFACTURING CO., South Hadley Falls, Mass.
Vulcan Ledger — (w) — DIEM & WING PAPER CO., Cincinnati, Ohio.
Vulcan Linen — (b) — writing—CAREW MANUFACTURING CO., South Hadley Falls, Mass.
Vulcan Linen Ledger — (w)—writing—CAREW MANUFACTURING CO., South Hadley Falls, Mass.
Vulcan Mills—(b)—A. STORRS & BEMENT CO., Boston.
Vulcan Mills—(b)—colored laid flat — R. P. ANDREWS PAPER CO., Washington, D. C.

W

"W"—(b)—HY. LINDENMEYR & SONS, New York.
Wabacoat—(b) — enamel book and cover, litho paper and blanks and folding bristol—WABASH COATING MILLS, Wabash, Ind.
Wabash Mills — (b) — THOS. W PRICE CO., Philadelphia.
Wabash Wove—(w)—WHITING PAPER CO., Holyoke, Mass.
Waconnah Mills—(w) — BYRON WESTON CO., Dalton, Mass.
Wadjo—(b) — HOLLINGSWORTH & WHITNEY CO., Boston.
Wafer Carbon Copy—(b) — BRADNER SMITH & CO., Chicago.
Wakefield—(b) — book — W. H. GEORGE, Philadelphia.
Waldo Mills—(b)—C. P. LESH PAPER CO., Indianapolis.
Waldo Mills—(b) — TROY PAPER CO., Troy, New York.
Waldorf—(b) — SCOTT PAPER CO., Philadelphia.
Waldorf Laid—(b)—book — LOUISVILLE PAPER CO., Louisville, Ky.
Wall Street Linen—(w) — F. W. ANDERSON & CO., New York.
Wallace — (b) — book—GRAHAM PAPER CO., St. Louis.
Walrus—(b)—ruled headings — CONROW BROS., New York.
Walton—(b)—PEERLESS MFG. CO., Norristown, Pa.
Walton—(b)—bristol — C. P. LESH PAPER CO., Indianapolis, Ind.
Wamesit Manila Tag—(b)—C. S. PROCTOR PAPER CO., Boston.
Wampum Linen—(b) — white laid—HENRY LINDENMEYR & SONS, New York.
Wang—(b)—toilet—H. NORWOOD EWING CO., New York.
Wantaga—(b)—MORGAN & HAMILTON CO., Nashville, Tenn.
Ward's Boston Bond — (w)—SAMUEL WARD MFG. CO., Boston.
Ward's Boston Ledger — (w)—SAMUEL WARD MFG. CO., Boston.
Ward's Boston Linen — (w)—SAMUEL WARD MFG. CO., Boston.
Ward's Bunker Hill Bond—(w)—SAMUEL WARD MFG. CO., Boston.
Ward's Bunker Hill Ledger—(w) —SAMUEL WARD MFG. CO., Boston.
Ward's Bunker Hill Linen—(w)—SAMUEL WARD MFG. CO., Boston.
Ward's Elsmere Linen — (w)—SAMUEL WARD MFG. CO., Boston.
Ward's Swaco Linen — (w)—SAMUEL WARD MFG. CO., Boston.
Ward's Trimount Bond — (w)—SAMUEL WARD MFG. CO., Boston.
Ward's Wardwove Linen — (w)—SAMUEL WARD MFG. CO., Boston.

Warewell Enamel — (b) — book — LOUISVILLE PAPER CO., Louisville, Ky.
Warhawk—(b) — gummed — LOUIS' PER CO., Louisville, Ky.
Warp and Woof—(w)—extra superfine—J. C. BLAIR CO., Huntingdon, Pa.
Warrantee Bond — (b)—white and colored bond—R. C. KASTNER PAPER CO., New York.
Warranty—(b)—J. C. BLAIR CO., Huntingdon, Pa.
Warren's Art Gravure—(b) —book —J. W. BUTLER PAPER CO., Chicago.
Warren's Cameo Plate—(b)—writing—J. W. BUTLER PAPER CO., Chicago.
Warren's Cameo Plate Coated—(b)—book—J. W. BUTLER PAPER CO., Chicago.
Warren's Cumberland Coated—book—S. & S. C. and M. F.—J. W. BUTLER PAPER CO., Chicago.
Warren's Lustro Coated — (b)— book—J. W. BUTLER PAPER CO., Chicago.
Warren's Printone—(b)—book — J. W. BUTLER PAPER CO., Chicago.
Warren's Superfine Coated—(b)— book—J. W. BUTLER PAPER CO., Chicago.
Warrentown—(w)—regular book, eggshell and "Med" finish, white—S. D. WARREN & CO., Boston.
Warrington — (b) — b o o k —W. H. GEORGE, Philadelphia.
Warrior—(b)—bristol—LOUISVILLE PAPER CO., Louisville, Ky.
Warsaw Ledger—(w) — WHITING-PATTERSON CO., Philadelphia.
Warsaw Mills—(b)—colored—THOS. W. PRICE CO., Philadelphia.
Warwick— (w) — ledger—L E S L I E-DONAHOWER CO., St. Paul.
Warwick—(b)—LOUISVILLE PAPER CO., Louisville, Ky.
Warwick—(w)—flats—W E S T E R N PAPER CO., Omaha, Neb.
Warwick Ledger—(w)—FOX RIVER PAPER CO., Appleton, Wis.
Warwick Linen — (w)—STRATHMORE PAPER CO., Mittineague, Mass.
Warwick Plate—(b)—bristol—J. C. PARKER PAPER CO., Louisville, Ky.
Warwick Superfine—(w) — WHITING PAPER CO., Holyoke, Mass.
Warwick Wedding Bristol—(b)— UNION PAPER & TWINE CO., Detroit, Mich.
Waseda Bond—(w) — KALAMAZOO PAPER CO., Kalamazoo, Mich.
Washington— (b) — b o x covering— DISTRICT OF COLUMBIA PAPER MFG. CO., Washington, D. C.
Washington—(b)—binders' trunk and friction board — GRAHAM PAPER CO., St. Louis.

Washington—(w) — writing — GRAHAM PAPER CO., St. Louis.
Washington Bond—(w)—LEE PAPER CO., Vicksburg, Mich.
Washington Brilliant — (b) — box coverings—DISTRICT OF COLUMBIA, Washington, D. C.
Washington C o v e r s— (b) —DISTRICT OF COLUMBIA PAPER MFG. CO., Washington, D. C.
Washington Mills—(b) — toilet— HALLETT BROS., Boston.
Washington Mills—(w) — HUDSON VALLEY PAPER CO., Albany, N. Y.
Washington Plate—(b)—SEYMOUR CO., New York.
Wateredge — (w)—bond—GRAHAM PAPER CO., St. Louis.
Watered Embossed—(b)—GEO. B. HURD & CO., New York.
Waterleaf—(b)—SOUTHERN PAPER COMPANY, Richmond, Va.
Waterleaf — (w) — mimeograph — GRAHAM PAPER CO., St. Louis.
Waterleaf—(b)—blotting — CHATFIELD & WOODS CO., Cincinnati.
Waterlite—(b)—vegetable parchment —MINNEAPOLIS PAPER CO., Minneapolis, Minn.
Waterways—(w)—writing — GRAHAM PAPER CO., St. Louis.
Waterways Bond—(w)—FOX RIVER PAPER CO., Appleton, Wis.
Waterways Bond — (w)—WRIGHT, BARRETT & STILWELL CO., St. Paul, Minn.
Watkins Press—Extra Quality— (w)—JOHN B. WATKINS CO., N. Y.
Waugumbaug—(b)—bond — SOUTH COVENTRY PAPER CO., South Coventry, Conn.
Waukon Bond—(b) — C. P. LESH PAPER CO., Indianapolis, Ind.
Wavene Cover—(b)—PENINSULAR PAPER CO., Ypsilanti, Mich.
Waverly — (b) — book — BEECHER, PECK & LEWIS, Detroit, Mich.
Waverly — (b) — coated blotting— ARNOLD-ROBERTS CO., Boston.
Waverly—(w)—flats—KANSAS CITY PAPER HOUSE, Kansas City, Mo.
Waverly—(b)—blotting — KANSAS CITY PAPER HOUSE, Kansas City.
Waverly—(b)—news—GRAHAM PAPER CO., St. Louis.
Waverly Bond — (b) — C. P. LESH PAPER CO., Indianapolis.
Waverly Egg Shell — (b) — book —BRADNER SMITH & CO., Chicago.
Waverly Linen—(w) — MERRIAM PAPER CO., New York.
Waverly M i l l s—(w) — B Y R O N WESTON CO., Dalton, Mass.
Waverly Vellum — (b) — JOHN CARTER & CO., Boston.
Wawasa—(b)—flat, bristol and book— J. W. BUTLER PAPER CO., Chicago.
Waybill—(b)—writing — GRAHAM PAPER CO., St. Louis.

Wayne—(b)—super book—CHATFIELD & WOODS CO., Cincinnati, O.
Wayne Mills—(b)—J. E. LINDE PAPER CO., New York.
Wayne Mills—(b)—white writing—JOHNSTON PAPER CO., Harrisburg, Pa.
Wayside—(b) — writing — UNION CARD AND PAPER CO., New York.
Wayside—(w) — writing — UNION CARD AND PAPER CO., N. Y.
Webster—(w)—HAMMERMILL PAPER CO., Erie, Pa.
Webster—(b)—book—GRAHAM PAPER CO., St. Louis.
Webster— (b) — book—LOUISVILLE PAPER CO., Louisville, Pa.
Webster Bond—(w)—HOWARD PAPER CO., Urbana, O.
Wecco Bond — (w) — WALKER, EVANS & COGSWELL CO., Charleston, S. C.
Wecco Superfine —(w)—WALKER, EVANS & COGSWELL CO., Charleston, S. C.
Wedgewood—(w) — white wove—UNITED STATES ENVELOPE CO. (Plimpton Mfg. Co. Division), Hartford, Conn.
Weldon Mills Fine—(w) — KEITH PAPER CO., Turners Falls, Mass.
Welfare Bond—(w and b)—bond, ledger—NEENAH PAPER CO., Neenah, Wis.
Welland Wove — (w)—writing—KINLEITH PAPER CO., LTD., St. Catharines, Ont.
Wellington—(w)—bond— MIDLAND PAPER CO., Chicago.
Wellington—(b) — writing — GRAHAM PAPER CO., St. Louis.
Wellington—(b)—toilet — UNITED STATES ENVELOPE CO. (Morgan Envelope Co. Division), Springfield.
Wellington — (b)—WHITAKER PAPER CO., Cincinnati, Ohio.
Wellington — (b) — flat—WHITING PAPER CO., Holyoke, Mass.
Wellington Check—(w)—writing — GRAHAM PAPER CO., St. Louis.
Wellington Colored Laid—(b) — J. E. LINDE PAPER CO., New York.
Wellington Wove — (w) — KINLEITH PAPER CO., Canada.
Wellmade Linen Ledger — (w) — HOWARD SMITH PAPER MILLS, LTD., Montreal, Can.
Wellworth—(b)—envelope—GRAHAM PAPER CO., St. Louis.
Welmaid—(b) — toilet — SCOTT PAPER CO., Philadelphia.
Wenlock Bond—(w)—ruled and flat —H. S. CROCKER CO., San Francisco.
Wenlock Linen—(w)—ruled and flat —H. S. CROCKER CO., San Francisco.
Wenlock Vellum — (w) — ruled and flat — H. S. CROCKER CO., San Francisco.
Wenonah Superfine — (w) — W. E. WROE & CO., Chicago.

Werner Bond—(w)—THE WERNER CO., Akron, Ohio.
Westend—(w)—flats—WESTERN PAPER CO., Omaha, Neb.
Westerly Writing—(b)—JUDD PAPER CO., Holyoke, Mass.
Western — (b)—toilet — NORTHERN PAPER MILLS, Green Bay, Wis.
Western King—(b) — ALEX. McARTHUR & CO., LTD., Montreal.
Western Blanks — (b) — McCLELLAN PAPER CO., Minneapolis, Minn.
Western Bond — (w) — KANSAS CITY PAPER CO., Kansas City, Mo.
Westfall—(b) — book and label — GRAHAM PAPER CO., St. Louis.
Westford Ledger—(b)—MILLER & WRIGHT PAPER CO., INC., New York.
Westgate Linen Ledger — (w)—BLUNDER-LYON CO., Chicago.
West Indian — (b) — cover—J. W. BUTLER PAPER CO., Chicago.
Westlaid Flats — (w) — WESTERN PAPER CO., Omaha, Neb.
Westlake—(w)—flats—WESTERN PAPER CO., Omaha, Neb.
Westlock Linen Record — (w)—KEITH PAPER CO., Turners Falls, Mass.
Westlock Superfine — (w)—KEITH PAPER CO., Turners Falls, Mass.
Westminster — (b)—cover—J. W. BUTLER PAPER CO., Chicago.
Westminster—(b)—GEO. T. JOHNSON CO., Boston.
Westminster, A. S. & B. Quality —(w)—A. STORRS & BEMENT CO., Boston.
Westminster Bond — (w)—flats—R. L. GREENE PAPER CO., Providence, R. I.
Westminster Linen—(w and b) — CUNNINGHAM, CURTISS & WELCH, Los Angeles.
Westminster Linen—(w) — CHAS. T. BAINBRIDGE'S SONS, INC., Brooklyn, New York.
Westmore—(w) — writing—BRYANT PAPER CO., Kalamazoo, Mich.
Westmont Enamel — (b) — WEST VIRGINIA PULP & PAPER CO., New York.
Weston—(b)—S. & S. C.—J. P. HEILBRONN CO., Manila, P. I.
Weston's Flexible Hinge Loose Leaf Ledger—(b)—BYRON WESTON CO., Dalton, Mass.
Weston's Linen Ledger and Record — (w) —BYRON WESTON CO., Dalton, Mass.
Westover—(b) — book — WM. H. GEORGE, Philadelphia.
Westover Mills — (b) — enamel—W. H. GEORGE, Philadelphia.
Westover Mills — (w) — No. 2 fine —OLD DOMINION PAPER CO., Norfolk, Va.
West Penna. Colored, Enameled, book—(b) — WESTERN PENNA. PAPER CO., Pittsburgh.

Carl Riordan; Mechanical Pulp Section, Chairman, J. H. A. Acer; Book and Writing Section, Chairman, R. S. Waldie; Board Section, Chairman, J. F. Taylor; Coated Section, Chairman, Geo. Pauline; Felt Section, Chairman, Geo. Graves; Technical Section, Chairman, Dr. J. S. Bates; Woodlands Section, Chairman, W. G. Power; Secretary-Treasurer, A. L. Dawe.

CARTON CLUB OF CHICAGO. President, Geo. J. Kroeck, Kroeck Paper Box Company, Chicago;; Vice-President, T. W. Ritchie, W. C. Ritchie & Co., Chicago; Secretary and Treasurer, Geo. H. Tompkins, 1915 City Hall Square Building, Chicago.

CENTRAL STATES PAPER DEALERS' ASSOCIATION. President: Harold Helmer, Beecher, Peck & Lewis, Detroit, Mich.; Treasurer, Harry C. Hanna, Central Ohio Paper Company, Columbus, Ohio; Secretary: C. E. Lyter, 503 First National Bank Bldg., Chicago.

CENTRAL PAPER BOX MANUFACTURERS' ASSOCIATION. President, E. P. Franke, George Franke & Sons, Baltimore, Md.; Vice-President, F. M. Howell, Elmira, N. Y.; Secretary and Treasurer, Frank Stone, Jesse Jones Paper Box Co., Philadelphia.

CHICAGO STATIONERS' ASSOCIATION. Chairman, John W. Ogren, 1647 Conway Bldg., Chicago.

CORRUGATED FIBRE ASSOCIATION. President: J. Sprigg McMahon. Corrugated Fibre Association, Schwind Building, Dayton, Ohio.; Treasurer and Traffic Commissioner, G. R. Browder, 608 S. Dearborn St., Chicago, Ill.; Secretary, A. J. Neumann, 608 S. Dearborn St., Chicago, Ill.

COVER PAPER MANUFACTURERS' ASSOCIATION. President, Sidney S. Rogers, Chemical Paper Manufacturing Co., Holyoke, Mass.; Secretary-Treasurer, Emmett Hay Naylor, 18 E. 41st St., New York City. Telephone 4198 Murray Hill.

EASTERN PAPERBOARD MANUFACTURERS' ASSOCIATION. Charles R. White, Secretary, Room 20, 1410 G St., Washington, D. C.

EMPIRE STATE PAPER ASSOCIATION. President, Harry J. Severance, Hubbs & Howe Paper Co., Buffalo, N. Y.; Vice-President, B. E. Reeves, Alling & Cory Co., Rochester, N. Y.; Secretary and Treasurer, Fred. D. Morgan, Fred. D. Morgan & Co., Rochester, N. Y.

FIBRE SHIPPING CONTAINER ASSOCIATION. Office, 2140 Transportation Bldg., 608 S. Dearborn St., Chicago. President, J. M. Richardson; Vice-President, M. W. Waldorf; Secretary, W. S. Salt; Chairman of Executive Committee, Thomas W. Ross.

FINE STATIONERY MANUFACTURERS' ASSOCIATION. Secretary-Treasurer, Mortimer W. Byers, 41 Park Row, New York. Telephone, 130 Cortlandt.

FOLDING BOX MANUFACTURERS' NATIONAL ASSOCIATION. President, J. E. Clenny, 1301 W. 35th St., Chicago; Vice-President, Wm. Ottmann, 85 N. 3d St., Brooklyn; Treasurer, H. C. Stevenson, Rochester Folding Box Company, Rochester. COMMITTEE ON COSTS AND AC-

COUNTING. Otto R. Rohr, Stecher Lithographic Company, Rochester; Robert Gair, Jr., Robert Gair Company, Brooklyn; H. C. Stevenson, Rochester Folding Box Company, Rochester. COMMITTEE ON TRADE CUSTOMS AND PRACTICES: John Omwake, The U. S. Ptg. & Lithograph Company, Cincinnati; Irving Randall, The Chicago Label & Box Company, Chicago; Chas. Borland, Fort Orange Paper Company, Castleton, N. Y DIRESTORS: District 1, G. T. F. Clarke, Manager Box Department, Brooks Bank Note Company, Springfield; District 2, Robert Gair, Jr., Vice-President Robert Gair Company, Brooklyn; District 3, H. C. Stevenson, Secreary-Treasurer Rochester Folding Box Co., Rochester; District 4, Henry Doeller, President The Simpson & Doeller Co., Baltimore; District 5, Arthur I. Harris, Vice-President Atlanta Paper Co., Atlanta; District 6, Wm. Ottmann, Vice-President The U. S. Ptg. & Lithograph Company, Cincinnati and Brooklyn; District 7, J. E. Clenny, Vice-President Sefton Manufacturing Corp., Chicago; District 8, Edw. G. Gereke, President Gereke-Allan Carton Co., St. Louis; District 9, Max Schmidt, President Schmidt Lithograph Company, San Francisco; District 10, Edward Newell, Vice-President and Managing Director Dominion Envelope & Carton Co., Ltd., Toronto.

GLAZED AND FANCY PAPER MANUFACTURERS' ASSOCIATION. President, W. H. Shuart, Springfield, Mass.; Secretary, F. O. Walther, 72 Duane St., New York; Treasurer, G. Frank Merriam, Springfield, Mass.

GRAPHIC ARTS BOARD OF TRADE. Actuary, Frederick M. Leonard; Secretary, Thomas P. Longmore; Membership Chairman, George P. Northrop, 291 Broadway, New York City. Telephone, Worth, 2203.

INTERNATIONAL BROTHERHOOD OF PAPER MAKERS. Headquarters, Papermakers Building, 25 South Hawk St., Albany, N. Y. President and Secretary, J. T. Carey; First Vice-President, George J. Schneider; Second Vice-President, M. H. Parker; Third Vice-President, Wm. B. Clements; Fourth Vice-President, Jas. E. Lockwood; Treasurer, Dominick McDermott; Auditor, Wm. Hanna.

INTERNATIONAL BROTHERHOOD OF PULP, SULPHITE AND PAPER MILL WORKERS. President and Secretary, John P. Burke, Fort Edward, N. Y.; First Vice-President, H. W. Sullivan, Orono, Me.; Second Vice-President, John Connelly, Palmer, N. Y.; Third Vice-President, Henry N. Moores, Woodland, Me.; Fourth Vice-President, Maurice La Belle, Sturgeon Falls, Ontario, Canada; Fifth Vice-President, Joseph Tylkoff, 944 Tiffany St., New York City; Treasurer, Michael Daley, 17 May St., Glens Falls, N. Y.; Auditor, George C. Brooks, Franklin, N. H.

KANSAS BOOK-DEALERS' ASSOCIATION. President, Mason McCarty, Emporia, Kans.; Vice-President, O. Scott Morgan, Baldwin, Kans.; Secretary-Treasurer, Phil M. Anderson, Newton, Kans.

LABEL MANUFACTURERS NATIONAL ASSOCIATION. President, Otto R. Rohr, Rochester, N. Y.; Treasurer, Frank N. Hoen, Baltimore, Md.; Secretary, H. A. Dickle, 1457 Broadway, New York City. Telephone, Bryant 9557.

METROPOLITAN BAG AND PAPER JOBBERS' ASSOCIATION, 66 Broadway, New York. President, A. E. MacAdam, Sr.; Vice-President, A. T. Wolf; Treasurer, Max Berger; Secretary, A. E. Foster, Jr. DIRECTORS: A. E. MacAdam, A. T. Wolf, Wm. Spreen, F. W. Hinrichs, W. E. Shuttleworth, Jos. Stein, Hyman Jacobs.

MIAMI VALLEY PAPER MANUFACTURERS' ASSOCIATION. President, John M. Richardson, Richardson Paper Co., Lockland, Ohio; Vice-President, E. T. Gardner, Colin Gardner Paper Co., Middletown, Ohio; Secretary and Treasurer, J. F. Dunifer, The Miami Paper Co., West Carrollton, Ohio.

MIDDLE STATES WRAPPING PAPER ASSOCIATION. President, Frank E. Floyd, Crescent Paper Company, Indianapolis, Ind.; First Vice-President, Walter Seinsheimer, The Seinsheimer Paper Company, Cincinnati, O.; Second Vice-President, T. F. Willis, Chatfield & Woods Company, Cincinnati, O.; Third Vice-President, T. P. Chapman, T. P. Chapman Paper Company, St. Louis, Mo.; Treasurer, R. Roesch, Union Paper & Twine Company, Cleveland, O.; Secretary, Curtis E. Lyter, First National Bank Building, Chicago, Ill.

MISSOURI VALLEY WRAPPING PAPER ASSOCIATION. President, S. J. Hodgens, Central Topeka Paper Company, Topeka, Kans.; Vice-President, Brinn & Jensen, Omaha, Neb.; Secretary, A. L. Lowenstein, St. Joseph Paper Company, St. Joseph, Mo.; Treasurer, E. C. Benedict, Benedict Paper Company, Kansas City, Mo.

NATIONAL ASSOCIATION MANUFACTURERS OF CORRUGATED FIBER BOXES. President, J. P. Brunt; Vice-President, W. G. Chapin; Vice-President, J. H. Hirsch; Treasurer, F. J. Kress; Secretary, B. C. Tamlin, 900 Lytton Bldg., Chicago.

NATIONAL ASSOCIATION OF STATIONERS AND MANUFACTURERS. President, William H. Brooks, Philadelphia, Pa.; First Vice-President, William Pitt, Kansas City, Mo.; Second Vice-President, William C. Whittemore, New York; Third Vice-President, Ralph S. Bauer, Lynn, Mass.; Treasurer, Henry W. Rogers, New York; Auditor, J. Ogden Pierson, New Orleans, La.; Secretary, Mortimer W. Byers, 41 Park Row, New York.

NATIONAL ASSOCIATION OF WASTE MATERIAL DEALERS. President, Emanuel Salomon, New York City; First Vice-President, James Rosenberg; Second Vice-President, Edward A. Stone; Third Vice-President, Henry Lissberger; ourth Vice-President, Ivan Reitler; Fifth Vice-President, F. W. Reidenbach; Sixth Vice-President, Paul H. Loewenthal; Treasurer, Mark Sherwin; Secretary, Charles M. Haskins. Chairman of the Paper Stock Division, Oscar Gumbinsky; Chairman Scrap Rubber Division, David Feinburg; Chairman Woolen Rag Divilson, Mark Sherwin; Chairman Metal Division, F. W. Reidenbach; Chairman Scrap Iron Division, Wm. Lewin; Chairman Waste Paper Division, A. J. Moran; Chairman Western Division, Ivan Reitler. Office of Secretary, 185 Summer St., Boston, Mass., Room 802.

NATIONAL FEDERATION OF PAPER BOX MANUFACTURERS' ASSOCIATIONS. President, W. C. Carlson, 400 Florida St., Milwaukee. Wis.; Vice-President, E. C. Wentworth, 30-36 Granite St., Haverhill, Mass.; Treasurer, H. L. Stortz, 321 New St., Philadelphia, Pa.; Secretary, Jas. L. Kalleen, Room 1211, Fidelity Mutual Life Insurance Bldg., 112 N. Broad St., Philadelphia, Pa.

NATIONAL PAPER TRADE ASSOCIATION OF THE UNITED STATES. President, George Olmsted, J. W. Butler Paper Company; Vice-President in Charge of the Fine Paper Division, R. P. Andrews, R. P. Andrews Paper Company, Washington, D. C.; Vice-President in Charge of the Coarse Paper Division, H. E. Platt, The J. L. N. Smythe Company, Philadelphia, Pa.; Treasurer, A. J. Corning, Hubbs and Corning Company, Baltimore, Md.; Secretary, Wm. C. Ridgway, 41 Park Row, New York; Assistant Secretary, Curtis E. Lyter, First National Bank Building, Chicago, Ill. BOARD OF DIRECTORS: Fine Paper Division: George Olmsted, J. W. Butler Paper Company, Chicago, Ill.; R. P. Andrews, R. P. Andrews Paper Company, Washington, D. C.; W. F. McQuillen, A. Storrs & Bement Company, Boston, Mass.; E. J. Merriam, Merriam Paper Company, New York; Morgan H. Thomas, Garrett-Buchanan Company, Philadelphia, Pa.; B. W. Wilson, B. W. Wilson Paper Company, Richmond, Va.; C. N. Bicknell, The Union Paper & Twine Company, Cleveland, Ohio; Forest Hopkins, The Paper Mills Company, Chicago, Ill.; C. F. Wright, Wright, Barrett & Stillwell, St. Paul, Minn.; B. E. Reeves, The Alling & Cory Company, Rochester, N. Y.; A. D. Tayloe, Tayloe Paper Company, Memphis, Tenn.; Mr. J. Y. Baruh, Zellerbach Paper Co., Los Angeles, Cal. BOARD OF DIRECTORS: Coarse Paper Division: H. E. Platt, J. L. N. Smythe Company, Philadelphia, Pa.; F. W. Power, Carter, Rice & Co., Boston, Mass.; Chas. G. Stott, Chas. G. Stott Company, Washington, D. C.; George E. Beggs, Hubbs & Hastings Company, Rochester, N. Y.; Simon Walter, Philadelphia, Pa., A. E. Dubey, Domestic Mills Paper Company, New York City; J. A. Carpenter, Kansas City Paper House, Kansas City, Mo.; Edw. F. Herrlinger, Herrlinger & Co., Cincinnati, Ohio; H. W. Mathewson, The Paper Supply Company, Minneapolis, Minn.; S. J. Hodgins, The Central Topeka Paper Company, Topeka, Kan.; T. M. McClellan, Birmingham Paper Company, Birmingham, Ala.; A. J. Corning, Hubbs & Corning Company, Baltimore, Md.; Frank G. Smith, Frank H. Smith & Co., Milwaukee, Wis.; A. B. Galloway, American Paper Company, Seattle, Wash. ADVISORY COUNCIL: O. A. Miller, Central Ohio Paper Company, Columbus, O.; W. F. McQuillan, A. Storrs & Bement Company, Boston, Mass.; E. U. Kimbark, The Paper Mills Company, Chicago, Ill.; John Leslie, John Leslie Paper Company, Minneapolis, Minn.; Jos. T. Alling, The Alling & Cory Company, Rochester, N. Y.; Thos. F. Smith, Louisville Paper Company, Louisville, Ky.

NATIONAL SAFETY COUNCIL, PAPER AND PULP SECTION. Chairman, G. E. Williamson, Strathmore Paper Co., Mittineague, Mass.; Vice-Chairman, G. Schenck, Jr., Superintendent Bureau of Economy, Great Northern Paper Co., Millinocket, Me.; Secretary, A. G. Pounsford, General Manager, Port Arthur Pulp & Paper Co., Ltd., Port Arthur, Ont., Canada.

NEW ENGLAND PAPER AND PULP TRAFFIC ASSOCIATION. Office,

766 Trade Associations

220 Devonshire St., Boston, Mass. Secretary and Traffic Manager, C. H. Tiffany; Counsel, Fred'k Manley Ives. EXECUTIVE COMMITTEE: Herbert W. Mason, Chairman and Treasurer; Amor Hollingsworth, H. B. Mills, G. F. Russell, Stuart W. Webb and G. W. Wheelwright, Jr.

NEW ENGLAND PAPER BOX MANUFACTURERS' ASSOCIATION. President, Austin M. Sweet, Norton, Mass.; First Vice-President, Jos. H. Perry, Cambridge Paper Box Company, Cambridge, Mass.; Second Vice-President, Donald G. Robbins, 33 Farnsworth St., Boston, Mass.; Secretary, Frank E. Vincent, Lynn, Mass.; Treasurer, Myrton O. Hill, 297 Congress St., Boston, Mass. EXECUTIVE COMMITTEE: Herbert C. Low, Brockton, Mass.; Charles F. Sprague, Lynn, Mass.; Charles K. Shaw, Pawtucket, R. I.

NEW ENGLAND PAPER MERCHANTS' ASSOCIATION, THE. President, F. W. Power, Boston, Mass.; Vice-President, F. B. Cummings, Boston, Mass.; Treasurer, R. M. Stone, Boston, Mass.; Secretary, F. B. Tracy, 145 High St., Boston, Mass.; Auditor, A. M. Eaton, Waltham, Mass. EXECUTIVE COMMITTEE: White Division, J. D. Snell and A. E. Ham; Manila Division, C. A. Shaw and L. H. Young; New England Division, C. L. Beckwith, Springfield, Mass.; Chairman Fine Paper Division, National Paper Trade Association, W. F. McQuillen; Chairman Coarse Paper Division, F. W. Power.

NEWS-PRINT SERVICE BUREAU. Justus A. B. Cowles, President; Maurice Hoopes, Vice-President; R. S. Kellogg, Secretary and Treasurer; John A. Davis, Chairman of Executive Committee, 18 East 41st St., New York City. Telephone, Murray Hill 8637.

NORTHWESTERN PAPER MERCHANTS' ASSOCIATION, Minneapolis, Minn. President, L. R. Boswell, Minneapolis Paper Co., Minneapolis, Minn.; Secretary-Treasurer, W. C. Wilson, McClellan Paper Co., Minneapolis, Minn. Representative on Executive Committees Fine and Coarse Paper Divisions of National Paper Trade Association: Fine Papers: Cushing R. Wright, Wright, Barrett & Stillwell Co., St. Paul, Minn.; Coarse Papers: H. W. Mathewson, Paper Supply Co., Minneapolis, Minn.

OMAHA STATIONERS' ASSOCIATION. President, Charles E. Moyer; Secretary, Charles C. Cope, Jr., Omaha Printing Co., 13th and Farnam Sts.; Treasurer, Guy C. McKenzie.

PACIFIC COAST PAPER BOX MANUFACTURERS' ASSOCIATION. President, H. M. Simmons, Northwestern Paper Box Company, Seattle, Wash.; VicePresident, Wm. J. O'Donnell, A. Fleishhacker & Co., San Francisco, Cal.; Secretary-Treasurer, A. J. Schoephoester, Union Paper Box Manufacturing Company, 2112 First Avenue, Seattle, Wash. EXECUTIVE COMMITTEE: A. Sidney Jones, Renshaw, Jones & Sutton, Los Angeles, Cal., and F. C. Stettler, F. C. Stettler Manufacturing Company, Portland, Ore.

PACIFIC NORTHWESTERN STATIONERS' ASSOCIATION. President, W. A. Montgomery, J. K. Gill Company, Portland, Ore.; Vice-President, H. B. Benson, Benson Office Supply Company, Aberdeen, Wash.; Secretary-Treasurer, Julius Marlitt, Pacific State Printing Company, Portland, Ore.

PAPER ASSOCIATION OF NEW YORK CITY. President, E. J. Merriam, 150 Lafayette Street; First Vice-President, A. E. Dubey, 96 Reade Street; Second Vice-President, Alfred Kinn, 90 Beekman Street; Treasurer, K. S. Warner, 85 John Street; Secretary, N. J. Barrett, 500 Broome Street; Assistant Secretary, W. C. Ridgway, 41 Park Row.

PAPER BOX CREDIT PROTECTIVE ASSOCIATION OF NEW YORK, INC. President, Nathan Lakin; Vice-President, Morris Lipp; Treasurer, Louis Levy; Secretary, Samuel Kaplan; Counsel, Samuel L. Wallerstein, 115 Broadway, New York.

PAPER BOX SUPPLY CREDIT BUREAU, THE, 291 Broadway, New York. Secretary, Frederick M. Leonard. EXECUTIVE COMMITTEE: Chairman, Chas. E. Daniel, United Paperboard Co., 171 Madison Av., New York; Eugene Boggs, D. J. O'Connell, Charles I. McLaughlin and C. T. Karasik.

PAPER MAKERS' ADVERTISING CLUB, Boston, Mass., P. O. Box 2828, President, C. W. Dearden; Secretary, Fred Webster; Treasurer, Philip W. Gridley. EXECUTIVE COMMITTEE: The Officers, H. M. Van Valkenburg and C. W. Chabot.

PAPER MILL SUPPLY DEALERS' ASSOCIATION OF NEW ENGLAND. President, H. B. Wilder; Vice-President, M. Feinberg; Treasurer, I. Feinberg; Secretary, J. J. Holland. EXECUTIVE COMMITTEE: A. S. Ford, M. J. Collins, M. F. Driscoll. Annual meeting second Monday in October.

PAPER TRADE ASSOCIATION OF PHILADELPHIA. President, George Ward; Vice-President, Allen Whiting; Treasurer, Harvey E. Platt; Secretary, Walter Matthias; Corresponding Secretary, Louis S. Megargee.

PHILADELPHIA PAPER STOCK DEALERS' ASSOCIATION. President, Evan G. Badger; Vice-President, William McGarity; Secretary and Treasurer, William L. Simmons, 30 South Marshall St. EXECUTIVE BOARD: The Officers, Simon Weil, Daniel I. Murphy and H. Feldman.

PHILADELPHIA STATIONERS' ASSOCIATION. President, Harry A. Prizer; First Vice-President, Frank R. Welsh; Second Vice-President, Lewis A. Hawkes; Treasurer, Dr. Philip Jaisohn; Secretary, Francis B. Irwin, 607 Chestnut St.

PITTSBURGH BOOKSELLERS AND STATIONERS ASSOCIATION. President, Charles H. Clough; Vice-President, F. C. Herget; Treasurer, John A. Brown; Recording Secretary, J. Albert Cooper; Corresponding Secretary, Geo. H. Alexander.

PULP MANUFACTURERS' ASSOCIATION. EXECUTIVE COMMITTEE: Chairman, James E. Campbell, Dexter, N. Y.; E. W. Kiefer, Port Huron, Mich.; T. J. Stevenson, Montreal, Can.; Secretary, H. H. Bishop, 18 E. 41st St., New York City.

RETAIL BOOKSELLERS' AND STATIONERS' ASSOCIATION OF ILLINOIS. President, Clifford Lloyde, Champaign, Ill.; Vice-President, Wm. Coe, Springfield, Ill.; Secretary, C. W. Follett, 323 S. Wabash Av., Chicago; Treasurer, Fred Greenwood, Kimbark Av., Chicago.

RETAIL BOOKSELLERS' AND STATIONERS' ASSOCIATION OF OHIO. President, John J. Wood, Cleveland; Vice-President, C. R. Comings, A. G. Comings & Son, Oberlin; Secretary, Fred E. Huntsberger, University Book Store, Delaware; Treasurer, V. E. Hardin, Hardin & Gallant, Delaware. EXECUTIVE COMMITTEE: John Frazer, Oxford; A. Schapiro, Portsmouth; L. W. Hazen, Marysville; S. T. Lemley, Delaware, and Ellis Gallant, Delaware.

ST. LOUIS STATIONERS' CLUB. Vice-President, H. J. Wantz; Secretary, Clarence R. Comfort, 804 Pine St.; Treasurer, Edw. T. Henkel, 315 N. 3d St.

ST. PAUL STATIONERS' ASSOCIATION. President, E. D. L. Sperry, of Brown, Blodgett & Sperry Company, 5th and Minnesota Sts.; Vice-President, Louis F. Dow, of Louis F. Dow Company, 381 Jackson St.; Secretary, John H. Boemer, of Henry E. Wedelstaedt Company, 91 East 6th St.; Treasurer, R. J. Maybell, of R. J. Maybell Stationery Company, 150 East 5th St.

SOUTHEASTERN WRAPPING PAPER ASSOCIATION. President, Sidney L. Wellhouse, National Paper Company, Atlanta, Ga.; Vice-President, T. M. McClellan, Birmingham Paper Company, Birmingham, Ala.; Treasurer, W. H. Weatherford, Archer Paper Company, Chattanooga, Tenn.: Secretary, E. Klein, Tennessee Paper & Bag Company, Memphis, Tenn.

STATIONERS & PUBLISHERS BOARD OF TRADE, INC., THE, 97 and 99 Nassau St., New York. President, Arthur P. Jackson, 38 Murray St., New York; First Vice-President, Louis V. Blanchet, 547 W. 27th St., New York; Second Vice-President, H. C. Bainbridge, 2 Cumberland St., Brooklyn; Secretary-Treasurer, Gordon Cameron, 99 Nassau St. (Telephone Cortlandt 282), New York.

STATIONERS' ASSOCIATION OF CALIFORNIA. Chairman, H. P. Dimond, 255 California St., San Francisco, Cal.

STATIONERS' ASSOCIATION OF ESSEX COUNTY. President, S. R. Baker, 251 Market St.; Vice-President, Reinhold Kniep, 3 South Orange Av.; Secretary, E. F. Sheridan, 927 Broad St.; Treasurer, R. Russell Brant, 237 Market St.; all of Newark, N. J.

STATIONERS' ASSOCIATION OF NEW YORK. President, Charles A. Lent, 90 William St.; First Vice-President, W. W. J. Warren, 129 Lafayette St.; Second Vice-President, E. E. Huber, 37 Greenpoint Av., Brooklyn; Third Vice-President, Mortimer W. Byers, 41 Park Row; Secretary, Henry Frank, 39 E. 20th St.; Treasurer, E. V. Brokaw, 54 New St., New York.

STATIONERS' CLUB OF COLUMBUS. President, John T. Gale; Vice-President, E. H. Sell; Treasurer, W. E. McDonald; Secretary, Wm. R. Diehl, c/o Diehl Office Equipment Co., Columbus, Ohio.

STATIONERS' CLUB OF DENVER. President, W. H. Kistler; Secretary, H. E. Bellamy, 801 16th St., Denver, Colo.

STATIONERS' CLUB OF INDIANAPOLIS. President, Walter E. Evans, 121 W. Georgia St.; Vice-President, W. W. Hampton, 220 East Ohio St.; Secretary and Treasurer, M. S. Thomas, 44 E. Washington St.

STATIONERS' ASSOCIATION OF SOUTHERN CALIFORNIA. President, Henry W. Stacey, Grimes-Stassforth Company; Vice-President, Arthur L. Stoll, Cunningham, Curtiss & Welch Company; Treasurer, Willard Goodwin, Fowler Brothers; Secretary, W. T. Yeazell, 446 Douglas Building, Los Angeles, Cal.

STATIONERS' ASSOCIATION OF NEW ORLEANS. Burt W. Henry, Chairman, 403 Weis Bldg.

STATIONERS' CLUB OF TOLEDO. President, Louis B. Busse, Franklin Ptg. & Eng. Co.; Vice-President, Leroy Barnes; Corresponding Secretary, Joseph Leroux; Recording Secretary, Frank Lang; Treasurer, Gerald Stephens. EXECUTIVE COMMITTEE: Louis Busse, Joseph Leroux, Frank Lang, N. B. Newton, Gerald Stephens, Leroy Barnes, Frank Palmer, D. E. Hand.

STATIONERS' SOCIAL CLUB OF CINCINNATI. President, John H. Gibson, Gibson & Perin Co.; Secretary, E. E. Davis, Sellers, Davis & Co.; Treasurer, Edward C. Mills, J. R. Mills Sons.

TECHNICAL ASSOCIATION OF THE PULP AND PAPER INDUSTRY. President, Henry P. Carruth, Mead Pulp and Paper Company, Chillicothe, Ohio; Vice-President, Henry F. Obermanns, Hammermill Paper Company, Erie, Pa.; Secretary-Treasurer, Thomas J. Keenan, Paper, Inc., 117 E. 24th St., New York City. EXECUTIVE COMMITTEE: Chairman, Henry P. Carruth, Henry F. Obermanns, Hammermill Paper Company, Erie, Pa.; Raymond S. Hatch, Crocker-McElwain Company, Holyoke, Mass.; Henry E. Fletcher, Fletcher Paper Company, Alpena, Mich.; Frederick C. Clark, U. S. Bureau of Standards, Washington, D. C.

TISSUE PAPER MANUFACTURERS' ASSOCIATION. President, A. D. Coffin, C. H. Dexter & Sons, Windsor Locks, Conn.; Secretary-Treasurer, Emmett Hay Naylor, 18 E. 41st St., New York City. Telephone, 4198 Murray Hill.

WALL PAPER MANUFACTURERS' ASSOCIATION OF THE UNITED STATES. President, Henry Burn, Robert Graves Co., Brooklyn, N. Y.; Vice-President, Frank M. Page, Becker, Smith & Page, Philadelphia, Pa.; Treasurer, John J. McCabe, Standard Wall Paper Co., Hudson Falls, N. Y.; Secretary, Fred B. Lindsay, 49 Liberty St., New York.

WASTE MERCHANTS' ASSOCIATION OF NEW YORK. President, Emanuel Saloman; Vice-President, Walter Clark; Treasurer, Alfred J. Moran; Albert T. Hicks, 15 Park Row.

WAXED PAPER MANUFACTURERS' ASSOCIATION. President, J. Kindleberger, Kalamazoo, Mich.; Secretary, J. W. Hurlbut, Bennington, Vt.

WESTCHESTER PURCHASING CO. (Formerly Westchester County Stationers' Assn.). President, Frank J. Chapman, New Rochelle; Secretary, George H. Mason, Yonkers; Treasurer, Samuel Shapiro, White Plains.

WESTERN PAPER BOX MANUFACTURERS' ASSOCIATION. President, George J. Kroeck, 220 Institute Place, Chicago, Ill.; Vice-President, Harry O. Alderman, 367 Orchard St., Rochester, N. Y.; Secretary and Treasurer, William W. Baird, 1400 E. 30th St., Cleveland, Ohio.

WESTERN PAPER MERCHANTS' ASSOCIATION. President, P. A. Van Vlack, Moser Paper Company, Chicago; First Vice-President, Arthur Fuhlage, Beacon Paper Company, St. Louis, Mo.; Second Vice-President, Clifton R. Field, Field-Hamilton-Smith Paper Company, Omaha, Neb.; Secretary, Walter N. Gillett, Chicago Paper Company, Chicago; Treasurer, John D. Swigart, Swigart Paper Company, Chicago.

WESTERN TRAFFIC ASSOCIATION (Pulp and Paper Manufacturers). President, W. M. Gilbert; Vice-President, F. J. Sensenbrenner; Secretary and Traffic Manager, W. D. Hurlbut, 28 E. Jackson Blvd., Chicago; Treasurer and Assistant Traffic Manager, J. E. Bryan, 28 E. Jackson Blvd., Chicago. EXECUTIVE COMMITTEE: W. M. Gilbert, F. J. Sensenbrenner, L. M. Alexander, George W. Mead.

WHOLESALE STATIONERS' ASSOCIATION OF THE U. S. A. President, J. H. Niedecken, H. Niedecken Company, Milwaukee, Wis.; Vice-President, W. A. Nuettell, Nuettell Bros. Company, Dubuque, Ia.; Treasurer, R. P. Andrews, R. P. Andrews Paper Company, Washington, D. C.; Secretary, John P. Black, Marcus W. Wolf Company, Baltimore, Md. EXECUTIVE COMMITTEE: Chairman, Wm. G. Whittemore, The American News Company, New York City; G. L. Davis, Adams, Cushing & Foster, Inc., Boston, Mass.; J. A. Hirshberg, The Hirshberg Company, Atlanta.

WISCONSIN PAPER DEALERS' ASSOCIATION. President, W. R. Mershon, Milwaukee; Vice-President, T. S. Morris, Madison; Secretary, A. E. Hansen, Green Bay; Treasurer, J. A. Wellensgard, Racine.

WRAPPING PAPER MANUFACTURERS' SERVICE BUREAU. President, W. L. Edmonds, Brokaw, Wis.; Vice-President, F. L. Moore, Watertown, N. Y. EXECUTIVE COMMITTEE: W. L. Edmonds; F. L. Moore; W. L. Davis, Eau Claire, Wis.; J. C. Schmidt, York, Pa.; A. W. Maynes, Lockland, Ohio. Secretary-Treasurer, A. J. Stewartson, 2 Rector St., New York, N. Y.

WRITING PAPER MANUFACTURERS' ASSOCIATION. President, W. J. Raybold, B. D. Rising Paper Company, Housatonic, Mass.; First Vice-President, R. F. McElwain, Crocker-McElwain Co., Holyoke, Mass.; Second Vice-President, Norman W. Wilson, Hammermill Paper Co., Erie, Pa.; Secretary-Treasurer, Emmett Hay Naylor, 18 E. 41st St., New York City. Telephone, 4198 Murray Hill.

WRITING TABLET MANUFACTURERS' ASSOCIATION. Secretary-Treasurer, Mortimer W. Beyers, 41 Park Row, New York. Telephone, 130 Cortlandt.

ADVERTISEMENTS

Machinery, Paper and Paper Makers' Supplies

See Classified Buyers' Guide, pages 9-26

Rag Cutters

Under the  Trade Mark

FOR EVERY KIND OF PAPER STOCK

Paper Bag, Envelope, Labeling and Gumming Machines of All Types

POTDEVIN MACHINE CO.
1221 Thirty-eighth Street   Brooklyn, N. Y.

WATER WHEELS HUNT-McCORMICK & HUNT-FRANCIS TURBINE TYPES

We are continually remodeling old equipments of our own and other makes of wheels by installing our latest design. Immense gains in power from same water used are realised, the power being in some cases nearly doubled.

PENSTOCK, HEADGATES, HOISTS, TEXTILE MACHINERY, ETC.

RODNEY HUNT MACHINE COMPANY
ORANGE, MASSACHUSETTS

CALENDERS

FURNISHED COMPLETE

WITH

ELECTRIC MOTOR LIFT,

HYDRAULIC LIFT

OR RATCHET LIFT,

ALL OPERATED FROM FLOOR.

Roll Grinding Machines
PROVIDED WITH
Patent Automatic Crowning Device

Lobdell Car Wheel Company
Wilmington, Delaware

PENNSYLVANIA PAPER STOCK COMPANY

PACKERS AND DEALERS IN

PAPER STOCK

26 GRADES OF PAPER

Main Office: 29th St. & Liberty Ave. Pittsburgh, Pa.

Wisconsin Wires
WISCONSIN WIRE WORKS
APPLETON   WISCONSIN

ACKNOWLEDGED BY ALL!

R. GOLDSTEIN & SON

LARGEST PACKERS

COTTON RAGS

ADVISE YOUR REQUIREMENTS TODAY

N. Y. OFFICE
200 5th AVE.

1162 Scott St., BALTO., MD.

STANDARD WIRE CO.

J. W. LAFFEY, Manager

MANUFACTURERS OF

FOURDRINIER WIRES and CYLINDER MOULDS

Cylinder Covers and Washer Wires. All Grades Wire Cloth for Paper Mill Use.
Cylinder Covering at Mills. Cylinder Repairs a Specialty.

WIRES FOR TISSUE and FINE GRADE PAPERS

FACTORY :: :: :: :: HARRISON, N. J.

ESTABLISHED 1842   INCORPORATED 1887

Cheney Bigelow Wire Works

SPRINGFIELD, MASS.

FOURDRINIER WIRES, DANDY ROLLS

CYLINDER MOULDS

ALSO MANUFACTURERS OF

Brass, Copper and Iron Cloth, Bank, Office Railing

and

WIRE SIGNS

SINCE 1878

BUCHANAN & BOLT WIRE CO.

HOLYOKE, MASS.

OUR SPECIALTY

Fine Wires for Magazine and Book Papers

DANDY ROLLS, CYLINDER COVERS
HIGHEST GRADE FOURDRINIER WIRES

BRASS WIRE CLOTH OF ALL MESHES FOR PAPER, PULP AND COATING MILLS

QUALITY GUARANTEED

Ultramarine Blue

is unequaled

FOR WHITE PAPERS

in

Brilliancy—Uniformity—Economy
Fastness to Sunlight—Ease of Application

The Ultramarine Company

NEW YORK

American Made Ultramarine Blues

1837 - - - - 1919

RICE, BARTON & FALES MACHINE & IRON COMPANY

WORCESTER, MASS.

For Over Eighty Years
DESIGNERS *and* BUILDERS

of

Pulp and Paper Mill Machinery

This Experience is at Your Command

NATRONA POROUS ALUM

AND ALL GRADES

SULPHATE OF ALUMINA

BLEACHING POWDER

AND

CAUSTIC SODA

MANUFACTURED BY

PENNSYLVANIA SALT MANUFACTURING COMPANY

PHILADELPHIA, PA.

BUSINESS ESTABLISHED 1773

J. RUSSEL MARBLE & CO.

BOSTON AND WORCESTER

NEW ENGLAND AGENTS FOR

Bleach and Caustic Soda

MADE BY THE

HOOKER ELECTROCHEMICAL CO.
NIAGARA FALLS

MANUFACTURERS' AGENTS FOR

ALKALI, CORN STARCH

Casein, Stearic Acid, Paraffine Wax

And All Materials For Coating Paper

FARREL FOUNDRY AND MACHINE CO.
ANSONIA, CONN., U. S. A.

CHILLED AND DRY SAND ROLLS FOR ALL PURPOSES

PATENTED HYDRAULIC LIFTING DEVICE

WITH this device the machine tender, standing at base of machine, can lift the entire stack except the bottom roll or any desired number of rolls, above the bottom roll the time required for operating, either lifting or lowering, being but two or three seconds when operated in connection with accumulator, and but a comparatively few seconds when operated by hand pump, as in cut above; a money-saving feature when rolls become "plugged." On large machines with old style lift four men were required to perform this operation and a large amount of paper was wasted.

Made with hand-operated pump attached to housing or with accumulator, as desired. High speed machines should have no other lift.

AMONG THE USERS OF THESE MACHINES ARE

Hollingsworth & Whitney Co.
Kimberly & Clark Co.
Great Northern Paper Co.
International Paper Co.
Piermont Paper Co.
Remington-Martin Co.
Nekoosa Paper Co.
Stony Brook Paper Co.
Racquette River Paper Co.
Berlin Mills Co.
West Virginia Pulp & Paper Co.
Haverhill Box Board Co.
Howe & Davidson.
Canada Paper Co.
Tonawanda Board & Paper Co.
S. D. Warren & Co.
St. George Pulp & Paper Co.
Roanoke Rapids Pulp & Paper Co.
N. H. Pulp & Board Co.
Crocker-Burbank Co.
Crown-Columbia Pulp & Paper Co.
Iroquois Paper Co.
Odell Mfg. Co.

J. C. Wilson & Co.
Cheboygan Paper Co.
Marietta Paper Mills.
Belgo-Canadian Pulp & Paper Co.
Hammermill Paper Co.
C. S. Garrett & Sons.
Finch, Pruyn & Co.
St. Croix Paper Co.
Continental Paper Co.
Henry Paper Co.
Ryegate Paper Co.
Willamette Pulp & Paper Co.
Watab Paper Co.
Wall Paper Manufacturers, Ltd.
Petit Parisien.
Papeterie Avot Vallee.
Darblay & Sons.
Varzenier Papier Fabriek.
Papeterie de Nanterre.
Minnesota & Ontario Power Co.
Anglo-Newfoundland Development Co.
Powell River Paper Co.
Marathon Paper Company.

FARREL FOUNDRY AND MACHINE CO.
ANSONIA, CONN., U. S. A.
MANUFACTURERS OF
ROLL GRINDING MACHINES

WITH
PATENT CROWNING DEVICE

Insuring Great Accuracy in Crowning Bottom or Other Rolls

PARTIAL LIST OF USERS OF THE FARREL ROLL GRINDING MACHINE
WITH THE "VINE" PATENT CROWNING DEVICE

International Paper Co.
Rice, Barton & Fales
Baltimore C. S. & R. Co.
Kimberly & Clark Co.
E. B. Eddy Company.
Northwest Paper Company.
Canada Paper Company.
S. D. Warren & Co.
Laurentide P. & P. Co.
American Brass Company.
Black-Clawson Company.
Williamette P. & P. Co.
Remington-Martin Co.
Manhattan Rubber Mfg. Co.
B. F. Goodrich Company.
Oxford Paper Company.
Aillmand, Ilves, France.
Dalton Paper Mills.
Interstate Steel Co.
Berlin Mills Company.
Seymour Manufacturing Co.
Imperial Paper Mills Co.
Boston Belting Company.
Belgo-Canadian P. & P. Co.
Fletcher Paper Company.
Great Northern Paper Co.
Pejepscot Paper Company.
Stora Kopparsberg, Sweden.
Rocky Mountain Paper Co.
F. A. Marsily & Co.
St. Regis Paper Company.
Outhenin-Chalandre, Paris.
Union Machine Company.
New York & Penn. Company
C. G. Haubold, Jr., Germany
Bevis & Shartle Machine Co.
Papeteries de L'Ouest.

Hollingsworth & Whitney Co.
Dells Pulp & Paper Co.
McKeesport Tin Plate Co
J. & J. Rogers.
W. Virginia P. & P. Co.
Neyret-Brenier, France.
The Duncan Company.
J. C. Wilson & Company.
Central Paper Company.
Detroit Sulphite F. Co
Hammermill Paper Company.
Munising Paper Company.
Tileston & Hollingsworth.
Rolland Paper Company
Royal Iron Works, Germany.
Finch, Pruyn & Co.
St. Croix Paper Company.
Canadian Rubber Company.
York Haven Paper Company.
Wausau Paper Company.
Petit Parisien, Paris.
J. R. Booth, Ottawa.
San Rafael, Mexico.
Keith Paper Company.
Mitsu-Bishi P. M. Co., Japan.
Minnesota & Ontario Power Co.
B. F. Perkins & Son.
American Wringer Co.
Bedford Pulp & Paper Co.
Papeterie Nanterre, France.
Okura & Co. (for Japan).
The Stanley Works.
American Tube & Stamping Co.
J. M. Voith, Germany
Crown-Columbia P. & P. Co
Papeterie de L'oa.
Papeterie de Roanne.

J. H. Horne (for Japan).
Cherry River Paper Co.
Wall Paper Mfrs., London.
Buffalo C. & B. R. Mills.
Rhinelander Paper Company.
Mitsui & Co. (for Japan).
Odell Mfg. Company.
Papeteries Darblay, France.
Thiry & Co., Belgium.
Anglo-Newfoundland D. Co.
Floriston P. & P. Co.
Cheboygan Paper Company.
Champion Coated P. Co.
Bardeen Paper Company.
F. W. Warren & E. Henry.
Revere Rubber Company.
Powell River Paper Co.
News Pulp & Paper Co.
Societe Anonyme des Papeteries, France.
Bayless Pulp & Paper Co.
Falulah Paper Co.
Valley Paper Co.
International Paper Co.
Price Brothers & Co., Ltd.
Mead Pulp & Paper Co.
Willamette Pulp & Paper Co.
Marathon Pulp & Paper Co.
Parks Paper Co.
Diana Paper Co.
Canton Sheet Steel Co.
Spanish River Pulp & Paper Co.
Racquette River Paper Co.
Union Bag & Paper Co.
Halifax Paper Corp.
Abitibi Power & Paper Co.

THE DRAPER MANUFACTURING CO.
Port Huron, Mich., U. S. A.

Manufacturers of

Hollow Balanced Brass Balls

for stuff pumps

Brass, Steel and Iron Balls

for all valve purposes

Ball Check Valves   Ball Unions

Valve Facing Tools

for Common Globe Valves, Flat Seat Valves, Pump Valve Seats, Etc.

Specify "DRAPER BALLS" when purchasing pumps

Write us when you have Balls needing repairs.   Send for catalog.

STANDARD REINFORCED SPIRAL PIPE
Continuous Interlocking Seam Smooth Inside

STANDARD SPIRAL PIPE WORKS   ROCKWELL AND WEST 48TH STREETS, CHICAGO

WILLIAM GANSCHOW CO.
1001 WEST WASHINGTON STREET, CHICAGO
GEARS FOR ALL PURPOSES
RAWHIDE AND BAKELITE PINIONS

THE PAPER TRADE JOURNAL

The medium which dominates its field. Circulation greater than combined circulations of all other mediums in its field.

The only publication in the Paper and Pulp Industry furnishing an A. B. C. report.

SUTHERLAND PAPER CO.
Manufacturers
Vegetable Parchment Paper, Waxed Paper and Paraffined Cartons
Inquiries for any of above solicited and will receive prompt attention
KALAMAZOO, MICHIGAN

SWENSON EVAPORATORS
have gradually become the recognized standard of the American Chemical Engineer.

We believe this popularity is partly due to the ease and quickness with which our machines can be erected, operated and kept clean— in a word, it is their simplicity that recommends them for recovery of soda or sulphate or concentration of waste sulphite liquor. *Catalog gratis.*

The Enormous Waste of Pulp Flowing into the Rivers through imperfect drainers is well known.

Save your Valuable Stock
by using the
SNELL ORAINER BOTTOM

Send for sample and price

SAMUEL SNELL CO. HOLYOKE MASS.

TICONDEROGA MACHINE WORKS
TICONDEROGA, N. Y., U. S. A.

Manufacturers of the

Improved WARREN Patent Double Drum WINDER

WARREN Improved Calender DOCTORS With
Flexible Blades, Universal Adjustment and Control (Patented)

And other Paper Mill Specialties   Send For Bulletins

DIAMOND TOOLS FOR TURNING CALENDER ROLLS

Special Shaped Carbon, Black Diamond, Pointed Tools for Turning Paper, Cotton, Husk, Rag, Brass, Hard and Soft Rubber Rolls, Fibre, Etc. Maintain their sharp cutting edges for many months of continuous use. The rolls are left exactly uniform in size and with a smooth, true finish.

MANUFACTURED BY   **THOS. L. DICKINSON**   **44 NASSAU STREET NEW YORK**
Successor to JOHN DICKINSON   Established 1796
Agents for Great Britain, C. W. BURTON, GRIFFITHS & CO., Ludgate Square, London

ESTABLISHED 1819

CHARLES LENNIG & CO., Inc.
MANUFACTURING CHEMISTS

Hyposulphite of Soda
Crystal Alum   Brown Sugar of Lead
Concentrated Alum   Nitrate of Lead
Paper Makers' Alum   Glaubers Salts
Water Filtration Alum   Muriatic Acid
Sulphate of Alumina   Nitric Acid
  (Iron Free)   Sulphuric Acid

Office: 112 South Front Street, Philadelphia, Pa.

THE WORLD STANDARD

THE MULLEN PAPER TESTER
The ADOPTED STANDARD OF THE U. S. GOVERNMENT and the Leading Manufacturers, Dealers and Publishers

We claim that two samples of paper, uniformly made of the same stock of equal weight, thickness and finish, tested on this machine, will show exactly uniform tests. The test results shown, not in some arbitrary scale, as with other testers, but in pounds pressure per square inch, a recognized standard the world over.

Send for Catalogue and References

B. F. PERKINS & SON, Inc.
Sole Manufacturers HOLYOKE, MASS.

Takes the Place of Several Men

ONE or two men with a Revolvator will do the work of several men in piling rolls of paper, cases, bales, barrels, etc.

This machine not only **saves labor** but enables you to utilise all your storage space. It permits piling goods clear to the ceiling.

Write for Bulletin PT42

REVOLVATOR CO.
357 Garfield Avenue
Jersey City, N. J.

Piling 2000 lb. rolls of paper 5 tiers high with a Revolvator

Sales Agent for N. Y. REVOLVING PORTABLE ELEVATOR CO.

Jos. O'Neill Wire Works
SOUTHPORT, CONN., U. S. A.
MANUFACTURERS OF

Durable Paper Machine and Cylinder Wires

IN SINGLE, DOUBLE, TRIPLE TWILLED AND TWISTED WEAVES OF BRASS OR PHOSPHOR BRONZE

Also Pulp Wires of Bronze, Monel and Nickel Alloy Metals.

Our Nickel Alloy Pulp Wires have the greatest wearing and acid-resisting qualities of any known metal.

Also Wire Cloth in all metals and weaves, up to and including No. 350 mesh.

INQUIRIES SOLICITED

WALTER IBBOTSON, Junr.
(M. K. IBBOTSON)

Station Buildings, ALTRINCHAM, Nr. Manchester

Formerly: 21 Cannon Street, Manchester   Established 1885

Agents in Dublin and Glasgow

Paper Merchants, Importers and Exporters

All qualities from STRAWBOARDS to the most expensive COPYING and TISSUES

BOOKBINDERS' CLOTHS, LABEL AND TAG CLOTHS, MULLS, CAMBRICS, LINEN BUCKRAMS, BLUE LININGS, LITHOGRAPHIC AND PHOTOGRAPHIC CLOTHS, BLUE AND BLACK LINE RAW.

SAMPLES FREE ON APPLICATION

T. WILLIAMSON & CO.

6, 8 and 8a Palace Square } MANCHESTER, ENGLAND   30-31 St. Swithens Lane
7 Peel Street   LONDON, E. C.

Telegrams: "Swiftness," Manchester, England

Hudson-Sharp Machine Co.
Green Bay, Wis.

Toilet Roll Winders, Automatic Collapsing Reels, Napkin Folders, Bundling and Bailing Presses, Crepe Machines.

GIBBS BROWN CO., New York, Selling Agents

OSWEGO MACHINE WORKS
NEIL GRAY, Jr., Proprietor

Cutting Machines Exclusively

One hundred different sizes and styles. All generally in stock for instant shipment. *Write.*

OSWEGO, NEW YORK, U. S. A.

C. K. WILLIAMS & CO. EASTON, PENNSYLVANIA

MINERS AND MANUFACTURERS OF

AGALITE & TALC

AND IMPORTERS AND MANUFACTURERS OF

CHINA CLAYS, YELLOW and RED OCHRES, TURKEY UMBERS, RED OXIDES, INDIAN and TUSCAN REDS, Etc.

Especially adapted for Paper Manufacturing—Daily Capacity over 100 Tons

ESTIMATES AND SAMPLES FURNISHED UPON APPLICATION Correspondence earnestly solicited

Telegrams: Kaolin, Manchester   ABC Code used

MANCHESTER CHINA CLAY CO., Ltd.

4 St. Ann's Square
MANCHESTER, ENGLAND

Mines: St. Austell and St. Dennis, Cornwall

Producers of all qualities and Shippers
to all parts of the World

Domestic Mills Paper Company

All Grades of Paper at Wholesale

Wrappings	Manifold
Writings	Specialties
Colored Textiles	Paper Towels
Tissues	Toilet Paper
Onion Skin	Liquid Soap
and Dispensers	

96-98 Reade St., New York, N. Y.

Increase Your Boiler Efficiency

Plibrico

is a plastic substance that makes a solid— one-piece fire-box lining without joints.

It will increase your boiler efficiency 15%. It will make your furnace gas and air tight and greatly reduce the cost of upkeep. Will outwear any firebrick made.

Write for further information

Jointless Fire Brick Company

1871-1879 Kingsbury St.
Chicago, Ill.

Canadian Agents:
Beveridge Paper Co., Ltd.,
17-21 Ste Therese Street,
Montreal Canada.

NORWOOD FILTERS
SPECIALLY DESIGNED TO MEET YOUR REQUIREMENTS

HIGH GRADE
Paper Finishing Machinery

WEB SUPERCALENDERS
SHEET SUPERCALENDERS   IMPROVED PLATERS

RAG THRASHERS   DUST-EXHAUSTING   RAG CUTTERS
RAILROAD DUSTERS   SYSTEMS   FAN DUSTERS

Norwood Engineering Company
FLORENCE, MASSACHUSETTS

Paper Cutters

Single,
Duplex
and
Diagonal

CUTTER KNIVES.

PATENT TOP SLITTERS.

Hamblet Machine Co.   -   Lawrence, Mass.

JAFFE & CO.
DEALERS AND PACKERS IN ALL GRADES OF
NEW CUTTINGS
236 South Street,   New York

Telephone 4334 Orchard

WE DO ALL OUR OWN PACKING

LUKE BOYLE
Established 1854

PAPER BOX BOARDS   Straw Chip, Plain & Lined, and News

Packer and Dealer in
PAPER STOCK

390 WEST BROADWAY - NEW YORK

GEORGE F. HILLS CO.
WHOLESALE AND RETAIL DEALERS IN
Paper and Paper Mfg. Supplies
108-110-112 Cliff St. and 9-11-13 Hague St.

NEW YORK

DAILY CAPACITY 300 TONS
MAIN PAPER STOCK CO.
INCORPORATED

SPECIAL GRADERS OF PAPER STOCK
NEW AND OLD COTTON RAGS

If you have special requirements we can certainly please you

Branch, 321 Pearl St.   25-27-29-31 Peck Slip   New York City

THE M. J. O'MALLEY CO.

MANUFACTURERS OF STENCIL BOARDS, OIL BOARDS
HIGH GRADE STOCK
WRITE FOR SAMPLES

SPRINGFIELD   MASSACHUSETTS

COPYING BOOKS, OIL TISSUE, TRAIN ORDER BLANKS

DOBLER & MUDGE

WHOLESALE PAPER

TWINE-BOARDS

BALTIMORE, MD.

ESTABLISHED 1898

Central Dyestuff and Chemical Company

MANUFACTURERS OF

Full line of ANILINE COLORS
for the PAPER TRADE

MAIN OFFICE AND WORKS, NEWARK, N. J.

James L. Carey
Paper Mill Architect and
Engineer

208 N. Laramie Ave.
Chicago, Ill.

New mills for paper or board.
Plans for repairing old mills.

THE D. M. BARE PAPER CO.
MANUFACTURERS OF
SUPER-CALENDERED AND
MACHINE FINISH
ANTIQUE LAID AND WOVE
BOOK PAPERS

Lithograph, White Flats and Mimeograph
Daily Capacity, 32 Tons

ROARING SPRING, - - PA.

FITCHBURG DUCK MILLS

ESTABLISHED 1844

MANUFACTURERS OF

STANDARD AND MULTIPLE

PLY DRYER FELTS

"TRIUNE" Three Ply Felt,
the one you can depend upon.

"BAKER" in two, three, four, five and six ply.
A fine faced felt for fine papers.
Absolutely no felt marks in the paper.

IN WIDTHS OF 60 INCHES TO 176 INCHES

FITCHBURG,   **MASS.**

F. BREDT & CO.

240 WATER ST., NEW YORK CITY

ANILINE COLORS and DYE-STUFFS for Paper Mills   Sole Agents for JOSEPH PORRITT & SONS

ULTRAMARINE BLUE
FOURDRINIER WIRES
CANVAS DRYER FELTS Felts and Jackets

---

"The House of Service"
FEDERAL PAPER STOCK CO.
Packers and Graders
Waste Paper and Rags

Quality Our Specialty   Write Us for Prices

St. Louis, Mo.

1790 SHRYOCK BROTHERS 1919
(INCORPORATED)

S. S. SHRYOCK, President.   S. S. SHRYOCK, Jr., Vice-President.
O. A. SHRYOCK, Secretary and Treasurer.

MANUFACTURERS
PAPER BOARDS

OFFICE AND WAREHOUSE
924-26-28 Cherry Street   PHILADELPHIA, PA.

H. P. & H. F. WILSON

SINGLE LOOP
TRIPLE LOOP
OPEN HOOK
CLOSED HOOK

MANUFACTURERS OF
Steel Wire
Bale Ties

For Baling Hay, Straw, Jute, Moss, Rags, Paper Stock and All Compressible Material.

542-544-546 W. 22nd St.
NEW YORK

Keith Paper Company
Turners Falls, Massachusetts

Bonds
Keith Parchment
Ravelstone
Cambrai
Tisrite

Onion Skin

Ledgers
Keith Linen
Ravelstone
Westlock
Tisrite

Writings
Keith Linen
 Wove and Laid
Keith Halftone
 Writing

Weddings
No. 1 Bridal White
Superior

Specialties
Onyx Covers and
 Bristols
Keith Covers
Keith Quality Tints
Keith Sheepskin
 Parchment

Manufacturers of
Standard Lines of

High Grade

Papers
and
Bristols

in a full assortment of colors, sizes and weights

The American Papeterie Company, of Albany, N. Y., is the sole manufacturer of Keith's Watermarked Papers in stationery form

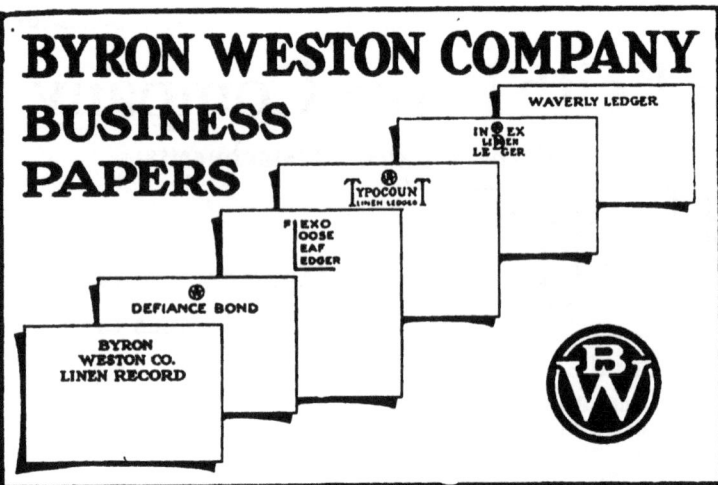

They Meet all Requirements

CELEBRATED for service, quality, finish and convenience, Byron Weston Company Business Papers are in a class by themselves. Each line combines, to the degree of perfection, all the qualities most desirable in the particular work for which it is designed.

Each Weston Company product has an unusual toughness of fibre which gives great strength, firmness and "life" to the paper, making it practically indestructible. The stock is then finished so that a perfect surface is obtained for writing, and ruling either by pen or machine. *Typocount*, the ledger paper for machine bookkeeping, is specially finished for typewriting.

Besides the four ledger papers—the famous Byron Weston Company Linen Ledger and Record Paper, Flexo Loose Leaf, Waverly Ledger and Typocount—there is Defiance Bond. This is a fine stock of the grade of the famous Linen Ledger, and is intended for stationery, booklets, folders, announcements and similar high-grade advertising purposes.

May we send you samples and prices?

BYRON WESTON COMPANY
DALTON, MASSACHUSETTS

Z. & W. M. Crane

Dalton, Massachusetts

Makers of

Crane's
Extra Superfine
Superfine and
Pasted Boards
and
Old Berkshire Mills
Brands

CRANE & CO.
DALTON, MASS.

Manufacturers of
Bond, Bank Note *and*
Parchment Deed
PAPERS

The American Stationer and Office Outfitter

THE BEST CIRCULATED and THE BEST READ medium, covering the commercial, wholesale and retail stationery and office supply fields.

Published by

LOCKWOOD TRADE JOURNAL CO., Inc.

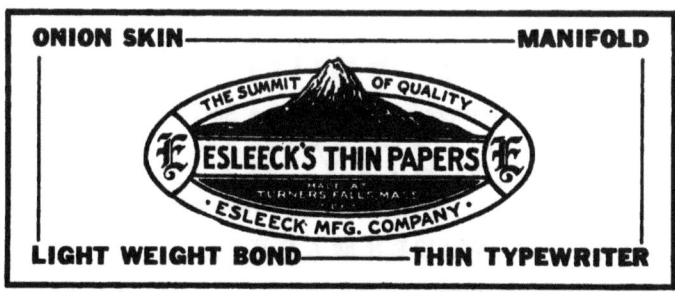

ONION SKIN ——————— MANIFOLD
LIGHT WEIGHT BOND ——— THIN TYPEWRITER

ORONO PULP & PAPER CO., Bangor, Me.

Makers of

Strong Sulphite Papers

Kraft (Brown and Colors)

Bag   Wrapping
Envelope   Manifold
Tissue

Specialties

Daily Product, 60 Tons Paper and 50 Tons Sulphite Pulp

MILLERS FALLS PAPER CO.
MILLERS FALLS, MASS.

Makers of

Old Veda Bond   Sales Record Ledger
Old Deerfield Bond   Extra Fine White Wove
Index Bristol

Established 1885 **C. H. Smith Co.** **Incorporated 1917**

Makers of the Famous SMITH

DANDY ROLL

Over 6000 now in use at the Best Paper Mills in the World

SHADED WATERMARKING COVERS

Intricate designs and letters now our specialties   Springfield, Mass.

RECORD FOUNDRY and MACHINE COMPANY
MACHINISTS and FOUNDERS

Paper, Pulp and Sulphite Transmission Machinery, Cast Iron Flanged Pipe and Fittings, all sizes. SAFETY FIRST DIGESTER BLOW PIPE, Cast Iron or Bronze, Conveying Machinery. Shaving Scuppers for Dutch Ovens, Centrifugal Pumps, Building and Bronze Castings, Bronze Bearing Metal, Stuff Chests, Water Penstocks, Blow Tanks, RECORD IMPROVED QUICK-OPENING GATE VALVES, PATENTED, for Sulphite, Paper and Pulp Mills.

LIVERMORE FALLS   -   -   -   -   MAINE

EDWIN RILEY, Pres.   RALPH J. RILEY, Sec. and Treas.   FRED E. RILEY, Mgr. and Engineer

---

JOS. J. PLANK & CO.
APPLETON, WISCONSIN

Dandy Roll Makers
EXCLUSIVELY

Unexcelled Watermarking

STRATHMORE
"QUALITY PAPERS"

Bond, Stationery, Ledger, Book and Cover Papers. Pasted Wedding Bristols and Pasted Cover Papers. Photo Mount and Mat Paper and Boards. Artist Paper and Boards. Bond, Book, Cover and Special Papers in Rolls.

FROM THE FINEST MADE TO MEDIUM GRADES.

STRATHMORE PAPER COMPANY
MITTINEAGUE MILLS, MITTINEAGUE, MASS., U. S. A.

WHITING PAPER CO.

MAKERS OF

The Standard Grades of Loft-Dried

Ledgers : Bonds : and : Writing : Papers

MILLS AT

HOLYOKE, MASSACHUSETTS

WAREHOUSES IN

NEW YORK   CHICAGO   PHILADELPHIA

BENNINGTON WAX PAPER COMPANY

MANUFACTURERS OF

All Grades ......of...... *PARAFFINE PAPERS*

Plain or printed in one or two colors

ALL CORRESPONDENCE CHEERFULLY RESPONDED TO—ASK US

BENNINGTON :: :: :: :: VERMONT

HAVERHILL BOX BOARD COMPANY

IN ADDITION TO REGULAR BOX BOARD LINES
WE MANUFACTURE

'CALNO' WALLBOARDS

"BEST FOR BUILDING"

HAVERHILL, MASS.

CHEMICAL PAPER MANUFACTURING COMPANY.

HOLYOKE, MASS.

Five Machines in Operation—3 Fourdriniers and 2 Cylinders

MAKERS OF

Tub-sized Writing and Envelope, Climax Detail, Ledger and Paramount Drawing, Index Bristol, Offset Paper and Bristol, Wedding, Kid and Linen Finished Papeterie, Chemco, No Protest, Cabinet, Cretonne, Old Holyoke and Sphinx Bonds, Chemco and Buyers' Ledger, Mimeograph, White and Colored Manifold, No. 1 Rag Onion Skin, Book, Interwoven Covers, Uwanta Cover, International Cover, Wicker Cover, White and Colored Patent Coated Folding Box Boards, Bristols, Silk Board, Chocolate Board, Mount Board, White Blanks and Specialties.

Advertisers Paper Mills

Makers in Holyoke of Fine Printing Papers

Our line of "Made in Holyoke" Covers and Book Papers is the most complete and comprehensive series of high class printing papers for advertisers made by any mill in America.

HOLYOKE

Taylor-Logan Co. Papermakers

Makers in Holyoke of
PUBLIC SERVICE BOND

HOLYOKE

The New York - New England Co.
HOLYOKE, MASSACHUSETTS

NYNEMILL LINES

WRITINGS, BONDS, BRISTOLS
ARTLOVERS' MARBLE PAPER

We specialize in

Pasting—Any thickness desired
Finishing—plain and fancy
Folding—Embossing and specialties

Inquiries solicited on any paper problems

Crocker-McElwain Co.
HOLYOKE, MASS.

SURETY BOND	LEDGER INDEX BRISTOL
TOKYO BOND	SUPERFINE INDEX BRISTOL
CERTIFICATE BOND	TABULAR INDEX BRISTOL
COMMUNITY BOND	SOCIETY PASTED BRISTOL
ECONOMIC LEDGER	WEDDING AND OTHER ENVELOPE PAPERS
HAMPTON COURT SUPERFINE	FINE FLATS
CROMAC OFFSET	CROMAC OFFSET BRISTOL

For Manufacturing Data see page 111

B. D. RISING PAPER COMPANY
HOUSATONIC, BERKSHIRE COUNTY, MASS., U. S. A.

Manufacturers of

Housatonic, Barrington, Danish
Twentieth Century and Finance Bonds
Twenty Carat Linen

Reference, Danish and Finance Ledgers, also
Wedding and Index Bristols

As a logical result of our development in the explosive and chemical industries, we are now undertaking the manufacture of synthetic dyestuffs and kindred products in a broad and comprehensive way.

The explosive and coal tar dye industries are closely allied. Both require intermediates which we manufacture in a large way; both are highly scientific and thoroughly developed and both require large technical and commercial organizations.

We start with (1) the necessary raw materials, products of this country, therefore not dependent upon Europe; (2) a chemical and engineering organization, second to none in magnitude and scientific attainment; (3) unequalled plant and laboratory facilities, and (4) an adequate commercial organization.

The construction of our dye plants is progressing satisfactorily and on schedule time. Some of the more important ones are now in commission; others will follow.

Back of our entry into the dyestuffs industry is the compelling force of the country's needs; if as the result of the combined efforts of all, the United States can in time become self-contained, the effort will have been well worth while.

E. I. DU PONT DE NEMOURS & CO.
Dyestuff Sales Department
WILMINGTON DELAWARE

■ ■ ■

THE DU PONT AMERICAN INDUSTRIES ARE:
E. I. du Pont de Nemours & Co., Wilmington, Del., Explosives
Du Pont Chemical Works, New York, N. Y., Pyroxylin and Coal Tar Chemicals
Du Pont Fabrikoid Company, Wilmington, Del., Leather Substitutes
The Arlington Works, 725 Broadway, N. Y., Ivory Py-ra-lin and Challenge Collars
Harrison Works, Philadelphia, Pa., Paints, Pigments, Acids and Chemicals
Du Pont Dye Works, Wilmington, Del., Coal Tar Dyestuffs

UNITED STATES PAPER CORPORATION

COARSE and FINE
PAPERS

727 So. FIFTH Ave.
CHICAGO.

Stratford Paper Company
ESTABLISHED 1876
Successors to JERSEY CITY PAPER COMPANY
Manufacturers of
High Grade Fourdrinier Tissues
"Crown" White, Colored and G. B. Silver
Crown Manifold Linen Typewriter Papers
Celluloid, Cigarette and Thin Carbon Tissues
170 CORNELISON AVE. :: JERSEY CITY, N. J.

The Smith Paper Company
MANUFACTURERS OF
TISSUE PAPERS
EXCLUSIVELY
LEE, - - MASS.
Cigarette Papers of Highest Quality
WRITE FOR SAMPLES AND PRICES

Watervliet Paper Company
WATERVLIET, MICHIGAN
W. M. Loveland, President
MANUFACTURERS OF
High Grade Coated Book *and* Coated Lithograph Papers

A SPLENDID "ALL-AROUND" PAPER

Snowdrift is a noticeably "different" stock.

Its texture is firm, with a soft, full body and a satiny finish that is perfect for writing or printing.

Snowdrift is a dazzling white—admittedly "the whitest paper made!"

For high-grade stationery, folders, booklets and similar business purposes.

Made in plain and deckle-edge (Featheredge) styles.

Moderate in price.

Send for samples and prices

Mountain Mill Paper Company
Lee, Berkshire County
Massachusetts

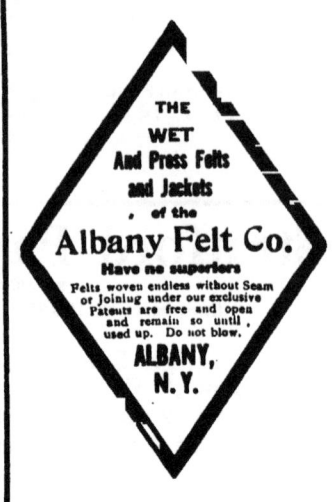

THE WET And Press Felts and Jackets of the **Albany Felt Co.** Have no superiors. Felts woven endless without Seam or Joining under our exclusive Patents are free and open and remain so until used up. Do not blow.
ALBANY, N.Y.

Pure Food Lunch Rolls and Family Packages

Roll Toilet Papers, Tissue Paper and Specialties

No. 1 White Tissue   No. 2 White Tissue
No. 1 Manila Tissue in reams

Richard S. Hoffman Company
BALDWINSVILLE   **NEW YORK**

"The Mill That Will"

PENINSULAR PAPER COMPANY
Manufacturers of Uncommon Cover Papers   Ypsilanti, Mich.

Folding Photo Mounts, Calendar Mounts and Cover Specialties

Also our mill brand covers as follows:
GIBRALTAR   PUBLICITY   PLATEFOLD   ORKID
     ONIMBO   COVENANT   NEAPOLITAN

ONE LINE { Paper Makers' Felts

ONE QUALITY { The Best

ONE TRIAL { Repeat Orders

ONE RESULT { Satisfaction

Lockport Felt Comp'y

NEWFANE, N. Y.

27 Years' experience

TO PAPER MANUFACTURERS

Please look over our list of waste paper assortments packed in power presses bales in minimum carloads.

Hard White Shavings
Soft White Book Shavings
Fly Leaf Shavings
Mixed Colored Shavings
Department Store Papers
No. 1 Mixed Papers
Over-issue News Papers
House News Papers
Blank News
Flat Book and Magazines
Light Book
Ledger and Writing Paper
Manilla Cuttings
Manilla Papers
Red Rope Paper
Kraft Paper
Mill Wrappers

PENN. PAPER AND STOCK COMPANY
206 N. Delaware Avenue
207 N. Water Street
PHILADELPHIA, PENN.

The Albemarle Paper Mfg. Co.

MAKERS OF BLOTTING AND ABSORPTIVE PAPERS EXCLUSIVELY

=======Richmond, Va., U. S. A.=======

OUR BRANDS ARE KNOWN AS THE STANDARDS OF QUALITY
"WORLD"   "HOLLYWOOD"   "RELIANCE"

SPECIALTIES.—"VIENNA MOIRE" and "DIRECTOIRE" fancy desk blotters, the most attractive fancy designs. "ALBEMARLE ENAMELED" and "ALBEMARLE HALF-TONE" Blottings, for color process, half-tone and lithograph work. Working samples furnished on request.

HOUSATONIC MILL

THE EATON-DIKEMAN CO.
LEE, - - - MASS.

Blotting Paper

Matrix, Interleaving, Filter and all grades of Absorbent Papers

MAGNET, COLUMBIAN, LENOX, ARLINGTON AND OTHER BRANDS OF BLOTTING CARRIED IN STOCK

Exact Size 8x9 inches—Outside Measure   Size of Dial 6 inches Diameter

AUTOMATIC MICROMETER
MADE IN U.S.A.

Each instrument is correctly adjusted before being shipped
Present price $36.00, securely packed, F. O. B. Chicago

E. J. CADY & COMPANY
326 WEST MADISON STREET   CHICAGO, ILL.

STANDARD PAPER COMPANY
Manufacturers of
BLANKS, BRISTOLS
and all the higher grades of
BOXBOARDS
Kalamazoo - - - - - - - Michigan

SCREEN PLATES   WATERMARKING
DANDY ROLLS   BRONZE CASTINGS

Central Mfg. Co.
Kalamazoo   Michigan

GENERAL PAPER STOCK COMPANY

SAINT LOUIS, MISSOURI

PACKERS OF ALL GRADES OF

Rags and Waste Paper

HARTFORD CITY PAPER COMPANY
HARTFORD CITY, INDIANA, U. S. A.

MANUFACTURERS OF HIGH GRADE

GREASEPROOF AND GLASSINE PAPER, GLAZED AND UNGLAZED ONION SKIN, MANIFOLD PAPERS, PLAIN EMBOSSED AND INK COLORED EMBOSSED GLASSINE.

Widest sheet made 96 inches; heaviest paper made 24x36-50 Lbs. to 480 sheets; lightest paper made 24x36-12½ Lbs. to 500 sheets. We are equipped to die cut circles and forms, and to do one, two and three color printing. Write us for quotations.

HARTFORD CITY PAPER COMPANY
HARTFORD CITY, INDIANA

DICK CROTTEAU
Paper Mill Agent

Mill Accounts Solicited
All Grades

Room 1262, Conway Building.   Chicago, Ill.

HOWARD BOND

WATERMARKED

Color Brilliant
Strength Wonderful

THE HOWARD PAPER CO.
URBANA, OHIO

Book and Catalogue
Bonds and Writings
Newsprint
Wrappings
Specialties

Warehouse Stock
Mill Shipments

A. C. Allen Paper Co.
122 South Michigan Ave.
Chicago

If It is an Envelope—
WE MAKE IT

Capacity—
2,750,000 Daily

ILLINOIS ENVELOPE CO.
General Office and Factory, Bryant Street
Kalamazoo, Michigan

Chicago Office—In charge of Mr. R. H. Vogdes

608 So. Dearborn St.   440 Transportation Bldg.

SEAMAN
Paper Company

Manufacturers and National Distributors of Quality

Book *and* Catalog Papers

Daily Capacity 1,000 Tons

■ ■ ■

Mills in both Eastern and Western Territories. Branches and Competent Selling Organizations in all Important Printing Centers. Large Supplies of Coated Papers, Coated Boards, Index Bristols, Bonds, etc., on hand at all times in Warehouses. :: Samples and Quotations on Request. :: Communicate with nearest Branch.

Chicago	New York	Buffalo
Philadelphia	St. Paul	Cincinnati
Milwaukee	Minneapolis	St. Louis

PAPER MILL SUPPLIES
"Service and Dependability"

High Quality Bleached and Unbleached Spruce Pulp—Kraft—Ground Wood. High Grade Domestic Coating and Filler Clays, Wire Products, Screen Plates, Dandy Rolls and Trimming Knives, Starch and Heavy Chemicals

Inquiries Solicited

CALE. B. FORSYTHE
902 Hanselman Building   Kalamazoo, Michigan

MID-STATES GUMMED PAPER CO.

MANUFACTURERS OF

Gummed Sealing, Stay and Veneer Tapes

Write for Prices and Samples

Factory and Office: 312 Union Park Court, CHICAGO

724-732 WEST LAKE STREET   CHICAGO

Manufacturers of **Merchandise, Envelopes, Paper Bags** (both Machine- and Hand-made), **Folding Boxes** and **Cartons, Glassine Bags** and Specialties of Paper, &c. Also General Dealers in **Wrapping Papers, Twines,** &c.

Designers and Builders of Calender Rolls, Dryers and other Paper Mill Machinery

Guyton & Cumfer Mfg. Co., Chicago, Ill.

U. & Z.
Patented Portable
Calender Roll
GRINDER

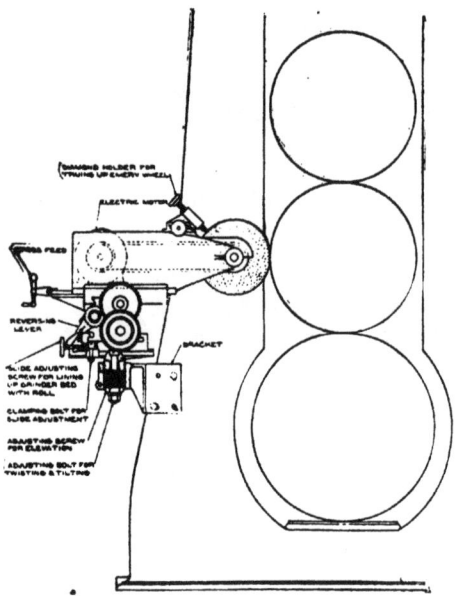

Write for U. & Z. Circular

B. S. ROY & SON CO.
Established 1868
Worcester, Mass., U. S. A.

MOREY AND COMPANY
Incorporated

27 Commercial Avenue
East Cambridge, Mass.

MORECO
TRADEMARK

Paper Manufacturers Supplies
English China Clay, Domestic Clay, Paper Stock, Rags, Deckle Webbing, Belting, Woolen Felt Cleaner, Chemicals, Soap Powder, Rubber Tissue, Talc.

Paper Box Manufacturers Supplies
PAPER
Glazed, Plated, Litho, Cheviot, Wrapping
BOXBOARD
Chip, News, Manila, Jute, Straw, Gummed Sealing and Stay Tapes

Lithographers and Printers Supplies
Bond, Book, Ledger, Coated, News, Tissue, Writing and Wrapping Papers

■ ■ ■

WIPING RAGS, BALING MACHINES, TIES

■ ■ ■

We Solicit Your Inquiries

MERRIMAC CHEMICAL CO.

MANUFACTURERS OF

ALUM

Oil Vitriol, Acids, Ammonia and Paper Makers' Chemicals

MERRIMAC POROUS AND FILTER ALUMS
ARE UNEXCELLED

Office: 148 State St., BOSTON, MASS.
PLEASE SEND FOR CATALOG

Tanks, Acid Towers, Blow Pipes
OF YELLOW PINE AND CYPRESS—Our Specialty

Nearly Seventy Years' Experience

Heavy Paper Mill Work A Specialty

OUR AIR-DRIED CYPRESS IS REMARKABLE FOR ITS GREAT DURABILITY

THE A. T. STEARNS LUMBER CO.
Established 1849   BOSTON, MASS.

 **Glazed and Coated Paper of every Description**
SILFOIL--The Great Economical Substitute for Tin Foil
INDIAN BRAND GUMMED PAPERS
GUMMED CLOTH and GUMMED BOX STAYS
WAXED PAPERS of EVERY DESCRIPTION
Nashua Gummed & Coated Paper Company, Nashua, N. H.

CHARLES D. BROWN & CO.
INCORPORATED
185 Devonshire Street, BOSTON, MASS.

Paper Stock   Dryer Felts
Paper Mill Supplies
AMERICAN AGENTS:
R. R. Whitehead & Bro., Woolen Felts

Stone & Forsyth Co.
67 KINGSTON ST., BOSTON, MASS.
PAPER, TWINE, BAGS, BOXES
HYGIENIC PAPER SPECIALTIES
Including Paper Drinking Cups, Towels, Cuspidors, Sputum Cups

FACTORY AT EVERETT, MASS.

Magnifying Manpower is what all manufacturers are striving to accomplish. It can't be done without labor-saving equipments. Therefore, as Transveyors really accomplish this object, you should be interested. We have a booklet fully covering this topic which is yours for the asking.

The Cowan Truck Company HOLYOKE Massachusetts

F. G. MARQUARDT, President   CHAS. E. RAND, Secretary
HUGO THUM, Vice-President   JAS. J. BOYD, Treasurer

F. G. Marquardt, Inc.

Paper and Paper Makers
Supplies

320 Broadway, New York

Packing House: Rockville Centre, N. Y.

OUR SPECIAL
PACKING and GRADING
Will certainly please you

J. G. SWIFT, Pres. and Gen. Manager   W. H. CLAFLIN, Treas.

W. H. CLAFLIN & CO., Inc.
Manufacturers' Agents and Wholesale Dealers in
ALL GRADES OF PAPERS
NEWS, BOOK and MANILA
General Sales Agents Continental Paper Bag Co.
332-340 SUMMER STREET   -   BOSTON, MASS.

W. R. ELLIOTT COMPANY
MASSACHUSETTS CORPORATION

Manufacturers of **Special Roll Paper**
For Recording and Computing Machines of All Kinds
ROLL PAPER SLITTING FOR THE TRADE
NARROW WIDTHS A SPECIALTY

78 India Street   BOSTON, MASS.

STONE & ANDREW, Inc.
270 CONGRESS STREET   **BOSTON, MASS.**

MANUFACTURERS AND DISTRIBUTORS OF S & A PAPERS
Book, Covers, Bonds, Ledgers, Writing and Envelopes

DIRECT BY MAIL
FOLDING COATED
Reg. U. S. Pat. Office

HANCOCK DULL FINISH BOOK AND POST CARD
Agents for both these lines in all large Cities in the United States

SOLE NEW ENGLAND DISTRIBUTORS for
Champion Coated Paper Company   Maine Coated Paper Company

Importers and Sole Agents in America for **RIVINGTON COVER**

BRANCH OFFICES:
Mediterranean Trading Company   886 Sumner Ave.   828 Industrial Trust Building
29 Broadway, New York City   Springfield, Mass.   Providence, R. I.

JOHN CARTER & CO., Incorporated
PAPER

A large complete stock for the
Printer, Publisher and Stationer

100 and 102 Federal Street   BOSTON, MASS.

S. W. BARTLETT, President   C. L. BAIRD, Treasurer

BAIRD & BARTLETT COMPANY
No. 63 HIGH STREET   BOSTON, MASS.

PAPER BOX BOARDS
OF EVERY DESCRIPTION

Binders Board, Coated Manila and Tag Boards. Laundry and Layer Boards. Paper Specialties. Regular stock sizes carried in Boston Warehouse.

CARTER, RICE & CO.
(CORPORATION)

The Most Complete Line of

FINE PAPERS

Cardboard, Envelopes, Book, News, Manila, Twines

246 Devonshire Street, Boston, Mass.

STIMPSON & CO.
WILLIAM W. JENKS, Manager,

Manufacturers' Agents and Jobbers of

Paper, Paper Bags and Twine, Skewers and Burlaps, Oval and Wired End Butter Trays, Oyster Pails.

Selling Agents for
UNION BAG AND PAPER CO.

MANILA PAPERS, TISSUES, TOILET PAPERS.

64 & 65 Chatham Street, - - BOSTON, MASS.

PERRY B. VON OLKER, Pres.   JOSEPH D. SNELL, Treas.

VON OLKER-SNELL PAPER CO.
112-114 Pearl Street, Boston, Mass.
TELEPHONE, FORT HILL 4142

WRITINGS	BOOK	MANILA	ENVELOPES
LEDGERS	NEWS	KRAFT	CARDBOARDS
BONDS	COVERS	TWINE	SPECIALTIES

Manufacturers VOSCO Paper Fuel Bags

D. F. MUNROE COMPANY
A. W. BLACKMAN, President and Treasurer   W. F. BROWN, Secretary

MANILA, KRAFT, NEWS, TISSUE
WAX AND TOILET PAPERS
FOLDING BOXES, TWINES AND

MILL SELLING AGENTS   PAPER BAGS   NEW MILL CONNECTIONS
AND JOBBERS   SOLICITED

MAIN OFFICE, 299 CONGRESS STREET, BOSTON, MASS.
Railroad Warehouse—Boynton's Yard, Boston, B. & M. Siding
Telephones, Main 5100, 5101, 5102

Francis L. Andrews, *President*   John F. Kuster, *Treasurer*
Frank H. Merrill, *Vice-President*   Frank C. Cate, *Secretary*

Andrews Paper Company
Exclusive Territory
Mill Accounts Solicited

MANILA, KRAFT TISSUE, TOILET, TWINE, PAPER TOWELS, PAPER
NAPKINS, FOLDING PAPER BOXES, OYSTER PAILS, PAPER BAGS
Hygienic Paper Specialties
Selling Agents for Union Bag and Paper Company
New England Agents for Dexter Sulphite Pulp and Paper Company

54-60 India Street   **BOSTON, MASS.**

C. E. PERRY COMPANY, Inc.
Successors to
Charles E. Perry Company

Roll Paper Manufacturers
Adding Machine Rolls   Fire Alarm and   Every Other Form
Police Register Rolls   Telegraph Tape   of Roll Paper

77 Washington Street, North   BOSTON, MASS.

HARRISON'S PAPER MAKERS' ALUM

(17% Al_2O_3)

For those paper manufacturers who want a dependable paper size. A product backed by a century-old reputation of the largest chemical organization in the world.

HARRISON WORKS

 35th and Gray's Ferry Road,
Philadelphia
New York Office, 21 E. 40th St.

Munroe Felt and Paper Co.

MANUFACTURERS OF

Parcel Post Kraft

For High Class Wrapping,
Bags, Envelopes, etc.
Tough, Elastic, Pliable,
Uniform.
Free from acid and adulterants.
Made From Pure Imported
Sulphate Pulp.

MAKERS ALSO OF

Blanks, Carpet Linings,
Cheviots, Crimps and other
Specialties.

C. W. RANTOUL CO.   Mills at Lawrence, Mass.
42nd Street Building   New York Agents   Office: 79 Summer Street
                                           BOSTON

SHEA, STURM CO.
MILL AGENTS

35 Warren St.,   New York City

TELEPHONE—BARCLAY 3780

PAPER SPECIALTIES and CORDAGE

Kraft	Wax Papers
Bogus	Plain and Printed
Fibres	Lunch Rolls
Sulphite Papers	Bread Wrappers
Parchment	Adding Machine Rolls
Glassine	Small Roll Papers
Blotting	Toilet Tissues
Bond and Ledgers	Envelopes
Papeteries	Gummed Papers

INQUIRIES
DOMESTIC ::   :: EXPORT
SOLICITED

Lightning Source UK Ltd.
Milton Keynes UK
UKHW011155180119
335792UK00011B/714/P